P9-DCW-682

Jim O'Keeffe
206 931 1209

www. C# Corner (good for info)

ADO.Net McGraw Hill

go thro → Programing/C#
Mcgraw & Hill.

ISBN 0072886250/
9780072

Lidia

Pro C# 2008 and the .NET 3.5 Platform

Fourth Edition

■■■

Andrew Troelsen

Apress®

Pro C# 2008 and the .NET 3.5 Platform, Fourth Edition

ISBN-13: 978-1-59059-884-9

ISBN-13 (electronic): 978-1-4302-0422-0

Printed and bound in the United States of America 9 8 7 6 5 4

Lead Editor: Ewan Buckingham
Technical Reviewer: Gavin Smyth
Editorial Board: Steve Anglin, Ewan Buckingham, Tony Campbell, Gary Cornell, Jonathan Gennick, Jason Gilmore, Kevin Goff, Jonathan Hassell, Matthew Moodie, Joseph Ottinger, Jeffrey Pepper, Ben Renow-Clarke, Dominic Shakeshaft, Matt Wade, Tom Welsh
Production Director | Project Manager: Grace Wong
Senior Copy Editors: Ami Knox, Nicole Flores
Associate Production Director: Kari Brooks-Copony
Production Editor: Ellie Fountain
Compositor: Dina Quan
Proofreaders: April Eddy and Liz Welch
Indexer: Broccoli Information Management
Artist: Kinetic Publishing Services, LLC
Cover Designer: Kurt Krames
Manufacturing Director: Tom Debolski

Distributed to the book trade worldwide by Springer-Verlag New York, Inc., 233 Spring Street, 6th Floor, New York, NY 10013. Phone 1-800-SPRINGER, fax 201-348-4505, e-mail `orders-ny@springer-sbm.com`, or visit `http://www.springeronline.com`.

For information on translations, please contact Apress directly at 2855 Telegraph Avenue, Suite 600, Berkeley, CA 94705. Phone 510-549-5930, fax 510-549-5939, e-mail `info@apress.com`, or visit `http://www.apress.com`.

The source code for this book is available to readers at `http://www.apress.com` in the Source Code/Download section. You will need to answer questions pertaining to this book in order to successfully download the code.

This edition of the text is dedicated to Mikko the wonder cat, life at 412, and my wonderful wife, Amanda, who patiently waited for me to finish yet another book.

Contents

Part 1 ■ ■ ■ Introducing C# and the .NET Platform

Part 2 ■ ■ ■ Core C# Programming Constructs

Part 5 ■ ■ ■ Introducing the .NET Base Class Libraries

About the Author

ANDREW TROELSEN is a Microsoft MVP (Visual C#) and a partner, trainer, and consultant with Intertech Training (`http://www.Intertech.com`), a .NET and J2EE developer education center. He is the author of numerous books, including *Developer's Workshop to COM and ATL 3.0* (Wordware Publishing, 2000), *COM and .NET Interoperability* (Apress, 2002), *Visual Basic .NET and the .NET Platform: An Advanced Guide* (Apress, 2001), and the award-winning *C# and the .NET Platform* (Apress, 2003). Andrew has also authored numerous articles on .NET for MSDN online, DevX, and *MacTech*, and is frequently a speaker at various .NET conferences and user groups.

Andrew lives in Minneapolis, Minnesota, with his wife, Amanda. He spends his free time waiting for the Wild to win the Stanley Cup, but has given up all hope of the Vikings winning a Super Bowl and feels quite strongly that the Timberwolves will never get back to the playoffs until current management is replaced.

About the Technical Reviewer

GAVIN SMYTH is a professional software engineer with more years of experience in development than he cares to admit on projects ranging from device drivers to distributed web applications; under platforms as diverse as 8-bit "bare metal," embedded real-time operating systems, Unix, and Windows; and in languages including assembler, C++, Ada, and C#, among a good many others. He has worked for clients such as BT and Nortel, and is currently employed by Microsoft. Gavin has published a few pieces of technical prose in the past (*EXE*, where are you now?) but finds criticizing other people's work much more fulfilling. Beyond that, when he's not battling weeds and ants in the garden, he tries to persuade LEGO robots to do what he wants them to do (it's for the kids' benefit—honest).

Acknowledgments

While I might be the only name seen on the front of this book, this text would never be printed without the aid of numerous talented people. Allow me to offer some heartfelt words of thanks to the many, many people who made this book possible.

First and foremost, thanks to all of the people at Apress, whom I have had the pleasure of working with for many years now. You are all extremely talented people who do a wonderful job of transforming my original Word documents into polished prose. Thank you so much. Looking forward to working with you all on the next book (well, after I take a sanity break from this book).

Special thanks to my technical editor, Gavin, who has offered me many words of wisdom that I feel make this edition of the book better than ever. As always, any remaining typos or technical errors are my responsibility alone.

Last but not least, thanks to my family, friends, and coworkers who put up with my occasional grumpy demeanor, which sadly presented itself once or twice during the final phases of this manuscript.

Introduction

This book has existed (in one form or another) since the first edition of *C# and the .NET Platform* was published in conjunction with the release of .NET 1.0 Beta 2, circa the summer of 2001. Since that point, I have been extremely happy and grateful to see that this text was very well received by the press and, most important, by readers. Over the years it was nominated as a Jolt Award finalist (I lost . . . crap!) and for the 2003 Referenceware Excellence Award in the programming book category (I won? Cool!).

Since that point, I have worked to keep the book current with each release of the .NET platform, including a limited printing of a Special Edition, which introduced the technologies of .NET 3.0 (Windows Presentation Foundation, Windows Communication Foundation, and Windows Workflow Foundation) as well as offered previews of several forthcoming technologies, which we now know as LINQ.

The fourth edition of this text, which you hold in your hands, is a massive retelling of the previous manuscript to account for all of the major changes that are found within .NET 3.5. Not only will you find numerous brand-new chapters, you will find many of the previous chapters have been expanded in great detail.

As with the earlier editions, this edition presents the C# programming language and .NET base class libraries using a friendly and approachable tone. I have never understood the need some technical authors have to spit out prose that reads more like a GRE vocabulary study guide than a readable book. As well, this new edition remains focused on providing you with the information you need to build software solutions today, rather than spending too much time examining esoteric details that few individuals will ever actually care about.

We're a Team, You and I

Technology authors write for a demanding group of people (I should know—I'm one of them). You know that building software solutions using any platform (.NET, J2EE, COM, etc.) is extremely detailed and is very specific to your department, company, client base, and subject matter. Perhaps you work in the electronic publishing industry, develop systems for the state or local government, or work at NASA or a branch of the military. Speaking for myself, I have developed children's educational software, various n-tier systems, and projects within the medical and financial industries. The chances are almost 100 percent that the code you write at your place of employment has little to do with the code I write at mine (unless we happened to work together previously!).

Therefore, in this book, I have deliberately chosen to avoid creating examples that tie the example code to a specific industry or vein of programming. Given this, I explain C#, OOP, the CLR, and the .NET 3.5 base class libraries using industry-agnostic examples. Rather than having every blessed example fill a grid with data, calculate payroll, or whatnot, I'll stick to subject matter we can all relate to: automobiles (with some geometric structures and employees thrown in for good measure). And that's where you come in.

My job is to explain the C# programming language and the core aspects of the .NET platform the best I possibly can. As well, I will do everything I can to equip you with the tools and strategies you need to continue your studies at this book's conclusion.

Your job is to take this information and apply it to your specific programming assignments. I obviously understand that your projects most likely don't revolve around automobiles with pet names, but that's what applied knowledge is all about! Rest assured, once you understand the concepts presented within this text, you will be in a perfect position to build .NET solutions that map to your own unique programming environment.

An Overview of This Book

Pro C# 2008 and the .NET 3.5 Platform, Fourth Edition is logically divided into eight distinct parts, each of which contains a number of related chapters. If you have read the earlier editions of this text, you will quickly notice a number of changes. For example, several topics (such as core C# constructs, object-oriented programming, and platform-independent .NET development) have been expanded into several dedicated chapters. Furthermore, this edition of the text contains numerous new chapters to account for .NET 3.0–3.5 programming features (LINQ, WCF, WPF, WF, etc.). Here is a part-by-part and chapter-by-chapter breakdown of the text.

Part 1: Introducing C# and the .NET Platform

The purpose of Part 1 is to acclimate you to the nature of the .NET platform and various development tools (many of which are open source) used during the construction of .NET applications. Along the way, you will also check out some basic details of the C# programming language and the .NET type system.

Chapter 1: The Philosophy of .NET

This first chapter functions as the backbone for the remainder of the text. We begin by examining the world of traditional Windows development and uncover the shortcomings with the previous state of affairs. The primary goal of this chapter, however, is to acquaint you with a number of .NET-centric building blocks, such as the common language runtime (CLR), Common Type System (CTS), Common Language Specification (CLS), and base class libraries. Here, you will take an initial look at the C# programming language and the .NET assembly format, and get an overview the platform-independent nature of the .NET platform (Appendix B will examine this topic in greater detail).

Chapter 2: Building C# Applications

The goal of this chapter is to introduce you to the process of compiling C# source code files using various tools and techniques. First, you will learn how to make use of the command-line compiler (`csc.exe`) and C# response files. Over the remainder of the chapter, you will examine numerous code editors and integrated development environments (IDEs), including TextPad, Notepad++, SharpDevelop, Visual C# 2008 Express, and Visual Studio 2008. As well, you will be exposed to a number of additional programming tools that any .NET developer should have in their back pocket.

Part 2: Core C# Programming Constructs

The topics presented in this part of the book are quite important, as they will be used regardless of which type of .NET software you intend to develop (web applications, desktop GUI applications, code libraries, Windows services, etc.). Here, you will come to understand the core constructs of the C# language, including the details of object-oriented programming (OOP). As well, this part will examine how to process runtime exceptions and dive into the details of .NET's garbage collection services.

Chapter 3: Core C# Programming Constructs, Part I

This chapter begins your formal investigation of the C# programming language. Here you will learn about the role of the `Main()` method and numerous details regarding the intrinsic data types of the .NET platform, including the manipulation of textual data using `System.String` and `System.Text.StringBuilder`. You will also examine iteration and decision constructs, narrowing and widening operations, and use of the `unchecked` keyword.

Chapter 4: Core C# Programming Constructs, Part II

This chapter completes your examination of the core aspects of C#, beginning with the construction of overloaded type methods and defining parameters via the `out`, `ref`, and `params` keywords. You will also learn how to create and manipulate arrays of data, define nullable data types (with the ? and ?? operators), and understand the distinction between *value types* (including enumerations and custom structures) and *reference types*.

Chapter 5: Defining Encapsulated Class Types

This chapter begins your examination of object-oriented programming (OOP) using the C# programming language. Once we qualify the pillars of OOP (encapsulation, inheritance, and polymorphism), the remainder of this chapter will examine how to build robust class types using constructors, properties, static members, constants, and read-only fields. We wrap up with an examination of partial type definitions and C#'s XML code documentation syntax.

Chapter 6: Understanding Inheritance and Polymorphism

Here, you will examine the remaining pillars of OOP (inheritance and polymorphism), which allow you to build families of related class types. During this time, you will examine the role of virtual methods, abstract methods (and abstract base classes), and the nature of the *polymorphic interface*. Last but not least, this chapter will explain the role of the supreme base class of the .NET platform, `System.Object`.

Chapter 7: Understanding Structured Exception Handling

The point of this chapter is to discuss how to handle runtime anomalies in your code base through the use of structured exception handling. Not only will you learn about the C# keywords that allow you to handle such problems (`try`, `catch`, `throw`, and `finally`), but you will also come to understand the distinction between application-level and system-level exceptions. In addition, this chapter examines various tools within Visual Studio 2008 that allow you to debug the exceptions that have escaped your view.

Chapter 8: Understanding Object Lifetime

The final chapter of this part examines how the CLR manages memory using the .NET garbage collector. Here you will come to understand the role of application roots, object generations, and the `System.GC` type. Once you understand the basics, the remainder of this chapter covers the topics of *disposable objects* (via the `IDisposable` interface) and the finalization process (via the `System.Object.Finalize()` method).

Part 3: Advanced C# Programming Constructs

This section of the book will deepen your understanding of the C# language, by examining a number of more advanced (but very important) concepts. Here, you will complete your examination of the .NET type system by examining interfaces and delegates. As well, you will learn about the role of generics and the numerous new language features of C# 2008, and take an initial look at Language Integrated Query (LINQ).

Chapter 9: Working with Interfaces

The material in this chapter builds upon your understanding of object-based development by covering the topic of interface-based programming. Here, you will learn how to define types that support multiple behaviors, how to discover these behaviors at runtime, and how to selectively hide particular behaviors using *explicit interface implementation*. In addition to examining a number of predefined .NET interface types, you will also learn how to make use of custom interfaces to build an ad hoc event architecture.

Chapter 10: Collections and Generics

This chapter begins by examining the collection types of the `System.Collections` namespace, which has been part of the .NET platform since its initial release. However, since the release of .NET 2.0, the C# programming language offers support for *generics*. As you will see, generic programming greatly enhances application performance and type safety. Not only will you explore various generic types within the `System.Collections.Generic` namespace, but you will also learn how to build your own generic methods and types (with and without constraints).

Chapter 11: Delegates, Events, and Lambdas

The purpose of Chapter 11 is to demystify the *delegate* type. Simply put, a .NET delegate is an object that "points" to other methods in your application. Using this pattern, you are able to build systems that allow multiple objects to engage in a two-way conversation. After you have examined the use of .NET delegates, you will then be introduced to the C# `event` keyword, which is used to simplify the manipulation of raw delegate programming. You wrap up by investigating the role of the C# 2008 lambda operator (`=>`) and exploring the connection between delegates, anonymous methods, and lambda expressions.

Chapter 12: Indexers, Operators, and Pointers

This chapter deepens your understanding of the C# programming language by introducing a number of advanced programming techniques. Here, you will learn how to overload operators and create custom conversion routines (both implicit and explicit) for your types. As well, you will learn how to build and interact with *type indexers*, and manipulate C-style pointers using an "unsafe" code context.

Chapter 13: C# 2008 Language Features

With the release of .NET 3.5, the C# language has been enhanced to support a great number of new programming constructs, many of which are used to enable the LINQ API (which you will begin to examine in Chapter 14). Here, you will learn the role of implicit typing of local variables, partial methods, automatic properties, extension methods, anonymous types, and object initialization syntax.

Chapter 14: An Introduction to LINQ

This chapter will begin your examination of Language Integrated Query (LINQ), which could easily be considered the most intriguing aspect of .NET 3.5. As you will see in this chapter, LINQ allows you to build strongly typed *query expressions*, which can be applied to a number of LINQ targets to manipulate "data" in the broadest sense of the word. Here, you will learn about LINQ to Objects, which allows you to apply LINQ expressions to containers of data (arrays, collections, custom types). This information will serve you well when we examine how to apply LINQ expressions to relational databases (via LINQ to ADO) and XML documents (à la LINQ to XML) later in Chapter 24.

Part 4: Programming with .NET Assemblies

Part 4 dives into the details of the .NET assembly format. Not only will you learn how to deploy and configure .NET code libraries, but you will also come to understand the internal composition of a .NET binary image. This part also explains the role of .NET attributes and the construction of multithreaded applications. Later chapters examine some fairly advanced topics such as object context, CIL code, and dynamic assemblies.

Chapter 15: Introducing .NET Assemblies

From a very high level, *assembly* is the term used to describe a managed `*.dll` or `*.exe` binary file. However, the true story of .NET assemblies is far richer than that. Here you will learn the distinction between single-file and multifile assemblies, and how to build and deploy each entity. You'll examine how private and shared assemblies may be configured using XML-based `*.config` files and publisher policy assemblies. Along the way, you will investigate the internal structure of the global assembly cache (GAC) and the role of the .NET Framework configuration utility.

Chapter 16: Type Reflection, Late Binding, and Attribute-Based Programming

Chapter 16 continues our examination of .NET assemblies by checking out the process of runtime type discovery via the `System.Reflection` namespace. Using these types, you are able to build applications that can read an assembly's metadata on the fly. You will learn how to dynamically load and create types at runtime using *late binding*. The final topic of this chapter explores the role of .NET attributes (both standard and custom). To illustrate the usefulness of each of these topics, the chapter concludes with the construction of an extendable Windows Forms application.

Chapter 17: Processes, AppDomains, and Object Contexts

Now that you have a solid understanding of assemblies, this chapter dives deeper into the composition of a loaded .NET executable. The goal of this chapter is to illustrate the relationship between processes, application domains, and contextual boundaries. These topics provide the proper foundation for the topic of the following chapter, where we examine the construction of multithreaded applications.

Chapter 18: Building Multithreaded Applications

This chapter examines how to build multithreaded applications and illustrates a number of techniques you can use to author thread-safe code. The chapter opens by revisiting the .NET delegate type in order to understand a delegate's intrinsic support for asynchronous method invocations. Next, you will investigate the types within the `System.Threading` namespace. You will look at numerous types (`Thread`, `ThreadStart`, etc.) that allow you to easily create additional threads of execution. We wrap up by examining the `BackgroundWorker` type, which greatly simplifies the creation of threads from within a desktop user interface.

Chapter 19: Understanding CIL and the Role of Dynamic Assemblies

The goal of the final chapter of this part is twofold. In the first half (more or less), you will examine the syntax and semantics of CIL in much greater detail than in previous chapters. The remainder of this chapter covers the role of the `System.Reflection.Emit` namespace. Using these types, you are able to build software that is capable of generating .NET assemblies in memory at runtime. Formally speaking, assemblies defined and executed in memory are termed *dynamic assemblies*.

Part 5: Introducing the .NET Base Class Libraries

By this point in the text, you have a solid handle on the C# language and the details of the .NET assembly format. Part 5 leverages your newfound knowledge by exploring a number of commonly used services found within the base class libraries, including file I/O and database access using ADO.NET. This part also covers the construction of distributed applications using Windows Communication Foundation (WCF) and workflow-enabled applications that make use of the Windows Workflow Foundation (WF) API.

Chapter 20: File I/O and Isolated Storage

The `System.IO` namespace allows you to interact with a machine's file and directory structure. Over the course of this chapter, you will learn how to programmatically create (and destroy) a directory system as well as move data into and out of various streams (file based, string based, memory based, etc.). The latter part of this chapter examines the role of *isolated storage*, which allows you to persist per-user data into a safe sandbox, regardless of the security settings of a target machine. To understand certain aspects of the `System.IO.IsolatedStorage` API, you will also receive an overview of Code Access Security (CAS).

Chapter 21: Introducing Object Serialization

This chapter examines the object serialization services of the .NET platform. Simply put, *serialization* allows you to persist the state of an object (or a set of related objects) into a stream for later use. *Deserialization* (as you might expect) is the process of plucking an object from the stream into memory for consumption by your application. Once you understand the basics, you will then learn how to customize the serialization process via the `ISerializable` interface and a set of .NET attributes.

Chapter 22: ADO.NET Part I: The Connected Layer

In this first of two database-centric chapters, you will learn about the ADO.NET programming API. Specifically, this chapter will introduce the role of .NET data providers and how to communicate with a relational database using the *connected layer* of ADO.NET, represented by connection objects, command objects, transaction objects, and data reader objects. Be aware that this chapter will also walk you through the creation of a custom database and a data access library that will be used throughout the remainder of this text.

Chapter 23: ADO.NET Part II: The Disconnected Layer

This chapter continues your study of database manipulation by examining the *disconnected layer* of ADO.NET. Here, you will learn the role of the `DataSet` type, data adapter objects, and numerous tools of Visual Studio 2008 that can greatly simplify the creation of data-driven applications. Along the way, you will learn how to bind `DataTable` objects to user interface elements, such as the `GridView` type of the Windows Forms API.

Chapter 24: Programming with the LINQ APIs

Chapter 14 introduced you to the LINQ programming model, specifically LINQ to Objects. Here, you will deepen your understanding of Language Integrated Query by examining how to apply LINQ queries to relational databases, `DataSet` objects, and XML documents. Along the way, you will learn the role of data context objects, the `sqlmetal.exe` utility, and various LINQ-specific aspects of Visual Studio 2008.

Chapter 25: Introducing Windows Communication Foundation

.NET 3.0 introduced a brand-new API, WCF, that allows you to build distributed applications, regardless of their underlying plumbing, in a symmetrical manner. This chapter will expose you to the construction of WCF services, hosts, and clients. As you will see, WCF services are extremely flexible, in that clients and hosts can leverage XML-based configuration files to declaratively specify addresses, bindings, and contracts.

Chapter 26: Introducing Windows Workflow Foundation

In addition to WCF, .NET 3.0 also introduced an API, WF, that allows you to define, execute, and monitor *workflows* to model complex business processes. Here, you will learn the overall purpose of Windows Workflow Foundation, as well as the role of activities, workflow designers, the workflow runtime engine, and the creation of workflow-enabled code libraries.

Part 6: Desktop User Interfaces

It is a common misconception for newcomers to the .NET platform to assume this framework is only concerned with the construction of web-based user interfaces (which I suspect is due to the term ".NET," as this tends to conjure up the notion of the "Internet" and therefore "web programs"). While it is true that .NET provides outstanding support for the construction of web applications, this part of the book focuses on traditional desktop user interfaces using two GUI frameworks, Windows Forms and Windows Presentation Foundation (WPF).

Chapter 27: Programming with Windows Forms

The original desktop GUI toolkit that shipped with the .NET platform is termed *Windows Forms*. This chapter will walk you through the role of this UI framework, and illustrate how to build main windows, dialog boxes, and menu systems. As well, you will understand the role of form inheritance and see how to render 2D graphical data using the `System.Drawing` namespace. To illustrate these topics using a cohesive example, we wrap up by building a (semicapable) painting application.

Chapter 28: Introducing Windows Presentation Foundation and XAML

.NET 3.0 introduced a brand-new GUI toolkit termed *WPF*. Essentially, WPF allows you to build extremely interactive and media-rich front ends for desktop applications (and indirectly, web applications). Unlike Windows Forms, this supercharged UI framework integrates a number of key services (2D and 3D graphics, animations, rich documents, etc.) into a single unified object model. In this chapter, you will begin your examination of WPF and the Extendable Application Markup Language (XAML). Here, you will learn how to build WPF programs XAML-free, using nothing but XAML, and a combination of each. We wrap up by building a custom XAML viewer, which will be used during the remainder of the WPF-centric chapters.

Chapter 29: Programming with WPF Controls

In this chapter, you will learn how to work with the WPF control content model as well as a number of related control-centric topics such as dependency properties and routed events. As you would hope, this chapter provides coverage of working with a number of WPF controls; however, more interestingly, this chapter will explain the use of layout managers, control commands, and the WPF data-binding model.

Chapter 30: WPF 2D Graphical Rendering, Resources, and Themes

The final chapter of this part will wrap up your examination of WPF by examining three seemingly independent topics. However, as you will see, WPF's graphical rendering services typically require you to define custom resources. Using these resources, you are able to generate custom WPF animations, and using graphics, resources, and animations, you are able to build custom themes for a WPF application. To pull all of these topics together, this chapter wraps up by illustrating how to apply custom graphical themes at runtime.

Part 7: Building Web Applications with ASP.NET

Part 7 is devoted to the examination of constructing web applications using the ASP.NET programming API. As you will see, ASP.NET was intentionally designed to model the creation of desktop user interfaces by layering on top of standard HTTP request/response an event-driven, object-oriented framework.

Chapter 31: Building ASP.NET Web Pages

This chapter begins your study of web application development using ASP.NET. As you will see, server-side scripting code has now been replaced with real object-oriented languages (such as C#, VB .NET, and the like). This chapter will examine the construction of an ASP.NET web page, the underlying programming model, and other key aspects of ASP.NET, such as your choice of web server and the use of `Web.config` files.

Chapter 32: ASP.NET Web Controls, Themes, and Master Pages

Whereas the previous chapter examined the construction of ASP.NET `Page` objects, this chapter is concerned with the controls that populate the internal control tree. Here, you will examine the core ASP.NET web controls, including validation controls, the intrinsic site navigation controls, and various data-binding operations. As well, this chapter will illustrate the role of *master pages* and the ASP.NET theme engine, which is a server-side alternative to traditional style sheets.

Chapter 33: ASP.NET State Management Techniques

This chapter extends your current understanding of ASP.NET by examining various ways to handle state management under .NET. Like classic ASP, ASP.NET allows you to easily create cookies, as well as application-level and session-level variables. However, ASP.NET also introduces a new state management technique: the application cache. Once you have looked at the numerous ways to handle state with ASP.NET, you will then come to learn the role of the `System.HttpApplication` base class (lurking within the `Global.asax` file) and how to dynamically alter the runtime behavior of your web application using the `Web.config` file.

Part 8: Appendixes

This final part of this book examines two important topics, which quite frankly did not seem to fit naturally within the bulk of the text, and have therefore been "appendix-ized." Here you will complete your examination of C# and the .NET platform by learning how to integrate legacy code into your .NET applications as well as how to take .NET development beyond the Windows family of operating systems.

Appendix A: COM and .NET Interoperability

If you have programmed the Windows operating system prior to using .NET, you are most likely aware of the Component Object Model (COM). While COM and .NET have nothing to do with each other (beyond the fact that they each originated from Microsoft), the .NET platform has an entire namespace (`System.Runtime.InteropServices`) that makes it possible for .NET software to make use of legacy COM components and vice versa. This appendix will examine the interoperability layer in quite a bit of detail, as this topic is quite important when looking for ways to leverage your existing code base as you build new .NET applications.

Appendix B: Platform-Independent .NET Development with Mono

Last but not least, Appendix B covers the use of an open source implementation of the .NET platform named *Mono*. Using Mono, it is possible to build feature-rich .NET applications that can be created, deployed, and executed upon a variety of operating systems, including Mac OS X, Solaris, AIX, and numerous Linux distributions. Given that Mono is largely comparable with Microsoft's .NET platform, you already know most of what Mono has to offer. Therefore, this appendix will focus on the Mono installation process, Mono development tools, and Mono runtime engine.

Diving Even Deeper with Five Free Chapters

As if a grand total of thirty-three chapters and two appendixes were not enough, those of you who purchase this book are eligible to download an additional five chapters for free. As you may be aware, previous editions of this text included three chapters devoted to Windows Forms development (including an examination of custom controls), another chapter that addressed the .NET remoting layer (`System.Runtime.Remoting` and friends), and a final chapter covering the construction of traditional XML web services using the ASP.NET Web Service project template.

This edition of the text does not provide printed versions of these five chapters. The major reason for doing so is due to the fact that the .NET 3.0 WCF and WPF APIs are poised to become the heirs apparent to .NET remoting/XML web services and Windows Forms APIs, respectively. If you wish to dig deeper into Windows Forms (beyond what is provided in Chapter 27) or to see how to make use of the (legacy?) .NET remoting and XML web service APIs, simply look up this book from the Apress website:

`http://apress.com/book/view/1590598849`

There you will find a link to download this book's supplemental chapters in a digital format, once you answer randomly generated questions regarding the text within this book.

Obtaining This Book's Source Code

All of the code examples contained within this book (including the five additional chapters that may be downloaded for free, as mentioned in the previous section) are available for free and immediate download from the Source Code/Download area of the Apress website. Simply navigate to `http://www.apress.com`, select the Source Code/Download link, and look up this title by name. Once you are on the home page for *Pro C# 2008 and the .NET 3.5 Platform, Fourth Edition*, you may download a self-extracting `*.zip` file. After you unzip the contents, you will find that the code has been logically divided by chapter.

Do be aware that Source Code notes like the following in the chapters are your cue that the example under discussion may be loaded into Visual Studio 2008 for further examination and modification:

Source Code This is a source code note referring you to a specific directory!

To do so, simply open the `*.sln` file found in the correct subdirectory. If you are not making use of Visual Studio 2008 (see Chapter 2 for additional IDEs), you can manually load the provided source code files into your development tool of choice.

Obtaining Updates for This Book

As you read through this text, you may find an occasional grammatical or code error (although I sure hope not). If this is the case, my apologies. Being human, I am sure that a glitch or two may be present, despite my best efforts. If this is the case, you can obtain the current errata list from the Apress website (located once again on the home page for this book) as well as information on how to notify me of any errors you might find.

Contacting Me

If you have any questions regarding this book's source code, are in need of clarification for a given example, or simply wish to offer your thoughts regarding the .NET platform, feel free to drop me a line at the following e-mail address (to ensure your messages don't end up in my junk mail folder, please include "C# FE" in the Subject line somewhere): `atroelsen@Intertech.com`.

Please understand that I will do my best to get back to you in a timely fashion; however, like yourself, I get busy from time to time. If I don't respond within a week or two, do know I am not trying to be a jerk or don't care to talk to you. I'm just busy (or, if I'm lucky, on vacation somewhere).

So, then! Thanks for buying this text (or at least looking at it in the bookstore while you try to decide if you will buy it). I hope you enjoy reading this book and putting your newfound knowledge to good use.

Take care,
Andrew Troelsen

PART 1

Introducing C# and the .NET Platform

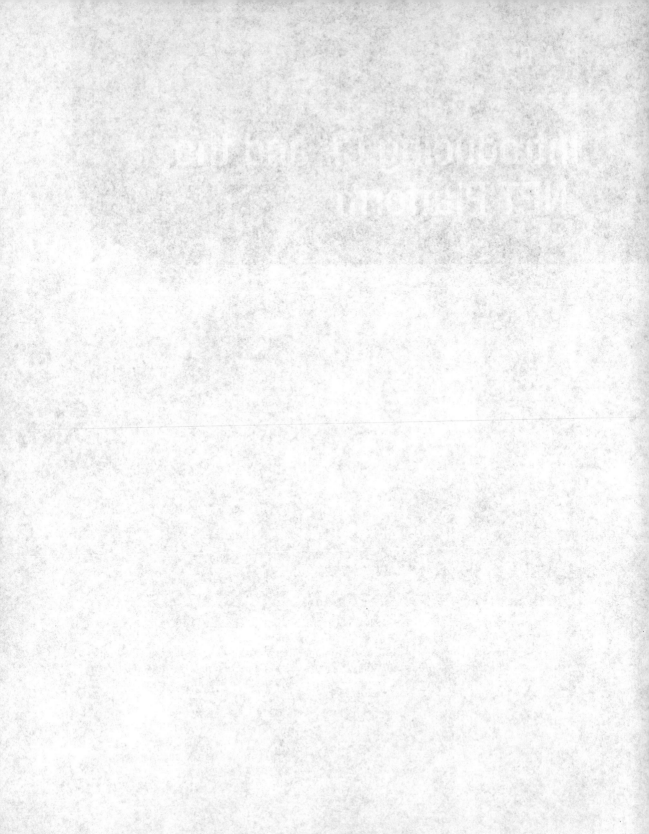

CHAPTER 1

The Philosophy of .NET

Every few years or so, the modern-day programmer must be willing to perform a self-inflicted knowledge transplant to stay current with the new technologies of the day. The languages (C++, Visual Basic 6.0, Java), frameworks (OWL, MFC, ATL, STL), architectures (COM, CORBA, EJB), and APIs (such as .NET's Windows Forms and GDI+ libraries) that were touted as the silver bullets of software development eventually become overshadowed by something better or at the very least something new. Regardless of the frustration you can feel when upgrading your internal knowledge base, it is frankly unavoidable. To this end, the goal of this book is to examine the details of Microsoft's current offering within the landscape of software engineering: the .NET platform and the C# programming language.

The point of this chapter is to lay the conceptual groundwork for the remainder of the book. Here you will find a high-level discussion of a number of .NET-related topics such as assemblies, the common intermediate language (CIL), and just-in-time (JIT) compilation. In addition to previewing some key features of the C# programming language, you will also come to understand the relationship between various aspects of the .NET Framework, such as the common language runtime (CLR), the Common Type System (CTS), and the Common Language Specification (CLS).

This chapter also provides you with a survey of the functionality supplied by the .NET base class libraries, sometimes abbreviated as the BCL or alternatively as the FCL (being the Framework class libraries). Finally, this chapter overviews the language-agnostic and platform-independent nature of the .NET platform (yes it's true, .NET is not confined to the Windows operating system). As you would hope, all of these topics are explored in further detail throughout the remainder of this text.

Understanding the Previous State of Affairs

Before examining the specifics of the .NET universe, it's helpful to consider some of the issues that motivated the genesis of Microsoft's current platform. To get in the proper mind-set, let's begin this chapter with a brief and painless history lesson to remember our roots and understand the limitations of the previous state of affairs (after all, admitting you have a problem is the first step toward finding a solution). After completing this quick tour of life as we knew it, we turn our attention to the numerous benefits provided by C# and the .NET platform.

Life As a C/Win32 API Programmer

Traditionally speaking, developing software for the Windows family of operating systems involved using the C programming language in conjunction with the Windows application programming interface (API). While it is true that numerous applications have been successfully created using this time-honored approach, few of us would disagree that building applications using the raw API is a complex undertaking.

The first obvious problem is that C is a very terse language. C developers are forced to contend with manual memory management, ugly pointer arithmetic, and ugly syntactical constructs. Furthermore, given that C is a structured language, it lacks the benefits provided by the object-oriented approach (can anyone say *spaghetti code*?). When you combine the thousands of global functions and data types defined by the Win32 API to an already formidable language, it is little wonder that there are so many buggy applications floating around today.

Life As a C++/MFC Programmer

One vast improvement over raw C/API development is the use of the C++ programming language. In many ways, C++ can be thought of as an object-oriented *layer* on top of C. Thus, even though C++ programmers benefit from the famed "pillars of OOP" (encapsulation, inheritance, and polymorphism), they are still at the mercy of the painful aspects of the C language (e.g., manual memory management, ugly pointer arithmetic, and ugly syntactical constructs).

Despite its complexity, many C++ frameworks exist today. For example, the Microsoft Foundation Classes (MFC) provide the developer with a set of C++ classes that facilitate the construction of Win32 applications. The main role of MFC is to wrap a "sane subset" of the raw Win32 API behind a number of classes, magic macros, and numerous code-generation tools (a.k.a. *wizards*). Regardless of the helpful assistance offered by the MFC framework (as well as many other C++-based windowing toolkits), the fact of the matter is that C++ programming remains a difficult and error-prone experience, given its historical roots in C.

Life As a Visual Basic 6.0 Programmer

Due to a heartfelt desire to enjoy a simpler lifestyle, many programmers have shifted away from the world of C(++)-based frameworks to kinder, gentler languages such as Visual Basic 6.0 (VB6). VB6 is popular due to its ability to build complex user interfaces, code libraries (e.g., COM servers), and data access logic with minimal fuss and bother. Even more than MFC, VB6 hides the complexities of the raw Win32 API from view using a number of integrated code wizards, intrinsic data types, classes, and VB-specific functions.

The major downfall of VB6 (which has been rectified given the advent of the .NET platform) is that it is not a fully object-oriented language; rather, it is "object aware." For example, VB6 does not allow the programmer to establish "is-a" relationships between types (i.e., no classical inheritance) and has no intrinsic support for parameterized class construction. Moreover, VB6 doesn't provide the ability to build multithreaded applications unless you are willing to drop down to low-level Win32 API calls (which is complex at best and dangerous at worst).

Life As a Java/J2EE Programmer

Enter Java. Java is an object-oriented programming language that has its syntactic roots in C++. As many of you are aware, Java's strengths are far greater than its support for platform independence. Java (as a language) cleans up many unsavory syntactical aspects of C++. Java (as a platform) provides programmers with a large number of predefined "packages" that contain various type definitions. Using these types, Java programmers are able to build "100% Pure Java" applications complete with database connectivity, messaging support, web-enabled front ends, and a rich desktop user interface.

Although Java is a very elegant language, one potential problem is that using Java typically means that you must use Java front-to-back during the development cycle. In effect, Java offers little hope of language integration, as this goes against the grain of Java's primary goal (a single programming language for every need). In reality, however, there are millions of lines of existing code out there in the world that would ideally like to commingle with newer Java code. Sadly, Java makes this task problematic. While Java does provide a limited ability to access non-Java APIs, there is little support for true cross-language integration.

Life As a COM Developer

The Component Object Model (COM) was Microsoft's previous application development framework. COM is an architecture that says in effect, "If you build your classes in accordance with the rules of COM, you end up with a block of *reusable binary code*."

The beauty of a binary COM server is that it can be accessed in a language-independent manner. Thus, C++ programmers can build COM classes that can be used by VB6. Delphi programmers can use COM classes built using C, and so forth. However, as you may be aware, COM's language independence is somewhat limited. For example, there is no way to derive a new COM class using an existing COM class (as COM has no support for classical inheritance). Rather, you must make use of the more cumbersome "has-a" relationship to reuse COM class types.

Another benefit of COM is its location-transparent nature. Using constructs such as application identifiers (AppIDs), stubs, proxies, and the COM runtime environment, programmers can avoid the need to work with raw sockets, RPC calls, and other low-level details. For example, consider the following VB6 COM client code:

```
' The MyCOMClass type could be written in
' any COM-aware language, and may be located anywhere
' on the network (including your local machine).
Dim obj as MyCOMClass
Set obj = New MyCOMClass    ' Location resolved using AppID.
obj.DoSomeWork
```

Although COM can be considered a very successful object model, it is extremely complex under the hood (at least until you have spent many months exploring its plumbing—especially if you happen to be a C++ programmer). To help simplify the development of COM binaries, numerous COM-aware frameworks have come into existence. For example, the Active Template Library (ATL) provides another set of C++ classes, templates, and macros to ease the creation of COM types.

Many other languages also hide a good part of the COM infrastructure from view. However, language support alone is not enough to hide the complexity of COM. Even when you choose a relatively simply COM-aware language such as VB6, you are still forced to contend with fragile registration entries and numerous deployment-related issues (collectively, and somewhat comically, termed *DLL hell*).

Life As a Windows DNA Programmer

To further complicate matters, there is a little thing called the Internet. Over the last several years, Microsoft has been adding more Internet-aware features into its family of operating systems and products. Sadly, building a web application using COM-based Windows Distributed interNet Applications Architecture (DNA) is also quite complex.

Some of this complexity is due to the simple fact that Windows DNA requires the use of numerous technologies and languages (ASP, HTML, XML, JScript, VBScript, and COM[+], as well as a data access API such as ADO). One problem is that many of these technologies are completely unrelated from a syntactic point of view. For example, JScript has a syntax much like C, while VBScript is a subset of VB6. The COM servers that are created to run under the COM+ runtime have an entirely different look and feel from the ASP pages that invoke them. The result is a highly confused mishmash of technologies.

Furthermore, and perhaps more important, each language and/or technology has its own type system (that may look nothing like another's type system). Beyond the fact that each API ships with its own collection of prefabricated code, even basic data types cannot always be treated identically. A `CComBSTR` in ATL is not quite the same as a `String` in VB6, both of which have nothing to do with a `char*` in C.

The .NET Solution

So much for the brief history lesson. The bottom line is that life as a Windows programmer has been tough. The .NET Framework is a rather radical and brute-force approach to making our lives easier. The solution proposed by .NET is "Change everything" (sorry, you can't blame the messenger for the message). As you will see during the remainder of this book, the .NET Framework is a completely new model for building systems on the Windows family of operating systems, as well as on numerous non-Microsoft operating systems such as Mac OS X and various Unix/Linux distributions. To set the stage, here is a quick rundown of some core features provided courtesy of .NET:

- *Comprehensive interoperability with existing code*: This is (of course) a good thing. Existing COM binaries can commingle (i.e., interop) with newer .NET binaries and vice versa. Also, Platform Invocation Services (PInvoke) allows you to call C-based libraries (including the underlying API of the operating system) from .NET code.
- *Complete and total language integration*: .NET supports cross-language inheritance, cross-language exception handling, and cross-language debugging of code.
- *A common runtime engine shared by all .NET-aware languages*: One aspect of this engine is a well-defined set of types that each .NET-aware language "understands."
- *A comprehensive base class library*: This library provides shelter from the complexities of raw API calls and offers a consistent object model used by all .NET-aware languages.
- *No more COM plumbing*: `IClassFactory`, `IUnknown`, `IDispatch`, IDL code, and the evil variant-compliant data types (`BSTR`, `SAFEARRAY`, and so forth) have no place in a .NET binary.
- *A truly simplified deployment model*: Under .NET, there is no need to register a binary unit into the system registry. Furthermore, .NET allows multiple versions of the same `*.dll` to exist in harmony on a single machine.

As you can most likely gather from the previous bullet points, the .NET platform has nothing to do with COM (beyond the fact that both frameworks originated from Microsoft). In fact, the only way .NET and COM types can interact with each other is using the interoperability layer.

■ **Note** Coverage of the .NET interoperability layer can be found in Appendix A.

Introducing the Building Blocks of the .NET Platform (the CLR, CTS, and CLS)

Now that you know some of the benefits provided by .NET, let's preview three key (and interrelated) entities that make it all possible: the CLR, CTS, and CLS. From a programmer's point of view, .NET can be understood as a runtime environment and a comprehensive base class library. The runtime layer is properly referred to as the *common language runtime*, or *CLR*. The primary role of the CLR is to locate, load, and manage .NET types on your behalf. The CLR also takes care of a number of low-level details such as memory management; creating application domains, threads, and object context boundaries; and performing various security checks.

Another building block of the .NET platform is the *Common Type System*, or *CTS*. The CTS specification fully describes all possible data types and programming constructs supported by the runtime, specifies how these entities can interact with each other, and details how they are represented in the .NET metadata format (more information on metadata later in this chapter; see Chapter 16 for complete details).

Understand that a given .NET-aware language might not support each and every feature defined by the CTS. The *Common Language Specification* (*CLS*) is a related specification that defines a subset of common types and programming constructs that all .NET programming languages can agree on. Thus, if you build .NET types that only expose CLS-compliant features, you can rest assured that all .NET-aware languages can consume them. Conversely, if you make use of a data type or programming construct that is outside of the bounds of the CLS, you cannot guarantee that every .NET programming language can interact with your .NET code library.

The Role of the Base Class Libraries

In addition to the CLR and CTS/CLS specifications, the .NET platform provides a base class library that is available to all .NET programming languages. Not only does this base class library encapsulate various primitives such as threads, file input/output (I/O), graphical rendering, and interaction with various external hardware devices, but it also provides support for a number of services required by most real-world applications.

For example, the base class libraries define types that facilitate database access, manipulation of XML documents, programmatic security, and the construction of web-enabled (as well as traditional desktop and console-based) front ends. From a high level, you can visualize the relationship between the CLR, CTS, CLS, and the base class library, as shown in Figure 1-1.

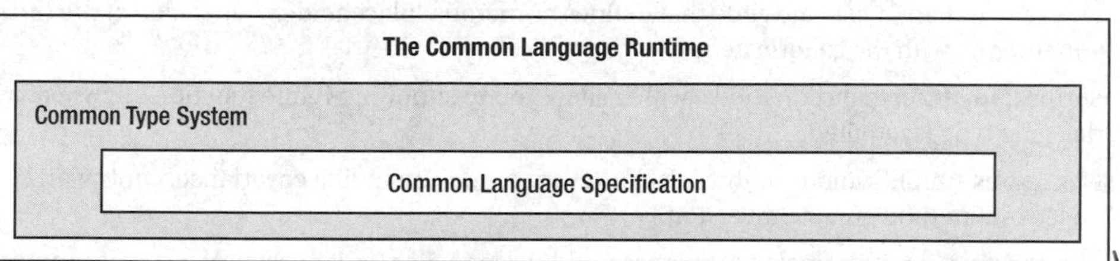

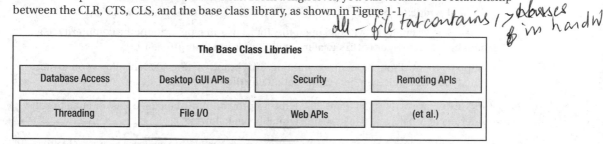

Figure 1-1. *The CLR, CTS, CLS, and base class library relationship*

What C# Brings to the Table

Given that .NET is such a radical departure from previous technologies, Microsoft crafted a new programming language, C# (pronounced "see sharp"), specifically for this new platform. C# is a programming language whose core syntax looks *very* similar to the syntax of Java. However, to call C# a

Java rip-off is inaccurate. Both C# and Java are members of the C family of programming languages (C, Objective C, C++, etc.) and therefore share a similar syntax. Just as Java is in many ways a cleaned-up version of C++, C# can be viewed as a cleaned-up version of Java.

The truth of the matter is that many of C#'s syntactic constructs are modeled after various aspects of Visual Basic 6.0 and C++. For example, like VB6, C# supports the notion of formal type properties (as opposed to traditional getter and setter methods) and the ability to declare methods taking a varying number of arguments (via parameter arrays). Like C++, C# allows you to overload operators, as well as to create structures, enumerations, and callback functions (via delegates).

■ **Note** As you will see in Chapter 13, C# 2008 has adopted a number of constructs traditionally found in various functional languages (e.g., LISP or Haskell). Furthermore, with the advent of LINQ (see Chapters 14 and 24), C# supports a number of programming constructs that make it quite unique in the programming landscape. Nevertheless, the crux of C# is indeed influenced by C-based languages.

Due to the fact that C# is a hybrid of numerous languages, the result is a product that is as syntactically clean—if not cleaner—than Java, is about as simple as VB6, and provides just about as much power and flexibility as C++ (without the associated ugly bits). Here is a partial list of core C# features that are found in all versions of the language:

- No pointers required! C# programs typically have no need for direct pointer manipulation (although you are free to drop down to that level if absolutely necessary).
- Automatic memory management through garbage collection. Given this, C# does not support a `delete` keyword.
- Formal syntactic constructs for classes, interfaces, structures, enumerations, and delegates.
- The C++-like ability to overload operators for a custom type, without the complexity (e.g., making sure to "return `*this` to allow chaining" is not your problem).
- Support for attribute-based programming. This brand of development allows you to annotate types and their members to further qualify their behavior.

With the release of .NET 2.0 (circa 2005), the C# programming language was updated to support numerous new bells and whistles, most notably the following:

- The ability to build generic types and generic members. Using generics, you are able to build very efficient and type-safe code that defines numerous "placeholders" specified at the time you interact with the generic item.
- Support for anonymous methods, which allow you to supply an inline function anywhere a delegate type is required.
- Numerous simplifications to the delegate/event model, including covariance, contravariance, and method group conversion.
- The ability to define a single type across multiple code files (or if necessary, as an in-memory representation) using the `partial` keyword.

As you might guess, .NET 3.5 adds even more functionality to the C# programming language (C# 2008, to be exact), including the following features:

- Support for strongly typed queries (a la LINQ, or Language Integrated Query) used to interact with various forms of data
- Support for anonymous types, which allow you to model the "shape" of a type rather than its behavior
- The ability to extend the functionality of an existing type using extension methods
- Inclusion of a lambda operator (=>), which even further simplifies working with .NET delegate types
- A new object initialization syntax, which allows you to set property values at the time of object creation

Perhaps the most important point to understand about the C# language is that it can only produce code that can execute within the .NET runtime (you could never use C# to build a native COM server or an unmanaged Win32 API application). Officially speaking, the term used to describe the code targeting the .NET runtime is *managed code*. The binary unit that contains the managed code is termed an *assembly* (more details on assemblies in just a bit in the section "An Overview of .NET Assemblies"). Conversely, code that cannot be directly hosted by the .NET runtime is termed *unmanaged code*.

Additional .NET-Aware Programming Languages

Understand that C# is not the only language that can be used to build .NET applications. When the .NET platform was first revealed to the general public during the 2000 Microsoft Professional Developers Conference (PDC), several vendors announced they were busy building .NET-aware versions of their respective compilers.

Since that point, dozens of different languages have undergone .NET enlightenment. In addition to the five languages that ship with the Microsoft .NET Framework 3.5 SDK (C#, Visual Basic .NET, J#, C++/CLI [previously termed "Managed Extensions for C++"], and JScript .NET), there are .NET compilers for Smalltalk, COBOL, and Pascal (to name a few). Although this book focuses (almost) exclusively on C#, be aware of the following website (please note that this URL is subject to change):

```
http://www.dotnetlanguages.net
```

If you click the Resources link at the top of the homepage, you will find a list of numerous .NET programming languages and related links where you are able to download various compilers (see Figure 1-2).

While I assume you are primarily interested in building .NET programs using the syntax of C#, I encourage you to visit this site, as you are sure to find many .NET languages worth investigating at your leisure (LISP .NET, anyone?).

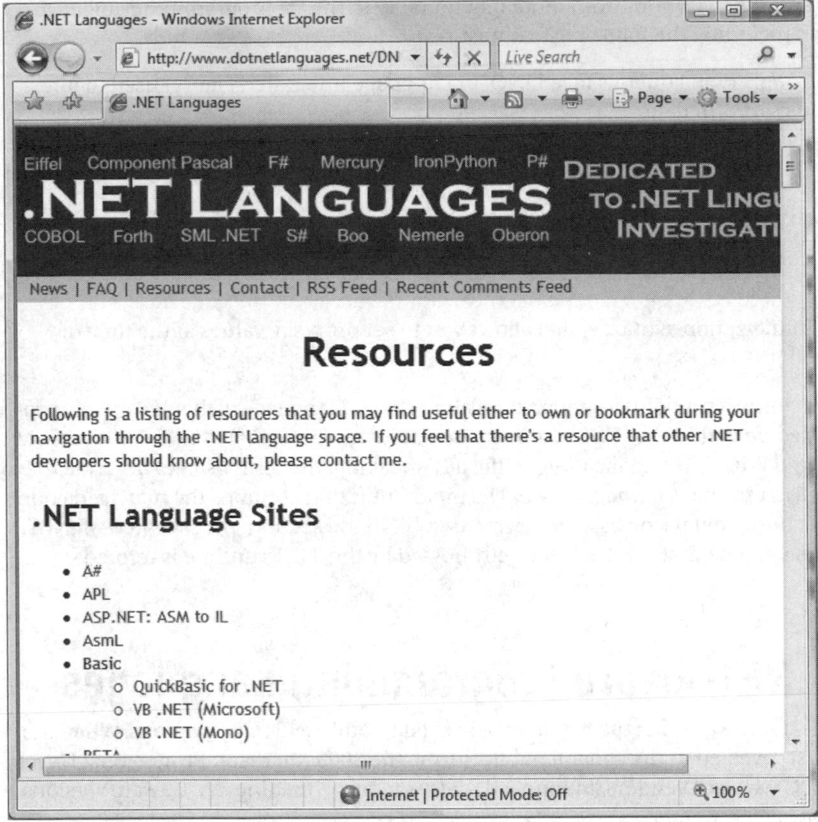

Figure 1-2. *www.DotNetLanguages.net is one of many sites documenting known .NET programming languages.*

Life in a Multilanguage World

As developers first come to understand the language-agnostic nature of .NET, numerous questions arise. The most prevalent of these questions would have to be, "If all .NET languages compile down to 'managed code,' why do we need more than one compiler?" There are a number of ways to answer this question. First, we programmers are a *very* particular lot when it comes to our choice of programming language (myself included). Some of us prefer languages full of semicolons and curly brackets, with as few language keywords as possible. Others enjoy a language that offers more "human-readable" syntactic tokens (such as Visual Basic). Still others may want to leverage their mainframe skills while moving to the .NET platform (via COBOL .NET).

Now, be honest. If Microsoft were to build a single "official" .NET language that was derived from the BASIC family of languages, can you really say all programmers would be happy with this choice? Or, if the only "official" .NET language was based on Fortran syntax, imagine all the folks out there who would ignore .NET altogether. Because the .NET runtime couldn't care less which language was used to build a block of managed code, .NET programmers can stay true to their syntactic preferences, and share the compiled assemblies among teammates, departments, and external organizations (regardless of which .NET language others choose to use).

Another excellent byproduct of integrating various .NET languages into a single unified software solution is the simple fact that all programming languages have their own sets of strengths and weaknesses. For example, some programming languages offer excellent intrinsic support for advanced mathematical processing. Others offer superior support for financial calculations, logical calculations, interaction with mainframe computers, and so forth. When you take the strengths of a particular programming language and then incorporate the benefits provided by the .NET platform, everybody wins.

Of course, in reality the chances are quite good that you will spend much of your time building software using your .NET language of choice. However, once you master the syntax of one .NET language, it is very easy to learn another. This is also quite beneficial, especially to the software consultants of the world. If your language of choice happens to be C#, but you are placed at a client site that has committed to Visual Basic .NET, you are still able to leverage the functionality of the .NET Framework, and you should be able to understand the overall structure of the code base with minimal fuss and bother. Enough said.

An Overview of .NET Assemblies

Regardless of which .NET language you choose to program with, understand that despite the fact that .NET binaries take the same file extension as COM servers and unmanaged Win32 binaries (`*.dll` or `*.exe`), they have absolutely no internal similarities. For example, `*.dll` .NET binaries do not export methods to facilitate communications with the COM runtime (given that .NET is *not* COM). Furthermore, .NET binaries are not described using COM type libraries and are not registered into the system registry. Perhaps most important, .NET binaries do not contain platform-specific instructions, but rather platform-agnostic *intermediate language* (*IL*) and type metadata. Figure 1-3 shows the big picture of the story thus far.

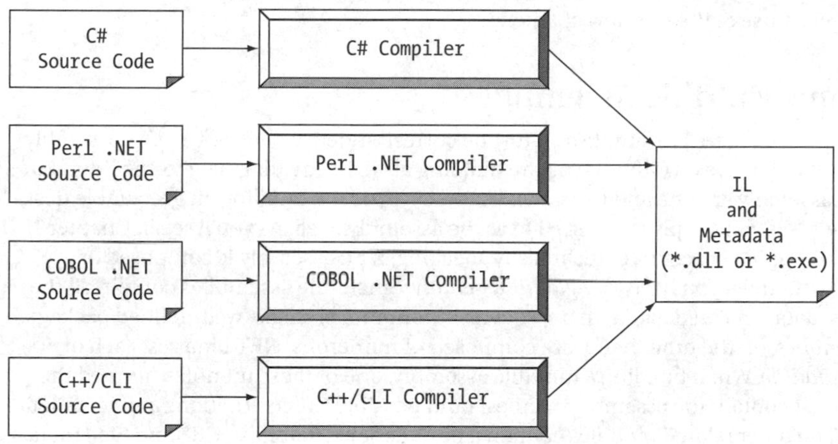

Figure 1-3. *All .NET-aware compilers emit IL instructions and metadata.*

■ **Note** There is one point to be made regarding the abbreviation "IL." During the development of .NET, the official term for IL was Microsoft intermediate language (MSIL). However with the final release of .NET, the term was changed to common intermediate language (CIL). Thus, as you read the .NET literature, understand that IL, MSIL, and CIL are all describing the same exact entity. In keeping with the current terminology, I will use the abbreviation "CIL" throughout this text.

When a *.dll or an *.exe has been created using a .NET-aware compiler, the resulting module is bundled into an *assembly*. You will examine numerous details of .NET assemblies in Chapter 15. However, to facilitate the discussion of the .NET runtime environment, you do need to understand some basic properties of this new file format.

As mentioned, an assembly contains CIL code, which is conceptually similar to Java bytecode in that it is not compiled to platform-specific instructions until absolutely necessary. Typically, "absolutely necessary" is the point at which a block of CIL instructions (such as a method implementation) is referenced for use by the .NET runtime.

In addition to CIL instructions, assemblies also contain *metadata* that describes in vivid detail the characteristics of every "type" living within the binary. For example, if you have a class named SportsCar, the type metadata describes details such as SportsCar's base class, which interfaces are implemented by SportsCar (if any), as well as a full description of each member supported by the SportsCar type.

.NET metadata is a dramatic improvement to COM type metadata. As you may already know, COM binaries are typically described using an associated type library (which is little more than a binary version of Interface Definition Language [IDL] code). The problems with COM type information are that it is not guaranteed to be present and the fact that IDL code has no way to document the externally referenced servers that are required for the correct operation of the current COM server. In contrast, .NET metadata is always present and is automatically generated by a given .NET-aware compiler.

Finally, in addition to CIL and type metadata, assemblies themselves are also described using metadata, which is officially termed a *manifest*. The manifest contains information about the current version of the assembly, culture information (used for localizing string and image resources), and a list of all externally referenced assemblies that are required for proper execution. You'll examine various tools that can be used to examine an assembly's types, metadata, and manifest information over the course of the next few chapters.

Single-File and Multifile Assemblies

In a great number of cases, there is a simple one-to-one correspondence between a .NET assembly and the binary file (*.dll or *.exe). Thus, if you are building a .NET *.dll, it is safe to consider that the binary and the assembly are one and the same. Likewise, if you are building an executable desktop application, the *.exe can simply be referred to as the assembly itself. As you'll see in Chapter 15, however, this is not completely accurate. Technically speaking, if an assembly is composed of a single *.dll or *.exe module, you have a *single-file assembly*. Single-file assemblies contain all the necessary CIL, metadata, and associated manifest in an autonomous, single, well-defined package.

Multifile assemblies, on the other hand, are composed of numerous .NET binaries, each of which is termed a *module*. When building a multifile assembly, one of these modules (termed the *primary module*) must contain the assembly manifest (and possibly CIL instructions and metadata for various types). The other related modules contain a module-level manifest, CIL, and type metadata. As you might suspect, the primary module documents the set of required secondary modules within the assembly manifest.

So, why would you choose to create a multifile assembly? When you partition an assembly into discrete modules, you end up with a more flexible deployment option. For example, if a user is referencing a remote assembly that needs to be downloaded onto his or her machine, the runtime will only download the required modules. Therefore, you are free to construct your assembly in such a way that less frequently required types (such as a class named HardDriveReformatter) are kept in a separate stand-alone module.

In contrast, if all your types were placed in a single-file assembly, the end user may end up downloading a large chunk of data that is not really needed (which is obviously a waste of time). Thus, as you can see, an assembly is really a *logical grouping* of one or more related modules that are intended to be initially deployed and versioned as a single unit.

The Role of the Common Intermediate Language

Let's examine CIL code, type metadata, and the assembly manifest in a bit more detail. CIL is a language that sits above any particular platform-specific instruction set. For example, the following C# code models a trivial calculator. Don't concern yourself with the exact syntax for now, but do notice the format of the Add() method in the Calc class:

```
// Calc.cs
using System;

namespace CalculatorExample
{
  // This class contains the app's entry point.
  class Program
  {
    static void Main()
    {
      Calc c = new Calc();
      int ans = c.Add(10, 84);
      Console.WriteLine("10 + 84 is {0}.", ans);

      // Wait for user to press the Enter key before shutting down.
      Console.ReadLine();
    }
  }

  // The C# calculator.
  class Calc
  {
    public int Add(int x, int y)
    { return x + y; }
  }
}
```

Once you compile this code file using the C# compiler (csc.exe), you end up with a single-file *.exe assembly that contains a manifest, CIL instructions, and metadata describing each aspect of the Calc and Program classes.

Note Chapter 2 examines the details of compiling code using the C# compiler, as well as the use of graphical IDEs such as Visual Studio, Visual C# Express, and SharpDevelop.

For example, if you were to open this assembly using ildasm.exe (examined a little later in this chapter), you would find that the Add() method is represented using CIL such as the following:

```
.method public hidebysig instance int32  Add(int32 x,
   int32 y) cil managed
{
  // Code size       9 (0x9)
  .maxstack  2
  .locals init (int32 V_0)
  IL_0000:  nop
  IL_0001:  ldarg.1
  IL_0002:  ldarg.2
  IL_0003:  add
  IL_0004:  stloc.0
```

```
  IL_0005:  br.s       IL_0007
  IL_0007:  ldloc.0
  IL_0008:  ret
} // end of method Calc::Add
```

Don't worry if you are unable to make heads or tails of the resulting CIL for this method—Chapter 19 will describe the basics of the CIL programming language. The point to concentrate on is that the C# compiler emits CIL, not platform-specific instructions.

Now, recall that this is true of all .NET-aware compilers. To illustrate, assume you created this same application using Visual Basic .NET, rather than C#:

```
' Calc.vb
Imports System

Namespace CalculatorExample
  ' A VB "Module" is a class that contains only
  ' static members.
  Module Program
    Sub Main()
      Dim c As New Calc
      Dim ans As Integer = c.Add(10, 84)
      Console.WriteLine("10 + 84 is {0}.", ans)
      Console.ReadLine()
    End Sub
  End Module

  Class Calc
    Public Function Add(ByVal x As Integer, ByVal y As Integer) As Integer
      Return x + y
    End Function
  End Class
End Namespace
```

If you examine the CIL for the Add() method, you find similar instructions (slightly tweaked by the VB .NET compiler, vbc.exe):

```
.method public instance int32  Add(int32 x,
  int32 y) cil managed
{
  // Code size       8 (0x8)
  .maxstack  2
  .locals init (int32 V_0)
  IL_0000:  ldarg.1
  IL_0001:  ldarg.2
  IL_0002:  add.ovf
  IL_0003:  stloc.0
  IL_0004:  br.s       IL_0006
  IL_0006:  ldloc.0
  IL_0007:  ret
} // end of method Calc::Add
```

Source Code The Calc.cs and Calc.vb code files are included under the Chapter 1 subdirectory.

Benefits of CIL

At this point, you might be wondering exactly what is gained by compiling source code into CIL rather than directly to a specific instruction set. One benefit is language integration. As you have already seen, each .NET-aware compiler produces nearly identical CIL instructions. Therefore, all languages are able to interact within a well-defined binary arena.

Furthermore, given that CIL is platform-agnostic, the .NET Framework itself is platform-agnostic, providing the same benefits Java developers have grown accustomed to (i.e., a single code base running on numerous operating systems). In fact, there is an international standard for the C# language, and a large subset of the .NET platform and implementations already exist for many non-Windows operating systems (more details in the section "The Platform-Independent Nature of .NET" toward the end of this chapter). In contrast to Java, however, .NET allows you to build applications using your language of choice.

Compiling CIL to Platform-Specific Instructions

Due to the fact that assemblies contain CIL instructions, rather than platform-specific instructions, CIL code must be compiled on the fly before use. The entity that compiles CIL code into meaningful CPU instructions is termed a *just-in-time (JIT) compiler*, which sometimes goes by the friendly name of *Jitter*. The .NET runtime environment leverages a JIT compiler for each CPU targeting the runtime, each optimized for the underlying platform.

For example, if you are building a .NET application that is to be deployed to a handheld device (such as a Pocket PC), the corresponding Jitter is well equipped to run within a low-memory environment. On the other hand, if you are deploying your assembly to a back-end server (where memory is seldom an issue), the Jitter will be optimized to function in a high-memory environment. In this way, developers can write a single body of code that can be efficiently JIT-compiled and executed on machines with different architectures.

Furthermore, as a given Jitter compiles CIL instructions into corresponding machine code, it will cache the results in memory in a manner suited to the target operating system. In this way, if a call is made to a method named `PrintDocument()`, the CIL instructions are compiled into platform-specific instructions on the first invocation and retained in memory for later use. Therefore, the next time `PrintDocument()` is called, there is no need to recompile the CIL.

■ **Note** It is also possible to perform a "pre-JIT" of an assembly when installing your application using the `ngen.exe` command-line tool that ships with the .NET Framework 3.5 SDK. Doing so may improve startup time for graphically intensive applications.

The Role of .NET Type Metadata

In addition to CIL instructions, a .NET assembly contains full, complete, and accurate metadata, which describes each and every type (class, structure, enumeration, and so forth) defined in the binary, as well as the members of each type (properties, methods, events, and so on). Thankfully, it is always the job of the compiler (not the programmer) to emit the latest and greatest type metadata. Because .NET metadata is so wickedly meticulous, assemblies are completely self-describing entities.

To illustrate the format of .NET type metadata, let's take a look at the metadata that has been generated for the `Add()` method of the C# `Calc` class you examined previously (the metadata generated for the VB .NET version of the `Add()` method is similar):

```
TypeDef #2 (02000003)
-------------------------------------------------------
  TypDefName: CalculatorExample.Calc  (02000003)
  Flags     : [NotPublic] [AutoLayout] [Class]
  [AnsiClass] [BeforeFieldInit]  (00100001)
  Extends   : 01000001 [TypeRef] System.Object
  Method #1 (06000003)
-------------------------------------------------------
  MethodName: Add (06000003)
  Flags     : [Public] [HideBySig] [ReuseSlot]  (00000086)
  RVA       : 0x00002090
  ImplFlags : [IL] [Managed]  (00000000)
  CallCnvntn: [DEFAULT]
  hasThis
  ReturnType: I4
    2 Arguments
    Argument #1:  I4
    Argument #2:  I4
    2 Parameters
    (1) ParamToken : (08000001) Name : x flags: [none] (00000000)
    (2) ParamToken : (08000002) Name : y flags: [none] (00000000)
```

Metadata is used by numerous aspects of the .NET runtime environment, as well as by various development tools. For example, the IntelliSense feature provided by tools such as Visual Studio 2008 is made possible by reading an assembly's metadata at design time. Metadata is also used by various object browsing utilities, debugging tools, and the C# compiler itself. To be sure, metadata is the backbone of numerous .NET technologies including Windows Communication Foundation (WCF), XML web services/the .NET remoting layer, reflection, late binding, and object serialization. Chapter 16 will formalize the role of .NET metadata.

The Role of the Assembly Manifest

Last but not least, remember that a .NET assembly also contains metadata that describes the assembly itself (technically termed a *manifest*). Among other details, the manifest documents all external assemblies required by the current assembly to function correctly, the assembly's version number, copyright information, and so forth. Like type metadata, it is always the job of the compiler to generate the assembly's manifest. Here are some relevant details of the manifest generated when compiling the `Calc.cs` code file shown earlier in this chapter (assume we instructed the compiler to name our assembly `Calc.exe`):

```
.assembly extern mscorlib
{
  .publickeytoken = (B7 7A 5C 56 19 34 E0 89 )
  .ver 2:0:0:0
}
.assembly Calc
{
  .hash algorithm 0x00008004
  .ver 0:0:0:0
}
.module Calc.exe
.imagebase 0x00400000
.subsystem 0x00000003
.file alignment 512
.corflags 0x00000001
```

In a nutshell, this manifest documents the list of external assemblies required by `Calc.exe` (via the `.assembly extern` directive) as well as various characteristics of the assembly itself (version number, module name, and so on). Chapter 15 will examine the usefulness of manifest data in much more detail.

Understanding the Common Type System

A given assembly may contain any number of distinct types. In the world of .NET, *type* is simply a general term used to refer to a member from the set {class, interface, structure, enumeration, delegate}. When you build solutions using a .NET-aware language, you will most likely interact with many of these types. For example, your assembly may define a single class that implements some number of interfaces. Perhaps one of the interface methods takes an enumeration type as an input parameter and returns a structure to the caller.

Recall that the CTS is a formal specification that documents how types must be defined in order to be hosted by the CLR. Typically, the only individuals who are deeply concerned with the inner workings of the CTS are those building tools and/or compilers that target the .NET platform. It is important, however, for all .NET programmers to learn about how to work with the five types defined by the CTS in their language of choice. Here is a brief overview.

CTS Class Types

Every .NET-aware language supports, at the very least, the notion of a *class type*, which is the cornerstone of object-oriented programming (OOP). A class may be composed of any number of members (such as properties, methods, and events) and data points (fields). In C#, classes are declared using the `class` keyword:

```
// A C# class type.
class Calc
{
  public int Add(int x, int y)
  { return x + y; }
}
```

Chapter 5 will begin your examination of building CTS class types with C#; however, Table 1-1 documents a number of characteristics pertaining to class types.

Table 1-1. *CTS Class Characteristics*

Class Characteristic	Meaning in Life
Is the class "sealed" or not?	Sealed classes cannot function as a base class to other classes.
Does the class implement any interfaces?	An *interface* is a collection of abstract members that provide a contract between the object and object user. The CTS allows a class or structure to implement any number of interfaces.
Is the class abstract or concrete?	*Abstract* classes cannot be directly created, but are intended to define common behaviors for derived types. *Concrete* classes can be created directly.
What is the "visibility" of this class?	Each class must be configured with a visibility attribute. Basically, this trait defines whether the class may be used by external assemblies or only from within the defining assembly.

CTS Interface Types

Interfaces are nothing more than a named collection of abstract member definitions, which may be supported (i.e., implemented) by a given class or structure. Unlike COM, .NET interfaces do *not* derive a common base interface such as IUnknown. In C#, interface types are defined using the interface keyword, for example:

```
// A C# interface type is usually
// declared as public, to allow types in other
// assemblies to implement their behavior.
public interface IDraw
{
  void Draw();
}
```

On their own, interfaces are of little use. However, when a class or structure implements a given interface in its unique way, you are able to request access to the supplied functionality using an interface reference in a polymorphic manner. Interface-based programming will be fully explored in Chapter 9.

CTS Structure Types

The concept of a structure is also formalized under the CTS. If you have a C background, you should be pleased to know that these user-defined types (UDTs) have survived in the world of .NET (although they behave a bit differently under the hood). Simply put, a *structure* can be thought of as a lightweight class type having value-based semantics. For more details on the subtleties of structures, see Chapter 4. Typically, structures are best suited for modeling geometric and mathematical data, and are created in C# using the struct keyword:

```
// A C# structure type.
struct Point
{
  // Structures can contain fields.
  public int xPos, yPos;

  // Structures can contain parameterized constructors.
  public Point(int x, int y)
  { xPos = x; yPos = y;}

  // Structures may define methods.
  public void Display()
  {
    Console.WriteLine("({0}, {1}", xPos, yPos);
  }
}
```

CTS Enumeration Types

Enumerations are handy programming constructs that allow you to group name/value pairs. For example, assume you are creating a video-game application that allows the player to select one of three character categories (Wizard, Fighter, or Thief). Rather than keeping track of raw numerical values to represent each possibility, you could build a custom enumeration using the enum keyword:

```
// A C# enumeration type.
enum CharacterType
{
```

```
    Wizard = 100,
    Fighter = 200,
    Thief = 300
}
```

By default, the storage used to hold each item is a 32-bit integer; however, it is possible to alter this storage slot if need be (e.g., when programming for a low-memory device such as a Pocket PC). Also, the CTS demands that enumerated types derive from a common base class, `System.Enum`. As you will see in Chapter 4, this base class defines a number of interesting members that allow you to extract, manipulate, and transform the underlying name/value pairs programmatically.

CTS Delegate Types

Delegates are the .NET equivalent of a type-safe C-style function pointer. The key difference is that a .NET delegate is a *class* that derives from `System.MulticastDelegate`, rather than a simple pointer to a raw memory address. In C#, delegates are declared using the `delegate` keyword:

```
// This C# delegate type can "point to" any method
// returning an integer and taking two integers as input.
delegate int BinaryOp(int x, int y);
```

Delegates are useful when you wish to provide a way for one entity to forward a call to another entity, and provide the foundation for the .NET event architecture. As you will see in Chapters 11 and 18, delegates have intrinsic support for multicasting (i.e., forwarding a request to multiple recipients) and asynchronous method invocations.

CTS Type Members

Now that you have previewed each of the types formalized by the CTS, realize that most types take any number of *members*. Formally speaking, a *type member* is constrained by the set {constructor, finalizer, static constructor, nested type, operator, method, property, indexer, field, read-only field, constant, event}.

The CTS defines various "adornments" that may be associated with a given member. For example, each member has a given visibility trait (e.g., public, private, protected, and so forth). Some members may be declared as abstract to enforce a polymorphic behavior on derived types as well as virtual to define a canned (but overridable) implementation. Also, most members may be configured as static (bound at the class level) or instance (bound at the object level). The construction of type members is examined over the course of the next several chapters.

■ **Note** As described in Chapter 10, the C# language also supports the construction of generic types and generic members.

Intrinsic CTS Data Types

The final aspect of the CTS to be aware of for the time being is that it establishes a well-defined set of fundamental data types. Although a given language typically has a unique keyword used to declare an intrinsic CTS data type, all language keywords ultimately resolve to the same type defined in an assembly named `mscorlib.dll`. Consider Table 1-2, which documents how key CTS data types are expressed in various .NET languages.

Table 1-2. *The Intrinsic CTS Data Types*

CTS Data Type	VB .NET Keyword	C# Keyword	C++/CLI Keyword
System.Byte	Byte	byte	unsigned char
System.SByte	SByte	sbyte	signed char
System.Int16	Short	short	short
System.Int32	Integer	int	int or long
System.Int64	Long	long	__int64
System.UInt16	UShort	ushort	unsigned short
System.UInt32	UInteger	uint	unsigned int or unsigned long
System.UInt64	ULong	ulong	unsigned __int64
System.Single	Single	float	Float
System.Double	Double	double	Double
System.Object	Object	object	Object^
System.Char	Char	char	wchar_t
System.String	String	string	String^
System.Decimal	Decimal	decimal	Decimal
System.Boolean	Boolean	bool	Bool

Given the fact that the unique keywords of a managed language are simply shorthand notations for a real type in the System namespace, we no longer have to worry about overflow/underflow conditions for numerical data, or how strings and Booleans are internally represented across different languages. Consider the following code snippets, which define 32-bit numerical variables in C# and VB .NET, using language keywords as well as the formal CTS type:

```
// Define some "ints" in C#.
int i = 0;
System.Int32 j = 0;

' Define some "ints" in VB .NET.
Dim i As Integer = 0
Dim j As System.Int32 = 0
```

Understanding the Common Language Specification

As you are aware, different languages express the same programming constructs in unique, language-specific terms. For example, in C# you denote string concatenation using the plus operator (+), while in VB .NET you typically make use of the ampersand (&). Even when two distinct languages express the same programmatic idiom (e.g., a function with no return value), the chances are very good that the syntax will appear quite different on the surface:

```
// C# method returning nothing.
public void MyMethod()
{
  // Some interesting code...
}
```

```
' VB method returning nothing.
Public Sub MyMethod()
  ' Some interesting code...
End Sub
```

As you have already seen, these minor syntactic variations are inconsequential in the eyes of the .NET runtime, given that the respective compilers (csc.exe or vbc.exe, in this case) emit a similar set of CIL instructions. However, languages can also differ with regard to their overall level of functionality. For example, a .NET language may or may not have a keyword to represent unsigned data, and may or may not support pointer types. Given these possible variations, it would be ideal to have a baseline to which all .NET-aware languages are expected to conform.

The CLS is a set of rules that describe in vivid detail the minimal and complete set of features a given .NET-aware compiler must support to produce code that can be hosted by the CLR, while at the same time be accessed in a uniform manner by all languages that target the .NET platform. In many ways, the CLS can be viewed as a *subset* of the full functionality defined by the CTS.

The CLS is ultimately a set of rules that compiler builders must conform to, if they intend their products to function seamlessly within the .NET universe. Each rule is assigned a simple name (e.g., "CLS Rule 6") and describes how this rule affects those who build the compilers as well as those who (in some way) interact with them. The crème de la crème of the CLS is the mighty Rule 1:

- *Rule 1*: CLS rules apply only to those parts of a type that are exposed outside the defining assembly.

Given this rule, you can (correctly) infer that the remaining rules of the CLS do not apply to the logic used to build the inner workings of a .NET type. The only aspects of a type that must conform to the CLS are the member definitions themselves (i.e., naming conventions, parameters, and return types). The implementation logic for a member may use any number of non-CLS techniques, as the outside world won't know the difference.

To illustrate, the following Add() method is not CLS-compliant, as the parameters and return values make use of unsigned data (which is not a requirement of the CLS):

```
class Calc
{
  // Exposed unsigned data is not CLS compliant!
  public ulong Add(ulong x, ulong y)
  { return x + y;}
}
```

However, if you were to simply make use of unsigned data internally as follows:

```
class Calc
{
  public int Add(int x, int y)
  {
    // As this ulong variable is only used internally,
    // we are still CLS compliant.
    ulong temp = 0;
    ...
    return x + y;
  }
}
```

you have still conformed to the rules of the CLS, and can rest assured that all .NET languages are able to invoke the Add() method.

Of course, in addition to Rule 1, the CLS defines numerous other rules. For example, the CLS describes how a given language must represent text strings, how enumerations should be represented internally (the base type used for storage), how to define static members, and so forth.

Luckily, you don't have to commit these rules to memory to be a proficient .NET developer. Again, by and large, an intimate understanding of the CTS and CLS specifications is only of interest to tool/compiler builders.

Ensuring CLS Compliance

As you will see over the course of this book, C# does define a number of programming constructs that are not CLS-compliant. The good news, however, is that you can instruct the C# compiler to check your code for CLS compliance using a single .NET attribute:

```
// Tell the C# compiler to check for CLS compliance.
[assembly: System.CLSCompliant(true)]
```

Chapter 16 dives into the details of attribute-based programming. Until then, simply understand that the `[CLSCompliant]` attribute will instruct the C# compiler to check each and every line of code against the rules of the CLS. If any CLS violations are discovered, you receive a compiler error and a description of the offending code.

Understanding the Common Language Runtime

In addition to the CTS and CLS specifications, the final TLA (three-letter abbreviation) to contend with at the moment is the CLR. Programmatically speaking, the term *runtime* can be understood as a collection of external services that are required to execute a given compiled unit of code. For example, when developers make use of the MFC to create a new application, they are aware that their program requires the MFC runtime library (i.e., `mfc42.dll`). Other popular languages also have a corresponding runtime. VB6 programmers are also tied to a runtime module or two (e.g., `msvbvm60.dll`). Java developers are tied to the Java Virtual Machine (JVM), and so forth.

The .NET platform offers yet another runtime system. The key difference between the .NET runtime and the various other runtimes I just mentioned is the fact that the .NET runtime provides a single well-defined runtime layer that is shared by *all* languages and platforms that are .NET-aware.

The crux of the CLR is physically represented by a library named `mscoree.dll` (a.k.a. the Common Object Runtime Execution Engine). When an assembly is referenced for use, `mscoree.dll` is loaded automatically, which in turn loads the required assembly into memory. The runtime engine is responsible for a number of tasks. First and foremost, it is the entity in charge of resolving the location of an assembly and finding the requested type within the binary by reading the contained metadata. The CLR then lays out the type in memory, compiles the associated CIL into platform-specific instructions, performs any necessary security checks, and then executes the code in question.

In addition to loading your custom assemblies and creating your custom types, the CLR will also interact with the types contained within the .NET base class libraries when required. Although the entire base class library has been broken into a number of discrete assemblies, the key assembly is `mscorlib.dll`. `mscorlib.dll` contains a large number of core types that encapsulate a wide variety of common programming tasks as well as the core data types used by all .NET languages. When you build .NET solutions, you automatically have access to this particular assembly.

Figure 1-4 illustrates the workflow that takes place between your source code (which is making use of base class library types), a given .NET compiler, and the .NET execution engine.

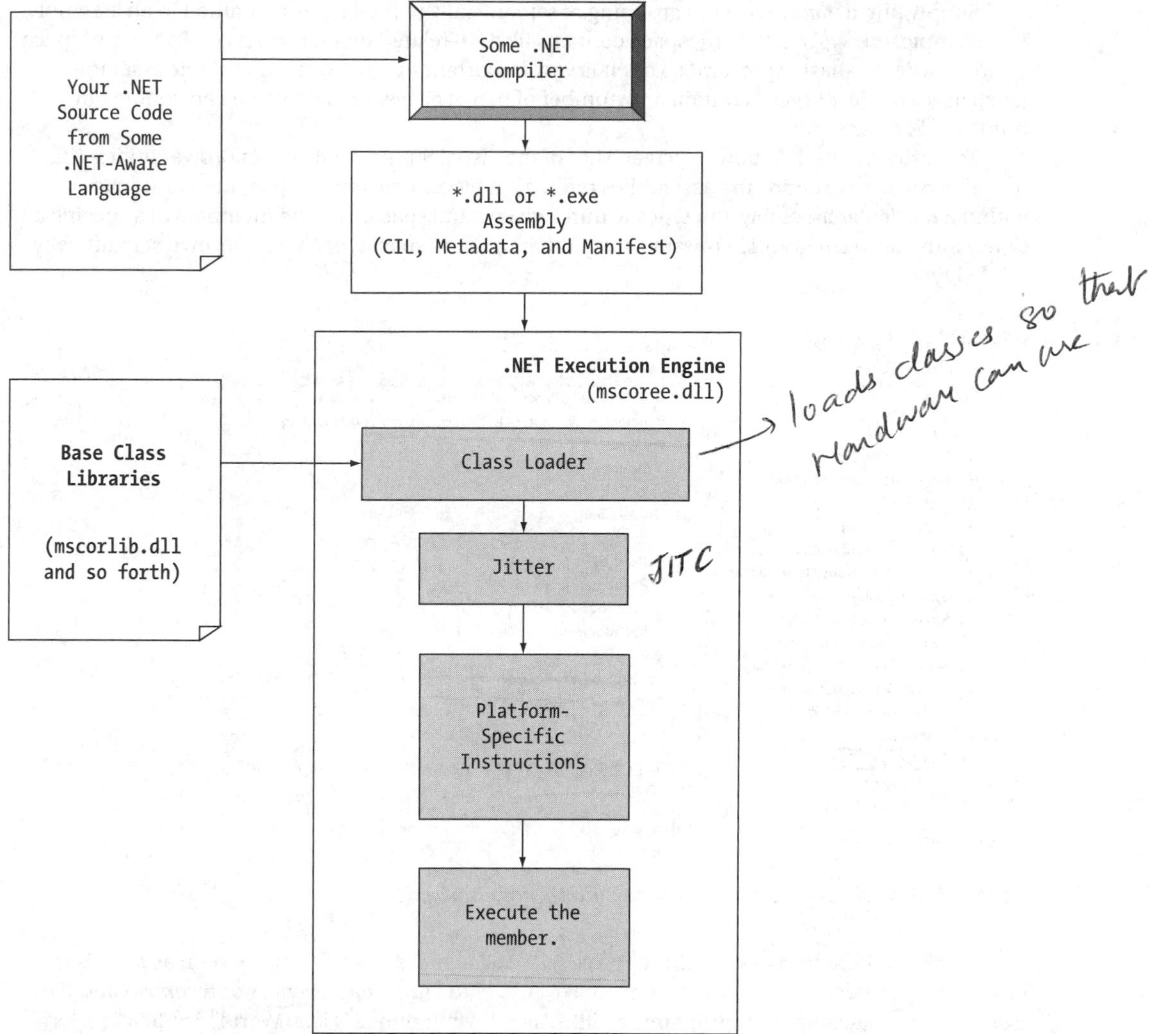

Figure 1-4. `mscoree.dll` *in action*

The Assembly/Namespace/Type Distinction

Each of us understands the importance of code libraries. The point of libraries such as MFC, J2EE, and ATL is to give developers a well-defined set of existing code to leverage in their applications. However, the C# language does not come with a language-specific code library. Rather, C# developers leverage the language-neutral .NET libraries. To keep all the types within the base class libraries well organized, the .NET platform makes extensive use of the *namespace* concept.

Simply put, a namespace is a grouping of semantically related types contained in an assembly. For example, the `System.IO` namespace contains file I/O–related types, the `System.Data` namespace defines basic database types, and so on. It is very important to point out that a single assembly (such as `mscorlib.dll`) can contain any number of namespaces, each of which can contain any number of types.

To clarify, Figure 1-5 shows a screen shot of the Visual Studio 2008 Object Brower utility. This tool allows you to examine the assemblies referenced by your current project, the namespaces within a particular assembly, the types within a given namespace, and the members of a specific type. Note that `mscorlib.dll` contains many different namespaces, each with its own semantically related types.

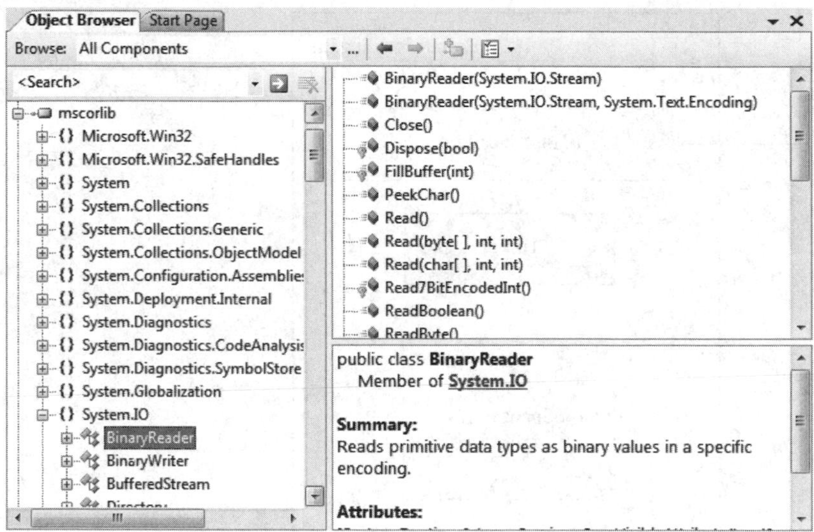

Figure 1-5. *A single assembly can have any number of namespaces.*

The key difference between this approach and a language-specific library such as MFC is that any language targeting the .NET runtime makes use of the *same* namespaces and *same* types. For example, the following three programs all illustrate the ubiquitous "Hello World" application, written in C#, VB .NET, and C++/CLI:

```
// Hello world in C#
using System;

public class MyApp
{
  static void Main()
  {
    Console.WriteLine("Hi from C#");
  }
}

' Hello world in VB
Imports System

Public Module MyApp
  Sub Main()
```

```
    Console.WriteLine("Hi from VB")
  End Sub
End Module

// Hello world in C++/CLI
#include "stdafx.h"
using namespace System;

int main(array<System::String ^> ^args)
{
  Console::WriteLine(L"Hi from C++/CLI");
  return 0;
}
```

Notice that each language is making use of the Console class defined in the System namespace. Beyond minor syntactic variations, these three applications look and feel very much alike, both physically and logically.

Clearly, your primary goal as a .NET developer is to get to know the wealth of types defined in the (numerous) .NET namespaces. The most fundamental namespace to get your hands around is named System. This namespace provides a core body of types that you will need to leverage time and again as a .NET developer. In fact, you cannot build any sort of functional C# application without at least making a reference to the System namespace, as the core data types (System.Int32, System.String, etc.) are defined here. Table 1-3 offers a rundown of some (but certainly not all) of the .NET namespaces grouped by related functionality.

Table 1-3. *A Sampling of .NET Namespaces*

.NET Namespace	Meaning in Life
System	Within System, you find numerous useful types dealing with intrinsic data, mathematical computations, random number generation, environment variables, and garbage collection, as well as a number of commonly used exceptions and attributes.
System.Collections System.Collections.Generic	These namespaces define a number of stock container types, as well as base types and interfaces that allow you to build customized collections.
System.Data System.Data.Odbc System.Data.OracleClient System.Data.OleDb System.Data.SqlClient	These namespaces are used for interacting with relational databases using ADO.NET.
System.IO System.IO.Compression System.IO.Ports	These namespaces define numerous types used to work with file I/O, compression of data, and port manipulation.
System.Reflection System.Reflection.Emit	These namespaces define types that support runtime type discovery as well as dynamic creation of types.
System.Runtime.InteropServices	This namespace provides facilities to allow .NET types to interact with "unmanaged code" (e.g., C-based DLLs and COM servers) and vice versa.
System.Drawing System.Windows.Forms	These namespaces define types used to build desktop applications using .NET's original UI toolkit (Windows Forms).

Continued

Table 1-3. *Continued*

.NET Namespace	Meaning in Life

`System.Windows`
`System.Windows.Controls`
`System.Windows.Shapes`
	The `System.Windows` namespace is the root for several namespaces that represent the Windows Presentation Foundation (WPF) UI toolkit.

`System.Linq`
`System.Xml.Linq`
`System.Data.Linq`
	These namespaces define types used when programming against the LINQ API.

`System.Web`	This is one of many namespaces that allow you to build ASP.NET web applications.
`System.ServiceModel`	This is one of many namespaces used to build distributed applications using the WCF API.
`System.Workflow.Runtime` `System.Workflow.Activities`	These are two of many namespaces that define types used to build "workflow-enabled" applications using the WCF API.
`System.Threading`	This namespace defines numerous types to build multithreaded applications.
`System.Security`	Security is an integrated aspect of the .NET universe. In the security-centric namespaces, you find numerous types dealing with permissions, cryptography, and so on.
`System.Xml`	The XML-centric namespaces contain numerous types used to interact with XML data.

The Role of the Microsoft Namespaces

I'm sure you noticed while reading over the listings in Table 1-3 that `System` is the root namespace for a good number of nested namespaces (`System.IO`, `System.Data`, etc.). As it turns out, however, the .NET base class library defines a number of topmost root namespaces beyond `System`, the most useful of which is named `Microsoft`.

In a nutshell, any namespace nested within `Microsoft` (e.g., `Microsoft.CSharp`, `Microsoft.Ink`, `Microsoft.ManagementConsole`, and `Microsoft.Win32`) contain types that are used to interact with services that are unique to the Windows operating system. Given this point, you should not assume that these types could be used successfully on other .NET-enabled operating systems such as Mac OS X. For the most part, this text will not dig into the details of the `Microsoft` rooted namespaces, so be sure to consult the documentation if you are so interested.

■ **Note** Chapter 2 will illustrate the use of the .NET Framework 3.5 SDK documentation, which provides details regarding every namespace, type, and member found within the base class libraries.

Accessing a Namespace Programmatically

It is worth reiterating that a namespace is nothing more than a convenient way for us mere humans to logically understand and organize related types. Consider again the `System` namespace. From your perspective, you can assume that `System.Console` represents a class named `Console` that is contained within a namespace called `System`. However, in the eyes of the .NET runtime, this is not so. The runtime engine only sees a single entity named `System.Console`.

In C#, the `using` keyword simplifies the process of referencing types defined in a particular namespace. Here is how it works. Let's say you are interested in building a traditional desktop application. The main window renders a bar chart based on some information obtained from a back-end database and displays your company logo. While learning the types each namespace contains takes study and experimentation, here are some possible candidates to reference in your program:

```
// Here are all the namespaces used to build this application.
using System;                   // General base class library types.
using System.Drawing;           // Graphical rendering types.
using System.Windows.Forms;     // Windows Forms GUI widget types.
using System.Data;              // General data-centric types.
using System.Data.SqlClient;    // MS SQL Server data access types.
```

Once you have specified some number of namespaces (and set a reference to the assemblies that define them), you are free to create instances of the types they contain. For example, if you are interested in creating an instance of the `Bitmap` class (defined in the `System.Drawing` namespace), you can write:

```
// Explicitly list the namespaces used by this file.
using System;
using System.Drawing;

class Program
{
  public void DisplayLogo()
  {
    // Create a 20 * 20 pixel bitmap.
    Bitmap companyLogo = new Bitmap(20, 20);
    ...
  }
}
```

Because your code file is referencing `System.Drawing`, the compiler is able to resolve the `Bitmap` class as a member of this namespace. If you did not specify the `System.Drawing` namespace, you would be issued a compiler error. However, you are free to declare variables using a *fully qualified name* as well:

```
// Not listing System.Drawing namespace!
using System;

class Program
{
  public void DisplayLogo()
  {
    // Using fully qualified name.
    System.Drawing.Bitmap companyLogo =
      new System.Drawing.Bitmap(20, 20);
    ...
  }
}
```

While defining a type using the fully qualified name provides greater readability, I think you'd agree that the C# `using` keyword reduces keystrokes. In this text, I will avoid the use of fully qualified names (unless there is a definite ambiguity to be resolved) and opt for the simplified approach of the C# `using` keyword.

However, always remember that the `using` keyword is simply a shorthand notation for specifying a type's fully qualified name, and either approach results in the *exact* same underlying CIL (given the fact that CIL code always makes use of fully qualified names) and has no effect on performance or the size of the assembly.

Referencing External Assemblies

In addition to specifying a namespace via the C# `using` keyword, you also need to tell the C# compiler the name of the assembly containing the actual CIL definition for the referenced type. As mentioned, many core .NET namespaces live within `mscorlib.dll`. However, the `System.Drawing.Bitmap` type is contained within a separate assembly named `System.Drawing.dll`. A vast majority of the .NET Framework assemblies are located under a specific directory termed the *global assembly cache* (GAC). On a Windows machine, this can be located by default under C:\Windows\Assembly, as shown in Figure 1-6.

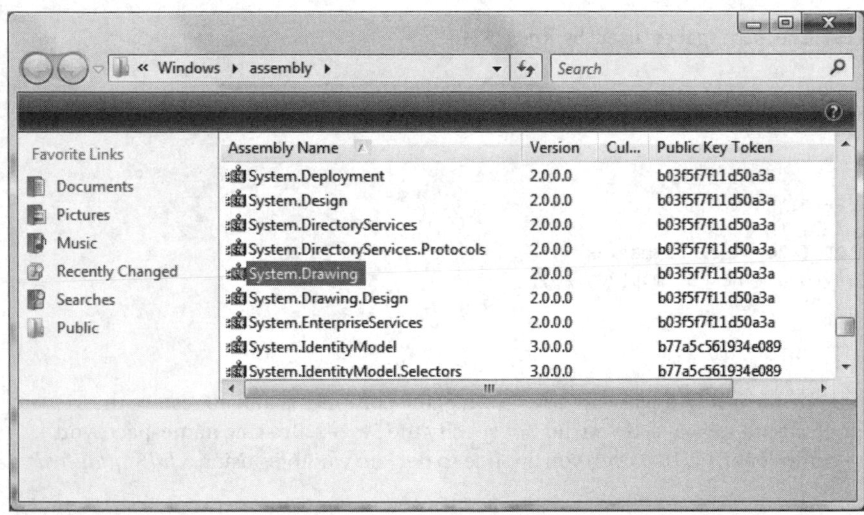

Figure 1-6. *The base class libraries reside in the GAC.*

Depending on the development tool you are using to build your .NET applications, you will have various ways to inform the compiler which assemblies you wish to include during the compilation cycle. You'll examine how to do so in the next chapter, so I'll hold off on the details for now.

Exploring an Assembly Using ildasm.exe

If you are beginning to feel a tad overwhelmed at the thought of gaining mastery over every namespace in the .NET platform, just remember that what makes a namespace unique is that it contains types that are somehow *semantically related*. Therefore, if you have no need for a user interface beyond a simple console application, you can forget all about the `System.Windows.Forms`, `System.Windows`, and `System.Web` namespaces (among others). If you are building a painting application, the database namespaces are most likely of little concern. Like any new set of prefabricated code, you learn as you go.

The Intermediate Language Disassembler utility (`ildasm.exe`), which ships with the .NET Framework 3.5 SDK, allows you to load up any .NET assembly and investigate its contents, including the associated manifest, CIL code, and type metadata. To load `ildasm.exe`, open a Visual Studio command prompt (using Start ➤ All Programs ➤ Microsoft Visual Studio 2008 ➤ Visual Studio Tools), type **ildasm** and press the Enter key.

Once you run this tool, proceed to the File ➤ Open menu command and navigate to an assembly you wish to explore. By way of illustration, here is the `Calc.exe` assembly generated based on the `Calc.cs` file shown earlier in this chapter (see Figure 1-7). `ildasm.exe` presents the structure of an assembly using a familiar tree-view format.

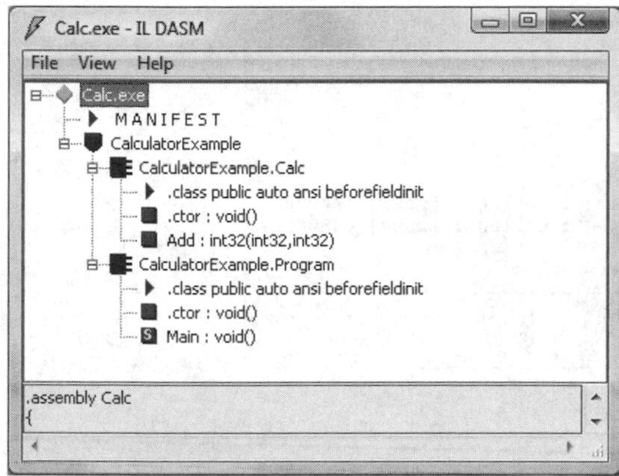

Figure 1-7. `ildasm.exe` *allows you to see the CIL code, manifest, and metadata within a .NET assembly.*

Viewing CIL Code

In addition to showing the namespaces, types, and members contained in a given assembly, `ildasm.exe` also allows you to view the CIL instructions for a given member. For example, if you were to double-click the `Main()` method of the `Program` class, a separate window would display the underlying CIL (see Figure 1-8).

CalculatorExample.CalcApp::Main : void()

Find Find Next

```
.method private hidebysig static void  Main() cil managed
{
  .entrypoint
  // Code size       42 (0x2a)
  .maxstack  3
  .locals init (class CalculatorExample.Calc V_0,
           int32 V_1)
  IL_0000:  nop
  IL_0001:  newobj     instance void CalculatorExample.Calc::.ctor()
  IL_0006:  stloc.0
  IL_0007:  ldloc.0
  IL_0008:  ldc.i4.s   10
  IL_000a:  ldc.i4.s   84
  IL_000c:  callvirt   instance int32 CalculatorExample.Calc::Add(int32,
                                                                  int32)
  IL_0011:  stloc.1
```

Figure 1-8. *Viewing the underlying CIL*

Viewing Type Metadata

If you wish to view the type metadata for the currently loaded assembly, press Ctrl+M. Figure 1-9 shows the metadata for the `Calc.Add()` method.

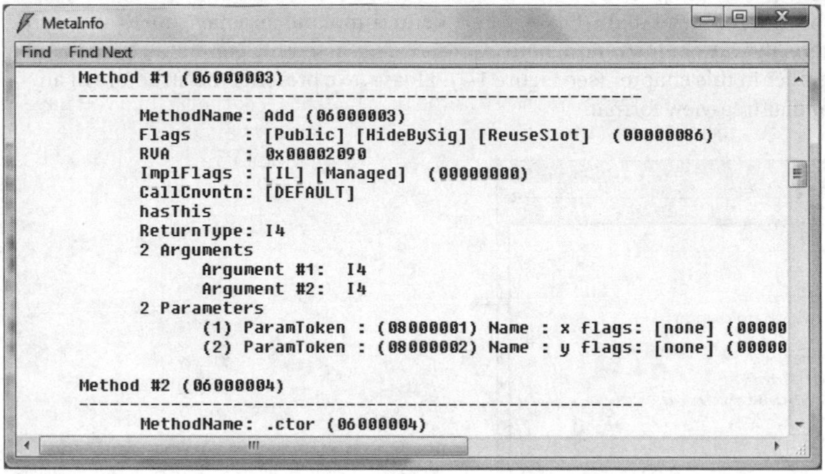

```
MetaInfo
Find  Find Next
    Method #1 (06000003)
    -------------------------------------------------------
          MethodName: Add (06000003)
          Flags     : [Public] [HideBySig] [ReuseSlot]  (00000086)
          RVA       : 0x00002090
          ImplFlags : [IL] [Managed]  (00000000)
          CallCnvntn: [DEFAULT]
          hasThis
          ReturnType: I4
          2 Arguments
                Argument #1:  I4
                Argument #2:  I4
          2 Parameters
                (1) ParamToken : (08000001) Name : x flags: [none] (00000
                (2) ParamToken : (08000002) Name : y flags: [none] (00000

    Method #2 (06000004)
    -------------------------------------------------------
          MethodName: .ctor (06000004)
```

Figure 1-9. *Viewing type metadata via* `ildasm.exe`

Viewing Assembly Metadata (a.k.a. the Manifest)

Finally, if you are interested in viewing the contents of the assembly's manifest, simply double-click the MANIFEST icon (see Figure 1-10).

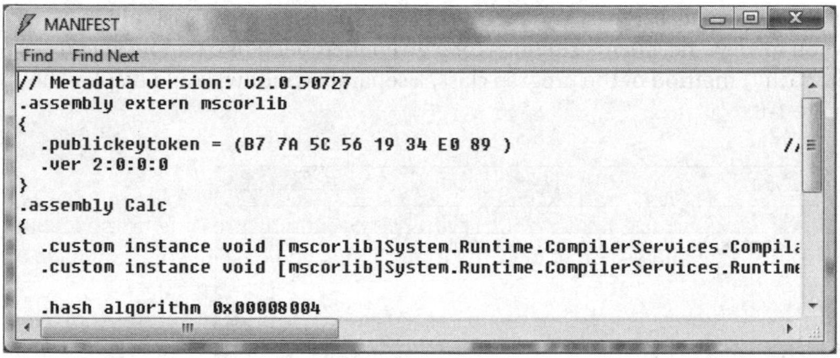

```
MANIFEST
Find  Find Next
// Metadata version: v2.0.50727
.assembly extern mscorlib
{
  .publickeytoken = (B7 7A 5C 56 19 34 E0 89 )                         //
  .ver 2:0:0:0
}
.assembly Calc
{
  .custom instance void [mscorlib]System.Runtime.CompilerServices.Compil
  .custom instance void [mscorlib]System.Runtime.CompilerServices.Runtim

  .hash algorithm 0x00008004
```

Figure 1-10. *Viewing manifest data via* `ildasm.exe`.

To be sure, `ildasm.exe` has more options than shown here, and I will illustrate additional features of the tool where appropriate in the text.

Exploring an Assembly Using Lutz Roeder's Reflector

While using `ildasm.exe` is a very common task when you wish to dig into the guts of a .NET binary, the one gotcha is that you are only able to view the underlying CIL code, rather than looking at an assembly's implementation using your managed language of choice. Thankfully, many .NET object browsers are available for download, including the very popular Reflector.

This free tool can be downloaded from `http://www.aisto.com/roeder/dotnet`. Once you have unzipped the archive, you are able to run the tool and plug in any assembly you wish using the File ➤ Open menu option. Figure 1-11 shows our `Calc.exe` application once again.

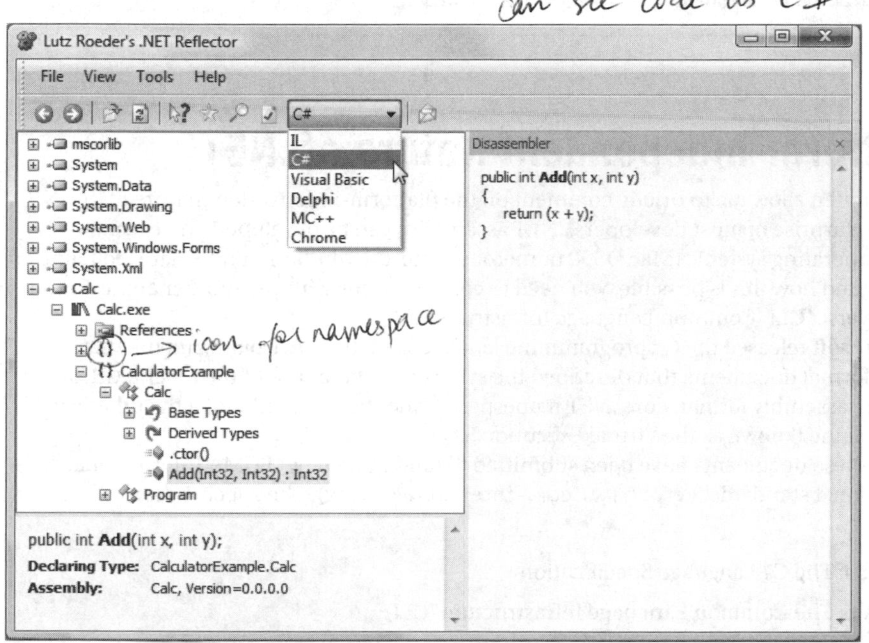

Figure 1-11. *Reflector is a very popular object browsing tool.*

Notice that `reflector.exe` supports a Disassembler window (opened by pressing the spacebar) as well as a drop-down list box that allows you to view the underlying code base in your language of choice (including, of course, CIL code).

I'll leave it up to you to check out the number of intriguing features found within this tool. Do be aware that over the course of the remainder of the book, I'll make use of both `ildasm.exe` as well as `reflector.exe` to illustrate various concepts.

Deploying the .NET Runtime

It should come as no surprise that .NET assemblies can be executed only on a machine that has the .NET Framework installed. For an individual who builds .NET software, this should never be an issue, as your development machine will be properly configured at the time you install the freely available .NET Framework 3.5 SDK (as well as commercial .NET development environments such as Visual Studio 2008).

However, if you deploy an assembly to a computer that does not have .NET installed, it will fail to run. For this reason, Microsoft provides a setup package named `dotnetfx3setup.exe` that can be freely shipped and installed along with your .NET software. This installation program can be freely downloaded from Microsoft from their .NET download area (`http://msdn.microsoft.com/netframework`). Once `dotNetFx35setup.exe` is installed, the target machine will now contain the .NET base class libraries, .NET runtime (`mscoree.dll`), and additional .NET infrastructure (such as the GAC).

■ **Note** The Vista operating system is preconfigured with the necessary .NET runtime infrastructure. However, if you are deploying your application to Windows XP or Windows Server 2003, you will want to ensure the target machine has the .NET runtime environment installed and configured.

The Platform-Independent Nature of .NET

To close this chapter, allow me to briefly comment on the platform-independent nature of the .NET platform. To the surprise of most developers, .NET assemblies can be developed and executed on non-Microsoft operating systems (Mac OS X, numerous Linux distributions, and Solaris, to name a few). To understand how this is possible, you need to come to terms with yet another abbreviation in the .NET universe: CLI (Common Language Infrastructure).

When Microsoft released the C# programming language and the .NET platform, they also crafted a set of formal documents that described the syntax and semantics of the C# and CIL languages, the .NET assembly format, core .NET namespaces, and the mechanics of a hypothetical .NET runtime engine (known as the Virtual Execution System, or VES).

Better yet, these documents have been submitted to (and ratified by) ECMA International as official international standards (`http://www.ecma-international.org`). The specifications of interest are

- *ECMA-334*: The C# Language Specification
- *ECMA-335*: The Common Language Infrastructure (CLI)

The importance of these documents becomes clear when you understand that they enable third parties to build distributions of the .NET platform for any number of operating systems and/or processors. ECMA-335 is perhaps the more "meaty" of the two specifications, so much so that is has been broken into various partitions, including those shown in Table 1-4.

Table 1-4. *Partitions of the CLI*

Partitions of ECMA-335	Meaning in Life
Partition I: Architecture	Describes the overall architecture of the CLI, including the rules of the CTS and CLS, and the mechanics of the .NET runtime engine
Partition II: Metadata	Describes the details of .NET metadata
Partition III: CIL	Describes the syntax and semantics of CIL code
Partition IV: Libraries	Gives a high-level overview of the minimal and complete class libraries that must be supported by a .NET distribution.
Partition V: Annexes	Provides a collection of "odds and ends" details such as class library design guidelines and the implementation details of a CIL compiler

Be aware that Partition IV (Libraries) defines only a *minimal* set of namespaces that represent the core services expected by a CLI distribution (collections, console I/O, file I/O, threading, reflection, network access, core security needs, XML manipulation, and so forth). The CLI does *not* define namespaces that facilitate web development (ASP.NET), database access (ADO.NET), or desktop graphical user interface (GUI) application development (Windows Forms/Windows Presentation Foundation).

The good news, however, is that the mainstream .NET distributions extend the CLI libraries with Microsoft-compatible equivalents of ASP.NET, ADO.NET, and Windows Forms in order to provide full-featured, production-level development platforms. To date, there are two major implementations of the CLI (beyond Microsoft's Windows-specific offering). Although this text focuses on the creation of .NET applications using Microsoft's .NET distribution, Table 1-5 provides information regarding the Mono and Portable .NET projects.

Table 1-5. *Open Source .NET Distributions*

Distribution	Meaning in Life
`http://www.mono-project.com`	The Mono project is an open source distribution of the CLI that targets various Linux distributions (e.g., SuSE, Fedora, and so on) as well as Win32 and Mac OS X.
`http://www.dotgnu.org`	Portable.NET is another open source distribution of the CLI that runs on numerous operating systems. Portable.NET aims to target as many operating systems as possible (Win32, AIX, BeOS, Mac OS X, Solaris, all major Linux distributions, and so on).

Both Mono and Portable.NET provide an ECMA-compliant C# compiler, .NET runtime engine, code samples, documentation, as well as numerous development tools that are functionally equivalent to the tools that ship with Microsoft's .NET Framework 3.5 SDK. Furthermore, Mono and Portable.NET collectively ship with a VB .NET, Java, and C complier.

Note Coverage of creating cross-platform .NET applications using Mono can be found in Appendix B.

Summary

The point of this chapter was to lay out the conceptual framework necessary for the remainder of this book. I began by examining a number of limitations and complexities found within the technologies prior to .NET, and followed up with an overview of how .NET and C# attempt to simplify the current state of affairs.

.NET basically boils down to a runtime execution engine (`mscoree.dll`) and base class library (`mscorlib.dll` and associates). The common language runtime (CLR) is able to host any .NET binary (a.k.a. assembly) that abides by the rules of managed code. As you have seen, assemblies contain CIL instructions (in addition to type metadata and the assembly manifest) that are compiled to platform-specific instructions using a just-in-time (JIT) compiler. In addition, you explored the role of the Common Language Specification (CLS) and Common Type System (CTS).

This was followed by an examination of the `ildasm.exe` and `reflector.exe` object browsing utilities, as well as coverage of how to configure a machine to host .NET applications using `dotnetfx3setup.exe`. I wrapped up by briefly addressing the platform-independent nature of C# and the .NET platform, a topic further examined in Appendix B.

CHAPTER 2

Building C# Applications

As a C# programmer, you may choose among numerous tools to build .NET applications. The point of this chapter is to provide a tour of various .NET development options, including, of course, Visual Studio 2008. The chapter opens, however, with an examination of working with the C# command-line compiler, `csc.exe`, and the simplest of all text editors, the Notepad application that ships with the Microsoft Windows OS.

Once you become comfortable compiling assemblies "IDE-free," you will then examine various lightweight editors (such as TextPad and Notepad++) that allow you to author C# source code files and interact with the compiler in a slightly more sophisticated manner.

While you could work through this entire text using nothing other than `csc.exe` and a basic text editor, I'd bet you are also interested in working with feature-rich integrated development environments (IDEs). To this end, you will be introduced to a free, open source .NET IDE named SharpDevelop. This IDE rivals the functionality of many commercial .NET development environments. After briefly examining the Visual C# 2008 Express IDE (which is also free), you will be given a guided tour of the key features of Visual Studio 2008. This chapter wraps up with a quick tour of a number of complementary .NET development tools (again, many of which are open source) and describes where to obtain them.

Note Over the course of this chapter, you will see a number of C# programming constructs we have not formally examined. If you are unfamiliar with the syntax, don't fret. Chapter 3 will formally begin your examination of the C# language.

The Role of the .NET Framework 3.5 SDK

One common misconception regarding .NET development is the belief that programmers must purchase a copy of Visual Studio in order to build their C# applications. The truth of the matter is that you are able to build any sort of .NET program using the freely downloadable .NET Framework 3.5 Software Development Kit (SDK). This SDK provides you with numerous managed compilers, command-line utilities, white papers, sample code, the .NET class libraries, and a complete documentation system.

Note The .NET Framework 3.5 SDK (`dotNetFx35setup.exe`) can be obtained from the .NET download website (`http://msdn.microsoft.com/netframework`).

If you are indeed going to be using Visual Studio 2008 or Visual C# 2008 Express, you have no need to manually install the .NET Framework 3.5 SDK. When you install either of these products, the SDK is installed automatically, thereby giving you everything you need out of the box. However, if you are *not* going to be using a Microsoft IDE as you work through this text, be sure to install the SDK before proceeding.

The Visual Studio 2008 Command Prompt

When you install the .NET Framework 3.5 SDK, Visual Studio 2008, or Visual C# 2008 Express, you will end up with a number of new directories on your local hard drive, each of which contains various .NET development tools. Many of these tools are driven from the command prompt, so if you wish to use these utilities from any Windows command window, you will need to register these paths with the operating system.

While you could update your PATH variable manually to do so, you can save yourself some time by simply making use of the Visual Studio 2008 Command Prompt that is accessible from the Start ➤ Programs ➤ Visual Studio 2008 ➤ Visual Studio Tools folder (see Figure 2-1).

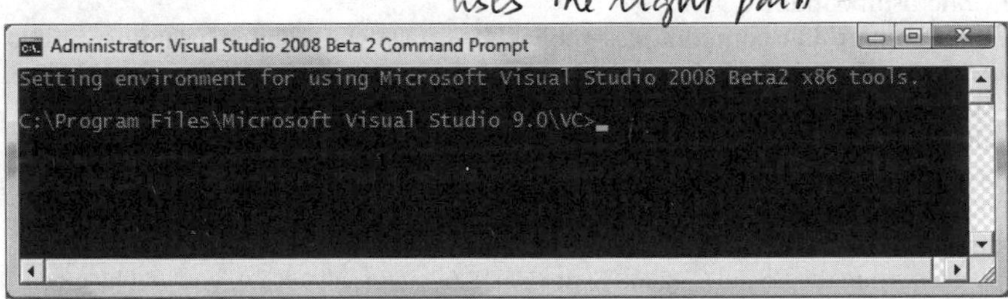

Figure 2-1. *The Visual Studio 2008 command prompt*

The benefit of using this particular command prompt is that it has been preconfigured to provide access to each of the .NET development tools. Assuming you have a .NET development environment installed, type the following command and press the Enter key:

```
csc -?
```

If all is well, you should see a list of command-line arguments of the C# command-line compiler (where csc stands for the *C-sharp compiler*).

Building C# Applications Using csc.exe

While it is true that you may never decide to build a large-scale application using the C# command-line compiler, it is important to understand the basics of how to compile your code files by hand. I can think of a few reasons you should get a grip on the process:

- The most obvious reason is the simple fact that you might not have a copy of Visual Studio 2008.
- You may be in a university setting where you are prohibited from using code generation tools/IDEs in the classroom.
- You plan to make use of automated build tools such as MSBuild or NAnt, which require you to know the command-line options of the tools you are utilizing.

- You want to deepen your understanding of C#. When you use graphical IDEs to build applications, you are ultimately instructing `csc.exe` how to manipulate your C# input files. In this light, it's edifying to see what takes place behind the scenes.

Another nice by-product of working with `csc.exe` in the raw is that you become that much more comfortable manipulating other command-line tools included with the .NET Framework 3.5 SDK. As you will see throughout this book, a number of important utilities are accessible only from the command line.

To illustrate how to build a .NET application IDE-free, we will build a simple executable assembly named `TestApp.exe` using the C# command-line compiler and Notepad. First, you need some source code. Open Notepad (using the Start ➤ Programs ➤ Accessories menu option) and enter the following trivial C# code:

```
// A simple C# application.
using System;

class TestApp
{
  static void Main()
  {
    Console.WriteLine("Testing! 1, 2, 3");
  }
}
```

Once you have finished, save the file in a convenient location (e.g., C:\CscExample) as `TestApp.cs`. Now, let's get to know the core options of the C# compiler.

■ **Note** As a convention, all C# code files take a `*.cs` file extension. The name of the file does not need to have any mapping to the name of the type (or types) it is defining.

Specifying Input and Output Targets

The first point of interest is to understand how to specify the name and type of assembly to create (e.g., a console application named `MyShell.exe`, a code library named `MathLib.dll`, a Windows Forms application named `Halo8.exe`, and so forth). Each possibility is represented by a specific flag passed into `csc.exe` as a command-line parameter (see Table 2-1).

Table 2-1. *Output Options of the C# Compiler*

Option	Meaning in Life
`/out`	This option is used to specify the name of the assembly to be created. By default, the assembly name is the same as the name of the initial input `*.cs` file.
`/target:exe`	This option builds an executable console application. This is the default assembly output type, and thus may be omitted when building this type of application.
`/target:library`	This option builds a single-file `*.dll` assembly.
`/target:module`	This option builds a *module*. Modules are elements of multifile assemblies (fully described in Chapter 15).
`/target:winexe`	Although you are free to build graphical user interface–based applications using the `/target:exe` option, `/target:winexe` prevents a console window from appearing in the background.

Note The options sent to the command-line compiler (as well as most other command-line tools) can be prefixed with either a dash (-?) or a slash (/?).

To compile `TestApp.cs` into a console application named `TestApp.exe`, change to the directory containing your source code file:

```
cd C:\CscExample
```

and enter the following command set (note that command-line flags must come before the name of the input files, not after):

```
csc /target:exe TestApp.cs
```

Here I did not explicitly specify an `/out` flag, therefore the executable will be named `TestApp.exe`, given that `TestApp` is the name of the input file. Also be aware that most of the C# compiler flags support an abbreviated version, such as `/t` rather than `/target` (you can view all abbreviations by entering `csc -?` at the command prompt).

```
csc /t:exe TestApp.cs
```

Furthermore, given that the `/t:exe` flag is the default output used by the C# compiler, you could also compile `TestApp.cs` simply by typing

```
csc TestApp.cs
```

`TestApp.exe` can now be run from the command line as shown in Figure 2-2.

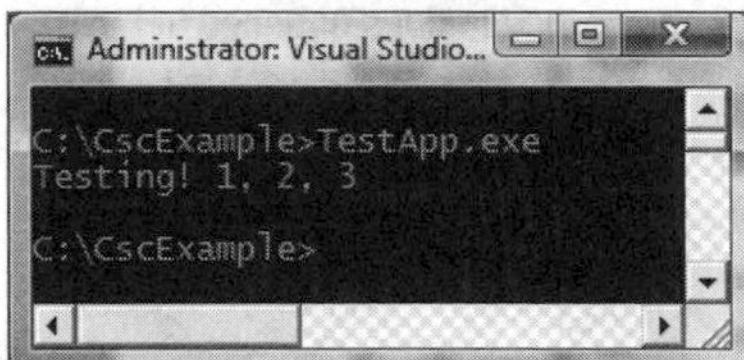

Figure 2-2. `TestApp.exe` *in action*

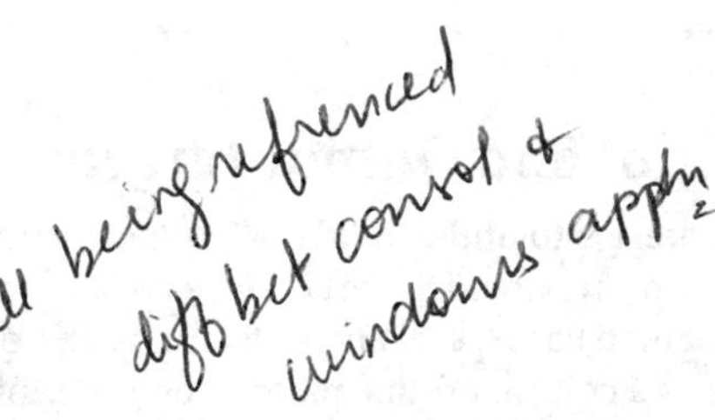

Referencing External Assemblies

Next, let's examine how to compile an application that makes use of types defined in a separate .NET assembly. Speaking of which, just in case you are wondering how the C# compiler understood your reference to the `System.Console` type, recall from Chapter 1 that `mscorlib.dll` is *automatically referenced* during the compilation process (if for some strange reason you wish to disable this behavior, you may specify the `/nostdlib` option of `csc.exe`).

Let's update the `TestApp` application to display a Windows Forms message box. Open your `TestApp.cs` file and modify it as follows:

```
using System;

// Add this!
using System.Windows.Forms;

class TestApp
{
```

```
    static void Main()
    {
      Console.WriteLine("Testing! 1, 2, 3");

      // Add this!
      MessageBox.Show("Hello...");
    }
}
```

Notice you are importing the `System.Windows.Forms` namespace via the C# `using` keyword (introduced in Chapter 1). Recall that when you explicitly list the namespaces used within a given `*.cs` file, you avoid the need to make use of fully qualified names of a type (which can lead to hand cramps).

At the command line, you must inform `csc.exe` which assembly contains the namespaces you are using. Given that you have made use of the `System.Windows.Forms.MessageBox` class, you must specify the `System.Windows.Forms.dll` assembly using the `/reference` flag (which can be abbreviated to `/r`):

```
csc /r:System.Windows.Forms.dll TestApp.cs
```

If you now rerun your application, you should see what appears in Figure 2-3 in addition to the console output.

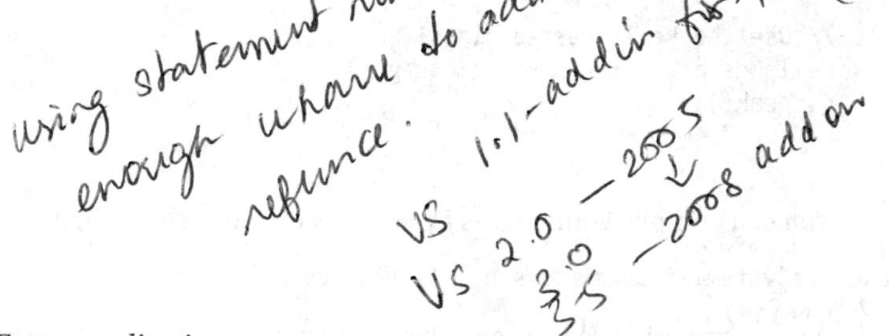

Figure 2-3. *Your first Windows Forms application*

Referencing Multiple External Assemblies

On a related note, what if you need to reference numerous external assemblies using `csc.exe`? Simply list each assembly using a semicolon-delimited list. You don't need to specify multiple external assemblies for the current example, but some sample usage follows:

```
csc /r:System.Windows.Forms.dll;System.Drawing.dll *.cs
```

Compiling Multiple Source Files

The current incarnation of the `TestApp.exe` application was created using a single `*.cs` source code file. While it is perfectly permissible to have all of your .NET types defined in a single `*.cs` file, most projects are composed of multiple `*.cs` files to keep your code base a bit more flexible. Assume you have authored an additional class contained in a new file named `HelloMsg.cs`:

```
// The HelloMessage class
using System;
using System.Windows.Forms;

class HelloMessage
{
```

```
  public void Speak()
  {
    MessageBox.Show("Hello...");
  }
}
```

Now, update your initial TestApp class to make use of this new class type, and comment out the previous Windows Forms logic:

```
using System;

// Don't need this anymore.
// using System.Windows.Forms;

class TestApp
{
  static void Main()
  {
    Console.WriteLine("Testing! 1, 2, 3");

    // Don't need this anymore either.
    // MessageBox.Show("Hello...");

    // Use the HelloMessage class!
    HelloMessage h = new HelloMessage();
    h.Speak();
  }
}
```

You can compile your C# files by listing each input file explicitly:

```
csc /r:System.Windows.Forms.dll TestApp.cs HelloMsg.cs
```

As an alternative, the C# compiler allows you to make use of the wildcard character (*) to inform csc.exe to include all *.cs files contained in the project directory as part of the current build:

```
csc /r:System.Windows.Forms.dll *.cs
```

When you run the program again, the output is identical. The only difference between the two applications is the fact that the current logic has been split among multiple files.

Working with C# Response Files

As you might guess, if you were to build a complex C# application at the command prompt, you would have to specify a tedious number of input options to inform the compiler how to process your source code. To help lessen your typing burden, the C# compiler honors the use of *response files*.

C# response files contain all the instructions to be used during the compilation of your current build. By convention, these files end in a *.rsp (response) extension. Assume that you have created a response file named TestApp.rsp that contains the following options (as you can see, comments are denoted with the # character):

```
# This is the response file
# for the TestApp.exe example
# of Chapter 2.
```

```
# External assembly references.
/r:System.Windows.Forms.dll

# output and files to compile (using wildcard syntax).
/target:exe /out:TestApp.exe *.cs
```

Now, assuming this file is saved in the same directory as the C# source code files to be compiled, you are able to build your entire application as follows (note the use of the @ symbol):

```
csc @TestApp.rsp
```

If the need should arise, you are also able to specify multiple `*.rsp` files as input (e.g., `csc @FirstFile.rsp @SecondFile.rsp @ThirdFile.rsp`). If you take this approach, do be aware that the compiler processes the command options as they are encountered! Therefore, command-line arguments in a later `*.rsp` file can override options in a previous response file.

Also note that flags listed explicitly on the command line before a response file will be overridden by the specified `*.rsp` file. Thus, if you were to enter the following:

```
csc /out:MyCoolApp.exe @TestApp.rsp
```

the name of the assembly would still be `TestApp.exe` (rather than `MyCoolApp.exe`), given the `/out:TestApp.exe` flag listed in the `TestApp.rsp` response file. However, if you list flags after a response file, the flag will override settings in the response file.

■ **Note** The effect of the `/reference` flag is cumulative. Regardless of where you specify external assemblies (before, after, or within a response file), the end result is a summation of each reference assembly.

The Default Response File (csc.rsp)

The final point to be made regarding response files is that the C# compiler has an associated default response file (`csc.rsp`), which is located in the same directory as `csc.exe` itself (which is by default installed under C:\Windows\Microsoft.NET\Framework\v3.5). If you were to open this file using Notepad, you will find that numerous .NET assemblies have already been specified using the `/r:` flag, including various libraries for web development, LINQ, data access, and other core libraries (beyond `mscorlib.dll`).

When you are building your C# programs using `csc.exe`, this response file will be automatically referenced, even when you supply a custom `*.rsp` file. Given the presence of the default response file, the current `TestApp.exe` application could be successfully compiled using the following command set (as `System.Windows.Forms.dll` is referenced within `csc.rsp`):

```
csc /out:TestApp.exe *.cs
```

In the event that you wish to disable the automatic reading of `csc.rsp`, you can specify the `/noconfig` option:

```
csc @TestApp.rsp /noconfig
```

■ **Note** If you reference assemblies (via the `/r` option) that you do not actually make use of; they are ignored by the compiler. Therefore, you have no need to worry about "code bloat."

Obviously, the C# command-line compiler has many other options that can be used to control how the resulting .NET assembly is to be generated. If you wish to learn more details regarding the functionality of `csc.exe`, look up my article titled "Working with the C# 2.0 Command Line Compiler" online at `http://msdn.microsoft.com`. While this article examines the options of the C# 2.0 compiler, thankfully the C# 2008 compiler supports the same set of features.

■ **Source Code** The CscExample application can be found under the Chapter 2 subdirectory.

Building .NET Applications Using TextPad

While Notepad is fine for creating simple .NET programs, it offers nothing in the way of developer productivity. It would be ideal to author `*.cs` files using an editor that supports (at a minimum) keyword coloring and integration with a C# compiler. As luck would have it, such a tool does exist: TextPad.

TextPad is an editor you can use to author code for numerous programming languages, including C#. The chief advantage of this product is the fact that it is very simple to use and provides just enough bells and whistles to enhance your coding efforts, without too many to obfuscate the learning process.

To obtain TextPad, navigate to `http://www.textpad.com` and download the latest version (5.0.3 at the time of this writing). Once you have installed the product, you will have a feature-complete version of TextPad; however, this tool is not freeware. Until you purchase a single-user license (for around US$30.00), you will be presented with a "friendly reminder" each time you run the application.

Enabling C# Keyword Coloring

TextPad is not equipped to understand C# keywords or work with `csc.exe` out of the box. To do so, you will need to register the `*.cs` file extension with the tool. Launch TextPad and perform the following tasks using the New Document Wizard:

1. Select the Configure ➤ New Document Class menu option.
2. Enter the name **C#** in the Document class name edit box.
3. In the next step, enter ***.cs** in the Class members edit box.
4. Finally, enable syntax highlighting, choose `csharp.syn` from the drop-down list box, and close the wizard.

■ **Note** Earlier versions of TextPad did not ship with the C# syntax file (`csharp.syn`); however, it could be downloaded from the TextPad website. In fact, syntax files for a variety of languages can be downloaded from the TextPad website.

You can now tweak TextPad's C# look and feel using the Document Classes node accessible from the Configure ➤ Preferences menu option (see Figure 2-4).

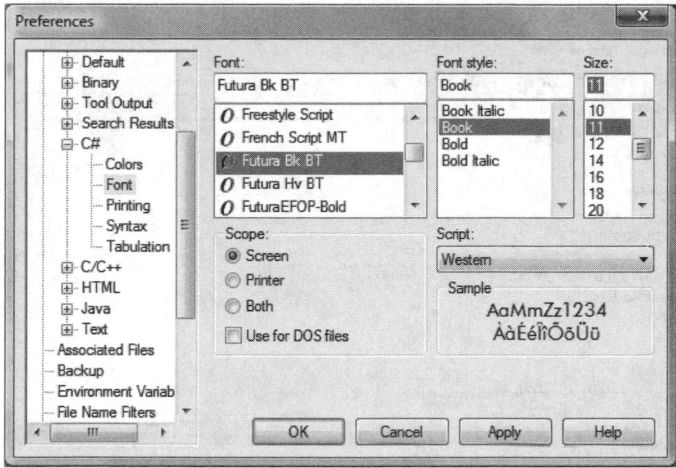

Figure 2-4. *Setting TextPad's C# preferences*

Configuring the *.cs File Filter

The next configuration detail is to create a filter for C# source code files displayed by the Open and Save dialog boxes:

1. Select the Configure ➤ Preferences menu option and select File Name Filters from the tree view control.
2. Click the New button, and enter **C#** into the Description field and ***.cs** into the Wild cards text box.
3. Move your new filter to the top of the list using the Move Up button and click OK.

Create a new file (using File ➤ New) and save it in a convenient location (such as C:\TextPadTestApp) as `TextPadTest.cs`. Next, enter a trivial class definition (see Figure 2-5).

Hooking Into csc.exe

The last configuration detail to contend with is to load `csc.exe` from within TextPad so you can compile your C# files. The first way to do so is using the Tools ➤ Run menu option. Here you are presented with a dialog box that allows you to specify the name of the tool to run and any necessary command-line flags. To compile `TextPadTest.cs` into a .NET console-based executable, follow these steps:

1. Enter the full path to `csc.exe` into the Command text box (e.g., C:\Windows\Microsoft.NET\Framework\v3.5\csc.exe).
2. Enter the command-line options you wish to specify within the Parameters text box (e.g., `/out:myApp.exe *.cs`). Recall that you can specify a custom response file to simplify matters (e.g., `@myInput.rsp`).
3. Enter the directory containing the input files via the Initial folder text box (for example, C:\TextPadTestApp).
4. If you wish TextPad to capture the compiler output directly (rather than within a separate command window), select the Capture Output check box.

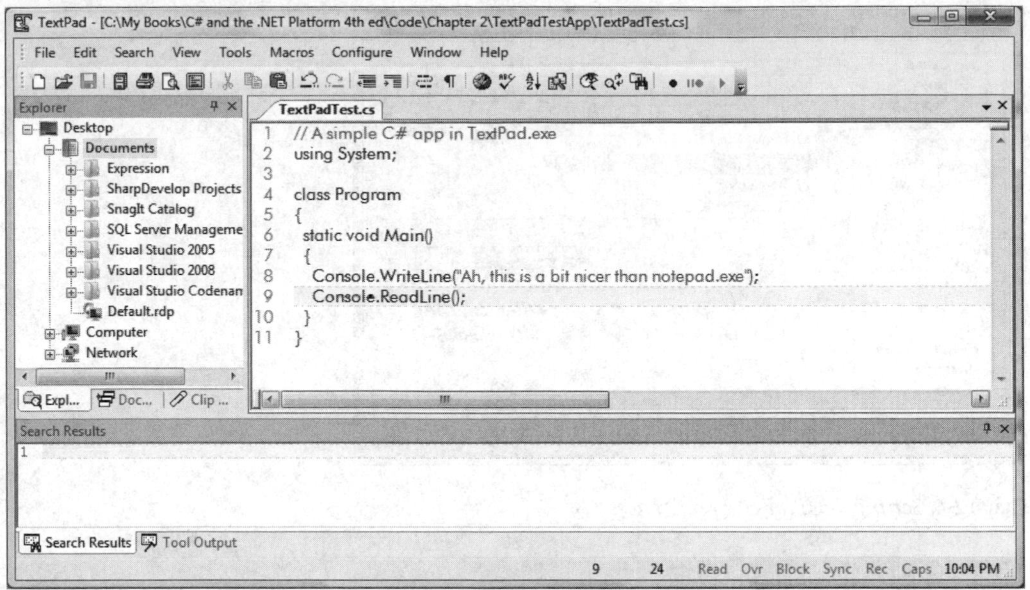

Figure 2-5. *TextPad in action*

Figure 2-6 shows some possible compilation settings.

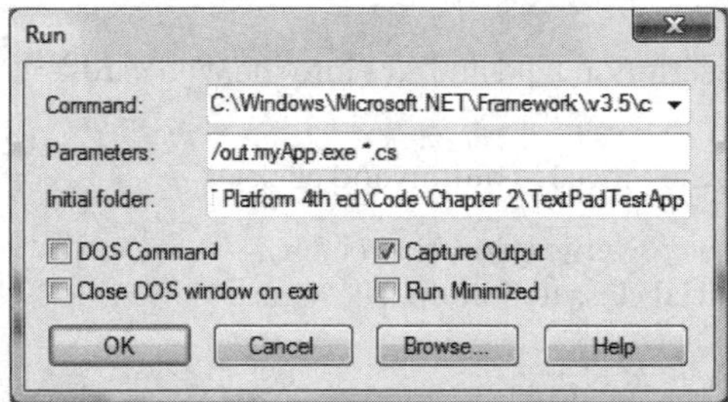

Figure 2-6. *Specifying a custom* `Run` *command*

At this point, you can either run your program by double-clicking the executable using Windows Explorer or leverage the Tools ➤ Run menu option once again to specify `myApp.exe` as the current command (see Figure 2-7).

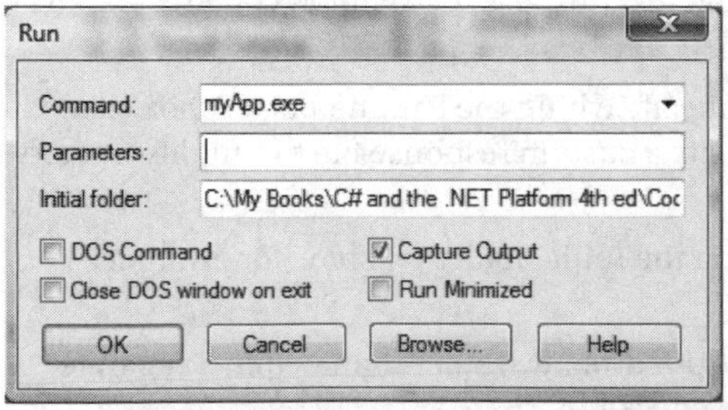

Figure 2-7. *Instructing TextPad to run* `myApp.exe`

When you click OK, you should see the program's output displayed in the Tool Output window.

Associating Run Commands with Menu Items

TextPad also allows you to create custom menu items that represent predefined run commands. Thus, rather than having to manually configure the tool, parameters, and starting folder each time you wish to run the command, you can essentially do so once and save the settings for later use. Let's create a custom item under the Tools menu named "Compile C# Code" that will compile all C# files in the current directory using a response file.

1. Select the Configure ➤ Preferences menu option and select Tools from the tree view control.
2. Using the Add button, select Program and specify the full path to `csc.exe` (again, C:\Windows\Microsoft.NET\Framework\v3.5 by default) using the resulting dialog box and click OK.
3. If you wish, rename your new menu item to a more descriptive label (Compile C#) by selecting the name of the tool in the list box (to activate it for editing).
4. Finally, select your tool name (Compile C#) from the Tools node, and specify `@build.rsp` as the sole value in the Parameters field; the `$FileDir` token in the Initial Folder field instructs TextPad to look in the folder of the active file (see Figure 2-8).

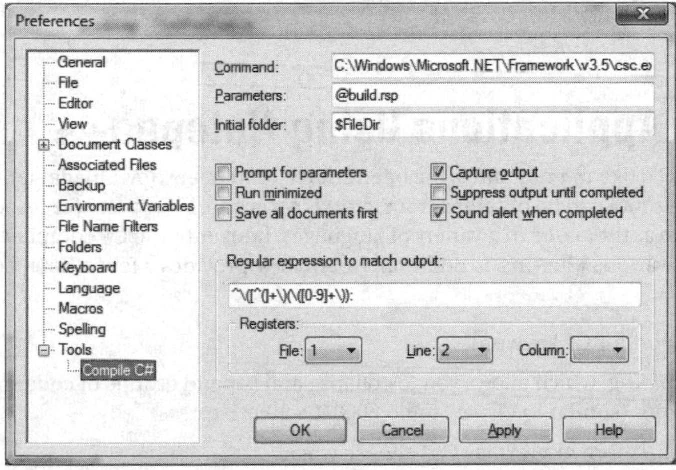

Figure 2-8. *Creating a Tools menu item*

With this, you can now compile all C# files in the current directory using your custom Tools menu item, provided that this same directory has a C# response file named `build.rsp`. Notice in Figure 2-9 the Document Selector pane can be used to see each file opened within TextPad at the current time. The Tool Output window shows the output of running our custom Tool menu.

This should be enough information regarding TextPad to get you in a good position for further exploration. As you might suspect, this tool is a very rich editor that supports many additional plug-in utilities (spell checkers, code formatters, clip libraries, autocompletion support, etc.). Check out `http://www.textpad.com/add-ons` for further details.

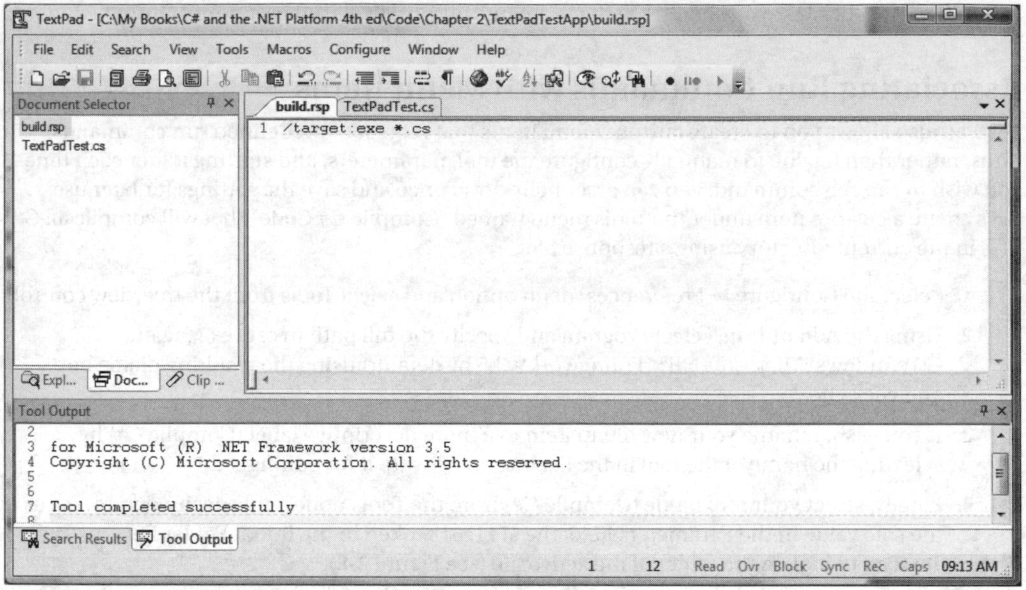

Figure 2-9. *Executing the C# compiler using TextPad*

Building .NET Applications Using Notepad++

The final simple text editor I'd like to point out is the open source (and freely downloadable) Notepad++ application. This tool can be obtained from `http://notepad-plus.sourceforge.net`, and like TextPad, it allows you to author code in a variety of languages, hook into the C# compiler (via the Run menu), and install various plug-ins. In addition, Notepad++ provides a few other niceties, including the following:

- Out-of-the-box support for C# keywords
- Support for *syntax folding*, which allows you to collapse and expand groups of code statements within the editor (similar to Visual Studio 2008/C# 2008 Express)
- The ability to zoom in/zoom out text via Ctrl-mouse wheel
- Configurable autocompletion for a variety of C# keywords and .NET namespaces

Regarding this last point, the Ctrl+space keyboard combination will activate C# autocompletion support (see Figure 2-10).

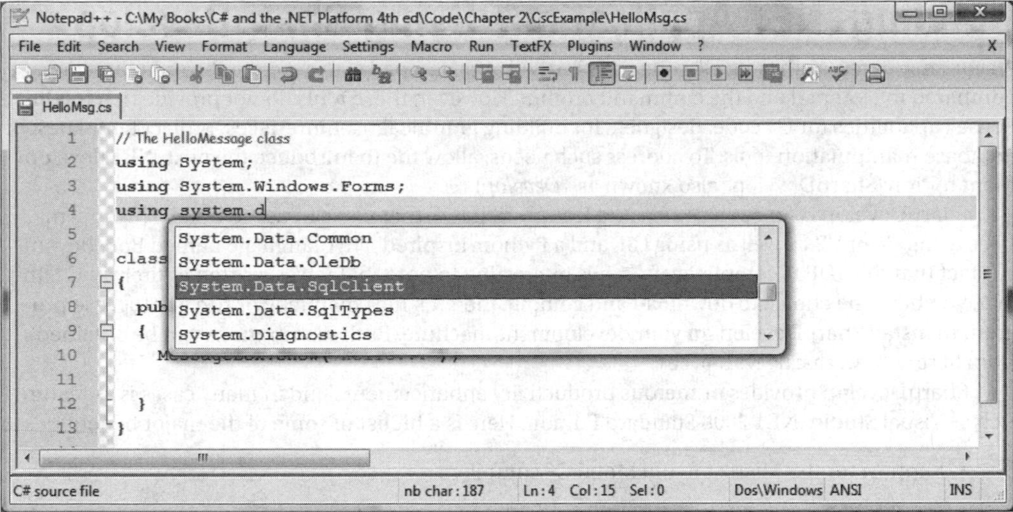

Figure 2-10. *Autocompletion using Notepad++*

Customizing the Autocompletion List

The list of options shown within the autocomplete window can be modified and extended. Simply open up the C:\Program Files\Notepad++\plugins\APIs\cs.api file for editing and add any additional entries. As you can see in Figure 2-11, each entry is listed on a single line.

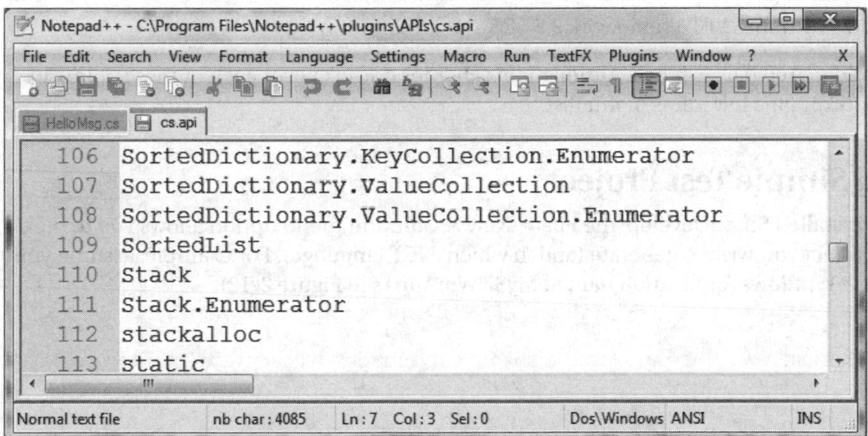

Figure 2-11. *Updating the autocompletion list of Notepad++*

I won't go into too many details of Notepad++ beyond what we have examined here, given that the functionality of this application is similar to that of TextPad. If you require more assistance, select the ? ➤ Online Help menu option.

Building .NET Applications Using SharpDevelop

As you may agree, authoring C# code with TextPad and Notepad++ is a step in the right direction, compared to Notepad and the command prompt. However, these tools do not provide rich IntelliSense capabilities for C# code, designers for building graphical user interfaces, project templates, or database manipulation tools. To address such needs, allow me to introduce the next .NET development option: SharpDevelop (also known as *#Develop*).

SharpDevelop is an open source and feature-rich IDE that you can use to build .NET assemblies using C# or VB as well as using CIL and a Python-inspired .NET language named Boo. Beyond the fact that this IDE is completely free, it is interesting to note that it was written entirely in C#. In fact, you have the choice to download and compile the `*.cs` files manually or run a `setup.exe` program to install SharpDevelop on your development machine. Both distributions can be obtained from `http://www.sharpdevelop.com`.

SharpDevelop provides numerous productivity enhancements and in many cases is as feature rich as Visual Studio .NET 2008 Standard Edition. Here is a hit list of some of the major benefits:

- Support for the Microsoft and Mono C# compilers
- IntelliSense, code completion, and code snippet capabilities
- An Add Reference dialog box to reference external assemblies, including assemblies deployed to the global assembly cache (GAC)
- A visual Windows Forms designer
- Integrated object browsing and code definition utilities
- Visual database designer utilities
- A C# to VB (and vice versa) code conversion utility
- Integration with the NUnit (a .NET unit testing utility) and NAnt (a .NET build utility)
- Integration with the .NET Framework 3.5 SDK documentation

Impressive for a free IDE, is it not? Although this chapter doesn't cover each of these points in detail, let's walk through a few items of interest.

Building a Simple Test Project

Once you have installed SharpDevelop, the File ➤ New ➤ Solution menu option allows you to pick which type of project you wish to generate (and in which .NET language). For example, assume you have created a C# Windows Application named MySDWinApp (see Figure 2-12).

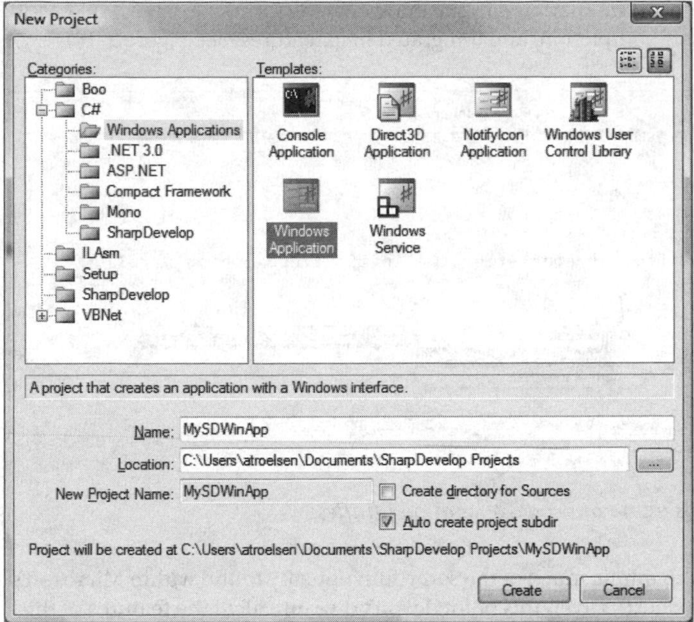

Figure 2-12. *The SharpDevelop New Project dialog box*

Like Visual Studio, you have a GUI designer, toolbox (to drag and drop controls onto the designer), and a Properties window to set up the look and feel of each UI item. Figure 2-13 illustrates configuring a Button type using the IDE.

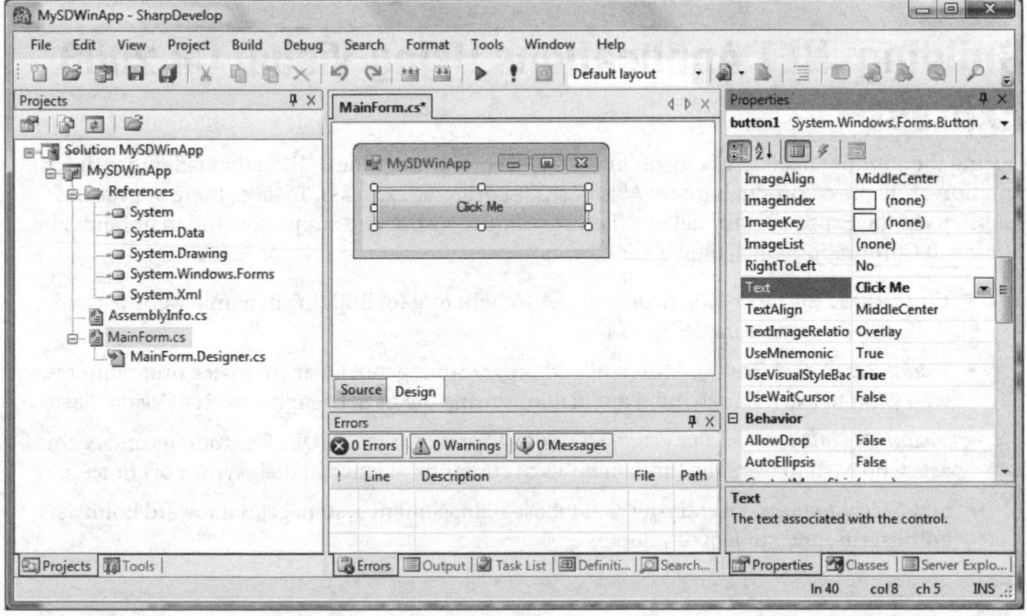

Figure 2-13. *Graphically designing a Windows Forms Application with SharpDevelop*

If you were to click the Source button mounted to the bottom of the form's designer, you would find the expected IntelliSense, code completion, and integrated help features (see Figure 2-14).

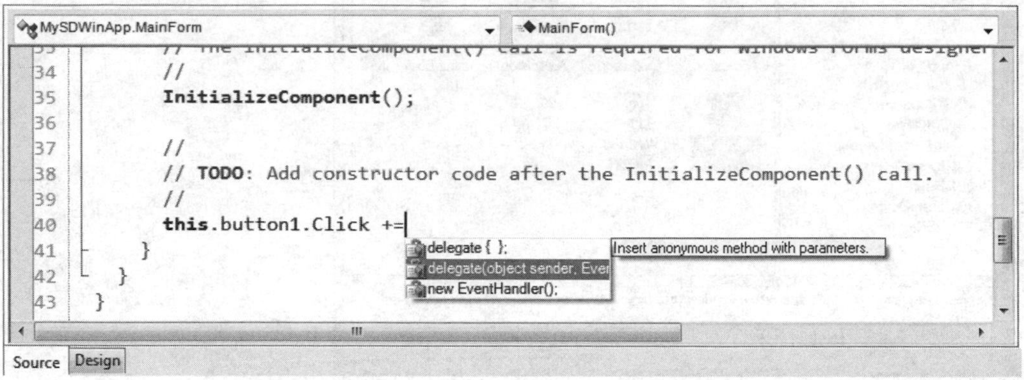

Figure 2-14. *SharpDevelop supports numerous code-generation utilities.*

SharpDevelop was designed to mimic much of the same functionality found within Microsoft's .NET IDEs (which we will examine next). Given this point, I won't dive into all of the features of this open source .NET IDE. If you require more information, simply use the provided Help menu.

■ **Note** Appendix B will examine building cross-platform .NET applications using the open source Mono .NET distribution. As you read over that appendix, be sure you remember that SharpDevelop is Mono-aware!

Building .NET Applications Using Visual C# 2008 Express

During the summer of 2004, Microsoft introduced a brand-new line of IDEs that fall under the designation of "Express" products (`http://msdn.microsoft.com/express`). To date, there are various members of the Express family (all of which are *completely free* and supported and maintained by Microsoft Corporation), including the following:

- *Visual Web Developer 2008 Express*: A lightweight tool for building dynamic websites and XML web services using ASP.NET
- *Visual Basic 2008 Express*: A streamlined programming tool ideal for novice programmers who want to learn how to build applications using the user-friendly syntax of Visual Basic
- *Visual C# 2008 Express and Visual C++ 2008 Express*: Targeted IDEs for students and enthusiasts who wish to learn the fundamentals of computer science in their syntax of choice
- *SQL Server Express*: An entry-level database management system geared toward hobbyists, enthusiasts, and student developers

Some Unique Features of Visual C# Express

By and large, the Express products are slimmed-down versions of their Visual Studio 2008 counterparts and are primarily targeted at .NET hobbyists and students. Like SharpDevelop, Visual C# 2008 Express provides various object browsing tools, a Windows Forms designer, the Add References dialog box, IntelliSense capabilities, and code expansion templates.

However, Visual C# 2008 Express offers a few (important) features currently not available in SharpDevelop, including the following:

- Rich support for Windows Presentation Foundation (WPF) XAML applications
- IntelliSense for new C# 2008 syntactical constructs including lambda expressions and LINQ query statements
- The ability to program Xbox 360 and PC video games using the freely available Microsoft XNA Game Studio

Consider Figure 2-15, which illustrates using Visual C# Express to author the XAML markup for a WPF project.

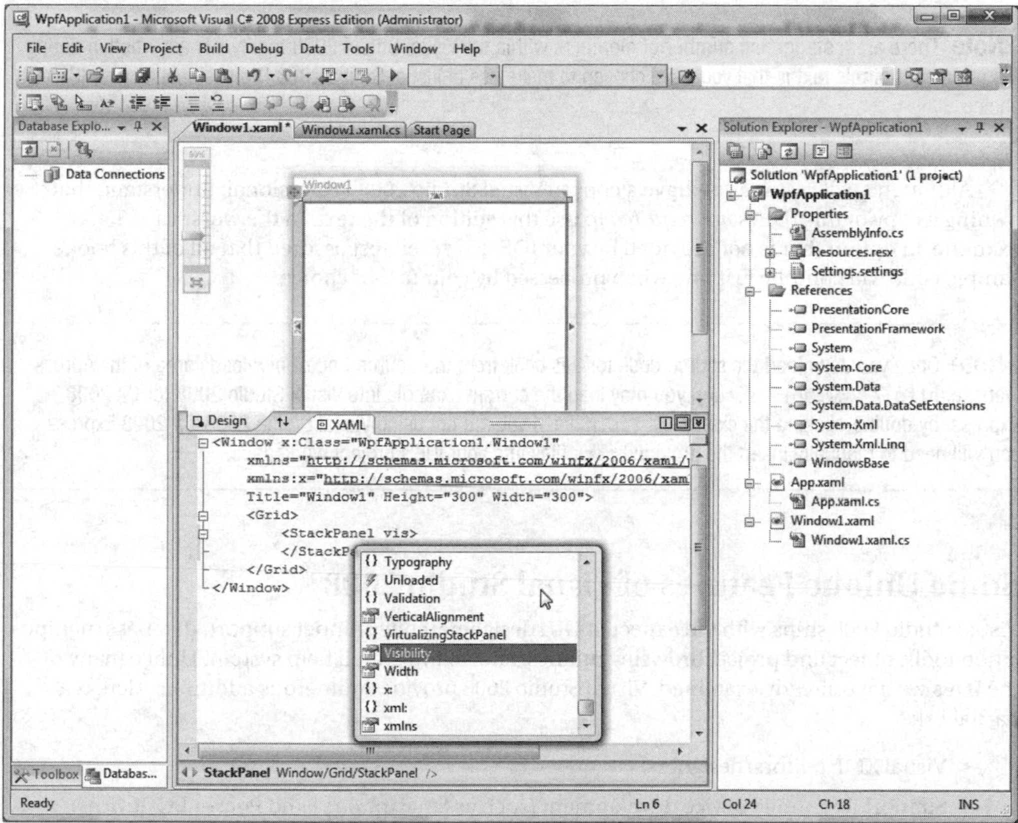

Figure 2-15. *Visual C# Express has integrated support for .NET 3.0 and .NET 3.5 APIs.*

Because the look and feel of Visual C# 2008 Express is so similar to that of Visual Studio 2008 (and, to some degree, SharpDevelop), I do not provide a walk-through of this particular IDE here. If you do wish to learn more about the product, look up my article "An Introduction to Programming Using Microsoft Visual C# 2005 Express Edition" online at `http://msdn.microsoft.com`. While this article is based on Visual C# 2005 Express, a majority of the topics are identical.

Building .NET Applications Using Visual Studio 2008

If you are a professional .NET software engineer, the chances are extremely good that your employer has purchased Microsoft's premier IDE, Visual Studio 2008, for your development endeavors (`http://msdn.microsoft.com/vstudio`). This tool is far and away the most feature-rich and enterprise-ready IDE examined in this chapter. Of course, this power comes at a price, which will vary based on the version of Visual Studio 2008 you purchase. As you might suspect, each version supplies a unique set of features.

■ **Note** There are a staggering number of members within the Visual Studio 2008 family. My assumption during the remainder of this text is that you have chosen to make use of Visual Studio 2008 Professional as your IDE of choice.

Although I will assume you have a copy of Visual Studio 2008 Professional, understand that owning a copy of this IDE is *not required* to use this edition of the text. In the worst case, I may examine an option that is not provided by your IDE. However, rest assured that all of this book's sample code will compile just fine when processed by your tool of choice.

■ **Note** Once you download the source code for this book from the Source Code/Downloads area of the Apress website (`http://www.apress.com`), you may load the current example into Visual Studio 2008 (or C# 2008 Express) by double-clicking the example's `*.sln` file. If you are not using Visual Studio 2008/C# 2008 Express, you will need to manually insert the provided `*.cs` files into your IDE's project workspace.

Some Unique Features of Visual Studio 2008

Visual Studio 2008 ships with the expected GUI designers, code snippet support, database manipulation tools, object and project browsing utilities, and an integrated help system. Unlike many of the IDEs we have already examined, Visual Studio 2008 provides numerous additions. Here is a partial list:

- Visual XML editors/designers
- Support for mobile device development (such as Smartphones and Pocket PC devices)
- Support for Microsoft Office development
- Designer support for Windows Workflow Foundation projects
- Integrated support for code refactoring

- Visual class design utilities
- The Object Test Bench window, which allows you to create objects and invoke their members directly within the IDE

To be completely honest, Visual Studio 2008 provides so many features that it would take an entire book (a rather large book at that) to fully describe every aspect of the IDE. *This is not that book.* However, I do want to point out some of the major features in the pages that follow. As you progress through the text, you'll learn more about the Visual Studio 2008 IDE where appropriate.

Targeting the .NET Framework Using the New Project Dialog Box

If you are following along, create a new C# Console Application (named Vs2008Example) using the File ➤ New ➤ Project menu item. As you can see in Figure 2-16, Visual Studio 2008 now *(finally)* supports the ability to select which version of the .NET Framework you wish to build against (2.0, 3.0, or 3.5) using the drop-down list box on the upper right of the New Project dialog box. For each project in this text, you can simply leave the default selection of .NET Framework 3.5.

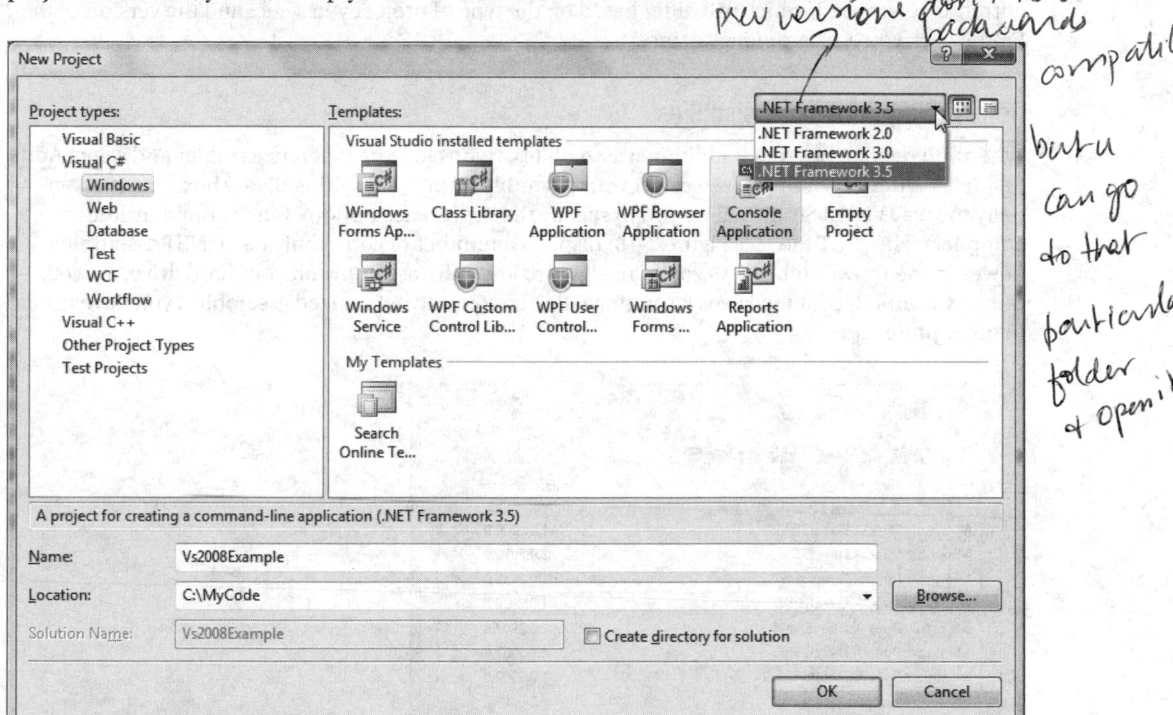

Figure 2-16. *Visual Studio 2008 now allows you to target a particular version of the .NET Framework.*

Using the Solution Explorer Utility

The Solution Explorer utility (accessible from the View menu) allows you to view the set of all content files and referenced assemblies that comprise the current project (see Figure 2-17).

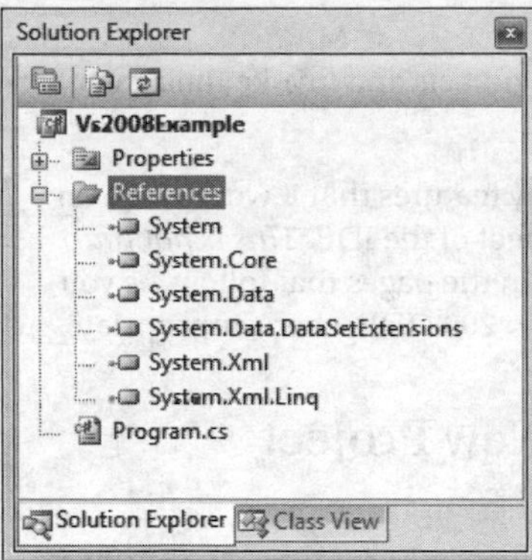

Figure 2-17. *The Solution Explorer utility*

Notice that the References folder of Solution Explorer displays a list of each assembly you have currently referenced, which will differ based on the type of project you select and the version of the Framework you are compiling against.

Referencing External Assemblies

When you need to reference additional assemblies, right-click the References folder and select Add Reference. At this point, you can select your assembly from the resulting dialog box (this is essentially the way Visual Studio allows you to specify the `/reference` option of the command-line compiler). The .NET tab (see Figure 2-18) displays a number of commonly used .NET assemblies; however, the Browse tab allows you to navigate to any .NET assembly on your hard drive. As well, the very useful Recent tab keeps a running tally of frequently referenced assemblies you have used in other projects.

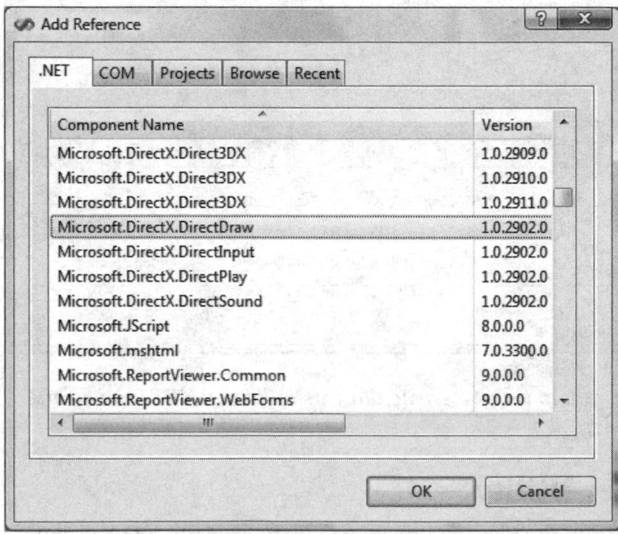

Figure 2-18. *The Add Reference dialog box*

Viewing Project Properties

Finally, notice an icon named Properties within Solution Explorer. When you double-click this item, you are presented with a sophisticated project configuration editor (see Figure 2-19).

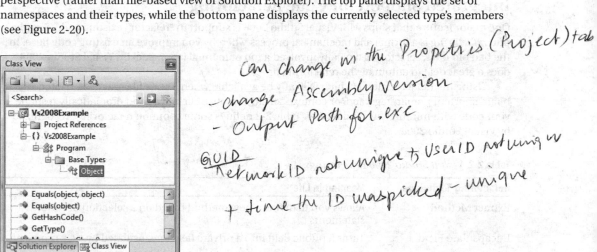

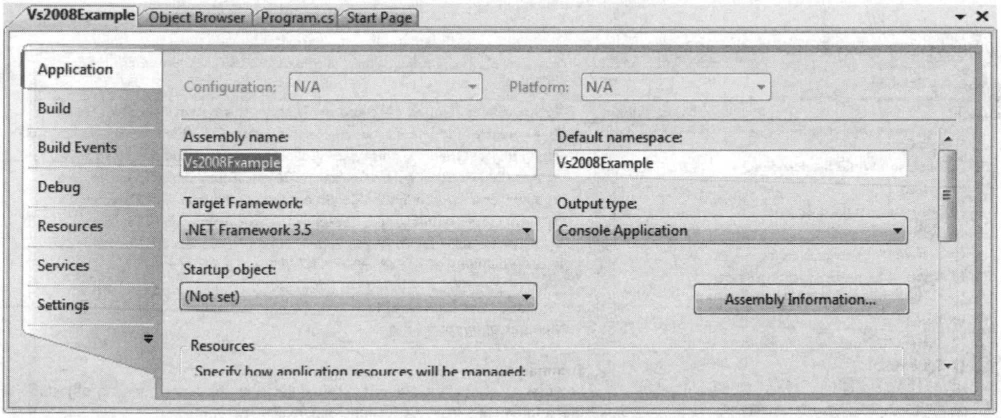

Figure 2-19. *The Project Properties window*

You will see various aspects of the Project Properties window as you progress through this book. However, if you take some time to poke around, you will see that you can establish various security settings, strongly name your assembly, deploy your application, insert application resources, and configure pre- and postbuild events.

The Class View Utility

The next tool to examine is the Class View utility, which you can load from the View menu. The purpose of this utility is to show all of the types in your current project from an object-oriented perspective (rather than file-based view of Solution Explorer). The top pane displays the set of namespaces and their types, while the bottom pane displays the currently selected type's members (see Figure 2-20).

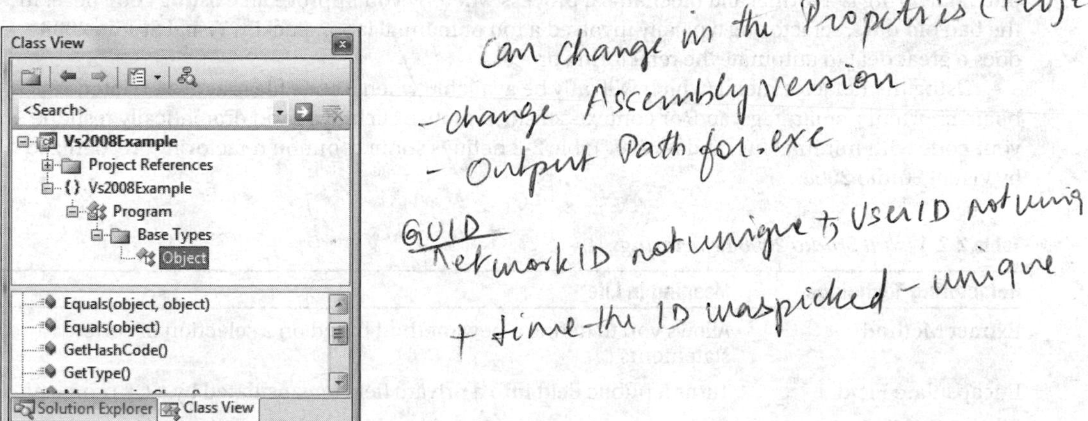

Figure 2-20. *The Class View utility*

The Object Browser Utility

Visual Studio 2008 also provides a utility to investigate the set of referenced assemblies within your current project. Activate the Object Browser using the View menu, and then select the assembly you wish to investigate (see Figure 2-21).

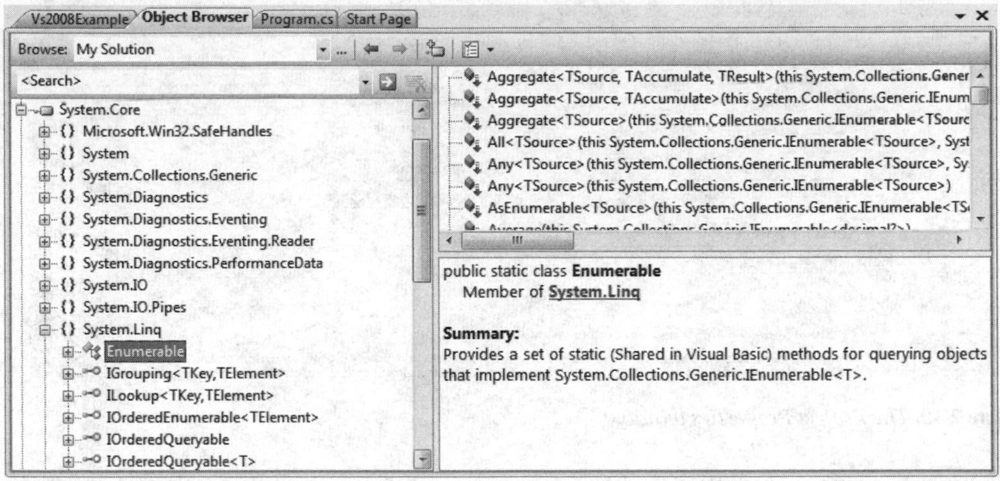

Figure 2-21. *The Object Browser utility*

Note If you double-click an assembly icon from the References folder of Solution Explorer, the Object Browser will open automatically with the selected assembly highlighted.

Integrated Support for Code Refactoring

One major feature that ships with Visual Studio 2008 is support to "refactor" existing code. Simply put, *refactoring* is a formal and mechanical process whereby you improve an existing code base. In the bad old days, refactoring typically involved a ton of manual labor. Luckily, Visual Studio 2008 does a great deal to automate the refactoring process.

Using the Refactor menu (which will only be available when a code file is active), related keyboard shortcuts, smart tags, and/or context-sensitive mouse clicks, you can dramatically reshape your code with minimal fuss and bother. Table 2-2 defines some common refactorings recognized by Visual Studio 2008.

Table 2-2. *Visual Studio 2008 Refactorings*

Refactoring Technique	Meaning in Life
Extract Method	Allows you to define a new method based on a selection of code statements
Encapsulate Field	Turns a public field into a private field encapsulated by a C# property
Extract Interface	Defines a new interface type based on a set of existing type members
Reorder Parameters	Provides a way to reorder member arguments
Remove Parameters	Removes a given argument from the current list of parameters (as you would expect)

Refactoring Technique	Meaning in Life
Rename	Allows you to rename a code token (method name, field, local variable, and so on) throughout a project
Promote Local Variable to Parameter	Moves a local variable to the parameter set of the defining method

To illustrate refactoring in action, update your `Main()` method with the following code:

```
static void Main(string[] args)
{
  // Set up Console UI (CUI)
  Console.Title = "My Rocking App";
  Console.ForegroundColor = ConsoleColor.Yellow;
  Console.BackgroundColor = ConsoleColor.Blue;
  Console.WriteLine("*************************************");
  Console.WriteLine("***** Welcome to My Rocking App *****");
  Console.WriteLine("*************************************");
  Console.BackgroundColor = ConsoleColor.Black;

  // Wait for Enter key to be pressed.
  Console.ReadLine();
}
```

While there is nothing wrong with the preceding code as it now stands, imagine that you want to display this welcome message at various places throughout your program. Rather than retyping the same exact console user interface logic, it would be ideal to have a helper function that could be called to do so. Given this, you will apply the Extract Method refactoring to your existing code.

First, select each code statement within `Main()` (except the final call to `Console.ReadLine()`) using the editor. Now, right-click the selected text and select the Extract Method option within the Refactor context menu (see Figure 2-22).

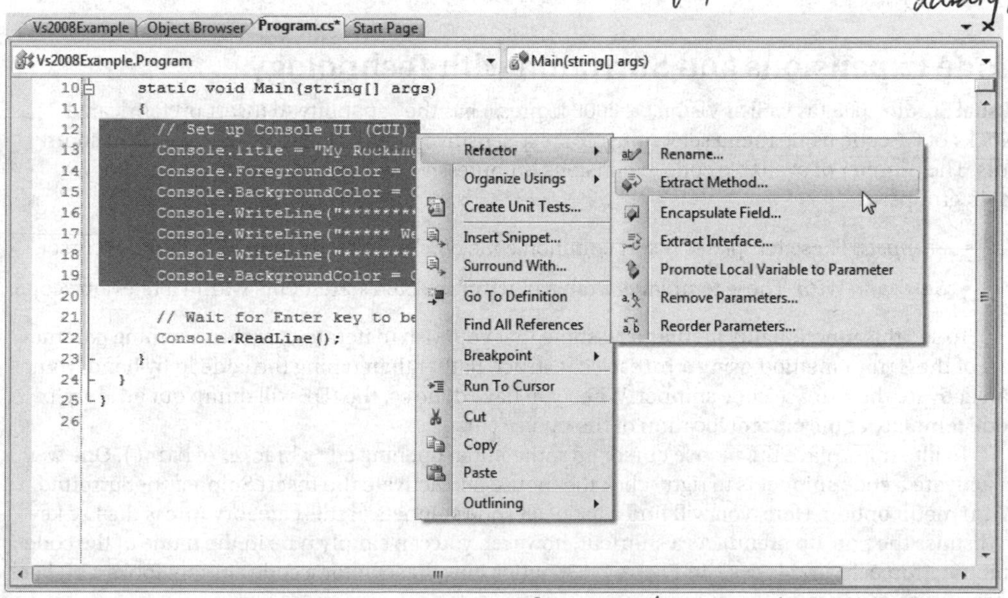

Figure 2-22. *Activating a code refactoring*

Name your new method `ConfigureCUI` using the resulting dialog box. When you have finished, you will find that your `Main()` method calls the newly generated `ConfigureCUI()` method, which now contains the previously selected code:

```
class Program
{
  static void Main(string[] args)
  {
    ConfigureCUI();

    // Wait for key press to close.
    Console.ReadLine();
  }

  private static void ConfigureCUI()
  {
    // Set up Console UI (CUI)
    Console.Title = "My Rocking App";
    Console.ForegroundColor = ConsoleColor.Yellow;
    Console.BackgroundColor = ConsoleColor.Blue;
    Console.WriteLine("**************************************");
    Console.WriteLine("***** Welcome to My Rocking App *****");
    Console.WriteLine("**************************************");
    Console.BackgroundColor = ConsoleColor.Black;
  }
}
```

This is a simple example of using the built-in refactorings of Visual Studio 2008, and you'll see additional examples here and there over the course of this text. However, if you are interested in more information on the refactoring process and a detailed walk-through of each refactoring supported by Visual Studio 2008, look up my article "Refactoring C# Code Using Visual Studio 2005" online at `http://msdn.microsoft.com` (again, while this article was written for Visual Studio 2005, Visual Studio 2008 has the same refactoring support).

Code Expansions and Surround with Technology

Visual Studio 2008 (as well as Visual C# 2008 Express) has the capability to insert prefabricated blocks of C# code using menu selections, context-sensitive mouse clicks, and/or keyboard shortcuts. The number of available code expansions is impressive and can be broken down into two main groups:

- *Snippets*: These templates insert common code blocks at the location of the mouse cursor.
- *Surround With*: These templates wrap a block of selected statements within a relevant scope.

To see this functionality firsthand, assume that you wish to iterate over the incoming parameters of the `Main()` method using a `foreach` construct. Rather than typing the code in by hand, you can activate the `foreach` code snippet. When you have done so, the IDE will dump out a `foreach` code template at the current location of the mouse cursor.

To illustrate, place the mouse cursor after the initial opening curly bracket of `Main()`. One way to activate a code snippet is to right-click the mouse and activate the Insert Snippet (or Surround With) menu option. Here, you will find a list of all code snippets of this category (press the Esc key to dismiss the pop-up menu). As a shortcut, however, you can simply type in the name of the code snippet, "foreach" in this case. In Figure 2-23, notice how the icon for a code snippet looks a bit like a torn piece of paper.

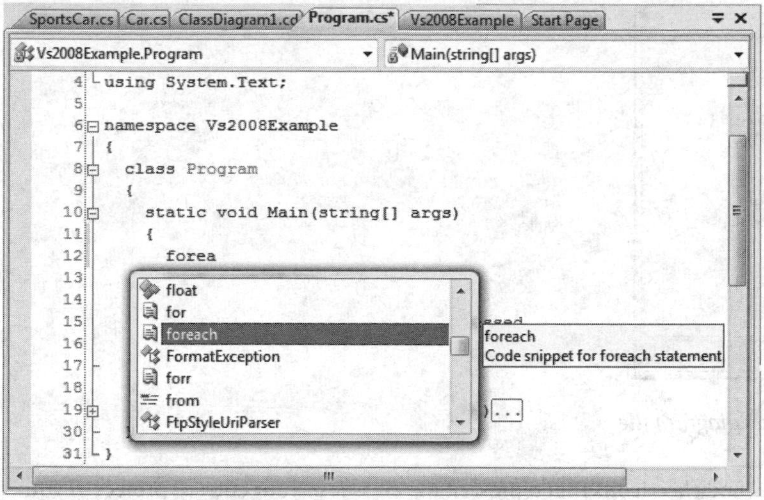

Figure 2-23. *Activating a code snippet*

Once you find the snippet you want to activate, press the Tab key twice. This will autocomplete the entire snippet and leave a set of *placeholders* that you can fill in to complete the snippet. If you press the Tab key, you can cycle between each placeholder and fill in the gaps (press the Esc key to exit the code snippet edit mode).

If you were to right-click and select the Surround With menu, you would likewise be presented with a list of options. Recall that when using Surround With snippets you typically first select a block of code statements to represent what should be used to wrap them (`try/catch` block, etc.). Be sure to take time to explore these predefined code expansion templates, as they can radically speed up the development process.

■ Note All code expansion templates are XML-based descriptions of the code to generate within the IDE. Using Visual Studio 2008 (as well as Visual C# 2008 Express), you can create your own custom code templates. Details of how to do so can be found in my article "Investigating Code Snippet Technology" at `http://msdn.microsoft.com`.

The Visual Class Designer

Visual Studio 2008 gives us the ability to design classes visually (this capability is not included in Visual C# 2008 Express). The Class Designer utility allows you to view and modify the relationships of the types (classes, interfaces, structures, enumerations, and delegates) in your project. Using this tool, you are able to visually add (or remove) members to (or from) a type and have your modifications reflected in the corresponding C# file. As well, as you modify a given C# file, changes are reflected in the class diagram.

To work with this aspect of Visual Studio 2008, the first step is to insert a new class diagram file. There are many ways to do so, one of which is to click the View Class Diagram button located on Solution Explorer's right side (see Figure 2-24).

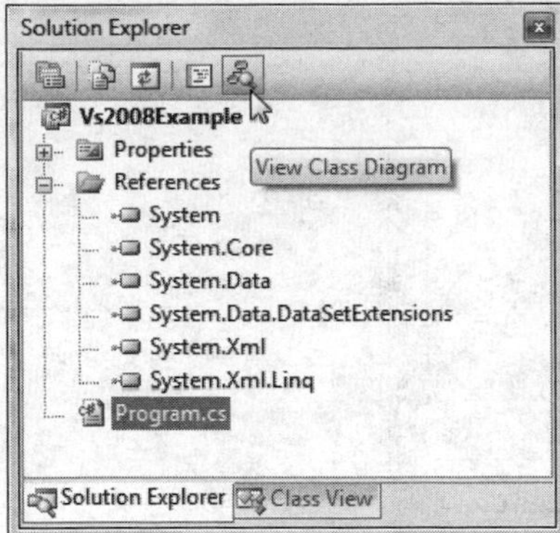

Figure 2-24. *Inserting a class diagram file*

Once you do, you will find class icons that represent the classes in your current project. If you click the arrow icon for a given type, you can show or hide the type's members. Using the Class Designer toolbar, you can fine-tune the display options of the designer surface (see Figure 2-25).

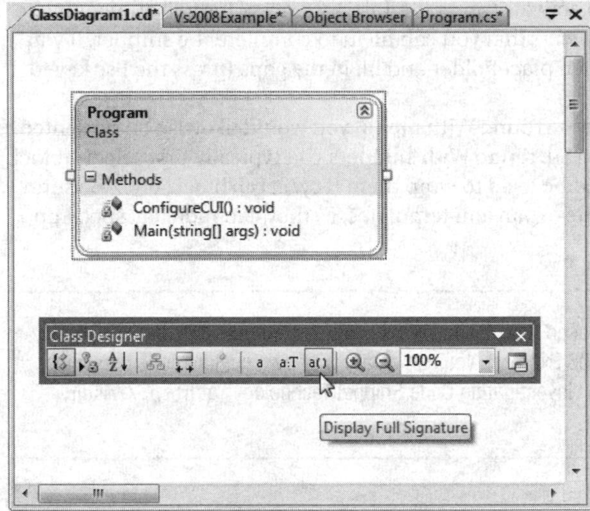

Figure 2-25. *The Class Diagram viewer*

This utility works in conjunction with two other aspects of Visual Studio 2008: the Class Details window (activated using the View ➤ Other Windows menu) and the Class Designer Toolbox (activated using the View ➤ Toolbox menu item). The Class Details window not only shows you the details of the currently selected item in the diagram, but also allows you to modify existing members and insert new members on the fly (see Figure 2-26).

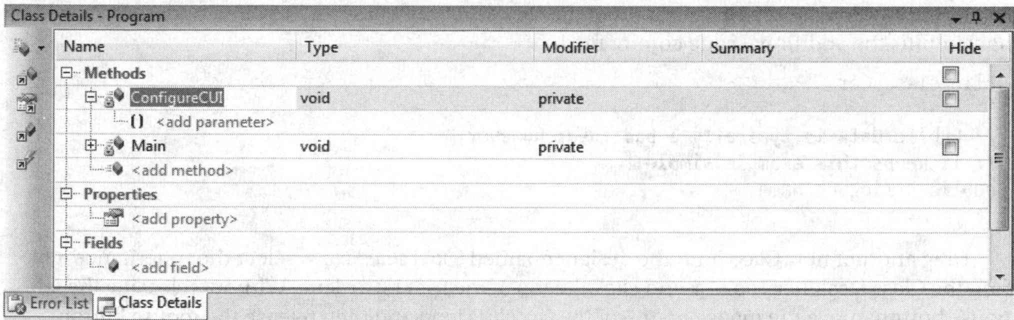

Figure 2-26. *The Class Details window*

The Class Designer Toolbox (see Figure 2-27) allows you to insert new types into your project (and create relationships between these types) visually. (Be aware you must have a class diagram as the active window to view this toolbox.) As you do so, the IDE automatically creates new C# type definitions in the background.

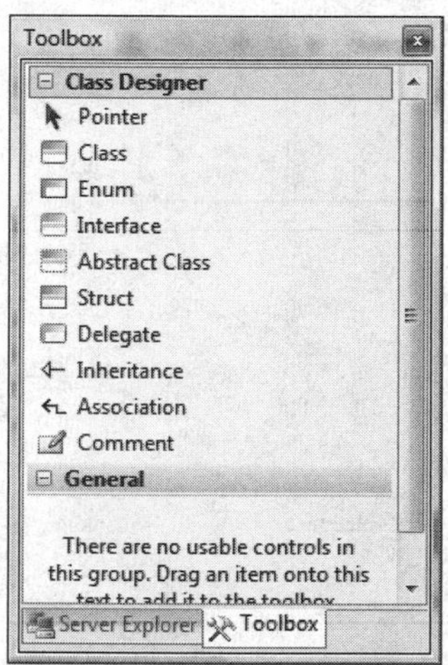

Figure 2-27. *The Class Designer Toolbox*

By way of example, drag a new Class from the Class Designer Toolbox onto your Class Designer. Name this class `Car` in the resulting dialog box. Now, using the Class Details window, add a public `string` field named `PetName` (see Figure 2-28).

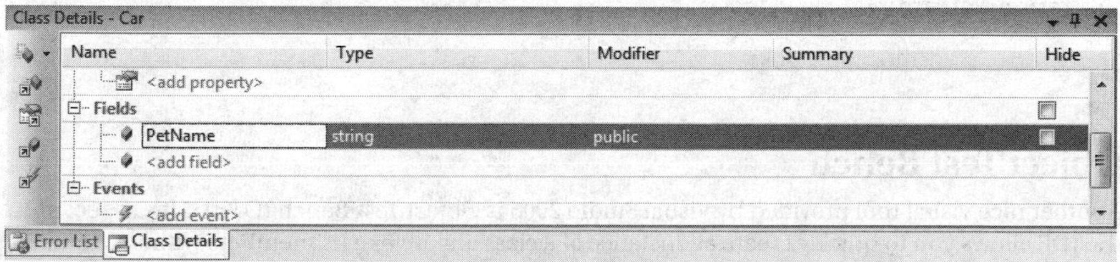

Figure 2-28. *Adding a field with the Class Details window*

If you now look at the C# definition of the Car class, you will see it has been updated accordingly (minus the additional code comments):

```
public class Car
{
  // Public data is typically a bad idea; however,
  // it keeps this example simple.
  public string PetName;
}
```

Drag another new Class onto the designer named SportsCar. Now, select the Inheritance icon from the Class Designer Toolbox and click the top of the SportsCar icon. Without releasing the left mouse button, move the mouse on top of the Car class icon and then release the mouse button. If you performed these steps correctly, you have just derived the SportsCar class from Car (see Figure 2-29).

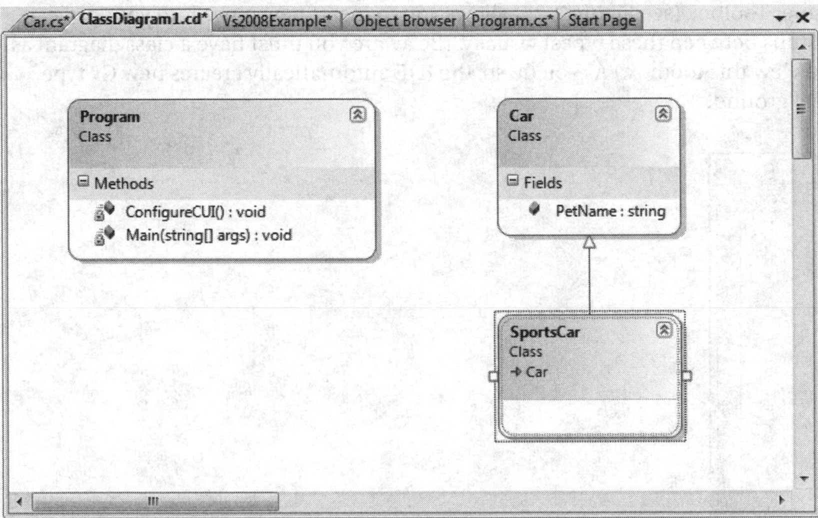

Figure 2-29. *Visually deriving from an existing class*

To complete this example, update the generated SportsCar class with a public method named GetPetName() authored as follows:

```
public class SportsCar : Car
{
  public string GetPetName()
  {
    PetName = "Fred";
    return PetName;
  }
}
```

Object Test Bench

Another nice visual tool provided by Visual Studio 2008 is Object Test Bench (OTB). This aspect of the IDE allows you to quickly create an instance of a class and invoke its members without running the entire application. This can be extremely helpful when you wish to test a specific method, but would rather not step through dozens of lines of code to do so. It is also very useful when you are building a .NET code library, and would rather not create a client application to test its functionality.

Note One limitation of the OTB is that it has no ability to handle incoming events sent from a given object. If you need to test the incoming events, you will be required to build a separate assembly to do so.

To work with OTB, right-click the type you wish to create using the Class Designer. For example, right-click the `SportsCar` type, and from the resulting context menu select Create Instance ➤ SportsCar(). This will display a dialog box that allows you to name your temporary object variable (and supply any constructor arguments if required). Once the process is complete, you will find your object hosted within the IDE. Right-click the object icon and invoke the `GetPetName()` method (see Figure 2-30).

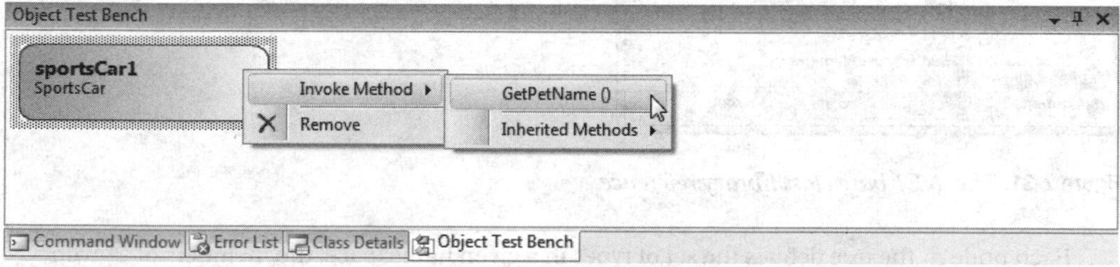

Figure 2-30. *The Visual Studio 2008 Object Test Bench*

Once you do, you will see the value `Fred` displayed in the Method Call Result dialog box. In fact, if you wish, you can save this value as a new object (of type `System.String`) on the OTB.

The Integrated .NET Framework 3.5 Documentation System

The final aspect of Visual Studio 2008 you *must* be comfortable with from the outset is the fully integrated help system. The .NET Framework 3.5 SDK documentation is extremely good, very readable, and full of useful information. Given the huge number of predefined .NET types (which number well into the thousands), you must be willing to roll up your sleeves and dig into the provided documentation. If you resist, you are doomed to a long, frustrating, and painful existence as a .NET developer.

Visual Studio 2008 provides the Dynamic Help window (accessible from the Help menu), which changes its contents based on what item (window, menu, source code keyword, etc.) is currently selected. For example, if you place the cursor on the `Console` class, the Dynamic Help window displays a set of links regarding the `System.Console` type.

Note Another great shortcut is to click once (but don't select) a C# keyword or .NET type and press the F1 key. This will automatically open the documentation for the item containing the blinking text cursor.

You should also be aware of a very important subdirectory of the .NET Framework 3.5 SDK documentation. Under the .NET Development ➤ .NET Framework SDK ➤ .NET Framework ➤ .NET Framework Class Library Reference node of the documentation, you will find complete documentation of each and every namespace in the .NET base class libraries (see Figure 2-31).

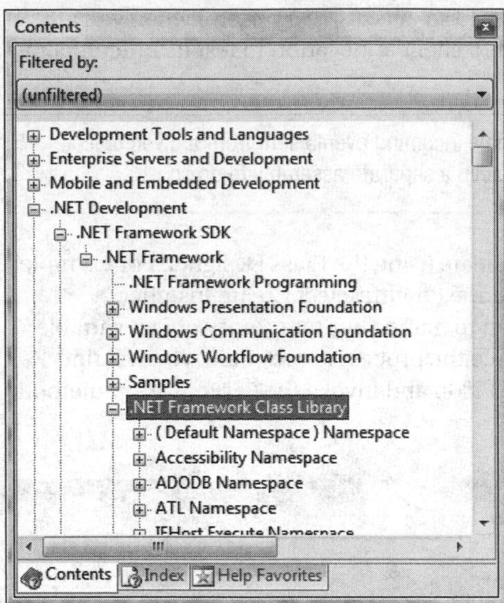

Figure 2-31. *The .NET base class library reference*

Each node in the tree defines the set of types in a given namespace, the members of a given type, and the parameters of a given member. Furthermore, when you view the help page for a given type, you will be told the name of the assembly and namespace that contains the type in question (located at the top of said page). As you read through the remainder of this book, I assume that you will dive into this *very, very* critical node to read up on additional details of the entity under examination.

■Note At the risk of sounding like a broken record, I really can't emphasize enough how important it is that you learn to use the .NET Framework 3.5 SDK documentation. No book, no matter how lengthy, can cover every aspect of the .NET platform. Make sure you take some time to get comfortable using the help system; you'll thank yourself later.

A Partial Catalog of Additional .NET Development Tools

To conclude this chapter, I would like to point out a number of .NET development tools that complement the functionality provided by your IDE of choice. Many of the tools mentioned here are open source, and all of them are free of charge. While I don't have the space to cover the details of these utilities, Table 2-3 lists a number of the tools I have found to be extremely helpful as well as URLs you can visit to find more information about them.

Table 2-3. *Select .NET Development Tools*

Tool	Meaning in Life	URL
FxCop	This is a must-have for any .NET developer interested in .NET best practices. FxCop will test any .NET assembly against the official Microsoft .NET best-practice coding guidelines.	`http://www.gotdotnet.com/team/fxcop`
Lutz Roeder's Reflector	This advanced .NET decompiler/object browser allows you to view the .NET implementation of any .NET type using a variety of languages.	`http://www.aisto.com/roeder/dotnet`
NAnt	NAnt is the .NET equivalent of Ant, the popular Java automated build tool. NAnt allows you to define and execute detailed build scripts using an XML-based syntax.	`http://sourceforge.net/projects/nant`
NDoc	NDoc is a tool that will generate code documentation files for C# code (or a compiled .NET assembly) in a variety of popular formats (MSDN's `*.chm`, XML, HTML, Javadoc, and LaTeX).	`http://sourceforge.net/projects/ndoc`
NUnit	NUnit is the .NET equivalent of the Java-centric JUnit unit testing tool. Using NUnit, you are able to facilitate the testing of your managed code.	`http://www.nunit.org`

Summary

So as you can see, you have many new toys at your disposal! The point of this chapter was to provide you with a tour of the major programming tools a C# programmer may leverage during the development process. You began the journey by learning how to generate .NET assemblies using nothing other than the free C# compiler and Notepad. Next, you were introduced to the TextPad and Notepad++ applications and walked through the process of using these tools to edit and compile `*.cs` code files.

You also examined three feature-rich IDEs, starting with the open source SharpDevelop, followed by Microsoft's Visual C# 2008 Express and Visual Studio 2008 Professional. While this chapter only scratched the surface of each tool's functionality, you should be in a good position to explore your chosen IDE at your leisure (and recall, you'll see additional features of Visual Studio 2008 as you progress through the book). The chapter wrapped up by examining various open source .NET development tools that extend the functionality of your IDE of choice.

PART 2

Core C# Programming Constructs

if u want the Continue option when u exe then use start without Debugging.

CHAPTER 3

Core C# Programming Constructs, Part I

This chapter begins your formal investigation of the C# programming language by presenting a number of bite-sized, stand-alone topics you must be comfortable with as you explore the .NET Framework. The first order of business is to understand how to build your program's *application object* and the composition of an executable program's entry point: the `Main()` method. Next, you will investigate the intrinsic C# data types (and their equivalent types in the `System` namespace) including an examination of the `System.String` and `System.Text.StringBuilder` class types.

Once you know the details of the fundamental .NET data types, you will then examine a number of data type conversion techniques, including narrowing operations, widening operations, and the use of the `unchecked` keyword. We wrap up this chapter by examining the core operators, iteration constructs, and decision constructs used to build valid C# code statements.

The Anatomy of a Simple C# Program

C# demands that all program logic be contained within a type definition (recall from Chapter 1 that *type* is a general term referring to a member of the set {class, interface, structure, enumeration, delegate}). Unlike many other languages, in C# it is not possible to create global functions or global points of data. Rather, all data members and methods must be contained within a type definition. To get the ball rolling, create a new Console Application project named SimpleCSharpApp. As you might agree, the initial code statements are rather uneventful:

```
using System;
using System.Collections.Generic;
using System.Text;
using System.Linq;

namespace SimpleCSharpApp
{
  class Program
  {
    static void Main(string[] args)
    {
    }
  }
}
```

Given this, update the `Main()` method with the following code statements:

```
class Program
{
  static void Main(string[] args)
  {
    // Display a simple message to the user.
    Console.WriteLine("***** My First C# App *****");
    Console.WriteLine("Hello World!");
    Console.WriteLine();

    // Wait for Enter key to be pressed before shutting down.
    Console.ReadLine();
  }
}
```

Here, we have a definition for a class type that supports a single method named `Main()`. By default, Visual Studio 2008 names the class defining `Main()` "Program"; however, you are free to change this if you so choose. Every executable C# application (console program, Windows desktop program, or Windows service) must contain a class defining a `Main()` method, which is used to signify the entry point of the application.

Formally speaking, the class that defines the `Main()` method is termed the *application object*. While it is possible for a single executable application to have more than one application object (which can be useful when performing unit tests), you must inform the compiler which `Main()` method should be used as the entry point via the `/main` option of the command-line compiler.

Note that the signature of `Main()` is adorned with the `static` keyword, which will be examined in detail in Chapter 5. For the time being, simply understand that static members are scoped to the class level (rather than the object level) and can thus be invoked without the need to first create a new class instance.

■ **Note** C# is a case-sensitive programming language. Therefore, "Main" is not the same as "main," and "Readline" is not the same as "ReadLine." Given this, be aware that all C# keywords are lowercase (`public`, `lock`, `class`, `global`, and so on), while namespaces, types, and member names begin (by convention) with an initial capital letter and have capitalized the first letter of any embedded words (e.g., `Console.WriteLine`, `System.Windows.Forms.MessageBox`, `System.Data.SqlClient`, and so on). As a rule of thumb, whenever you receive a compiler error regarding "undefined symbols," be sure to check your spelling!

In addition to the `static` keyword, this `Main()` method has a single parameter, which happens to be an array of strings (`string[] args`). Although you are not currently bothering to process this array, this parameter may contain any number of incoming command-line arguments (you'll see how to access them momentarily). Finally, this `Main()` method has been set up with a `void` return value, meaning we do not explicitly define a return value using the `return` keyword before exiting the method scope.

The logic of `Program` is within `Main()` itself. Here, you make use of the `Console` class, which is defined within the `System` namespace. Among its set of members is the static `WriteLine()` which, as you might assume, pumps a text string and carriage return to the standard output. You also make a call to `Console.ReadLine()` to ensure the command prompt launched by the Visual Studio 2008 IDE remains visible during a debugging session until you press the Enter key.

Variations on the Main() Method

By default, Visual Studio 2008 will generate a `Main()` method that has a `void` return value and an array of `string` types as the single input parameter. This is not the only possible form of `Main()`, however. It is permissible to construct your application's entry point using any of the following signatures (assuming it is contained within a C# class or structure definition):

```
// int return type, array of strings as the argument.
static int Main(string[] args)
{
}

// No return type, no arguments.
static void Main()
{
}

// int return type, no arguments.
static int Main()
{
}
```

■ **Note** The `Main()` method may also be defined as public as opposed to private, which is assumed if you do not supply a specific access modifier. Visual Studio 2008 automatically defines a program's `Main()` method as implicitly private. Doing so ensures other applications cannot directly invoke the entry point of another.

Obviously, your choice of how to construct `Main()` will be based on two questions. First, do you want to return a value to the system when `Main()` has completed and your program terminates? If so, you need to return an `int` data type rather than `void`. Second, do you need to process any user-supplied command-line parameters? If so, they will be stored in the array of `string`s. Let's examine all of our options.

Specifying an Application Error Code

While a vast majority of your `Main()` methods will return `void` as the return value, the ability to return an `int` from `Main()` keeps C# consistent with other C-based languages. By convention, returning the value `0` indicates the program has terminated successfully, while another value (such as `-1`) represents an error condition (do be aware that the value `0` is automatically returned, even if you construct a `Main()` method prototyped to return `void`).

On the Windows operating system, an application's return value is stored within a system environment variable named `%ERRORLEVEL%`. If you were to create an application that programmatically launches another executable (a topic examined in Chapter 17), you can obtain the value of `%ERRORLEVEL%` using the static `System.Diagnostics.Process.ExitCode` property.

Given that an application's return value is passed to the system at the time the application terminates, it is obviously not possible for an application to obtain and display its final error code while running. However, to illustrate how to view this error level upon program termination, begin by updating the `Main()` method as follows:

```
// Note we are now returning an int, rather than void.
static int Main(string[] args)
{
  // Display a message and wait for Enter key to be pressed.
```

```
    Console.WriteLine("***** My First C# App *****");
    Console.WriteLine("Hello World!");
    Console.WriteLine();
    Console.ReadLine();

    // Return an arbitrary error code.
    return -1;
  }
```

Let's now capture Main()'s return value with the help of a batch file. Using the Windows Explorer, navigate to the folder containing your compiled application (for example, C:\SimpleCSharpApp\bin\Debug). Add a new text file (named SimpleCSharpApp.bat) to the Debug folder that contains the following instructions (if you have not authored *.bat files before, don't concern yourself with the details; this is a test . . . this is only a test):

```
@echo off

rem A batch file for SimpleCSharpApp.exe
rem which captures the app's return value.

SimpleCSharpApp
@if "%ERRORLEVEL%" == "0" goto success

:fail
  echo This application has failed!
  echo return value = %ERRORLEVEL%
  goto end
:success
  echo This application has succeeded!
  echo return value = %ERRORLEVEL%
  goto end
:end
  echo All Done.
```

At this point, open a command prompt and navigate to the folder containing your executable and new *.bat file (again, for example, C:\SimpleCSharpApp\bin\Debug). Execute the batch logic by typing its name and pressing the Enter key. You should find the following output, given that your Main() method is returning -1 (see Figure 3-1). Had the Main() method returned 0, you would see the message "This application has succeeded!" print to the console.

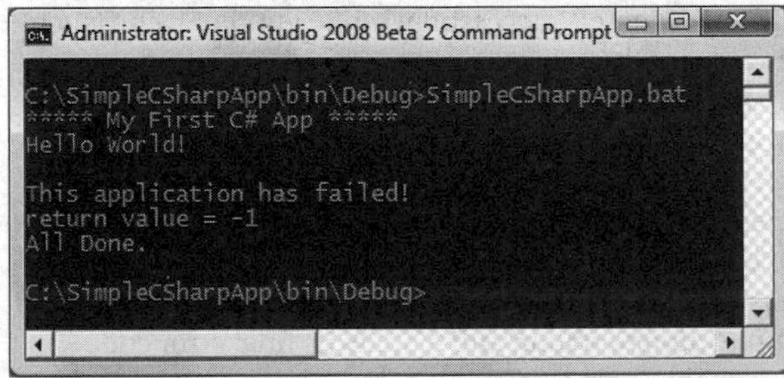

Figure 3-1. *Capturing an application's return value via a batch file*

Again, a vast majority (if not all) of your C# applications will use void as the return value from Main(), which as you recall implicitly returns the error code of zero. To this end, the Main() methods used in this text will indeed return void (and the remaining projects will certainly not need to make use of batch files to capture return codes!).

Processing Command-Line Arguments

Now that you better understand the return value of the Main() method, let's examine the incoming array of string data. Assume that you now wish to update your application to process any possible command-line parameters. One way to do so is using a C# for loop (do note that C#'s iteration constructs will be examined in some detail near the end of this chapter):

```
static int Main(string[] args)
{
...
  // Process any incoming args.
  for(int i = 0; i < args.Length; i++)
    Console.WriteLine("Arg: {0}", args[i]);

  Console.ReadLine();
  return -1;
}
```

Here, you are checking to see whether the array of strings contains some number of items using the Length property of System.Array. As you'll see in Chapter 4, all C# arrays actually alias the System.Array type, and therefore share a common set of members. As you loop over each item in the array, its value is printed to the console window. Supplying the arguments at the command line is equally as simple, as shown in Figure 3-2.

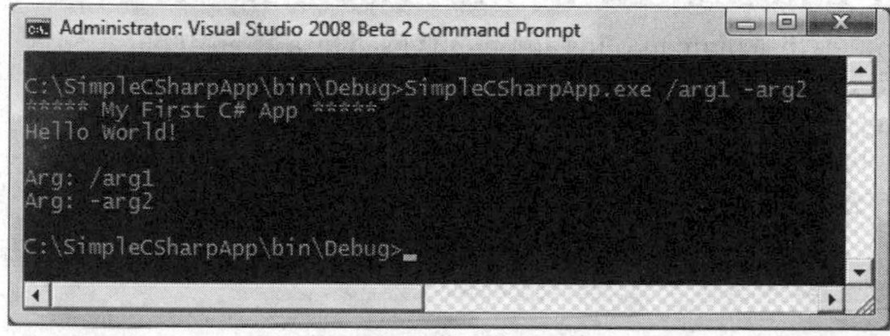

Figure 3-2. *Supplying arguments at the command line*

As an alternative to the standard for loop, you may iterate over an incoming string array using the C# foreach keyword. Here is some sample usage:

```
// Notice you have no need to check the size of the array when using "foreach".
static int Main(string[] args)
{
...
  // Process any incoming args using foreach.
  foreach(string arg in args)
    Console.WriteLine("Arg: {0}", arg);

  Console.ReadLine();
  return -1;
}
```

Finally, you are also able to access command-line arguments using the static `GetCommandLineArgs()` method of the `System.Environment` type. The return value of this method is an array of `strings`. The first index identifies the name of the application itself, while the remaining elements in the array contain the individual command-line arguments (note that when using this approach, it is no longer necessary to define `Main()` as taking a `string` array as the input parameter, although there is no harm in doing so):

```
static int Main(string[] args)
{
...
  // Get arguments using System.Environment.
  string[] theArgs = Environment.GetCommandLineArgs();
  foreach(string arg in theArgs)
    Console.WriteLine("Arg: {0}", arg);

  Console.ReadLine();
  return -1;
}
```

Of course, it is up to you to determine which command-line arguments your program will respond to (if any) and how they must be formatted (such as with a - or / prefix). Here we simply passed in a series of options that were printed directly to the command prompt. Assume, however, you were creating a new video game and programmed your application to process an option named `-godmode`. If the user starts your application with the flag, you know the user is in fact *a cheater*, and can take an appropriate course of action.

Specifying Command-Line Arguments with Visual Studio 2008

In the real world, an end user supplies the command-line arguments used by a given application when starting the program. However, during the development cycle, you may wish to specify possible command-line flags for testing purposes. To do so with Visual Studio 2008, double-click the Properties icon from Solution Explorer and select the Debug tab on the left side. From here, specify values using the Command line arguments text box (see Figure 3-3).

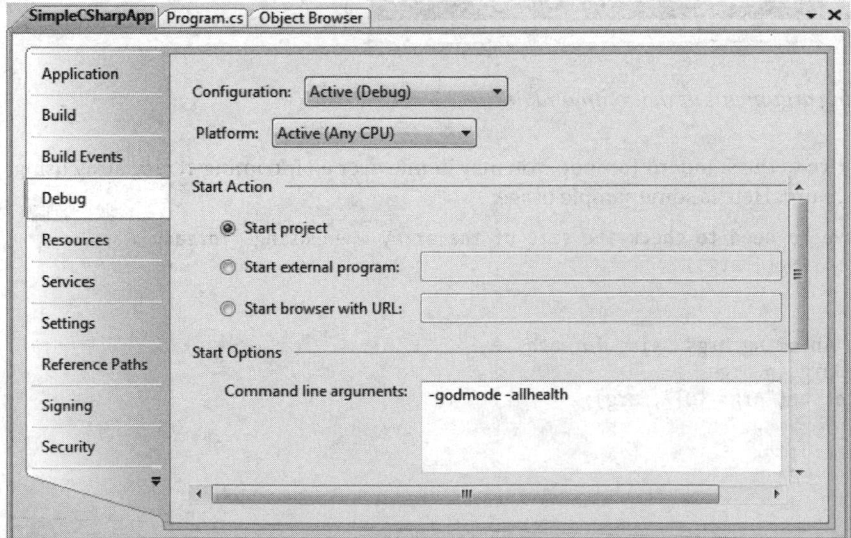

Figure 3-3. *Setting command arguments via Visual Studio 2008*

An Interesting Aside: Some Additional Members of the System.Environment Class

The Environment type exposes a number of extremely helpful methods beyond GetCommandLineArgs(). Specifically, this class allows you to obtain a number of details regarding the operating system currently hosting your .NET application using various static members. To illustrate the usefulness of System.Environment, update your Main() method to call a helper method named ShowEnvironmentDetails():

```
static int Main(string[] args)
{
...
  // Helper method within the Program class.
  ShowEnvironmentDetails();

  Console.ReadLine();
  return -1;
}
```

Implement this method within your Program class to call various members of the Environment type. For example:

```
static void ShowEnvironmentDetails()
{
  // Print out the drives on this machine,
  // and other interesting details.
  foreach (string drive in Environment.GetLogicalDrives())
    Console.WriteLine("Drive: {0}", drive);

  Console.WriteLine("OS: {0}", Environment.OSVersion);
  Console.WriteLine("Number of processors: {0}",
    Environment.ProcessorCount);
  Console.WriteLine(".NET Version: {0}",
    Environment.Version);
}
```

Figure 3-4 shows a possible test run of invoking this method (if you did not specify command-line arguments via Visual Studio 2008's Debug tab, you will not find them printed to the console).

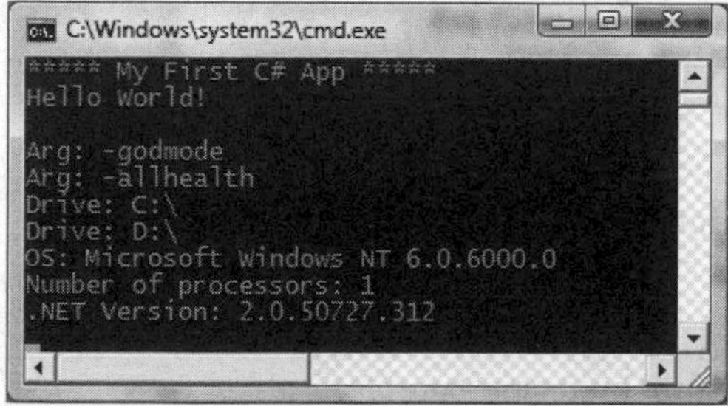

Figure 3-4. *Displaying system environment variables*

The Environment type defines members other than those shown in the previous example. Table 3-1 documents some additional properties of interest; however, be sure to check out the .NET Framework 3.5 SDK documentation for full details.

Table 3-1. *Select Properties of* `System.Environment`

Property	Meaning in Life
`ExitCode`	Gets or sets the exit code anywhere within the application
`MachineName`	Gets the name of the current machine
`NewLine`	Gets the newline symbol for the current environment
`StackTrace`	Gets the current stack trace information for the application
`SystemDirectory`	Returns the full path to the system directory
`UserName`	Returns the name of the user that started this application

■ **Source Code** The SimpleCSharpApp project is located under the Chapter 3 subdirectory.

The System.Console Class

Almost all of the example applications created over the course of the initial chapters of this book make extensive use of the `System.Console` class. While it is true that a console user interface (CUI) is not as enticing as a graphical user interface (GUI) or web-based front end, restricting the early examples to console programs will allow us to keep focused on the syntax of C# and the core aspects of the .NET platform, rather than dealing with the complexities of building GUIs.

As its name implies, the `Console` class encapsulates input, output, and error-stream manipulations for console-based applications. Table 3-2 lists some (but definitely not all) members of interest.

Table 3-2. *Select Members of* `System.Console`

Member	Meaning in Life
`Beep()`	This method forces the console to emit a beep of a specified frequency and duration.
`BackgroundColor` `ForegroundColor`	These properties set the background/foreground colors for the current output. They may be assigned any member of the `ConsoleColor` enumeration.
`BufferHeight` `BufferWidth`	These properties control the height/width of the console's buffer area.
`Title`	This property sets the title of the current console.

`WindowHeight`
`WindowWidth`
`WindowTop`
`WindowLeft`
	These properties control the dimensions of the console in relation to the established buffer.

`Clear()`	This method clears the established buffer and console display area.

Basic Input and Output with the Console Class

In addition to the members in Table 3-2, the `Console` type defines a set of methods to capture input and output, all of which are static and are therefore called by prefixing the name of the class

(Console) to the method name. As you have seen, WriteLine() pumps a text string (including a carriage return) to the output stream. The Write() method pumps text to the output stream without a carriage return. ReadLine() allows you to receive information from the input stream up until the Enter key is pressed, while Read() is used to capture a single character from the input stream.

To illustrate basic I/O using the Console class, create a new Console Application project named BasicConsoleIO and update your Main() method to call a helper method named GetUserData():

```
class Program
{
  static void Main(string[] args)
  {
    Console.WriteLine("***** Basic Console I/O *****");
    GetUserData();
    Console.ReadLine();
  }
}
```

Implement this method within the Program class with logic that prompts the user for some bits of information and echoes each item to the standard output stream. For example, we could ask the user for his or her name and age (which we will treat as a text value for simplicity, rather than the expected numerical value) as follows:

```
static void GetUserData()
{
  // Get name and age.
  Console.Write("Please enter your name: ");
  string userName = Console.ReadLine();
  Console.Write("Please enter your age: ");
  string userAge = Console.ReadLine();

  // Change echo color, just for fun.
  ConsoleColor prevColor = Console.ForegroundColor;
  Console.ForegroundColor = ConsoleColor.Yellow;

  // Echo to the console.
  Console.WriteLine("Hello {0}!  You are {1} years old.",
    userName, userAge);

  // Restore previous color.
  Console.ForegroundColor = prevColor;
}
```

Not surprisingly, when you run this application, the input data is printed to the console (using a custom color to boot!).

Formatting Console Output

During these first few chapters, you may have noticed numerous occurrences of the tokens {0}, {1}, and the like embedded within various string literals. The .NET platform introduces a style of string formatting slightly akin to the printf() statement of C. Simply put, when you are defining a string literal that contains segments of data whose value is not known until runtime, you are able to specify a placeholder within the literal using this curly-bracket syntax. At runtime, the value(s) passed into Console.WriteLine() are substituted for each placeholder.

The first parameter to WriteLine() represents a string literal that contains optional placeholders designated by {0}, {1}, {2}, and so forth. Be very aware that the first ordinal number of a curly-bracket placeholder always begins with 0. The remaining parameters to WriteLine() are simply the values to be inserted into the respective placeholders.

■ **Note** If you have a mismatch between the number of uniquely numbered curly-bracket placeholders and fill arguments, you will receive a FormatException exception at runtime.

It is also permissible for a given placeholder to repeat within a given string. For example, if you are a Beatles fan and want to build the string "9, Number 9, Number 9", you would write

```
// John says...
Console.WriteLine("{0}, Number {0}, Number {0}", 9);
```

Also know that it is possible to position each placeholder in any location within a string literal, and it need not follow an increasing sequence. For example, consider the following code snippet:

```
// Prints: 20, 10, 30
Console.WriteLine("{1}, {0}, {2}", 10, 20, 30);
```

Formatting Numerical Data

If you require more elaborate formatting for numerical data, each placeholder can optionally contain various format characters. Table 3-3 shows your core formatting options.

Table 3-3. *.NET Numerical Format Characters*

String Format Character	Meaning in Life
C or c	Used to format currency. By default, the flag will prefix the local cultural symbol (a dollar sign [$] for US English).
D or d	Used to format decimal numbers. This flag may also specify the minimum number of digits used to pad the value.
E or e	Used for exponential notation. Casing controls whether the exponential constant is uppercase (E) or lowercase (e).
F or f	Used for fixed-point formatting. This flag may also specify the minimum number of digits used to pad the value.
G or g	Stands for *general.* This character can be used to format a number to fixed or exponential format.
N or n	Used for basic numerical formatting (with commas).
X or x	Used for hexadecimal formatting. If you use an uppercase X, your hex format will also contain uppercase characters.

These format characters are suffixed to a given placeholder value using the colon token (e.g., {0:C}, {1:d}, {2:X}, and so on). To illustrate, update the Main() method to call a new helper function named FormatNumericalData(). Implement this method to format a fixed value in a variety of ways, for example:

```
// Now make use of some format tags.
static void FormatNumericalData()
{
  Console.WriteLine("The value 99999 in various formats:");
  Console.WriteLine("c format: {0:c}", 99999);
  Console.WriteLine("d9 format: {0:d9}", 99999);
  Console.WriteLine("f3 format: {0:f3}", 99999);
  Console.WriteLine("n format: {0:n}", 99999);
```

```
    // Notice that upper- or lowercasing for hex
    // determines if letters are upper- or lowercase.
    Console.WriteLine("E format: {0:E}", 99999);
    Console.WriteLine("e format: {0:e}", 99999);
    Console.WriteLine("X format: {0:X}", 99999);
    Console.WriteLine("x format: {0:x}", 99999);
}
```

Figure 3-5 shows the output for our current application.

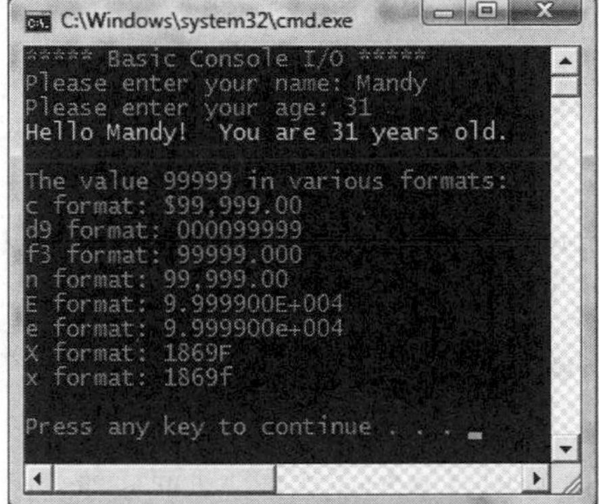

Figure 3-5. *Basic console I/O (with .NET string formatting)*

Beyond controlling how numerical data is formatted, the .NET platform provides additional tokens that may appear in a string literal that controls spacing and positioning of content. Furthermore, the tokens applied to numerical data can be applied to other data types (such as enumerations or the `DateTime` type) to control data formatting. Also be aware that it is possible to build a custom class (or structure) that defines a custom formatting scheme through the implementation of the `ICustomFormatter` interface.

You'll see additional formatting examples where required throughout this text; however, if you are interested in digging into .NET string formatting further, look up the topic "Formatting Types" within the .NET Framework 3.5 SDK documentation.

■ **Source Code** The BasicConsoleIO project is located under the Chapter 3 subdirectory.

Formatting Numerical Data Beyond Console Applications

On a final note, be aware that the use of the .NET string formatting characters is not limited to console programs! This same formatting syntax can be used when calling the static `string.Format()` method. This can be helpful when you need to compose textual data at runtime for use in any application type (desktop GUI app, ASP.NET web app, XML web services, and so on).

By way of a quick example, assume you are building a graphical desktop application and need to format a string for display in a message box:

```
void DisplayMessage()
{
    // Using string.Format() to format a string literal.
```

```
    string userMessage = string.Format("100000 in hex is {0:x}",
      100000);

    // You would need to reference System.Windows.Forms.dll
    // in order to compile this line of code!
    System.Windows.Forms.MessageBox.Show(userMessage);
}
```

Notice how `string.Format()` returns a new `string` object, which is formatted according to the provided flags. After this point, you are free to use the textual data as you see fit.

System Data Types and C# Shorthand Notation

Like any programming language, C# defines an intrinsic set of data types, which are used to represent local variables, member variables, return values, and input parameters. Unlike other programming languages, however, these keywords are much more than simple compiler-recognized tokens. Rather, the C# data type keywords are actually shorthand notations for full-blown types in the `System` namespace. Table 3-4 lists each system data type, its range, the corresponding C# keyword, and the type's compliance with the Common Language Specification (CLS).

■ Note Recall from Chapter 1 that CLS-compliant .NET code can be used by any managed programming language. If you expose non–CLS-compliant data from your programs, other languages may not be able to make use of it.

Table 3-4. *The Intrinsic Data Types of C#*

C# Shorthand	CLS Compliant?	System Type	Range	Meaning in Life
`bool`	Yes	`System.Boolean`	True or false	Represents truth or falsity
`sbyte`	No	`System.SByte`	–128 to 127	Signed 8-bit number
`byte`	Yes	`System.Byte`	0 to 255	Unsigned 8-bit number
`short`	Yes	`System.Int16`	–32,768 to 32,767	Signed 16-bit number
`ushort`	No	`System.UInt16`	0 to 65,535	Unsigned 16-bit number
`int`	Yes	`System.Int32`	–2,147,483,648 to 2,147,483,647	Signed 32-bit number
`uint`	No	`System.UInt32`	0 to 4,294,967,295	Unsigned 32-bit number
`long`	Yes	`System.Int64`	–9,223,372,036,854,775,808 to 9,223,372,036,854,775,807	Signed 64-bit number
`ulong`	No	`System.UInt64`	0 to 18,446,744,073,709,551,615	Unsigned 64-bit number
`char`	Yes	`System.Char`	U+0000 to U+ffff	Single 16-bit Unicode character

C# Shorthand	CLS Compliant?	System Type	Range	Meaning in Life
float	Yes	System.Single	±1.5 × 10–45 to ±3.4 × 1038	32-bit floating-point number
double	Yes	System.Double	±5.0 × 10–324 to ±1.7 × 10308	64-bit floating-point number
decimal	Yes	System.Decimal	±1.0 × 10e–28 to ±7.9 × 10e28	96-bit signed number
string	Yes	System.String	Limited by system memory	Represents a set of Unicode characters
object	Yes	System.Object	Can store any type in an object variable	The base class of all types in the .NET universe

■ **Note** By default, a real numeric literal on the right-hand side of the assignment operator is treated as `double`. Therefore, to initialize a `float` variable, use the suffix `f` or `F` (for example, `5.3F`).

Each of the numerical types (`short`, `int`, and so forth) map to a corresponding *structure* in the `System` namespace. In a nutshell, structures are "value types" allocated on the stack. On the other hand, `string` and `object` are "reference types," meaning the variable is allocated on the managed heap. You will examine full details of value and reference types in Chapter 4; however, for the time being, simply understand that value types can be allocated into memory very quickly and have a very fixed and predictable lifetime.

Variable Declaration and Initialization

When you are declaring a data type as a local variable (e.g., a variable within a member scope), you do so by specifying the data type followed by the variable's name. You'll see how this is done by way of a few examples. Create a new Console Application project named BasicDataTypes. Update the `Program` class with the following helper method that is called from within `Main()`:

```
static void LocalVarDeclarations()
{
  Console.WriteLine("=> Data Declarations:");
  // Local variables are declared as so:
  // dataType varName;
  int myInt;
  string myString;
  Console.WriteLine();
}
```

Do be aware that it is a *compiler error* to make use of a local variable before assigning an initial value. Given this, it is good practice to assign an initial value to your local data points at the time of declaration. You may do so on a single line, or by separating the declaration and assignment into two code statements:

```
static void LocalVarDeclarations()
{
  Console.WriteLine("=> Data Declarations:");
  // Local variables are declared and initialized as follows:
```

```
  // dataType varName = initialValue;
  int myInt = 0;

  // You can also declare and assign on two lines.
  string myString;
  myString = "This is my character data";
  Console.WriteLine();
}
```

It is also permissible to declare multiple variables of the same underlying type on a single line of code:

```
static void LocalVarDeclarations()
{
  Console.WriteLine("=> Data Declarations:");
  int myInt = 0;
  string myString;
  myString = "This is my character data";

  // Declare 3 bools on a single line.
  bool b1 = true, b2 = false, b3 = b1;
  Console.WriteLine();
}
```

As well, since the C# bool keyword is simply a shorthand notation for the System.Boolean structure, it is possible to allocate any data type using its full name (of course, the same point holds true for any C# data type keyword). Here is the final implementation of LocalVarDeclarations():

```
static void LocalVarDeclarations()
{
  Console.WriteLine("=> Data Declarations:");
  // Local variables are declared and initialized as follows:
  // dataType varName = initialValue;
  int myInt = 0;

  string myString;
  myString = "This is my character data";

  // Declare 3 bools on a single line.
  bool b1 = true, b2 = false, b3 = b1;

  // Very verbose manner in which to declare a bool.
  System.Boolean b4 = false;

  Console.WriteLine("Your data: {0}, {1}, {2}, {3}, {4}, {5}",
      myInt, myString, b1, b2, b3, b4);
  Console.WriteLine();
}
```

"New-ing" Intrinsic Data Types

All intrinsic data types support what is known as a *default constructor* (see Chapter 5). In a nutshell, this feature allows you to create a variable using the new keyword, which automatically sets the variable to its default value:

- bool types are set to false.
- Numeric data is set to 0 (or 0.0 in the case of floating-point data types).

- `char` types are set to a single empty character.
- `DateTime` types are set to `1/1/0001 12:00:00 AM`.
- Object references (including `string`s) are set to `null`.

Although it is more cumbersome to use the new keyword when creating a basic data type variable, the following is syntactically well-formed C# code:

```
static void NewingDataTypes()
{
  Console.WriteLine("=> Using new to create intrinsic data types:");
  bool b = new bool();              // Set to false.
  int i = new int();                // Set to 0.
  double d = new double();          // Set to 0.
  DateTime dt = new DateTime();     // Set to 1/1/0001 12:00:00 AM
  Console.WriteLine("{0}, {1}, {2}, {3}", b, i, d, dt);
  Console.WriteLine();
}
```

The Data Type Class Hierarchy

It is very interesting to note that even the primitive .NET data types are arranged in a "class hierarchy." If you are new to the world of inheritance, you will discover the full details in Chapter 6. Until then, just understand that types at the top of a class hierarchy provide some default behaviors that are granted to the derived types. The relationship between these core system types can be understood as shown in Figure 3-6.

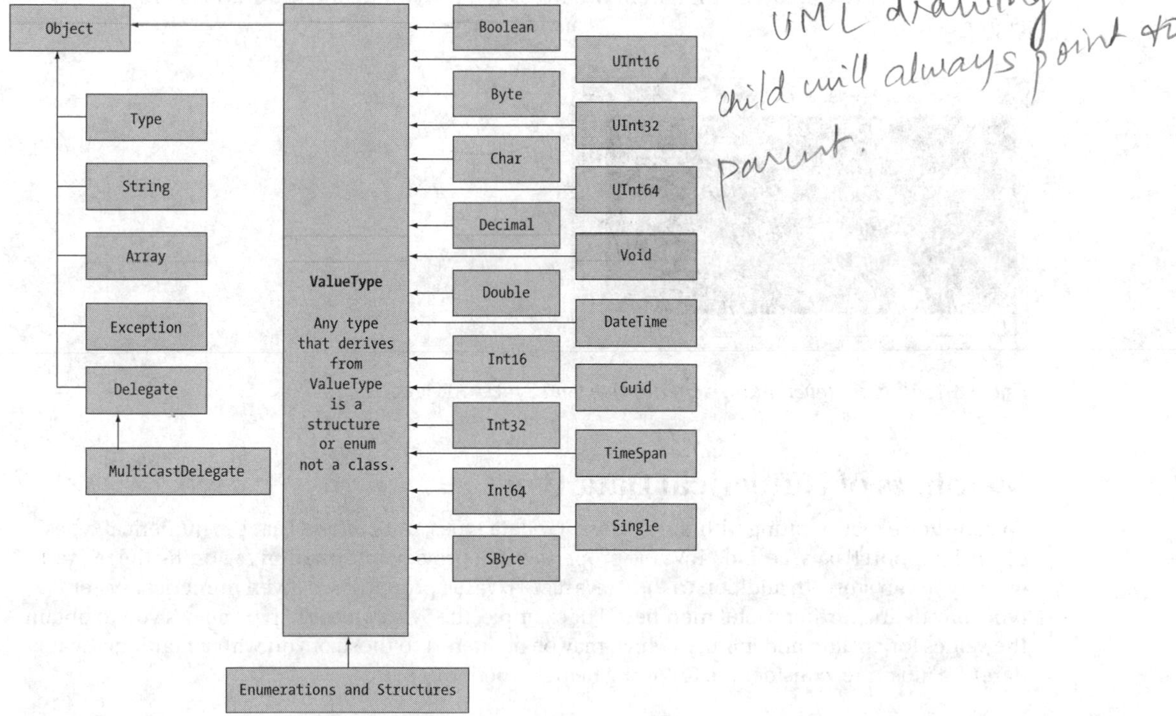

Figure 3-6. *The class hierarchy of system types*

Notice that each of these types ultimately derives from `System.Object`, which defines a set of methods (`ToString()`, `Equals()`, `GetHashCode()`, and so forth) common to all types in the .NET base class libraries (these methods are fully detailed in Chapter 6).

Also note that many numerical data types derive from a class named `System.ValueType`. Descendents of `ValueType` are automatically allocated on the stack and therefore have a very predictable lifetime and are quite efficient. On the other hand, types that do not have `System.ValueType` in their inheritance chain (such as `System.Type`, `System.String`, `System.Array`, `System.Exception`, and `System.Delegate`) are not allocated on the stack, but on the garbage-collected heap.

Without getting too hung up on the details of `System.Object` and `System.ValueType` for the time being (again, more details in Chapter 4), just understand that because a C# keyword (such as `int`) is simply shorthand notation for the corresponding system type (in this case, `System.Int32`), the following is perfectly legal syntax, given that `System.Int32` (the C# `int`) eventually derives from `System.Object`, and therefore can invoke any of its public members, as illustrated by this additional helper function:

```
static void ObjectFunctionality()
{
  Console.WriteLine("=> System.Object Functionality:");
  // A C# int is really a shorthand for System.Int32.
  // which inherits the following members from System.Object.
  Console.WriteLine("12.GetHashCode() = {0}", 12.GetHashCode());
  Console.WriteLine("12.Equals(23) = {0}", 12.Equals(23));
  Console.WriteLine("12.ToString() = {0}", 12.ToString());
  Console.WriteLine("12.GetType() = {0}", 12.GetType());
  Console.WriteLine();
}
```

If you were to call this method from within `Main()`, you would find the output shown in Figure 3-7.

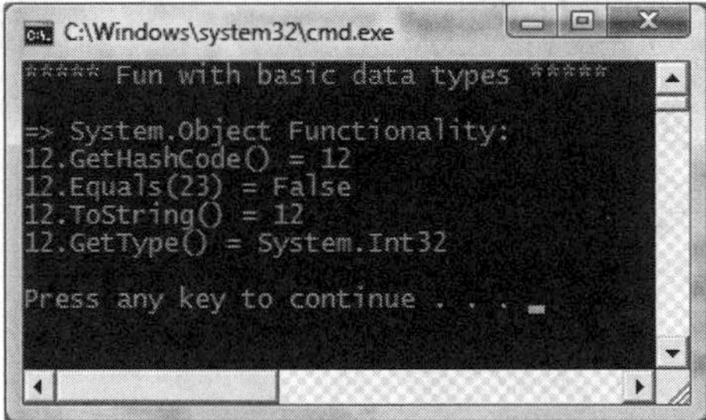

Figure 3-7. *All types (even numerical data) extend* `System.Object`

Members of Numerical Data Types

To continue experimenting with the intrinsic C# data types, understand that the numerical types of .NET support `MaxValue` and `MinValue` properties that provide information regarding the range a given type can store. In addition to the `MinValue`/`MaxValue` properties, a given numerical system type may define further useful members. For example, the `System.Double` type allows you to obtain the values for epsilon and infinity (which may be of interest to those of you with a mathematical flare). To illustrate, consider the following helper function:

```
static void DataTypeFunctionality()
{
  Console.WriteLine("=> Data type Functionality:");
  Console.WriteLine("Max of int: {0}", int.MaxValue);
  Console.WriteLine("Min of int: {0}", int.MinValue);
  Console.WriteLine("Max of double: {0}", double.MaxValue);
  Console.WriteLine("Min of double: {0}", double.MinValue);
  Console.WriteLine("double.Epsilon: {0}", double.Epsilon);
  Console.WriteLine("double.PositiveInfinity: {0}",
    double.PositiveInfinity);
  Console.WriteLine("double.NegativeInfinity: {0}",
    double.NegativeInfinity);
  Console.WriteLine();
}
```

Members of System.Boolean

Next, consider the `System.Boolean` data type. The only valid assignment a C# `bool` can take is from the set {`true | false`}. Given this point, it should be clear that `System.Boolean` does not support a `MinValue`/`MaxValue` property set, but rather `TrueString`/`FalseString` (which yields the string `"True"` or `"False"`, respectively). Add the following code statements to the `DataTypeFunctionality()` helper method:

```
Console.WriteLine("bool.FalseString: {0}", bool.FalseString);
Console.WriteLine("bool.TrueString: {0}", bool.TrueString);
```

Figure 3-8 shows the output of invoking `DataTypeFunctionality()` from within `Main()`.

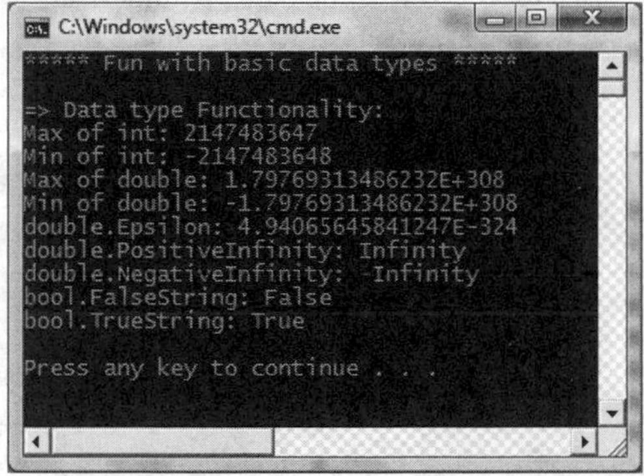

Figure 3-8. *Select functionality of various data types*

Members of System.Char

C# textual data is represented by the intrinsic `string` and `char` keywords, which are simple shorthand notations for `System.String` and `System.Char`, both of which are Unicode under the hood. As you most likely already know, a `string` represents a contiguous set of characters (e.g., `"Hello"`), while the `char` can represent a single slot in a `string` type (e.g., `'H'`).

The System.Char type provides you with a great deal of functionality beyond the ability to hold a single point of character data. Using the static methods of System.Char, you are able to determine whether a given character is numerical, alphabetical, a point of punctuation, or whatnot. Consider the following method:

```
static void CharFunctionality()
{
  Console.WriteLine("=> char type Functionality:");
  char myChar = 'a';
  Console.WriteLine("char.IsDigit('a'): {0}", char.IsDigit(myChar));
  Console.WriteLine("char.IsLetter('a'): {0}", char.IsLetter(myChar));
  Console.WriteLine("char.IsWhiteSpace('Hello There', 5): {0}",
    char.IsWhiteSpace("Hello There", 5));
  Console.WriteLine("char.IsWhiteSpace('Hello There', 6): {0}",
    char.IsWhiteSpace("Hello There", 6));
  Console.WriteLine("char.IsPunctuation('?'): {0}",
    char.IsPunctuation('?'));
  Console.WriteLine();
}
```

As illustrated in the previous code snippet, the members of System.Char have two calling conventions: a single character or a string with a numerical index that specifies the position of the character to test.

Parsing Values from String Data

The .NET data types provide the ability to generate a variable of their underlying type given a textual equivalent (e.g., parsing). This technique can be extremely helpful when you wish to convert a bit of user input data (such as a selection from a GUI-based drop-down list box) into a numerical value. Consider the following parsing logic within a method named ParseFromStrings():

```
static void ParseFromStrings()
{
  Console.WriteLine("=> Data type parsing:");
  bool b = bool.Parse("True");
  Console.WriteLine("Value of b: {0}", b);
  double d = double.Parse("99.884");
  Console.WriteLine("Value of d: {0}", d);
  int i = int.Parse("8");
  Console.WriteLine("Value of i: {0}", i);
  char c = Char.Parse("w");
  Console.WriteLine("Value of c: {0}", c);
  Console.WriteLine();
}
```

■ **Source Code** The BasicDataTypes project is located under the Chapter 3 subdirectory.

Understanding the System.String Type

System.String provides a number of methods you would expect from such a utility class, including methods that return the length of the character data, find substrings within the current string, convert to and from uppercase/lowercase, and so forth. Table 3-5 lists some (but by no means all) of the interesting members.

Table 3-5. *Select Members of* `System.String`

String Member	Meaning in Life
`Length`	This property returns the length of the current string.
`Compare()`	This method compares two strings.
`Contains()`	This method determines whether a string contains a specific substring.
`Equals()`	This method tests whether two string objects contain identical character data.
`Format()`	This method formats a string using other primitives (e.g., numerical data, other strings) and the `{0}` notation examined earlier in this chapter.
`Insert()`	This method inserts a string within a given string.
`PadLeft()` `PadRight()`	These methods are used to pad a string with some characters.
`Remove()` `Replace()`	Use these methods to receive a copy of a string, with modifications (characters removed or replaced).
`Split()`	This method returns a `String` array containing the substrings in this instance that are delimited by elements of a specified `Char` or `String` array.
`Trim()`	This method removes all occurrences of a set of specified characters from the beginning and end of the current string.
`ToUpper()` `ToLower()`	These methods create a copy of the current string in uppercase or lowercase format, respectively.

Basic String Manipulation

Working with the members of `System.String` is as you would expect. Simply create a `string` data type and make use of the provided functionality via the dot operator. Do be aware that a few of the members of `System.String` are static members, and are therefore called at the class (rather than the object) level. Assume you have created a new Console Application project named FunWithStrings. Author the following method, which is called from within `Main()`:

```
static void BasicStringFunctionality()
{
  Console.WriteLine("=> Basic String functionality:");
  string firstName = "Freddy";
  Console.WriteLine("Value of firstName: {0}", firstName);
  Console.WriteLine("firstName has {0} characters.", firstName.Length);
  Console.WriteLine("firstName in uppercase: {0}", firstName.ToUpper());
  Console.WriteLine("firstName in lowercase: {0}", firstName.ToLower());
  Console.WriteLine("firstName contains the letter y?: {0}",
    firstName.Contains("y"));
  Console.WriteLine("firstName after replace: {0}", firstName.Replace("dy", ""));
  Console.WriteLine();
}
```

Not too much to say here, as this method simply invokes various members (`ToUpper()`, `Contains()`, etc.) on a local `string` variable to yield various formats and transformations. Figure 3-9 shows the initial output.

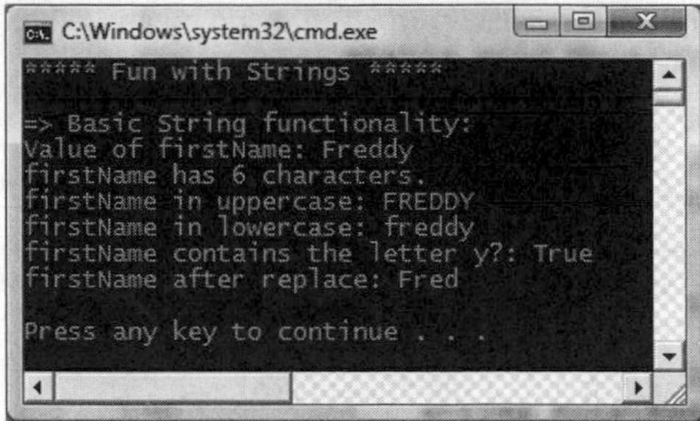

Figure 3-9. *Basic string manipulation*

String Concatenation

`String` variables can be connected together to build larger `string` types via the C# + operator. As you may know, this technique is formally termed *string concatenation*. Consider the following new helper function:

```
static void StringConcatenation()
{
  Console.WriteLine("=> String concatenation:");
  string s1 = "Programming the ";
  string s2 = "PsychoDrill (PTP)";
  string s3 = s1 + s2;
  Console.WriteLine(s3);
  Console.WriteLine();
}
```

You may be interested to know that the C# + symbol is processed by the compiler to emit a call to the static `String.Concat()` method. In fact, if you were to compile the previous code and open the assembly within `ildasm.exe` (see Chapter 1), you would find the CIL code shown in Figure 3-10.

```
FunWithStrings.Program::StringConcatenation : void()
Find  Find Next
.method private hidebysig static void  StringConcatenation() cil managed
{
  // Code size       29 (0x1d)
  .maxstack  2
  .locals init ([0] string s1,
           [1] string s2,
           [2] string s3)
  IL_0000:  nop
  IL_0001:  ldstr      "Programming the "
  IL_0006:  stloc.0
  IL_0007:  ldstr      "PsychoDrill (PTP)"
  IL_000c:  stloc.1
  IL_000d:  ldloc.0
  IL_000e:  ldloc.1
  IL_000f:  call       string [mscorlib]System.String::Concat(string,
                                                              string)
  IL_0014:  stloc.2
  IL_0015:  ldloc.2
  IL_0016:  call       void [mscorlib]System.Console::WriteLine(string)
  IL_001b:  nop
  IL_001c:  ret
} // end of method Program::StringConcatenation
```

Figure 3-10. *The C# + operator results in a call to* `String.Concat()`.

Given this, it is possible to perform string concatenation by calling `String.Concat()` directly (although you really have not gained anything by doing so—in fact, you have incurred additional keystrokes!):

```
static void StringConcatenation()
{
  Console.WriteLine("=> String concatenation:");
  string s1 = "Programming the ";
  string s2 = "PsychoDrill (PTP)";
  string s3 = String.Concat(s1, s2);
  Console.WriteLine(s3);
  Console.WriteLine();
}
```

Escape Characters

Like in other C-based languages, C# string literals may contain various *escape characters*, which qualify how the character data should be printed to the output stream. Each escape character begins with a backslash, followed by a specific token. In case you are a bit rusty on the meanings behind these escape characters, Table 3-6 lists the more common options.

Table 3-6. *String Literal Escape Characters*

Character	Meaning in Life
`\'`	Inserts a single quote into a string literal.
`\"`	Inserts a double quote into a string literal.
`\\`	Inserts a backslash into a string literal. This can be quite helpful when defining file paths.
`\a`	Triggers a system alert (beep). For console programs, this can be an audio clue to the user.
`\n`	Inserts a new line (on Win32 platforms).
`\r`	Inserts a carriage return.
`\t`	Inserts a horizontal tab into the string literal.

For example, to print a string that contains a tab between each word, you can make use of the `\t` escape character. As another example, assume you wish to create a string literal that contains quotation marks, another that defines a directory path, and a final string literal that inserts three blank lines after printing the character data. To do so without compiler errors, you would need to make use of the `\"`, `\\`, and `\n` escape characters. As well, to annoy any person within a 10 foot radius from you, notice that I have embedded an alarm within each string literal (to trigger a beep). Consider the following:

```
static void EscapeChars()
{
  Console.WriteLine("=> Escape characters:\a");
  string strWithTabs = "Model\tColor\tSpeed\tPet Name\a ";
  Console.WriteLine(strWithTabs);

  Console.WriteLine("Everyone loves \"Hello World\"\a ");
  Console.WriteLine("C:\\MyApp\\bin\\Debug\a ");
```

```
// Adds a total of 4 blank lines (then beep again!).
Console.WriteLine("All finished.\n\n\n\a ");
Console.WriteLine();
}
```

Defining Verbatim Strings

When you prefix a string literal with the @ symbol, you have created what is termed a *verbatim string*. Using verbatim strings, you disable the processing of a literal's escape characters and print out a string as is. This can be most useful when working with strings representing directory and network paths. Therefore, rather than making use of \\ escape characters, you can simply write the following:

```
// The following string is printed verbatim
// thus, all escape characters are displayed.
Console.WriteLine(@"C:\MyApp\bin\Debug");
```

Also note that verbatim strings can be used to preserve white space for strings that flow over multiple lines:

```
// White space is preserved with verbatim strings.
string myLongString = @"This is a very
     very
          very
               long string";
Console.WriteLine(myLongString);
```

Using verbatim strings, you can also directly insert a double quote into a literal string by doubling the " token, for example:

```
Console.WriteLine(@"Cerebus said ""Darrr! Pret-ty sun-sets""");
```

Figure 3-11 shows the result of invoking EscapeChars().

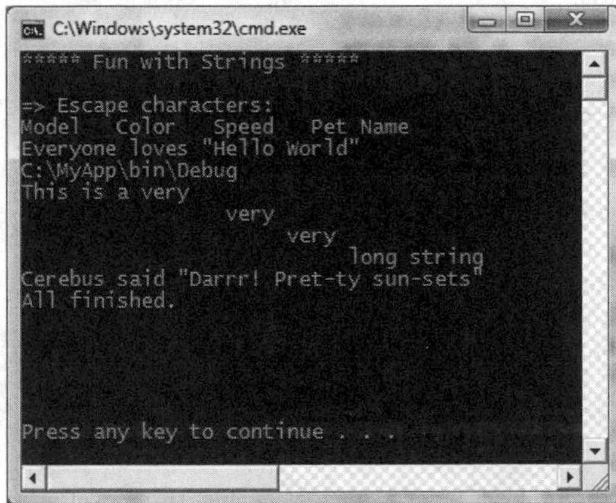

Figure 3-11. *Escape characters and verbatim strings in action*

Strings and Equality

As fully explained in Chapter 4, a *reference type* is an object allocated on the garbage-collected managed heap. By default, when you perform a test for equality on reference types (via the C# == and != operators), you will be returned true if the references are pointing to the same object in memory. However, even though the string data type is indeed a reference type, the equality operators have been redefined to compare the *values* of string objects, not the object in memory to which they refer:

```
static void StringEquality()
{
  Console.WriteLine("=> String equality:");
  string s1 = "Hello!";
  string s2 = "Yo!";
  Console.WriteLine("s1 = {0}", s1);
  Console.WriteLine("s2 = {0}", s2);
  Console.WriteLine();

  // Test these strings for equality.
  Console.WriteLine("s1 == s2: {0}", s1 == s2);
  Console.WriteLine("s1 == Hello!: {0}", s1 == "Hello!");
  Console.WriteLine("s1 == HELLO!: {0}", s1 == "HELLO!");
  Console.WriteLine("s1 == hello!: {0}", s1 == "hello!");
  Console.WriteLine("s1.Equals(s2): {0}", s1.Equals(s2));
  Console.WriteLine("Yo.Equals(s2): {0}", "Yo!".Equals(s2));
  Console.WriteLine();
}
```

Notice that the C# equality operators perform a case-sensitive, character-by-character equality test. Therefore, "Hello!" is not equal to "HELLO!", which is different from "hello!". Also, keeping the connection between string and System.String in mind, notice that we are able to test for equality using the Equals() method of String as well as the baked-in equality operators. Finally, given that every string literal (such as "Yo") is a valid System.String instance, we are able to access string-centric functionality from a fixed sequence of characters.

Strings Are Immutable

One of the interesting aspects of System.String is that once you assign a string object with its initial value, the character data *cannot be changed*. At first glance, this might seem like a flat-out lie, given that we are always reassigning strings to new values and due to the fact that the System.String type defines a number of methods that appear to modify the character data in one way or another (uppercasing, lowercasing, etc.). However, if you look more closely at what is happening behind the scenes, you will notice the methods of the string type are in fact returning you a brand-new string object in a modified format:

```
static void StringAreImmutable()
{
  // Set initial string value.
  string s1 = "This is my string.";
  Console.WriteLine("s1 = {0}", s1);

  // Uppercase s1?
  string upperString = s1.ToUpper();
  Console.WriteLine("upperString = {0}", upperString);

  // Nope! s1 is in the same format!
  Console.WriteLine("s1 = {0}", s1);
}
```

If you examine the relevant output in Figure 3-12, you can verify that the original `string` object (`s1`) is not uppercased when calling `ToUpper()`, rather you are returned a *copy* of the `string` in a modified format.

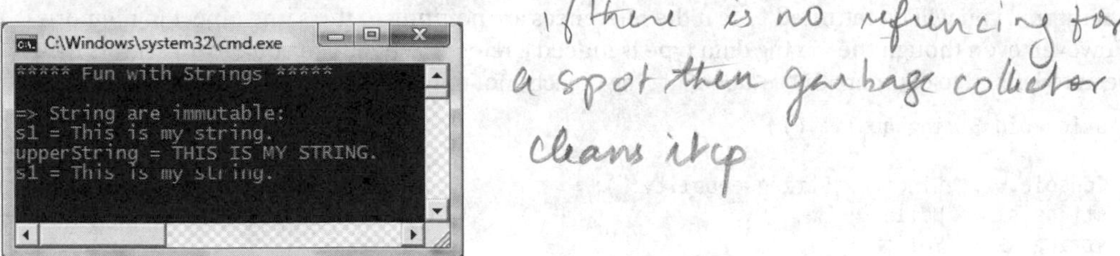

Figure 3-12. *Strings are immutable!*

The same law of immutability holds true when you use the C# assignment operator. To illustrate, comment out (or delete) any existing code within `StringAreImmutable()` (to decrease the amount of generated CIL code) and add the following code statements:

```
static void StringAreImmutable()
{
  string s2 = "My other string";
  s2 = "New string value";
}
```

Now, compile your application and load the assembly into `ildasm.exe` (again, see Chapter 1). If you were to double-click the `Main()` method, you would find the CIL code shown in Figure 3-13.

```
FunWithStrings.Program::StringAreImmutable : void()
Find  Find Next
.method private hidebysig static void  StringAreImmutable() cil managed
{
  // Code size       14 (0xe)
  .maxstack  1
  .locals init ([0] string s2)
  IL_0000:  nop
  IL_0001:  ldstr      "My other string"
  IL_0006:  stloc.0
  IL_0007:  ldstr      "New string value"
  IL_000c:  stloc.0
  IL_000d:  ret
} // end of method Program::StringAreImmutable
```

Figure 3-13. *Assigning a value to a string object results in a new string object.*

Although we have yet to examine the low-level details of the Common Intermediate Language (CIL), do note that the `Main()` method makes numerous calls to the `ldstr` (load string) opcode. Simply put, the `ldstr` opcode of CIL loads a new `string` object on the managed heap. The previous `string` object that contained the value `"My other string."` will eventually be garbage collected.

So, what exactly are we to gather from this insight? In a nutshell, the `string` type can be inefficient and result in bloated code if misused, especially when performing string concatenation. If you need to represent basic character data such as a US Social Security number (SSN), first or last names, or simple string literals used within your application, the `string` data type is the perfect choice.

However, if you are building an application that makes heavy use of textual data (such as a word processing program), it would be a very bad idea to represent the word processing data using string types, as you will most certainly (and often indirectly) end up making unnecessary copies of string data. So what is a programmer to do? Glad you asked.

The System.Text.StringBuilder Type

Given that the string type can be inefficient when used with reckless abandon, the .NET base class libraries provide the System.Text namespace. Within this (relatively small) namespace lives a class named StringBuilder. Like the System.String class, StringBuilder defines methods that allow you to replace or format segments and so forth. When you wish to use this type in your C# code files, your first step is to import the correct namespace:

```
// StringBuilder lives here!
using System.Text;
```

What is unique about the StringBuilder is that when you call members of this type, you are directly modifying the object's internal character data (and is thus more efficient), not obtaining a copy of the data in a modified format. When you create an instance of the StringBuilder, you can supply the object's initial startup values via one of many *constructors*. If you are new to the topic of constructors, simply understand that constructors allow you to create an object with an initial state when you apply the new keyword. Consider the following usage of StringBuilder:

```
static void FunWithStringBuilder()
{
  Console.WriteLine("=> Using the StringBuilder:");
  StringBuilder sb = new StringBuilder("**** Fantastic Games ****");
  sb.Append("\n");
  sb.AppendLine("Half Life");
  sb.AppendLine("Beyond Good and Evil");
  sb.AppendLine("Deus Ex 2");
  sb.AppendLine("System Shock");
  Console.WriteLine(sb.ToString());

  sb.Replace("2", "Invisible War");
  Console.WriteLine(sb.ToString());
  Console.WriteLine("sb as {0} chars.", sb.Length);
  Console.WriteLine();
}
```

Here we have constructed a StringBuilder set to the initial value "**** Fantastic Games ****". As you can see, we are appending to the internal buffer, and are able to replace (or remove) characters at will. By default, a StringBuilder is only able to hold a string of 16 characters or less; however, this initial value can be changed via an additional constructor argument:

```
// Make a StringBuilder with an initial size of 256.
StringBuilder sb = new StringBuilder("**** Fantastic Games ****", 256);
```

If you append more characters than the specified limit, the StringBuilder object will copy its data into a new instance and grow the buffer by the specified limit. Figure 3-14 shows the output of the current helper function.

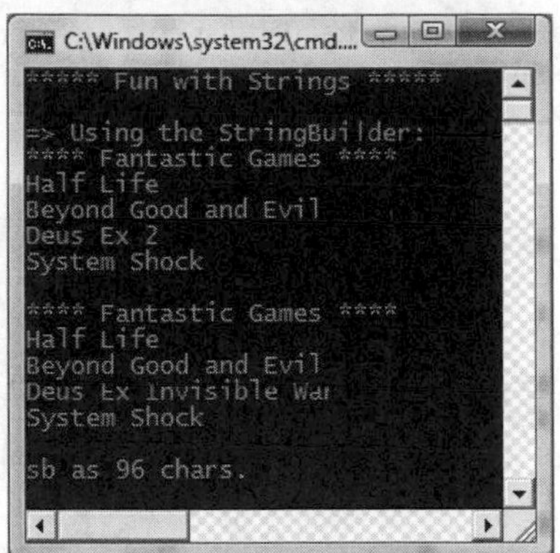

Figure 3-14. *The* `StringBuilder` *is more efficient than* `string`.

Source Code The FunWithStrings project is located under the Chapter 3 subdirectory.

System.DateTime and System.TimeSpan

To wrap up our examination of core data types, allow me to point out the fact that the `System` namespace defines a few useful data types for which there is no C# keyword—specifically, the `DateTime` and `TimeSpan` structures (I'll leave the investigation of `System.Guid` and `System.Void`, as shown in Figure 3-6, to interested readers).

The `DateTime` type contains data that represents a specific date (month, day, year) and time value, both of which may be formatted in a variety of ways using the supplied members. By way of a simple example, ponder the following statements:

```
// This constructor takes (year, month, day)
DateTime dt = new DateTime(2004, 10, 17);

// What day of the month is this?
Console.WriteLine("The day of {0} is {1}", dt.Date, dt.DayOfWeek);
dt = dt.AddMonths(2);  // Month is now December.
Console.WriteLine("Daylight savings: {0}", dt.IsDaylightSavingTime());
```

The `TimeSpan` structure allows you to easily define and transform units of time using various members, for example:

```
// This constructor takes (hours, minutes, seconds)
TimeSpan ts = new TimeSpan(4, 30, 0);
Console.WriteLine(ts);

// Subtract 15 minutes from the current TimeSpan and
// print the result.
Console.WriteLine(ts.Subtract(new TimeSpan(0, 15, 0)));
```

At this point, I hope you understand that each data type keyword of C# has a corresponding type in the .NET base class libraries, each of which exposes a fixed functionality. While I have not detailed each member of these core types, you are in a great position to dig into the details as you see fit. Be sure to consult the .NET Framework 3.5 SDK documentation for full details regarding the intrinsic .NET data types.

Narrowing and Widening Data Type Conversions

Now that you understand how to interact with intrinsic data types, let's examine the related topic of *data type conversion*. Assume you have a new Console Application project (named TypeConversions) that defines the following class type:

```
class Program
{
  static void Main(string[] args)
  {
    Console.WriteLine("***** Fun with type conversions *****");

    // Add two shorts and print the result.
    short numb1 = 9, numb2 = 10;
    Console.WriteLine("{0} + {1} = {2}",
      numb1, numb2, Add(numb1, numb2));
    Console.ReadLine();
  }

  static int Add(int x, int y)
  { return x + y; }
}
```

Notice that the `Add()` method expects to be sent two `int` parameters. However, the `Main()` method is in fact sending in two `short` variables. While this might seem like a complete and total mismatch of data types, the program compiles and executes without error, returning the expected result of 19.

The reason that the compiler treats this code as syntactically sound is due to the fact that there is no possibility for loss of data. Given that the maximum value of a `short` (32,767) is well within the range of an `int` (2,147,483,647), the compiler implicitly *widens* each `short` to an `int`. Formally speaking, *widening* is the term used to define an implicit "upward cast" that does not result in a loss of data.

■ **Note** Look up the topic "Type Conversion Tables" within the .NET Framework 3.5 SDK documentation if you wish to see permissible widening conversions for each C# data type.

Although this implicit widening worked in our favor for the previous example, other times this "feature" can be the source of compile-time errors. For example, assume that you have set values to `numb1` and `numb2` that (when added together) overflow the maximum value of a `short`. As well, assume you are storing the return value of the `Add()` method within a new local `short` variable, rather than directly printing the result to the console:

```
static void Main(string[] args)
{
  Console.WriteLine("***** Fun with type conversions *****");

  // Compiler error below!
  short numb1 = 30000, numb2 = 30000;
  short answer = Add(numb1, numb2);
  Console.WriteLine("{0} + {1} = {2}",
    numb1, numb2, answer);
  Console.ReadLine();
}
```

In this case, the compiler reports the following error:

```
Cannot implicitly convert type 'int' to 'short'. An explicit conversion exists
(are you missing a cast?)
```

The problem is that although the `Add()` method is capable of returning an `int` with the value 60,000 (as this fits within the range of a `System.Int32`), the value cannot be stored in a `short` (as it overflows the bounds of this data type). Formally speaking, the CLR was unable to apply a *narrowing operation*. As you can guess, narrowing is the logical opposite of widening, in that a larger value is stored within a smaller variable.

It is important to point out that all narrowing conversions result in a compiler error, even when you can reason that the narrowing conversion should indeed succeed. For example, the following code also results in a compiler error:

```
// Another compiler error!
static void NarrowingAttempt()
{
  byte myByte = 0;
  int myInt = 200;
  myByte = myInt;
  Console.WriteLine("Value of myByte: {0}", myByte);
}
```

Here, the value contained within the `int` variable (`myInt`) is safely within the range of a `byte`, therefore you would expect the narrowing operation to not result in a runtime error. However, given that C# is a language built with type safety in mind, we do indeed receive a compiler error. When you wish to inform the compiler than you are willing to deal with a possible loss of data due to a narrowing operation, you must apply an *explicit cast* using the C# casting operator `()`. Consider the following update to the `Program` type and resulting output in Figure 3-15.

```
class Program
{
  static void Main(string[] args)
  {
    Console.WriteLine("***** Fun with type conversions *****");
    short numb1 = 30000, numb2 = 30000;

    // Explicitly cast the int into a short (and allow loss of data).
    short answer = (short)Add(numb1, numb2);

    Console.WriteLine("{0} + {1} = {2}",
      numb1, numb2, answer);
    NarrowingAttempt();
    Console.ReadLine();
  }

  static int Add(int x, int y)
  { return x + y; }

  static void NarrowingAttempt()
  {
    byte myByte = 0;
    int myInt = 200;
```

```
    // Explicitly cast the int into a byte (no loss of data).
    myByte = (byte)myInt;
    Console.WriteLine("Value of myByte: {0}", myByte);
  }
}
```

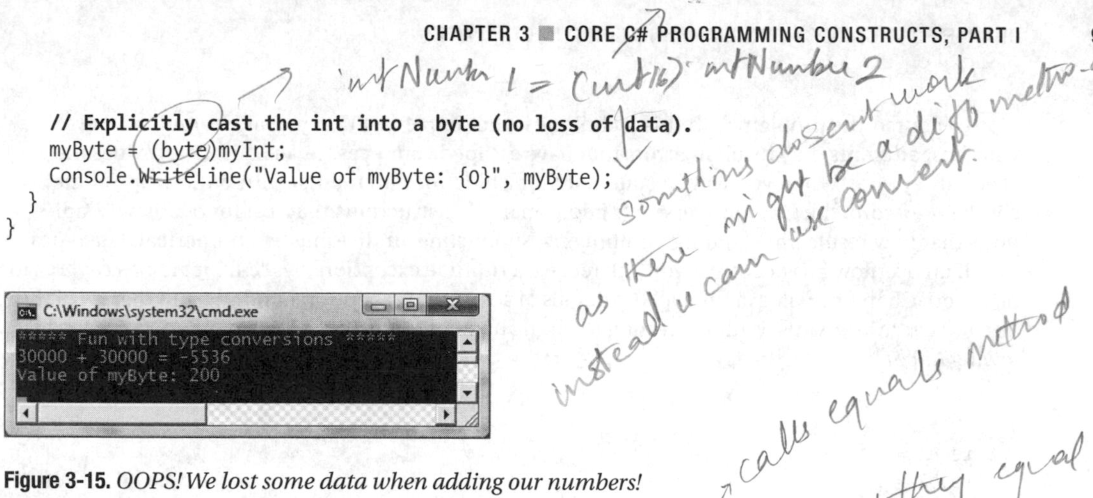

Figure 3-15. *OOPS! We lost some data when adding our numbers!*

Trapping Narrowing Data Conversions

As you have just witnessed, an explicit cast allows you to force the compiler to apply a narrowing conversion, even when doing so may result in a loss of data. In the case of the `NarrowingAttempt()` method, this was not a problem, as the value 200 can fit snuggly within the range of a `byte`. However, in the case of adding the two `shorts` within `Main()`, the end result is completely unacceptable (30,000 + 30,000 = –5536?). If you are building an application where loss of data is always unacceptable, C# provides the `checked` and `unchecked` keywords to ensure data loss does not escape undetected.

To illustrate the use of these keywords, assume you have a new method within `Program` that attempts to add two `bytes`, each of which has been assigned a value that is safely below the maximum (255). If you were to add the values of these types (casting the returned `int` to a `byte`), you would assume that the result would be the exact sum of each member:

```
static void ProcessBytes()
{
  byte b1 = 100;
  byte b2 = 250;
  byte sum = (byte)Add(b1, b2);

  // sum should hold the value 350. However, we find the value 94!
  Console.WriteLine("sum = {0}", sum);
}
```

If you were to view the output of this application, you might be surprised to find that `sum` contains the value 94 (rather than the expected 350). The reason is simple. Given that a `System.Byte` can hold a value only between 0 and 255 (inclusive, for a grand total of 256 slots), `sum` now contains the overflow value (350 – 256 = 94). By default, if you take no corrective course of action, overflow/underflow conditions occur without error.

To handle overflow or underflow conditions in your application, you have two options. Your first choice is to leverage your wits and programming skills to handle all overflow/underflow conditions manually. Assuming you were indeed able to find each overflow condition in your program, you could resolve the previous overflow error as follows:

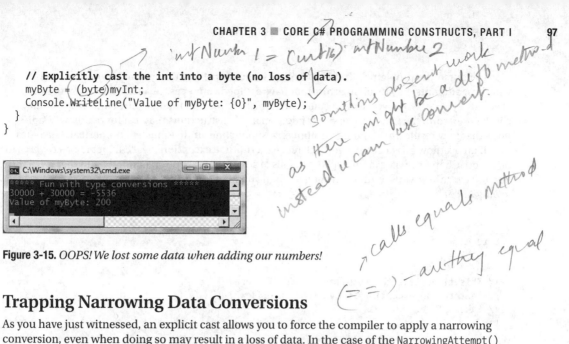

```
// Store sum in an int to prevent overflow.
byte b1 = 100;
byte b2 = 250;
int sum = (byte)Add(b1, b2);
```

Of course, the problem with this technique is the simple fact that you are human, and even your best attempts may result in errors that have escaped your eyes. Given this, C# provides the `checked` keyword. When you wrap a statement (or a block of statements) within the scope of the `checked` keyword, the C# compiler emits additional CIL instructions that test for overflow conditions that may result when adding, multiplying, subtracting, or dividing two numerical data types.

If an overflow has occurred, you will receive a runtime exception (`System.OverflowException` to be exact). Chapter 7 will examine all the details of structured exception handling and the use of the `try` and `catch` keywords. Without getting too hung up on the specifics at this point, observe the following update:

```
static void ProcessBytes()
{
  byte b1 = 100;
  byte b2 = 250;

  // This time, tell the compiler to add CIL code
  // to throw an exception if overflow/underflow
  // takes place.
  try
  {
    byte sum = checked((byte)Add(b1, b2));
    Console.WriteLine("sum = {0}", sum);
  }
  catch (OverflowException ex)
  {
    Console.WriteLine(ex.Message);
  }
}
```

Notice that the return value of `Add()` has been wrapped within the scope of the `checked` keyword. Since the sum is greater than a `byte`, we trigger a runtime exception. Notice the error message printed out via the `Message` property in Figure 3-16.

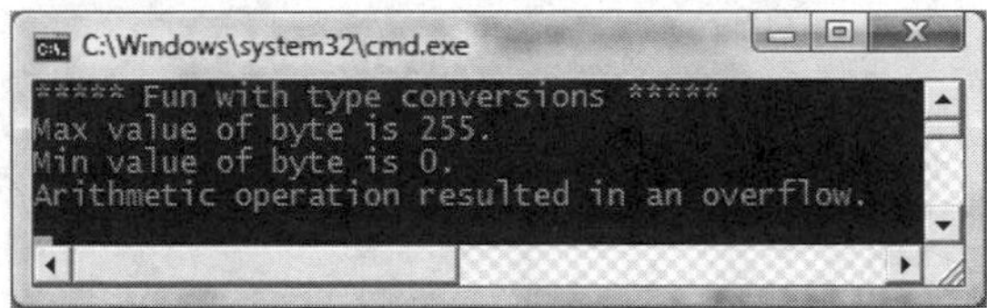

C:\Windows\system32\cmd.exe
***** Fun with type conversions *****
Max value of byte is 255.
Min value of byte is 0.
Arithmetic operation resulted in an overflow.

Figure 3-16. *The* `checked` *keyword forces runtime exceptions to be thrown when data loss occurs.*

If you wish to force overflow checking to occur over a block of code statements, you can do so by defining a *checked scope* as follows:

```
try
{
  checked
  {
    byte sum = (byte)Add(b1, b2);
    Console.WriteLine("sum = {0}", sum);
  }
}
catch (OverflowException ex)
{
  Console.WriteLine(ex.Message);
}
```

In either case, the code in question will be evaluated for possible overflow conditions automatically, which will trigger an overflow exception if encountered.

Setting Projectwide Overflow Checking

If you are creating an application that should never allow silent overflow to occur, you may find yourself in the annoying position of wrapping numerous lines of code within the scope of the checked keyword. As an alternative, the C# compiler supports the /checked flag. When enabled, all of your arithmetic will be evaluated for overflow without the need to make use of the C# checked keyword. If overflow has been discovered, you will still receive a runtime exception.

To enable this flag using Visual Studio 2008, open your project's property page and click the Advanced button on the Build tab. From the resulting dialog box, select the Check for arithmetic overflow/underflow check box (see Figure 3-17).

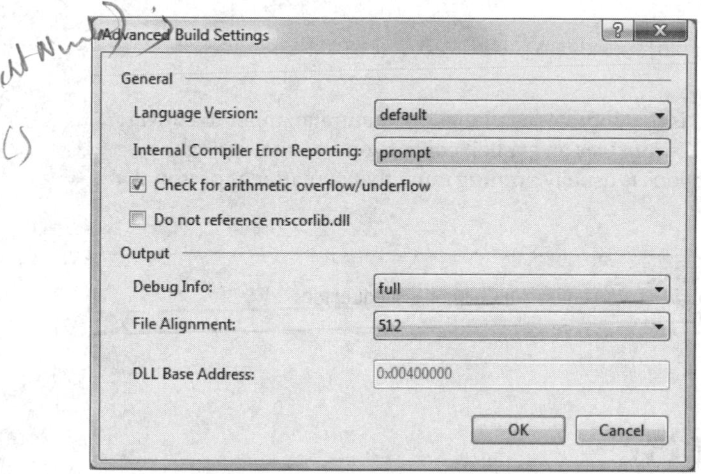

Figure 3-17. *Enabling projectwide overflow/underflow data checking*

Enabling this setting can be very helpful when you're creating a debug build. Once all of the overflow exceptions have been squashed out of the code base, you're free to disable the /checked flag for subsequent builds (which will increase the runtime performance of your application).

The unchecked Keyword

Now, assuming you have enabled this projectwide setting, what are you to do if you have a block of code where data loss *is* acceptable? Given that the /checked flag will evaluate all arithmetic logic, C# provides the unchecked keyword to disable the throwing of an overflow exception on a case-by-case basis. This keyword's use is identical to that of the checked keyword in that you can specify a single statement or a block of statements, for example:

```
// Assuming /checked is enabled,
// this block will not trigger
// a runtime exception.
unchecked
{
  byte sum = (byte)(b1 + b2);
  Console.WriteLine("sum = { 0} ", sum);
}
```

So, to summarize the C# checked and unchecked keywords, remember that the default behavior of the .NET runtime is to ignore arithmetic overflow. When you want to selectively handle discrete statements, make use of the checked keyword. If you wish to trap overflow errors throughout your application, enable the /checked flag. Finally, the unchecked keyword may be used if you have a block of code where overflow is acceptable (and thus should not trigger a runtime exception).

The Role of System.Convert

To wrap up the topic of data type conversions, I'd like to point out the fact that the System namespace defines a class named Convert that can also be used to widen or narrow data:

```
static void NarrowWithConvert()
{
  byte myByte = 0;
  int myInt = 200;
  myByte = Convert.ToByte(myInt);
  Console.WriteLine("Value of myByte: {0}", myByte);
}
```

One benefit of using System.Convert is that it provides a language-neutral manner to convert between data types. However, given that C# provides an explicit conversion operator, using the Convert type to do your data type conversions is usually nothing more than a matter of personal preference.

■ **Source Code** The TypeConversions project is located under the Chapter 3 subdirectory.

C# Iteration Constructs

All programming languages provide ways to repeat blocks of code until a terminating condition has been met. Regardless of which language you have used in the past, the C# iteration statements should not raise too many eyebrows and should require little explanation. C# provides the following four iteration constructs:

- for loop
- foreach/in loop
- while loop
- do/while loop

Let's quickly examine each looping construct in turn, using a new Console Application project named IterationsAndDecisions.

The for Loop

When you need to iterate over a block of code a fixed number of times, the for statement provides a good deal of flexibility. In essence, you are able to specify how many times a block of code repeats itself, as well as the terminating condition. Without belaboring the point, here is a sample of the syntax:

```
// A basic for loop.
static void ForAndForEachLoop()
{
  // Note! "i" is only visible within the scope of the for loop.
  for(int i = 0; i < 4; i++)
  {
    Console.WriteLine("Number is: {0} ", i);
  }
  // "i" is not visible here.
}
```

All of your old C, C++, and Java tricks still hold when building a C# `for` statement. You can create complex terminating conditions, build endless loops, and make use of the `goto`, `continue`, and `break` keywords. I'll assume that you will bend this iteration construct as you see fit. Consult the .NET Framework 3.5 SDK documentation if you require further details on the C# `for` keyword.

The foreach Loop

The C# `foreach` keyword allows you to iterate over all items within an array, without the need to test for the array's upper limit. Here are two examples using `foreach`, one to traverse an array of strings and the other to traverse an array of integers:

```
// Iterate array items using foreach.
static void ForAndForEachLoop()
{
...
  string[] carTypes = {"Ford", "BMW", "Yugo", "Honda" };
  foreach (string c in carTypes)
    Console.WriteLine(c);

  int[] myInts = { 10, 20, 30, 40 };
  foreach (int i in myInts)
    Console.WriteLine(i);
}
```

In addition to iterating over simple arrays, `foreach` is also able to iterate over system-supplied or user-defined collections. I'll hold off on the details until Chapter 9, as this aspect of the `foreach` keyword entails an understanding of interface-based programming and the role of the `IEnumerator` and `IEnumerable` interfaces.

The while and do/while Looping Constructs

The `while` looping construct is useful should you wish to execute a block of statements until some terminating condition has been reached. Within the scope of a `while` loop, you will, of course, need to ensure this terminating event is indeed established; otherwise, you will be stuck in an endless loop. In the following example, the message "In while loop" will be continuously printed until the user terminates the loop by entering **yes** at the command prompt:

```
static void ExecuteWhileLoop()
{
  string userIsDone = "";

  // Test on a lower-class copy of the string.
  while(userIsDone.ToLower() != "yes")
  {
    Console.Write("Are you done? [yes] [no]: ");
```

```
    userIsDone = Console.ReadLine();
    Console.WriteLine("In while loop");
  }
}
```

Closely related to the while loop is the do/while statement. Like a simple while loop, do/while is used when you need to perform some action an undetermined number of times. The difference is that do/while loops are guaranteed to execute the corresponding block of code at least once (in contrast, it is possible that a simple while loop may never execute if the terminating condition is false from the onset).

```
static void ExecuteDoWhileLoop()
{
  string userIsDone = "";

  do
  {
    Console.WriteLine("In do/while loop");
    Console.Write("Are you done? [yes] [no]: ");
    userIsDone = Console.ReadLine();
  }while(userIsDone.ToLower() != "yes"); // Note the semicolon!
}
```

Decision Constructs and the Relational/Equality Operators

Now that you can iterate over a block of statements, the next related concept is how to control the flow of program execution. C# defines two simple constructs to alter the flow of your program, based on various contingencies:

- The if/else statement
- The switch statement

The if/else Statement

First up is our good friend the if/else statement. Unlike in C and C++, however, the if/else statement in C# operates only on Boolean expressions, not ad hoc values such as –1, 0. Given this, if/else statements typically involve the use of the C# operators shown in Table 3-7 in order to obtain a literal Boolean value.

Table 3-7. *C# Relational and Equality Operators*

C# Equality/Relational Operator	Example Usage	Meaning in Life
==	if(age == 30)	Returns true only if each expression is the same
!=	if("Foo" != myStr)	Returns true only if each expression is different

<
>
<=
>=
	if(bonus < 2000)
	if(bonus > 2000)
	if(bonus <= 2000)
	if(bonus >= 2000)
		Returns true if expression A is less than, greater than, less than or equal to, or greater than or equal to expression B

Again, C and C++ programmers need to be aware that the old tricks of testing a condition for a value "not equal to zero" will not work in C#. Let's say you want to see whether the `string` you are working with is longer than zero characters. You may be tempted to write

```
static void ExecuteIfElse()
{
  // This is illegal, given that Length returns an int, not a bool.
  string stringData = "My textual data";
  if(stringData.Length)
  {
    Console.WriteLine("string is greater than 0 characters");
  }
}
```

If you wish to make use of the `String.Length` property to determine truth or falsity, you need to modify your conditional expression to resolve to a Boolean. For example:

```
// Legal, as this resolves to either true or false.
if(stringData.Length > 0)
{
  Console.WriteLine("string is greater than 0 characters");
}
```

An `if` statement may be composed of complex expressions as well and can contain `else` statements to perform more complex testing. The syntax is identical to C(++) and Java (and not too far removed from Visual Basic). To build complex expressions, C# offers an expected set of conditional operators, as shown in Table 3-8.

Table 3-8. *C# Conditional Operators*

Operator	Example	Meaning in Life
`&&`	`if((age == 30) && (name == "Fred"))`	Conditional AND operator
`||`	`if((age == 30) || (name == "Fred"))`	Conditional OR operator
`!`	`if(!myBool)`	Conditional NOT operator

The switch Statement

The other simple selection construct offered by C# is the `switch` statement. As in other C-based languages, the `switch` statement allows you to handle program flow based on a predefined set of choices. For example, the following `Main()` logic prints a specific string message based on one of two possible selections (the `default` case handles an invalid selection):

```
// Switch on a numerical value.
static void ExecuteSwitch()
{
  Console.WriteLine("1 [C#], 2 [VB]");
  Console.Write("Please pick your language preference: ");

  string langChoice = Console.ReadLine();
  int n = int.Parse(langChoice);

  switch (n)
  {
    case 1:
```

```
      Console.WriteLine("Good choice, C# is a fine language.");
    break;
    case 2:
      Console.WriteLine("VB .NET: OOP, multithreading, and more!");
    break;
    default:
      Console.WriteLine("Well...good luck with that!");
    break;
  }
}
```

■ **Note** C# demands that each case (including `default`) that contains executable statements have a terminating `break` or `goto` to avoid fall-through.

One nice feature of the C# `switch` statement is that you can evaluate string data in addition to numeric data. Here is an updated `switch` statement that does this very thing (notice we have no need to parse the user data into a numeric value with this approach):

```
static void ExecuteSwitchOnString()
{
  Console.WriteLine("C# or VB");
  Console.Write("Please pick your language preference: ");

  string langChoice = Console.ReadLine();
  switch (langChoice)
  {
    case "C#":
      Console.WriteLine("Good choice, C# is a fine language.");
    break;
    case "VB":
      Console.WriteLine("VB .NET: OOP, multithreading and more!");
    break;
    default:
      Console.WriteLine("Well...good luck with that!");
    break;
  }
}
```

■ **Source Code** The IterationsAndDecisions project is located under the Chapter 3 subdirectory.

Summary

The goal of this chapter was to expose you to numerous core aspects of the C# programming language. Here, we examined the constructs that will be commonplace in any application you may be interested in building. After examining the role of an application object, you learned that every C# executable program must have a type defining a `Main()` method, which serves as the program's entry point. Within the scope of `Main()`, you typically create any number of objects that work together to breathe life into your application.

Next, we dove into the details of the built-in data types of C#, and came to understand that each data type keyword (e.g., `int`) is really a shorthand notation for a full-blown type in the `System` namespace (`System.Int32` in this case). Given this, each C# data type has a number of built-in members. Along the same vein, you also learned about the role of *widening* and *narrowing* as well as the role of the `checked` and `unchecked` keywords.

We wrapped up by checking out the various iteration and decision constructs supported by C#. Now that you have an understanding of some of the basic nuts and bolts, the next chapter completes our examination of core language features. After this point, you will be well prepared to examine the object-oriented features of C#.

when u use Form1's static methods u have to reference it with the class its from as the object is always created!

can change label's autosize option

Accept + Cancel Button property

Tab index - highlights items as u click Tab

Those which are interacting with user put in 1 block

Enter - Accept Button

Esc - Cancel Button

when u dbl click button accidentally can also delete from events when you delete from 2 text files.

CHAPTER 4

Core C# Programming Constructs, Part II

This chapter picks up where the previous chapter left off, and completes your investigation of the core aspects of the C# programming language. We begin by examining various details regarding the construction of C# methods, exploring the `out`, `ref`, and `params` keywords along the way. Once you examine the topic of *method overloading*, the next task is to investigate the details behind manipulating array types using the syntax of C# and get to know the functionality contained within the related `System.Array` class type.

In addition, this chapter provides a discussion regarding the construction of enumeration and structure types, including a fairly detailed examination of the distinction between a *value type* and a *reference type*. We wrap this up by examining the role of nullable data types and the ? and ?? operators.

Methods and Parameter Modifiers

To begin this chapter, let's examine the details of defining type methods. Just like the `Main()` method (see Chapter 3), your custom methods may or may not take parameters and may or may not return values. As you will see over the next several chapters, methods can be implemented within the scope of classes or structures (and prototyped within interface types) and may be decorated with various keywords (`internal`, `virtual`, `public`, `new`, etc.) to qualify their behavior. At this point in the text, each of our methods has followed this basic format:

```
// Recall that static methods can be called directly
// without creating a class instance.
class Program
{
  // static returnVal MethodName(args) {...}
  static int Add(int x, int y){ return x + y; }
}
```

While the definition of a method in C# is quite straightforward, there are a handful of keywords that you can use to control how arguments are passed to the method in question, and these are listed in Table 4-1.

Table 4-1. *C# Parameter Modifiers*

Parameter Modifier	Meaning in Life
(None)	If a parameter is not marked with a parameter modifier, it is assumed to be passed by value, meaning the called method receives a copy of the original data.
`out`	Output parameters must be assigned by the method being called (and therefore are passed by reference). If the called method fails to assign output parameters, you are issued a compiler error.
`ref`	The value is initially assigned by the caller and may be optionally reassigned by the called method (as the data is also passed by reference). No compiler error is generated if the called method fails to assign a `ref` parameter.
`params`	This parameter modifier allows you to send in a variable number of arguments as a single logical parameter. A method can have only a single `params` modifier, and it must be the final parameter of the method.

To illustrate the use of these keywords, create a new Console Application project named `FunWithMethods`. Now, let's walk through the role of each keyword in turn.

The Default Parameter-Passing Behavior

The default manner in which a parameter is sent into a function is *by value*. Simply put, if you do not mark an argument with a parameter-centric modifier, a copy of the data is passed into the function. As explained at the end of this chapter, exactly *what* is copied will depend on whether the parameter is a value type or a reference type. For the time being, assume the following method within the `Program` class that operates on two numerical data types passed by value:

```
// Arguments are passed by value by default.
static int Add(int x, int y)
{
  int ans = x + y;

  // Caller will not see these changes
  // as you are modifying a copy of the
  // original data.
  x = 10000; y = 88888;
  return ans;
}
```

Numerical data falls under the category of value types. Therefore, if you change the values of the parameters within the scope of the member, the caller is blissfully unaware, given that you are changing the values on a copy of the caller's data:

```
static void Main(string[] args)
{
  Console.WriteLine("***** Fun with Methods *****");

  // Pass two variables in by value.
  int x = 9, y = 10;
  Console.WriteLine("Before call: X: {0}, Y: {1}", x, y);
  Console.WriteLine("Answer is: {0}", Add(x, y));
  Console.WriteLine("After call: X: {0}, Y: {1}", x, y);
  Console.ReadLine();
}
```

As you would hope, the values of x and y remain identical before and after the call to Add(), as shown in Figure 4-1.

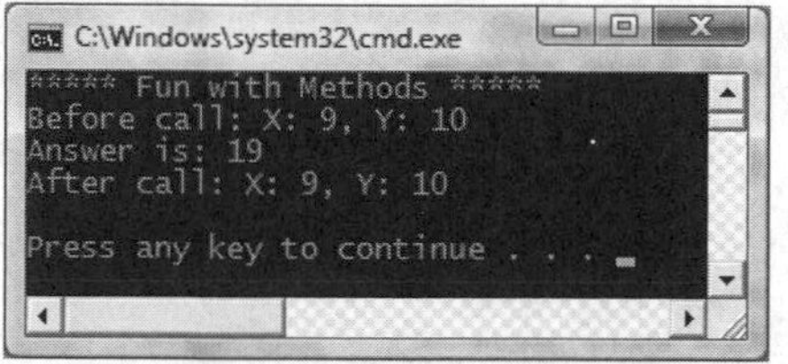

Figure 4-1. *By default, parameters are passed by value.*

The out Modifier

Next, we have the use of *output parameters*. Methods that have been defined to take output parameters (via the out keyword) are under obligation to assign them to an appropriate value before exiting the method in question (if you fail to do so, you will receive compiler errors).

To illustrate, here is an alternative version of the Add() method that returns the sum of two integers using the C# out modifier (note the physical return value of this method is now void):

```
// Output parameters must be assigned by the called method.
static void Add(int x, int y, out int ans)
{
  ans = x + y;
}
```

Calling a method with output parameters also requires the use of the out modifier. Recall that local variables passed as output variables are not required to be assigned before use (if you do so, the original value is lost after the call), for example:

```
static void Main(string[] args)
{
  Console.WriteLine("***** Fun with Methods *****");
...
  // No need to assign initial value to local variables
  // used as output parameters.
  int ans;
  Add(90, 90, out ans);
  Console.WriteLine("90 + 90 = {0}", ans);
  Console.ReadLine();
}
```

The previous example is intended to be illustrative in nature; you really have no reason to return the value of your summation using an output parameter. However, the C# out modifier does serve a very useful purpose: it allows the caller to obtain multiple return values from a single method invocation.

```
// Returning multiple output parameters.
static void FillTheseValues(out int a, out string b, out bool c)
{
  a = 9;
  b = "Enjoy your string.";
  c = true;
}
```

The caller would be able to invoke the following method:

```
static void Main(string[] args)
{
  Console.WriteLine("***** Fun with Methods *****");
...
  int i; string str; bool b;

  FillTheseValues(out i, out str, out b);
  Console.WriteLine("Int is: {0}", i);
  Console.WriteLine("String is: {0}", str);
  Console.WriteLine("Boolean is: {0}", b);
  Console.ReadLine();
}
```

Finally, remember that methods that define output parameters *must* assign the parameter to a valid value before exiting the methods. Therefore, the following method will result in a compiler error, as the integer parameter has not been assigned within the method scope:

```
static void ThisWontCompile(out int a)
{
  Console.WriteLine("This is an error...");
}
```

The ref Modifier

Now consider the use of the C# `ref` parameter modifier. Reference parameters are necessary when you wish to allow a method to operate on (and usually change the values of) various data points declared in the caller's scope (such as a sorting or swapping routine). Note the distinction between output and reference parameters:

- Output parameters do not need to be initialized before they passed to the method. The reason for this? The method must assign output parameters before exiting.
- Reference parameters must be initialized before they are passed to the method. The reason for this? You are passing a reference to an existing variable. If you don't assign it to an initial value, that would be the equivalent of operating on an unassigned local variable.

Let's check out the use of the `ref` keyword by way of a method that swaps two strings:

```
// Reference parameters.
public static void SwapStrings(ref string s1, ref string s2)
{
  string tempStr = s1;
  s1 = s2;
  s2 = tempStr;
}
```

This method can be called as follows:

```
static void Main(string[] args)
{
  Console.WriteLine("***** Fun with Methods *****");
...
  string s1 = "Flip";
  string s2 = "Flop";
  Console.WriteLine("Before: {0}, {1} ", s1, s2);
  SwapStrings(ref s1, ref s2);
```

```
  Console.WriteLine("After: {0}, {1} ", s1, s2);
  Console.ReadLine();
}
```

Here, the caller has assigned an initial value to local string data (s and s2). Once the call to SwapStrings() returns, s1 now contains the value "Flop", while s2 reports the value "Flip" (see Figure 4-2).

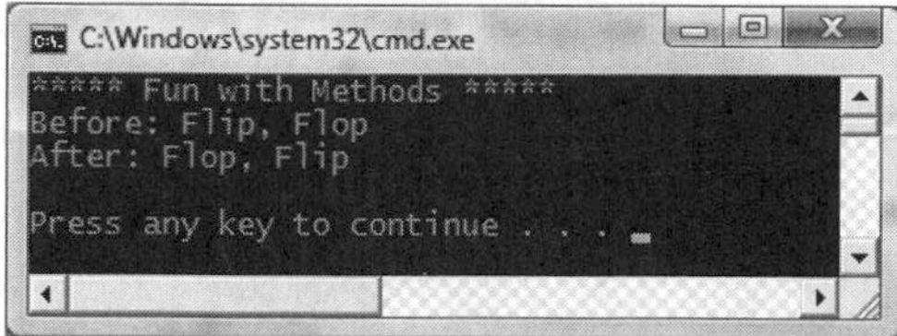

Figure 4-2. *Reference parameters can be changed by the called method.*

Note The C# ref keyword will be revisited later in this chapter in the section "Understanding Value Types and Reference Types." As you will see, the behavior of this keyword changes just a bit depending on whether the argument is a "value type" (structure) or "reference type" (class).

The params Modifier

Last but not least, C# supports the use of *parameter arrays*. To understand the role of the params keyword, you must (as the name implies) understand how to manipulate C# arrays. If this is not the case, you may wish to return to this section once you have finished this chapter, as we will formally examine the System.Array type a bit later in this chapter in the section "Array Manipulation in C#."

The params keyword allows you to pass into a method a variable number of parameters (of the same type) as a *single logical parameter*. As well, arguments marked with the params keyword can be processed if the caller sends in a strongly typed array or a comma-delimited list of items. Yes, this can be confusing! To clear things up, assume you wish to create a function that allows the caller to pass in any number of arguments and return the calculated average.

If you were to prototype this method to take an array of doubles, this would force the caller to first define the array, then fill the array, and finally pass it into the method. However, if you define CalculateAverage() to take a params of integer data types, the caller can simply pass a comma-delimited list of doubles. The .NET runtime will automatically package the set of doubles into an array of type double behind the scenes:

```
// Return average of "some number" of doubles.
static double CalculateAverage(params double[] values)
{
  Console.WriteLine("You sent me {0} doubles.", values.Length);

  double sum = 0;
  if(values.Length == 0)
    return sum;

  for (int i = 0; i < values.Length; i++)
    sum += values[i];
  return (sum / values.Length);
}
```

This method has been defined to take a parameter array of doubles. What this method is in fact saying is, "Send me any number of doubles and I'll compute the average." Given this, you can call CalculateAverage() in any of the following ways (if you did not make use of the params modifier in the definition of CalculateAverage(), the first invocation of this method would result in a compiler error):

```
static void Main(string[] args)
{
  Console.WriteLine("***** Fun with Methods *****");
...
  // Pass in a comma-delimited list of doubles...
  double average;
  average = CalculateAverage(4.0, 3.2, 5.7, 64.22, 87.2);
  Console.WriteLine("Average of data is: {0}", average);

  // ...or pass an array of doubles.
  double[] data = { 4.0, 3.2, 5.7 };
  average = CalculateAverage(data);
  Console.WriteLine("Average of data is: {0}", average);

  // Average of 0 is 0!
  Console.WriteLine("Average of data is: {0}", CalculateAverage());

  Console.ReadLine();
}
```

Note To avoid any ambiguity, C# demands a method only support a single params argument, which must be the final argument in the parameter list.

As you might guess, this technique is nothing more than a convenience for the caller, given that the array is created by the CLR as necessary. By the time the array is within the scope of the method being called, you are able to treat it as a full-blown .NET array that contains all the functionality of the System.Array base class library type. Figure 4-3 illustrates the output.

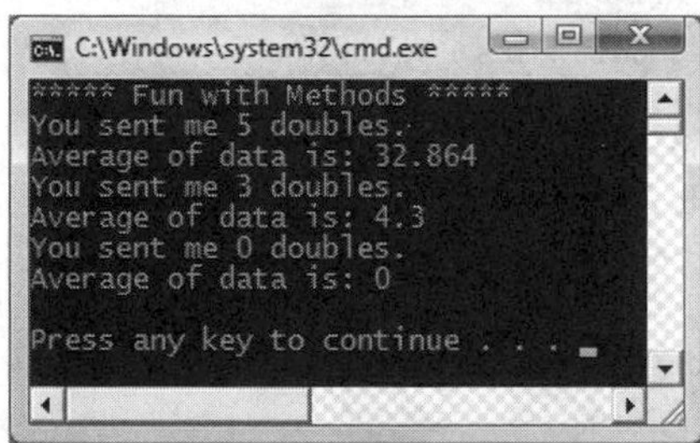

Figure 4-3. *The* params *keyword allows you to build methods with a variable number of arguments.*

Source Code The FunWithMethods application is located under the Chapter 4 subdirectory.

Understanding Member Overloading

Like other modern object-oriented languages, C# allows a method to be *overloaded*. Simply put, when you define a set of identically named members that differ by the number (or type) of parameters, the member in question is said to be overloaded. To check this out firsthand, create a new Console Application project named MethodOverloading.

To understand why overloading is so useful, consider life as a Visual Basic 6.0 developer. Assume you are using VB6 to build a set of methods that return the sum of various incoming types (Integers, Doubles, and so on). Given that VB6 does not support method overloading, you would be required to define a unique set of methods that essentially do the same thing (return the sum of the arguments):

```
' VB6 code.
Public Function AddInts(ByVal x As Integer, ByVal y As Integer) As Integer
  AddInts = x + y
End Function
Public Function AddDoubles(ByVal x As Double, ByVal y As Double) As Double
  AddDoubles = x + y
End Function
Public Function AddLongs(ByVal x As Long, ByVal y As Long) As Long
  AddLongs = x + y
End Function
```

Not only can code such as this become tough to maintain, but the caller must now be painfully aware of the name of each method. Using overloading, we are able to allow the caller to call a single method named Add(). Again, the key is to ensure that each version of the method has a distinct set of arguments (members differing only by return type are *not* unique enough). Consider the following class definition:

```
// C# code.
class Program
{
  static void Main(string[] args) { }

  // Overloaded Add() method.
  static int Add(int x, int y)
  { return x + y; }
  static double Add(double x, double y)
  { return x + y; }
  static long Add(long x, long y)
  { return x + y; }
}
```

Note As explained in Chapter 10, it is possible to build generic methods that take the concept of overloading to the next level. Using generics, you can define "placeholders" for a method implementation that are specified at the time you invoke the member.

The caller can now simply invoke Add() with the required arguments and the compiler is happy to comply, given the fact that the compiler is able to resolve the correct implementation to invoke given the provided arguments:

```
static void Main(string[] args)
{
  Console.WriteLine("***** Fun with Method Overloading *****");
```

```
    // Calls int version of Add()
    Console.WriteLine(Add(10, 10));
    // Calls long version of Add()
    Console.WriteLine(Add(900000000000, 900000000000));
    // Calls double version of Add()
    Console.WriteLine(Add(4.3, 4.4));
    Console.ReadLine();
}
```

The Visual Studio 2008 IDE provides assistance when calling overloaded members to boot. When you type in the name of an overloaded method (such as our good friend `Console.WriteLine()`), IntelliSense will list each version of the method in question. Note that you are able to cycle through each version of an overloaded method using the up and down arrow keys shown in Figure 4-4.

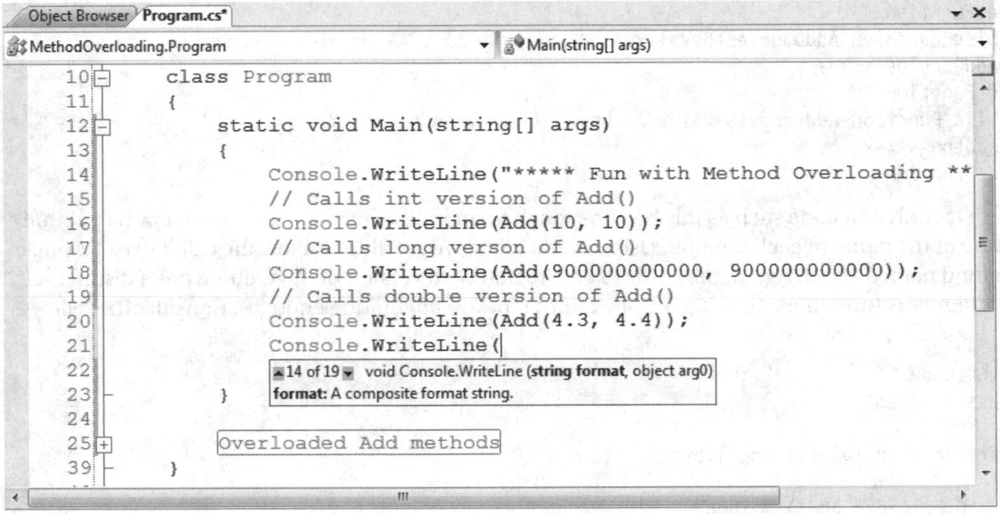

```
Object Browser  Program.cs*
MethodOverloading.Program          Main(string[] args)
    class Program
    {
        static void Main(string[] args)
        {
            Console.WriteLine("***** Fun with Method Overloading **
            // Calls int version of Add()
            Console.WriteLine(Add(10, 10));
            // Calls long verson of Add()
            Console.WriteLine(Add(900000000000, 900000000000));
            // Calls double version of Add()
            Console.WriteLine(Add(4.3, 4.4));
            Console.WriteLine(
            14 of 19  void Console.WriteLine (string format, object arg0)
        }   format: A composite format string.

        Overloaded Add methods
    }
```

Figure 4-4. *Visual Studio IntelliSense for overloaded members*

■ Source Code The MethodOverloading application is located under the Chapter 4 subdirectory.

That wraps up our initial examination of building methods using the syntax of C#. Next up, let's check out how to build and manipulate arrays, enumerations, and structures.

Array Manipulation in C#

As I would guess you are already aware, an *array* is a set of data items, accessed using a numerical index. More specifically, an array is a set of contiguous data points of the same type (an array of `int`s, an array of `string`s, an array of `SportsCar`s, and so on). Declaring an array with C# is quite straightforward. To illustrate, create a new Console Application project (named FunWithArrays) that contains a helper method named `SimpleArrays()`, invoked from within `Main()`:

```
class Program
{
  static void Main(string[] args)
  {
    Console.WriteLine("***** Fun with Arrays *****");
    SimpleArrays();
  }

  static void SimpleArrays()
  {
    Console.WriteLine("=> Simple Array Creation.");
    // Assign an array ints containing 3 elements {0 - 2}
    int[] myInts = new int[3];

    // Initialize a 100 item string array, numbered {0 - 99}
    string[] booksOnDotNet = new string[100];
    Console.WriteLine();
  }
}
```

Look closely at the previous code comments. When declaring a C# array using this syntax, the number used in the array declaration represents the total number of items, not the upper bound. Also note that the lower bound of an array always begins at `0`. Thus, when you write `int[] myInts[3]`, you end up with a array holding three elements (`{0, 1, 2}`).

Once you have defined an array, you are then able to fill the elements index by index as shown in the updated `SimpleArrays()` method:

```
static void SimpleArrays()
{
  Console.WriteLine("=> Simple Array Creation.");
  // Create and fill an array of 3 Integers
  int[] myInts = new int[3];
  myInts[0] = 100;
  myInts[1] = 200;
  myInts[2] = 300;

  // Now print each value.
  foreach(int i in myInts)
    Console.WriteLine(i);
  Console.WriteLine();
}
```

Note Do be aware that if you declare an array, but do not explicitly fill each index, each item will be set to the default value of the data type (e.g., an array of `bools` will be set to `false`, an array of `ints` will be set to `0`, and so forth).

C# Array Initialization Syntax

In addition to filling an array element by element, you are also able to fill the items of an array using C# array initialization syntax. To do so, specify each array item within the scope of curly brackets (`{}`). This syntax can be helpful when you are creating an array of a known size and wish to quickly specify the initial values. For example, consider the following alternative array declarations:

```
static void ArrayInitialization()
{
  Console.WriteLine("=> Array Initialization.");

  // Array initialization syntax using the new keyword.
  string[] stringArray = new string[]
    { "one", "two", "three" };
  Console.WriteLine("stringArray has {0} elements", stringArray.Length);

  // Array initialization syntax without using the new keyword.
  bool[] boolArray = { false, false, true };
  Console.WriteLine("boolArray has {0} elements", boolArray.Length);

  // Array initialization with new keyword and size.
  int[] intArray = new int[4] { 20, 22, 23, 0 };
  Console.WriteLine("intArray has {0} elements", intArray.Length);
  Console.WriteLine();
}
```

Notice that when you make use of this "curly bracket" syntax, you do not need to specify the size of the array (seen when constructing the `stringArray` type), given that this will be inferred by the number of items within the scope of the curly brackets. Also notice that use of the `new` keyword is optional (shown when constructing the `boolArray` type).

In the case of the `intArray` declaration, again recall the numeric value specified represents the number of elements in the array, not the value of the upper bound. If there is a mismatch between the declared size and the number of initializers, you are issued a compile-time error:

```
// OOPS! Mismatch of size and elements!
int[] intArray = new int[2] { 20, 22, 23, 0 };
```

Defining an Array of Objects

As mentioned, when you define an array, you do so by specifying the type of item that can be within the array variable. While this seems quite straightforward, there is one notable twist. As you will come to understand in Chapter 6, `System.Object` is the ultimate base class to each and every type (including fundamental data types) in the .NET type system. Given this fact, if you were to define an array of `object`s, the subitems could be anything at all. Consider the following `ArrayOfObjects()` method (which again can be invoked from `Main()` for testing):

```
static void ArrayOfObjects()
{
  Console.WriteLine("=> Array of Objects.");

  // An array of objects can be anything at all.
  object[] myObjects = new object[4];
  myObjects[0] = 10;
  myObjects[1] = false;
  myObjects[2] = new DateTime(1969, 3, 24);
  myObjects[3] = "Form & Void";

  foreach (object obj in myObjects)
  {
    // Print the type and value for each item in array.
    Console.WriteLine("Type: {0}, Value: {1}", obj.GetType(), obj);
  }
  Console.WriteLine();
}
```

Here, as we are iterating over the contents of `myObjects`, we print out the underlying type of each item using the `GetType()` method of `System.Object` as well as the value of the current item. Without going into too much detail regarding `System.Object.GetType()` at this point in the text, simply understand that this method can be used to obtain the fully qualified name of the item (Chapter 16 fully examines the topic of type information and reflection services). Figure 4-5 shows the output of the previous snippet.

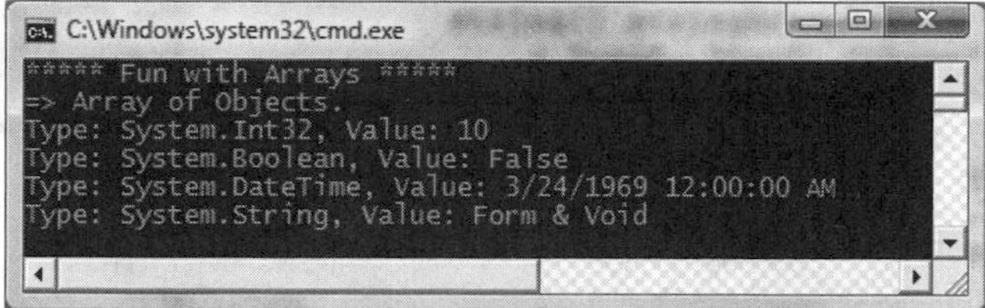

Figure 4-5. *Arrays of type* `object` *can hold anything at all.*

Working with Multidimensional Arrays

In addition to the single-dimension arrays you have seen thus far, C# also supports two varieties of multidimensional arrays. The first of these is termed a *rectangular array*, which is simply an array of multiple dimensions, where each row is of the same length. To declare and fill a multidimensional rectangular array, proceed as follows:

```
static void RectMultidimensionalArray()
{
  Console.WriteLine("=> Rectangular multidimensional array.");
  // A rectangular MD array.
  int[,] myMatrix;
  myMatrix = new int[6,6];

  // Populate (6 * 6) array.
  for(int i = 0; i < 6; i++)
    for(int j = 0; j < 6; j++)
      myMatrix[i, j] = i * j;

  // Print (6 * 6) array.
  for(int i = 0; i < 6; i++)
  {
    for(int j = 0; j < 6; j++)
      Console.Write(myMatrix[i, j] + "\t");
    Console.WriteLine();
  }
  Console.WriteLine();
}
```

The second type of multidimensional array is termed a *jagged array*. As the name implies, jagged arrays contain some number of inner arrays, each of which may have a unique upper limit, for example:

```
static void JaggedMultidimensionalArray()
{
  Console.WriteLine("=> Jagged multidimensional array.");
  // A jagged MD array (i.e., an array of arrays).
```

```
  // Here we have an array of 5 different arrays.
  int[][] myJagArray = new int[5][];

  // Create the jagged array.
  for (int i = 0; i < myJagArray.Length; i++)
    myJagArray[i] = new int[i + 7];

  // Print each row (remember, each element is defaulted to zero!)
  for(int i = 0; i < 5; i++)
  {
    for(int j = 0; j < myJagArray[i].Length; j++)
      Console.Write(myJagArray[i][j] + " ");
    Console.WriteLine();
  }
  Console.WriteLine();
}
```

Figure 4-6 shows the output of calling each of these methods within Main().

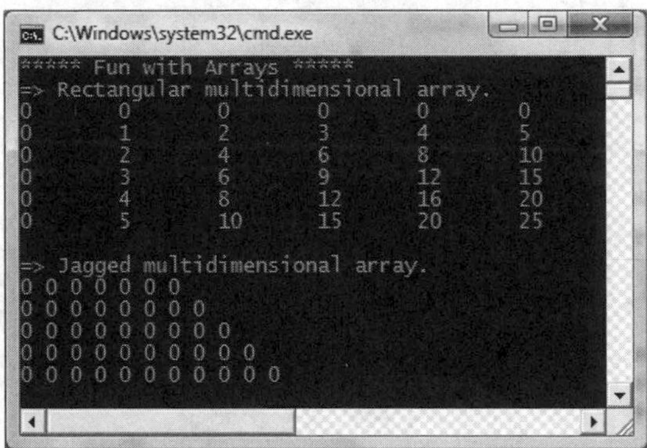

Figure 4-6. *Rectangular and jagged multidimensional arrays*

Arrays As Parameters (and Return Values)

Once you have created an array, you are free to pass it as a parameter and receive it as a member return value. For example, the following PrintArray() method takes an incoming array of ints and prints each member to the console, while the GetStringArray() method populates an array of strings and returns it to the caller:

```
static void PrintArray(int[] myInts)
{
  for(int i = 0; i < myInts.Length; i++)
    Console.WriteLine("Item {0} is {1}", i, myInts[i]);
}

static string[] GetStringArray()
{
  string[] theStrings = {  "Hello", "from", "GetStringArray" };
  return theStrings;
}
```

These methods may be invoked as you would expect:

```
static void PassAndReceiveArrays()
{
  Console.WriteLine("=>Arrays as params and return values.");
  // Pass array as parameter.
  int[] ages = {20, 22, 23, 0} ;
  PrintArray(ages);

  // Get array as return value.
  string[] strs = GetStringArray();
  foreach(string s in strs)
    Console.WriteLine(s);

  Console.WriteLine();
}
```

So, at this point you hopefully feel comfortable with the process of defining, filling, and examining the contents of a C# array type. To complete the picture, let's now examine the role of the System.Array class.

The System.Array Base Class

Every array you create gathers much of its functionality from the System.Array class. Using these common members, we are able to operate on an array using a consistent object model. Table 4-2 gives a rundown of some of the more interesting members (be sure to check the .NET Framework 3.5 SDK for full details).

Table 4-2. *Select Members of* System.Array

Member of Array Class	Meaning in Life
Clear()	This static method sets a range of elements in the array to empty values (0 for value items, static for object references).
CopyTo()	This method is used to copy elements from the source array into the destination array.
GetEnumerator()	This method returns the IEnumerator interface for a given array. I address interfaces in Chapter 9, but for the time being, keep in mind that this interface is required by the foreach construct.
Length	This property returns the number of items within the array.
Rank	This property returns the number of dimensions of the current array.
Reverse()	This static method reverses the contents of a one-dimensional array.
Sort()	This static method sorts a one-dimensional array of intrinsic types. If the elements in the array implement the IComparer interface, you can also sort your custom types (see Chapter 9).

Let's see some of these members in action. The following helper method makes use of the static Reverse() and Clear() methods to pump out information about an array of string types to the console:

```
static void SystemArrayFunctionality()
{
  Console.WriteLine("=> Working with System.Array.");
  // Initialize items at startup.
  string[] gothicBands = {"Tones on Tail", "Bauhaus", "Sisters of Mercy"};
```

```
    // Print out names in declared order.
    Console.WriteLine(" -> Here is the array:");
    for (int i = 0; i <= gothicBands.GetUpperBound(0); i++)
    {
      // Print a name
      Console.Write(gothicBands[i] + " ");
    }
    Console.WriteLine("\n");

    // Reverse them...
    Array.Reverse(gothicBands);
    Console.WriteLine(" -> The reversed array");
    // ... and print them.
    for (int i = 0; i <= gothicBands.GetUpperBound(0); i++)
    {
      // Print a name
      Console.Write(gothicBands[i] + " ");
    }
    Console.WriteLine("\n");

    // Clear out all but the final member.
    Console.WriteLine(" -> Cleared out all but one...");
    Array.Clear(gothicBands, 1, 2);
    for (int i = 0; i <= gothicBands.GetUpperBound(0); i++)
    {
      // Print a name
      Console.Write(gothicBands[i] + " ");
    }
    Console.WriteLine();
  }
```

If you invoke this method from within `Main()`, you will get the output shown in Figure 4-7.

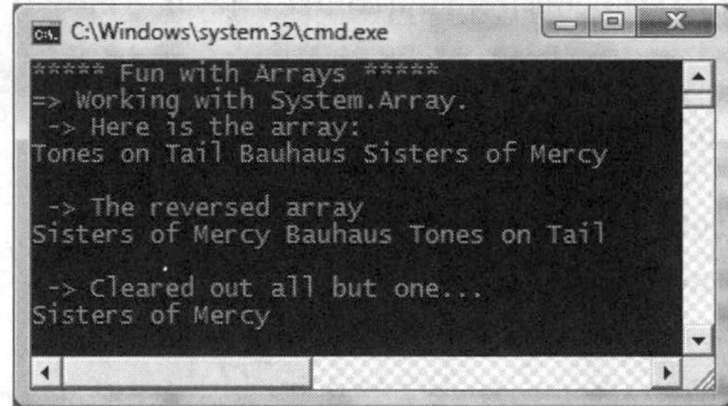

Figure 4-7. *The* `System.Array` *class provides functionality to all .NET arrays.*

Notice that many members of `System.Array` are defined as static members and are therefore called at the class level (for example, the `Array.Sort()` or `Array.Reverse()` methods). Methods such as these are passed in the array you wish to process. Other methods of `System.Array` (such as the `GetUpperBound()` method or `Length` property) are bound at the object level, and thus you are able to invoke the member directly on the array.

■ Source Code The FunWithArrays application is located under the Chapter 4 subdirectory.

Understanding the Enum Type

Recall from Chapter 1 that the .NET type system is composed of classes, structures, enumerations, interfaces, and delegates. To begin our exploration of these types, let's check out the role of the *enumeration* (or simply, *enums*) using a new Console Application project named FunWithEnums.

When building a system, it is often convenient to create a set of symbolic names that map to known numerical values. For example, if you are creating a payroll system, you may want to refer to the type of employees using constants such as vice president, manager, contractor, and grunt. C# supports the notion of custom enumerations for this very reason. For example, here is an enumeration named EmpType:

```
// A custom enumeration.
enum EmpType
{
  Manager,       // = 0
  Grunt,         // = 1
  Contractor,    // = 2
  VicePresident  // = 3
}
```

The EmpType enumeration defines four named constants, corresponding to discrete numerical values. By default, the first element is set to the value zero (0), followed by an *n+1* progression. You are free to change the initial value as you see fit. For example, if it made sense to number the members of EmpType as 102 through 105, you could do so as follows:

```
// Begin with 102.
enum EmpType
{
  Manager = 102,
  Grunt,         // = 103
  Contractor,    // = 104
  VicePresident  // = 105
}
```

Enumerations do not necessarily need to follow a sequential ordering, and need not have unique values. If (for some reason or another) it makes sense to establish your EmpType as shown here, the compiler continues to be happy:

```
// Elements of an enumeration need not be sequential!
enum EmpType
{
  Manager = 10,
  Grunt = 1,
  Contractor = 100,
  VicePresident = 9
}
```

Controlling the Underlying Storage for an Enum

By default, the storage type used to hold the values of an enumeration is a System.Int32 (the C# int); however, you are free to change this to your liking. C# enumerations can be defined in a similar manner for any of the core system types (byte, short, int, or long). For example, if you want to set the underlying storage value of EmpType to be a byte rather than an int, you can write the following:

```
// This time, EmpType maps to an underlying byte.
enum EmpType : byte
{
  Manager = 10,
  Grunt = 1,
  Contractor = 100,
  VicePresident = 9
}
```

Changing the underlying type of an enumeration can be helpful if you are building a .NET application that will be deployed to a low-memory device (such as a .NET-enabled cell phone or PDA) and need to conserve memory wherever possible. Of course, if you do establish your enumeration to use a byte as storage, each value must be within its range!

Declaring and Using Enums

Once you have established the range and storage type of your enumeration, you can use it in place of so-called magic numbers. Because enumerations are nothing more than a user-defined type, you are able to use them as function return values, method parameters, local variables, and so forth. Assume you have a method named AskForBonus(), taking an EmpType variable as the sole parameter. Based on the value of the incoming parameter, you will print out a fitting response to the pay bonus request:

```
class Program
{
  static void Main(string[] args)
  {
    Console.WriteLine("**** Fun with Enums *****");
    // Make a contractor type.
    EmpType emp = EmpType.Contractor;
    AskForBonus(emp);
    Console.ReadLine();
  }

  // Enums as parameters.
  static void AskForBonus(EmpType e)
  {
    switch (e)
    {
      case EmpType.Manager:
        Console.WriteLine("How about stock options instead?");
      break;
      case EmpType.Grunt:
        Console.WriteLine("You have got to be kidding...");
      break;
      case EmpType.Contractor:
        Console.WriteLine("You already get enough cash...");
      break;
      case EmpType.VicePresident:
        Console.WriteLine("VERY GOOD, Sir!");
      break;
    }
  }
}
```

Notice that when you are assigning a value to an enum variable, you must scope the enum name (EmpType) to the value (Grunt). Because enumerations are a fixed set of name/value pairs, it is illegal to set an enum variable to a value that is not defined directly by the enumerated type:

```
static void Main(string[] args)
{
  Console.WriteLine("**** Fun with Enums *****");

  // Error! SalesManager is not in the EmpType enum!
  EmpType emp = EmpType.SalesManager;

  // Error! Forgot to scope Grunt value to EmpType enum!
  emp= Grunt;

  Console.ReadLine();
}
```

The System.Enum Type

The interesting thing about .NET enumerations is that they gain functionality from the System.Enum class type. This class defines a number of methods that allow you to interrogate and transform a given enumeration. One helpful method is the static Enum.GetUnderlyingType(), which as the name implies returns the data type used to store the values of the enumerated type (System.Byte in the case of the current EmpType declaration).

```
static void Main(string[] args)
{
  Console.WriteLine("**** Fun with Enums *****");
  // Make a contractor type.
  EmpType emp = EmpType.Contractor;
  AskForBonus(emp);

  // Print storage for the enum.
  Console.WriteLine("EmpType uses a {0} for storage",
    Enum.GetUnderlyingType(emp.GetType()));
  Console.ReadLine();
}
```

If you were to consult the Visual Studio 2008 object browser, you would be able to verify that the Enum.GetUnderlyingType() method requires you to pass in a System.Type as the first parameter. As fully examined in Chapter 16, Type represents the metadata description of a given .NET entity.

One possible way to obtain metadata (as shown previously) is to use the GetType() method, which is common to all types in the .NET base class libraries. Another approach is to make use of the C# typeof operator. One benefit of doing so is that you do not need to have a variable of the entity you wish to obtain a metadata description of:

```
// This time use typeof to extract a Type.
Console.WriteLine("EmpType uses a {0} for storage",
    Enum.GetUnderlyingType(typeof(EmpType)));
```

Dynamically Discovering an Enum's Name/Value Pairs

Beyond the Enum.GetUnderlyingType() method, all C# enumerations support a method named ToString(), which returns the string name of the current enumeration's value. For example:

```
static void Main(string[] args)
{
  Console.WriteLine("**** Fun with Enums *****");
  EmpType emp = EmpType.Contractor;

  // Prints out "emp is a Contractor".
  Console.WriteLine("emp is a {0}.", emp.ToString());
  Console.ReadLine();
}
```

If you are interested in discovering the value of a given enumeration variable, rather than its name, you can simply cast the enum variable against the underlying storage type. For example:

```
static void Main(string[] args)
{
  Console.WriteLine("**** Fun with Enums *****");
  EmpType emp = EmpType.Contractor;

  // Prints out "Contractor = 100".
  Console.WriteLine("{0} = {1}", emp.ToString(), (byte)emp);
  Console.ReadLine();
}
```

■ **Note** The static `Enum.Format()` method provides a finer level of formatting options by specifying a desired format flag. Consult the .NET Framework 3.5 SDK documentation for full details of the `System.Enum.Format()` method.

`System.Enum` also defines another static method named `GetValues()`. This method returns an instance of `System.Array`. Each item in the array corresponds to a member of the specified enumeration. Consider the following method, which will print out each name/value pair within any enumeration you pass in as a parameter:

```
// This method will print out the details of any enum.
static void EvaluateEnum(System.Enum e)
{
  Console.WriteLine("=> Information about {0}", e.GetType().Name);

  Console.WriteLine("Underlying storage type: {0}",
    Enum.GetUnderlyingType(e.GetType()));

  // Get all name/value pairs for incoming parameter.
  Array enumData = Enum.GetValues(e.GetType());
  Console.WriteLine("This enum has {0} members.", enumData.Length);

  // Now show the string name and associated value.
  for(int i = 0; i < enumData.Length; i++)
  {
    Console.WriteLine("Name: {0}, Value: {0:D}",
      enumData.GetValue(i));
  }
  Console.WriteLine();
}
```

To test this new method, update your `Main()` method to create variables of several enumeration types declared in the `System` namespace (as well as an `EmpType` enumeration for good measure). For example:

```
static void Main(string[] args)
{
  Console.WriteLine("**** Fun with Enums *****");
  EmpType e2;

  // These types are enums in the System namespace.
  DayOfWeek day;
  ConsoleColor cc;

  EvaluateEnum(e2);
  EvaluateEnum(day);
  EvaluateEnum(cc);
  Console.ReadLine();
}
```

The output is shown in Figure 4-8.

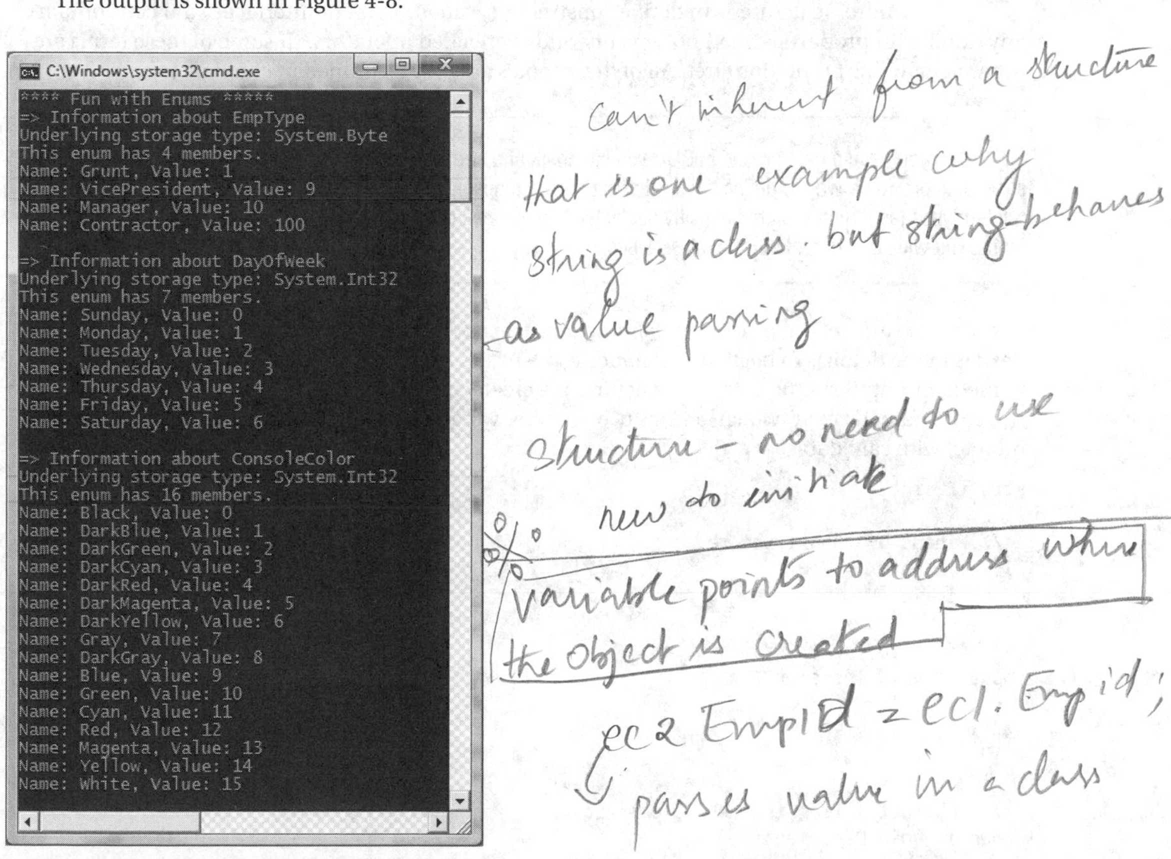

Figure 4-8. *Dynamically discovering name/value pairs of enumeration types.*

As you will see over the course of this text, enumerations are used extensively throughout the .NET base class libraries. For example, ADO.NET makes use of numerous enumerations to represent the state of a database connection (opened, closed, etc.), the state of a row in a DataTable (changed, new, detached, etc.), and so forth. Therefore, when you make use of any enumeration, always remember that you are able to interact with the name/value pairs using the members of System.Enum.

■ **Source Code** The FunWithEnums project is located under the Chapter 4 subdirectory.

Understanding the Structure Type

Now that you understand the role of enumeration types, let's examine the use of .NET *structures* (or simply *structs*). Structure types are well suited for modeling mathematical, geometrical, and other "atomic" entities in your application. A structure (like an enumeration) is a user-defined type; however, structures are not simply a collection of name/value pairs. Rather, structures are types that can contain any number of data fields and members that operate on these fields.

Furthermore, structures can define constructors, can implement interfaces, and can contain any number of properties, methods, events, and overloaded operators. (If some of these terms are unfamiliar at this point, don't fret. All of these topics are fully examined in chapters to come.)

■ **Note** If you have a background in OOP, you can think of a structure as a "lightweight class type," given that structures provide a way to define a type that supports encapsulation, but cannot be used to build a family of related types (as structures are implicitly sealed). When you need to build a family of related types through inheritance, you will need to make use of class types.

On the surface, the process of defining and using structures is very simple, but as they say, the devil is in the details. To begin understanding the basics of structure types, create a new project named FunWithStructures. In C#, structures are created using the struct keyword. Define a new structure named Point, which defines two member variables of type int and a set of methods to interact with said data:

```
struct Point
{
  // Fields of the structure.
  public int X;
  public int Y;

  // Add 1 to the (X, Y) position.
  public void Increment()
  {
    X++; Y++;
  }

  // Subtract 1 from the (X, Y) position.
  public void Decrement()
  {
    X--; Y--;
  }

  // Display the current position.
  public void Display()
```

```
  {
    Console.WriteLine("X = {0}, Y = {1}", X, Y);
  }
}
```

Here, we have defined our two integer data types (X and Y) using the public keyword, which is an access control modifier (full details in the next chapter). Declaring data with the public keyword ensures the caller has direct access to the data from a given Point variable (via the dot operator).

■ **Note** It is typically considered bad style to define public data within a class or structure. Rather, you will want to define *private* data, which can be accessed and changed using *public* properties. These details will be examined in Chapter 5.

Here is a Main() method that takes our Point type out for a test drive. Figure 4-9 shows the program's output.

```
static void Main(string[] args)
{
  Console.WriteLine("***** A First Look at Structures *****");
  // Create an initial Point.
  Point myPoint;
  myPoint.X = 349;
  myPoint.Y = 76;
  myPoint.Display();

  // Adjust the X and Y values.
  myPoint.Increment();
  myPoint.Display();
  Console.ReadLine();
}
```

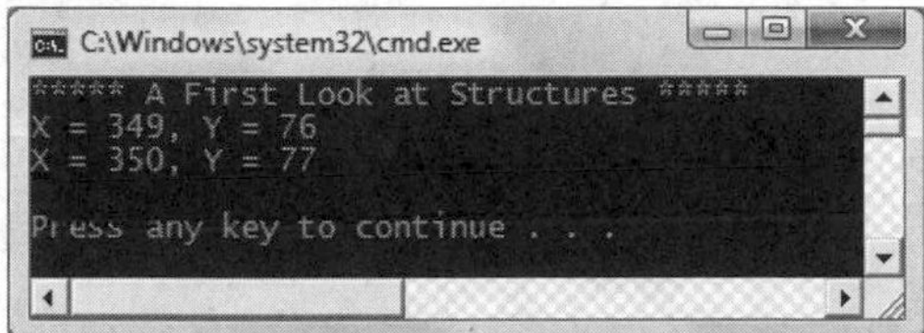

Figure 4-9. *Our* Point *structure in action*

Creating Structure Variables

When you wish to create a structure variable, you have a variety of options. Here, we simply create a Point variable and assign each piece of public field data before invoking its members. If we do *not* assign each piece of public field data (X and Y in our case) before making use of the structure, we will receive a compiler error:

```
// Error! Did not assign Y value.
Point p1;
p1.X = 10;
p1.Display();
```

```
// OK! Both fields assigned before use.
Point p2;
p2.X = 10;
p2.Y = 10;
p2.Display();
```

As an alternative, we can create structure variables using the C# new keyword, which will invoke the structure's *default constructor*. By definition, a default constructor takes any input parameters. The benefit of invoking the default constructor of a structure is that each piece of field data is automatically set to its default value:

```
// Set all fields to default values
// using the default constructor.
Point p1 = new Point();

// Prints X=0,Y=0
p1.Display();
```

It is also possible to design a structure with a *custom constructor*. This allows you to specify the values of field data upon variable creation, rather than having to set each data member field by field. Chapter 5 will provide a detailed examination of constructors; however, to illustrate, update the Point structure with the following code:

```
struct Point
{
  // Fields of the structure.
  public int X;
  public int Y;

  // A custom constructor.
  public Point(int XPos, int YPos)
  {
    X = XPos;
    Y = YPos;
  }
...
}
```

With this, we could now create Point types as follows:

```
// Call custom constructor.
Point p2 = new Point(50, 60);

// Prints X=50,Y=60
p2.Display();
```

As mentioned, working with structures on the surface is quite simple. However, to deepen your understanding of this type, we need to explore the distinction between a .NET value type and a .NET reference type.

■ **Source Code** The FunWithStructures project is located under the Chapter 4 subdirectory.

Understanding Value Types and Reference Types

Note The following discussion of value types and reference types assumes that you have a background in object-oriented programming. We will examine a number of topics that assume you have a background in object-oriented programming. If this is not the case, you may wish to reread this section once you have completed Chapters 5 and 6.

Unlike arrays, strings, or enumerations, C# structures do not have an identically named representation in the .NET library (that is, there is no `System.Structure` class), but are implicitly derived from `System.ValueType`. Simply put, the role of `System.ValueType` is to ensure that the derived type (e.g., any structure) is allocated on the *stack* rather than the garbage collected *heap*.

Functionally, the only purpose of `System.ValueType` is to "override" the virtual methods defined by `System.Object` to use value-based, versus reference-based, semantics. As you may know, overriding is the process of changing the implementation of a virtual (or possibly abstract) method defined within a base class. The base class of `ValueType` is `System.Object`. In fact, the instance methods defined by `System.ValueType` are identical to those of `System.Object`:

```
// Structures and enumerations extend System.ValueType.
public abstract class ValueType : object
{
  public virtual bool Equals(object obj);
  public virtual int GetHashCode();
  public Type GetType();
  public virtual string ToString();
}
```

Given the fact that value types are using value-based semantics, the lifetime of a structure (which includes all numerical data types [`int`, `float`, etc.], as well as any enum or custom structure) is very predictable. When a structure variable falls out of the defining scope, it is removed from memory immediately:

```
// Local structures are popped off
// the stack when a method returns.
static void LocalValueTypes()
{
  // Recall! "int" is really a System.Int32 structure.
  int i = 0;

  // Recall! Point is a structure type.
  Point p = new Point();
} // "i" and "p" popped off the stack here!
```

Value Types, References Types, and the Assignment Operator

When you assign one value type to another, a member-by-member copy of the field data is achieved. In the case of a simple data type such as `System.Int32`, the only member to copy is the numerical value. However, in the case of our `Point`, the `X` and `Y` values are copied into the new structure variable. To illustrate, create a new Console Application project named ValueAndReferenceTypes and copy your previous `Point` definition into your new namespace. Now, add the following method to your `Program` type:

```
// Assigning two intrinsic value types results in
// two independent variables on the stack.
static void ValueTypeAssignment()
{
  Console.WriteLine("Assigning value types\n");

  Point p1 = new Point(10, 10);
  Point p2 = p1;

  // Print both points.
  p1.Display();
  p2.Display();

  // Change p1.X and print again. p2.X is not changed.
  p1.X = 100;
  Console.WriteLine("\n=> Changed p1.X\n");
  p1.Display();
  p2.Display();
}
```

Here you have created a variable of type `Point` (named `p1`) that is then assigned to another `Point` (`p2`). Because `Point` is a value type, you have two copies of the `MyPoint` type on the stack, each of which can be independently manipulated. Therefore, when you change the value of `p1.X`, the value of `p2.X` is unaffected. Figure 4-10 shows the output once this method is called from `Main()`.

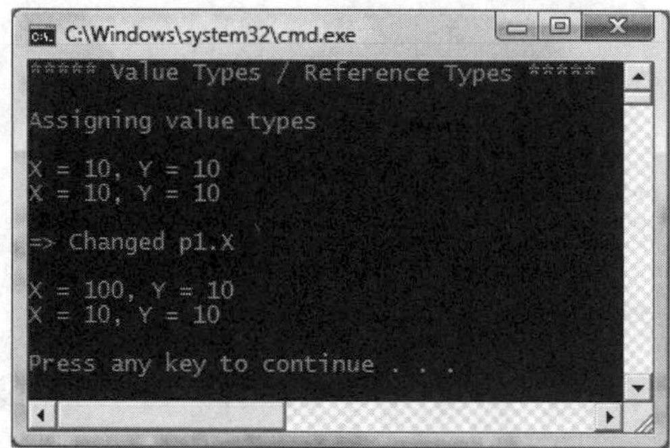

Figure 4-10. *Assignment of value types results in a verbatim copy of each field.*

In stark contrast to value types, when you apply the assignment operator to reference types (meaning all class instances), you are redirecting what the reference variable points to in memory. To illustrate, create a new class type named `PointRef` that has the exact same members as the `Point` structures, beyond renaming the constructor to match the class name:

```
// Classes are always reference types.
class PointRef
{
  // Same members as the Point structure.

  // Be sure to change your constructor name to PointRef!
  public PointRef(int XPos, int YPos)
  {
    X = XPos;
```

```
    Y = YPos;
  }
}
```

Now, make use of your `PointRef` type within the following new method (note the code is identical to the `ValueTypeAssignment()` method). Assuming you have called this new method within `Main()`, your output should look like that in Figure 4-11.

```
static void ReferenceTypeAssignment()
{
  Console.WriteLine("Assigning reference types\n");
  PointRef p1 = new PointRef(10, 10);
  PointRef p2 = p1;

  // Print both point refs.
  p1.Display();
  p2.Display();

  // Change p1.X and print again.
  p1.X = 100;
  Console.WriteLine("\n=> Changed p1.X\n");
  p1.Display();
  p2.Display();
}
```

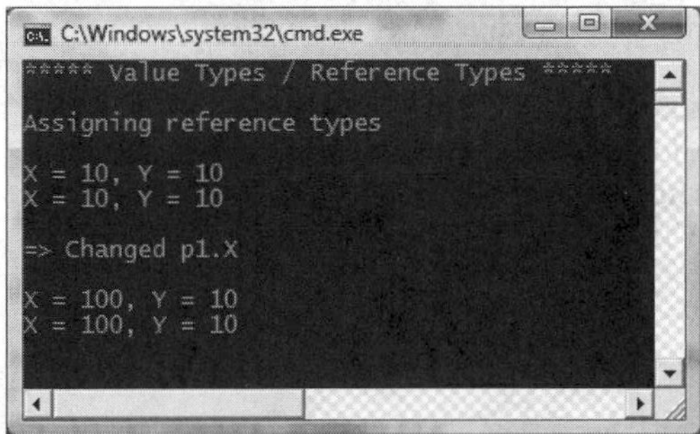

Figure 4-11. *Assignment of reference types copies the reference.*

In this case, you have two references pointing to the *same object* on the managed heap. Therefore, when you change the value of `X` using the `p2` reference, `p1.X` reports the same value.

Value Types Containing Reference Types

Now that you have a better feeling for the core differences between value types and reference types, let's examine a more complex example. Assume you have the following reference (class) type that maintains an informational `string` that can be set using a custom constructor:

```
class ShapeInfo
{
  public string infoString;
  public ShapeInfo(string info)
  { infoString = info; }
}
```

Now assume that you want to contain a variable of this class type within a value type named Rectangle. To allow the caller to set the value of the inner ShapeInfo member variable, you also provide a custom constructor. Here is the complete definition of the Rectangle type:

```
struct Rectangle
{
  // The Rectangle structure contains a reference type member.
  public ShapeInfo rectInfo;

  public int rectTop, rectLeft, rectBottom, rectRight;

  public Rectangle(string info, int top, int left, int bottom, int right)
  {
    rectInfo = new ShapeInfo(info);
    rectTop = top;  rectBottom = bottom;
    rectLeft = left; rectRight = right;
  }

  public void Display()
  {
    Console.WriteLine("String = {0}, Top = {1}, Bottom = {2}," +
      "Left = {3}, Right = {4}",
      rectInfo.infoString, rectTop, rectBottom, rectLeft, rectRight);
  }
}
```

At this point, you have contained a reference type within a value type. The million-dollar question now becomes, What happens if you assign one Rectangle variable to another? Given what you already know about value types, you would be correct in assuming that the integer data (which is indeed a structure) should be an independent entity for each Rectangle variable. But what about the internal reference type? Will the object's state be fully copied, or will the reference to that object be copied? To answer this question, define the following method and invoke it from Main(). Check out Figure 4-12 for the answer.

```
static void ValueTypeContainingRefType()
{
  // Create the first Rectangle.
  Console.WriteLine("-> Creating r1");
  Rectangle r1 = new Rectangle("First Rect", 10, 10, 50, 50);

  // Now assign a new Rectangle to r1.
  Console.WriteLine("-> Assigning r2 to r1");
  Rectangle r2 = r1;

  // Change some values of r2.
  Console.WriteLine("-> Changing values of r2");
  r2.rectInfo.infoString = "This is new info!";
  r2.rectBottom = 4444;

  // Print values of both rectangles.
  r1.Display();
  r2.Display();
}
```

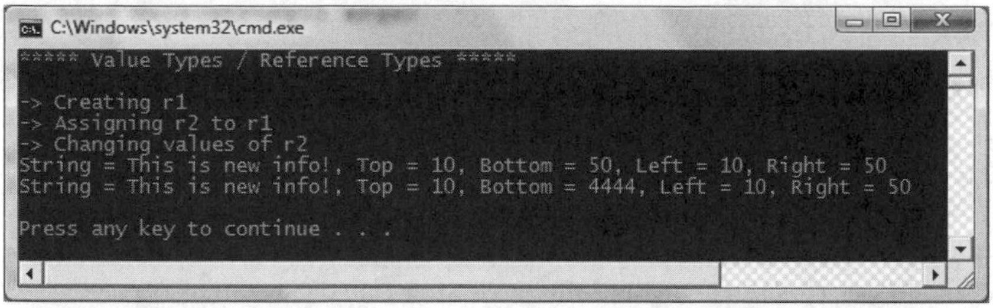

```
C:\Windows\system32\cmd.exe
***** Value Types / Reference Types *****

-> Creating r1
-> Assigning r2 to r1
-> Changing values of r2
String = This is new info!, Top = 10, Bottom = 50, Left = 10, Right = 50
String = This is new info!, Top = 10, Bottom = 4444, Left = 10, Right = 50

Press any key to continue . . .
```

Figure 4-12. *The internal references point to the same object!*

As you can see, when you change the value of the informational string using the r2 reference, the r1 reference displays the same value. By default, when a value type contains other reference types, assignment results in a copy of the references. In this way, you have two independent structures, each of which contains a reference pointing to the same object in memory (i.e., a "shallow copy"). When you want to perform a "deep copy," where the state of internal references is fully copied into a new object, one approach is to implement the ICloneable interface (as you will do in Chapter 9).

■ **Source Code** The ValueAndReferenceTypes project is located under the Chapter 4 subdirectory.

Passing Reference Types by Value

Reference types or value types can obviously be passed as parameters to type members. However, passing a reference type (e.g., a class) by reference is quite different from passing it by value. To understand the distinction, assume you have a simple Person class defined in a new Console Application project named RefTypeValTypeParams, defined as follows:

```
class Person
{
  public string personName;
  public int personAge;

  // Constructors.
  public Person(string name, int age)
  {
    personName = name;
    personAge = age;
  }
  public Person(){}

  public void Display()
  {
    Console.WriteLine("Name: {0}, Age: {1}", personName, personAge);
  }
}
```

Now, what if you create a method that allows the caller to send in the Person type by value (note the lack of parameter modifiers):

```
static void SendAPersonByValue(Person p)
{
  // Change the age of "p"?
  p.personAge = 99;

  // Will the caller see this reassignment?
  p = new Person("Nikki", 99);
}
```

Notice how the SendAPersonByValue() method attempts to reassign the incoming Person reference to a new object as well as change some state data. Now let's test this method using the following Main() method:

```
static void Main(string[] args)
{
  // Passing ref-types by value.
  Console.WriteLine("***** Passing Person object by value *****");
  Person fred = new Person("Fred", 12);
  Console.WriteLine("\nBefore by value call, Person is:");
  fred.Display();

  SendAPersonByValue(fred);
  Console.WriteLine("\nAfter by value call, Person is:");
  fred. Display();
  Console.ReadLine();
}
```

Figure 4-13 shows the output of this call.

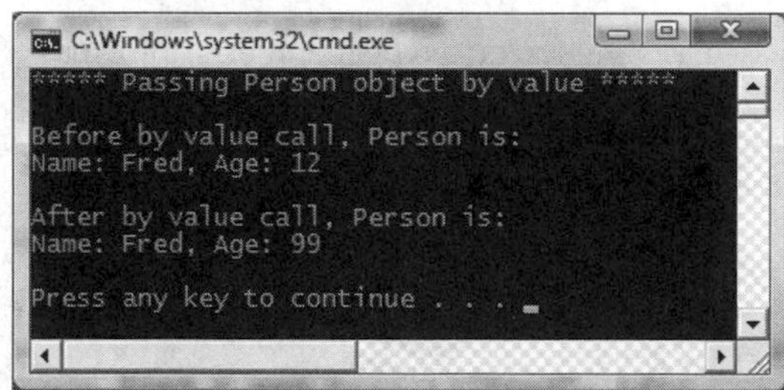

Figure 4-13. *Passing reference types by value locks the reference in place.*

As you can see, the value of personAge has been modified. This behavior seems to fly in the face of what it means to pass a parameter "by value." Given that you were able to change the state of the incoming Person, what was copied? The answer: a copy of the reference to the caller's object. Therefore, as the SendAPersonByValue() method is pointing to the same object as the caller, it is possible to alter the object's state data. What is not possible is to reassign what the reference is pointing to.

Passing Reference Types by Reference

Now assume you have a SendAPersonByReference() method, which passes a reference type by reference (note the ref parameter modifier):

```
static void SendAPersonByReference(ref Person p)
{
  // Change some data of "p".
  p.personAge = 555;
```

```
  // "p" is now pointing to a new object on the heap!
  p = new Person("Nikki", 999);
}
```

As you might expect, this allows complete flexibility of how the callee is able to manipulate the incoming parameter. Not only can the callee change the state of the object, but if it so chooses, it may also reassign the reference to a new Person type. Now ponder the following updated Main() method and check Figure 4-14 for output:

```
static void Main(string[] args)
{
  // Passing ref-types by ref.
  Console.WriteLine("\n***** Passing Person object by reference *****");
  Person mel = new Person("Mel", 23);
  Console.WriteLine("Before by ref call, Person is:");
  mel.Display();

  SendAPersonByReference(ref mel);
  Console.WriteLine("After by ref call, Person is:");
  mel.Display();
  Console.ReadLine();
}
```

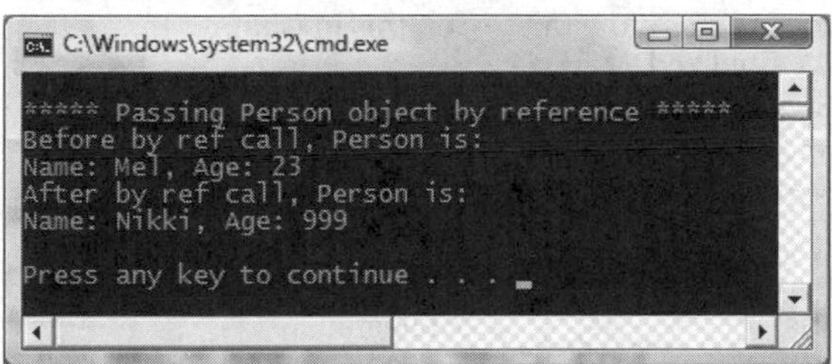

Figure 4-14. *Passing reference types by reference allows the reference to be redirected.*

As you can see, an object named Mel returns after the call as a type named Nikki, as the method was able to change what the incoming reference pointed to in memory. The golden rule to keep in mind when passing reference types:

- If a reference type is passed by reference, the callee may change the values of the object's state data as well as the object it is referencing.
- If a reference type is passed by value, the callee may change the values of the object's state data but not the object it is referencing.

■ **Source Code** The RefTypeValTypeParams project is located under the Chapter 4 subdirectory.

Value and Reference Types: Final Details

To wrap up this topic, consider the information in Table 4-3, which summarizes the core distinctions between value types and reference types.

Table 4-3. *Value Types and Reference Types Side by Side*

Intriguing Question	Value Type	Reference Type
Where is this type allocated?	Allocated on the stack.	Allocated on the managed heap.
How is a variable represented?	Value type variables are local copies.	Reference type variables are pointing to the memory occupied by the allocated instance.
What is the base type?	Must derive from `System.ValueType`.	Can derive from any other type (except `System.ValueType`), as long as that type is not "sealed" (more details on this in Chapter 6).
Can this type function as a base to other types?	No. Value types are always sealed and cannot be extended.	Yes. If the type is not sealed, it may function as a base to other types.
What is the default parameter passing behavior?	Variables are passed by value (i.e., a copy of the variable is passed into the called function).	Variables are passed by reference (i.e., the address of the variable is passed into the called function).
Can this type override `System.Object.Finalize()`?	No. Value types are never placed onto the heap and therefore do not need to be finalized.	Yes, indirectly (more details on this in Chapter 8).
Can I define constructors for this type?	Yes, but the default constructor is reserved (i.e., your custom constructors must all have arguments).	But of course!
When do variables of this type die?	When they fall out of the defining scope.	When the object is garbage collected.

Despite their differences, value types and reference types both have the ability to implement interfaces and may support any number of fields, methods, overloaded operators, constants, properties, and events.

Understanding C# Nullable Types

To wrap up this chapter, let's examine the role of *nullable data type* using a final Console Application named NullableTypes. As you know, CLR data types have a fixed range and are represented as a type in the `System` namespace. For example, the `System.Boolean` data type can be assigned a value from the set {`true, false`}. Now, recall that all of the numerical data types (as well as the `Boolean` data type) are *value types*. As a rule, value types can never be assigned the value of `null`, as that is used to establish an empty object reference:

```
static void Main(string[] args)
{
  // Compiler errors!
  // Value types cannot be set to null!
  bool myBool = null;
  int myInt = null;
```

```
  // OK! Strings are reference types.
  string myString = null;
}
```

Since the release of .NET 2.0, it has been possible to create nullable data types. Simply put, a nullable type can represent all the values of its underlying type, plus the value `null`. Thus, if we declare a nullable `System.Boolean`, it could be assigned a value from the set `{true, false, null}`. This can be extremely helpful when working with relational databases, given that it is quite common to encounter undefined columns in database tables. Without the concept of a nullable data type, there is no convenient manner in C# to represent a numerical data point with no value.

To define a nullable variable type, the question mark symbol (?) is suffixed to the underlying data type. Do note that this syntax is only legal when applied to value types. If you attempt to create a nullable reference type (including `strings`), you are issued a compile-time error. Like a nonnullable variable, local nullable variables must be assigned an initial value:

```
static void LocalNullableVariables()
{
  // Define some local nullable types.
  int? nullableInt = 10;
  double? nullableDouble = 3.14;
  bool? nullableBool = null;
  char? nullableChar = 'a';
  int?[] arrayOfNullableInts = new int?[10];

  // Error! Strings are reference types!
  // string? s = "oops";
}
```

In C#, the ? suffix notation is a shorthand for creating an instance of the generic `System.Nullable<T>` structure type. Although we will not examine generics until Chapter 10, it is important to understand that the `System.Nullable<T>` type provides a set of members that all nullable types can make use of.

For example, you are able to programmatically discover whether the nullable variable indeed has been assigned a `null` value using the `HasValue` property or the `!=` operator. The assigned value of a nullable type may be obtained directly or via the `Value` property. Given that the ? suffix is just a shorthand for using `Nullable<T>`, you could implement your `LocalNullableVariables()` method as follows:

```
static void LocalNullableVariables()
{
  // Define some local nullable types using Nullable<T>.
  Nullable<int> nullableInt = 10;
  Nullable<double> nullableDouble = 3.14;
  Nullable<bool> nullableBool = null;
  Nullable<char> nullableChar = 'a';
  Nullable<int>[] arrayOfNullableInts = new int?[10];
}
```

Working with Nullable Types

As stated, nullable data types can be particularly useful when you are interacting with databases, given that columns in a data table may be intentionally empty (e.g., undefined). To illustrate, assume the following class, which simulates the process of accessing a database that has a table containing two columns that may be `null`. Note that the `GetIntFromDatabase()` method is not assigning a value to the nullable integer member variable, while GetBoolFromDatabase() is assigning a valid value to the bool? member:

```
class DatabaseReader
{
  // Nullable data field.
  public int? numericValue = null;
  public bool? boolValue = true;

  // Note the nullable return type.
  public int? GetIntFromDatabase()
  { return numericValue; }

  // Note the nullable return type.
  public bool? GetBoolFromDatabase()
  { return boolValue; }
}
```

Now, assume the following Main() method, which invokes each member of the DatabaseReader class, and discovers the assigned values using the HasValue and Value members as well as using the C# equality operator (not-equal, to be exact):

```
static void Main(string[] args)
{
  Console.WriteLine("***** Fun with Nullable Data *****\n");
  DatabaseReader dr = new DatabaseReader();

  // Get int from "database".
  int? i = dr.GetIntFromDatabase();
  if (i.HasValue)
    Console.WriteLine("Value of 'i' is: {0}", i.Value);
  else
    Console.WriteLine("Value of 'i' is undefined.");

  // Get bool from "database".
  bool? b = dr.GetBoolFromDatabase();
  if (b != null)
    Console.WriteLine("Value of 'b' is: {0}", b.Value);
  else
    Console.WriteLine("Value of 'b' is undefined.");
  Console.ReadLine();
}
```

The ?? Operator

The final aspect of nullable types to be aware of is that they can make use of the C# ?? operator. This operator allows you to assign a value to a nullable type if the retrieved value is in fact null. For this example, assume you wish to assign a local nullable integer to 100 if the value returned from GetIntFromDatabase() is null (of course, this method is programmed to *always* return null, but I am sure you get the general idea):

```
static void Main(string[] args)
{
  Console.WriteLine("***** Fun with Nullable Data *****\n");
  DatabaseReader dr = new DatabaseReader();
...
  // If the value from GetIntFromDatabase() is null,
```

```
    // assign local variable to 100.
    int? myData = dr.GetIntFromDatabase() ?? 100;
    Console.WriteLine("Value of myData: {0}", myData.Value);
    Console.ReadLine();
}
```

Source Code The NullableTypes application is located under the Chapter 4 subdirectory.

Summary

This chapter began with an examination of several C# keywords that allow you to build custom methods. Recall that by default, parameters are passed by value; however, you may pass a parameter by reference if you mark it with `ref.` or `out`. You also learned about the role of optional parameters and how to define and invoke methods taking parameter arrays.

Once we investigated the topic of method overloading, the bulk of this chapter examined several details regarding how arrays, enumerations, and structures are defined in C# and represented within the .NET base class libraries. Along the way, you examined several details regarding value types and reference types, including how they respond when passing them as parameters to methods, and how to interact with nullable data types using the ? and ?? operators. With this, our initial investigation of the C# programming language is complete! In the next chapter, we will begin to dig into the details of object-oriented development.

CHAPTER 5

Defining Encapsulated Class Types

In the previous two chapters, you investigated a number of core syntactical constructs that are commonplace to any .NET application you may be developing. Here, you will begin your examination of the object-oriented capabilities of C#. The first order of business is to examine the process of building well-defined class types that support any number of *constructors*. Once you understand the basics of defining classes and allocating objects, the remainder of this chapter will examine the role of *encapsulation*. Along the way you will understand how to define class properties as well as the role of static fields and members, read-only fields, and constant data. We wrap up by examining the role of XML code documentation syntax.

Introducing the C# Class Type

As far as the .NET platform is concerned, the most fundamental programming construct is the *class type*. Formally, a class is a user-defined type that is composed of field data (often called *member variables*) and members that operate on this data (such as constructors, properties, methods, events, and so forth). Collectively, the set of field data represents the "state" of a class instance (otherwise known as an *object*). The power of object-based languages such as C# is that by grouping data and related functionality in a class definition, you are able to model your software after entities in the real world.

To get the ball rolling, create a new C# Console Application named SimpleClassExample. Next, insert a new class file (named `Car.cs`) into your project using the Project ➤ Add Class menu selection, choose the Class icon from the resulting dialog box as shown in Figure 5-1, and click the Add button.

A class is defined in C# using the `class` keyword. Here is the simplest possible declaration:

```
class Car
{
}
```

Once you have defined a class type, you will need to consider the set of member variables that will be used to represent its state. For example, you may decide that cars maintain an `int` data type to represent the current speed and a `string` data type to represent the car's friendly pet name. Given these initial design notes, update your `Car` class as follows:

```
class Car
{
  // The 'state' of the Car.
  public string petName;
  public int currSpeed;
}
```

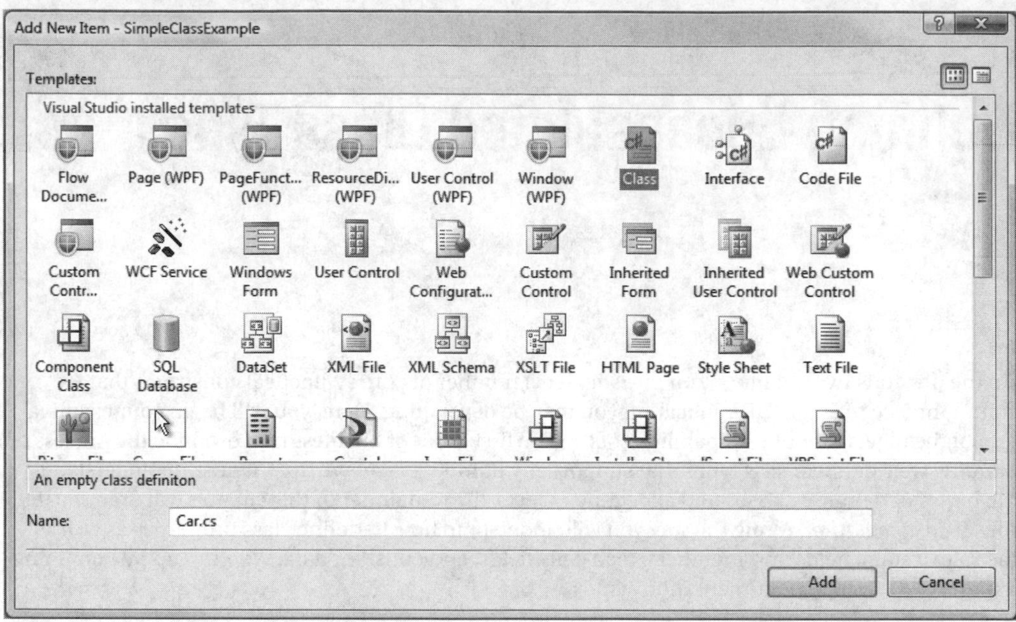

Figure 5-1. *Inserting a new C# class type*

Notice that these member variables are declared using the `public` access modifier. Public members of a class are directly accessible once an *object* of this type has been created. As you may already know, the term "object" is used to represent an instance of a given class type created using the `new` keyword.

Note Field data of a class should seldom (if ever) be defined as public. To preserve the integrity of your state data, it is a far better design to define data as private (or possibly protected) and allow controlled access to the data via type properties (as shown later in this chapter). However, to keep this first example as simple as possible, public data fits the bill.

After you have defined the set of member variables that represent the state of the type, the next design step is to establish the members that model its behavior. For this example, the `Car` class will define one method named `SpeedUp()` and another named `PrintState()`:

```
class Car
{
  // The 'state' of the Car.
  public string petName;
  public int currSpeed;

  // The functionality of the Car.
  public void PrintState()
  {
    Console.WriteLine("{0} is going {1} MPH.", petName, currSpeed);
  }
  public void SpeedUp(int delta)
  {
```

```
    currSpeed += delta;
  }
}
```

As you can see, PrintState() is more or less a diagnostic function that will simply dump the current state of a given Car object to the command window. SpeedUp() will increase the speed of the Car by the amount specified by the incoming int parameter. Now, update your Main() method with the following code:

```
static void Main(string[] args)
{
  Console.WriteLine("***** Fun with Class Types *****\n");
  // Allocate and configure a Car object.
  Car myCar = new Car();
  myCar.petName = "Henry";
  myCar.currSpeed = 10;

  // Speed up the car a few times and print out the
  // new state.
  for (int i = 0; i <= 10; i++)
  {
    myCar.SpeedUp(5);
    myCar.PrintState();
  }
  Console.ReadLine();
}
```

Once you run your program, you will see that the Car object (myCar) maintains its current state throughout the life of the application, as shown in Figure 5-2.

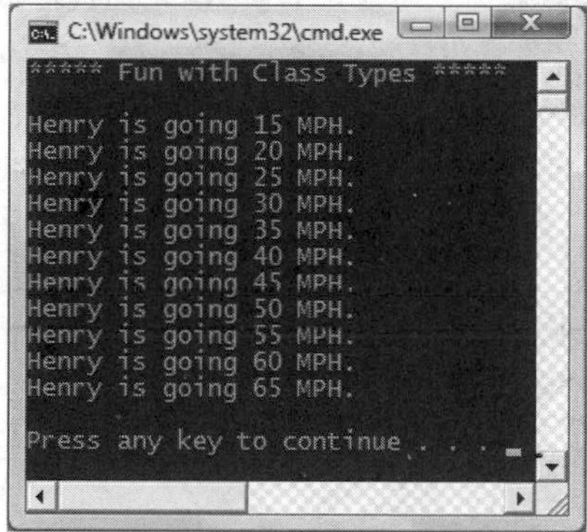

Figure 5-2. *Taking the* Car *for a test drive (pun intended)*

Allocating Objects with the new Keyword

As shown in the previous code example, objects must be allocated into memory using the new keyword. If you do not make use of the new keyword and attempt to make use of your class variable in a subsequent code statement, you will receive a compiler error:

```
static void Main(string[] args)
{
  // Error! Forgot to use 'new'!
  Car myCar;
```

```
    myCar.petName = "Fred";
}
```

To correctly create a class type variable, you may define and allocate a Car object on a single line of code:

```
static void Main(string[] args)
{
  Car myCar = new Car();
  myCar.petName = "Fred";
}
```

As an alternative, if you wish to define and allocate an object on separate lines of code, you may do so as follows:

```
static void Main(string[] args)
{
  Car myCar;
  myCar = new Car();
  myCar.petName = "Fred";
}
```

Here, the first code statement simply declares *a reference* to a yet-to-be-determined Car object. It is not until you assign a reference to an object via the new keyword that this reference points to a valid class instance in memory.

In any case, at this point we have a trivial class type that defines a few points of data and some basic methods. To enhance the functionality of the current Car type, we need to understand the role of *class constructors*.

Understanding Class Constructors

Given that objects have state (represented by the values of an object's member variables), the object user will typically want to assign relevant values to the object's field data before use. Currently, the Car type demands that the petName and currSpeed fields be assigned on a field-by-field basis. For the current example, this is not too problematic, given that we have only two public data points. However, it is not uncommon for a class to have dozens of fields to contend with. Clearly, it would be undesirable to author 20 initialization statements to set 20 points of data.

Thankfully, C# supports the use of *class constructors*, which allow the state of an object to be established at the time of creation. A constructor is a special method of a class that is called indirectly when creating an object using the new keyword. However, unlike a "normal" method, constructors never have a return value (not even void) and are always named identically to the class they are constructing.

■ Note As shown in Chapter 13, C# 2008 provides a new object initialization syntax, which allows you to set the values of public fields and invoke public properties at the time of construction.

The Role of the Default Constructor

Every C# class is provided with a freebee *default constructor* that you may redefine if need be. By definition, a default constructor never takes arguments. Beyond allocating the new object into memory, the default constructor ensures that all field data is set to an appropriate default value (see Chapter 3 for information regarding the default values of C# data types).

If you are not satisfied with these default assignments, you may redefine the default constructor to suit your needs. To illustrate, update your C# Car class as follows:

```
class Car
{
  // The 'state' of the Car.
  public string petName;
  public int currSpeed;

  // A custom default constructor.
  public Car()
  {
    petName = "Chuck";
    currSpeed = 10;
  }
...
}
```

In this case, we are forcing all Car objects to begin life named Chuck at a rate of 10 mph. With this, you are able to create a Car object set to these default values as follows:

```
static void Main(string[] args)
{
  // Invoking the default constructor.
  Car chuck = new Car();

  // Prints "Chuck is going 10 MPH."
  chuck.PrintState();
}
```

Defining Custom Constructors

Typically, classes define additional constructors beyond the default. In doing so, you provide the object user with a simple and consistent way to initialize the state of an object directly at the time of creation. Ponder the following update to the Car class, which now supports a total of three class constructors:

```
class Car
{
  // The 'state' of the Car.
  public string petName;
  public int currSpeed;

  // A custom default constructor.
  public Car()
  {
    petName = "Chuck";
    currSpeed = 10;
  }

  // Here, currSpeed will receive the
  // default value of an int (zero).
  public Car(string pn)
  {
    petName = pn;
  }
```

```
    // Let caller set the full 'state' of the Car.
    public Car(string pn, int cs)
    {
      petName = pn;
      currSpeed = cs;
    }
...
}
```

Keep in mind that what makes one constructor different from another (in the eyes of the C# compiler) is the number of and type of constructor arguments. Recall from Chapter 4, when you define a method of the same name that differs by the number or type of arguments, you have *overloaded* the method. Thus, the `Car` type has *overloaded* the constructor to provide a number of ways to create the object at the time of declaration. In any case, you are now able to create `Car` objects using any of the public constructors. For example:

```
static void Main(string[] args)
{
  // Make a Car called Chuck going 10 MPH.
  Car chuck = new Car();
  chuck.PrintState();

  // Make a Car called Mary going 0 MPH.
  Car mary = new Car("Mary");
  mary.PrintState();

  // Make a Car called Daisy going 75 MPH.
  Car daisy = new Car("Daisy", 75);
  daisy.PrintState();
}
```

The Default Constructor Revisited

As you have just learned, all classes are endowed with a free default constructor. Thus, if you insert a new class into your current project named `Motorcycle`, defined like so:

```
class Motorcycle
{
  public void PopAWheely()
  {
    Console.WriteLine("Yeeeeeee Haaaaaeewww!");
  }
}
```

you are able to create an instance of the `Motorcycle` type via the default constructor out of the box:

```
static void Main(string[] args)
{
  Motorcycle mc = new Motorcycle();
  mc.PopAWheely();
}
```

However, as soon as you define a custom constructor, the default constructor is *silently removed* from the class and is no longer available! Think of it this way: if you do not define a custom constructor, the C# compiler grants you a default in order to allow the object user to allocate an instance of your type with field data set to the correct default values. However, when you define a unique constructor, the compiler assumes you have taken matters into your own hands.

Therefore, if you wish to allow the object user to create an instance of your type with the default constructor, as well as your custom constructor, you must *explicitly* redefine the default. To this end, understand that in a vast majority of cases, the implementation of the default constructor of a class is intentionally empty, as all you require is the ability to create an object with default values. Consider the following update to the `Motorcycle` class:

```
class Motorcycle
{
  public int driverIntensity;

  public void PopAWheely()
  {
    for (int i = 0; i <= driverIntensity; i++)
    {
      Console.WriteLine("Yeeeeeee Haaaaaeewww!");
    }
  }

  // Put back the default constructor.
  public Motorcycle() {}

  // Our custom constructor.
  public Motorcycle(int intensity)
  { driverIntensity = intensity; }
}
```

The Role of the this Keyword

Like other C-based languages, C# supplies a `this` keyword that provides access to the current class instance. One possible use of the `this` keyword is to resolve scope ambiguity, which can arise when an incoming parameter is named identically to a data field of the type. Of course, ideally you would simply adopt a naming convention that does not result in such ambiguity; however, to illustrate this use of the `this` keyword, update your `Motorcycle` class with a new `string` field (named `name`) to represent the driver's name. Next, add a method named `SetDriverName()` implemented as follows:

```
class Motorcycle
{
  public int driverIntensity;
  public string name;

  public void SetDriverName(string name)
  { name = name; }
...
}
```

Although this code will compile just fine, if you update `Main()` to call `SetDriverName()` and then print out the value of the `name` field, you may be surprised to find that the value of the `name` field is an empty string!

```
// Make a Motorcycle with a rider named Tiny?
Motorcycle c = new Motorcycle(5);
c.SetDriverName("Tiny");
c.PopAWheely();
Console.WriteLine("Rider name is {0}", c.name); // Prints an empty name value!
```

The problem is that the implementation of SetDriverName() is assigning the incoming parameter *back to itself* given that the compiler assumes name is referring to the variable currently in the method scope rather than the name field at the class scope. To inform the compiler that you wish to set the current object's name data field to the incoming name parameter, simply use this to resolve the ambiguity:

```
public void SetDriverName(string name)
{ this.name = name; }
```

Do understand that if there is no ambiguity, you are not required to make use of the this keyword when a class wishes to access its own data or members. For example, if we rename the string data member to driverName, the use of this is optional as there is no longer a scope ambiguity:

```
class Motorcycle
{
  public int driverIntensity;
  public string driverName;

  public void SetDriverName(string name)
  {
    // These two statements are functionally the same.
    driverName = name;
    this.driverName = name;
  }
...
}
```

Even though there is little to be gained when using this in unambiguous situations, you may still find this keyword useful when implementing members, as IDEs such as SharpDevelop and Visual Studio 2008 will enable IntelliSense when this is specified. This can be very helpful when you have forgotten the name of a class member and want to quickly recall the definition. Consider Figure 5-3.

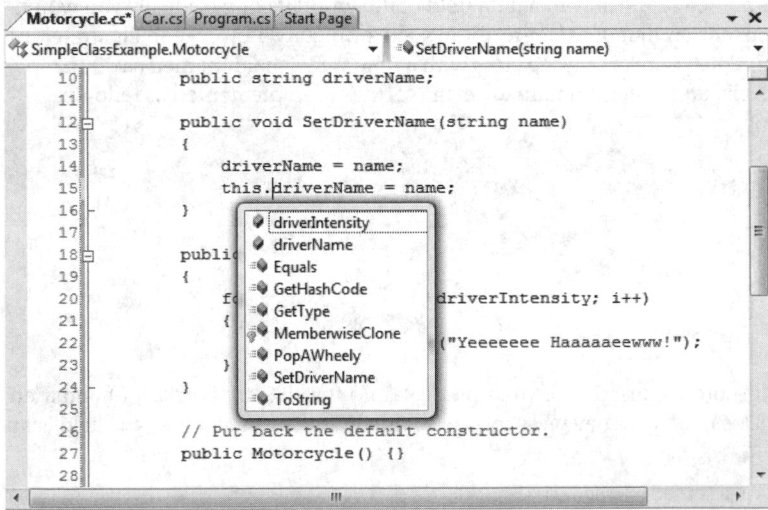

Figure 5-3. *The IntelliSense of* this

■Note It is a compiler error to use the `this` keyword within the implementation of a static member (explained shortly). As you will see, static members operate on the class (not object) level, and therefore at the class level, there is no current object (thus no `this`)!

Chaining Constructor Calls Using this

Another use of the `this` keyword is to design a class using a technique termed *constructor chaining*. This design pattern is helpful when you have a class that defines multiple constructors. Given the fact that constructors often validate the incoming arguments to enforce various business rules, it can be quite common to find redundant validation logic within a class's constructor set. Consider the following updated `Motorcycle`:

```
class Motorcycle
{
  public int driverIntensity;
  public string driverName;

  public Motorcycle() { }

  // Redundent constructor logic!
  public Motorcycle(int intensity)
  {
    if (intensity > 10)
    {
      intensity = 10;
    }
    driverIntensity = intensity;
  }

  public Motorcycle(int intensity, string name)
  {
    if (intensity > 10)
    {
      intensity = 10;
    }
    driverIntensity = intensity;
    driverName = name;
  }
...
}
```

Here (perhaps in an attempt to ensure the safety of the rider), each constructor is ensuring that the intensity level is never greater than 10. While this is all well and good, we do have redundant code statements in two constructors. This is less than ideal, as we are now required to update code in multiple locations if our rules change (for example, if the intensity should not be greater than 5).

One way to improve the current situation is to define a method in the `Motorcycle` class that will validate the incoming argument(s). If we were to do so, each constructor could make a call to this method before making the field assignment(s). While this approach does allow us to isolate the code we need to update when the business rules change, we are now dealing with the following redundancy:

```
class Motorcycle
{
  public int driverIntensity;
  public string driverName;

  // Constructors.
  public Motorcycle() { }

  public Motorcycle(int intensity)
  {
    SetIntensity(intensity);
  }
  public Motorcycle(int intensity, string name)
  {
    SetIntensity(intensity);
    driverName = name;
  }

  public void SetIntensity(int intensity)
  {
    if (intensity > 10)
    {
      intensity = 10;
    }
    driverIntensity = intensity;
  }
...
}
```

A cleaner approach is to designate the constructor that takes the *greatest number of arguments* as the "master constructor" and have its implementation perform the required validation logic. The remaining constructors can make use of the `this` keyword to forward the incoming arguments to the master constructor and provide any additional parameters as necessary. In this way, we only need to worry about maintaining a single constructor for the entire class, while the remaining constructors are basically empty.

Here is the final iteration of the `Motorcycle` class (with one additional constructor for the sake of illustration). When chaining constructors, note how the `this` keyword is "dangling" off the constructor's declaration (via a colon operator) outside the scope of the constructor itself:

```
class Motorcycle
{
  public int driverIntensity;
  public string driverName;

  // Constructor chaining.
  public Motorcycle() {}
  public Motorcycle(int intensity)
    : this(intensity, "") {}
  public Motorcycle(string name)
    : this(0, name) {}

  // This is the 'master' constructor that does all the real work.
  public Motorcycle(int intensity, string name)
  {
    if (intensity > 10)
    {
      intensity = 10;
```

```
      }
      driverIntensity = intensity;
      driverName = name;
    }
  ...
}
```

Understand that using the this keyword to chain constructor calls is never mandatory. However, when you make use of this technique, you do tend to end up with a more maintainable and concise class definition. Again, using this technique you can simplify your programming tasks, as the real work is delegated to a single constructor (typically the constructor that has the most parameters), while the other constructors simply "pass the buck."

Observing Constructor Flow

On a final note, do know that once a constructor passes arguments to the designated master constructor (and that constructor has processed the data), the constructor invoked originally by the caller will finish executing any remaining code statements. To clarify, update each of the constructors of the Motorcycle class with a fitting call to Console.WriteLine():

```
class Motorcycle
{
  public int driverIntensity;
  public string driverName;

  // Constructor chaining.
  public Motorcycle()
  {
    Console.WriteLine("In default ctor");
  }
  public Motorcycle(int intensity)
    : this(intensity, "")
  {
    Console.WriteLine("In ctor taking an int");
  }

  public Motorcycle(string name)
    : this(0, name)
  {
    Console.WriteLine("In ctor taking a string");
  }

  // This is the 'master' constructor that does all the real work.
  public Motorcycle(int intensity, string name)
  {
    Console.WriteLine("In master ctor ");
    if (intensity > 10)
    {
      intensity = 10;
    }
    driverIntensity = intensity;
    driverName = name;
  }
...
}
```

Now, ensure your `Main()` method exercises a `Motorcycle` object as follows:

```
static void Main(string[] args)
{
  Console.WriteLine("***** Fun with class Types *****\n");

  // Make a Motorcycle.
  Motorcycle c = new Motorcycle(5);
  c.SetDriverName("Tiny");
  c.PopAWheely();
  Console.WriteLine("Rider name is {0}", c.driverName);
  Console.ReadLine();
}
```

With this, ponder the output in Figure 5-4.

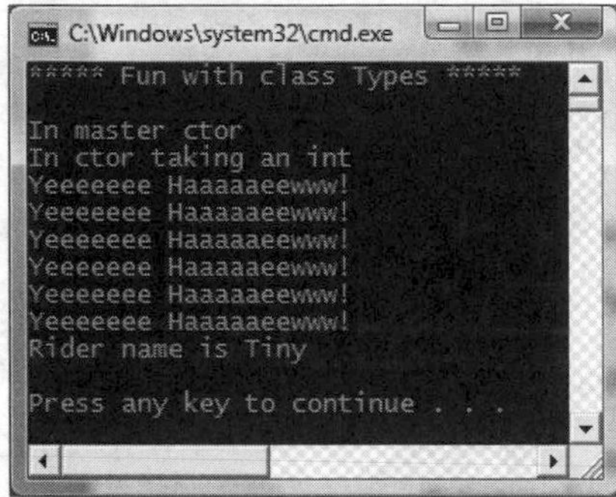

Figure 5-4. *Constructor chaining at work*

As you can see, the flow of constructor logic is as follows:

- We create our object by invoking the constructor requiring a single `int`.
- This constructor forwards the supplied data to the master constructor and provides any additional startup arguments not specified by the caller.
- The master constructor assigns the incoming data to the object's field data.
- Control is returned to the constructor originally called, and executes any remaining code statements.

Great! At this point you are able to define a class with field data (aka member variables) and various members that can be created using any number of constructors. Next up, let's formalize the role of the `static` keyword.

■ **Source Code** The SimpleClassExample project is included under the Chapter 5 subdirectory.

Understanding the static Keyword

A C# class (or structure) may define any number of *static members* via the `static` keyword. When you do so, the member in question must be invoked directly from the class level, rather than from a type instance. To illustrate the distinction, consider our good friend System.Console. As you have seen, you do not invoke the WriteLine() method from the object level:

```
// Error!  WriteLine() is not an instance level method!
Console c = new Console();
c.WriteLine("I can't be printed...");
```

but instead simply prefix the type name to the static WriteLine() member:

```
// Correct!  WriteLine() is a static method.
Console.WriteLine("Thanks...");
```

Simply put, static members are items that are deemed (by the type designer) to be so commonplace that there is no need to create an instance of the type when invoking the member. While any class (or structure) can define static members, they are most commonly found within "utility classes." For example, if you were to use the Visual Studio 2008 object browser (via the View ➤ Object Browser menu item) and examine the members of System.Console, System.Math, System.Environment, or System.GC (to name a few), you will find that all of their functionality is exposed from static members.

Defining Static Methods (and Fields)

Assume you have a new Console Application project named StaticMethods and have inserted a class named Teenager that defines a static method named Complain(). This method returns a random string, obtained in part by calling a static helper function named GetRandomNumber():

```
class Teenager
{
  public static Random r = new Random();

  public static int GetRandomNumber(short upperLimit)
  {
    return r.Next(upperLimit);
  }

  public static string Complain()
  {
    string[] messages = {"Do I have to?", "He started it!",
      "I'm too tired...", "I hate school!",
      "You are sooooooo wrong!"};
    return messages[GetRandomNumber(5)];
  }
}
```

Notice that the System.Random member variable and the GetRandomNumber() helper function method have also been declared as static members of the Teenager class, given the rule that static members can operate only on other static members.

■ **Note** Allow me to repeat myself: static members can operate only on static data and call static methods of the defining class. If you attempt to make use of nonstatic class data or call a nonstatic method of the class within a static member's implementation, you'll receive compile-time errors.

Like any static member, to call `Complain()`, prefix the name of the defining class:

```
static void Main(string[] args)
{
  Console.WriteLine("***** Fun with Static Methods *****\n");
  for(int i =0; i < 5; i++)
    Console.WriteLine(Teenager.Complain());
  Console.ReadLine();
}
```

Source Code The StaticMethods application is located under the Chapter 5 subdirectory.

Defining Static Data

In addition to static members, a type may also define static field data (such as the `Random` member variable seen in the previous `Teenager` class). Understand that when a class defines nonstatic data (properly referred to as *instance data*), each object of this type maintains an independent copy of the field. For example, assume a class that models a savings account is defined in a new Console Application project named StaticData:

```
// A simple savings account class.
class SavingsAccount
{
  public double currBalance;
  public SavingsAccount(double balance)
  {
    currBalance = balance;
  }
}
```

When you create `SavingsAccount` objects, memory for the `currBalance` field is allocated for each class instance. Static data, on the other hand, is allocated once and shared among all objects of the same type. To illustrate the usefulness of static data, add a static point of data named `currInterestRate` to the `SavingsAccount` class, which is set to a default value of 0.04:

```
// A simple savings account class.
class SavingsAccount
{
  public double currBalance;

  // A static point of data.
  public static double currInterestRate = 0.04;

  public SavingsAccount(double balance)
  {
    currBalance = balance;
  }
}
```

If you were to create three instances of `SavingsAccount` as follows:

```
static void Main(string[] args)
{
  Console.WriteLine("***** Fun with Static Data *****\n");
```

```
  Dim s1 As new SavingsAccount(50);
  Dim s2 As new SavingsAccount(100);
  Dim s3 As new SavingsAccount(10000.75);
  Console.ReadLine();
}
```

the in-memory data allocation would look something like Figure 5-5.

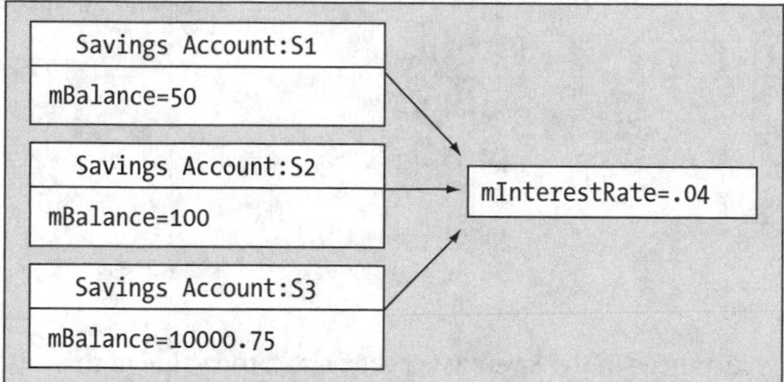

Figure 5-5. *Static data is allocated once and shared among all instances of the class.*

Let's update the SavingsAccount class to define two static methods to get and set the interest rate value:

```
// A simple savings account class.
class SavingsAccount
{
  public double currBalance;

  // A static point of data.
  public static double currInterestRate = 0.04;

  public SavingsAccount(double balance)
  {
    currBalance = balance;
  }

  // Static members to get/set interest rate.
  public static void SetInterestRate(double newRate )
  { currInterestRate = newRate; }
  public static double GetInterestRate()
  { return currInterestRate; }
}
```

Now, observe the following usage and the output in Figure 5-6:

```
static void Main(string[] args)
{
  Console.WriteLine("***** Fun with Static Data *****\n");
  SavingsAccount s1 = new SavingsAccount(50);
  SavingsAccount s2 = new SavingsAccount(100);

  // Print the current interest rate.
  Console.WriteLine("Interest Rate is: {0}", SavingsAccount.GetInterestRate());
```

```
  // Make new object, this does NOT 'reset' the interest rate.
  SavingsAccount s3 = new SavingsAccount(10000.75);
  Console.WriteLine("Interest Rate is: {0}", SavingsAccount.GetInterestRate());
  Console.ReadLine();
}
```

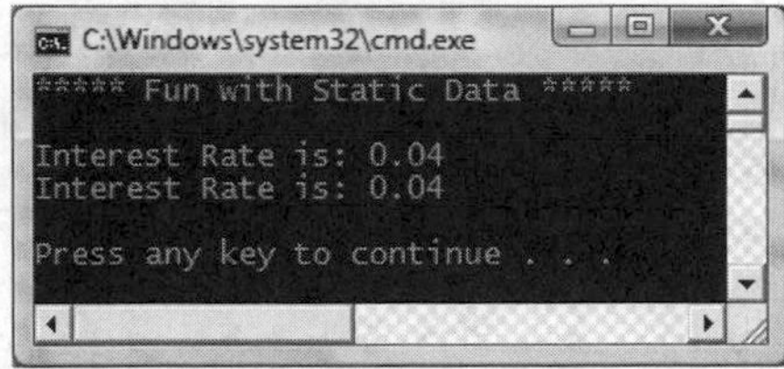

Figure 5-6. *Static data is allocated only once.*

As you can see, when you create new instances of the `SavingsAccount` class, the value of the static data is not reset, as the CLR will allocate the data into memory exactly one time. After that point, all objects of type `SavingsAccount` operate on the same value.

As stated, static methods can operate only on static data. However, a nonstatic method can make use of both static and nonstatic data. This should make sense, given that static data is available to all instances of the type. To illustrate, update `SavingsAccount` with the following instance-level members:

```
class SavingsAccount
{
  public double currBalance;
  public static double currInterestRate = 0.04;

  // Instance members to get/set interest rate.
  public void SetInterestRateObj(double newRate)
  { currInterestRate = newRate; }
  public double GetInterestRateObj()
  { return currInterestRate; }
...
}
```

Here, `SetInterestRateObj()` and `GetInterestRateObj()` are operating on the same static field as the static `SetInterestRate()`/`GetInterestRate()` methods. Thus, if one object were to change the interest rate, all other objects report the same value:

```
static void Main(string[] args)
{
  Console.WriteLine("***** Fun with Static Data *****\n");
  SavingsAccount.SetInterestRate(0.09);
  SavingsAccount s1 = new SavingsAccount(50);
  SavingsAccount s2 = new SavingsAccount(100);

  // All three lines print out "Interest Rate is: 0.09"
  Console.WriteLine("Interest Rate is: {0}", s1.GetInterestRateObj());
  Console.WriteLine("Interest Rate is: {0}", s2.GetInterestRateObj());
  Console.WriteLine("Interest Rate is: {0}", SavingsAccount.GetInterestRate());
  Console.ReadLine();
}
```

In this case, the value 0.09 is returned regardless of which `SavingsAccount` object we ask (including asking via the static `GetInterestRate()` method).

Defining Static Constructors

As explained earlier in this chapter, constructors are used to set the value of a type's data at the time of creation. Thus, if you were to assign a value to a static data member within an instance-level constructor, you may be surprised to find that the value is reset each time you create a new object! For example, assume you have updated the `SavingsAccount` class as follows:

```
class SavingsAccount
{
  public double currBalance;
  public static double currInterestRate;

  public SavingsAccount(double balance)
  {
    currInterestRate = 0.04;
    currBalance = balance;
  }
...
}
```

If you execute the previous `Main()` method, notice how the `currInterestRate` variable is reset each time you create a new `SavingsAccount` object (see Figure 5-7).

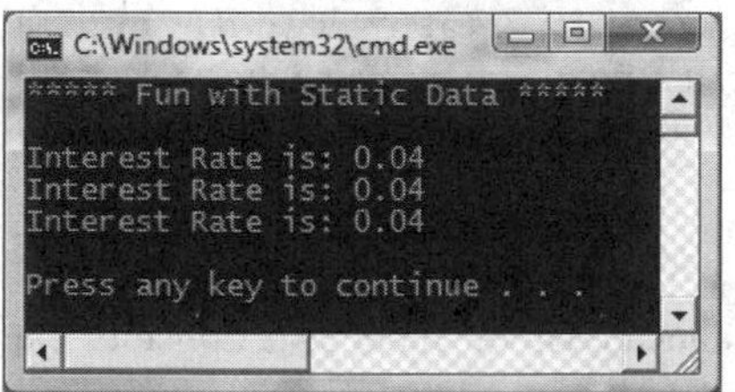

Figure 5-7. *Assigning static data in an instance level constructor "resets" the value.*

While you are always free to establish the initial value of static data using the member initialization syntax, what if the value for your static data needed to be obtained from a database or external file? To perform such tasks requires a method scope (such as a constructor) to execute the code statements. For this very reason, C# allows you to define a *static constructor*:

```
class SavingsAccount
{
  public double currBalance;
  public static double currInterestRate;

  public SavingsAccount(double balance)
  {
    currBalance = balance;
  }

  // A static constructor.
  static SavingsAccount()
  {
    Console.WriteLine("In static ctor!");
```

```
    currInterestRate = 0.04;
  }
...
}
```

Simply put, a static constructor is a special constructor that is an ideal place to initialize the values of static data when the value is not known at compile time (e.g., you need to read in the value from an external file, generate a random number, etc.). Here are a few points of interest regarding static constructors:

- A given class (or structure) may define only a single static constructor.
- A static constructor does not take an access modifier and cannot take any parameters.
- A static constructor executes exactly one time, regardless of how many objects of the type are created.
- The runtime invokes the static constructor when it creates an instance of the class or before accessing the first static member invoked by the caller.
- The static constructor executes before any instance-level constructors.

Given this modification, when you create new `SavingsAccount` objects, the value of the static data is preserved, as the static member is set only one time within the static constructor, regardless of the number of objects created.

Defining Static Classes

Since the release of .NET 2.0, the C# language expanded the scope of the `static` keyword by introducing *static classes*. When a class has been defined as static, it is not creatable using the `new` keyword, and it can contain only members or fields marked with the `static` keyword (if this is not the case, you receive compiler errors).

At first glance, this might seem like a fairly useless feature, given that a class that cannot be created does not appear all that helpful. However, if you create a class that contains nothing but static members and/or constant data, the class has no need to be allocated in the first place. Consider the following new static class type:

```
// Static classes can only
// contain static members!
static class TimeUtilClass
{
  public static void PrintTime()
  { Console.WriteLine(DateTime.Now.ToShortTimeString()); }
  public static void PrintDate()
  { Console.WriteLine(DateTime.Today.ToShortDateString()); }
}
```

Given that this class has been defined with the `static` keyword, we cannot create an instance of `TimeUtilClass` using the `new` keyword:

```
static void Main(string[] args)
{
  Console.WriteLine("***** Fun with Static Data *****\n");
  TimeUtilClass.PrintDate();

  // Compiler error! Can't create static classes.
  TimeUtilClass u = new TimeUtilClass ();
...
}
```

Prior to .NET 2.0, the only way to prevent the creation of a class type was to either redefine the default constructor as private or mark the class as an abstract type using the C# abstract keyword (full details regarding abstract types are in Chapter 6):

```
class TimeUtilClass
{
  // Redefine the default ctor as private
  // to prevent creation.
  private TimeUtilClass (){}

  public static void PrintTime()
  { Console.WriteLine(DateTime.Now.ToShortTimeString()); }
  public static void PrintDate()
  { Console.WriteLine(DateTime.Today.ToShortDateString()); }
}

// Define type as abstract to prevent
// creation
abstract class TimeUtilClass
{
  public static void PrintTime()
  { Console.WriteLine(DateTime.Now.ToShortTimeString()); }
  public static void PrintDate()
  { Console.WriteLine(DateTime.Today.ToShortDateString()); }
}
```

While these constructs are still permissible, the use of static classes is a cleaner solution and more type-safe, given that the previous two techniques allowed nonstatic members to appear within the class definition without error.

On a related note, a project's application object (e.g., the class defining the Main() method) is often defined as a static class, to ensure it only contains static members and cannot be directly created. For example:

```
// Define the application object as static.
static class Program
{
  static void Main(string[] args)
  {
    ...
  }
}
```

At this point in the chapter you hopefully feel comfortable defining simple class types containing constructors, fields, and various static (and nonstatic) members. Now that you have the basics under your belt, we can formally investigate the three pillars of object-oriented programming.

Source Code The StaticData project is located under the Chapter 5 subdirectory.

Defining the Pillars of OOP

All object-based languages must contend with three core principals of object-oriented programming, often called the "pillars of object-oriented programming (OOP)":

- *Encapsulation*: How does this language hide an object's internal implementation details and preserve data integrity?
- *Inheritance*: How does this language promote code reuse?
- *Polymorphism*: How does this language let you treat related objects in a similar way?

Before digging into the syntactic details of each pillar, it is important that you understand the basic role of each. Here is an overview of each pillar, which will be examined in full detail over the remainder of this chapter and the next.

The Role of Encapsulation

The first pillar of OOP is called *encapsulation*. This trait boils down to the language's ability to hide unnecessary implementation details from the object user. For example, assume you are using a class named `DatabaseReader`, which has two primary methods: `Open()` and `Close()`:

```
// This type encapsulates the details of opening and closing a database.
DatabaseReader dbReader = new DatabaseReader();
dbReader.Open(@"C:\MyCars.mdf");

// Do something with data file and close the file.
dbReader.Close();
```

The fictitious `DatabaseReader` class encapsulates the inner details of locating, loading, manipulating, and closing the data file. Object users love encapsulation, as this pillar of OOP keeps programming tasks simpler. There is no need to worry about the numerous lines of code that are working behind the scenes to carry out the work of the `DatabaseReader` class. All you do is create an instance and send the appropriate messages (e.g., "Open the file named `MyCars.mdf` located on my C drive").

Closely related to the notion of encapsulating programming logic is the idea of data hiding. Ideally, an object's state data should be specified using the `private` (or possibly `protected`) keyword. In this way, the outside world must ask politely in order to change or obtain the underlying value. This is a good thing, as publicly declared data points can easily become corrupted (hopefully by accident rather than intent!). You will formally examine this aspect of encapsulation in just a bit.

The Role of Inheritance

The next pillar of OOP, *inheritance*, boils down to the language's ability to allow you to build new class definitions based on existing class definitions. In essence, inheritance allows you to extend the behavior of a base (or *parent*) class by inheriting core functionality into the derived subclass (also called a *child class*). Figure 5-8 shows a simple example.

You can read the diagram in Figure 5-8 as "A Hexagon is-a Shape that is-an Object." When you have classes related by this form of inheritance, you establish *"is-a" relationships* between types. The "is-a" relationship is termed *classical inheritance*.

Here, you can assume that `Shape` defines some number of members that are common to all descendents. Given that the `Hexagon` class extends `Shape`, it inherits the core functionality defined by `Shape` and `Object`, as well as defines additional hexagon-related details of its own (whatever those may be).

■ **Note** Under the .NET platform, `System.Object` is always the topmost parent in any class hierarchy, which defines some bare-bones functionality fully described in Chapter 6.

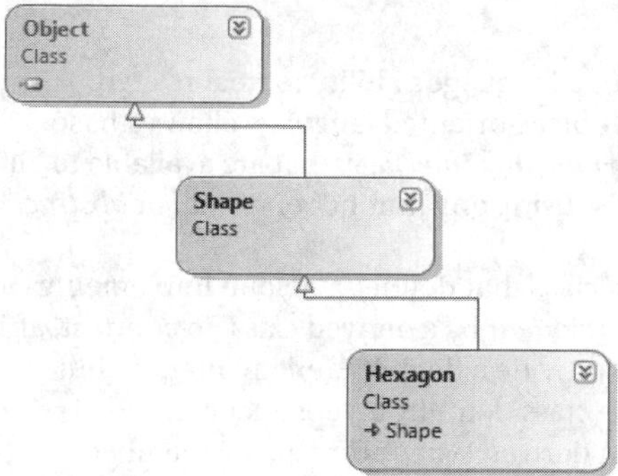

Figure 5-8. *The "is-a" relationship*

There is another form of code reuse in the world of OOP: the containment/delegation model (also known as the *"has-a" relationship* or *aggregation*). This form of reuse is *not* used to establish parent/child relationships. Rather, the "has-a" relationship allows one class to define a member variable of another class and expose its functionality (if required) to the object user indirectly.

For example, assume you are again modeling an automobile. You might want to express the idea that a car "has-a" radio. It would be illogical to attempt to derive the Car class from a Radio, or vice versa (a Car "is-a" Radio? I think not!). Rather, you have two independent classes working together, where the Car class creates and exposes the Radio's functionality:

```
class Radio
{
  public void Power(bool turnOn)
  {
    Console.WriteLine("Radio on: {0}", turnOn);
  }
}

class Car
{
  // Car 'has-a' Radio
  private Radio myRadio = new Radio();
  public void TurnOnRadio(bool onOff)
  {
    // Delegate call to inner object.
    myRadio.Power(onOff);
  }
}
```

Notice that the object user has no clue that the Car class is making use of an inner Radio object.

```
static void Main(string[] args)
{
  // Call is forwarded to Radio internally.
  Car viper = new Car();
  viper.TurnOnRadio(false);
}
```

The Role of Polymorphism

The final pillar of OOP is *polymorphism*. This trait captures a language's ability to treat related objects in a similar manner. Specifically, this tenant of an object-oriented language allows a base class to define a set of members (formally termed the *polymorphic interface*) that are available to all descendents. A class's polymorphic interface is constructed using any number of *virtual* or *abstract* members (see Chapter 6 for full details).

In a nutshell, a *virtual member* is a member in a base class that defines a default implementation that may be changed (or more formally speaking, *overridden*) by a derived class. In contrast, an *abstract method* is a member in a base class that does *not* provide a default implementation, but does provide a signature. When a class derives from a base class defining an abstract method, it *must* be overridden by a derived type. In either case, when derived types override the members defined by a base class, they are essentially redefining how they respond to the same request.

To preview polymorphism, let's provide some details behind the shapes hierarchy shown in Figure 5-8. Assume that the Shape class has defined a virtual method named Draw() that takes no parameters. Given the fact that every shape needs to render itself in a unique manner, subclasses (such as Hexagon and Circle) are free to override this method to their own liking (see Figure 5-9).

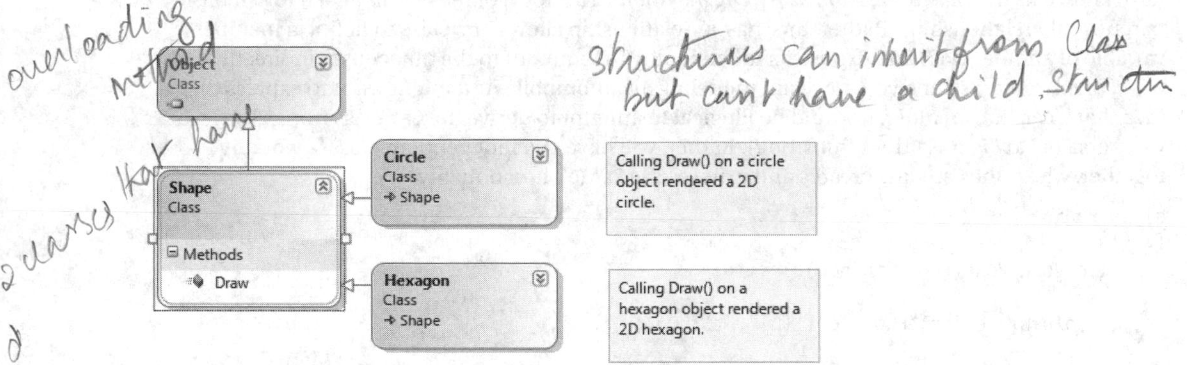

Figure 5-9. *Classical polymorphism*

Once a polymorphic interface has been designed, you can begin to make various assumptions in your code. For example, given that Hexagon and Circle derive from a common parent (Shape), an array of Shape types could contain anything deriving from this base class. Furthermore, given that Shape defines a polymorphic interface to all derived types (the Draw() method in this example), we can assume each member in the array has this functionality.

Consider the following Main() method, which instructs an array of Shape-derived types to render themselves using the Draw() method:

```
class Program
{
  static void Main(string[] args)
  {
    Shape[] myShapes = new Shape[3];
    myShapes[0] = new Hexagon();
    myShapes[1] = new Circle();
    myShapes[2] = new Hexagon();

    foreach (Shape s in myShapes)
    {
      s.Draw();
    }
```

```
        Console.ReadLine();
    }
}
```

This wraps up our brisk overview of the pillars of OOP. Now that you have the theory in your mind, the remainder of this chapter explores further details of how encapsulation is handled under C#. The next chapter will tackle the details of inheritance and polymorphism.

C# Access Modifiers

When working with encapsulation, you must always take into account which aspects of a type are visible to various parts of your application. Specifically, types (classes, interfaces, structures, enumerations, delegates) and their members (properties, methods, constructors, fields, and so forth) are always defined using a specific keyword to control how "visible" the item is to other parts of your application. Although C# defines numerous keywords to control access, they differ on where they can be successfully applied (type or member). Table 5-1 documents the role of each access modifier and where it may be applied.

Table 5-1. *C# Access Modifiers*

C# Access Modifier	May Be Applied To	Meaning in Life
`public`	Types or type members	Public items have no access restrictions. A public member can be accessed from an object as well as any derived class. A public type can be accessed from other external assemblies.
`private`	Type members or nested types	Private items can only be accessed by the class (or structure) that defines the item.
`protected`	Type members or nested types	Protected items are not directly accessible from an object variable; however, they are accessible by the defining type as well as by derived classes.
`internal`	Types or type members	Internal items are accessible only within the current assembly. Therefore, if you define a set of internal types within a .NET class library, other assemblies are not able to make use of them.
`protected internal`	Type members or nested types	When the `protected` and `internal` keywords are combined on an item, the item is accessible within the defining assembly, the defining class, and by derived classes.

In this chapter, we are only concerned with the `public` and `private` keywords. Later chapters will examine the role of the `internal` and `protected internal` modifiers (useful when you build .NET code libraries) and the `protected` modifier (useful when you are creating class hierarchies).

The Default Access Modifiers

By default, type members are *implicitly private* while types are *implicitly internal*. Thus, the following class definition is automatically set to internal, while the type's default constructor is automatically set to private:

```
// An internal class with a private default constructor.
class Radio
{
  Radio(){}
}
```

Thus, to allow other types to invoke members of an object, you must mark them as publically accessible. As well, if you wish to expose the Radio to external assemblies (again, useful when building .NET code libraries; see Chapter 15) you will need to add the public modifier.

```
// A public class with a public default constructor.
public class Radio
{
  public Radio(){}
}
```

Access Modifiers and Nested Types

As mentioned in Table 5-1, the private, protected, and protected internal access modifiers can be applied to a *nested type*. Chapter 6 will examine nesting in detail. What you need to know at this point, however, is that a nested type is a type declared directly within the scope of class or structure. By way of example, here is a private enumeration (named Color) nested within a public class (named SportsCar):

```
public class SportsCar
{
  // OK!  Nested types can be marked private.
  private enum CarColor
  {
    Red, Green, Blue
  }
}
```

Here, it is permissible to apply the private access modifier on the nested type. However, nonnested types (such as the SportsCar) can only be defined with the public or internal modifiers. Therefore, the following class definition is illegal:

```
// Error! Nonnested types cannot be marked private!
private class SportsCar
{}
```

The First Pillar: C#'s Encapsulation Services

The concept of encapsulation revolves around the notion that an object's internal data should not be directly accessible from an object instance. Rather, if the caller wants to alter the state of an object, the user does so indirectly using accessor (i.e., "getter") and mutator (i.e., "setter") methods. In C#, encapsulation is enforced at the syntactic level using the public, private, internal, and protected keywords. To illustrate the need for encapsulation services, assume you have created the following class definition:

```
// A class with a single public field.
class Book
{
  public int numberOfPages;
}
```

The problem with public field data is that the items have no ability to intrinsically "understand" whether the current value to which they are assigned is valid with regard to the current business rules of the system. As you know, the upper range of a C# int is quite large (2,147,483,647). Therefore, the compiler allows the following assignment:

```
// Humm. That is one heck of a mini-novel!
static void Main(string[] args)
{
  Book miniNovel = new Book();
  miniNovel.numberOfPages = 30000000;
}
```

Although you have not overflowed the boundaries of an int data type, it should be clear that a mini-novel with a page count of 30,000,000 pages is a bit unreasonable. As you can see, public fields do not provide a way to trap logical upper (or lower) limits. If your current system has a business rule that states a book must be between 1 and 1,000 pages, you are at a loss to enforce this programmatically. Because of this, public fields typically have no place in a production-level class definition.

Encapsulation provides a way to preserve the integrity of an object's state data. Rather than defining public fields (which can easily foster data corruption), you should get in the habit of defining *private data*, which is indirectly manipulated using one of two main techniques:

- Define a pair of accessor (get) and mutator (set) methods.
- Define a type property.

Additionally, C# provides the readonly keyword, which also delivers a level of data protection. Whichever technique you choose, the point is that a well-encapsulated class should hide the details of how it operates from the prying eyes of the outside world. This is often termed *black box programming*. The beauty of this approach is that an object is free to change how a given method is implemented under the hood. It does this without breaking any existing code making use of it, provided that the signature of the method remains constant.

Encapsulation Using Traditional Accessors and Mutators

Over the remaining pages in this chapter, we will be building a fairly complete class that models a general employee. To get the ball rolling, create a new Console Application named EmployeeApp and insert a new class file (named Employee.cs) using the Project ➤ Add class menu item. Update the Employee class with the following fields, methods, and constructors:

```
class Employee
{
  // Field data.
  private string empName;
  private int empID;
  private float currPay;

  // Constructors.
  public Employee() {}
  public Employee(string name, int id, float pay)
  {
    empName = name;
```

```
    empID = id;
    currPay = pay;
  }

  // Members.
  public void GiveBonus(float amount)
  {
    currPay += amount;
  }
  public void DisplayStats()
  {
    Console.WriteLine("Name: {0}", empName);
    Console.WriteLine("ID: {0}", empID);
    Console.WriteLine("Pay: {0}", currPay);
  }
}
```

Notice that the fields of the Employee class are currently defined using the private access keyword. Given this, the empName, empID, and currPay fields are not directly accessible from an object variable:

```
static void Main(string[] args)
{
  // Error! Cannot directly access private members
  // from an object!
  Employee emp = new Employee();
  emp.empName = "Marv";
}
```

If you want the outside world to interact with your private string representing a worker's full name, tradition dictates defining an accessor (get method) and a mutator (set method). For example, to encapsulate the empName field, you could add the following public members to the existing Employee class type:

```
class Employee
{
  // Field data.
  private string empName;
  ...
  // Accessor (get method)
  public string GetName()
  {
    return empName;
  }

  // Mutator (set method)
  public void SetName(string name)
  {
    // Remove any illegal characters (!,@,#,$,%),
    // check maximum length or case before making assignment.
    empName = name;
  }
}
```

This technique requires two uniquely named methods to operate on a single data point. To illustrate, update your Main() method as follows:

```
static void Main(string[] args)
{
  Console.WriteLine("***** Fun with Encapsulation *****\n");
  Employee emp = new Employee("Marvin", 456, 30000);
  emp.GiveBonus(1000);
  emp.DisplayStats();

  // Use the get/set methods to interact with the object's name.
  emp.SetName("Marv");
  Console.WriteLine("Employee is named: {0}", emp.GetName());
  Console.ReadLine();
}
```

Encapsulation Using Type Properties

Although you can encapsulate a piece of field data using traditional get and set methods, .NET languages prefer to enforce data protection using *properties*. First of all, understand that properties always map to "real" accessor and mutator methods in terms of CIL code. Therefore, as a class designer, you are still able to perform any internal logic necessary before making the value assignment (e.g., uppercase the value, scrub the value for illegal characters, check the bounds of a numerical value, and so on).

Here is the updated `Employee` class, now enforcing encapsulation of each field using property syntax rather than traditional get and set methods:

```
class Employee
{
  // Field data.
  private string empName;
  private int empID;
  private float currPay;

  // Properties.
  public string Name
  {
    get { return empName; }
    set { empName = value; }
  }

  public int ID
  {
    get { return empID; }
    set { empID = value; }
  }

  public float Pay
  {
    get { return currPay; }
    set { currPay = value; }
  }
...
}
```

A C# property is composed by defining a `get` scope (accessor) and `set` scope (mutator) directly within the property scope itself. Once we have these properties in place, it appears to the caller that it is getting and setting a *public point* of data; however, the correct `get` and `set` block is called behind the scenes to preserve encapsulation:

```
static void Main(string[] args)
{
  Console.WriteLine("***** Fun with Encapsulation *****\n");
  Employee emp = new Employee("Marvin", 456, 30000);
  emp.GiveBonus(1000);
  emp.DisplayStats();

  // Set and get the Name property.
  emp.Name = "Marv";
  Console.WriteLine("Employee is named: {0}", emp.Name);
  Console.ReadLine();
}
```

Properties (as opposed to accessors and mutators) also make your types easier to manipulate, in that properties are able to respond to the intrinsic operators of C#. To illustrate, assume that the `Employee` class type has an internal private member variable representing the age of the employee. Here is the relevant update:

```
class Employee
{
...
  private int empAge;
  public int Age
  {
    get { return empAge; }
    set { empAge = value; }
  }

  // Constructors
  public Employee() {}
  public Employee(string name, int age, int id, float pay)
  {
    empName = name;
    empID = id;
    empAge = age;
    currPay = pay;
  }

  public void DisplayStats()
  {
    Console.WriteLine("Name: {0}", empName);
    Console.WriteLine("ID: {0}", empID);
    Console.WriteLine("Age: {0}", empAge);
    Console.WriteLine("Pay: {0}", currPay);
  }
}
```

Now assume you have created an `Employee` object named `joe`. On his birthday, you wish to increment the age by one. Using traditional accessor and mutator methods, you would need to write code such as the following:

```
Employee joe = new Employee();
joe.SetAge(joe.GetAge() + 1);
```

However, if you encapsulate `empAge` using a property named `Age`, you are able to simply write

```
Employee joe = new Employee();
joe.Age++;
```

Internal Representation of Properties

Many programmers (especially those who program with a C-based language such as C++) tend to name traditional accessor and mutator methods using `get_` and `set_` prefixes (e.g., `get_Name()` and `set_Name()`). This naming convention itself is not problematic as far as C# is concerned. However, it is important to understand that under the hood, a property is represented in CIL code using these same prefixes.

For example, if you open up the `EmployeeApp.exe` assembly using `ildasm.exe`, you see that each property is mapped to hidden `get_XXX()/set_XXX()` methods called internally by the CLR (see Figure 5-10).

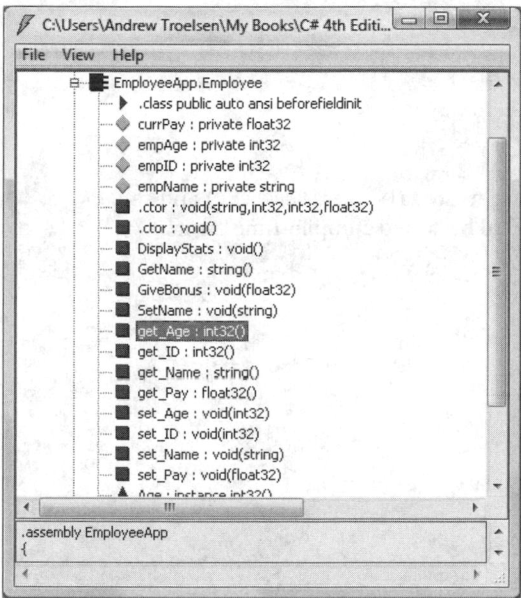

Figure 5-10. *A property is represented by get/set methods internally.*

Assume the `Employee` type now has a private member variable named `empSSN` to represent an individual's Social Security number, which is manipulated by a property named `SocialSecurityNumber` (and also assume you have updated your type's custom constructor and `DisplayStats()` method to account for this new piece of field data).

```
// Add support for a new field representing the employee's SSN.
class Employee
{
...
  private string empSSN;
  public string SocialSecurityNumber
  {
    get { return empSSN; }
    set { empSSN = value; }
  }

  // Constructors
  public Employee() {}
  public Employee(string name, int age, int id, float pay, string ssn)
```

```
  {
    empName = name;
    empID = id;
    empAge = age;
    currPay = pay;
    empSSN = ssn;
  }
  public void DisplayStats()
  {
    Console.WriteLine("Name: {0}", empName);
    Console.WriteLine("ID: {0}", empID);
    Console.WriteLine("Age: {0}", empAge);
    Console.WriteLine("SSN: {0}", empSSN);
    Console.WriteLine("Pay: {0}", currPay);
  }
...
}
```

If you were to also define two methods named `get_SocialSecurityNumber()` and `set_SocialSecurityNumber()` in the same class, you would be issued compile-time errors:

```
// Remember, a property really maps to a get_/set_ pair!
class Employee
{
...
  public string get_SocialSecurityNumber()
  {
    return empSSN;
  }
  public void set_SocialSecurityNumber(string ssn)
  {
    empSSN = ssn;
  }
}
```

■ Note The .NET base class libraries always favor type properties over traditional accessor and mutator methods when encapsulating field data. Therefore, if you wish to build custom types that integrate well with the .NET platform, avoid defining traditional get and set methods.

Controlling Visibility Levels of Property Get/Set Statements

Prior to .NET 2.0, the visibility of get and set logic was solely controlled by the access modifier of the property declaration:

```
// The get and set logic is both public,
// given the declaration of the property.
public string SocialSecurityNumber
{
  get { return empSSN; }
  set { empSSN = value; }
}
```

In some cases, it would be useful to specify unique accessibility levels for get and set logic. To do so, simply prefix an accessibility keyword to the appropriate get or set keyword (the unqualified scope takes the visibility of the property's declaration):

```
// Object users can only get the value, however
// the Employee class and derived types can set the value.
public string SocialSecurityNumber
{
  get { return empSSN; }
  protected set { empSSN = value; }
}
```

In this case, the set logic of SocialSecurityNumber can only be called by the current class and derived classes and therefore cannot be called from an object instance. Again, the protected keyword will be formally detailed in the next chapter when we examine inheritance and polymorphism.

Read-Only and Write-Only Properties

When encapsulating data, you may wish to configure a *read-only property*. To do so, simply omit the set block. Likewise, if you wish to have a *write-only property*, omit the get block. For example, here is how the SocialSecurityNumber property could be retrofitted as read-only:

```
public string SocialSecurityNumber
{
  get { return empSSN; }
}
```

Given this adjustment, the only manner in which an employee's US Social Security number can be set is through a constructor argument. Therefore it would now be a compiler error to attempt to set an employee's SSN value as so:

```
static void Main(string[] args)
{
  Console.WriteLine("***** Fun with Encapsulation *****\n");
  Employee emp = new Employee("Marvin", 24, 456, 30000, "111-11-1111");
  emp.GiveBonus(1000);
  emp.DisplayStats();

  // Error!  SSN is read only!
  emp.SocialSecurityNumber = "222-22-2222";

  Console.ReadLine();
}
```

Static Properties

C# also supports static properties. Recall from earlier in this chapter that static members are accessed at the class level, not from an instance (object) of that class. For example, assume that the Employee type defines a static point of data to represent the name of the organization employing these workers. You may encapsulate a static property as follows:

```
// Static properties must operate on static data!
class Employee
{
...
  private static string companyName;
```

```
  public static string Company
  {
    get { return companyName; }
    set { companyName = value; }
  }
  ...
}
```

Static properties are manipulated in the same manner as static methods, as shown here:

```
// Interact with the static property.
static void Main(string[] args)
{
  Console.WriteLine("***** Fun with Encapsulation *****\n");

  // Set company.
  Employee.Company = "Intertech Training";
  Console.WriteLine("These folks work at {0}.", Employee.Company);

  Employee emp = new Employee("Marvin", 24, 456, 30000, "111-11-1111");
  emp.GiveBonus(1000);
  emp.DisplayStats();

  Console.ReadLine();
}
```

Finally, recall that classes can support static constructors. Thus, if you wanted to ensure that the name of the static `companyName` field was always assigned to "Intertech Training," you would write the following:

```
// Static constructors are used to initialize static data.
public class Employee
{
  private Static companyName As string
...
  static Employee()
  {
    companyName = "Intertech Training";
  }
}
```

Using this approach, there is no need to explicitly call the `Company` property to set the initial value:

```
// Automatically set to "Intertech Training" via static constructor.
static void Main(string[] args)
{
  Console.WriteLine("These folks work at {0}", Employee.Company);
}
```

To wrap up the examination of encapsulation using C# properties, understand that these syntactic entities are used for the same purpose as traditional accessor (get)/mutator (set) methods. The benefit of properties is that the users of your objects are able to manipulate the internal data point using a single named item.

■ Note In Chapter 13 you will examine a new C# 2008 construct called *automatic properties*. This feature allows you to define a property definition and the related private member variable using a very concise syntax.

Understanding Constant Data

Now that you can create fields that can be modified using type properties, allow me to illustrate how to define data that can never change after the initial assignment. C# offers the `const` keyword to define constant data. As you might guess, this can be helpful when you are defining a set of known values for use in your applications that are logically connected to a given class or structure.

Turning away from the `Employee` example for a moment, assume you are building a utility class named `MyMathClass` that needs to define a value for the value PI (which we will assume to be 3.14). Begin by creating a new Console Application project named ConstData. Given that we would not want to allow other developers to change this value in code, PI could be modeled with the following constant:

```
namespace ConstData
{
  class MyMathClass
  {
    public const double PI = 3.14;
  }

  class Program
  {
    static void Main(string[] args)
    {
      Console.WriteLine("***** Fun with Const *****\n");
      Console.WriteLine("The value of PI is: {0}", MyMathClass.PI);

      // Error! Can't change a constant!
      MyMathClass.PI = 3.1444;

      Console.ReadLine();
    }
  }
}
```

Notice that we are referencing the constant data defined by `MyMathClass` using a class name prefix (i.e., `MyMathClass.PI`). This is due to the fact that constant fields of a class or structure are implicitly *static*. However, it is permissible to define and access a local constant variable within a type member. By way of example:

```
static void LocalConstStringVariable()
{
  // A local constant data point can be directly accessed.
  const string fixedStr = "Fixed string Data";
  Console.WriteLine(fixedStr);

  // Error!
  fixedStr = "This will not work!";
}
```

Regardless of where you define a constant piece of data, the one point to always remember is that the initial value assigned to the constant must be specified at the time you define the constant. Thus, if you were to modify your `MyMathClass` in such a way that the value of PI is assigned in a class constructor as follows:

```
class MyMathClass
{
  // Try to set PI in ctor?
  public const double PI;

  public MyMathClass()
  {
    // Error!
    PI = 3.14;
  }
}
```

you would receive a compile-time error. The reason for this restriction has to do with the fact the value of constant data must be known *at compile time*. Constructors, as you know, are invoked *at runtime*.

Understanding Read-Only Fields

Closely related to constant data is the notion of *read-only field data* (which should not be confused with a read-only property). Like a constant, a read-only field cannot be changed after the initial assignment. However, unlike a constant, the value assigned to a read-only field can be determined at runtime, and therefore can legally be assigned within the scope of a constructor (but nowhere else).

This can be very helpful when you don't know the value of a field until runtime (perhaps because you need to read an external file to obtain the value), but wish to ensure that the value will not change after that point. For the sake of illustration, assume the following update to `MyMathClass`:

```
class MyMathClass
{
  // Read-only fields can be assigned in ctors,
  // but nowhere else.
  public readonly double PI;
  public MyMathClass ()
  {
    PI = 3.14;
  }
}
```

Again, any attempt to make assignments to a field marked `readonly` outside the scope of a constructor results in a compiler error:

```
class MyMathClass
{
  public readonly double PI;
  public MyMathClass ()
  {
    PI = 3.14;
  }

  // Error!
  public void ChangePI()
  { PI = 3.14444;}
}
```

Static Read-Only Fields

Unlike a constant field, read-only fields are *not* implicitly static. Thus, if you wish to expose `PI` from the class level, you must explicitly make use of the `static` keyword. If you know the value of a static read-only field at compile time, the initial assignment looks very similar to that of a constant:

```
class MyMathClass
{
  public static readonly double PI = 3.14;
}

class Program
{
  static void Main(string[] args)
  {
    Console.WriteLine("***** Fun with Const *****");
    Console.WriteLine("The value of PI is: {0}", MyMathClass.PI);
    Console.ReadLine();
  }
}
```

However, if the value of a static read-only field is not known until runtime, you must make use of a static constructor as described earlier in this chapter:

```
class MyMathClass
{
  public static readonly double PI;

  static MyMathClass()
  { PI = 3.14; }
}
```

Now that we have examined the role of constant data and read-only fields, we can return to the `Employee` example and put the wraps on this chapter.

■ **Source Code** The ConstData project is included under the Chapter 5 subdirectory.

Understanding Partial Types

Classes and structures can be defined with a type modifier named `partial` that allows you to define a type across multiple `*.cs` files. Earlier versions of the language required all code for a given type be defined within a single `*.cs` file. Given the fact that a production-level C# class may be hundreds of lines of code (or more), this can end up being a mighty lengthy file indeed.

In these cases, it may be beneficial to partition a type's implementation across numerous `*.cs` files in order to separate code that is in some way more important from other aspects of the type definition. For example, using the `partial` class modifier, you could place all of the `Employee` constructors and properties into a new file named `Employee.Internals.cs`:

```
partial class Employee
{
  // Constructors
...
  // Properties
...
}
```

while the private field data and type methods are defined within the initial Employee.cs:

```
partial class Employee
{
  // Field data.
  private string empName;
  private int empID;
  private float currPay;
  private int empAge;
  private string empSSN;
  private static string companyName;

  public void GiveBonus(float amount)
  {
    currPay += amount;
  }

  public void DisplayStats()
  {
    Console.WriteLine("Name: {0}", empName);
    Console.WriteLine("ID: {0}", empID);
    Console.WriteLine("Age: {0}", empAge);
    Console.WriteLine("SSN: {0}", empSSN);
    Console.WriteLine("Pay: {0}", currPay);
  }
}
```

As you might guess, this can be helpful to new team members who need to quickly learn about the public interface of the type. Rather than reading through a single (lengthy) C# file to find the members of interest, they can focus on the public members. Of course, once these files are compiled by the C# compiler, the end result is a single unified type. To this end, the partial modifier is purely a design-time construct.

Also know that the names you give to the files that contain partial type definitions are entirely up to you. Here, Employee.Internal.cs was chosen simply to indicate that this file contains grungy infrastructure code that most developers can ignore. The only requirement when defining partial types is that the type's name (Employee in this case) is identical and defined within the same .NET namespace.

■ **Note** Visual Studio 2008 makes use of the partial keyword to partition code generated by the IDE's designer tools (such as various GUI designers). Using this approach, you can keep focused on your current solution, and be blissfully unaware of the designer-generated code.

Documenting C# Source Code via XML

The final task of this chapter is to examine a specific way to comment your code that yields XML-based code documentation. If you have worked with the Java programming language, you may be familiar with the javadoc utility. Using javadoc, you are able to turn Java source code into a corresponding HTML representation (provided the *.java file contains the correct code comment syntax). The C# documentation model is slightly different, in that the code-comments-to-XML conversion process is the job of the C# compiler (via the /doc option) rather than a stand-alone utility.

So, why use XML to document our type definitions rather than HTML? The main reason is that XML is a very "enabling technology." Given that XML separates the definition of data from the presentation of that data, we can apply any number of XML transformations to the underlying XML to display the code documentation in a variety of formats (MSDN format, HTML, etc.).

When you wish to document your C# types in XML, your first step is to make use of the new triple slash (///) code comment notations. Once a documentation comment has been declared, you are free to use any well-formed XML elements, including the recommended set shown in Table 5-2.

Table 5-2. *Recommended Code Comment XML Elements*

Predefined XML Documentation Element	Meaning in Life
`<c>`	Indicates that the following text should be displayed in a specific "code font"
`<code>`	Indicates multiple lines should be marked as code
`<example>`	Mocks up a code example for the item you are describing
`<exception>`	Documents which exceptions a given class may throw
`<list>`	Inserts a list or table into the documentation file
`<param>`	Describes a given parameter
`<paramref>`	Associates a given XML tag with a specific parameter
`<permission>`	Documents the security constraints for a given member
`<remarks>`	Builds a description for a given member
`<returns>`	Documents the return value of the member
`<see>`	Cross-references related items in the document
`<seealso>`	Builds an "also see" section within a description
`<summary>`	Documents the "executive summary" for a given member
`<value>`	Documents a given property

If you are making use of the new C# XML code comment notation, do be aware the Visual Studio 2008 IDE will generate documentation skeletons on your behalf. For example, if you add a triple slash above the definition of your `Employee` class, you end up with the following skeleton:

```
/// <summary>
///
/// </summary>
partial class Employee
{
 ...
}
```

Simply fill in the blanks with your custom content:

```
/// <summary>
///  This class represents an Employee.
/// </summary>
partial class Employee
{
 ...
}
```

By way of another example, insert a triple slash code comment to your custom five-argument constructor. This time the comment builder utility has been kind enough to add <param> elements:

```
/// <summary>
///
/// </summary>
/// <param name="name"></param>
/// <param name="age"></param>
/// <param name="id"></param>
/// <param name="pay"></param>
/// <param name="ssn"></param>
public Employee(string name, int age, int id, float pay, string ssn)
{
    empName = name;
    empID = id;
    empAge = age;
    currPay = pay;
    empSSN = ssn;
}
```

Also be aware that these XML code comments can be entered using the Class Details window (see Chapter 2) of Visual Studio 2008, as shown in Figure 5-11.

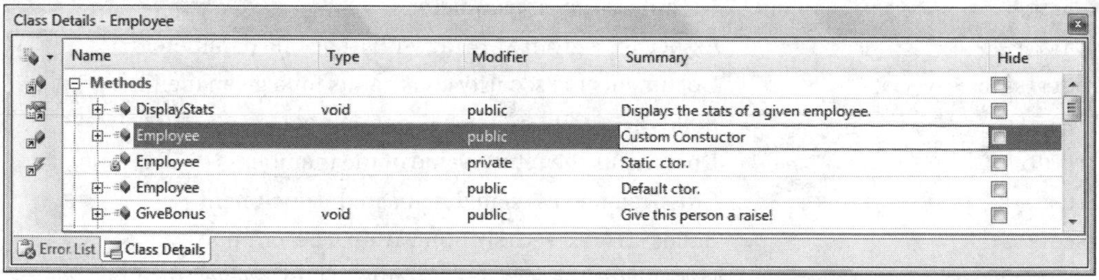

Figure 5-11. *Entering XML comments using the Class Details window*

One benefit of annotating your code with XML comments is that you are able to view this information from within Visual Studio's IntelliSense (see Figure 5-12). As you would guess, this can be helpful to other members on your team who might not know the role of a given type member.

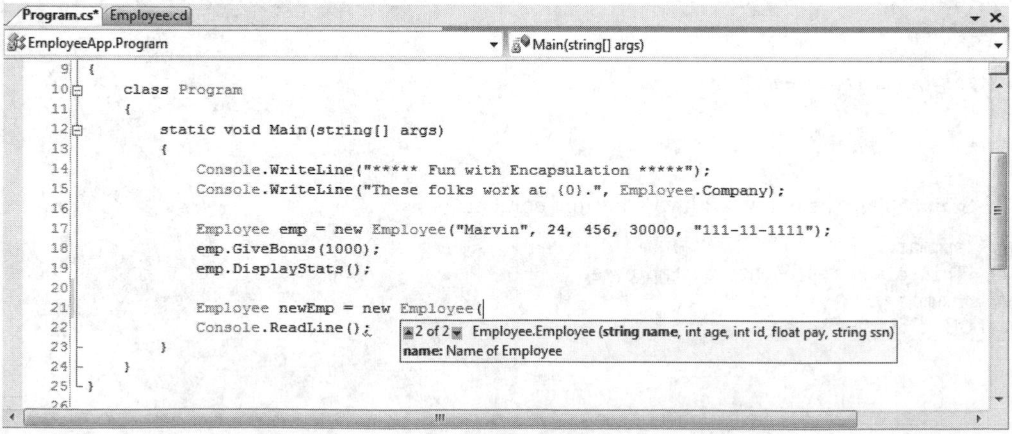

Figure 5-12. *XML comments are viewable via IntelliSense.*

Generating the XML File

In any case, once you have documented your code with XML comments, the next step is to generate a corresponding *.xml file based on the XML data. If you are building your C# programs using the command-line compiler (csc.exe), the /doc flag is used to generate a specified *.xml file based on your XML code comments:

```
csc /doc:XmlCarDoc.xml *.cs
```

Visual Studio 2008 projects allow you to specify the name of an XML documentation file using the Generate XML documentation file check box option found on the Build tab of the Properties window (see Figure 5-13).

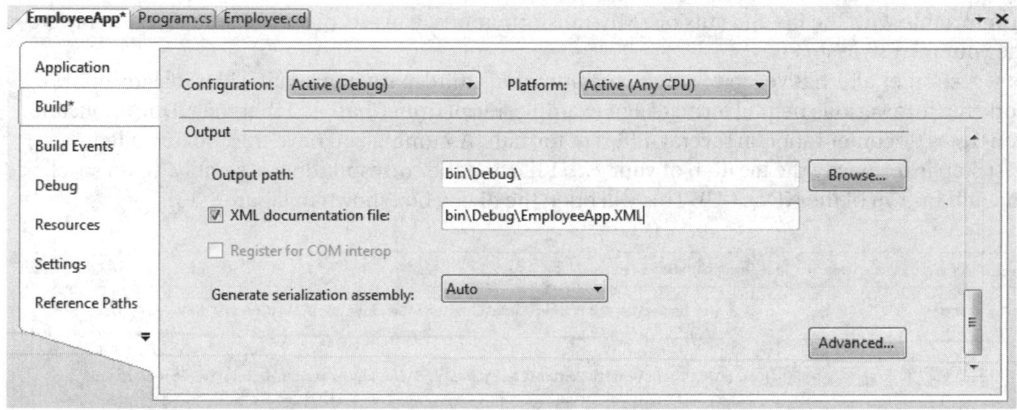

Figure 5-13. *Generating an XML code comment file via Visual Studio 2008*

Once you have enabled this behavior, the compiler will place the generated *.xml file within your project's \bin\Debug folder. You can verify this for yourself by clicking the Show All Files button on the Solution Explorer, generating the result in Figure 5-14.

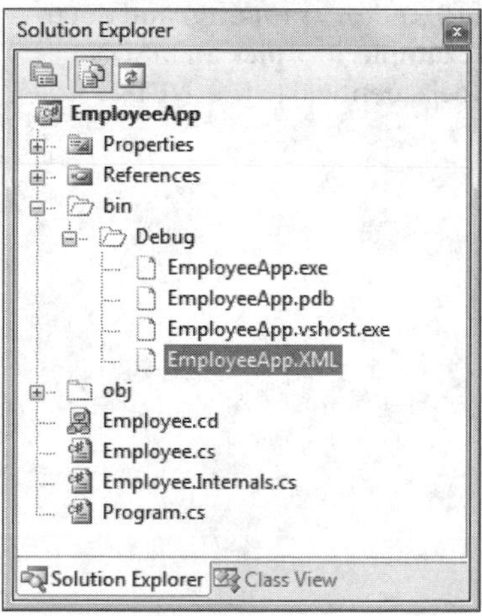

Figure 5-14. *Locating the generated XML documentation file*

■ **Note** There are many other elements and notations that may appear in C# XML code comments. If you are interested in more details, look up the topic "XML Documentation Comments (C# Programming Guide)" within the .NET Framework SDK 3.5 documentation.

Transforming XML Code Comments via NDoc

Now that you have generated an `*.xml` file that contains your source code comments, you may be wondering exactly what to do with it. Sadly, Visual Studio 2008 does not provide a built-in utility that transforms XML data into a more user-friendly help format (such as an HTML page). If you are comfortable with the ins and outs of XML transformations, you are, of course, free to manually create your own style sheets.

A simpler alternative, however, are the numerous third-party tools that will translate an XML code file into various helpful formats. For example, recall from Chapter 2 that the NDoc application generates documentation in several different formats. Assuming you have this tool installed, the first step is to specify the location of your `*.xml` file and the corresponding assembly. To do so, click the Add button of the NDoc GUI. This will open the dialog box shown in Figure 5-15.

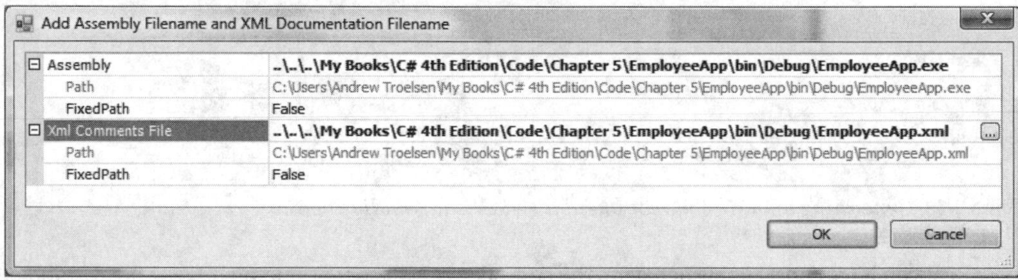

Figure 5-15. *Specifying the XML file and corresponding assembly*

At this point, you can select for output location (via the `OutputDirectory` property) and document type (via the Documentation Type drop-down list). For this example, let's pick an MSDN-CHM format, which will generate documentation that looks and feels identical to the .NET Framework 3.5 documentation (see Figure 5-16).

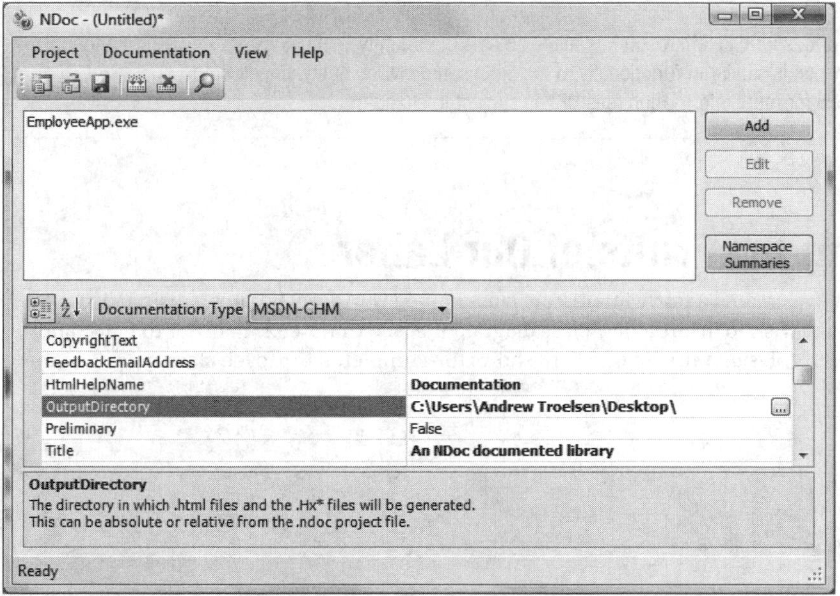

Figure 5-16. *Specifying the output directory and documentation format*

Obviously, we could establish other settings using the NDoc GUI, however once you select the Documentation ➤ Build menu option, NDoc will generate a full help system for your application. Figure 5-17 shows the end result.

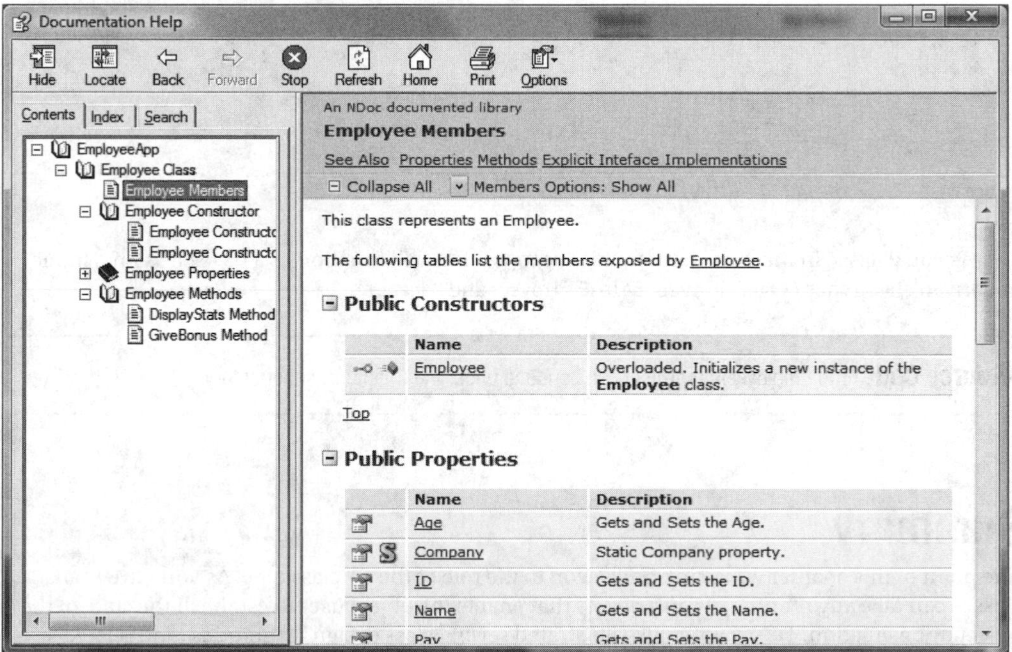

Figure 5-17. *Our MSDN-style help system for the EmployeeApp project*

■ **Note** At the time of this writing, Microsoft has released as a Community Technology Preview (CTP) a tool named Sandcastle, which is similar in functionally to the open source NDoc utility. Check out `http://www.sandcastledocs.com` for more information (this URL is subject to change).

Visualizing the Fruits of Our Labor

At this point, you have created a fairly interesting class named `Employee`. If you are using Visual Studio 2008, you may wish to insert a new class diagram file (see Chapter 2) in order to view (and maintain) your class at design time. Figure 5-18 shows the completed `Employee` class type.

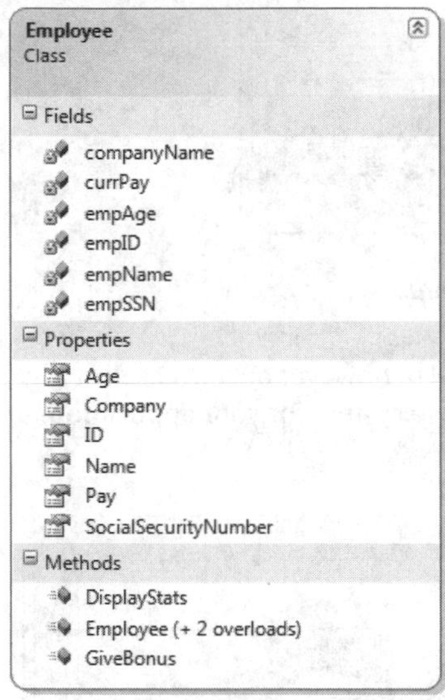

Figure 5-18. *The completed* `Employee` *class*

As you will see in the next chapter, this `Employee` class will function as a base class for a family of derived class types (`WageEmployee`, `SalesEmployee`, and `Manager`).

■ **Source Code** The EmployeeApp project can be found under the Chapter 5 subdirectory.

Summary

The point of this chapter was to introduce you to the role of the C# class type. As you have seen, classes can take any number of *constructors* that enable the object user to establish the state of the object upon creation. This chapter also illustrated several class design techniques (and related keywords). Recall that the `this` keyword can be used to obtain access to the current object, the `static` keyword allows you to define fields and members that are bound at the class (not object) level, and the `const` keyword (and `readonly` modifier) allows you to define a point of data that can never change after the initial assignment.

The bulk of this chapter dug into the details of the first pillar of OOP: encapsulation. Here you learned about the access modifiers of C# and the role of type properties, partial classes, and XML code documentation. With this behind us, we are now able to turn to the next chapter where you will learn to build a family of related classes using inheritance and polymorphism.

Tabular Data Stream (Protocol) that
talks between SQL Serv + App'n

CHAPTER 6

Understanding Inheritance and Polymorphism

The previous chapter examined the first pillar of OOP: encapsulation. At that time you learned how to build a single well-defined class type with constructors and various members (fields, properties, constants, read-only fields, etc.). This chapter will focus on the remaining two pillars of OOP: inheritance and polymorphism.

First, you will learn how to build families of related classes using *inheritance*. As you will see, this form of code reuse allows you to define common functionality in a parent class that can be leveraged (and possibly altered) by child classes. Along the way, you will learn how to establish a *polymorphic interface* into the class hierarchies using virtual and abstract members. We wrap up by examining the role of the ultimate parent class in the .NET base class libraries: `System.Object`.

The Basic Mechanics of Inheritance

Recall from the previous chapter that *inheritance* is the aspect of OOP that facilitates code reuse. Specifically speaking, code reuse comes in two flavors: classical inheritance (the "is-a" relationship) and the containment/delegation model (the "has-a" relationship). Let's begin this chapter by examining the classical "is-a" inheritance model.

When you establish "is-a" relationships between classes, you are building a dependency between two or more class types. The basic idea behind classical inheritance is that new classes may leverage (and possibly extend) the functionality of existing classes. To begin with a very simple example, create a new Console Application project named BasicInheritance. Now assume you have designed a simple class named `Car` that models some basic details of an automobile:

```
// A simple base class.
class Car
{
  public readonly int maxSpeed;
  private int currSpeed;

  public Car(int max)
  {
    maxSpeed = max;
  }
  public Car()
  {
    maxSpeed = 55;
  }
```

```
  public int Speed
  {
    get { return currSpeed; }
    set
    {
      currSpeed += value;
      if (currSpeed > maxSpeed)
      {
        currSpeed = maxSpeed;
      }
    }
  }
}
```

Notice that the Car class is making use of encapsulation services to control access to the private currSpeed field using a public property named Speed. At this point you can exercise your Car type as follows:

```
static void Main(string[] args)
{
  Console.WriteLine("***** Basic Inheritance *****\n");
  // Make a Car type.
  Car myCar = new Car(80);
  myCar.Speed = 50;
  Console.WriteLine("My car is going {0} MPH", myCar.Speed);
  Console.ReadLine();
}
```

Specifying a Class Type's Parent Class

Now assume you wish to build a new class named MiniVan. Like a basic Car, you wish to define the MiniVan class to support a maximum speed, current speed, and a property named Speed to allow the object user to modify the object's state. Clearly, the Car and MiniVan classes are related; in fact we can say that a MiniVan "*is-a*" Car. The "is-a" relationship (formally termed *classical inheritance*) allows you to build new class definitions that extend the functionality of an existing class.

The existing class that will serve as the basis for the new class is termed a *base* or *parent* class. The role of a base class is to define all the common data and members for the classes that extend it. The extending classes are formally termed *derived* or *child* classes. In C#, we make use of the colon operator on the class definition to establish an "is-a" relationship between classes:

```
// MiniVan 'is-a' Car.
class MiniVan : Car
{
}
```

So, what have we gained by extending our MiniVan from the Car base class? Simply put, MiniVan objects now have access to each public member defined within the parent class. Given the relation between these two class types, we could now make use of the MiniVan type like so:

```
static void Main(string[] args)
{
  Console.WriteLine("***** Basic Inheritance *****\n");
...
  // Make a MiniVan type.
  MiniVan myVan = new MiniVan();
  myVan.Speed = 10;
  Console.WriteLine("My van is going {0} MPH",
```

```
    myVan.Speed);
  Console.ReadLine();
}
```

Notice that although we have not added any members to the MiniVan class, we have direct access to the public Speed property of our parent class, and have thus reused code. Recall, however, that encapsulation is preserved; therefore the following code results in a compiler error:

```
static void Main(string[] args)
{
  Console.WriteLine("***** Basic Inheritance *****\n");
...
  // Make a MiniVan type.
  MiniVan myVan = new MiniVan();
  myVan.Speed = 10;
  Console.WriteLine("My van is going {0} MPH",
    myVan.Speed);

  // Error! Can't access private members using an object reference!
  myVan.currSpeed = 55;
  Console.ReadLine();
}
```

On a related note, if the MiniVan defined its own set of members, it would not be able to access any private member of the Car base class:

```
// MiniVan derives from Car.
class MiniVan : Car
{
  public void TestMethod()
  {
    // OK! Can access public members
    // of a parent within a derived type.
    Speed = 10;

    // Error! Cannot access private
    // members of parent within a derived type.
    currSpeed = 10;
  }
}
```

Regarding Multiple Base Classes

Speaking of base classes, it is important to keep in mind that the .NET platform demands that a given class have exactly *one* direct base class. It is not possible to create a class type that directly derives from two or more base classes (this technique [which is supported in other C-based languages, such as unmanaged C++] is known as *multiple inheritance*, or simply *MI*):

```
// Illegal! The .NET platform does not allow
// multiple inheritance for classes!
class WontWork
  : BaseClassOne, BaseClassTwo
{}
```

As you will see in Chapter 9, the .NET platform does allow a given class (or structure) type to implement any number of discrete interfaces. In this way, a C# type can exhibit a number of behaviors while avoiding the complexities associated with MI. On a related note, while a class can have only one direct base class, it is permissible for an interface to directly derive from multiple interfaces. Using this technique, you can build sophisticated interface hierarchies that model complex behaviors (again, see Chapter 9).

The sealed Keyword

C# supplies another keyword, `sealed`, that *prevents* inheritance from occurring. When you mark a class as `sealed`, the compiler will not allow you to derive from this type. For example, assume you have decided that it makes no sense to further extend the `MiniVan` class:

```
// This class cannot be extended!
sealed class MiniVan : Car
{
}
```

If you (or a teammate) were to attempt to derive from this class, you would receive a compile-time error:

```
// Error! Cannot extend
// a class marked with the sealed keyword!
class DeluxeMiniVan
  : MiniVan
{}
```

Most often, sealing a class makes the best sense when you are designing a utility class. For example, the `System` namespace defines numerous sealed classes. You can verify this for yourself by opening up the Visual Studio 2008 Object Browser (via the View menu) and selecting the `System.String` type defined within the `mscorlib.dll` assembly. Notice in Figure 6-1 the use of the `sealed` keyword highlighted in the Summary window.

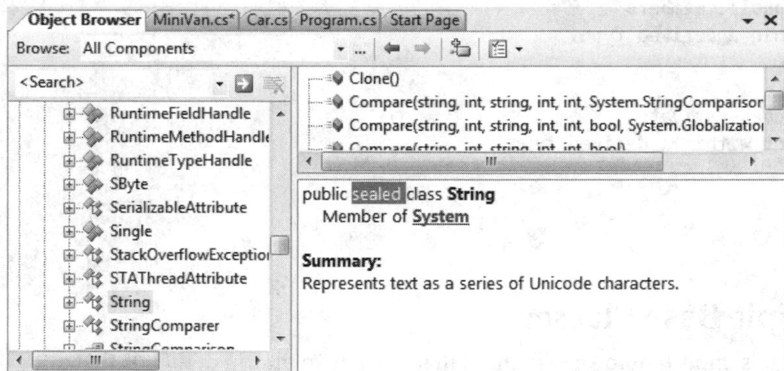

Figure 6-1. *The base class libraries define numerous sealed types.*

Thus, just like the `MiniVan`, if you attempted to build a new class that extends `System.String`, you will receive a compile-time error:

```
// Another error! Cannot extend
// a class marked as sealed!
class MyString
  : String
{}
```

■ Note In Chapter 4 you learned that C# structures are always implicitly sealed (see Table 4-3). Therefore, you can never derive one structure from another structure, a class from a structure or a structure from a class.

As you would guess, there are many more details to inheritance that you will come to know during the remainder of this chapter. For now, simply keep in mind that the colon operator allows you to establish base/derived class relationships, while the `sealed` keyword prevents inheritance from occurring.

■ Note C# 2008 introduces the concept of *extension methods*. As you will see in Chapter 13, this technique makes it possible to add new functionality to precompiled types (including sealed types) within your current project.

Revising Visual Studio Class Diagrams

Back in Chapter 2, I briefly mentioned that Visual Studio 2008 allows you to establish base/derived class relationships visually at design time. To leverage this aspect of the IDE, your first step is to include a new class diagram file into your current project. To do so, access the Project ➤ Add New Item menu option and select the Class Diagram icon (in Figure 6-2, I renamed the file from `ClassDiagram1.cd` to `Cars.cd`).

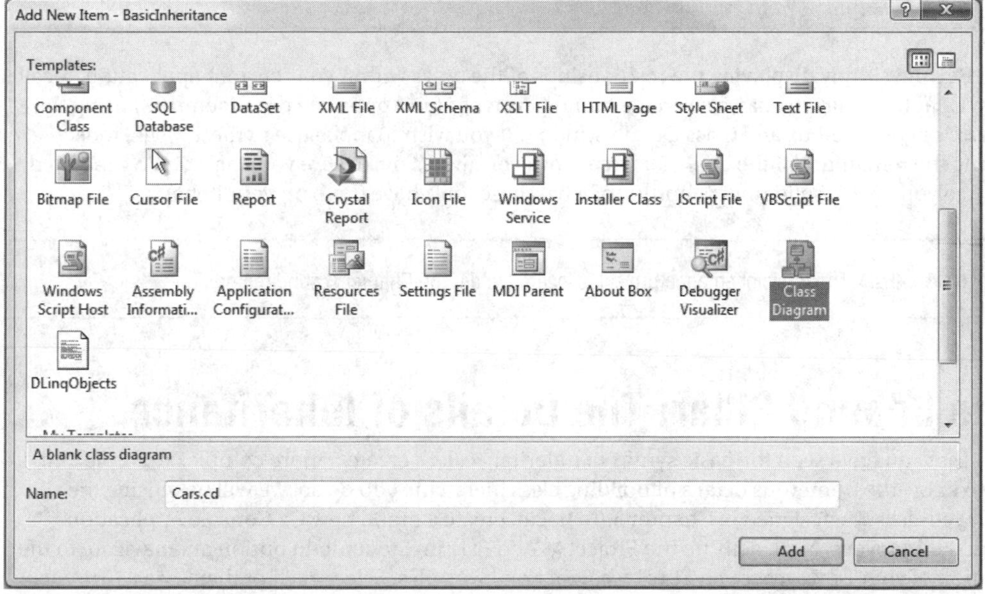

Figure 6-2. *Inserting a new class diagram*

Once you click the Add button, you will be presented with a blank designer surface. To add types to a class designer, simply drag each file from the Solution Explorer window onto the surface. When you do so, the IDE responds by automatically including all types on the designer surface.

Realize that if you delete an item from the visual designer, this will not delete the associated source code, but simply take it off the designer surface. Our current class hierarchy is shown in Figure 6-3.

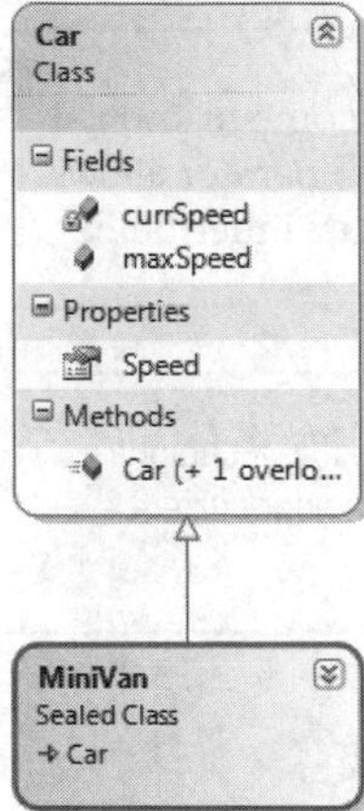

Figure 6-3. *The visual designer of Visual Studio*

■ Note As a shortcut, if you wish to automatically add all of your project's types to a designer surface, select the Project node within the Solution Explorer and click the View Class Diagram button in the upper right of the Solution Explorer window.

Beyond simply displaying the relationships of the types within your current application, recall from Chapter 2 that you can also create brand new types (and populate their members) using the Class Designer toolbox and Class Details window. If you wish to make use of these visual tools during the remainder of the book, feel free. However, always make sure you analyze the generated code so you have a solid understanding of what these tools have done on your behalf.

■ Source Code The BasicInheritance project is located under the Chapter 6 subdirectory.

The Second Pillar: The Details of Inheritance

Now that you have seen the basic syntax of inheritance, let's create a more complex example and get to know the numerous details of building class hierarchies. To do so, we will be reusing the `Employee` class we designed in Chapter 5. To begin, create a brand new C# Console Application named Employees. Next, activate the Project ➤ Add Existing Item menu option and navigate to the location of your `Employee.cs` and `Employee.Internals.cs` files. Select each of them (via a Ctrl-click) and click the OK button. Visual Studio 2008 responds by copying each file into the current project.

Before we start to build derived classes, you have one detail to attend to. Because the `Employee` class was created in a project named EmployeeApp, the type has been wrapped within an identically named .NET namespace scope. Chapter 15 will examine namespaces in detail; however for simplicity, rename the current namespace (in both file locations) to `Employee` in order to match your new project name:

```
// Be sure to change the namespace name in both files!
namespace Employees
{
  /// <summary>
  /// This class represents an Employee.
  /// </summary>
  partial class Employee
  {...}
}
```

Our goal is to create a family of classes that model various types of employees in a company. Assume that you wish to leverage the functionality of the `Employee` class to create two new classes (`SalesPerson` and `Manager`). The class hierarchy we will be building initially looks something like what you see in Figure 6-4.

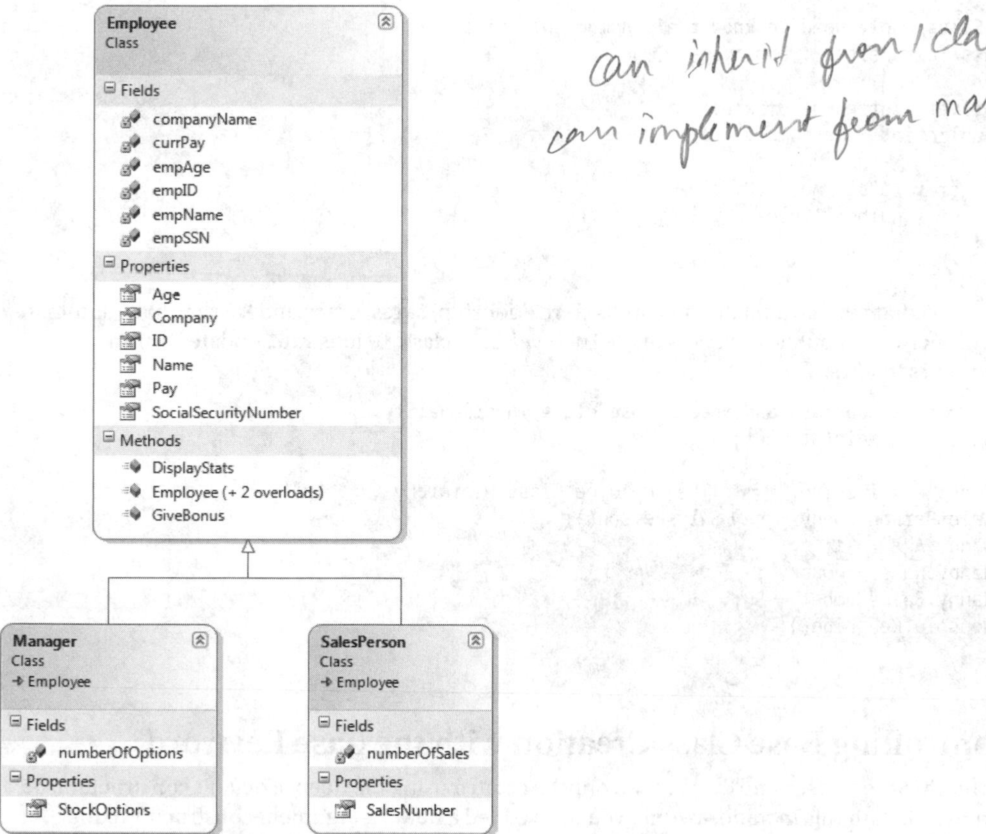

Figure 6-4. *The initial Employees hierarchy*

As illustrated in Figure 6-4, you can see that a `SalesPerson` "is-a" `Employee` (as is a `Manager`). Remember that under the classical inheritance model, base classes (such as `Employee`) are used to define general characteristics that are common to all descendents. Subclasses (such as `SalesPerson` and `Manager`) extend this general functionality while adding more specific behaviors.

For our example, we will assume that the Manager class extends Employee by recording the number of stock options, while the SalesPerson class maintains the number of sales made. Insert a new class file (Manager.cs) that defines the Manager type as follows:

```
// Managers need to know their number of stock options.
class Manager : Employee
{
  private int numberOfOptions;
  public int StockOptions
  {
    get { return numberOfOptions; }
    set { numberOfOptions = value; }
  }
}
```

Next, add another new class file (SalesPerson.cs) that defines the SalesPerson type:

```
// Salespeople need to know their number of sales.
class SalesPerson : Employee
{
  private int numberOfSales;
  public int SalesNumber
  {
    get { return numberOfSales; }
    set { numberOfSales = value; }
  }
}
```

Now that you have established an "is-a" relationship, SalesPerson and Manager have automatically inherited all public members of the Employee base class. To illustrate, update your Main() method as follows:

```
// Create a subclass and access base class functionality.
static void Main(string[] args)
{
  Console.WriteLine("***** The Employee Class Hierarchy *****\n");
  SalesPerson danny = new SalesPerson();
  danny.Age = 31;
  danny.Name = "Danny";
  danny.SalesNumber = 50;
  Console.ReadLine();
}
```

Controlling Base Class Creation with the base Keyword

Currently, SalesPerson and Manager can only be created using the freebee default constructor (see Chapter 5). With this in mind, assume you have added a new six-argument constructor to the Manager type, which is invoked as follows:

```
static void Main(string[] args)
{
...
  // Assume Manager has a constructor matching this signature:
  // (string fullName, int age, int empID,
  //  float currPay, string ssn, int numbOfOpts)
  Manager chucky = new Manager("Chucky", 50, 92, 100000, "333-23-2322", 9000);
  Console.ReadLine();
}
```

If you look at the argument list, you can clearly see that most of these parameters should be stored in the member variables defined by the Employee base class. To do so, you might implement this custom constructor on the Manager class as follows:

```
public Manager(string fullName, int age, int empID,
  float currPay, string ssn, int numbOfOpts)
{
  // This field is defined by the Manager class.
  numberOfOptions = numbOfOpts;

  // Assign incoming parameters using the
  // inherited properties of the parent class.
  ID = empID;
  Age = age;
  Name = fullName;
  Pay = currPay;

  // OOPS! This would be a compiler error,
  // as the SSN property is read-only!
  SocialSecurityNumber = ssn;
}
```

The first issue with this approach is that we defined the SocialSecurityNumber property in the parent as read-only; therefore we are unable to assign the incoming string parameter to this field, as seen in the final code statement of this custom constructor.

The second issue is that we have indirectly created a rather inefficient constructor, given the fact that under C#, unless you say otherwise, the default constructor of a base class is called automatically before the logic of the derived constructor is executed. After this point, the current implementation accesses numerous public properties of the Employee base class to establish its state. Thus, you have really made seven hits (five inherited properties and two constructor calls) during the creation of a Manager object!

To help optimize the creation of a derived class, you will do well to implement your subclass constructors to explicitly call an appropriate custom base class constructor, rather than the default. In this way, you are able to reduce the number of calls to inherited initialization members (which saves processing time). Let's retrofit the custom constructor of the Manager type to do this very thing using the base keyword:

```
public Manager(string fullName, int age, int empID,
  float currPay, string ssn, int numbOfOpts)
  : base(fullName, age, empID, currPay, ssn)
{
  // This field is defined by the Manager class.
  numberOfOptions = numbOfOpts;
}
```

Here, the base keyword is hanging off the constructor signature (much like the syntax used to chain constructors on a single class using the this keyword; see Chapter 5), which always indicates a derived constructor is passing data to the immediate parent constructor. In this situation, you are explicitly calling the five-argument constructor defined by Employee and saving yourself unnecessary calls during the creation of the child class. The custom SalesPerson constructor looks almost identical:

```
// As a general rule, all subclasses should explicitly call an appropriate
// base class constructor.
public SalesPerson(string fullName, int age, int empID,
  float currPay, string ssn, int numbOfSales)
  : base(fullName, age, empID, currPay, ssn)
```

```
{
  // This belongs with us!
  numberOfSales = numbOfSales;
}
```

Also be aware that you may use the base keyword anytime a subclass wishes to access a public or protected member defined by a parent class. Use of this keyword is not limited to constructor logic. You will see examples using base in this manner during our examination of polymorphism later in this chapter.

Finally, recall that once you add a custom constructor to a class definition, the default constructor is silently removed. Therefore, be sure to redefine the default constructor for the SalesPerson and Manager types, for example:

```
// Add back the default ctor
// in the Manager class as well.
public SalesPerson() {}
```

Keeping Family Secrets: The protected Keyword

As you already know, public items are directly accessible from anywhere, while private items cannot be accessed from any object beyond the class that has defined it. Recall from Chapter 5 that C# takes the lead of many other modern object languages and provides an additional keyword to define member accessibility: protected.

When a base class defines protected data or protected members, it establishes a set of items that can be accessed directly by any descendent. If you wish to allow the SalesPerson and Manager child classes to directly access the data sector defined by Employee, you can update the original Employee class definition as follows:

```
// protected state data.
partial class Employee
{
  // Derived classes can now directly access this information.
  protected string empName;
  protected int empID;
  protected float currPay;
  protected int empAge;
  protected string empSSN;
  protected static string companyName;
...
}
```

The benefit of defining protected members in a base class is that derived types no longer have to access the data indirectly using public methods or properties. The possible downfall, of course, is that when a derived type has direct access to its parent's internal data, it is very possible to accidentally bypass existing business rules found within public properties. When you define protected members, you are creating a level of trust between the parent and child class, as the compiler will not catch any violation of your type's business rules.

Finally, understand that as far as the object user is concerned, protected data is regarded as private (as the user is "outside" of the family). Therefore, the following is illegal:

```
static void Main(string[] args)
{
  // Error! Can't access protected data from object instance.
  Employee emp = new Employee();
  emp.empName = "Fred";
}
```

■Note Although `protected` field data can break encapsulation, it is quite safe (and useful) to define `protected` methods. When building class hierarchies, it is very common to define a set of methods that are only for use by derived types.

Adding a Sealed Class

Recall that a *sealed* class cannot be extended by other classes. As mentioned, this technique is most often used when you are designing a utility class. However, when building class hierarchies, you might find that a certain branch in the inheritance chain should be "capped off," as it makes no sense to further extend the linage. For example, assume you have added yet another class to your program (PTSalesPerson) that extends the existing SalesPerson type. Figure 6-5 shows the current update.

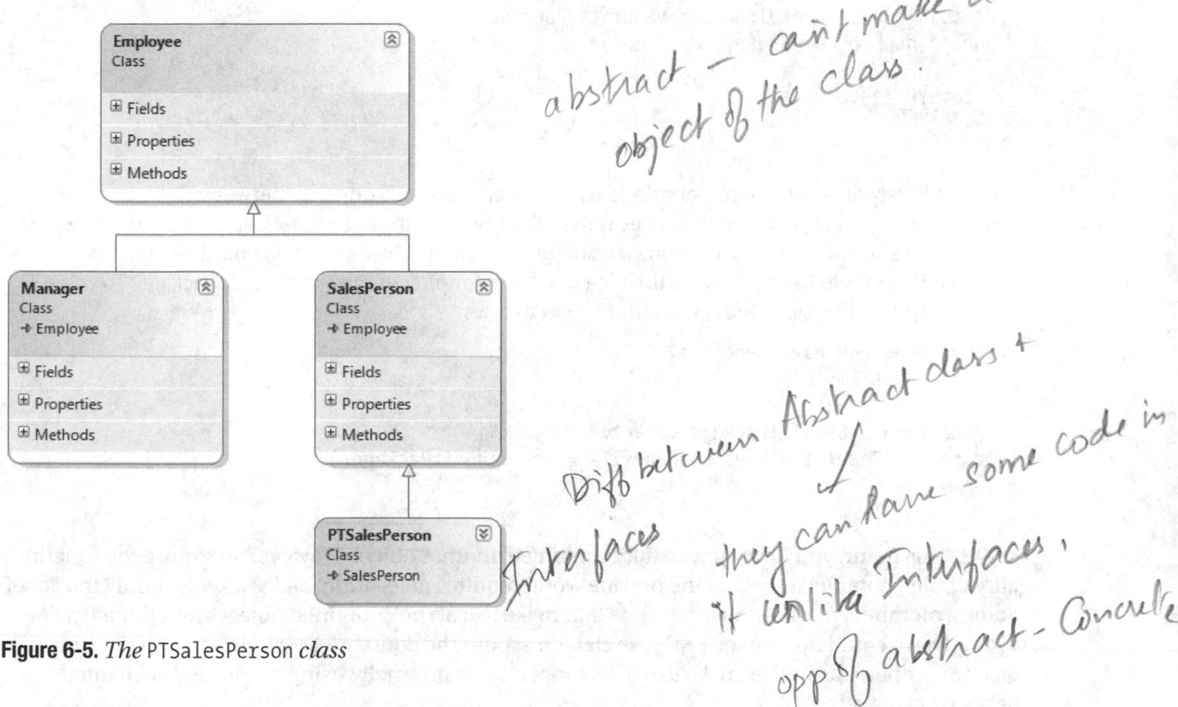

Figure 6-5. *The* PTSalesPerson *class*

PTSalesPerson is a class representing (of course) a part-time salesperson. For the sake of argument, let's say that you wish to ensure that no other developer is able to subclass from PTSalesPerson. (After all, how much more part-time can you get than "part-time"?) Again, to prevent others from extending a class, make use of the sealed keyword:

```
sealed class PTSalesPerson : SalesPerson
{
  public PTSalesPerson(string fullName, int age, int empID,
    float currPay, string ssn, int numbOfSales)
    :base (fullName, age, empID, currPay, ssn, numbOfSales)
  {
  }
    // Assume other members here...
}
```

Given that sealed classes cannot be extended, you may wonder if it is possible to reuse the code within a class marked sealed. If you wish to build a new class that leverages the functionality of a sealed class, your only option is to forego classical inheritance and make use of the containment/delegation model (aka the "has-a" relationship).

Programming for Containment/Delegation

As noted a bit earlier in this chapter, code reuse comes in two flavors. We have just explored the classical "is-a" relationship. Before we examine the third pillar of OOP (polymorphism), let's examine the "has-a" relationship (also known as the *containment/delegation model* or *aggregation*). Assume you have created a new class that models an employee benefits package:

```
// This type will function as a contained class.
class BenefitPackage
{
  // Assume we have other members that represent
  // 401K plans, dental/health benefits, and so on.
  public double ComputePayDeduction()
  {
    return 125.0;
  }
}
```

Obviously, it would be rather odd to establish an "is-a" relationship between the BenefitPackage class and the employee types. (Employee "is-a" BenefitPackage? I don't think so.) However, it should be clear that some sort of relationship between the two could be established. In short, you would like to express the idea that each employee "has-a" BenefitPackage. To do so, you can update the Employee class definition as follows:

```
// Employees now have benefits.
partial class Employee
{
  // Contain a BenefitPackage object.
  protected BenefitPackage empBenefits = new BenefitPackage();
...
}
```

At this point, you have successfully contained another object. However, to expose the functionality of the contained object to the outside world requires delegation. *Delegation* is simply the act of adding members to the containing class that make use of the contained object's functionality. For example, we could update the Employee class to expose the contained empBenefits object using a custom property as well as make use of its functionality internally using a new method named GetBenefitCost():

```
public partial class Employee
{
  // Contain a BenefitPackage object.
  protected BenefitPackage empBenefits = new BenefitPackage();

  // Expose certain benefit behaviors of object.
  public double GetBenefitCost()
  { return empBenefits.ComputePayDeduction(); }

  // Expose object through a custom property.
  public BenefitPackage Benefits
  {
```

```
    get { return empBenefits; }
    set { empBenefits = value; }
  }
...
}
```

In the following updated Main() method, notice how we can interact with the internal BenefitsPackage type defined by the Employee type:

```
static void Main(string[] args)
{
  Console.WriteLine("***** The Employee Class Hierarchy *****\n");
  Manager chucky = new Manager("Chucky", 50, 92, 100000, "333-23-2322", 9000);
  double cost = chucky.GetBenefitCost();
  Console.ReadLine();
}
```

Understanding Nested Type Definitions

The previous chapter briefly mentioned the concept of nested types, which is a spin on the "has-a" relationship we have just examined. In C# (as well as other .NET languages), it is possible to define a type (enum, class, interface, struct, or delegate) directly within the scope of a class or structure. When you have done so, the nested (or "inner") type is considered a member of the nesting (or "outer") class, and in the eyes of the runtime can be manipulated like any other member (fields, properties, methods, events, etc.). The syntax used to nest a type is quite straightforward:

```
public class OuterClass
{
  // A public nested type can be used by anybody.
  public class PublicInnerClass {}

  // A private nested type can only be used by members
  // of the containing class.
  private class PrivateInnerClass {}
}
```

Although the syntax is clean, understanding why you might do this is not readily apparent. To understand this technique, ponder the following traits of nesting a type:

- Nested types allow you to gain complete control over the access level of the inner type, as they may be declared privately (recall that nonnested classes cannot be declared using the private keyword).
- Because a nested type is a member of the containing class, it can access private members of the containing class.
- Oftentimes, a nested type is only useful as a helper for the outer class, and is not intended for use by the outside world.

When a type nests another class type, it can create member variables of the type, just as it would for any point of data. However, if you wish to make use of a nested type from outside of the containing type, you must qualify it by the scope of the nesting type. Consider the following code:

```
static void Main(string[] args)
{
  // Create and use the public inner class. OK!
  OuterClass.PublicInnerClass inner;
  inner = new OuterClass.PublicInnerClass();
```

```
  // Compiler Error! Cannot access the private class.
  OuterClass.PrivateInnerClass inner2;
  inner2 = new OuterClass.PrivateInnerClass();
}
```

To make use of this concept within our employees example, assume we have now nested the BenefitPackage directly within the Employee class type:

```
partial class Employee
{
  public class BenefitPackage
  {
    // Assume we have other members that represent
    // 401K plans, dental/health benefits, and so on.
    public double ComputePayDeduction()
    {
      return 125.0;
    }
  }
...
}
```

The nesting process can be as "deep" as you require. For example, assume we wish to create an enumeration named BenefitPackageLevel, which documents the various benefit levels an employee may choose. To programmatically enforce the tight connection between Employee, BenefitPackage, and BenefitPackageLevel, we could nest the enumeration as follows:

```
// Employee nests BenefitPackage.
public partial class Employee
{
  // BenefitPackage nests BenefitPackageLevel.
  public class BenefitPackage
  {
    public enum BenefitPackageLevel
    {
      Standard, Gold, Platinum
    }
    public double ComputePayDeduction()
    {
      return 125.0;
    }
  }
...
}
```

Because of the nesting relationships, note how we are required to make use of this enumeration:

```
static void Main(string[] args)
{
...
  // Define my benefit level.
  Employee.BenefitPackage.BenefitPackageLevel myBenefitLevel =
    Employee.BenefitPackage.BenefitPackageLevel.Platinum;
  Console.ReadLine()
}
```

Excellent! At this point you have been exposed to a number of keywords (and concepts) that allow you to build hierarchies of related types via classical inheritance, containment, and nested types. If the details aren't crystal clear at this point, don't sweat it. You will be building a number of additional hierarchies over the remainder of this text. Next up, let's examine the final pillar of OOP: polymorphism.

The Third Pillar: C#'s Polymorphic Support

Recall that the Employee base class defined a method named GiveBonus(), which was originally implemented as follows:

```
public partial class Employee
{
  public void GiveBonus(float amount)
  {
    currPay += amount;
  }
...
}
```

Because this method has been defined with the public keyword, you can now give bonuses to salespeople and managers (as well as part-time salespeople):

```
static void Main(string[] args)
{
  Console.WriteLine("***** The Employee Class Hierarchy *****\n");

  // Give each employee a bonus?
  Manager chucky = new Manager("Chucky", 50, 92, 100000, "333-23-2322", 9000);
  chucky.GiveBonus(300);
  chucky.DisplayStats();
  Console.WriteLine();

  SalesPerson fran = new SalesPerson("Fran", 43, 93, 3000, "932-32-3232", 31);
  fran.GiveBonus(200);
  fran.DisplayStats();
  Console.ReadLine();
}
```

The problem with the current design is that the publicly inherited GiveBonus() method operates identically for all subclasses. Ideally, the bonus of a salesperson or part-time salesperson should take into account the number of sales. Perhaps managers should gain additional stock options in conjunction with a monetary bump in salary. Given this, you are suddenly faced with an interesting question: "How can related types respond differently to the same request?" Glad you asked!

The virtual and override Keywords

Polymorphism provides a way for a subclass to define its own version of a method defined by its base class, using the process termed *method overriding*. To retrofit your current design, you need to understand the meaning of the virtual and override keywords. If a base class wishes to define a method that *may be* (but does not have to be) overridden by a subclass, it must mark the method with the virtual keyword:

```
partial class Employee
{
  // This method can now be 'overridden' by a derived class.
  public virtual void GiveBonus(float amount)
```

```
  {
    currPay += amount;
  }
...
}
```

■ **Note** Methods that have been marked with the `virtual` keyword are (not surprisingly) termed *virtual methods*.

When a subclass wishes to change the implementation details of a virtual method, it does so using the `override` keyword. For example, the `SalesPerson` and `Manager` could override `GiveBonus()` as follows (assume that `PTSalesPerson` will not override `GiveBonus()` and therefore simply inherit the version defined by `SalesPerson`):

```
class SalesPerson : Employee
{
...
  // A salesperson's bonus is influenced by the number of sales.
  public override void GiveBonus(float amount)
  {
    int salesBonus = 0;
    if (numberOfSales >= 0 && numberOfSales <= 100)
    { salesBonus = 10; }
    else
    {
      if (numberOfSales >= 101 && numberOfSales <= 200)
      {
        salesBonus = 15;
      }
      else
      { salesBonus = 20; }
    }
    base.GiveBonus(amount * salesBonus);
  }
}

class Manager : Employee
{
...
  public override void GiveBonus(float amount)
  {
    base.GiveBonus(amount);
    Random r = new Random();
    numberOfOptions += r.Next(500);
  }
}
```

Notice how each overridden method is free to leverage the default behavior using the `base` keyword. In this way, you have no need to completely reimplement the logic behind `GiveBonus()`, but can reuse (and possibly extend) the default behavior of the parent class.

Also assume that the current `DisplayStats()` method of the `Employee` class has been declared virtually. By doing so, each subclass can override this method to account for displaying the number of sales (for salespeople) and current stock options (for managers). For example, consider the `Manager`'s version of the `DisplayStats()` method (the `SalesPerson` class would implement `DisplayStats()` in a similar manner):

```
public override void DisplayStats()
{
  base.DisplayStats();
  Console.WriteLine("Number of Stock Options: {0}", numberOfOptions);
}
```

Now that each subclass can interpret what these virtual methods means to itself, each object instance behaves as a more independent entity:

```
static void Main(string[] args)
{
  Console.WriteLine("***** The Employee Class Hierarchy *****\n");

  // A better bonus system!
  Manager chucky = new Manager("Chucky", 50, 92, 100000, "333-23-2322", 9000);
  chucky.GiveBonus(300);
  chucky.DisplayStats();
  Console.WriteLine();

  SalesPerson fran = new SalesPerson("Fran", 43, 93, 3000, "932-32-3232", 31);
  fran.GiveBonus(200);
  fran.DisplayStats();
  Console.ReadLine();
}
```

Figure 6-6 shows a possible test run of our application thus far.

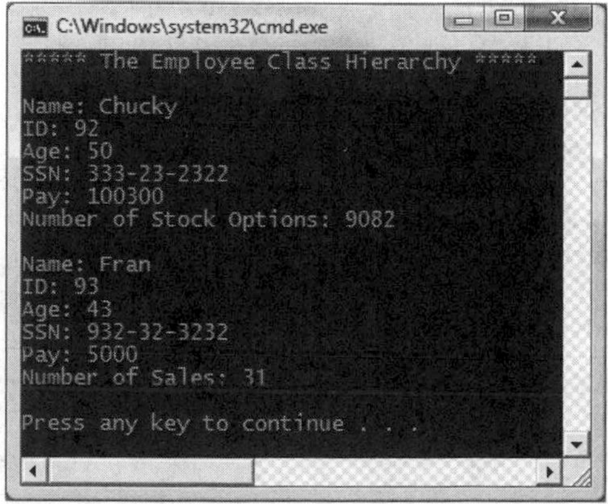

Figure 6-6. *Output of the current Employees application*

Overriding Virtual Members Using Visual Studio 2008

As you may have already noticed, when you are overriding a member, you must recall the type of each and every parameter—not to mention the method name and parameter passing conventions (`ref`, `params`, etc.). Visual Studio 2008 has a very helpful feature that you can make use of when overriding a virtual member. If you type the word "override" within the scope of a class type, IntelliSense will automatically display a list of all the overridable members defined in your parent classes, as you see in Figure 6-7.

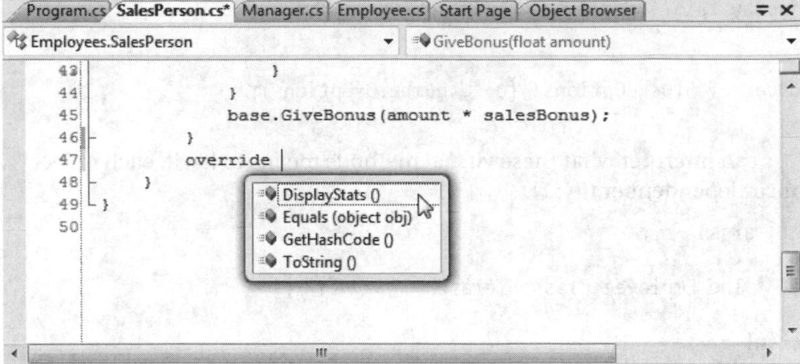

Figure 6-7. *Quickly viewing overridable methods à la Visual Studio 2008*

When you select a member and hit the Enter key, the IDE responds by automatically filling in the method stub on your behalf. Note that you also receive a code statement that calls your parent's version of the virtual member (you are free to delete this line if it is not required):

```
public override void DisplayStats()
{
  base.DisplayStats();
}
```

Sealing Virtual Members

Recall that the `sealed` keyword can be applied to a class type to prevent other types from extending its behavior via inheritance. As you may remember, we sealed `PTSalesPerson` as we assumed it made no sense for other developers to extend this line of inheritance any further.

On a related note, sometimes you may not wish to seal an entire class, but simply want to prevent derived types from overriding particular virtual methods. For example, assume we do not want part-time salespeople to obtain customized bonuses. To prevent the `PTSalesPerson` class from overriding the virtual `GiveBonus()` method, we could effectively seal this method in the `SalesPerson` class as follows:

```
// SalesPerson has sealed the GiveBonus() method!
class SalesPerson : Employee
{
...
  public override sealed void GiveBonus(float amount)
  {
    ...
  }
}
```

Here, `SalesPerson` has indeed overridden the virtual `GiveBonus()` method defined in the `Employee` class; however, it has explicitly marked it as sealed. Thus, if we attempted to override this method in the `PTSalesPerson` class:

```
sealed class PTSalesPerson : SalesPerson
{
  public PTSalesPerson(string fullName, int age, int empID,
   float currPay, string ssn, int numbOfSales)
   :base (fullName, age, empID, currPay, ssn, numbOfSales)
  {
  }

  // No bonus for you! Error!
  public override void GiveBonus(float amount)
  {
    // Rats. Can't change this method any further.
  }
}
```

we receive compile-time errors.

Understanding Abstract Classes

Currently, the Employee base class has been designed to supply protected member variables for its descendents, as well as supply two virtual methods (GiveBonus() and DisplayStats()) that may be overridden by a given descendent. While this is all well and good, there is a rather odd byproduct of the current design; you can directly create instances of the Employee base class:

```
// What exactly does this mean?
Employee X = new Employee();
```

In this example, the only real purpose of the Employee base class is to define common members for all subclasses. In all likelihood, you did not intend anyone to create a direct instance of this class, reason being that the Employee type itself is too general of a concept. For example, if I were to walk up to you and say, "I'm an employee!" I would bet your very first question to me would be, "What *kind* of employee are you?" (a consultant, trainer, admin assistant, copy editor, White House aide, etc.).

Given that many base classes tend to be rather nebulous entities, a far better design for our example is to prevent the ability to directly create a new Employee object in code. In C#, you can enforce this programmatically by using the abstract keyword, thus creating an *abstract base class*:

```
// Update the Employee class as abstract
// to prevent direct instantiation.
abstract partial class Employee
{
  ...
}
```

With this, if you now attempt to create an instance of the Employee class, you are issued a compile-time error:

```
// Error! Cannot create an abstract class!
Employee X = new Employee();
```

At this point you have constructed a fairly interesting employee hierarchy. We will add a bit more functionality to this application later in this chapter when examining C# casting rules. Until then, Figure 6-8 illustrates the core design of our current types.

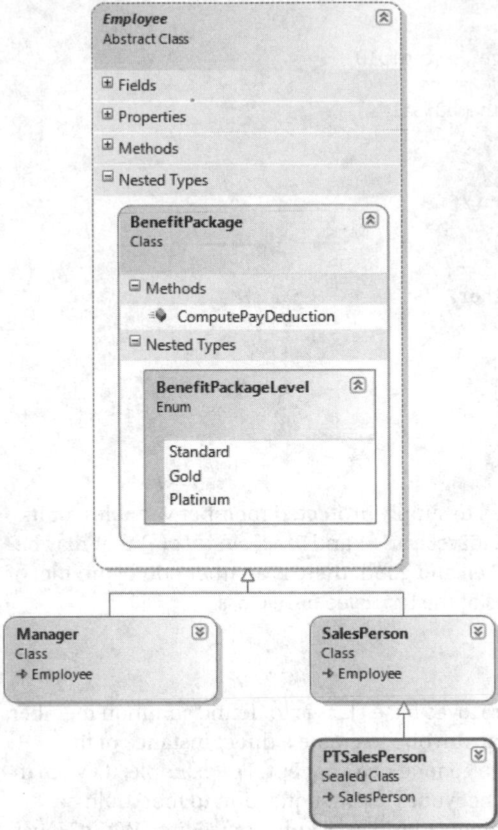

Figure 6-8. *The Employee hierarchy*

■ **Source Code** The Employees project is included under the Chapter 6 subdirectory.

Building a Polymorphic Interface

When a class has been defined as an abstract base class (via the `abstract` keyword), it may define any number of *abstract members*. Abstract members can be used whenever you wish to define a member that does *not* supply a default implementation. By doing so, you enforce a *polymorphic interface* on each descendent, leaving them to contend with the task of providing the details behind your abstract methods.

Simply put, an abstract base class's polymorphic interface simply refers to its set of virtual and abstract methods. This is much more interesting than first meets the eye, as this trait of OOP allows us to build very extendable and flexible software applications. To illustrate, we will be implementing (and slightly modifying) the hierarchy of shapes briefly examined in Chapter 5 during our overview of the pillars of OOP. To begin, create a new C# Console Application project named Shapes.

In Figure 6-9, notice that the `Hexagon` and `Circle` types each extend the `Shape` base class. Like any base class, `Shape` defines a number of members (a `PetName` property and `Draw()` method in this case) that are common to all descendents.

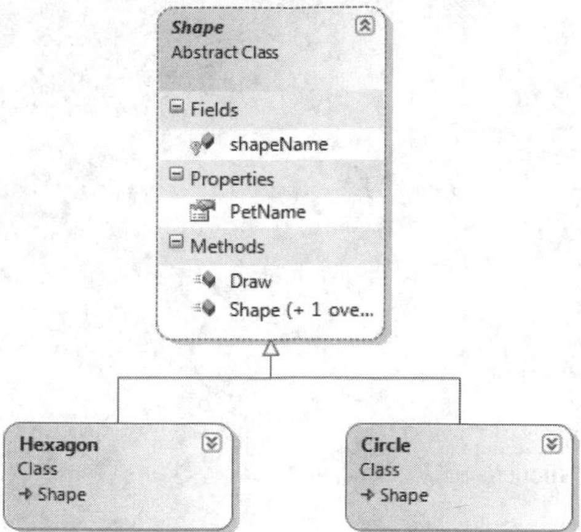

Figure 6-9. *The shapes hierarchy*

Much like the employee hierarchy, you should be able to tell that you don't want to allow the object user to create an instance of Shape directly, as it is too abstract of a concept. Again, to prevent the direct creation of the Shape type, you could define it as an abstract class. As well, given that we wish the derived types to respond uniquely to the Draw() method, let's mark it as virtual and define a default implementation:

```
// The abstract base class of the hierarchy.
abstract class Shape
{
  protected string shapeName;

  public Shape()
  { shapeName = "NoName"; }

  public Shape(string s)
  { shapeName = s; }

  // A single virtual method.
  public virtual void Draw()
  {
    Console.WriteLine("Inside Shape.Draw()");
  }

  public string PetName
  {
    get { return shapeName; }
    set { shapeName = value; }
  }
}
```

Notice that the virtual Draw() method provides a default implementation that simply prints out a message that informs us we are calling the Draw() method within the Shape base class. Now recall that when a method is marked with the virtual keyword, the method provides a default implementation that all derived types automatically inherit. If a child class so chooses, it *may* override the method but does not *have* to. Given this, consider the following implementation of the Circle and Hexagon types:

```
// Circle DOES NOT override Draw().
class Circle : Shape
{
  public Circle() {}
  public Circle(string name) : base(name){}
}

// Hexagon DOES override Draw().
class Hexagon : Shape
{
  public Hexagon() {}
  public Hexagon(string name) : base(name){}
  public override void Draw()
  {
    Console.WriteLine("Drawing {0} the Hexagon", shapeName);
  }
}
```

The usefulness of abstract methods becomes crystal clear when you once again remember that subclasses are never required to override virtual methods (as in the case of `Circle`). Therefore, if you create an instance of the `Hexagon` and `Circle` types, you'd find that the `Hexagon` understands how to "draw" itself correctly (or at least print out an appropriate message to the console). The `Circle`, however, is more than a bit confused (see Figure 6-10 for output):

```
static void Main(string[] args)
{
  Console.WriteLine("***** Fun with Polymorphism *****\n");

  Hexagon hex = new Hexagon("Beth");
  hex.Draw();

  Circle cir = new Circle("Cindy");
  // Calls base class implementation!
  cir.Draw();
  Console.ReadLine();
}
```

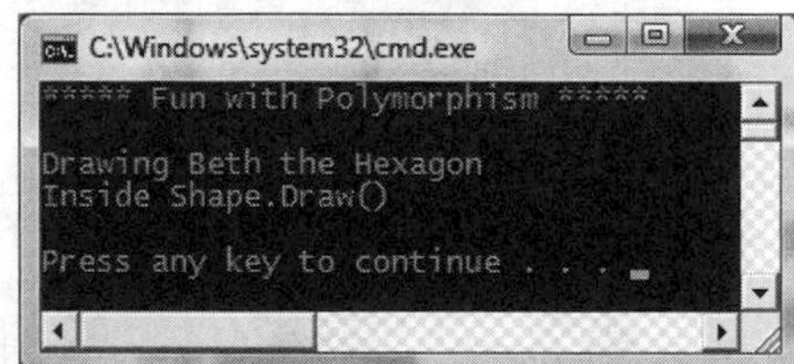

Figure 6-10. *Hmm . . . something is not quite right.*

Clearly, this is not a very intelligent design for the current hierarchy. To force each child class to override the `Draw()` method, you can define `Draw()` as an abstract method of the `Shape` class, which by definition means you provide no default implementation whatsoever. To mark a method as abstract in C#, you use the `abstract` keyword. Notice that abstract members do *not* provide any implementation whatsoever:

```
// Force all child classes to define how to be rendered.
public abstract class Shape
{
  public abstract void Draw();
  ...
}
```

■Note Abstract methods can only be defined in abstract classes. If you attempt to do otherwise, you will be issued a compiler error.

Methods marked with abstract are pure protocol. They simply define the name, return value (if any), and argument set (if required). Here, the abstract Shape class informs the derived types "I have a subroutine named Draw() that takes no arguments. If you derive from me, you figure out the details."

Given this, we are now obligated to override the Draw() method in the Circle class. If you do not, Circle is also assumed to be a noncreatable abstract type that must be adorned with the abstract keyword (which is obviously not very useful in this example). Here is the code update:

```
// If we did not implement the abstract Draw() method, Circle would also be
// considered abstract, and would have to be marked abstract!
class Circle : Shape
{
  public Circle() {}
  public Circle(string name) : base(name) {}
  public override void Draw()
  {
    Console.WriteLine("Drawing {0} the Circle", shapeName);
  }
}
```

The short answer is that we can now make the assumption that anything deriving from Shape does indeed have a unique version of the Draw() method. To illustrate the full story of polymorphism, consider the following code:

```
static void Main(string[] args)
{
  Console.WriteLine("***** Fun with Polymorphism *****\n");

  // Make an array of Shape-compatible objects.
  Shape[] myShapes = {new Hexagon(), new Circle(), new Hexagon("Mick"),
    new Circle("Beth"), new Hexagon("Linda")};

  // Loop over each item and interact with the
  // polymorphic interface.
  foreach (Shape s in myShapes)
  {
    s.Draw();
  }
  Console.ReadLine();
}
```

Figure 6-11 shows the output.

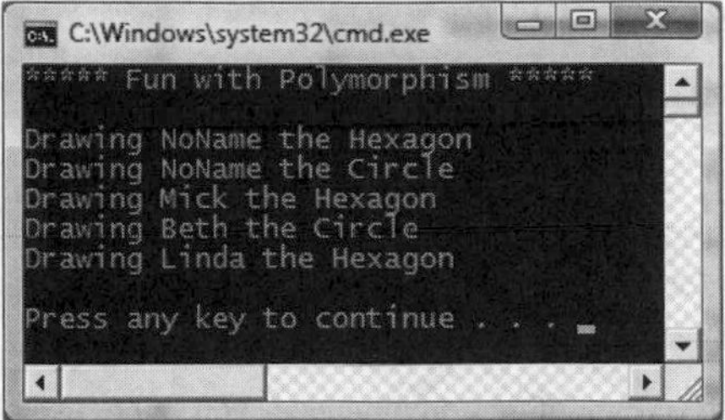

Figure 6-11. *Polymorphism in action*

This Main() method illustrates polymorphism at its finest. Although it is not possible to *directly* create an abstract base class (the Shape), you are able to freely store references to any subclass with an abstract base variable. Therefore, when you are creating an array of Shapes, the array can hold any object deriving from the Shape base class (if you attempt to place Shape-incompatible objects into the array, you receive a compiler error).

Given that all items in the myShapes array do indeed derive from Shape, we know they all support the same polymorphic interface (or said more plainly, they all have a Draw() method). As you iterate over the array of Shape references, it is at runtime that the underlying type is determined. At this point, the correct version of the Draw() method is invoked.

This technique also makes it very simple to safely extend the current hierarchy. For example, assume we derived five more classes from the abstract Shape base class (Triangle, Square, etc.). Due to the polymorphic interface, the code within our for loop would not have to change in the slightest as the compiler enforces that only Shape-compatible types are placed within the myShapes array.

Understanding Member Shadowing

C# provides a facility that is the logical opposite of method overriding termed *shadowing*. Formally speaking, if a derived class defines a member that is identical to a member defined in a base class, the derived class has *shadowed* the parent's version. In the real world, the possibility of this occurring is the greatest when you are subclassing from a class you (or your team) did not create yourselves (for example, if you purchase a third-party .NET software package).

For the sake of illustration, assume you receive a class named ThreeDCircle from a coworker (or classmate) that defines a subroutine named Draw() taking no arguments:

```
class ThreeDCircle
{
  public void Draw()
  {
    Console.WriteLine("Drawing a 3D Circle");
  }
}
```

You figure that a ThreeDCircle "is-a" Circle, so you derive from your existing Circle type:

```
class ThreeDCircle : Circle
{
  public void Draw()
  {
    Console.WriteLine("Drawing a 3D Circle");
  }
}
```

Once you recompile, you find a warning in the Visual Studio 2008 error window (see Figure 6-12).

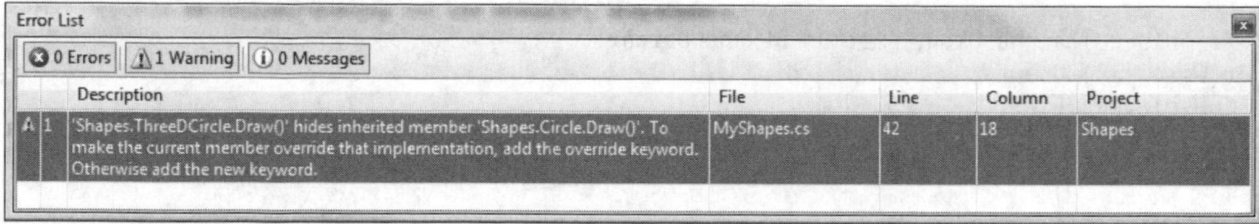

Figure 6-12. *Oops! We just shadowed a member in our parent class.*

To address this issue, you have two options. You could simply update the parent's version of `Draw()` using the `override` keyword (as suggested by the compiler). With this approach, the `ThreeDCircle` type is able to extend the parent's default behavior as required. However, if you don't have access to the code defining the base class (again, as would be the case in many third-party libraries), you would be unable to modify the `Draw()` method as a virtual member, as you don't have access to the code file!

As an alternative, you can include the `new` keyword to the offending `Draw()` member of the derived type (`ThreeDCircle` in this example). Doing so explicitly states that the derived type's implementation is intentionally designed to hide the parent's version (again, in the real world, this can be helpful if external .NET software somehow conflicts with your current software).

```
// This class extends Circle and hides the inherited Draw() method.
class ThreeDCircle : Circle
{
  // Hide any Draw() implementation above me.
  public new void Draw()
  {
    Console.WriteLine("Drawing a 3D Circle");
  }
}
```

You can also apply the `new` keyword to any member type inherited from a base class (field, constant, static member, property, etc.). As a further example, assume that `ThreeDCircle` wishes to hide the inherited `shapeName` field:

```
// This class extends Circle and hides the inherited Draw() method.
class ThreeDCircle : Circle
{
  // Hide the shapeName field above me.
  protected new string shapeName;

  // Hide any Draw() implementation above me.
  public new void Draw()
  {
    Console.WriteLine("Drawing a 3D Circle");
  }
}
```

Finally, be aware that it is still possible to trigger the base class implementation of a shadowed member using an explicit cast (described in the next section). For example:

```
static void Main(string[] args)
{
...
```

```
  // This calls the Draw() method of the ThreeDCircle.
  ThreeDCircle o = new ThreeDCircle();
  o.Draw();

  // This calls the Draw() method of the parent!
  ((Circle)o).Draw();
  Console.ReadLine();
}
```

■ **Source Code** The Shapes project can be found under the Chapter 6 subdirectory.

Understanding Base Class/Derived Class Casting Rules

Now that you can build a family of related class types, you need to learn the laws of class type casting operations. To do so, let's return to the Employees hierarchy created earlier in this chapter. Under the .NET platform, the ultimate base class in the system is `System.Object`. Therefore, everything "is-a" `Object` and can be treated as such. Given this fact, it is legal to store an instance of any type within an object variable:

```
// A Manager "is-a" System.Object.
object frank = new Manager("Frank Zappa", 9, 3000, 40000, "111-11-1111", 5);
```

In the `Employees` system, `Managers`, `SalesPerson`, and `PTSalesPerson` types all extend `Employee`, so we can store any of these objects in a valid base class reference. Therefore, the following statements are also legal:

```
// A Manager "is-an" Employee too.
Employee moonUnit = new Manager("MoonUnit Zappa", 2, 3001, 20000, "101-11-1321", 1);

// A PTSalesPerson "is-a" SalesPerson.
SalesPerson jill = new PTSalesPerson("Jill", 834, 3002, 100000, "111-12-1119", 90);
```

The first law of casting between class types is that when two classes are related by an "is-a" relationship, it is always safe to store a derived type within a base class reference. Formally, this is called an *implicit cast,* as "it just works" given the laws of inheritance. This leads to some powerful programming constructs. For example, assume you have defined a new method within your current `Program` class:

```
static void FireThisPerson(Employee emp)
{
  // Remove from database...
  // Get key and pencil sharpener from fired employee...
}
```

Because this method takes a single parameter of type `Employee`, you can effectively pass any descendent from the `Employee` class into this method directly, given the "is-a" relationship:

```
// Streamline the staff.
FireThisPerson(moonUnit);   // "moonUnit" was declared as an Employee.
FireThisPerson(jill);       // "jill" was declared as a SalesPerson.
```

The previous code compiles given the implicit cast from the base class type (Employee) to the derived type. However, what if you also wanted to fire Frank Zappa (currently stored in a generic System.Object reference)? If you pass the frank object directly into FireThisPerson() as follows:

```
// Error!
object frank = new Manager("Frank Zappa", 9, 3000, 40000, "111-11-1111", 5);
FireThisPerson(frank);
```

you will find a compiler error. As you can see, however, the object reference is pointing to an Employee-compatible object. You can satisfy the compiler by performing an explicit cast. This is the second law of casting: you must explicitly downcast using the C# casting operator. Thus, the previous problem can be avoided as follows:

```
// OK!
FireThisPerson((Manager)frank);
```

The C# as Keyword

Be very aware that explicit casting is evaluated at *runtime*, not compile time. Therefore, if you were to author the following C# code:

```
// Ack! You can't cast frank to a Hexagon!
Hexagon hex = (Hexagon)frank;
```

you would receive a runtime error, or more formally a *runtime exception*. Chapter 7 will examine the full details of structured exception handling; however, it is worth pointing out for the time being when you are performing an explicit cast, you can trap the possibility of an invalid cast using the try and catch keywords (again, don't fret over the details):

```
// Catch a possible invalid cast.
try
{
  Hexagon hex = (Hexagon)frank;
}
catch (InvalidCastException ex)
{
  Console.WriteLine(ex.Message);
}
```

While this is a fine example of defensive programming, C# provides the as keyword to quickly determine at runtime whether a given type is compatible with another. When you use the as keyword, you are able to determine compatibility by checking against a null return value. Consider the following:

```
// Use 'as' to test compatability.
Hexagon hex2 = frank as Hexagon;
if (hex2 == null)
  Console.WriteLine("Sorry, frank is not a Hexagon...");
```

The C# is Keyword

Given that the FireThisPerson() method has been designed to take any possible type derived from Employee, one question on your mind may be how this method can determine which derived type was sent into the method. On a related note, given that the incoming parameter is of type Employee, how can you gain access to the specialized members of the SalesPerson and Manager types?

In addition to the as keyword, the C# language provides the is keyword to determine whether two items are compatible. Unlike the as keyword, however, the is keyword returns false, rather than a null reference, if the types are incompatible. Consider the following implementation of the FireThisPerson() method:

```
static void FireThisPerson(Employee emp)
{
  if (emp is SalesPerson)
  {
    Console.WriteLine("Lost a sales person named {0}", emp.Name);
    Console.WriteLine("{0} made {1} sale(s)...", emp.Name,
      ((SalesPerson)emp).SalesNumber);
    Console.WriteLine();
  }
  if (emp is Manager)
  {
    Console.WriteLine("Lost a suit named {0}", emp.Name);
    Console.WriteLine("{0} had {1} stock options...", emp.Name,
      ((Manager)emp).StockOptions);
    Console.WriteLine();
  }
}
```

Here you are performing a runtime check to determine what the incoming base class reference is actually pointing to in memory. Once you determine whether you received a SalesPerson or Manager type, you are able to perform an explicit cast to gain access to the specialized members of the class. Also notice that you are not required to wrap your casting operations within a try/catch construct, as you know that the cast is safe if you enter either if scope, given our conditional check.

The Master Parent Class: System.Object

To wrap up this chapter, I'd like to examine the details of the master parent class in the .NET platform: Object. As you were reading the previous section, you may have noticed that the base classes in our hierarchies (Car, Shape, Employee) never explicitly specify their parent classes:

```
// Who is the parent of Car?
class Car
{...}
```

In the .NET universe, every type ultimately derives from a base class named System.Object. The Object class defines a set of common members for every type in the framework. In fact, when you do build a class that does not explicitly define its parent, the compiler automatically derives your type from Object. If you want to be very clear in your intentions, you are free to define classes that derive from Object as follows:

```
// Here we are explicitly deriving from System.Object.
class Car : object
{...}
```

Like any class, System.Object defines a set of members. In the following formal C# definition, note that some of these items are declared virtual, which specifies that a given member may be overridden by a subclass, while others are marked with static (and are therefore called at the class level):

```
public class Object
{
  // Virtual members.
  public virtual bool Equals(object obj);
  protected virtual void Finalize();
```

```
    public virtual int GetHashCode();
    public virtual string ToString();

    // Instance level, nonvirtual members.
    public Type GetType();
    protected object MemberwiseClone();

    // Static members.
    public static bool Equals(object objA, object objB);
    public static bool ReferenceEquals(object objA, object objB);
  }
```

Table 6-1 offers a rundown of the functionality provided by each method.

Table 6-1. *Core Members of* `System.Object`

Instance Method of Object Class	Meaning in Life
`Equals()`	By default, this method returns `true` only if the items being compared refer to the exact same item in memory. Thus, `Equals()` is used to compare object references, not the state of the object. Typically, this method is overridden to return `true` only if the objects being compared have the same internal state values (that is, value-based semantics). Be aware that if you override `Equals()`, you should also override `GetHashCode()`, as these methods are used internally by `Hashtable` types to retrieve subobjects from the container.
`GetHashCode()`	This method returns an `int` that identifies a specific object instance.
`GetType()`	This method returns a `Type` object that fully describes the object you are currently referencing. In short, this is a Runtime Type Identification (RTTI) method available to all objects (discussed in greater detail in Chapter 16).
`ToString()`	This method returns a string representation of this object, using the `<namespace>.<type name>` format (termed the *fully qualified name*). This method can be overridden by a subclass to return a tokenized string of name/value pairs that represent the object's internal state, rather than its fully qualified name.
`Finalize()`	For the time being, you can understand this method (when overridden) is called to free any allocated resources before the object is destroyed. I talk more about the CLR garbage collection services in Chapter 8.
`MemberwiseClone()`	This method exists to return a member-by-member copy of the current object, which is often used when cloning an object (see Chapter 9).

To illustrate some of the default behavior provided by the `Object` base class, create a new C# Console Application named ObjectOverrides. Insert a new C# class type that contains the following empty class definition for a type named `Person`:

```
// Remember! Person extends Object.
class Person {}
```

Now, update your `Main()` method to interact with the inherited members of `System.Object` as follows:

```
class Program
{
  static void Main(string[] args)
  {
    Console.WriteLine("***** Fun with System.Object *****\n");
    Person p1 = new Person();

    // Use inherited members of System.Object.
    Console.WriteLine("ToString: {0}", p1.ToString());
    Console.WriteLine("Hash code: {0}", p1.GetHashCode());
    Console.WriteLine("Type: {0}", p1.GetType());

    // Make some other references to p1.
    Person p2 = p1;
    object o = p2;

    // Are the references pointing to the same object in memory?
    if (o.Equals(p1) && p2.Equals(o))
    {
      Console.WriteLine("Same instance!");
    }
    Console.ReadLine();
  }
}
```

Figure 6-13 shows the output.

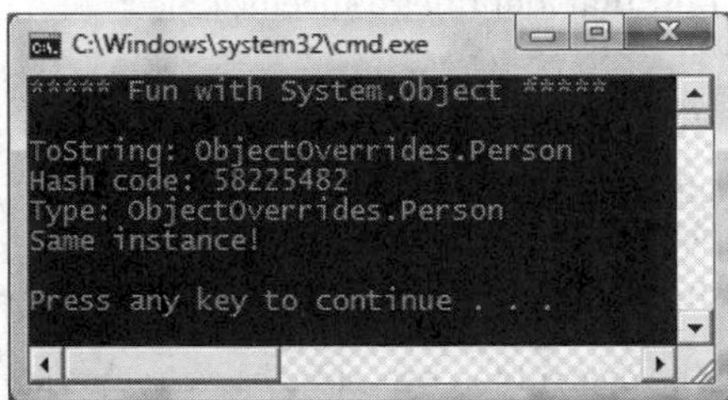

Figure 6-13. *Invoking the inherited members of* `System.Object`

First, notice how the default implementation of `ToString()` returns the fully qualified name of the current type (`ObjectOverrides.Person`). As you will see later during our examination of building custom namespaces (Chapter 15), every C# project defines a "root namespace," which has the same name of the project itself. Here, we created a project named ObjectOverrides; thus the `Person` type (as well as the `Program` class) have both been placed within the `ObjectOverrides` namespace.

The default behavior of `Equals()` is to test whether two variables are pointing to the same object in memory. Here, you create a new `Person` variable named `p1`. At this point, a new `Person` object is placed on the managed heap. `p2` is also of type `Person`. However, you are not creating a *new* instance, but rather assigning this variable to reference `p1`. Therefore, `p1` and `p2` are both pointing to the same object in memory, as is the variable `o` (of type `object`, which was thrown in for good measure). Given that `p1`, `p2`, and `o` all point to the same memory location, the equality test succeeds.

Although the canned behavior of `System.Object` can fit the bill in a number of cases, it is quite common for your custom types to override some of these inherited methods. To illustrate, update the `Person` class to support some state data representing an individual's first name, last name, and age, each of which can be set by a custom constructor:

```
// Remember! Person extends Object.
class Person
{
  // Public only for simplicity. Properties and private data
  // would obviously be preferred.
  public string fName;
  public string lName;
  public byte personAge;

  public Person(string firstName, string lastName, byte age)
  {
    fName = firstName;
    lName = lastName;
    personAge = age;
  }
  public Person(){}
}
```

Overriding System.Object.ToString()

Many classes (and structures) that you create can benefit from overriding `ToString()` in order to return a string textual representation of the type's current state. This can be quite helpful for purposes of debugging (among other reasons). How you choose to construct this string is a matter of personal choice; however, a recommended approach is to separate each name/value pair with semicolons and wrap the entire string within square brackets (many types in the .NET base class libraries follow this approach). Consider the following overridden `ToString()` for our `Person` class:

```
public override string ToString()
{
  string myState;
  myState = string.Format("[First Name: {0}; Last Name: {1}; Age: {2}]",
    fName, lName, personAge);
  return myState;
}
```

This implementation of `ToString()` is quite straightforward, given that the `Person` class only has three pieces of state data. However, always remember that a proper `ToString()` override should also account for any data defined up the chain of inheritance. When you override `ToString()` for a class extending a custom base class, the first order of business is to obtain the `ToString()` value from your parent using `base`. Once you have obtained your parent's string data, you can append the derived class's custom information.

Overriding System.Object.Equals()

Let's also override the behavior of `Object.Equals()` to work with *value-based semantics*. Recall that by default, `Equals()` returns `true` only if the two objects being compared reference the same object instance in memory. For the `Person` class, it may be helpful to implement `Equals()` to return `true` if the two variables being compared contain the same state values (e.g., first name, last name, and age).

First of all, notice that the incoming argument of the `Equals()` method is a generic `System.Object`. Given this, our first order of business is to ensure the caller has indeed passed in a `Person` type, and as an extra safeguard, to make sure the incoming parameter is not an unallocated object.

Once we have established the caller has passed us an allocated Person, one approach to implement Equals() is to perform a field-by-field comparison against the data of the incoming object to the data of the current object:

```
public override bool Equals(object obj)
{
  if (obj is Person && obj != null)
  {
    Person temp;
    temp = (Person)obj;
    if (temp.fName == this.fName && temp.lName == this.fName
       && temp.personAge == this.personAge)
    {
      return true;
    }
    else
    {
      return false;
    }
  }
  return false;
}
```

Here, you are examining the values of the incoming object against the values of our internal values (note the use of the this keyword). If the name and age of each are identical, you have two objects with the exact same state data and therefore return true. Any other possibility results in returning false.

While this approach does indeed work, you can certainly imagine how labor intensive it would be to implement a custom Equals() method for nontrivial types that may contain dozens of data fields. One common shortcut is to leverage your own implementation of ToString(). If a class has a prim-and-proper implementation of ToString() that accounts for all field data up the chain of inheritance, you can simply perform a comparison of the object's string data:

```
public override bool Equals(object obj)
{
  // No need to cast 'obj' to a Person anymore,
  // as everything has a ToString() method.
  return obj.ToString() == this.ToString();
}
```

Overriding System.Object.GetHashCode()

When a class overrides the Equals() method, you should also override the default implementation of GetHashCode(). Simply put, a *hash code* is a numerical value that represents an object as a particular state. For example, if you create two string objects that hold the value Hello, you would obtain the same hash code. However, if one of the string objects were in all lowercase (hello), you would obtain different hash codes.

By default, System.Object.GetHashCode() uses your object's current location in memory to yield the hash value. However, if you are building a custom type that you intend to store in a Hashtable type (within the System.Collections namespace), you should always override this member, as the Hashtable will be internally invoking Equals() and GetHashCode() to retrieve the correct object.

Although we are not going to place our Person into a System.Collections.Hashtable, for completion, let's override GetHashCode(). There are many algorithms that can be used to create a hash code, some fancy, others not so fancy. Most of the time, you are able to generate a hash code value by leveraging the System.String's GetHashCode() implementation.

Given that the String class already has a solid hash code algorithm that is using the character data of the String to compute a hash value, if you can identify a piece of field data on your class that should be unique for all instances (such as the Social Security number), simply call GetHashCode() on that point of field data. If this is not the case, but you have overridden ToString(), call GetHashCode() on your own string representation:

```
// Return a hash code based on the person's ToString() value.
public override int GetHashCode()
{
  return this.ToString().GetHashCode();
}
```

Testing Our Modified Person Class

Now that we have overridden the virtual members of Object, update Main() to test your updates (see Figure 6-14 for output).

```
static void Main(string[] args)
{
  Console.WriteLine("***** Fun with System.Object *****\n");

  // NOTE:  We want these to be identical to test
  // the Equals() and GetHashCode() methods.
  Person p1 = new Person("Homer", "Simpson", 50);
  Person p2 = new Person("Homer", "Simpson", 50);

  // Get stringified version of objects.
  Console.WriteLine("p1.ToString() = {0}", p1.ToString());
  Console.WriteLine("p2.ToString() = {0}", p2.ToString());

  // Test Overridden Equals()
  Console.WriteLine("p1 = p2?: {0}", p1.Equals(p2));

  // Test hash codes.
  Console.WriteLine("Same hash codes?: {0}", p1.GetHashCode() == p2.GetHashCode());
  Console.WriteLine();

  // Change age of p2 and test again.
  p2.personAge = 45;
  Console.WriteLine("p1.ToString() = {0}", p1.ToString());
  Console.WriteLine("p2.ToString() = {0}", p2.ToString());
  Console.WriteLine("p1 = p2?: {0}", p1.Equals(p2));
  Console.WriteLine("Same hash codes?: {0}", p1.GetHashCode() == p2.GetHashCode());
  Console.ReadLine();
}
```

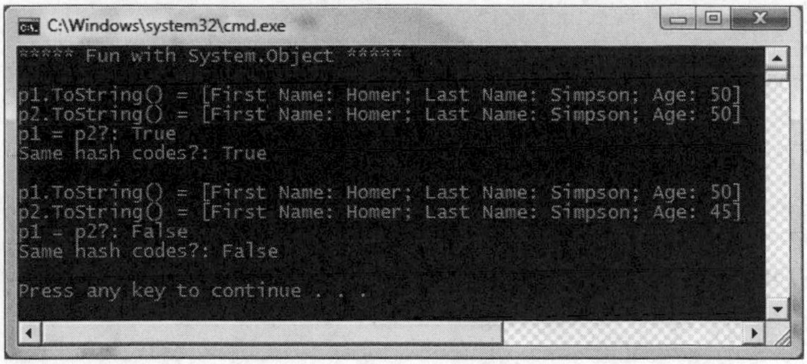

```
C:\Windows\system32\cmd.exe
***** Fun with System.Object *****

p1.ToString() = [First Name: Homer; Last Name: Simpson; Age: 50]
p2.ToString() = [First Name: Homer; Last Name: Simpson; Age: 50]
p1 = p2?: True
Same hash codes?: True

p1.ToString() = [First Name: Homer; Last Name: Simpson; Age: 50]
p2.ToString() = [First Name: Homer; Last Name: Simpson; Age: 45]
p1 = p2?: False
Same hash codes?: False

Press any key to continue . . .
```

Figure 6-14. *Our customized* `Person` *type*

The Static Members of System.Object

In addition to the instance-level members you have just examined, `System.Object` does define two (very helpful) static members that also test for value-based or reference-based equality. Consider the following code:

```
static void SharedMembersOfObject()
{
  // Static members of System.Object.
  Person p3 = new Person("Sally", "Jones", 4);
  Person p4 = new Person("Sally", "Jones", 4);
  Console.WriteLine("P3 and P4 have same state: {0}", object.Equals(p3, p4));
  Console.WriteLine("P3 and P4 are pointing to same object: {0}",
    object.ReferenceEquals(p3, p4));
}
```

Here, you are able to simply send in two objects (of any type) and allow the `System.Object` class to determine the details automatically. These methods can be very helpful when you have redefined equality for a custom type, yet still need to quickly determine whether two reference variables point to the same location in memory (via the static `ReferenceEquals()` method).

■ **Source Code** The ObjectOverrides project is located under the Chapter 6 subdirectory.

Summary

This chapter explored the role and details of inheritance and polymorphism. Over these pages you were introduced to numerous new keywords and tokens to support each of these techniques. For example, recall that the colon token is used to establish the parent class of a given type. Parent types are able to define any number of virtual and/or abstract members to establish a polymorphic interface. Derived types override such members using the `override` keyword.

In addition to building numerous class hierarchies, this chapter also examined how to explicitly cast between base and derived types, and wrapped up by diving into the details of the cosmic parent class in the .NET base class libraries: `System.Object`.

CHAPTER 7

Understanding Structured Exception Handling

The point of this chapter is to understand how to handle runtime anomalies in your C# code base through the use of *structured exception handling*. Not only will you learn about the C# keywords that allow you to handle such matters (`try`, `catch`, `throw`, `finally`), but you will also come to understand the distinction between application-level and system-level exceptions and learn the role of the `System.Exception` base class. This discussion will also provide a lead-in to the topic of building custom exceptions, as well as how to leverage the exception-centric debugging tools of Visual Studio 2008.

Ode to Errors, Bugs, and Exceptions

Despite what our (sometimes inflated) egos may tell us, no programmer is perfect. Writing software is a complex undertaking, and given this complexity, it is quite common for even the best software to ship with various . . . *problems*. Sometimes the problem is caused by "bad code" (such as overflowing the bounds of an array). Other times, a problem is caused by bogus user input that has not been accounted for in the application's code base (e.g., a phone number input field assigned to the value "Chucky"). Now, regardless of the cause of said problem, the end result is that your application does not work as expected. To help frame the upcoming discussion of structured exception handling, allow me to provide definitions for three commonly used anomaly-centric terms:

- *Bugs*: These are, simply put, errors on the part of the programmer. For example, assume you are programming with unmanaged C++. If you fail to delete dynamically allocated memory (resulting in a memory leak), you have a bug.
- *User errors*: Unlike bugs, user errors are typically caused by the individual running your application, rather than by those who created it. For example, an end user who enters a malformed string into a text box could very well generate an error *if* you fail to handle this faulty input in your code base.
- *Exceptions*: Exceptions are typically regarded as runtime anomalies that are difficult, if not impossible, to account for while programming your application. Possible exceptions include attempting to connect to a database that no longer exists, opening a corrupted file, or contacting a machine that is currently offline. In each of these cases, the programmer (and end user) has little control over these "exceptional" circumstances.

Given the previous definitions, it should be clear that .NET structured *exception* handling is a technique well suited to deal with runtime *exceptions*. However, as for the bugs and user errors that have escaped your view, the CLR will often generate a corresponding exception that identifies the problem at hand.

The .NET base class libraries define numerous exceptions such as FormatException, IndexOutOfRangeException, FileNotFoundException, ArgumentOutOfRangeException, and so forth. Within the .NET nomenclature, an "exception" accounts for bugs, bogus user input, and runtime errors, even though we programmers may view each possibility as a distinct issue. However, before we get too far ahead of ourselves, let's formalize the role of structured exception handling and check out how it differs from traditional error-handling techniques.

■ Note To make the code examples used in this book as clean as possible, I will not catch every possible exception that may be thrown by a given method in the base class libraries. In your production-level projects, you should, of course, make liberal use of the techniques presented in this chapter.

The Role of .NET Exception Handling

Prior to .NET, error handling under the Windows operating system was a confused mishmash of techniques. Many programmers rolled their own error-handling logic within the context of a given application. For example, a development team may define a set of numerical constants that represent known error conditions, and make use of them as method return values. By way of an example, ponder the following partial C code:

```
/* A very C-style error trapping mechanism. */
#define E_FILENOTFOUND 1000

int SomeFunction()
{
  // Assume something happens in this f(x)
  // that causes the following return value.
  return E_FILENOTFOUND;
}

void main()
{
  int retVal = SomeFunction();
  if(retVal == E_FILENOTFOUND)
    printf("Cannot find file...");
}
```

This approach is less than ideal, given the fact that the constant E_FILENOTFOUND is little more than a numerical value, and is far from being a helpful agent regarding how to deal with the problem. Ideally, you would like to wrap the error's name, a descriptive message, and other helpful information regarding this error condition into a single, well-defined package (which is exactly what happens under structured exception handling).

In addition to a developer's ad hoc techniques, the Windows API defines hundreds of error codes that come by way of #defines, HRESULTs, and far too many variations on the simple Boolean (bool, BOOL, VARIANT_BOOL, and so on). Also, many C++ COM developers (and indirectly, many VB6 COM developers) have made use of a small set of standard COM interfaces (e.g., ISupportErrorInfo, IErrorInfo, ICreateErrorInfo) to return meaningful error information to a COM client.

The obvious problem with these previous techniques is the tremendous lack of symmetry. Each approach is more or less tailored to a given technology, a given language, and perhaps even a given project. In order to put an end to this madness, the .NET platform provides a standard technique to send and trap runtime errors: structured exception handling (SEH).

The beauty of this approach is that developers now have a unified approach to error handling, which is common to all languages targeting the .NET platform. Therefore, the way in which a C# programmer handles errors is syntactically similar to that of a VB .NET programmer, and a C++ programmer using managed extensions. As an added bonus, the syntax used to throw and catch exceptions across assemblies and machine boundaries is identical.

Another bonus of .NET exceptions is the fact that rather than receiving a cryptic numerical value that identifies the problem at hand, exceptions are objects that contain a human-readable description of the problem, as well as a detailed snapshot of the call stack that triggered the exception in the first place. Furthermore, you are able to provide the end user with help link information that points the user to a URL that provides detailed information regarding the error at hand as well as custom programmer-defined data.

The Atoms of .NET Exception Handling

Programming with structured exception handling involves the use of four interrelated entities:

- A class type that represents the details of the exception
- A member that *throws* an instance of the exception class to the caller
- A block of code on the caller's side that invokes the exception-prone member
- A block of code on the caller's side that will process (or *catch*) the exception should it occur

The C# programming language offers four keywords (`try`, `catch`, `throw`, and `finally`) that allow you to throw and handle exceptions. The type that represents the problem at hand is a class derived from `System.Exception` (or a descendent thereof). Given this fact, let's check out the role of this exception-centric base class.

The System.Exception Base Class

All user- and system-defined exceptions ultimately derive from the `System.Exception` base class, which in turn derives from `System.Object`. Here is the crux of this type (note that some of these members are virtual and may thus be overridden by derived classes):

```
public class Exception : ISerializable, _Exception
{
  // Public constructors
  public Exception(string message, Exception innerException);
  public Exception(string message);
  public Exception();

  // Methods
  public virtual Exception GetBaseException();
  public virtual void GetObjectData(SerializationInfo info,
    StreamingContext context);

  // Properties
  public virtual IDictionary Data { get; }
  public virtual string HelpLink { get; set; }
  public System.Exception InnerException { get; }
  public virtual string Message { get; }
  public virtual string Source { get; set; }
  public virtual string StackTrace { get; }
  public MethodBase TargetSite { get; }
}
```

As you can see, many of the properties defined by `System.Exception` are read-only in nature. This is due to the simple fact that derived types will typically supply default values for each property (for example, the default message of the `IndexOutOfRangeException` type is "Index was outside the bounds of the array").

■Note The `Exception` class implements two .NET interfaces. Although we have yet to examine interfaces (see Chapter 9), simply understand that the `_Exception` interface allows a .NET exception to be processed by an unmanaged code base (such as a COM application), while the `ISerializable` interface allows an exception object to be persisted across boundaries (such as a machine boundary).

Table 7-1 describes the details of some (but not all) of the members of `System.Exception`.

Table 7-1. *Core Members of the* `System.Exception` *Type*

System.Exception Property	Meaning in Life
`Data`	This property retrieves a collection of key/value pairs (represented by an object implementing `IDictionary`) that provides additional, programmer-defined information about the exception. By default, this collection is empty (e.g., `null`).
`HelpLink`	This property returns a URL to a help file or website describing the error in full detail.
`InnerException`	This read-only property can be used to obtain information about the previous exception(s) that caused the current exception to occur. The previous exception(s) are recorded by passing them into the constructor of the most current exception.
`Message`	This read-only property returns the textual description of a given error. The error message itself is set as a constructor parameter.
`Source`	This property returns the name of the assembly that threw the exception.
`StackTrace`	This read-only property contains a string that identifies the sequence of calls that triggered the exception. As you might guess, this property is very useful during debugging or if you wish to dump the error to an external error log.
`TargetSite`	This read-only property returns a `MethodBase` type, which describes numerous details about the method that threw the exception (invoking `ToString()` will identify the method by name).

The Simplest Possible Example

To illustrate the usefulness of structured exception handling, we need to create a type that may throw an exception under the correct circumstances. Assume we have created a new C# Console Application project (named SimpleException) that defines two class types (`Car` and `Radio`) associated by the "has-a" relationship. The `Radio` type defines a single method that turns the radio's power on or off:

```
class Radio
{
  public void TurnOn(bool on)
```

```
  {
    if(on)
      Console.WriteLine("Jamming...");
    else
      Console.WriteLine("Quiet time...");
  }
}
```

In addition to leveraging the Radio type via containment/delegation, the Car type is defined in such a way that if the user accelerates a Car object beyond a predefined maximum speed (specified using a constant member variable named MaxSpeed), its engine explodes, rendering the Car unusable (captured by a bool member variable named carIsDead).

Beyond these points, the Car type has a few member variables to represent the current speed and a user supplied "pet name" as well as various constructors to set the state of a new Car object. Here is the complete definition (with code annotations):

```
class Car
{
  // Constant for maximum speed.
  public const int MaxSpeed = 100;

  // Internal state data.
  private int currSpeed;
  private string petName;

  // Is the car still operational?
  private bool carIsDead;

  // A car has-a radio.
  private Radio theMusicBox = new Radio();

  // Constructors.
  public Car() {}
  public Car(string name, int currSp)
  {
    currSpeed = currSp;
    petName = name;
  }

  public void CrankTunes(bool state)
  {
    // Delegate request to inner object.
    theMusicBox.TurnOn(state);
  }

  // See if Car has overheated.
  public void Accelerate(int delta)
  {
    if (carIsDead)
      Console.WriteLine("{0} is out of order...", petName);
    else
    {
      currSpeed += delta;
      if (currSpeed > MaxSpeed)
      {
        Console.WriteLine("{0} has overheated!", petName);
        currSpeed = 0;
```

```
        carIsDead = true;
      }
      else
        Console.WriteLine("=> CurrSpeed = {0}", currSpeed);
    }
  }
}
```

Now, if we were to implement a `Main()` method that forces a `Car` object to exceed the predefined maximum speed as shown here:

```
static void Main(string[] args)
{
  Console.WriteLine("***** Simple Exception Example *****");
  Console.WriteLine("=> Creating a car and stepping on it!");
  Car myCar = new Car("Zippy", 20);
  myCar.CrankTunes(true);

  for (int i = 0; i < 10; i++)
    myCar.Accelerate(10);
  Console.ReadLine();
}
```

we would see the output displayed in Figure 7-1.

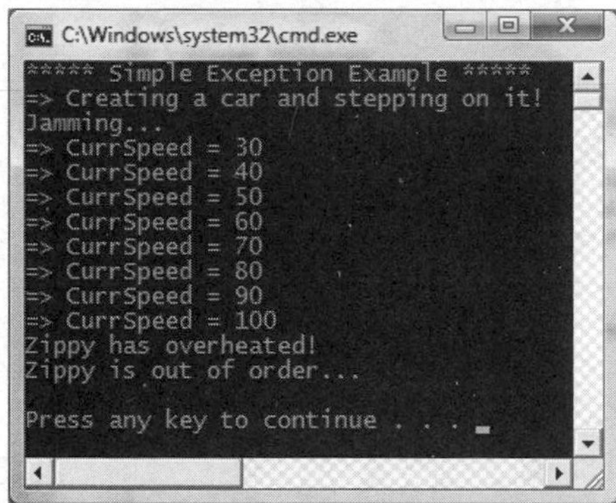

Figure 7-1. *The* `Car` *in action*

Throwing a Generic Exception

Now that we have a functional `Car` type, I'll illustrate the simplest way to throw an exception. The current implementation of `Accelerate()` simply displays an error message if the caller attempts to speed up the `Car` beyond its upper limit.

To retrofit this method to throw an exception if the user attempts to speed up the automobile after it has met its maker, you want to create and configure a new instance of the `System.Exception` class, setting the value of the read-only `Message` property via the class constructor. When you wish to send the error object back to the caller, make use of the C# `throw` keyword. Here is the relevant code update to the `Accelerate()` method:

```
// This time, throw an exception if the user speeds up beyond MaxSpeed.
public void Accelerate(int delta)
{
```

```
  if (carIsDead)
    Console.WriteLine("{0} is out of order...", petName);
  else
  {
    currSpeed += delta;
    if (currSpeed >= MaxSpeed)
    {
      carIsDead = true;
      currSpeed = 0;

      // Use the "throw" keyword to raise an exception.
      throw new Exception(string.Format("{0} has overheated!", petName));
    }
    else
      Console.WriteLine("=> CurrSpeed = {0}", currSpeed);
  }
}
```

Before examining how a caller would catch this exception, a few points of interest. First of all, when you are throwing an exception, it is always up to you to decide exactly what constitutes the error in question, and when it should be thrown. Here, you are making the assumption that if the program attempts to increase the speed of a car that has expired, a `System.Exception` type should be thrown to indicate the `Accelerate()` method cannot continue (which may or may not be a valid assumption).

Alternatively, you could implement `Accelerate()` to recover automatically without needing to throw an exception in the first place. By and large, exceptions should be thrown only when a more terminal condition has been met (for example, not finding a necessary file, failing to connect to a database, and whatnot). Deciding exactly what constitutes throwing an exception is a design issue you must always contend with. For our current purposes, assume that asking a doomed automobile to increase its speed justifies a cause to throw an exception.

Catching Exceptions

Because the `Accelerate()` method now throws an exception, the caller needs to be ready to handle the exception should it occur. When you are invoking a method that may throw an exception, you make use of a `try/catch` block. Once you have caught the exception object, you are able to invoke the members of the `System.Exception` type to extract the details of the problem. What you do with this data is largely up to you. You may wish to log this information to a report file, write the data to the Windows event log, e-mail a system administrator, or display the problem to the end user. Here, you will simply dump the contents to the console window:

```
// Handle the thrown exception.
static void Main(string[] args)
{
  Console.WriteLine("***** Simple Exception Example *****");
  Console.WriteLine("=> Creating a car and stepping on it!");
  Car myCar = new Car("Zippy", 20);
  myCar.CrankTunes(true);

  // Speed up past the car's max speed to
  // trigger the exception.
  try
  {
    for(int i = 0; i < 10; i++)
      myCar. Accelerate(10);
```

```
    }
    catch(Exception e)
    {
      Console.WriteLine("\n*** Error! ***");
      Console.WriteLine("Method: {0}", e.TargetSite);
      Console.WriteLine("Message: {0}", e.Message);
      Console.WriteLine("Source: {0}", e.Source);
    }

    // The error has been handled, processing continues with the next statement.
    Console.WriteLine("\n***** Out of exception logic *****");
    Console.ReadLine();
  }
```

In essence, a try block is a section of statements that may throw an exception during execution. If an exception is detected, the flow of program execution is sent to the appropriate catch block. On the other hand, if the code within a try block does not trigger an exception, the catch block is skipped entirely, and all is right with the world. Figure 7-2 shows a test run of this program.

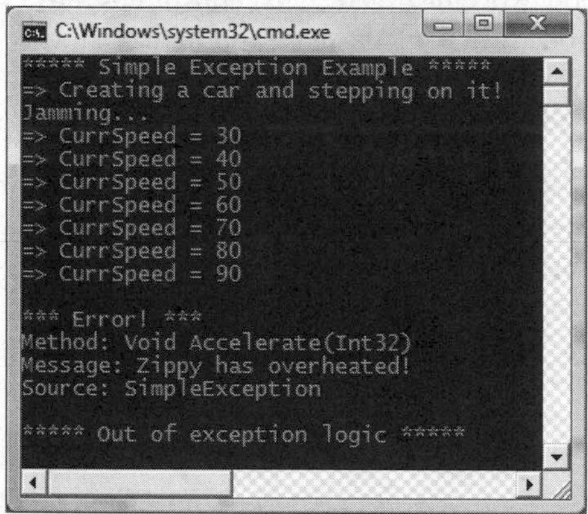

Figure 7-2. *Dealing with the error using structured exception handling*

As you can see, once an exception has been handled, the application is free to continue on from the point after the catch block. In some circumstances, a given exception may be critical enough to warrant the termination of the application. However, in a good number of cases, the logic within the exception handler will ensure the application will be able to continue on its merry way (although it may be slightly less functional, such as the case of not being able to connect to a remote data source).

Configuring the State of an Exception

Currently, the System.Exception object configured within the Accelerate() method simply establishes a value exposed to the Message property (via a constructor parameter). As shown previously in Table 7-1, however, the Exception class also supplies a number of additional members (TargetSite, StackTrace, HelpLink, and Data) that can be useful in further qualifying the nature of the problem. To spruce up our current example, let's examine further details of these members on a case-by-case basis.

The TargetSite Property

The System.Exception.TargetSite property allows you to determine various details about the method that threw a given exception. As shown in the previous Main() method, printing the value of TargetSite will display the return value, name, and parameters of the method that threw the exception. However, TargetSite does not simply return a vanilla-flavored string, but a strongly typed System.Reflection.MethodBase object. This type can be used to gather numerous details regarding the offending method as well as the class that defines the offending method. To illustrate, assume the previous catch logic has been updated as follows:

```
static void Main(string[] args)
{
...
  // TargetSite actually returns a MethodBase object.
  catch(Exception e)
  {
    Console.WriteLine("\n*** Error! ***");
    Console.WriteLine("Member name: {0}", e.TargetSite);
    Console.WriteLine("Class defining member: {0}",
      e.TargetSite.DeclaringType);
    Console.WriteLine("Member type: {0}", e.TargetSite.MemberType);
    Console.WriteLine("Message: {0}", e.Message);
    Console.WriteLine("Source: {0}", e.Source);
  }
  Console.WriteLine("\n***** Out of exception logic *****");
  Console.ReadLine();
}
```

This time, you make use of the MethodBase.DeclaringType property to determine the fully qualified name of the class that threw the error (SimpleException.Car in this case) as well as the MemberType property of the MethodBase object to identify the type of member (such as a property vs. a method) where this exception originated. Figure 7-3 shows the updated output.

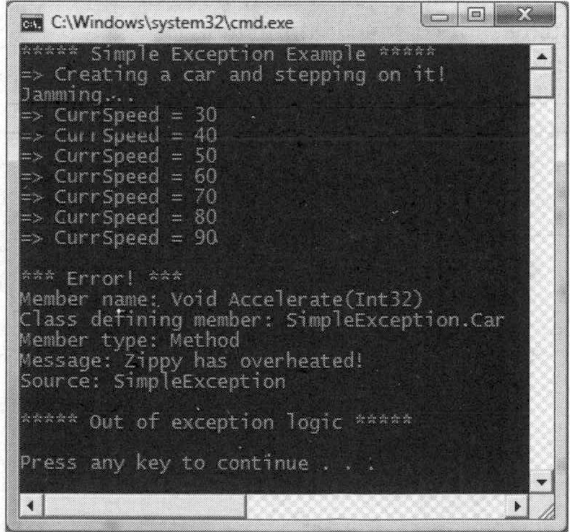

Figure 7-3. *Obtaining aspects of the target site*

The StackTrace Property

The `System.Exception.StackTrace` property allows you to identify the series of calls that resulted in the exception. Be aware that you never set the value of `StackTrace` as it is established automatically at the time the exception is created. To illustrate, assume you have once again updated your `catch` logic:

```
catch(Exception e)
{
  ...
  Console.WriteLine("Stack: {0}", e.StackTrace);
}
```

If you were to run the program, you would find the following stack trace is printed to the console (your line numbers and file paths may differ, of course):

```
Stack: at SimpleException.Car.Accelerate(Int32 delta)
in c:\MyApps\SimpleException\car.cs:line 65 at SimpleException.Program.Main()
in c:\MyApps\SimpleException\Program.cs:line 21
```

The string returned from `StackTrace` documents the sequence of calls that resulted in the throwing of this exception. Notice how the bottommost line number of this string identifies the first call in the sequence, while the topmost line number identifies the exact location of the offending member. Clearly, this information can be quite helpful during the debugging or logging of a given application, as you are able to "follow the flow" of the error's origin.

The HelpLink Property

While the `TargetSite` and `StackTrace` properties allow programmers to gain an understanding of a given exception, this information is of little use to the end user. As you have already seen, the `System.Exception.Message` property can be used to obtain human-readable information that may be displayed to the current user. In addition, the `HelpLink` property can be set to point the user to a specific URL or standard Windows help file that contains more detailed information.

By default, the value managed by the `HelpLink` property is an empty string. If you wish to fill this property with a more interesting value, you will need to do so before throwing the `System.Exception` type. Here are the relevant updates to the `Car.Accelerate()` method:

```
public void Accelerate(int delta)
{
  if (carIsDead)
    Console.WriteLine("{0} is out of order...", petName);
  else
  {
    currSpeed += delta;
    if (currSpeed >= MaxSpeed)
    {
      carIsDead = true;
      currSpeed = 0;

      // We need to call the HelpLink property, thus we need to
      // create a local variable before throwing the Exception object.
      Exception ex =
        new Exception(string.Format("{0} has overheated!", petName));
      ex.HelpLink = "http://www.CarsRUs.com";
      throw ex;
    }
```

```
    else
      Console.WriteLine("=> CurrSpeed = {0}", currSpeed);
  }
}
```

The catch logic could now be updated to print out this help link information as follows:

```
catch(Exception e)
{
  ...
  Console.WriteLine("Help Link: {0}", e.HelpLink);
}
```

The Data Property

The Data property of System.Exception allows you to fill an exception object with relevant auxiliary information (such as a time stamp or what have you). The Data property returns an object implementing an interface named IDictionary, defined in the System.Collections namespace. Chapter 9 examines the role of interface-based programming as well as the System.Collections namespace. For the time being, just understand that dictionary collections allow you to create a set of values that are retrieved using a specific key. Observe the next update to the Car.Accelerate() method:

```
public void Accelerate(int delta)
{
  if (carIsDead)
    Console.WriteLine("{0} is out of order...", petName);
  else
  {
    currSpeed += delta;
    if (currSpeed >= MaxSpeed)
    {
      carIsDead = true;
      currSpeed = 0;

      // We need to call the HelpLink property, thus we need
      // to create a local variable before throwing the Exception object.
      Exception ex =
        new Exception(string.Format("{0} has overheated!", petName));
      ex.HelpLink = "http://www.CarsRUs.com";

      // Stuff in custom data regarding the error.
      ex.Data.Add("TimeStamp",
        string.Format("The car exploded at {0}", DateTime.Now));
      ex.Data.Add("Cause", "You have a lead foot.");
      throw ex;
    }
    else
      Console.WriteLine("=> CurrSpeed = {0}", currSpeed);
  }
}
```

To successfully enumerate over the key/value pairs, you first must make sure to specify a using directive for the System.Collections namespace, given we will make use of a DictionaryEntry type in the file containing the class implementing your Main() method:

```
using System.Collections;
```

Next, we need to update the catch logic to test that the value returned from the Data property is not null (the default value). After this point, we make use of the Key and Value properties of the DictionaryEntry type to print the custom data to the console:

```
catch (Exception e)
{
...
  // By default, the data field is empty, so check for null.
  Console.WriteLine("\n-> Custom Data:");
  if (e.Data != null)
  {
    foreach (DictionaryEntry de in e.Data)
      Console.WriteLine("-> {0}: {1}", de.Key, de.Value);
  }
}
```

With this, we would now find the update shown in Figure 7-4.

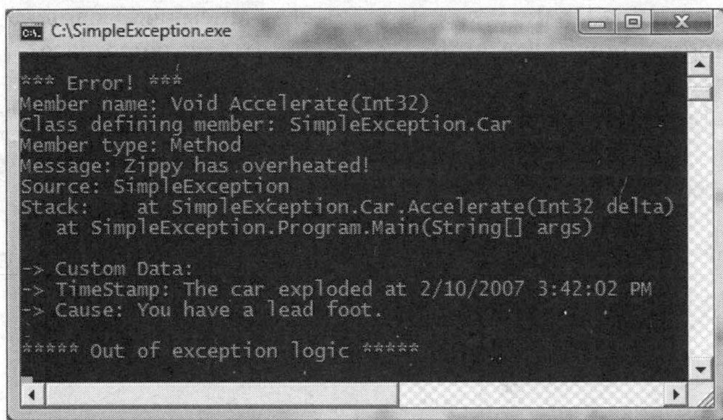

Figure 7-4. *Obtaining programmer-defined data*

The Data property is very useful in that it allows us to pack in custom information regarding the error at hand without requiring us to build a brand-new class type extending the Exception base class (which, prior to .NET 2.0, was our only option!). As helpful as the Data property may be, however, it is still common for .NET developers to build strongly typed exception classes, which account for custom data using strongly typed properties.

This approach allows the caller to catch a specific Exception-derived type, rather than having to dig into a data collection to obtain additional details. To understand how to do so, we need to examine the distinction between system-level and application-level exceptions.

Source Code The SimpleException project is included under the Chapter 7 subdirectory.

System-Level Exceptions (System.SystemException)

The .NET base class libraries define many classes which ultimately derive from System.Exception. For example, the System namespace defines core error objects such as ArgumentOutOfRangeException,

IndexOutOfRangeException, StackOverflowException, and so forth. Other namespaces define exceptions that reflect the behavior of that namespace (e.g., System.Drawing.Printing defines printing exceptions, System.IO defines IO-based exceptions, System.Data defines database-centric exceptions, and so forth).

Exceptions that are thrown by the .NET platform are (appropriately) called *system exceptions*. These exceptions are regarded as nonrecoverable, fatal errors. System exceptions derive directly from a base class named System.SystemException, which in turn derives from System.Exception (which derives from System.Object):

```
public class SystemException : Exception
{
  // Various constructors.
}
```

Given that the System.SystemException type does not add any additional functionality beyond a set of custom constructors, you might wonder why SystemException exists in the first place. Simply put, when an exception type derives from System.SystemException, you are able to determine that the .NET runtime is the entity that has thrown the exception, rather than the code base of the executing application. You can verify this quite simply using the is keyword:

```
// True! NullReferenceException is-a SystemException.
NullReferenceException nullRefEx = new NullReferenceException();

Console.WriteLine("NullReferenceException is-a SystemException? : {0}",
  nullRefEx is SystemException);
```

Application-Level Exceptions (System.ApplicationException)

Given that all .NET exceptions are class types, you are free to create your own application-specific exceptions. However, due to the fact that the System.SystemException base class represents exceptions thrown from the CLR, you may naturally assume that you should derive your custom exceptions from the System.Exception type. While you could do so, best practice dictates that you instead derive from the System.ApplicationException type:

```
public class ApplicationException : Exception
{
  // Various constructors.
}
```

Like SystemException, ApplicationException does not define any additional members beyond a set of constructors. Functionally, the only purpose of System.ApplicationException is to identify the source of the error. When you handle an exception deriving from System.ApplicationException, you can assume the exception was raised by the code base of the executing application, rather than by the .NET base class libraries or .NET runtime engine.

Building Custom Exceptions, Take One

While you can always throw instances of System.Exception to signal a runtime error (as shown in our first example), it is sometimes advantageous to build a *strongly typed exception* that represents the unique details of your current problem. For example, assume you wish to build a custom exception (named CarIsDeadException) to represent the error of speeding up a doomed automobile. The first step is to derive a new class from System.ApplicationException (by convention, all exception classes end with the "Exception" suffix; in fact, this is a .NET best practice).

■ **Note** As a rule, all custom exception classes should be defined as public types (recall, the default access modifier of a non-nested type is internal). The reason is that exceptions are often passed outside of assembly boundaries, and should therefore be accessible to the calling code base.

Create a new Console Application project named CustomException, and copy the previous `Car` and `Radio` definitions into your new project using the Project ➤ Add Existing Item menu option (be sure to change the namespace that defines the `Car` and `Radio` types from `SimpleException` to `CustomException`). Next, add the following class definition:

```
// This custom exception describes the details of the car-is-dead condition.
public class CarIsDeadException : ApplicationException
{}
```

Like any class, you are free to include any number of custom members that can be called within the `catch` block of the calling logic. You are also free to override any virtual members defined by your parent classes. For example, we could implement `CarIsDeadException` by overriding the virtual `Message` property.

As well, rather than filling the data collection (via the `Data` property) when throwing our exception, our constructor allows the sender to pass in a time stamp and reason for the error. Finally, the time stamp data and cause of the error can be obtained using strongly typed properties:

```
public class CarIsDeadException : ApplicationException
{
  private string messageDetails;
  private DateTime errorTimeStamp;
  private string causeOfError;

  public DateTime TimeStamp
  {
    get {return errorTimeStamp;}
    set {errorTimeStamp = value;}
  }

  public string Cause
  {
    get {return causeOfError;}
    set {causeOfError = value;}
  }

  public CarIsDeadException(){}
  public CarIsDeadException(string message,
    string cause, DateTime time)
  {
    messageDetails = message;
    causeOfError = cause;
    errorTimeStamp = time;
  }

  // Override the Exception.Message property.
  public override string Message
  {
    get
    {
```

```
      return string.Format("Car Error Message: {0}", messageDetails);
    }
  }
}
```

Here, the CarIsDeadException type maintains a private data member (messageDetails) that represents data regarding the current exception, which can be set using a custom constructor. Throwing this error from the Accelerate() method is straightforward. Simply allocate, configure, and throw a CarIsDeadException type rather than a System.Exception (notice that in this case, we no longer need to fill the data collection manually):

```
// Throw the custom CarIsDeadException.
public void Accelerate(int delta)
{
...
  CarIsDeadException  ex =
   new CarIsDeadException (string.Format("{0} has overheated!", petName),
   "You have a lead foot", DateTime.Now);
  ex.HelpLink = "http://www.CarsRUs.com";
  throw ex;
...
}
```

To catch this incoming exception, your catch scope can now be updated to catch a specific CarIsDeadException type (however, given that CarIsDeadException "is-a" System.Exception, it is still permissible to catch a System.Exception as well):

```
static void Main(string[] args)
{
  Console.WriteLine("***** Fun with Custom Exceptions *****\n");
  Car myCar = new Car("Rusty", 90);

  try
  {
    // Trip exception.
    myCar.Accelerate(50);
  }
  catch (CarIsDeadException e)
  {
    Console.WriteLine(e.Message);
    Console.WriteLine(e.TimeStamp);
    Console.WriteLine(e.Cause);
  }
  Console.ReadLine();
}
```

So, now that you understand the basic process of building a custom exception, you may wonder when you are required to do so. Typically, you only need to create custom exceptions when the error is tightly bound to the class issuing the error (for example, a custom file-centric class that throws a number of file-related errors, a Car class that throws a number of car-related errors, and so forth). In doing so, you provide the caller with the ability to handle numerous exceptions on a descriptive error-by-error basis.

Building Custom Exceptions, Take Two

The current CarIsDeadException type has overridden the System.Exception.Message property in order to configure a custom error message and supplied two custom properties to account for additional bits of data. In reality, however, we are not required to override the virtual Message property, as we could simply pass the incoming message to our parent's constructor as follows:

```
public class CarIsDeadException : ApplicationException
{
  private DateTime errorTimeStamp;
  private string causeOfError;

  public DateTime TimeStamp
  {
    get { return errorTimeStamp; }
    set { errorTimeStamp = value; }
  }

  public string Cause
  {
    get { return causeOfError; }
    set { causeOfError = value; }
  }

  public CarIsDeadException() { }

  // Feed message to parent constructor.
  public CarIsDeadException(string message,
    string cause, DateTime time)
    :base(message)
  {
    causeOfError = cause;
    errorTimeStamp = time;
  }
}
```

Notice that this time you have *not* defined a string variable to represent the message, and have *not* overridden the Message property. Rather, you are simply passing the parameter to your base class constructor. With this design, a custom exception class is little more than a uniquely named class deriving from System.ApplicationException, devoid of any base class overrides.

Don't be surprised if most (if not all) of your custom exception classes follow this simple pattern. Many times, the role of a custom exception is not necessarily to provide additional functionality beyond what is inherited from the base classes, but to provide a *strongly named type* that clearly identifies the nature of the error.

Building Custom Exceptions, Take Three

If you wish to build a truly prim-and-proper custom exception class, you would want to make sure your type adheres to the exception-centric .NET best practices. Specifically, this requires that your custom exception

- Derives from Exception/ApplicationException
- Is marked with the [System.Serializable] attribute
- Defines a default constructor

- Defines a constructor that sets the inherited `Message` property
- Defines a constructor to handle "inner exceptions"
- Defines a constructor to handle the serialization of your type

Now, based on your current background with .NET, you may have no idea regarding the role of attributes or object serialization, which is just fine. I'll address these topics later in the text (see Chapter 16 for information on attributes and Chapter 21 for details on serialization services). However, to finalize our examination of building custom exceptions, here is the final iteration of `CarIsDeadException`, which accounts for each of these special constructors:

```
[Serializable]
public class CarIsDeadException : ApplicationException
{
  public CarIsDeadException() { }
  public CarIsDeadException(string message) : base( message ) { }
  public CarIsDeadException(string message,
    System.Exception inner) : base( message, inner ) { }
  protected CarIsDeadException(
    System.Runtime.Serialization.SerializationInfo info,
    System.Runtime.Serialization.StreamingContext context)
      : base( info, context ) { }

  // Any additional custom properties, constructors and data members...
}
```

Given that building custom exceptions that adhere to .NET best practices really only differ by their name, you will be happy to know that Visual Studio 2008 provides a code snippet template named "Exception" (see Figure 7-5), which will autogenerate a new exception class that adheres to .NET best practices (see Chapter 2 for an explanation of code snippet templates).

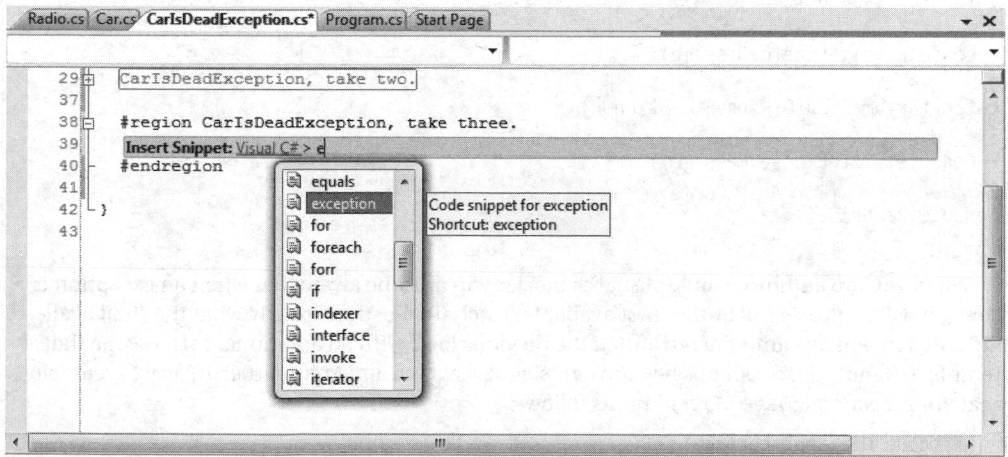

Figure 7-5. *The Exception code snippet template*

Source Code The CustomException project is included under the Chapter 7 subdirectory.

Processing Multiple Exceptions

In its simplest form, a try block has a single catch block. In reality, you often run into a situation where the statements within a try block could trigger *numerous* possible exceptions. Create a new C# Console Application project named ProcessMultipleExceptions, add your existing Car, Radio, and CarIsDeadException classes to the new project (via Project ➤ Add Existing Item), and update your namespace names accordingly.

Now, update the Car's Accelerate() method to also throw a base class library–predefined ArgumentOutOfRangeException if you pass an invalid parameter (which we will assume is any value less than zero):

```
// Test for invalid argument before proceeding.
public void Accelerate(int delta)
{
  if(delta < 0)
    throw new ArgumentOutOfRangeException("Speed must be greater than zero!");
  ...
}
```

The catch logic could now specifically respond to each type of exception:

```
static void Main(string[] args)
{
  Console.WriteLine("***** Handling Multiple Exceptions *****\n");
  Car myCar = new Car("Rusty", 90);

  try
  {
    // Trip Arg out of range exception.
    myCar.Accelerate(-10);
  }
  catch (CarIsDeadException e)
  {
    Console.WriteLine(e.Message);
  }
  catch (ArgumentOutOfRangeException e)
  {
    Console.WriteLine(e.Message);
  }
  Console.ReadLine();
}
```

When you are authoring multiple catch blocks, you must be aware that when an exception is thrown, it will be processed by the "first available" catch. To illustrate exactly what the "first available" catch means, assume you retrofitted the previous logic with an additional catch scope that attempts to handle all exceptions beyond CarIsDeadException and ArgumentOutOfRangeException by catching a general System.Exception as follows:

```
// This code will not compile!
static void Main(string[] args)
{
  Console.WriteLine("***** Handling Multiple Exceptions *****\n");
  Car myCar = new Car("Rusty", 90);

  try
  {
    // Trip Arg out of range exception.
    myCar.Accelerate(-10);
```

```
  }
  catch(Exception e)
  {
    // Process all other exceptions?
    Console.WriteLine(e.Message);
  }
  catch (CarIsDeadException e)
  {
    Console.WriteLine(e.Message);
  }
  catch (ArgumentOutOfRangeException e)
  {
    Console.WriteLine(e.Message);
  }
  Console.ReadLine();
}
```

This exception-handling logic generates compile-time errors. The problem is due to the fact that the first catch block can handle *anything* derived from System.Exception (given the "is-a" relationship), including the CarIsDeadException and ArgumentOutOfRangeException types. Therefore, the final two catch blocks are unreachable!

The rule of thumb to keep in mind is to make sure your catch blocks are structured such that the very first catch is the most specific exception (i.e., the most derived type in an exception type inheritance chain), leaving the final catch for the most general (i.e., the base class of a given exception inheritance chain, in this case System.Exception).

Thus, if you wish to define a catch block that will handle any errors beyond CarIsDeadException and ArgumentOutOfRangeException, you would write the following:

```
// This code compiles just fine.
static void Main(string[] args)
{
  Console.WriteLine("***** Handling Multiple Exceptions *****\n");
  Car myCar = new Car("Rusty", 90);
  try
  {
    // Trip Arg out of range exception.
    myCar.Accelerate(-10);
  }
  catch (CarIsDeadException e)
  {
    Console.WriteLine(e.Message);
  }
  catch (ArgumentOutOfRangeException e)
  {
    Console.WriteLine(e.Message);
  }
  // This will catch any other exception
  // beyond CarIsDeadException or
  // ArgumentOutOfRangeException.
  catch(Exception e)
  {
    Console.WriteLine(e.Message);
  }
  Console.ReadLine();
}
```

Generic catch Statements

C# also supports a "generic" catch scope that does not explicitly receive the exception object thrown by a given member:

```
// A generic catch.
static void Main(string[] args)
{
  Console.WriteLine("***** Handling Multiple Exceptions *****\n");
  Car myCar = new Car("Rusty", 90);
  try
  {
    myCar.Accelerate(90);
  }
  catch
  {
    Console.WriteLine("Something bad happened...");
  }
  Console.ReadLine();
}
```

Obviously, this is not the most informative way to handle exceptions, given that you have no way to obtain meaningful data about the error that occurred (such as the method name, call stack, or custom message). Nevertheless, C# does allow for such a construct, which can be helpful when you wish to handle all errors in a very generic fashion.

Rethrowing Exceptions

Be aware that it is permissible for logic in a try block to *rethrow* an exception up the call stack to the previous caller. To do so, simply make use of the throw keyword within a catch block. This passes the exception up the chain of calling logic, which can be helpful if your catch block is only able to partially handle the error at hand:

```
// Passing the buck.
static void Main(string[] args)
{
...
  try
  {
    // Speed up car logic...
  }
  catch(CarIsDeadException e)
  {
    // Do any partial processing of this error and pass the buck.
    throw;
  }
...
}
```

Be aware that in this example code, the ultimate receiver of CarIsDeadException is the CLR, given that it is the Main() method rethrowing the exception. Given this point, your end user is presented with a system-supplied error dialog box. Typically, you would only rethrow a partial handled exception to a caller that has the ability to handle the incoming exception more gracefully.

Also notice that we are not explicitly rethrowing the CarIsDeadException object, but rather making use of the throw keyword with no argument. Doing so preserves the context of the original target.

Inner Exceptions

As you may suspect, it is entirely possible to trigger an exception at the time you are handling another exception. For example, assume that you are handling a CarIsDeadException within a particular catch scope, and during the process you attempt to record the stack trace to a file on your C drive named carErrors.txt (you must specify you are using the System.IO namespace to gain access to these I/O-centric types):

```
catch(CarIsDeadException e)
{
  // Attempt to open a file named carErrors.txt on the C drive.
  FileStream fs = File.Open(@"C:\carErrors.txt", FileMode.Open);
  ...
}
```

Now, if the specified file is not located on your C drive, the call to File.Open() results in a FileNotFoundException! Later in this text, you will learn all about the System.IO namespace where you will discover how to programmatically determine whether a file exists on the hard drive before attempting to open the file in the first place (thereby avoiding the exception altogether). However, to keep focused on the topic of exceptions, assume the exception has been raised.

When you encounter an exception while processing another exception, best practice states that you should record the new exception object as an "inner exception" within a new object of the same type as the initial exception (that was a mouthful). The reason we need to allocate a new object of the exception being handled is that the only way to document an inner exception is via a constructor parameter. Consider the following code:

```
catch (CarIsDeadException e)
{
  try
  {
    FileStream fs = File.Open(@"C:\carErrors.txt", FileMode.Open);
    ...
  }
  catch (Exception e2)
  {
    // Throw an exception that records the new exception,
    // as well as the message of the first exception.
    throw new CarIsDeadException(e.Message, e2);
  }
}
```

Notice in this case, we have passed in the FileNotFoundException object as the second parameter to the CarIsDeadException constructor. Once we have configured this new object, we throw it up the call stack to the next caller, which in this case would be the Main() method.

Given that there is no "next caller" after Main() to catch the exception, we would be again presented with an error dialog box. Much like the act of rethrowing an exception, recording inner exceptions is usually only useful when the caller has the ability to gracefully catch the exception in the first place. If this is the case, the caller's catch logic can make use of the InnerException property to extract the details of the inner exception object.

The Finally Block

A try/catch scope may also define an optional finally block. The motivation behind a finally block is to ensure that a set of code statements will *always* execute, exception (of any type) or not.

To illustrate, assume you wish to always power down the car's radio before exiting `Main()`, regardless of any handled exception:

```
static void Main(string[] args)
{
  Console.WriteLine("***** Handling Multiple Exceptions *****\n");
  Car myCar = new Car("Rusty", 90);
  myCar.CrankTunes(true);

  try
  {
    // Speed up car logic.
  }
  catch(CarIsDeadException e)
  {
    // Process CarIsDeadException.
  }
  catch(ArgumentOutOfRangeException e)
  {
    // Process ArgumentOutOfRangeException.
  }
  catch(Exception e)
  {
    // Process any other Exception.
  }
  finally
  {
    // This will always occur. Exception or not.
    myCar.CrankTunes(false);
  }
  Console.ReadLine();
}
```

If you did not include a `finally` block, the radio would not be turned off if an exception is encountered (which may or may not be problematic). In a more real-world scenario, when you need to dispose of objects, close a file, detach from a database (or whatever), a `finally` block ensures a location for proper cleanup.

Who Is Throwing What?

Given that a method in the .NET Framework could throw any number of exceptions (under various circumstances), a logical question would be "How do I know which exceptions may be thrown by a given base class library method?" The ultimate answer is simple: consult the .NET Framework 3.5 SDK documentation. Each method in the help system documents the exceptions a given member may throw. As a quick alternative, Visual Studio 2008 allows you to view the list of all exceptions thrown by a base class library member (if any) simply by hovering your mouse cursor over the member name in the code window (see Figure 7-6).

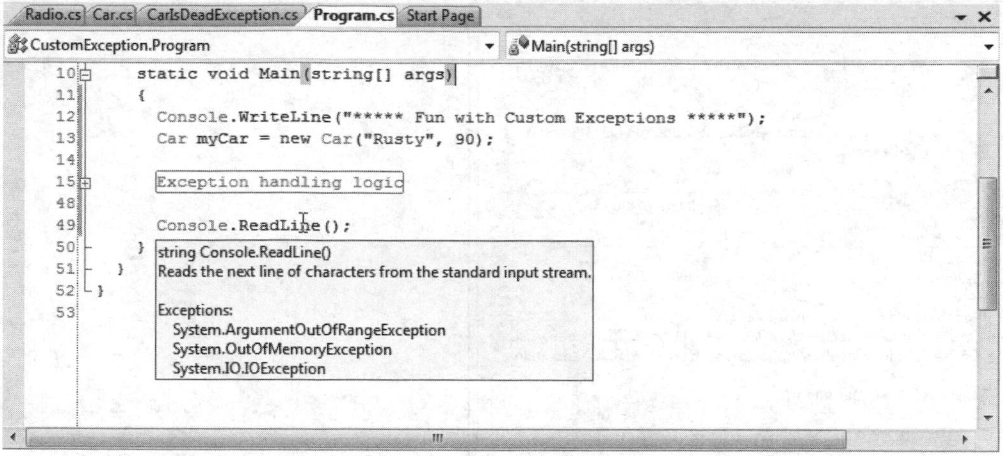

Figure 7-6. *Identifying the exceptions thrown from a given method*

For those coming to .NET from a Java background, understand that type members are *not* prototyped with the set of exceptions it may throw (in other words, .NET does not support checked exceptions). For better or for worse, you are *not* required to handle each and every exception thrown from a given member. In many cases, you can handle all possible errors thrown from a set scope by catching a single `System.Exception`:

```
static void Main(string[] args)
{
  try
  {
    File.Open("IDontExist.txt", FileMode.Open);
  }
  catch(Exception ex)
  {
    Console.WriteLine(ex.Message);
  }
}
```

However, if you do wish to handle specific exceptions uniquely, just make use of multiple catch blocks as shown throughout this chapter.

The Result of Unhandled Exceptions

At this point, you might be wondering what would happen if you do not handle an exception thrown your direction. Assume that the logic in `Main()` increases the speed of the `Car` object beyond the maximum speed, without the benefit of `try`/`catch` logic. The result of ignoring an exception would be highly obstructive to the end user of your application, as an “unhandled exception” dialog box is displayed (see Figure 7-7).

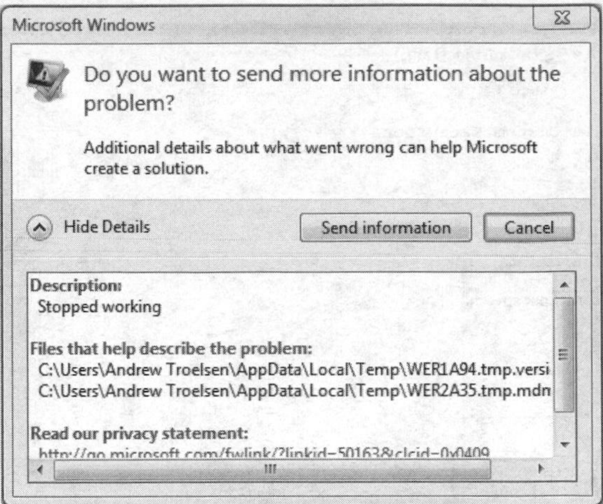

Figure 7-7. *The result of not dealing with exceptions*

■ **Source Code** The ProcessMultipleExceptions project is included under the Chapter 7 subdirectory.

Debugging Unhandled Exceptions Using Visual Studio

To wrap things up, do be aware that Visual Studio 2008 provides a number of tools that help you debug unhandled custom exceptions. Again, assume you have increased the speed of a `Car` object beyond the maximum. If you were to start a debugging session (using the Debug ➤ Start menu selection), Visual Studio automatically breaks at the time the uncaught exception is thrown. Better yet, you are presented with a window (see Figure 7-8) displaying the value of the `Message` property.

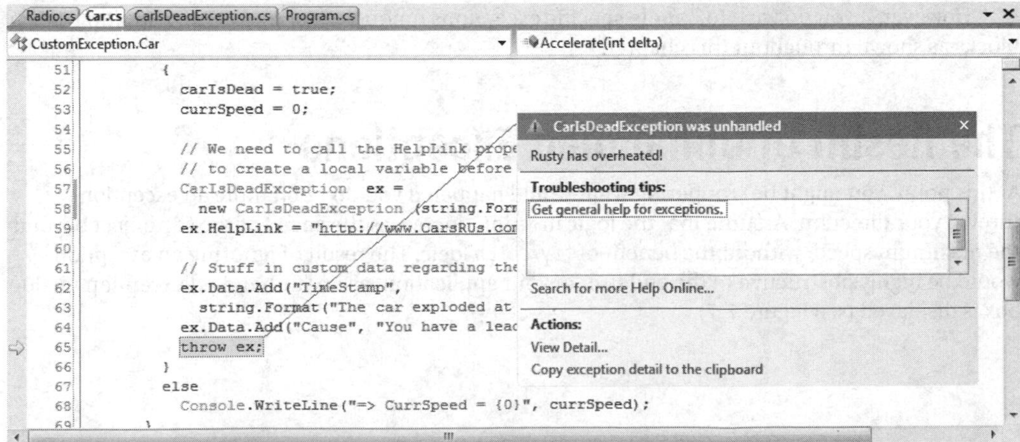

Figure 7-8. *Debugging unhandled custom exceptions with Visual Studio 2008*

If you click the View Detail link, you will find the details regarding the state of the object (see Figure 7-9).

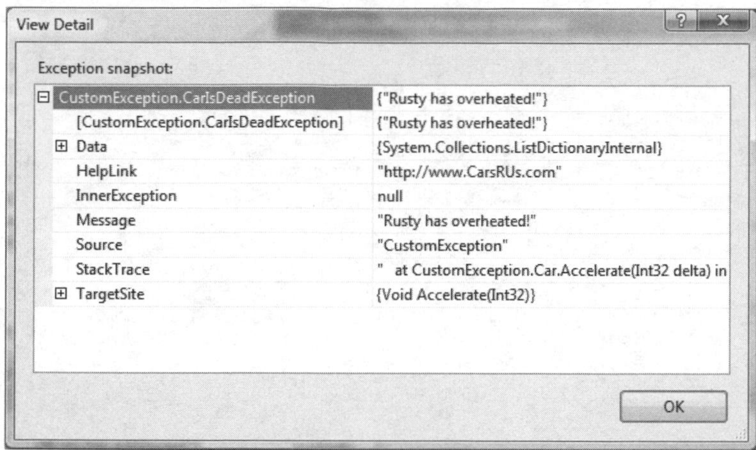

Figure 7-9. *Viewing exception details*

■Note If you fail to handle an exception thrown by a method in the .NET base class libraries, the Visual Studio 2008 debugger breaks at the statement that called the offending method.

Summary

In this chapter, you examined the role of structured exception handling. When a method needs to send an error object to the caller, it will allocate, configure, and throw a specific `System.Exception` derived type via the C# `throw` keyword. The caller is able to handle any possible incoming exceptions using the C# `catch` keyword and an optional `finally` scope.

When you are creating your own custom exceptions, you ultimately create a class type deriving from `System.ApplicationException`, which denotes an exception thrown from the currently executing application. In contrast, error objects deriving from `System.SystemException` represent critical (and fatal) errors thrown by the CLR. Last but not least, this chapter illustrated various tools within Visual Studio 2008 that can be used to create custom exceptions (according to .NET best practices) as well as debug exceptions.

CHAPTER 8

Understanding Object Lifetime

At this point in the text, you have learned a great deal about how to build custom class types using C#. Here, you will come to understand how the CLR is managing allocated objects via *garbage collection*. C# programmers never directly deallocate a managed object from memory (recall there is no delete keyword in the C# language). Rather, .NET objects are allocated onto a region of memory termed the *managed heap*, where they will be automatically destroyed by the garbage collector "sometime in the future."

Once you have examined the core details of the collection process, you will learn how to programmatically interact with the garbage collector using the System.GC class type. Next you examine how the virtual System.Object.Finalize() method and IDisposable interface can be used to build types that release internal *unmanaged resources* in a timely manner. By the time you have completed this chapter, you will have a solid understanding of how .NET objects are managed by the CLR.

Classes, Objects, and References

To frame the topics examined in this chapter, it is important to further clarify the distinction between classes, objects, and references. Recall that a class is nothing more than a blueprint that describes how an instance of this type will look and feel in memory. Classes, of course, are defined within a code file (which in C# takes a *.cs extension by convention). Consider a simple Car class defined within a new C# Console Application project named SimpleGC:

```
// Car.cs
public class Car
{
  private int currSp;
  private string petName;

  public Car(){}
  public Car(string name, int speed)
  {
    petName = name;
    currSp = speed;
  }
  public override string ToString()
  {
    return string.Format("{0} is going {1} MPH",
      petName, currSp);
  }
}
```

Once a class is defined, you can allocate any number of objects using the C# new keyword. Understand, however, that the new keyword returns a *reference* to the object on the heap, not the actual object itself. This reference variable is stored on the stack for further use in your application. When you wish to invoke members on the object, apply the C# dot operator to the stored reference:

```
class Program
{
  static void Main(string[] args)
  {
    // Create a new Car object on
    // the managed heap. We are
    // returned a reference to this
    // object ("refToMyCar").
    Car refToMyCar = new Car("Zippy", 50);

    // The C# dot operator (.) is used
    // to invoke members on the object
    // using our reference variable.
    Console.WriteLine(refToMyCar.ToString());
    Console.ReadLine();
  }
}
```

Figure 8-1 illustrates the class, object, and reference relationship.

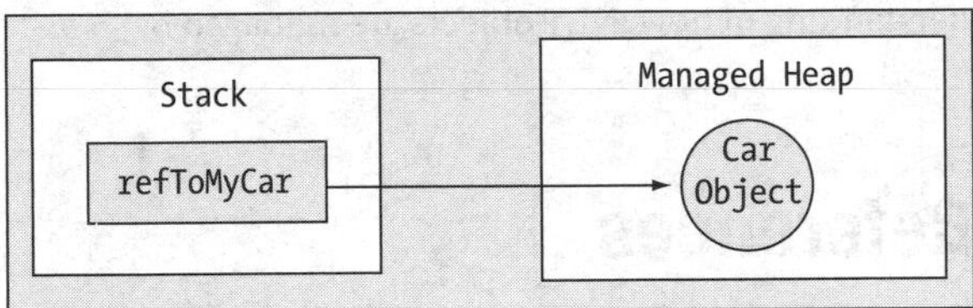

Figure 8-1. *References to objects on the managed heap*

The Basics of Object Lifetime

When you are building your C# applications, you are correct to assume that the managed heap will take care of itself without your direct intervention. In fact, the golden rule of .NET memory management is simple:

■ **Rule** Allocate an object onto the managed heap using the new keyword and forget about it.

Once instantiated, the garbage collector will destroy the object when it is no longer needed. The next obvious question, of course, is, "How does the garbage collector determine when an object is no longer needed?" The short (i.e., incomplete) answer is that the garbage collector removes an object from the heap when it is *unreachable* by any part of your code base. Assume you have a method in your Program class that allocates a local Car object:

```
static void MakeACar()
{
  // If myCar is the only reference to the Car object,
  // it *may* be destroyed when this method returns.
  Car myCar = new Car();
}
```

Notice that the Car reference (myCar) has been created directly within the MakeACar() method and has not been passed outside of the defining scope (via a return value or ref/out parameters). Thus, once this method call completes, the myCar reference is no longer reachable, and the associated Car object is now a candidate for garbage collection. Understand, however, that you cannot guarantee that this object will be reclaimed from memory immediately after MakeACar() has completed. All you can assume at this point is that when the CLR performs the next garbage collection, the myCar object could be safely destroyed.

As you will most certainly discover, programming in a garbage-collected environment will greatly simplify your application development. In stark contrast, C++ programmers are painfully aware that if they fail to manually delete heap-allocated objects, memory leaks are never far behind. In fact, tracking down memory leaks is one of the most time-consuming (and tedious) aspects of programming with unmanaged languages. By allowing the garbage collector to be in charge of destroying objects, the burden of memory management has been taken from your shoulders and placed onto those of the CLR.

■ **Note** If you happen to have a background in COM development, do know that .NET objects do not maintain an internal reference counter, and therefore managed objects do not expose methods such as AddRef() or Release().

The CIL of new

When the C# compiler encounters the new keyword, it will emit a CIL newobj instruction into the method implementation. If you were to compile the current example code and investigate the resulting assembly using ildasm.exe, you would find the following CIL statements within the MakeACar() method:

```
.method public hidebysig static void MakeACar() cil managed
{
  // Code size  7 (0x7)
  .maxstack  1
  .locals init ([0] class SimpleGC.Car c)
  IL_0000:  newobj instance void  SimpleGC.Car::.ctor()
  IL_0005:  stloc.0
  IL_0006:  ret
} // end of method Program::MakeACar
```

Before we examine the exact rules that determine when an object is removed from the managed heap, let's check out the role of the CIL newobj instruction in a bit more detail. First, understand that the managed heap is more than just a random chunk of memory accessed by the CLR. The .NET garbage collector is quite a tidy housekeeper of the heap, given that it will compact empty blocks of memory (when necessary) for purposes of optimization. To aid in this endeavor, the managed heap maintains a pointer (commonly referred to as the *next object pointer* or *new object pointer*) that identifies exactly where the next object will be located.

These things being said, the newobj instruction informs the CLR to perform the following core tasks:

- Calculate the total amount of memory required for the object to be allocated (including the necessary memory required by the type's data members and the type's base classes).
- Examine the managed heap to ensure that there is indeed enough room to host the object to be allocated. If this is the case, the type's constructor is called, and the caller is ultimately returned a reference to the new object in memory, whose address just happens to be identical to the last position of the next object pointer.
- Finally, before returning the reference to the caller, advance the next object pointer to point to the next available slot on the managed heap.

The basic process is illustrated in Figure 8-2.

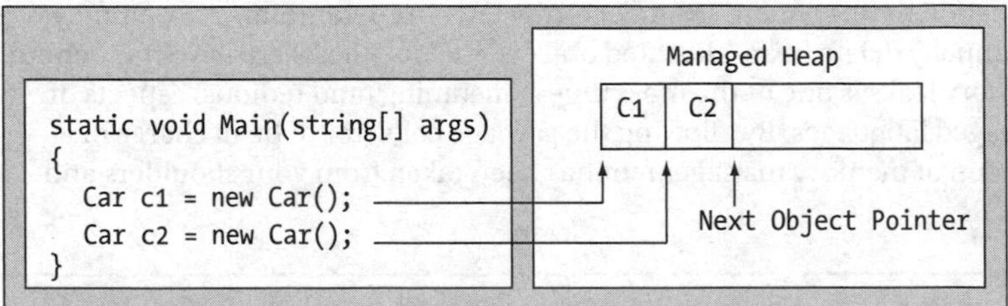

Figure 8-2. *The details of allocating objects onto the managed heap*

As your application is busy allocating objects, the space on the managed heap may eventually become full. When processing the newobj instruction, if the CLR determines that the managed heap does not have sufficient memory to allocate the requested type, it will perform a garbage collection in an attempt to free up memory. Thus, the next rule of garbage collection is also quite simple:

■ **Rule** If the managed heap does not have sufficient memory to allocate a requested object, a garbage collection will occur.

When a collection does take place, the garbage collector temporarily suspends all active *threads* within the current process to ensure that the application does not access the heap during the collection process. We will examine the topic of threads in Chapter 18; however, for the time being, simply regard a thread as a path of execution within a running executable. Once the garbage collection cycle has completed, the suspended threads are permitted to carry on their work. Thankfully, the .NET garbage collector is highly optimized; you will seldom (if ever) notice this brief interruption in your application.

Setting Object References to null

Those of you who have created COM objects using Visual Basic 6.0 were well aware that it was always preferable to set their references to Nothing when you were finished using them. Under the covers, the reference count of the COM object was decremented by one, and may be removed from memory if the object's reference count equaled 0. In a similar fashion, C/C++ programmers often set pointer variables to null to ensure they are no longer referencing unmanaged memory.

Given these facts, you might wonder what the end result is of assigning object references to null under C#. For example, assume the MakeACar() subroutine has now been updated as follows:

```
static void MakeACar()
{
  Car myCar = new Car();
  myCar = null;
}
```

When you assign object references to null, the compiler will generate CIL code that ensures the reference (myCar in this example) no longer points to any object. If you were once again to make use of ildasm.exe to view the CIL code of the modified MakeACar(), you would find the ldnull opcode (which pushes a null value on the virtual execution stack) followed by a stloc.0 opcode (which sets the null reference on the allocated Car):

```
.method private hidebysig static void MakeACar() cil managed
{
  // Code size       10 (0xa)
  .maxstack  1
  .locals init ([0] class SimpleGC.Car myCar)
  IL_0000:  nop
  IL_0001:  newobj instance void SimpleGC.Car::.ctor()
  IL_0006:  stloc.0
  IL_0007:  ldnull
  IL_0008:  stloc.0
  IL_0009:  ret
} // end of method Program::MakeACar
```

What you must understand, however, is that assigning a reference to null does not in any way force the garbage collector to fire up at that exact moment and remove the object from the heap. The only thing you have accomplished is explicitly clipping the connection between the reference and the object it previously pointed to. Given this point, setting references to null under C# is far less consequential than doing so in other C-based languages (or VB 6.0); however, doing so will certainly not cause any harm.

The Role of Application Roots

Now, back to the topic of how the garbage collector determines when an object is "no longer needed." To understand the details, you need to be aware of the notion of *application roots*. Simply put, a *root* is a storage location containing a reference to an object on the heap. Strictly speaking, a root can fall into any of the following categories:

- References to global objects (while not allowed in C#, CIL code does permit allocation of global objects)
- References to any static objects/static fields
- References to local objects within an application's code base
- References to object parameters passed into a method
- References to objects waiting to be *finalized* (described later in this chapter)
- Any CPU register that references an object

During a garbage collection process, the runtime will investigate objects on the managed heap to determine whether they are still reachable (aka *rooted*) by the application. To do so, the CLR will build an *object graph*, which represents each reachable object on the heap. Object graphs will be explained in some detail during our discussion of object serialization (Chapter 21). For now, just understand that object graphs are used to document all reachable objects. As well, be aware that the garbage collector will never graph the same object twice, thus avoiding the nasty circular reference count found in COM programming.

Assume the managed heap contains a set of objects named A, B, C, D, E, F, and G. During a garbage collection, these objects (as well as any internal object references they may contain) are examined for active roots. Once the graph has been constructed, unreachable objects (which we will assume are objects C and F) are marked as garbage. Figure 8-3 diagrams a possible object graph for the scenario just described (you can read the directional arrows using the phrase *depends on* or *requires*, for example, "E depends on G and indirectly B," "A depends on nothing," and so on).

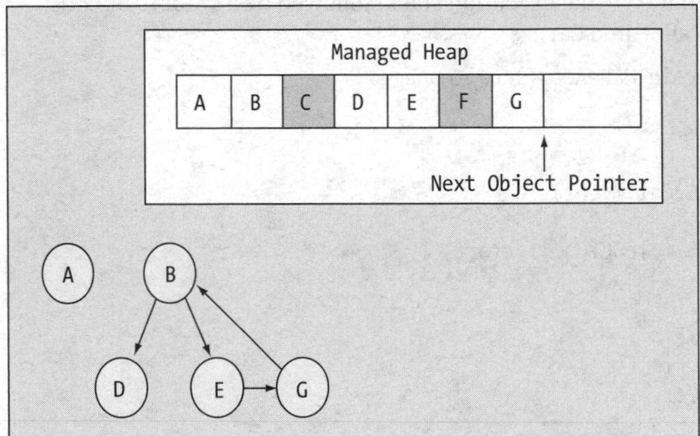

Figure 8-3. *Object graphs are constructed to determine which objects are reachable by application roots.*

Once an object has been marked for termination (C and F in this case—as they are not accounted for in the object graph), they are swept from memory. At this point, the remaining space on the heap is compacted, which in turn will cause the CLR to modify the set of active application roots (and the underlying pointers) to refer to the correct memory location (this is done automatically and transparently). Last but not least, the next object pointer is readjusted to point to the next available slot. Figure 8-4 illustrates the resulting readjustment.

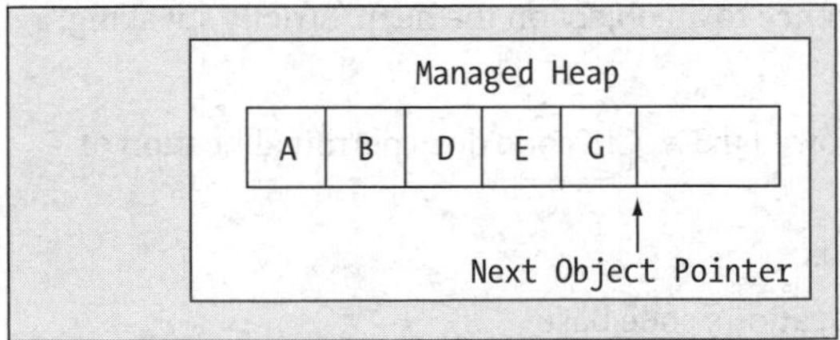

Figure 8-4. *A clean and compacted heap*

■ **Note** Strictly speaking, the garbage collector makes use of two distinct heaps, one of which is specifically used to store very large objects. This heap is less frequently consulted during the collection cycle, given possible performance penalties involved with relocating large objects. Regardless of this fact, it is safe to consider the "managed heap" as a single region of memory.

Understanding Object Generations

When the CLR is attempting to locate unreachable objects, is does *not* literally examine each and every object placed on the managed heap. Obviously, doing so would involve considerable time, especially in larger (i.e., real-world) applications.

To help optimize the process, each object on the heap is assigned to a specific "generation." The idea behind generations is simple: the longer an object has existed on the heap, the more likely it is to stay there. For example, the object implementing `Main()` will be in memory until the program terminates. Conversely, objects that have been recently placed on the heap (such as an object allocated within a method scope) are likely to be unreachable rather quickly. Given these assumptions, each object on the heap belongs to one of the following generations:

- *Generation 0*: Identifies a newly allocated object that has never been marked for collection
- *Generation 1*: Identifies an object that has survived a garbage collection (i.e., it was marked for collection, but was not removed due to the fact that the sufficient heap space was acquired)
- *Generation 2*: Identifies an object that has survived more than one sweep of the garbage collector

The garbage collector will investigate all generation 0 objects first. If marking and sweeping these objects results in the required amount of free memory, any surviving objects are promoted to generation 1. To illustrate how an object's generation affects the collection process, ponder Figure 8-5, which diagrams how a set of surviving generation 0 objects (A, B, and E) are promoted once the required memory has been reclaimed.

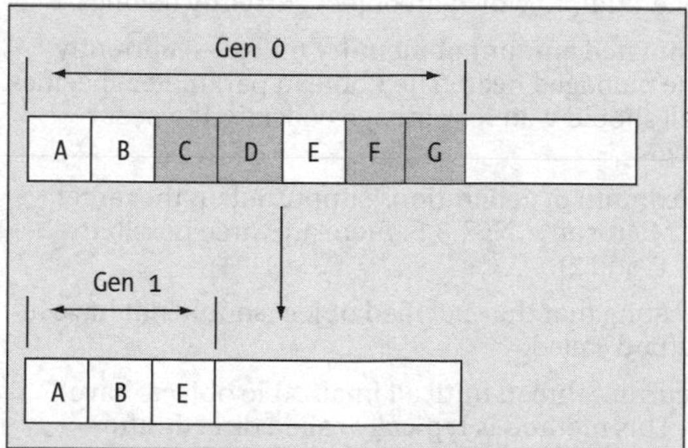

Figure 8-5. *Generation 0 objects that survive a garbage collection are promoted to generation 1.*

If all generation 0 objects have been evaluated, but additional memory is still required, generation 1 objects are then investigated for their "reachability" and collected accordingly. Surviving generation 1 objects are then promoted to generation 2. If the garbage collector *still* requires additional memory, generation 2 objects are then evaluated for their reachability. At this point, if a generation 2 object survives a garbage collection, it remains a generation 2 object given the predefined upper limit of object generations.

The bottom line is that by assigning a generational value to objects on the heap, newer objects (such as local variables) will be removed quickly, while older objects (such as a program's application object) are not "bothered" as often.

The System.GC Type

The base class libraries provide a class type named `System.GC` that allows you to programmatically interact with the garbage collector using a set of static members. Now, do be very aware that you will seldom (if ever) need to make use of this type directly in your code. Typically speaking, the only time you will make use of the members of `System.GC` is when you are creating types that make use of *unmanaged resources*. Table 8-1 provides a rundown of some of the more interesting members (consult the .NET Framework 3.5 SDK documentation for complete details).

Table 8-1. *Select Members of the* `System.GC` *Type*

System.GC Member	Meaning in Life
`AddMemoryPressure()` `RemoveMemoryPressure()`	Allow you to specify a numerical value that represents the calling object's "urgency level" regarding the garbage collection process. Be aware that these methods should alter pressure *in tandem* and thus never remove more pressure than the total amount you have added.
`Collect()`	Forces the GC to perform a garbage collection. This method has been overloaded to specify a generation to collect, as well as the mode of collection (via the `GCCollectionMode` enumeration).
`CollectionCount()`	Returns a numerical value representing how many times a given generation has been swept.
`GetGeneration()`	Returns the generation to which an object currently belongs.
`GetTotalMemory()`	Returns the estimated amount of memory (in bytes) currently allocated on the managed heap. The Boolean parameter specifies whether the call should wait for garbage collection to occur before returning.
`MaxGeneration`	Returns the maximum of generations supported on the target system. Under Microsoft's .NET 3.5, there are three possible generations (0, 1, and 2).
`SuppressFinalize()`	Sets a flag indicating that the specified object should not have its `Finalize()` method called.
`WaitForPendingFinalizers()`	Suspends the current thread until all finalizable objects have been finalized. This method is typically called directly after invoking `GC.Collect()`.

To illustrate how the `System.GC` type can be used to obtain various garbage collection–centric details, consider the following `Main()` method, which makes use of several members of `GC`:

```
static void Main(string[] args)
{
  Console.WriteLine("***** Fun with System.GC *****");

  // Print out estimated number of bytes on heap.
  Console.WriteLine("Estimated bytes on heap: {0}",
    GC.GetTotalMemory(false));

  // MaxGeneration is zero based, so add 1 for display purposes.
  Console.WriteLine("This OS has {0} object generations.\n",
    (GC.MaxGeneration + 1));

  Car refToMyCar = new Car("Zippy", 100);
  Console.WriteLine(refToMyCar.ToString());

  // Print out generation of refToMyCar object.
  Console.WriteLine("Generation of refToMyCar is: {0}",
    GC.GetGeneration(refToMyCar));

  Console.ReadLine();
}
```

Forcing a Garbage Collection

Again, the whole purpose of the .NET garbage collector is to manage memory on our behalf. However, under some very rare circumstances, it may be beneficial to programmatically force a garbage collection using `GC.Collect()`. Specifically:

- Your application is about to enter into a block of code that you do not wish to be interrupted by a possible garbage collection.
- Your application has just finished allocating an extremely large number of objects and you wish to remove as much of the acquired memory as possible.

If you determine it may be beneficial to have the garbage collector check for unreachable objects, you could explicitly trigger a garbage collection, as follows:

```
static void Main(string[] args)
{
...
  // Force a garbage collection and wait for
  // each object to be finalized.
  GC.Collect();
  GC.WaitForPendingFinalizers();
...
}
```

When you manually force a garbage collection, you should always make a call to `GC.WaitForPendingFinalizers()`. With this approach, you can rest assured that all *finalizable objects* have had a chance to perform any necessary cleanup before your program continues forward. Under the hood, `GC.WaitForPendingFinalizers()` will suspend the calling "thread" during the collection process. This is a good thing, as it ensures your code does not invoke methods on an object currently being destroyed!

The `GC.Collect()` method can also be supplied a numerical value that identifies the oldest generation on which a garbage collection will be performed. For example, if you wished to instruct the CLR to only investigate generation 0 objects, you would write the following:

```
static void Main(string[] args)
{
...
  // Only investigate generation 0 objects.
  GC.Collect(0);
  GC.WaitForPendingFinalizers();
...
}
```

As well, as of .NET 3.5, the Collect() method can also be passed in a value of the GCCollectionMode enumeration as a second parameter, to fine-tune exactly how the runtime should force the garbage collection. This enum defines the following values:

```
public enum GCCollectionMode
{
  Default,    // Forced is the current default.
  Forced,     // Tells the runtime to collect immediately!
  Optimized   // Allows the runtime to determine
              // whether the current time is optimal to reclaim objects.
}
```

Like any garbage collection, calling GC.Collect() will promote surviving generations. To illustrate, assume that our Main() method has been updated as follows:

```
static void Main(string[] args)
{
  Console.WriteLine("***** Fun with System.GC *****");

  // Print out estimated number of bytes on heap.
  Console.WriteLine("Estimated bytes on heap: {0}",
    GC.GetTotalMemory(false));

  // MaxGeneration is zero based.
  Console.WriteLine("This OS has {0} object generations.\n",
    (GC.MaxGeneration + 1));

  Car refToMyCar = new Car("Zippy", 100);
  Console.WriteLine(refToMyCar.ToString());

  // Print out generation of refToMyCar.
  Console.WriteLine("\nGeneration of refToMyCar is: {0}",
    GC.GetGeneration(refToMyCar));

  // Make a ton of objects for testing purposes.
  object[] tonsOfObjects = new object[50000];
  for (int i = 0; i < 50000; i++)
    tonsOfObjects[i] = new object();

  // Collect only gen 0 objects.
  GC.Collect(0, GCCollectionMode.Forced);
  GC.WaitForPendingFinalizers();

  // Print out generation of refToMyCar.
  Console.WriteLine("Generation of refToMyCar is: {0}",
    GC.GetGeneration(refToMyCar));
```

```
    // See if tonsOfObjects[9000] is still alive.
    if (tonsOfObjects[9000] != null)
    {
      Console.WriteLine("Generation of tonsOfObjects[9000] is: {0}",
        GC.GetGeneration(tonsOfObjects[9000]));
    }
    else
      Console.WriteLine("tonsOfObjects[9000] is no longer alive.");

    // Print out how many times a generation has been swept.
    Console.WriteLine("\nGen 0 has been swept {0} times",
      GC.CollectionCount(0));
    Console.WriteLine("Gen 1 has been swept {0} times",
      GC.CollectionCount(1));
    Console.WriteLine("Gen 2 has been swept {0} times",
      GC.CollectionCount(2));
    Console.ReadLine();
  }
```

Here, we have purposely created a very large array of `object` types (50,000 to be exact) for testing purposes. As you can see from the output shown in Figure 8-6, even though this `Main()` method only made one explicit request for a garbage collection (via the `GC.Collect()` method), the CLR performed a number of them in the background.

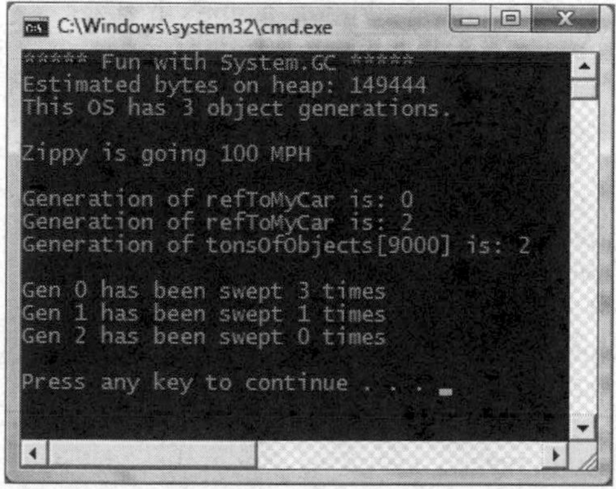

Figure 8-6. *Interacting with the CLR garbage collector via* `System.GC`

At this point in the chapter, I hope you feel more comfortable regarding the details of object lifetime. The remainder of this chapter examines the garbage collection process a bit further by addressing how you can build *finalizable objects* as well as *disposable objects*. Be very aware that the following techniques will only be useful if you are building managed classes that maintain internal unmanaged resources.

Source Code The SimpleGC project is included under the Chapter 8 subdirectory.

Building Finalizable Objects

In Chapter 6, you learned that the supreme base class of .NET, `System.Object`, defines a virtual method named `Finalize()`. The default implementation of this method does nothing whatsoever:

```
// System.Object
public class Object
{
  ...
  protected virtual void Finalize() {}
}
```

When you override `Finalize()` for your custom classes, you establish a specific location to perform any necessary cleanup logic for your type. Given that this member is defined as protected, it is not possible to directly call an object's `Finalize()` method from a class instance via the dot operator. Rather, the *garbage collector* will call an object's `Finalize()` method (if supported) before removing the object from memory.

■ **Note** It is illegal to override `Finalize()` on structure types. This makes perfect sense given that structures are value types, which are never allocated on the heap to begin with, and therefore are not garbage collected!

Of course, a call to `Finalize()` will (eventually) occur during a "natural" garbage collection or when you programmatically force a collection via `GC.Collect()`. In addition, a type's finalizer method will automatically be called when the *application domain* hosting your application is unloaded from memory. Based on your current background in .NET, you may know that application domains (or simply AppDomains) are used to host an executable assembly and any necessary external code libraries. If you are not familiar with this .NET concept, you will be by the time you've finished Chapter 17. The short answer is that when your AppDomain is unloaded from memory, the CLR automatically invokes finalizers for every finalizable object created during its lifetime.

Now, despite what your developer instincts may tell you, a *vast majority* of your C# classes will not require any explicit cleanup logic and will not need a custom finalizer. The reason is simple: if your types are simply making use of other managed objects, everything will eventually be garbage collected. The only time you would need to design a class that can clean up after itself is when you are making use of *unmanaged resources* (such as raw OS file handles, raw unmanaged database connections, chunks of unmanaged memory, or other unmanaged resources). Under the .NET platform, unmanaged resources are obtained by directly calling into the API of the operating system using Platform Invocation Services (PInvoke) or due to some very elaborate COM interoperability scenarios. Given this, consider the next rule of garbage collection:

■ **Rule** The only reason to override `Finalize()` is if your C# class is making use of unmanaged resources via PInvoke or complex COM interoperability tasks (typically via various members defined by the `System.Runtime.InteropServices.Marshal` type).

Overriding System.Object.Finalize()

In the rare case that you do build a C# class that makes use of unmanaged resources, you will obviously wish to ensure that the underlying memory is released in a predictable manner. Assume you have created a new C# Console Application named SimpleFinalize and inserted a class named `MyResourceWrapper` that makes use of an unmanaged resource (whatever that may be) and you wish to override Finalize(). The odd thing about doing so in C# is that you cannot do so using the expected override keyword:

```
public class MyResourceWrapper
{
  // Compile-time error!
  protected override void Finalize(){ }
}
```

Rather, when you wish to configure your custom C# class types to override the Finalize() method, you make use of a (C++-like) destructor syntax to achieve the same effect. The reason for this alternative form of overriding a virtual method is that when the C# compiler processes the finalizer syntax, it will automatically add a good deal of required infrastructure within the implicitly overridden Finalize() method (shown in just a moment).

C# finalizers look very similar to a constructor in that they are named identically to the class they are defined within. In addition, finalizers are prefixed with a tilde symbol (~). Unlike a constructor, however, finalizers never take an access modifier (they are implicitly protected), never take parameters and cannot be overloaded (only one finalizer per class).

Here is a custom finalizer for MyResourceWrapper that will issue a system beep when invoked. Obviously this is only for instructional purposes. A real-world finalizer would do nothing more than free any unmanaged resources and would *not* interact with other managed objects, even those referenced by the current object, as you cannot assume they are still alive at the point the garbage collector invokes your Finalize() method:

```
// Override System.Object.Finalize() via finalizer syntax.
class MyResourceWrapper
{
  ~MyResourceWrapper()
  {
    // Clean up unmanaged resources here.

    // Beep when destroyed (testing purposes only!)
    Console.Beep();
  }
}
```

If you were to examine this C# destructor using ildasm.exe, you will see that the compiler inserts some necessary error checking code. First, the code statements within the scope of your Finalize() method are placed within a try block (see Chapter 7). The related finally block ensures that your base classes' Finalize() method will always execute, regardless of any exceptions encountered within the try scope:

```
.method family hidebysig virtual instance void
  Finalize() cil managed
{
  // Code size       13 (0xd)
  .maxstack  1
  .try
  {
    IL_0000:  ldc.i4     0x4e20
    IL_0005:  ldc.i4     0x3e8
    IL_000a:  call
    void [mscorlib]System.Console::Beep(int32, int32)
    IL_000f:  nop
    IL_0010:  nop
    IL_0011:  leave.s    IL_001b
  }  // end .try
```

```
  finally
  {
    IL_0013:  ldarg.0
    IL_0014:
      call instance void [mscorlib]System.Object::Finalize()
    IL_0019:  nop
    IL_001a:  endfinally
  }  // end handler
  IL_001b:  nop
  IL_001c:  ret
} // end of method MyResourceWrapper::Finalize
```

If you were to now test the MyResourceWrapper type, you would find that a system beep occurs when the application terminates, given that the CLR will automatically invoke finalizers upon AppDomain shutdown:

```
static void Main(string[] args)
{
  Console.WriteLine("***** Fun with Finalizers *****\n");
  Console.WriteLine("Hit the return key to shut down this app");
  Console.WriteLine("and force the GC to invoke Finalize()");
  Console.WriteLine("for finalizable objects created in this AppDomain.");
  Console.ReadLine();
  MyResourceWrapper rw = new MyResourceWrapper();
}
```

■ **Source Code** The SimpleFinalize project is included under the Chapter 8 subdirectory.

Detailing the Finalization Process

Not to beat a dead horse, but always remember that the role of the `Finalize()` method is to ensure that a .NET object can clean up unmanaged resources when garbage collected. Thus, if you are building a type that does not make use of unmanaged entities (by far the most common case), finalization is of little use. In fact, if at all possible, you should design your types to avoid supporting a `Finalize()` method for the very simple reason that finalization takes time.

When you allocate an object onto the managed heap, the runtime automatically determines whether your object supports a custom `Finalize()` method. If so, the object is marked as *finalizable*, and a pointer to this object is stored on an internal queue named the *finalization queue*. The finalization queue is a table maintained by the garbage collector that points to each and every object that must be finalized before it is removed from the heap.

When the garbage collector determines it is time to free an object from memory, it examines each entry on the finalization queue and copies the object off the heap to yet another managed structure termed the *finalization reachable* table (often abbreviated as freachable, and pronounced "eff-reachable"). At this point, a separate thread is spawned to invoke the `Finalize()` method for each object on the freachable table *at the next garbage collection*. Given this, it will take at the very least *two* garbage collections to truly finalize an object.

The bottom line is that while finalization of an object does ensure an object can clean up unmanaged resources, it is still nondeterministic in nature, and due to the extra behind-the-curtains processing, considerably slower.

Building Disposable Objects

As you have seen, finalizers can be used to release unmanaged resources when the garbage collector kicks in. However, given that many unmanaged objects are "precious items" (such as database or file handles), it may be valuable to release them as soon as possible instead of relying on a garbage collection to occur. As an alternative to overriding `Finalize()`, your class could implement the `IDisposable` interface, which defines a single method named `Dispose()`:

```
public interface IDisposable
{
  void Dispose();
}
```

If you are new to interface-based programming, Chapter 9 will take you through the details. In a nutshell, an interface as a collection of abstract members a class or structure may support. When you do support the `IDisposable` interface, the assumption is that when the *object user* is finished using the object, it manually calls `Dispose()` before allowing the object reference to drop out of scope. In this way, an object can perform any necessary cleanup of unmanaged resources without incurring the hit of being placed on the finalization queue and without waiting for the garbage collector to trigger the class's finalization logic.

Note Structures and class types can both implement `IDisposable` (unlike overriding `Finalize()`, which is reserved for class types), as the object user (not the garbage collector) invokes the `Dispose()` method.

To illustrate the use of this interface, create a new C# Console Application named SimpleDispose. Here is an updated `MyResourceWrapper` class that now implements `IDisposable`, rather than overriding `System.Object.Finalize()`:

```
// Implementing IDisposable.
public class MyResourceWrapper : IDisposable
{
  // The object user should call this method
  // when they finish with the object.
  public void Dispose()
  {
    // Clean up unmanaged resources...

    // Dispose other contained disposable objects...

    // Just for a test.
    Console.WriteLine("***** In Dispose! *****");
  }
}
```

Notice that a `Dispose()` method is not only responsible for releasing the type's unmanaged resources, but should also call `Dispose()` on any other contained disposable methods. Unlike `Finalize()`, it is perfectly safe to communicate with other managed objects within a `Dispose()` method. The reason is simple: the garbage collector has no clue about the `IDisposable` interface and will never call `Dispose()`. Therefore, when the object user calls this method, the object is still living a productive life on the managed heap and has access to all other heap-allocated objects. The calling logic is straightforward:

```
public class Program
{
  static void Main()
  {
    Console.WriteLine("***** Fun with Dispose *****\n");

    // Create a disposable object and call Dispose()
    // to free any internal resources.
    MyResourceWrapper rw = new MyResourceWrapper();
    rw.Dispose();
    Console.ReadLine();
  }
}
```

Of course, before you attempt to call `Dispose()` on an object, you will want to ensure the type supports the `IDisposable` interface. While you will typically know which base class library types implement `IDisposable` by consulting the .NET Framework 3.5 SDK documentation, a programmatic check can be accomplished using the `is` or `as` keywords discussed in Chapter 6:

```
public class Program
{
  static void Main()
  {
    Console.WriteLine("***** Fun with Dispose *****\n");
    MyResourceWrapper rw = new MyResourceWrapper();
    if (rw is IDisposable)
      rw.Dispose();
    Console.ReadLine();
  }
}
```

This example exposes yet another rule of working with garbage-collected types.

■ **Rule** Always call `Dispose()` on any object you directly create if the object supports `IDisposable`. The assumption you should make is that if the class designer chose to support the `Dispose()` method, the type has some cleanup to perform.

There is one caveat to the previous rule. A number of types in the base class libraries that do implement the `IDisposable` interface provide a (somewhat confusing) alias to the `Dispose()` method, in an attempt to make the disposal-centric method sound more natural for the defining type. By way of an example, while the `System.IO.FileStream` class implements `IDisposable` (and therefore supports a `Dispose()` method), it *also* defines a `Close()` method that is used for the same purpose:

```
// Assume you have imported
// the System.IO namespace...
static void DisposeFileStream()
{
  FileStream fs = new FileStream("myFile.txt", FileMode.OpenOrCreate);

  // Confusing, to say the least!
  // These method calls do the same thing!
  fs.Close();
  fs.Dispose();
}
```

While it does feel more natural to "close" a file rather than "dispose" of one, you may agree that this doubling up of disposal-centric methods is confusing. For the few types that do provide an alias, just remember that if a type implements IDisposable, calling Dispose() is always a correct course of action.

Reusing the C# using Keyword

When you are handling a managed object that implements IDisposable, it will be quite common to make use of structured exception handling to ensure the type's Dispose() method is called in the event of a runtime exception:

```
static void Main(string[] args)
{
  Console.WriteLine("***** Fun with Dispose *****\n");
  MyResourceWrapper rw = new MyResourceWrapper ();
  try
  {
    // Use the members of rw.
  }
  finally
  {
    // Always call Dispose(), error or not.
    rw.Dispose();
  }
}
```

While this is a fine example of defensive programming, the truth of the matter is that few developers are thrilled by the prospects of wrapping each and every disposable type within a try/finally block just to ensure the Dispose() method is called. To achieve the same result in a much less obtrusive manner, C# supports a special bit of syntax that looks like this:

```
static void Main(string[] args)
{
  Console.WriteLine("***** Fun with Dispose *****\n");
  // Dispose() is called automatically when the
  // using scope exits.
  using(MyResourceWrapper rw = new MyResourceWrapper())
  {
    // Use rw object.
  }
}
```

If you were to look at the CIL code of the Main() method using ildasm.exe, you will find the using syntax does indeed expand to try/final logic, with the expected call to Dispose():

```
.method private hidebysig static void Main(string[] args) cil managed
{
...
  .try
  {
    ...
  } // end .try
  finally
  {
...
  IL_0012:  callvirt instance void
    SimpleFinalize.MyResourceWrapper::Dispose()
  } // end handler
```

```
...
} // end of method Program::Main
```

Note If you attempt to "use" an object that does not implement `IDisposable`, you will receive a compiler error.

While this syntax does remove the need to manually wrap disposable objects within `try/finally` logic, the C# `using` keyword unfortunately now has a double meaning (specifying namespaces and invoking a `Dispose()` method). Nevertheless, when you are working with .NET types that support the `IDisposable` interface, this syntactical construct will ensure that the object "being used" will automatically have its `Dispose()` method called once the `using` block has exited.

Also, be aware that it is possible to declare multiple objects *of the same type* within a using scope. As you would expect, the compiler will inject code to call `Dispose()` on each declared object:

```
static void Main(string[] args)
{
  Console.WriteLine("***** Fun with Dispose *****\n");

  // Use a comma-delimited list to declare multiple objects to dispose.
  using(MyResourceWrapper rw = new MyResourceWrapper(),
        rw2 = new MyResourceWrapper())
  {
    // Use rw and rw2 objects.
  }
}
```

Source Code The SimpleDispose project is included under the Chapter 8 subdirectory.

Building Finalizable and Disposable Types

At this point, we have seen two different approaches to construct a class that cleans up internal unmanaged resources. On the one hand, we could override `System.Object.Finalize()`. Using this technique, we have the peace of mind that comes with knowing the object cleans itself up when garbage collected (whenever that may be) without the need for user interaction. On the other hand, we could implement `IDisposable` to provide a way for the object user to clean up the object as soon as it is finished. However, if the caller forgets to call `Dispose()`, the unmanaged resources may be held in memory indefinitely.

As you might suspect, it is possible to blend both techniques into a single class definition. By doing so, you gain the best of both models. If the object user does remember to call `Dispose()`, you can inform the garbage collector to bypass the finalization process by calling `GC.SuppressFinalize()`. If the object user *forgets* to call `Dispose()`, the object will eventually be finalized and have a chance to free up the internal resources. The good news is that the object's internal unmanaged resources will be freed one way or another.

Here is the next iteration of `MyResourceWrapper`, which is now finalizable and disposable, defined in a C# Console Application named FinalizableDisposableClass:

```
// A sophisticated resource wrapper.
public class MyResourceWrapper : IDisposable
{
  // The garbage collector will call this method if the
  // object user forgets to call Dispose().
  ~ MyResourceWrapper()
  {
    // Clean up any internal unmanaged resources.
    // Do **not** call Dispose() on any managed objects.
  }

  // The object user will call this method to clean up
  // resources ASAP.
  public void Dispose()
  {
    // Clean up unmanaged resources here.
    // Call Dispose() on other contained disposable objects.

    // No need to finalize if user called Dispose(),
    // so suppress finalization.
    GC.SuppressFinalize(this);
  }
}
```

Notice that this Dispose() method has been updated to call GC.SuppressFinalize(), which informs the CLR that it is no longer necessary to call the destructor when this object is garbage collected, given that the unmanaged resources have already been freed via the Dispose() logic.

A Formalized Disposal Pattern

The current implementation of MyResourceWrapper does work fairly well; however, we are left with a few minor drawbacks. First, the Finalize() and Dispose() methods each have to clean up the same unmanaged resources. This could result in duplicate code, which can easily become a nightmare to maintain. Ideally, you would define a private helper function that is called by either method.

Next, you would like to make sure that the Finalize() method does not attempt to dispose of any managed objects, while the Dispose() method should do so. Finally, you would also like to make sure that the object user can safely call Dispose() multiple times without error. Currently, our Dispose() method has no such safeguards.

To address these design issues, Microsoft has defined a formal, prim-and-proper disposal pattern that strikes a balance between robustness, maintainability, and performance. Here is the final (and annotated) version of MyResourceWrapper, which makes use of this official pattern:

```
public class MyResourceWrapper : IDisposable
{
  // Used to determine if Dispose()
  // has already been called.
  private bool disposed = false;

  public void Dispose()
  {
    // Call our helper method.
    // Specifying "true" signifies that
    // the object user triggered the cleanup.
    CleanUp(true);
```

```
    // Now suppress finalization.
    GC.SuppressFinalize(this);
  }

  private void CleanUp(bool disposing)
  {
    // Be sure we have not already been disposed!
    if (!this.disposed)
    {
      // If disposing equals true, dispose all
      // managed resources.
      if (disposing)
      {
        // Dispose managed resources.
      }
      // Clean up unmanaged resources here.
    }
    disposed = true;
  }

  ~MyResourceWrapper()
  {
    // Call our helper method.
    // Specifying "false" signifies that
    // the GC triggered the cleanup.
    CleanUp(false);
  }
}
```

Notice that MyResourceWrapper now defines a private helper method named CleanUp(). When specifying true as an argument, we are signifying that the object user has initiated the cleanup, therefore we should clean up all managed *and* unmanaged resources. However, when the garbage collector initiates the cleanup, we specify false when calling CleanUp() to ensure that internal disposable objects are *not* disposed (as we can't assume they are still in memory!). Last but not least, our bool member variable (disposed) is set to true before exiting CleanUp() to ensure that Dispose() can be called numerous times without error.

To test our final iteration of MyResourceWrapper, add a call to Console.Beep() within the scope of your finalizer:

```
~MyResourceWrapper()
{
  Console.Beep();
  // Call our helper method.
  // Specifying "false" signifies that
  // the GC triggered the cleanup.
  CleanUp(false);
}
```

Next, update Main() as follows:

```
static void Main(string[] args)
{
  Console.WriteLine("***** Dispose() / Destructor Combo Platter *****");

  // Call Dispose() manually, this will not call the finalizer.
  MyResourceWrapper rw = new MyResourceWrapper();
  rw.Dispose();
```

```
    // Don't call Dispose(), this will trigger the finalizer
    // and cause a beep.
    MyResourceWrapper rw2 = new MyResourceWrapper();
}
```

Notice that we are explicitly calling Dispose() on the rw object, therefore the destructor call is suppressed. However, we have "forgotten" to call Dispose() on the rw2 object, and therefore when the application terminates, we hear a single beep. If you were to comment out the call to Dispose() on the rw object, you would hear two beeps.

Source Code The FinalizableDisposableClass project is included under the Chapter 8 subdirectory.

That wraps up our investigation of how the CLR is managing your objects via garbage collection. While there are additional (fairly esoteric) details regarding the collection process I have not examined here (such as weak references and object resurrection), you are certainly in a perfect position for further exploration on your own terms.

Summary

The point of this chapter was to demystify the garbage collection process. As you have seen, the garbage collector will only run when it is unable to acquire the necessary memory from the managed heap (or when a given AppDomain unloads from memory). When a collection does occur, you can rest assured that Microsoft's collection algorithm has been optimized by the use of object generations, secondary threads for the purpose of object finalization, and a managed heap dedicated to host large objects.

This chapter also illustrated how to programmatically interact with the garbage collector using the System.GC class type. As mentioned, the only time when you will really need to do so is when you are building finalizable or disposable class types that operate upon unmanaged resources.

Recall that finalizable types are classes that have overridden the virtual System.Object.Finalize() method to clean up unmanaged resources at the time of garbage collection. Disposable objects, on the other hand, are classes (or structures) that implement the IDisposable interface, which should be called by the object user when it is finished using said object. Finally, you learned about an official "disposal" pattern that blends both approaches.

PART 3

Advanced C# Programming Constructs

CHAPTER 9

Working with Interfaces

This chapter builds on your current understanding of object-oriented development by examining the topic of interface-based programming. Here you learn how to define and implement interfaces, and come to understand the benefits of building types that support "multiple behaviors." Along the way, a number of related topics are also discussed, such as obtaining interface references, explicit interface implementation, and the construction of interface hierarchies.

The remainder of this chapter is spent examining a number of standard interfaces defined within the .NET base class libraries. As you will see, your custom types are free to implement these predefined interfaces to support a number of advanced behaviors such as object cloning, object enumeration, and object sorting. We wrap up the chapter by examining how interface types can be used to establish a callback mechanism, allowing two objects in memory to communicate in a bidirectional manner.

Understanding Interface Types

To begin this chapter, allow me to provide a formal definition of the interface type. An *interface* is nothing more than a named set of *abstract members*. Recall from Chapter 6 that abstract methods are pure protocol in that they do not provide a default implementation. The specific members defined by an interface depend on the exact behavior it is modeling. Yes, it's true. An interface expresses a *behavior* that a given class or structure may choose to implement. Furthermore, as you will see in this chapter, a class (or structure) can support as many interfaces as necessary, thereby supporting (in essence) multiple behaviors.

As you might guess, the .NET base class libraries ship with hundreds of predefined interface types that are implemented by various classes and structures. For example, as you will see in Chapter 22, ADO.NET ships with multiple data providers that allow you to communicate with a particular database management system. Thus, unlike COM-based ADO, under ADO.NET we have numerous connection objects we may choose between (`SqlConnection`, `OracleConnection`, `OdbcConnection`, etc.).

Regardless of the fact that each connection object has a unique name, is defined within a different namespace, and (in some cases) is bundled within a different assembly, all connection objects implement a common interface named `IDbConnection`:

```
// The IDbConnection interface defines a common
// set of members supported by all connection objects.
public interface IDbConnection : IDisposable
{
  // Methods
  IDbTransaction BeginTransaction();
  IDbTransaction BeginTransaction(IsolationLevel il);
  void ChangeDatabase(string databaseName);
  void Close();
```

```
    IDbCommand CreateCommand();
    void Open();

    // Properties
    string ConnectionString { get; set;}
    int ConnectionTimeout { get; }
    string Database { get; }
    ConnectionState State { get; }
}
```

■ **Note** By convention, .NET interface types are prefixed with a capital letter "I." When you are creating your own custom interfaces, it is considered a best practice to do the same.

Don't concern yourself with the details of what these members actually do at this point. Simply understand that the IDbConnection interface defines a set of members that are common to all ADO.NET connection objects. Given this, you are guaranteed that each and every connection object supports members such as Open(), Close(), CreateCommand(), and so forth. Furthermore, given that interface members are always abstract, each connection object is free to implement these methods in its own unique manner.

Another example: the System.Windows.Forms namespace defines a class named Control, which is a base class to a number of Windows Forms UI widgets (DataGridView, Label, StatusBar, TreeView, etc.). The Control class implements an interface named IDropTarget, which defines basic drag-and-drop functionality:

```
public interface IDropTarget
{
    // Methods
    void OnDragDrop(DragEventArgs e);
    void OnDragEnter(DragEventArgs e);
    void OnDragLeave(EventArgs e);
    void OnDragOver(DragEventArgs e);
}
```

Based on this interface, we can now correctly assume that any class that extends System.Windows.Forms.Control supports four subroutines named OnDragDrop(), OnDragEnter(), OnDragLeave(), and OnDragOver().

As you work through the remainder of this text, you will be exposed to dozens of interfaces that ship with the .NET base class libraries. As you will see, these interfaces can be implemented on your own custom classes and structures to define types that integrate tightly within the framework.

Contrasting Interface Types to Abstract Base Classes

Given your work in Chapter 6, the interface type may seem very similar to an abstract base class. Recall that when a class is marked as abstract, it *may* define any number of abstract members to provide a polymorphic interface to all derived types. However, even when a class type does define a set of abstract members, it is also free to define any number of constructors, field data, nonabstract members (with implementation), and so on. Interfaces, on the other hand, *only* contain abstract members.

The polymorphic interface established by an abstract parent class suffers from one major limitation in that *only derived types* support the members defined by the abstract parent. However, in larger software systems, it is very common to develop multiple class hierarchies that have no common parent beyond System.Object. Given that abstract members in an abstract base class only apply to derived types, we have no way to configure types in different hierarchies to support the same polymorphic interface. By way of an illustrative example, assume you have defined the following abstract class:

```
abstract class CloneableType
{
  // Only derived types can support this
  // "polymorphic interface." Classes in other
  // heirarchies have no access to this abstract
  // member.
  public abstract object Clone();
}
```

Given this definition, only members that extend `CloneableType` are able to support the `Clone()` method. If you create a new collection of classes that do not extend this base class, you are unable to gain this polymorphic interface. As you would guess, interface types come to the rescue. Once an interface has been defined, it can be implemented by any type, in any hierarchy, within any namespaces or any assembly (written in any .NET programming language). Given this, interfaces are *highly* polymorphic. Consider the standard .NET interface named `ICloneable` defined in the `System` namespace. This interface defines a single method named `Clone()`:

```
public interface ICloneable
{
  object Clone();
}
```

If you were to examine the .NET Framework 3.5 SDK documentation, you would find that a large number of seemingly unrelated types (`System.Array`, `System.Data.SqlClient.SqlConnection`, `System.OperatingSystem`, `System.String`, etc.) all implement this interface. Although these types have no common parent (other than `System.Object`), we can treat them polymorphically via the `ICloneable` interface type.

For example, if we had a method named `CloneMe()` that took an `ICloneable` interface parameter, we could pass this method any object that implements said interface. Consider the following simple `Program` class defined within a Console Application named ICloneableExample:

```
class Program
{
  static void Main(string[] args)
  {
    Console.WriteLine("***** A First Look at Interfaces *****\n");

    // All of these types support the ICloneable interface.
    string myStr = "Hello";
    OperatingSystem unixOS = new OperatingSystem(PlatformID.Unix, new Version());
    System.Data.SqlClient.SqlConnection sqlCnn =
      new System.Data.SqlClient.SqlConnection();

    // Therefore, they can all be passed into a method taking ICloneable.
    CloneMe(myStr);
    CloneMe(unixOS);
    CloneMe(sqlCnn);
    Console.ReadLine();
  }

  private static void CloneMe(ICloneable c)
  {
    // Clone whatever we get and print out the name.
```

```
    object theClone = c.Clone();
    Console.WriteLine("Your clone is a: {0}",
      theClone.GetType().Name);
  }
}
```

When you run this application, you will find the full name of each class print out to the console, via the GetType() method you inherit from System.Object (Chapter 16 will provide full coverage of this method and .NET reflection services).

Source Code The ICloneableExample project is located under the Chapter 9 subdirectory.

Another limitation of traditional abstract base classes is that *each and every derived type* must contend with the set of abstract members and provide an implementation. To see this problem, recall the shapes hierarchy we defined in Chapter 6. Assume we defined a new abstract method in the Shape base class named GetNumberOfPoints(), which allows derived types to return the number of points required to render the shape:

```
abstract class Shape
{
...
  // Every derived class must now support this method!
  public abstract byte GetNumberOfPoints();
}
```

Clearly, the only type that has any points in the first place is Hexagon. However, with this update, *every* derived type (Circle, Hexagon, and ThreeDCircle) must now provide a concrete implementation of this function even if it makes no sense to do so.

Again, the interface type provides a solution. If we were to define an interface that represents the behavior of "having points," we could simply plug it into the Hexagon type, leaving Circle and ThreeDCircle untouched.

Defining Custom Interfaces

Now that you better understand the overall role of interface types, let's see an example of defining custom interfaces. To begin, create a brand-new Console Application named CustomInterface. Using the Project ➤ Add Existing Item menu option, insert the files containing your shape type definitions (MyShapes.cs and Shape.cs in the book's solution code) created back in Chapter 6 during the Shapes example. Once you have done so, rename the namespace that defines your shape-centric types to CustomInterface (simply to avoid having to import namespace definitions within your new project):

```
namespace CustomInterface
{
  // Your previous shape types defined here...
}
```

Now, insert a new interface into your project named IPointy using the Project ➤ Add New Item menu option, as shown in Figure 9-1.

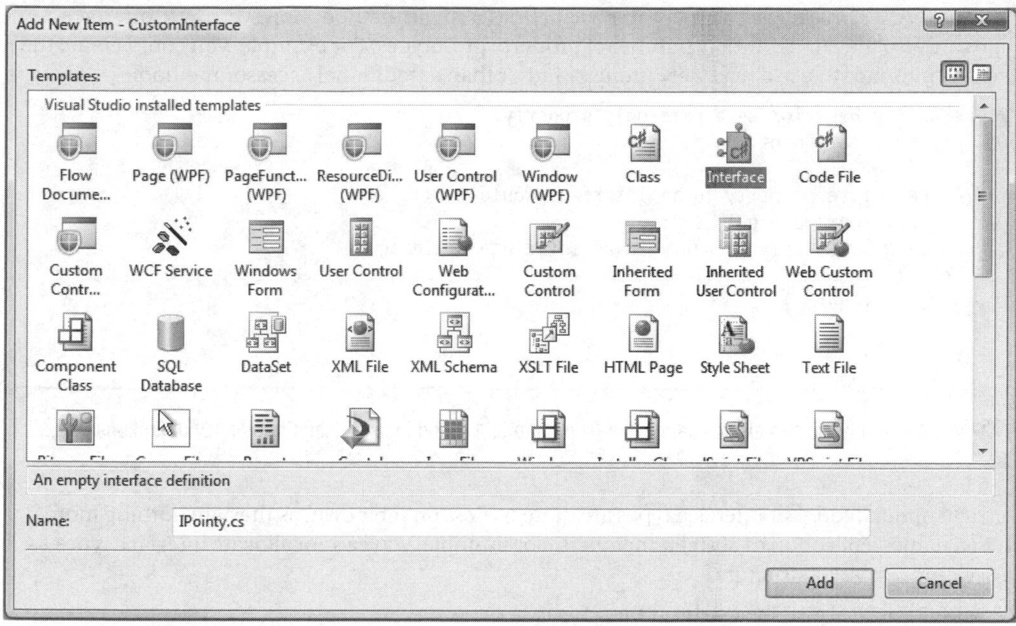

Figure 9-1. *Interfaces, like classes, can be defined in any* `*.cs` *file.*

At a syntactic level, an interface is defined using the C# `interface` keyword. Unlike other .NET types, interfaces never specify a base class (not even `System.Object`) and their members never specify an access modifier (as all interface members are implicitly public and abstract). To get the ball rolling, here is a custom interface defined in C#:

```
// This interface defines the behavior of "having points."
public interface IPointy
{
  // Implicitly public and abstract.
  byte GetNumberOfPoints();
}
```

Notice that when you define interface members, you do *not* define an implementation scope for the member in question. Interfaces are pure protocol, and therefore never define an implementation (that is up to the supporting class or structure). Therefore, the following version of `IPointy` would result in various compiler errors:

```
// Ack! Errors abound!
public interface IPointy
{
  // Error! Interfaces cannot have fields!
  public int numbOfPoints;

  // Error! Interfaces do not have constructors!
  public IPointy() { numbOfPoints = 0;};

  // Error! Interfaces don't provide an implementation!
  byte GetNumberOfPoints() { return numbOfPoints; }
}
```

In any case, this initial IPointy interface defines a single method. However, .NET interface types are also able to define any number of property prototypes. For example, you could create the IPointy interface to use a read-only property rather than a traditional accessor method:

```
// The pointy behavior as a read-only property.
public interface IPointy
{
  // A read-write property in an interface would look like
  // retVal PropName { get; set; }
  // while a write-only property in an interface would be
  // retVal PropName { set; }
  byte Points{ get; }
}
```

Note Interface types can also contain event (see Chapter 11) and indexer (see Chapter 12) definitions.

Do understand that interface types are quite useless on their own, as they are nothing more than a named collection of abstract members. For example, you cannot allocate interface types as you would a class or structure:

```
// Ack! Illegal to allocate interface types.
static void Main(string[] args)
{
  IPointy p = new IPointy();  // Compiler error!
}
```

Interfaces do not bring much to the table until they are implemented by a class or structure. Here, IPointy is an interface that expresses the behavior of "having points." The idea is simple: some classes in the shapes hierarchy have points (such as the Hexagon), while others (such as the Circle) do not.

Implementing an Interface

When a class (or structure) chooses to extend its functionality by supporting interface types, it does so using a comma-delimited list in the type definition. Be aware that the direct base class must be the first item listed after the colon operator. When your class type derives directly from System.Object, you are free to simply list the interface(s) supported by the class, as the C# compiler will extend your types from System.Object if you do not say otherwise. On a related note, given that structures always derive from System.ValueType (see Chapter 4 for full details), simply list each interface directly after the structure definition. Ponder the following examples:

```
// This class derives from System.Object and
// implements a single interface.
public class Pencil : IPointy
{...}

// This class also derives from System.Object
// and implements a single interface.
public class SwitchBlade : object, IPointy
{...}
```

```
// This class derives from a custom base class
// and implements a single interface.
public class Fork : Utensil, IPointy
{...}

// This struct implicitly derives from System.ValueType and
// implements two interfaces.
public struct Arrow : IClonable, IPointy
{...}
```

Understand that implementing an interface is an all-or-nothing proposition. The supporting type is not able to selectively choose which members it will implement. Given that the `IPointy` interface defines a single read-only property, this is not too much of a burden.

However, if you are implementing an interface that defines ten members (such as the `IDbConnection` interface seen earlier), the type is now responsible for fleshing out the details of all ten abstract entities.

For this example, insert a new class type named `Triangle` which "is-a" `Shape` and supports `IPointy`:

```
// New Shape derived class named Triangle.
public class Triangle : Shape, IPointy
{
  public Triangle() { }
  public Triangle(string name) : base(name) { }
  public override void Draw()
  { Console.WriteLine("Drawing {0} the Triangle", PetName); }

  // IPointy Implementation.
  public byte Points
  {
    get { return 3; }
  }
}
```

Now, update your existing `Hexagon` type to also support the `IPointy` interface type:

```
// Hexagon now implements IPointy.
public class Hexagon : Shape, IPointy
{
  public Hexagon(){ }
  public Hexagon(string name) : base(name){ }
  public override void Draw()
  { Console.WriteLine("Drawing {0}  the Hexagon", PetName); }

  // IPointy Implementation.
  public byte Points
  {
    get { return 6; }
  }
}
```

To sum up the story so far, the Visual Studio 2008 class diagram shown in Figure 9-2 illustrates `IPointy`-compatible classes using the popular "lollipop" notation. Notice again that `Circle` and `ThreeDCircle` do not implement `IPointy`, as this behavior makes no sense for these particular types.

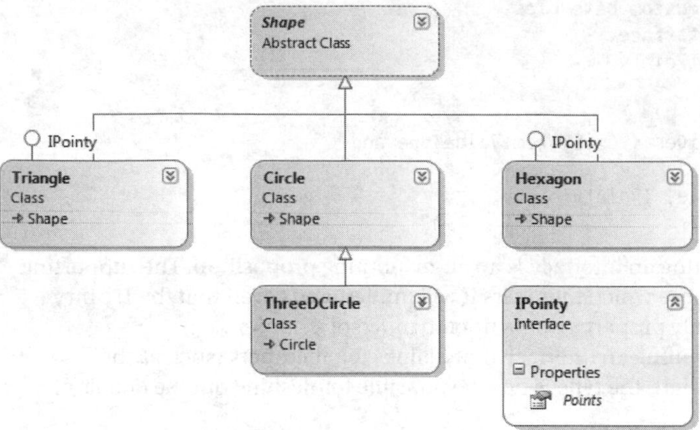

Figure 9-2. *The shapes hierarchy (now with interfaces)*

■ **Note** To display or hide interface names on the class designer, right-click on the interface icon and select Collapse or Expand.

Invoking Interface Members at the Object Level

Now that you have a set of types that support the `IPointy` interface, the next question is how you interact with the new functionality. The most straightforward way to interact with functionality supplied by a given interface is to invoke the methods directly from the object level (provided the interface members are not implemented explicitly; more details later in the section "Resolving Name Clashes via Explicit Interface Implementation"). For example, consider the following `Main()` method:

```
static void Main(string[] args)
{
  Console.WriteLine("***** Fun with Interfaces *****\n");
  // Call Points property defined by IPointy.
  Hexagon hex = new Hexagon();
  Console.WriteLine("Points: {0}", hex.Points);
  Console.ReadLine();
}
```

This approach works fine in this particular case, given that you are well aware that the `Hexagon` type has implemented the interface in question and therefore has a `Points` property. Other times, however, you may not be able to determine which interfaces are supported by a given type. For example, assume you have an array containing 50 `Shape`-compatible types, only some of which support `IPointy`. Obviously, if you attempt to invoke the `Points` property on a type that has not implemented `IPointy`, you receive an error. Next question: how can we dynamically determine the set of interfaces supported by a type?

One way to determine at runtime whether a type supports a specific interface is to make use of an explicit cast. If the type does not support the requested interface, you receive an `InvalidCastException`. To handle this possibility gracefully, make use of structured exception handling, for example:

```
static void Main(string[] args)
{
...
  // Catch a possible InvalidCastException.
  Circle c = new Circle("Lisa");
  IPointy itfPt = null;
  try
  {
    itfPt = (IPointy)c;
    Console.WriteLine(itfPt.Points);
  }
  catch (InvalidCastException e)
  { Console.WriteLine(e.Message); }
  Console.ReadLine();
}
```

While you could make use of `try/catch` logic and hope for the best, it would be ideal to determine which interfaces are supported before invoking the interface members in the first place. Let's see two ways of doing so.

Obtaining Interface References: The as Keyword

The second way you can determine whether a given type supports an interface is to make use of the `as` keyword, which was first introduced in Chapter 6. If the object can be treated as the specified interface, you are returned a reference to the interface in question. If not, you receive a `null` reference. Therefore, be sure to check against a `null` value before proceeding:

```
static void Main(string[] args)
{
...
  // Can we treat hex2 as IPointy?
  Hexagon hex2 = new Hexagon("Peter");
  IPointy itfPt2 = hex2 as IPointy;

  if(itfPt2 != null)
    Console.WriteLine("Points: {0}", itfPt2.Points);
  else
    Console.WriteLine("OOPS! Not pointy...");
  Console.ReadLine();
}
```

Notice that when you make use of the `as` keyword, you have no need to make use of `try/catch` logic, given that if the reference is not `null`, you know you are calling on a valid interface reference.

Obtaining Interface References: The is Keyword

You may also check for an implemented interface using the `is` keyword (also first seen in Chapter 6). If the object in question is not compatible with the specified interface, you are returned the value `false`. On the other hand, if the type is compatible with the interface in question, you can safely call the members without needing to make use of `try/catch` logic.

To illustrate, assume we have an array of `Shape` types containing some members that implement `IPointy`. Notice how we are able to determine which item in the array supports this interface using the `is` keyword, as shown in this retrofitted `Main()` method:

```
static void Main(string[] args)
{
  Console.WriteLine("***** Fun with Interfaces *****\n");

  // Make an array of Shapes.
  Shape[] s = { new Hexagon(), new Circle(), new Triangle("Joe"),
    new Circle("JoJo")} ;

  for(int i = 0; i < s.Length; i++)
  {
    // Recall the Shape base class defines an abstract Draw()
    // member, so all shapes know how to draw themselves.
    s[i].Draw();

    // Who's pointy?
    if(s[i] is IPointy)
      Console.WriteLine("-> Points: {0}", ((IPointy)s[i]).Points);
    else
      Console.WriteLine("-> {0}\'s not pointy!", s[i].PetName);
    Console.WriteLine();
  }
  Console.ReadLine();
}
```

The output follows in Figure 9-3.

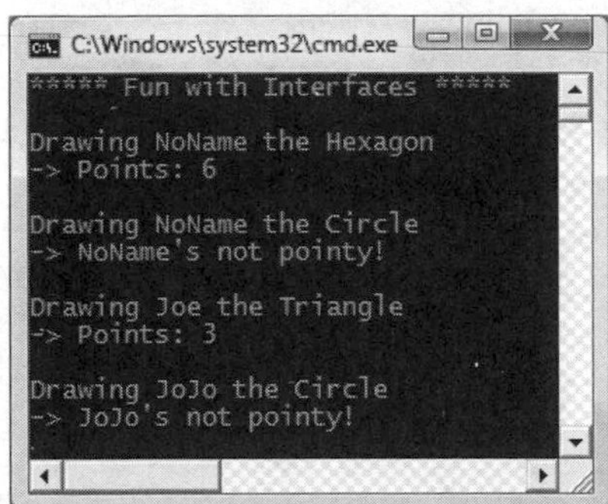

Figure 9-3. *Dynamically determining implemented interfaces*

Interfaces As Parameters

Given that interfaces are valid .NET types, you may construct methods that take interfaces as parameters as illustrated by the `CloneMe()` method earlier in this chapter. For the current example, assume you have defined another interface named `IDraw3D`:

```
// Models the ability to render a type in stunning 3D.
public interface IDraw3D
{
  void Draw3D();
}
```

Next, assume that two of your three shapes (Circle and Hexagon) have been configured to support this new behavior:

```
// Circle supports IDraw3D.
public class Circle : Shape, IDraw3D
{
...
  public void Draw3D()
  {  Console.WriteLine("Drawing Circle in 3D!"); }
}

// Hexagon supports IPointy and IDraw3D.
public class Hexagon : Shape, IPointy, IDraw3D
{
...
  public void Draw3D()
  {  Console.WriteLine("Drawing Hexagon in 3D!"); }
}
```

Figure 9-4 presents the updated Visual Studio 2008 class diagram.

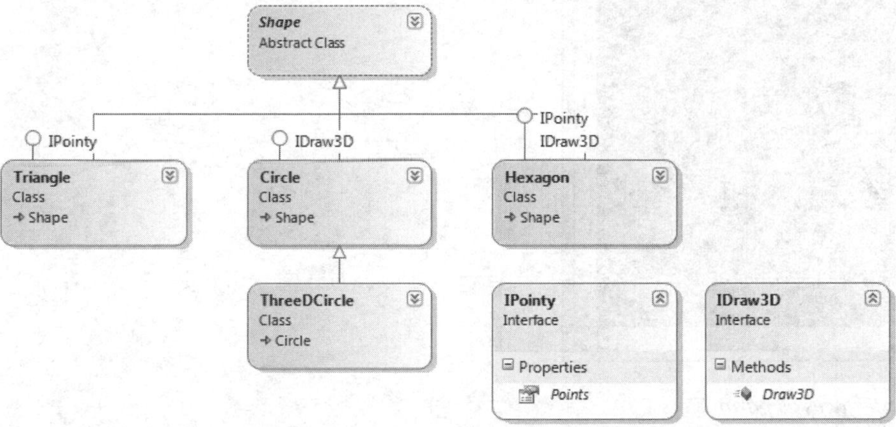

Figure 9-4. *The updated shapes hierarchy*

If you now define a method taking an IDraw3D interface as a parameter, you are able to effectively send in any object implementing IDraw3D (if you attempt to pass in a type not supporting the necessary interface, you receive a compile-time error). Consider the following method defined within your Program type:

```
// I'll draw anyone supporting IDraw3D.
static void DrawIn3D(IDraw3D itf3d)
{
  Console.WriteLine("-> Drawing IDraw3D compatible type");
  itf3d.Draw3D();
}
```

We could now test whether an item in the Shape array supports this new interface, and if so, pass it into the DrawIn3D() method for processing:

```
static void Main()
{
  Console.WriteLine("***** Fun with Interfaces *****\n");
  Shape[] s = { new Hexagon(), new Circle(),
    new Triangle(), new Circle("JoJo") } ;

  for(int i = 0; i < s.Length; i++)
  {
    ...
    // Can I draw you in 3D?
    if(s[i] is IDraw3D)
      DrawIn3D((IDraw3D)s[i]);
  }
}
```

Notice that the `Triangle` type is never drawn in 3D, as it is not `IDraw3D`-compatible (see Figure 9-5).

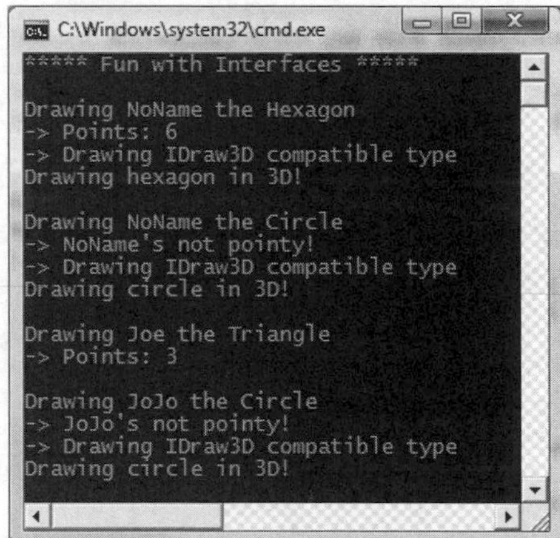

Figure 9-5. *Interfaces as parameters*

Interfaces As Return Values

Interfaces can also be used as method return values. For example, you could write a method that takes any `System.Object`, checks for `IPointy` compatibility, and returns a reference to the extracted interface (if supported):

```
// This method tests for IPointy compatibility and,
// if able, returns an interface reference.
static IPointy ExtractPointyness(object o)
{
  if (o is IPointy)
    return (IPointy)o;
  else
    return null;
}
```

We could interact with this method as follows:

```
static void Main(string[] args)
{
...
  // Attempt to get IPointy from array of ints.
  int[] myInts = {10, 20, 30};
  IPointy itfPt = ExtractPointyness(myInts);
  if(itfPt != null)
    Console.WriteLine("Object has {0} points.", itfPt.Points);
  else
    Console.WriteLine("This object does not implement IPointy");
  Console.ReadLine();
}
```

Arrays of Interface Types

Recall that the same interface can be implemented by numerous types, even if they are not within the same class hierarchy and do not have a common parent class beyond `System.Object`. This can yield some very powerful programming constructs. For example, assume that you have developed three new class types within your current project modeling kitchen utensils (via `Knife` and `Fork` classes) and another modeling gardening equipment (à la `PitchFork`). Consider Figure 9-6.

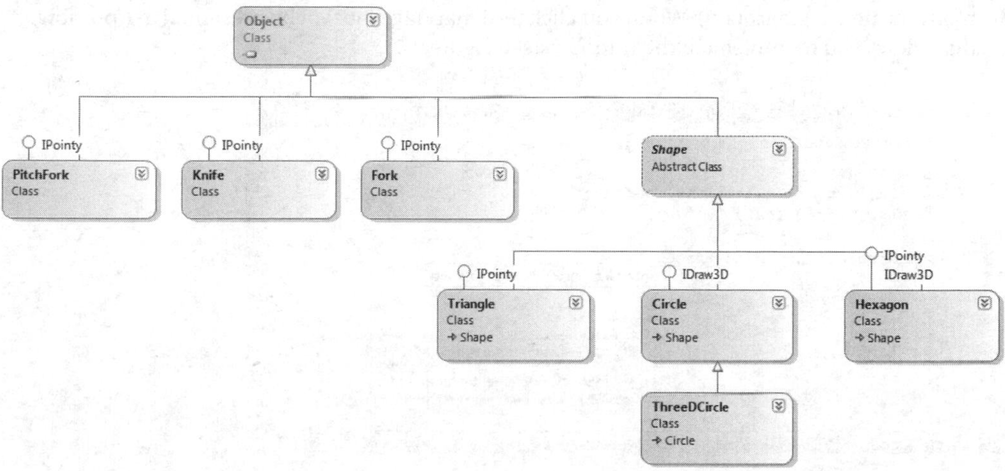

Figure 9-6. *Recall that interfaces can be "plugged into" any type in any part of a class hierarchy.*

If you did define the `PitchFork`, `Fork`, and `Knife` types, you could now define an array of `IPointy`-compatible objects. Given that these members all support the same interface, you are able to iterate through the array and treat each item as an `IPointy`-compatible object, regardless of the overall diversity of the class hierarchies:

```
static void Main(string[] args)
{
...
  // This array can only contain types that
  // implement the IPointy interface.
  IPointy[] myPointyObjects = {new Hexagon(), new Knife(),
    new Triangle(), new Fork(), new PitchFork()};
```

```
  foreach(IPointy i in myPointyObjects)
    Console.WriteLine("Object has {0} points.", i.Points);
  Console.ReadLine();
}
```

■ **Source Code** The CustomInterface project is located under the Chapter 9 subdirectory.

Implementing Interfaces Using Visual Studio 2008

Although interface-based programming is a very powerful programming technique, implementing interfaces may entail a healthy amount of typing. Given that interfaces are a named set of abstract members, you will be required to type in the definition and implementation for *each* interface method on *each* type that supports the behavior.

As you would hope, Visual Studio 2008 does support various tools that make the task of implementing interfaces less burdensome. By way of a simple test, insert a final class into your current project named PointyTestClass. When you implement IPointy (or any interface for that matter) on a type, you might have noticed that when you complete typing the interface's name (or when you position the mouse cursor on the interface name in the code window), the first letter is underlined (formally termed a "smart tag"). When you click the smart tag, you will be presented a drop-down list that allows you to implement the interface (see Figure 9-7).

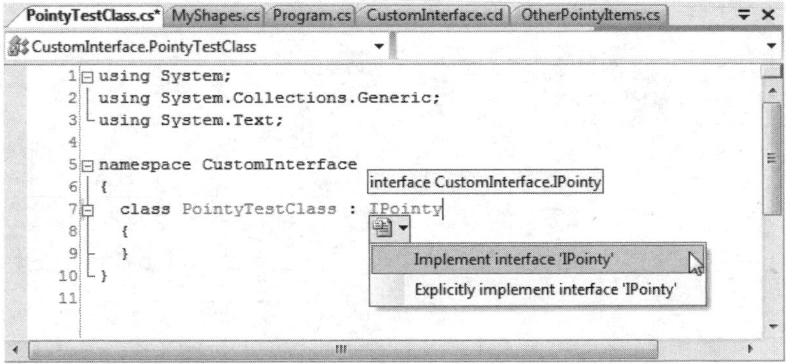

Figure 9-7. *Implementing interfaces using Visual Studio 2008*

Notice you are presented with two options, the second of which (explicit interface implementation) will be examined in the next section. For the time being, once you select the first option, you will see that Visual Studio 2008 has built generated stub code (within a named code region) for you to update (note that the default implementation throws a System.Exception, which can obviously be deleted).

```
namespace CustomInterface
{
  class PointyTestClass : IPointy
  {
    #region IPointy Members
    public byte Points
    {
```

```
      get { throw new Exception("The method or operation is not implemented."); }
    }
    #endregion
  }
}
```

■ **Note** Visual Studio 2008 also supports an extract interface refactoring, available from the Refactoring menu. This allows you to pull out a new interface definition from an existing class definition. See my MSDN article "Refactoring C# Code Using Visual Studio 2005" (the same holds true for Visual Studio 2008) for further details.

Resolving Name Clashes via Explicit Interface Implementation

As shown earlier in this chapter, a single class or structure can implement any number of interfaces. Given this, there is always a possibility that you may implement interfaces that contain identically named members, and therefore have a name clash to contend with. To illustrate various manners in which you can resolve this issue, create a new Console Application named InterfaceNameClash. Now design three custom interfaces that represent various locations to which an implementing type could render its output:

```
// Draw image to a Form.
public interface IDrawToForm
{
  void Draw();
}

// Draw to buffer in memory.
public interface IDrawToMemory
{
  void Draw();
}

// Render to the printer.
public interface IDrawToPrinter
{
  void Draw();
}
```

Notice that each interface defines a method named `Draw()`. If you now wish to support each of these interfaces on a single class type named `Octagon`, the compiler would allow the following definition:

```
class Octagon : IDrawToForm, IDrawToMemory, IDrawToPrinter
{
  public void Draw()
  {
    // Shared drawing logic.
    Console.WriteLine("Drawing the Octagon...");
  }
}
```

Although the code compiles cleanly, you may agree we do have a possible problem. Simply put, providing a single implementation of the Draw() method does not allow us to take unique courses of action based on which interface is obtained from an Octagon object. For example, the following code will invoke the same Draw() method, regardless of which interface we obtain:

```
static void Main(string[] args)
{
  Console.WriteLine("***** Fun with Interface Name Clashes *****\n");
  // All of these invocations call the
  // same Draw() method!
  Octagon oct = new Octagon();
  oct.Draw();
  IDrawToForm itfForm = (IDrawToForm)oct;
  itfForm.Draw();
  IDrawToPrinter itfPriner = (IDrawToPrinter)oct;
  itfPriner.Draw();
  IDrawToMemory itfMemory = (IDrawToMemory)oct;
  itfMemory.Draw();
  Console.ReadLine();
}
```

Clearly, the sort of code required to render the image to a window is quite different from the code needed to render the image to a networked printer or a region of memory. When you implement a collection of interfaces that have identical members, you can resolve this sort of name clash using *explicit interface implementation* syntax. Consider the following update to the Octagon type:

```
class Octagon : IDrawToForm, IDrawToMemory, IDrawToPrinter
{
  // Explicitly bind Draw() implementations
  // to a given interface.
  void IDrawToForm.Draw()
  {
    Console.WriteLine("Drawing to form...");
  }
  void IDrawToMemory.Draw()
  {
    Console.WriteLine("Drawing to memory...");
  }
  void IDrawToPrinter.Draw()
  {
    Console.WriteLine("Drawing to a printer...");
  }
}
```

As you can see, when explicitly implementing an interface member, the general pattern breaks down to

```
returnValue InterfaceName.MethodName(args)
```

Note that when using this syntax, you do not supply an access modifier; explicitly implemented members are automatically private. For example, the following is illegal syntax:

```
// Error! No access modifer!
public void IDrawToForm.Draw()
{
  Console.WriteLine("Drawing to form...");
}
```

Because explicitly implemented members are always implicitly private, these members are no longer available from the object level. In fact, if you were to apply the dot operator to an `Octagon` type, you will find that IntelliSense will not show you any of the `Draw()` members (see Figure 9-8).

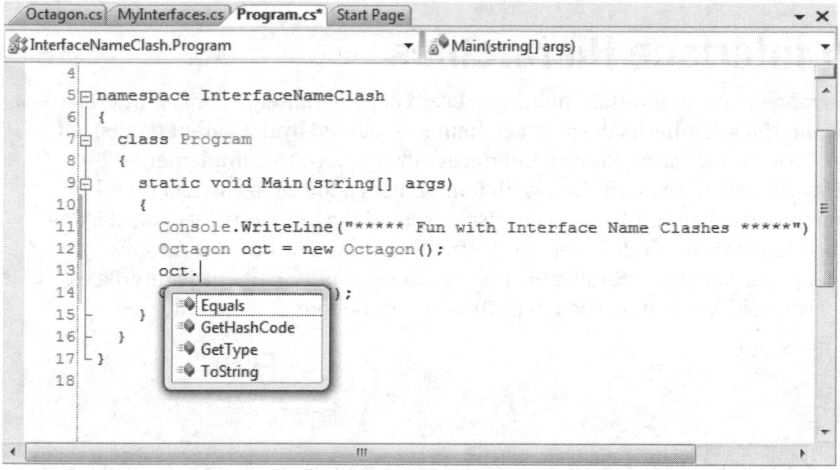

Figure 9-8. *Explicitly implemented interface members are not exposed from the object level.*

As expected, you must make use of explicit casting to access the required functionality. For example:

```
static void Main(string[] args)
{
  Console.WriteLine("***** Fun with Interface Name Clashes *****\n");
  Octagon oct = new Octagon();

  // We now must use casting to access the Draw()
  // members.
  IDrawToForm itfForm = (IDrawToForm)oct;
  itfForm.Draw();

  // Shorthand notation if you don't need
  // the interface variable for later use.
  ((IDrawToPrinter)oct).Draw();

  // Could also use the "as" keyword.
  if(oct is IDrawToMemory)
    ((IDrawToMemory)oct).Draw();

  Console.ReadLine();
}
```

While this syntax is quite helpful when you need to resolve name clashes, you are able to use explicit interface implementation simply to hide more "advanced" members from the object level. In this way, when the object user applies the dot operator, he or she will only see a subset of the type's overall functionality. However, those who require the more advanced behaviors can extract out the desired interface via an explicit cast.

■ **Source Code** The InterfaceNameClash project is located under the Chapter 9 subdirectory.

Designing Interface Hierarchies

Interfaces can be arranged into an interface hierarchy. Like a class hierarchy, when an interface extends an existing interface, it inherits the abstract members defined by the parent type(s). Of course, unlike class-based inheritance, derived interfaces never inherit true implementation. Rather, a derived interface simply extends its own definition with additional abstract members.

Interface hierarchies can be useful when you wish to extend the functionality of an existing interface without breaking existing code bases. To illustrate, create a new Console Application named InterfaceHierarchy. Now, let's redesign the previous set of rendering-centric interfaces (from the InterfaceNameClash example) such that `IDrawable` is the root of the family tree:

```
public interface IDrawable
{
  void Draw();
}
```

Given that `IDrawable` defines a basic drawing behavior, we could now create a derived interface that extends this type with the ability to render its output to the printer. Assume this method is called `Print()`:

```
public interface IPrintable : IDrawable
{
  void Print();
}
```

And just for good measure, we could define a final interface named `IRenderToMemory`, which extends `IPrintable` with a new member named `Render()`:

```
public interface IRenderToMemory : IPrintable
{
  void Render();
}
```

Given this design, if a type were to implement `IRenderToMemory`, we would now be required to implement each and every member defined up the chain of inheritance (specifically, the `Render()`, `Print()`, and `Draw()` methods). On the other hand, if a type were to only implement `IPrintable`, we would only need to contend with `Print()` and `Draw()`. For example:

```
public class SuperShape : IRenderToMemory
{
  public void Draw()
  {
    Console.WriteLine("Drawing...");
  }

  public void Print()
  {
    Console.WriteLine("Printing...");
  }

  public void Render()
  {
```

```
    Console.WriteLine("Rendering...");
  }
}
```

Now, when we make use of the SuperShape, we are able to invoke each method at the object level (as they are all public) as well as extract out a reference to each supported interface explicitly via casting:

```
static void Main(string[] args)
{
  Console.WriteLine("***** The SuperShape *****");
  // Call from object level.
  SuperShape myShape = new SuperShape();
  myShape.Draw();

  // Get IPrintable explicitly.
  // (and IDrawable implicitly!)
  IPrintable iPrint;
  iPrint = (IPrintable)myShape;
  iPrint.Draw();
  iPrint.Print();
  Console.ReadLine();
}
```

Source Code The InterfaceHierarchy project is located under the Chapter 9 subdirectory.

Multiple Inheritance with Interface Types

Unlike class types, it is possible for a single interface to extend multiple base interfaces. This allows us to design some very powerful and flexible abstractions. Create a new Console Application project named MIInterfaceHierarchy. Here is a brand-new collection of interfaces that model various rendering and shape-centric abstractions. Notice that the IShape interface is extending both IDrawable and IPrintable:

```
// Multiple inheritance for interface types is a-okay.
public interface IDrawable
{
   void Draw();
}

public interface IPrintable
{
   void Print();
   void Draw(); // <-- Note possible name clash here!
}

// Multiple interface inheritance. OK!
public interface IShape : IDrawable, IPrintable
{
   int GetNumberOfSides();
}
```

Figure 9-9 illustrates the current interface hierarchy.

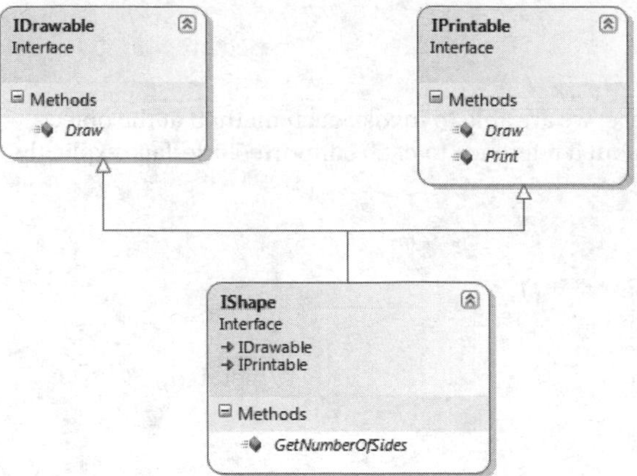

Figure 9-9. *Unlike classes, interfaces can extend multiple interface types.*

Now, the million dollar question is, if we have a class supporting IShape, how many methods will it be required to implement? The answer: it depends. If we wish to provide a simple implementation of the Draw() method, we only need to provide three members, as shown in the following Rectangle type:

```
class Rectangle : IShape
{
  public int GetNumberOfSides()
  { return 4; }

  public void Draw()
  { Console.WriteLine("Drawing..."); }

  public void Print()
  { Console.WriteLine("Prining..."); }
}
```

If you would rather have specific implementations for each Draw() method (which in this case would make the most sense), you can resolve the name clash using explicit interface implementation, as shown in the following Square type:

```
class Square : IShape
{
  // Using explicit implementation to handle member name clash.
  void IPrintable.Draw()
  { // Draw to printer ...
  }
  void IDrawable.Draw()
  { // Draw to screen ...
  }
  public void Print()
  { // Print ...
  }
  public int GetNumberOfSides()
  { return 4; }
}
```

So at this point, you hopefully feel more comfortable with the process of defining and implementing custom interfaces using the syntax of C#. To be honest, interface-based programming can take awhile to get comfortable with, so if you are in fact still scratching your head just a bit, this is a perfectly normal reaction.

Do be aware, however, that interfaces are a fundamental aspect of the .NET Framework. Regardless of the type of application you are developing (web-based, desktop GUIs, data access libraries, etc.), working with interfaces will be part of the process. To summarize the story thus far, remember that interfaces can be extremely useful when

- You have a single hierarchy where only a subset of the derived types support a common behavior.
- You need to model a common behavior that is found across multiple hierarchies with no common parent class beyond `System.Object`.

Now that you have drilled into the specifics of building and implementing custom interfaces, the remainder of the chapter examines a number of predefined interfaces contained within the .NET base class libraries.

■ **Source Code** The MIInterfaceHierarchy project is located under the Chapter 9 subdirectory.

Building Enumerable Types (IEnumerable and IEnumerator)

To begin examining the process of implementing existing .NET interfaces, let's first look at the role of `IEnumerable` and `IEnumerator`. Recall that C# supports a keyword named `foreach`, which allows you to iterate over the contents of any array type:

```
// Iterate over an array of items.
int[] myArrayOfInts = {10, 20, 30, 40};
foreach(int i in myArrayOfInts)
{
  Console.WriteLine(i);
}
```

While it may seem that only array types can make use of this construct, the truth of the matter is any type supporting a method named `GetEnumerator()` can be evaluated by the `foreach` construct. To illustrate, begin by creating a new Console Application project named CustomEnumerator. Next, add the `Car.cs` and `Radio.cs` files defined in the SimpleException example of Chapter 7 (via the Project ➤ Add Existing Item menu option) and update the current class definition with two new properties (named `PetName` and `Speed`) that wrap the existing `currSpeed` and `petName` member variables:

```
public class Car
{
  private int currSpeed;
  private string petName;

  public int Speed
  {
    get { return currSpeed; }
```

```
    set { currSpeed = value; }
  }
  public string PetName
  {
    get { return petName; }
    set { petName = value; }
  }
...
}
```

■ **Note** You may wish to rename the namespace containing the Car and Radio types to CustomEnumerator, simply to avoid having to import the CustomException namespace within this new project.

Now, insert a new class named Garage that stores a set of Car types within a System.Array:

```
// Garage contains a set of Car objects.
public class Garage
{
  private Car[] carArray = new Car[4];

  // Fill with some Car objects upon startup.
  public Garage()
  {
    carArray[0] = new Car("Rusty", 30);
    carArray[1] = new Car("Clunker", 55);
    carArray[2] = new Car("Zippy", 30);
    carArray[3] = new Car("Fred", 30);
  }
}
```

Ideally, it would be convenient to iterate over the Garage object's subitems using the C# foreach construct, just like an array of data values:

```
// This seems reasonable...
public class Program
{
  static void Main(string[] args)
  {
    Console.WriteLine("***** Fun with IEnumerable / IEnumerator *****\n");
    Garage carLot = new Garage();

    // Hand over each car in the collection?
    foreach (Car c in carLot)
    {
      Console.WriteLine("{0} is going {1} MPH",
        c.PetName, c.Speed);
    }
    Console.ReadLine();
  }
}
```

Sadly, the compiler informs you that the Garage class does not implement a method named GetEnumerator(). This method is formalized by the IEnumerable interface, which is found lurking within the System.Collections namespace. Types that support this behavior advertise that they are able to expose contained subitems to the caller (in this example, the foreach keyword itself):

```
// This interface informs the caller
// that the object's subitems can be enumerated.
public interface IEnumerable
{
  IEnumerator GetEnumerator();
}
```

As you can see, the GetEnumerator() method returns a reference to yet another interface named System.Collections.IEnumerator. This interface provides the infrastructure to allow the caller to traverse the internal objects contained by the IEnumerable-compatible container:

```
// This interface allows the caller to
// obtain a container's subitems.
public interface IEnumerator
{
  bool MoveNext ();          // Advance the internal position of the cursor.
  object Current { get;}     // Get the current item (read-only property).
  void Reset ();             // Reset the cursor before the first member.
}
```

If you wish to update the Garage type to support these interfaces, you could take the long road and implement each method manually. While you are certainly free to provide customized versions of GetEnumerator(), MoveNext(), Current, and Reset(), there is a simpler way. As the System.Array type (as well as many other types) already implements IEnumerable and IEnumerator, you can simply delegate the request to the System.Array as follows:

```
using System.Collections;
...
public class Garage : IEnumerable
{
  // System.Array already implements IEnumerator!
  private Car[] carArray = new Car[4];

  public Garage()
  {
    carArray[0] = new Car("FeeFee", 200, 0);
    carArray[1] = new Car("Clunker", 90, 0);
    carArray[2] = new Car("Zippy", 30, 0);
    carArray[3] = new Car("Fred", 30, 0);
  }

  public IEnumerator GetEnumerator()
  {
    // Return the array object's IEnumerator.
    return carArray.GetEnumerator();
  }
}
```

Once you have updated your Garage type, you can now safely use the type within the C# foreach construct. Furthermore, given that the GetEnumerator() method has been defined publicly, the object user could also interact with the IEnumerator type:

```
// Manually work with IEnumerator.
IEnumerator i = carLot.GetEnumerator();
i.MoveNext();
Car myCar = (Car)i.Current;
Console.WriteLine("{0} is going {1} MPH", myCar.PetName, myCar.Speed);
```

However, if you would prefer to hide the functionality of IEnumerable from the object level, simply make use of explicit interface implementation:

```
IEnumerator IEnumerable.GetEnumerator()
{
  // Return the array object's IEnumerator.
  return carArray.GetEnumerator();
}
```

By doing so, the causal object user will not find the Garage's GetEnumerator() method, while the foreach construct will obtain the interface in the background when necessary.

Source Code The CustomEnumerator project is located under the Chapter 9 subdirectory.

Building Iterator Methods with the yield Keyword

Historically, when you wished to build a custom collection (such as Garage) that supported foreach enumeration, implementing the IEnumerable interface (and possibly the IEnumerator interface) was your only option. However, since the release of .NET 2.0, we are provided with an alternative way to build types that work with the foreach loop via *iterators*.

Simply put, an iterator is a member that specifies how a container's internal items should be returned when processed by foreach. While the iterator method must still be named GetEnumerator(), and the return value must still be of type IEnumerator, your custom class does not need to implement any of the expected interfaces.

To illustrate, create a new Console Application project named CustomEnumeratorWithYield and insert the Car, Radio, and Garage types from the previous example (again, renaming your namespace definitions to the current project if you so choose). Now, retrofit the current Garage type as follows:

```
public class Garage
{
  private Car[] carArray = new Car[4];
  ...
  // Iterator method.
  public IEnumerator GetEnumerator()
  {
    foreach (Car c in carArray)
    {
      yield return c;
    }
  }
}
```

Notice that this implementation of GetEnumerator() iterates over the subitems using internal foreach logic and returns each Car to the caller using the yield return syntax. The yield keyword is used to specify the value (or values) to be returned to the caller's foreach construct. When the yield return statement is reached, the current location is stored, and execution is restarted from this location the next time the iterator is called.

Iterator methods are not required to make use of the foreach keyword to return its contents. It is also permissible to define this iterator method as follows:

```
public IEnumerator GetEnumerator()
{
  yield return carArray[0];
```

```
    yield return carArray[1];
    yield return carArray[2];
    yield return carArray[3];
}
```

In this implementation, notice that the `GetEnumerator()` method is explicitly returning a new value to the caller with each pass through. Doing so for this example makes little sense, given that if we were to add more objects to the `carArray` member variable, our `GetEnumerator()` method would now be out of sync. Nevertheless, this syntax can be useful when you wish to return local data from a method for processing by the `foreach` syntax.

Building a Named Iterator

It is also interesting to note that the `yield` keyword can technically be used within any method, regardless of its name. These methods (which are technically called *named iterators*) are also unique in that they can take any number of arguments. When building a named iterator, be very aware that the method will return the `IEnumerable` interface, rather than the expected `IEnumerator`-compatible type. To illustrate, we could add the following method to the `Garage` type:

```
public IEnumerable GetTheCars(bool ReturnRevesed)
{
  // Return the items in reverse.
  if (ReturnRevesed)
  {
    for (int i = carArray.Length; i != 0; i--)
    {
      yield return carArray[i-1];
    }
  }
  else
  {
    // Return the items as placed in the array.
    foreach (Car c in carArray)
    {
      yield return c;
    }
  }
}
```

Notice that our new method allows the caller to obtain the subitems in a sequential order, as well as in reverse order, if the incoming parameter has the value `true`. We could now interact with our new method as follows:

```
static void Main(string[] args)
{
  Console.WriteLine("***** Fun with the Yield Keyword *****\n");
  Garage carLot = new Garage();

  // Get items using GetEnumerator().
  foreach (Car c in carLot)
  {
    Console.WriteLine("{0} is going {1} MPH",
      c.PetName, c.Speed);
  }

  Console.WriteLine();
```

```
  // Get items (in reverse!) using named iterator.
  foreach (Car c in carLot.GetTheCars(true))
  {
    Console.WriteLine("{0} is going {1} MPH",
      c.PetName, c.Speed);
  }
  Console.ReadLine();
}
```

Named iterators are helpful constructs, in that a single custom container can define multiple ways to request the returned set.

Internal Representation of an Iterator Method

When the C# compiler encounters an iterator method, it will dynamically generate a nested class definition within the scope of the defining type (Garage in this case). The autogenerated nested class implements the GetEnumerator(), MoveNext(), and Current members on your behalf (oddly, the Reset() method is not, and you will receive a runtime exception if you attempt to call it). If you were to load the current application into ildasm.exe, you would find two nested types, each of which accounts for the logic required by a specific iterator method. Notice in Figure 9-10 that these compiler-generated types have been named <GetEnumerator>d__0 and <GetTheCars>d__5.

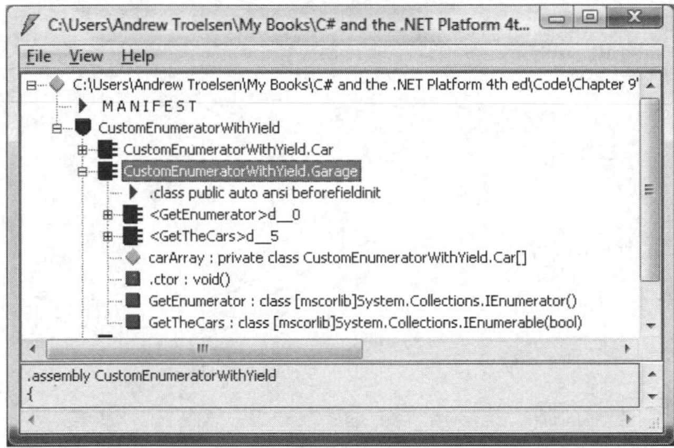

Figure 9-10. *Iterator methods are internally implemented with the help of an autogenerated nested class.*

If you used ildasm.exe to view the implementation of the GetEnumerator() method of the Garage type, you'd find that it has been implemented to make use of the <GetEnumerator>d__0 type behind the scenes (the nested <GetTheCars>d__5 type is used by the GetTheCars() method in a similar manner).

```
.method public hidebysig instance class
    [mscorlib]System.Collections.IEnumerator
    GetEnumerator() cil managed
{
...
  newobj instance void
    CustomEnumeratorWithYield.Garage/'<GetEnumerator>d__0'::.ctor(int32)
...
} // end of method Garage::GetEnumerator
```

So, to wrap up our look at building enumerable objects, remember that in order for your custom types to work with the C# foreach keyword, the container must define a method named GetEnumerator(), which has been formalized by the IEnumerable interface type. The implementation of this method is typically achieved by simply delegating it to the internal member that is holding onto the subobjects; however, it is also possible to make use of the yield return syntax to provide multiple "named iterator" methods.

■ **Source Code** The CustomEnumeratorWithYield project is located under the Chapter 9 subdirectory.

Building Cloneable Objects (ICloneable)

As you recall from Chapter 6, System.Object defines a member named MemberwiseClone(). This method is used to obtain a *shallow copy* of the current object. Object users do not call this method directly (as it is protected); however, a given object may call this method itself during the *cloning* process. To illustrate, create a new Console Application named CloneablePoint that defines a class named Point:

```
// A class named Point.
public class Point
{
  // Public for easy access.
  public int x, y;
  public Point(int x, int y) { this.x = x; this.y = y;}
  public Point(){}

  // Override Object.ToString().
  public override string ToString()
  {  return string.Format("X = {0}; Y = {1}", x, y ); }
}
```

Given what you already know about reference types and value types (Chapter 4), you are aware that if you assign one reference variable to another, you have two references pointing to the same object in memory. Thus, the following assignment operation results in two references to the same Point object on the heap; modifications using either reference affect the same object on the heap:

```
static void Main(string[] args)
{
  Console.WriteLine("***** Fun with Object Cloning *****\n");
  // Two references to same object!
  Point p1 = new Point(50, 50);
  Point p2 = p1;
  p2.x = 0;
  Console.WriteLine(p1);
  Console.WriteLine(p2);
  Console.ReadLine();
}
```

When you wish to equip your custom types to support the ability to return an identical copy of itself to the caller, you may implement the standard ICloneable interface. As shown at the start of this chapter, this type defines a single method named Clone():

```
public interface ICloneable
{
  object Clone();
}
```

■Note The usefulness of the `ICloneable` interface is currently under debate within the .NET community. The problem has to do with the fact that the official specification does not explicitly say that objects implementing this interface must return a *deep copy* of the object (i.e., internal reference types of an object result in brand-new objects with identical state). Thus, it is technically possible that objects implementing `ICloneable` actually return a *shallow copy* of the interface (i.e., internal references point to the same object on the heap), which clearly generates a good deal of confusion. In our example, I am assuming we are implementing `Clone()` to return a full, deep copy of the object.

Obviously, the implementation of the `Clone()` method varies between objects. However, the basic functionality tends to be the same: copy the values of your member variables into a new object instance of the same type, and return it to the user. To illustrate, ponder the following update to the `Point` class:

```
// The Point now supports "clone-ability."
public class Point : ICloneable
{
  public int x, y;
  public Point(){ }
  public Point(int x, int y) { this.x = x; this.y = y;}

  // Return a copy of the current object.
  public object Clone()
  { return new Point(this.x, this.y); }

  public override string ToString()
  { return string.Format("X = {0}; Y = {1}", x, y ); }
}
```

In this way, you can create exact stand-alone copies of the `Point` type, as illustrated by the following code:

```
static void Main(string[] args)
{
  Console.WriteLine("***** Fun with Object Cloning *****\n");
  // Notice Clone() returns a generic object type.
  // You must perform an explicit cast to obtain the derived type.
  Point p3 = new Point(100, 100);
  Point p4 = (Point)p3.Clone();

  // Change p4.x (which will not change p3.x).
  p4.x = 0;

  // Print each object.
  Console.WriteLine(p3);
  Console.WriteLine(p4);
  Console.ReadLine();
}
```

While the current implementation of Point fits the bill, you can streamline things just a bit. Because the Point type does not contain any internal reference type variables, you could simplify the implementation of the Clone() method as follows:

```
public object Clone()
{
  // Copy each field of the Point member by member.
  return this.MemberwiseClone();
}
```

Be aware, however, that if the Point did contain any reference type member variables, MemberwiseClone() will copy the references to those objects (aka a *shallow copy*). If you wish to support a true deep copy, you will need to create a new instance of any reference type variables during the cloning process. Let's see an example.

A More Elaborate Cloning Example

Now assume the Point class contains a reference type member variable of type PointDescription. This class maintains a point's friendly name as well as an identification number expressed as a System.Guid (if you don't come from a COM background, know that a globally unique identifier [GUID] is a statistically unique 128-bit number). Here is the implementation:

```
// This class describes a point.
public class PointDescription
{
  // Exposed publicly for simplicity.
  public string petName;
  public Guid pointID;

  public PointDescription()
  {
    this.petName = "No-name";
    pointID = Guid.NewGuid();
  }
}
```

The initial updates to the Point class itself included modifying ToString() to account for these new bits of state data, as well as defining and creating the PointDescription reference type. To allow the outside world to establish a pet name for the Point, you also update the arguments passed into the overloaded constructor:

```
public class Point : ICloneable
{
  public int x, y;
  public PointDescription desc = new PointDescription();

  public Point(){}
  public Point(int x, int y)
  {
    this.x = x; this.y = y;
  }
  public Point(int x, int y, string petname)
  {
    this.x = x;
    this.y = y;
    desc.petName = petname;
  }
```

```
  public object Clone()
  { return this.MemberwiseClone(); }

  public override string ToString()
  {
    return string.Format("X = {0}; Y = {1}; Name = {2};\nID = {3}\n",
      x, y, desc.petName, desc.pointID);
  }
}
```

Notice that you did not yet update your `Clone()` method. Therefore, when the object user asks for a clone using the current implementation, a shallow (member-by-member) copy is achieved. To illustrate, assume you have updated `Main()` as follows:

```
static void Main(string[] args)
{
  Console.WriteLine("***** Fun with Object Cloning *****\n");
  Console.WriteLine("Cloned p3 and stored new Point in p4");
  Point p3 = new Point(100, 100, "Jane");
  Point p4 = (Point)p3.Clone();

  Console.WriteLine("Before modification:");
  Console.WriteLine("p3: {0}", p3);
  Console.WriteLine("p4: {0}", p4);
  p4.desc.petName = "My new Point";
  p4.x = 9;

  Console.WriteLine("\nChanged p4.desc.petName and p4.x");
  Console.WriteLine("After modification:");
  Console.WriteLine("p3: {0}", p3);
  Console.WriteLine("p4: {0}", p4);
  Console.ReadLine();
}
```

Figure 9-11 shows the output. Notice that while the value types have indeed been changed, the internal reference types maintain the same values, as they are "pointing" to the same objects in memory.

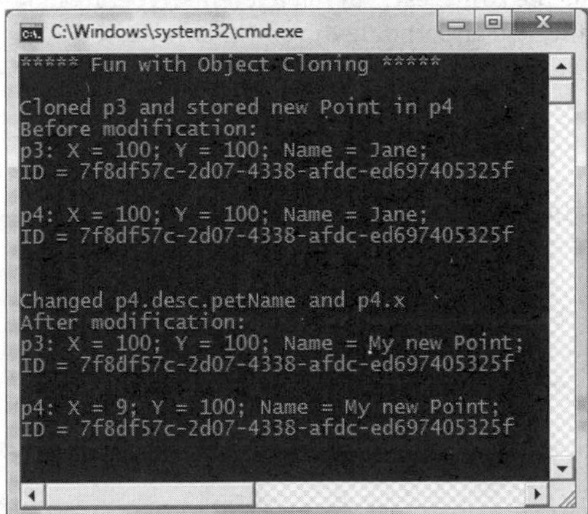

Figure 9-11. `MemberwiseClone()` *returns a shallow copy of the current object.*

In order for your Clone() method to make a complete deep copy of the internal reference types, you need to configure the object returned by MemberwiseClone() to account for the current point's name (the System.Guid type is in fact a structure, so the numerical data is indeed copied). Here is one possible implementation:

```
// Now we need to adjust for the PointDescription member.
public object Clone()
{
  // First get a shallow copy.
  Point newPoint = (Point)this.MemberwiseClone();

  // Then fill in the gaps.
  PointDescription currentDesc = new PointDescription();
  currentDesc.petName = this.desc.petName;
  newPoint.desc = currentDesc;
  return newPoint;
}
```

If you rerun the application once again as shown in Figure 9-12, you see that the Point returned from Clone() does copy its internal reference type member variables (note the pet name is now unique for both p3 and p4).

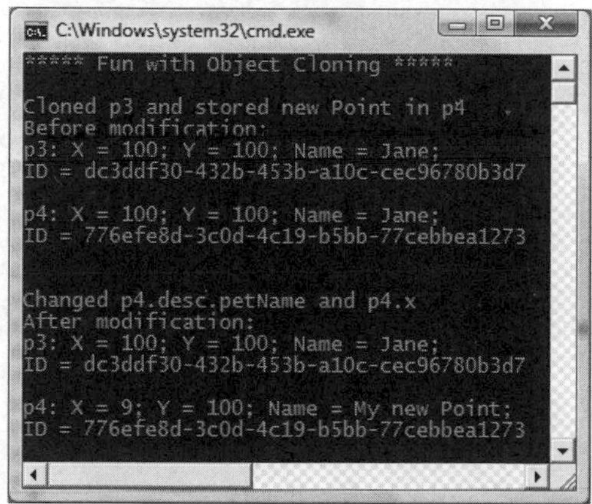

Figure 9-12. *Now you have a true deep copy of the object.*

To summarize the cloning process, if you have a class or structure that contains nothing but value types, implement your Clone() method using MemberwiseClone(). However, if you have a custom type that maintains other reference types, you need to establish a new type that takes into account each reference type member variable.

■ **Source Code** The CloneablePoint project is located under the Chapter 9 subdirectory.

Building Comparable Objects (IComparable)

The System.IComparable interface specifies a behavior that allows an object to be sorted based on some specified key. Here is the formal definition:

```
// This interface allows an object to specify its
// relationship between other like objects.
public interface IComparable
{
  int CompareTo(object o);
}
```

Let's assume you have a new Console Application named ComparableCar that defines the following updated Car type (notice that we have basically just added a new member variable to represent a unique ID for each car as well as ways to get and set the value):

```
public class Car
{
...
  private int carID;
  public int ID
  {
    get { return carID; }
    set { carID = value; }
  }
  public Car(string name, int currSp, int id)
  {
    currSpeed = currSp;
    petName = name;
    carID = id;
  }
...
}
```

Now assume you have an array of Car types as follows:

```
static void Main(string[] args)
{
  Console.WriteLine("***** Fun with Object Sorting *****\n");
  // Make an array of Car types.
  Car[] myAutos = new Car[5];
  myAutos[0] = new Car("Rusty", 80, 1);
  myAutos[1] = new Car("Mary", 40, 234);
  myAutos[2] = new Car("Viper", 40, 34);
  myAutos[3] = new Car("Mel", 40, 4);
  myAutos[4] = new Car("Chucky", 40, 5);
  Console.ReadLine();
}
```

The System.Array class defines a static method named Sort(). When you invoke this method on an array of intrinsic types (int, short, string, etc.), you are able to sort the items in the array in numeric/alphabetic order as these intrinsic data types implement IComparable. However, what if you were to send an array of Car types into the Sort() method as follows?

```
// Sort my cars?
Array.Sort(myAutos);
```

If you run this test, you would find that an ArgumentException exception is thrown by the runtime, with the following message:

```
"At least one object must implement IComparable."
```

When you build custom types, you can implement IComparable to allow arrays of your types to be sorted. When you flesh out the details of CompareTo(), it will be up to you to decide what the baseline of the ordering operation will be. For the Car type, the internal carID seems to be the logical candidate:

```
// The iteration of the Car can be ordered
// based on the CarID.
public class Car : IComparable
{
...
  // IComparable implementation.
  int IComparable.CompareTo(object obj)
  {
    Car temp = (Car)obj;
    if(this.carID > temp.carID)
      return 1;
    if(this.carID < temp.carID)
      return -1;
    else
      return 0;
  }
}
```

As you can see, the logic behind CompareTo() is to test the incoming type against the current instance based on a specific point of data. The return value of CompareTo() is used to discover whether this type is less than, greater than, or equal to the object it is being compared with (see Table 9-1).

Table 9-1. CompareTo() *Return Values*

CompareTo() Return Value	Meaning in Life
Any number less than zero	This instance comes before the specified object in the sort order.
Zero	This instance is equal to the specified object.
Any number greater than zero	This instance comes after the specified object in the sort order.

We can streamline the previous implementation of CompareTo() given the fact that the C# int data type (which is just a shorthand notation for the CLR System.Int32) implements IComparable; you could implement the Car's CompareTo() as follows:

```
int IComparable.CompareTo(object obj)
{
  Car temp = (Car)obj;
  return this.carID.CompareTo(temp.carID);
}
```

In either case, so that your Car type understands how to compare itself to like objects, you can write the following user code:

```
// Exercise the IComparable interface.
static void Main(string[] args)
{
  // Make an array of Car types.
...
  // Display current array.
  Console.WriteLine("Here is the unordered set of cars:");
```

```
    foreach(Car c in myAutos)
      Console.WriteLine("{0} {1}", c.ID, c.PetName);

    // Now, sort them using IComparable!
    Array.Sort(myAutos);
    Console.WriteLine();

    // Display sorted array.
    Console.WriteLine("Here is the ordered set of cars:");
    foreach(Car c in myAutos)
      Console.WriteLine("{0} {1}", c.ID, c.PetName);
    Console.ReadLine();
  }
```

Figure 9-13 illustrates a test run.

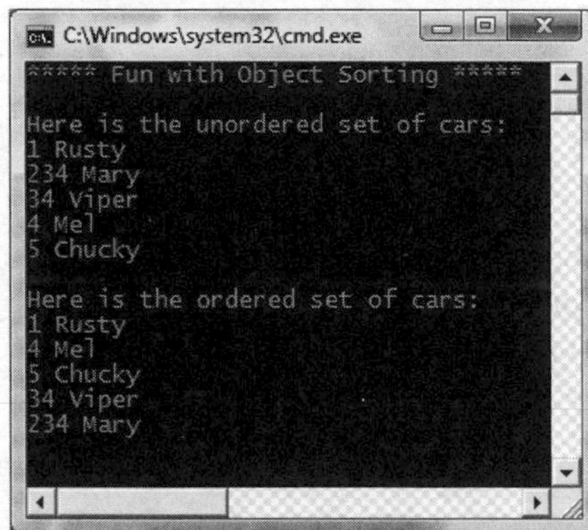

Figure 9-13. *Comparing automobiles based on car ID*

Specifying Multiple Sort Orders (IComparer)

In this version of the Car type, you made use of the car's ID to function as the baseline of the sort order. Another design might have used the pet name of the car as the basis of the sorting algorithm (to list cars alphabetically). Now, what if you wanted to build a Car that could be sorted by ID *as well as* by pet name? If this is the behavior you are interested in, you need to make friends with another standard interface named IComparer, defined within the System.Collections namespace as follows:

```
// A generic way to compare two objects.
interface IComparer
{
  int Compare(object o1, object o2);
}
```

Unlike the IComparable interface, IComparer is typically *not* implemented on the type you are trying to sort (i.e., the Car). Rather, you implement this interface on any number of helper classes, one for each sort order (pet name, car ID, etc.). Currently, the Car type already knows how to compare itself against other cars based on the internal car ID. Therefore, allowing the object user to sort an array of Car types by pet name will require an additional helper class that implements IComparer. Here's the code:

```
// This helper class is used to sort an array of Cars by pet name.
using System.Collections;

public class PetNameComparer : IComparer
{
  // Test the pet name of each object.
  int IComparer.Compare(object o1, object o2)
  {
    Car t1 = (Car)o1;
    Car t2 = (Car)o2;
    return String.Compare(t1.PetName, t2.PetName);
  }
}
```

The object user code is able to make use of this helper class. `System.Array` has a number of overloaded `Sort()` methods, one that just happens to take an object implementing `IComparer`. Figure 9-14 shows the output of sorting by a car's pet name.

```
static void Main(string[] args)
{
...
  // Now sort by pet name.
  Array.Sort(myAutos, new PetNameComparer());

  // Dump sorted array.
  Console.WriteLine("Ordering by pet name:");
  foreach(Car c in myAutos)
    Console.WriteLine("{0} {1}", c.ID, c.PetName);
...
}
```

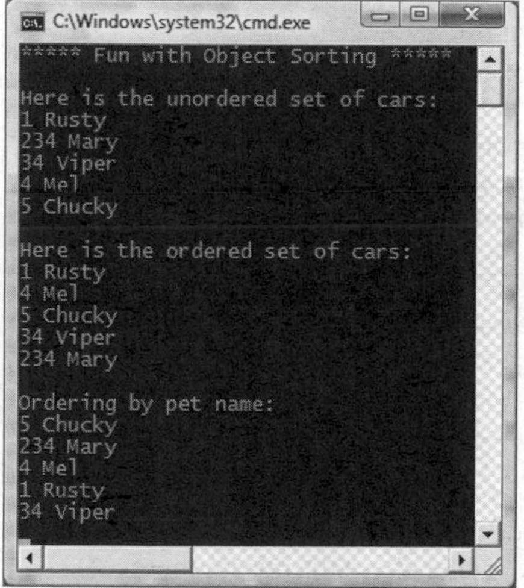

Figure 9-14. *Sorting automobiles by pet name*

Custom Properties, Custom Sort Types

It is worth pointing out that you can make use of a custom static property in order to help the object user along when sorting your Car types by a specific data point. Assume the Car class has added a static read-only property named SortByPetName that returns an instance of an object implementing the IComparer interface (PetNameComparer, in this case):

```
// We now support a custom property to return
// the correct IComparer interface.
public class Car : IComparable
{
  ...
  // Property to return the SortByPetName comparer.
  public static IComparer SortByPetName
  { get { return (IComparer)new PetNameComparer(); } }
}
```

The object user code can now sort by pet name using a strongly associated property, rather than just "having to know" to use the stand-alone PetNameComparer class type:

```
// Sorting by pet name made a bit cleaner.
Array.Sort(myAutos, Car.SortByPetName);
```

Source Code The ComparableCar project is located under the Chapter 9 subdirectory.

Hopefully at this point, you not only understand how to define and implement interface types, but can understand their usefulness. To be sure, interfaces will be found within every major .NET namespace. To wrap up this chapter, let's check out the interfaces that can be used to enable callback mechanisms.

Understanding Callback Interfaces

Beyond using interfaces to establish polymorphism across diverse class hierarchies, namespaces, and assemblies, interfaces may also be used as a *callback mechanism*. This technique enables objects to engage in a two-way conversation using a common set of members.

Note The .NET platform provides a formal fabric used to build events (which is quite different from the technique that will be shown here). As you will see in Chapter 11, delegates, events, and lambdas are the standard way to enable objects to chit-chat back and forth.

To illustrate the use of callback interfaces, let's update the now familiar Car type in such a way that it is able to inform the caller when it is about to explode (the current speed is 10 miles below the maximum speed) and has exploded (the current speed is at or above the maximum speed).

Begin by creating a new Console Application named CallbackInterface. The ability to send and receive these events will be facilitated with a new custom interface named IEngineNotification:

```
// The callback interface.
public interface IEngineNotification
{
```

```
    void AboutToBlow(string msg);
    void Exploded(string msg);
}
```

Callback interfaces are often not implemented by the object directly interested in receiving the events, but rather by a helper object called a *sink object*. The sender of the events (the Car type in this case) will make calls on the sink under the appropriate circumstances. Assume the sink class is called CarEventSink. When this object is notified of the various incoming events, it will simply print out the incoming messages to the console. Furthermore, our sink will also maintain a string member variable that represents its friendly name (you'll see how this can be useful as you move through the example):

```
// Car event sink.
public class CarEventSink : IEngineNotification
{
  private string name;
  public CarEventSink(){}
  public CarEventSink(string sinkName)
  { name = sinkName; }

  public void AboutToBlow(string msg)
  {
    Console.WriteLine("{0} reporting: {1}", name, msg);
  }
  public void Exploded(string msg)
  {
    Console.WriteLine("{0} reporting: {1}", name, msg);
  }
}
```

Now that you have a sink object that implements the callback interface, your next task is to pass a reference to this sink into the Car type. The Car holds onto the reference and makes calls back on the sink when appropriate. In order to allow the Car to obtain a reference to the sink, we will need to add a public helper member to the Car type that we will call Advise(). Likewise, if the caller wishes to detach from the event source, it may call another helper method on the Car type named Unadvise(). Finally, in order to allow the caller to register multiple event sinks (for the purposes of multicasting), the Car now maintains an ArrayList to represent each outstanding connection.

■Note The ArrayList class is contained within the System.Collections namespace of the mscorlib.dll assembly. Be sure to import this namespace within the file containing your Car definition. Collections (and generics for that matter) will be examined in detail in Chapter 10.

```
// This Car and caller can now communicate
// using the IEngineNotification interface.
public class Car
{
  // The set of connected sinks.
  ArrayList clientSinks = new ArrayList();

  // Attach or disconnect from the source of events.
  public void Advise(IEngineNotification sink)
  {
    clientSinks.Add(sink);
  }
```

```
  public void Unadvise(IEngineNotification sink)
  {
    clientSinks.Remove(sink);
  }
...
}
```

To actually send the events, let's update the `Car.Accelerate()` method to iterate over the list of connections maintained by the `ArrayList` and fire the correct notification when appropriate. First of all, add a new `Boolean` member variable named `carIsDead` to represent the engine's state:

```
class Car
{
  // Is the car alive or dead?
  bool carIsDead;
...
}
```

Next, update your current `Accelerate()` method to make use of this new member variable as follows:

```
public void Accelerate(int delta)
{
  // If the car is dead, send Exploded event.
  if (carIsDead)
  {
    foreach (IEngineNotification sink in clientSinks)
      sink.Exploded("Sorry, this car is dead...");
  }
  else
  {
    currSpeed += delta;

    // Almost dead?
    if (10 == (maxSpeed - currSpeed))
    {
      foreach (IEngineNotification sink in clientSinks)
        sink.AboutToBlow("Careful buddy!  Gonna blow!");
    }

    // Still OK!
    if (currSpeed >= maxSpeed)
      carIsDead = true;
    else
      Console.WriteLine("->CurrSpeed = " + currSpeed);
  }
}
```

With our infrastructure in place, we can now implement our `Main()` method to receive the events sent from the `Car` type as follows:

```
// Make a car and listen to the events.
static void Main(string[] args)
{
  Console.WriteLine("***** Interfaces as event enablers *****\n");
  Car c1 = new Car("SlugBug", 100, 10);

  // Make sink object.
  CarEventSink sink = new CarEventSink();
```

```
    // Pass the Car a reference to the sink.
    c1.Advise(sink);

    // Speed up (this will trigger the events).
    for(int i = 0; i < 10; i++)
      c1.Accelerate(20);

    // Detach from event source.
    c1.Unadvise(sink);
    Console.ReadLine();
}
```

Figure 9-15 shows the end result of this interface-based event protocol.

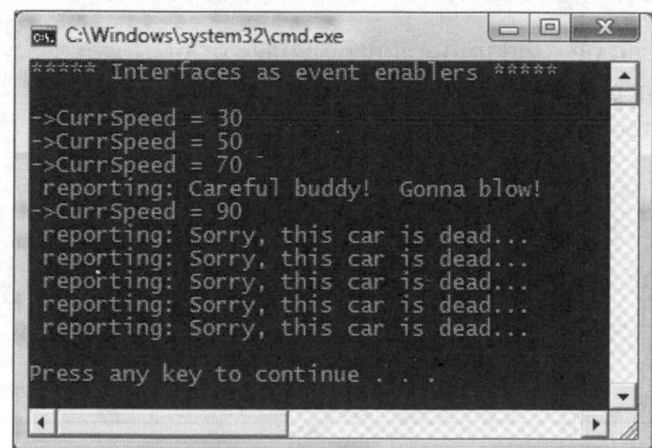

Figure 9-15. *Receiving event notifications using callback interfaces*

Do note that the `Unadvise()` method can be very helpful in that it allows the caller to selectively detach from an event source at will. Here, you call `Unadvise()` before exiting `Main()`, although this is not technically necessary. However, assume that the application now wishes to register two sinks, dynamically remove a particular sink during the flow of execution, and continue processing the program at large:

```
static void Main(string[] args)
{
  Console.WriteLine("***** Interfaces as event enablers *****\n");
  Car c1 = new Car("SlugBug", 100, 10);

  // Make 2 sink objects.
  Console.WriteLine("***** Creating sinks *****");
  CarEventSink sink = new CarEventSink("First sink");
  CarEventSink myOtherSink = new CarEventSink("Other sink");

  // Hand sinks to Car.
  Console.WriteLine("\n***** Sending 2 sinks into Car *****");
  c1.Advise(sink);
  c1.Advise(myOtherSink);

  // Speed up (this will generate the events).
  Console.WriteLine("\n***** Speeding up *****");
  for(int i = 0; i < 10; i++)
    c1.Accelerate(20);
```

```
    // Detach first sink from events.
    Console.WriteLine("\n***** Removing first sink *****");
    c1.Unadvise(sink);

    // Speed up again (only myOtherSink will be called).
    Console.WriteLine("\n***** Speeding up again *****");
    for(int i = 0; i < 10; i++)
      c1.Accelerate(20);

    // Detach other sink from events.
    Console.WriteLine("\n***** Removing second sink *****");
    c1.Unadvise(myOtherSink);
    Console.ReadLine();
}
```

Callback interfaces can be helpful in that they can be used under any language or platform (.NET, J2EE, or otherwise) that supports interface-based programming. However, as mentioned, Chapter 11 will examine a number of event-centric techniques that are specific to the .NET platform.

■ **Source Code** The CallbackInterface project is located under the Chapter 9 subdirectory.

Summary

An interface can be defined as a named collection of *abstract members*. Because an interface does not provide any implementation details, it is common to regard an interface as a behavior that may be supported by a given type. When two or more classes implement the same interface, you are able to treat each type the same way (aka interface-based polymorphism) even if the types are defined within unique class hierarchies.

C# provides the `interface` keyword to allow you to define a new interface. As you have seen, a type can support as many interfaces as necessary using a comma-delimited list. Furthermore, it is permissible to build interfaces that derive from multiple base interfaces.

In addition to building your custom interfaces, the .NET libraries define a number of standard (i.e., framework-supplied) interfaces. As you have seen, you are free to build custom types that implement these predefined interfaces to gain a number of desirable traits such as cloning, sorting, and enumerating. Finally, you spent some time investigating how interface types can be used to establish bidirectional communications between two objects in memory.

CHAPTER 10

Collections and Generics

The most primitive container within the .NET platform is the System.Array type. As you have seen over the course of the previous chapters, C# arrays allow you to define a set of identically typed items (including an array of System.Objects, which essentially represents an array of any types) of a fixed upper limit. While this will often fit the bill, there are many other times where you require more flexible data structures, such as a dynamically growing and shrinking container, or a container that can hold only items that meet a specific criteria (e.g., only items deriving from a given base class, items implementing a particular interface, or whatnot). To begin understanding the task of building flexible and type-safe containers, this chapter will first examine the System.Collections namespace that has been part of the .NET base class libraries since the initial release.

However, since the release of .NET 2.0, the C# programming language was enhanced to support a new feature of the CTS termed *generics*. Many of the generics you will use on a daily basis are found within the System.Collections.Generic namespace. As shown over this chapter, generic containers are in many ways far superior to their nongeneric counterparts in that they provide greater type safety and performance benefits. Once you've seen generic support within the base class libraries, in the remainder of this chapter you'll examine how you can build your own generic members, classes, structures, and interfaces.

Note It is also possible to create generic delegate types, which will be addressed in the next chapter.

The Interfaces of the System.Collections Namespace

The most primitive container construct would have to be our good friend System.Array. As you have already seen in Chapter 4, this class provides a number of services (e.g., reversing, sorting, clearing, and enumerating). However, the simple Array class has a number of limitations; most notably, it does not automatically resize itself as you add or clear items. When you need to contain types in a more flexible container, one option is to leverage the types defined within the System.Collections namespace.

The System.Collections namespace defines a number of interfaces (some of which you have already implemented during Chapter 9). A majority of the classes within System.Collections implement these interfaces to provide access to their contents. Table 10-1 gives a breakdown of the core collection-centric interfaces.

Table 10-1. *Interfaces of* `System.Collections`

System.Collections Interface	Meaning in Life
`ICollection`	Defines general characteristics (e.g., size, enumeration, thread safety) for all nongeneric collection types.
`IComparer`	Allows two objects to be compared.
`IDictionary`	Allows a nongeneric collection object to represent its contents using name/value pairs.
`IDictionaryEnumerator`	Enumerates the contents of a type supporting `IDictionary`.
`IEnumerable`	Returns the `IEnumerator` interface for a given object.
`IEnumerator`	Enables `foreach` style iteration of subtypes.
`IHashCodeProvider`	Returns the hash code for the implementing type using a customized hash algorithm.
`IList`	Provides behavior to add, remove, and index items in a list of objects. Also, this interface defines members to determine whether the implementing collection type is read-only and/or a fixed-size container.

Many of these interfaces are related by an interface hierarchy, while others are stand-alone entities. Figure 10-1 illustrates the relationship between each type (recall from Chapter 9 that it is permissible for a single interface to derive from multiple interfaces).

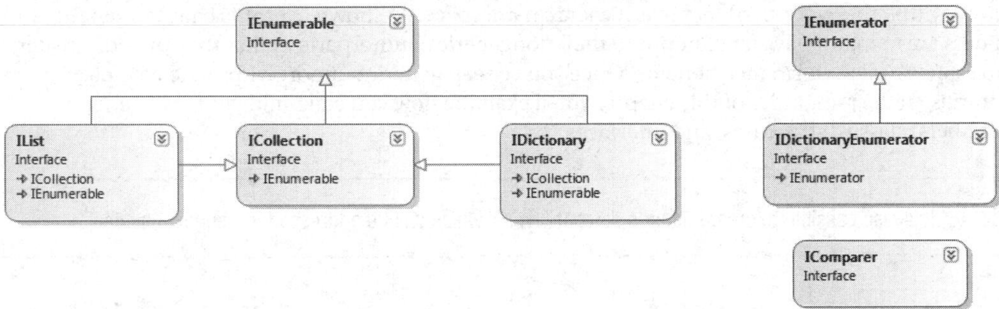

Figure 10-1. *The* `System.Collections` *interface hierarchy*

The Role of ICollection

The `ICollection` interface is the most primitive interface of the `System.Collections` namespace in that it defines a behavior supported by a collection type. In a nutshell, this interface provides a small set of members that allow you to determine (a) the number of items in the container, (b) the thread safety of the container, as well as (c) the ability to copy the contents into a `System.Array` type. Formally, `ICollection` is defined as follows (note that `ICollection` extends `IEnumerable`):

```
public interface ICollection : IEnumerable
{
  int Count { get; }
  bool IsSynchronized { get; }
  object SyncRoot { get; }
  void CopyTo(Array array, int index);
}
```

The Role of IDictionary

A *dictionary* is simply a collection that maintains a set of name/value pairs. For example, you could build a custom type that implements IDictionary such that you can store Car types (the values) that may be retrieved by ID or pet name (e.g., names). Given this functionality, you can see that the IDictionary interface defines a Keys and Values property as well as Add(), Remove(), and Contains() methods. The individual items may be obtained by the type indexer, which is a construct that allows you to interact with subitems using an arraylike syntax. Here is the formal definition:

```
public interface IDictionary :
  ICollection, IEnumerable
{
  bool IsFixedSize { get; }
  bool IsReadOnly { get; }

  // Type indexer; see Chapter 12 for full details.
  object this[object key] { get; set; }

  ICollection Keys { get; }
  ICollection Values { get; }
  void Add(object key, object value);
  void Clear();
  bool Contains(object key);
  IDictionaryEnumerator GetEnumerator();
  void Remove(object key);
}
```

The Role of IDictionaryEnumerator

If you were paying attention in the previous section, you may have noted that IDictionary.GetEnumerator() returns an instance of the IDictionaryEnumerator type. IDictionaryEnumerator is simply a strongly typed enumerator, given that it extends IEnumerator by adding the following functionality:

```
public interface IDictionaryEnumerator : IEnumerator
{
  DictionaryEntry Entry { get; }
  object Key { get; }
  object Value { get; }
}
```

Notice how IDictionaryEnumerator allows you to enumerate over items in the dictionary via the generalized Entry property, which returns a System.Collections.DictionaryEntry class type. In addition, you are also able to traverse the name/value pairs using the Key/Value properties.

The Role of IList

The final core interface of System.Collections is IList, which provides the ability to insert, remove, and index items into (or out of) a container:

```
public interface IList :
  ICollection, IEnumerable
{
  bool IsFixedSize { get; }
  bool IsReadOnly { get; }
  object this[ int index ] { get; set; }
```

```
  int Add(object value);
  void Clear();
  bool Contains(object value);
  int IndexOf(object value);
  void Insert(int index, object value);
  void Remove(object value);
  void RemoveAt(int index);
}
```

The Class Types of System.Collections

As explained in the previous chapter, interfaces by themselves are not very useful until they are implemented by a given class or structure. Table 10-2 provides a rundown of the core classes in the `System.Collections` namespace and the key interfaces they support.

Table 10-2. *Classes of* `System.Collections`

System.Collections Class	Meaning in Life	Key Implemented Interfaces
`ArrayList`	Represents a dynamically sized array of objects.	`IList`, `ICollection`, `IEnumerable`, and `ICloneable`
`Hashtable`	Represents a collection of objects identified by a numerical key. Custom types stored in a `Hashtable` should always override `System.Object.GetHashCode()`.	`IDictionary`, `ICollection`, `IEnumerable`, and `ICloneable`
`Queue`	Represents a standard first-in, first-out (FIFO) queue.	`ICollection`, `ICloneable`, and `IEnumerable`
`SortedList`	Like a dictionary; however, the elements can also be accessed by ordinal position (e.g., index).	`IDictionary`, `ICollection`, `IEnumerable`, and `ICloneable`
`Stack`	A last-in, first-out (LIFO) queue providing push and pop (and peek) functionality.	`ICollection`, `ICloneable`, and `IEnumerable`

In addition to these key types, `System.Collections` defines some minor players (at least in terms of their day-to-day usefulness) such as `BitArray`, `CaseInsensitiveComparer`, and `CaseInsensitiveHashCodeProvider`. Furthermore, this namespace also defines a small set of abstract base classes (`CollectionBase`, `ReadOnlyCollectionBase`, and `DictionaryBase`) that can be used to build strongly typed containers.

As you begin to experiment with the `System.Collections` types, you will find they all tend to share common functionality (that's the point of interface-based programming). Thus, rather than listing out the members of each and every collection class, the next task of this chapter is to illustrate how to interact with three common collection types: `ArrayList`, `Queue`, and `Stack`.

Once you understand the functionality of these types, gaining an understanding of the remaining collection classes (such as the `Hashtable`) should naturally follow; especially since each of the types is fully documented within the .NET Framework 3.5 documentation.

Working with the ArrayList Type

To illustrate working with these collection types, create a new Console Application project named CollectionTypes. Our `ArrayList` will maintain a set of simple `Car` objects, defined as follows:

```
class Car
{
  // Public fields for simplicity.
  public string PetName;
  public int Speed;

  // Constructors.
  public Car(){}
  public Car(string name, int currentSpeed)
  { PetName = name; Speed = currentSpeed;}
}
```

Next, update your project's initial C# file to specify you are using the `System.Collections` namespace:

```
using System.Collections;
```

The `ArrayList` type is bound to be your most frequently used type in the `System.Collections` namespace in that it allows you to dynamically resize the contents at your whim. To illustrate the basics of this type, ponder the following method to your `Program` class, which leverages the `ArrayList` to manipulate a set of `Car` objects:

```
static void ArrayListTest()
{
  Console.WriteLine("\n=> ArrayList Test:\n");
  // Create ArrayList and fill with some initial values.
  ArrayList carArList = new ArrayList();
  carArList.AddRange(new Car[] { new Car("Fred", 90, 10),
    new Car("Mary", 100, 50), new Car("MB", 190, 11)});

  // Print out # of items in ArrayList.
  Console.WriteLine("Items in carArList: {0}", carArList.Count);

  // Print out current values.
  foreach(Car c in carArList)
    Console.WriteLine("Car pet name: {0}", c.PetName);

  // Insert a new item.
  Console.WriteLine("->Inserting new Car.");
  carArList.Insert(2, new Car("TheNewCar", 0, 12));
  Console.WriteLine("Items in carArList: {0}", carArList.Count);

  // Get object array from ArrayList and print again.
  object[] arrayOfCars = carArList.ToArray();
  for(int i = 0; i < arrayOfCars.Length; i++)
  {
    Console.WriteLine("Car pet name: {0}",
      ((Car)arrayOfCars[i]).PetName);
  }
}
```

Here you are making use of the AddRange() method to populate your ArrayList with an array of Car types (which is basically a shorthand notation for calling Add() *n* number of times). Once you print out the number of items in the collection (as well as enumerate over each item to obtain the pet name), you invoke Insert(). As you can see, Insert() allows you to plug a new item into the ArrayList at a specified index.

Finally, notice the call to the ToArray() method, which returns an array of System.Object types based on the contents of the original ArrayList. From this array, we loop over the items once again using the array's indexer syntax. If you call this method from within Main(), you will find the ArrayList has indeed grown by one item to account for the new Car object.

Working with the Queue Type

Queues are containers that ensure items are accessed using a first-in, first-out manner. Sadly, we humans are subject to queues all day long: lines at the bank, lines at the movie theater, and lines at the morning coffeehouse. When you are modeling a scenario in which items are handled on a first-come, first-served basis, System.Collections.Queue fits the bill. In addition to the functionality provided by the supported interfaces, Queue defines the key members shown in Table 10-3.

Table 10-3. *Members of the* Queue *Type*

Member of System.Collection.Queue	Meaning in Life
Dequeue()	Removes and returns the object at the beginning of the Queue
Enqueue()	Adds an object to the end of the Queue
Peek()	Returns the object at the beginning of the Queue without removing it

To illustrate these methods, we will leverage our automobile theme once again and build a Queue object that simulates a line of cars waiting to enter a car wash. First, assume the following static helper method:

```
static void WashCar(Car c)
{
  Console.WriteLine("Cleaning {0}", c.PetName);
}
```

Now assume this additional helper method, which calls WashCar() internally:

```
static void QueueTest()
{
  Console.WriteLine("\n=> Queue Test:\n");
  // Make a Q with three items.
  Queue carWashQ = new Queue();
  carWashQ.Enqueue(new Car("FirstCar", 10));
  carWashQ.Enqueue(new Car("SecondCar", 20));
  carWashQ.Enqueue(new Car("ThirdCar", 30));

  // Peek at first car in Q.
  Console.WriteLine("First in Q is {0}",
    ((Car)carWashQ.Peek()).PetName);

  // Remove each item from Q.
  WashCar((Car)carWashQ.Dequeue());
```

```
  WashCar((Car)carWashQ.Dequeue());
  WashCar((Car)carWashQ.Dequeue());

  // Try to de-Q again?
  try
  { WashCar((Car)carWashQ.Dequeue()); }
  catch(Exception e)
  { Console.WriteLine("Error!! {0}", e.Message);}
}
```

Here, you insert three items into the Queue type via its Enqueue() method. The call to Peek() allows you to view (but not remove) the first item currently in the Queue, which in this case is the object named FirstCar. Finally, the call to Dequeue() removes the item from the line and sends it into the WashCar() helper function for processing. Do note that if you attempt to remove items from an empty queue, a runtime exception is thrown.

Working with the Stack Type

The System.Collections.Stack type represents a collection that maintains items using a last-in, first-out manner. As you would expect, Stack defines a member named Push() and Pop() (to place items onto or remove items from the stack). The following stack example makes use of the standard System.String:

```
static void StackTest()
{
  Console.WriteLine("\n=> Stack Test:\n");
  Stack stringStack = new Stack();
  stringStack.Push("One");
  stringStack.Push("Two");
  stringStack.Push("Three");

  // Now look at the top item, pop it, and look again.
  Console.WriteLine("Top item is: {0}", stringStack.Peek());
  Console.WriteLine("Popped off {0}", stringStack.Pop());
  Console.WriteLine("Top item is: {0}", stringStack.Peek());
  Console.WriteLine("Popped off {0}", stringStack.Pop());
  Console.WriteLine("Top item is: {0}", stringStack.Peek());
  Console.WriteLine("Popped off {0}", stringStack.Pop());

  try
  {
    Console.WriteLine("Top item is: {0}", stringStack.Peek());
    Console.WriteLine("Popped off {0}", stringStack.Pop());
  }
  catch(Exception e)
  { Console.WriteLine("Error!! {0}", e.Message);}
}
```

Here, you build a stack that contains three string types (named according to their order of insertion). As you peek into the stack, you will always see the item at the very top, and therefore the first call to Peek() reveals the third string. After a series of Pop() and Peek() calls, the stack is eventually empty, at which time additional Peek()/Pop() calls raise a system exception.

■ **Source Code** The CollectionTypes project can be found under the Chapter 10 subdirectory.

System.Collections.Specialized Namespace

In addition to the types defined within the System.Collections namespace, you should also be aware that the .NET base class libraries provide the System.Collections.Specialized namespace defined in the System.dll assembly, which defines another set of types that are more (pardon the redundancy) specialized. For example, the StringDictionary and ListDictionary types each provide a stylized implementation of the IDictionary interface. Table 10-4 documents the key class types.

Table 10-4. *Types of the* System.Collections.Specialized *Namespace*

Member of System.Collections.Specialized	Meaning in Life
BitVector32	A simple structure that stores Boolean values and small integers in 32 bits of memory.
CollectionsUtil	Creates collections that ignore the case in strings.
HybridDictionary	Implements IDictionary by using a ListDictionary while the collection is small, and then switching to a Hashtable when the collection gets large.
ListDictionary	Implements IDictionary using a singly linked list. Recommended for collections that typically contain ten items or fewer.
NameValueCollection	Represents a sorted collection of associated String keys and String values that can be accessed either with the key or with the index.
StringCollection	Represents a collection of strings.
StringDictionary	Implements a hashtable with the key strongly typed to be a string rather than an object.
StringEnumerator	Supports a simple iteration over a StringCollection.

Now that you have had a chance to examine some of the basic collection types within the System.Collections (and System.Collections.Specialized) namespace, you might be surprised when I tell you that these types are basically regarded as *legacy types* that should not be used for new project developments for .NET 2.0 or higher. The reason is not because these types are somehow dangerous, but due to the fact that they suffer from performance issues and a lack of type safety.

New projects should ignore these legacy container types in favor of related types in the System.Collections.Generic namespace. However, before we examine how to make use of generic types, it is very helpful to understand exactly what problems generics intend to solve in the first place. To begin, we must examine the role of *boxing* and *unboxing*.

The Boxing, Unboxing, and System.Object Relationship

As you recall from Chapter 4, the .NET platform supports two broad groups of data types, termed *value types* and *reference types*. Given that .NET defines two major categories of types, you may occasionally need to represent a variable of one category as a variable of the other category. To do so, C# provides a very simple mechanism, termed *boxing*, to convert a value type to a reference type. Assume that you have created a variable of type short:

```
// Make a short value type.
short s = 25;
```

If during the course of your application you wish to represent this value type as a reference type, you would box the value as follows:

```
// Box the value into an object reference.
object objShort = s;
```

Boxing can be formally defined as the process of explicitly converting a value type into a corresponding reference type by storing the variable in a System.Object. When you box a value, the CLR allocates a new object on the heap and copies the value type's value (in this case, 25) into that instance. What is returned to you is a reference to the newly allocated object. Using this technique, .NET developers have no need to make use of a set of wrapper classes used to temporarily treat stack data as heap-allocated objects.

The opposite operation is also permitted through *unboxing*. Unboxing is the process of converting the value held in the object reference back into a corresponding value type on the stack. The unboxing operation begins by verifying that the receiving data type is equivalent to the boxed type, and if so, it copies the value back into a local stack-based variable. For example, the following unboxing operations work successfully, given that the underlying type of the objShort is indeed a short:

```
// Unbox the reference back into a corresponding short.
short anotherShort = (short)objShort;
```

Again, it is mandatory that you unbox into an appropriate data type. Thus, the following unboxing logic generates an InvalidCastException exception:

```
// Illegal unboxing.
static void Main(string[] args)
{
  short s = 25;
  object objShort = s;

  try
  {
    // The type contained in the box is NOT an int, but a short!
    int i = (int)objShort;
  }
  catch(InvalidCastException e)
  {
    Console.WriteLine("OOPS!\n{0} ", e.ToString());
  }
}
```

At first glance, boxing/unboxing may seem like a rather uneventful language feature that is more academic than practical. In reality, the (un)boxing process is very helpful in that it allows us to assume everything can be treated as a System.Object, while the CLR takes care of the memory-related details on our behalf.

To see a practical use of this technique, assume you have created a System.Collections.ArrayList to hold numeric (stack-allocated) data. If you were to examine the members of ArrayList, you would find they are typically prototyped to receive and return System.Object types:

```
public class System.Collections.ArrayList : object,
  System.Collections.IList,
  System.Collections.ICollection,
```

```
  System.Collections.IEnumerable,
  ICloneable
{
...
  public virtual int Add(object value);
  public virtual void Insert(int index, object value);
  public virtual void Remove(object obj);
  public virtual object this[int index] {get; set; }
}
```

However, rather than forcing programmers to manually wrap the stack-based integer in a related object wrapper, the runtime will automatically do so via a boxing operation:

```
static void Main(string[] args)
{
  // Value types are automatically boxed when
  // passed to a member requesting an object.
  ArrayList myInts = new ArrayList();
  myInts.Add(10);
  Console.ReadLine();
}
```

If you wish to retrieve this value from the ArrayList object using the type indexer, you must unbox the heap-allocated object into a stack-allocated integer using a casting operation:

```
static void Main(string[] args)
{
...
  // Value is now unboxed.
  int i = (int)myInts[0];

  // Now it is reboxed, as WriteLine() requires object types!
  Console.WriteLine("Value of your int: {0}", i);
  Console.ReadLine();
}
```

When the C# compiler transforms a boxing operation into terms of CIL code, you find the box opcode is used internally. Likewise, the unboxing operation is transformed into a CIL unbox operation. Here is the relevant CIL code for the previous Main() method (which can be viewed using ildasm.exe):

```
.method private hidebysig static void  Main(string[] args) cil managed
{
...
  box  [mscorlib]System.Int32
  callvirt  instance int32 [mscorlib]System.Collections.ArrayList::Add(object)
  pop
  ldstr  "Value of your int: {0}"
  ldloc.0
  ldc.i4.0
  callvirt  instance object [mscorlib]
    System.Collections.ArrayList::get_Item(int32)
  unbox  [mscorlib]System.Int32
  ldind.i4
  box  [mscorlib]System.Int32
  call  void [mscorlib]System.Console::WriteLine(string, object)
...
}
```

Note that the stack-allocated System.Int32 is boxed prior to the call to ArrayList.Add() in order to pass in the required System.Object. Also note that the System.Object is unboxed back into a System.Int32 once retrieved from the ArrayList using the type indexer (which maps to the hidden get_Item() method), only to be *boxed again* when it is passed to the Console.WriteLine() method, as this method is operating on System.Object types.

The Problem with (Un)Boxing Operations

Although boxing and unboxing are very convenient from a programmer's point of view, this simplified approach to stack/heap memory transfer comes with the baggage of performance issues (in both speed of execution and code size) and a lack of type safety. To understand the performance issues, ponder the steps that must occur to box and unbox a simple integer:

1. A new object must be allocated on the managed heap.
2. The value of the stack-based data must be transferred into that memory location.
3. When unboxed, the value stored on the heap-based object must be transferred back to the stack.
4. The now unused object on the heap will (eventually) be garbage collected.

Although the current Main() method won't cause a major bottleneck in terms of performance, you could certainly feel the impact if an ArrayList contained thousands of integers that are manipulated by your program on a somewhat regular basis.

Now consider the lack of type safety regarding unboxing operations. As previously explained, to unbox a value using the syntax of C#, you make use of the casting operator. However, the success or failure of a cast is not known until *runtime*. Therefore, if you attempt to unbox a value into the wrong data type, you receive an InvalidCastException:

```
static void Main(string[] args)
{
  ArrayList myInts = new ArrayList();
  myInts.Add(10);

  // Runtime exception!
  short i = (int)myInts[0];

  // Now it is reboxed as WriteLine() requires object types!
  Console.WriteLine("Value of your int: {0}", i);
  Console.ReadLine();
}
```

In an ideal world, the C# compiler would be able to resolve these illegal unboxing operations at compile time, rather than at runtime. On a related note, in a *really* ideal world, we could store sets of value types in a container that did not require boxing in the first place. Generics are the solution to each of these issues.

The Issue of Type Safety and Strongly Typed Collections

The final major collection-centric issue we have in a generic-free programming world is the fact that a majority of the types of System.Collections can typically hold anything whatsoever, as their members are prototyped to operate on System.Objects:

```
static void Main(string[] args)
{
  // The ArrayList can hold anything at all.
  ArrayList allMyObject = new ArrayList();
  allMyObjects.Add(true);
  allMyObjects.Add(new Car());
  allMyObjects.Add(66);
  allMyObjects.Add(3.14);
}
```

In some cases, you will require an extremely flexible container that can hold literally anything. However, most of the time you desire a *type-safe* container that can only operate on a particular type of data point. For example, you might need a container that can only hold database connections, bitmaps, IPointy-compatible objects, or what have you.

Building a Custom Collection

Prior to the introduction of generics in .NET 2.0, programmers attempted to address type safety by manually building custom strongly typed collections. To illustrate why this can be problematic, create a new Console Application project named CustomNonGenericCollection. Once you have done so, be sure you import the System.Collections namespace. Now, assume you wish to create a custom collection that can only contain objects of type Person:

```
public class Person
{
  // Made public for simplicity.
  public int Age;
  public string FirstName, LastName;

  public Person(){}
  public Person(string firstName, string lastName, int age)
  {
    Age = age;
    FirstName = firstName;
    LastName = lastName;
  }

  public override string ToString()
  {
    return string.Format("Name: {0} {1}, Age: {2}",
      FirstName, LastName, Age);
  }
}
```

To build a person collection, you could define a System.Collections.ArrayList member variable within a class named PeopleCollection and configure all members to operate on strongly typed Person objects, rather than on System.Object types:

```
public class PeopleCollection : IEnumerable
{
  private ArrayList arPeople = new ArrayList();
  public PeopleCollection(){}

  // Cast for caller.
  public Person GetPerson(int pos)
  { return (Person)arPeople[pos]; }
```

```
  // Only insert Person types.
  public void AddPerson(Person p)
  { arPeople.Add(p); }

  public void ClearPeople()
  { arPeople.Clear(); }

  public int Count
  { get { return arPeople.Count; } }

  // Foreach enumeration support.
  IEnumerator IEnumerable.GetEnumerator()
  { return arPeople.GetEnumerator(); }
}
```

Notice that the PeopleCollection type implements the IEnumerable interface, to allow foreach-like iteration over each contained item. Also notice that our GetPerson() and AddPerson() method has been prototyped to only operate on Person objects (not bitmaps, strings, database connections, or other items). With these types defined, you are now assured of type safety, given that the C# compiler will be able to determine any attempt to insert an incompatible type:

```
static void Main(string[] args)
{
  Console.WriteLine("***** Custom Person Collection *****\n");
  PeopleCollection myPeople = new PeopleCollection();
  myPeople.AddPerson(new Person("Homer", "Simpson", 40));
  myPeople.AddPerson(new Person("Marge", "Simpson", 38));
  myPeople.AddPerson(new Person("Lisa", "Simpson", 9));
  myPeople.AddPerson(new Person("Bart", "Simpson", 7));
  myPeople.AddPerson(new Person("Maggie", "Simpson", 2));

  // This would be a compile-time error!
  // myPeople.AddPerson(new Car());

  foreach (Person p in myPeople)
    Console.WriteLine(p);
  Console.ReadLine();
}
```

While custom collections do ensure type safety, this approach leaves you in a position where you must create an (almost identical) custom collection for each type you wish to contain. Thus, if you need a custom collection that will be able to operate only on classes deriving from the Car base class, you need to build a very similar type:

```
public class CarCollection : IEnumerable
{
  private ArrayList arCars = new ArrayList();
  public CarCollection(){}

  // Cast for caller.
  public Car GetCar(int pos)
  { return (Car) arCars[pos]; }

  // Only insert Car types.
  public void AddCar(Car c)
  { arCars.Add(c); }
```

```
  public void ClearCars()
  { arCars.Clear(); }

  public int Count
  { get { return arCars.Count; } }

  // Foreach enumeration support.
  IEnumerator IEnumerable.GetEnumerator()
  { return arCars.GetEnumerator(); }
}
```

As you may know from firsthand experience, the process of creating multiple strongly typed collections to account for various types is not only labor intensive, but also a nightmare to maintain. Generic collections allow us to delay the specification of the contained type until the time of creation. Don't fret about the syntactic details just yet, however. Consider the following code, which makes use of a generic class named `System.Collections.Generic.List<T>` to create two type-safe container objects:

```
static void Main(string[] args)
{
  // Use the generic List type to hold only people.
  List<Person> morePeople = new List<Person>();
  morePeople.Add(new Person());

  // Use the generic List type to hold only cars.
  List<Car> moreCars = new List<Car>();

  // Compile-time error!
  moreCars.Add(new Person());
}
```

Boxing Issues and Strongly Typed Collections

Strongly typed collections are found throughout the .NET base class libraries and are very useful programming constructs. However, these custom containers do little to solve the issue of boxing penalties. Even if you were to create a custom collection named `IntCollection` that was constructed to operate only on `System.Int32` data types, you would have to allocate some type of object to hold the data (`System.Array`, `System.Collections.ArrayList`, etc.):

```
public class IntCollection : IEnumerable
{
  private ArrayList arInts = new ArrayList();
  public IntCollection() { }

  // Unbox for caller.
  public int GetInt(int pos)
  { return (int)arInts[pos]; }

  // Boxing operation!
  public void AddInt(int i)
  { arInts.Add(i); }

  public void ClearInts()
  { arInts.Clear(); }
```

```
  public int Count
  { get { return arInts.Count; } }

  IEnumerator IEnumerable.GetEnumerator()
  { return arInts.GetEnumerator(); }
}
```

Regardless of which type you may choose to hold the integers (`System.Array`, `System.Collections.ArrayList`, etc.), you cannot escape the boxing dilemma using nongeneric containers. As you might guess, generics come to the rescue again. The following code leverages the `System.Collections.Generic.List<T>` type to create a container of integers that does *not* incur any boxing or unboxing penalties when inserting or obtaining the value type:

```
static void Main(string[] args)
{
  // No boxing!
  List<int> myInts = new List<int>();
  myInts.Add(5);

  // No unboxing!
  int i = myInts[0];
}
```

Just to prove the point, the previous `Main()` method results in the following CIL code (note the lack of any `box` or `unbox` opcodes):

```
.method private hidebysig static void Main(string[] args) cil managed
{
  .entrypoint
  .maxstack  2
  .locals init ([0] class [mscorlib]System.Collections.Generic.'List`1'<int32>
    myInts, [1] int32 i)
  newobj instance void class
    [mscorlib]System.Collections.Generic.'List`1'<int32>::.ctor()
  stloc.0
  ldloc.0
  ldc.i4.5
  callvirt instance void class [mscorlib]
    System.Collections.Generic.'List`1'<int32>::Add(!0)
  nop
  ldloc.0
  ldc.i4.0
  callvirt instance !0 class [mscorlib]
    System.Collections.Generic.'List`1'<int32>::get_Item(int32)
  stloc.1
  ret
}
```

In summary, generic containers provide the following benefits over their nongeneric counterparts:

- Generics provide better performance, as they do not result in boxing or unboxing penalties.
- Generics are more type safe, as they can only contain the "type of type" you specify.
- Generics greatly reduce the need to build custom collection types, as the base class library provides several prefabricated containers.

■ **Source Code** The CustomNonGenericCollection project is located under the Chapter 10 directory.

The System.Collections.Generic Namespace

Generic types are found sprinkled throughout the .NET base class libraries; however, the System.Collections.Generic namespace is chock-full of them (as its name implies). Like its nongeneric counterpart (System.Collections), the System.Collections.Generic namespace contains numerous class and interface types that allow you to contain subitems in a variety of containers. Not surprisingly, the generic interfaces mimic the corresponding nongeneric types in the System.Collections namespace:

- ICollection<T>
- IComparer<T>
- IDictionary<TKey, TValue>
- IEnumerable<T>
- IEnumerator<T>
- IList<T>

■ **Note** By convention, generic types specify their placeholders using common names. Although any letter (or word) will do, typically T is used to represent types, TKey is used for keys, and TValue is used for values.

The System.Collections.Generic namespace also defines a number of classes that implement many of these key interfaces. Table 10-5 describes the core class types of this namespace, the interfaces they implement, and any corresponding type in the System.Collections namespace.

Table 10-5. *Classes of* System.Collections.Generic

Nongeneric Counterpart	Generic Class in System.Collections	Meaning in Life
Collection<T>	CollectionBase	The basis for a generic collection
Comparer<T>	Comparer	Compares two generic objects for equality
Dictionary<TKey, TValue>	Hashtable	A generic collection of name/value pairs
List<T>	ArrayList	A dynamically resizable list of items
Queue<T>	Queue	A generic implementation of a first-in, first-out (FIFO) list
SortedDictionary<TKey, TValue>	SortedList	A generic implementation of a sorted set of name/value pairs
Stack<T>	Stack	A generic implementation of a last-in, first-out (LIFO) list

Nongeneric Counterpart	Generic Class in System.Collections	Meaning in Life
LinkedList<T>	N/A	A generic implementation of a doubly linked list
ReadOnlyCollection<T>	ReadOnlyCollectionBase	A generic implementation of a set of read-only items

The System.Collections.Generic namespace also defines a number of auxiliary classes and structures that work in conjunction with a specific container. For example, the LinkedListNode<T> type represents a node within a generic LinkedList<T>, the KeyNotFoundException exception is raised when attempting to grab an item from a container using a nonexistent key, and so forth.

As you can see from Table 10-5, many of the generic collection classes have a nongeneric counterpart in the System.Collections namespace (some of which are identically named). Because the generic classes mimic their nongeneric types so closely, I will not provide a detailed examination of each generic item (once you understand how to work with a given container, the remaining items are quite straightforward). Instead, I'll make use of List<T> to illustrate the process of working with generics. If you require details regarding other members of the System.Collections.Generic namespace, consult the .NET Framework 3.5 documentation.

Examining the List<T> Type

Like nongeneric classes, generic classes are created with the new keyword and any required constructor arguments. In addition, you are required to specify the type(s) to be substituted for the type parameter(s) defined by the generic type. For example, System.Collections.Generic.List<T> requires you to specify a single value that describes the type of item the List<T> will operate upon. Therefore, if you wish to create three List<T> objects to contain integers and SportsCar and Person objects, you would write the following:

```
static void Main(string[] args)
{
  // Create a List containing integers.
  List<int> myInts = new List<int>();

  // Create a List containing SportsCar objects.
  List<SportsCar> myCars = new List<SportsCar>();

  // Create a List containing Person objects.
  List<Person> myPeople = new List<Person>();
}
```

At this point, you might wonder what exactly becomes of the specified placeholder value. If you were to make use of the Visual Studio 2008 Code Definition window (see Chapter 2), you will find that the placeholder T is used throughout the definition of the List<T> type. Here is a partial listing (note the items in **bold**):

```
// A partial listing of the List<T> type.
namespace System.Collections.Generic
{
  public class List<T> :
    IList<T>, ICollection<T>, IEnumerable<T>,
    IList, ICollection, IEnumerable
  {
...
    public void Add(T item);
```

```
    public IList<T> AsReadOnly();
    public int BinarySearch(T item);
    public bool Contains(T item);
    public void CopyTo(T[] array);
    public int FindIndex(System.Predicate<T> match);
    public T FindLast(System.Predicate<T> match);
    public bool Remove(T item);
    public int RemoveAll(System.Predicate<T> match);
    public T[] ToArray();
    public bool TrueForAll(System.Predicate<T> match);
    public T this[int index] { get; set; }
  }
}
```

When you create a List<T> specifying SportsCar types, it is as if the List<T> type were really defined as follows:

```
namespace System.Collections.Generic
{
  public class List<SportsCar> :
    IList<SportsCar>, ICollection<SportsCar>, IEnumerable<SportsCar>,
    IList, ICollection, IEnumerable
  {
...
    public void Add(SportsCar item);
    public IList<SportsCar> AsReadOnly();
    public int BinarySearch(SportsCar item);
    public bool Contains(SportsCar item);
    public void CopyTo(SportsCar[] array);
    public int FindIndex(System.Predicate<SportsCar> match);
    public SportsCar FindLast(System.Predicate<SportsCar> match);
    public bool Remove(SportsCar item);
    public int RemoveAll(System.Predicate<SportsCar> match);
    public SportsCar [] ToArray();
    public bool TrueForAll(System.Predicate<SportsCar> match);
    public SportsCar this[int index] { get; set; }
  }
}
```

Of course, when you create a generic List<T>, the compiler does not literally create a brand-new implementation of the List<T> type. Rather, it will address only the members of the generic type you actually invoke. To solidify this point, assume you exercise a List<T> of SportsCar objects as follows:

```
static void Main(string[] args)
{
  // Exercise a List containing SportsCars
  List<SportsCar> myCars = new List<SportsCar>();
  myCars.Add(new SportsCar());
  Console.WriteLine("Your List contains {0} item(s).", myCars.Count);
}
```

If you examine the generated CIL code using ildasm.exe, you will find the following substitutions:

```
.method private hidebysig static void Main(string[] args) cil managed
{
  .entrypoint
  .maxstack  2
```

```
  .locals init ([0] class [mscorlib]System.Collections.Generic.'List`1'
    <class SportsCar> myCars)
  newobj instance void class [mscorlib]System.Collections.Generic.'List`1'
    <class SportsCar>::.ctor()
  stloc.0
  ldloc.0
  newobj instance void CollectionGenerics.SportsCar::.ctor()
  callvirt instance void class [mscorlib]System.Collections.Generic.'List`1'
    <class SportsCar>::Add(!0)
   nop
  ldstr "Your List contains {0} item(s)."
  ldloc.0
  callvirt  instance int32 class [mscorlib]System.Collections.Generic.'List`1'
    <class SportsCar>::get_Count()
  box [mscorlib]System.Int32
  call void [mscorlib]System.Console::WriteLine(string, object)
  nop
  ret
}
```

Now that you've looked at the process of working with generic types provided by the base class libraries, in the remainder of this chapter you'll examine how to create your own generic methods, types, and collections.

Creating Custom Generic Methods

While most developers will typically make use of the existing generic types within the base class libraries, it is certainly possible to build your own generic members and custom generic types. To learn how to incorporate generics into your own projects, the first task is to build a generic swap method. Begin by creating a new Console Application named GenericMethod.

The goal of this example is to build a swap method that can operate on any possible data type (value-based or reference-based) using a single type parameter. Due to the nature of swapping algorithms, the incoming parameters will be sent by reference (via the C# `ref` keyword). Here is the full implementation of our generic swap method, contained within the initial `Program` class:

```
// This method will swap any two items.
// as specified by the type parameter <T>.
static void Swap<T>(ref T a, ref T b)
{
  Console.WriteLine("You sent the Swap() method a {0}",
    typeof(T));
  T temp;
  temp = a;
  a = b;
  b = temp;
}
```

Notice how a generic method is defined by specifying the type parameter after the method name but before the parameter list. Here, you're stating that the `Swap()` method can operate on any two parameters of type `<T>`. Just to spice things up a bit, you're printing out the type name of the supplied placeholder to the console using the C# `typeof()` operator. Now consider the following `Main()` method that swaps integer and string types:

```
static void Main(string[] args)
{
  Console.WriteLine("***** Fun with Custom Generic Methods *****\n");
```

```
    // Swap 2 ints.
    int a = 10, b = 90;
    Console.WriteLine("Before swap: {0}, {1}", a, b);
    Swap<int>(ref a, ref b);
    Console.WriteLine("After swap: {0}, {1}", a, b);
    Console.WriteLine();

    // Swap 2 strings.
    string s1 = "Hello", s2 = "There";
    Console.WriteLine("Before swap: {0} {1}!", s1, s2);
    Swap<string>(ref s1, ref s2);
    Console.WriteLine("After swap: {0} {1}!", s1, s2);
    Console.ReadLine();
  }
```

Inference of Type Parameters

When you invoke generic methods such as `Swap<T>`, you can optionally omit the type parameter if (and only if) the generic method requires arguments, as the compiler can infer the type parameter based on the member parameters. For example, you could swap two `System.Boolean` types by adding the following code to `Main()`:

```
// Compiler will infer System.Boolean.
bool b1 = true, b2 = false;
Console.WriteLine("Before swap: {0}, {1}", b1, b2);
Swap(ref b1, ref b2);
Console.WriteLine("After swap: {0}, {1}", b1, b2);
```

However, if you had another generic method named `DisplayBaseClass<T>` that did not take any incoming parameters, as follows:

```
static void DisplayBaseClass<T>()
{
  Console.WriteLine("Base class of {0} is: {1}.",
    typeof(T), typeof(T).BaseType);
}
```

you are required to supply the type parameter upon invocation:

```
static void Main(string[] args)
{
...
  // Must supply type parameter if
  // the method does not take params.
  DisplayBaseClass<int>();
  DisplayBaseClass<string>();

  // Compiler error! No params? Must supply placeholder!
  // DisplayBaseClass();
  Console.ReadLine();
}
```

Figure 10-2 shows the current output of this application.

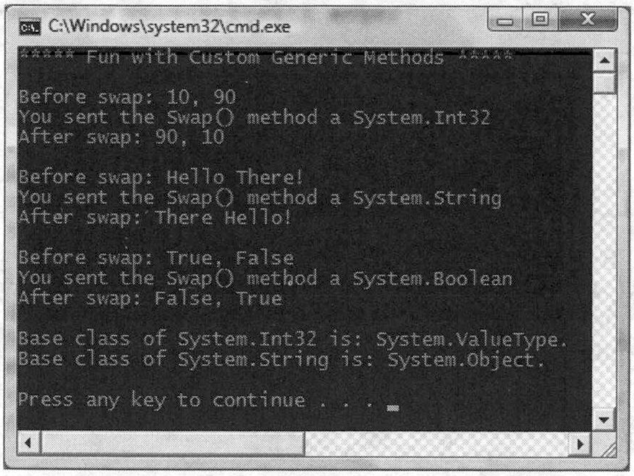

```
C:\Windows\system32\cmd.exe
***** Fun with Custom Generic Methods *****

Before swap: 10, 90
You sent the Swap() method a System.Int32
After swap: 90, 10

Before swap: Hello There!
You sent the Swap() method a System.String
After swap: There Hello!

Before swap: True, False
You sent the Swap() method a System.Boolean
After swap: False, True

Base class of System.Int32 is: System.ValueType.
Base class of System.String is: System.Object.

Press any key to continue . . .
```

Figure 10-2. *Generic methods in action*

Currently, the generic `Swap<T>` and `DisplayBaseClass<T>` methods have been defined within the application object (i.e., the type defining the `Main()` method). Of course, like any method, if you would rather define these members in a separate class type (`MyGenericMethods`), you are free to do so:

```
public static class MyGenericMethods
{
  public static void Swap<T>(ref T a, ref T b)
  {
    Console.WriteLine("You sent the Swap() method a {0}",
      typeof(T));
    T temp;
    temp = a;
    a = b;
    b = temp;
  }

  public static void DisplayBaseClass<T>()
  {
    Console.WriteLine("Base class of {0} is: {1}.",
      typeof(T), typeof(T).BaseType);
  }
}
```

Because the static `Swap<T>` and `DisplayBaseClass<T>` methods have been scoped within a new static class type, you will need to specify the type's name when invoking either member, for example:

```
MyGenericMethods.Swap<int>(ref a, ref b);
```

Of course, generic methods do not need to be static. If `Swap<T>` and `DisplayBaseClass<T>` were instance level (and defined in a nonstatic class), you would simply make an instance of `MyGenericMethods` and invoke them off the object variable:

```
MyGenericMethods c = new MyGenericMethods();
c.Swap<int>(ref a, ref b);
```

■ **Source Code** The GenericMethod project is located under the Chapter 10 directory.

Creating Generic Structures and Classes

Now that you understand how to define and invoke generic methods, let's turn our attention to the construction of a generic structure (the process of building a generic class is identical) within a new Console Application project named GenericPoint. Assume you have built a generic `Point` structure that supports a single type parameter representing the underlying storage for the (*x*, *y*) coordinates. The caller would then be able to create `Point<T>` types as follows:

```
// Point using ints.
Point<int> p = new Point<int>(10, 10);

// Point using double.
Point<double> p2 = new Point<double>(5.4, 3.3);
```

Here is the complete definition of `Point<T>`, with analysis to follow:

```
// A generic Point structure.
public struct Point<T>
{
  // Generic state date.
  private T xPos;
  private T yPos;

  // Generic constructor.
  public Point(T xVal, T yVal)
  {
    xPos = xVal;
    yPos = yVal;
  }

  // Generic properties.
  public T X
  {
    get { return xPos; }
    set { xPos = value; }
  }

  public T Y
  {
    get { return yPos; }
    set { yPos = value; }
  }

  public override string ToString()
  {
    return string.Format("[{0}, {1}]", xPos, yPos);
  }

  // Reset fields to the default value of the
  // type parameter.
  public void ResetPoint()
  {
```

```
    xPos = default(T);
    yPos = default(T);
  }
}
```

The default Keyword in Generic Code

As you can see, Point<T> leverages its type parameter in the definition of the field data, constructor arguments, and property definitions. Notice that in addition to overriding ToString(), Point<T> defines a method named ResetPoint() that makes use of some new syntax:

```
// The "default" keyword is overloaded in C#.
// When used with generics, it represents the default
// value of a type parameter.
public void ResetPoint()
{
  xPos = default(T);
  yPos = default(T);
}
```

With the introduction of generics, the C# default keyword has been given a dual identity. In addition to its use within a switch construct, it can be used to set a type parameter to its default value. This is clearly helpful given that a generic type does not know the actual placeholders up front and therefore cannot safely assume what the default value will be. The defaults for a type parameter are as follows:

- Numeric values have a default value of 0.
- Reference types have a default value of null.
- Fields of a structure are set to 0 (for value types) or null (for reference types).

For Point<T>, you could simply set xPos and yPos to 0 directly, given that it is safe to assume the caller will supply only numerical data. However, by using the default(T) syntax, you increase the overall flexibility of the generic type. In any case, you can now exercise the methods of Point<T> as follows:

```
static void Main(string[] args)
{
  Console.WriteLine("***** Fun with Generic Structures *****\n");

  // Point using ints.
  Point<int> p = new Point<int>(10, 10);
  Console.WriteLine("p.ToString()={0}", p.ToString());
  p.ResetPoint();
  Console.WriteLine("p.ToString()={0}", p.ToString());
  Console.WriteLine();

  // Point using double.
  Point<double> p2 = new Point<double>(5.4, 3.3);
  Console.WriteLine("p2.ToString()={0}", p2.ToString());
  p2.ResetPoint();
  Console.WriteLine("p2.ToString()={0}", p2.ToString());

  Console.ReadLine();
}
```

Figure 10-3 shows the output.

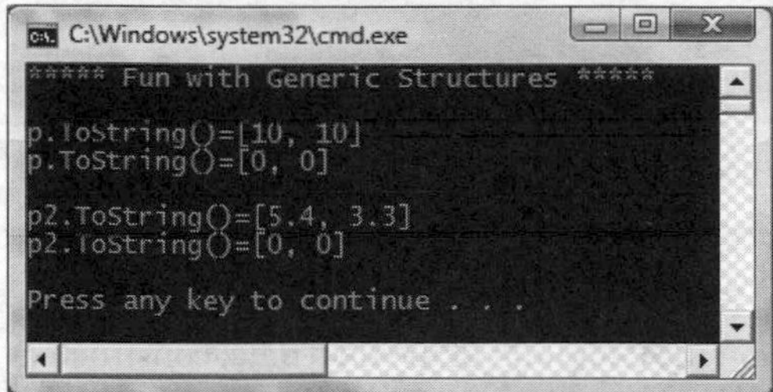

Figure 10-3. *Using the generic* `Point` *type*

■ Source Code The GenericPoint project is located under the Chapter 10 subdirectory.

Creating a Custom Generic Collection

As you have seen, the `System.Collections.Generic` namespace provides numerous types that allow you to create type-safe and efficient containers. Given the set of available choices, the chances are quite good that you will not need to build custom collection types when programming with the .NET platform. Nevertheless, to illustrate how you could build a stylized generic container, the next task is to build a generic collection class named `CarCollection<T>` (and see exactly what, if anything, this buys us). Begin by creating a new Console Application named CustomGenericCollection.

Like the nongeneric `CarCollection` created earlier in this chapter, this iteration will leverage an existing collection type to hold the subitems (a `List<T>` in this case). As well, you will support `foreach` iteration by implementing the generic `IEnumerable<T>` interface. Do note that `IEnumerable<T>` extends the nongeneric `IEnumerable` interface; therefore, the compiler expects you to implement *two* versions of the `GetEnumerator()` method. Here is the update:

```
public class CarCollection<T> : IEnumerable<T>
{
  private List<T> arCars = new List<T>();

  public T GetCar(int pos)
  { return arCars[pos]; }

  public void AddCar(T c)
  { arCars.Add(c); }

  public void ClearCars()
  { arCars.Clear(); }

  public int Count
  { get { return arCars.Count; } }

  // IEnumerable<T> extends IEnumerable, therefore
  // we need to implement both versions of GetEnumerator().
  IEnumerator<T> IEnumerable<T>.GetEnumerator()
  { return arCars.GetEnumerator(); }
```

```
  System.Collections.IEnumerator System.Collections.IEnumerable.GetEnumerator()
  { return arCars.GetEnumerator(); }
}
```

You could now make use of this updated `CarCollection<T>` as follows (assuming you had a simple `Car` definition within your current project):

```
static void Main(string[] args)
{
  Console.WriteLine("***** Custom Generic Collection *****\n");

  // Make a collection of Cars.
  CarCollection<Car> myCars = new CarCollection<Car>();
  myCars.AddCar(new Car("Rusty", 20));
  myCars.AddCar(new Car("Zippy", 90));

  foreach (Car c in myCars)
  {
    Console.WriteLine("PetName: {0}, Speed: {1}",
    c.PetName, c.Speed);
  }
  Console.ReadLine();
}
```

Here you are creating a `CarCollection<T>` type that contains only `Car` types. Again, you could achieve a similar end result if you make use of the `List<T>` type directly. The major benefit at this point is the fact that you are free to add uniquely named methods (`AddCar()`, `GetCar()`, etc.) to the `CarCollection` that delegate the request to the internal `List<T>`.

Limitations of Custom Generic Collections

Currently, the `CarCollection<T>` class does not buy you much beyond uniquely named public methods. Furthermore, an object user could create an instance of `CarCollection<T>` and specify a completely unrelated type parameter:

```
// This is syntactically correct, but confusing at best!
CarCollection<int> myInts = new CarCollection<int>();
myInts.AddCar(5);
myInts.AddCar(11);

foreach (int i in myInts)
{
  Console.WriteLine("Int value: {0}", i);
}
```

So, why does the compiler allow such code? Well, remember that generics are, in fact, *generic*. A type parameter can be anything whatsoever, even if it completely makes no sense within the context of the generic type (e.g., a car collection holding integers).

To illustrate another form of generics abuse, assume that you have now created two new classes (`SportsCar` and `MiniVan`) that derive from the `Car` type:

```
public class SportsCar : Car
{
  public SportsCar(string p, int s)
    : base(p, s){}
  // Assume additional SportsCar methods.
}
```

```
public class MiniVan : Car
{
  public MiniVan(string p, int s)
    : base(p, s){}
  // Assume additional MiniVan methods.
}
```

Given the laws of inheritance, it is permissible to add a MiniVan or SportsCar type directly into a CarCollection<T> created with a type parameter of Car:

```
// CarCollection<Car> can hold any type deriving from Car.
CarCollection<Car> myAutos = new CarCollection<Car>();
myAutos.AddCar(new MiniVan("Family Truckster", 55));
myAutos.AddCar(new SportsCar("Crusher", 40));
```

Although this is syntactically valid code, what if you wished to update CarCollection<T> with a new public method named PrintPetName()? This seems simple enough—just access the correct item in the List<T> and pluck out the PetName value:

```
// Error! System.Object does not have a
// property named PetName.
public void PrintPetName(int pos)
{
  Console.WriteLine(arCars[pos].PetName);
}
```

However, this will not compile, given that the true identity of T is not yet known, and you cannot say for certain whether the item contained within the List<T> type has a PetName property. When a type parameter is not constrained in any way (as is the case here), the generic type is said to be *unbound*. By design, unbound type parameters are assumed to have only the members of System.Object (which clearly does not provide a PetName property).

You may try to trick the compiler by casting the item returned from the List<T>'s indexer method into a strongly typed Car and invoking PetName from the returned object:

```
// Error!
// Cannot convert type "T" to "Car"
public void PrintPetName(int pos)
{
  Console.WriteLine(((Car)arCars[pos]).PetName);
}
```

This again does not compile, given that the compiler does not yet know the value of the type parameter <T> and cannot guarantee the cast would be legal. Given the issues we have just examined, you might rightly wonder when (if ever) would you need to create a custom generic container? Glad you asked!

Constraining Type Parameters Using the where Keyword

The major reason developers would author a custom generic collection type is to enforce *constraints* upon type parameters in order to build extremely type-safe containers. In C#, constraints are applied using the where keyword, which can control the various characteristics of a type parameter (see Table 10-6).

Table 10-6. *Possible Constraints for Generic Type Parameters*

Generic Constraint	Meaning in Life
`where T : struct`	The type parameter <T> must have `System.ValueType` in its chain of inheritance.
`where T : class`	The type parameter <T> must *not* have `System.ValueType` in its chain of inheritance (e.g., <T> must be a reference type).
`where T : new()`	The type parameter <T> must have a default constructor. This is very helpful if your generic type must create an instance of the type parameter, as you cannot assume the format of custom constructors. Note that this constraint must be listed last on a multiconstrained type.
`where T :` *`NameOfBaseClass`*	The type parameter <T> must be derived from the class specified by *`NameOfBaseClass`*.
`where T :` *`NameOfInterface`*	The type parameter <T> must implement the interface specified by *`NameOfInterface`*. Multiple interfaces can be separated as a comma-delimited list.

When constraints are applied using the `where` keyword, the constraint list is placed after the generic type's base class and interface list. By way of a few concrete examples, consider the following constraints of a generic class named `MyGenericClass`:

```
// MyGenericClass derives from Object, while
// contained items must have a default ctor.
public class MyGenericClass<T> where T : new()
{...}

// MyGenericClass derives from Object, while
// contained items must be a class implementing IDrawable
// and support a default ctor.
public class MyGenericClass<T> where T : class, IDrawable, new()
{...}

// MyGenericClass derives from MyBase and implements ISomeInterface,
// while the contained items must be structures.
public class MyGenericClass<T> : MyBase, ISomeInterface where T : struct
{...}
```

On a related note, if you are building a generic type that specifies multiple type parameters, you can specify a unique set of constraints for each:

```
// <K> must have a default ctor, while <T> must
// implement the generic IComparable interface.
public class MyGenericClass<K, T> where K : new()
    where T : IComparable<T>
{...}
```

To see the usefulness of applying constraints, if you wish to update `CarCollection<T>` to ensure that only `Car`-derived types can be placed within it, you could write the following:

```
public class CarCollection<T> : IEnumerable<T> where T : Car
{
...
  public void PrintPetName(int pos)
  {
    // Because all subitems must be in the Car family,
    // we can now directly call the PetName property.
```

```
    Console.WriteLine(arCars[pos].PetName);
  }
}
```

Notice that once you constrain CarCollection<T> such that it can contain only Car-derived types, the implementation of PrintPetName() is straightforward, given that the compiler now assumes <T> is a Car-derived type. Furthermore, if the specified type parameter is not Car-compatible, you are issued a compiler error:

```
// Compiler error!
CarCollection<int> myInts = new CarCollection<int>();
```

Do be aware that generic methods can also leverage the where keyword. For example, if you wish to ensure that only System.ValueType-derived types are passed into the Swap() method created previously in this chapter, update the code accordingly:

```
// This method will swap any value type, but not classes.
static void Swap<T>(ref T a, ref T b) where T : struct
{
  ...
}
```

Understand that if you were to constrain the Swap() method in this manner, you would no longer be able to swap string types (as done in the sample code) as they are reference types.

The Lack of Operator Constraints

When you are creating generic methods, it may come as a surprise to you that it is a *compiler error* to apply any C# operators (+, -, *, ==, etc.) on the type parameters. As an example, I am sure you could imagine the usefulness of a class that can Add(), Subtract(), Multiply(), and Divide() generic types:

```
// Compiler error! Cannot apply
// operators to type parameters!
public class BasicMath<T>
{
  public T Add(T arg1, T arg2)
  { return arg1 + arg2; }
  public T Subtract(T arg1, T arg2)
  { return arg1 - arg2; }
  public T Multiply(T arg1, T arg2)
  { return arg1 * arg2; }
  public T Divide(T arg1, T arg2)
  { return arg1 / arg2; }
}
```

Sadly, the preceding BasicMath<T> class will not compile. While this may seem like a major restriction, you need to again remember that generics *are* generic. Of course, the System.Int32 type can work just fine with the binary operators of C#. However, for the sake of argument, if <T> were a custom class or structure type, the compiler cannot assume it has overloaded the +, -, *, and / operators. Ideally, C# would allow a generic type to be constrained by supported operators, for example:

```
// Illustrative code only!
// This is not legal code under C# 2008.
public class BasicMath<T> where T : operator +, operator -,
  operator *, operator /
{
  public T Add(T arg1, T arg2)
```

```
  { return arg1 + arg2; }
  public T Subtract(T arg1, T arg2)
  { return arg1 - arg2; }
  public T Multiply(T arg1, T arg2)
  { return arg1 * arg2; }
  public T Divide(T arg1, T arg2)
  { return arg1 / arg2; }
}
```

Alas, operator constraints are not supported under the current version of C#. If you were to make use of generic interface types, you could simulate the notion of applying operators on type parameters. You'll see this approach in just a moment.

■ **Source Code** The CustomGenericCollection project is located under the Chapter 10 subdirectory.

Creating Generic Base Classes

Before we examine generic interfaces, it is worth pointing out that generic classes can be the base class to other classes, and can therefore define any number of virtual or abstract methods. However, the derived types must abide by a few rules to ensure that the nature of the generic abstraction flows through. First of all, if a nongeneric class extends a generic class, the derived class must specify a type parameter:

```
// Assume you have created a custom
// generic list class.
public class MyList<T>
{
  private List<T> listOfData = new List<T>();
}

// Concrete types must specify the type
// parameter when deriving from a
// generic base class.
public class MyStringList : MyList<string>
{}
```

Furthermore, if the generic base class defines generic virtual or abstract methods, the derived type must override the generic methods using the specified type parameter:

```
// A generic class with a virtual method.
public class MyList<T>
{
  private List<T> listOfData = new List<T>();
  public virtual void PrintList(T data) { }
}

public class MyStringList : MyList<string>
{
  // Must substitute the type parameter used in the
  // parent class in derived methods.
  public override void PrintList(string data) { }
}
```

If the derived type is generic as well, the child class can (optionally) reuse the type placeholder in its definition. Be aware, however, that any constraints placed on the base class must be honored by the derived type, for example:

```
// Note that we now have a default constructor constraint.
public class MyList<T> where T : new()
{
  private List<T> listOfData = new List<T>();

  public virtual void PrintList(T data) { }
}

// Derived type must honor constraints.
public class MyReadOnlyList<T> : MyList<T> where T : new()
{
    public override void PrintList(T data) { }
}
```

Again, in your day-to-day programming tasks, creating custom generic class hierarchies will most likely not be a very common task. Nevertheless, doing so is completely possible (as long as you abide by the rules).

Creating Generic Interfaces

As you saw earlier in the chapter during the examination of the `System.Collections.Generic` namespace, generic interfaces are also permissible (e.g., `IEnumerable<T>`). You are, of course, free to define your own generic interfaces (with or without constraints). Assume you wish to define an interface that can perform binary operations on a generic type parameter:

```
public interface IBinaryOperations<T> where T : struct
{
  T Add(T arg1, T arg2);
  T Subtract(T arg1, T arg2);
  T Multiply(T arg1, T arg2);
  T Divide(T arg1, T arg2);
}
```

Of course, interfaces are more or less useless until they are implemented by a class or structure. When you implement a generic interface, the supporting type specifies the placeholder type:

```
public class BasicMath : IBinaryOperations<int>
{
  public int Add(int arg1, int arg2)
  { return arg1 + arg2; }

  public int Subtract(int arg1, int arg2)
  { return arg1 - arg2; }

  public int Multiply(int arg1, int arg2)
  { return arg1 * arg2; }

  public int Divide(int arg1, int arg2)
  { return arg1 / arg2; }
}
```

At this point, you make use of BasicMath as you would expect:

```
static void Main(string[] args)
{
  Console.WriteLine("***** Generic Interfaces *****\n");
  BasicMath m = new BasicMath();
  Console.WriteLine("1 + 1 = {0}", m.Add(1, 1));
  Console.ReadLine();
}
```

If you would rather create a BasicMath class that operates on floating-point numbers, you could specify the type parameter as follows:

```
public class BasicMath : IBinaryOperations<float>
{
  public float Add(float arg1, float arg2)
  { return arg1 + arg2; }
...
}
```

In this case, the compiler will ensure that we pass in a float to each method of the BasicMath class. You may recall from Chapter 3 that floating-point literal values default to a double, therefore we must add the suffix F to inform the compiler we do indeed require a float:

```
static void Main(string[] args)
{
  Console.WriteLine("***** Generic Interfaces *****\n");
  BasicMath m = new BasicMath();
  Console.WriteLine("1.98 + 1.3 = {0}", m.Add(1.98F, 1.3F));
  Console.ReadLine();
}
```

■ **Source Code** The GenericInterface project is located under the Chapter 10 subdirectory.

This wraps up our initial look at building custom generic types. In the next chapter, we will pick up the topic of generics once again, when we examine the .NET delegate type.

Summary

This chapter began by examining the use of the "classic" containers found within the System.Collections namespace. While these types will still be supported for purposes of backward compatibility, new .NET applications will benefit from instead making use of the generic counterparts within the System.Collections.Generic namespace.

As you have seen, a generic item allows you to specify "placeholders" (i.e., type parameters) that are specified at the time of creation (or invocation, in the case of generic methods). Essentially, generics provide a solution to the boxing and type-safety issues that plagued .NET 1.1 software development. In addition, generic types by and large remove the need to build custom collection types.

While you will most often simply make use of the generic types provided in the .NET base class libraries, you are also able to create your own generic types. When you do so, you have the option of specifying any number of constraints (via the where keyword) to increase the level of type safety and ensure that you are performing operations on types of a "known quantity."

CHAPTER 11

■ ■ ■

Delegates, Events, and Lambdas

Up to this point in the text, most of the applications you have developed added various bits of code to `Main()`, which, in some way or another, sent requests to a given object. In Chapter 9, you examined how the interface type can be used to build objects that can "talk back" to the entity that created it. While callback interfaces can be used to configure objects that engage in two-way conversations, the .NET delegate type is the preferred manner to define and respond to callbacks under the .NET platform.

Essentially, the .NET delegate type is a type-safe object that "points to" a method, or if you wish, a list of methods, that can be invoked at a later time. Unlike a traditional C++ function pointer, however, .NET delegates are classes that have built-in support for multicasting and asynchronous method invocation.

Once you learn how to create and manipulate delegate types, you then investigate the C# `event` keyword, which streamlines the process of working with delegate types. Along the way you will also examine several delegate-and-event-centric language features of C#, including anonymous methods and method group conversions.

I wrap up this chapter by investigating a new C# 2008 language feature termed *lambda expressions*. Using the new lambda operator (`=>`), it is now possible to specify a block of code statements (and the parameters to pass to said code statements) wherever a strongly typed delegate is required. As you will see, a lambda expression is little more than an anonymous method in disguise.

Understanding the .NET Delegate Type

Before formally defining .NET delegates, let's gain a bit of perspective. Historically speaking, the Windows API made frequent use of C-style function pointers to create entities termed *callback functions* or simply *callbacks*. Using callbacks, programmers were able to configure one function to report back to (call back) another function in the application. Using this approach, Win32 developers were able to handle button clicking, mouse moving, menu selecting, and general bidirectional communications between two programming entities.

The problem with standard C-style callback functions is that they represent little more than a raw address in memory. Ideally, callbacks could be configured to include additional type-safe information such as the number of (and types of) parameters and the return value (if any) of the method pointed to. Sadly, this is not the case in traditional callback functions, and, as you may suspect, can therefore be a frequent source of bugs, hard crashes, and other runtime disasters. Nevertheless, callbacks are useful entities.

In the .NET Framework, callbacks are still possible, and their functionality is accomplished in a much safer and more object-oriented manner using *delegates*. In essence, a delegate is a type-safe object that points to another method (or possibly a list of methods) in the application, which can be invoked at a later time. Specifically speaking, a delegate object maintains three important pieces of information:

- The *address* of the method on which it makes calls
- The *arguments* (if any) of this method
- The *return value* (if any) of this method

■ **Note** Unlike C(++) function pointers, .NET delegates can point to either static or instance methods.

Once a delegate has been created and provided the necessary information, it may dynamically invoke the method(s) it points to at runtime. As you will see, every delegate in the .NET Framework (including your custom delegates) is automatically endowed with the ability to call its methods *synchronously* or *asynchronously*. This fact greatly simplifies programming tasks, given that we can call a method on a secondary thread of execution without manually creating and managing a Thread object.

■ **Note** We will examine the asynchronous behavior of delegate types during our investigation of the System.Threading namespace in Chapter 18.

Defining a Delegate in C#

When you want to create a delegate in C#, you make use of the delegate keyword. The name of your delegate can be whatever you desire. However, you must define the delegate to match the signature of the method it will point to. For example, assume you wish to build a delegate named BinaryOp that can point to any method that returns an integer and takes two integers as input parameters:

```
// This delegate can point to any method,
// taking two integers and returning an integer.
public delegate int BinaryOp(int x, int y);
```

When the C# compiler processes delegate types, it automatically generates a sealed class deriving from System.MulticastDelegate. This class (in conjunction with its base class, System.Delegate) provides the necessary infrastructure for the delegate to hold onto a list of methods to be invoked at a later time. For example, if you examine the BinaryOp delegate using ildasm.exe, you would find the class shown in Figure 11-1.

As you can see, the compiler-generated BinaryOp class defines three public methods. Invoke() is perhaps the core method, as it is used to invoke each method maintained by the delegate type in a *synchronous* manner, meaning the caller must wait for the call to complete before continuing on its way. Strangely enough, the synchronous Invoke() method need not be called explicitly from your C# code. As you will see in just a bit, Invoke() is called behind the scenes when you make use of the appropriate C# syntax.

BeginInvoke() and EndInvoke() provide the ability to call the current method *asynchronously* on a separate thread of execution. If you have a background in multithreading, you are aware that one of the most common reasons developers create secondary threads of execution is to invoke methods that require time to complete. Although the .NET base class libraries provide an entire namespace devoted to multithreaded programming (System.Threading), delegates provide this functionality out of the box.

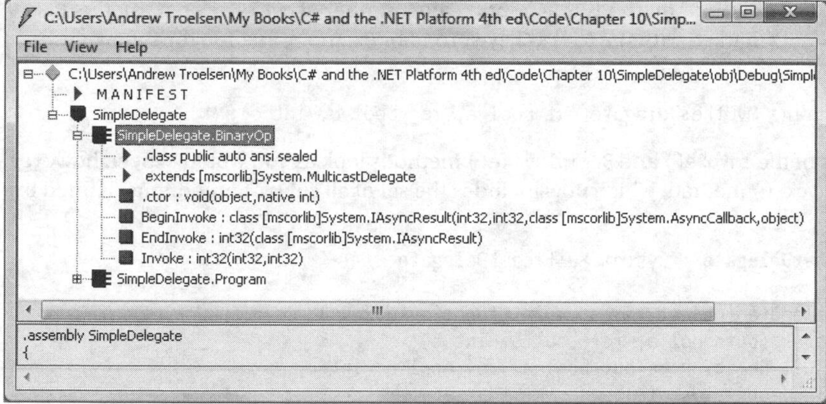

Figure 11-1. *The C#* `delegate` *keyword represents a sealed class deriving from* `System.MulticastDelegate`.

Now, how exactly does the compiler know how to define the `Invoke()`, `BeginInvoke()`, and `EndInvoke()` methods? To understand the process, here is the crux of the compiler-generated `BinaryOp` class type (**bold** marks the items specified by the defined delegate type):

```
sealed class BinaryOp : System.MulticastDelegate
{
  public BinaryOp(object target, uint functionAddress);
  public int Invoke(int x, int y);
  public IAsyncResult BeginInvoke(int x, int y,
    AsyncCallback cb, object state);
  public int EndInvoke(IAsyncResult result);
}
```

First, notice that the parameters and return value defined for the `Invoke()` method exactly match the definition of the `BinaryOp` delegate. The initial parameters to `BeginInvoke()` members (two integers in our case) are also based on the `BinaryOp` delegate; however, `BeginInvoke()` will always provide two final parameters (of type `AsyncCallback` and `object`) that are used to facilitate asynchronous method invocations. Finally, the return value of `EndInvoke()` is identical to the original delegate declaration and will always take as a sole parameter an object implementing the `IAsyncResult` interface.

Let's see another example. Assume you have defined a delegate type that can point to any method returning a `string` and receiving three `System.Boolean` input parameters:

```
public delegate string MyDelegate(bool a, bool b, bool c);
```

This time, the compiler-generated class breaks down as follows:

```
sealed class MyDelegate : System.MulticastDelegate
{
  public MyDelegate(object target, uint functionAddress);
  public string Invoke(bool a, bool b, bool c);
  public IAsyncResult BeginInvoke(bool a, bool b, bool c,
    AsyncCallback cb, object state);
  public string EndInvoke(IAsyncResult result);
}
```

Delegates can also "point to" methods that contain any number of out or ref parameters (as well as array parameters marked with the params keyword). For example, assume the following delegate type:

```
public delegate string MyOtherDelegate(out bool a, ref bool b, int c);
```

The signatures of the Invoke() and BeginInvoke() methods look as you would expect; however, check out the EndInvoke() method, which now includes the set of all out/ref arguments defined by the delegate type:

```
sealed class MyOtherDelegate : System.MulticastDelegate
{
  public MyOtherDelegate (object target, uint functionAddress);
  public string Invoke(out bool a, ref bool b, int c);
  public IAsyncResult BeginInvoke(out bool a, ref bool b, int c,
    AsyncCallback cb, object state);
  public string EndInvoke(out bool a, ref bool b, IAsyncResult result);
}
```

To summarize, a C# delegate definition results in a sealed class with three compiler-generated methods whose parameter and return types are based on the delegate's declaration. The following pseudo-code approximates the basic pattern:

```
// This is only pseudo-code!
public sealed class DelegateName : System.MulticastDelegate
{
  public DelegateName (object target, uint functionAddress);

  public delegateReturnValue Invoke(allDelegateInputRefAndOutParams);

  public IAsyncResult BeginInvoke(allDelegateInputRefAndOutParams,
    AsyncCallback cb, object state);

  public delegateReturnValue EndInvoke(allDelegateRefAndOutParams,
    IAsyncResult result);
}
```

The System.MulticastDelegate and System.Delegate Base Classes

So, when you build a type using the C# delegate keyword, you indirectly declare a class type that derives from System.MulticastDelegate. This class provides descendents with access to a list that contains the addresses of the methods maintained by the delegate type, as well as several additional methods (and a few overloaded operators) to interact with the invocation list. Here are some select members of System.MulticastDelegate:

```
public abstract class MulticastDelegate : Delegate
{
  // Returns the list of methods "pointed to."
  public sealed override Delegate[] GetInvocationList();

  // Overloaded operators.
  public static bool operator ==(MulticastDelegate d1, MulticastDelegate d2);
  public static bool operator !=(MulticastDelegate d1, MulticastDelegate d2);
```

```
  // Used internally to manage the list of methods maintained by the delegate.
  private IntPtr _invocationCount;
  private object _invocationList;
}
```

System.MulticastDelegate obtains additional functionality from its parent class, System.Delegate. Here is a partial snapshot of the class definition:

```
public abstract class Delegate : ICloneable, ISerializable
{
  // Methods to interact with the list of functions.
  public static Delegate Combine(params Delegate[] delegates);
  public static Delegate Combine(Delegate a, Delegate b);
  public static Delegate Remove(Delegate source, Delegate value);
  public static Delegate RemoveAll(Delegate source, Delegate value);

  // Overloaded operators.
  public static bool operator ==(Delegate d1, Delegate d2);
  public static bool operator !=( Delegate d1, Delegate d2);

  // Properties that expose the delegate target.
  public MethodInfo Method { get; }
  public object Target { get; }
}
```

Now, understand that you can never directly derive from these base classes in your code (it is a compiler error to do so). Nevertheless, when you use the delegate keyword, you have indirectly created a class that "is-a" MulticastDelegate. Table 11-1 documents the core members commonplace to all delegate types.

Table 11-1. *Select Members of* System.MultcastDelegate/System.Delegate

Inherited Member	Meaning in Life
Method	This property returns a System.Reflection.MethodInfo type that represents details of a static method maintained by the delegate.
Target	If the method to be called is defined at the object level (rather than a static method), Target returns an object that represents the method maintained by the delegate. If the value returned from Target equals null, the method to be called is a static member.
Combine()	This static method adds a method to the list maintained by the delegate. In C#, you trigger this method using the overloaded += operator as a shorthand notation.
GetInvocationList()	This method returns an array of System.Delegate types, each representing a particular method that may be invoked.
Remove() RemoveAll()	These static methods remove a method (or all methods) from the delegate's invocation list. In C#, the Remove() method can be called indirectly using the overloaded -= operator.

The Simplest Possible Delegate Example

Delegates can tend to cause a great deal of confusion when encountered for the first time. Thus, to get the ball rolling, let's take a look at a very simple Console Application program (named

SimpleDelegate) that makes use of the BinaryOp delegate type you've seen previously. Here is the complete code, with analysis to follow:

```
namespace SimpleDelegate
{
  // This delegate can point to any method,
  // taking two integers and returning an integer.
  public delegate int BinaryOp(int x, int y);

  // This class contains methods BinaryOp will
  // point to.
  public class SimpleMath
  {
    public static int Add(int x, int y)
    { return x + y; }
    public static int Subtract(int x, int y)
    { return x - y; }
  }

  class Program
  {
    static void Main(string[] args)
    {
      Console.WriteLine("***** Simple Delegate Example *****\n");

      // Create a BinaryOp object that
      // "points to" SimpleMath.Add().
      BinaryOp b = new BinaryOp(SimpleMath.Add);

      // Invoke Add() method indirectly using delegate object.
      Console.WriteLine("10 + 10 is {0}", b(10, 10));
      Console.ReadLine();
    }
  }
}
```

Again, notice the format of the BinaryOp delegate, which can point to any method taking two integers and returning an integer (the actual name of the method pointed to is irrelevant). Here, we have created a class named SimpleMath, which defines two static methods that (surprise, surprise) match the pattern defined by the BinaryOp delegate.

When you want to insert the target method to a given delegate, simply pass in the name of the method to the delegate's constructor. At this point, you are able to invoke the member pointed to using a syntax that looks like a direct function invocation:

```
// Invoke() is really called here!
Console.WriteLine("10 + 10 is {0}", b(10, 10));
```

Under the hood, the runtime actually calls the compiler-generated Invoke() method. You can verify this fact for yourself if you open your assembly in ildasm.exe and investigate the CIL code within the Main() method:

```
.method private hidebysig static void Main(string[] args) cil managed
{
...
  callvirt instance int32 SimpleDelegate.BinaryOp::Invoke(int32, int32)
}
```

Although C# does not require you to explicitly call Invoke() within your code base, you are free to do so. Thus, the following code statement is permissible:

```
Console.WriteLine("10 + 10 is {0}", b.Invoke(10, 10));
```

Recall that .NET delegates are *type safe*. Therefore, if you attempt to pass a delegate a method that does not "match the pattern," you receive a compile-time error. To illustrate, assume the SimpleMath class now defines an additional method named SquareNumber(), which takes a single integer as input:

```
public class SimpleMath
{
...
  public static int SquareNumber(int a)
  { return a * a; }
}
```

Given that the BinaryOp delegate can *only* point to methods that take two integers and return an integer, the following code is illegal and will not compile:

```
// Error! Method does not match delegate pattern!
BinaryOp b2 = new BinaryOp(SimpleMath.SquareNumber);
```

Investigating a Delegate Object

Let's spice up the current example by creating a static method (named DisplayDelegateInfo()) within the Program type. This method will print out names of the methods maintained by the incoming delegate type as well as the name of the class defining the method. To do so, we will iterate over the System.Delegate array returned by GetInvocationList(), invoking each object's Target and Method properties:

```
static void DisplayDelegateInfo(Delegate delObj)
{
  // Print the names of each member in the
  // delegate's invocation list.
  foreach (Delegate d in delObj.GetInvocationList())
  {
    Console.WriteLine("Method Name: {0}", d.Method);
    Console.WriteLine("Type Name: {0}", d.Target);
  }
}
```

Assuming you have updated your Main() method to actually call this new helper method, you would find the output shown in Figure 11-2.

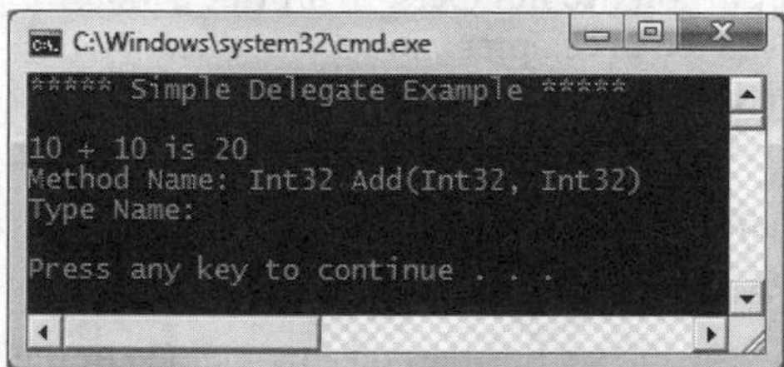

Figure 11-2. *Examining a delegate's invocation list*

Notice that the name of the type (SimpleMath) is currently not displayed by the Target property. The reason has to do with the fact that our BinaryOp delegate is pointing to a *static* method and therefore there is no object to reference! However, if we update the Add() and Subtract() methods to be nonstatic (simply by deleting the static keywords), we could create an instance of the SimpleMath type and specify the methods to invoke using the object reference:

```
static void Main(string[] args)
{
  Console.WriteLine("***** Simple Delegate Example *****\n");

  // .NET delegates can also point to instance methods as well.
  SimpleMath m = new SimpleMath();
  BinaryOp b = new BinaryOp(m.Add);

  // Show information about this object.
  DisplayDelegateInfo(b);

  Console.WriteLine("10 + 10 is {0}", b(10, 10));
  Console.ReadLine();
}
```

In this case, we would find the output shown in Figure 11-3.

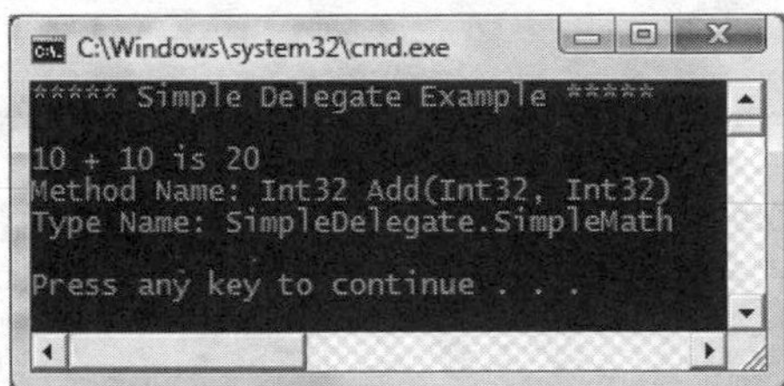

Figure 11-3. *Examining a delegate's invocation list (once again)*

Source Code The SimpleDelegate project is located under the Chapter 11 subdirectory.

Retrofitting the Car Type with Delegates

Clearly, the previous SimpleDelegate example was intended to be purely illustrative in nature, given that there would be no reason to build a delegate simply to add two numbers. To provide a more realistic use of delegate types, let's retrofit the Car type created in Chapter 9 to send notifications using .NET delegates rather than a custom callback interface. Beyond no longer implementing IEngineNotification, here are the basic steps we will need to take:

- Define new delegate types that will send notifications to the caller.
- Declare a member variable of these delegate types in the Car class.
- Create helper functions on the Car that allow the caller to set the methods maintained by the delegate member variables.
- Update the Accelerate() method to invoke the delegate's invocation list under the correct circumstances.

To begin, create a new Console Application project named CarDelegate and insert your previous Car and Radio definitions from the CallbackInterface example of Chapter 9 (you may wish to change the namespace containing these types to the current project name or import the CallbackInterface namespace as an alternative). Consider the following updates to the Car class, which address the first three points:

```
public class Car
{
  // Define the delegate types.
  public delegate void AboutToBlow(string msg);
  public delegate void Exploded (string msg);

  // Define member variables of each delegate type.
  private AboutToBlow almostDeadList;
  private Exploded explodedList;

  // Add members to the invocation lists using helper methods.
  public void OnAboutToBlow(AboutToBlow clientMethod)
  { almostDeadList = clientMethod; }

  public void OnExploded(Exploded clientMethod)
  { explodedList = clientMethod; }
...
}
```

Notice in this example that we define the delegate types directly within the scope of the Car type. As you explore the base class libraries, you will find it is quite common to define a delegate within the scope of the type it naturally works with. On a related note, given that the compiler transforms a delegate into a full class definition, what we have actually done is create two nested classes (AboutToBlow and Exploded) within the Car class.

Next, note that we declare two private member variables (one for each delegate type) and two helper functions (OnAboutToBlow() and OnExploded()) that allow the client to add a method to the delegate's invocation list. In concept, these methods are similar to the Advise() and Unadvise() methods we created during the CallbackInterface example. Of course, in this case, the incoming parameter is a client-allocated delegate object rather than a class implementing a custom interface.

■ **Note** Strictly speaking, we could have defined our delegate member variables as public, therefore avoiding the need to create additional registration methods. However, by defining the members as private, we are enforcing encapsulation services and providing a more type-safe solution. You'll revisit the risk of public delegate member variables later in this chapter when examining the C# event keyword.

At this point, we need to update the Accelerate() method to invoke each delegate, rather than iterate over an ArrayList of client-side sinks (as we did in the CallbackInterface example). Here is the update:

```
public void Accelerate(int delta)
{
  // If the car is dead, fire Exploded event.
  if (carIsDead)
  {
    if (explodedList != null)
      explodedList("Sorry, this car is dead...");
  }
  else
```

```
  {
    currSpeed += delta;

    // Almost dead?
    if (10 == maxSpeed - currSpeed
      && almostDeadList != null)
    {
      almostDeadList("Careful buddy!  Gonna blow!");
    }

    // Still OK!
    if (currSpeed >= maxSpeed)
      carIsDead = true;
    else
      Console.WriteLine("->CurrSpeed = {0}", currSpeed);
  }
}
```

Notice that before we invoke the methods maintained by the almostDeadList and explodedList member variables, we are checking them against a null value. The reason is that it will be the job of the caller to allocate these objects by calling the OnAboutToBlow() and OnExploded() helper methods. If the caller does not call these methods, and we attempt to invoke the delegate's invocation list, we will trigger a NullReferenceException and bomb at runtime (which would obviously be a bad thing!). Now that we have the delegate infrastructure in place, observe the updates to the Program class:

```
class Program
{
  static void Main(string[] args)
  {
    Console.WriteLine("***** Delegates as event enablers *****\n");

    // Make a car as usual.
    Car c1 = new Car("SlugBug", 100, 10);

    // Register event handlers with Car type.
    c1.OnAboutToBlow(new Car.AboutToBlow(CarAboutToBlow));
    c1.OnExploded(new Car.Exploded(CarExploded));

    // Speed up (this will trigger the events).
    Console.WriteLine("***** Speeding up *****");
    for (int i = 0; i < 6; i++)
      c1.Accelerate(20);
    Console.ReadLine();
  }

  // The Car will call these methods.
  public static void CarAboutToBlow(string msg)
  { Console.WriteLine(msg); }

  public static void CarExploded(string msg)
  { Console.WriteLine(msg); }
}
```

The only major point to be made here is the fact that the caller is the entity that assigns the delegate member variables via the helper registration methods. Also, because the AboutToBlow and Exploded delegates are nested within the Car class, we must allocate them using their full name (e.g., Car.AboutToBlow). Like any delegate constructor, we pass in the name of the method to add to the invocation list, which in this case are two static members on the Program class (if you wanted to wrap these methods in a new class, it would look very similar to the CarEventSink type of the CallbackInterface example).

Enabling Multicasting

Recall that .NET delegates have the intrinsic ability to *multicast*. In other words, a delegate object can maintain a list of methods to call, rather than a single method. When you wish to add multiple methods to a delegate object, you simply make use of the overloaded += operator, rather than a direct assignment. To enable multicasting on the Car type, we could update the OnAboutToBlow() and OnExploded() methods as follows:

```
public class Car
{
  // Add member to the invocation lists.
  public void OnAboutToBlow(AboutToBlow clientMethod)
  { almostDeadList += clientMethod; }

  public void OnExploded(Exploded clientMethod)
  { explodedList += clientMethod; }
...
}
```

With this, the caller can now register multiple targets for the same callback:

```
class Program
{
  static void Main(string[] args)
  {
    Console.WriteLine("***** Delegates as event enablers *****\n");
    Car c1 = new Car("SlugBug", 100, 10);

    // Register multiple event handlers!
    c1.OnAboutToBlow(new Car.AboutToBlow(CarAboutToBlow));
    c1.OnAboutToBlow(new Car.AboutToBlow(CarIsAlmostDoomed));

    c1.OnExploded(new Car.Exploded(CarExploded));
  ...
  }

  // Car will call these.
  public static void CarAboutToBlow(string msg)
  { Console.WriteLine(msg); }
  public static void CarIsAlmostDoomed(string msg)
  { Console.WriteLine("Critical Message from Car: {0}", msg); }
  public static void CarExploded(string msg)
  { Console.WriteLine(msg); }
}
```

In terms of CIL code, the += operator resolves to a call to the static Delegate.Combine() method (in fact, you could call Delegate.Combine() directly, but the += operator offers a simpler alternative). Ponder the following CIL implementation of OnAboutToBlow():

```
.method public hidebysig instance void OnAboutToBlow
  (class CarDelegate.Car/AboutToBlow clientMethod) cil managed
{
  .maxstack 8
```

```
  ldarg.0
  dup
  ldfld class CarDelegate.Car/AboutToBlow CarDelegate.Car::almostDeadList
  ldarg.1
  call class [mscorlib]System.Delegate
    [mscorlib]System.Delegate::Combine(
      class [mscorlib]System.Delegate,
      class [mscorlib]System.Delegate)
  castclass  CarDelegate.Car/AboutToBlow
  stfld class CarDelegate.Car/AboutToBlow CarDelegate.Car::almostDeadList
  ret
}
```

The Delegate class also defines a static Remove() method that allows a caller to dynamically remove a member from the invocation list. C# developers can leverage the overloaded -= operator as a shorthand notation.

■ **Note** Be aware that the object passed into Remove() must match the associated signature, but not necessarily the actual delegate instance you wish to remove. In other words, you are *not* actually required to hold on to the exact delegate object you added to the collection in order to precisely remove that instance; you can create a new delegate object pointing to the same function on the same instance and pass it to Remove(). The delegate will match the previous delegate referencing the same objects.

If you wish to allow the caller the option to detach from the AboutToBlow and Exploded notifications, you could add the following additional helper methods to the Car type (note the -= operators at work):

```
public class Car
{
  // Remove member from the invocation lists.
  public void RemoveAboutToBlow(AboutToBlow clientMethod)
  { almostDeadList -= clientMethod; }

  public void RemoveExploded(Exploded clientMethod)
  { explodedList -= clientMethod; }
...
}
```

Again, the -= syntax is simply a shorthand notation for manually calling the static Delegate.Remove() method, as illustrated by the following CIL code for the RemoveAboutToBlow() member of the Car type:

```
.method public hidebysig instance void  RemoveAboutToBlow(class
CarDelegate.Car/AboutToBlow clientMethod) cil managed
{
  .maxstack  8
  ldarg.0
  dup
  ldfld class CarDelegate.Car/AboutToBlow CarDelegate.Car::almostDeadList
  ldarg.1
  call class [mscorlib]System.Delegate
    [mscorlib]System.Delegate::Remove(
    class [mscorlib]System.Delegate,
    class [mscorlib]System.Delegate)
  castclass CarDelegate.Car/AboutToBlow
```

```
   stfld class CarDelegate.Car/AboutToBlow CarDelegate.Car::almostDeadList
   ret
}
```

Removing a Target from a Delegate's Invocation List

With the current updates to the Car class, we could stop receiving the Exploded notification by updating Main() as follows:

```
static void Main(string[] args)
{
  Console.WriteLine("***** Delegates as event enablers *****\n");
  Car c1 = new Car("SlugBug", 100, 10);

  // Hold onto Car.Exploded delegate object for later use.
  Car.Exploded d = new Car.Exploded(CarExploded);
  c1.OnExploded(d);
...
  // Remove CarExploded method
  // from invocation list.
  c1.RemoveExploded(d);
...
}
```

The output of our CarDelegate application can be seen in Figure 11-4.

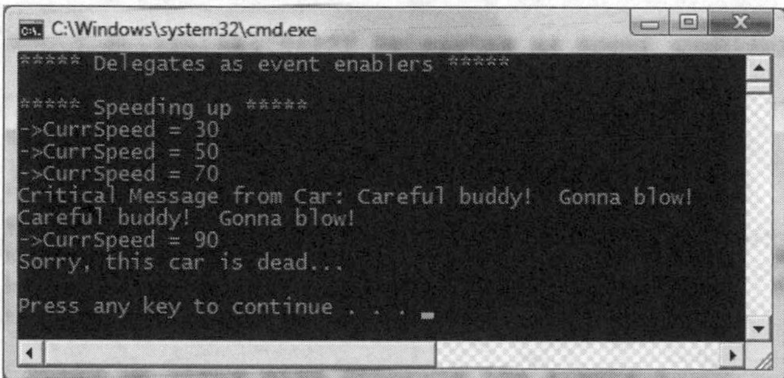

Figure 11-4. *The CarDelegate application at work*

Source Code The CarDelegate project is located under the Chapter 11 subdirectory.

A More Elaborate Delegate Example

To illustrate a more advanced use of delegates, create a new Console Application named CarGarage (be sure to include your Car/Radio type definitions into this new project). Let's begin by updating the Car class to include two new Boolean member variables. The first is used to determine whether the automobile is due for a wash (isDirty); the other represents whether the car in question is in need of a tire rotation (shouldRotate). To enable the object user to interact with this new state data, Car also defines some additional properties and an updated constructor. Here is the story so far:

```
// Updated Car class.
public class Car
{
...
  // Are we in need of a wash? Need to rotate tires?
  private bool isDirty;
  private bool shouldRotate;

  // Extra params to set bools.
  public Car(string name, int max, int curr,
    bool washCar, bool rotateTires)
  {
    ...
    isDirty = washCar;
    shouldRotate = rotateTires;
  }
  public bool Dirty
  {
    get{  return isDirty; }
    set{  isDirty = value; }
  }
  public bool Rotate
  {
    get{  return shouldRotate; }
    set{  shouldRotate = value; }
  }
}
```

Now, also assume the Car type nests a new delegate type named CarMaintenanceDelegate:

```
// Car defines yet another delegate.
public class Car
{
  // Can call any method taking a Car as
  // a parameter and returning nothing.
  public delegate void CarMaintenanceDelegate (Car c);
...
}
```

Notice that the CarMaintenanceDelegate type can point to any function taking a Car as a parameter and returns nothing.

Delegates As Parameters

Now that you have a new delegate type that points to methods taking a Car parameter and returning nothing, you can create other functions that take this delegate as a parameter. To illustrate, assume you have a new class named Garage. This type maintains a collection of Car types contained in a List<T>. Upon creation, the List<T> is filled with some initial Car types (be sure to import the System.Collections.Generic namespace into your new code file):

```
// The Garage class maintains a list of Car types.
public class Garage
{
  // A list of all cars in the garage.
  private List<Car> theCars = new List<Car>();
```

```
  // Create the cars in the garage.
  public Garage()
  {
    // Recall, we updated the ctor to set isDirty and shouldRotate.
    theCars.Add(new Car("Viper", 100, 0, true, false));
    theCars.Add(new Car("Fred", 100, 0, false, false));
    theCars.Add(new Car("BillyBob", 100, 0, false, true));
  }
}
```

The Garage class also defines a public ProcessCars() method, which takes a single argument of our new delegate type (Car.CarMaintenanceDelegate). In the implementation of ProcessCars(), you pass each Car in your collection as a parameter to the "function pointed to" by the delegate. ProcessCars() also makes use of the Target and Method members of System.MulticastDelegate to determine exactly which function the delegate is currently pointing to:

```
// The Garage class has a method that makes use of the CarMaintenanceDelegate.
public class Garage
{
...
  public void ProcessCars(Car.CarMaintenanceDelegate proc)
  {
    // Where are we forwarding the call?
    Console.WriteLine("***** Calling: {0}  *****",
      proc.Method);

    // Are we calling an instance method or a static method?
    if(proc.Target != null)
      Console.WriteLine("-->Target: {0} ", proc.Target);
    else
      Console.WriteLine("-->Target is a static method");

    // Call the method "pointed to," passing in each car.
    foreach (Car c in theCars)
    {
      Console.WriteLine("\n-> Processing a Car");
      proc(c);
    }
  }
}
```

Like any delegate operation, when calling ProcessCars(), we send in the address of the method that should handle this request (via a delegate type). Recall that a delegate may point to either static or instance-level methods. For the sake of argument, assume these are instance members named WashCar() and RotateTires() that are defined by a new class named ServiceDepartment. Notice that these two methods are making use of the new Rotate and Dirty properties of the Car type.

```
// This class defines method to be invoked by
// the Car.CarMaintenanceDelegate type.
public class ServiceDepartment
{
  public void WashCar(Car c)
  {
    if(c.Dirty)
      Console.WriteLine("Cleaning a car");
    else
      Console.WriteLine("This car is already clean...");
  }
```

```
  public void RotateTires(Car c)
  {
    if(c.Rotate)
      Console.WriteLine("Tires have been rotated");
    else
      Console.WriteLine("Don't need to be rotated...");
  }
}
```

Now, to illustrate the interplay between the new Car.CarMaintenanceDelegate, Garage, and ServiceDepartment types, consider the following usage:

```
// The Garage delegates all work orders to the ServiceDepartment
// (finding a good mechanic is always a problem...)
static void Main(string[] args)
{
  Console.WriteLine("*****Delegates as Parameters *****\n");

  // Make the garage.
  Garage g = new Garage();

  // Make the service department.
  ServiceDepartment sd = new ServiceDepartment();

  // Wash all dirty cars.
  g.ProcessCars(new Car.CarMaintenanceDelegate(sd.WashCar));

  // Rotate the tires.
  g.ProcessCars(new Car.CarMaintenanceDelegate(sd.RotateTires));
  Console.ReadLine();
}
```

Figure 11-5 shows the current output.

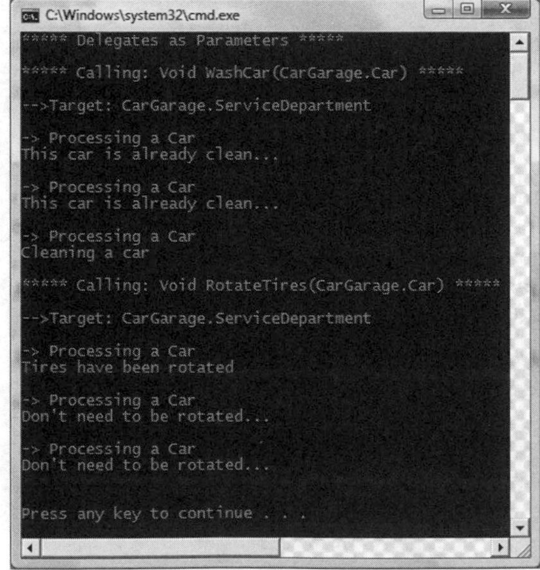

Figure 11-5. *Passing the buck*

Analyzing the Delegation Code

The Main() method begins by creating an instance of the Garage and ServiceDepartment types. Now, when you write the following:

```
// Wash all dirty cars.
g.ProcessCars(new Car.CarMaintenanceDelegate(sd.WashCar));
```

what you are effectively saying is, "Insert the address of the ServiceDepartment.WashCar() method to a Car.CarMaintenanceDelegate object, and pass this object to Garage.ProcessCars()." Like most real-world garages, the real work is delegated to the service department (which explains why a 30-minute oil change takes 2 hours). Given this, ProcessCars() can be understood as

```
// CarDelegate points to the ServiceDepartment.WashCar function.
public void ProcessCars(Car.CarMaintenanceDelegate proc)
{
...
  foreach(Car c in theCars)
    proc(c);      // proc(c) => ServiceDepartment.WashCar(c)
}
```

Likewise, if you say the following:

```
// Rotate the tires.
g.ProcessCars(new Car.CarMaintenanceDelegate(sd.RotateTires));
```

then ProcessCars() can be understood as

```
// CarDelegate points to the ServiceDepartment.RotateTires function:
public void ProcessCars(Car.CarMaintenanceDelegate proc)
{
  foreach(Car c in theCars)
    proc(c);      // proc(c) => ServiceDepartment.RotateTires(c)
...
}
```

Source Code The CarGarage project is located under the Chapter 11 subdirectory.

So at this point in the chapter, you have seen three examples of delegates at work. The first example (SimpleDelegate) illustrated the basics of defining and manipulating delegate types. As shown, a delegate simply maintains a list of methods to call at a later time when you call (implicitly or explicitly) the Invoke() method. Our second example (CarDelegate) illustrated how delegates can be used to establish an event architecture (in place of .NET interface types). Finally, the example we just completed pointed out that delegates can be used as method parameters just like any other .NET type.

Note As you explore the .NET collection types, you will notice that delegates are commonly used as parameters to provide sorting and filtering of subitems.

Collectively, these examples have illustrated the core nuts and bolts of the delegate type. To deepen your understanding of this programming construct, let's now address the role of covariance.

Understanding Delegate Covariance

As you may have noticed, each of the delegates created thus far point to methods returning simple numerical data types (or void). However, assume you have a new Console Application named DelegateCovariance that defines a delegate that can point to methods returning a custom class type (be sure to include your Car/Radio type definitions into this new project):

```
// Define a delegate pointing to methods that return Car types.
public delegate Car ObtainCarDelegate();
```

Of course, you would be able to define a target for the delegate as expected:

```
class Program
{
  public delegate Car ObtainCarDelegate();

  public static Car GetBasicCar()
  { return new Car("Zippy", 150, 50, false, false); }

  static void Main(string[] args)
  {
    ObtainCarDelegate targetA = new ObtainCarDelegate(GetBasicCar);
    Car c = targetA();
    Console.WriteLine("Obtained a {0}", c);
    Console.ReadLine();
  }
}
```

Now, what if you were to derive a new class from the Car type named SportsCar and wish to create a delegate type that can point to methods returning this class type? Prior to .NET 2.0, you would be required to define an entirely new delegate to do so, given that delegates were *so* type safe that they did not honor the basic laws of inheritance:

```
// A new delegate pointing to targets returning SportsCar types.
public delegate SportsCar ObtainSportsCarDelegate();
```

As we now have two delegate types, we now must create an instance of each to obtain Car and SportsCar types:

```
class Program
{
  public delegate Car ObtainCarDelegate();
  public delegate SportsCar ObtainSportsCarDelegate();

  public static Car GetBasicCar()
  { return new Car(); }

  public static SportsCar GetSportsCar()
  { return new SportsCar(); }

  static void Main(string[] args)
  {
    ObtainCarDelegate targetA = new ObtainCarDelegate(GetBasicCar);
    Car c = targetA();
    Console.WriteLine("Obtained a {0}", c);

    ObtainSportsCarDelegate targetB =
      new ObtainSportsCarDelegate(GetSportsCar);
    SportsCar sc = targetB();
```

```
    Console.WriteLine("Obtained a {0}", sc);
    Console.ReadLine();
  }
}
```

Given the laws of classic inheritance, it would be ideal to build a single delegate type that can point to methods returning either Car or SportsCar objects (after all, a SportsCar "is-a" Car). *Covariance* (which also goes by the term *relaxed delegates*) allows for this very possibility. Simply put, covariance allows you to build a single delegate that can point to methods returning class types related by classical inheritance:

```
class Program
{
  // Define a single delegate that may return a Car
  // or SportsCar.
  public delegate Car ObtainVehicalDelegate();

  public static Car GetBasicCar()
  { return new Car(); }

  public static SportsCar GetSportsCar()
  { return new SportsCar(); }

  static void Main(string[] args)
  {
    Console.WriteLine("***** Delegate Covariance *****\n");
    ObtainVehicalDelegate targetA = new ObtainVehicalDelegate(GetBasicCar);
    Car c = targetA();
    Console.WriteLine("Obtained a {0}", c);

    // Covariance allows this target assignment.
    ObtainVehicalDelegate targetB = new ObtainVehicalDelegate(GetSportsCar);
    SportsCar sc = (SportsCar)targetB();
    Console.WriteLine("Obtained a {0}", sc);
    Console.ReadLine();
  }
}
```

Notice that the ObtainVehicalDelegate delegate type has been defined to point to methods returning a strongly typed Car type. Given covariance, however, we can point to methods returning derived types as well. To obtain access to the members of the derived type, simply perform an explicit cast.

■ **Note** In a similar vein, contravariance allows you to create a single delegate that can point to numerous methods that receive objects related by classical inheritance. Consult the .NET Framework 3.5 SDK documentation for further details.

■ **Source Code** The DelegateCovariance project is located under the Chapter 11 subdirectory.

Creating Generic Delegates

Recall from the previous chapter that C# does allow you to define generic delegate types. For example, assume you wish to define a delegate that can call any method returning void and receiving a single argument. If the argument in question may differ, you could model this using a type parameter. To illustrate, consider the following code within a new Console Application named GenericDelegate:

```
namespace GenericDelegate
{
  // This generic delegate can call any method
  // returning void and taking a single parameter.
  public delegate void MyGenericDelegate<T>(T arg);

  class Program
  {
    static void Main(string[] args)
    {
      Console.WriteLine("***** Generic Delegates *****\n");

      // Register targets.
      MyGenericDelegate<string> strTarget =
        new MyGenericDelegate<string>(StringTarget);
      strTarget("Some string data");

      MyGenericDelegate<int> intTarget =
        new MyGenericDelegate<int>(IntTarget);
      intTarget(9);
      Console.ReadLine();
    }

    static void StringTarget(string arg)
    {
      Console.WriteLine("arg in uppercase is: {0}", arg.ToUpper());
    }

    static void IntTarget(int arg)
    {
      Console.WriteLine("++arg is: {0}", ++arg);
    }
  }
}
```

Notice that MyGenericDelegate<T> defines a single type parameter that represents the argument to pass to the delegate target. When creating an instance of this type, you are required to specify the value of the type parameter as well as the name of the method the delegate will invoke. Thus, if you specified a string type, you send a string value to the target method:

```
// Create an instance of MyGenericDelegate<T>
// with string as the type parameter.
MyGenericDelegate<string> strTarget =
  new MyGenericDelegate<string>(StringTarget);
strTarget("Some string data");
```

Given the format of the strTarget object, the StringTarget() method must now take a single string as a parameter:

```
static void StringTarget(string arg)
{
  Console.WriteLine("arg in uppercase is: {0}", arg.ToUpper());
}
```

Simulating Generic Delegates Without Generics

Generic delegates offer a more flexible way to specify the method to be invoked in a type-safe manner. Prior to the introduction to generics (with the release of .NET 2.0), you could achieve a similar end result using a generic `System.Object`:

```
public delegate void MyDelegate(object arg);
```

Although this allows you to send any type of data to a delegate target, you do so without type safety and with possible boxing penalties. For instance, assume you have created two instances of `MyDelegate`, both of which point to the same method, `MyTarget`. Note the boxing/unboxing penalties as well as the inherent lack of type safety:

```
class Program
{
  static void Main(string[] args)
  {
...
    // Register target with "traditional" delegate syntax.
    MyDelegate d = new MyDelegate(MyTarget);
    d("More string data");

    // Method group conversion syntax (explained later in this chapter)
    MyDelegate d2 = MyTarget;
    d2(9);  // Boxing penalty.
    Console.ReadLine();
  }

  // Due to a lack of type safety, we must
  // determine the underlying type before casting.
  static void MyTarget(object arg)
  {
    if(arg is int)
    {
      int i = (int)arg;  // Unboxing penalty.
      Console.WriteLine("++arg is: {0}", ++i);
    }
    if(arg is string)
    {
      string s = (string)arg;
      Console.WriteLine("arg in uppercase is: {0}", s.ToUpper());
    }
  }
}
```

When you send out a value type to the target site, the value is boxed and unboxed once it is received by the target method. As well, given that the incoming parameter could be anything at all, you must dynamically check the underlying type before casting. Using generic delegates, you can still obtain the desired flexibility without the "issues."

Source Code The GenericDelegate project is located under the Chapter 11 directory.

That wraps up our initial look at the .NET delegate type. We will revisit some additional details of working with delegates at the conclusion of this chapter and once again in Chapter 18 during our examination of multithreading. Until then, let's move on to the related topic of the C# event keyword.

Understanding C# Events

Delegates are fairly interesting constructs in that they enable objects in memory to engage in a two-way conversation. As you may agree, however, working with delegates in the raw can entail some boilerplate code (defining the delegate, declaring necessary member variables, and creating custom registration/unregistration methods to preserve encapsulation, etc.).

Typing time aside, another issue with using delegates in the raw as your application's callback mechanism is the fact that *if* you do not define a class's delegate member variables as private, the caller will have direct access to the delegate objects. If this were the case, the caller would be able to reassign the variable to a new delegate object (effectively deleting the current list of functions to call) and worse yet, the caller would be able to directly invoke the delegate's invocation list. To illustrate this problem, consider the following reworking (and simplification) of the previous CarDelegate example:

```
public class Car
{
  // A single delegate
  public delegate void Exploded(string msg);

  // Now public! No more helper functions!
  public Exploded explodedList;

  // Just fire out the Exploded notification.
  public void Accelerate(int delta)
  {
    if (explodedList != null)
      explodedList("Sorry, this car is dead...");
  }
}
```

Notice that we no longer have private delegate member variables encapsulated with custom registration methods. Because these members are indeed public, the caller can directly access the explodedList member and resign this type to new Exploded objects and invoke the delegate whenever it so chooses:

```
class Program
{
  static void Main(string[] args)
  {
    Console.WriteLine("***** Agh!  No Encapsulation! *****\n");
    // Make a Car.
    Car myCar = new Car();
```

```
    // We have direct access to the delegate!
    myCar.explodedList = new Car.Exploded(CallWhenExploded);
    myCar.Accelerate(10);

    // We can now assign to a whole new object...
    // confusing at best.
    myCar.explodedList = new Car.Exploded(CallHereToo);
    myCar.Accelerate(10);

    // The caller can also directly invoke the delegate!
    myCar.explodedList.Invoke("hee, hee, hee...");
  }

  static void CallWhenExploded(string msg)
  { Console.WriteLine(msg); }
  static void CallHereToo(string msg)
  { Console.WriteLine(msg); }
}
```

Exposing public delegate members breaks encapsulation, which not only can lead to code that is hard to maintain (and debug), but could also open your application to possible security risks! Obviously, you would not want to give other applications the power to change what a delegate is pointing to or the power to invoke the members without your permission.

Source Code The PublicDelegateProblem project is located under the Chapter 11 subdirectory.

The Event Keyword

As a shortcut to having to build custom methods to add or remove methods to a delegate's invocation list, C# provides the `event` keyword. When the compiler processes the `event` keyword, you are automatically provided with registration and unregistration methods as well as any necessary member variables for your delegate types. These delegate member variables are *always* declared private, and therefore they are not directly exposed from the object firing the event. To be sure, the `event` keyword is little more than syntactic sugar in that it simply saves you some typing time.

Defining an event is a two-step process. First, you need to define a delegate that will hold the list of methods to be called when the event is fired. Next, you declare an event (using the C# `event` keyword) in terms of the related delegate.

To illustrate the `event` keyword, this iteration of the `Car` type will define two events (named identically to the previous `AboutToBlow` and `Exploded` delegates). These events are associated to a single delegate type named `CarEventHandler`. Here are the initial updates to the `Car` type:

```
public class Car
{
  // This delegate works in conjunction with the
  // Car's events.
  public delegate void CarEventHandler(string msg);

  // This car can send these events.
  public event CarEventHandler Exploded;
  public event CarEventHandler AboutToBlow;
 ...
}
```

Sending an event to the caller is as simple as specifying the event by name as well as any required parameters as defined by the associated delegate. To ensure that the caller has indeed registered with the event, you will want to check the event against a `null` value before invoking the delegate's method set. These things being said, here is the new iteration of the `Car`'s `Accelerate()` method:

```
public void Accelerate(int delta)
{
  // If the car is dead, fire Exploded event.
  if (carIsDead)
  {
    if (Exploded != null)
      Exploded("Sorry, this car is dead...");
  }
  else
  {
    currSpeed += delta;

    // Almost dead?
    if (10 == maxSpeed - currSpeed
      && AboutToBlow != null)
    {
      AboutToBlow("Careful buddy!  Gonna blow!");
    }

    // Still OK!
    if (currSpeed >= maxSpeed)
      carIsDead = true;
    else
      Console.WriteLine("->CurrSpeed = {0}", currSpeed);
  }
}
```

With this, you have configured the car to send two custom events without the need to define custom registration functions or declare delegate member variables. You will see the usage of this new automobile in just a moment, but first, let's check the event architecture in a bit more detail.

Events Under the Hood

A C# event actually expands into two hidden public methods, one having an `add_` prefix, the other having a `remove_` prefix. This prefix is followed by the name of the C# event. For example, the `Exploded` event results in two CIL methods named `add_Exploded()` and `remove_Exploded()`. In addition to the `add_XXX()` and `remove_XXX()` methods, the CIL-level event definition associates the correct delegate to a given event.

If you were to check out the CIL instructions behind `add_AboutToBlow()`, you would find code that looks just about identical to the `OnAboutToBlow()` helper method you wrote previously in the `CarDelegate` example (note the call to `Delegate.Combine()`):

```
.method public hidebysig specialname instance void
  add_AboutToBlow(class CarEvents.Car/CarEventHandler 'value')
  cil managed synchronized
{
  .maxstack  8
  ldarg.0
  ldarg.0
```

```
  ldfld class CarEvents.Car/CarEventHandler CarEvents.Car::AboutToBlow
  ldarg.1
  call class [mscorlib]System.Delegate
  [mscorlib]System.Delegate::Combine(
    class [mscorlib]System.Delegate, class [mscorlib]System.Delegate)
  castclass CarEvents.Car/CarEventHandler
  stfld class CarEvents.Car/CarEventHandler CarEvents.Car::AboutToBlow
  ret
}
```

As you would expect, remove_AboutToBlow() will indirectly call Delegate.Remove() and is more or less identical to the previous RemoveAboutToBlow() helper method:

```
.method public hidebysig specialname instance void
  remove_AboutToBlow(class CarEvents.Car/CarEventHandler 'value')
  cil managed synchronized
{
  .maxstack  8
  ldarg.0
  ldarg.0
  ldfld class CarEvents.Car/CarEventHandler CarEvents.Car::AboutToBlow
  ldarg.1
  call class [mscorlib]System.Delegate
    [mscorlib]System.Delegate::Remove(
      class [mscorlib]System.Delegate, class [mscorlib]System.Delegate)
  castclass CarEvents.Car/CarEventHandler
  stfld class CarEvents.Car/CarEventHandler CarEvents.Car::AboutToBlow
  ret
}
```

Finally, the CIL code representing the event itself makes use of the .addon and .removeon directives to map the names of the correct add_*XXX*() and remove_*XXX*() methods to invoke:

```
.event CarEvents.Car/EngineHandler AboutToBlow
{
  .addon void CarEvents.Car::add_AboutToBlow
    (class CarEvents.Car/CarEngineHandler)
  .removeon void CarEvents.Car::remove_AboutToBlow
    (class CarEvents.Car/CarEngineHandler)
}
```

Now that you understand how to build a class that can send C# events (and are aware that events are little more than a typing time-saver), the next big question is how to "listen to" the incoming events on the caller's side.

Listening to Incoming Events

C# events also simplify the act of registering the caller-side event handlers. Rather than having to specify custom helper methods, the caller simply makes use of the += and -= operators directly (which triggers the correct add_*XXX*() or remove_*XXX*() method in the background). When you wish to register with an event, follow the pattern shown here:

```
// ObjectVariable.EventName +=
// new AssociatedDelegate(functionToCall);
Car.EngineHandler d = new Car.CarEventHandler(CarExplodedEventHandler)
myCar.Exploded += d;
```

When you wish to detach from a source of events, use the -= operator:

```
// ObjectVariable.EventName -= delegateObject;
myCar.Exploded -= d;
```

Given these very predictable patterns, here is the refactored Main() method, now using the C# event registration syntax:

```
class Program
{
  static void Main(string[] args)
  {
    Console.WriteLine("***** Fun with Events *****\n");
    Car c1 = new Car("SlugBug", 100, 10);

    // Register event handlers.
    c1.AboutToBlow += new Car.CarEventHandler(CarIsAlmostDoomed);
    c1.AboutToBlow += new Car.CarEventHandler(CarAboutToBlow);

    Car.CarEventHandler d = new Car.CarEventHandler(CarExploded);
    c1.Exploded += d;

    Console.WriteLine("***** Speeding up *****");
     for (int i = 0; i < 6; i++)
       c1.Accelerate(20);

      // Remove CarExploded method
      // from invocation list.
      c1.Exploded -= d;

      Console.WriteLine("\n***** Speeding up *****");
      for (int i = 0; i < 6; i++)
        c1.Accelerate(20);
      Console.ReadLine();
  }

  public static void CarAboutToBlow(string msg)
  { Console.WriteLine(msg); }
  public static void CarIsAlmostDoomed(string msg)
  { Console.WriteLine("Critical Message from Car: {0}", msg); }
  public static void CarExploded(string msg)
  { Console.WriteLine(msg); }
}
```

Simplifying Event Registration Using Visual Studio 2008

Visual Studio 2008 offers assistance with the process of registering event handlers. When you apply the += syntax during the act of event registration, you will find an IntelliSense window is displayed inviting you to hit the Tab key to autofill the associated delegate instance (see Figure 11-6).

```
Program.cs*
CarEvents.Program                    Main(string[] args)

            // Make a car as usual.
            Car c1 = new Car("SlugBug", 100, 10);

            // Register event handlers.
            c1.AboutToBlow += new Car.CarEventHandler(CarIsAlmostDoomed);
            c1.AboutToBlow += new Car.CarEventHandler(CarAboutToBlow);
            c1.AboutToBlow +=
            Car.CarEventHandl new Car.CarEventHandler(c1_AboutToBlow);  (Press TAB to insert) loded);
            c1.Exploded += d;
```

Figure 11-6. *Delegate selection IntelliSense*

Once you do hit the Tab key, you are then invited to enter the name of the event handler to be generated (or simply accept the default name) as shown in Figure 11-7.

```
Program.cs*
CarEvents.Program                    Main(string[] args)

            // Make a car as usual.
            Car c1 = new Car("SlugBug", 100, 10);

            // Register event handlers.
            c1.AboutToBlow += new Car.CarEventHandler(CarIsAlmostDoomed);
            c1.AboutToBlow += new Car.CarEventHandler(CarAboutToBlow);
            c1.AboutToBlow +=new Car.CarEventHandler(c1_AboutToBlow);
            Car.CarEventHandler d = new Car.CarEventH Press TAB to generate handler 'c1_AboutToBlow' in this class
            c1.Exploded += d;
```

Figure 11-7. *Delegate target format IntelliSense*

Once you hit the Tab key again, you will be provided with stub code in the correct format of the delegate target (note that this method has been declared static due to the fact that the event was registered within the static `Main()` method):

```
static void c1_AboutToBlow(string msg)
{
  // Add your code!
}
```

This IntelliSense feature is available to all .NET events in the base class libraries. This IDE feature is a massive time-saver, given that this removes you from the act of needing to search the .NET help system to figure out the correct delegate to use with a particular event as well as the format of the delegate target.

■ **Source Code** The CarEvents project is located under the Chapter 11 subdirectory.

A "Prim-and-Proper" Event

Truth be told, there is one final enhancement we could make to the current iteration of the `Car` type that mirrors Microsoft's recommended event pattern. As you begin to explore the events sent by a given type in the base class libraries, you will find that the first parameter of the underlying delegate is a `System.Object`, while the second parameter is a type deriving from `System.EventArgs`.

The System.Object argument represents a reference to the object that sent the event (such as the Car), while the second parameter represents information regarding the event at hand. The System.EventArgs base class represents an event that is not sending any custom information:

```
public class EventArgs
{
  public static readonly System.EventArgs Empty;
  public EventArgs();
}
```

For simple events, you can pass an instance of EventArgs directly. However, when you wish to pass along custom data, you should build a suitable class deriving from EventArgs. For our example, assume we have a class named CarEventArgs, which maintains a string representing the message sent to the receiver:

```
public class CarEventArgs : EventArgs
{
  public readonly string msg;
  public CarEventArgs(string message)
  {
    msg = message;
  }
}
```

With this, we would now update the CarEventHandler delegate as follows (the events would be unchanged):

```
public class Car
{
  public delegate void CarEventHandler(object sender, CarEventArgs e);
...
}
```

Here, when firing our events from within the Accelerate() method, we would now need to supply a reference to the current Car (via the this keyword) and an instance of our CarEventArgs type. For example, consider the following update:

```
public void Accelerate(int delta)
{
  // If the car is dead, fire Exploded event.
  if (carIsDead)
  {
    if (Exploded != null)
      Exploded(this, new CarEventArgs("Sorry, this car is dead..."));
  }
...
}
```

On the caller's side, all we would need to do is update our event handlers to receive the incoming parameters and obtain the message via our read-only field. For example:

```
public static void CarAboutToBlow(object sender, CarEventArgs e)
{
  Console.WriteLine("{0} says: {1}", sender, e.msg);
}
```

If the receiver wishes to interact with the object that sent the event, we can explicitly cast the System.Object. Thus, if we wish to power down the radio when the Car object is about to meet its maker, we could author an event handler looking something like the following:

```
public static void CarIsAlmostDoomed(object sender, CarEventArgs e)
{
  // Just to be safe, perform a
  // runtime check before casting.
  if (sender is Car)
  {
    Car c = (Car)sender;
    c.CrankTunes(false);
  }
  Console.WriteLine("Critical Message from {0}: {1}", sender, e.msg);
}
```

Source Code The PrimAndProperCarEvents project is located under the Chapter 11 subdirectory.

The Generic EventHandler<T> Delegate

Given that so many custom delegates take an object as the first parameter and an EventArgs descendent as the second, you could further streamline the previous example by using the generic EventHandler<T> type, where T is your custom EventArgs type. Consider the following update to the Car type (notice how we no longer need to build a custom delegate type at all):

```
public class Car
{
  public event EventHandler<CarEventArgs> Exploded;
  public event EventHandler<CarEventArgs> AboutToBlow;
...
}
```

The Main() method could then make use of EventHandler<CarEventArgs> anywhere we previously specified CarEventHandler:

```
static void Main(string[] args)
{
  Console.WriteLine("***** Prim and Proper Events *****\n");

  // Make a car as usual.
  Car c1 = new Car("SlugBug", 100, 10);

  // Register event handlers.
  c1.AboutToBlow += new EventHandler<CarEventArgs>(CarIsAlmostDoomed);
  c1.AboutToBlow += new EventHandler<CarEventArgs>(CarAboutToBlow);

  EventHandler<CarEventArgs> d = new EventHandler<CarEventArgs>(CarExploded);
  c1.Exploded += d;
...
}
```

Source Code The PrimAndProperCarEvents (Generic) project is located under the Chapter 11 subdirectory.

Understanding C# Anonymous Methods

Traditionally speaking, when a caller wishes to listen to incoming events, it must define a unique method that matches the signature of the associated delegate, for example:

```
class Program
{
  static void Main(string[] args)
  {
    SomeType t = new SomeType();

    // Assume "SomeDeletage" can point to methods taking no
    // args and returning void.
    t.SomeEvent += new SomeDelegate(MyEventHandler);
  }

  // Typically only called by the SomeDelegate object.
  public static void MyEventHandler()
  {
    // Do something when event is fired.
  }
}
```

When you think about it, however, methods such as `MyEventHandler()` are seldom intended to be called by any part of the program other than the invoking delegate. As far as productivity is concerned, it is a bit of a bother (though in no way a showstopper) to manually define a separate method to be called by the delegate object.

To address this point, it is possible to associate a delegate directly to a block of code statements at the time of event registration. Formally, such code is termed an *anonymous method*. To illustrate the syntax, check out the following `Main()` method, which handles the events sent from the `Car` type using anonymous methods, rather than specifically named event handlers:

```
class Program
{
  static void Main(string[] args)
  {
    Console.WriteLine("***** Anonymous Methods *****\n");
    Car c1 = new Car("SlugBug", 100, 10);

    // Register event handlers as anonymous methods.
    c1.AboutToBlow += delegate {
      Console.WriteLine("Eek! Going too fast!");
    };

    c1.AboutToBlow += delegate(object sender, CarEventArgs e) {
      Console.WriteLine("Message from Car: {0}", e.msg);
    };

    c1.Exploded += delegate(object sender, CarEventArgs e) {
      Console.WriteLine("Fatal Message from Car: {0}", e.msg);
    };
    ...
  }
}
```

Note The final curly bracket of an anonymous method must be terminated by a semicolon. If you fail to do so, you are issued a compilation error.

Again, notice that the Program type no longer defines specific static event handlers such as CarAboutToBlow() or CarExploded(). Rather, the unnamed (aka anonymous) methods are defined inline at the time the caller is handling the event using the += syntax. The basic syntax of an anonymous method matches the following pseudo-code:

```
class Program
{
  static void Main(string[] args)
  {
    SomeType t = new SomeType();
    t.SomeEvent += delegate (optionallySpecifiedDelegateArgs)
    { /* statements */ };
  }
}
```

When handling the first AboutToBlow event within the previous Main() method, notice that you are not specifying the arguments passed from the delegate:

```
c1.AboutToBlow += delegate {
  Console.WriteLine("Eek! Going too fast!");
};
```

Strictly speaking, you are not required to receive the incoming arguments sent by a specific event. However, if you wish to make use of the possible incoming arguments, you will need to specify the parameters prototyped by the delegate type (as shown in the second handling of the AboutToBlow and Exploded events). For example:

```
c1.AboutToBlow += delegate(object sender, CarEventArgs e) {
  Console.WriteLine("Critical Message from Car: {0}", e.msg);
};
```

Accessing "Outer" Variables

Anonymous methods are interesting in that they are able to access the local variables of the method that defines them. Formally speaking, such variables are termed *outer variables* of the anonymous method.

Note An anonymous method cannot access ref or out parameters of the defining method.

Assume our Main() method defined a local integer named aboutToBlowCounter. Within the anonymous methods that handle the AboutToBlow event, we will increment this counter by 1 and print out the tally before Main() completes:

```
static void Main(string[] args)
{
...
  int aboutToBlowCounter = 0;

  // Make a car as usual.
  Car c1 = new Car("SlugBug", 100, 10);
```

```
  // Register event handlers as anonymous methods.
  c1.AboutToBlow += delegate
  {
    aboutToBlowCounter++;
    Console.WriteLine("Eek!  Going too fast!");
  };

  c1.AboutToBlow += delegate(string msg)
  {
    aboutToBlowCounter++;
    Console.WriteLine("Critical Message from Car: {0}", msg);
  };
...
  Console.WriteLine("AboutToBlow event was fired {0} times.",
    aboutToBlowCounter);
  Console.ReadLine();
}
```

Once you run this updated `Main()` method, you will find the final `Console.WriteLine()` reports the `AboutToBlow` event was fired twice.

Source Code The AnonymousMethods project is located under the Chapter 11 subdirectory.

Understanding Method Group Conversions

Another delegate-and-event-centric feature of C# is termed *method group conversion*. This feature allows you to register the "simple" name of an event handler (in fact, you may have noticed that this syntax was actually used earlier in this chapter during the GenericDelegate example). To illustrate, let's revisit the `SimpleMath` type examined earlier in this chapter, which is now updated with a new event named `ComputationFinished`:

```
public class SimpleMath
{
  // Not bothering to create a System.EventArgs
  // derived type here.
  public delegate void MathMessage(string msg);
  public event MathMessage ComputationFinished;

  public int Add(int x, int y)
  {
    ComputationFinished("Adding complete.");
    return x + y;
  }

  public int Subtract(int x, int y)
  {
    ComputationFinished("Subtracting complete.");
    return x - y;
  }
}
```

If we are not using anonymous method syntax, you know that the way we would handle the ComputationComplete event is as follows:

```
class Program
{
  static void Main(string[] args)
  {
    SimpleMath m = new SimpleMath();
    m.ComputationFinished +=
      new SimpleMath.MathMessage(ComputationFinishedHandler);
    Console.WriteLine("10 + 10 is {0}", m.Add(10, 10));
    Console.ReadLine();
  }

  static void ComputationFinishedHandler(string msg)
  { Console.WriteLine(msg); }
}
```

However, we can register the event handler with a specific event like this (the remainder of the code is identical):

```
m.ComputationFinished += ComputationFinishedHandler;
```

Notice that we are not directly allocating the associated delegate object, but rather simply specifying a method that matches the delegate's expected signature (a method returning void and taking a single System.String in this case). Understand that the C# compiler is still ensuring type safety. Thus, if the ComputationFinishedHandler() method did not take a System.String and return void, we would be issued a compiler error.

It is also possible to explicitly convert an event handler into an instance of the delegate it relates to. This can be helpful if you need to obtain the underlying delegate to interact with the inherited members of System.MulticastDelegate. For example:

```
// Event handlers to be converted into
// their underlying delegate.
SimpleMath.MathMessage mmDelegate =
    (SimpleMath.MathMessage)ComputationFinishedHandler;
Console.WriteLine(mmDelegate.Method);
```

If you executed this code, the final Console.WriteLine() prints out the signature of ComputationFinishedHandler, as shown in Figure 11-8.

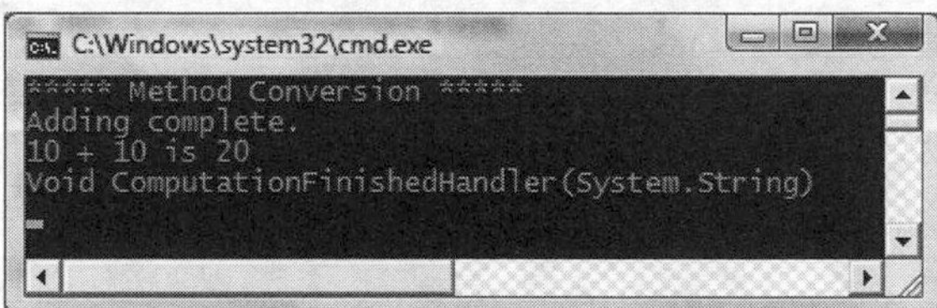

Figure 11-8. *You can extract a delegate from the related event handler.*

Source Code The MethodGroupConversion project is located under the Chapter 11 subdirectory.

The C# 2008 Lambda Operator

To conclude our look at the .NET event architecture, we will close with an examination of C# 2008 *lambda expressions*. As explained earlier in this chapter, C# supports the ability to handle events "inline" by assigning a block of code statements directly to an event (using anonymous methods), rather than building a stand-alone method to be called by the underlying delegate. Lambda expressions are nothing more than a more concise way to author anonymous methods and ultimately simplify how we work with the .NET delegate type.

■Note C# 2008 also allows you to represent lambda expressions as an in-memory object using *expression trees*. This can be very useful for third parties who are building software that needs to extend the functionality of existing lambdas, as well as when programming with Language Integrated Query (LINQ). Consult the .NET Framework 3.5 SDK documentation.

To set the stage for our examination of lambda expressions, create a new Console Application named SimpleLambdaExpressions. Now, consider the `FindAll()` method of the generic `List<T>` type. This method is expecting a generic delegate of type `System.Predicate<T>`, used to wrap any method returning a Boolean and taking a specified `T` as the only input parameter. Add a method (named `TraditionalDelegateSyntax()`) within your `Program` type that interacts with the `System.Predicate<T>` type to discover the even numbers in a `List<T>` of integers:

```
class Program
{
  static void Main(string[] args)
  {
    Console.WriteLine("***** Fun with Lambdas *****\n");
    TraditionalDelegateSyntax();

    Console.ReadLine();
  }

  static void TraditionalDelegateSyntax()
  {
    // Make a list of integers.
    List<int> list = new List<int>();
    list.AddRange(new int[] { 20, 1, 4, 8, 9, 44 });

    // Call FindAll() using traditional delegate syntax.
    Predicate<int> callback = new Predicate<int>(IsEvenNumber);
    List<int> evenNumbers = list.FindAll(callback);

    Console.WriteLine("Here are your even numbers:");
    foreach (int evenNumber in evenNumbers)
    {
      Console.Write("{0}\t", evenNumber);
    }
    Console.WriteLine();
  }

  // Target for the Predicate<> delegate.
  static bool IsEvenNumber(int i)
  {
    // Is it an even number?
```

```
    return (i % 2) == 0;
  }
}
```

Here, we have a method (IsEvenNumber()) that is in charge of testing the incoming integer parameter to see whether it is even or odd via the C# modulo operator, %. If you execute your application, you will find the numbers 20, 4, 8, and 44 print out to the console.

While this traditional approach to working with delegates works as expected, the IsEvenNumber() method, however, is only invoked under very limited circumstances; specifically, when we call FindAll(), which leaves us with the baggage of a full method definition. If we were to instead use an anonymous method, our code would clean up considerably. Consider the following new method of the Program type:

```
static void AnonymousMethodSyntax()
{
  // Make a list of integers.
  List<int> list = new List<int>();
  list.AddRange(new int[] { 20, 1, 4, 8, 9, 44 });

  // Now, use an anonymous method.
  List<int> evenNumbers = list.FindAll(delegate(int i)
    { return (i % 2) == 0; } );

  Console.WriteLine("Here are your even numbers:");
  foreach (int evenNumber in evenNumbers)
  {
    Console.Write("{0}\t", evenNumber);
  }
  Console.WriteLine();
}
```

In this case, rather than directly creating a Predicate<T> delegate type, and then authoring a stand-alone method, we are able to inline a method anonymously. While this is a step in the right direction, we are still required to use the delegate keyword (or a strongly typed Predicate<T>), and must ensure that the parameter list is a dead-on match. As well, as you may agree, the syntax used to define an anonymous method can be viewed as being a bit hard on the eyes, which is even more apparent here:

```
List<int> evenNumbers = list.FindAll(
  delegate(int i)
  {
    return (i % 2) == 0;
  }
);
```

Lambda expressions can be used to simplify our call to FindAll() even more. When we make use of this new syntax, there is no trace of the underlying delegate whatsoever. Consider the following update to our code base:

```
static void LambdaExpressionSyntax()
{
  // Make a list of integers.
  List<int> list = new List<int>();
  list.AddRange(new int[] { 20, 1, 4, 8, 9, 44 });

  // Now, use a C# 2008 lambda expression.
  List<int> evenNumbers = list.FindAll(i => (i % 2) == 0);
```

```
  Console.WriteLine("Here are your even numbers:");
  foreach (int evenNumber in evenNumbers)
  {
    Console.Write("{0}\t", evenNumber);
  }
  Console.WriteLine();
}
```

In this case, notice the rather strange statement of code passed into the `FindAll()` method, which is in fact a lambda expression. Notice that in this iteration of the example, there is no trace whatsoever of the `Predicate<T>` delegate (or the `delegate` keyword for that matter). All we have specified is the lambda expression: `i => (i % 2) == 0`.

Before we break this syntax down, at this level simply understand that lambda expressions can be used anywhere you would have used an anonymous method or a strongly typed delegate (typically with far fewer keystrokes). Under the hood, the C# compiler translates our expression into a standard anonymous method making use of the `Predicate<T>` delegate type (which can be verified using `ildasm.exe` or `reflector.exe`). Specifically, the following code statement:

```
// This lambda expression...
List<int> evenNumbers = list.FindAll(i => (i % 2) == 0);
```

is compiled into the following approximate C# code:

```
// ...becomes this anonymous method.
List<int> evenNumbers = list.FindAll(delegate (int i)
{
  return (i % 2) == 0;
});
```

Dissecting a Lambda Expression

A lambda expression is written by first defining a parameter list, followed by the => token (C#'s token for the lambda operator found in the *lambda calculus*), followed by a set of statements (or a single statement) that will process these arguments. From a very high level, a lambda expression can be understood as follows:

```
ArgumentsToProcess => StatementsToProcessThem
```

Within our `LambdaExpressionSyntax()` method, things break down like so:

```
// "i" is our parameter list.
// "(i % 2) == 0" is our statement set to process "i".
List<int> evenNumbers = list.FindAll(i => (i % 2) == 0);
```

The parameters of a lambda expression can be explicitly or implicitly typed. Currently, the underlying data type representing the `i` parameter (an integer) is determined implicitly. The compiler is able to figure out that `i` is an integer based on the context of the overall lambda expression and the underlying delegate. However, it is also possible to explicitly define the type of each parameter in the expression, by wrapping the data type and variable name in a pair of parentheses as follows:

```
// Now, explicitly state what the parameter type.
List<int> evenNumbers = list.FindAll((int i) => (i % 2) == 0);
```

As you have seen, if a lambda expression has a single, implicitly typed parameter, the parentheses may be omitted from the parameter list. If you wish to be consistent regarding your use of lambda parameters, you are free to *always* wrap the parameter list within parentheses, leaving us with this expression:

```
List<int> evenNumbers = list.FindAll((i) => (i % 2) == 0);
```

Finally, notice that currently our expression has not been wrapped in parentheses (we have of course wrapped the modulo statement to ensure it is executed first before the test for equality). Lambda expressions do allow for the statement to be wrapped as follows:

```
// Now, wrap the expression as well.
List<int> evenNumbers = list.FindAll((i) => ((i % 2) == 0));
```

Now that you have seen the various ways to build a lambda expression, how can we read this lambda statement in human-friendly terms? Leaving the raw mathematics behind, the following explanation fits the bill:

```
// My list of parameters (in this case a single integer named i)
// will be processed by the expression (i % 2) == 0.
List<int> evenNumbers = list.FindAll((i) => ((i % 2) == 0));
```

Processing Arguments Within Multiple Statements

Our first lambda expression was a single statement that ultimately evaluated to a Boolean. However, as you know full well, many delegate targets must perform a number of code statements. For this reason, C# 2008 allows you to build lambda expressions using multiple statement blocks. When your expression must process the parameters using multiple lines of code, you can do so by denoting a scope for these statements using the expected curly brackets. Consider the following example update to our `LambdaExpressionSyntax()` method:

```
static void LambdaExpressionSyntax()
{
  // Make a list of integers.
  List<int> list = new List<int>();
  list.AddRange(new int[] { 20, 1, 4, 8, 9, 44 });

  // Now process each argument within a group of
  // code statements.
  List<int> evenNumbers = list.FindAll((i) =>
  {
    Console.WriteLine("value of i is currently: {0}", i);
    bool isEven = ((i % 2) == 0);
    return isEven;
  });

  Console.WriteLine("Here are your even numbers:");
  foreach (int evenNumber in evenNumbers)
  {
    Console.Write("{0}\t", evenNumber);
  }
  Console.WriteLine();
}
```

In this case, our parameter list (again, a single integer named `i`) is being processed by a set of code statements. Beyond the calls to `Console.WriteLine()`, our modulo statement has been broken into two code statements for increased readability. Assuming each of these three methods are called from within `Main()`:

```
static void Main(string[] args)
{
  Console.WriteLine("***** Fun with Lambdas *****\n");
  TraditionalDelegateSyntax();
```

```
  AnonymousMethodSyntax();
  Console.WriteLine();
  LambdaExpressionSyntax();
  Console.ReadLine();
}
```

we will find the output in Figure 11-9.

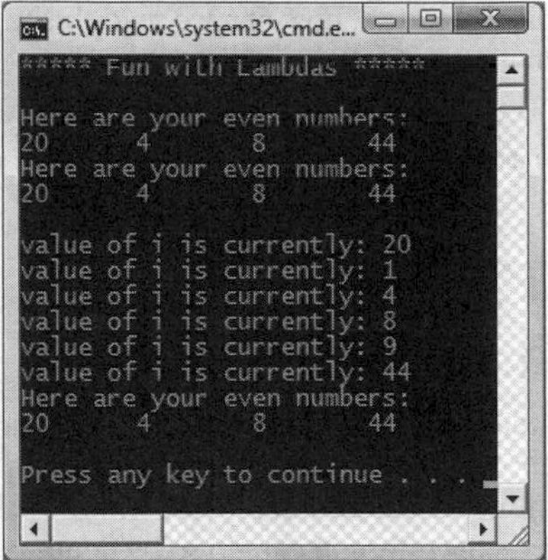

Figure 11-9. *The output of your first lambda expression*

■ **Source Code** The SimpleLambdaExpressions project can be found under the Chapter 11 subdirectory.

Retrofitting the CarDelegate Example Using Lambda Expressions

Given that the whole reason for lambda expressions is to provide a clean, concise manner to define an anonymous method (and therefore indirectly a manner to simplify working with delegates), let's retrofit the CarDelegate project we created earlier in this chapter. Here is a simplified version of that project's `Program` class, which makes use of "normal" delegate syntax to respond to each callback:

```
class Program
{
  static void Main(string[] args)
  {
    Console.WriteLine("***** More Fun with Lambdas *****\n");

    // Make a car as usual.
    Car c1 = new Car("SlugBug", 100, 10);

    // Normal delegate syntax.
    c1.OnAboutToBlow(new Car.AboutToBlow(CarAboutToBlow));
    c1.OnExploded(new Car.Exploded(CarExploded));

    // Speed up (this will generate the events).
    Console.WriteLine("\n***** Speeding up *****");
    for (int i = 0; i < 6; i++)
      c1.SpeedUp(20);
```

```
    Console.ReadLine();
  }

  // Delegate targets.
  public static void CarAboutToBlow(string msg)
  { Console.WriteLine(msg); }

  public static void CarExploded(string msg)
  { Console.WriteLine(msg); }
}
```

Here again is the Main() method now making use of anonymous methods:

```
static void Main(string[] args)
{
  Console.WriteLine("***** More Fun with Lambdas *****\n");

  // Make a car as usual.
  Car c1 = new Car("SlugBug", 100, 10);

  // Now use anonymous methods.
  c1.OnAboutToBlow(delegate(string msg) { Console.WriteLine(msg); });
  c1.OnExploded(delegate(string msg) { Console.WriteLine(msg); });

  // Speed up (this will generate the events.)
  Console.WriteLine("\n***** Speeding up *****");
  for (int i = 0; i < 6; i++)
    c1.SpeedUp(20);

  Console.ReadLine();
}
```

And finally, here is the Main() method now using lambda expressions:

```
static void Main(string[] args)
{
  Console.WriteLine("***** More Fun with Lambdas *****\n");

  // Make a car as usual.
  Car c1 = new Car("SlugBug", 100, 10);

  // Now with lambdas!
  c1.OnAboutToBlow(msg => { Console.WriteLine(msg); });
  c1.OnExploded(msg => { Console.WriteLine(msg); });

  // Speed up (this will generate the events).
  Console.WriteLine("\n***** Speeding up *****");
  for (int i = 0; i < 6; i++)
    c1.SpeedUp(20);

  Console.ReadLine();
}
```

Source Code The CarDelegateWithLambdas project can be found under the Chapter 11 subdirectory.

Lambda Expressions with Multiple (or Zero) Parameters

Each of the lambda expressions you have seen here processed a single parameter. This is not a requirement, however, as a lambda expression may process multiple arguments or provide no arguments whatsoever. To illustrate the first scenario, create a final Console Application named LambdaExpressionsMultipleParams. Next, assume the following incarnation of the SimpleMath type:

```
public class SimpleMath
{
  public delegate void MathMessage(string msg, int result);
  private MathMessage mmDelegate;

  public void SetMathHandler(MathMessage target)
  {mmDelegate = target; }

  public void Add(int x, int y)
  {
    if (mmDelegate != null)
      mmDelegate.Invoke("Adding has completed!", x + y);
  }
}
```

Notice that the MathMessage delegate is expecting two parameters. To represent them as a lambda expression, our Main() method might be written as follows:

```
static void Main(string[] args)
{
  // Register w/ delegate as a lambda expression.
  SimpleMath m = new SimpleMath();
  m.SetMathHandler((msg, result) =>
    {Console.WriteLine("Message: {0}, Result: {1}", msg, result);});

  // This will execute the lambda expression.
  m.Add(10, 10);
  Console.ReadLine();
}
```

Here, we are leveraging type inference, as our two parameters have not been strongly typed for simplicity. However, we could call SetMathHandler() as follows:

```
m.SetMathHandler((string msg, int result) =>
  {Console.WriteLine("Message: {0}, Result: {1}", msg, result);});
```

Finally, if you are using a lambda expression to interact with a delegate taking no parameters at all, you may do so by supplying a pair of empty parentheses as the parameter. Thus, assuming you have defined the following delegate type:

```
public delegate string VerySimpleDelegate();
```

you could handle the result of the invocation as follows:

```
// Prints "Enjoy your string!" to the console.
VerySimpleDelegate d = new VerySimpleDelegate( () => {return "Enjoy your string!";} );
Console.WriteLine(d.Invoke());
```

So hopefully at this point you can see the overall role of lambda expressions and understand how they provide a "functional manner" to work with anonymous methods and delegate types. Although the new lambda operator (=>) might take a bit to get used to, always remember a lambda expression can be broken down to the following simple equation:

```
ArgumentsToProcess => StatementsToProcessThem
```

It is worth pointing out that the LINQ programming model also makes substantial use of lambda expressions to help simplify your coding efforts. You will examine LINQ beginning in Chapter 14.

Source Code The LambdaExpressionsMultipleParams project can be found under the Chapter 11 subdirectory.

Summary

In this chapter, you have examined a number of ways in which multiple objects can partake in a bidirectional conversation. First, you examined the C# `delegate` keyword, which is used to indirectly construct a class derived from `System.MulticastDelegate`. As you have seen, a delegate is simply an object that maintains a list of methods to call when told to do so. These invocations may be made synchronously (using the `Invoke()` method) or asynchronously (via the `BeginInvoke()` and `EndInvoke()` methods). Again, the asynchronous nature of .NET delegate types will be examined in Chapter 18.

You then examined the C# `event` keyword which, when used in conjunction with a delegate type, can simplify the process of sending your event notifications to awaiting callers. As shown via the resulting CIL, the .NET event model maps to hidden calls on the `System.Delegate`/`System.MulticastDelegate` types. In this light, the C# `event` keyword is purely optional in that it simply saves you some typing time.

This chapter also examined a C# language feature termed *anonymous methods*. Using this syntactic construct, you are able to directly associate a block of code statements to a given event. As you have seen, anonymous methods are free to ignore the parameters sent by the event and have access to the "outer variables" of the defining method. You also examined a simplified way to register events using *method group conversion*.

Finally, we wrapped things up by examining the C# 2008 *lambda operator*, `=>`. As shown, this syntax is a great shorthand notation for authoring anonymous methods, where a stack of arguments can be passed into a group of statements for processing.

CHAPTER 12

Indexers, Operators, and Pointers

In this chapter, you'll deepen your understanding of the C# programming language by examining a handful of advanced syntactic constructs. To begin, you'll learn how to construct and use an *indexer method*. This C# mechanism enables you to build custom types that provide access to internal subtypes using an array-like syntax. Once you learn how to build an indexer method, you'll then examine how to overload various operators (+, -, <, >, and so forth), and how to create custom explicit and implicit conversion routines for your types (and you'll learn why you may wish to do so).

The remainder of this chapter examines a small set of lesser used (but nonetheless interesting) C# keywords. For example, you'll learn how to create an "unsafe" code context in order to directly manipulate pointer types using C# and make use of various preprocessor directives.

Understanding Indexer Methods

As programmers, we are very familiar with the process of accessing individual items contained within a standard array using the index operator ([]), for example:

```
static void Main(string[] args)
{
  // Loop over incoming start up params.
  for(int i = 0; i < args.Length; i++)
    Console.WriteLine("Args: {0}", args[i]);

  // Declare an array of local integers.
  int[] myInts = { 10, 9, 100, 432, 9874};

  // Use the [] operator to access each element.
  for(int j = 0; j < myInts.Length; j++)
    Console.WriteLine("Index {0}  = {1} ", j,  myInts[j]);
  Console.ReadLine();
}
```

The previous code is by no means a major newsflash. However, the C# language provides the capability to design custom classes and structures that may be indexed just like a standard array, by defining an *indexer method*. This particular language feature is most useful when you are creating custom collection types (generic or nongeneric).

Before examining how to create such a construct, let's begin by seeing one in action. Assume you have added support for an indexer method to the custom PeopleCollection type developed in Chapter 10 (specifically, the CustomNonGenericCollection project). Observe the following usage within a new Console Application named SimpleIndexer:

```
// Indexers allow you to access items in an array-like fashion.
class Program
{
  static void Main(string[] args)
  {
    Console.WriteLine("***** Fun with Indexers *****\n");

    PeopleCollection myPeople = new PeopleCollection();

    // Add objects with indexer syntax.
    myPeople[0] = new Person("Homer", "Simpson", 40);
    myPeople[1] = new Person("Marge", "Simpson", 38);
    myPeople[2] = new Person("Lisa", "Simpson", 9);
    myPeople[3] = new Person("Bart", "Simpson", 7);
    myPeople[4] = new Person("Maggie", "Simpson", 2);

    // Now obtain and display each item using indexer.
    for (int i = 0; i < myPeople.Count; i++)
    {
      Console.WriteLine("Person number: {0}", i);
      Console.WriteLine("Name: {0} {1}",
        myPeople[i].FirstName, myPeople[i].LastName);
      Console.WriteLine("Age: {0}", myPeople[i].Age);
      Console.WriteLine();
    }
  }
}
```

As you can see, indexers behave much like a custom collection supporting the IEnumerator and IEnumerable interfaces in that they provide access to a container's subitems. The major difference of course is that rather than accessing the contents using the foreach construct, you are able to manipulate the internal collection of sub-objects just like a standard array.

Now for the big question: How do you configure the PeopleCollection class (or any class/ structure) to support this functionality? An indexer is represented as a slightly mangled C# property. In its simplest form, an indexer is created using the this[] syntax. Here is the required update for the PeopleCollection class:

```
// Add the indexer to the existing class definition.
public class PeopleCollection : IEnumerable
{
  private ArrayList arPeople = new ArrayList();

  // Custom indexer for this class.
  public Person this[int index]
  {
    get { return (Person)arPeople[index]; }
    set { arPeople.Insert(index, value); }
  }
...
}
```

Beyond the use of the this keyword, the indexer looks just like any other C# property declaration. For example, the role of the get scope is to return the correct object to the caller. Here, we are in fact doing so by using the indexer of the ArrayList object! The set scope is in charge of placing the incoming object into the container at the specified index; in this example, this is achieved by calling the Insert() method of the ArrayList.

As you can see, indexers are yet another form of syntactic sugar, given that this functionality can also be achieved using "normal" public methods such as `AddPerson()` or `GetPerson()`. Nevertheless, when you support indexer methods on your custom collection types, they integrate well into the fabric of the .NET base class libraries.

While building indexer methods is quite commonplace when you are building custom collections, do remember that generic types give you this very functionality out of the box. Consider the following method, which makes use of a generic `List<T>` of `Person` objects. Note we are able to simply use the indexer of `List<T>` directly, for example:

```
static void UseGenericListOfPeople()
{
  List<Person> myPeople = new List<Person>();
  myPeople.Add(new Person("Lisa", "Simpson", 9));
  myPeople.Add(new Person("Bart", "Simpson", 7));

  // Change first person with indexer.
  myPeople[0] = new Person("Maggie", "Simpson", 2);

  // Now obtain and display each item using indexer.
  for (int i = 0; i < myPeople.Count; i++)
  {
    Console.WriteLine("Person number: {0}", i);
    Console.WriteLine("Name: {0} {1}", myPeople[i].FirstName,
      myPeople[i].LastName);
    Console.WriteLine("Age: {0}", myPeople[i].Age);
    Console.WriteLine();
  }
}
```

■ **Source Code** The SimpleIndexer project is located under the Chapter 12 subdirectory.

Indexing Objects Using String Values

The current `PeopleCollection` type defined an indexer that allowed the caller to identify subitems using a numerical value. Understand, however, that this is not a requirement of an indexer method. Assume you would rather contain the `Person` objects using a `System.Collections.Generic.Dictionary<TKey, TValue>` rather than an `ArrayList`. Given that `ListDictionary` types allow access to the contained types using a string token (such as a person's first name), you could define an indexer as follows:

```
public class PeopleCollection : IEnumerable
{
  private Dictionary<string, Person> listPeople =
    new Dictionary<string, Person>();

  // This indexer returns a person based on a string index.
  public Person this[string name]
  {
    get { return (Person)listPeople[name]; }
    set { listPeople[name] = value; }
  }
```

```
  public void ClearPeople()
  { listPeople.Clear(); }

  public int Count
  { get { return listPeople.Count; } }

  IEnumerator IEnumerable.GetEnumerator()
  { return listPeople.GetEnumerator(); }
}
```

The caller would now be able to interact with the internal Person objects as shown here:

```
static void Main(string[] args)
{
  Console.WriteLine("***** Fun with Indexers *****\n");

  PeopleCollection myPeople = new PeopleCollection();

  myPeople["Homer"] = new Person("Homer", "Simpson", 40);
  myPeople["Marge"] = new Person("Marge", "Simpson", 38);

  // Get "Homer" and print data.
  Person homer = myPeople["Homer"];
  Console.WriteLine(homer.ToString());
  Console.ReadLine();
}
```

Again, if you were to make use of the generic `Dictionary<TKey, TValue>` type directly, you could gain the indexer method functionality out of the box.

■ **Source Code** The StringIndexer project is located under the Chapter 12 subdirectory.

Overloaded Indexer Methods

Understand that indexer methods may be overloaded. Thus, if it made sense to allow the caller to access subitems using a numerical index *or* a string value, you might define multiple indexers for a single type. By way of example, if you have ever programmed with ADO.NET (.NET's native database access API), you may recall that the DataSet type supports a property named Tables, which returns to you a strongly typed DataTableCollection type. As it turns out, DataTableCollection defines three indexers to get and set DataTable objects; one by ordinal position, and the others by a friendly string moniker and optional containing namespace:

```
public sealed class DataTableCollection : InternalDataCollectionBase
{
...
  // Overloaded indexers!
  public DataTable this[string name] { get; }
  public DataTable this[string name, string tableNamespace] { get; }
  public DataTable this[int index] { get; }
}
```

To be sure, a number of types in the base class libraries support indexer methods. Therefore, even if your current project does not require you to build custom indexers for your classes and structures, be aware that many types already support this syntax.

Internal Representation of Indexer Methods

Now that you have seen a few variations on the C# indexer method, you may be wondering how indexers are represented in terms of CIL. If you were to open up the indexer of the current `PeopleCollection` type, you would find that the C# compiler has created a property named `Item`, which maps to the correct getter/setter methods:

```
.property instance class StringIndexer.Person Item(string)
{
  .get instance class StringIndexer.Person
    StringIndexer.PeopleCollection::get_Item(string)
  .set instance void StringIndexer.PeopleCollection::set_Item(string,
    class StringIndexer.Person)
} // end of property PeopleCollection::Item
```

The `get_Item()` and `set_Item()` methods are implemented like any other .NET property; for example, consider the following set logic:

```
.method public hidebysig specialname instance void
  set_Item(string name,
   class StringIndexer.Person 'value') cil managed
{
  // Code size       16 (0x10)
  .maxstack  8
  IL_0000:  nop
  IL_0001:  ldarg.0
  IL_0002:  ldfld  class [System]System.Collections.Specialized.ListDictionary
    StringIndexer.PeopleCollection::listPeople
  IL_0007:  ldarg.1
  IL_0008:  ldarg.2
  IL_0009:  callvirt instance void
  [System]System.Collections.Specialized.ListDictionary::Add(object, object)
  IL_000e:  nop
  IL_000f:  ret
} // end of method PeopleCollection::set_Item
```

■ **Note** The .NET Framework SDK 3.5 documentation will list indexer methods of a class or structure as a property named `Item`. However, the Visual Studio Object Browser will show indexers as properties defined using expected `this[]` syntax.

Indexers with Multiple Dimensions

It is also permissible to create an indexer method that takes multiple parameters. Assume you have a custom collection that stores subitems in a 2D array. If this is the case, you may configure an indexer method as follows:

```
public class SomeContainer
{
  private int[,] my2DintArray = new int[10, 10];

  public int this[int row, int column]
  {  /* get or set value from 2D array */  }
}
```

Indexer Definitions on Interface Types

Finally, understand that indexers can be defined on a given .NET interface type to allow supporting types to provide a custom implementation. Such an interface is as follows:

```
public interface IStringContainer
{
  // This interface defines an indexer that returns
  // strings based on a numerical index.
  string this[int index] { get; set; }
}
```

With this interface definition, any class or structure that implements this interface must now support a read/write indexer that manipulates subitems using a numerical value. As well, you could design a generic interface where the type indexer allows the implementer to determine what will be used to get or set the subobjects:

```
public interface IStringContainer<Key>
{
  string this[int Key] { get; set; }
}
```

Here would be an implementation using a numerical indexer:

```
class MyStrings : IStringContainer<int>
{
  string[] strings = { "First", "Second" };

  public string this[int Key]
  {
    get
    {
      return strings[Key];
    }
    set
    {
      strings[Key] = value;
    }
  }
}
```

Understanding Operator Overloading

C#, like any programming language, has a canned set of tokens that are used to perform basic operations on intrinsic types. For example, you know that the + operator can be applied to two integers in order to yield a larger integer:

```
// The + operator with ints.
int a = 100;
int b = 240;
int c = a + b;  // c is now 340
```

Again, this is no major newsflash, but have you ever stopped and noticed how the same + operator can be applied to most intrinsic C# data types? For example, consider this code:

```
// + operator with strings.
string s1 = "Hello";
string s2 = " world!";
string s3 = s1 + s2;  // s3 is now "Hello world!"
```

In essence, the + operator functions in unique ways based on the supplied data types (strings or integers in this case). When the + operator is applied to numerical types, the result is the summation of the operands. However, when the + operator is applied to string types, the result is string concatenation.

The C# language provides the capability for you to build custom classes and structures that also respond uniquely to the same set of basic tokens (such as the + operator). Be aware that you cannot overload each and every intrinsic C# operator. Table 12-1 outlines the "overloadability" of the core operators.

Table 12-1. *Overloadability of C# Operators*

<table>
<tr><th>C# Operator</th><th>Overloadability</th></tr>
<tr><td>+, -, !, ~, ++, --, true, false</td><td>This set of unary operators can be overloaded.</td></tr>
<tr><td>+, -, *, /, %, &, |, ^, <<, >></td><td>These binary operators can be overloaded.</td></tr>
<tr><td>==, !=, <, >, <=, >=</td><td>The comparison operators can be overloaded. C# will demand that "like" operators (i.e., < and >, <= and >=, == and !=) are overloaded together.</td></tr>
<tr><td>[]</td><td>The [] operator cannot be overloaded. As you saw earlier in this chapter, however, the indexer construct provides the same functionality.</td></tr>
<tr><td>()</td><td>The () operator cannot be overloaded. As you will see later in this chapter, however, custom conversion methods provide the same functionality.</td></tr>
<tr><td>+=, -=, *=, /=, %=, &=, |=, ^=, <<=, >>=</td><td>Shorthand assignment operators cannot be overloaded; however, you receive them as a freebie when you overload the related binary operator.</td></tr>
</table>

■ Note In C#, `true` and `false` can be used as operators in addition to literals. This functionality can be useful when building custom types that represent true, false, and null (meaning neither true nor false).

Overloading Binary Operators

To illustrate the process of overloading binary operators, assume the following simple `Point` structure defined in a new Console Application named OverloadedOps:

```
// Just a simple everyday C# struct.
public struct Point
{
  private int x, y;
  public Point(int xPos, int yPos)
  {
    x = xPos;
    y = yPos;
  }

  public override string ToString()
  {
    return string.Format("[{0}, {1}]", this.x, this.y);
  }
}
```

Now, logically speaking, it makes sense to add Points together. For example, if you added together two Point variables, you should receive a new Point that is the summation of the x and y values. On a related note, it may be helpful to subtract one Point from another. Ideally, you would like to be able to author the following code:

```
// Adding and subtracting two points?
static void Main(string[] args)
{
  Console.WriteLine("***** Fun with Overloaded Operators *****\n");

  // Make two points.
  Point ptOne = new Point(100, 100);
  Point ptTwo = new Point(40, 40);
  Console.WriteLine("ptOne = {0}", ptOne);
  Console.WriteLine("ptTwo = {0}", ptTwo);

  // Add the points to make a bigger point?
  Console.WriteLine("ptOne + ptTwo: {0} ", ptOne + ptTwo);

  // Subtract the points to make a smaller point?
  Console.WriteLine("ptOne - ptTwo: {0} ", ptOne - ptTwo);
  Console.ReadLine();
}
```

However, as our Point now stands, we will receive compile-time errors, as the Point type does not know how to respond to the + or - operators (see Figure 12-1).

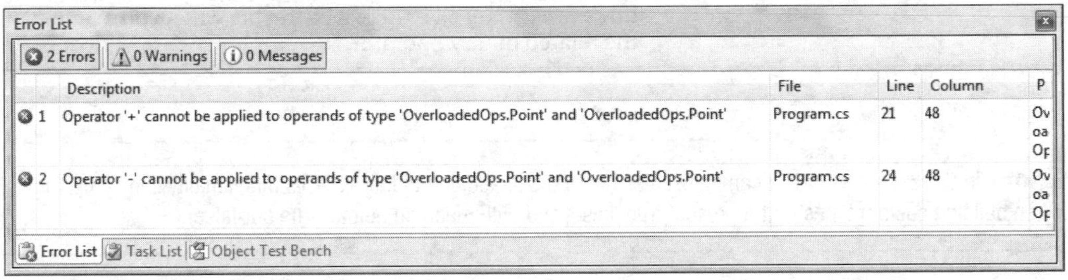

Error List

2 Errors | 0 Warnings | 0 Messages

	Description	File	Line	Column	P
1	Operator '+' cannot be applied to operands of type 'OverloadedOps.Point' and 'OverloadedOps.Point'	Program.cs	21	48	Ov oa Op
2	Operator '-' cannot be applied to operands of type 'OverloadedOps.Point' and 'OverloadedOps.Point'	Program.cs	24	48	Ov oa Op

Error List | Task List | Object Test Bench

Figure 12-1. *By default, custom classes/structures do not support custom operators.*

To equip a custom type to respond uniquely to intrinsic operators, C# provides the operator keyword, which you can use only in conjunction with *static* methods. When you are overloading a binary operator (such as + and -), you will most often pass in two arguments that are the same type as the defining class (a Point in this example), as illustrated in the following code update:

```
// A more intelligent Point type.
public struct Point
{
...
  // overloaded operator +
  public static Point operator + (Point p1, Point p2)
  { return new Point(p1.x + p2.x, p1.y + p2.y); }

  // overloaded operator -
  public static Point operator - (Point p1, Point p2)
  { return new Point(p1.x - p2.x, p1.y - p2.y); }
}
```

The logic behind operator + is simply to return a brand new `Point` based on the summation of the fields of the incoming `Point` parameters. Thus, when you write `pt1 + pt2`, under the hood you can envision the following hidden call to the static operator + method:

```
// Point p3 = Point.operator+ (p1, p2)
Point p3 = p1 + p2;
```

Likewise, `p1 – p2` maps to the following:

```
// Point p4 = Point.operator- (p1, p2)
Point p4 = p1 - p2;
```

With this update, our program now compiles, and we find we are able to add and subtract `Point` objects (see Figure 12-2).

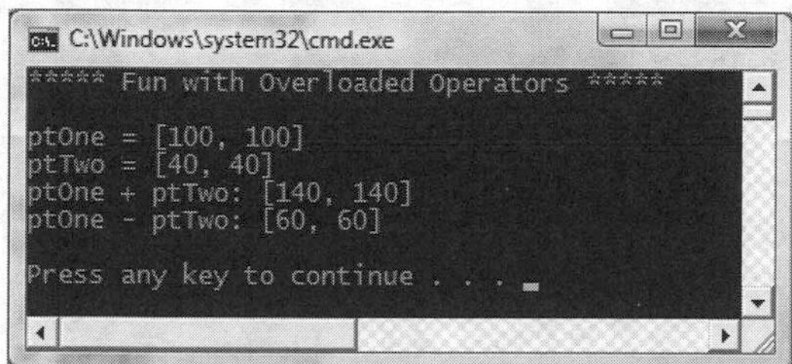

Figure 12-2. *Redefining + and - for the* `Point` *type*

Strictly speaking, when you are overloading a binary operator, you are not required to pass in two parameters of the same type. If it makes sense to do so, one of the arguments can differ. For example, here is an overloaded operator +, which allows the caller to obtain a new `Point` that is based on a numerical adjustment:

```
public struct Point
{
...
  public static Point operator +(Point p1, int change)
  {
    return new Point(p1.x + change, p1.y + change);
  }
  public static Point operator +(int change, Point p1)
  {
    return new Point(p1.x + change, p1.y + change);
  }
}
```

We would now be able to use these new versions of operator + as follows:

```
// Prints [110, 110]
Point biggerPoint = ptOne + 10;
Console.WriteLine("ptOne + 10 = {0}", biggerPoint);

// Prints [120, 120]
Console.WriteLine("10 + biggerPoint = {0}", 10 + biggerPoint);
Console.WriteLine();
```

And What of the += and –+ Operators?

If you are coming to C# from a C++ background, you may lament the loss of overloading the shorthand assignment operators (+=, -=, and so forth). Fear not. In terms of C#, the shorthand assignment operators are automatically simulated if a type overloads the related binary operator. Thus, given that the Point structure has already overloaded the + and - operators, you are able to write the following:

```
// Overloading binary operators results in a freebie shorthand operator.
static void Main(string[] args)
{
...
  // Freebie +=
  Point ptThree = new Point(90, 5);
  Console.WriteLine("ptThree = {0}", ptThree);
  Console.WriteLine("ptThree += ptTwo: {0}", ptThree += ptTwo);

  // Freebie -=
  Point ptFour = new Point(0, 500);
  Console.WriteLine("ptFour = {0}", ptFour);
  Console.WriteLine("ptFour -= ptThree: {0}", ptFour -= ptThree);
  Console.ReadLine();
}
```

Overloading Unary Operators

C# also allows you to overload various unary operators, such as ++ and --. When you overload a unary operator, you will also define a static method via the operator keyword; however, in this case you will simply pass in a single parameter that is the same type as the defining class/structure. For example, if you were to update the Point with the following overloaded operators:

```
public struct Point
{
...
  // Add 1 to the incoming Point.
  public static Point operator ++(Point p1)
  { return new Point(p1.x+1, p1.y+1); }

  // Subtract 1 from the incoming Point.
  public static Point operator --(Point p1)
  { return new Point(p1.x-1, p1.y-1); }
}
```

you could increment and decrement Point's x and y values as follows:

```
static void Main(string[] args)
{
...
  // Applying the ++ and -- unary operators to a Point.
  Point ptFive = new Point(1, 1);
  Console.WriteLine("++ptFive = {0}", ++ptFive);  // [2, 2]
  Console.WriteLine("--ptFive = {0}", --ptFive);  // [1, 1]

  // Apply same operators as postincrement/decrement.
  Point ptSix = new Point(20, 20);
```

```
  Console.WriteLine("ptSix++ = {0}", ptSix++);  // [20, 20]
  Console.WriteLine("ptSix-- = {0}", ptSix--);  // [21, 21]
  Console.ReadLine();
}
```

Notice in the previous code example we are applying our custom ++ and -- operators in two unique manners. In C++, it is possible to overload pre- and postincrement/decrement operators separately. This is not possible in C#; however, the return value of the increment/decrement is automatically handled “correctly” free of charge (i.e., for an overloaded ++ operator, pt++ has the value of the unmodified object as its value within an expression, while ++pt has the new value applied before use in the expression).

Overloading Equality Operators

As you may recall from Chapter 6, `System.Object.Equals()` can be overridden to perform value-based (rather than referenced-based) comparisons between types. If you choose to override `Equals()` (and the often related `System.Object.GetHashCode()` method), it is trivial to overload the equality operators (== and !=). To illustrate, here is the updated `Point` type:

```
// This incarnation of Point also overloads the == and != operators.
public struct Point
{
...
  public override bool Equals(object o)
  {
    return o.ToString() == this.ToString();
  }

  public override int GetHashCode()
  {  return this.ToString().GetHashCode(); }

  // Now let's overload the == and != operators.
  public static bool operator ==(Point p1, Point p2)
  {  return p1.Equals(p2); }

  public static bool operator !=(Point p1, Point p2)
  {  return !p1.Equals(p2); }
}
```

Notice how the implementation of operator == and operator != simply makes a call to the overridden `Equals()` method to get the bulk of the work done. Given this, you can now exercise your `Point` class as follows:

```
// Make use of the overloaded equality operators.
static void Main(string[] args)
{
...
  Console.WriteLine("ptOne == ptTwo : {0}", ptOne == ptTwo);
  Console.WriteLine("ptOne != ptTwo : {0}", ptOne != ptTwo);
  Console.ReadLine();
}
```

As you can see, it is quite intuitive to compare two objects using the well-known == and != operators rather than making a call to `Object.Equals()`. If you do overload the equality operators for a given class, keep in mind that C# demands that if you override the == operator, you *must* also override the != operator (if you forget, the compiler will let you know).

Overloading Comparison Operators

In Chapter 9, you learned how to implement the IComparable interface in order to compare the relative relationship between two like objects. Additionally, you may also overload the comparison operators (<, >, <=, and >=) for the same class. Like the equality operators, C# demands that if you overload <, you must also overload >. The same holds true for the <= and >= operators. If the Point type overloaded these comparison operators, the object user could now compare Points as follows:

```
// Using the overloaded < and > operators.
static void Main(string[] args)
{
...
  Console.WriteLine("ptOne < ptTwo : {0}", ptOne < ptTwo);
  Console.WriteLine("ptOne > ptTwo : {0}", ptOne > ptTwo);
  Console.ReadLine();
}
```

Assuming you have implemented the IComparable interface, overloading the comparison operators is trivial. Here is the updated class definition:

```
// Point is also comparable using the comparison operators.
public struct Point : IComparable
{
...
  public int CompareTo(object obj)
  {
    if (obj is Point)
    {
      Point p = (Point)obj;
      if (this.x > p.x && this.y > p.y)
        return 1;
      if (this.x < p.x && this.y < p.y)
        return -1;
      else
        return 0;
    }
    else
      throw new ArgumentException();
  }

  public static bool operator <(Point p1, Point p2)
  { return (p1.CompareTo(p2) < 0); }

  public static bool operator >(Point p1, Point p2)
  { return (p1.CompareTo(p2) > 0); }

  public static bool operator <=(Point p1, Point p2)
  { return (p1.CompareTo(p2) <= 0); }

  public static bool operator >=(Point p1, Point p2)
  { return (p1.CompareTo(p2) >= 0); }
}
```

The Internal Representation of Overloaded Operators

Like any C# programming element, overloaded operators are represented using specific CIL syntax. To begin examining what takes place behind the scenes, open the OverloadedOps.exe assembly using ildasm.exe. As you can see from Figure 12-3, the overloaded operators are internally expressed via hidden methods (e.g., op_Addition(), op_Subtraction(), op_Equality(), and so on).

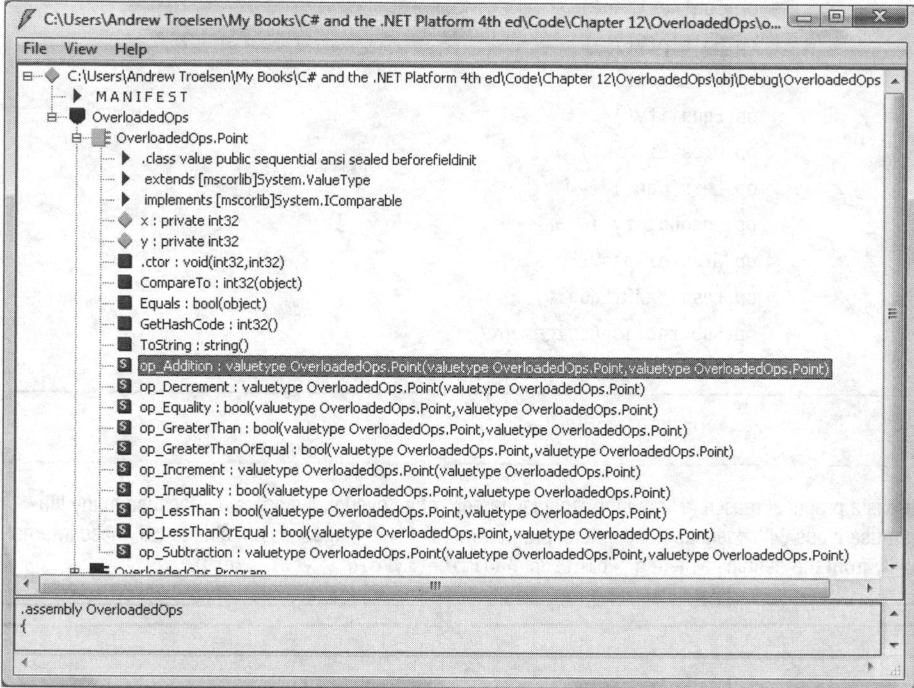

Figure 12-3. *In terms of CIL, overloaded operators map to hidden methods.*

Now, if you were to examine the specific CIL instructions for the op_Addition method, you would find that the specialname method decoration has also been inserted by csc.exe:

```
.method public hidebysig specialname static
  valuetype OverloadedOps.Point
  op_Addition(valuetype OverloadedsOps.Point p1,
              valuetype OverloadedOps.Point p2) cil managed
{
  ...
}
```

The truth of the matter is that any operator that you may overload equates to a specially named method in terms of CIL. Table 12-2 documents the C# operator-to-CIL mapping for the most common C# operators.

Table 12-2. *C# Operator-to-CIL Special Name Road Map*

Intrinsic C# Operator	CIL Representation
--	op_Decrement()
++	op_Increment()
+	op_Addition()

Continued

Table 12-2. *Continued*

Intrinsic C# Operator	CIL Representation
`-`	`op_Subtraction()`
`*`	`op_Multiply()`
`/`	`op_Division()`
`==`	`op_Equality()`
`>`	`op_GreaterThan()`
`<`	`op_LessThan()`
`!=`	`op_Inequality()`
`>=`	`op_GreaterThanOrEqual()`
`<=`	`op_LessThanOrEqual()`
`-=`	`op_SubtractionAssignment()`
`+=`	`op_AdditionAssignment()`

Note There is a practical reason to know the "special names" of an overloaded operator. Because many languages cannot use types with overloaded operators, programmers of said languages are able to call these internal names statically from the defining type (e.g., `Point.op_Addition(myPoint, yourPoint)`).

Final Thoughts Regarding Operator Overloading

As you have seen, C# provides the capability to build types that can respond uniquely to various intrinsic, well-known operators. Now, before you go and retrofit all your classes to support such behavior, you must be sure that the operator(s) you are about to overload make some sort of logical sense in the world at large.

For example, let's say you overloaded the multiplication operator for the `MiniVan` class. What exactly would it mean to multiply two `MiniVan` objects? Not much. In fact, it would be very confusing for teammates to see the following use of `MiniVan` objects.

```
// Huh?! This is far from intuitive...
MiniVan newVan = myVan * yourVan;
```

Overloading operators is generally only useful when you're building utility types. Strings, points, rectangles, fractions, and hexagons make good candidates for operator overloading. People, managers, cars, database connections, and web pages do not. As a rule of thumb, if an overloaded operator makes it *harder* for the user to understand a type's functionality, don't do it. Use this feature wisely.

Also be aware that even if you do not tend to overload operators for your custom classes, numerous types in the base class libraries have already done so. For example, the `System.Drawing.dll` assembly provides an "official" `Point` definition that overloads numerous operators. Notice the operator icon from the Visual Studio 2008 Object Browser (see Figure 12-4).

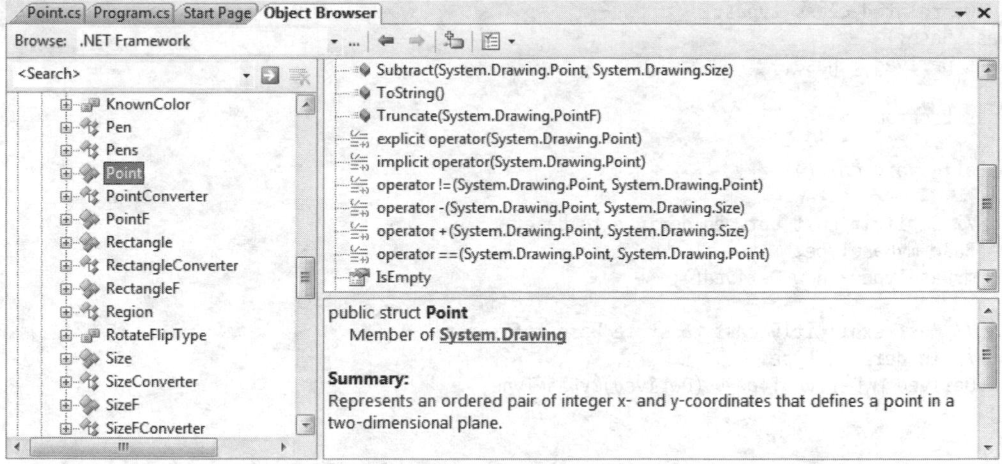

Figure 12-4. *Numerous types in the base class libraries have already-overloaded operators.*

Source Code The OverloadedOps project is located under the Chapter 12 subdirectory.

Understanding Custom Type Conversions

Let's now examine a topic closely related to operator overloading: custom type conversions. To set the stage for the discussion to follow, let's quickly review the notion of explicit and implicit conversions between numerical data and related class types.

Recall: Numerical Conversions

In terms of the intrinsic numerical types (`sbyte`, `int`, `float`, etc.), an *explicit conversion* is required when you attempt to store a larger value in a smaller container, as this may result in a loss of data. Basically, this is your way to tell the compiler, "Leave me alone, I know what I am trying to do." Conversely, an *implicit conversion* happens automatically when you attempt to place a smaller type in a destination type that will not result in a loss of data:

```
static void Main()
{
  int a = 123;
  long b = a;       // Implicit conversion from int to long
  int c = (int) b;  // Explicit conversion from long to int
}
```

Recall: Conversions Among Related Class Types

As shown in Chapter 6, class types may be related by classical inheritance (the "is-a" relationship). In this case, the C# conversion process allows you to cast up and down the class hierarchy. For example, a derived class can always be implicitly cast to a base type. However, if you wish to store a base class type in a derived variable, you must perform an explicit cast:

```
// Two related class types.
class Base{}
class Derived : Base{}

class Program
{
  static void Main()
  {
    // Implicit cast between derived to base.
    Base myBaseType;
    myBaseType = new Derived();

    // Must explicitly cast to store base reference
    // in derived type.
    Derived myDerivedType = (Derived)myBaseType;
  }
}
```

This explicit cast works due to the fact that the Base and Derived classes are related by classical inheritance. However, what if you have two class types in *different hierarchies* with no common parent (other than System.Object) that requires conversions? Given that they are not related by classical inheritance, explicit casting offers no help.

On a related note, consider value types (e.g., structures). Assume you have two .NET structures named Square and Rectangle. Given that structures cannot leverage classic inheritance (as they are always sealed), you have no natural way to cast between these seemingly related types.

While you could build helper methods in the structures (such as Rectangle.ToSquare()), C# allows you to build custom conversion routines that allow your types to respond to the () casting operator. Therefore, if you configured the structures correctly, you would be able to use the following syntax to explicitly convert between them as follows:

```
// Convert a Rectangle to a Square!
Rectangle rect;
rect.Width = 3;
rect.Height = 10;
Square sq = (Square)rect;
```

Creating Custom Conversion Routines

Begin by creating a new Console Application named CustomConversions. C# provides two keywords, explicit and implicit, that you can use to control how your types respond during an attempted conversion. Assume you have the following structure definitions:

```
public struct Rectangle
{
  // Public for ease of use;
  // however, feel free to encapsulate with properties.
  public int Width, Height;

  public Rectangle(int w, int h)
  {
    Width = w; Height = h;
  }

  public void Draw()
  {
    for (int i = 0; i < Height; i++)
```

```
    {
      for (int j = 0; j < Width; j++)
      {
        Console.Write("*");
      }
      Console.WriteLine();
    }
  }

  public override string ToString()
  {
    return string.Format("[Width = {0}; Height = {1}]",
      Width, Height);
  }
}

public struct Square
{
  public int Length;
  public Square(int l)
  {
    Length = l;
  }

  public void Draw()
  {
    for (int i = 0; i < Length; i++)
    {
      for (int j = 0; j < Length; j++)
      {
        Console.Write("*");
      }
      Console.WriteLine();
    }
  }

  public override string ToString()
  { return string.Format("[Length = {0}]", Length); }

  // Rectangles can be explicitly converted
  // into Squares.
  public static explicit operator Square(Rectangle r)
  {
    Square s;
    s.Length = r.Height;
    return s;
  }
}
```

Notice that this iteration of the Square type defines an explicit conversion operator. Like the process of overloading an operator, conversion routines make use of the C# operator keyword (in conjunction with the explicit or implicit keyword) and must be defined as static. The incoming parameter is the entity you are converting *from,* while the operator type is the entity you are converting *to.*

In this case, the assumption is that a square (being a geometric pattern in which all sides are of equal length) can be obtained from the height of a rectangle. Thus, you are free to convert a `Rectangle` into a `Square` as follows:

```
static void Main(string[] args)
{
  Console.WriteLine("***** Fun with Conversions *****\n");

  // Make a Rectangle.
  Rectangle r = new Rectangle(15, 4);
  Console.WriteLine(r.ToString());
  r.Draw();

  Console.WriteLine();

  // Convert r into a Square,
  // based on the height of the Rectangle.
  Square s = (Square)r;
  Console.WriteLine(s.ToString());
  s.Draw();
  Console.ReadLine();
}
```

The output can be seen in Figure 12-5.

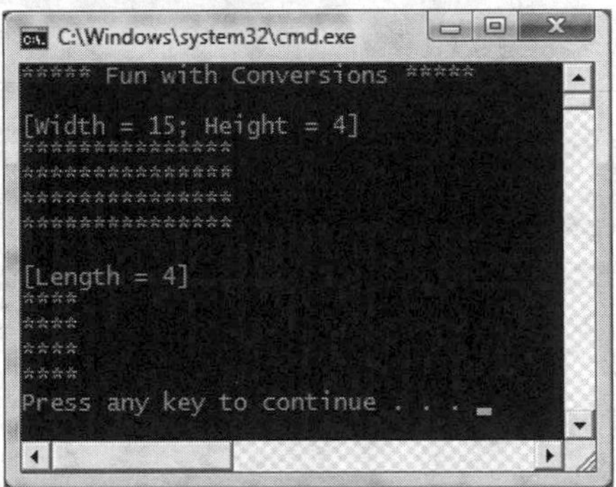

Figure 12-5. *Converting a* `Rectangle` *structure to a* `Square` *structure*

While it may not be all that helpful to convert a `Rectangle` into a `Square` within the same scope, assume you have a function that has been designed to take `Square` parameters.

```
// This method requires a Square type.
static void DrawSquare(Square sq)
{
  Console.WriteLine(sq.ToString());
  sq.Draw();
}
```

Using your explicit conversion operation on the `Square` type, you can now pass in `Rectangle` types for processing using an explicit cast:

```
static void Main(string[] args)
{
...
  // Convert Rectangle to Square to invoke method.
```

```
    Rectangle rect = new Rectangle(10, 5);
    DrawSquare((Square)rect);
    Console.ReadLine();
}
```

Additional Explicit Conversions for the Square Type

Now that you can explicitly convert Rectangles into Squares, let's examine a few additional explicit conversions. Given that a square is symmetrical on each side, it might be helpful to provide an explicit conversion routine that allows the caller to cast from a System.Int32 type into a Square (which, of course, will have a side length equal to the incoming integer). Likewise, what if you were to update Square such that the caller can cast *from* a Square into a System.Int32? Here is the calling logic:

```
static void Main(string[] args)
{
...
  // Converting a System.Int32 to a Square.
  Square sq2 = (Square)90;
  Console.WriteLine("sq2 = {0}", sq2);

  // Converting a Square to a System.Int32.
  int side = (int)sq2;
  Console.WriteLine("Side length of sq2 = {0}", side);
  Console.ReadLine();
}
```

and here is the update to the Square type:

```
public struct Square
{
...
  public static explicit operator Square(int sideLength)
  {
    Square newSq;
    newSq.Length = sideLength;
    return newSq;
  }

  public static explicit operator int (Square s)
  {return s.Length;}
}
```

To be honest, converting from a Square into a System.Int32 may not be the most intuitive (or useful) operation. However, this does point out a very important fact regarding custom conversion routines: the compiler does not care what you convert to or from, as long as you have written syntactically correct code. Thus, as with overloading operators, just because you can create an explicit cast operation for a given type does not mean you should. Typically, this technique will be most helpful when you're creating .NET structure types, given that they are unable to participate in classical inheritance (where casting comes for free).

Defining Implicit Conversion Routines

Thus far, you have created various custom *explicit* conversion operations. However, what about the following *implicit* conversion?

```
static void Main(string[] args)
{
...
  // Attempt to make an implicit cast?
  Square s3;
  s3.Length = 83;
  Rectangle rect2 = s3;
  Console.ReadLine();
}
```

This code will not compile, given that you have not provided an implicit conversion routine for the Rectangle type. Now here is the catch: it is illegal to define explicit and implicit conversion functions on the same type, if they do not differ by their return type or parameter set. This might seem like a limitation; however, the second catch is that when a type defines an *implicit* conversion routine, it is legal for the caller to make use of the *explicit* cast syntax!

Confused? To clear things up, let's add an implicit conversion routine to the Rectangle structure using the C# implicit keyword (note that the following code assumes the width of the resulting Rectangle is computed by multiplying the side of the Square by 2):

```
public struct Rectangle
{
...
  public static implicit operator Rectangle(Square s)
  {
    Rectangle r;
    r.Height = s.Length;

    // Assume the length of the new Rectangle with
    // (Length x 2)
    r.Width = s.Length * 2;
    return r;
  }
}
```

With this update, you are now able to convert between types as follows:

```
static void Main(string[] args)
{
...
  // Implicit cast OK!
  Square s3;
  s3.Length= 7;
  Rectangle rect2 = s3;
  Console.WriteLine("rect2 = {0}", rect2);
  DrawSquare(s3);

  // Explicit cast syntax still OK!
  Square s4;
  s4.Length = 3;
  Rectangle rect3 = (Rectangle)s4;
  Console.WriteLine("rect3 = {0}", rect3);
  Console.ReadLine();
}
```

Again, be aware that it is permissible to define explicit and implicit conversion routines for the same type as long as their signatures differ. Thus, you could update the Square as follows:

```
public struct Square
{
...
  // Can call as:
  // Square sq2 = (Square)90;
  // or as:
  // Square sq2 = 90;
  public static implicit operator Square(int sideLength)
  {
    Square newSq;
    newSq.Length = sideLength;
    return newSq;
  }

  // Must call as:
  // int side = (int)mySquare;
  public static explicit operator int (Square s)
  { return s.Length; }
}
```

The Internal Representation of Custom Conversion Routines

Like overloaded operators, methods that are qualified with the `implicit` or `explicit` keywords have "special" names in terms of CIL: `op_Implicit` and `op_Explicit`, respectively (see Figure 12-6).

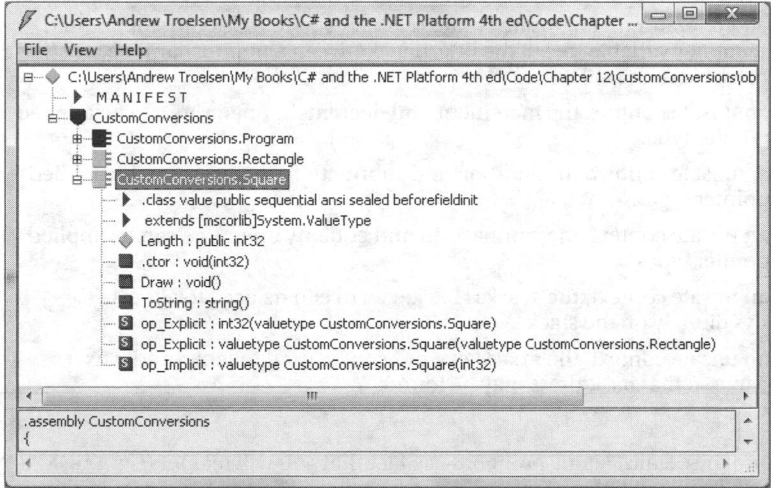

Figure 12-6. *CIL representation of user-defined conversion routines*

Note The Visual Studio 2008 Object Browser shows custom conversion operators using the "explicit operator" and "implicit operator" icons.

That wraps up our examination of defining custom conversion routines. As with overloaded operators, remember that this bit of syntax is simply a shorthand notation for "normal" member functions, and in this light it is always optional. When used correctly, however, your custom structures can be used more naturally, as they can be treated as true class types related by inheritance.

■ **Source Code** The CustomConversions project is located under the Chapter 12 subdirectory.

Working with Pointer Types

In Chapter 4, you learned that the .NET platform defines two major categories of data: value types and reference types. Truth be told, however, there is a third category: *pointer types*. To work with pointer types, we are provided with specific operators and keywords that allow us to bypass the CLR's memory management scheme and take matters into our own hands (see Table 12-3).

Table 12-3. *Pointer-Centric C# Operators and Keywords*

Operator/Keyword	Meaning in Life
`*`	This operator is used to create a *pointer variable* (i.e., a variable that represents a direct location in memory). As in C(++), this same operator is used for pointer indirection.
`&`	This operator is used to obtain the address of a variable in memory.
`->`	This operator is used to access fields of a type that is represented by a pointer (the unsafe version of the C# dot operator).
`[]`	The `[]` operator (in an unsafe context) allows you to index the slot pointed to by a pointer variable (recall the interplay between a pointer variable and the `[]` operator in C(++)!).
`++, --`	In an unsafe context, the increment and decrement operators can be applied to pointer types.
`+, -`	In an unsafe context, the addition and subtraction operators can be applied to pointer types.
`==, !=, <, >, <=, =>`	In an unsafe context, the comparison and equality operators can be applied to pointer types.
`stackalloc`	In an unsafe context, the `stackalloc` keyword can be used to allocate C# arrays directly on the stack.
`fixed`	In an unsafe context, the `fixed` keyword can be used to temporarily fix a variable so that its address may be found.

Now, before we dig into the details, let me point out the fact that you will *seldom if ever* need to make use of pointer types. Although C# does allow you to drop down to the level of pointer manipulations, understand that the .NET runtime has absolutely no clue of your intentions. Thus, if you mismanage a pointer, you are the one in charge of dealing with the consequences. Given these warnings, when exactly would you need to work with pointer types? There are two common situations:

- You are looking to optimize select parts of your application by directly manipulating memory outside the management of the CLR.
- You are calling methods of a C-based `*.dll` or COM server that demand pointer types as parameters. Even in this case, you can often bypass the use of pointer types in favor of the `System.IntPtr` type and members of the `System.Runtime.InteropServices.Marshal` type.

In the event that you do decide to make use of this C# language feature, you will be required to inform the C# compiler (`csc.exe`) of your intentions by enabling your project to support "unsafe code." To do so at the command line, simply supply the `/unsafe` flag as an argument:

```
csc /unsafe *.cs
```

From Visual Studio 2008, you will need to access your project's Properties page and check the Allow Unsafe Code check box from the Build tab (see Figure 12-7). To experiment with pointer types, create a new Console Application project named UnsafeCode and enable unsafe code.

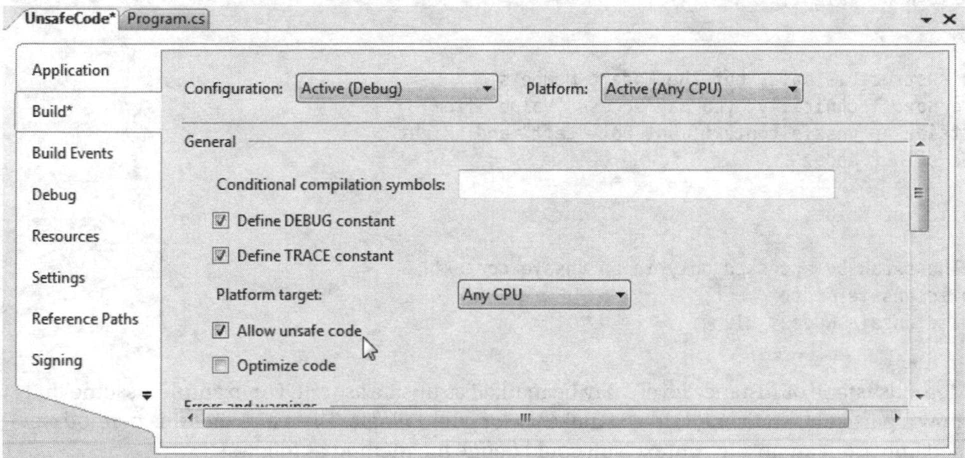

Figure 12-7. *Enabling unsafe code using Visual Studio 2008*

■ Note In the examples that follow, I'm assuming that you have some background in C(++) pointer manipulations. If this is not true in your case, feel free to skip this topic entirely. Again, writing unsafe code will not be a common task for a vast majority of C# applications.

The unsafe Keyword

When you wish to work with pointers in C#, you must specifically declare a block of "unsafe code" using the `unsafe` keyword (any code that is not marked with the `unsafe` keyword is considered "safe" automatically). For example, the following `Program` class declares a scope of unsafe code within the safe `Main()` method:

```
class Program
{
  static void Main(string[] args)
  {
    unsafe
    {
      // Work with pointer types here!
    }
    // Can't work with pointers here!
  }
}
```

In addition to declaring a scope of unsafe code within a method, you are able to build structures, classes, type members, and parameters that are "unsafe." Here are a few examples to gnaw on (no need to define these types in your current project):

```
// This entire structure is "unsafe" and can
// be used only in an unsafe context.
public unsafe struct Node
{
  public int Value;
  public Node* Left;
  public Node* Right;
}

// This struct is safe, but the Node2* members
// are not. Technically, you may access "Value" from
// outside an unsafe context, but not "Left" and "Right".
public struct Node2
{
  public int Value;

  // These can be accessed only in an unsafe context!
  public unsafe Node2* Left;
  public unsafe Node2* Right;
}
```

Methods (static or instance level) may be marked as unsafe as well. For example, assume that you know a particular static method will make use of pointer logic. To ensure that this method can be called only from an unsafe context, you could define the method as follows:

```
unsafe static void SquareIntPointer(int* myIntPointer)
{
  // Square the value just for a test.
  *myIntPointer *= *myIntPointer;
}
```

The configuration of our method demands that the caller invoke `SquareIntPointer()` as follows:

```
static void Main(string[] args)
{
  unsafe
  {
    int myInt = 10;
    // OK, because we are in an unsafe context.
    SquareIntPointer(&myInt);
    Console.WriteLine("myInt: {0}", myInt);
  }

  int myInt2 = 5;
  // Compiler error! Must be in unsafe context!
  SquareIntPointer(&myInt2);
  Console.WriteLine("myInt: {0}", myInt2);
}
```

If you would rather not force the caller to wrap the invocation within an unsafe context, you could update `Main()` with the `unsafe` keyword. In this case, the following code would compile:

```
unsafe static void Main(string[] args)
{
  int myInt2 = 5;
  SquareIntPointer(&myInt2);
  Console.WriteLine("myInt: {0}", myInt2);
}
```

Working with the * and & Operators

Once you have established an unsafe context, you are then free to build pointers to data types using the * operator and obtain the address of said pointer using the & operator. Unlike in C or C++, using C#, the * operator is applied to the underlying type only, not as a prefix to each pointer variable name. For example, consider the following code, which illustrates the correct and incorrect way to declare pointers to integer variables:

```
// No! This is incorrect under C#!
int *pi, *pj;

// Yes! This is the way of C#.
int* pi, pj;
```

Consider the following unsafe method:

```
unsafe static void PrintValueAndAddress()
{
  int myInt;

  // Define an int pointer, and
  // assign it the address of myInt.
  int* ptrToMyInt = &myInt;

  // Assign value of myInt using pointer indirection.
  *ptrToMyInt = 123;

  // Print some stats.
  Console.WriteLine("Value of myInt {0}", myInt);
  Console.WriteLine("Address of myInt {0:X}", (int)&ptrToMyInt);
}
```

An Unsafe (and Safe) Swap Function

Of course, declaring pointers to local variables simply to assign their value (as shown in the previous example) is never required and not altogether useful. To illustrate a more practical example of unsafe code, assume you wish to build a swap function using pointer arithmetic:

```
unsafe public static void UnsafeSwap(int* i, int* j)
{
  int temp = *i;
  *i = *j;
  *j = temp;
}
```

Very C-like, don't you think? However, given your work in Chapter 4 you should be aware that you could write the following safe version of your swap algorithm using the C# `ref` keyword:

```
public static void SafeSwap(ref int i, ref int j)
{
  int temp = i;
  i = j;
  j = temp;
}
```

The functionality of each method is identical, thus reinforcing the point that direct pointer manipulation is not a mandatory task under C#. Here is the calling logic using a safe `Main()`, with an unsafe context:

```
static void Main(string[] args)
{
  Console.WriteLine("***** Calling method with unsafe code *****");

  // Values for swap.
  int i = 10, j = 20;

  // Swap values "safely."
  Console.WriteLine("\n***** Safe swap *****");
  Console.WriteLine("Values before safe swap: i = {0}, j = {1}", i, j);
  SafeSwap(ref i, ref j);
  Console.WriteLine("Values after safe swap: i = {0}, j = {1}", i, j);

  // Swap values "unsafely."
  Console.WriteLine("\n***** Unsafe swap *****");
  Console.WriteLine("Values before unsafe swap: i = {0}, j = {1}", i, j);
  unsafe { UnsafeSwap(&i, &j); }
  Console.WriteLine("Values after unsafe swap: i = {0}, j = {1}", i, j);
  Console.ReadLine();
}
```

Field Access via Pointers (the -> Operator)

Now assume that you have defined a simple safe `Point` structure as follows:

```
struct Point
{
  public int x;
  public int y;
  public override string ToString()
  { return string.Format("({0}, {1})", x, y);}
}
```

If you declare a pointer to a `Point` type, you will need to make use of the pointer-field access operator (represented by `->`) to access its public members. As shown in Table 12-3, this is the unsafe version of the standard (safe) dot operator (`.`). In fact, using the pointer indirection operator (*), it is possible to dereference a pointer to (once again) apply the dot operator notation. Check out the unsafe method:

```
unsafe static void UsePointerToPoint()
{
  // Access members via pointer.
  Point point;
  Point* p = &point;
  p->x = 100;
  p->y = 200;
  Console.WriteLine(p->ToString());
```

```
  // Access members via pointer indirection.
  Point point2;
  Point* p2 = &point2;
  (*p2).x = 100;
  (*p2).y = 200;
  Console.WriteLine((*p2).ToString());
}
```

The stackalloc Keyword

In an unsafe context, you may need to declare a local variable that allocates memory directly from the call stack (and is therefore not subject to .NET garbage collection). To do so, C# provides the `stackalloc` keyword, which is the C# equivalent to the `_alloca` function of the C runtime library. Here is a simple example:

```
unsafe  static void UnsafeStackAlloc()
{
  char* p = stackalloc char[256];
  for (int k = 0; k < 256; k++)
    p[k] = (char)k;
}
```

Pinning a Type via the fixed Keyword

As you saw in the previous example, allocating a chunk of memory within an unsafe context may be facilitated via the `stackalloc` keyword. By the very nature of this operation, the allocated memory is cleaned up as soon as the allocating method has returned (as the memory is acquired from the stack). However, assume a more complex example. During our examination of the `->` operator, you created a value type named `Point`. Like all value types, the allocated memory is popped off the stack once the executing scope has terminated. For the sake of argument, assume `Point` was instead defined as a *reference* type:

```
class PointRef  // <= Renamed and retyped.
{
  public int x;
  public int y;
  public override string ToString()
  { return string.Format("({0}, {1})", x, y);}
}
```

As you are well aware, if the caller declares a variable of type `Point`, the memory is allocated on the garbage-collected heap. The burning question then becomes, "What if an unsafe context wishes to interact with this object (or any object on the heap)?" Given that garbage collection can occur at any moment, imagine the problems encountered when accessing the members of `Point` at the very point in time at which a sweep of the heap is under way. Theoretically, it is possible that the unsafe context is attempting to interact with a member that is no longer accessible or has been repositioned on the heap after surviving a generational sweep (which is an obvious problem).

To lock a reference type variable in memory from an unsafe context, C# provides the `fixed` keyword. The `fixed` statement sets a pointer to a managed type and "pins" that variable during the execution of statement. Without `fixed`, pointers to managed variables would be of little use, since garbage collection could relocate the variables unpredictably. (In fact, the C# compiler will not allow you to set a pointer to a managed variable except in a `fixed` statement.)

Thus, if you create a Point type (now redesigned as a class) and want to interact with its members, you must write the following code (or receive a compiler error):

```
unsafe public static void UseAndPinPoint()
{
  PointRef pt = new PointRef ();
  pt.x = 5;
  pt.y = 6;

  // pin pt in place so it will not
  // be moved or GC-ed.
  fixed (int* p = &pt.x)
  {
    // Use int* variable here!
  }

  // pt is now unpinned, and ready to be GC-ed.
  Console.WriteLine ("Point is: {0}", pt);
}
```

In a nutshell, the fixed keyword allows you to build a statement that locks a reference variable in memory, such that its address remains constant for the duration of the statement. To be sure, any time you interact with a reference type from within the context of unsafe code, pinning the reference is a must.

The sizeof Keyword

The final unsafe-centric C# keyword to consider is sizeof. As in C(++), the C# sizeof keyword is used to obtain the size in bytes for a value type (never a reference type), and it may only be used within an unsafe context. As you may imagine, this ability may prove helpful when you're interacting with unmanaged C-based APIs. Its usage is straightforward:

```
unsafe static void UseSizeOfOperator()
{
  Console.WriteLine("The size of short is {0}.", sizeof(short));
  Console.WriteLine("The size of int is {0}.", sizeof(int));
  Console.WriteLine("The size of long is {0}.", sizeof(long));
}
```

As sizeof will evaluate the number of bytes for any System.ValueType-derived entity, you are able to obtain the size of custom structures as well. For example, we could pass the Point structure into sizeof as follows:

```
unsafe static void UseSizeOfOperator()
{
...
  Console.WriteLine("The size of Point is {0}.", sizeof(Point));
}
```

■ **Source Code** The UnsafeCode project can be found under the Chapter 12 subdirectory.

C# Preprocessor Directives

Like many other languages in the C family, C# supports the use of various symbols that allow you to interact with the compilation process. Before examining various C# preprocessor directives, let's get our terminology correct. The term "C# preprocessor directive" is not entirely accurate. In reality, this term is used only for consistency with the C and C++ programming languages. In C#, there is no separate preprocessing step. Rather, preprocessing directives are processed as part of the lexical analysis phase of the compiler.

In any case, the syntax of the C# preprocessor directives is very similar to that of the other members of the C family, in that the directives are always prefixed with the pound sign (#). Table 12-4 defines some of the more commonly used directives (consult the .NET Framework 3.5 SDK documentation for complete details).

Table 12-4. *Common C# Preprocessor Directives*

Directives	Meaning in Life
`#region, #endregion`	Used to mark sections of collapsible source code
`#define, #undef`	Used to define and undefine conditional compilation symbols
`#if, #elif, #else, #endif`	Used to conditionally skip sections of source code (based on specified compilation symbols)

Specifying Code Regions

Perhaps some of the most useful of all preprocessor directives are `#region` and `#endregion`. Using these tags, you are able to specify a block of code that may be hidden from view and identified by a friendly textual marker. Use of regions can help keep lengthy `*.cs` files more manageable. For example, you could create one region for a type's constructors, another for type properties, and so forth:

```
class Car
{
  private string petName;
  private int currSp;

  #region Constructors
  public Car()
  { ... }
  public Car (int currSp, string petName)
  { ... }
  #endregion

  #region Properties
  public int Speed
  { ... }
  public string Name
  { ... }
  #endregion
}
```

When you place your mouse cursor over a collapsed region, you are provided with a snapshot of the code lurking behind (see Figure 12-8).

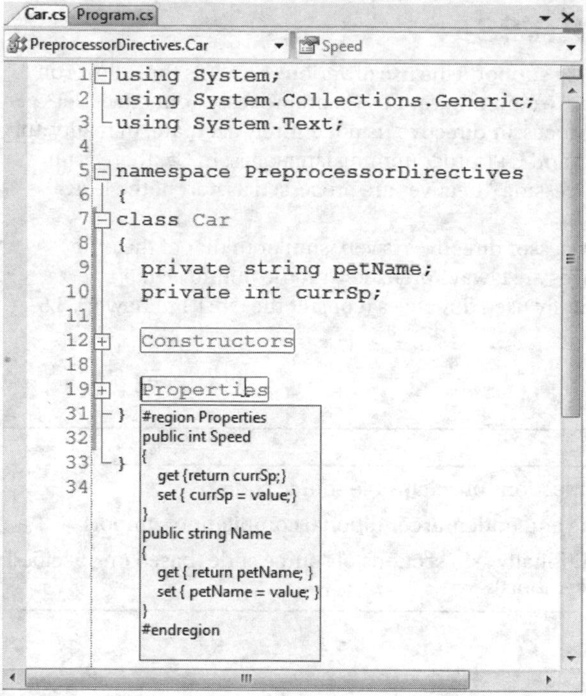

Figure 12-8. *Regions at work*

Conditional Code Compilation

The next batch of preprocessor directives (`#if`, `#elif`, `#else`, `#endif`) allows you to conditionally compile a block of code, based on predefined symbols. The classic use of these directives is to identify a block of code that is compiled only under a debug (rather than a release) build:

```
class Program
{
  static void Main(string[] args)
  {
    #region Print machine info under DEBUG build
    // This code will only execute if the project is
    // compiled as a debug build.
    #if DEBUG
    Console.WriteLine("App directory: {0}",
      Environment.CurrentDirectory);
    Console.WriteLine("Box: {0}",
      Environment.MachineName);
    Console.WriteLine("OS: {0}",
      Environment.OSVersion);
    Console.WriteLine(".NET Version: {0}",
      Environment.Version);
    #endif
    #endregion
  }
}
```

Here, you are checking for a symbol named DEBUG. If it is present, you dump out a number of interesting statistics using some static members of the System.Environment class. If the DEBUG symbol is not defined, the code placed between #if and #endif will not be compiled into the resulting assembly, and it will be effectively ignored.

Note The System.Diagnostics namespace provides the [Conditional] attribute, which can be applied to a class or method. Chapter 16 will explain the role of attributes in detail; however, for now, simply know that if you use [Conditional], you are not required to use the related preprocessor symbols.

By default, Visual Studio 2008 always defines a DEBUG symbol; however, this can be prevented by deselecting the Define DEBUG constant check box option located under the Build tab of your project's Properties page. Assuming you did disable this autogenerated DEBUG symbol, you could now define this symbol on a file-by-file basis using the #define preprocessor directive:

```
#define DEBUG
using System;

namespace PreprocessorDirectives
{
  class Program
  {
    static void Main(string[] args)
    {
      // Same code as before...
    }
  }
}
```

Note #define directives must be listed before anything else in a C# code file.

You are also able to define your own custom preprocessor symbols. For example, assume you have authored a C# class that should be compiled a bit differently under the Mono distribution of .NET (see Appendix B). Using #define, you can define a symbol named MONO_BUILD on a file-by-file basis:

```
#define DEBUG
#define MONO_BUILD

using System;

namespace PreprocessorDirectives
{
  class Program
  {
    static void Main(string[] args)
    {
      #if MONO_BUILD
        Console.WriteLine("Compiling under Mono!");
      #else
        Console.WriteLine("Compiling under Microsoft .NET");
```

```
        #endif
    }
  }
}
```

To create a project-wide symbol, make use of the Conditional compilation symbols text box located on the Build tab of your project's Properties page (see Figure 12-9).

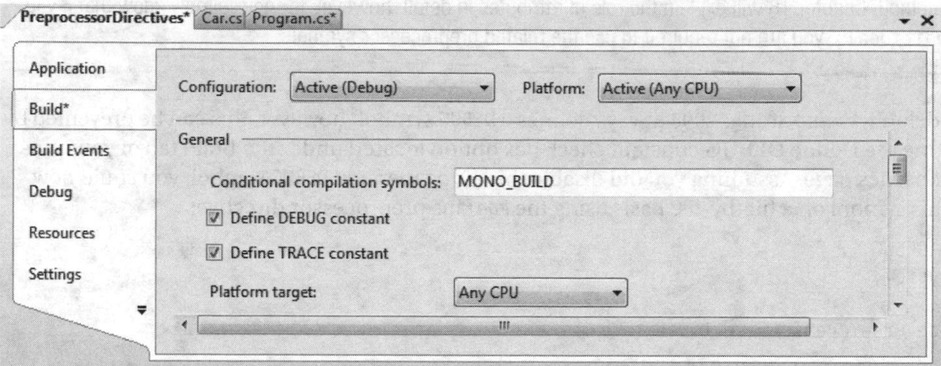

Figure 12-9. *Defining a projectwide preprocessor symbol*

■ **Source Code** The PreprocessorDirectives project can be found under the Chapter 12 subdirectory.

Summary

The purpose of this chapter is to deepen your understanding of the C# programming language. You began by investigating various advanced type construction techniques (indexer methods, overloaded operators, and custom conversion routines). You spent the remainder of this chapter examining a small set of lesser-known keywords (e.g., `sizeof`, `checked`, `unsafe`, and so forth), and during the process came to learn how to work with raw pointer types. As stated throughout the chapter's examination of pointer types, a vast majority of your C# applications will *never* need to make use of them.

We wrapped up with an examination of the core C# preprocessor directives, which allow you to interact with the compiler (or in the case of `#region`/`#endregion`, Visual Studio 2008) regarding the compilation of your code files.

CHAPTER 13

C# 2008 Language Features

C# 2008, the current release of Microsoft's flagship .NET programming language, introduces a large number of new syntactic constructs, one of which (the lambda operator) you have already explored in Chapter 11. This chapter will complete your investigation of the new language features offered by C# 2008. Specifically, you will examine implicit data typing, automatic properties, extension methods, partial methods, object initializers, and the role of anonymous types.

While many of these new language features can be used directly out of the box to help build robust and highly functional .NET software, it is also worth pointing out that many of these new constructs are most helpful when interacting with the LINQ technology set, which you'll begin to examine in Chapter 14. Given this fact, don't be too concerned if the usefulness of some of these new constructs is not immediately obvious. Once you understand the role of LINQ, the role of many of these new features will become crystal clear.

Understanding Implicitly Typed Local Variables

The first new language feature of C# 2008 we will examine is the *implicit typing* of local variables, using a new Console Application aptly named ImplicitlyTypedLocalVars. As you have learned since the very beginning of this text, local variables (such as variables declared in a method scope) are declared in a very predictable (and *explicit*) manner:

```
static void DeclareExplicitVars()
{
  // Explicitly typed local variables
  // are declared as follows:
  // dataType variableName = initialValue;
  int myInt = 0;
  bool myBool = true;
  string myString = "Time, marches on...";
}
```

C# 2008 now provides a new keyword, `var`, which you can use in place of specifying a formal data type (such as `int`, `bool`, or `string`). When you do so, the compiler will automatically infer the underlying data type based on the initial value used to initialize the local data point. For example, the previous variables can now be declared as follows:

```
static void DeclareImplicitVars()
{
  // Implicitly typed local variables
  // are declared as follows:
  // var variableName = initialValue;
```

```
  var myInt = 0;
  var myBool = true;
  var myString = "Time, marches on...";
}
```

Note Strictly speaking, var is not a C# keyword. It is permissible to declare variables, parameters, and fields named "var" without compile-time errors. However, when the var token is used as a data type, it is contextually treated as a keyword by the compiler. For simplicity, I will use the term "var keyword," rather than the more cumbersome "contextual var token."

In this case, the compiler is able to infer that myInt is in fact a System.Int32, myBool is a System.Boolean, and myString is indeed of type System.String, given the initially assigned value. You can verify this by printing out the type name via reflection:

```
static void DeclareImplicitVars()
{
  // Implicitly typed local variables.
  var myInt = 0;
  var myBool = true;
  var myString = "Time, marches on...";

  // Print out the underlying type.
  Console.WriteLine("myInt is a: {0}", myInt.GetType().Name);
  Console.WriteLine("myBool is a: {0}", myBool.GetType().Name);
  Console.WriteLine("myString is a: {0}", myString.GetType().Name);
}
```

Be aware that you can use this implicit typing for any type including arrays, generic types, and your own custom types:

```
static void DeclareImplicitVars()
{
...
  // More implicitly typed local variables.
  var evenNumbers = new int[] { 2, 4, 6, 8 };
  var myMinivans = new List<MiniVan>();
  var myCar = new SportsCar();

  Console.WriteLine("evenNumbers is a: {0}", evenNumbers.GetType().Name);
  Console.WriteLine("myMinivans is a: {0}", myMinivans.GetType().Name);
  Console.WriteLine("myCar is a: {0}", myCar.GetType().Name);
}
```

If you were to call the DeclareImplicitVars() method from within Main(), you'd find the output shown in Figure 13-1.

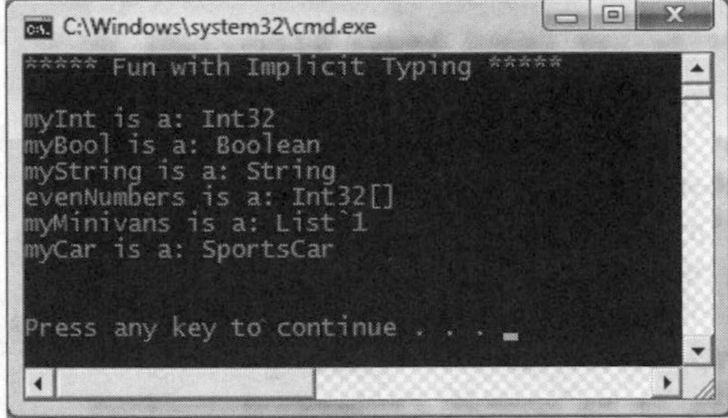

Figure 13-1. *Reflecting over implicitly defined local variables*

Use of var Within foreach Constructs

It is also possible to make use of implicit typing within a `foreach` looping construct. As you would expect, the compiler will correctly infer the correct "type of type." Consider the following method, which iterates over an implicitly typed local array of integers:

```
static void VarInForeachLoop()
{
  var evenNumbers = new int[] { 2, 4, 6, 8 };

  // Use "var" in a standard foreach loop.
  foreach (var item in evenNumbers)
  {
    Console.WriteLine("Item value: {0}", item);
  }
}
```

Understand, however, that a `foreach` loop can make use of a strongly typed iterator when processing an implicitly defined local array. Thus, the following code is also syntactically correct:

```
static void VarInForeachLoop()
{
  var evenNumbers = new int[] { 2, 4, 6, 8 };

  // Use a strongly typed System.Int32 to iterate over contents.
  foreach (int item in evenNumbers)
  {
    Console.WriteLine("Item value: {0}", item);
  }
}
```

Restrictions on Implicitly Typed Variables

There are, of course, various restrictions regarding the use of the `var` keyword. First and foremost, implicit typing applies *only* to local variables in a method or property scope. It is illegal to use the `var` keyword to define return values, parameters, or field data of a type:

```
class ThisWillNeverCompile
{
  // Error! var cannot be used as field data!
  private var myInt = 10;
```

```
  // Error! var cannot be used as a return value
  // or parameter type!
  public var MyMethod(var x, var y){}
}
```

As well, local variables declared with the var keyword *must* be assigned an initial value at the exact time of declaration and *cannot* be assigned the initial value of null. The first restriction makes the act of defining an implicitly typed variable look and feel like the process of defining a constant data point with the const keyword (see Chapter 5). This last restriction should make sense, given that the compiler cannot infer what sort of type in memory the variable would be pointing to based only on null:

```
// Error! Must assign a value!
var myData;

// Error! Must assign value at exact time of declaration!
var myInt;
myInt = 0;

// Error! Can't assign null as initial value!
var myObj = null;
```

It is permissible, however, to assign an inferred local variable to null after its initial assignment (provided it is a reference type):

```
// OK, is SportsCar is a reference type!
var myCar = new SportsCar();
myCar = null;
```

Furthermore, it is permissible to assign the value of an implicitly typed local variable to the value of other variables, implicitly typed or not:

```
// Also OK!
var myInt = 0;
var anotherInt = myInt;

string myString = "Wake up!";
var myData = myString;
```

As well, it is permissible to return an implicitly typed local variable to the caller, provided that the method return type is the same underlying type as the var-defined data point:

```
static int GetAnInt()
{
  var retVal = 9;
  return retVal;
}
```

Last but not least, be aware that it is illegal to define a nullable implicitly typed local variable using the C# ? token (see Chapter 4 for details on nullable data types):

```
// Nope, can't define nullable implicit variables,
// as implicit variables can never be initially assigned
// null to begin with!
var? nope = new SportsCar();
var? stillNo = 12;
var? noWay = null;
```

Implicitly Typed Local Arrays

Closely related to the topic of implicitly typed local variables is the subject of *implicitly typed local arrays*. Using this technique, you can allocate a new array type without specifying the type contained within the array itself:

```
static void DeclareImplicitArrays()
{
  // a is really int[].
  var a = new[] { 1, 10, 100, 1000 };
  Console.WriteLine("a is a: {0}", a.ToString());

  // b is really double[].
  var b = new[] { 1, 1.5, 2, 2.5 };
  Console.WriteLine("b is a: {0}", b.ToString());

  // c is really string[].
  var c = new[] { "hello", null, "world" };
  Console.WriteLine("c is a: {0}", c.ToString());

  // myCars is really SportsCar[].
  var myCars = new[] { new SportsCar(), new SportsCar() };
  Console.WriteLine("myCars is a: {0}", myCars.ToString());
  Console.WriteLine();
}
```

Of course, just as when you allocate an array using explicit C# syntax, the items in the array's initialization list must be of the same underlying type (all ints, all strings, all SportsCars, etc.). Unlike what you might be expecting, an implicitly typed local array does not default to System.Object; thus the following generates a compile-time error:

```
// Error! Mixed types!
var d = new[] { 1, "one", 2, "two", false };
```

Implicit Typed Data Is Strongly Typed Data

Be very aware that implicit typing of local variables results in *strongly typed data*. Therefore, use of the var keyword is *not* the same technique used with scripting languages (such as VBScript or Perl) or the COM Variant data type, where a variable can hold values of different types over its lifetime in a program (often termed "dynamic typing").

Rather, type inference keeps the strongly typed aspect of the C# language and affects only the declaration of variables at compile time. After that point, the data point is treated as if it were declared with that type; assigning a value of a different type into that variable will result in a compile-time error:

```
static void ImplicitTypingIsStrongTyping()
{
  // The compiler knows "s" is a System.String.
  var s = "This variable can only hold string data!";
  s = "This is fine...";

  // Can invoke any member of the underlying type.
  string upper = s.ToUpper();

  // Error! Can't assign numerical data to a a string!
  s = 44;
}
```

Usefulness of Implicitly Typed Local Variables

Now that you have seen the syntax used to declare implicitly typed local variables, I am sure you are wondering when to make use of this construct? First and foremost, using var to declare local variables simply for the sake of doing so really brings little to the table. Doing so can be confusing to others reading your code, as it becomes harder to quickly determine the underlying data type (and therefore more difficult to understand the overall functionality of the variable). Therefore, if you know you need an int, declare an int!

However, as you will see beginning in Chapter 14, the LINQ technology set makes use of *query expressions* that can yield dynamically created result sets based on the format of the query itself. In these cases, implicit typing is extremely helpful, as we do not need to explicitly define the type that a query may return, which in some cases would be literally impossible to do. Don't get hung up on the following LINQ example code; however, see if you can figure out the underlying data type of subset:

```
static void QueryOverInts()
{
  int[] numbers = { 10, 20, 30, 40, 1, 2, 3, 8 };
  var subset = from i in numbers where i < 10 select i;

  Console.Write("Values in subset: ");
  foreach (var i in subset)
  {
    Console.Write("{0} ", i);
  }
  Console.WriteLine();

  // Hmm...what type is subset?
  Console.WriteLine("subset is a: {0}", subset.GetType().Name);
  Console.WriteLine("subset is defined in: {0}", subset.GetType().Namespace);
}
```

I'll let the interested reader verify the type-of-type of subset by executing the preceding code (and it is not an array of integers!). In any case, it should be clear that implicit typing does have its place within the LINQ technology set. In fact, it could be argued that the *only* time one would make use of the var keyword is when defining data returned from a LINQ query.

■ **Source Code** The ImplicitlyTypedLocalVars project can be found under the Chapter 13 subdirectory.

Understanding Automatic Properties

As you learned in Chapter 5 during our examination of encapsulation services, .NET programming languages prefer the use of type properties to safely obtain and assign private data fields of a type, rather than using traditional Get*XXX*() and Set*XXX*() methods. Consider the following encapsulated string type:

```
// A Car type using standard property
// syntax.
class Car
{
  private string carName = string.Empty;
  public int PetName
```

```
  {
    get { return carName; }
    set { carName = value; }
  }
}
```

While defining a C# property is not too problematic, you may agree that when your properties simply assign and return the value straightaway as you see here, it is rather verbose to define backing fields and simple property definitions multiple times. By way of an example, if you are modeling a type that requires 15 private points of field data, you end up authoring 15 related properties that are little more than thin wrappers for encapsulation services.

To streamline the process of providing simple encapsulation of field data, C# 2008 now provides *automatic property syntax*. As the name implies, this feature will offload the work of defining a private backing field and the related C# property member to the compiler using a new bit of syntax. To illustrate, under C# 2008, the previous `Car` type could now be defined as follows:

```
class Car
{
  // Automatic property syntax.
  public string PetName { get; set; }
}
```

Note The Visual Studio 2008 "Prop" code snippet has been rewritten to make use of automatic property syntax, rather than the traditional C# property logic (see Chapter 2 for an explanation of code snippets).

At first glance, automatic property syntax might seem as if you were defining an abstract property to be overridden by derived types, given the presence of unimplemented `get` and `set` scopes. However, this is not the case. If you did intend to define an abstract property in the `Car` type, you would need to make use of the C# `abstract` keyword as follows:

```
abstract class Car
{
  // Abstract property in an abstract base class.
  public abstract string PetName { get; set; }
}
```

When defining automatic properties, you simply specify the access modifier, underlying data type, property name, and empty get/set scopes. At compile time, your type will be provided with an autogenerated private backing field and a fitting implementation of the get/set logic.

Note The name of the autogenerated private backing field is not visible within your C# code base. The only way to see it is to make use of a tool such as `ildasm.exe`.

Unlike traditional C# properties, however, it is *not* possible to build read-only or write-only automatic properties. While you might think you can just omit the `get;` or `set;` within your property declaration as follows:

```
// Read-only property? Error!
public int MyReadOnlyProp { get; }

// Write only property? Error!
public int MyWriteOnlyProp { set; }
```

this will result in a compiler error. When you are defining an automatic property, it must support both read and write functionality.

Interacting with Automatic Properties

Because the compiler will define the private backing field at compile time, the class defining automatic properties will always need to use property syntax to get and set the underlying value. This is important to note because many programmers make direct use of the private fields *within* a class definition, which is not possible in this case. For example, if the Car type were to override ToString(), you would need to implement this method using the property name:

```
class Car
{
  public string PetName { get; set; }

  public override string ToString()
  {
    // No access to the private member in the defining
    // class. Must use properties!
    return string.Format("PetName = {0}", PetName);
  }
}
```

When you are using an object defined with automatic properties, you will be able to assign and obtain the values using the expected property syntax:

```
static void Main(string[] args)
{
  Console.WriteLine("***** Fun with Automatic Properties *****");
  Car c = new Car();
  c.PetName = "Frank";
  Console.WriteLine("Your car is named {0}?  That's odd...",
    c.PetName);
  Console.ReadLine();
}
```

Restricting Access on Automatic Properties

Recall that a "normal" .NET property can be constructed in such a way that the get and set logic is assigned a unique access modifier. For example, it is possible to define a public get scope and a more restrictive protected scope as follows:

```
// Anyone can get the PetName value, but
// only the defining type and the children can set it.
public int PetName
{
  get { return carName; }
  protected set { carName = value; }
}
```

This same possibility is allowed using automatic property syntax as follows:

```
public string PetName { get; protected set; }
```

Of course, with this update, the previous Main() method would now generate a compiler error when attempting to assign the value of the PetName property:

```
static void Main(string[] args)
{
  ...
  // Error! Setting the PetName is only possible
  // from within the Car type or by a child type!
  c.PetName = "Frank";

  // Getting the value is still OK.
  Console.WriteLine("Your car is named {0}?  That's odd...",
    c.PetName);
  Console.ReadLine();
}
```

Regarding Automatic Properties and Default Values

When you use automatic properties to encapsulate numerical or Boolean data, you are able to use the autogenerated type properties straightaway within your code base, as the hidden backing fields will be assigned a safe default value that can be used directly. However, be very aware that if you use automatic property syntax to wrap a reference type, the hidden private reference type will also be set to a default value of `null`:

```
class Garage
{
  // The hidden int backing field is set to zero!
  public int NumberOfCars { get; set; }

  // The hidden Car backing field is set to null!
  public Car MyAuto { get; set; }
}
```

Given C#'s default values for field data, you would be able to print out the value of `NumberOfCars` as is (as it is automatically assigned the value of zero), but if you directly invoke `MyAuto`, you will receive a null reference exception:

```
static void Main(string[] args)
{
  ...
  Garage g = new Garage();

  // OK, prints defualt value of zero.
  Console.WriteLine("Number of Cars: {0}", g.NumberOfCars);

  // Runtime error! Backing field is currently null!
  Console.WriteLine(g.MyAuto.PetName);
  Console.ReadLine();
}
```

Given that the private backing fields are created at compile time, you will be unable to make use of C# field initialization syntax to allocate the reference type directly with the `new` keyword. Therefore, this work will need to be done with type constructors to ensure the object comes to life in a safe manner. For example:

```
class Garage
{
  // The hidden backing field is set to zero!
  public int NumberOfCars { get; set; }
```

```
  // The hidden backing field is set to null!
  public Car MyAuto { get; set; }

  // Must use constructors to override default
  // values assigned to hidden backing fields.
  public Garage()
  {
    MyAuto = new Car();
    NumberOfCars = 1;
  }
  public Garage(Car car, int number)
  {
    MyAuto = car;
    NumberOfCars = number;
  }
}
```

As you most likely agree, this is a very nice extension to the C# programming language, as you can define a number of properties for a class using a streamlined syntax. Be aware of course that if you are building a property that requires additional code beyond getting and setting the underlying private field (such as data validation logic, writing to an event log, communicating with a database, etc.), you will be required to define a "normal" .NET property type by hand. C# 2008 automatic properties never do more than provide simple encapsulation for an underlying data type.

■ **Source Code** The AutomaticProperties project can be found under the Chapter 13 subdirectory.

Understanding Extension Methods

The next C# 2008 language feature we will examine is the use of *extension methods*. As you know, once a type is defined and compiled into a .NET assembly, its definition is, more or less, final. The only way to add new members, update members, or remove members is to recode and recompile the code base into an updated assembly (or take more drastic measures, such as using the `System.Reflection.Emit` namespace to dynamically reshape a compiled type in memory).

Under C# 2008, it is now possible to define extension methods. In a nutshell, extension methods allow existing compiled types (specifically, classes, structures, or interface implementations) as well as types currently being compiled (such as types in a project that contains extension methods) to gain new functionality without needing to directly update the type being extended.

This technique can be quite helpful when you need to inject new functionality into types for which you do not have an existing code base. It can also be quite helpful when you need to force a type to support a set of members (in the interest of polymorphism), but cannot modify the original type declaration. Using extension methods, you can add functionality to precompiled types while providing the illusion these methods were there all along.

■ **Note** Understand that extension methods do not literally change the compiled code base! This technique only adds members to a type within the context of the current application.

When you define extension methods, the first restriction is that they must be defined within a *static class* (see Chapter 5), and therefore each extension method must also be declared with the static keyword. The second point is that all extension methods are marked as such by using the this keyword as a modifier on the first (and only the first) parameter of the method in question. The third point is that every extension method can be called either from the correct instance in memory or *statically* via the defining static class! Sound strange? Let's look at a full example to clarify matters.

Defining Extension Methods

Create a new Console Application named ExtensionMethods. Now, assume you are authoring a utility class named MyExtensions that defines two extension methods. The first method allows any object in the .NET base class libraries to have a brand-new method named DisplayDefiningAssembly() that makes use of types in the System.Reflection namespace to display the assembly of the specified type.

The second extension method, named ReverseDigits(), allows any System.Int32 to obtain a new version of itself where the value is reversed digit by digit. For example, if an integer with the value 1234 called ReverseDigits(), the integer returned is set to the value 4321. Consider the following class implementation:

```
static class MyExtensions
{
  // This method allows any object to display the assembly
  // it is defined in.
  public static void DisplayDefiningAssembly(this object obj)
  {
    Console.WriteLine("{0} lives here:\n\t->{1}\n", obj.GetType().Name,
      Assembly.GetAssembly(obj.GetType()));
  }

  // This method allows any integer to reverse its digits.
  // For example, 56 would return 65.
  public static int ReverseDigits(this int i)
  {
    // Translate int into a string, and then
    // get all the characters.
    char[] digits = i.ToString().ToCharArray();

    // Now reverse items in the array.
    Array.Reverse(digits);

    // Put back into string.
    string newDigits = new string(digits);

    // Finally, return the modified string back as an int.
    return int.Parse(newDigits);
  }
}
```

Again, note how the first parameter of each extension method has been qualified with the this keyword, before defining the parameter type. It is always the case that the first parameter of an extension method represents the type being extended. Given that DisplayDefiningAssembly() has been prototyped to extend System.Object, any type in any assembly now has this new member. However, ReverseDigits() has been prototyped to only extend integer types, and therefore if anything other than an integer attempts to invoke this method, you will receive a compile-time error.

Understand that a given extension method could have multiple parameters, but *only* the first parameter can be qualified with this. For example, here is an overloaded extension method defined in another utility class, named simply TesterUtilClass:

```
static class TesterUtilClass
{
  // Every Int32 now has a Foo() method...
  public static void Foo(this int i)
  { Console.WriteLine("{0} called the Foo() method.", i); }

  // ...which has been overloaded to take a string!
  public static void Foo(this int i, string msg)
  { Console.WriteLine("{0} called Foo() and told me: {1}", i, msg); }
}
```

Invoking Extension Methods on an Instance Level

Now that we have these extension methods, look at how all objects (which of course means everything in the .NET base class libraries) have a new method named `DisplayDefiningAssembly()`, while `System.Int32` types (and only integers) have methods named `ReverseDigits()` and `Foo()`:

```
static void Main(string[] args)
{
  Console.WriteLine("***** Fun with Extension Methods *****\n");

  // The int has assumed a new identity!
  int myInt = 12345678;
  myInt.DisplayDefiningAssembly();

  // So has the DataSet!
  System.Data.DataSet d = new System.Data.DataSet();
  d.DisplayDefiningAssembly();

  // And the SoundPlayer!
  System.Media.SoundPlayer sp = new System.Media.SoundPlayer();
  sp.DisplayDefiningAssembly();

  // Use new integer functionality.
  Console.WriteLine("Value of myInt: {0}", myInt);
  Console.WriteLine("Reversed digits of myInt: {0}", myInt.ReverseDigits());
  myInt.Foo();
  myInt.Foo("Ints that Foo?  Who would have thought it!");

  bool b2 = true;

  // Error! Booleans don't have the Foo() method!
  // b2.Foo();

  Console.ReadLine();
}
```

Figure 13-2 shows the output.

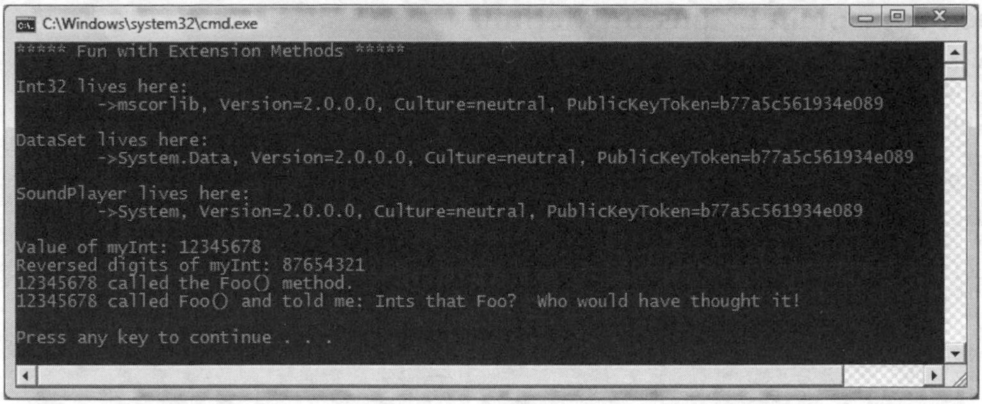

```
C:\Windows\system32\cmd.exe
***** Fun with Extension Methods *****

Int32 lives here:
        ->mscorlib, Version=2.0.0.0, Culture=neutral, PublicKeyToken=b77a5c561934e089

DataSet lives here:
        ->System.Data, Version=2.0.0.0, Culture=neutral, PublicKeyToken=b77a5c561934e089

SoundPlayer lives here:
        ->System, Version=2.0.0.0, Culture=neutral, PublicKeyToken=b77a5c561934e089

Value of myInt: 12345678
Reversed digits of myInt: 87654321
12345678 called the Foo() method.
12345678 called Foo() and told me: Ints that Foo?  Who would have thought it!

Press any key to continue . . .
```

Figure 13-2. *Extension methods in action*

Invoking Extension Methods Statically

Recall that the first parameter of an extension method is marked with the `this` keyword, followed by the type of item the method is applicable to. If we peek at what is happening behind the scenes (as verified by a tool such as `ildasm.exe`), we will find that the compiler simply calls the "normal" static method, passing in the variable calling the method as a parameter (e.g., it is the value of `this`). Consider the following C# code, which approximates the code substitution that took place:

```
private static void Main(string[] args)
{
  Console.WriteLine("***** Fun with Extension Methods *****\n");
  int myInt = 12345678;
  MyExtensions.DisplayDefiningAssembly(myInt);

  DataSet d = new DataSet();
  MyExtensions.DisplayDefiningAssembly(d);

  SoundPlayer sp = new SoundPlayer();
  MyExtensions.DisplayDefiningAssembly(sp);

  Console.WriteLine("Value of myInt: {0}", myInt);
  Console.WriteLine("Reversed digits of myInt: {0}",
    MyExtensions.ReverseDigits(myInt));
  TesterUtilClass.Foo(myInt);
  TesterUtilClass.Foo(myInt, "Ints that Foo?  Who would have thought it!");
  Console.ReadLine();
}
```

Given that calling an extension method from an object (thereby making it seem that the method is in fact an instance-level method) is just some smoke-and-mirrors effect provided by the compiler, you are always free to call extension methods as normal static methods using the expected C# syntax (as just shown).

The Scope of an Extension Method

As just explained, extension methods are essentially static methods that can be invoked from an instance of the extended type. Given this flavor of syntactic sugar, it is really important to point out that unlike a "normal" method, extension methods do not have direct access to the members of the type they are extending; said another way, *extending* is not *inheriting*. Consider the following simple Car type:

```
public class Car
{
  public int Speed;
  public int SpeedUp()
  {
    return ++Speed;
  }
}
```

If you were to build an extension method for the Car type named SlowDown(), you do not have direct access to the members of Car within the scope of the extension method as we are not performing an act of classical inheritance. Therefore, the following would result in a compiler error:

```
public static class CarExtensions
{
  public static int SlowDown(this Car c)
  {
    // Error! This method is not deriving from Car!
    return --Speed;
  }
}
```

The problem here is that the static SlowDown() extension method is attempting to access the Speed field of the Car type; however, because SlowDown() is a static member of the CarExtensions class, Speed does not exist in this context! What is permissible, however, is to make use of the this-qualified parameter to access all public members (and *only* the public members) of the type being extending. Thus, the following code compiles as expected:

```
public static class CarExtensions
{
  public static int SlowDown(this Car c)
  {
    // OK!
    return --c.Speed;
  }
}
```

At this point, you could create a Car object and invoke the SpeedUp() and SlowDown() methods as follows:

```
static void UseCar()
{
  Car c = new Car();
  Console.WriteLine("Speed: {0}", c.SpeedUp());
  Console.WriteLine("Speed: {0}", c.SlowDown());
}
```

Importing Types That Define Extension Methods

When you partition a set of static classes containing extension methods in a unique namespace, other namespaces in that assembly will make use of the standard C# `using` keyword to import not only the static classes themselves, but also each of the supported extension methods. This is important to remember, because if you do not explicitly import the correct namespace, the extension methods are not available for that C# code file.

In effect, although it can appear on the surface that extension methods are global in nature, they are in fact limited to the namespaces that define them or the namespaces that import them. Thus, if we wrap the definitions of our static classes (`MyExtensions`, `TesterUtilClass`, and `CarExtensions`) into a namespace named `MyExtensionMethods` as follows:

```
namespace MyExtensionMethods
{
  static class MyExtensions
  {
    ...
  }

  static class TesterUtilClass
  {
    ...
  }

  static class CarExtensions
  {
    ...
  }
}
```

other namespaces in the project would need to explicitly import the `MyExtensionMethods` namespace to gain the extension methods defined by these types. Therefore, the following is a compiler error:

```
// Here is our only using directive.
using System;

namespace MyNewApp
{
  class JustATest
  {
    void SomeMethod()
    {
      // Error! Need to import MyExtensionMethods
      // namespace to extend int with Foo()!
      int i = 0;
      i.Foo();
    }
  }
}
```

The IntelliSense of Extension Methods

Given the fact that extension methods are not literally defined on the type being extended, it is certainly possible to become confused when examining an existing code base. For example, assume you have imported a namespace that defined some number of extension methods authored by a teammate. As you are authoring your code, you might create a variable of the extended type, apply the dot operator, and find dozens of new methods that are not members of the original class definition!

Thankfully, Visual Studio's IntelliSense mechanism marks all extension methods with a unique "downward arrow" icon (see Figure 13-3), which appears blue on your screen.

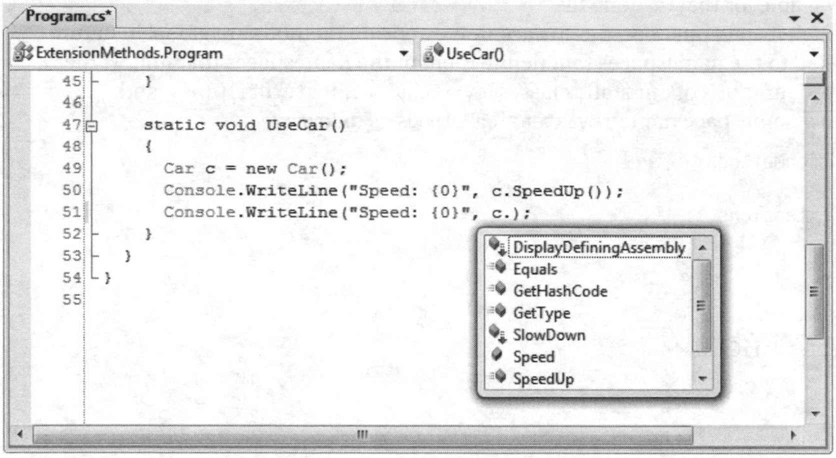

```
static void UseCar()
{
  Car c = new Car();
  Console.WriteLine("Speed: {0}", c.SpeedUp());
  Console.WriteLine("Speed: {0}", c.);
}
  }
}
```

Figure 13-3. *The IntelliSense of extension methods*

Any method marked with this visual icon is a friendly reminder that the method is defined outside of the original class definition via an extension method.

■ **Source Code** The ExtensionMethods project can be found under the Chapter 13 subdirectory.

Building and Using Extension Libraries

The previous example extended the functionality of various types (such as the `System.Int32` type) for use by the current console application. However, I am sure you could imagine the usefulness of building a.NET code library that defines numerous extensions that can be referenced by multiple applications. As luck would have it, doing so is very straightforward.

To illustrate, create a new Class Library project (named MyExtensionsLibrary). Next, rename your initial C# code file to `MyExtensions.cs`, and copy the `MyExtensions` class definition in your new namespace:

```
namespace MyExtensionsLibrary
{
  // Be sure to import System.Reflection.
  public static class MyExtensions
  {
    // Same implementation as before.
    public static void DisplayDefiningAssembly(this object obj)
    {...}
```

```
    // Same implementation as before.
    public static int ReverseDigits(this int i)
    {...}
  }
}
```

Note If you wish to export extension methods from a .NET code library, the defining type must be declared publically (recall the default access modifier for a type is internal).

At this point, you can compile your library and reference the `MyExtensionsLibrary.dll` assembly within new .NET projects. When you do so, the new functionality provided to `System.Object` and `System.Int32` can be used by any application that references the library.

To test this out, add a new Console Application project (named MyExtensionsLibraryClient). Next, add a reference to the `MyExtensionsLibrary.dll` assembly. Within the initial code file, specify that you are using the `MyExtensionsLibrary` namespace, and author some simple code that invokes these new methods on a local integer:

```
using System;
// Import our custom namespace.
using MyExtensionsLibrary;

namespace MyExtnesionsLibraryClient
{
  class Program
  {
    static void Main(string[] args)
    {
      Console.WriteLine("***** Using Library with Extensions *****\n");
      // This time, these extension methods
      // have been defined within an external
      // .NET class library.
      int myInt = 987;
      myInt.DisplayDefiningAssembly();
      Console.WriteLine("{0} is reversed to {1}",
        myInt, myInt.ReverseDigits());
      Console.ReadLine();
    }
  }
}
```

Microsoft recommends placing types that have extension methods in a dedicated assembly (within a dedicated namespace). The reason is simply to reduce cluttering of your programming environment. By way of example, if you were to author a core library for your company that every application was expected to make use of, and if the root namespace of that library defined 30 extension methods, the end result would be that all applications would now find these methods pop up in IntelliSense (even if they are not required).

Source Code The MyExtensionsLibrary and MyExtensionsLibraryClient projects can be found under the Chapter 13 subdirectory.

Extending Interface Types via Extension Methods

At this point, you have seen how to extend classes (and, indirectly, structures that follow the same syntax) with new functionality via extension methods. To wrap up our investigation of C# 2008 extension methods, allow me to point out that it is possible to extend an interface type with new methods; however, the semantics of such an action are sure to be a bit different from what you might expect.

Create a new Console Application named InterfaceExtensions and define a simple interface type (IBasicMath) that contains a single method named Add(). Next, implement this interface on a class type (MyCalc) in a fitting manner. For example:

```
// Define a normal CLR interface in C#.
interface IBasicMath
{
  int Add(int x, int y);
}

// Implementation of IBasicMath.
class MyCalc : IBasicMath
{
  public int Add(int x, int y)
  {
    return x + y;
  }
}
```

Now, assume you do not have access to the code definition of IBasicMath, but wish to add a new member (such as a subtraction method) to expand its behavior. You might attempt to author the following extension class to do so:

```
static class MathExtensions
{
  // Extend IBasicMath with subtraction method?
  public static int Subtract(this IBasicMath itf,
    int x, int y);
}
```

However, this will result in compile-time errors. When you extend an interface with new members, you must *also supply an implementation* of these members! This seems to fly in the face of the very nature of interface types, as interfaces do not provide implementations, only definitions. Nevertheless, we are required to define our MathExtensions class as follows:

```
static class MathExtensions
{
  // Extend IBasicMath this method and this
  // implementation.
  public static int Subtract(this IBasicMath itf,
    int x, int y)
  {
    return x - y;
  }
}
```

At this point, you might assume you could create a variable of type IBasicMath and directly invoke Subtract(). Again, if this were possible (which it is not), this would destroy the nature of .NET interface types. In reality, what we have actually said here is "Any class in my project implementing IBasicMath now has a Subtract() method, implemented in this manner." As before, all the basic rules apply, therefore the namespace defining MyCalc must have access to the namespace defining MathExtensions. Consider the following Main() method:

```
static void Main(string[] args)
{
  Console.WriteLine("***** Extending an interface *****\n");

  // Call IBasicMath members from MyCalc object.
  MyCalc c = new MyCalc();
  Console.WriteLine("1 + 2 = {0}", c.Add(1, 2));
  Console.WriteLine("1 - 2 = {0}", c.Subtract(1, 2));

  // Can also cast into IBasicMath to invoke extension.
  Console.WriteLine("30 - 9 = {0}",
    ((IBasicMath)c).Subtract(30, 9));

  // This would NOT work!
  // IBasicMath itfBM = new IBasicMath();
  // itfBM.Subtract(10, 10);
  Console.ReadLine();
}
```

That wraps up our examination of C# 2008 extension methods. Remember that this particular language feature can be very useful whenever you wish to extend the functionality of a type, even if you do not have access to the original source code, for the purposes of polymorphism. And, much like implicitly typed local variables, extension methods are a key element of working with the LINQ API. As you will see in the next chapter, numerous existing types in the base class libraries have been extended with new functionality (via extension methods) to allow them to integrate with the LINQ programming model.

Source Code The InterfaceExtension project can be found under the Chapter 13 subdirectory.

Understanding Partial Methods

Since the release of .NET 2.0, we have been able to build partial class definitions using the partial keyword (see Chapter 5). Recall that this bit of syntax allows us to partition the full implementation of a type across multiple code files (or other locations, such as in memory). As long as each aspect of the partial type has the same fully qualified name, the end result is a single "normal" compiled class type in the assembly being constructed.

C# 2008 widens the scope of the partial keyword in that it can now be applied on the method level. In a nutshell, this allows you to prototype a method in one file, yet implement it in another file. If you have a C++ background, this might remind you of the concept of a C++ header/implementation file; however, C# partial methods have a number of important restrictions:

- Partial methods can only be defined within a partial class.
- Partial methods must return void.
- Partial methods can be static or instance level.
- Partial methods can have arguments (including parameters modified by this, ref, or params—but not with the out modifier).
- Partial methods are always implicitly private.

Even stranger is the fact that a partial method may or may not be emitted into the compiled assembly!

A First Look at Partial Methods

To see the implications of defining a partial method, create a new Console Application project named PartialMethods. Now, define a new class named `CarLocator` within a C# file named `CarLocator.cs`:

```
// CarLocator.cs
partial class CarLocator
{
  // This member will always be part of the
  // CarLocator class.
  public bool CarAvailableInZipCode(string zipCode)
  {
    // This call *may* be part of this method
    // implementation.
    VerifyDuplicates(zipCode);

    // Assume some interesting database logic
    // here...
    return true;
  }

  // This member *may* be part of the CarLocator class!
  partial void VerifyDuplicates(string make);
}
```

Notice that the `VerifyDuplicates()` method has been defined with the `partial` modifier and does not define a method body within this file. Also notice that the `CarAvailableInZipCode()` method is making a call to `VerifyDuplicates()` within its implementation.

If you were to compile this application as it now stands and open the compiled assembly into a tool such as `ildasm.exe` or `reflector.exe`, you will find *no trace* of the `VerifyDuplicates()` method in the `CarLocator` class, and *no trace* of the call to `VerifyDuplicates()` within `CarAvailableInZipCode()`! Given the project as it now stands, you *really* authored the following definition of the `CarLocator` class as far as the compiler is concerned:

```
internal class CarLocator
{
  public bool CarAvailableInZipCode(string zipCode)
  {
    return true;
  }
}
```

The reason for this strange stripping away of code has to do with the fact that our partial `VerifyDuplicates()` method was never given a true implementation. If we were to now add a new file to our project (named perhaps `CarLocatorImpl.cs`) that defined the remainder of our partial method:

```
// CarLocatorImpl.cs
partial class CarLocator
{
  partial void VerifyDuplicates(string make)
  {
    // Assume some expensive data validation
```

```
    // takes place here...
  }
}
```

We would now find that the full scope of the CarLocator class is taken into account at compile time (as shown in the following approximate C# code):

```
internal class CarLocator
{
  public bool CarAvailableInZipCode(string zipCode)
  {
    this.VerifyDuplicates(zipCode);
    return true;
  }

  private void VerifyDuplicates(string make)
  {
  }
}
```

As you can see, when a method is defined with the partial keyword, the compiler will determine if it should be emitted into the assembly based on whether the method has a method body or is simply an empty signature. If there is no method body, all traces of the method (invocations, metadata descriptions, prototypes) are stripped out during the compilation cycle.

In some ways, C# partial methods are a strongly typed version of *conditional code compilation* (via the #if, #elif, #else, and #endif preprocessor directives; see Chapter 12). The major difference, however, is that a partial method will be completely ignored during the compilation cycle (regardless of build settings) if there is not a supporting implementation.

Uses of Partial Methods

Given the restrictions that come with a partial method, most notably the fact that they must be implicitly private and always return void, it is hard to see many useful applications of this new language feature. Truth be told, out of all of the language features found with C# 2008, partial methods will more likely than not be the least used among them.

In the current example, the VerifyDuplicates() method was marked as partial for illustrative purposes; however, imagine that this method, if implemented, had to perform some very intensive calculations.

By marking this method with the partial modifier, other class builders have the *option* of providing implementation details if they so choose. In this case, partial methods provide a cleaner solution than using preprocessor directives, supplying "dummy" implementations to virtual methods or throwing NotImplementedException objects.

The most common use of this syntax is to define what are termed *lightweight events*. This technique enables class designers to provide method hooks, similar to event handlers, that developers may choose to implement or not. As a naming convention, such lightweight event-handling methods take an On prefix, for example:

```
// CarLocator.EventHandler.cs
partial class CarLocator
{
  public bool CarAvailableInZipCode(string zipCode)
  {
    ...
    OnZipCodeLookup(zipCode);
    return true;
  }
```

```
  ...
  // A "lightweight" event handler.
  partial void OnZipCodeLookup(string make);
}
```

If a class builder wishes to be informed when the `CarAvailableInZipCode()` method has been called, they can provide an implementation of the `OnZipCodeLookup()` method. If they do not care, they simply do nothing.

■ **Source Code** The PartialMethods project can be found under the Chapter 13 subdirectory.

Understanding Object Initializer Syntax

C# 2008 offers a new way to hydrate the state of a new class or structure variable termed *object initializer syntax*. Using this technique, it is possible to create a new type variable and assign a slew of properties and/or public fields in a few lines of code. Syntactically, an object initializer consists of a comma-delimited list of specified values, enclosed by the { and } tokens. Each member in the initialization list maps to the name of a public field or public property of the object being initialized.

To see this new syntax in action, create a new Console Application named ObjectInitializers. Now, consider the various geometric types created over the course of this text (`Point`, `Rectangle`, `Hexagon`, etc.). For example, recall our simple `Point` type (which did not make use of C# 2008 automatic properties):

```
public class Point
{
  private int xPos, yPos;

  public Point(int x, int y)
  {  xPos = x; yPos = y; }
  public Point(){}

  public int X
  {
    get { return xPos; }
    set { xPos = value; }
  }
  public int Y
  {
    get { return yPos; }
    set { yPos = value; }
  }

  public override string ToString()
  { return string.Format("[{0}, {1}]", xPos, yPos); }
}
```

Under C# 2008, we could now make `Points` using any of the following approaches:

```
static void Main(string[] args)
{
  Console.WriteLine("***** Fun with Object Init Syntax *****\n");
  // Make a Point by setting each property manually...
  Point firstPoint = new Point();
```

```
    firstPoint.X = 10;
    firstPoint.Y = 10;

    // ...or make a Point via a custom constructor...
    Point anotherPoint = new Point(20, 20);

    // ...or make some Point types using the new object init syntax.
    var yetAnotherPoint = new Point { X = 30, Y = 30 };
    Point finalPoint = new Point { X = 30, Y = 30 };
    Console.ReadLine();
}
```

The final two Point types (one of which is implicitly typed, just for the purpose of illustration) are not making use of a custom type constructor (as one might do traditionally), but are rather setting values to the public X and Y properties. Behind the scenes, the type's default constructor is invoked, followed by setting the values to the specified properties. To this end, yetAnotherPoint and finalPoint are just shorthand notations for the syntax used to create the firstPoint variable (going property by property).

Now recall that this same syntax can be used to set public fields of a type, which Point currently does not support. However, for the sake of argument, assume that the xPos and yPos member variables have been declared publicly. We could now set values to these fields as follows:

```
var p = new Point {xPos = 2, yPos = 3};
```

Given that Point now has four public members, the following syntax is also legal. However, try to figure out the actual final values of xPos and yPos:

```
var p = new Point {xPos = 2, yPos = 3, X = 900};
```

As you might guess, xPos is set to 900, while yPos is the value 3. From this, you can correctly infer that object initialization is performed in a left-to-right manner. To clarify, the previous initialization of p using standard object constructor syntax would appear as follows:

```
Point p = new Point();
p.xPos = 2;
p.yPos = 3;
p.X = 900;
```

Calling Custom Constructors with Initialization Syntax

The previous examples initialized Point types by implicitly calling the default constructor on the type:

```
// Here, the default constructor is called implicitly.
Point finalPoint = new Point { X = 30, Y = 30 };
```

If you wish to be very clear about this, it is permissible to explicitly call the default constructor as follows:

```
// Here, the default constructor is called explicitly.
Point finalPoint = new Point() { X = 30, Y = 30 };
```

Do be aware that when you are constructing a type using the new initialization syntax, you are able to invoke *any* constructor defined by the class or structure. Our Point type currently defines a two-argument constructor to set the (*x*, *y*) position. Therefore, the following Point declaration results in an X value of 100 and a Y value of 100, regardless of the fact that our constructor arguments specified the values 10 and 16:

```
// Calling a custom constructor.
Point pt = new Point(10, 16) { X = 100, Y = 100 };
```

Given the current definition of our Point type, calling the custom constructor while using initialization syntax is not terribly useful (and more than a bit verbose). However, if our Point type provides a new constructor that allows the caller to establish a color (via a custom enumeration named PointColor), the combination of custom constructors and object initialization syntax becomes clear. Assume we have updated Point as follows:

```
public enum PointColor
{ LightBlue, BloodRed, Gold }

public class Point
{
  public int xPos, yPos;
  private PointColor c;

  public Point(PointColor color)
  {
    xPos = 0; yPos = 0;
    c = color;
  }
  public Point(){}
  public Point(int x, int y)
  {
    xPos = x; yPos = y;
    c = PointColor.Gold;
  }
  ...
  public override string ToString()
  { return string.Format("[{0}, {1}, Color = {2}]", xPos, yPos, c); }
}
```

With this new constructor, we can now create a golden point (positioned at 90, 20) as follows:

```
// Calling a more interesting custom constructor with init syntax.
Point goldPoint = new Point(PointColor.Gold){ X = 90, Y = 20 };
Console.WriteLine("Value of Point is: {0}", goldPoint);
```

Initializing Inner Types

Recall from Chapter 6 that the "has-a" relationship allows us to compose new types by defining member variables of existing types. For example, assume we now have a Rectangle class, which makes use of the Point type to represent its upper-left/bottom-right coordinates:

```
public class Rectangle
{
  private Point topLeft = new Point();
  private Point bottomRight = new Point();

  public Point TopLeft
  {
    get { return topLeft; }
    set { topLeft = value; }
  }
  public Point BottomRight
  {
```

```
    get { return bottomRight; }
    set { bottomRight = value; }
  }

  public override string ToString()
  {
    return string.Format("[TopLeft: {0}, {1}, BottomRight: {2}, {3}]", topLeft.X,
      topLeft.Y, bottomRight.X, bottomRight.Y);
  }
}
```

Using object initialization syntax, we could create a new Rectangle type and set the inner Points as follows:

```
// Create and initialize a Rectangle.
Rectangle myRect = new Rectangle
{
  TopLeft = new Point { X = 10, Y = 10 },
  BottomRight = new Point { X = 200, Y = 200}
};
```

Again, the benefit of this new syntax is that it basically decreases the number of keystrokes (assuming there is not a suitable constructor). Here is the traditional approach to establishing a similar Rectangle:

```
// Old-school approach.
Rectangle r = new Rectangle();
Point p1 = new Point();
p1.X = 10;
p1.Y = 10;
r.TopLeft = p1;
Point p2 = new Point();
p2.X = 200;
p2.Y = 200;
r.BottomRight = p2;
```

Understanding Collection Initialization

Closely related to the concept of object initialization syntax is *collection initialization*. This syntax makes it possible to populate a container (such as ArrayList or List<T>) with items using a syntax that models that of a simple array. Consider the following examples:

```
// Init a standard array.
int[] myArrayOfInts = { 0, 1, 2, 3, 4, 5, 6, 7, 8, 9 };

// Init a generic List<> of ints.
List<int> myGenericList = new List<int> { 0, 1, 2, 3, 4, 5, 6, 7, 8, 9 };

// Init an ArrayList with numerical data.
ArrayList myList = new ArrayList { 0, 1, 2, 3, 4, 5, 6, 7, 8, 9 };
```

If your container is managing a collection of object types, you can blend object initialization syntax with collection initialization syntax to provide the following:

```
List<Point> myListOfPoints = new List<Point>
{
  new Point { X = 2, Y = 2 },
  new Point { X = 3, Y = 3 },
```

```
  new Point(PointColor.BloodRed){ X = 4, Y = 4 }
};

foreach (var pt in myListOfPoints)
{
  Console.WriteLine(pt);
}
```

Again, the benefit of this syntax is that you save yourself numerous keystrokes. While the nested curly brackets can become difficult to read if you don't mind your formatting, imagine the amount of code that would be required to fill the following `List<T>` of `Rectangles` if we did not have collection initialization syntax:

```
List<Rectangle> myListOfRects = new List<Rectangle>
{
  new Rectangle {TopLeft = new Point { X = 10, Y = 10 },
                 BottomRight = new Point { X = 200, Y = 200}},
  new Rectangle {TopLeft = new Point { X = 2, Y = 2 },
                 BottomRight = new Point { X = 100, Y = 100}},
  new Rectangle {TopLeft = new Point { X = 5, Y = 5 },
                 BottomRight = new Point { X = 90, Y = 75}}
};

foreach (var r in myListOfRects)
{
  Console.WriteLine(r);
}
```

Source Code The ObjectInitializers project can be found under the Chapter 13 subdirectory.

Understanding Anonymous Types

As an OO programmer, you know the benefits of defining classes to represent the state and functionality of a given programming entity. To be sure, whenever you need to define a class that is intended to be reused across projects and provides numerous bits of functionality through a set of methods, events, properties, and custom constructors, creating a new C# class is common practice and often mandatory.

However, there are other times in programming when you would like to define a class simply to model a set of encapsulated (and somehow related) data points without any associated methods, events, or other custom functionality. Furthermore, what if this type is only used internally to your current application and it's not intended to be reused? If you need such a "temporary" type, earlier versions of C# would require you to nevertheless build a new class definition by hand:

```
internal class SomeClass
{
  // Define a set of private member variables...

  // Make a property for each member variable...

  // Override ToString() to account for each member variable...

  // Override GetHashCode() and Equals() to work with value based equality...
}
```

While building such a class is not rocket science, it can be rather labor intensive if you are attempting to encapsulate more than a handful of members (although automatic properties do help in this regard). As of C# 2008, we are now provided with a massive shortcut for this very situation termed *anonymous types*, which in many ways is a natural extension of C#'s anonymous methods syntax (examined in Chapter 11).

When you define an anonymous type, you do so by making use of the new var keyword in conjunction with the object initialization syntax you have just examined. To illustrate, create a new Console Application named AnonymousTypes. Now, update Main() with the following anonymous class, which models a simple car type:

```
static void Main(string[] args)
{
  Console.WriteLine("***** Fun with Anonymous Types *****\n");

  // Make an anonymous type representing a car.
  var myCar = new { Color = "Bright Pink", Make = "Saab", CurrentSpeed = 55 };

  // Now show the color and make.
  Console.WriteLine("My car is a {0} {1}.", myCar.Color, myCar.Make);
  Console.ReadLine();
}
```

Again note that the myCar variable must be implicitly typed, which makes good sense, as we are not modeling the concept of an automobile using a strongly typed class definition. At compile time, the C# compiler will autogenerate a uniquely named class on our behalf. Given the fact that this class name is not visible from C#, the use of implicit typing using the var keyword is mandatory.

Also notice that we have to specify (using object initialization syntax) the set of properties that model the data we are attempting to encapsulate. Once defined, these values can then be obtained using standard C# property invocation syntax.

The Internal Representation of Anonymous Types

All anonymous types are automatically derived from System.Object, and therefore support each of the members provided by this base class. Given this, we could invoke ToString(), GetHashCode(), Equals(), or GetType() on the implicitly typed myCar object. Assume our Program class defines the following static helper function:

```
static void ReflectOverAnonymousType(object obj)
{
  Console.WriteLine("obj is an instance of: {0}", obj.GetType().Name);
  Console.WriteLine("Base class of {0} is {1}",
    obj.GetType().Name,
    obj.GetType().BaseType);
  Console.WriteLine("obj.ToString() = {0}", obj.ToString());
  Console.WriteLine("obj.GetHashCode() = {0}", obj.GetHashCode());
  Console.WriteLine();
}
```

Now assume we invoke this method from Main(), passing in the myCar object as the parameter:

```
static void Main(string[] args)
{
  Console.WriteLine("***** Fun with Anonymous types *****\n");

  // Make an anonymous type representing a car.
  var myCar = new {Color = "Bright Pink", Make = "Saab", CurrentSpeed = 55};
```

```
  // Reflect over what the compiler generated.
  ReflectOverAnonymousType(myCar);
  Console.ReadLine();
}
```

Check out the output shown in Figure 13-4.

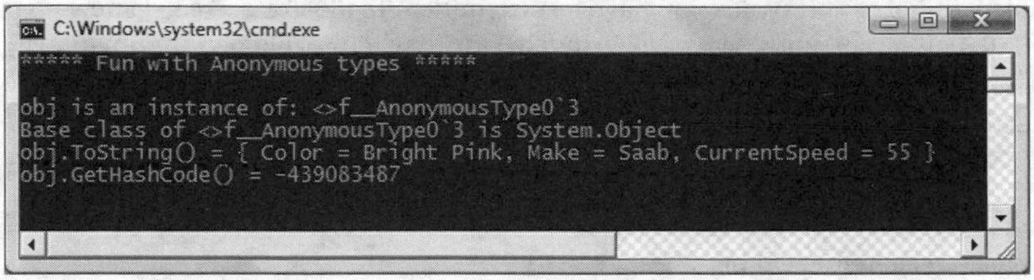

```
C:\Windows\system32\cmd.exe
***** Fun with Anonymous types *****

obj is an instance of: <>f__AnonymousType0`3
Base class of <>f__AnonymousType0`3 is System.Object
obj.ToString() = { Color = Bright Pink, Make = Saab, CurrentSpeed = 55 }
obj.GetHashCode() = -439083487
```

Figure 13-4. *Anonymous types are represented by a compiler-generated class type.*

First of all, notice that in this example, the myCar object is of type <>f__AnonymousType0`3 (your name may differ). Remember that the assigned type name is completely determined by the compiler and is not directly accessible in your C# code base.

Perhaps most important, notice that each name/value pair defined using the object initialization syntax is mapped to an identically named read-only property and a corresponding private read-only backing field. The following C# code approximates the compiler-generated class used to represent the myCar object (which again can be verified using tools such as reflector.exe or ildasm.exe):

```
internal sealed class <>f__AnonymousType0<<Color>j__TPar,
  <Make>j__TPar, <CurrentSpeed>j__TPar>
{
  // Read-only fields
  private readonly <Color>j__TPar <Color>i__Field;
  private readonly <CurrentSpeed>j__TPar <CurrentSpeed>i__Field;
  private readonly <Make>j__TPar <Make>i__Field;

  // Default constructor
  public <>f__AnonymousType0(<Color>j__TPar Color,
    <Make>j__TPar Make, <CurrentSpeed>j__TPar CurrentSpeed);

  // Overridden methods
  public override bool Equals(object value);
  public override int GetHashCode();
  public override string ToString();

  // Read-only properties
  public <Color>j__TPar Color { get; }
  public <CurrentSpeed>j__TPar CurrentSpeed { get; }
  public <Make>j__TPar Make { get; }
}
```

The Implementation of ToString() and GetHashCode()

All anonymous types automatically derive from System.Object and are provided with an overridden version of Equals(), GetHashCode(), and ToString(). The ToString() implementation simply builds a string from each name/value pair, for example:

```
public override string ToString()
{
  StringBuilder builder = new StringBuilder();
  builder.Append("{ Color = ");
  builder.Append(this.<Color>i__Field);
  builder.Append(", Make = ");
  builder.Append(this.<Make>i__Field);
  builder.Append(", CurrentSpeed = ");
  builder.Append(this.<CurrentSpeed>i__Field);
  builder.Append(" }");
  return builder.ToString();
}
```

The GetHashCode() implementation computes a hash value using each anonymous type's member variables as input to the System.Collections.Generic.EqualityComparer<T> type. Using this implementation of GetHashCode(), two anonymous types will yield the same hash value if (and only if) they have the same set of properties that have been assigned the same values. Given this implementation, anonymous types are well suited to be contained within a Hashtable container.

The Semantics of Equality for Anonymous Types

While the implementation of the overridden ToString() and GetHashCode() methods is fairly straightforward, you may be wondering how the Equals() method has been implemented. For example, if we were to define two "anonymous cars" variables that specify the same name/value pairs, would these two variables be considered equal or not? To see the results firsthand, update your Program type with the following new method:

```
static void EqualityTest()
{
  // Make 2 anonymous classes with identical name/value pairs.
  var firstCar = new { Color = "Bright Pink", Make = "Saab", CurrentSpeed = 55 };
  var secondCar = new { Color = "Bright Pink", Make = "Saab", CurrentSpeed = 55 };

  // Are they considered equal when using Equals()?
  if (firstCar.Equals(secondCar))
    Console.WriteLine("Same anonymous object!");
  else
    Console.WriteLine("Not the same anonymous object!");

  // Are they considered equal when using ==?
  if (firstCar == secondCar)
    Console.WriteLine("Same anonymous object!");
  else
    Console.WriteLine("Not the same anonymous object!");

  // Are these objects the same underlying type?
  if (firstCar.GetType().Name == secondCar.GetType().Name)
    Console.WriteLine("We are both the same type!");
  else
    Console.WriteLine("We are different types!");

  // Show all the details.
  Console.WriteLine();
  ReflectOverAnonymousType(firstCar);
  ReflectOverAnonymousType(secondCar);
}
```

Assuming you have called this method from within `Main()`, Figure 13-5 shows the (somewhat surprising) output.

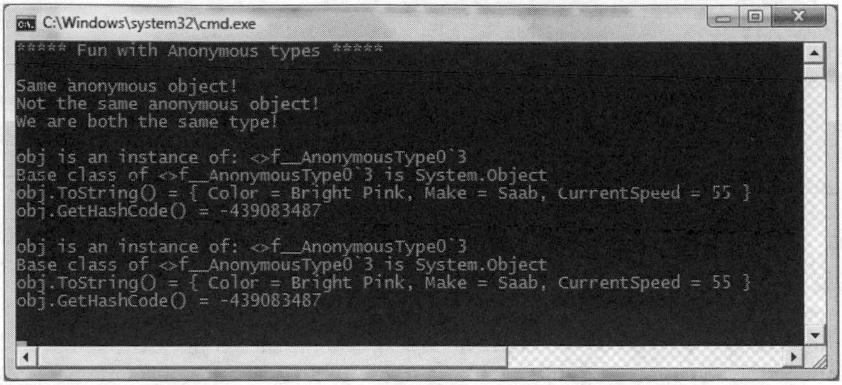

```
C:\Windows\system32\cmd.exe
***** Fun with Anonymous types *****

Same anonymous object!
Not the same anonymous object!
We are both the same type!

obj is an instance of: <>f__AnonymousType0`3
Base class of <>f__AnonymousType0`3 is System.Object
obj.ToString() = { Color = Bright Pink, Make = Saab, CurrentSpeed = 55 }
obj.GetHashCode() = -439083487

obj is an instance of: <>f__AnonymousType0`3
Base class of <>f__AnonymousType0`3 is System.Object
obj.ToString() = { Color = Bright Pink, Make = Saab, CurrentSpeed = 55 }
obj.GetHashCode() = -439083487
```

Figure 13-5. *The equality of anonymous types*

When you run this test code, you will see that the first conditional test where you are calling `Equals()` returns `true`, and therefore the message "Same anonymous object!" prints out to the screen. This is because the compiler-generated `Equals()` method makes use of *value-based semantics* when testing for equality (e.g., checking the value of each field for the objects being compared).

However, the second conditional test (which makes use of the C# equality operator, `==`) prints out "Not the same anonymous object!", which may seem at first glance to be a bit counterintuitive. This is due to the fact that anonymous types do *not receive* overloaded versions of the C# equality operators (`==` and `!=`). Given this, when you test for equality of anonymous types using the C# equality operators (rather than the `Equals()` method), the *references*, not the values maintained by the objects, are being tested for equality. Recall from Chapter 12 that this is the default behavior for all class types until you overload the operators directly in your code (something that is not possible for anonymous types, as you don't define the type!).

Last but not least, in our final conditional test (where we are examining the underlying type name), we find that the anonymous types are instances of the same compiler-generated class type (in this example, `<>f__AnonymousType0`3`), due to the fact that `firstCar` and `secondCar` have the same properties (`Color`, `Make`, and `CurrentSpeed`).

This illustrates an important but subtle point: the compiler will only generate a new class definition when an anonymous type contains *unique* names of the anonymous type. Thus, if you were to declare identical anonymous types (again, meaning the same names) within the same assembly, the compiler only generates a single anonymous type definition.

Anonymous Types Containing Anonymous Types

It is possible to create an anonymous type that is composed of additional anonymous types. For example, assume you wish to model a purchase order that consists of a timestamp, a price point, and the automobile purchased. Here is a new (slightly more sophisticated) anonymous type representing such an entity:

```
// Make an anonymous type that is composed of another.
var purchaseItem = new {
  TimeBought = DateTime.Now,
```

```
  ItemBought = new {Color = "Red", Make = "Saab", CurrentSpeed = 55},
  Price = 34.000};

ReflectOverAnonymousType(purchaseItem);
```

At this point, you should understand the syntax used to define anonymous types, but you may still be wondering exactly where (and when) to make use of this new language feature. To be blunt, the use of anonymous type declarations should be used sparingly, typically only when making use of the LINQ technology set (see Chapter 14). You would never want to abandon the use of strongly typed classes/structures simply for the sake of doing so, given anonymous types' numerous limitations, which include the following:

- You don't control the name of the anonymous type.
- Anonymous types always extend `System.Object`.
- The fields and properties of an anonymous type are always read-only.
- Anonymous types cannot support events, custom methods, custom operators, or custom overrides.
- Anonymous types are always implicitly sealed.
- Anonymous types are always created using the default constructor.

However, when programming with the LINQ technology set, you will find that in many cases this syntax can be very helpful when you wish to quickly model the overall *shape* of an entity rather than its functionality.

Source Code The AnonymousTypes project can be found under the Chapter 13 subdirectory.

Summary

C# 2008 provides a number of very interesting features that bring C# into the family of *functional languages*. This chapter walked you through each of the core updates, beginning with the notion of implicitly typed local variables. While the vast majority of your local variables will not need to be declared with the `var` keyword, as you will see in the next chapter doing so can greatly simplify your interactions with the LINQ family of technologies.

This chapter also described the role of automatic properties, partial methods, extension methods (which allow you to add new functionality to a compiled type), and the syntax of object initialization (which can be used to assign property values at the time of construction).

The chapter wrapped up by examining the use of anonymous types. This language feature allows you to define the "shape" of a type rather than its functionality. This can be very helpful when you need to model a type for limited usage within a program, given that a majority of the workload is offloaded to the compiler.

CHAPTER 14

An Introduction to LINQ

The previous chapter introduced you to numerous C# 2008 programming constructs. As you have seen, features such as implicitly typed local variables, anonymous types, object initialization syntax, and lambda expressions (examined in Chapter 11) allow us to build very functional C# code. Recall that while many of these features can be used directly as is, their benefits are much more apparent when used within the context of the Language Integrated Query (LINQ) technology set.

This chapter will introduce you to the LINQ model and its role in the .NET platform. Here, you will come to learn the role of *query operators* and *query expressions*, which allow you to define statements that will interrogate a data source to yield the requested result set. Along the way, you will build numerous LINQ examples that interact with data contained within arrays as well as various collection types (both generic and nongeneric) and understand the assemblies and types that enable LINQ.

Note Chapter 24 will examine additional LINQ-centric APIs that allow you to interact with relational databases and XML documents.

Understanding the Role of LINQ

As software developers, it is hard to deny that the vast majority of our programming time is spent obtaining and manipulating *data*. When speaking of "data," it is very easy to immediately envision information contained within relational databases. However, another popular location in which data exists is within XML documents (`*.config` files, locally persisted `DataSets`, in-memory data returned from XML web services, etc.).

Data can be found in numerous places beyond these two common homes for information. For instance, say you have a generic `List<T>` type containing 300 integers, and you want to obtain a subset that meets a given criterion (e.g., only the odd or even members in the container, only prime numbers, only nonrepeating numbers greater than 50, etc.). Or perhaps you are making use of the reflection APIs and need to obtain only metadata descriptions for each class deriving from a particular parent class within an array of `Types`. Indeed, data is everywhere.

Prior to .NET 3.5, interacting with a particular flavor of data required programmers to make use of diverse APIs. Consider, for example, Table 14-1, which illustrates several common APIs used to access various types of data.

Table 14-1. *Ways to Manipulate Various Types of Data*

The Data We Want	How to Obtain It
Relational data	`System.Data.dll`, `System.Data.SqlClient.dll`, etc.
XML document data	`System.Xml.dll`
Metadata tables	The `System.Reflection` namespace
Collections of objects	`System.Array` and the `System.Collections`/`System.Collections.Generic` namespaces

Of course, nothing is wrong with these approaches to data manipulation. In fact, when programming with .NET 3.5/C# 2008, you can (and will) certainly make direct use of ADO.NET, the XML namespaces, reflection services, and the various collection types. However, the basic problem is that each of these APIs is an island unto itself, which offers very little in the way of integration. True, it is possible (for example) to save an ADO.NET `DataSet` as XML, and then manipulate it via the `System.Xml` namespaces, but nonetheless, data manipulation remains rather asymmetrical.

The LINQ API is an attempt to provide a consistent, *symmetrical* manner in which programmers can obtain and manipulate "data" in the broad sense of the term. Using LINQ, we are able to create directly within the C# programming language entities called *query expressions*. These query expressions are based on numerous *query operators* that have been intentionally designed to look and feel very similar (but not quite identical) to a SQL expression.

The twist, however, is that a query expression can be used to interact with numerous types of data—even data that has nothing to do with a relational database. Specifically, LINQ allows query expressions to manipulate any object that implements the `IEnumerable<T>` interface (directly or indirectly via extension methods), relational databases, `DataSets`, or XML documents in a consistent manner.

■ **Note** Strictly speaking, "LINQ" is the term used to describe this overall approach to data access. LINQ to Objects is LINQ over objects implementing `IEnumerable<T>`, LINQ to SQL is LINQ over relational data, LINQ to DataSet is a superset of LINQ to SQL, and LINQ to XML is LINQ over XML documents. In the future, you are sure to find other APIs that have been injected with LINQ functionality (in fact, there are already other LINQ-centric projects under development at Microsoft).

LINQ Expressions Are Strongly Typed and Extendable

It is also very important to point out that a LINQ query expression (unlike a traditional SQL statement) is *strongly typed*. Therefore, the C# compiler will keep us honest and make sure that these expressions are syntactically well formed. On a related note, query expressions have metadata representation within the assembly that makes use of them. Tools such as Visual Studio 2008 can use this metadata for useful features such as IntelliSense, autocompletion, and so forth.

Also, before we dig into the details of LINQ, one final point is that LINQ is designed to be an extendable technology. While this initial release of LINQ is targeted for relational databases/`DataSets`, XML documents, and objects implementing `IEnumerable<T>`, third parties can incorporate new query operators (or redefine existing operators) using extension methods (see Chapter 13) to account for addition forms of data.

Note Before you continue reading over this chapter, I wholeheartedly recommend that you first feel comfortable with the material presented in Chapter 13 (which covered C# 2008 specific constructs). As you will see, LINQ programming makes use of several of the new C# features to simplify coding tasks.

The Core LINQ Assemblies

As mentioned in Chapter 2, the New Project dialog of Visual Studio 2008 now has the option of selecting which version of the .NET platform you wish to compile against, using the drop-down list box mounted on the upper-right corner. When you opt to compile against the .NET Framework 3.5, each of the project templates will automatically reference the key LINQ assemblies. For example, if you were to create a new .NET 3.5 Console Application, you will find the assemblies shown in Figure 14-1 visible within the Solution Explorer.

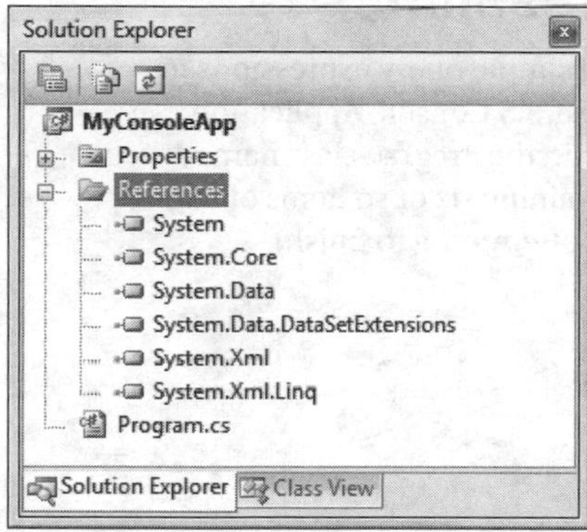

Figure 14-1. *.NET 3.5 project types automatically reference key LINQ assemblies.*

Table 14-2 documents the role of the core LINQ-specific assemblies.

Table 14-2. *Core LINQ-centric Assemblies*

Assembly	Meaning in Life
`System.Core.dll`	Defines the types that represent the core LINQ API. This is the one assembly you must have access to.
`System.Data.Linq.dll`	Provides functionality for using LINQ with relational databases (LINQ to SQL).
`System.Data.DataSetExtensions.dll`	Defines a handful of types to integrate ADO.NET types into the LINQ programming paradigm (LINQ to DataSet).
`System.Xml.Linq.dll`	Provides functionality for using LINQ with XML document data (LINQ to XML).

When you wish to do any sort of LINQ programming, you will at the very least need to import the `System.Linq` namespace (defined within `System.Core.dll`), which is typically accounted for by new Visual Studio 2008 project files; for example, here is the starting code for a new .NET 3.5 Console Application project:

```
using System;
using System.Collections.Generic;
using System.Linq;
using System.Text;

namespace MyConsoleApp
{
  class Program
  {
    static void Main(string[] args)
    {
    }
  }
}
```

A First Look at LINQ Query Expressions

To begin examining the LINQ programming model, let's build simple query expressions to manipulate data contained within various arrays. Create a .NET 3.5 Console Application named LinqOverArray, and define a static helper method within the `Program` class named `QueryOverStrings()`. In this method, create a string array containing six or so items of your liking (here, I listed out a batch of video games I am currently attempting to finish).

```
static void QueryOverStrings()
{
  // Assume we have an array of strings.
  string[] currentVideoGames = {"Morrowind", "BioShock",
    "Half Life 2: Episode 1", "The Darkness",
    "Daxter", "System Shock 2"};
  Console.ReadLine();
}
```

Now, update `Main()` to invoke `QueryOverStrings()`:

```
static void Main(string[] args)
{
  Console.WriteLine("***** Fun with LINQ *****\n");
  QueryOverStrings();
  Console.ReadLine();
}
```

When you have any array of data, it is very common to extract a subset of items based on a given requirement. Maybe you want to obtain only the items with names that contain a number (e.g., System Shock 2 and Half Life 2: Episode 1), have more than some number of characters, or don't have embedded spaces (e.g., Morrowind). While you could certainly perform such tasks using members of the `System.Array` type and a bit of elbow grease, LINQ query expressions can greatly simplify the process.

Going on the assumption that we wish to obtain a subset from the array that contains items with names consisting of more than six characters, we could build the following query expression:

```
static void QueryOverStrings()
{
  // Assume we have an array of strings.
  string[] currentVideoGames = {"Morrowind", "BioShock",
    "Half Life 2: Episode 1", "The Darkness",
    "Daxter", "System Shock 2"};
```

```
  // Build a query expression to represent the items in the array
  // that have more than 6 letters.
  IEnumerable<string> subset = from g in currentVideoGames
                      where g.Length > 6 orderby g select g;

  // Print out the results.
  foreach (string s in subset)
    Console.WriteLine("Item: {0}", s);
}
```

Notice that the query expression created here makes use of the `from`, `in`, `where`, `orderby`, and `select` LINQ query operators. We will dig into the formalities of query expression syntax in just a bit, but even now you should be able to parse this statement as "Give me the items inside of `currentVideoGames` that have more than six characters, ordered alphabetically." Here, each item that matches the search criteria has been given the name "g" (as in "game"); however, any valid C# variable name would do:

```
IEnumerable<string> subset = from game in currentVideoGames
  where game.Length > 6 orderby game select game;
```

Notice that the "result set" variable, `subset`, is represented by an object that implements the generic version of `IEnumerable<T>`, where `T` is of type `System.String` (after all, we are querying an array of strings). Once we obtain the result set, we then simply print out each item using a standard `foreach` construct.

Before we see the results of our query, assume the `Program` class defines an additional helper function named `ReflectOverQueryResults()` that will print out various details of the LINQ result set (note the parameter is a `System.Object`, to account for multiple types of result sets):

```
static void ReflectOverQueryResults(object resultSet)
{
  Console.WriteLine("***** Info about your query *****");
  Console.WriteLine("resultSet is of type: {0}", resultSet.GetType().Name);
  Console.WriteLine("resultSet location: {0}", resultSet.GetType().Assembly);
}
```

Assuming you have called this method within `QueryOverStrings()` directly after printing out the obtained subset, if you run the application, you will see the `subset` is really an instance of the generic `OrderedEnumerable<TElement, TKey>` type (represented in terms of CIL code as ``OrderedEnumerable`2``), which is an internal abstract type residing in the `System.Core.dll` assembly (see Figure 14-2).

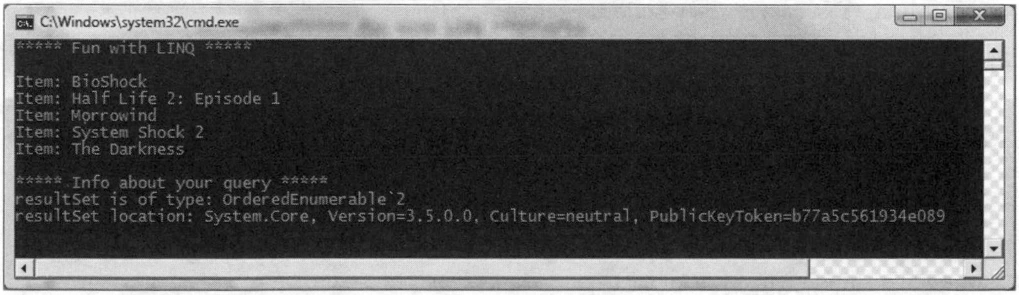

```
C:\Windows\system32\cmd.exe
***** Fun with LINQ *****

Item: BioShock
Item: Half Life 2: Episode 1
Item: Morrowind
Item: System Shock 2
Item: The Darkness

***** Info about your query *****
resultSet is of type: OrderedEnumerable`2
resultSet location: System.Core, Version=3.5.0.0, Culture=neutral, PublicKeyToken=b77a5c561934e089
```

Figure 14-2. *The result of our LINQ query*

■ **Note** Many of the types that represent a LINQ result are hidden by the Visual Studio 2008 object browser. Make use of `ildasm.exe` or `reflector.exe` to see these internal, hidden types.

LINQ and Implicitly Typed Local Variables

While the current sample program makes it relatively easy to determine that the result set is enumerable as a string collection, I would guess that it is *not* clear that `subset` is really of type `OrderedEnumerable<TElement, TKey>`. Given the fact that LINQ result sets can be represented using a good number of types in various LINQ-centric namespaces, it would be tedious to define the proper type to hold a result set, because in many cases the underlying type may not be obvious or directly accessible from your code base (and as you will see, in some cases the type is generated at compile time).

To further accentuate this point, consider the following additional helper method defined within the `Program` class (which I assume you will invoke from within the `Main()` method):

```
static void QueryOverInts()
{
  int[] numbers = {10, 20, 30, 40, 1, 2, 3, 8};

  // Only print items less than 10.
  IEnumerable<int> subset = from i in numbers where i < 10 select i;

  foreach (int i in subset)
    Console.WriteLine("Item: {0}", i);
  ReflectOverQueryResults(subset);
}
```

In this case, the `subset` variable is obtained (under the covers) by calling the `System.Linq.Enumerable.Where<T>` method, passing in a *compiler-generated anonymous method* as the second parameter. Here is the crux of the internal definition of the `subset` variable generated by the compiler (assume the anonymous method has been named `9__CachedAnonymousMethodDelegate8`):

```
// The following LINQ query expression:
//
// IEnumerable<int> subset = from i in numbers where i < 10 select i;
//
// Is transformed into a call to the Enumerable.Where<int>() method:
//
IEnumerable<int> subset = Enumerable.Where<int>(numbers,
  Program.<>9__CachedAnonymousMethodDelegate8);
```

■ **Note** I would recommend that you load LINQ-based applications into a decompiler such as `ildasm.exe` or `reflector.exe`. These sorts of tools can greatly strengthen your understanding of LINQ internals.

Without diving too deeply into the use of `Enumerable.Where<T>` at this point, do note that in Figure 14-3, the underlying type for each query expression is indeed unique, based on the format of our LINQ query expression.

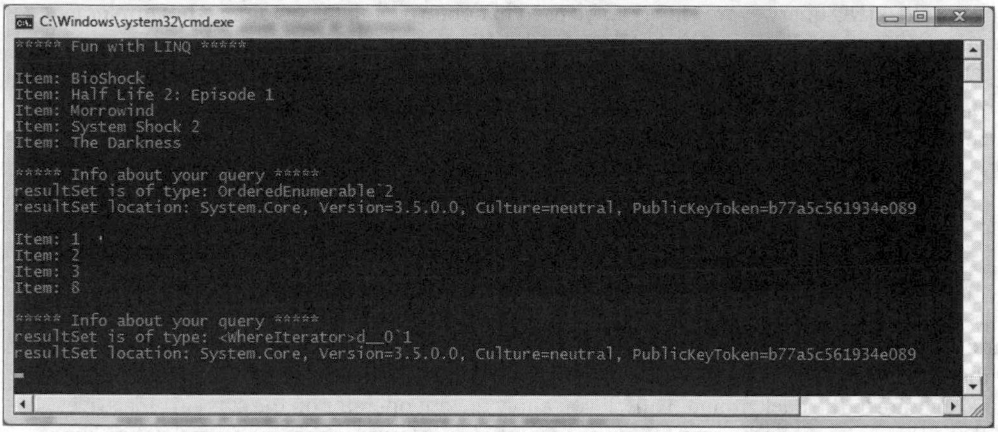

```
C:\Windows\system32\cmd.exe
***** Fun with LINQ *****

Item: BioShock
Item: Half Life 2: Episode 1
Item: Morrowind
Item: System Shock 2
Item: The Darkness

***** Info about your query *****
resultSet is of type: OrderedEnumerable`2
resultSet location: System.Core, Version=3.5.0.0, Culture=neutral, PublicKeyToken=b77a5c561934e089

Item: 1
Item: 2
Item: 3
Item: 8

***** Info about your query *****
resultSet is of type: <WhereIterator>d__0`1
resultSet location: System.Core, Version=3.5.0.0, Culture=neutral, PublicKeyToken=b77a5c561934e089
```

Figure 14-3. *LINQ query expressions can return numerous result sets.*

Given the fact that the exact underlying type of a LINQ query is certainly not obvious, the current example has represented the query results as local `IEnumerable<T>` variable. Given that `IEnumerable<T>` extends the nongeneric `IEnumerable` interface, it would also be permissible to capture the result of a LINQ query as follows:

```
System.Collections.IEnumerable subset =
  from i in numbers where i < 10 select i;
```

While this is syntactically correct, implicit typing cleans things up considerably when working with LINQ queries:

```
static void QueryOverInts()
{
  int[] numbers = {10, 20, 30, 40, 1, 2, 3, 8};

  // Use implicit typing here...
  var subset = from i in numbers where i < 10 select i;

  // ...and here.
  foreach (var i in subset)
    Console.WriteLine("Item: {0} ", i);

  ReflectOverQueryResults(subset);
}
```

Recall that the `var` keyword should not be confused with the legacy COM `Variant` or loosely typed variable declaration found in many scripting languages. The underlying type is determined by the compiler based on the result of the initial assignment. After that point, it is a compiler error to attempt to change the "type of type." Furthermore, given the fact that in many cases the underlying type is the result of a dynamically generated anonymous type, it is commonplace to use implicit typing whenever you wish to capture a LINQ result set.

LINQ and Extension Methods

Recall from the previous chapter that *extension methods* make it possible to add new members to a previously compiled type within the scope of a given project. Although the current example does not have you author any extension methods directly, you are in fact using them seamlessly in the background. LINQ query expressions can be used to iterate over data containers that implement the generic `IEnumerable<T>` interface. However, the .NET `System.Array` class type (used to represent our array of strings and array of integers) does *not* implement this behavior:

```
// The System.Array type does not seem to implement the correct
// infrastructure for query expressions!
public abstract class Array : ICloneable, IList, ICollection, IEnumerable
{
  ...
}
```

While `System.Array` does not directly implement the `IEnumerable<T>` interface, it indirectly gains the required functionality of this type (as well as many other LINQ-centric members) via the static `System.Linq.Enumerable` class type. This type defined a good number of generic extension methods (such as `Aggregate<T>()`, `First<T>()`, `Max<T>()`, etc.), which `System.Array` (and other types) acquire in the background. Thus, if you apply the dot operator on the `currentVideoGames` local variable, you will find a good number of members *not* found within the formal definition of `System.Array` (see Figure 14-4).

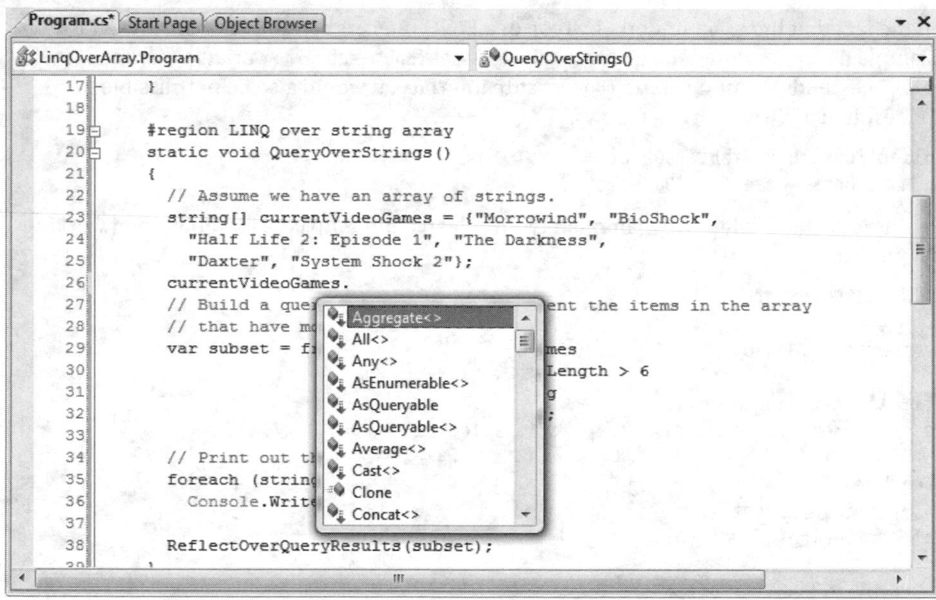

Figure 14-4. *The* `System.Array` *type has been extended with members of* `System.Linq.Enumerable`.

The Role of Differed Execution

Another important point regarding LINQ query expressions is that they are not actually evaluated until you iterate over their contents. Formally speaking, this is termed *differed execution*. The benefit of this approach is that you are able to apply the same LINQ query multiple times to the same container, and rest assured you are obtaining the latest and greatest results. Consider the following update to the `QueryOverInts()` method:

```
static void QueryOverInts()
{
  int[] numbers = { 10, 20, 30, 40, 1, 2, 3, 8 };
```

```
    // Get numbers less than ten.
    var subset = from i in numbers where i < 10 select i;

    // LINQ statement evaluated here!
    foreach (var i in subset)
      Console.WriteLine("{0} < 10", i);
    Console.WriteLine();

    // Change some data in the array.
    numbers[0] = 4;

    // Evaluate again.
    foreach (var j in subset)
      Console.WriteLine("{0} < 10", j);
    ReflectOverQueryResults(subset);
  }
```

If you were to execute the program yet again, you will find the output shown in Figure 14-5.

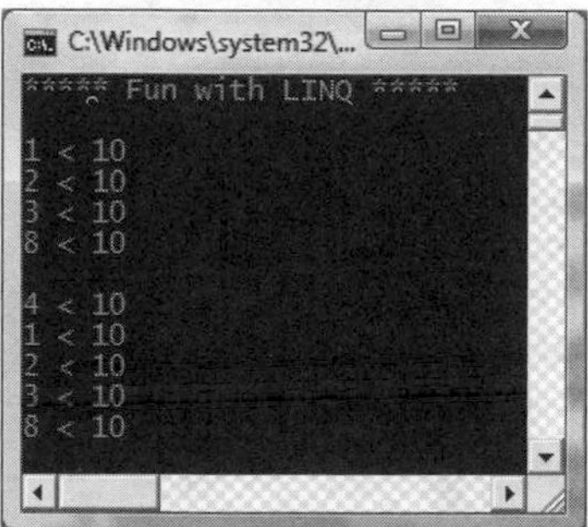

C:\Windows\system32\...
***** Fun with LINQ *****
1 < 10
2 < 10
3 < 10
8 < 10
4 < 10
1 < 10
2 < 10
3 < 10
8 < 10

Figure 14-5. *LINQ expressions are executed when evaluated.*

One very useful aspect of Visual Studio 2008 is that if you set a breakpoint before the evaluation of a LINQ query, you are able to view the contents during a debugging session. Simply locate your mouse cursor above the LINQ result set variable (`subset` in Figure 14-6). When you do, you will be given the option of evaluating the query at that time by expanding the Results View option.

```
LinqOverArray.Program                    QueryOverStrings()
      // that have more than 6 letters.
      var subset = from g in currentVideoGames
   subset {System.Linq.OrderedEnumerable<string,string>}
     [System.Linq.OrderedEnumerable<string,string>]  {System.Linq.OrderedEnumerable<string,string>}
     Results View   Expanding the Results View will enumerate the IEnumerable

      // Print out the results.
      foreach (string s in subset)
        Console.WriteLine("Item: {0}", s);
      Console.WriteLine();
      ReflectOverQueryResults(subset);
    }
```

Figure 14-6. *Debugging LINQ expressions*

The Role of Immediate Execution

When you wish to evaluate a LINQ expression from outside the confines of foreach logic, you are able to call any number of extension methods defined by the Enumerable type to do so. Enumerable defines a number of extension methods such as ToArray<T>(), ToDictionary<TSource,TKey>(), and ToList<T>(), which allow you to capture a LINQ query result set in a strongly typed container. Once you have done so, the container is no longer "connected" to the LINQ expression, and may be independently manipulated:

```
static void ImmediateExecution()
{
  int[] numbers = { 10, 20, 30, 40, 1, 2, 3, 8 };

  // Get data RIGHT NOW as int[].
  int[] subsetAsIntArray =
    (from i in numbers where i < 10 select i).ToArray<int>();

  // Get data RIGHT NOW as List<int>.
  List<int> subsetAsListOfInts =
    (from i in numbers where i < 10 select i).ToList<int>();
}
```

Notice that the entire LINQ expression is wrapped within parentheses to cast it into the correct underlying type (whatever that may be) in order to call the extension methods of Enumerable.

Also recall from Chapter 10 that when the C# compiler can unambiguously determine the type parameter of a generic item, you are not required to specify the type parameter. Thus, we could also call ToArray<T>() (or ToList<T>() for that matter) as follows:

```
int[] subsetAsIntArray =
  (from i in numbers where i < 10 select i).ToArray();
```

■ **Source Code** The LinqOverArray project can be found under the Chapter 14 subdirectory.

LINQ and Generic Collections

Beyond pulling results from a simple array of data, LINQ query expressions can also manipulate data within members of the System.Collections.Generic namespace, such as the List<T> type. Create a new .NET 3.5 Console Application project named LinqOverCustomObjects, and define a basic Car type that maintains a current speed, color, make, and pet name (public fields are used to easily set the string fields to empty text. Feel free to make use of automatic properties and class constructors if you wish):

```
class Car
{
  public string PetName = string.Empty;
  public string Color = string.Empty;
  public int Speed;
  public string Make = string.Empty;
}
```

Now, within your Main() method, define a local List<T> variable of type Car, and make use of the new object initialization syntax (see Chapter 13) to fill the list with a handful of new Car objects:

```
static void Main(string[] args)
{
  Console.WriteLine("***** More fun with LINQ Expressions *****\n");

  // Make a List<> of Car objects
  // using object init syntax.
  List<Car> myCars = new List<Car>() {
    new Car{ PetName = "Henry", Color = "Silver", Speed = 100, Make = "BMW"},
    new Car{ PetName = "Daisy", Color = "Tan", Speed = 90, Make = "BMW"},
    new Car{ PetName = "Mary", Color = "Black", Speed = 55, Make = "VW"},
    new Car{ PetName = "Clunker", Color = "Rust", Speed = 5, Make = "Yugo"},
    new Car{ PetName = "Melvin", Color = "White", Speed = 43, Make = "Ford"}
  };
}
```

Applying a LINQ Expression

Our goal is to build a query expression to select only the items within the myCars list, where the speed is greater than 55. Once we get the subset, we will print out the name of each Car object. Assume you have the following helper method (taking a List<Car> parameter), which is called from within Main():

```
static void GetFastCars(List<Car> myCars)
{
  // Create a query expression.
  var fastCars = from c in myCars where c.Speed > 55 select c;

  foreach (var car in fastCars)
  {
    Console.WriteLine("{0} is going too fast!", car.PetName);
  }
}
```

Notice that our query expression is only grabbing items from the List<T> where the Speed property is greater than 55. If we run the application, we will find that "Henry" and "Daisy" are the only two items that match the search criteria.

If we want to build a more complex query, we might wish to only find the BMWs that have a Speed value above 90. To do so, simply build a compound Boolean statement using the C# && operator:

```
// Create a query expression.
var fastCars = from c in myCars where
  c.Speed > 90 && c.Make == "BMW" select c;
```

In this case, the only pet name printed out is "Henry".

■ **Source Code** The LinqOverCustomObjects project can be found under the Chapter 14 subdirectory.

LINQ and Nongeneric Collections

Recall that the query operators of LINQ are designed to work with any type implementing IEnumerable<T> (either directly or via extension methods). Given that System.Array has been provided with such necessary infrastructure, it may surprise you that the legacy (nongeneric) containers within `System.Collections` have *not*. Thankfully, it is still possible to iterate over data contained within nongeneric collections using the generic `Enumerable.OfType<T>()` method.

The `OfType<T>()` method is one of the few members of `Enumerable` that does not extend generic types. When calling this member off a nongeneric container implementing the `IEnumerable` interface (such as the `ArrayList`), simply specify the type of item within the container to extract a compatible `IEnumerable<T>` object. Assume we have a new Console Application named LinqOverArrayList that defines the following `Main()` method (note that we are making use of the previously defined `Car` type and be sure to import the `System.Collections` namespace).

```
static void Main(string[] args)
{
  Console.WriteLine("***** LINQ over ArrayList *****\n");

  // Here is a nongeneric collection of cars.
  ArrayList myCars = new ArrayList() {
    new Car{ PetName = "Henry", Color = "Silver", Speed = 100, Make = "BMW"},
    new Car{ PetName = "Daisy", Color = "Tan", Speed = 90, Make = "BMW"},
    new Car{ PetName = "Mary", Color = "Black", Speed = 55, Make = "VW"},
    new Car{ PetName = "Clunker", Color = "Rust", Speed = 5, Make = "Yugo"},
    new Car{ PetName = "Melvin", Color = "White", Speed = 43, Make = "Ford"}
  };

  // Transform ArrayList into an IEnumerable<T>-compatible type.
  IEnumerable<Car> myCarsEnum = myCars.OfType<Car>();

  // Create a query expression.
  var fastCars = from c in myCarsEnum where c.Speed > 55 select c;

  foreach (var car in fastCars)
  {
    Console.WriteLine("{0} is going too fast!", car.PetName);
  }
}
```

Filtering Data Using OfType<T>()

As you know, nongeneric types are capable of containing any combination of items, as the members of these containers (again, such as the `ArrayList`) are prototyped to receive `System.Objects`. For example, assume an `ArrayList` contains a variety of items, only a subset of which are numerical. If we want to obtain a subset that contains only numerical data, we can do so using `OfType<T>()`, since it filters out each element whose type is different from the given type during the iterations:

```
// Extract the ints from the ArrayList.
ArrayList myStuff = new ArrayList();
myStuff.AddRange(new object[] { 10, 400, 8, false, new Car(), "string data" });
IEnumerable<int> myInts = myStuff.OfType<int>();

// Prints out 10, 400, and 8.
foreach (int i in myInts)
{
  Console.WriteLine("Int value: {0}", i);
}
```

Source Code The LinqOverArrayList project can be found under the Chapter 14 subdirectory.

Now that you have seen how to use LINQ to manipulate data contained within various arrays and collections, let's dig in a bit deeper to see what is happening behind the scenes.

The Internal Representation of LINQ Query Operators

So at this point you have been briefly introduced to the process of building query expressions using various C# query operators (such as from, in, where, orderby, and select). When compiled, the C# compiler actually translates these tokens into calls on various methods of the System.Linq.Enumerable type (and possibly other types, based on your LINQ query).

As it turns out, a great many of the methods of Enumerable have been prototyped to take delegates as arguments. In particular, many methods require a generic delegate of type Func<>, defined within the System namespace of System.Core.dll. For example, consider the following members of Enumerable that extend the IEnumerable<T> interface:

```
// Overloaded versions of the Enumerable.Where<T>() method.
// Note the second parameter is of type System.Func<>.
public static IEnumerable<TSource> Where<TSource>(this IEnumerable<TSource> source,
  System.Func<TSource,int,bool> predicate)

public static IEnumerable<TSource> Where<TSource>(this IEnumerable<TSource> source,
  System.Func<TSource,bool> predicate)
```

This delegate (as the name implies) represents a pattern for a given *func*tion with a set of arguments and a return value. If you were to examine this type using the Visual Studio 2008 object browser, you'll notice that the Func<> delegate can take between zero and four input arguments (here typed T0, T1, T2, and T3 and named arg0, arg1, arg2, and arg3), and a return type denoted by TResult:

```
// The various formats of the Func<> delegate.
public delegate TResult Func<T0,T1,T2,T3,TResult>(
  T0 arg0, T1 arg1, T2 arg2, T3 arg3)
public delegate TResult Func<T0,T1,T2,TResult>(T0 arg0, T1 arg1, T2 arg2)
public delegate TResult Func<T0,T1,TResult>(T0 arg0, T1 arg1)
public delegate TResult Func<T0,TResult>(T0 arg0)
public delegate TResult Func<TResult>()
```

Given that many members of System.Linq.Enumerable demand a delegate as input, when invoking them, we can either manually create a new delegate type and author the necessary target methods, make use of a C# anonymous method, or define a proper lambda expression. Regardless of which approach you take, the end result is identical.

While it is true that making use of C# LINQ query operators is far and away the simplest way to build a LINQ query expression, let's walk through each of these possible approaches just so you can see the connection between the C# query operators and the underlying Enumerable type.

Building Query Expressions with Query Operators (Revisited)

To begin, create a new Console Application named LinqUsingEnumerable. The Program class will define a series of static helper methods (each of which is called within the Main() method) to illustrate the various manners in which we can build LINQ query expressions. The first method, `QueryStringsWithOperators()`, offers the most straightforward way to build a query expression and is identical to the code seen in the previous LinqOverArray example:

```
static void QueryStringWithOperators()
{
  Console.WriteLine("***** Using Query Operators *****");
  string[] currentVideoGames = {"Morrowind", "BioShock",
    "Half Life 2: Episode 1", "The Darkness",
    "Daxter", "System Shock 2"};

  // Build a query expression using query operators.
  var subset = from g in currentVideoGames
               where g.Length > 6 orderby g select g;

  // Print out the results.
  foreach (var s in subset)
    Console.WriteLine("Item: {0}", s);
}
```

The obvious benefit of using C# query operators to build query expressions is the fact that the `Func<>` delegates and calls on the `Enumerable` type are out of sight and out of mind, as it is the job of the C# compiler to perform this translation. To be sure, building LINQ expressions using various query operators (`from`, `in`, `where`, `orderby`, etc.) is the most common and most straightforward approach.

Building Query Expressions Using the Enumerable Type and Lambdas

Keep in mind that the LINQ query operators used here are simply shorthand versions for calling various extension methods defined by the `Enumerable` type. Consider the following `QueryStringsWithEnumerableAndLambdas()` method, which is processing the local string array now making direct use of the `Enumerable` extension methods:

```
static void QueryStringsWithEnumerableAndLambdas()
{
  Console.WriteLine("***** Using Enumerable / Lambda Expressions *****");

  string[] currentVideoGames = {"Morrowind", "BioShock",
    "Half Life 2: Episode 1", "The Darkness",
    "Daxter", "System Shock 2"};

  // Build a query expression using extension methods
  // granted to the Array via the Enumerable type.
  var subset = currentVideoGames.Where(game => game.Length > 6)
    .OrderBy(game => game).Select(game => game);

  // Print out the results.
  foreach (var game in subset)
    Console.WriteLine("Item: {0}", game);
  Console.WriteLine();
}
```

Here, we are calling the generic `Where()` method off the string array object, granted to the `Array` type as an extension method defined by `Enumerable`. The `Enumerable.Where<T>()` method makes use of the `System.Func<T0, TResult>` delegate type. The first type parameter of this delegate represents the IEnumerable<T>-compatible data to process (an array of strings in this case), while the second type parameter represents the method that will process said data.

Given that we have opted for a lambda expression (rather than directly creating an instance of Func<T> or crafting an anonymous method), we are specifying that the "game" parameter is processed by the statement game.Length > 6, which results in a Boolean return type.

The return value of the Where<T>() method has implicitly typed, but under the covers we are operating on an OrderedEnumerable type. From this resulting object, we call the generic OrderBy<T, K>() method, which also requires a Func<T, K> delegate parameter. Finally, from the result of the specified lambda expression, we select each element, using once again a Func<T, K> under the covers.

It is also worth remembering that extension methods are unique in that they can be called as instance-level members upon the type they are extending (System.Array in this case) *or* as static members using the type they were defined within. Given this, we could also author our query expression as follows:

```
var subset = Enumerable.Where(currentVideoGames, game => game.Length > 6)
  .OrderBy(game => game).Select(game => game);
```

As you may agree, building a LINQ query expression using the methods of the Enumerable type directly is much more verbose than making use of the C# query operators. As well, given that the methods of Enumerable require delegates as parameters, you will typically need to author lambda expressions to allow the input data to be processed by the underlying delegate target.

Building Query Expressions Using the Enumerable Type and Anonymous Methods

Given that C# 2008 lambda expressions are simply shorthand notations for working with anonymous methods, consider the third query expression created within the QueryStringsWithAnonymousMethods() helper function:

```
static void QueryStringsWithAnonymousMethods()
{
  Console.WriteLine("***** Using Anonymous Methods *****");

  string[] currentVideoGames = {"Morrowind", "BioShock",
    "Half Life 2: Episode 1", "The Darkness",
    "Daxter", "System Shock 2"};

  // Build the necessary Func<> delegates using anonymous methods.
  Func<string, bool> searchFilter =
    delegate(string game) { return game.Length > 6; };
  Func<string, string> itemToProcess = delegate(string s) { return s; };

  // Pass the delegates into the methods of Enumerable.
  var subset = currentVideoGames.Where(searchFilter)
    .OrderBy(itemToProcess).Select(itemToProcess);

  // Print out the results.
  foreach (var game in subset)
    Console.WriteLine("Item: {0}", game);
  Console.WriteLine();
}
```

This iteration of the query expression is even more verbose, because we are manually creating the Func<> delegates used by the Where(), OrderBy(), and Select() methods of the Enumerable type.

On the plus side, the anonymous method syntax does keep all the processing contained within a single method definition. Nevertheless, this method is functionally equivalent to the QueryStringsWithEnumerableAndLambdas() and QueryStringsWithOperators() methods created in the previous sections.

Building Query Expressions Using the Enumerable Type and Raw Delegates

Finally, if we want to build a query expression using the *really verbose approach,* we could avoid the use of lambdas/anonymous method syntax and directly create delegate targets for each Func<> type. Here is the final iteration of our query expression, modeled within a new class type named VeryComplexQueryExpression:

```
class VeryComplexQueryExpression
{
  public static void QueryStringsWithRawDelegates()
  {
    Console.WriteLine("***** Using Raw Delegates *****");

    string[] currentVideoGames = {"Morrowind", "BioShock",
      "Half Life 2: Episode 1", "The Darkness",
      "Daxter", "System Shock 2"};

    // Build the necessary Func<> delegates using anonymous methods.
    Func<string, bool> searchFilter = new Func<string, bool>(Filter);
    Func<string, string> itemToProcess = new Func<string,string>(ProcessItem);

    // Pass the delegates into the methods of Enumerable.
    var subset = currentVideoGames
      .Where(searchFilter).OrderBy(itemToProcess).Select(itemToProcess);

    // Print out the results.
    foreach (var game in subset)
      Console.WriteLine("Item: {0}", game);
    Console.WriteLine();
  }

  // Delegate targets.
  public static bool Filter(string s) {return s.Length > 6;}
  public static string ProcessItem(string s) { return s; }
}
```

We can test this iteration of our string processing logic by calling this method within Main() method of the Program class as follows:

```
VeryComplexQueryExpression.QueryStringsWithRawDelegates();
```

If you were to now run the application to test each possible approach, it should not be too surprising that the output is identical regardless of the path taken. Keep the following points in mind regarding how LINQ query expressions are represented under the covers:

- Query expressions are created using various C# query operators.
- Query operators are simply shorthand notations for invoking extension methods defined by the System.Linq.Enumerable type.
- Many methods of Enumerable require delegates (Func<> in particular) as parameters.

- Under C# 2008, any method requiring a delegate parameter can instead be passed a lambda expression.
- Lambda expressions are simply anonymous methods in disguise (which greatly improve readability).
- Anonymous methods are shorthand notations for allocating a raw delegate and manually building a delegate target method.

Whew! That might have been a bit deeper under the hood than you wish to have gone, but I hope this discussion has helped you understand what the user-friendly C# query operators are actually doing behind the scenes. Let's now turn our attention to the operators themselves.

■ **Source Code** The LinqOverArrayUsingEnumerable project can be found under the Chapter 14 subdirectory.

Investigating the C# LINQ Query Operators

C# defines a good number of query operators out of the box. Table 14-3 documents some of the more commonly used query operators.

■ **Note** The .NET Framework 3.5 SDK documentation provides full details regarding each of the C# LINQ operators. Look up the topic "LINQ General Programming Guide" for more information.

Table 14-3. *Various LINQ Query Operators*

Query Operators	Meaning in Life
`from`, `in`	Used to define the backbone for any LINQ expression, which allows you to extract a subset of data from a fitting container.
`where`	Used to define a restriction for which items to extract from a container.
`select`	Used to select a sequence from the container.
`join`, `on`, `equals`, `into`	Performs joins based on specified key. Remember, these "joins" do not need to have anything to do with data in a relational database.
`orderby`, `ascending`, `descending`	Allows the resulting subset to be ordered in ascending or descending order.
`group`, `by`	Yields a subset with data grouped by a specified value.

In addition to the partial list of operators shown in Table 14-3, the `Enumerable` type provides a set of methods that do not have a direct C# query operator shorthand notation, but are instead exposed as extension methods. These generic methods can be called to transform a result set in various manners (`Reverse<>()`, `ToArray<>()`, `ToList<>()`, etc.). Some are used to extract singletons from a result set, others perform various set operations (`Distinct<>()`, `Union<>()`, `Intersect<>()`, etc.), and still others aggregate results (`Count<>()`, `Sum<>()`, `Min<>()`, `Max<>()`, etc.).

Obtaining Counts Using Enumerable

Using these query operators (and auxiliary members of the `System.Linq.Enumerable` type), you are able to build very expressive query expressions in a strongly typed manner. To invoke the `Enumerable` extension methods, you typically wrap the LINQ expression within parentheses to cast the result to an `IEnumerable<T>`-compatible object to invoke the `Enumerable` extension method.

You have already done so during our examination of immediate execution; however, here is another example that allows you to discover the number of items returned by a LINQ query:

```
static void GetCount()
{
  string[] currentVideoGames = {"Morrowind", "BioShock",
    "Half Life 2: Episode 1", "The Darkness",
    "Daxter", "System Shock 2"};

  // Get count from the query.
  int numb = (from g in currentVideoGames
              where g.Length > 6
              orderby g
              select g).Count<string>();

  // numb is the value 5.
  Console.WriteLine("{0} items honor the LINQ query.", numb);
}
```

Building a New Test Project

To begin digging into more intricate LINQ queries, create a new Console Application named FunWithLinqExpressions. Next, define a trivial `Car` type, this time sporting a custom `ToString()` implementation to quickly view the object's state:

```
class Car
{
  public string PetName = string.Empty;
  public string Color = string.Empty;
  public int Speed;
  public string Make = string.Empty;

  public override string ToString()
  {
    return string.Format("Make={0}, Color={1}, Speed={2}, PetName={3}",
      Make, Color, Speed, PetName);
  }
}
```

Now populate an array with the following `Car` objects within your `Main()` method:

```
static void Main(string[] args)
{
  Console.WriteLine("***** Fun with Query Expressions *****\n");

  // This array will be the basis of our testing...
  Car[] myCars = new [] {
    new Car{ PetName = "Henry", Color = "Silver", Speed = 100, Make = "BMW"},
    new Car{ PetName = "Daisy", Color = "Tan", Speed = 90, Make = "BMW"},
    new Car{ PetName = "Mary", Color = "Black", Speed = 55, Make = "VW"},
    new Car{ PetName = "Clunker", Color = "Rust", Speed = 5, Make = "Yugo"},
```

```
    new Car{ PetName = "Hank", Color = "Tan", Speed = 0, Make = "Ford"},
    new Car{ PetName = "Sven", Color = "White", Speed = 90, Make = "Ford"},
    new Car{ PetName = "Mary", Color = "Black", Speed = 55, Make = "VW"},
    new Car{ PetName = "Zippy", Color = "Yellow", Speed = 55, Make = "VW"},
    new Car{ PetName = "Melvin", Color = "White", Speed = 43, Make = "Ford"}
  };

  // We will call various methods here!
  Console.ReadLine();
}
```

Basic Selection Syntax

Because LINQ query expressions are validated at compile time, you need to remember that the ordering of these operators is critical. In the simplest terms, every LINQ query expression is built using the from, in, and select operators:

```
var result = from item in container select item;
```

In this case, our query expression is doing nothing more than selecting every item in the container (similar to a Select * SQL statement). Consider the following:

```
static void BasicSelection(Car[] myCars)
{
  // Get everything.
  Console.WriteLine("All cars:");
  var allCars = from c in myCars select c;
  foreach (var c in allCars)
  {
    Console.WriteLine(c.ToString());
  }
}
```

Again, this query expression is not entirely useful, given that our subset is identical to that of the data in the incoming parameter. If we wish, we could use this incoming parameter to extract only the PetName values of each car using the following selection syntax:

```
// Now get only the names of the cars.
Console.WriteLine("Only PetNames:");
var names = from c in myCars select c.PetName;

foreach (var n in names)
{
  Console.WriteLine("Name: {0}", n);
}
```

In this case, names is really an internal type that implements IEnumerable<string>, given that we are selecting only the values of the PetName property for each Car object. Again, using implicit typing via the var keyword, our coding task is simplified.

Now consider the following task. What if you'd like to obtain and display the makes of each vehicle? If you author the following query expression:

```
var makes = from c in myCars select c.Make;
```

you will end up with a number of redundant listings, as you will find BMW, Ford, and VW accounted for multiple times. You can use the Enumerable.Distinct<T>() method to eliminate such duplication:

```
var makes = (from c in myCars select c.Make).Distinct<string>();
```

When calling any extension method defined by Enumerable, you can do so either at the time you build the query expression (as shown in the previous example) or via an extension method on a compatible underlying array type. Thus, the following code yields identical output:

```
var makes = from c in myCars select c.Make;
Console.WriteLine("Distinct makes:");
foreach (var m in makes.Distinct<string>())
{
  Console.WriteLine("Make: {0}", m);
}
```

Figure 14-7 shows the result of calling BasicSelections().

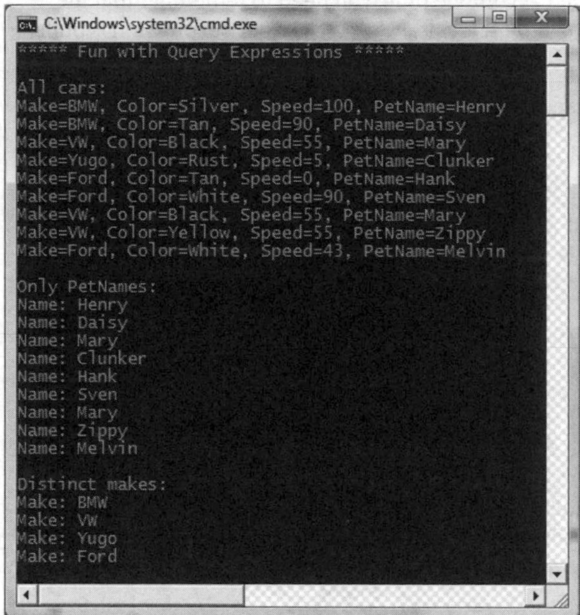

Figure 14-7. *Selecting basic data from the* Car[] *parameter*

Obtaining Subsets of Data

To obtain a specific subset from a container, you can make use of the where operator. When doing so, the general template now becomes as follows:

```
var result = from item in container where Boolean expression select item;
```

Notice that the where operator expects an expression that resolves to a Boolean. For example, to extract from the Car[] parameter only the items that have "BMW" as the value assigned to the Make field, you could author the following code within a new method named GetSubsets():

```
static void GetSubsets(Car[] myCars)
{
  // Now get only the BMWs.
  var onlyBMWs = from c in myCars where c.Make == "BMW" select c;
```

```
  foreach (Car c in onlyBMWs)
  {
    Console.WriteLine(c.ToString());
  }
}
```

As seen earlier in this chapter, when you are building a `where` clause, it is permissible to make use of any valid C# operators to build complex expressions. For example, consider the following query that only extracts out the BMWs going at least 100 mph:

```
// Get BMWs going at least 100 mph.
var onlyFastBMWs = from c in myCars
                   where c.Make == "BMW" && c.Speed >= 100
                   select c;

foreach (Car c in onlyFastBMWs)
{
  Console.WriteLine("{0} is going {1} MPH", c.PetName, c.Speed);
}
```

Projecting New Data Types

It is also possible to project new forms of data from an existing data source. Let's assume that you wish to take the incoming `Car[]` parameter and obtain a result set that accounts only for the make and color of each vehicle. To do so, you can define a `select` statement that dynamically yields new types via C# 2008 *anonymous types*. Recall from Chapter 13 that the compiler defines a read-only property and a read-only backing field for each specified name, and also is kind enough to override `ToString()`, `GetHashCode()`, and `Equals()`:

```
var makesColors = from c in myCars select new {c.Make, c.Color};
foreach (var o in makesColors)
{
  // Could also use Make and Color properties directly.
  Console.WriteLine(o.ToString());
}
```

Figure 14-8 shows the output of each of these new queries.

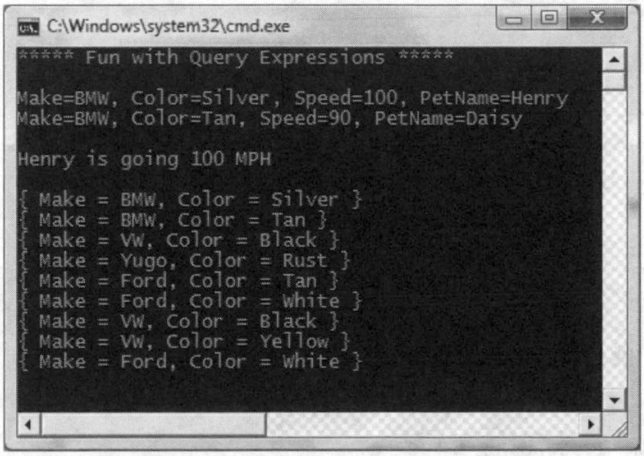

```
C:\Windows\system32\cmd.exe
***** Fun with Query Expressions *****

Make=BMW, Color=Silver, Speed=100, PetName=Henry
Make=BMW, Color=Tan, Speed=90, PetName=Daisy

Henry is going 100 MPH

{ Make = BMW, Color = Silver }
{ Make = BMW, Color = Tan }
{ Make = VW, Color = Black }
{ Make = Yugo, Color = Rust }
{ Make = Ford, Color = Tan }
{ Make = Ford, Color = White }
{ Make = VW, Color = Black }
{ Make = VW, Color = Yellow }
{ Make = Ford, Color = White }
```

Figure 14-8. *Enumerating over subsets*

Reversing Result Sets

You can reverse the items within a result set quite simply using the generic Reverse<T>() method of the Enumerable type. For example, the following method selects all items from the incoming Car[] parameter in reverse:

```
static void ReversedSelection(Car[] myCars)
{
  // Get everything in reverse.
  Console.WriteLine("All cars in reverse:");
  var subset = (from c in myCars select c).Reverse<Car>();
  foreach (Car c in subset)
  {
    Console.WriteLine("{0} is going {1} MPH", c.PetName, c.Speed);
  }
}
```

Here, we called the Reverse<T>() method at the time we constructed our query. Again, as an alternative, we could invoke this method on the myCars array as follows:

```
static void ReversedSelection(Car[] myCars)
{
  // Get everything in reverse.
  Console.WriteLine("All cars in reverse:");
  var subset = from c in myCars select c;
  foreach (Car c in subset.Reverse<Car>())
  {
    Console.WriteLine(c.ToString());
  }
}
```

Sorting Expressions

As you have seen over this chapter's initial examples, a query expression can take an orderby operator to sort items in the subset by a specific value. By default, the order will be ascending; thus, ordering by a string would be alphabetical, ordering by numerical data would be lowest to highest, and so forth. If you wish to view the results in a descending order, simply include the descending operator. Ponder the following method:

```
static void OrderedResults(Car[] myCars)
{
  // Order all the cars by PetName.
  var subset = from c in myCars orderby c.PetName select c;

  Console.WriteLine("Ordered by PetName:");
  foreach (Car c in subset)
  {
    Console.WriteLine(c.ToString());
  }

  // Now find the cars that are going less than 55 mph,
  // and order by descending PetName
  subset = from c in myCars
    where c.Speed > 55 orderby  c.PetName descending select c;
  Console.WriteLine("\nCars going faster than 55, ordered by PetName:");
  foreach (Car c in subset)
  {
```

```
    Console.WriteLine(c.ToString());
  }
}
```

Although ascending order is the default, you are able to make your intentions very clear by making use of the ascending operator:

```
var subset = from c in myCars
  orderby c.PetName ascending select c;
```

Given these examples, you can now understand the format of a basic sorting query expression as follows:

```
var result = from item in container orderby value
  ascending/descending select item;
```

Finding Differences

The last LINQ query we will examine for the time being involves obtaining a result set that determines the differences between two `IEnumerable<T>` compatible containers. Consider the following method, which makes use of the `Enumerable.Except()` method to yield (in this example) a Yugo:

```
static void GetDiff()
{
  List<string> myCars = new List<String>
  { "Yugo", "Aztec", "BMW"};

  List<string> yourCars = new List<String>
  { "BMW", "Saab", "Aztec" };

  var carDiff =(from c in myCars select c)
    .Except(from c2 in yourCars select c2);

  Console.WriteLine("Here is what you don't have, but I do:");
  foreach (string s in carDiff)
    Console.WriteLine(s); // Prints Yugo.
}
```

These examples should give you enough knowledge to feel comfortable with the process of building LINQ query expressions. Chapter 24 will explore the related topics of LINQ to ADO (which is a catch-all term describing LINQ to SQL and LINQ to DataSet) and LINQ to XML. However, before wrapping the current chapter, let's examine the topic LINQ queries as method return values.

■ **Source Code** The FunWithLinqExpressions project can be found under the Chapter 14 subdirectory.

LINQ Queries: An Island unto Themselves?

You may have noticed that each of the LINQ queries seen over the course of this chapter were all defined within the scope of a local method. Moreover, to simplify our programming, the variable used to hold the result set was stored in an implicitly typed local variable (in fact, in the case of projections, this is mandatory). Recall from Chapter 13 that implicitly typed local variables *cannot* be used to define parameters, return values, or fields of a class type.

Given this point, you may wonder exactly how you could return a query result to an external caller. The answer is it depends. If you have a result set consisting of strongly typed data (such as an array of strings, a `List<T>` of `Car`s, or whatnot), you could abandon the use of the `var` keyword and using a proper `IEnumerable<T>` or `IEnumerable` type (again, as `IEnumerable<T>` extends `IEnumerable`). Consider the following example for a new .NET 3.5 Console Application named LinqRetValues:

```
class Program
{
  static void Main(string[] args)
  {
    Console.WriteLine("***** LINQ Transformations *****\n");
    IEnumerable<string> subset = GetStringSubset();
    foreach (string item in subset)
    {
      Console.WriteLine(item);
    }
    Console.ReadLine();
  }

  static IEnumerable<string> GetStringSubset()
  {
    string[] currentVideoGames = {"Morrowind", "BioShock",
      "Half Life 2: Episode 1", "The Darkness",
      "Daxter", "System Shock 2"};

    // Note subset is an IEnumerable<string> compatible object.
    IEnumerable<string> subset = from g in currentVideoGames
                                 where g.Length > 6
                                 orderby g
                                 select g;
    return subset;
  }
}
```

This example works as expected, only because the return value of the `GetStringSubset()` and the LINQ query within this method has been strongly typed. If you used the `var` keyword to define the subset variable, it would be permissible to return the value *only* if the method is still prototyped to return `IEnumerable<string>` (and if the implicitly typed local variable is in fact compatible with the specified return type).

However, always remember that when you have a LINQ query that makes use of a projection, you have no way of knowing the underlying data type, as this is determined at compile time. In these cases, the `var` keyword is mandatory; therefore, the following code method would not compile:

```
// Error! Can't return a var data type!
static var GetProjectedSubset()
{
  Car[] myCars = new Car[] {
    new Car{ PetName = "Henry", Color = "Silver", Speed = 100, Make = "BMW"},
    new Car{ PetName = "Daisy", Color = "Tan", Speed = 90, Make = "BMW"},
    new Car{ PetName = "Mary", Color = "Black", Speed = 55, Make = "VW"},
    new Car{ PetName = "Clunker", Color = "Rust", Speed = 5, Make = "Yugo"},
    new Car{ PetName = "Melvin", Color = "White", Speed = 43, Make = "Ford"}
  };
```

```
  var makesColors = from c in myCars select new { c.Make, c.Color };
  return makesColors;  // Nope!
}
```

Given that return values cannot be implicitly typed, how can we return the makesColors object to an external caller?

Transforming Query Results to Array Types

When you wish to return projected data to a caller, one approach is to transform the query result into a standard CLR Array object using the ToArray<T>() extension method. Thus, if we were to update our query expression as follows:

```
// Return value is now an Array.
static Array GetProjectedSubset()
{
  Car[] myCars = new Car[]{
    new Car{ PetName = "Henry", Color = "Silver", Speed = 100, Make = "BMW"},
    new Car{ PetName = "Daisy", Color = "Tan", Speed = 90, Make = "BMW"},
    new Car{ PetName = "Mary", Color = "Black", Speed = 55, Make = "VW"},
    new Car{ PetName = "Clunker", Color = "Rust", Speed = 5, Make = "Yugo"},
    new Car{ PetName = "Melvin", Color = "White", Speed = 43, Make = "Ford"}
  };

  var makesColors = from c in myCars select new { c.Make, c.Color };

  // Map set of anonymous objects to an Array object.
  // Here were are relying on type inference of the generic
  // type parameter, as we don't know the type of type!
  return makesColors.ToArray();
}
```

we could invoke and process the data from Main() as follows:

```
Array objs = GetProjectedSubset();
foreach (object o in objs)
{
  Console.WriteLine(o);  // Calls ToString() on each anonymous object.
}
```

Note that we have to use a literal System.Array object and cannot make use of the C# array declaration syntax, given that we don't know the underlying type of type! Also note that we are not specifying the type parameter to the generic ToArray<T>() method, as we (once again) don't know the underlying data type until compile time (which is too late for our purposes).

The obvious problem is that we lose any strong typing, as each item in the Array object is assumed to be of type Object. Nevertheless, when you need to return a LINQ result set which is the result of a projection operation, transforming the data into an Array type (or another suitable container via other members of the Enumerable type) is mandatory.

■ **Source Code** The LinqRetValues project can be found under the Chapter 14 subdirectory.

Summary

LINQ is a set of related technologies that attempts to provide a single, symmetrical manner to interact with diverse forms of data. As explained over the course of this chapter, LINQ can interact with any type implementing the `IEnumerable<T>` interface, including simple arrays as well as generic and nongeneric collections of data.

As you have seen over the course of this chapter, working with LINQ technologies is accomplished using several new C# 2008 language features. For example, given the fact that LINQ query expressions can return any number of result sets, it is common to make use of the `var` keyword to represent the underlying data type. As well, lambda expressions, object initialization syntax, and anonymous types can all be used to build very functional and compact LINQ queries.

More importantly, you have seen how the C# LINQ query operators are simply shorthand notations for making calls on static members of the `System.Linq.Enumerable` type. As shown, most members of `Enumerable` operate on `Func<T>` delegate types, which can take literal method addresses, anonymous methods, or lambda expressions as input to evaluate the query.

PART 4

Programming with .NET Assemblies

CHAPTER 15

Introducing .NET Assemblies

Each of the applications developed in this book's first fourteen chapters were along the lines of traditional "stand-alone" applications, given that all of your custom programming logic was contained within a single executable file (*.exe). However, one major aspect of the .NET platform is the notion of *binary reuse*, where applications make use of the types contained within various external assemblies (aka code libraries). The point of this chapter is to examine the core details of creating, deploying, and configuring .NET assemblies.

In this chapter, you'll first learn the construction of .NET namespaces followed by the distinction between single-file and multifile assemblies, as well as "private" and "shared" assemblies. Next, you'll examine exactly how the .NET runtime resolves the location of an assembly and come to understand the role of the global assembly cache (GAC), application configuration files (*.config files), publisher policy assemblies, and the role of the System.Configuration namespace.

Defining Custom Namespaces

Before diving into the details of assembly deployment and configuration, it is very important to examine the topic of creating custom .NET namespaces. Up to this point in the text, you have been building small test programs leveraging existing namespaces in the .NET universe (System in particular). However, when you build your own custom applications, it can be very helpful to group your related types into custom namespaces. In C#, this is accomplished using the namespace keyword. This is even more important when creating .NET *.dll assemblies, as other developers will need to import your custom namespaces to make use of your types.

Assume you are developing a collection of geometric classes named Square, Circle, and Hexagon. Given their similarities, you would like to group them all together into a common custom namespace. You have two basic approaches. First, you may choose to define each class within a single file (ShapesLib.cs) as follows:

```
// shapeslib.cs
using System;

namespace MyShapes
{
  // Circle class
  class Circle{  /* Interesting methods... */ }
  // Hexagon class
  class Hexagon{ /* More interesting methods... */ }
  // Square class
  class Square{  /* Even more interesting methods... */ }
}
```

Notice how the MyShapes namespace acts as the conceptual "container" of these types. Alternatively, you can split a single namespace into multiple C# files. To do so, simply wrap the given class definitions in the same namespace:

```
// circle.cs
using System;

namespace MyShapes
{
  // Circle class
  class Circle{ }
}

// hexagon.cs
using System;

namespace MyShapes
{
  // Hexagon class
  class Hexagon{ }
}

// square.cs
using System;

namespace MyShapes
{
  // Square class
  class Square{ }
}
```

When another namespace wishes to use objects within a distinct namespace, the using keyword can be used as follows:

```
// Make use of types defined the MyShape namespace.
using System;
using MyShapes;

namespace MyApp
{
  class ShapeTester
  {
    static void Main(string[] args)
    {
      Hexagon h = new Hexagon();
      Circle c = new Circle();
      Square s = new Square();
    }
  }
}
```

A Type's Fully Qualified Name

Technically speaking, you are not required to make use of the C# using keyword when declaring a type defined in an external namespace. You could make use of the fully qualified name of the type, which as you recall from Chapter 1 is the type's name prefixed with the defining namespace:

```
// Note we are not "using" MyShapes anymore.
using System;

namespace MyApp
{
  class ShapeTester
  {
    static void Main(string[] args)
    {
      MyShapes.Hexagon h = new MyShapes.Hexagon();
      MyShapes.Circle c = new MyShapes.Circle();
      MyShapes.Square s = new MyShapes.Square();
    }
  }
}
```

Typically there is no need to use a fully qualified name. Not only does it require a greater number of keystrokes, but also it makes no difference whatsoever in terms of code size or execution speed. In fact, in CIL code, types are *always* defined with the fully qualified name. In this light, the C# `using` keyword is simply a typing time-saver.

However, fully qualified names can be very helpful (and sometimes necessary) to avoid name clashes that may occur when using multiple namespaces that contain identically named types. Assume you have a new namespace termed `My3DShapes`, which defines three classes capable of rendering a shape in stunning 3D:

```
// Another shapes namespace...
using System;

namespace My3DShapes
{
  // 3D Circle class
  class Circle{ }
  // 3D Hexagon class
  class Hexagon{ }
  // 3D Square class
  class Square{ }
}
```

If you update `ShapeTester` as was done here, you are issued a number of compile-time errors, because both namespaces define identically named types:

```
// Ambiguities abound!
using System;
using MyShapes;
using My3DShapes;

namespace MyApp
{
  class ShapeTester
  {
    static void Main(string[] args)
    {
      // Which namespace do I reference?
      Hexagon h = new Hexagon(); // Compiler error!
      Circle c = new Circle();   // Compiler error!
      Square s = new Square();   // Compiler error!
    }
  }
}
```

The ambiguity can be resolved using the type's fully qualified name:

```
// We have now resolved the ambiguity.
static void Main(string[] args)
{
  My3DShapes.Hexagon h = new My3DShapes.Hexagon();
  My3DShapes.Circle c = new My3DShapes.Circle();
  MyShapes.Square s = new MyShapes.Square();
}
```

Defining using Aliases

The C# using keyword can also be used to create an alias to a type's fully qualified name. When you do so, you are able to define a token that is substituted with the type's full name at compile time, for example:

```
using System;
using MyShapes;
using My3DShapes;

// Resolve the ambiguity using a custom alias.
using The3DHexagon = My3DShapes.Hexagon;

namespace MyApp
{
  class ShapeTester
  {
    static void Main(string[] args)
    {
      // This is really creating a My3DShapes.Hexagon type.
      The3DHexagon h2 = new The3DHexagon();
...
    }
  }
}
```

This alternative using syntax can also be used to create an alias to a lengthy namespace. One of the longer namespaces in the base class library would have to be System.Runtime.Serialization.Formatters.Binary, which contains a member named BinaryFormatter. If you wish, you could create an instance of the BinaryFormatter as follows:

```
using MyAlias = System.Runtime.Serialization.Formatters.Binary;

namespace MyApp
{
  class ShapeTester
  {
    static void Main(string[] args)
    {
      MyAlias.BinaryFormatter b = new MyAlias.BinaryFormatter();
    }
  }
}
```

as well as with a traditional using directive:

```
using System.Runtime.Serialization.Formatters.Binary;

namespace MyApp
{
  class ShapeTester
  {
    static void Main(string[] args)
    {
      BinaryFormatter b = new BinaryFormatter();
    }
  }
}
```

■ **Note** C# also provides a mechanism that can be used to resolve name clashes between identically named `namespaces` using the namespace alias qualifier (`::`) and `global` token. Thankfully, this type of name collision is rare. If you require more information regarding this topic, look up my article "Working with the C# 2.0 Command Line Compiler" from `http://msdn.microsoft.com`.

Creating Nested Namespaces

When organizing your types, you are free to define namespaces within other namespaces. The .NET base class libraries do so in numerous places to provide an even deeper level of type organization. For example, the `Collections` namespace is nested within `System`, to yield `System.Collections`. If you wish to create a root namespace that contains the existing `My3DShapes` namespace, you can update your code as follows:

```
// Nesting a namespace.
namespace Chapter15
{
  namespace My3DShapes
  {
    // 3D Circle class
    class Circle{ }
    // 3D Hexagon class
    class Hexagon{ }
    // 3D Square class
    class Square{ }
  }
}
```

In many cases, the role of a root namespace is simply to provide a further level of scope, and therefore may not define any types directly within its scope (as in the case of the `Chapter15` namespace). If this is the case, a nested namespace can be defined using the following compact form:

```
// Nesting a namespace (take two).
namespace Chapter15.My3DShapes
{
  // 3D Circle class
  class Circle{ }
  // 3D Hexagon class
  class Hexagon{ }
  // 3D Square class
  class Square{ }
}
```

Given that you have now nested the `My3DShapes` namespace within the `Chapter15` root namespace, you need to update any existing `using` directives and type aliases:

```
using Chapter15.My3DShapes;
using The3DHexagon = Chapter15.My3DShapes.Hexagon;
```

The "Default Namespace" of Visual Studio 2008

On a final namespace-related note, it is worth pointing out that by default, when you create a new C# project using Visual Studio 2008, the name of your application's default namespace will be identical to the project name. From this point on, when you insert new items using the Project ➤ Add New Item menu selection, types will automatically be wrapped within the default namespace. If you wish to change the name of the default namespace (e.g., to be your company name), simply access the Default namespace option using the Application tab of the project's Properties window (see Figure 15-1).

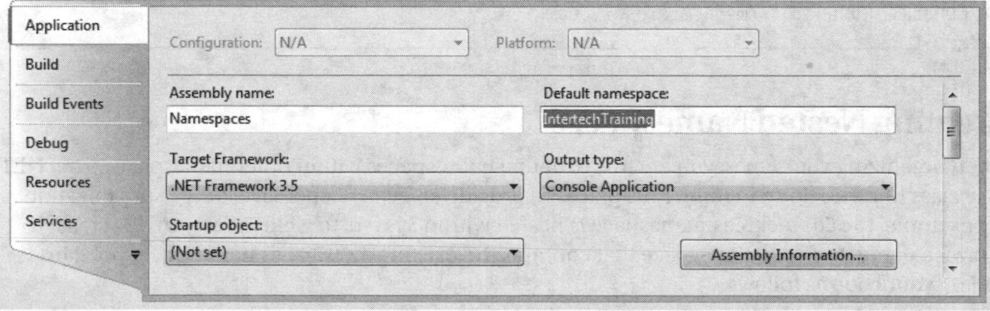

Figure 15-1. *Configuring the default namespace*

With this update, any new item inserted into the project will be wrapped within the `IntertechTraining` namespace (and, obviously, if another namespace wishes to use these types, the correct `using` directive must be applied).

Source Code The Namespaces project is located under the Chapter 15 subdirectory.

The Role of .NET Assemblies

.NET applications are constructed by piecing together any number of *assemblies*. Simply put, an assembly is a versioned, self-describing binary file hosted by the CLR. Now, despite the fact that .NET assemblies have exactly the same file extensions (`*.exe` or `*.dll`) as previous Win32 binaries (including legacy COM servers), they have very little in common under the hood. Thus, to set the stage for the information to come, let's consider some of the benefits provided by the assembly format.

Assemblies Promote Code Reuse

As you have been building your Console Applications over the previous chapters, it may have seemed that *all* of the applications' functionality was contained within the executable assembly you were constructing. In reality, your applications were leveraging numerous types contained within the always accessible .NET code library, `mscorlib.dll` (recall that the C# compiler references `mscorlib.dll` automatically), and in the case of some examples, `System.Windows.Forms.dll`.

As you may know, a *code library* (also termed a *class library*) is a `*.dll` that contains types intended to be used by external applications. When you are creating executable assemblies, you will no doubt be leveraging numerous system-supplied and custom code libraries as you create the application at hand. Do be aware, however, that a code library need not take a `*.dll` file extension. It is perfectly possible for an executable assembly to make use of types defined within an external executable file. In this light, a referenced `*.exe` can also be considered a "code library."

Regardless of how a code library is packaged, the .NET platform allows you to reuse types in a language-independent manner. For example, you could create a code library in C# and reuse that library in any other .NET programming language. It is possible to not only allocate types across languages, but also derive from them. A base class defined in C# could be extended by a class authored in Visual Basic. Interfaces defined in Pascal .NET can be implemented by structures defined in C#, and so forth. The point is that when you begin to break apart a single monolithic executable into numerous .NET assemblies, you achieve a *language-neutral* form of code reuse.

Assemblies Establish a Type Boundary

To begin this chapter, you learned about the formalities behind .NET namespaces. Recall that a type's *fully qualified name* is composed by prefixing the type's namespace (e.g., `System`) to its name (e.g., `Console`). Strictly speaking however, the assembly in which a type resides further establishes a type's identity. For example, if you have two uniquely named assemblies (say, `MyCars.dll` and `YourCars.dll`) that both define a namespace (`CarLibrary`) containing a class named `SportsCar`, they are considered unique types in the .NET universe.

Assemblies Are Versionable Units

.NET assemblies are assigned a four-part numerical version number of the form *<major>*.*<minor>*.*<build>*.*<revision>* (if you do not explicitly provide a version number, the assembly is automatically assigned a version of 0.0.0.0). This number, in conjunction with an optional *public key value*, allows multiple versions of the same assembly to coexist in harmony on a single machine. Formally speaking, assemblies that provide public key information are termed *strongly named*. As you will see in this chapter, using a strong name, the CLR is able to ensure that the correct version of an assembly is loaded on behalf of the calling client.

Assemblies Are Self-Describing

Assemblies are regarded as *self-describing* in part because they record every external assembly it must have access to in order to function correctly. Thus, if your assembly requires `System.Windows.Forms.dll` and `System.Drawing.dll`, they will be documented in the assembly's *manifest*. Recall from Chapter 1 that a manifest is a blob of metadata that describes the assembly itself (name, version, required external assemblies, etc.).

In addition to manifest data, an assembly contains metadata that describes the composition (member names, implemented interfaces, base classes, constructors, and so forth) of every contained type. Given that an assembly is documented in such vivid detail, the CLR does *not* consult the Win32 system registry to resolve its location (quite the radical departure from Microsoft's legacy COM programming model). As you will discover during this chapter, the CLR makes use of an entirely new scheme to resolve the location of external code libraries.

Assemblies Are Configurable

Assemblies can be deployed as "private" or "shared." Private assemblies reside in the same directory (or possibly a subdirectory) as the client application making use of them. Shared assemblies, on the other hand, are libraries intended to be consumed by numerous applications on a single machine and are deployed to a specific directory termed the *global assembly cache*, or *GAC*.

Regardless of how you deploy your assemblies, you are free to author XML-based configuration files. Using these configuration files, the CLR can be instructed to "probe" for assemblies under a specific location, load a specific version of a referenced assembly for a particular client, or consult an arbitrary directory on your local machine, your network location, or a web-based URL. You'll learn a good deal more about XML configuration files throughout this chapter.

Understanding the Format of a .NET Assembly

Now that you've learned about several benefits provided by the .NET assembly, let's shift gears and get a better idea of how an assembly is composed under the hood. Structurally speaking, a .NET assembly (`*.dll` or `*.exe`) consists of the following elements:

- A Win32 file header
- A CLR file header
- CIL code
- Type metadata
- An assembly manifest
- Optional embedded resources

While the first two elements (the Win32 and CLR headers) are blocks of data that you can typically ignore, they do deserve some brief consideration. This being said, an overview of each element follows.

The Win32 File Header

The Win32 file header establishes the fact that the assembly can be loaded and manipulated by the Windows family of operating systems. This header data also identifies the kind of application (console-based, GUI-based, or `*.dll` code library) to be hosted by the Windows operating system. If you open a .NET assembly using the `dumpbin.exe` utility (via a Visual Studio 2008 command prompt) and specify the `/headers` flag, you can view an assembly's Win32 header information. Figure 15-2 shows (partial) Win32 header information for the `CarLibrary.dll` assembly you will build a bit later in this chapter.

Administrator: Visual Studio 2008 Beta 2 Command Prompt

```
C:\>dumpbin CarLibrary.dll /headers
Microsoft (R) COFF/PE Dumper Version 9.00.20706.01
Copyright (C) Microsoft Corporation.  All rights reserved.


Dump of file CarLibrary.dll

PE signature found

File Type: DLL

FILE HEADER VALUES
             14C machine (x86)
               3 number of sections
        46086AC3 time date stamp Mon Mar 26 19:52:19 2007
               0 file pointer to symbol table
               0 number of symbols
              E0 size of optional header
            210E characteristics
                   Executable
                   Line numbers stripped
```

Figure 15-2. *An assembly's Win32 file header information*

The CLR File Header

The CLR header is a block of data that all .NET files must support (and do support, courtesy of the C# compiler) in order to be hosted by the CLR. In a nutshell, this header defines numerous flags that enable the runtime to understand the layout of the managed file. For example, flags exist that identify the location of the metadata and resources within the file, the version of the runtime the assembly was built against, the value of the (optional) public key, and so forth. If you supply the `/clrheader` flag to `dumpbin.exe`, you are presented with the internal CLR header information for a given .NET assembly, as shown in Figure 15-3.

Administrator: Visual Studio 2008 Beta 2 Command Prompt

```
C:\>dumpbin CarLibrary.dll /clrheader
Microsoft (R) COFF/PE Dumper Version 9.00.20706.01
Copyright (C) Microsoft Corporation.  All rights reserved.


Dump of file CarLibrary.dll

File Type: DLL

  clr Header:

              48 cb
            2.05 runtime version
            21E4 [     9FC] RVA [size] of MetaData Directory
               9 flags
                   IL Only
                   Strong Name Signed
               0 entry point token
               0 [       0] RVA [size] of Resources Directory
            2050 [      80] RVA [size] of StrongNameSignature Directory
               0 [       0] RVA [size] of CodeManagerTable Directory
               0 [       0] RVA [size] of VTableFixups Directory
               0 [       0] RVA [size] of ExportAddressTableJumps Directory
               0 [       0] RVA [size] of ManagedNativeHeader Directory


  Summary

        2000 .reloc
        2000 .rsrc
        2000 .text

C:\>
```

Figure 15-3. *An assembly's CLR file header information*

Again, as a .NET developer you will not need to concern yourself with the gory details of Win32 or CLR header information (unless perhaps you are building a compiler for a new managed language!). Just understand that every .NET assembly contains this data, which is used behind the scenes by the .NET runtime and Win32 operating system.

CIL Code, Type Metadata, and the Assembly Manifest

At its core, an assembly contains CIL code, which as you recall is a platform- and CPU-agnostic intermediate language. At runtime, the internal CIL is compiled on the fly (using a just-in-time [JIT] compiler) to platform- and CPU-specific instructions. Given this architecture, .NET assemblies can indeed execute on a variety of architectures, devices, and operating systems. Although you can live a happy and productive life without understanding the details of the CIL programming language, Chapter 19 offers an introduction to the syntax and semantics of CIL.

An assembly also contains metadata that completely describes the format of the contained types as well as the format of external types referenced by this assembly. The .NET runtime uses this metadata to resolve the location of types (and their members) within the binary, lay out types in memory, and facilitate remote method invocations. You'll check out the details of the .NET metadata format in Chapter 16 during our examination of reflection services.

An assembly must also contain an associated *manifest* (also referred to as *assembly metadata*). The manifest documents each module within the assembly, establishes the version of the assembly, and also documents any *external* assemblies referenced by the current assembly (unlike legacy COM type libraries, which did not provide a way to document external dependencies). As you will see over the course of this chapter, the CLR makes extensive use of an assembly's manifest during the process of locating external assembly references.

■ **Note** Needless to say by this point in the book, when you wish to view an assembly's CIL code, type metadata, or manifest, `ildasm.exe` or `reflector.exe` are the tools of choice. I will assume you will make extensive use of these tools as you work through the code examples in this chapter.

Optional Assembly Resources

Finally, a .NET assembly may contain any number of embedded resources such as application icons, image files, sound clips, or string tables. In fact, the .NET platform supports *satellite assemblies* that contain nothing but localized resources. This can be useful if you wish to partition your resources based on a specific culture (English, German, etc.) for the purposes of building international software. The topic of building satellite assemblies is outside the scope of this text; however, you will learn how to embed application resources into an assembly during our examination of Windows Presentation Foundation.

Single-File and Multifile Assemblies

Technically speaking, an assembly can be composed of multiple *modules*. A module is really nothing more than a generic term for a valid .NET binary file. In most situations, an assembly is in fact composed of a single module. In this case, there is a one-to-one correspondence between the (logical) assembly and the underlying (physical) binary (hence the term *single-file assembly*).

Single-file assemblies contain all of the necessary elements (header information, CIL code, type metadata, manifest, and required resources) in a single `*.exe` or `*.dll` package. Figure 15-4 illustrates the composition of a single-file assembly.

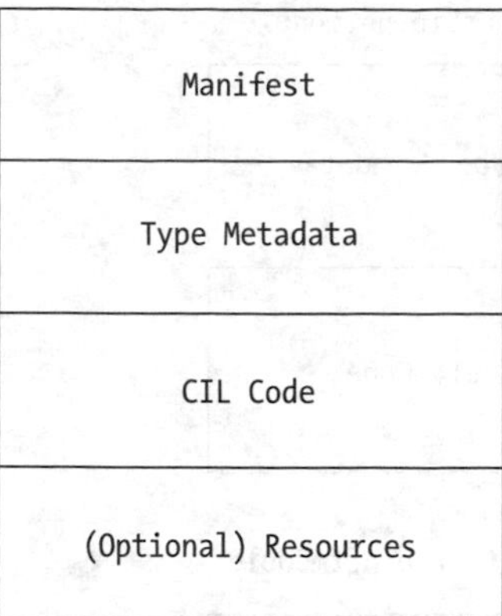

Figure 15-4. *A single-file assembly*

A multifile assembly, on the other hand, is a set of .NET `*.dll`s that are deployed and versioned as a single logic unit. Formally speaking, one of these `*.dll`s is termed the *primary module* and contains the assembly-level manifest (as well as any necessary CIL code, metadata, header information, and optional resources). The manifest of the primary module records each of the related `*.dll` files it is dependent upon.

As a naming convention, the secondary modules in a multifile assembly take a `*.netmodule` file extension; however, this is not a requirement of the CLR. Secondary `*.netmodule`s also contain CIL code and type metadata, as well as a *module-level manifest*, which simply records the externally required assemblies of that specific module.

The major benefit of constructing multifile assemblies is that they provide a very efficient way to download content. For example, assume you have a machine that is referencing a remote multifile assembly composed of three modules, where the primary module is installed on the client. If the client requires a type within a secondary remote `*.netmodule`, the CLR will download the binary to the local machine on demand to a specific location termed the *download cache*. If each `*.netmodule` is 5MB, I'm sure you can see the benefit (compared with downloading a single 15MB file).

Another benefit of multifile assemblies is that they enable modules to be authored using multiple .NET programming languages (which is very helpful in larger corporations, where individual departments tend to favor a specific .NET language). Once each of the individual modules has been compiled, the modules can be logically "connected" into a logical assembly using the C# command-line compiler.

In any case, do understand that the modules that compose a multifile assembly are *not* literally linked together into a single (larger) file. Rather, multifile assemblies are only logically related by information contained in the primary module's manifest. Figure 15-5 illustrates a multifile assembly composed of three modules, each authored using a unique .NET programming language.

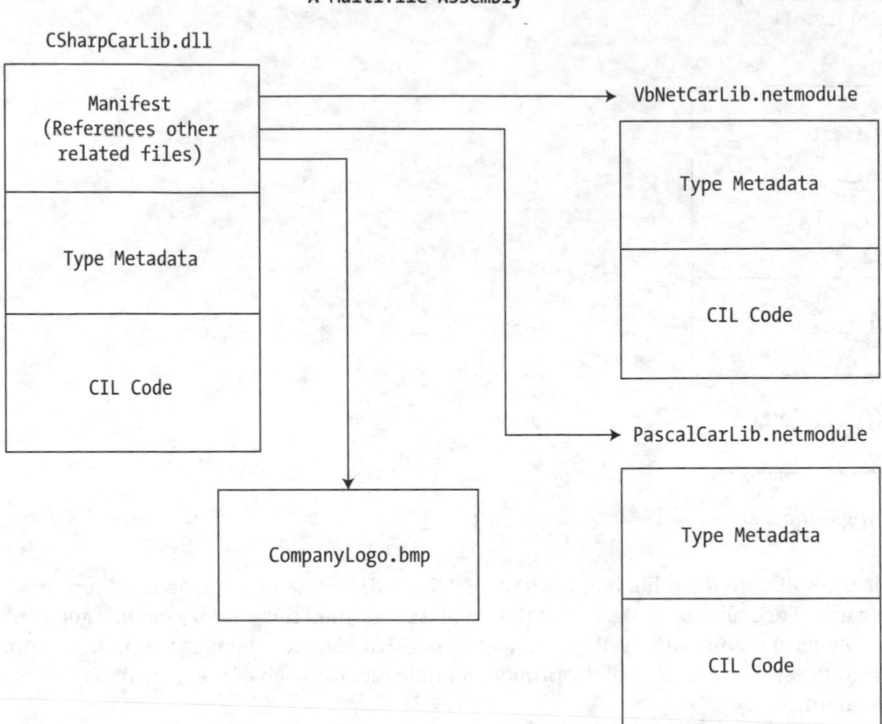

Figure 15-5. *The primary module records secondary modules in the assembly manifest.*

At this point you (hopefully) have a better understanding about the internal composition of a .NET binary file. With this necessary preamble out of the way, we are ready to dig into the details of building and configuring a variety of code libraries.

Building and Consuming a Single-File Assembly

To begin exploring the world of .NET assemblies, you'll first create a single-file `*.dll` assembly (named `CarLibrary`) that contains a small set of public types. To build a code library using Visual Studio 2008, simply select the Class Library project workspace (see Figure 15-6).

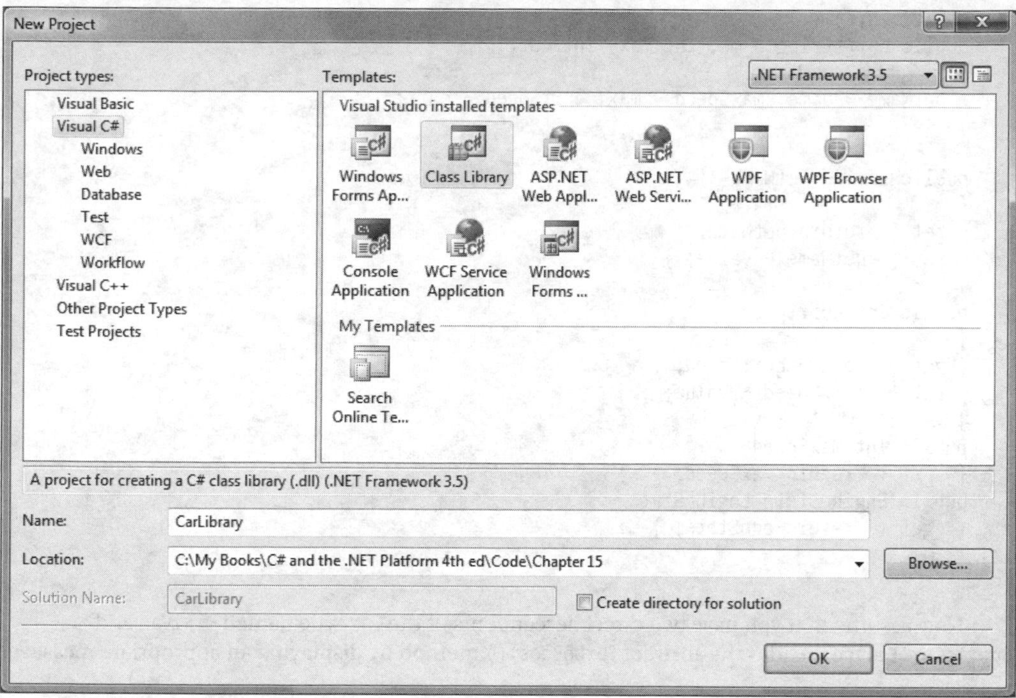

Figure 15-6. *Creating a C# code library*

The design of your automobile library begins with an abstract base class named `Car` that defines a number of protected data members exposed through custom properties (feel free to use automatic property syntax if you wish; see Chapter 13). This class has a single abstract method named `TurboBoost()`, which makes use of a custom enumeration (`EngineState`) representing the current condition of the car's engine:

```
using System;

namespace CarLibrary
{
  // Represents the state of the engine.
  public enum EngineState
  { engineAlive, engineDead }

  // The abstract base class in the hierarchy.
  public abstract class Car
  {
    protected string petName;
    protected int currSpeed;
    protected int maxSpeed;
    protected EngineState egnState = EngineState.engineAlive;

    public abstract void TurboBoost();
```

```
    public Car(){}
    public Car(string name, int max, int curr)
    {
      petName = name; maxSpeed = max; currSpeed = curr;
    }

    public string PetName
    {
      get {  return petName; }
      set {  petName = value; }
    }
    public int CurrSpeed
    {
      get {  return currSpeed; }
      set {  currSpeed = value; }
    }
    public int MaxSpeed
    {  get {  return maxSpeed; }  }
    public EngineState EngineState
    {  get {  return egnState; }  }
  }
}
```

Now assume that you have two direct descendents of the `Car` type named `MiniVan` and `SportsCar`. Each overrides the abstract `TurboBoost()` method by displaying an appropriate message.

```
using System;
using System.Windows.Forms;

namespace CarLibrary
{
  public class SportsCar : Car
  {
    public SportsCar(){ }
    public SportsCar(string name, int max, int curr)
      : base (name, max, curr){ }

    public override void TurboBoost()
    {
      MessageBox.Show("Ramming speed!", "Faster is better...");
    }
  }

  public class MiniVan : Car
  {
    public MiniVan(){ }
    public MiniVan(string name, int max, int curr)
      : base (name, max, curr){ }

    public override void TurboBoost()
    {
      // Minivans have poor turbo capabilities!
      egnState = EngineState.engineDead;
      MessageBox.Show("Time to call AAA", "Your car is dead");
    }
  }
}
```

Notice how each subclass implements `TurboBoost()` using the Windows Form's `MessageBox` class, which is defined in the `System.Windows.Forms.dll` assembly. For your assembly to make use of the types defined within this external assembly, the CarLibrary project must set a reference to this binary via the Add Reference dialog box (see Figure 15-7), which you can access through the Visual Studio Project ➤ Add Reference menu selection.

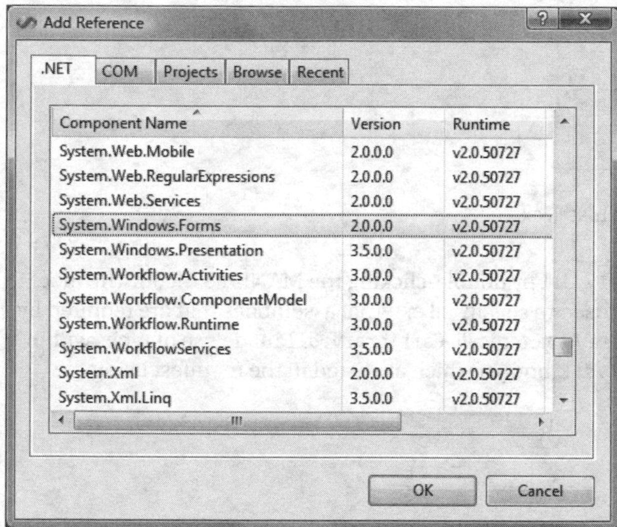

Figure 15-7. *Referencing external .NET assemblies begins here.*

It is *really* important to understand that the assemblies displayed in the .NET tab of the Add Reference dialog box do not represent each and every assembly on your machine. The Add Reference dialog box will *not* display your custom assemblies, and it does *not* display all assemblies located in the GAC. Rather, this dialog box simply presents a list of common assemblies that Visual Studio 2008 is preprogrammed to display. When you are building applications that require the use of an assembly not listed within the Add Reference dialog box, you need to click the Browse tab to manually navigate to the `*.dll` or `*.exe` in question.

■ **Note** Be aware that the Recent tab of the Add Reference dialog box keeps a running list of previously referenced assemblies. This can be handy, as many .NET projects tend to use the same core set of external libraries.

Exploring the Manifest

Before making use of `CarLibrary.dll` from a client application, let's check out how the code library is composed under the hood. Assuming you have compiled this project, load `CarLibrary.dll` into `ildasm.exe` (see Figure 15-8).

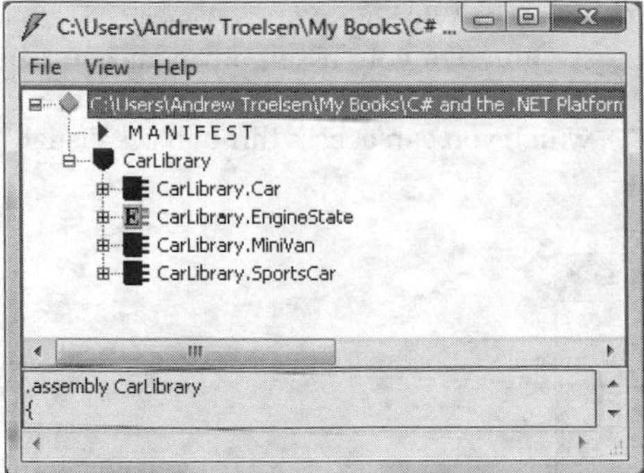

Figure 15-8. `CarLibrary.dll` *loaded into* `ildasm.exe`

Now, open the manifest of `CarLibrary.dll` by double-clicking the MANIFEST icon. The first code block encountered in a manifest is used to specify all external assemblies that are required by the current assembly to function correctly. As you recall, `CarLibrary.dll` made use of types within `mscorlib.dll` and `System.Windows.Forms.dll`, both of which are listed in the manifest using the `.assembly extern` token:

```
.assembly extern mscorlib
{
  .publickeytoken = (B7 7A 5C 56 19 34 E0 89 )
  .ver 2:0:0:0
}
.assembly extern System.Windows.Forms
{
  .publickeytoken = (B7 7A 5C 56 19 34 E0 89 )
  .ver 2:0:0:0
}
```

Here, each `.assembly extern` block is qualified by the `.publickeytoken` and `.ver` directives. The `.publickeytoken` instruction is present only if the assembly has been configured with a *strong name* (more details on strong names in the section "Understanding Strong Names" later in this chapter). The `.ver` token defines (of course) the numerical version identifier.

After cataloging each of the external references, you will find a number of `.custom` tokens that identify assembly-level attributes. If you examine the `AssemblyInfo.cs` file created by Visual Studio (which can be viewed by expanding the Properties icon of the Solution Explorer), you will find these attributes represent basic characteristics about the assembly such as company name, trademark, and so forth.

Chapter 16 examines attributes in detail, so don't sweat the details at this point. Do be aware, however, that the attributes defined in `AssemblyInfo.cs` update the manifest with various `.custom` tokens, such as `[AssemblyTitle]`:

```
.assembly CarLibrary
{
...
  .custom instance void [mscorlib]
    System.Reflection.AssemblyTitleAttribute::.ctor(string) =
  ( 01 00 0A 43 61 72 4C 69 62 72 61 72 79 00 00 )    // ...CarLibrary..
   .hash algorithm 0x00008004
  .ver 1:0:0:0
}
.module CarLibrary.dll
```

Finally, you can also see that the .assembly token is used to mark the friendly name of your assembly (CarLibrary), while the .module token specifies the name of the module itself (CarLibrary.dll). The .ver token defines the version number assigned to this assembly, as specified by the [AssemblyVersion] attribute within AssemblyInfo.cs.

Exploring the CIL

Recall that an assembly does not contain platform-specific instructions; rather, it contains platform-agnostic common intermediate language (CIL) instructions. When the .NET runtime loads an assembly into memory, the underlying CIL is compiled (using the JIT compiler) into instructions that can be understood by the target platform. If you double-click the TurboBoost() method of the SportsCar class, ildasm.exe will open a new window showing the CIL tokens that implement this method:

```
.method public hidebysig virtual instance void
  TurboBoost() cil managed
{
  // Code size       18 (0x12)
  .maxstack  8
  IL_0000:  nop
  IL_0001:  ldstr  "Ramming speed!"
  IL_0006:  ldstr  "Faster is better..."
  IL_000b:  call  valuetype [System.Windows.Forms]System.Windows.Forms.DialogResult
    [System.Windows.Forms]System.Windows.Forms.MessageBox::Show(string, string)
  IL_0010:  pop
  IL_0011:  ret
} // end of method SportsCar::TurboBoost
```

Notice that the .method tag is used to identify a method defined by the SportsCar type. Member variables defined by a type are marked with the .field tag. Recall that the Car class defined a set of protected data, such as currSpeed:

```
.field family int32 currSpeed
```

Properties are marked with the .property tag. Here is the CIL describing the public CurrSpeed property (note that the read/write nature of a property is marked by .get and .set tags):

```
.property instance int32 CurrSpeed()
{
  .get instance int32 CarLibrary.Car::get_CurrSpeed()
  .set instance void CarLibrary.Car::set_CurrSpeed(int32)
} // end of property Car::CurrSpeed
```

As you can see, the get/set scopes of a property simply delegate to normal (and hidden) methods within the assembly (get_CurrSpeed() and set_currSpeed() in this case). Again, while most .NET developers do not need to be deeply concerned with the details of CIL, Chapter 19 will provide more details on the syntax and semantics of the common intermediate language.

Exploring the Type Metadata

Finally, if you now press Ctrl+M, ildasm.exe displays the metadata for each type within the CarLibrary.dll assembly (see Figure 15-9).

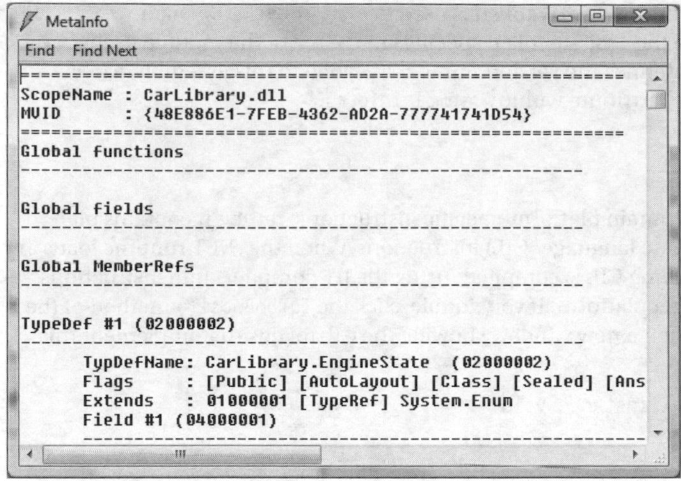

Figure 15-9. *Type metadata for the types within* `CarLibrary.dll`

As explained in the next chapter, an assembly's metadata is a very important trait of the .NET platform, and serves as the backbone for numerous technologies (object serialization, late binding, extendable applications, etc.). In any case, now that you have looked inside the `CarLibrary.dll` assembly, you can build some client applications that make use of your types.

Source Code The CarLibrary project is located under the Chapter 15 subdirectory.

Building a C# Client Application

Because each of the `CarLibrary` types has been declared using the `public` keyword, other assemblies are able to make use of them. Recall that you may also define types using the C# `internal` keyword (in fact, this is the default C# access mode). Internal types can be used only by the assembly in which they are defined. External clients can neither see nor create types marked with the `internal` keyword.

Note .NET does provides a way to specify "friend assemblies" that allow internal types to be consumed by a set of specified assemblies. Look up the `InternalsVisibleToAttribute` class in the .NET Framework 3.5 SDK documentation for details.

To consume these types, create a new C# Console Application project (CSharpCarClient). Once you have done so, set a reference to `CarLibrary.dll` using the Browse tab of the Add Reference dialog box (if you compiled `CarLibrary.dll` using Visual Studio, your assembly is located under the \bin\Debug subdirectory of the CarLibrary project folder). At this point you can build your client application to make use of the external types. Update your initial C# file as follows:

```
using System;

// Don't forget to import the CarLibrary namespace!
using CarLibrary;

namespace CSharpCarClient
{
  public class Program
  {
    static void Main(string[] args)
    {
      Console.WriteLine("***** C# CarLibrary Client App *****");
      // Make a sports car.
      SportsCar viper = new SportsCar("Viper", 240, 40);
      viper.TurboBoost();

      // Make a minivan.
      MiniVan mv = new MiniVan();
      mv.TurboBoost();
      Console.ReadLine();
    }
  }
}
```

This code looks just like the code of the other applications developed thus far in the text. The only point of interest is that the C# client application is now making use of types defined within a separate custom assembly. Go ahead and run your program. As you would expect, the execution of this program results in the display of various message boxes.

It is also important to point out that Visual Studio 2008 has also placed a copy of `CarLibrary.dll` into the \bin\Debug folder of the CSharpCarClient project folder. This can be verified by clicking the Show All Files button of the Solution Explorer (see Figure 15-10).

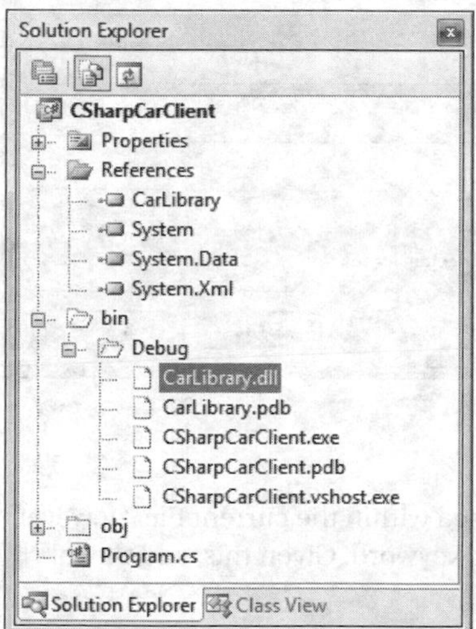

Figure 15-10. *Visual Studio 2008 copies private assemblies to the client's directory.*

As explained later in this chapter, `CarLibrary.dll` has been deployed as a "private" assembly. Therefore the CLR loads the local copy of the .NET binary on behalf of the current client (`CSharpCarClient.exe`).

Source Code The CSharpCarClient project is located under the Chapter 15 subdirectory.

Building a Visual Basic Client Application

To illustrate the language-agnostic attitude of the .NET platform, let's create another Console Application (VbNetCarClient), this time using Visual Basic (see Figure 15-11). Once you have created the project, set a reference to `CarLibrary.dll` using the Add Reference dialog box, which can be activated by the Project ➤ Add Reference menu option.

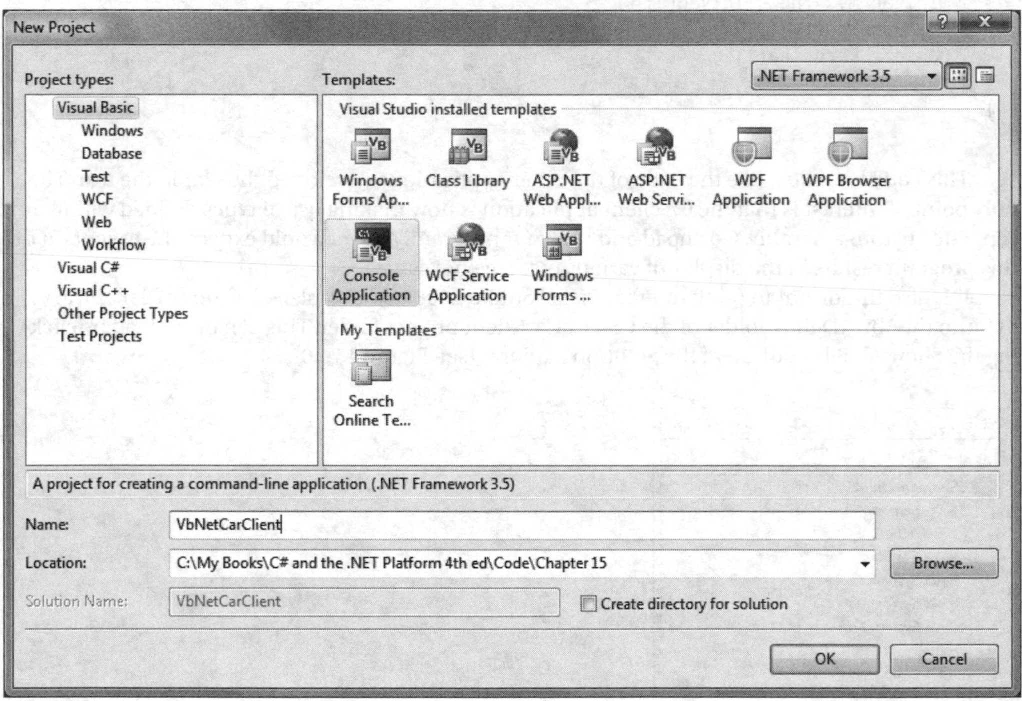

Figure 15-11. *Creating a Visual Basic Console Application*

Like C#, Visual Basic requires you to list each namespace used within the current file. However, Visual Basic offers the `Imports` keyword rather than the C# `using` keyword. Given this, add the following `Imports` statement within the `Module1.vb` code file:

```
Imports CarLibrary

Module Module1
  Sub Main()
  End Sub
End Module
```

Notice that the `Main()` method is defined within a Visual Basic module type (which has nothing to do with a `*.netmodule` file for a multifile assembly). In a nutshell, modules are a Visual Basic notation for defining a sealed class that can contain only static methods. In any case, to exercise the `MiniVan` and `SportsCar` types using the syntax of Visual Basic, update your `Main()` method as follows:

```
Sub Main()
  Console.WriteLine("***** VB CarLibrary Client App *****")

  ' Local variables are declared using the Dim keyword.
  Dim myMiniVan As New MiniVan()
  myMiniVan.TurboBoost()

  Dim mySportsCar As New SportsCar()
  mySportsCar.TurboBoost()
  Console.ReadLine()
End Sub
```

When you compile and run your application, you will once again find a series of message boxes displayed. Furthermore, this new client application has its own local copy of `CarLibrary.dll` located under the bin\Debug folder.

Cross-Language Inheritance in Action

A very enticing aspect of .NET development is the notion of *cross-language inheritance*. To illustrate, let's create a new Visual Basic class that derives from `SportsCar` (which was authored using C#). First, add a new class file to your current Visual Basic application (by selecting the Project ➤ Add Class menu option) named `PerformanceCar.vb`. Update the initial class definition by deriving from the `SportsCar` type using the `Inherits` keyword. Furthermore, override the abstract `TurboBoost()` method using the `Overrides` keyword:

```
Imports CarLibrary

' This VB type is deriving from the C# SportsCar.
Public Class PerformanceCar
  Inherits SportsCar
  Public Overrides Sub TurboBoost()
    Console.WriteLine("Zero to 60 in a cool 4.8 seconds...")
  End Sub
End Class
```

To test this new class type, update the module's `Main()` method as follows:

```
Sub Main()
...
  Dim dreamCar As New PerformanceCar()

  ' Use Inherited property.
  dreamCar.PetName = "Hank"
  dreamCar.TurboBoost()
  Console.ReadLine()
End Sub
```

Notice that the `dreamCar` object is able to invoke any public member (such as the `PetName` property) found up the chain of inheritance, regardless of the fact that the base class has been defined in a completely different language and is defined in a completely different assembly.

■ **Source Code** The VbNetCarClient project is located under the Chapter 15 subdirectory.

Building and Consuming a Multifile Assembly

Now that you have constructed and consumed a single-file assembly, let's examine the process of building a multifile assembly. Recall that a multifile assembly is simply a collection of related modules that is deployed and versioned as a single logical unit. At the time of this writing, the Visual Studio IDE does not support a C# multifile assembly project template. Therefore, you will need to make use of the command-line compiler (csc.exe) if you wish to build such a beast.

To illustrate the process, you will build a multifile assembly named AirVehicles. The primary module (airvehicles.dll) will contain a single class type named Helicopter. The related manifest (also contained in airvehicles.dll) catalogs an additional *.netmodule file named ufo.netmodule, which contains another class type named (of course) Ufo. Although both class types are physically contained in separate binaries, you will group them into a single namespace named AirVehicles. Finally, both classes are created using C# (although you could certainly mix and match languages if you desire).

To begin, open a simple text editor (such as Notepad) and create the following Ufo class definition saved to a file named ufo.cs:

```
using System;

namespace AirVehicles
{
  public class Ufo
  {
    public void AbductHuman()
    {
      Console.WriteLine("Resistance is futile");
    }
  }
}
```

To compile this class into a .NET module, navigate to the folder containing ufo.cs and issue the following command to the C# compiler (the module option of the /target flag instructs csc.exe to produce a *.netmodule as opposed to a *.dll or an *.exe file):

```
csc.exe /t:module ufo.cs
```

If you now look in the folder that contains the ufo.cs file, you should see a new file named ufo.netmodule (take a peek). Next, create a new file named helicopter.cs that contains the following class definition:

```
using System;

namespace AirVehicles
{
  public class Helicopter
  {
    public void TakeOff()
    {
      Console.WriteLine("Helicopter taking off!");
```

```
    }
  }
}
```

Given that airvehicles.dll is the intended name of the primary module of this multifile assembly, you will need to compile helicopter.cs using the /t:library and /out: options. To enlist the ufo.netmodule binary into the assembly manifest, you must also specify the /addmodule flag. The following command does the trick:

```
csc /t:library /addmodule:ufo.netmodule /out:airvehicles.dll helicopter.cs
```

At this point, your directory should contain the primary airvehicles.dll module as well as the secondary ufo.netmodule binaries.

Exploring the ufo.netmodule File

Now, using ildasm.exe, open ufo.netmodule. As you can see, *.netmodules contain a *module-level manifest*; however, its sole purpose is to list each external assembly referenced by the code base. Given that the Ufo class did little more than make a call to Console.WriteLine(), you find the following:

```
.assembly extern mscorlib
{
  .publickeytoken = (B7 7A 5C 56 19 34 E0 89 )
  .ver 2:0:0:0
}
.module ufo.netmodule
```

Exploring the airvehicles.dll File

Next, using ildasm.exe, open the primary airvehicles.dll module and investigate the assembly-level manifest. Notice that the .file token documents the associated modules in the multifile assembly (ufo.netmodule in this case). The .class extern tokens are used to document the names of the external types referenced for use from the secondary module (Ufo):

```
.assembly extern mscorlib
{
  .publickeytoken = (B7 7A 5C 56 19 34 E0 89 )
  .ver 2:0:0:0
}
.assembly airvehicles
{
...
  .hash algorithm 0x00008004
  .ver 0:0:0:0
}
.file ufo.netmodule
...
.class extern public AirVehicles.Ufo
{
  .file ufo.netmodule
  .class 0x02000002
}
.module airvehicles.dll
```

Again, realize that the only entity that links together airvehicles.dll and ufo.netmodule is the assembly manifest. These two binary files have not been merged into a single, larger *.dll.

Consuming a Multifile Assembly

The consumers of a multifile assembly couldn't care less that the assembly they are referencing is composed of numerous modules. To keep things simple, let's create a new C# client application at the command line. Create a new file named Client.cs with the following module definition. When you are done, save it in the same location as your multifile assembly.

```
using System;
using AirVehicles;

class Program
{
  static void Main()
  {
    Console.WriteLine("***** Multifile Assembly Client *****");
    Helicopter h  = new Helicopter();
    h.TakeOff();

    // This will load the *.netmodule on demand.
    Ufo u = new Ufo();
    u.AbductHuman();
    Console.ReadLine();
  }
}
```

To compile this executable assembly at the command line, you will make use of the Visual Basic .NET command-line compiler, csc.exe, with the following command set:

```
csc /r:airvehicles.dll Client.cs
```

Notice that when you are referencing a multifile assembly, the compiler needs to be supplied only with the name of the primary module (the *.netmodules are loaded on demand by the CLR when used by the client's code base). In and of themselves, *.netmodules do not have an individual version number and cannot be directly loaded by the CLR. Individual *.netmodules can be loaded only by the primary module (e.g., the file that contains the assembly manifest).

■ **Note** Visual Studio 2008 also allows you to reference a multifile assembly. Simply use the Add References dialog box and select the primary module. Any related *.netmodules are copied during the process.

At this point, you should feel comfortable with the process of building both single-file and multifile assemblies. To be completely honest, chances are that 99.99 percent of your assemblies will be single-file entities. Nevertheless, multifile assemblies can prove helpful when you wish to break a large physical binary into more modular units (and they are quite useful for remote download scenarios). Next up, let's formalize the concept of a private assembly.

■ **Source Code** The MultifileAssembly project is included under the Chapter 15 subdirectory.

Understanding Private Assemblies

Technically speaking, the assemblies you've created thus far in this chapter have been deployed as *private assemblies*. Private assemblies are required to be located within the same directory as the client application (termed the *application directory*) or a subdirectory thereof. Recall that when you set a reference to `CarLibrary.dll` while building the `CSharpCarClient.exe` and `VbNetCarClient.exe` applications, Visual Studio 2008 responded by placing a copy of `CarLibrary.dll` within the client's application directory (at least, after the first compilation).

When a client program uses the types defined within this external assembly, the CLR simply loads the local copy of `CarLibrary.dll`. Because the .NET runtime does not consult the system registry when searching for referenced assemblies, you can relocate the `CSharpCarClient.exe` (or `VbNetCarClient.exe`) and `CarLibrary.dll` assemblies to a new location on your machine and run the application (this is often termed *Xcopy deployment*).

Uninstalling (or replicating) an application that makes exclusive use of private assemblies is a no-brainer: simply delete (or copy) the application folder. Unlike with COM applications, you do not need to worry about dozens of orphaned registry settings. More important, you do not need to worry that the removal of private assemblies will break any other applications on the machine.

The Identity of a Private Assembly

The full identity of a private assembly consists of the friendly name and numerical version, both of which are recorded in the assembly manifest. The *friendly name* simply is the name of the module that contains the assembly's manifest minus the file extension. For example, if you examine the manifest of the `CarLibrary.dll` assembly, you find the following:

```
.assembly CarLibrary
{
...
  .ver 1:0:0:0
}
```

Given the isolated nature of a private assembly, it should make sense that the CLR does not bother to make use of the version number when resolving its location. The assumption is that private assemblies do not need to have any elaborate version checking, as the client application is the only entity that "knows" of its existence. Given this, it is (very) possible for a single machine to have multiple copies of the same private assembly in various application directories.

Understanding the Probing Process

The .NET runtime resolves the location of a private assembly using a technique termed *probing*, which is much less invasive than it sounds. Probing is the process of mapping an external assembly request to the location of the requested binary file. Strictly speaking, a request to load an assembly may be either *implicit* or *explicit*. An implicit load request occurs when the CLR consults the manifest in order to resolve the location of an assembly defined using the `.assembly extern` tokens:

```
// An implicit load request.
.assembly extern CarLibrary
{ ... }
```

An explicit load request occurs programmatically using the `Load()` or `LoadFrom()` method of the `System.Reflection.Assembly` class type, typically for the purposes of late binding and dynamic invocation of type members. You'll examine these topics further in Chapter 16, but for now you can see an example of an explicit load request in the following code:

```
// An explicit load request based on a friendly name.
Assembly asm = Assembly.Load("CarLibrary");
```

In either case, the CLR extracts the friendly name of the assembly and begins probing the client's application directory for a file named CarLibrary.dll. If this file cannot be located, an attempt is made to locate an executable assembly based on the same friendly name (CarLibrary.exe). If neither of these files can be located in the application directory, the runtime gives up and throws a FileNotFoundException exception at runtime.

■ **Note** Technically speaking, if a copy of the requested assembly cannot be found within the client's application directory, the CLR will also attempt to locate a client subdirectory with the exact same name as the assembly's friendly name (e.g., C:\MyClient\CarLibrary). If the requested assembly resides within this subdirectory, the CLR will load the assembly into memory.

Configuring Private Assemblies

While it is possible to deploy a .NET application by simply copying all required assemblies to a single folder on the user's hard drive, you will most likely wish to define a number of subdirectories to group related content. For example, assume you have an application directory named C:\MyApp that contains CSharpCarClient.exe. Under this folder might be a subfolder named MyLibraries that contains CarLibrary.dll.

Regardless of the intended relationship between these two directories, the CLR will *not* probe the MyLibraries subdirectory unless you supply a configuration file. Configuration files contain various XML elements that allow you to influence the probing process. Configuration files must have the same name as the launching application and take a *.config file extension, and they must be deployed in the client's application directory. Thus, if you wish to create a configuration file for CSharpCarClient.exe, it must be named CSharpCarClient.exe.config and located (for this example) under the C:\MyApp directory.

To illustrate the process, create a new directory on your C drive named MyApp using Windows Explorer. Next, copy CSharpCarClient.exe and CarLibrary.dll to this new folder, and run the program by double-clicking the executable. Your program should run successfully at this point (remember, the assemblies are not registered!). Next, create a new subdirectory under C:\MyApp named MyLibraries (see Figure 15-12), and move CarLibrary.dll to this location.

Try to run your client program again. Because the CLR could not locate an assembly named "CarLibrary" directly within the application directory, you are presented with a rather nasty unhandled FileNotFoundException exception.

To instruct the CLR to probe under the MyLibraries subdirectory, create a new configuration file named CSharpCarClient.exe.config and save it in the *same* folder containing the CSharpCarClient.exe application, which in this example would be C:\MyApp. Open this file and enter the following content exactly as shown (be aware that XML is case sensitive!):

```
<configuration>
  <runtime>
    <assemblyBinding xmlns="urn:schemas-microsoft-com:asm.v1">
      <probing privatePath="MyLibraries"/>
    </assemblyBinding>
  </runtime>
</configuration>
```

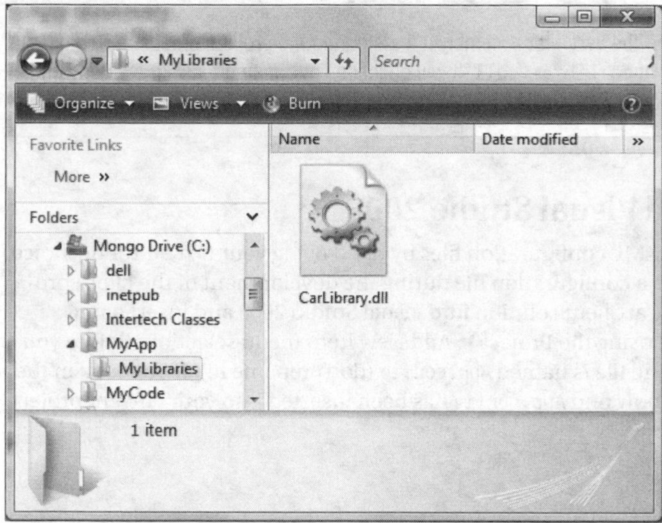

Figure 15-12. `CarLibrary.dll` *now resides under the MyLibraries subdirectory.*

.NET `*.config` files always open with a root element named `<configuration>`. The nested `<runtime>` element may specify an `<assemblyBinding>` element, which nests a further element named `<probing>`. The `privatePath` attribute is the key point in this example, as it is used to specify the subdirectories relative to the application directory where the CLR should probe.

Do note that the `<probing>` element does not specify *which* assembly is located under a given subdirectory. In other words, you cannot say, "CarLibrary is located under the MyLibraries subdirectory, but MathUtils is located under the Bin subdirectory." The `<probing>` element simply instructs the CLR to investigate all specified subdirectories for the requested assembly until the first match is encountered.

■ Note Be very aware that the `privatePath` attribute cannot be used to specify an absolute (C:\SomeFolder\SomeSubFolder) or relative (..\\SomeFolder\\AnotherFolder) path! If you wish to specify a directory outside the client's application directory, you will need to make use of a completely different XML element named `<codeBase>` (more details on this element later in the chapter).

Multiple subdirectories can be assigned to the `privatePath` attribute using a semicolon-delimited list. You have no need to do so at this time, but here is an example that informs the CLR to consult the MyLibraries and MyLibraries\Tests client subdirectories:

```
<probing privatePath="MyLibraries; MyLibraries\Tests"/>
```

Once you've finished creating `CSharpCarClient.exe.config`, run the client by double-clicking the executable in Windows Explorer. You should find that `CSharpCarClient.exe` executes without a hitch (if this is not the case, double-check your `*.config` file for typos).

Next, for testing purposes, change the name of your configuration file (in one way or another) and attempt to run the program once again. The client application should now fail. Remember that `*.config` files must be prefixed with the same name as the related client application. By way of a final test, open your configuration file for editing and capitalize any of the XML elements. Once the file is saved, your client should fail to run once again (as XML is case sensitive).

■Note Understand that the CLR will load the very first assembly it finds during the probing process. For example, if the C:\MyApp folder did contain a copy of `CarLibrary.dll`, it will be loaded into memory, while the copy under MyLibraries is effectively ignored.

Configuration Files and Visual Studio 2008

While you are always able to create XML configuration files by hand using your text editor of choice, Visual Studio 2008 allows you create a configuration file during the development of the client program. To illustrate, load the CSharpCarClient solution into Visual Studio 2008 and insert a new Application Configuration File item using the Project ➤ Add New Item menu selection. Before you click the OK button, take note that the file is named `App.config` (don't rename it!). If you look in the Solution Explorer window, you will now find `App.config` has been inserted into your current project (see Figure 15-13).

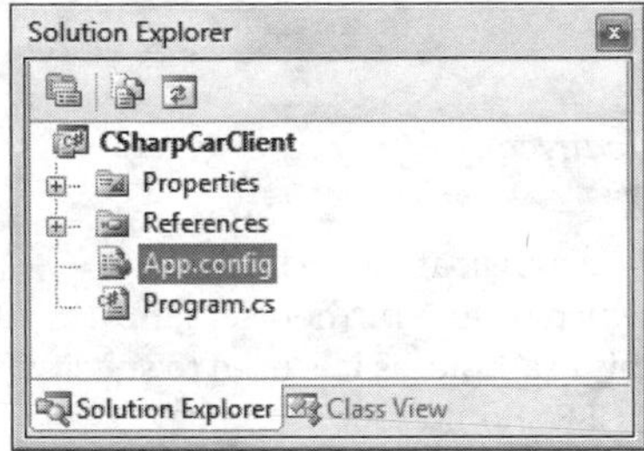

Figure 15-13. *The Visual Studio 2008* `App.config` *file*

At this point, you are free to enter the necessary XML elements for the client you happen to be creating. Now, here is the cool thing. Each time you compile your project, Visual Studio 2008 will automatically copy the data in `App.config` to the \bin\Debug directory using the proper naming convention (such as `CSharpCarClient.exe.config`). However, this behavior will happen only if your configuration file is indeed named `App.config`.

Using this approach, all you need to do is maintain `App.config`, and Visual Studio 2008 will ensure your application directory contains the latest and greatest configuration data (even if you happen to rename your project).

■Note Using `App.config` files within Visual Studio 2008 is always recommended. If you were to manually add a `*config` file to your bin\Debug folder via the Windows Explorer, Visual Studio 2008 may delete your file upon the next compilation!

Introducing the .NET Framework Configuration Utility

Although authoring a `*.config` file by hand is not too traumatic, the .NET Framework 3.5 SDK does ship with a tool that allows you to build XML configuration files using a friendly GUI. You can find the .NET Framework Configuration utility under the Administrative Tools folder of your Control Panel (if you are running Vista, click the Classic View link in the left-hand pane to quickly find the Administrative Tools folder). Once you launch this tool, you will find a number of configuration options (see Figure 15-14).

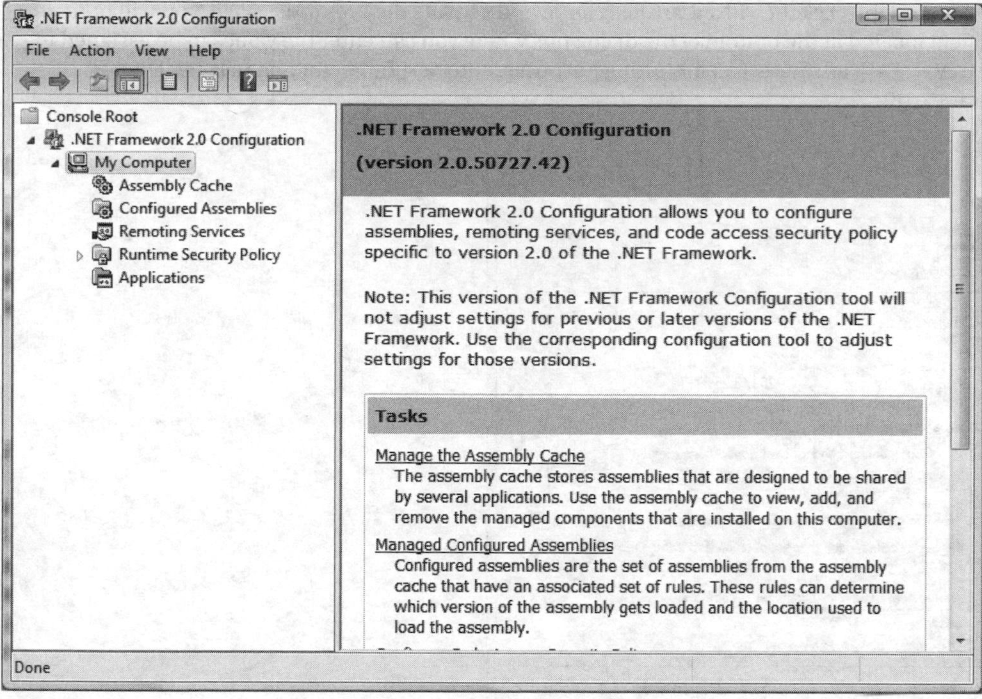

Figure 15-14. *The .NET Framework Configuration utility*

To generate a client `*.config` file using this utility, your first step is to add the application to configure by right-clicking the Applications node and selecting Add. In the resulting dialog box, click the Other button and navigate to the location of the client program you wish to configure. For this example, select the `VbNetCarClient.exe` application created earlier in this chapter (look under the bin\Debug folder of that project). Once you have done so, you will now find a new subnode, as shown in Figure 15-15.

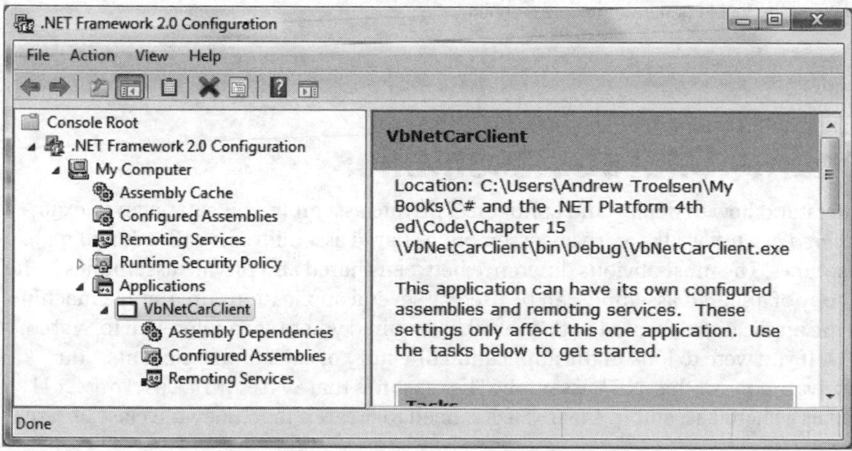

Figure 15-15. *Preparing to configure* `VbNetCarClient.exe`

If you right-click the VbNetCarClient node and activate the Properties page, you will notice a text field located at the bottom of the dialog box where you can enter the values to be assigned to the `privatePath` attribute. Just for testing purposes, enter a subdirectory named TestDir (see Figure 15-16).

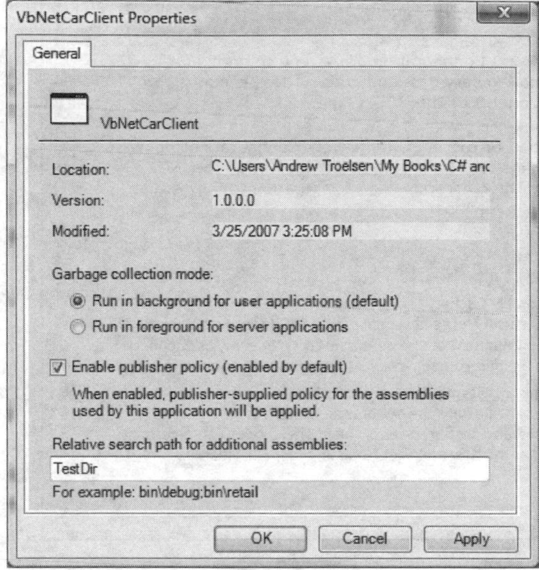

Figure 15-16. *Configuring a private probing path graphically*

Once you click the OK button, you can examine the VbNetCarClient\bin\Debug directory and find that the `*.config` file has been updated with the correct `<probing>` element.

Note As you may guess, you can copy the XML content generated by the .NET Framework Configuration utility into a Visual Studio `App.config` file for further editing. Using this approach, you can certainly decrease your typing burden by allowing the tool to generate the initial content.

Understanding Shared Assemblies

Now that you understand how to deploy and configure a private assembly, you can begin to examine the role of a *shared assembly*. Like a private assembly, a shared assembly is a collection of types and (optional) resources. The most obvious difference between shared and private assemblies is the fact that a single copy of a shared assembly can be used by several applications on a single machine.

Consider all the applications created in this text that required you to set a reference to `System.Windows.Forms.dll`. If you were to look in the application directory of each of these clients, you would *not* find a private copy of this .NET assembly. The reason is that `System.Windows.Forms.dll` has been deployed as a shared assembly. Clearly, if you need to create a machinewide class library, this is the way to go.

As suggested in the previous paragraph, a shared assembly is not deployed within the same directory as the application making use of it. Rather, shared assemblies are installed into the GAC.

The GAC is located under a subdirectory of your Windows directory named Assembly (e.g., C:\Windows\Assembly), as shown in Figure 15-17.

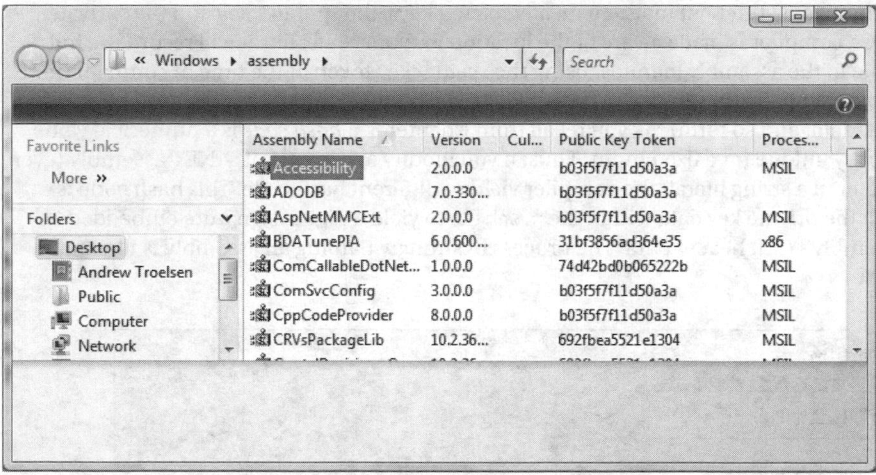

Figure 15-17. *The global assembly cache*

■Note You cannot install executable assemblies (`*.exe`) into the GAC. Only assemblies that take the `*.dll` file extension can be deployed as a shared assembly.

Understanding Strong Names

Before you can deploy an assembly to the GAC, you must assign it a *strong name,* which is used to uniquely identify the publisher of a given .NET binary. Understand that a "publisher" could be an individual programmer, a department within a given company, or an entire company at large.

In some ways, a strong name is the modern day .NET equivalent of the COM globally unique identifier (GUID) identification scheme. If you have a COM background, you may recall that AppIDs are GUIDs that identify a particular COM application. Unlike COM GUID values (which are nothing more than 128-bit numbers), strong names are based (in part) on two cryptographically related keys (termed the *public key* and the *private key*), which are much more unique and resistant to tampering than a simple GUID.

Formally, a strong name is composed of a set of related data, much of which is specified using assembly-level attributes:

- The friendly name of the assembly (which you recall is the name of the assembly minus the file extension)
- The version number of the assembly (assigned using the `[AssemblyVersion]` attribute)
- The public key value (assigned using the `[AssemblyKeyFile]` attribute)
- An optional culture identity value for localization purposes (assigned using the `[AssemblyCulture]` attribute)
- An embedded *digital signature* created using a hash of the assembly's contents and the private key value

To provide a strong name for an assembly, your first step is to generate public/private key data using the .NET Framework 3.5 SDK's `sn.exe` utility (which you'll do momentarily). The `sn.exe` utility responds by generating a file (typically ending with the `*.snk` [Strong Name Key] file extension) that contains data for two distinct but mathematically related keys, the "public" key and the "private" key. Once the C# compiler is made aware of the location for your `*.snk` file, it will record the full public key value in the assembly manifest using the `.publickey` token at the time of compilation.

The C# compiler will also generate a hash code based on the contents of the entire assembly (CIL code, metadata, and so forth). As you recall from Chapter 6, a *hash code* is a numerical value that is statistically unique for a fixed input. Thus, if you modify any aspect of a .NET assembly (even a single character in a string literal) the compiler yields a different hash code. This hash code is combined with the private key data within the `*.snk` file to yield a digital signature embedded within the assembly's CLR header data. The process of strongly naming an assembly is illustrated in Figure 15-18.

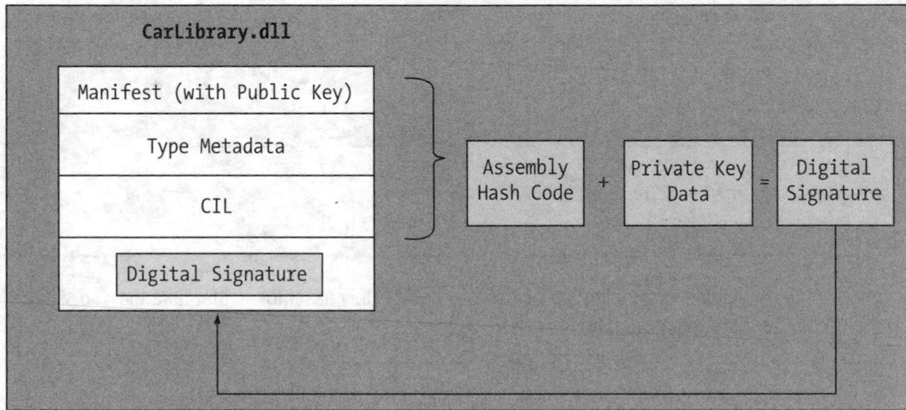

Figure 15-18. *At compile time, a digital signature is generated and embedded into the assembly based in part on public and private key data.*

Understand that the actual *private key* data is not listed anywhere within the manifest, but is used only to digitally sign the contents of the assembly (in conjunction with the generated hash code). Again, the whole idea of making use of public/private key data is to ensure that no two companies, departments, or individuals have the same identity in the .NET universe. In any case, once the process of assigning a strong name is complete, the assembly may be installed into the GAC.

■Note Strong names also provide a level of protection against potential evildoers tampering with your assembly's contents. Given this point, it is considered a .NET best practice to strongly name every assembly (including `*.exe` assemblies) regardless of whether it is deployed to the GAC.

Strongly Naming CarLibrary.dll

Let's walk through the process of assigning a strong name to the CarLibrary assembly created earlier in this chapter. The first order of business is to generate the required key data using the sn.exe utility. Although this tool has numerous command-line options, all you need to concern yourself with for the moment is the -k flag, which instructs the tool to generate a new file containing the public/private key information. Create a new folder on your C drive named MyTestKeyPair and change to that directory using the Visual Studio 2008 command prompt. Next, issue the following command to generate a file named MyTestKeyPair.snk:

```
sn -k MyTestKeyPair.snk
```

Now that you have your key data, you need to inform the C# compiler exactly where MyTestKeyPair.snk is located. When you create any new C# project workspace using Visual Studio 2008, you will notice that one of your initial project files (located under the Properties node of Solution Explorer) is named AssemblyInfo.cs. This file contains a number of attributes that describe the assembly itself. The [AssemblyKeyFile] assembly-level attribute can be used to inform the compiler of the location of a valid *.snk file. Simply specify the path as a string parameter, for example:

```
[assembly: AssemblyKeyFile(@"C:\MyTestKeyPair\MyTestKeyPair.snk")]
```

■ **Note** When you manually specify the [AssemblyKeyFile] attribute, Visual Studio 2008 will generate a warning informing you to make use of the /keyfile option of csc.exe or establish the key file via the Visual Studio 2008 Properties window. You'll use the IDE to do so in just a moment (so feel free to ignore the generated warning).

Given that the version of a shared assembly is one aspect of a strong name, selecting a version number for CarLibrary.dll is a necessary detail. In the AssemblyInfo.cs file, you will find another attribute named [AssemblyVersion]. Initially the value is set to 1.0.0.0:

```
[assembly: AssemblyVersion("1.0.0.0")]
```

A .NET version number is composed of the four parts (*<major>.<minor>.<build>.<revision>*). While specifying a version number is entirely up to you, you can instruct Visual Studio 2008 to automatically increment the build and revision numbers as part of each compilation using the wildcard token, rather than with a specific build and revision value. We have no need to do so for this example; however, consider the following:

```
// Format: <Major number>.<Minor number>.<Build number>.<Revision number>
// Valid values for each part of the version number are between 0 and 65535.
[assembly: AssemblyVersion("1.0.*")]
```

At this point, the C# compiler has all the information needed to generate strong name data (as you are not specifying a unique culture value via the [AssemblyCulture] attribute, you "inherit" the culture of your current machine, which in my case would be US English). Compile your CarLibrary code library and open the manifest using ildasm.exe. You will now see a new .publickey tag is used to document the full public key information, while the .ver token records the version specified via the [AssemblyVersion] attribute (see Figure 15-19).

```
MANIFEST
Find  Find Next
   // --- The following custom attribute is added automatically, do not unco
   //  .custom instance void [mscorlib]System.Diagnostics.DebuggableAttribut

   .custom instance void [mscorlib]System.Runtime.CompilerServices.Compilati
   .custom instance void [mscorlib]System.Runtime.CompilerServices.RuntimeCo

   .publickey = (00 24 00 00 04 80 00 00 94 00 00 00 06 02 00 00   // .$....
                 00 24 00 00 52 53 41 31 00 04 00 00 01 00 01 00   // .$..RS
                 47 A5 86 7D 7B 90 04 7E 7C 89 6E BC 61 E4 94 A6   // G..}{.
                 E9 94 F7 95 05 28 3A 37 34 D0 55 A8 8C 40 13 0E   // .....(
                 12 14 49 43 97 E6 71 3A 41 CE B9 5F AA 8B AD 8F   // ..IC..
                 49 8D B2 0A 8B 5F 88 E5 C9 F6 63 FB 70 DE F3 D6   // I....
                 17 5A E1 37 FA 92 6B A5 A3 D2 F2 06 BA B2 BA 87   // .Z.7..
                 2A 43 72 B4 8E CC C9 28 81 4A 45 E1 15 57 D8 3A   // *Cr...
                 FE B8 BA 04 DB C7 A3 B4 19 2D 82 A6 80 CE CD E4   // ......
                 47 B2 DE 9E 04 17 5D 79 2E 70 86 A9 42 51 C4 B6 ) // G.....
   .hash algorithm 0x00008004
   .ver 1:0:0:0
}
.module CarLibrary.dll
// MVID: {5E039B0B-9F86-4B13-9BAD-0F36D3354B41}
.imagebase 0x00400000
```

Figure 15-19. *A strongly named assembly records the public key in the manifest.*

Assigning Strong Names Using Visual Studio 2008

Before you deploy `CarLibrary.dll` to the GAC, let me point out that Visual Studio 2008 allows you to specify the location of your `*.snk` file using the project's Properties page (as well as generate a new `*.snk` file rather than running `sn.exe` manually). We have no need to do so for the CarLibrary project; however, to illustrate, select the Signing node, supply the path to the `*.snk` file, and select the Sign the assembly check box (see Figure 15-20).

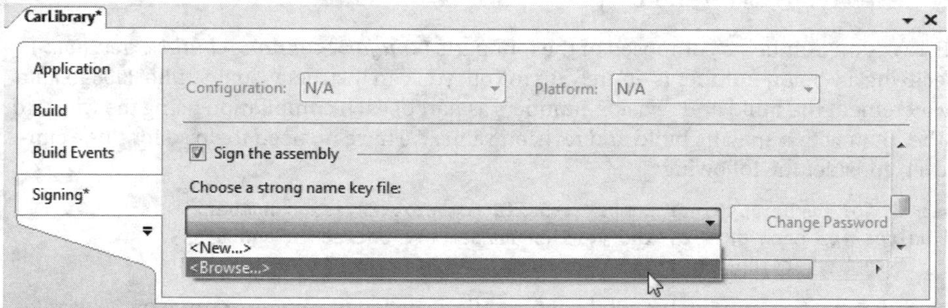

Figure 15-20. *Specifying a* `*.snk` *file via the Properties page*

■ **Note** The Application tab of the Properties editor provides a button named Assembly Information. When clicked, you will see a dialog box that allows you to establish numerous assembly-level attributes including the version number, copyright information, and so forth.

Installing/Removing Shared Assemblies to/from the GAC

The final step is to install the (now strongly named) `CarLibrary.dll` into the GAC. The simplest way to install a shared assembly into the GAC is to drag and drop the assembly to C:\Windows\Assembly using Windows Explorer (which is ideal for a quick test). Do be aware that copying/pasting the assembly into the GAC window will *not work*. You must literally drag and drop the `*.dll` from one window into the GAC window.

While dragging and dropping an assembly is just fine for local testing, the .NET Framework 3.5 SDK provides a command-line utility named `gacutil.exe` that allows you to administer the contents of the GAC. Table 15-1 documents some relevant options of `gacutil.exe` (specify the `/?` flag to see each option).

Table 15-1. *Various Options of* `gacutil.exe`

Option	Meaning in Life
`/i`	Installs a strongly named assembly into the GAC
`/u`	Uninstalls an assembly from the GAC
`/l`	Displays the assemblies (or a specific assembly) in the GAC

Using either technique, deploy `CarLibrary.dll` to the GAC. Once you've finished, you should see your library present and accounted for (see Figure 15-21).

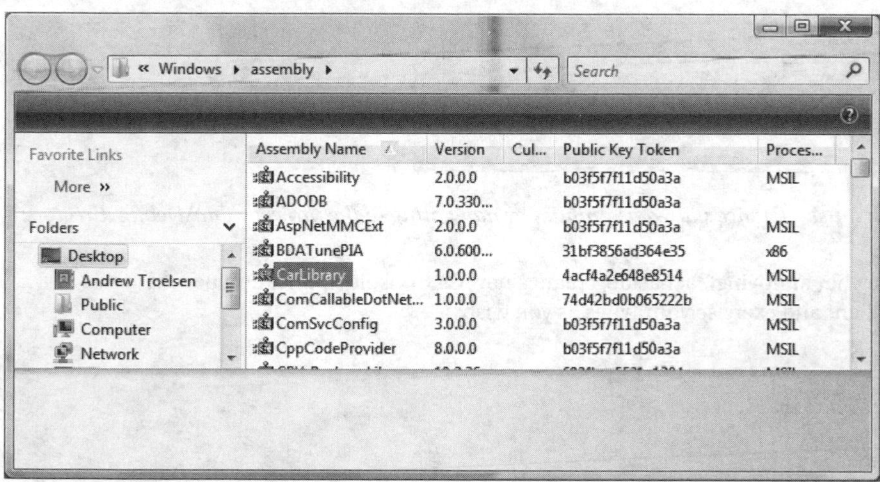

Figure 15-21. *The strongly named, shared CarLibrary (version 1.0.0.0)*

■ **Note** You may right-click any assembly icon to pull up its Properties page, and you may also uninstall a specific version of an assembly altogether from the right-click context menu (the GUI equivalent of supplying the `/u` flag to `gacutil.exe`).

Consuming a Shared Assembly

When you are building applications that make use of a shared assembly, the only difference from consuming a private assembly is in how you reference the library using Visual Studio 2008. In reality, there is no difference as far as the tool is concerned (you still make use of the Add Reference dialog box). What you must understand is that this dialog box will *not* allow you to reference the assembly by browsing to the C:\Windows\Assembly folder. Any efforts to do so will be in vain, as you cannot reference the assembly you have highlighted.

When you need to reference an assembly that has been deployed to the GAC, you will need to browse to the \bin\Debug directory of the *original* project via the Browse tab (see Figure 15-22).

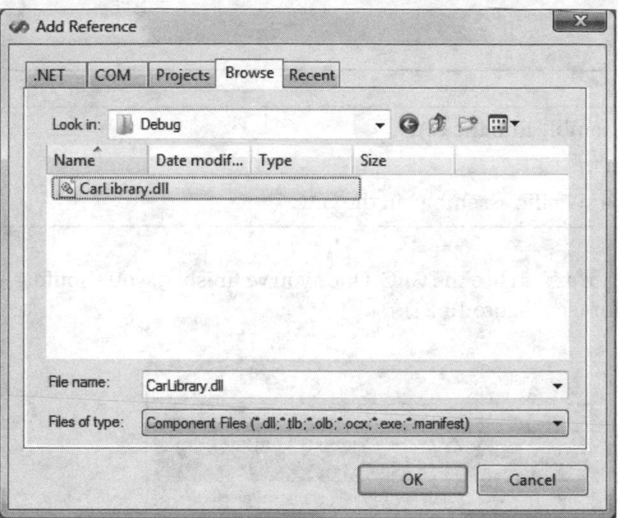

Figure 15-22. *You must reference shared assemblies by navigating to the project's \bin\Debug directory.*

This (somewhat annoying) fact aside, create a new C# Console Application named SharedCarLibClient and exercise your types as you wish:

```
using CarLibrary;

namespace SharedCarLibClient
{
  class Program
  {
    static void Main(string[] args)
    {
      Console.WriteLine("***** Shared Assembly Client *****");
      SportsCar c = new SportsCar();
      c.TurboBoost();
      Console.ReadLine();
    }
  }
}
```

Once you have compiled your client application, navigate to the directory that contains SharedCarLibClient.exe using Windows Explorer and notice that Visual Studio 2008 has *not* copied CarLibrary.dll to the client's application directory. When you reference an assembly whose manifest contains a .publickey value, Visual Studio 2008 assumes the strongly named assembly will most likely be deployed to the GAC, and therefore does not bother to copy the binary.

As a quick side note, if you wish to have Visual Studio 2008 copy a shared assembly to the client directory, you can select an assembly from the References node of Solution Explorer and set the Copy Local property to True using the Properties window (see Figure 15-23). Once you do, the *.dll will be copied to the client folder upon the next compilation.

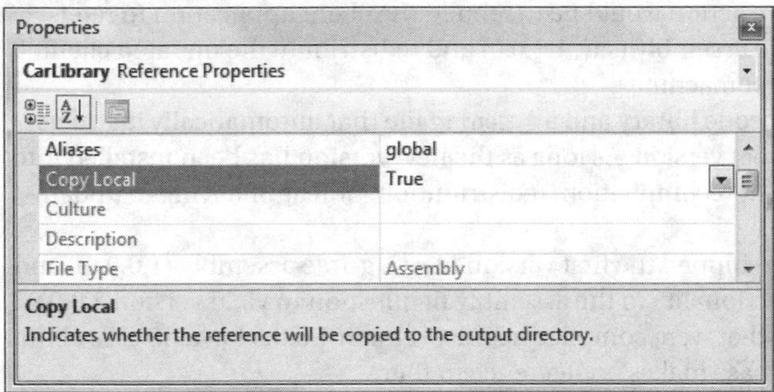

Figure 15-23. *The Copy Local property can force a copy of a strongly named code library.*

Exploring the Manifest of SharedCarLibClient

Recall that when you generate a strong name for an assembly, the entire public key is recorded in the assembly manifest. On a related note, when a client references a strongly named assembly, its manifest records a condensed hash value of the full public key, denoted by the .publickeytoken tag. If you were to open the manifest of SharedCarLibClient.exe using ildasm.exe, you would find the following (your public key token value will of course differ, as it is computed based on the public key value):

```
.assembly extern CarLibrary
{
  .publickeytoken = (21 9E F3 80 C9 34 8A 38)
  .ver 1:0:0:0
}
```

If you compare the value of the public key token recorded in the client manifest with the public key token value shown in the GAC, you will find a dead-on match. Recall that a public key represents one aspect of the strongly named assembly's identity. Given this, the CLR will only load version 1.0.0.0 of an assembly named CarLibrary that has a public key that can be hashed down to the value 219EF380C9348A38. If the CLR does not find an assembly meeting this description in the GAC (and did not find a private assembly named CarLibrary in the client's directory), a FileNotFoundException exception is thrown.

■ **Source Code** The SharedCarLibClient application can be found under the Chapter 15 subdirectory.

Configuring Shared Assemblies

Like a private assembly, shared assemblies can be configured using a client `*.config` file. Of course, because shared assemblies are deployed to a well-known location (the GAC), you will not use the `<privatePath>` element as you did for private assemblies (although if the client is using both shared and private assemblies, the `<privatePath>` element may still exist in the `*.config` file).

You can use application configuration files in conjunction with shared assemblies whenever you wish to instruct the CLR to bind to a *different* version of a specific assembly, effectively bypassing the value recorded in the client's manifest. This can be useful for a number of reasons. For example, imagine that you have shipped version 1.0.0.0 of an assembly and discover a major bug some time after the fact. One corrective action would be to rebuild the client application to reference the correct version of the bug-free assembly (say, 1.1.0.0) and redistribute the updated client and new library to each and every target machine.

Another option is to ship the new code library and a `*.config` file that automatically instructs the runtime to bind to the new (bug-free) version. As long as the new version has been installed into the GAC, the original client runs without recompilation, redistribution, or fear of having to update your resume.

Here's another example: you have shipped the first version of a bug-free assembly (1.0.0.0), and after a month or two, you add new functionality to the assembly in question to yield version 2.0.0.0. Obviously, existing client applications that were compiled against version 1.0.0.0 have no clue about these new types, given that their code base makes no reference to them.

New client applications, however, wish to make reference to the new functionality found in version 2.0.0.0. Under .NET, you are free to ship version 2.0.0.0 to the target machines, and have version 2.0.0.0 run alongside the older version 1.0.0.0. If necessary, existing clients can be dynamically redirected to load version 2.0.0.0 (to gain access to the implementation refinements), using an application configuration file without needing to recompile and redeploy the client application.

Freezing the Current Shared Assembly

To illustrate how to dynamically bind to a specific version of a shared assembly, open Windows Explorer and copy the current version of the compiled CarLibrary project (1.0.0.0) into a distinct subdirectory (I called mine "CarLibrary Version 1.0.0.0") to symbolize the freezing of this version (see Figure 15-24).

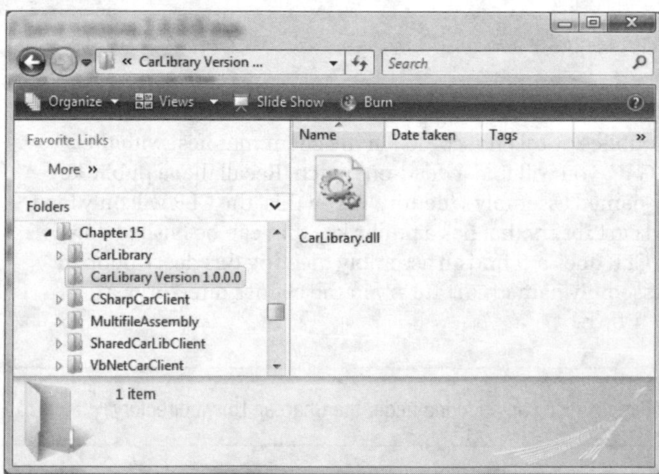

Figure 15-24. *Freezing the current version of* `CarLibrary.dll`

Building Shared Assembly Version 2.0.0.0

Now, open your existing CarLibrary project and update your code base with a new enum named `MusicMedia` that defines four possible musical devices:

```
// Holds source of music.
public enum MusicMedia
{
  musicCd,
  musicTape,
  musicRadio,
  musicMp3
}
```

As well, add a new public method to the `Car` type that allows the caller to turn on one of the given media players (be sure to import the `System.Windows.Forms` namespace within `Car.cs` if necessary):

```
public abstract class Car
{
...
  public void TurnOnRadio(bool musicOn, MusicMedia mm)
  {
    if(musicOn)
      MessageBox.Show(string.Format("Jamming {0}", mm));
    else
      MessageBox.Show("Quiet time...");
  }
...
}
```

Update the constructors of the `Car` class to display a `MessageBox` that verifies you are indeed using CarLibrary 2.0.0.0:

```
public abstract class Car
{
...
  public Car()
  {
    MessageBox.Show("CarLibrary Version 2.0!");
  }
  public Car(string name, short max, short curr)
  {
    MessageBox.Show("CarLibrary Version 2.0!");
    petName = name; maxSpeed = max; currSpeed = curr;
  }
...
}
```

Finally, before you recompile, be sure to update this version of this assembly to 2.0.0.0 by updating the value passed to the `[AssemblyVersion]` attribute:

```
// CarLibrary version 2.0.0.0 (now with music!)
[assembly: AssemblyVersion("2.0.0.0")]
```

If you look in your project's \bin\Debug folder, you'll see that you have a new version of this assembly (2.0.0.0), while version 1.0.0.0 is safe in storage under the CarLibrary Version 1.0.0.0 directory. Install this new assembly into the GAC as described earlier in this chapter. Notice that you now have two versions of the same assembly (see Figure 15-25).

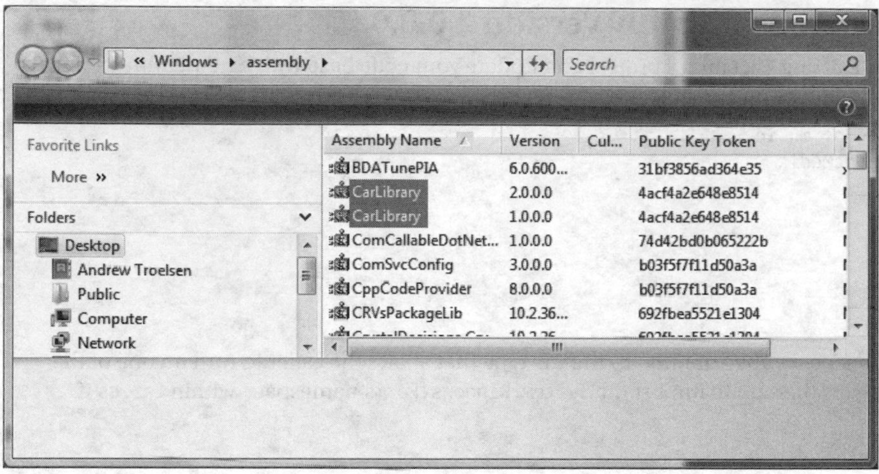

Figure 15-25. *Side-by-side execution of a shared assembly*

If you were to run the current SharedCarLibClient.exe program by double-clicking the icon using Windows Explorer, you should *not* see the "CarLibrary Version 2.0!" message box appear, as the manifest is specifically requesting version 1.0.0.0. How then can you instruct the CLR to bind to version 2.0.0.0? Glad you asked!

■ **Note** Visual Studio 2008 will automatically reset references when you compile your applications! Therefore, if you were to run your SharedCarLibClient.exe application within Visual Studio 2008, it will grab CarLibrary.dll version 2.0.0.0! If you accidentally ran your application in this way, simply delete the current CarLibrary.dll reference and select version 1.0.0.0 (which I suggested you place in a folder named CarLibrary Version 1.0.0.0).

Dynamically Redirecting to Specific Versions of a Shared Assembly

When you wish to inform the CLR to load a version of a shared assembly other than the version listed in its manifest, you may build a *.config file that contains a <dependentAssembly> element. When doing so, you will need to create an <assemblyIdentity> subelement that specifies the friendly name of the assembly listed in the client manifest (CarLibrary, for this example) and an optional culture attribute (which can be assigned an empty string or omitted altogether if you wish to specify the default culture for the machine). Moreover, the <dependentAssembly> element will define a <bindingRedirect> subelement to define the version *currently* in the manifest (via the oldVersion attribute) and the version in the GAC to load instead (via the newVersion attribute).

Create a new configuration file in the application directory of SharedCarLibClient named SharedCarLibClient.exe.config that contains the following XML data. Of course, the value of your public key token will be different from what you see in the following markup, and it can be obtained either by examining the client manifest using ildasm.exe or via the GAC.

```
<configuration>
  <runtime>
    <assemblyBinding xmlns="urn:schemas-microsoft-com:asm.v1">
      <dependentAssembly>
```

```
      <assemblyIdentity name="CarLibrary"
                        publicKeyToken="219ef380c9348a38"
                        culture="neutral"/>
      <bindingRedirect oldVersion= "1.0.0.0"
                       newVersion= "2.0.0.0"/>
    </dependentAssembly>
  </assemblyBinding>
 </runtime>
</configuration>
```

Now run the SharedCarLibClient.exe program by double-clicking the executable from the Windows Explorer. You should see the message that displays version 2.0.0.0 has loaded.

Multiple <dependentAssembly> elements can appear within a client's configuration file. Although you have no need to do so for this example, assume that the manifest of SharedCarLibClient.exe also referenced version 2.5.0.0 of an assembly named MathLibrary. If you wished to redirect to version 3.0.0.0 of MathLibrary (in addition to version 2.0.0.0 of CarLibrary), the SharedCarLibClient.exe.config file would look like the following:

```
<configuration>
 <runtime>
  <assemblyBinding xmlns="urn:schemas-microsoft-com:asm.v1">
      <!-- Controls Binding to CarLibrary -->
    <dependentAssembly>
      <assemblyIdentity name="CarLibrary"
                        publicKeyToken="219ef380c9348a38"
                        culture=""/>
      <bindingRedirect oldVersion= "1.0.0.0" newVersion= "2.0.0.0"/>
    </dependentAssembly>

      <!-- Controls Binding to MathLibrary -->
    <dependentAssembly>
      <assemblyIdentity name="MathLibrary"
                        publicKeyToken="219ef380c9348a38"
                        culture=""/>
      <bindingRedirect oldVersion= "2.5.0.0" newVersion= "3.0.0.0"/>
    </dependentAssembly>
  </assemblyBinding>
 </runtime>
</configuration>
```

■ **Note** It is possible to specify a range of old version numbers via the oldVersion attribute; for example, <bindingRedirect oldVersion="1.0.0.0-1.2.0.0" newVersion="2.0.0.0"/> informs the CLR to use version 2.0.0.0 for any older version within the range of 1.0.0.0 to 1.2.0.0.

Revisiting the .NET Framework Configuration Utility

As you would hope, you can generate configuration details for shared assemblies using the graphical .NET Framework Configuration utility. Like the process of building a *.config file for private assemblies, the first step is to reference the *.exe to configure. To illustrate, delete the SharedCarLibClient.exe.config you just authored. Now, add a reference to SharedCarLibClient.exe by right-clicking the Applications node. Once you do, expand the plus sign (+) icon and select the

Configured Assemblies subnode. From here, click the Configure an Assembly link on the right side of the utility.

At this point, you are presented with a dialog box that allows you to establish a <dependentAssembly> element using a number of friendly UI elements. First, select the "Choose an assembly from the list of assemblies this application uses" radio button and click the Choose Assembly button.

A dialog box now displays that shows you not only the assemblies specifically listed in the client manifest, but also the assemblies referenced by these assemblies. For this example's purposes, select CarLibrary. When you click the Finish button, you will be shown a Properties page for this one small aspect of the client's manifest. Here, you can generate the <dependentAssembly> using the Binding Policy tab.

Once you select the Binding Policy tab, you can set the `oldVersion` attribute (1.0.0.0) via the Requested Version text field and the `newVersion` attribute (2.0.0.0) using the New Version text field. Once you have committed the settings, you will find the following configuration file is generated for you:

```
<?xml version="1.0"?>
<configuration>
  <runtime>
    <assemblyBinding xmlns="urn:schemas-microsoft-com:asm.v1">
      <dependentAssembly>
        <assemblyIdentity name="CarLibrary"
           publicKeyToken="219ef380c9348a38" />
        <publisherPolicy apply="yes" />
        <bindingRedirect oldVersion="1.0.0.0" newVersion="2.0.0.0" />
      </dependentAssembly>
    </assemblyBinding>
  </runtime>
</configuration>
```

Investigating the Internal Composition of the GAC

At this point, you have deployed and configured private and shared assemblies. Before we turn to the topic of publisher policy, let's investigate the internal composition of the GAC itself. When you view the GAC using Windows Explorer, you find a number of icons representing each version of a shared assembly. This graphical shell is provided courtesy of a COM server named `shfusion.dll`. As you may suspect, however, beneath these icons is an elaborate (but predictable) directory structure.

To understand what the GAC really boils down to, open a command prompt and change to the Assembly directory:

```
cd c:\windows\assembly
```

Issue a `dir` command from the command line. Here you will find a folder named GAC_MISL (see Figure 15-26).

```
Administrator: Visual Studio 2005 Command Prompt

c:\Windows\assembly>dir
 Volume in drive C is Mongo Drive
 Volume Serial Number is E832-4719

 Directory of c:\Windows\assembly

03/22/2007  06:20 PM    <DIR>          GAC
03/17/2007  09:44 AM    <DIR>          GAC_32
03/25/2007  05:15 PM    <DIR>          GAC_MSIL
03/15/2007  10:36 PM    <DIR>          NativeImages_v2.0.50727_32
03/23/2007  10:36 PM    <DIR>          temp
03/26/2007  08:44 PM    <DIR>          tmp
               0 File(s)              0 bytes
               6 Dir(s)  43,945,603,072 bytes free

c:\Windows\assembly>
```

Figure 15-26. *The hidden GAC_MSIL subdirectory*

Change to the GAC_MSIL directory and issue a `dir` command once more. You will now be presented with a list of a number of subdirectories that happen to have the same exact name as the icons displayed by `shfusion.dll`. Change to the CarLibrary subdirectory and again issue a `dir` command (see Figure 15-27).

```
Administrator: Visual Studio 2005 Command Prompt

c:\Windows\assembly\GAC_MSIL\CarLibrary>dir
 Volume in drive C is Mongo Drive
 Volume Serial Number is E832-4719

 Directory of c:\Windows\assembly\GAC_MSIL\CarLibrary

03/26/2007  08:44 PM    <DIR>          .
03/26/2007  08:44 PM    <DIR>          ..
03/25/2007  05:15 PM    <DIR>          1.0.0.0__4acf4a2e648e8514
03/26/2007  08:44 PM    <DIR>          2.0.0.0__4acf4a2e648e8514
               0 File(s)              0 bytes
               4 Dir(s)  43,945,816,064 bytes free

c:\Windows\assembly\GAC_MSIL\CarLibrary>
```

Figure 15-27. *Inside the hidden CarLibrary subdirectory*

As you can see, the GAC maintains a subdirectory for each version of a shared assembly, which follows the naming convention *`<versionOfAssembly>__PublicKeyToken`*. If you were again to change the current directory to version 1.0.0.0 of CarLibrary, you would indeed find a copy of the code library (see Figure 15-28).

```
Administrator: Visual Studio 2005 Command Prompt

c:\Windows\assembly\GAC_MSIL\CarLibrary\1.0.0.0__4acf4a2e648e8514>dir
 Volume in drive C is Mongo Drive
 Volume Serial Number is E832-4719

 Directory of c:\Windows\assembly\GAC_MSIL\CarLibrary\1.0.0.0__4acf4a2e648e8514

03/25/2007  05:15 PM    <DIR>          .
03/25/2007  05:15 PM    <DIR>          ..
03/25/2007  05:15 PM            16,384 CarLibrary.dll
               1 File(s)         16,384 bytes
               2 Dir(s)  43,944,820,736 bytes free

c:\Windows\assembly\GAC_MSIL\CarLibrary\1.0.0.0__4acf4a2e648e8514>
```

Figure 15-28. *Behold! The GAC's internal copy of* `CarLibrary.dll`.

When you install a strongly named assembly into the GAC, the operating system responds by extending the directory structure beneath the Assembly subdirectory. Using this approach, the CLR is able to manipulate multiple versions of a specific assembly while avoiding the expected name clashes resulting from identically named `*.dll`s.

Understanding Publisher Policy Assemblies

The next configuration issue you'll examine is the role of *publisher policy assemblies*. As you've just seen, `*.config` files can be constructed to bind to a specific version of a shared assembly, thereby bypassing the version recorded in the client manifest. While this is all well and good, imagine you're an administrator who now needs to reconfigure *all* client applications on a given machine to rebind to version 2.0.0.0 of the `CarLibrary.dll` assembly. Given the strict naming convention of a configuration file, you would need to duplicate the same XML content in numerous locations (assuming you are, in fact, aware of the locations of the executables using CarLibrary!). Clearly this would be a maintenance nightmare.

Publisher policy allows the publisher of a given assembly (you, your department, your company, or what have you) to ship a binary version of a `*.config` file that is installed into the GAC along with the newest version of the associated assembly. The benefit of this approach is that client application directories do *not* need to contain specific `*.config` files. Rather, the CLR will read the current manifest and attempt to find the requested version in the GAC. However, if the CLR finds a publisher policy assembly, it will read the embedded XML data and perform the requested redirection *at the level of the GAC.*

Publisher policy assemblies are created at the command line using a .NET utility named `al.exe` (the assembly linker). While this tool provides a large number of options, building a publisher policy assembly requires you only to pass in the following input parameters:

- The location of the `*.config` or `*.xml` file containing the redirecting instructions
- The name of the resulting publisher policy assembly
- The location of the `*.snk` file used to sign the publisher policy assembly
- The version numbers to assign the publisher policy assembly being constructed

If you wish to build a publisher policy assembly that controls `CarLibrary.dll`, the command set is as follows (which must be entered on a single line within the command window):

```
al /link: CarLibraryPolicy.xml /out:policy.1.0.CarLibrary.dll
/keyf:C:\MyKey\myKey.snk /v:1.0.0.0
```

Here, the XML content is contained within a file named CarLibraryPolicy.xml. The name of the output file (which must be in the format *policy.<major>.<minor>.assemblyToConfigure*) is specified using the obvious /out flag. In addition, note that the name of the file containing the public/private key pair will also need to be supplied via the /keyf option. Remember, publisher policy files are shared, and therefore must have a strong name!

Once the al.exe tool has executed, the result is a new assembly that can be placed into the GAC to force all clients to bind to version 2.0.0.0 of CarLibrary.dll, without the use of a specific client application configuration file. Using this technique, you are able to design a "machinewide" redirection for all applications using a specific version (or range of versions) of an existing assembly.

Disabling Publisher Policy

Now, assume you (as a system administrator) have deployed a publisher policy assembly (and the latest version of the related assembly) to the GAC of a client machine. As luck would have it, nine of the ten affected applications rebind to version 2.0.0.0 without error. However, the remaining client application (for whatever reason) blows up when accessing CarLibrary.dll 2.0.0.0 (as we all know, it is next to impossible to build backward-compatible software that works 100 percent of the time).

In such a case, it is possible to build a configuration file for a specific troubled client that instructs the CLR to *ignore* the presence of any publisher policy files installed in the GAC. The remaining client applications that are happy to consume the newest .NET assembly will simply be redirected via the installed publisher policy assembly. To disable publisher policy on a client-by-client basis, author a (properly named) *.config file that makes use of the <publisherPolicy> element and set the apply attribute to no. When you do so, the CLR will load the version of the assembly originally listed in the client's manifest.

```
<configuration>
  <runtime>
    <assemblyBinding xmlns="urn:schemas-microsoft-com:asm.v1">
      <publisherPolicy apply="no" />
    </assemblyBinding>
  </runtime>
</configuration>
```

Understanding the <codeBase> Element

Application configuration files can also specify *code bases*. The <codeBase> element can be used to instruct the CLR to probe for dependent assemblies located at arbitrary locations (such as network end points, or an arbitrary local directory outside a client's application directory).

If the value assigned to a <codeBase> element is located on a remote machine, the assembly will be downloaded on demand to a specific directory in the GAC termed the *download cache*. Given what you have learned about deploying assemblies to the GAC, it should make sense that assemblies loaded from a <codeBase> element will need to be assigned a strong name (after all, how else could the CLR install remote assemblies to the GAC?). If you are interested, you can view the content of your machine's download cache by supplying the /ldl option to gacutil.exe:

```
gacutil /ldl
```

■ **Note** Technically speaking, the <codeBase> element can be used to probe for assemblies that do not have a strong name. However, the assembly's location must be relative to the client's application directory (and thus is little more than an alternative to the <privatePath> element).

To see the <codeBase> element in action, create a Console Application named CodeBaseClient, set a reference to CarLibrary.dll version 2.0.0.0, and update the initial file as follows:

```
using CarLibrary;

namespace CodeBaseClient
{
  class Program
  {
    static void Main(string[] args)
    {
      Console.WriteLine("***** Fun with CodeBases *****");
      SportsCar c = new SportsCar();
      Console.WriteLine("Sports car has been allocated.");
      Console.ReadLine();
    }
  }
}
```

Given that CarLibrary.dll has been deployed to the GAC, you are able to run the program as is. However, to illustrate the use of the <codeBase> element, create a new folder under your C drive (perhaps C:\MyAsms) and place a copy of CarLibrary.dll version 2.0.0.0 into this directory.

Now, add an App.config file to the CodeBaseClient project (as explained earlier in this chapter) and author the following XML content (remember that your .publickeytoken value will differ; consult your GAC as required):

```
<configuration>
  <runtime>
    <assemblyBinding xmlns="urn:schemas-microsoft-com:asm.v1">
      <dependentAssembly>
        <assemblyIdentity name=" CarLibrary" publicKeyToken="219ef380c9348a38" />
        <codeBase version="2.0.0.0" href="file:///C:/MyAsms/CarLibrary.dll" />
      </dependentAssembly>
    </assemblyBinding>
  </runtime>
</configuration>
```

As you can see, the <codeBase> element is nested within the <assemblyIdentity> element, which makes use of the name and publicKeyToken attributes to specify the friendly name as associated publicKeyToken values. The <codeBase> element itself specifies the version and location (via the href property) of the assembly to load. If you were to delete version 2.0.0.0 of CarLibrary.dll from the GAC, this client would still run successfully, as the CLR is able to locate the external assembly under C:\MyAsms.

Note If you place assemblies at random locations on your development machine, you are in effect re-creating the system registry (and the related DLL hell), given that if you move or rename the folder containing your binaries, the current bind will fail. Given this point, use <codeBase> with caution.

The <codeBase> element can also be helpful when referencing assemblies located on a remote networked machine. Assume you have permission to access a folder located at http://www.IntertechTraining.com. To download the remote *.dll to the GAC's download cache on your location machine, you could update the <codeBase> element as follows:

```
<codeBase version="2.0.0.0"
  href="http://www.IntertechTraining.com/Assemblies/CarLibrary.dll" />
```

■ **Source Code** The CodeBaseClient application can be found under the Chapter 15 subdirectory.

The System.Configuration Namespace

Currently, all of the `*.config` files shown in this chapter have made use of well-known XML elements that are read by the CLR to resolve the location of external assemblies. In addition to these recognized elements, it is perfectly permissible for a client configuration file to contain application-specific data that has nothing to do with binding heuristics. Given this, it should come as no surprise that the .NET Framework provides a namespace that allows you to programmatically read the data within a client configuration file.

The `System.Configuration` namespace provides a small set of types you may use to read custom data from a client's `*.config` file. These custom settings must be contained within the scope of an `<appSettings>` element. The `<appSettings>` element contains any number of `<add>` elements that define a key/value pair to be obtained programmatically.

For example, assume you have an `App.config` file for a Console Application named AppConfigReaderApp that defines a database connection string and a point of data named `timesToSayHello`:

```
<configuration>
  <appSettings>
    <add key="appConStr" value=
      "Data Source=localhost;Initial Catalog=AutoLot;Integrated Security=True" />
    <add key="timesToSayHello" value="8" />
  </appSettings>
</configuration>
```

Reading these values for use by the client application is as simple as calling the instance-level `GetValue()` method of the `System.Configuration.AppSettingsReader` type. As shown in the following code, the first parameter to `GetValue()` is the name of the key in the `*.config` file, whereas the second parameter is the underlying type of the key (obtained via the C# `typeof` operator):

```
using System.Configuration;

class Program
{
  static void Main(string[] args)
  {
    Console.WriteLine("***** Reading <appSettings> Data *****\n");
    // Create a reader and get the connection string value.
    AppSettingsReader ar = new AppSettingsReader();
    Console.WriteLine(ar.GetValue("appConStr", typeof(string)));

    // Now get the number of times to say hello, and then do it!
    int numbOfTimes = (int)ar.GetValue("timesToSayHello", typeof(int));
    for(int i = 0; i < numbOfTimes; i++)
      Console.WriteLine("Howdy!");
    Console.ReadLine();
  }
}
```

The `AppSettingsReader` class type does *not* provide a way to write application-specific data to a `*.config` file. However, if you ever needed to programmatically add new `<appSettings>` elements to the *.config file, you can do so using the System.Configuration.Configuration class type. Consult the .NET Framework 3.5 SDK documentation for complete details.

■ **Source Code** The AppConfigReaderApp application can be found under the Chapter 15 subdirectory.

The Machine Configuration File

The configuration files you've examined in this chapter have a common theme: they apply only to a specific application (that is why they have the same name as the launching application). In addition, each .NET-aware machine has a file named machine.config that contains a vast number of configuration details (many of which have nothing to do with resolving external assemblies) that control how a specific version of the .NET platform operates.

The .NET platform maintains a separate *.config file for each version of the framework installed on the local machine. For example, the machine.config file for .NET 2.0 can be found under the C:\WINDOWS\Microsoft.NET\Framework\v2.0.50727\CONFIG directory (your version may differ). If you were to open this file, you would find numerous XML elements that control ASP.NET settings, various security details, debugging support, and so forth. However, if you wish to update the machine.config file with machinewide application settings (via an <appSettings> element), you are free to do so.

Although this file can be directly edited using Notepad, be warned that if you alter this file incorrectly, you may cripple the ability of a specific version of the runtime to function correctly. This scenario can be far more painful than a malformed application *.config file, given that XML errors in an application configuration file affect only a single application, but erroneous XML in the machine.config file can break a specific version of the .NET platform.

Summary

This chapter drilled down into the details of how the CLR resolves the location of externally referenced assemblies. You began by examining the content within an assembly: headers, metadata, manifests, and CIL. Then you constructed single-file and multifile assemblies and a handful of client applications (written in a language-agnostic manner).

As you have seen, assemblies may be private or shared. Private assemblies are copied to the client's subdirectory, whereas shared assemblies are deployed to the GAC, provided they have been assigned a strong name. Finally, as you have seen, private and shared assemblies can be configured using a client-side XML configuration file or, alternatively, via a publisher policy assembly.

CHAPTER 16

Type Reflection, Late Binding, and Attribute-Based Programming

As shown in the previous chapter, assemblies are the basic unit of deployment in the .NET universe. Using the integrated object browsers of Visual Studio 2008 (and numerous other IDEs), you are able to examine the types within a project's referenced set of assemblies. Furthermore, external tools such as `ildasm.exe` and `reflector.exe` allow you to peek into the underlying CIL code, type metadata, and assembly manifest for a given .NET binary. In addition to this design-time investigation of .NET assemblies, you are also able to *programmatically* obtain this same information using the `System.Reflection` namespace. To this end, the first task of this chapter is to define the role of reflection and the necessity of .NET metadata.

The remainder of the chapter examines a number of closely related topics, all of which hinge upon reflection services. For example, you'll learn how a .NET client may employ dynamic loading and late binding to activate types it has no compile-time knowledge of. You'll also learn how to insert custom metadata into your .NET assemblies through the use of system-supplied and custom attributes. To put all of these (seemingly esoteric) topics into perspective, the chapter closes by demonstrating how to build several "snap-in objects" that you can plug into an extendable Windows Forms application.

The Necessity of Type Metadata

The ability to fully describe types (classes, interfaces, structures, enumerations, and delegates) using metadata is a key element of the .NET platform. Numerous .NET technologies, such as object serialization, .NET remoting, XML web services, and Windows Communication Foundation (WCF), require the ability to discover the format of types at runtime. Furthermore, cross-language interoperability, numerous compiler services, and an IDE's IntelliSense capabilities all rely on a concrete description of *type*.

Regardless of (or perhaps due to) its importance, metadata is not a new idea supplied by the .NET Framework. Java, CORBA, and COM all have similar concepts. For example, COM type libraries (which are little more than compiled IDL code) are used to describe the types contained within a COM server. Like COM, .NET code libraries also support type metadata. Of course, .NET metadata has no syntactic similarities to COM IDL.

Recall that the `ildasm.exe` utility allows you to view an assembly's type metadata using the Ctrl+M keyboard option (see Chapter 1). Thus, if you were to open any of the `*.dll` or `*.exe` assemblies created over the course of this book (such as the `CarLibrary.dll` created in the previous chapter) using `ildasm.exe` and press Ctrl+M, you would find the relevant type metadata (see Figure 16-1).

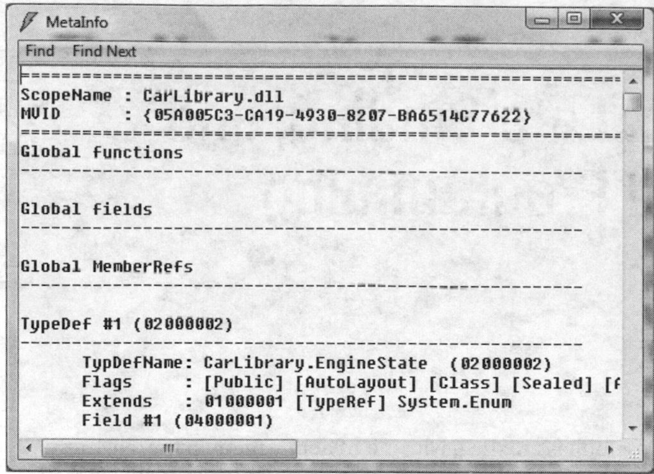

Figure 16-1. *Viewing an assembly's metadata*

As you can see, `ildasm.exe`'s display of .NET type metadata is very verbose (the actual binary format is much more compact). In fact, if I were to list the entire metadata description representing the `CarLibrary.dll` assembly, it would span several pages. Given that this act would be a woeful waste of paper, let's just glimpse into some key metadata descriptions of the `CarLibrary.dll` assembly.

Viewing (Partial) Metadata for the EngineState Enumeration

Each type defined within the current assembly is documented using a `TypeDef #n` token (where `TypeDef` is short for *type definition*). If the type being described uses a type defined within a separate .NET assembly, the referenced type is documented using a `TypeRef #n` token (where `TypeRef` is short for *type reference*). A `TypeRef` token is a pointer (if you will) to the referenced type's full metadata definition in an external library. In a nutshell, .NET metadata is a set of tables that clearly mark all type definitions (`TypeDefs`) and referenced entities (`TypeRefs`), all of which can be viewed using `ildasm.exe`'s metadata window.

As far as `CarLibrary.dll` goes, one `TypeDef` we encounter is the metadata description of the `CarLibrary.EngineState` enumeration (your number may differ; `TypeDef` numbering is based on the order in which the C# compiler processes the file):

```
TypeDef #1
-------------------------------------------------------
  TypDefName: CarLibrary.EngineState  (02000002)
  Flags     : [Public] [AutoLayout] [Class] [Sealed] [AnsiClass]  (00000101)
  Extends   : 01000001 [TypeRef] System.Enum
...
  Field #2
  -------------------------------------------------------
  Field Name: engineAlive (04000002)
  Flags     : [Public] [Static] [Literal] [HasDefault]  (00008056)
  DefltValue: (I4) 0
  CallCnvntn: [FIELD]
  Field type:  ValueClass CarLibrary.EngineState
...
```

Here, the TypDefName token is used to establish the name of the given type. The Extends metadata token is used to document the base class of a given .NET type (in this case, the referenced type, System.Enum). Each field of an enumeration is marked using the Field #*n* token. For brevity, I have simply listed the metadata for EngineState.engineAlive.

Viewing (Partial) Metadata for the Car Type

Here is a partial dump of the Car type that illustrates the following:

- How fields are defined in terms of .NET metadata
- How methods are documented via .NET metadata
- How a single type property is mapped to two discrete member functions

```
TypeDef #3
-------------------------------------------------------
  TypDefName: CarLibrary.Car  (02000004)
  Flags     : [Public] [AutoLayout] [Class] [Abstract] [AnsiClass]  (00100081)
  Extends   : 01000002 [TypeRef] System.Object
  Field #1
  -------------------------------------------------------
    Field Name: petName (04000008)
    Flags     : [Family]  (00000004)
    CallCnvntn: [FIELD]
    Field type:  String
...
  Method #1
  -------------------------------------------------------
    MethodName: .ctor (06000001)
    Flags     : [Public] [HideBySig] [ReuseSlot] [SpecialName]
    [RTSpecialName] [.ctor]  (00001886)
    RVA       : 0x00002050
    ImplFlags : [IL] [Managed]  (00000000)
    CallCnvntn: [DEFAULT]
    hasThis
    ReturnType: Void
    No arguments.
...
  Property #1
  -------------------------------------------------------
    Prop.Name : PetName (17000001)
    Flags     : [none] (00000000)
    CallCnvntn: [PROPERTY]
    hasThis
    ReturnType: String
    No arguments.
    DefltValue:
    Setter    : (06000004) set_PetName
    Getter    : (06000003) get_PetName
    0 Others
 ...
```

First, note that the Car class metadata marks the type's base class and includes various flags that describe how this type was constructed (e.g., [public], [abstract], and whatnot). Methods (such as our Car's constructor) are described in regard to their parameters, return value, and name.

Finally, note how properties are mapped to their internal get/set methods using the .NET metadata `Setter`/`Getter` tokens. As you would expect, the derived `Car` types (`SportsCar` and `MiniVan`) are described in a similar manner.

Examining a TypeRef

Recall that an assembly's metadata will describe not only the set of internal types (`Car`, `EngineState`, etc.), but also any external types the internal types reference. For example, given that `CarLibrary.dll` has defined two enumerations, you find a `TypeRef` block for the `System.Enum` type:

```
TypeRef #1 (01000001)
-------------------------------------------------------
Token:              0x01000001
ResolutionScope:    0x23000001
TypeRefName:        System.Enum
  MemberRef #1
  -------------------------------------------------------
  Member: (0a00000f) ToString:
  CallCnvntn: [DEFAULT]
  hasThis
  ReturnType: String
  No arguments.
```

Documenting the Defining Assembly

The `ildasm.exe` metadata window also allows you to view the .NET metadata that describes the assembly itself using the `Assembly` token. As you can see from the following (partial) listing, information documented within the `Assembly` table is (surprise, surprise!) the same information that can be viewable via the MANIFEST icon. Here is a partial dump of the manifest of `CarLibrary.dll` (version 2.0.0.0):

```
Assembly
-------------------------------------------------------
  Token: 0x20000001
  Name : CarLibrary
  Public Key    : 00 24 00 00 04 80 00 00  // Etc...

  Hash Algorithm : 0x00008004
  Major Version: 0x00000002
  Minor Version: 0x00000000
  Build Number: 0x00000000
  Revision Number: 0x00000000
  Locale: <null>
  Flags : [SideBySideCompatible]  (00000000)
```

Documenting Referenced Assemblies

In addition to the `Assembly` token and the set of `TypeDef` and `TypeRef` blocks, .NET metadata also makes use of `AssemblyRef #n` tokens to document each external assembly. Given that the `CarLibrary.dll` makes use of the `MessageBox` type, you find an `AssemblyRef` for `System.Windows.Forms`, for example:

```
AssemblyRef #2
-------------------------------------------------------
  Token: 0x23000002
  Public Key or Token: b7 7a 5c 56 19 34 e0 89
  Name: System.Windows.Forms
  Version: 2.0.3600.0
  Major Version: 0x00000002
  Minor Version: 0x00000000
  Build Number: 0x00000e10
  Revision Number: 0x00000000
  Locale: <null>
  HashValue Blob:
  Flags: [none] (00000000)
```

Documenting String Literals

The final point of interest regarding .NET metadata is the fact that each and every string literal in your code base is documented under the `User Strings` token, for example:

```
User Strings
-------------------------------------------------------
70000001 : (11) L"Jamming {0}"
70000019 : (13) L"Quiet time..."
70000035 : (23) L"CarLibrary Version 2.0!"
70000065 : (14) L"Ramming speed!"
70000083 : (19) L"Faster is better..."
700000ab : (16) L"Time to call AAA"
700000cd : (16) L"Your car is dead"
```

Now, don't be too concerned with the exact syntax of each and every piece of .NET metadata. The bigger point to absorb is that .NET metadata is very descriptive and lists each internally defined (and externally referenced) type found within a given code base.

The next question on your mind may be (in the best-case scenario) "How can I leverage this information in my applications?" or (in the worst-case scenario) "Why should I care about metadata?" To address both points of view, allow me to introduce .NET reflection services. Be aware that the usefulness of the topics presented over the pages that follow may be a bit of a head-scratcher until this chapter's endgame. So hang tight.

■ **Note** You will also find a number of `CustomAttribute` tokens displayed by the MetaInfo window, which documents the attributes applied within the code base. You'll learn about the role of .NET attributes later in this chapter.

Understanding Reflection

In the .NET universe, *reflection* is the process of runtime type discovery. Using reflection services, you are able to programmatically obtain the same metadata information displayed by `ildasm.exe` using a friendly object model. For example, through reflection, you can obtain a list of all types contained within a given assembly (or `*.netmodule`), including the methods, fields, properties, and events defined by a given type. You can also dynamically discover the set of interfaces supported by a given type, the parameters of a method, and other related details (base classes, namespace information, manifest data, and so forth).

Like any namespace, System.Reflection contains a number of related types. Table 16-1 lists some of the core items you should be familiar with.

Table 16-1. *A Sampling of Members of the* System.Reflection *Namespace*

Type	Meaning in Life
Assembly	This class contains a number of methods that allow you to load, investigate, and manipulate an assembly.
AssemblyName	This class allows you to discover numerous details behind an assembly's identity (version information, culture information, and so forth).
EventInfo	This class holds information for a given event.
FieldInfo	This class holds information for a given field.
MemberInfo	This is the abstract base class that defines common behaviors for the EventInfo, FieldInfo, MethodInfo, and PropertyInfo types.
MethodInfo	This class contains information for a given method.
Module	This class allows you to access a given module within a multifile assembly.
ParameterInfo	This class holds information for a given parameter.
PropertyInfo	This class holds information for a given property.

To understand how to leverage the System.Reflection namespace to programmatically read .NET metadata, you need to first come to terms with the System.Type class.

The System.Type Class

The System.Type class defines a number of members that can be used to examine a type's metadata, a great number of which return types from the System.Reflection namespace. For example, Type.GetMethods() returns an array of MethodInfo types, Type.GetFields() returns an array of FieldInfo types, and so on. The complete set of members exposed by System.Type is quite expansive; however, Table 16-2 offers a partial snapshot of the members supported by System.Type (see the .NET Framework 3.5 SDK documentation for full details).

Table 16-2. *Select Members of* System.Type

Type	Meaning in Life
IsAbstract IsArray IsClass IsCOMObject IsEnum IsGenericTypeDefinition IsGenericParameter IsInterface IsPrimitive IsNestedPrivate IsNestedPublic IsSealedIsValueType	These properties (among others) allow you to discover a number of basic traits about the Type you are referring to (e.g., if it is an abstract method, an array, a nested class, and so forth).

Type	Meaning in Life
GetConstructors() GetEvents() GetFields() GetInterfaces() GetMembers() GetMethods() GetNestedTypes() GetProperties()	These methods (among others) allow you to obtain an array representing the items (interface, method, property, etc.) you are interested in. Each method returns a related array (e.g., GetFields() returns a FieldInfo array, GetMethods() returns a MethodInfo array, etc.). Be aware that each of these methods has a singular form (e.g., GetMethod(), GetProperty(), etc.) that allows you to retrieve a specific item by name, rather than an array of all related items.
FindMembers()	This method returns an array of MemberInfo types based on search criteria.
GetType()	This static method returns a Type instance given a string name.
InvokeMember()	This method allows late binding to a given item.

Obtaining a Type Reference Using System.Object.GetType()

You can obtain an instance of the Type class in a variety of ways. However, the one thing you cannot do is directly create a Type object using the new keyword, as Type is an abstract class. Regarding your first choice, recall that System.Object defines a method named GetType(), which returns an instance of the Type class that represents the metadata for the current object:

```
// Obtain type information using a SportsCar instance.
SportsCar sc = new SportsCar();
Type t = sc.GetType();
```

Obviously, this approach will only work if you have compile-time knowledge of the type (SportsCar in this case) and currently have an instance of the type in memory. Given this restriction, it should make sense that tools such as ildasm.exe do not obtain type information by directly calling System.Object.GetType() for each type, given the ildasm.exe was not compiled against your custom assemblies!

Obtaining a Type Reference Using System.Type.GetType()

To obtain type information in a more flexible manner, you may call the static GetType() member of the System.Type class and specify the fully qualified string name of the type you are interested in examining. Using this approach, you do *not* need to have compile-time knowledge of the type you are extracting metadata from, given that Type.GetType() takes an instance of the omnipresent System.String.

■ Note When I say you do not need compile-time knowledge when calling Type.GetType(), I am referring to the fact that this method can take any string value whatsoever (rather than a strongly typed variable). Of course, you would still need to know the name of the type in a stringified format!

The Type.GetType() method has been overloaded to allow you to specify two Boolean parameters, one of which controls whether an exception should be thrown if the type cannot be found, and the other of which establishes the case sensitivity of the string. To illustrate, ponder the following:

```
// Obtain type information using the static Type.GetType() method
// (don't throw an exception if SportsCar cannot be found and ignore case).
Type t = Type.GetType("CarLibrary.SportsCar", false, true);
```

In the previous example, notice that the string you are passing into GetType() makes no mention of the assembly containing the type. In this case, the assumption is that the type is defined within the currently executing assembly. However, when you wish to obtain metadata for a type within an external private assembly, the string parameter is formatted using the type's fully qualified name, followed by the friendly name of the assembly containing the type (each of which is separated by a comma):

```
// Obtain type information for a type within an external assembly.
Type t = Type.GetType("CarLibrary.SportsCar, CarLibrary");
```

As well, do know that the string passed into Type.GetType() may specify a plus token (+) to denote a *nested type*. Assume you wish to obtain type information for an enumeration (SpyOptions) nested within a class named JamesBondCar. To do so, you would write the following:

```
// Obtain type information for a nested enumeration
// within the current assembly.
Type t =  Type.GetType("CarLibrary.JamesBondCar+SpyOptions");
```

Obtaining a Type Reference Using typeof()

The final way to obtain type information is using the C# typeof operator:

```
// Get the Type using typeof.
Type t = typeof(SportsCar);
```

Like Type.GetType(), the typeof operator is helpful in that you do not need to first create an object instance to extract type information. However, your code base must still have compile-time knowledge of the type you are interested in examining, as typeof expects the strongly typed name of the type, rather than a textual representation of the type.

Building a Custom Metadata Viewer

To illustrate the basic process of reflection (and the usefulness of System.Type), let's create a Console Application named MyTypeViewer. This program will display details of the methods, properties, fields, and supported interfaces (in addition to some other points of interest) for any type within mscorlib.dll (recall all .NET applications have automatic access to this core framework class library) or a type within MyTypeViewer itself. Once the application has been created, be sure to import the System.Reflection namespace.

```
using System.Reflection;
```

Reflecting on Methods

The Program class will be updated to define a number of static methods, each of which takes a single System.Type parameter and returns void. First you have ListMethods(), which (as you might guess) prints the name of each method defined by the incoming type. Notice how Type.GetMethods() returns an array of System.Reflection.MethodInfo types:

```
// Display method names of type.
static void ListMethods(Type t)
{
  Console.WriteLine("***** Methods *****");
  MethodInfo[] mi = t.GetMethods();
  foreach(MethodInfo m in mi)
```

```
    Console.WriteLine("->{0}", m.Name);
  Console.WriteLine();
}
```

Here, you are simply printing the name of the method using the `MethodInfo.Name` property. As you might guess, `MethodInfo` has many additional members that allow you to determine whether the method is static, virtual, generic, or abstract. As well, the `MethodInfo` type allows you to obtain the method's return value and parameter set. You'll spruce up the implementation of `ListMethods()` in just a bit.

Reflecting on Fields and Properties

The implementation of `ListFields()` is similar. The only notable difference is the call to `Type.GetFields()` and the resulting `FieldInfo` array. Again, to keep things simple, you are printing out only the name of each field.

```
// Display field names of type.
static void ListFields(Type t)
{
  Console.WriteLine("***** Fields *****");
  FieldInfo[] fi = t.GetFields();
  foreach(FieldInfo field in fi)
    Console.WriteLine("->{0}", field.Name);
  Console.WriteLine();
}
```

The logic to display a type's properties is similar:

```
// Display property names of type.
static void ListProps(Type t)
{
  Console.WriteLine("***** Properties *****");
  PropertyInfo[] pi = t.GetProperties();
  foreach(PropertyInfo prop in pi)
    Console.WriteLine("->{0}", prop.Name);
  Console.WriteLine();
}
```

Reflecting on Implemented Interfaces

Next, you will author a method named `ListInterfaces()` that will print out the names of any interfaces supported on the incoming type. The only point of interest here is that the call to `GetInterfaces()` returns an array of `System.Types`! This should make sense given that interfaces are, indeed, types:

```
// Display implemented interfaces.
static void ListInterfaces(Type t)
{
  Console.WriteLine("***** Interfaces *****");
  Type[] ifaces = t.GetInterfaces();
  foreach(Type i in ifaces)
    Console.WriteLine("->{0}", i.Name);
}
```

Displaying Various Odds and Ends

Last but not least, you have one final helper method that will simply display various statistics (indicating whether the type is generic, what the base class is, whether the type is sealed, and so forth) regarding the incoming type:

```
// Just for good measure.
static void ListVariousStats(Type t)
{
  Console.WriteLine("***** Various Statistics *****");
  Console.WriteLine("Base class is: {0}", t.BaseType);
  Console.WriteLine("Is type abstract? {0}", t.IsAbstract);
  Console.WriteLine("Is type sealed? {0}", t.IsSealed);
  Console.WriteLine("Is type generic? {0}", t.IsGenericTypeDefinition);
  Console.WriteLine("Is type a class type? {0}", t.IsClass);
  Console.WriteLine();
}
```

Implementing Main()

The `Main()` method of the `Program` class prompts the user for the fully qualified name of a type. Once you obtain this string data, you pass it into the `Type.GetType()` method and send the extracted `System.Type` into each of your helper methods. This process repeats until the user enters **Q** to terminate the application:

```
static void Main(string[] args)
{
  Console.WriteLine("***** Welcome to MyTypeViewer *****");
  string typeName = "";
  bool userIsDone = false;

  do
  {
    Console.WriteLine("\nEnter a type name to evaluate");
    Console.Write("or enter Q to quit: ");

    // Get name of type.
    typeName = Console.ReadLine();

    // Does user want to quit?
    if (typeName.ToUpper() == "Q")
    {
      userIsDone = true;
      break;
    }

    // Try to display type.
    try
    {
      Type t = Type.GetType(typeName);
      Console.WriteLine("");
      ListVariousStats(t);
```

```
      ListFields(t);
      ListProps(t);
      ListMethods(t);
      ListInterfaces(t);
    }
    catch
    {
      Console.WriteLine("Sorry, can't find type");
    }
  } while (!userIsDone);
}
```

At this point, MyTypeViewer.exe is ready to take out for a test drive. For example, run your application and enter the following fully qualified names (be aware that the manner in which you invoked Type.GetType() requires case-sensitive string names):

- System.Int32
- System.Collections.ArrayList
- System.Threading.Thread
- System.Void
- System.IO.BinaryWriter
- System.Math
- System.Console
- MyTypeViewer.Program

Figure 16-2 shows the partial output when specifying System.Math.

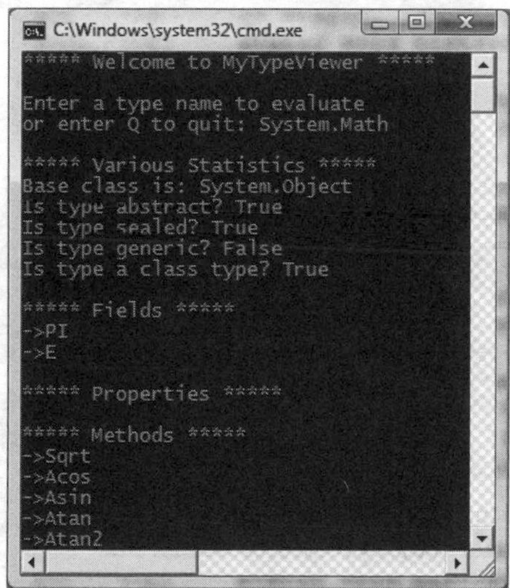

Figure 16-2. *Reflecting on* System.Math

Reflecting on Generic Types

When you call Type.GetType() in order to obtain metadata descriptions of generic types, you must make use of a special syntax involving a "back tick" character (`) followed by a numerical value that represents the number of type parameters the type supports. For example, if you wish to print out the metadata description of List<T>, you would need to pass the following string into your application:

```
System.Collections.Generic.List`1
```

Here, we are using the numerical value of 1, given that List<T> has only one type parameter. However, if you wish to reflect over Dictionary<TKey, TValue>, you would supply the value 2:

```
System.Collections.Generic.Dictionary`2
```

Reflecting on Method Parameters and Return Values

So far, so good! Let's make one minor enhancement to the current application. Specifically, you will update the ListMethods() helper function to list not only the name of a given method, but also the return value and incoming parameters. The MethodInfo type provides the ReturnType property and GetParameters() method for these very tasks. In the following code, notice that you are building a string type that contains the type and name of each parameter using a nested foreach loop:

```
static void ListMethods(Type t)
{
  Console.WriteLine("***** Methods *****");
  MethodInfo[] mi = t.GetMethods();
  foreach (MethodInfo m in mi)
  {
    // Get return value.
    string retVal = m.ReturnType.FullName;
    string paramInfo = "(";

    // Get params.
    foreach (ParameterInfo pi in m.GetParameters())
    {
      paramInfo += string.Format("{0} {1} ", pi.ParameterType, pi.Name);
    }
    paramInfo += ")";

    // Now display the basic method sig.
    Console.WriteLine("->{0} {1} {2}", retVal, m.Name, paramInfo);
  }
  Console.WriteLine();
}
```

If you now run this updated application, you will find that the methods of a given type are much more detailed. Figure 16-3 shows the method metadata of the System.Globalization.GregorianCalendar type.

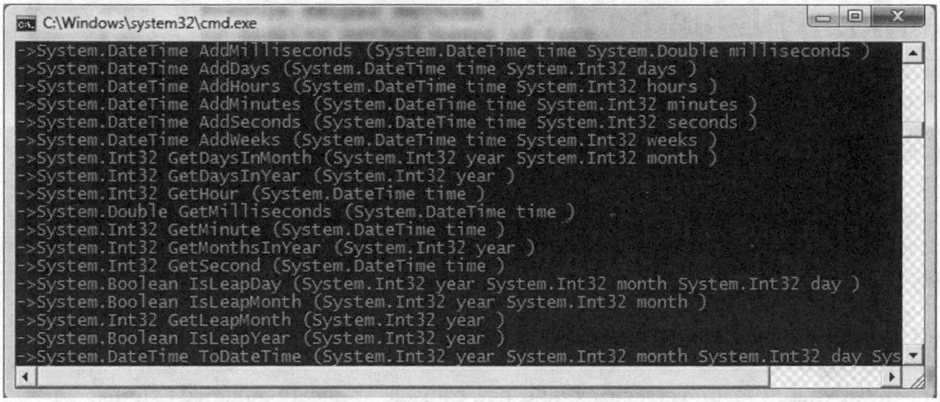

```
C:\Windows\system32\cmd.exe
->System.DateTime AddMilliseconds (System.DateTime time System.Double milliseconds )
->System.DateTime AddDays (System.DateTime time System.Int32 days )
->System.DateTime AddHours (System.DateTime time System.Int32 hours )
->System.DateTime AddMinutes (System.DateTime time System.Int32 minutes )
->System.DateTime AddSeconds (System.DateTime time System.Int32 seconds )
->System.DateTime AddWeeks (System.DateTime time System.Int32 weeks )
->System.Int32 GetDaysInMonth (System.Int32 year System.Int32 month )
->System.Int32 GetDaysInYear (System.Int32 year )
->System.Int32 GetHour (System.DateTime time )
->System.Double GetMilliseconds (System.DateTime time )
->System.Int32 GetMinute (System.DateTime time )
->System.Int32 GetMonthsInYear (System.Int32 year )
->System.Int32 GetSecond (System.DateTime time )
->System.Boolean IsLeapDay (System.Int32 year System.Int32 month System.Int32 day )
->System.Boolean IsLeapMonth (System.Int32 year System.Int32 month )
->System.Int32 GetLeapMonth (System.Int32 year )
->System.Boolean IsLeapYear (System.Int32 year )
->System.DateTime ToDateTime (System.Int32 year System.Int32 month System.Int32 day Sys
```

Figure 16-3. *Method details of* `System.Globalization.GregorianCalendar`

The current implementation of `ListMethods()` is helpful, in that you can directly investigate each parameter and method return value using the `System.Reflection` object model. As an extreme shortcut, be aware that each of the *XXX*`Info` types (`MethodInfo`, `PropertyInfo`, `EventInfo`, etc.) have overridden `ToString()` to display the signature of the item requested. Thus, we could also implement `ListMethods()` as follows:

```
public static void ListMethods(Type t)
{
  Console.WriteLine("***** Methods *****");
  MethodInfo[] mi = t.GetMethods();
  foreach (MethodInfo m in mi)
  {
    // Could also simply say "Console.WriteLine(m)" as well,
    // as ToString() is called automatically by WriteLine().
    Console.WriteLine(m.ToString());
  }
  Console.WriteLine();
}
```

Interesting stuff, huh? Clearly the `System.Reflection` namespace and `System.Type` class allow you to reflect over many other aspects of a type beyond what `MyTypeViewer` is currently displaying. As you would hope, you can obtain a type's events, get the list of any generic parameters for a given member, and glean dozens of other details.

Nevertheless, at this point you have created a (somewhat capable) object browser. The major limitation, of course, is that you have no way to reflect beyond the current assembly (`MyTypeViewer`) or the always accessible `mscorlib.dll`. This begs the question, "How can I build applications that can load (and reflect over) assemblies not referenced at compile time?"

■ **Source Code** The MyTypeViewer project can be found under the Chapter 16 subdirectory.

Dynamically Loading Assemblies

In the previous chapter, you learned all about how the CLR consults the assembly manifest when probing for an externally referenced assembly. However, there will be many times when you need to load assemblies on the fly programmatically, even if there is no record of said assembly in the manifest. Formally speaking, the act of loading external assemblies on demand is known as a *dynamic load*.

System.Reflection defines a class named Assembly. Using this type, you are able to dynamically load an assembly as well as discover properties about the assembly itself. Using the Assembly type, you are able to dynamically load private or shared assemblies, as well as load an assembly located at an arbitrary location. In essence, the Assembly class provides methods (Load() and LoadFrom() in particular) that allow you to programmatically supply the same sort of information found in a client-side *.config file.

To illustrate dynamic loading, create a brand-new Console Application named External AssemblyReflector. Your task is to construct a Main() method that prompts for the friendly name of an assembly to load dynamically. You will pass the Assembly reference into a helper method named DisplayTypes(), which will simply print the names of each class, interface, structure, enumeration, and delegate it contains. The code is refreshingly simple:

```
using System;
using System.Reflection;
using System.IO;  // For FileNotFoundException definition.

namespace ExternalAssemblyReflector
{
  class Program
  {
    static void DisplayTypesInAsm(Assembly asm)
    {
      Console.WriteLine("\n***** Types in Assembly *****");
      Console.WriteLine("->{0}", asm.FullName);
      Type[] types = asm.GetTypes();
      foreach (Type t in types)
        Console.WriteLine("Type: {0}", t);
      Console.WriteLine("");
    }

    static void Main(string[] args)
    {
      Console.WriteLine("***** External Assembly Viewer *****");

      string asmName = "";
      bool userIsDone = false;
      Assembly asm = null;

      do
      {
        Console.WriteLine("\nEnter an assembly to evaluate");
        Console.Write("or enter Q to quit: ");

        // Get name of assembly.
        asmName = Console.ReadLine();
```

```
        // Does user want to quit?
        if (asmName.ToUpper() == "Q")
        {
          userIsDone = true;
          break;
        }

        // Try to load assembly.
        try
        {
          asm = Assembly.Load(asmName);
          DisplayTypesInAsm(asm);
        }
        catch
        {
          Console.WriteLine("Sorry, can't find assembly.");
        }
      } while (!userIsDone);
    }
  }
}
```

Notice that the static `Assembly.Load()` method has been passed only the friendly name of the assembly you are interested in loading into memory. Thus, if you wish to reflect over `CarLibrary.dll`, you will need to copy the `CarLibrary.dll` binary to the \bin\Debug directory of the External AssemblyReflector application to run this program. Once you do, you will find output similar to Figure 16-4.

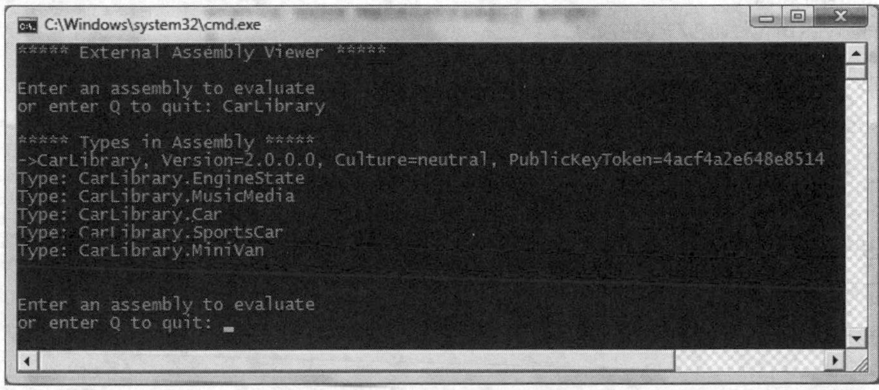

Figure 16-4. *Reflecting on the external* `CarLibrary` *assembly*

If you wish to make ExternalAssemblyReflector more flexible, you can update your code to load the external assembly using `Assembly.LoadFrom()` rather than `Assembly.Load()`. By doing so, you can enter an absolute path to the assembly you wish to view (e.g., C:\MyApp\MyAsm.dll). Essentially, `Assembly.LoadFrom()` allows you to programmatically supply a `<codeBase>` value.

Source Code The ExternalAssemblyReflector project is included in the Chapter 16 subdirectory.

Reflecting on Shared Assemblies

The `Assembly.Load()` method has been overloaded a number of times. One variation allows you to specify a culture value (for localized assemblies) as well as a version number and public key token value (for shared assemblies). Collectively speaking, the set of items identifying an assembly is termed the *display name*. The format of a display name is a comma-delimited string of name/value pairs that begins with the friendly name of the assembly, followed by optional qualifiers (that may appear in any order). Here is the template to follow (optional items appear in parentheses):

```
Name (,Version = major.minor.build.revision) (,Culture = culture token)
(,PublicKeyToken= public key token)
```

When you're crafting a display name, the convention `PublicKeyToken=null` indicates that binding and matching against a non–strongly named assembly is required. Additionally, `Culture=""` indicates matching against the default culture of the target machine, for example:

```
// Load version 1.0.982.23972 of CarLibrary using the default culture.
Assembly a = Assembly.Load(
  @"CarLibrary, Version=1.0.982.23972, PublicKeyToken=null, Culture=""");
```

Also be aware that the `System.Reflection` namespace supplies the `AssemblyName` type, which allows you to represent the preceding string information in a handy object variable. Typically, this class is used in conjunction with `System.Version`, which is an OO wrapper around an assembly's version number. Once you have established the display name, it can then be passed into the overloaded `Assembly.Load()` method:

```
// Make use of AssemblyName to define the display name.
AssemblyName asmName;
asmName = new AssemblyName();
asmName.Name = "CarLibrary";
Version v = new Version("1.0.982.23972");
asmName.Version = v;
Assembly a = Assembly.Load(asmName);
```

To load a shared assembly from the GAC, the `Assembly.Load()` parameter must specify a `PublicKeyToken` value. For example, assume you wish to load version 2.0.0.0 of the `System.Windows.Forms.dll` assembly provided by the .NET base class libraries. Given that the number of types in this assembly is quite large, the following application only prints out the names of public enums, using a simple LINQ query:

```
using System;
using System.Reflection;
using System.IO;
using System.Linq;

namespace SharedAsmReflector
{
  public class SharedAsmReflector
  {
    private static void DisplayInfo(Assembly a)
    {
      Console.WriteLine("***** Info about Assembly *****");
      Console.WriteLine("Loaded from GAC? {0}", a.GlobalAssemblyCache);
      Console.WriteLine("Asm Name: {0}", a.GetName().Name);
      Console.WriteLine("Asm Version: {0}", a.GetName().Version);
      Console.WriteLine("Asm Culture: {0}",
        a.GetName().CultureInfo.DisplayName);
      Console.WriteLine("\nHere are the public enums:");
```

```
    // Use a LINQ query to find the public enums.
    Type[] types = a.GetTypes();
    var publicEnums = from pe in types where pe.IsEnum &&
      pe.IsPublic select pe;

    foreach (var pe in publicEnums)
    {
      Console.WriteLine(pe);
    }
  }

  static void Main(string[] args)
  {
    Console.WriteLine("***** The Shared Asm Reflector App *****\n");

    // Load System.Windows.Forms.dll from GAC.
    string displayName = null;
    displayName = "System.Windows.Forms," +
      "Version=2.0.0.0," +
      "PublicKeyToken=b77a5c561934e089," +
      @"Culture=""";
    Assembly asm = Assembly.Load(displayName);
    DisplayInfo(asm);
    Console.WriteLine("Done!");
    Console.ReadLine();
  }
 }
}
```

Source Code The SharedAsmReflector project is included in the Chapter 16 subdirectory.

At this point you should understand how to use some of the core types defined within the System.Reflection namespace to discover metadata at runtime. Of course, I realize despite the "cool factor," you likely will not need to build custom object browsers at your place of employment. Do recall, however, that reflection services are the foundation for a number of very common programming activities, including *late binding*.

Understanding Late Binding

Simply put, *late binding* is a technique in which you are able to create an instance of a given type and invoke its members at runtime without having hard-coded compile-time knowledge of its existence. When you are building an application that binds late to a type in an external assembly, you have no reason to set a reference to the assembly; therefore, the caller's manifest has no direct listing of the assembly.

At first glance, it is not easy to see the value of late binding. It is true that if you can "bind early" to a type (e.g., set an assembly reference and allocate the type using the C# new keyword), you should opt to do so. For one reason, early binding allows you to determine errors at compile time, rather than at runtime. Nevertheless, late binding does have a critical role in any extendable application you may be building. You will have a chance to build such an "extendable" program at the end of this chapter in the section "Building an Extendable Application"; until then, we need to examine the role of the Activator type.

The System.Activator Class

The `System.Activator` class is the key to the .NET late binding process. Beyond the methods inherited from `System.Object`, `Activator` defines only a small set of members, many of which have to do with the .NET remoting API. For our current example, we are only interested in the `Activator.CreateInstance()` method, which is used to create an instance of a type à la late binding.

This method has been overloaded numerous times to provide a good deal of flexibility. The simplest variation of the `CreateInstance()` member takes a valid `Type` object that describes the entity you wish to allocate on the fly. Create a new Console Application named LateBindingApp, and update the `Main()` method as follows (be sure to place a copy of `CarLibrary.dll` in the project's \bin\Debug directory):

```
// Create a type dynamically.
public class Program
{
  static void Main(string[] args)
  {
    Console.WriteLine("***** Fun with Late Binding *****");
    // Try to load a local copy of CarLibrary.
    Assembly a = null;
    try
    {
      a = Assembly.Load("CarLibrary");
    }
    catch(FileNotFoundException e)
    {
      Console.WriteLine(e.Message);
      return;
    }

    // Get metadata for the Minivan type.
    Type miniVan = a.GetType("CarLibrary.MiniVan");

    // Create the Minivan on the fly.
    object obj = Activator.CreateInstance(miniVan);
    Console.WriteLine("Created a {0} using late binding!", obj);
    Console.ReadLine();
  }
}
```

Notice that the `Activator.CreateInstance()` method returns a `System.Object` rather than a strongly typed `MiniVan`. Therefore, if you apply the dot operator on the `obj` variable, you will fail to see any members of the `MiniVan` type. At first glance, you may assume you can remedy this problem with an explicit cast; however, this program has no clue what a `MiniVan` is in the first place (and if you did, why use late binding at all)!

Remember that the whole point of late binding is to create instances of objects for which there is no compile-time knowledge. Given this, how can you invoke the underlying methods of the `MiniVan` object stored in the `System.Object` variable? The answer, of course, is by using reflection.

Invoking Methods with No Parameters

Assume you wish to invoke the `TurboBoost()` method of the `MiniVan`. As you recall, this method will set the state of the engine to "dead" and display an informational message box. The first step is to obtain a `MethodInfo` type for the `TurboBoost()` method using `Type.GetMethod()`. From the resulting

MethodInfo, you are then able to call MiniVan.TurboBoost using Invoke(). MethodInfo.Invoke() requires you to send in all parameters that are to be given to the method represented by MethodInfo. These parameters are represented by an array of System.Object types (as the parameters for a given method could be any number of various entities).

Given that TurboBoost() does not require any parameters, you can simply pass null (meaning "this method has no parameters"). Update your Main() method as follows:

```
static void Main(string[] args)
{
...
  // Get metadata for the Minivan type.
  Type miniVan = a.GetType("CarLibrary.MiniVan");

  // Create the Minivan on the fly.
  object obj = Activator.CreateInstance(miniVan);
  Console.WriteLine("Created a {0} using late binding!", obj);

  // Get info for TurboBoost.
  MethodInfo mi = miniVan.GetMethod("TurboBoost");

  // Invoke method ('null' for no parameters).
  mi.Invoke(obj, null);
  Console.ReadLine();
}
```

At this point you are happy to see the message box in Figure 16-5.

Figure 16-5. *Late-bound method invocation*

Invoking Methods with Parameters

To illustrate how to dynamically invoke a method that does take some number of parameters, assume you have updated the MiniVan type created in the previous chapter with a new method named TellChildToBeQuiet():

```
// Quiet down the troops...
public void TellChildToBeQuiet(string kidName, int shameIntensity)
{
  for(int i = 0 ; i < shameIntensity; i++)
    MessageBox.Show(string.Format("Be quiet {0} !!", kidName));
}
```

TellChildToBeQuiet() takes two parameters: a string representing the child's name and an integer representing your current level of frustration. When using late binding, parameters are packaged as an array of System.Objects. To invoke the new method, update the Main() method as follows:

```
static void Main(string[] args)
{
...
  // Get metadata for the Minivan type.
  Type miniVan = a.GetType("CarLibrary.MiniVan");

  // Create the Minivan on the fly.
  object obj = Activator.CreateInstance(miniVan);
  Console.WriteLine("Created a {0} using late binding!", obj);

  // Bind late to a method taking params.
  object[] paramArray = new object[2];
  paramArray[0] = "Fred";  // Child name.
  paramArray[1] = 4;       // Shame Intensity.
  mi = miniVan.GetMethod("TellChildToBeQuiet");
  mi.Invoke(obj, paramArray);
  Console.ReadLine();
}
```

If you run this program, you will see four message boxes pop up, shaming young Fred. Hopefully at this point you can see the relationships among reflection, dynamic loading, and late binding. Again, you still may wonder exactly *when* you might make use of these techniques in your own applications. The conclusion of this chapter should shed light on this question; however, the next topic under investigation is the role of .NET attributes.

■ **Source Code** The LateBindingApp project is included in the Chapter 16 subdirectory.

Understanding Attributed Programming

As illustrated at beginning of this chapter, one role of a .NET compiler is to generate metadata descriptions for all defined and referenced types. In addition to this standard metadata contained within any assembly, the .NET platform provides a way for programmers to embed additional metadata into an assembly using *attributes*. In a nutshell, attributes are nothing more than code annotations that can be applied to a given type (class, interface, structure, etc.), member (property, method, etc.), assembly, or module.

The idea of annotating code using attributes is not new. COM IDL provided numerous predefined attributes that allowed developers to describe the types contained within a given COM server. However, COM attributes were little more than a set of keywords. If a COM developer needed to create a custom attribute, he or she could do so, but it was referenced in code by a 128-bit number (GUID), which was cumbersome at best.

Unlike COM IDL attributes (which again were simply keywords), .NET attributes are class types that extend the abstract `System.Attribute` base class. As you explore the .NET namespaces, you will find many predefined attributes that you are able to make use of in your applications. Furthermore, you are free to build custom attributes to further qualify the behavior of your types by creating a new type deriving from `Attribute`.

Understand that when you apply attributes in your code, the embedded metadata is essentially useless until another piece of software explicitly reflects over the information. If this is not the case, the blurb of metadata embedded within the assembly is ignored and completely harmless.

Attribute Consumers

As you would guess, the .NET 3.5 Framework SDK ships with numerous utilities that are indeed on the lookout for various attributes. The C# compiler (`csc.exe`) itself has been preprogrammed to discover the presence of various attributes during the compilation cycle. For example, if the C# compiler encounters the `[CLSCompliant]` attribute, it will automatically check the attributed item to ensure it is exposing only CLS-compliant constructs. By way of another example, if the C# compiler discovers an item attributed with the `[Obsolete]` attribute, it will display a compiler warning in the Visual Studio 2008 Error List window.

In addition to development tools, numerous methods in the .NET base class libraries are preprogrammed to reflect over specific attributes. For example, if you wish to persist the state of an object to file, all you are required to do is annotate your class with the `[Serializable]` attribute. If the `Serialize()` method of the `BinaryFormatter` class encounters this attribute, the object is automatically persisted to file in a compact binary format.

The .NET CLR is also on the prowl for the presence of certain attributes. Perhaps the most famous .NET attribute is `[WebMethod]`. If you wish to expose a method via HTTP requests and automatically encode the method return value as XML, simply apply `[WebMethod]` to the method and the CLR handles the details. Beyond web service development, attributes are critical to the operation of the .NET security system, Windows Communication Foundation, and COM/.NET interoperability (and so on).

Finally, you are free to build applications that are programmed to reflect over your own custom attributes as well as any attribute in the .NET base class libraries. By doing so, you are essentially able to create a set of "keywords" that are understood by a specific set of assemblies.

Applying Attributes in C#

As previously mentioned, the .NET base class library provides a number of attributes in various namespaces. Table 16-3 gives a snapshot of some—but by *absolutely* no means all—predefined attributes.

Table 16-3. *A Tiny Sampling of Predefined Attributes*

Attribute	Meaning in Life
`[CLSCompliant]`	Enforces the annotated item to conform to the rules of the Common Language Specification (CLS). Recall that CLS-compliant types are guaranteed to be used seamlessly across all .NET programming languages.
`[DllImport]`	Allows .NET code to make calls to any unmanaged C- or C++-based code library, including the API of the underlying operating system. Do note that `[DllImport]` is not used when communicating with COM-based software.
`[Obsolete]`	Marks a deprecated type or member. If other programmers attempt to use such an item, they will receive a compiler warning describing the error of their ways.
`[Serializable]`	Marks a class or structure as being "serializable," meaning it is able to persist its current state into a stream.
`[NonSerialized]`	Specifies that a given field in a class or structure should not be persisted during the serialization process.
`[WebMethod]`	Marks a method as being invokable via HTTP requests and instructs the CLR to serialize the method return value as XML.

To illustrate the process of applying attributes in C#, assume you wish to build a class named `Motorcycle` that can be persisted in a binary format. To do so, simply apply the `[Serializable]` attribute to the class definition. If you have a field that should not be persisted, you may apply the `[NonSerialized]` attribute:

```
// This class can be saved to disk.
[Serializable]
public class Motorcycle
{
  // However this field will not be persisted.
  [NonSerialized]
  float weightOfCurrentPassengers;

  // These fields are still serializable.
  bool hasRadioSystem;
  bool hasHeadSet;
  bool hasSissyBar;
}
```

■ **Note** An attribute only applies to the "very next" item. For example, the only nonserialized field of the `Motorcycle` class is `weightOfCurrentPassengers`. The remaining fields are serializable given that the entire class has been annotated with `[Serializable]`.

At this point, don't concern yourself with the actual process of object serialization (Chapter 21 examines the details). Just notice that when you wish to apply an attribute, the name of the attribute is sandwiched between square brackets.

Once this class has been compiled, you can view the extra metadata using `ildasm.exe`. Notice that these attributes are recorded using the `serializable` and `notserialized` tokens (see Figure 16-6).

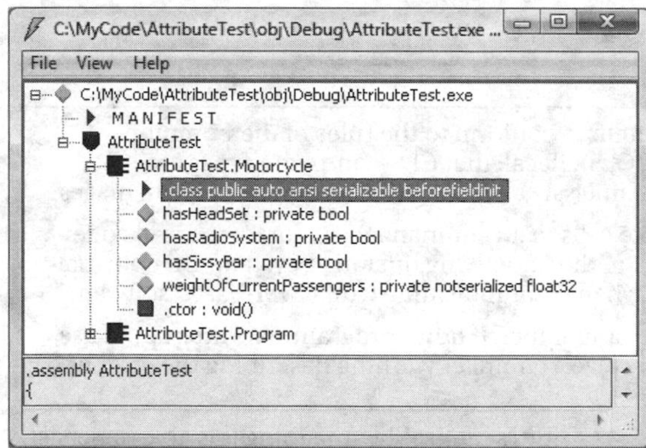

Figure 16-6. *Attributes shown in* `ildasm.exe`

As you might guess, a single item can be attributed with multiple attributes. Assume you have a legacy C# class type (`HorseAndBuggy`) that was marked as serializable, but is now considered obsolete for current development. Rather than deleting the class definition from your code base (and risk breaking existing software), you can mark the class with the `[Obsolete]` attribute. To apply multiple attributes to a single item, simply use a comma-delimited list:

```
[Serializable, Obsolete("Use another vehicle!")]
public class HorseAndBuggy
{
  // ...
}
```

As an alternative, you can also apply multiple attributes on a single item by stacking each attribute as follows (the end result is identical):

```
[Serializable]
[Obsolete("Use another vehicle!")]
public class HorseAndBuggy
{
  // ...
}
```

Specifying Constructor Parameters for Attributes

Notice that the [Obsolete] attribute is able to accept what appears to be a constructor parameter. If you view the formal definition of the [Obsolete] attribute using the Code Definition window of Visual Studio 2008, you will find that this class indeed provides a constructor receiving a System.String:

```
public sealed class ObsoleteAttribute : System.Attribute
{
  public bool IsError { get; }
  public string Message { get; }
  public ObsoleteAttribute(string message, bool error);
  public ObsoleteAttribute(string message);
  public ObsoleteAttribute();
}
```

Understand that when you supply constructor parameters to an attribute, the attribute is *not* allocated into memory until the parameters are reflected upon by another type or an external tool. The string data defined at the attribute level is simply stored within the assembly as a blurb of metadata.

The Obsolete Attribute in Action

Now that HorseAndBuggy has been marked as obsolete, if you were to allocate an instance of this type:

```
static void Main(string[] args)
{
  HorseAndBuggy mule = new HorseAndBuggy();
}
```

you would find that the supplied string data is extracted and displayed within the Error List window of Visual Studio 2008 (see Figure 16-7).

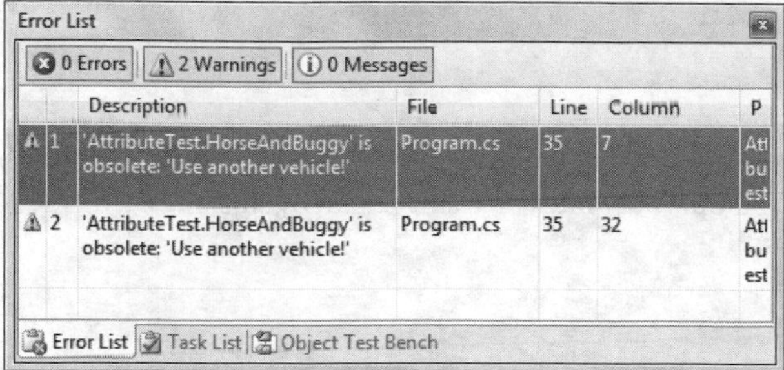

Figure 16-7. *Attributes in action*

In this case, the "other piece of software" that is reflecting on the [Obsolete] attribute is the C# compiler.

C# Attribute Shorthand Notation

If you were reading closely, you may have noticed that the actual class name of the [Obsolete] attribute is ObsoleteAttribute, not Obsolete. As a naming convention, all .NET attributes (including custom attributes you may create yourself) are suffixed with the Attribute token. However, to simplify the process of applying attributes, the C# language does not require you to type in the Attribute suffix. Given this, the following iteration of the HorseAndBuggy type is identical to the previous (it just involves a few more keystrokes):

```
[SerializableAttribute]
[ObsoleteAttribute("Use another vehicle!")]
public class HorseAndBuggy
{
  // ...
}
```

Be aware that this is a courtesy provided by C#. Not all .NET-enabled languages support this shorthand attribute syntax. In any case, at this point you should hopefully understand the following key points regarding .NET attributes:

- Attributes are classes that derive from System.Attribute.
- Attributes result in embedded metadata.
- Attributes are basically useless until another agent reflects upon them.
- Attributes are applied in C# using square brackets.

Next up, let's examine how you can build your own custom attributes and a piece of custom software that reflects over the embedded metadata.

Building Custom Attributes

The first step in building a custom attribute is to create a new class deriving from System.Attribute. Keeping in step with the automobile theme used throughout this book, assume you have created a brand new C# class library named AttributedCarLibrary. This assembly will define a handful of vehicles (some of which you have already seen in this text), each of which is described using a custom attribute named VehicleDescriptionAttribute:

```
// A custom attribute.
public sealed class VehicleDescriptionAttribute : System.Attribute
{
  private string msgData;

  public VehicleDescriptionAttribute(string description)
  { msgData = description;}
  public VehicleDescriptionAttribute(){ }

  public string Description
  {
    get { return msgData; }
    set { msgData = value; }
  }
}
```

As you can see, VehicleDescriptionAttribute maintains a private internal string (msgData) that can be set using a custom constructor and manipulated using a type property (Description). Beyond the fact that this class derived from System.Attribute, there is nothing unique to this class definition.

■ **Note** For security reasons, it is considered a .NET best practice to design all custom attributes as sealed. In fact, Visual Studio 2008 provides a code snippet named Attribute that will dump out a new System.Attribute-derived class into your code window. See Chapter 2 for an explication of using code snippets.

Applying Custom Attributes

Given that VehicleDescriptionAttribute is derived from System.Attribute, you are now able to annotate your vehicles as you see fit. For testing purposes, add the following class definitions to your new class library:

```
// Assign description using a "named property."
[Serializable]
[VehicleDescription(Description = "My rocking Harley")]
public class Motorcycle
{
}

[SerializableAttribute]
[ObsoleteAttribute("Use another vehicle!")]
[VehicleDescription("The old gray mare, she ain't what she used to be...")]
public class HorseAndBuggy
{
}

[VehicleDescription("A very long, slow, but feature-rich auto")]
public class Winnebago
{
}
```

Named Property Syntax

Notice that the description of the `Motorcycle` is assigned a description using a new bit of attribute-centric syntax termed a *named property*. In the constructor of the first `[VehicleDescription]` attribute, you set the underlying `System.String` using a name/value pair. If this attribute is reflected upon by an external agent, the value is fed into the `Description` property (named property syntax is legal only if the attribute supplies a writable .NET property).

In contrast, the `HorseAndBuggy` and `Winnebago` types are not making use of named property syntax and are simply passing the string data via the custom constructor. In any case, once you compile the `AttributedCarLibrary` assembly, you can make use of `ildasm.exe` to view the injected metadata descriptions for your type. For example, Figure 16-8 shows an embedded description of the `Winnebago` type.

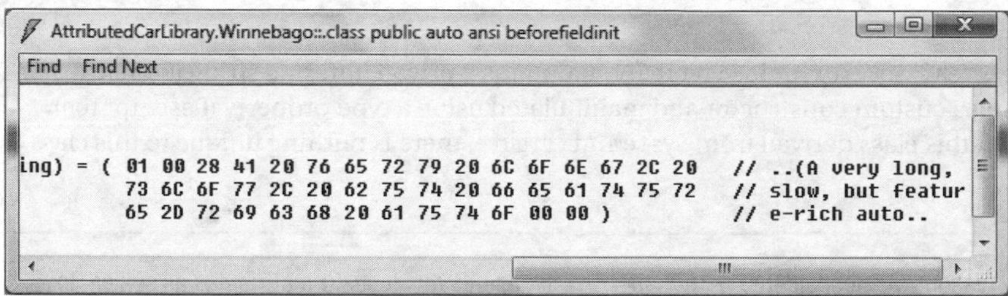

Figure 16-8. *Embedded vehicle description data*

Restricting Attribute Usage

By default, custom attributes can be applied to just about any aspect of your code (methods, classes, properties, and so on). Thus, if it made sense to do so, you could use `VehicleDescription` to qualify methods, properties, or fields (among other things):

```
[VehicleDescription("A very long, slow, but feature-rich auto")]
public class Winnebago
{
  [VehicleDescription("My rocking CD player")]
  public void PlayMusic(bool On)
  {
    ...
  }
}
```

In some cases, this is exactly the behavior you require. Other times, however, you may want to build a custom attribute that can be applied only to select code elements. If you wish to constrain the scope of a custom attribute, you will need to apply the `[AttributeUsage]` attribute on the definition of your custom attribute. The `[AttributeUsage]` attribute allows you to supply any combination of values (via an OR operation) from the `AttributeTargets` enumeration:

```
// This enumeration defines the possible targets of an attribute.
public enum AttributeTargets
{
  All, Assembly, Class, Constructor,
  Delegate, Enum, Event, Field,
  Interface, Method, Module, Parameter,
  Property, ReturnValue, Struct
}
```

Furthermore, [AttributeUsage] also allows you to optionally set a named property (AllowMultiple) that specifies whether the attribute can be applied more than once on the same item. As well, [AttributeUsage] allows you to establish whether the attribute should be inherited by derived classes using the Inherited named property.

To establish that the [VehicleDescription] attribute can be applied only once on a class or structure (and the value is not inherited by derived types), you can update the VehicleDescriptionAttribute definition as follows:

```
// This time, we are using the AttributeUsage attribute
// to annotate our custom attribute.
[AttributeUsage(AttributeTargets.Class | AttributeTargets.Struct,
 AllowMultiple = false, Inherited = false)]
public sealed class VehicleDescriptionAttribute : System.Attribute
{
...
}
```

With this, if a developer attempted to apply the [VehicleDescription] attribute on anything other than a class or structure, he or she is issued a compile-time error.

■ **Tip** Always get in the habit of explicitly marking the usage flags for any custom attribute you may create, as not all .NET programming languages honor the use of unqualified attributes!

Assembly-Level (and Module-Level) Attributes

It is also possible to apply attributes on all types within a given module (for a multifile assembly) or all modules within a given assembly using the [module:] and [assembly:] tags, respectively. For example, assume you wish to ensure that every public type defined within your assembly is CLS compliant. To do so, simply add the following line in any one of your C# source code files (do note that assembly-level attributes must be outside the scope of a namespace definition):

```
// Enforce CLS compliance for all public types in this assembly.
[assembly:System.CLSCompliantAttribute(true)]
```

If you now add a bit of code that falls outside the CLS specification (such as an exposed point of unsigned data):

```
// Ulong types don't jibe with the CLS.
public class Winnebago
{
  public ulong notCompliant;
}
```

you are issued a compiler warning.

The Visual Studio 2008 AssemblyInfo.cs File

By default, Visual Studio 2008 projects receive a file named AssemblyInfo.cs, which can be viewed by expanding the Properties icon of the Solution Explorer (see Figure 16-9).

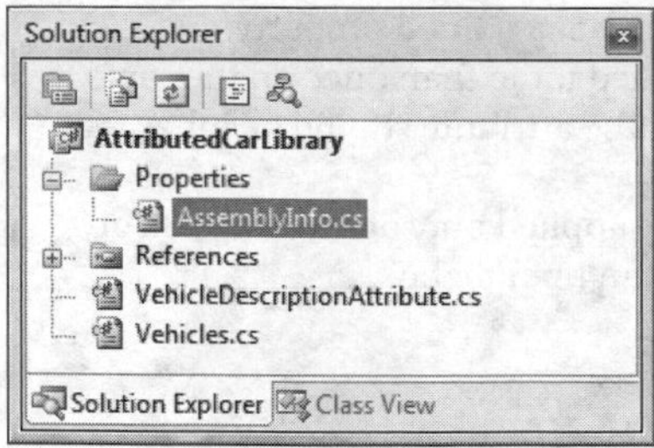

Figure 16-9. *The* `AssemblyInfo.cs` *file*

This file is a handy place to put attributes that are to be applied at the assembly level. You may recall from Chapter 15, during our examination of .NET assemblies, that the manifest contains assembly-level metadata, much of which comes from the assembly-level attributes shown in Table 16-4.

Table 16-4. *Select Assembly-Level Attributes*

Attribute	Meaning in Life
`AssemblyCompanyAttribute`	Holds basic company information
`AssemblyCopyrightAttribute`	Holds any copyright information for the product or assembly
`AssemblyCultureAttribute`	Provides information on what cultures or languages the assembly supports
`AssemblyDescriptionAttribute`	Holds a friendly description of the product or modules that make up the assembly
`AssemblyKeyFileAttribute`	Specifies the name of the file containing the key pair used to sign the assembly (i.e., establish a strong name)
`AssemblyOperatingSystemAttribute`	Provides information on which operating system the assembly was built to support
`AssemblyProcessorAttribute`	Provides information on which processors the assembly was built to support
`AssemblyProductAttribute`	Provides product information
`AssemblyTrademarkAttribute`	Provides trademark information
`AssemblyVersionAttribute`	Specifies the assembly's version information, in the format `<major.minor.build.revision>`

■ **Source Code** The AttributedCarLibrary project is included in the Chapter 16 subdirectory.

Reflecting on Attributes Using Early Binding

As mentioned in this chapter, an attribute is quite useless until some piece of software reflects over its values. Once a given attribute has been discovered, that piece of software can take whatever course of action necessary. Now, like any application, this "other piece of software" could discover the presence of a custom attribute using either early binding or late binding. If you wish to make use of early binding, you'll require the client application to have a compile-time definition of the attribute in question (VehicleDescriptionAttribute in this case). Given that the AttributedCarLibrary assembly has defined this custom attribute as a public class, early binding is the best option.

To illustrate the process of reflecting on custom attributes, create a new C# Console Application named VehicleDescriptionAttributeReader. Next, set a reference to the AttributedCarLibrary assembly. Finally, update your initial *.cs file with the following code:

```
// Reflecting on custom attributes using early binding.
using System;
using AttributedCarLibrary;

public class Program
{
  static void Main(string[] args)
  {
    // Get a Type representing the Winnebago.
    Type t = typeof(Winnebago);

    // Get all attributes on the Winnebago.
    object[] customAtts = t.GetCustomAttributes(false);

    // Print the description.
    Console.WriteLine("***** Value of VehicleDescriptionAttribute *****\n");
    foreach(VehicleDescriptionAttribute v in customAtts)
      Console.WriteLine("-> {0}\n", v.Description);
    Console.ReadLine();
  }
}
```

As the name implies, Type.GetCustomAttributes() returns an object array that represents all the attributes applied to the member represented by the Type (the Boolean parameter controls whether the search should extend up the inheritance chain). Once you have obtained the list of attributes, iterate over each VehicleDescriptionAttribute class and print out the value obtained by the Description property.

■ **Source Code** The VehicleDescriptionAttributeReader project is included under the Chapter 16 subdirectory.

Reflecting on Attributes Using Late Binding

The previous example made use of early binding to print out the vehicle description data for the Winnebago type. This was possible due to the fact that the VehicleDescriptionAttribute class type was defined as a public member in the AttributedCarLibrary assembly. It is also possible to make use of dynamic loading and late binding to reflect over attributes.

Create a new project called VehicleDescriptionAttributeReaderLateBinding and copy AttributedCarLibrary.dll to the project's \bin\Debug directory. Now, update your Main() method as follows:

```
using System.Reflection;
```

```
class Program
{
  static void Main(string[] args)
  {
    Console.WriteLine("***** Descriptions of Your Vehicles *****\n");

    // Load the local copy of AttributedCarLibrary.
    Assembly asm = Assembly.Load("AttributedCarLibrary");

    // Get type info of VehicleDescriptionAttribute.
    Type vehicleDesc =
      asm.GetType("AttributedCarLibrary.VehicleDescriptionAttribute");

    // Get type info of the Description property.
    PropertyInfo propDesc = vehicleDesc.GetProperty("Description");

    // Get all types in the assembly.
    Type[] types = asm.GetTypes();

    // Iterate over each type and obtain any VehicleDescriptionAttributes.
    foreach (Type t in types)
    {
      object[] objs = t.GetCustomAttributes(vehicleDesc, false);

      // Iterate over each VehicleDescriptionAttribute and print
      // the description using late binding.
      foreach (object o in objs)
      {
        Console.WriteLine("-> {0}: {1}\n",
          t.Name, propDesc.GetValue(o, null));
      }
    }
    Console.ReadLine();
  }
}
```

If you were able to follow along with the examples in this chapter, this `Main()` method should be (more or less) self-explanatory. The only point of interest is the use of the `PropertyInfo.GetValue()` method, which is used to trigger the property's accessor. Figure 16-10 shows the output.

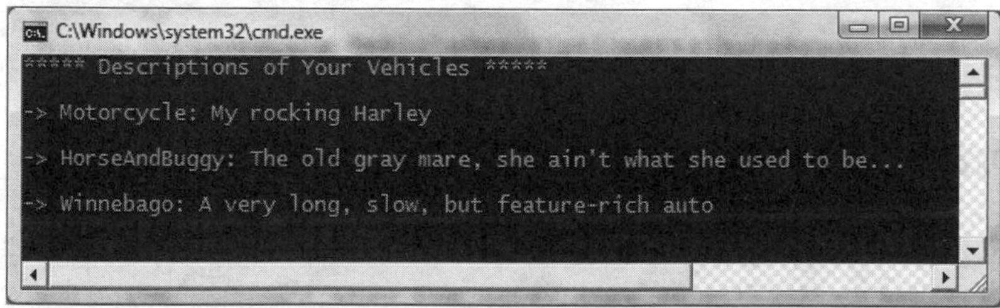

Figure 16-10. *Reflecting on attributes using late binding*

■ Source Code The VehicleDescriptionAttributeReaderLateBinding project is included under the Chapter 16 subdirectory.

Putting Reflection, Late Binding, and Custom Attributes in Perspective

Even though you have seen numerous examples of these techniques in action, you may still be wondering when to make use of reflection, dynamic loading, late binding, and custom attributes in your programs. To be sure, these topics can seem a bit on the academic side of programming (which may or may not be a bad thing, depending on your point of view). To help map these topics to a real-world situation, you need a solid example. Assume for the moment that you are on a programming team that is building an application with the following requirement:

- The product must be extendable by the use of additional third-party tools.

So, what exactly is meant by *extendable*? Consider the Visual Studio 2008 IDE. When this application was developed, various "hooks" were inserted to allow other software vendors to snap custom modules into the IDE. Obviously, the Visual Studio 2008 development team had no way to set references to external .NET assemblies it had not developed yet (thus, no early binding), so how exactly would an application provide the required hooks? Here is one possible way to solve this problem:

- First, an extendable application must provide some input vehicle to allow the user to specify the module to plug in (such as a dialog box or command-line flag). This requires *dynamic loading*.
- Second, an extendable application must be able to determine whether the module supports the correct functionality (such as a set of required interfaces) in order to be plugged into the environment. This requires *reflection*.
- Finally, an extendable application must obtain a reference to the required infrastructure (such as a set of interface types) and invoke the members to trigger the underlying functionality. This may require *late binding*.

Simply put, if the extendable application has been preprogrammed to query for specific interfaces, it is able to determine at runtime whether the type can be activated. Once this verification test has been passed, the type in question may support additional interfaces that provide a polymorphic fabric to their functionality. This is the exact approach taken by the Visual Studio 2008 team, and despite what you may be thinking, is not at all difficult.

Building an Extendable Application

In the sections that follow, I will take you through a complete example that illustrates the process of building an extendable Windows Forms application that can be augmented by the functionality of external assemblies. What I will not do at this point is comment on the process of programming Windows Forms applications (see Chapter 27 for an overview of the Windows Forms API). So, if you are not familiar with the process of building Windows Forms applications, feel free to simply open up the supplied sample code and follow along. To serve as a road map, our extendable application entails the following assemblies:

- CommonSnappableTypes.dll: This assembly contains type definitions that will be used by each snap-in object and will be directly referenced by the Windows Forms application.
- CSharpSnapIn.dll: A snap-in written in C#, which leverages the types of CommonSnappableTypes.dll.
- VbNetSnapIn.dll: A snap-in written in Visual Basic, which leverages the types of CommonSnappableTypes.dll.
- MyExtendableApp.exe: This Windows Forms application will be the entity that may be extended by the functionality of each snap-in.

Again, this application will make use of dynamic loading, reflection, and late binding to dynamically gain the functionality of assemblies it has no prior knowledge of.

Building CommonSnappableTypes.dll

The first order of business is to create an assembly that contains the types that a given snap-in must leverage to be plugged into the expandable Windows Forms application. The CommonSnappable-Types Class Library project defines two types:

```
namespace CommonSnappableTypes
{
  public interface IAppFunctionality
  {
    void DoIt();
  }

  [AttributeUsage(AttributeTargets.Class)]
  public sealed class CompanyInfoAttribute : System.Attribute
  {
    private string companyName;
    private string companyUrl;
    public CompanyInfoAttribute(){}

    public string Name
    {
      get { return companyName; }
      set { companyName = value; }
    }
    public string Url
    {
      get { return companyUrl; }
      set { companyUrl = value; }
    }
  }
}
```

The IAppFunctionality interface provides a polymorphic interface for all snap-ins that can be consumed by the extendable Windows Forms application. Given that this example is purely illustrative, you supply a single method named DoIt(). A more realistic interface (or a set of interfaces) might allow the object to generate scripting code, render an image onto the application's toolbox, or integrate into the main menu of the hosting application.

The CompanyInfoAttribute type is a custom attribute that will be applied on any class type that wishes to be snapped in to the container. As you can tell by the definition of this class, [CompanyInfo] allows the developer of the snap-in to provide some basic details about the component's point of origin.

Building the C# Snap-In

Next up, you need to create a type that implements the IAppFunctionality interface. Again, to focus on the overall design of an extendable application, a trivial type is in order. Assume a new C# Class Library project named CSharpSnapIn defines a class type named CSharpModule. Given that this class must make use of the types defined in CommonSnappableTypes, be sure to set a reference to this binary (as well as System.Windows.Forms.dll to display a noteworthy message). This being said, here is the code:

```
using System;
using CommonSnappableTypes;
using System.Windows.Forms;

namespace CSharpSnapIn
{
  [CompanyInfo(Name = "Intertech Training",
             Url = "www.intertech.com")]
  public class CSharpModule : IAppFunctionality
  {
    void IAppFunctionality.DoIt()
    {
      MessageBox.Show("You have just used the C# snap in!");
    }
  }
}
```

Notice that I choose to make use of explicit interface implementation when supporting the IAppFunctionality interface. This is not required; however, the idea is that the only part of the system that needs to directly interact with this interface type is the hosting Windows application. By explicitly implementing this interface, the DoIt() method is not directly exposed from the CSharpModule type.

Building the Visual Basic Snap-In

Now, to simulate the role of a third-party vendor who prefers Visual Basic over C#, create a new Visual Basic code library (VbNetSnapIn) that references the same external assemblies as the previous CSharpSnapIn project. The code is (again) intentionally simple:

```
Imports System.Windows.Forms
Imports CommonSnappableTypes

<CompanyInfo(Name:="Chucky's Software", Url:="www.ChuckySoft.com")> _
Public Class VbNetSnapIn
    Implements IAppFunctionality

    Public Sub DoIt() Implements CommonSnappableTypes.IAppFunctionality.DoIt
        MessageBox.Show("You have just used the VB .NET snap in!")
    End Sub
End Class
```

Notice that applying attributes in the syntax of Visual Basic requires angle brackets (< >) rather than square brackets ([ ]). Also notice that the Implements keyword is used to implement interface types on a given class or structure.

Building an Extendable Windows Forms Application

The final step is to create a new Windows Forms application (MyExtendableApp) that allows the user to select a snap-in using a standard Windows Open dialog box. Next, set a reference to the CommonSnappableTypes.dll assembly, but *not* the CSharpSnapIn.dll or VbNetSnapIn.dll code libraries. Remember that the whole goal of this application is to make use of late binding and reflection to determine the "snapability" of independent binaries created by third-party vendors.

Again, I won't bother to examine all the details of Windows Forms development at this point in the text. However, assuming you have placed a MenuStrip component onto the forms designer, define a topmost menu item named File that provides a single submenu named Snap In Module. As well, the main window will contain a ListBox type (which I renamed as lstLoadedSnapIns) that will be used to display the names of each snap-in loaded by the user. Figure 16-11 shows the final GUI.

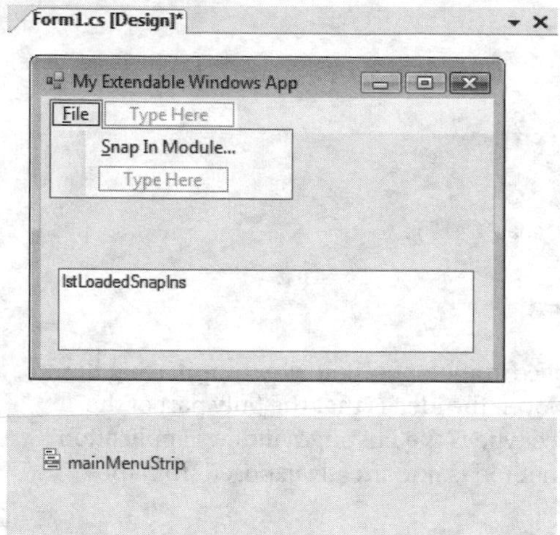

Figure 16-11. *GUI for MyExtendableApp*

The code that handles the Click event for the File ➤ Snap In Module menu item (which may be created simply by double-clicking the menu item from the design-time editor) displays a File Open dialog box and extracts the path to the selected file. Assuming the user did not select the CommonSnappableTypes.dll assembly (as this is purely infrastructure), the path is then sent into a helper function named LoadExternalModule() for processing. This method will return false when it is unable to find a class implementing IAppFunctionality:

```
private void snapInModuleToolStripMenuItem_Click(object sender,
  EventArgs e)
{
  // Allow user to select an assembly to load.
  OpenFileDialog dlg = new OpenFileDialog();

  if (dlg.ShowDialog() == DialogResult.OK)
  {
    if(dlg.FileName.Contains("CommonSnappableTypes"))
      MessageBox.Show("CommonSnappableTypes has no snap-ins!");
    else if(!LoadExternalModule(dlg.FileName))
      MessageBox.Show("Nothing implements IAppFunctionality!");
  }
}
```

The LoadExternalModule() method performs the following tasks:

- Dynamically loads the selected assembly into memory
- Determines whether the assembly contains any types implementing IAppFunctionality
- Creates the type using late binding

If a type implementing IAppFunctionality is found, the DoIt() method is called, and the fully qualified name of the type is added to the ListBox (note that the foreach loop will iterate over all types in the assembly to account for the possibility that a single assembly has multiple snap-ins). Finally, notice that we are making use of a LINQ query to obtain IAppFunctionality-compatible class types.

```
private bool LoadExternalModule(string path)
{
  bool foundSnapIn = false;
  Assembly theSnapInAsm = null;

  try
  {
    // Dynamically load the selected assembly.
    theSnapInAsm = Assembly.LoadFrom(path);
  }
  catch(Exception ex)
  {
    MessageBox.Show(ex.Message);
    return foundSnapIn;
  }

  // Get all IAppFunctionality compatible classes in assembly.
  var theClassTypes = from t in theSnapInAsm.GetTypes()
                      where t.IsClass &&
                      (t.GetInterface("IAppFunctionality") != null)
                      select t;

  // Now, create the object and call DoIt() method.
  foreach (Type t in theClassTypes)
  {
    foundSnapIn = true;
    // Use late binding to create the type.
    IAppFunctionality itfApp =
      (IAppFunctionality)theSnapInAsm.CreateInstance(t.FullName, true);
    itfApp.DoIt();
    lstLoadedSnapIns.Items.Add(t.FullName);
  }
  return foundSnapIn;
}
```

At this point, you can run your application. When you select the CSharpSnapIn.dll or VbNetSnapIn.dll assemblies, you should see the correct message displayed. The final task is to display the metadata provided by the [CompanyInfo] attribute. To do so, update LoadExternalModule() to call a new helper function named DisplayCompanyData() before exiting the foreach scope. Notice this method takes a single System.Type parameter.

```
private bool LoadExternalModule(string path)
{
...
  foreach (Type t in theClassTypes)
```

```
  {
...
    // Show company info.
    DisplayCompanyData(t);
  }
  return foundSnapIn;
}
```

Using the incoming type, simply reflect over the [CompanyInfo] attribute:

```
private void DisplayCompanyData(Type t)
{
  // Get [CompanyInfo] data.
  var compInfo = from ci in t.GetCustomAttributes(false) where
                 (ci.GetType() == typeof(CompanyInfoAttribute))
                 select ci;

  // Show data.
  foreach (CompanyInfoAttribute c in compInfo)
  {
    MessageBox.Show(c.Url,
      string.Format("More info about {0} can be found at", c.Name));
  }
}
```

Figure 16-12 shows one possible run.

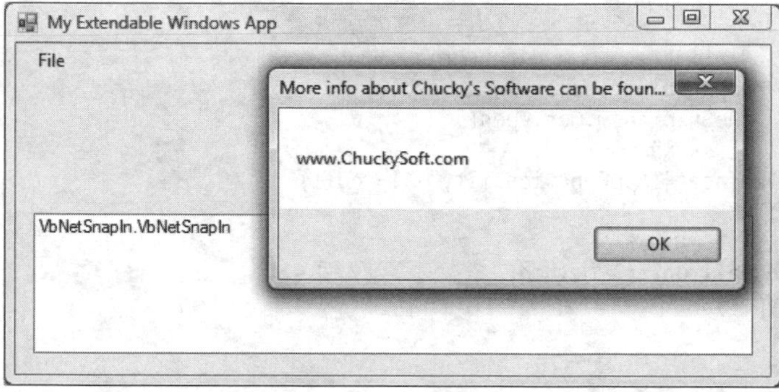

Figure 16-12. *Snapping in external assemblies*

Excellent! That wraps up the example application. I hope at this point you can see that the topics presented in this chapter can be quite helpful in the real world and are not limited to the tool builders of the world.

Source Code The CommonSnappableTypes, CSharpSnapIn, VbNetSnapIn, and MyExtendableApp projects are included under the Chapter 16 subdirectory.

Summary

Reflection is a very interesting aspect of a robust OO environment. In the world of .NET, the keys to reflection services revolve around the `System.Type` class and the `System.Reflection` namespace. As you have seen, reflection is the process of placing a type under the magnifying glass at runtime to understand the who, what, where, when, why, and how of a given item.

Late binding is the process of creating a type and invoking its members without prior knowledge of the specific names of said members. Late binding is often a direct result of *dynamic loading*, which allows you to load a .NET assembly into memory programmatically. As shown during this chapter's extendable application example, this is a very powerful technique used by tool builders as well as tool consumers. This chapter also examined the role of attribute-based programming. When you adorn your types with attributes, the result is the augmentation of the underlying assembly metadata.

CHAPTER 17

Processes, AppDomains, and Object Contexts

In the previous two chapters, you examined the steps taken by the CLR to resolve the location of an externally referenced assembly as well as the role of .NET metadata. In this chapter, you'll drill deeper into the details of how an assembly is hosted by the CLR and come to understand the relationship between processes, application domains, and object contexts.

In a nutshell, *application domains* (or simply *AppDomains*) are logical subdivisions within a given process that host a set of related .NET assemblies. As you will see, an AppDomain is further subdivided into *contextual boundaries*, which are used to group together like-minded .NET objects. Using the notion of context, the CLR is able to ensure that objects with special runtime requirements are handled appropriately.

Reviewing Traditional Win32 Processes

The concept of a "process" has existed within Windows-based operating systems well before the release of the .NET platform. Simply put, *process* is the term used to describe the set of resources (such as external code libraries and the primary thread) and the necessary memory allocations used by a running application. For each `*.exe` loaded into memory, the OS creates a separate and isolated process for use during its lifetime. Using this approach to application isolation, the result is a much more robust and stable runtime environment, given that the failure of one process does not affect the functioning of another.

Now, every Win32 process is assigned a unique process identifier (PID) and may be independently loaded and unloaded by the OS as necessary (as well as programmatically using Win32 API calls). As you may be aware, the Processes tab of the Windows Task Manager utility (activated via the Ctrl+Shift+Esc keystroke combination) allows you to view various statistics regarding the processes running on a given machine, including its PID and image name (see Figure 17-1).

Note The View ➤ Select Columns menu option of the Windows Task Manager allows you to select which columns (PID, User Name, etc.) you wish to have displayed.

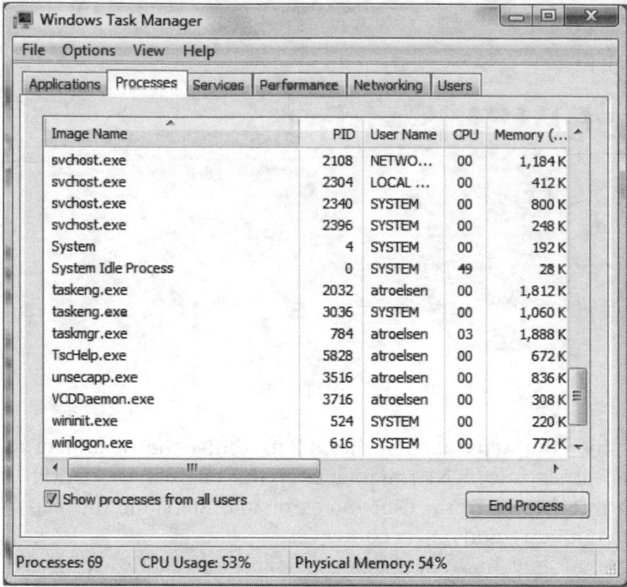

Figure 17-1. *The Windows Task Manager*

An Overview of Threads

Every Win32 process has exactly one main "thread" that functions as the entry point for the application. The next chapter examines how to create threads under the .NET platform using the `System.Threading` namespace; however, to facilitate the topics presented here, we need a few working definitions. First of all, a *thread* is a path of execution within a process. Formally speaking, the first thread created by a process's entry point is termed the *primary thread*. Win32 API GUI desktop applications define the `WinMain()` method as the application's entry point. On the other hand, a console-based program provides the `Main()` method for the same purpose.

Processes that contain a single primary thread of execution are intrinsically *thread safe*, given the fact that there is only one thread that can access the data in the application at a given time. However, a single-threaded process (especially one that is GUI-based) will often appear a bit unresponsive to the user if this single thread is performing a complex operation (such as printing out a lengthy text file, performing a mathematically intensive calculation, or attempting to connect to a remote server located thousands of miles away).

Given this potential drawback of single-threaded applications, the Win32 API (as well as the .NET platform) makes it possible for the primary thread to spawn additional secondary threads (also termed *worker threads*) using a handful of Win32 API functions such as `CreateThread()`. Each thread (primary or secondary) becomes a unique path of execution in the process and has concurrent access to all shared points of data.

As you may have guessed, developers typically create additional threads to help improve the program's overall responsiveness. Multithreaded processes provide the illusion that numerous activities are happening at more or less the same time. For example, an application may spawn a worker thread to perform a labor-intensive unit of work (again, such as printing a large text file).

As this secondary thread is churning away, the main thread is still responsive to user input, which gives the entire process the potential of delivering greater performance. However, this may not actually be the case: using too many threads in a single process can actually *degrade* performance, as the CPU must switch between the active threads in the process (which takes time).

In reality, it is always worth keeping in mind that multithreading is most commonly an illusion provided by the OS. Machines that host a single (nonhyperthreaded) CPU do not have the ability to literally handle multiple threads at the same exact time. Rather, a single CPU will execute one thread for a unit of time (called a *time slice*) based in part on the thread's priority level. When a thread's time slice is up, the existing thread is suspended to allow another thread to perform its business. For a thread to remember what was happening before it was kicked out of the way, each thread is given the ability to write to Thread Local Storage (TLS) and is provided with a separate call stack, as illustrated in Figure 17-2.

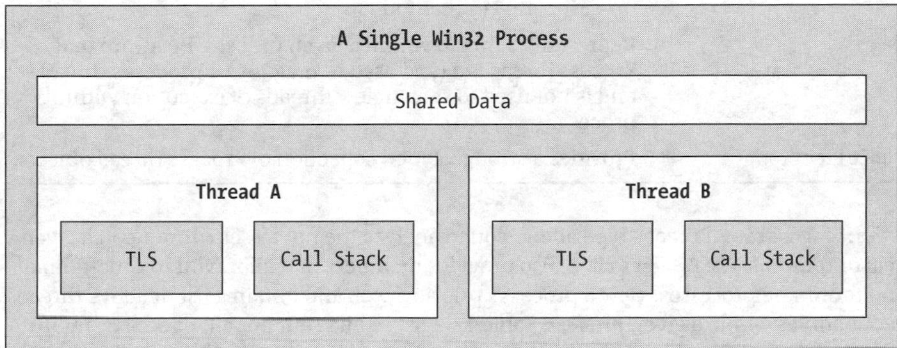

Figure 17-2. *The Win32 process/thread relationship*

If the subject of threads is new to you, don't sweat the details. At this point, just remember that a thread is a unique path of execution within a Win32 process. Every process has a primary thread (created via the executable's entry point) and may contain additional threads that have been programmatically created.

Interacting with Processes Under the .NET Platform

Although processes and threads are nothing new, the manner in which we interact with these primitives under the .NET platform has changed quite a bit (for the better). To pave the way to understanding the world of building multithreaded assemblies (see Chapter 18), let's begin by checking out how to interact with processes using the .NET base class libraries.

The `System.Diagnostics` namespace defines a number of types that allow you to programmatically interact with processes and various diagnostic-related types such as the system event log and performance counters. In this chapter, we are only concerned with the process-centric types defined in Table 17-1.

Table 17-1. *Select Members of the* System.Diagnostics *Namespace*

Process-Centric Types of the System.Diagnostics Namespace	Meaning in Life
Process	The Process class provides access to local and remote processes and also allows you to programmatically start and stop processes.
ProcessModule	This type represents a module (*.dll or *.exe) that is loaded into a particular process. Understand that the ProcessModule type can represent *any* module—COM-based, .NET-based, or traditional C-based binaries.
ProcessModuleCollection	Provides a strongly typed collection of ProcessModule objects.
ProcessStartInfo	Specifies a set of values used when starting a process via the Process.Start() method.
ProcessThread	Represents a thread within a given process. Be aware that ProcessThread is a type used to diagnose a process's thread set and is not used to spawn new threads of execution within a process.
ProcessThreadCollection	Provides a strongly typed collection of ProcessThread objects.

The System.Diagnostics.Process type allows you to analyze the processes running on a given machine (local or remote). The Process class also provides members that allow you to programmatically start and terminate processes, view a process's priority level, and obtain a list of active threads and/or loaded modules within a given process. Table 17-2 lists some (but not all) of the key members of System.Diagnostics.Process.

Table 17-2. *Select Members of the* Process *Type*

Members	Meaning in Life
ExitCode	This property gets the value that the associated process specified when it terminated. Do note that you will be required to handle the Exited event (for asynchronous notification) or call the WaitForExit() method (for synchronous notification) to obtain this value.
ExitTime	This property gets the timestamp associated with the process that has terminated (represented with a DateTime type).
Handle	This property returns the handle associated to the process by the OS.
HandleCount	This property returns the number of handles opened by the process.
Id	This property gets the PID for the associated process.
MachineName	This property gets the name of the computer the associated process is running on.
MainModule	This property gets the ProcessModule type that represents the main module for a given process.
MainWindowTitle MainWindowHandle	MainWindowTitle gets the caption of the main window of the process (if the process does not have a main window, you receive an empty string). MainWindowHandle gets the underlying handle (represented via a System.IntPtr type) of the associated window. If the process does not have a main window, the IntPtr type is assigned the value System.IntPtr.Zero.
Modules	This property provides access to the strongly typed ProcessModuleCollection type, which represents the set of modules (*.dll or *.exe) loaded within the current process.

Members	Meaning in Life
PriorityBoostEnabled	This property determines whether the OS should temporarily boost the process if the main window has the focus.
PriorityClass	This property allows you to read or change the overall priority for the associated process.
ProcessName	This property gets the name of the process (which, as you would assume, is the name of the application itself).
Responding	This property gets a value indicating whether the user interface of the process is responding to user input (or is currently "hung").
StartTime	This property gets the time that the associated process was started (via a DateTime type).
Threads	This property gets the set of threads that are running in the associated process (represented via an array of ProcessThread types).
CloseMainWindow()	This method closes a process that has a user interface by sending a close message to its main window.
GetCurrentProcess()	This static method returns a new Process type that represents the currently active process.
GetProcesses()	This static method returns an array of new Process components running on a given machine.
Kill()	This method immediately stops the associated process.
Start()	This method starts a process.

Enumerating Running Processes

To illustrate the process of manipulating Process types (pardon the redundancy), assume you have a C# Console Application named ProcessManipulator that defines the following static helper method within the Program class (be sure you import the System.Diagnostics namespace):

```
static void ListAllRunningProcesses()
{
  // Get all the processes on the local machine.
  Process[] runningProcs = Process.GetProcesses(".");

  // Print out PID and name of each process.
  foreach(Process p in runningProcs)
  {
    string info = string.Format("-> PID: {0}\tName: {1}",
      p.Id, p.ProcessName);
    Console.WriteLine(info);
  }
  Console.WriteLine("************************************\n");
}
```

Notice how the static Process.GetProcesses() method returns an array of Process types that represent the running processes on the target machine (the dot notation shown here represents the local computer). Once you have obtained the array of Process types, you are able to trigger any of the members seen in Table 17-2. Here, you are simply displaying the PID and the name of each process. Assuming the Main() method has been updated to call ListAllRunningProcesses(), you will see something like the output shown in Figure 17-3.

```
C:\Windows\system32\cmd.exe
***** Fun with Processes *****

-> PID: 1176    Name: svchost
-> PID: 1372    Name: svchost
-> PID: 5340    Name: ProcessManipulator.vshost
-> PID: 2028    Name: mqsvc
-> PID: 384     Name: smss
-> PID: 3140    Name: sidebar
-> PID: 2548    Name: SMSvcHost
-> PID: 2152    Name: svchost
-> PID: 772     Name: svchost
-> PID: 1756    Name: inetinfo
-> PID: 1952    Name: unsecapp
-> PID: 552     Name: sidebar
-> PID: 568     Name: lsm
-> PID: 1552    Name: svchost
-> PID: 4112    Name: wmpnetwk
-> PID: 4896    Name: ProcessManipulator
-> PID: 560     Name: lsass
-> PID: 1148    Name: SLsvc
-> PID: 2128    Name: sqlwriter
-> PID: 548     Name: services
```

Figure 17-3. *Enumerating running processes*

Investigating a Specific Process

In addition to obtaining a full and complete list of all running processes on a given machine, the static `Process.GetProcessById()` method allows you to obtain a single `Process` type via the associated PID. If you request access to a nonexistent PID, an `ArgumentException` exception is thrown. For example, if you were interested in obtaining a `Process` object representing a process with the PID of 987, you could write the following:

```
// If there is no process with the PID of 987, a
// runtime exception will be thrown.
static void GetSpecificProcess()
{
  Process theProc =  null;
  try
  {
    theProc = Process.GetProcessById(987);
  }
  catch  // Generic catch for used simplicity.
  {
    Console.WriteLine("-> Sorry...bad PID!");
  }
}
```

Investigating a Process's Thread Set

The `Process` class type also provides a manner to programmatically investigate the set of all threads currently used by a specific process. The set of threads is represented by the strongly typed `ProcessThreadCollection` collection, which contains some number of individual `ProcessThread` types. To illustrate, assume the following additional static helper function has been added to your current application:

```
static void EnumThreadsForPid(int pID)
{
  Process theProc = null;
  try
  {
    theProc = Process.GetProcessById(pID);
  }
  catch
  {
    Console.WriteLine("-> Sorry...bad PID!");
    Console.WriteLine("************************************\n");
    return;
  }

  // List out stats for each thread in the specified process.
  Console.WriteLine("Here are the threads used by: {0}",
    theProc.ProcessName);
  ProcessThreadCollection theThreads = theProc.Threads;
  foreach(ProcessThread pt in theThreads)
  {
    string info =
      string.Format("-> Thread ID: {0}\tStart Time {1}\tPriority {2}",
        pt.Id , pt.StartTime.ToShortTimeString(), pt.PriorityLevel);
    Console.WriteLine(info);
  }
  Console.WriteLine("************************************\n");
}
```

As you can see, the `Threads` property of the `System.Diagnostics.Process` type provides access to the `ProcessThreadCollection` class. Here, you are printing out the assigned thread ID, start time, and priority level of each thread in the process specified by the client. Thus, if you update your program's `Main()` method to prompt the user for a PID to investigate, as follows:

```
static void Main(string[] args)
{
...
  // Prompt user for a PID and print out the set of active threads.
  Console.WriteLine("***** Enter PID of process to investigate *****");
  Console.Write("PID: ");
  string pID = Console.ReadLine();
  int theProcID = int.Parse(pID);

  EnumThreadsForPid(theProcID);
  Console.ReadLine();
}
```

you would find output along the lines of that shown in Figure 17-4.

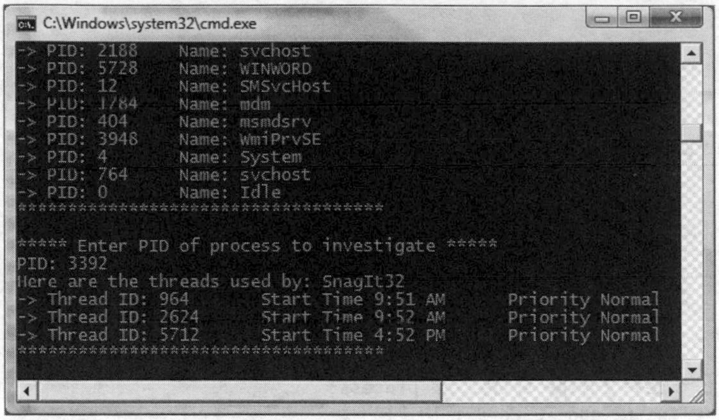

```
C:\Windows\system32\cmd.exe
-> PID: 2188     Name: svchost
-> PID: 5728     Name: WINWORD
-> PID: 12       Name: SMSvcHost
-> PID: 1784     Name: mdm
-> PID: 404      Name: msmdsrv
-> PID: 3948     Name: WmiPrvSE
-> PID: 4        Name: System
-> PID: 764      Name: svchost
-> PID: 0        Name: Idle
************************************

***** Enter PID of process to investigate *****
PID: 3392
Here are the threads used by: SnagIt32
-> Thread ID: 964       Start Time 9:51 AM      Priority Normal
-> Thread ID: 2624      Start Time 9:52 AM      Priority Normal
-> Thread ID: 5712      Start Time 4:52 PM      Priority Normal
************************************
```

Figure 17-4. *Enumerating the threads within a running process*

The ProcessThread type has additional members of interest beyond Id, StartTime, and PriorityLevel. Table 17-3 documents some members of interest.

Table 17-3. *Select Members of the* ProcessThread *Type*

Member	Meaning in Life
BasePriority	Gets the base priority of the thread
CurrentPriority	Gets the current priority of the thread
Id	Gets the unique identifier of the thread
IdealProcessor	Sets the preferred processor for this thread to run on
PriorityLevel	Gets or sets the priority level of the thread
ProcessorAffinity	Sets the processors on which the associated thread can run
StartAddress	Gets the memory address of the function that the operating system called that started this thread
StartTime	Gets the time that the operating system started the thread
ThreadState	Gets the current state of this thread
TotalProcessorTime	Gets the total amount of time that this thread has spent using the processor
WaitReason	Gets the reason that the thread is waiting

Before you read any further, be very aware that the ProcessThread type is *not* the entity used to create, suspend, or kill threads under the .NET platform. Rather, ProcessThread is a vehicle used to obtain diagnostic information for the active Win32 threads within a running process. Again, you will investigate how to build multithreaded applications using the System.Threading namespace in Chapter 18.

Investigating a Process's Module Set

Next up, let's check out how to iterate over the number of loaded modules that are hosted within a given process. Recall that a *module* is a generic name used to describe a given `*.dll` (or the `*.exe` itself) that is hosted by a specific process. When you access the `ProcessModuleCollection` via the `Process.Module` property, you are able to enumerate over *all modules* hosted within a process: .NET-based, COM-based, or traditional C-based libraries. Ponder the following additional helper function that will enumerate the modules in a specific process based on the PID:

```
static void EnumModsForPid(int pID)
{
  Process theProc = null;
  try
  {
    theProc = Process.GetProcessById(pID);
  }
  catch
  {
    Console.WriteLine("-> Sorry...bad PID!");
    Console.WriteLine("************************************\n");
    return;
  }
  Console.WriteLine("Here are the loaded modules for: {0}",
    theProc.ProcessName);
  try
  {
    ProcessModuleCollection theMods = theProc.Modules;
    foreach(ProcessModule pm in theMods)
    {
      string info = string.Format("-> Mod Name: {0}", pm.ModuleName);
      Console.WriteLine(info);
    }
  Console.WriteLine("************************************\n");
  }
  catch
  {
    Console.WriteLine("No mods!");
  }
}
```

To see some possible output, let's check out the loaded modules for the process hosting the current example program (ProcessManipulator). To do so, run the application, identify the PID assigned to `ProcessManipulator.exe` (via the Task Manager) and pass this value to the `EnumModsForPid()` method (be sure to update your `Main()` method accordingly). Once you do, you may be surprised to see the list of `*.dll`s used for a simple Console Application (`GDI32.dll`, `USER32.dll`, `ole32.dll`, and so forth). Figure 17-5 shows a test run.

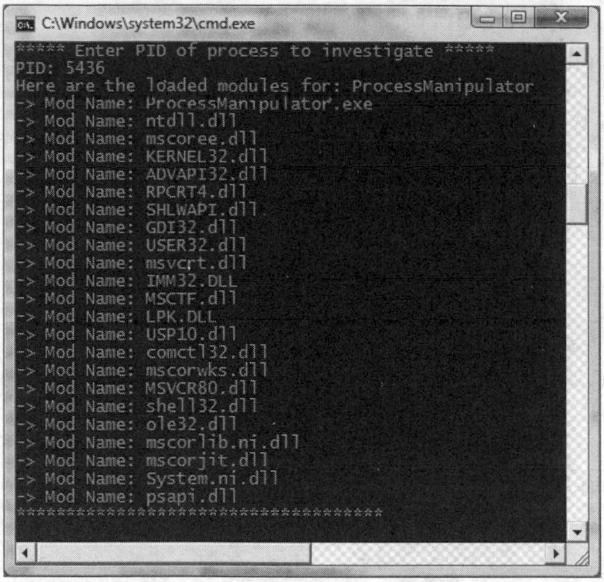

```
C:\Windows\system32\cmd.exe
***** Enter PID of process to investigate *****
PID: 5436
Here are the loaded modules for: ProcessManipulator
-> Mod Name: ProcessManipulator.exe
-> Mod Name: ntdll.dll
-> Mod Name: mscoree.dll
-> Mod Name: KERNEL32.dll
-> Mod Name: ADVAPI32.dll
-> Mod Name: RPCRT4.dll
-> Mod Name: SHLWAPI.dll
-> Mod Name: GDI32.dll
-> Mod Name: USER32.dll
-> Mod Name: msvcrt.dll
-> Mod Name: IMM32.DLL
-> Mod Name: MSCTF.dll
-> Mod Name: LPK.DLL
-> Mod Name: USP10.dll
-> Mod Name: comctl32.dll
-> Mod Name: mscorwks.dll
-> Mod Name: MSVCR80.dll
-> Mod Name: shell32.dll
-> Mod Name: ole32.dll
-> Mod Name: mscorlib.ni.dll
-> Mod Name: mscorjit.dll
-> Mod Name: System.ni.dll
-> Mod Name: psapi.dll
*************************************
```

Figure 17-5. *Enumerating the loaded modules within a running process*

Starting and Stopping Processes Programmatically

The final aspects of the `System.Diagnostics.Process` type examined here are the `Start()` and `Kill()` methods. As you can gather by their names, these members provide a way to programmatically launch and terminate a process, respectively. For example, consider the static `StartAndKillProcess()` helper method:

```
static void StartAndKillProcess()
{
  // Launch Internet Explorer.
  Process ieProc = Process.Start("IExplore.exe",  "www.intertech.com");

  Console.Write("--> Hit enter to kill {0}...", ieProc.ProcessName);
  Console.ReadLine();

  // Kill the iexplore.exe process.
  try
  {
    ieProc.Kill();
  }
  catch{}   // In case the user already killed it...
}
```

The static `Process.Start()` method has been overloaded a few times. At minimum, you will need to specify the friendly name of the process you wish to launch (such as Microsoft Internet Explorer, `iexplore.exe`). This example makes use of a variation of the `Start()` method that allows you to specify any additional arguments to pass into the program's entry point (i.e., the `Main()` method).

The Start() method also allows you to pass in a System.Diagnostics.ProcessStartInfo type to specify additional bits of information regarding how a given process should come to life. Here is the formal definition of ProcessStartInfo (see the .NET Framework 3.5 SDK documentation for full details):

```
public sealed class System.Diagnostics.ProcessStartInfo :
    object
{
  public ProcessStartInfo();
  public ProcessStartInfo(string fileName);
  public ProcessStartInfo(string fileName, string arguments);
  public string Arguments { get; set; }
  public bool CreateNoWindow { get; set; }
  public StringDictionary EnvironmentVariables { get; }
  public bool ErrorDialog { get; set; }
  public IntPtr ErrorDialogParentHandle { get; set; }
  public string FileName { get; set; }
  public bool RedirectStandardError { get; set; }
  public bool RedirectStandardInput { get; set; }
  public bool RedirectStandardOutput { get; set; }
  public bool UseShellExecute { get; set; }
  public string Verb { get; set; }
  public string[] Verbs { get; }
  public ProcessWindowStyle WindowStyle { get; set; }
  public string WorkingDirectory { get; set; }
  public virtual bool Equals(object obj);
  public virtual int GetHashCode();
  public Type GetType();
  public virtual string ToString();
}
```

Regardless of which version of the Process.Start() method you invoke, do note that you are returned a reference to the newly activated process. When you wish to terminate the process, simply call the instance-level Kill() method.

Source Code The ProcessManipulator project is included under the Chapter 17 subdirectory.

Understanding .NET Application Domains

Now that you understand the role of Win32 processes and how to interact with them from managed code, we need to investigate the concept of a .NET application domain. Under the .NET platform, executables are not hosted directly within a process (as is the case in traditional Win32 applications). Rather, a .NET executable is hosted by a logical partition within a process termed an *application domain*. As you will see, a single process may contain multiple application domains, each of which is hosting a .NET executable. This additional subdivision of a traditional Win32 process offers several benefits, some of which are as follows:

- AppDomains are a key aspect of the OS-neutral nature of the .NET platform, given that this logical division abstracts away the differences in how an underlying OS represents a loaded executable.
- AppDomains are far less expensive in terms of processing power and memory than a full-blown process. Thus, the CLR is able to load and unload application domains much quicker than a formal process.
- AppDomains provide a deeper level of isolation for hosting a loaded application. If one AppDomain within a process fails, the remaining AppDomains remain functional.

As suggested in the previous hit list, a single process can host any number of AppDomains, each of which is fully and completely isolated from other AppDomains within this process (or any other process). Given this fact, be very aware that an application running in one AppDomain is unable to obtain data of any kind (global variables or static fields) within another AppDomain unless they make use of a distributed programming protocol (such as Windows Communication Foundation).

While a single process *may* host multiple AppDomains, this is not typically the case. At the very least, an OS process will host what is termed the *default application domain*. This specific application domain is automatically created by the CLR at the time the process launches. After this point, the CLR creates additional application domains on an as-needed basis.

If the need should arise (which it most likely *will not* for the majority of your .NET endeavors), you are also able to programmatically create application domains at runtime within a given process using static methods of the `System.AppDomain` class. This class is also useful for low-level control of application domains. Key members of this class are shown in Table 17-4.

Table 17-4. *Select Members of AppDomain*

Member	Meaning in Life
`CreateDomain()`	This static method creates a new AppDomain in the current process. Understand that the CLR will create new application domains as necessary, and thus the chance of you absolutely needing to call this member is slim to none.
`GetCurrentThreadId()`	This static method returns the ID of the active thread in the current application domain.
`Unload()`	This is another static method that allows you to unload a specified AppDomain within a given process.
`BaseDirectory`	This property returns the base directory used to probe for dependent assemblies.
`CreateInstance()`	This method creates an instance of a specified type defined in a specified assembly file.
`ExecuteAssembly()`	This method executes an assembly within an application domain, given its file name.
`GetAssemblies()`	This method gets the set of .NET assemblies that have been loaded into this application domain (COM-based or C-based binaries are ignored).
`Load()`	This method is used to dynamically load an assembly into the current application domain.

In addition, the `AppDomain` type also defines a small set of events that correspond to various aspects of an application domain's life cycle, as shown in Table 17-5.

Table 17-5. *Events of the AppDomain Type*

Event	Meaning in Life
AssemblyLoad	Occurs when an assembly is loaded
AssemblyResolve	Occurs when the resolution of an assembly fails
DomainUnload	Occurs when an AppDomain is about to be unloaded
ProcessExit	Occurs on the default application domain when the default application domain's parent process exits
ResourceResolve	Occurs when the resolution of a resource fails
TypeResolve	Occurs when the resolution of a type fails
UnhandledException	Occurs when an exception is not caught by an event handler

Enumerating a Process's AppDomains

To illustrate how to interact with .NET application domains programmatically, assume you have a new C# Console Application named AppDomainManipulator that defines a static method named `PrintAllAssembliesInAppDomain()` within the `Program` type. This helper method makes use of `AppDomain.GetAssemblies()` to obtain a list of all .NET binaries hosted within the application domain in question.

This list is represented by an array of `System.Reflection.Assembly` types, and thus you are required to use the `System.Reflection` namespace (see Chapter 16). Once you acquire the assembly array, you iterate over the array and print out the friendly name and version of each assembly:

```
static void PrintAllAssembliesInAppDomain(AppDomain ad)
{
  Assembly[] loadedAssemblies = ad.GetAssemblies();
  Console.WriteLine("***** Here are the assemblies loaded in {0} *****\n",
    ad.FriendlyName);
  foreach(Assembly a in loadedAssemblies)
  {
    Console.WriteLine("-> Name: {0}", a.GetName().Name);
    Console.WriteLine("-> Version: {0}\n", a.GetName().Version);
  }
}
```

Now let's update the `Main()` method to obtain a reference to the current application domain before invoking `PrintAllAssembliesInAppDomain()`, using the `AppDomain.CurrentDomain` property.

To make things a bit more interesting, notice that the `Main()` method launches a Windows Forms message box to force the CLR to load the `System.Windows.Forms.dll`, `System.Drawing.dll`, and `System.dll` assemblies (so be sure to set a reference to these assemblies and update your `using` statements appropriately):

```
static void Main(string[] args)
{
  Console.WriteLine("***** Fun with AppDomains *****\n");

  // Get info for current AppDomain.
  AppDomain defaultAD= AppDomain.CurrentDomain;
```

```
  // This call is simply to load additional
  // assemblies into this app domain.
  MessageBox.Show("Hello");
  PrintAllAssembliesInAppDomain(defaultAD);

  Console.ReadLine();
}
```

Figure 17-6 shows the output.

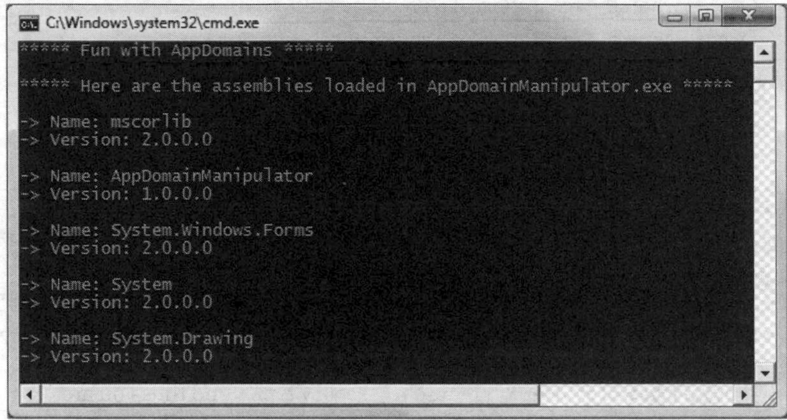

Figure 17-6. *Enumerating assemblies within the current application domain*

Programmatically Creating New AppDomains

Recall that a single process is capable of hosting multiple AppDomains. While it is true that you will seldom (if ever) need to manually create AppDomains in code, you are able to do so via the static `CreateDomain()` method. As you would guess, `AppDomain.CreateDomain()` has been overloaded a number of times. At minimum, you will specify the friendly name of the new application domain, as shown here:

```
static void Main(string[] args)
{
...
  // Make a new AppDomain in the current process.
  AppDomain anotherAD = AppDomain.CreateDomain("SecondAppDomain");
  PrintAllAssembliesInAppDomain(anotherAD);

  Console.ReadLine();
}
```

Now, if you run the application again (see Figure 17-7), notice that the `System.Windows.Forms.dll`, `System.Drawing.dll`, and `System.dll` assemblies are only loaded within the default application domain. This may seem counterintuitive if you have a background in traditional Win32 (as you might suspect, both application domains have access to the same assembly set). Recall, however, that an assembly loads into an *application domain*, not directly into the process itself.

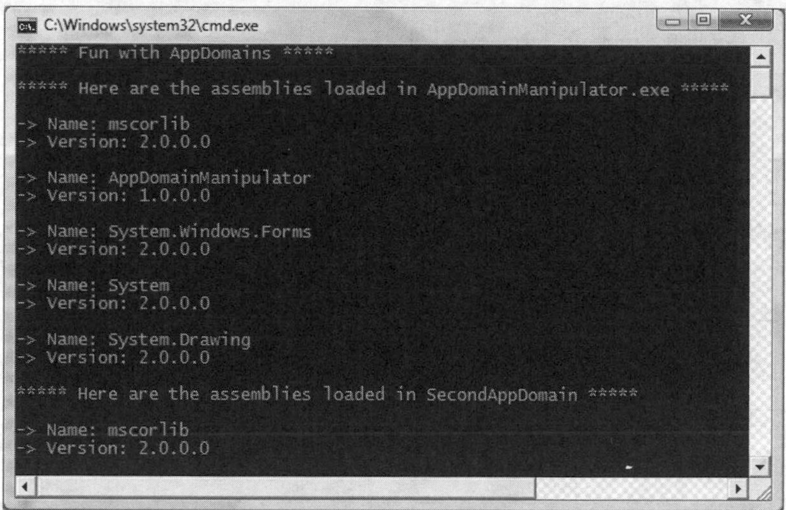

Figure 17-7. *A single process with two application domains*

Next, notice how the SecondAppDomain application domain automatically contains its own copy of `mscorlib.dll`, as this key assembly is automatically loaded by the CLR for each and every application domain. This begs the question, "How can I programmatically load an assembly into an application domain?" Answer: with the `AppDomain.Load()` method (or, alternatively, `AppDomain.ExecuteAssembly()` to load and execute the `Main()` method of an `*.exe` assembly).

Assuming you have copied `CarLibrary.dll` to the application directory of `AppDomainManipulator.exe`, you may load `CarLibrary.dll` into the SecondAppDomain application domain as follows:

```
static void Main(string[] args)
{
  ...
  // Load CarLibrary.dll into the new AppDomain.
  AppDomain anotherAD = AppDomain.CreateDomain("SecondAppDomain");
  try
  {
    anotherAD.Load("CarLibrary");
    PrintAllAssembliesInAppDomain(anotherAD);
  }
  catch(Exception ex)
  {
    Console.WriteLine(ex.Message);
  }
  Console.ReadLine();
}
```

To solidify the relationship between processes, application domains, and assemblies, Figure 17-8 diagrams the internal composition of the `AppDomainManipulator.exe` process just constructed.

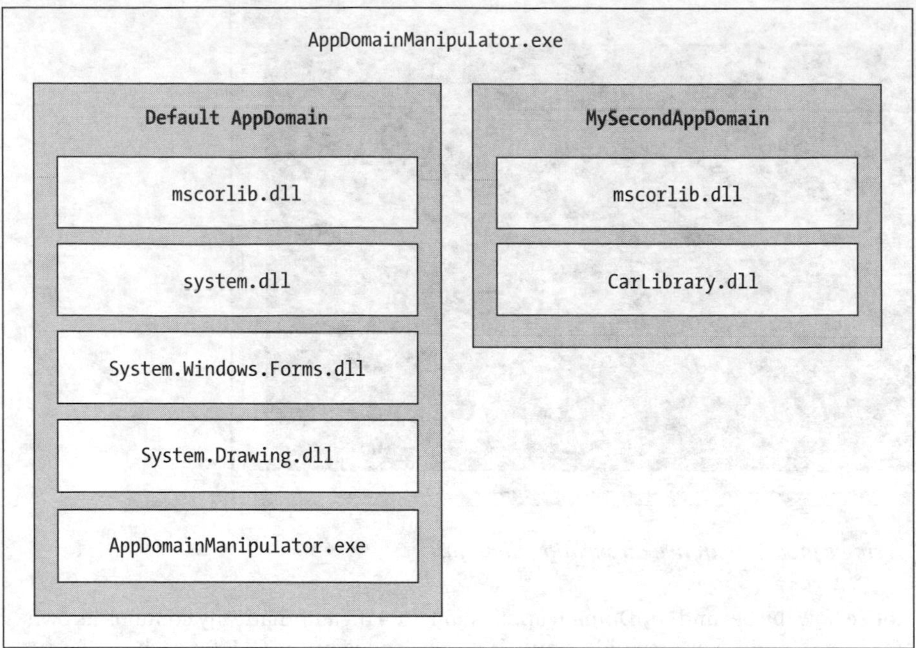

Figure 17-8. *The* `AppDomainManipulator.exe` *process under the hood*

Note If you debug this project (via F5), you will find many additional assemblies are loaded into each AppDomain which are used by the Visual Studio debugging process. Running this project (via Ctrl + F5) will display only the assemblies directly by each app domain.

Programmatically Unloading AppDomains

It is important to point out that the CLR does not permit unloading individual .NET assemblies. However, using the `AppDomain.Unload()` method, you are able to selectively unload a given application domain from its hosting process. When you do so, the application domain will unload each assembly in turn.

Recall that the `AppDomain` type defines a small set of events, one of which is `DomainUnload`. This event is fired when a (nondefault) AppDomain is unloaded from the containing process. Another event of interest is the `ProcessExit` event, which is fired when the default application domain is unloaded from the process (which obviously entails the termination of the process itself). Thus, if you wish to programmatically unload `anotherAD` from the `AppDomainManipulator.exe` process and be notified when the associated application domain is torn down, you are able to write the following event logic:

```
static void Main(string[] args)
{
...
  // Hook into DomainUnload event.
  anotherAD.DomainUnload +=
    new EventHandler(anotherAD_DomainUnload);
```

```
  // Now unload anotherAD.
  AppDomain.Unload(anotherAD);
  Console.ReadLine();
}
```

Notice that the DomainUnload event works in conjunction with the System.EventHandler delegate, and therefore the format of anotherAD_DomainUnload() takes the following arguments:

```
static void anotherAD_DomainUnload(object sender, EventArgs e)
{
  Console.WriteLine("***** Unloaded anotherAD! *****\n");
}
```

If you wish to be notified when the default AppDomain is unloaded, modify your Main() method to handle the ProcessEvent event of the default application domain:

```
static void Main(string[] args)
{
  Console.WriteLine("***** Fun with AppDomains *****\n");

  AppDomain defaultAD = AppDomain.CurrentDomain;
  defaultAD.ProcessExit +=new EventHandler(defaultAD_ProcessExit);
...
}
```

and define an appropriate event handler:

```
static void defaultAD_ProcessExit(object sender, EventArgs e)
{
  Console.WriteLine("***** Unloaded defaultAD! *****\n");
}
```

Source Code The AppDomainManipulator project is included under the Chapter 17 subdirectory.

Understanding Object Context Boundaries

As you have just seen, AppDomains are logical partitions within a process used to host .NET assemblies. On a related note, a given application domain may be further subdivided into numerous context boundaries. In a nutshell, a .NET context provides a way for a single AppDomain to establish a "specific home" for a given object.

Using context, the CLR is able to ensure that objects that have special runtime requirements are handled in an appropriate and consistent manner by intercepting method invocations into and out of a given context. This layer of interception allows the CLR to adjust the current method invocation to conform to the contextual settings of a given object. For example, if you define a C# class type that requires automatic thread safety (using the [Synchronization] attribute), the CLR will create a "synchronized context" during allocation.

Just as a process defines a default AppDomain, every application domain has a default context. This default context (sometimes referred to as *context 0*, given that it is always the first context created within an application domain) is used to group together .NET objects that have no specific or unique contextual needs. As you may expect, a vast majority of .NET objects are loaded into context 0. If the CLR determines a newly created object has special needs, a new context boundary is created within the hosting application domain. Figure 17-9 illustrates the process/AppDomain/context relationship.

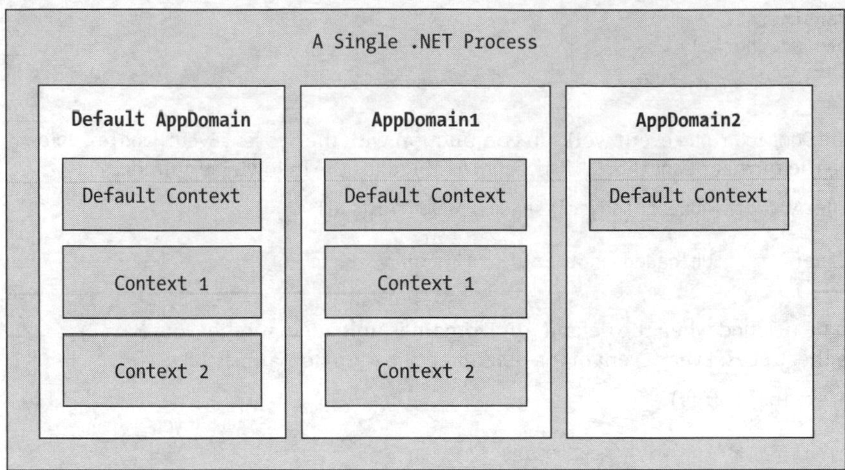

Figure 17-9. *Processes, application domains, and context boundaries*

Context-Agile and Context-Bound Types

.NET types that do not demand any special contextual treatment are termed *context-agile* objects. These objects can be accessed from anywhere within the hosting AppDomain without interfering with the object's runtime requirements. Building context-agile objects is a no-brainer, given that you simply do nothing (specifically, you do not adorn the type with any contextual attributes and do not derive from the `System.ContextBoundObject` base class):

```
// A context-agile object is loaded into context 0.
class SportsCar{}
```

On the other hand, objects that do demand contextual allocation are termed *context-bound* objects, and they *must* derive from the `System.ContextBoundObject` base class. This base class solidifies the fact that the object in question can function appropriately only within the context in which it was created. Given the role of .NET context, it should stand to reason that if a context-bound object were to somehow end up in an incompatible context, bad things would be guaranteed to occur at the most inopportune times.

In addition to deriving from `System.ContextBoundObject`, a context-sensitive type will also be adorned by a special category of .NET attributes termed (not surprisingly) *context attributes*. All context attributes derive from the `ContextAttribute` base class, which is defined within the `System.Runtime.Remoting.Contexts` namespace:

```
public class ContextAttribute :
  Attribute, IContextAttribute, IContextProperty
{
 public ContextAttribute(string name);
 public string Name { virtual get; }
 public object TypeId { virtual get; }
 public virtual bool Equals(object o);
 public virtual void Freeze(System.Runtime.Remoting.Contexts.Context newContext);
 public virtual int GetHashCode();
 public virtual void GetPropertiesForNewContext(
  System.Runtime.Remoting.Activation.IConstructionCallMessage ctorMsg);
 public Type GetType();
 public virtual bool IsContextOK(
```

```
    System.Runtime.Remoting.Contexts.Context ctx,
    System.Runtime.Remoting.Activation.IConstructionCallMessage ctorMsg);
  public virtual bool IsDefaultAttribute();
  public virtual bool IsNewContextOK(
    System.Runtime.Remoting.Contexts.Context newCtx);
  public virtual bool Match(object obj);
  public virtual string ToString();
}
```

Given that the ContextAttribute class is not sealed, it is possible for you to build your own custom contextual attribute (simply derive from ContextAttribute and override the necessary virtual methods). Once you have done so, you are able to build a custom piece of software that can respond to the contextual settings.

■ **Note** This book doesn't dive into the details of building custom object contexts; however, if you are interested in learning more, check out *Applied .NET Attributes*, by Jason Bock and Tom Barnaby (Apress, 2003).

Defining a Context-Bound Object

Assume that you wish to define a class (SportsCarTS) that is automatically thread safe in nature, even though you have not hard-coded thread synchronization logic within the member implementations. To do so, derive from ContextBoundObject and apply the [Synchronization] attribute as follows:

```
using System.Runtime.Remoting.Contexts;

// This context-bound type will only be loaded into a
// synchronized (hence thread-safe) context.
[Synchronization]
class SportsCarTS : ContextBoundObject
{}
```

Types that are attributed with the [Synchronization] attribute are loaded into a thread-safe context. Given the special contextual needs of the MyThreadSafeObject class type, imagine the problems that would occur if an allocated object were moved from a synchronized context into a nonsynchronized context. The object is suddenly no longer thread safe and thus becomes a candidate for massive data corruption, as numerous threads are attempting to interact with the (now thread-volatile) reference object. To ensure the CLR does not move SportsCarTS objects outside of a synchronized context, simply derive from ContextBoundObject.

Inspecting an Object's Context

Although very few of the applications you will write will need to programmatically interact with context, here is an illustrative example. Create a new Console Application named ContextManipulator. This application defines one context-agile class (SportsCar) and a single context-bound type (SportsCarTS):

```
using System.Runtime.Remoting.Contexts;  // For Context type.
using System.Threading;  // For Thread type.

// SportsCar has no special contextual
// needs and will be loaded into the
// default context of the app domain.
```

```
class SportsCar
{
  public SportsCar()
  {
    // Get context information and print out context ID.
    Context ctx = Thread.CurrentContext;
    Console.WriteLine("{0} object in context {1}",
      this.ToString(), ctx.ContextID);
    foreach(IContextProperty itfCtxProp in ctx.ContextProperties)
      Console.WriteLine("-> Ctx Prop: {0}", itfCtxProp.Name);
  }
}

// SportsCarTS demands to be loaded in
// a synchronization context.
[Synchronization]
class SportsCarTS : ContextBoundObject
{
  public SportsCarTS()
  {
    // Get context information and print out context ID.
    Context ctx = Thread.CurrentContext;
    Console.WriteLine("{0} object in context {1}",
      this.ToString(), ctx.ContextID);
    foreach(IContextProperty itfCtxProp in ctx.ContextProperties)
      Console.WriteLine("-> Ctx Prop: {0}", itfCtxProp.Name);
  }
}
```

Notice that each constructor obtains a `Context` type from the current thread of execution, via the static `Thread.CurrentContext` property. Using the `Context` object, you are able to print out statistics about the contextual boundary, such as its assigned ID, as well as a set of descriptors obtained via `Context.ContextProperties`. This property returns an object implementing the `IContextProperty` interface, which exposes each descriptor through the `Name` property. Now, update `Main()` to allocate an instance of each class type:

```
static void Main(string[] args)
{
  Console.WriteLine("***** Fun with Object Context *****\n");

  // Objects will display contextual info upon creation.
  SportsCar sport = new SportsCar();
  Console.WriteLine();

  SportsCar sport2 = new SportsCar();
  Console.WriteLine();

  SportsCarTS synchroSport = new SportsCarTS();
  Console.ReadLine();
}
```

As the objects come to life, the class constructors will dump out various bits of context-centric information (see Figure 17-10).

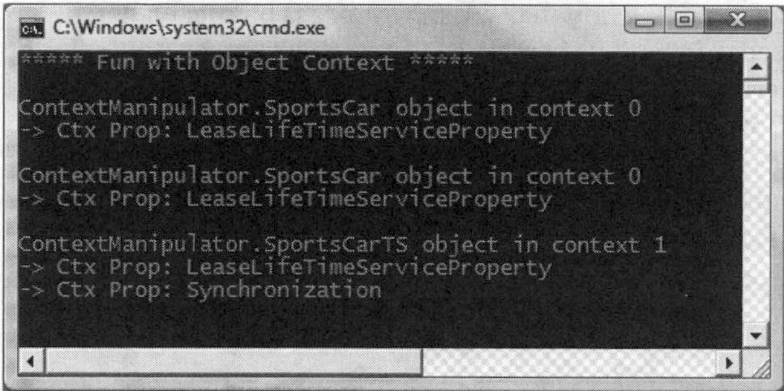

Figure 17-10. *Investigating an object's context*

Given that the `SportsCar` class has not been qualified with a context attribute, the CLR has allocated `sport` and `sport2` into context 0 (i.e., the default context). However, the `SportsCarTS` object is loaded into a unique contextual boundary (which has been assigned a context ID of 1), given the fact that this context-bound type was adorned with the `[Synchronization]` attribute.

Source Code The ContextManipulator project is included under the Chapter 17 subdirectory.

Summarizing Processes, AppDomains, and Context

At this point, you hopefully have a much better idea about how a .NET assembly is hosted by the CLR. To summarize the key points:

- A .NET process hosts one to many application domains. Each AppDomain is able to host any number of related .NET assemblies. AppDomains may be independently loaded and unloaded by the CLR (or programmatically via the `System.AppDomain` type).
- A given AppDomain consists of one to many contexts. Using a context, the CLR is able to place a "special needs" object into a logical container, to ensure that its runtime requirements are honored.

If the previous pages have seemed to be a bit too low level for your liking, fear not. For the most part, the .NET runtime automatically deals with the details of processes, application domains, and contexts on your behalf. The good news, however, is that this information provides a solid foundation for understanding multithreaded programming under the .NET platform.

Summary

The point of this chapter was to examine exactly how a .NET-executable image is hosted by the .NET platform. As you have seen, the long-standing notion of a Win32 process has been altered under the hood to accommodate the needs of the CLR. A single process (which can be programmatically manipulated via the `System.Diagnostics.Process` type) is now composed of multiple application domains, which represent isolated and independent boundaries within a process.

As you have seen, a single process can host multiple application domains, each of which is capable of hosting and executing any number of related assemblies. Furthermore, a single application domain can contain any number of contextual boundaries. Using this additional level of type isolation, the CLR can ensure that special-need objects are handled correctly.

CHAPTER 18

Building Multithreaded Applications

In the previous chapter, you examined the relationship between processes, application domains, and contexts. This chapter builds on your newfound knowledge by examining how the .NET platform allows you to build multithreaded applications and examines various ways to keep shared resources thread-safe.

You'll begin by revisiting the .NET delegate type and come to understand its intrinsic support for asynchronous method invocations. As you'll see, this technique allows you to invoke a method on a secondary thread of execution automatically. Next, you'll investigate the types within the `System.Threading` namespace. Here you'll examine numerous types (`Thread`, `ThreadStart`, etc.) that allow you to easily create additional threads of execution. As well, you will come to understand the use of the `BackgroundWorker` type, which simplifies the task of performing background operations within the context of a GUI-based application.

Of course, the complexity of multithreaded development isn't in the creation of threads, but in ensuring that your code base is well equipped to handle concurrent access to shared resources. Given this, the chapter also examines various synchronization primitives that the .NET Framework provides.

The Process/AppDomain/Context/Thread Relationship

In the previous chapter, a *thread* was defined as a path of execution within an executable application. While many .NET applications can live happy and productive single-threaded lives, an assembly's primary thread (spawned by the CLR when `Main()` executes) may create secondary threads of execution to perform additional units of work. By implementing additional threads, you can build more responsive (but not necessarily faster executing on single-core machines) applications.

Note These days it is quite common for new computers to make use of multicore processors (or at very least a hyperthreaded single-core processor). Without making use of multiple threads, developers are unable to exploit the full power of multicore machines.

The `System.Threading` namespace contains various types that allow you to create multithreaded applications. The `Thread` class is perhaps the core type, as it represents a given thread. If you wish to programmatically obtain a reference to the thread currently executing a given member, simply call the static `Thread.CurrentThread` property:

```
static void ExtractExecutingThread()
{
  // Get the thread currently
  // executing this method.
  Thread currThread = Thread.CurrentThread;
}
```

Under the .NET platform, there is *not* a direct one-to-one correspondence between application domains and threads. In fact, a given AppDomain can have numerous threads executing within it at any given time. Furthermore, a particular thread is not confined to a single application domain during its lifetime. Threads are free to cross application domain boundaries as the Win32 thread scheduler and CLR see fit.

Although active threads can be moved between AppDomain boundaries, a given thread can execute within only a single application domain at any point in time (in other words, it is impossible for a single thread to be doing work in more than one AppDomain at once). When you wish to programmatically gain access to the AppDomain that is hosting the current thread, call the static `Thread.GetDomain()` method:

```
static void ExtractAppDomainHostingThread()
{
  // Obtain the AppDomain hosting the current thread.
  AppDomain ad = Thread.GetDomain();
}
```

A single thread may also be moved into a particular context at any given time, and it may be relocated within a new context at the whim of the CLR. When you wish to obtain the current context a thread happens to be executing in, make use of the static `Thread.CurrentContext` property:

```
static void ExtractCurrentThreadContext()
{
  // Obtain the context under which the
  // current thread is operating.
  Context ctx = Thread.CurrentContext;
}
```

Again, the CLR is the entity that is in charge of moving threads into (and out of) application domains and contexts. As a .NET developer, you can usually remain blissfully unaware where a given thread ends up (or exactly when it is placed into its new boundary). Nevertheless, you should be aware of the various ways of obtaining the underlying primitives.

The Problem of Concurrency

One of the many "joys" (read: painful aspects) of multithreaded programming is that you have little control over how the underlying operating system or the CLR makes use of its threads. For example, if you craft a block of code that creates a new thread of execution, you cannot guarantee that the thread executes immediately. Rather, such code only instructs the OS to execute the thread as soon as possible (which is typically when the thread scheduler gets around to it).

Furthermore, given that threads can be moved between application and contextual boundaries as required by the CLR, you must be mindful of which aspects of your application are *thread-volatile* (e.g., subject to multithreaded access) and which operations are *atomic* (thread-volatile operations are the dangerous ones!). To illustrate the problem, assume a thread is invoking a method of a specific object. Now assume that this thread is instructed by the thread scheduler to suspend its activity, in order to allow another thread to access the same method of the same object.

If the original thread was not completely finished with its operation, the second incoming thread may be viewing an object in a partially modified state. At this point, the second thread is basically reading bogus data, which is sure to give way to extremely odd (and very hard to find) bugs, which are even harder to replicate and debug.

Atomic operations, on the other hand, are always safe in a multithreaded environment. Sadly, there are very few operations in the .NET base class libraries that are guaranteed to be atomic. Even the act of assigning a value to a member variable is not atomic! Unless the .NET Framework 3.5 SDK documentation specifically says an operation is atomic, you must assume it is thread-volatile and take precautions.

The Role of Thread Synchronization

At this point, it should be clear that multithreaded application domains are in themselves quite volatile, as numerous threads can operate on the shared functionality at (more or less) the same time. To protect an application's resources from possible corruption, .NET developers must make use of any number of threading primitives (such as locks, monitors, and the `[Synchronization]` attribute) to control access among the executing threads.

Although the .NET platform cannot make the difficulties of building robust multithreaded applications completely disappear, the process has been simplified considerably. Using types defined within the `System.Threading` namespace, you are able to spawn additional threads with minimal fuss and bother. Likewise, when it is time to lock down shared points of data, you will find additional types that provide the same functionality as the Win32 API threading primitives (using a much cleaner object model).

However, the `System.Threading` namespace is not the only way to build multithreaded .NET programs. During our examination of the .NET delegate (see Chapter 11), it was mentioned that all delegates have the ability to invoke members asynchronously. This is a *major* benefit of the .NET platform, given that one of the most common reasons a developer creates threads is for the purpose of invoking methods in a nonblocking (a.k.a. asynchronous) manner. Although you could make use of the `System.Threading` namespace to achieve a similar result, delegates make the whole process much easier.

A Brief Review of the .NET Delegate

Recall that the .NET delegate type is essentially a type-safe object-oriented function pointer. When you declare a .NET delegate, the C# compiler responds by building a sealed class that derives from `System.MulticastDelegate` (which in turn derives from `System.Delegate`). These base classes provide every delegate with the ability to maintain a list of method addresses, all of which may be invoked at a later time. Consider the `BinaryOp` delegate first defined in Chapter 11:

```
// A C# delegate type.
public delegate int BinaryOp(int x, int y);
```

Based on its definition, `BinaryOp` can point to any method taking two integers (by value) as arguments and returning an integer. Once compiled, the defining assembly now contains a full-blown class definition that is dynamically generated based on the delegate declaration. In the case of `BinaryOp`, this class looks more or less like the following (shown in pseudo-code):

```
public sealed class BinaryOp : System.MulticastDelegate
{
  public BinaryOp(object target, uint functionAddress);
  public void Invoke(int x, int y);
  public IAsyncResult BeginInvoke(int x, int y,
    AsyncCallback cb, object state);
  public int EndInvoke(IAsyncResult result);
}
```

Recall that the generated Invoke() method is used to invoke the methods maintained by a delegate object in a synchronous manner. Therefore, the calling thread (such as the primary thread of the application) is forced to wait until the delegate invocation completes. Also recall that in C#, the Invoke() method does not need to be directly called in code, but can be triggered indirectly under the hood when applying "normal" method invocation syntax. Consider the following console program (SyncDelegateReview), which invokes the static Add() method in a synchronous (a.k.a. blocking) manner:

```
// Need this for the Thread.Sleep() call.
using System.Threading;
using System;

namespace SyncDelegate
{
  public delegate int BinaryOp(int x, int y);

  class Program
  {
    static void Main(string[] args)
    {
      Console.WriteLine("***** Synch Delegate Review *****");

      // Print out the ID of the executing thread.
      Console.WriteLine("Main() invoked on thread {0}.",
        Thread.CurrentThread.ManagedThreadId);

      // Invoke Add() in a synchronous manner.
      BinaryOp b = new BinaryOp(Add);

      // Could also write b.Invoke(10, 10);
      int answer = b(10, 10);

      // These lines will not execute until
      // the Add() method has completed.
      Console.WriteLine("Doing more work in Main()!");
      Console.WriteLine("10 + 10 is {0}.", answer);
      Console.ReadLine();
    }

    static int Add(int x, int y)
    {
      // Print out the ID of the executing thread.
      Console.WriteLine("Add() invoked on thread {0}.",
        Thread.CurrentThread.ManagedThreadId);

      // Pause to simulate a lengthy operation.
      Thread.Sleep(5000);
      return x + y;
    }
  }
}
```

Notice first of all that this program is making use of the System.Threading namespace to gain access to the Thread type. Within the Add() method, you are invoking the static Thread.Sleep() method to suspend the calling thread for approximately five seconds to simulate a lengthy task. Given that you are invoking the Add() method in a *synchronous* manner, the Main() method will not print out the result of the operation until the Add() method has completed.

Next, note that the Main() method is obtaining access to the current thread (via Thread.CurrentThread) and printing out the ID of the thread via the ManagedThreadId property. This same logic is repeated in the static Add() method. As you might suspect, given that all the work in this application is performed exclusively by the primary thread, you find the same ID value displayed to the console (see Figure 18-1).

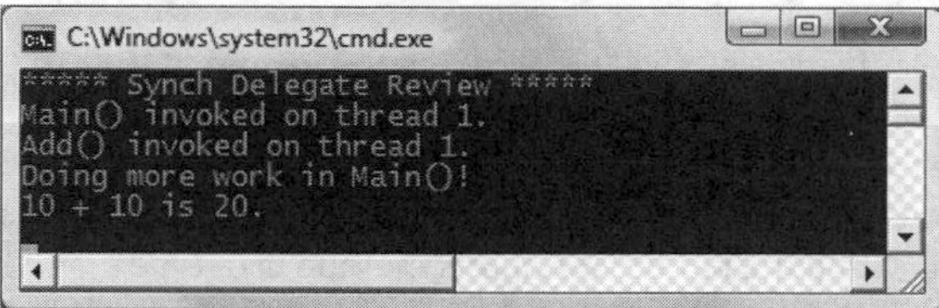

Figure 18-1. *Synchronous method invocations are "blocking" calls.*

When you run this program, you should notice that a five-second delay takes place before you see the final Console.WriteLine() logic in Main() execute. Although many (if not most) methods may be called synchronously without ill effect, .NET delegates can be instructed to call their methods asynchronously if necessary.

Source Code The SyncDelegateReview project is located under the Chapter 18 subdirectory.

The Asynchronous Nature of Delegates

If you are new to the topic of multithreading, you may wonder what exactly an *asynchronous* method invocation is all about. As you are no doubt fully aware, some programming operations take time. Although the previous Add() was purely illustrative in nature, imagine that you built a single-threaded application that is invoking a method on a remote object, performing a long-running database query, downloading a large document, or writing 500 lines of text to an external file. While performing these operations, the application will appear to hang for some amount of time. Until the task at hand has been processed, all other aspects of this program (such as menu activation, toolbar clicking, or console output) are unresponsive.

The question therefore is, how can you tell a delegate to invoke a method on a separate thread of execution to simulate numerous tasks performing "at the same time"? The good news is that every .NET delegate type is automatically equipped with this capability. The even better news is that you are *not* required to directly dive into the details of the System.Threading namespace to do so (although these entities can quite naturally work hand in hand).

The BeginInvoke() and EndInvoke() Methods

When the C# compiler processes the delegate keyword, the dynamically generated class defines two methods named BeginInvoke() and EndInvoke(). Given our definition of the BinaryOp delegate, these methods are prototyped as follows:

```
public sealed class BinaryOp : System.MulticastDelegate
{
...
  // Used to invoke a method asynchronously.
```

```
  public IAsyncResult BeginInvoke(int x, int y,
    AsyncCallback cb, object state);

  // Used to fetch the return value
  // of the invoked method.
  public int EndInvoke(IAsyncResult result);
}
```

The first stack of parameters passed into `BeginInvoke()` will be based on the format of the C# delegate (two integers in the case of `BinaryOp`). The final two arguments will always be `System.AsyncCallback` and `System.Object`. We'll examine the role of these parameters shortly; for the time being, though, we'll supply `null` for each. Also note that the return value of `EndInvoke()` is an integer, based on the definition of `BinaryOp`, while the parameter of this method is of type `IAsyncResult`.

The System.IAsyncResult Interface

The `BeginInvoke()` method always returns an object implementing the `IAsyncResult` interface, while `EndInvoke()` requires an `IAsyncResult`-compatible type as its sole parameter. The `IAsyncResult`-compatible object returned from `BeginInvoke()` is basically a coupling mechanism that allows the calling thread to obtain the result of the asynchronous method invocation at a later time via `EndInvoke()`. The `IAsyncResult` interface (defined in the `System` namespace) is defined as follows:

```
public interface IAsyncResult
{
  object AsyncState { get; }
  WaitHandle AsyncWaitHandle { get; }
  bool CompletedSynchronously { get; }
  bool IsCompleted { get; }
}
```

In the simplest case, you are able to avoid directly invoking these members. All you have to do is cache the `IAsyncResult`-compatible object returned by `BeginInvoke()` and pass it to `EndInvoke()` when you are ready to obtain the result of the method invocation. As you will see, you are able to invoke the members of an `IAsyncResult`-compatible object when you wish to become "more involved" with the process of fetching the method's return value.

■ **Note** If you asynchronously invoke a method that provides a `void` return value, you can simply "fire and forget." In such cases, you will never need to cache the `IAsyncResult`-compatible object or call `EndInvoke()` in the first place (as there is no return value to retrieve).

Invoking a Method Asynchronously

To instruct the `BinaryOp` delegate to invoke `Add()` asynchronously, you can update the previous `Main()` method as follows:

```
static void Main(string[] args)
{
  Console.WriteLine("***** Async Delegate Invocation *****");

  // Print out the ID of the executing thread.
  Console.WriteLine("Main() invoked on thread {0}.",
```

```
    Thread.CurrentThread.ManagedThreadId);

  // Invoke Add() on a secondary thread.
  BinaryOp b = new BinaryOp(Add);
  IAsyncResult iftAR = b.BeginInvoke(10, 10, null, null);

  // Do other work on primary thread...
  Console.WriteLine("Doing more work in Main()!");

  // Obtain the result of the Add()
  // method when ready.
  int answer = b.EndInvoke(iftAR);
  Console.WriteLine("10 + 10 is {0}.", answer);
  Console.ReadLine();
}
```

If you run this application, you will find that two unique thread IDs are displayed, given that there are in fact multiple threads working within the current AppDomain (see Figure 18-2).

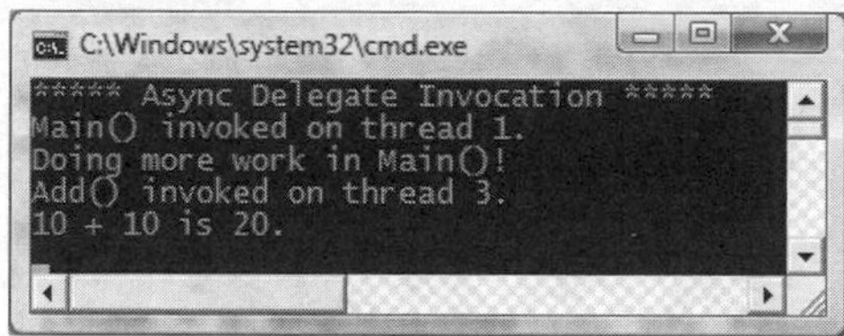

Figure 18-2. *Methods invoked asynchronously are done so on a unique thread.*

In addition to the unique ID values, you will also notice upon running the application that the `Doing more work in Main()!` message displays immediately, while the secondary thread is occupied attending to its business.

Synchronizing the Calling Thread

If you ponder the current implementation of `Main()`, you might have realized that the time span between calling `BeginInvoke()` and `EndInvoke()` is clearly less than five seconds. Therefore, once `Doing more work in Main()!` prints to the console, the calling thread is now blocked and waiting for the secondary thread to complete before being able to obtain the result of the `Add()` method. Therefore, you are effectively making yet another *synchronous call*:

```
static void Main(string[] args)
{
...
  BinaryOp b = new BinaryOp(Add);
  IAsyncResult iftAR = b.BeginInvoke(10, 10, null, null);

  // This call takes far less than five seconds!
  Console.WriteLine("Doing more work in Main()!");

  // The calling thread is now blocked until
  // BeginInvoke() completes.
  int answer = b.EndInvoke(iftAR);
...
}
```

Obviously, asynchronous delegates would lose their appeal if the calling thread had the potential of being blocked under various circumstances. To allow the calling thread to discover if the asynchronously invoked method has completed its work, the `IAsyncResult` interface provides the `IsCompleted` property. Using this member, the calling thread is able to determine whether the asynchronous call has indeed completed before calling `EndInvoke()`. If the method has not completed, `IsCompleted` returns `false`, and the calling thread is free to carry on its work. If `IsCompleted` returns `true`, the calling thread is able to obtain the result in the "least blocking manner" possible. Ponder the following update to the `Main()` method:

```
static void Main(string[] args)
{
...
  BinaryOp b = new BinaryOp(Add);
  IAsyncResult iftAR = b.BeginInvoke(10, 10, null, null);

  // This message will keep printing until
  // the Add() method is finished.
  while(!iftAR.IsCompleted)
  {
    Console.WriteLine("Doing more work in Main()!");
    Thread.Sleep(1000);
  }

  // Now we know the Add() method is complete.
  int answer = b.EndInvoke(iftAR);
...
}
```

Here, you enter a loop that will continue processing the `Console.WriteLine()` statement until the secondary thread has completed. Once this has occurred, you can obtain the result of the `Add()` method knowing full well the method has indeed completed. The call to `Thread.Sleep(1000)` is not necessary for this particular application to function correctly; however, by forcing the primary thread to wait for approximately one second during each iteration, it prevents the same message from printing hundreds of times.

In addition to the `IsCompleted` property, the `IAsyncResult` interface provides the `AsyncWaitHandle` property for more flexible waiting logic. This property returns an instance of the `WaitHandle` type, which exposes a method named `WaitOne()`. The benefit of `WaitHandle.WaitOne()` is that you can specify the maximum wait time. If the specified amount of time is exceeded, `WaitOne()` returns `false`. Ponder the following updated `while` loop, which no longer makes use of a call to `Thread.Sleep()`:

```
while (!iftAR.AsyncWaitHandle.WaitOne(1000, true))
{
  Console.WriteLine("Doing more work in Main()!");
}
```

While these properties of `IAsyncResult` do provide a way to synchronize the calling thread, they are not the most efficient approach. In many ways, the `IsCompleted` property is much like a really annoying manager (or classmate) who is constantly asking, "Are you done yet?" Thankfully, delegates provide a number of additional (and more elegant) techniques to obtain the result of a method that has been called asynchronously.

■ **Source Code** The AsyncDelegate project is located under the Chapter 18 subdirectory.

The Role of the AsyncCallback Delegate

Rather than polling a delegate to determine whether an asynchronously invoked method has completed, it would be more efficient to have the secondary thread inform the calling thread when the task is finished. When you wish to enable this behavior, you will need to supply an instance of the System.AsyncCallback delegate as a parameter to BeginInvoke(), which up until this point has been null. However, when you do supply an AsyncCallback object, the delegate will call the specified method automatically when the asynchronous call has completed.

Like any delegate, AsyncCallback can only invoke methods that match a specific pattern, which in this case is a method taking IAsyncResult as the sole parameter and returning nothing:

```
// Targets of AsyncCallback must match the following pattern.
void MyAsyncCallbackMethod(IAsyncResult itfAR)
```

Assume you have another application making use of the BinaryOp delegate. This time, however, you will not poll the delegate to determine whether the Add() method has completed. Rather, you will define a static method named AddComplete() to receive the notification that the asynchronous invocation is finished:

```
namespace AsyncCallbackDelegate
{
  public delegate int BinaryOp(int x, int y);

  class Program
  {
    static void Main(string[] args)
    {
      Console.WriteLine("***** AsyncCallbackDelegate Example *****");
      Console.WriteLine("Main() invoked on thread {0}.",
        Thread.CurrentThread.ManagedThreadId);

      BinaryOp b = new BinaryOp(Add);
      IAsyncResult iftAR = b.BeginInvoke(10, 10,
        new AsyncCallback(AddComplete), null);

      // Other work performed here...

      Console.ReadLine();
    }

    static void AddComplete(IAsyncResult itfAR)
    {
      Console.WriteLine("AddComplete() invoked on thread {0}.",
        Thread.CurrentThread.ManagedThreadId);
      Console.WriteLine("Your addition is complete");
    }

    static int Add(int x, int y)
    {
      Console.WriteLine("Add() invoked on thread {0}.",
      Thread.CurrentThread.ManagedThreadId);
      Thread.Sleep(5000);
      return x + y;
    }
  }
}
```

Again, the static `AddComplete()` method will be invoked by the `AsyncCallback` delegate when the `Add()` method has completed. If you run this program, you can confirm that the secondary thread is the thread invoking the `AddComplete()` callback (see Figure 18-3).

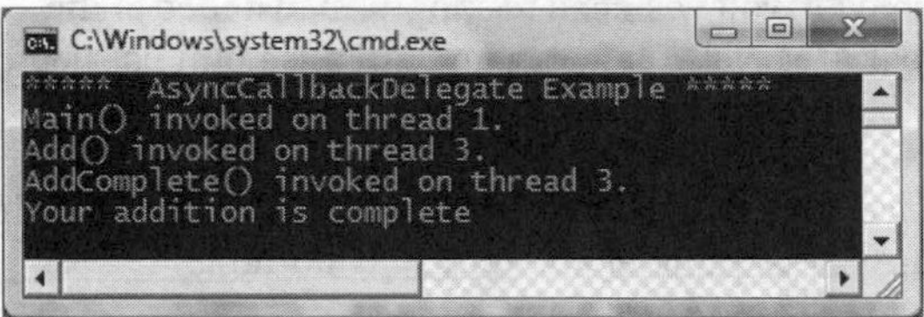

Figure 18-3. *The* `AsyncCallback` *delegate in action*

The Role of the AsyncResult Class

You may have noticed in the current example that the `Main()` method is not caching the `IAsyncResult` type returned from `BeginInvoke()` and is no longer calling `EndInvoke()`. The reason is that the target of the `AsyncCallback` delegate (`AddComplete()` in this example) does not have access to the original `BinaryOp` delegate created in the scope of `Main()`. While you could simply declare the `BinaryOp` variable as a static member variable in the class to allow both methods to access the same object, a more elegant solution is to use the incoming `IAsyncResult` parameter.

The incoming `IAsyncResult` parameter passed into the target of the `AsyncCallback` delegate is actually an instance of the `AsyncResult` class (note the lack of an `I` prefix) defined in the `System.Runtime.Remoting.Messaging` namespace. The static `AsyncDelegate` property returns a reference to the original asynchronous delegate that was created elsewhere. Therefore, if you wish to obtain a reference to the `BinaryOp` delegate object allocated within `Main()`, simply cast the `System.Object` returned by the `AsyncDelegate` property into type `BinaryOp`. At this point, you can trigger `EndInvoke()` as expected:

```
// Don't forget to import
// System.Runtime.Remoting.Messaging!
static void AddComplete(IAsyncResult itfAR)
{
  Console.WriteLine("AddComplete() invoked on thread {0}.",
    Thread.CurrentThread.ManagedThreadId);
  Console.WriteLine("Your addition is complete");

  // Now get the result.
  AsyncResult ar = (AsyncResult)itfAR;
  BinaryOp b = (BinaryOp)ar.AsyncDelegate;
  Console.WriteLine("10 + 10 is {0}.", b.EndInvoke(itfAR));
}
```

Passing and Receiving Custom State Data

The final aspect of asynchronous delegates we need to address is the final argument to the `BeginInvoke()` method (which has been `null` up to this point). This parameter allows you to pass additional state information to the callback method from the primary thread. Because this argument is prototyped as a `System.Object`, you can pass in any type of data whatsoever, as long as the callback method knows what to expect. Assume for the sake of demonstration that the primary thread wishes to pass in a custom text message to the `AddComplete()` method:

```
static void Main(string[] args)
{
...
  IAsyncResult iftAR = b.BeginInvoke(10, 10,
    new AsyncCallback(AddComplete),
    "Main() thanks you for adding these numbers.");
...
}
```

To obtain this data within the scope of `AddComplete()`, make use of the `AsyncState` property of the incoming `IAsyncResult` parameter. Notice that an explicit cast will be required; therefore the primary and secondary threads must agree on the underlying type returned from `AsyncState`.

```
static void AddComplete(IAsyncResult itfAR)
{
...
  // Retrieve the informational object and cast it to string.
  string msg = (string)itfAR.AsyncState;
  Console.WriteLine(msg);
}
```

Figure 18-4 shows the output of the current application.

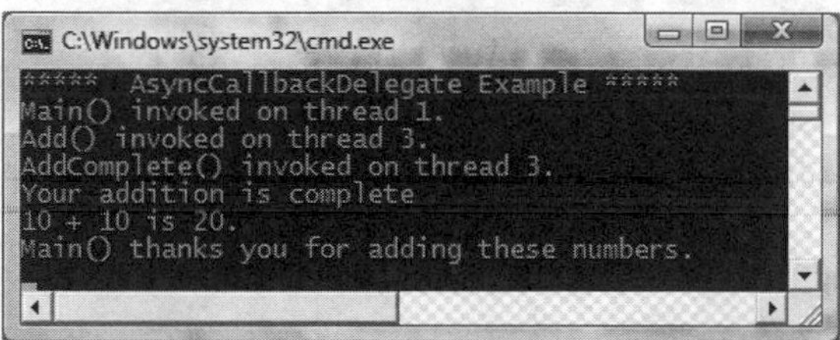

Figure 18-4. *Passing and receiving custom state data*

Now that you understand how a .NET delegate can be used to automatically spin off a secondary thread of execution to handle an asynchronous method invocation, let's turn our attention to directly interacting with threads using the `System.Threading` namespace.

Source Code The AsyncCallbackDelegate project is located under the Chapter 18 subdirectory.

The System.Threading Namespace

Under the .NET platform, the `System.Threading` namespace provides a number of types that enable the direct construction of multithreaded applications. In addition to providing types that allow you to interact with a particular CLR thread, this namespace defines types that allow access to the CLR maintained thread pool, a simple (non–GUI-based) `Timer` class, and numerous types used to provide synchronized access to shared resources. Table 18-1 lists some of the core members of this namespace. (Be sure to consult the .NET Framework 3.5 SDK documentation for full details.)

Table 18-1. *Select Types of the* `System.Threading` *Namespace*

Type	Meaning in Life
`Interlocked`	This type provides atomic operations for types that are shared by multiple threads.
`Monitor`	This type provides the synchronization of threading objects using locks and wait/signals. The C# `lock` keyword makes use of a `Monitor` type under the hood.
`Mutex`	This synchronization primitive can be used for synchronization between application domain boundaries.
`ParameterizedThreadStart`	This delegate allows a thread to call methods that take any number of arguments.
`Semaphore`	This type allows you to limit the number of threads that can access a resource, or a particular type of resource, concurrently.
`Thread`	This type represents a thread that executes within the CLR. Using this type, you are able to spawn additional threads in the originating AppDomain.
`ThreadPool`	This type allows you to interact with the CLR-maintained thread pool within a given process.
`ThreadPriority`	This enum represents a thread's priority level (`Highest`, `Normal`, etc.).
`ThreadStart`	This delegate is used to specify the method to call for a given thread. Unlike the `ParameterizedThreadStart` delegate, targets of `ThreadStart` must match a fixed prototype.
`ThreadState`	This enum specifies the valid states a thread may take (`Running`, `Aborted`, etc.).
`Timer`	This type provides a mechanism for executing a method at specified intervals.
`TimerCallback`	This delegate type is used in conjunction with `Timer` types.

The System.Threading.Thread Class

The most primitive of all types in the `System.Threading` namespace is `Thread`. This class represents an object-oriented wrapper around a given path of execution within a particular AppDomain. This type also defines a number of methods (both static and shared) that allow you to create new threads within the current AppDomain, as well as to suspend, stop, and destroy a particular thread. Consider the list of core static members in Table 18-2.

Table 18-2. *Key Static Members of the* `Thread` *Type*

Static Member	Meaning in Life
`CurrentContext`	This read-only property returns the context in which the thread is currently running.
`CurrentThread`	This read-only property returns a reference to the currently running thread.
`GetDomain()` `GetDomainID()`	These methods return a reference to the current AppDomain or the ID of this domain in which the current thread is running.
`Sleep()`	This method suspends the current thread for a specified time.

The Thread class also supports several instance-level members, some of which are shown in Table 18-3.

Table 18-3. *Select Instance-Level Members of the* Thread *Type*

Instance-Level Member	Meaning in Life
IsAlive	Returns a Boolean that indicates whether this thread has been started.
IsBackground	Gets or sets a value indicating whether or not this thread is a "background thread" (more details in just a moment).
Name	Allows you to establish a friendly text name of the thread.
Priority	Gets or sets the priority of a thread, which may be assigned a value from the ThreadPriority enumeration.
ThreadState	Gets the state of this thread, which may be assigned a value from the ThreadState enumeration.
Abort()	Instructs the CLR to terminate the thread as soon as possible.
Interrupt()	Interrupts (e.g., wakes) the current thread from a suitable wait period.
Join()	Blocks the calling thread until the specified thread (the one on which Join() is called) exits.
Resume()	Resumes a thread that has been previously suspended.
Start()	Instructs the CLR to execute the thread ASAP.
Suspend()	Suspends the thread. If the thread is already suspended, a call to Suspend() has no effect.

■ **Note** Aborting or suspending an active thread is generally considered a bad idea. When you do so, there is a chance (however small) that a thread could "leak" its workload when disturbed or terminated.

Obtaining Statistics About the Current Thread

Recall that the entry point of an executable assembly (i.e., the Main() method) runs on the primary thread of execution. To illustrate the basic use of the Thread type, assume you have a new Console Application named ThreadStats. As you know, the static Thread.CurrentThread property retrieves a Thread type that represents the currently executing thread. Once you have obtained the current thread, you are able to print out various statistics:

```
// Be sure to import the System.Threading namespace.
static void Main(string[] args)
{
  Console.WriteLine("***** Primary Thread stats *****\n");

  // Obtain and name the current thread.
  Thread primaryThread = Thread.CurrentThread;
  primaryThread.Name = "ThePrimaryThread";

  // Show details of hosting AppDomain/Context.
  Console.WriteLine("Name of current AppDomain: {0}",
    Thread.GetDomain().FriendlyName);
```

```
  Console.WriteLine("ID of current Context: {0}",
    Thread.CurrentContext.ContextID);

  // Print out some stats about this thread.
  Console.WriteLine("Thread Name: {0}",
    primaryThread.Name);
  Console.WriteLine("Has thread started?: {0}",
    primaryThread.IsAlive);
  Console.WriteLine("Priority Level: {0}",
    primaryThread.Priority);
  Console.WriteLine("Thread State: {0}",
    primaryThread.ThreadState);
  Console.ReadLine();
}
```

Figure 18-5 shows the output for the current application.

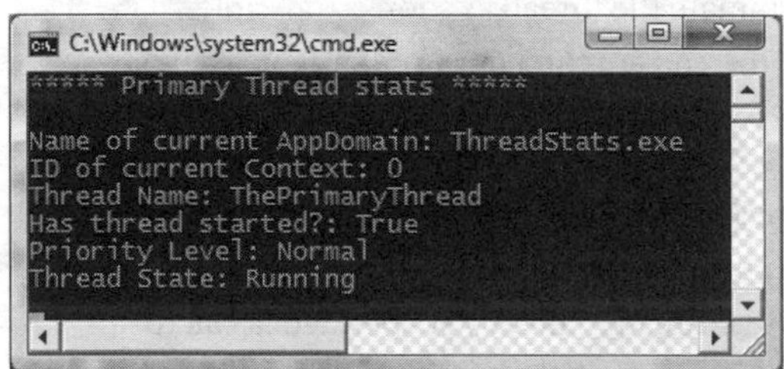

Figure 18-5. *Gathering thread statistics*

The Name Property

While this code is more or less self-explanatory, do notice that the `Thread` class supports a property called `Name`. If you do not set this value, `Name` will return an empty string. However, once you assign a friendly string moniker to a given `Thread` object, you can greatly simplify your debugging endeavors. If you are making use of Visual Studio 2008, you may access the Threads window during a debugging session (select Debug ➤ Windows ➤ Threads). As you can see from Figure 18-6, you can quickly identify the thread you wish to diagnose.

Threads

ID	Name	Location	Priority	Suspend
2768				0
960	<No Name>		Highest	0
5436	<No Name>		Normal	0
5584				0
5992	<No Name>		Normal	0
5716	.NET SystemEvents		Normal	0
4752	ThePrimaryThread	ThreadStats.Program.Main	Normal	0

Figure 18-6. *Debugging a thread with Visual Studio 2008*

The Priority Property

Next, notice that the Thread type defines a property named Priority. By default, all threads have a priority level of Normal. However, you can change this at any point in the thread's lifetime using the ThreadPriority property and the related System.Threading.ThreadPriority enumeration:

```
public enum ThreadPriority
{
  AboveNormal,
  BelowNormal,
  Highest,
  Idle,
  Lowest,
  Normal,    // Default value.
  TimeCritical
}
```

If you were to assign a thread's priority level to a value other than the default (ThreadPriority.Normal), understand that you would have no direct control over when the thread scheduler switches between threads. In reality, a thread's priority level offers a hint to the CLR regarding the importance of the thread's activity. Thus, a thread with the value ThreadPriority.Highest is not necessarily guaranteed to be given the highest precedence.

Again, if the thread scheduler is preoccupied with a given task (e.g., synchronizing an object, switching threads, or moving threads), the priority level will most likely be altered accordingly. However, all things being equal, the CLR will read these values and instruct the thread scheduler how to best allocate time slices. Threads with an identical thread priority should each receive the same amount of time to perform their work.

In most cases, you will seldom (if ever) need to directly alter a thread's priority level. In theory, it is possible to jack up the priority level on a set of threads, thereby preventing lower-priority threads from executing at their required levels (so use caution).

■ **Source Code** The ThreadStats project is included under the Chapter 18 subdirectory.

Programmatically Creating Secondary Threads

When you wish to programmatically create additional threads to carry on some unit of work, you will follow a very predictable process:

1. Create a type method to be the entry point for the new thread.
2. Create a new ParameterizedThreadStart (or legacy ThreadStart) delegate, passing the address of the method defined in step 1 to the constructor.
3. Create a Thread object, passing the ParameterizedThreadStart/ThreadStart delegate as a constructor argument.
4. Establish any initial thread characteristics (name, priority, etc.).
5. Call the Thread.Start() method. This starts the thread at the method referenced by the delegate created in step 2 as soon as possible.

As stated in step 2, you may make use of two distinct delegate types to "point to" the method that the secondary thread will execute. The ThreadStart delegate has been part of the System.

Threading namespace since .NET 1.0, and it can point to any method that takes no arguments and returns nothing. This delegate can be helpful when the method is designed to simply run in the background without further interaction.

The obvious limitation of ThreadStart is that you are unable to pass in parameters for processing. As of .NET 2.0, we were provided with the ParameterizedThreadStart delegate type, which allows a single parameter of type System.Object. Given that anything can be represented as a System.Object, you can pass in any number of parameters via a custom class or structure. Do note, however, that the ParameterizedThreadStart delegate can only point to methods that return void.

Working with the ThreadStart Delegate

To illustrate the process of building a multithreaded application (as well as to demonstrate the usefulness of doing so), assume you have a Console Application (SimpleMultiThreadApp) that allows the end user to choose whether the application will perform its duties using the single primary thread or split its workload using two separate threads of execution.

Assuming you have imported the System.Threading namespace, your first step is to define a type method to perform the work of the (possible) secondary thread. To keep focused on the mechanics of building multithreaded programs, this method will simply print out a sequence of numbers to the console window, pausing for approximately two seconds with each pass. Here is the full definition of the Printer class:

```
public class Printer
{
  public void PrintNumbers()
  {
    // Display Thread info.
    Console.WriteLine("-> {0} is executing PrintNumbers()",
      Thread.CurrentThread.Name);

    // Print out numbers.
    Console.Write("Your numbers: ");
    for(int i = 0; i < 10; i++)
    {
      Console.Write("{0}, ", i);
      Thread.Sleep(2000);
    }
    Console.WriteLine();
  }
}
```

Now, within Main(), you will first prompt the user to determine whether one or two threads will be used to perform the application's work. If the user requests a single thread, you will simply invoke the PrintNumbers() method within the primary thread. However, if the user specifies two threads, you will create a ThreadStart delegate that points to PrintNumbers(), pass this delegate object into the constructor of a new Thread object, and call Start() to inform the CLR this thread is ready for processing.

To begin, set a reference to the System.Windows.Forms.dll assembly and display a message within Main() using MessageBox.Show() (you'll see the point of doing so once you run the program). Here is the complete implementation of Main():

```
static void Main(string[] args)
{
  Console.WriteLine("***** The Amazing Thread App *****\n");
  Console.Write("Do you want [1] or [2] threads? ");
  string threadCount = Console.ReadLine();
```

```
    // Name the current thread.
    Thread primaryThread = Thread.CurrentThread;
    primaryThread.Name = "Primary";

    // Display Thread info.
    Console.WriteLine("-> {0} is executing Main()",
    Thread.CurrentThread.Name);

    // Make worker class.
    Printer p = new Printer();

    switch(threadCount)
    {
      case  "2":
        // Now make the thread.
        Thread backgroundThread =
          new Thread(new ThreadStart(p.PrintNumbers));
        backgroundThread.Name = "Secondary";
        backgroundThread.Start();
      break;
      case "1":
        p.PrintNumbers();
      break;
      default:
        Console.WriteLine("I don't know what you want...you get 1 thread.");
        goto case "1";
    }

    // Do some additional work.
    MessageBox.Show("I'm busy!", "Work on main thread...");
    Console.ReadLine();
  }
```

Now, if you run this program with a single thread, you will find that the final message box will not display the message until the entire sequence of numbers has printed to the console. As you are explicitly pausing for approximately two seconds after each number is printed, this will result in a less-than-stellar end-user experience. However, if you select two threads, the message box displays instantly, given that a unique Thread object is responsible for printing out the numbers to the console (see Figure 18-7).

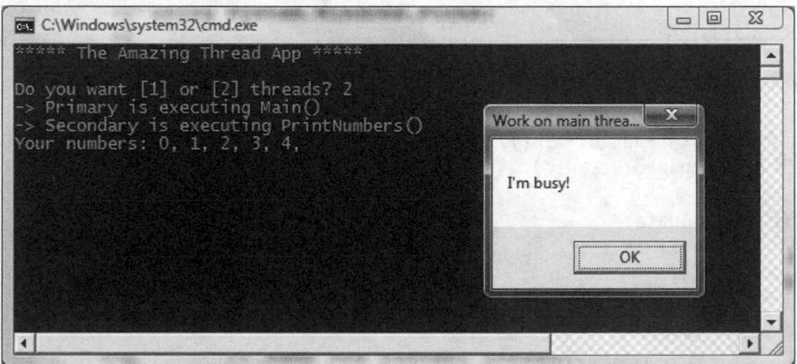

Figure 18-7. *Multithreaded applications provide results in more responsive applications.*

Before we move on, it is important to note that when you build multithreaded applications (which includes the use of asynchronous delegates to do so) on single CPU machines, you do not end up with an application that *runs* any faster, as that is a function of a machine's CPU. When running this application using either one or two threads, the numbers are still displaying at the same pace. In reality, multithreaded applications result in *more responsive* applications. To the end user, it may appear that this particular program is "faster," but this is not the case. Threads have no power to make `foreach` loops execute quicker, to make paper print faster, or to force numbers to be added together at rocket speed. Multithreaded applications simply allow multiple threads to share the workload.

■ **Source Code** The SimpleMultiThreadApp project is included under the Chapter 18 subdirectory.

Working with the ParameterizedThreadStart Delegate

Recall that the `ThreadStart` delegate can point only to methods that return `void` and take no arguments. While this may fit the bill in many cases, if you wish to pass data to the method executing on the secondary thread, you will need to make use of the `ParameterizedThreadStart` delegate type. To illustrate, let's re-create the logic of the `AsyncCallbackDelegate` project created earlier in this chapter, this time making use of the `ParameterizedThreadStart` delegate type.

To begin, create a new Console Application named AddWithThreads and import the `System.Threading` namespace. Now, given that `ParameterizedThreadStart` can point to any method taking a `System.Object` parameter, you will create a custom type containing the numbers to be added:

```
class AddParams
{
  public int a, b;

  public AddParams(int numb1, int numb2)
  {
    a = numb1;
    b = numb2;
  }
}
```

Next, create a static method in the `Program` class that will take an `AddParams` type and print out the summation of each value:

```
static void Add(object data)
{
  if (data is AddParams)
  {
    Console.WriteLine("ID of thread in Main(): {0}",
      Thread.CurrentThread.ManagedThreadId);

    AddParams ap = (AddParams)data;
    Console.WriteLine("{0} + {1} is {2}",
      ap.a, ap.b, ap.a + ap.b);
  }
}
```

The code within `Main()` is straightforward. Simply use `ParameterizedThreadStart` rather than `ThreadStart`:

```
static void Main(string[] args)
{
  Console.WriteLine("***** Adding with Thread objects *****");
  Console.WriteLine("ID of thread in Main(): {0}",
    Thread.CurrentThread.ManagedThreadId);

  // Make an AddParams object to pass to the secondary thread.
  AddParams ap = new AddParams(10, 10);
  Thread t = new Thread(new ParameterizedThreadStart(Add));
  t.Start(ap);
...
}
```

Source Code The AddWithThreads project is included under the Chapter 18 subdirectory.

Foreground Threads and Background Threads

Now that you have seen how to programmatically create new threads of execution using the `System.Threading` namespace, let's formalize the distinction between foreground threads and background threads:

- *Foreground threads* have the ability to prevent the current application from terminating. The CLR will not shut down an application (which is to say, unload the hosting AppDomain) until all foreground threads have ended.
- *Background threads* (sometimes called *daemon threads*) are viewed by the CLR as expendable paths of execution that can be ignored at any point in time (even if they are currently laboring over some unit of work). Thus, if all foreground threads have terminated, any and all background threads are automatically killed when the application domain unloads.

It is important to note that foreground and background threads are *not* synonymous with primary and worker threads. By default, every thread you create via the `Thread.Start()` method is automatically a *foreground* thread. Again, this means that the AppDomain will not unload until all threads of execution have completed their units of work. In most cases, this is exactly the behavior you require.

For the sake of argument, however, assume that you wish to invoke `Printer.PrintNumbers()` on a secondary thread that should behave as a background thread. Again, this means that the method pointed to by the `Thread` type (via the `ThreadStart` or `ParameterizedThreadStart` delegate) should be able to halt safely as soon as all foreground threads are done with their work. Configuring such a thread is as simple as setting the `IsBackground` property to `true`:

```
static void Main(string[] args)
{
  Console.WriteLine("***** Background Threads *****\n");

  Printer p = new Printer();
  Thread bgroundThread =
    new Thread(new ThreadStart(p.PrintNumbers));

  // This is now a background thread.
  bgroundThread.IsBackground = true;
  bgroundThread.Start();
}
```

Notice that this `Main()` method is *not* making a call to `Console.ReadLine()` to force the console to remain visible until you press the Enter key. Thus, when you run the application, it will shut down immediately because the `Thread` object has been configured as a background thread. Given that the `Main()` method triggers the creation of the primary *foreground* thread, as soon as the logic in `Main()` completes, the AppDomain unloads before the secondary thread is able to complete its work. However, if you comment out the line that sets the `IsBackground` property, you will find that each number prints to the console, as all foreground threads must finish their work before the AppDomain is unloaded from the hosting process.

For the most part, configuring a thread to run as a background type can be helpful when the worker thread in question is performing a noncritical task that is no longer needed when the main task of the program is finished.

■ **Source Code** The BackgroundThread project is included under the Chapter 18 subdirectory.

The Issue of Concurrency

All the multithreaded sample applications you have written over the course of this chapter have been thread-safe, given that only a single `Thread` object was executing the method in question. While some of your applications may be this simplistic in nature, a good deal of your multithreaded applications may contain numerous secondary threads. Given that all threads in an AppDomain have concurrent access to the shared data of the application, imagine what might happen if multiple threads were accessing the same point of data. As the thread scheduler will force threads to suspend their work at random, what if thread A is kicked out of the way before it has fully completed its work? Thread B is now reading unstable data.

To illustrate the problem of concurrency, let's build another C# Console Application project named MultiThreadedPrinting. This application will once again make use of the `Printer` class created previously, but this time the `PrintNumbers()` method will force the current thread to pause for a randomly generated amount of time:

```
public class Printer
{
  public void PrintNumbers()
  {
...
    for (int i = 0; i < 10; i++)
    {
      // Put thread to sleep for a random amount of time.
      Random r = new Random();
      Thread.Sleep(1000 * r.Next(5));
      Console.Write("{0}, ", i);
    }
    Console.WriteLine();
  }
}
```

The `Main()` method is responsible for creating an array of ten (uniquely named) `Thread` objects, each of which is making calls on the *same instance* of the `Printer` object:

```
class Program
{
  static void Main(string[] args)
```

```
  {
    Console.WriteLine("*****Synchronizing Threads *****\n");

    Printer p = new Printer();

    // Make 10 threads that are all pointing to the same
    // method on the same object.
    Thread[] threads = new Thread[10];
    for (int i = 0; i < 10; i++)
    {
      threads[i] =
        new Thread(new ThreadStart(p.PrintNumbers));
      threads[i].Name = string.Format("Worker thread #{0}", i);
    }

    // Now start each one.
    foreach (Thread t in threads)
      t.Start();
    Console.ReadLine();
  }
}
```

Before looking at some test runs, let's recap the problem. The primary thread within this AppDomain begins life by spawning ten secondary worker threads. Each worker thread is told to make calls on the `PrintNumbers()` method on the *same* `Printer` instance. Given that you have taken no precautions to lock down this object's shared resources (the console), there is a good chance that the current thread will be kicked out of the way before the `PrintNumbers()` method is able to print out the complete results. Because you don't know exactly when (or if) this might happen, you are bound to get unpredictable results. For example, you might find the output shown in Figure 18-8.

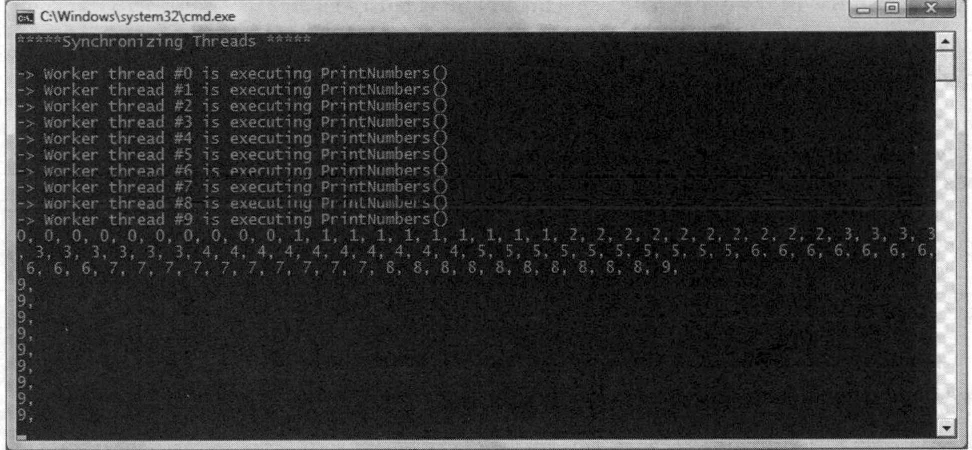

Figure 18-8. *Concurrency in action, take one*

Now run the application a few more times. Figure 18-9 shows another possibility (your results will obviously differ).

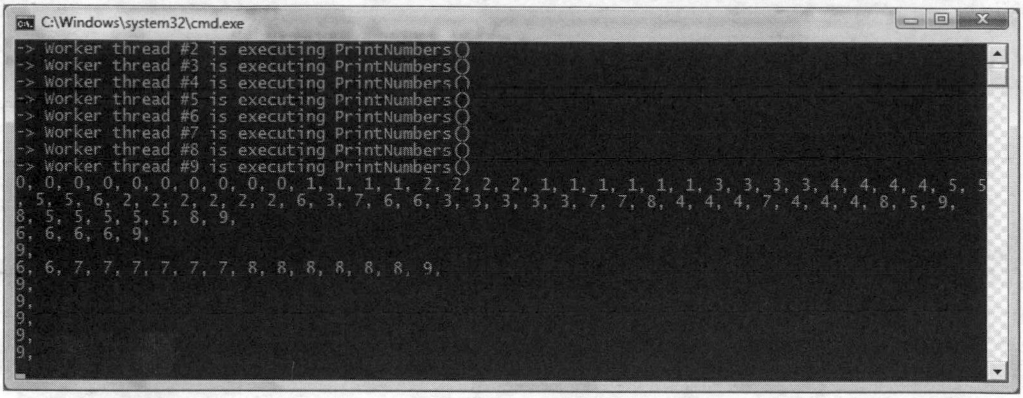

```
C:\Windows\system32\cmd.exe
-> Worker thread #2 is executing PrintNumbers()
-> Worker thread #3 is executing PrintNumbers()
-> Worker thread #4 is executing PrintNumbers()
-> Worker thread #5 is executing PrintNumbers()
-> Worker thread #6 is executing PrintNumbers()
-> Worker thread #7 is executing PrintNumbers()
-> Worker thread #8 is executing PrintNumbers()
-> Worker thread #9 is executing PrintNumbers()
0, 0, 0, 0, 0, 0, 0, 0, 0, 0, 1, 1, 1, 1, 2, 2, 2, 2, 1, 1, 1, 1, 1, 1, 3, 3, 3, 3, 4, 4, 4, 4, 5, 5
, 5, 5, 6, 2, 2, 2, 2, 2, 2, 6, 3, 7, 6, 6, 3, 3, 3, 3, 3, 7, 7, 8, 4, 4, 4, 7, 4, 4, 4, 8, 5, 9,
8, 5, 5, 5, 5, 5, 8, 9,
6, 6, 6, 6, 9,
9,
6, 6, 7, 7, 7, 7, 7, 7, 8, 8, 8, 8, 8, 8, 9,
9,
9,
9,
9,
9,
```

Figure 18-9. *Concurrency in action, take two*

■ **Note** If you are unable to generate unpredictable outputs, increase the number of threads from 10 to 100 (for example) or introduce another call to `Thread.Sleep()` within your program. Eventually, you will encounter the concurrency issue.

There are clearly some problems here. As each thread is telling the `Printer` to print out the numerical data, the thread scheduler is happily swapping threads in the background. The result is inconsistent output. What we need is a way to programmatically enforce synchronized access to the shared resources. As you would guess, the `System.Threading` namespace provides a number of synchronization-centric types. The C# programming language also provides a particular keyword for the very task of synchronizing shared data in multithreaded applications.

Synchronization Using the C# lock Keyword

The first technique you can use to synchronize access to shared resources is the C# `lock` keyword. This keyword allows you to define a scope of statements that must be synchronized between threads. By doing so, incoming threads cannot interrupt the current thread, preventing it from finishing its work. The `lock` keyword requires you to specify a *token* (an object reference) that must be acquired by a thread to enter within the lock scope. When you are attempting to lock down a *private* instance-level method, you can simply pass in a reference to the current type:

```
private void SomePrivateMethod()
{
  // Use the current object as the thread token.
  lock(this)
  {
    // All code within this scope is thread-safe.
  }
}
```

However, if you are locking down a region of code within a *public* member, it is safer (and a best practice) to declare a private `object` member variable to serve as the lock token:

```
public class Printer
{
  // Lock token.
  private object threadLock = new object();
```

```
  public void PrintNumbers()
  {
    // Use the lock token.
    lock (threadLock)
    {
      ...
    }
  }
}
```

In any case, if you examine the PrintNumbers() method, you can see that the shared resource the threads are competing to gain access to is the console window. Therefore, if you scope all interactions with the Console type within a lock scope as follows:

```
public void PrintNumbers()
{
  // Use the private object lock token.
  lock (threadLock)
  {
    // Display Thread info.
    Console.WriteLine("-> {0} is executing PrintNumbers()",
      Thread.CurrentThread.Name);

    // Print out numbers.
    Console.Write("Your numbers: ");
    for (int i = 0; i < 10; i++)
    {
      Random r = new Random();
      Thread.Sleep(1000 * r.Next(5));
      Console.Write("{0}, ", i);
    }
    Console.WriteLine();
  }
}
```

you have effectively designed a method that will allow the current thread to complete its task. Once a thread enters into a lock scope, the lock token (in this case, a reference to the current object) is inaccessible by other threads until the lock is released once the lock scope has exited. Thus, if thread A has obtained the lock token, other threads are unable to enter the scope until thread A relinquishes the lock token.

■ **Note** If you are attempting to lock down code in a static method, simply declare a private static object member variable to serve as the lock token.

If you now run the application, you can see that each thread has ample opportunity to finish its business (see Figure 18-10).

■ **Source Code** The MultiThreadedPrinting project is included under the Chapter 18 subdirectory.

```
*****Synchronizing Threads *****

-> Worker thread #0 is executing PrintNumbers()
Your numbers: 0, 1, 2, 3, 4, 5, 6, 7, 8, 9,
-> Worker thread #1 is executing PrintNumbers()
Your numbers: 0, 1, 2, 3, 4, 5, 6, 7, 8, 9,
-> Worker thread #2 is executing PrintNumbers()
Your numbers: 0, 1, 2, 3, 4, 5, 6, 7, 8, 9,
-> Worker thread #3 is executing PrintNumbers()
Your numbers: 0, 1, 2, 3, 4, 5, 6, 7, 8, 9,
-> Worker thread #4 is executing PrintNumbers()
Your numbers: 0, 1, 2, 3, 4, 5, 6, 7, 8, 9,
-> Worker thread #5 is executing PrintNumbers()
Your numbers: 0, 1, 2, 3, 4, 5, 6, 7, 8, 9,
-> Worker thread #6 is executing PrintNumbers()
Your numbers: 0, 1, 2, 3, 4, 5, 6, 7, 8, 9,
-> Worker thread #7 is executing PrintNumbers()
Your numbers: 0, 1, 2, 3, 4, 5, 6, 7, 8, 9,
-> Worker thread #8 is executing PrintNumbers()
Your numbers: 0, 1, 2, 3, 4, 5, 6, 7, 8, 9,
-> Worker thread #9 is executing PrintNumbers()
Your numbers: 0, 1, 2, 3, 4, 5, 6, 7, 8, 9,
```

Figure 18-10. *All threads are now synchronized.*

Synchronization Using the System.Threading.Monitor Type

The C# `lock` statement is really just a shorthand notation for working with the `System.Threading.Monitor` class type. Once processed by the C# compiler, a lock scope actually resolves to the following (which you can verify using `ildasm.exe` or `reflector.exe`):

```
public void PrintNumbers()
{
  Monitor.Enter(threadLock);
  try
  {
    // Display Thread info.
    Console.WriteLine("-> {0} is executing PrintNumbers()",
      Thread.CurrentThread.Name);

    // Print out numbers.
    Console.Write("Your numbers: ");
    for (int i = 0; i < 10; i++)
    {
      Random r = new Random();
      Thread.Sleep(1000 * r.Next(5));
      Console.Write("{0}, ", i);
    }
    Console.WriteLine();
  }
  finally
  {
    Monitor.Exit(threadLock);
  }
}
```

First, notice that the `Monitor.Enter()` method is the ultimate recipient of the thread token you specified as the argument to the `lock` keyword. Next, all code within a lock scope is wrapped within a `try` block. The corresponding `finally` clause ensures that the thread token is released (via the

`Monitor.Exit()` method), regardless of any possible runtime exception. If you were to modify the MultiThreadSharedData program to make direct use of the `Monitor` type (as just shown), you will find the output is identical.

Now, given that the `lock` keyword seems to require less code than making explicit use of the `System.Threading.Monitor` type, you may wonder about the benefits of using the `Monitor` type directly. The short answer is control. If you make use of the `Monitor` type, you are able to instruct the active thread to wait for some duration of time (via the `Wait()` method), inform waiting threads when the current thread is completed (via the `Pulse()` and `PulseAll()` methods), and so on.

As you would expect, in a great number of cases, the C# `lock` keyword will fit the bill. However, if you are interested in checking out additional members of the `Monitor` class, consult the .NET Framework 3.5 SDK documentation.

Synchronization Using the System.Threading.Interlocked Type

Although it always is hard to believe until you look at the underlying CIL code, assignments and simple arithmetic operations are *not atomic*. For this reason, the `System.Threading` namespace provides a type that allows you to operate on a single point of data atomically with less overhead than with the `Monitor` type. The `Interlocked` class type defines the static members shown in Table 18-4.

Table 18-4. *Members of the* `System.Threading.Interlocked` *Type*

Member	Meaning in Life
`CompareExchange()`	Safely tests two values for equality and, if equal, changes one of the values with a third
`Decrement()`	Safely decrements a value by 1
`Exchange()`	Safely swaps two values
`Increment()`	Safely increments a value by 1

Although it might not seem like it from the onset, the process of atomically altering a single value is quite common in a multithreaded environment. Assume you have a method named `AddOne()` that increments an integer member variable named `intVal`. Rather than writing synchronization code such as the following:

```
public void AddOne()
{
  lock(myLockToken)
  {
    intVal++;
  }
}
```

you can simplify your code via the static `Interlocked.Increment()` method. Simply pass in the variable to increment by reference. Do note that the `Increment()` method not only adjusts the value of the incoming parameter, but also returns the new value:

```
public void AddOne()
{
  int newVal = Interlocked.Increment(ref intVal);
}
```

In addition to `Increment()` and `Decrement()`, the `Interlocked` type allows you to atomically assign numerical and object data. For example, if you wish to assign the value of a member variable to the value 83, you can avoid the need to use an explicit lock statement (or explicit Monitor logic) and make use of the Interlocked.Exchange() method:

```
public void SafeAssignment()
{
  Interlocked.Exchange(ref myInt, 83);
}
```

Finally, if you wish to test two values for equality to change the point of comparison in a thread-safe manner, you are able to leverage the Interlocked.CompareExchange() method as follows:

```
public void CompareAndExchange()
{
  // If the value of i is currently 83, change i to 99.
  Interlocked.CompareExchange(ref i, 99, 83);
}
```

Synchronization Using the [Synchronization] Attribute

The final synchronization primitive examined here is the [Synchronization] attribute, which is a member of the System.Runtime.Remoting.Contexts namespace. In essence, this class-level attribute effectively locks down *all* instance member code of the object for thread safety. When the CLR allocates objects attributed with [Synchronization], it will place the object within a synchronized context. As you may recall from Chapter 17, objects that should not be removed from a contextual boundary should derive from ContextBoundObject. Therefore, if you wish to make the Printer class type thread-safe (without explicitly writing thread-safe code within the class members), you could update the definition as follows:

```
using System.Runtime.Remoting.Contexts;
...

// All methods of Printer are now thread-safe!
[Synchronization]
public class Printer : ContextBoundObject
{
  public void PrintNumbers()
  {
    ...
  }
}
```

In some ways, this approach can be seen as the lazy way to write thread-safe code, given that you are not required to dive into the details about which aspects of the type are truly manipulating thread-sensitive data. The major downfall of this approach, however, is that even if a given method is not making use of thread-sensitive data, the CLR will *still* lock invocations to the method. Obviously, this could degrade the overall functionality of the type, so use this technique with care.

At this point, you have seen a number of ways you are able to provide synchronized access to shared blocks of data. To be sure, additional synchronization types are available within the System.Threading namespace, which I will encourage you to explore at your leisure. To wrap up our examination of thread programming, allow me to introduce four additional types: TimerCallback, Timer, ThreadPool, and BackgroundWorker.

Programming with Timer Callbacks

Many applications have the need to call a specific method during regular intervals of time. For example, you may have an application that needs to display the current time on a status bar via a given helper function. As another example, you may wish to have your application call a helper function every so often to perform noncritical background tasks such as checking for new e-mail messages. For situations such as these, you can use the `System.Threading.Timer` type in conjunction with a related delegate named `TimerCallback`.

■Note The Windows Forms API provides a GUI-based `Timer` control that provides the same functionality of the `TimerCallback` type. In fact, the GUI-based `Timer` type is typically simpler to use, as it can be configured at design time.

To illustrate, assume you have a Console Application (TimerApp) that will print the current time every second until the user presses a key to terminate the application. The first obvious step is to write the method that will be called by the `Timer` type:

```
class Program
{
  static void PrintTime(object state)
  {
    Console.WriteLine("Time is: {0}",
      DateTime.Now.ToLongTimeString());
  }

  static void Main(string[] args)
  {
  }
}
```

Notice how this method has a single parameter of type `System.Object` and returns `void`. This is not optional, given that the `TimerCallback` delegate can only call methods that match this signature. The value passed into the target of your `TimerCallback` delegate can be any bit of information whatsoever (in the case of the e-mail example, this parameter might represent the name of the Microsoft Exchange server to interact with during the process). Also note that given that this parameter is indeed a `System.Object`, you are able to pass in multiple arguments using a `System.Array` or custom class/structure.

The next step is to configure an instance of the `TimerCallback` delegate and pass it into the `Timer` object. In addition to configuring a `TimerCallback` delegate, the `Timer` constructor allows you to specify the optional parameter information to pass into the delegate target (defined as a `System.Object`), the interval to poll the method, and the amount of time to wait (in milliseconds) before making the first call, for example:

```
static void Main(string[] args)
{
  Console.WriteLine("***** Working with Timer type *****\n");

  // Create the delegate for the Timer type.
  TimerCallback timeCB = new TimerCallback(PrintTime);

  // Establish timer settings.
  Timer t = new Timer(
    timeCB,     // The TimerCallback delegate type.
    null,       // Any info to pass into the called method (null for no info).
```

```
    0,          // Amount of time to wait before starting.
    1000);      // Interval of time between calls (in milliseconds).

  Console.WriteLine("Hit key to terminate...");
  Console.ReadLine();
}
```

In this case, the PrintTime() method will be called roughly every second and will pass in no additional information to said method. If you did wish to send in some information for use by the delegate target, simply substitute the null value of the second constructor parameter with the appropriate information:

```
// Establish timer settings.
Timer t = new Timer(timeCB, "Hello From Main", 0, 1000);
```

We can then obtain the incoming data as follows:

```
static void PrintTime(object state)
{
  Console.WriteLine("Time is: {0}, Param is: {1}",
    DateTime.Now.ToLongTimeString(), state.ToString());
}
```

Figure 18-11 shows the output.

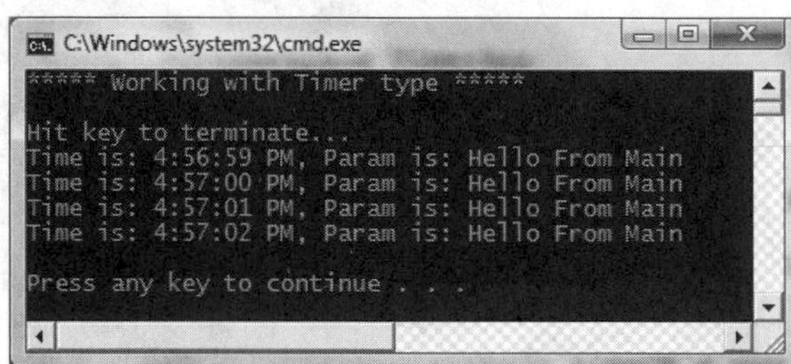

Figure 18-11. *Timers at work*

Source Code The TimerApp project is included under the Chapter 18 subdirectory.

Understanding the CLR ThreadPool

The next thread-centric topic we will examine in this chapter is the role of the CLR thread pool. When you invoke a method asynchronously using delegate types (via the BeginInvoke() method), the CLR does not literally create a brand-new thread. For purposes of efficiency, a delegate's BeginInvoke() method leverages a pool of worker threads that is maintained by the runtime. To allow you to interact with this pool of waiting threads, the System.Threading namespace provides the ThreadPool class type.

If you wish to queue a method call for processing by a worker thread in the pool, you can make use of the ThreadPool.QueueUserWorkItem() method. This method has been overloaded to allow you to specify an optional System.Object for custom state data in addition to an instance of the WaitCallback delegate:

```
public sealed class ThreadPool
{
  ...
  public static bool QueueUserWorkItem(WaitCallback callBack);
  public static bool QueueUserWorkItem(WaitCallback callBack,
    object state);
}
```

The WaitCallback delegate can point to any method that takes a System.Object as its sole parameter (which represents the optional state data) and returns nothing. Do note that if you do not provide a System.Object when calling QueueUserWorkItem(), the CLR automatically passes a null value. To illustrate queuing methods for use by the CLR thread pool, ponder the following program, which makes use of the Printer type once again. In this case, however, you are not manually creating an array of Thread types; rather, you are assigning members of the pool to the PrintNumbers() method:

```
class Program
{
  static void Main(string[] args)
  {
    Console.WriteLine("***** Fun with the CLR Thread Pool *****\n");

    Console.WriteLine("Main thread started. ThreadID = {0}",
      Thread.CurrentThread.ManagedThreadId);

    Printer p = new Printer();

    WaitCallback workItem = new WaitCallback(PrintTheNumbers);

    // Queue the method ten times.
    for (int i = 0; i < 10; i++)
    {
      ThreadPool.QueueUserWorkItem(workItem, p);
    }
    Console.WriteLine("All tasks queued");
    Console.ReadLine();
  }

  static void PrintTheNumbers(object state)
  {
    Printer task = (Printer)state;
    task.PrintNumbers();
  }
}
```

At this point, you may be wondering if it would be advantageous to make use of the CLR-maintained thread pool rather than explicitly creating Thread objects. Consider these benefits of leveraging the thread pool:

- The thread pool manages threads efficiently by minimizing the number of threads that must be created, started, and stopped.
- By using the thread pool, you can focus on your business problem rather than the application's threading infrastructure.

However, using manual thread management is preferred in some cases, for example:

- If you require foreground threads or must set the thread priority. Pooled threads are *always* background threads with default priority (`ThreadPriority.Normal`).
- If you require a thread with a fixed identity in order to abort it, suspend it, or discover it by name.

■ **Source Code** The ThreadPoolApp project is included under the Chapter 18 subdirectory.

The Role of the BackgroundWorker Component

The final threading type we will examine here is `BackgroundWorker`, defined in the `System.ComponentModel` namespace (of `mscorlib.dll`). `BackgroundWorker` is a class that is very helpful when you are building a graphical Windows Forms desktop application and need to execute a long-running task (invoking a remote web service, performing a database transaction, downloading a large file, etc.) on a thread different from your application's main UI thread.

While you are most certainly able to build multithreaded GUI applications by making direct use of the `System.Threading` types as seen in this chapter, `BackgroundWorker` allows you to get the job done with much less fuss and bother. Thankfully, the programming model of this type leverages much of the same threading syntax we find with asynchronous delegates, so learning how to use this type is very straightforward.

To use a `BackgroundWorker`, you simply tell it what method to execute in the background and call `RunWorkerAsync()`. The calling thread (typically the primary thread) continues to run normally while the worker method runs asynchronously. When the time-consuming method has completed, the `BackgroundWorker` type informs the calling thread by firing the `RunWorkerCompleted` event. The associated event hander provides an incoming argument that allows you to obtain the results of the operation (if any exist).

■ **Note** The following example assumes you have some familiarity with GUI desktop development using Windows Forms. If this is not the case, you may wish to return to this section once you have completed reading Chapter 27.

Working with the BackgroundWorker Type

To illustrate using this UI threading component, begin by creating a new Windows Forms application named WinFormsBackgroundWorkerThread. Staying true to the same numerical operation examples used here, construct a simple UI that allows the user to input two values to process (via `TextBox` types) and a `Button` type to begin the background operation. Be sure to give each UI element a fitting name using the `Name` property of the Properties window. Figure 18-12 shows one possible layout.

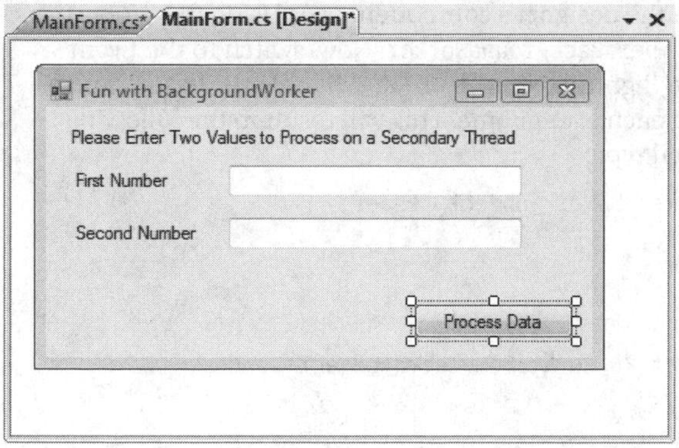

Figure 18-12. *Layout of the Windows Forms UI application*

After you have designed your UI layout, handle the `Click` event of the `Button` type by double-clicking the control on the form designer. This will result in a new event handler that we will implement in just a bit:

```
private void btnProcessData_Click(object sender, EventArgs e)
{
}
```

Now, open the Components region of your Toolbox, locate the `BackgroundWorker` component (see Figure 18-13), and drag an instance of this type onto your form designer.

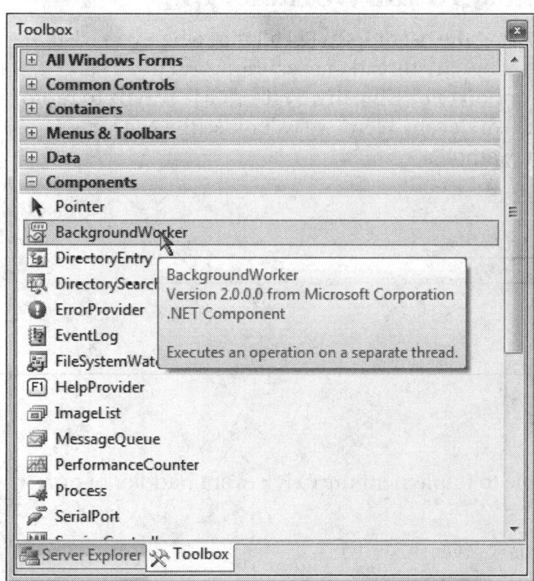

Figure 18-13. *The* `BackgroundWorker` *type*

You will now see a variable of this type on the designer's component tray. Using the Properties window, rename this component to ProcessNumbersBackgroundWorker. Now, switch to the Event pane of the Properties window (by clicking the "lightning bolt" icon) and handle the DoWork and RunWorkerCompleted events by double-clicking each event name. This will result in the following new handlers added to your initial Form-derived type:

```
private void ProcessNumbersBackgroundWorker_DoWork(object sender,
  DoWorkEventArgs e)
{
}

private void ProcessNumbersBackgroundWorker_RunWorkerCompleted(object sender,
  RunWorkerCompletedEventArgs e)
{
}
```

The DoWork event handler represents the method that will be called by the BackgroundWorker on the secondary thread of execution. Notice that the second parameter of the handler is a DoWorkEventArgs type, which will contain any arguments required by the secondary thread to complete its work. As you'll see in just a moment, when you call the RunWorkerAsync() method to spawn this thread, you have the option of passing in this related data (quite similar to working with the ParameterizedThreadStart delegate type used previously in this chapter).

The RunWorkerCompleted event represents the method that the BackgroundWorker will invoke once the background operation has completed. Using the RunWorkerCompletedEventArgs type, you are able to scrape out any return value of the asynchronous operation.

Processing Our Data with the BackgroundWorker Type

At this point, we can flesh out the details of processing the user input. Recall that when you wish to inform the BackgroundWorker type to spin up a secondary thread of execution, you must call RunWorkerAsync(). When you do so, you have the option of passing in a System.Object type to represent any data to pass the method invoked by the DoWork event. Here, we will reuse the AddParams class we created in the ParameterizedThreadStart example:

```
class AddParams
{
  public int a, b;

  public AddParams(int numb1, int numb2)
  {
    a = numb1;
    b = numb2;
  }
}
```

With this helper class in place, we are now able to implement the Click event handler of our Button type as follows:

```
private void btnProcessData_Click(object sender, EventArgs e)
{
  try
  {
    // First get the user data (as numerical).
    int numbOne = int.Parse(txtFirstNumber.Text);
    int numbTwo = int.Parse(this.txtSecondNumber.Text);
    AddParams args = new AddParams(numbOne, numbTwo);
```

```
    // Now spin up the new thread and pass args variable.
    ProcessNumbersBackgroundWorker.RunWorkerAsync(args);
  }
  catch(Exception ex)
  {
    MessageBox.Show(ex.Message);
  }
}
```

As soon as you call `RunWorkerAsync()`, the `DoWork` event fires, which will be captured by your handler. Implement this type to scrape out the `AddParams` object using the `Argument` property of the incoming `DoWorkEventArgs`. Again, to simulate a lengthy operation, we will put the current thread to sleep for approximately five seconds. After this point, we will return the value using the `Result` property of the `DoWorkEventArgs` type:

```
private void ProcessNumbersBackgroundWorker_DoWork(object sender,
  DoWorkEventArgs e)
{
  // Get the incoming AddParam object.
  AddParams args = (AddParams)e.Argument;

  // Artificial lag.
  System.Threading.Thread.Sleep(5000);

  // Return the value.
  e.Result = args.a + args.b;
}
```

Finally, once the `BackgroundWorker` type has exited the scope of the `DoWork` handler, the `RunWorkerCompleted` event will fire. Our registered handler will simply display the result of the operation using the `RunWorkerCompletedEventArgs.Result` property:

```
private void ProcessNumbersBackgroundWorker_RunWorkerCompleted(
  object sender, RunWorkerCompletedEventArgs e)
{
  MessageBox.Show(e.Result.ToString(), "Your result is");
}
```

If you were to now run your application, you will find that while the data is being processed, the thread hosting the UI is still completely responsive (for example, the window can be resized, moved, minimized, etc.). If you wish to accentuate this point, you might want to add a new `TextBox` to the form and verify you are able to enter data within the UI area while the five-second addition operation performs asynchronously in the background.

■ **Source Code** The WinFormsBackgroundWorkerThread project is included under the Chapter 18 subdirectory.

That wraps up our examination of multithreaded programming under .NET. To be sure, the `System.Threading` namespace defines numerous types beyond what I had the space to cover in this chapter. Nevertheless, at this point you should have a solid foundation to build on.

Summary

This chapter began by examining how .NET delegate types can be configured to execute a method in an asynchronous manner. As you have seen, the `BeginInvoke()` and `EndInvoke()` methods allow you to indirectly manipulate a background thread with minimum fuss and bother. During this discussion, you were also introduced to the `IAsyncResult` interface and `AsyncResult` class type. As you learned, these types provide various ways to synchronize the calling thread and obtain possible method return values.

The remainder of this chapter examined the role of the `System.Threading` namespace. As you learned, when an application creates additional threads of execution, the result is that the program in question is able to carry out numerous tasks at (what appears to be) the same time. You also examined several manners in which you can protect thread-sensitive blocks of code to ensure that shared resources do not become unusable units of bogus data.

This chapter also pointed out that the CLR maintains an internal pool of threads for the purposes of performance and convenience. Last but not least, you examined the use of the `BackgroundWorker` type, which allows you to easily spin up new threads of execution within a GUI-based application.

CHAPTER 19

Understanding CIL and the Role of Dynamic Assemblies

The goal of this chapter is twofold. In the first half, you will have a chance to examine the syntax and semantics of the common intermediate language (CIL) in much greater detail than in previous chapters. Now, to be perfectly honest, you are able to live a happy and productive life as a .NET programmer without concerning yourself too much with the details of CIL code. However, once you learn the basics of CIL, you will gain a much deeper understanding of how some of the "magical" aspects of .NET (such as cross-language inheritance) actually work.

In the remainder of this chapter, you will examine the role of the `System.Reflection.Emit` namespace. Using these types, you are able to build software that is capable of generating .NET assemblies in memory at runtime. Formally speaking, assemblies defined and executed in memory are termed *dynamic assemblies*. As you might guess, this particular aspect of .NET development requires you to speak the language of CIL, given that you will be required to specify the CIL instruction set that will be used during the assembly's construction.

Reflecting on the Nature of CIL Programming

CIL is the true mother tongue of the .NET platform. When you build a .NET assembly using your managed language of choice (C#, VB, COBOL.NET, etc.), the associated compiler translates your source code into terms of CIL. Like any programming language, CIL provides numerous structural and implementation-centric tokens. Given that CIL is just another .NET programming language, it should come as no surprise that it is possible to build your .NET assemblies directly using CIL and the CIL compiler (`ilasm.exe`) that ships with the .NET Framework 3.5 SDK.

Now while it is true that few programmers would choose to build an entire .NET application directly with CIL, CIL is still an extremely interesting intellectual pursuit. Simply put, the more you understand the grammar of CIL, the better able you are to move into the realm of advanced .NET development. By way of some concrete examples, individuals who possess an understanding of CIL are capable of the following:

- Talking intelligently about how different .NET programming languages map their respective keywords to CIL tokens.
- Disassembling an existing .NET assembly, editing the CIL code, and recompiling the updated code base into a modified .NET binary.
- Building dynamic assemblies using the `System.Reflection.Emit` namespace.

- Leveraging aspects of the CTS that are not supported by higher-level managed languages, but do exist at the level of CIL. To be sure, CIL is the only .NET language that allows you to access each and every aspect of the CTS. For example, using raw CIL, you are able to define global-level members and fields (which are not permissible in C#).

Again, to be perfectly clear, if you choose *not* to concern yourself with the details of CIL code, you are absolutely able to gain mastery of C# and the .NET base class libraries. In many ways, knowledge of CIL is analogous to a C(++) programmer's understanding of assembly language. Those who know the ins and outs of the low-level "goo" are able to create rather advanced solutions for the task at hand and gain a deeper understanding of the underlying programming (and runtime) environment. So, if you are up for the challenge, let's begin to examine the details of CIL.

■ **Note** Understand that this chapter is not intended to be a comprehensive treatment of the syntax and semantics of CIL. If you require a full examination of the topic, check out *CIL Programming: Under the Hood of .NET* by Jason Bock (Apress, 2002).

Examining CIL Directives, Attributes, and Opcodes

When you begin to investigate low-level languages such as CIL, you are guaranteed to find new (and often intimidating-sounding) names for very familiar concepts. For example, at this point in the text, if you were shown the following set of items:

```
{new, public, this, base, get, set, explicit, unsafe, enum, operator, partial}
```

you would most certainly understand them to be keywords of the C# language (which is correct). However, if you look more closely at the members of this set, you may be able to see that while each item is indeed a C# keyword, it has radically different semantics. For example, the `enum` keyword defines a `System.Enum`-derived type, while the `this` and `base` keywords allow you to reference the current object or the object's parent class, respectively. The `unsafe` keyword is used to establish a block of code that cannot be directly monitored by the CLR, while the `operator` keyword allows you to build a hidden (specially named) method that will be called when you apply a specific C# operator (such as the plus sign).

In stark contrast to a higher-level language such as C#, CIL does not just simply define a generic set of keywords, *per se*. Rather, the token set understood by the CIL compiler is subdivided into three broad categories based on semantics:

- CIL directives
- CIL attributes
- CIL operation codes (opcodes)

Each category of CIL token is expressed using a particular syntax, and the tokens are combined to build a valid .NET assembly.

The Role of CIL Directives

First up, we have a set of well-known CIL tokens that are used to describe the overall structure of a .NET assembly. These tokens are called *directives*. CIL directives are used to inform the CIL compiler how to define the namespaces(s), type(s), and member(s) that will populate an assembly.

Directives are represented syntactically using a single dot (`.`) prefix (e.g., `.namespace`, `.class`, `.publickeytoken`, `.method`, `.assembly`, etc.). Thus, if your `*.il` file (the conventional extension for a file containing CIL code) has a single `.namespace` directive and three `.class` directives, the CIL compiler will generate an assembly that defines a single .NET namespace containing three .NET class types.

The Role of CIL Attributes

In many cases, CIL directives in and of themselves are not descriptive enough to fully express the definition of a given .NET type or type member. Given this fact, many CIL directives can be further specified with various CIL *attributes* to qualify how a directive should be processed. For example, the `.class` directive can be adorned with the `public` attribute (to establish the type visibility), the `extends` attribute (to explicitly specify the type's base class), and the `implements` attribute (to list the set of interfaces supported by the type).

The Role of CIL Opcodes

Once a .NET assembly, namespace, and type set have been defined in terms of CIL using various directives and related attributes, the final remaining task is to provide the type's implementation logic. This is a job for *operation codes*, or simply *opcodes*. In the tradition of other low-level languages, many CIL opcodes tend to be cryptic and completely unpronounceable by us mere humans. For example, if you need to define a string variable, you don't use a friendly opcode named `LoadString`, but rather `ldstr`.

Now, to be fair, some CIL opcodes do map quite naturally to their C# counterparts (e.g., `box`, `unbox`, `throw`, and `sizeof`). As you will see, the opcodes of CIL are always used within the scope of a member's implementation, and unlike CIL directives, they are never written with a dot prefix.

The CIL Opcode/CIL Mnemonic Distinction

As just explained, opcodes such as `ldstr` are used to implement the members of a given type. In reality, however, tokens such as `ldstr` are *CIL mnemonics* for the actual *binary CIL opcodes*. To clarify the distinction, assume you have authored the following method in C#:

```
static int Add(int x, int y)
{
  return x + y;
}
```

The act of adding two numbers is expressed in terms of the CIL opcode `0X58`. In a similar vein, subtracting two numbers is expressed using the opcode `0X59`, and the act of allocating a new object on the managed heap is achieved using the `0X73` opcode. Given this reality, understand that the "CIL code" processed by a JIT compiler is actually nothing more than blobs of binary data.

Thankfully, for each binary opcode of CIL, there is a corresponding mnemonic. For example, the `add` mnemonic can be used rather than `0X58`, `sub` rather than `0X59`, and `newobj` rather than `0X73`. Given this opcode/mnemonic distinction, realize that CIL decompilers such as `ildasm.exe` translate an assembly's binary opcodes into their corresponding CIL mnemonics. For example, here would be the CIL presented by `ildasm.exe` for the previous C# `Add()` method:

```
.method private hidebysig static int32  Add(int32 x,
 int32 y) cil managed
{
 // Code size    9 (0x9)
 .maxstack 2
 .locals init ([0] int32 CS$1$0000)
```

```
  IL_0000: nop
  IL_0001: ldarg.0
  IL_0002: ldarg.1
  IL_0003: add
  IL_0004: stloc.0
  IL_0005: br.s    IL_0007
  IL_0007: ldloc.0
  IL_0008: ret
} // end of method MathStuff::Add
```

Unless you're building some extremely low-level .NET software (such as a custom managed compiler), you'll never need to concern yourself with the literal numeric binary opcodes of CIL. For all practical purposes, when .NET programmers speak about "CIL opcodes" they're referring to the set of friendly string token mnemonics (as I've done within this text, and will do for the remainder of this chapter) rather than the underlying numerical values.

Pushing and Popping: The Stack-Based Nature of CIL

Higher-level .NET languages (such as C#) attempt to hide low-level CIL grunge from view as much as possible. One aspect of .NET development that is particularly well hidden is the fact that CIL is a stack-based programming language. Recall from our examination of the collection namespaces (see Chapter 10) that the `System.Collections.Stack` type can be used to push a value onto a stack as well as pop the topmost value off of the stack for use. Of course, CIL developers do not literally use an object of type `System.Collections.Stack` to load and unload the values to be evaluated; however, the same pushing and popping mind-set still applies.

Formally speaking, the entity used to hold a set of values to be evaluated is termed the *virtual execution stack*. As you will see, CIL provides a number of opcodes that are used to push a value onto the stack; this process is termed *loading*. As well, CIL defines a number of additional opcodes that transfer the topmost value on the stack into memory (such as a local variable) using a process termed *storing*.

In the world of CIL, it is impossible to access a point of data directly, including locally defined variables, incoming method arguments, or field data of a type. Rather, you are required to explicitly load the item onto the stack, only to then pop it off for later use (keep this point in mind, as it will help explain why a given block of CIL code can look a bit redundant).

■ **Note** Recall that CIL is not directly executed, but compiled on demand. During the compilation of CIL code, many of these implementation redundancies are optimized away. Furthermore, if you enable the code optimization option for your current project (using the Build tab of the Visual Studio Project Properties window), the compiler will also remove various CIL redundancies.

To understand how CIL leverages a stack-based processing model, consider a simple C# method, `PrintMessage()`, which takes no arguments and returns `void`. Within the implementation of this method, you will simply print out the value of a local string variable to the standard output stream:

```
public void PrintMessage()
{
  string myMessage = "Hello.";
  Console.WriteLine(myMessage);
}
```

If you were to examine how the C# compiler translates this method in terms of CIL, you would first find that the PrintMessage() method defines a storage slot for a local variable using the .locals directive. The local string is then loaded and stored in this local variable using the ldstr (load string) and stloc.0 opcodes (which can be read as "store the current value in a local variable at index zero").

The value (again, at index 0) is then loaded into memory using the ldloc.0 ("load the local argument at index 0") opcode for use by the System.Console.WriteLine() method invocation (specified using the call opcode). Finally, the function returns via the ret opcode. Here is the (annotated) CIL code for the PrintMessage() method:

```
.method public hidebysig instance void PrintMessage() cil managed
{
  .maxstack  1
  // Define a local string variable (at index 0).
  .locals init ([0] string myMessage)
  // Load a string on to the stack with the value "Hello."
  ldstr  " Hello."
  // Store string value on the stack in the local variable.
  stloc.0
  // Load the value at index 0.
  ldloc.0
  // Call method with current value.
  call  void [mscorlib]System.Console::WriteLine(string)
  ret
}
```

■ **Note** As you can see, CIL supports code comments using the double-slash syntax (as well as the /*...*/ syntax, for that matter). As in C#, code comments are completely ignored by the CIL compiler.

Now that you have the basics of CIL in your mind, let's see a practical use of CIL programming, beginning with the topic of "round-trip engineering."

Understanding Round-Trip Engineering

You are aware of how to use ildasm.exe to view the CIL code generated by the C# compiler (see Chapter 1). What you may not know, however, is that ildasm.exe allows you to dump the CIL contained within an assembly loaded into ildasm.exe to an external file. Once you have the CIL code at your disposal, you are free to edit and recompile the code base using the CIL compiler, ilasm.exe.

■ **Note** Also recall that reflector.exe can be used to view the CIL code of a given assembly, as well as to translate the CIL code into an approximate C# code base. However, if an assembly contains CIL constructs that do not have a C# equivalent, you will need to fall back on the use of ildasm.exe.

Formally speaking, this technique is termed *round-trip engineering*, and it can be useful under a number of circumstances:

- You need to modify an assembly for which you no longer have the source code.
- You are working with a less-than-perfect .NET language compiler that has emitted ineffective (or flat-out incorrect) CIL code, and you wish to modify the code base.

- You are building COM interoperability assemblies and wish to account for some IDL attributes that have been lost during the conversion process (such as the COM [helpstring] attribute).

To illustrate the process of round-tripping, begin by creating a new C# code file (HelloProgram.cs) using a simple text editor, and define the following class type (you are free to use Visual Studio 2008's Console Application project if you wish; however, be sure to delete the AssemblyInfo.cs file to decrease the amount of generated CIL code):

```
// A simple C# console app.
using System;

class Program
{
  static void Main(string[] args)
  {
    Console.WriteLine("Hello CIL code!");
    Console.ReadLine();
  }
}
```

Save your file to a convenient location (for example, C:\HelloCilCode) and compile your program using csc.exe:

```
csc HelloProgram.cs
```

Now, open HelloProgram.exe with ildasm.exe and, using the File ➤ Dump menu option, save the raw CIL code to a new *.il file (HelloProgram.il) in the same folder containing your compiled assembly (all of the default values of the resulting dialog box are fine as is).

■ **Note** ildasm.exe will also generate a *.res file when dumping the contents of an assembly to file. These resource files can be ignored (and deleted) throughout this chapter, as we will not be making use of them.

Now you are able to view this file using your text editor of choice. Here is the (slightly reformatted and annotated) result:

```
// Referenced Assemblies.
.assembly extern mscorlib
{
  .publickeytoken = (B7 7A 5C 56 19 34 E0 89 )
  .ver 2:0:0:0
}

// Our assembly.
.assembly HelloProgram
{
  .hash algorithm 0x00008004
  .ver 0:0:0:0
}
.module HelloProgram.exe
.imagebase 0x00400000
.file alignment 0x00000200
.stackreserve 0x00100000
.subsystem 0x0003
.corflags 0x00000001
```

```
// Definition of Program class.
.class private auto ansi beforefieldinit Program
  extends [mscorlib]System.Object
{
  .method private hidebysig static void  Main(string[] args) cil managed
  {
    // Marks this method as the entry point of the
    // executable.
    .entrypoint
    .maxstack  8
    IL_0000:  nop
    IL_0001:  ldstr  "Hello CIL code!"
    IL_0006:  call void [mscorlib]System.Console::WriteLine(string)
    IL_000b:  nop
    IL_000c:  call string [mscorlib]System.Console::ReadLine()
    IL_0011:  pop
    IL_0012:  ret
  }

  // The default constructor.
  .method public hidebysig specialname rtspecialname
    instance void  .ctor() cil managed
  {
    .maxstack  8
    IL_0000:  ldarg.0
    IL_0001:  call instance void [mscorlib]System.Object::.ctor()
    IL_0006:  ret
  }
}
```

First, notice that the `*.il` file opens by declaring each externally referenced assembly the current assembly is compiled against. Here, you can see a single `.assembly extern` token set for the always present `mscorlib.dll`. Of course, if your class library made use of types within other referenced assemblies, you would find additional `.assembly extern` directives.

Next, you find the formal definition of your `HelloProgram.exe` assembly, which has been assigned a default version of 0.0.0.0 (given that you did not specify a value using the `[AssemblyVersion]` attribute). The assembly is further described using various CIL directives (such as `.module`, `.imagebase`, and so forth).

After documenting the externally referenced assemblies and defining the current assembly, you find a definition of the `Program` type. Note that the `.class` directive has various attributes (many of which are actually optional) such as `extends`, which marks the base class of the type:

```
.class private auto ansi beforefieldinit Program
  extends [mscorlib]System.Object
{ ... }
```

The bulk of the CIL code represents the implementation of the class's default constructor and the `Main()` method, both of which are defined (in part) with the `.method` directive. Once the members have been defined using the correct directives and attributes, they are implemented using various opcodes.

It is critical to understand that when interacting with .NET types (such as `System.Console`) in CIL, you will *always* need to use the type's fully qualified name. Furthermore, the type's fully qualified name must *always* be prefixed with the friendly name of the defining assembly (in square brackets). Consider the CIL implementation of `Main()`:

```
.method private hidebysig static void  Main(string[] args) cil managed
{
  .entrypoint
  .maxstack  8
  IL_0000:  nop
  IL_0001:  ldstr "Hello CIL code!"
  IL_0006:  call void [mscorlib]System.Console::WriteLine(string)
  IL_000b:  nop
  IL_000c:  call string [mscorlib]System.Console::ReadLine()
  IL_0011:  pop
  IL_0012:  ret
}
```

The implementation of the default constructor in terms of CIL code makes use of yet another "load-centric" instruction (`ldarg.0`). In this case, the value loaded onto the stack is not a custom variable specified by us, but the current object reference (more details on this later). Also note that the default constructor explicitly makes a call to the base class constructor:

```
.method public hidebysig specialname rtspecialname
  instance void  .ctor() cil managed
{
  .maxstack  8
  IL_0000:  ldarg.0
  IL_0001:  call instance void [mscorlib]System.Object::.ctor()
  IL_0006:  ret
}
```

The Role of CIL Code Labels

One thing you certainly have noticed is that each line of implementation code is prefixed with a token of the form `IL_`*XXX*`:` (e.g., `IL_0000:`, `IL_0001:`, and so on). These tokens are called *code labels* and may be named in any manner you choose (provided they are not duplicated within the same member scope). When you dump an assembly to file using `ildasm.exe`, it will automatically generate code labels that follow an `IL_`*XXX*`:` naming convention. However, you may change them to reflect a more descriptive marker:

```
.method private hidebysig static void  Main(string[] args) cil managed
{
  .entrypoint
  .maxstack  8
  Nothing_1:  nop
  Load_String:  ldstr  "Hello CIL code!"
  PrintToConsole: call void [mscorlib]System.Console::WriteLine(string)
  Nothing_2:  nop
  WaitFor_KeyPress: call string [mscorlib]System.Console::ReadLine()
  RemoveValueFromStack:  pop
  Leave_Function:  ret
}
```

The truth of the matter is that most code labels are completely optional. The only time code labels are truly mandatory is when you are authoring CIL code that makes use of various branching or looping constructs, as you can specify where to direct the flow of logic via these code labels. For our current example, you can remove these autogenerated labels altogether with no ill effect:

```
.method private hidebysig static void  Main(string[] args) cil managed
{
  .entrypoint
```

```
  .maxstack  8
  nop
  ldstr  "Hello CIL code!"
  call void [mscorlib]System.Console::WriteLine(string)
  nop
  call string [mscorlib]System.Console::ReadLine()
  pop
  ret
}
```

Interacting with CIL: Modifying an *.il File

Now that you have a better understanding of how a basic CIL file is composed, let's complete our round-tripping experiment. The goal here is to update the CIL within the existing `*.il` file as follows:

- Add a reference to the `System.Windows.Forms.dll` assembly.
- Load a local string within `Main()`.
- Call the `System.Windows.Forms.MessageBox.Show()` method using the local string variable as an argument.

The first step is to add a new `.assembly` directive (qualified with the `extern` attribute) that specifies your assembly requires the `System.Windows.Forms.dll` assembly. To do so, update the `*.il` file with the following logic after the external reference to `mscorlib`:

```
.assembly extern System.Windows.Forms
{
  .publickeytoken = (B7 7A 5C 56 19 34 E0 89)
  .ver 2:0:0:0
}
```

Be aware that the value assigned to the `.ver` directive may differ depending on which version of the .NET platform you have installed on your development machine. Here, you see that `System.Windows.Forms.dll` version 2.0.0.0 is used and has the public key token of B77A5C561934E089. If you open the GAC (see Chapter 15) and locate your version of the `System.Windows.Forms.dll` assembly, you can simply copy the correct version and public key token value through the assembly's Properties page (via a right-click of your mouse).

Next, you need to alter the current implementation of the `Main()` method. Locate this method within the `*.il` file and remove the current implementation code (the `.maxstack` and `.entrypoint` directives should remain intact; I'll describe them later):

```
.method private hidebysig static void  Main(string[] args) cil managed
{
  .entrypoint
  .maxstack  8
  // ToDo: Write new CIL code!
}
```

Again, the goal is to push a new string onto the stack and call the `MessageBox.Show()` method (rather than the `Console.WriteLine()` method). Recall that when you specify the name of an external type, you must make use of the type's fully qualified name (in conjunction with the friendly name of the assembly). Keeping this in mind, update the `Main()` method as follows:

```
.method private hidebysig static void Main(string[] args) cil managed
{
  .entrypoint
```

```
  .maxstack  8
  ldstr  "CIL is way cool"
  call valuetype [System.Windows.Forms]
    System.Windows.Forms.DialogResult
    [System.Windows.Forms]
    System.Windows.Forms.MessageBox::Show(string)
  pop
  ret
}
```

In effect, you have just updated the CIL code to correspond to the following C# class definition:

```
class Program
{
  static void Main(string[] args)
  {
    System.Windows.Forms.MessageBox.Show("CIL is way cool");
  }
}
```

Compiling CIL Code Using ilasm.exe

Assuming you have saved this modified `*.il` file, you can compile a new .NET assembly using the `ilasm.exe` (CIL compiler) utility. While the CIL compiler has numerous command-line options (all of which can be seen by specifying the -? option), Table 19-1 shows the core flags of interest.

Table 19-1. *Common* `ilasm.exe` *Command-Line Flags*

Flag	Meaning in Life
`/debug`	Includes debug information (such as local variable and argument names, as well as line numbers).
`/dll`	Produces a `*.dll` file as output.
`/exe`	Produces an `*.exe` file as output. This is the default setting and may be omitted.
`/key`	Compiles the assembly with a strong name using a given `*.snk` file.
`/noautoinherit`	Prevents class types from automatically inheriting from `System.Object` when a specific base class is not defined.
`/output`	Specifies the output file name and extension. If you do not make use of the `/output` flag, the resulting file name (minus the file extension) is the same as the name of the first source file.

To compile your updated `HelloProgram.il` file into a new .NET `*.exe`, you can issue the following command within a Visual Studio 2008 command prompt:

```
ilasm /exe HelloProgram.il /output=NewAssembly.exe
```

Assuming things have worked successfully, you will see the report shown in Figure 19-1.

```
Administrator: Visual Studio 2008 Beta 2 Command Prompt

C:\Chapter 19\HelloCilCode>ilasm /exe HelloProgram.il /output=NewAssembly.exe

Microsoft (R) .NET Framework IL Assembler.  Version 2.0.50727.1378
Copyright (c) Microsoft Corporation.  All rights reserved.
Assembling 'HelloProgram.il'  to EXE --> 'NewAssembly.exe'
Source file is UTF-8

Assembled method Program::Main
Assembled method Program::.ctor
Creating PE file

Emitting classes:
Class 1:        Program

Emitting fields and methods:
Global
Class 1 Methods: 2;

Emitting events and properties:
Global
Class 1
Writing PE file
Operation completed successfully

C:\Chapter 19\HelloCilCode>_
```

Figure 19-1. *Compiling* `*.il` *files using* `ilasm.exe`

At this point, you can run your new application. Sure enough, rather than showing a message within the console window, you will now see a message box displaying your message (see Figure 19-2).

Figure 19-2. *The result of the round-trip*

Compiling CIL Code Using SharpDevelop

When working with `*.il` files, you may wish to make use of the freely available SharpDevelop IDE (see Chapter 2). When you create a new solution (via the File ➤ New Solution menu option), one of your choices is to create a CIL project workspace (see Figure 19-3).

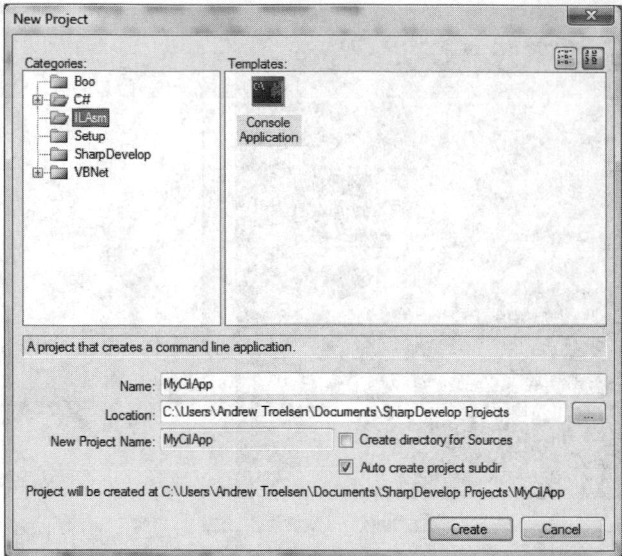

Figure 19-3. *The SharpDevelop CIL project template*

While SharpDevelop does not have IntelliSense support for CIL projects, CIL tokens are color-coded, and you are able to compile and run your application directly within the IDE (rather than running `ilasm.exe` from a command prompt). Consider Figure 19-4.

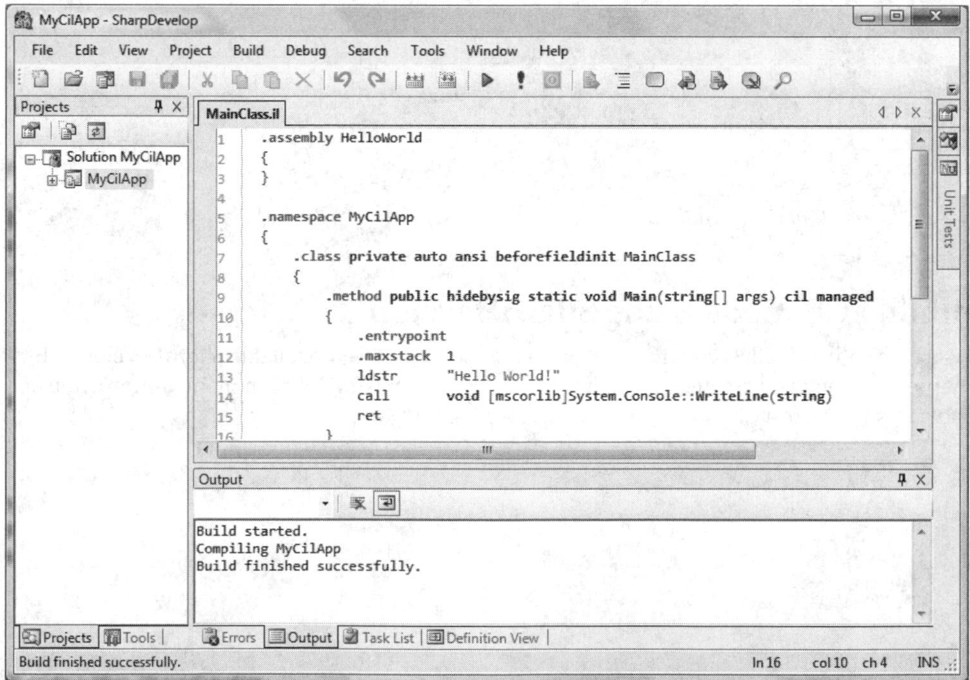

Figure 19-4. *Authoring CIL code within SharpDevelop*

The Role of peverify.exe

When you are building or modifying assemblies using CIL code, it is always advisable to verify that the compiled binary image is a well-formed .NET image using the `peverify.exe` command-line tool:

```
peverify MyNewAssembly.exe
```

This tool will examine all opcodes within the specified assembly for valid CIL code. For example, in terms of CIL code, the evaluation stack must always be empty before exiting a function. If you forget to pop off any remaining values, the `ilasm.exe` compiler will still generate a valid assembly (given that compilers are concerned only with *syntax*). `peverify.exe`, on the other hand, is concerned with *semantics*. If you did forget to clear the stack before exiting a given function, `peverify.exe` will let you know before you try running your code base.

■ **Source Code** The HelloCilCode example is included under the Chapter 19 subdirectory.

Understanding CIL Directives and Attributes

Now that you have seen how `ildasm.exe` and `ilasm.exe` can be used to perform a round-trip, we can get down to the business of checking out the syntax and semantics of CIL itself. The next sections will walk you through the process of authoring a custom namespace containing a set of types. However, to keep things simple, these types will not contain any implementation logic for their members. Once you understand how to create empty types, you can then turn your attention to the process of providing "real" members using CIL opcodes.

Specifying Externally Referenced Assemblies in CIL

Create a new file named `CilTypes.il` using your editor of choice. The first task a CIL project will require is to list the set of external assemblies used by the current assembly. For this example, you will only make use of types found within `mscorlib.dll`. To do so, the `.assembly` directive will be qualified using the `external` attribute. When you are referencing a strongly named assembly, such as `mscorlib.dll`, you'll want to specify the `.publickeytoken` and `.ver` directives as well:

```
.assembly extern mscorlib
{
  .publickeytoken = (B7 7A 5C 56 19 34 E0 89 )
  .ver 2:0:0:0
}
```

■ **Note** Strictly speaking, you are not required to explicitly reference `mscorlib.dll` as an external reference, as `ilasm.exe` will do so automatically.

Defining the Current Assembly in CIL

The next order of business is to define the assembly you are interested in building using the `.assembly` directive. At the simplest level, an assembly can be defined by specifying the friendly name of the binary:

```
// Our assembly.
.assembly CILTypes { }
```

While this indeed defines a new .NET assembly, you will typically place additional directives within the scope of the assembly declaration. For this example, update your assembly definition to include a version number of 1.0.0.0 using the `.ver` directive (note that each numerical identifier is separated by *colons*, not the C#-centric dot notation):

```
// Our assembly.
.assembly CILTypes
{
  .ver 1:0:0:0
}
```

Given that the `CILTypes` assembly is a single-file assembly, you will finish up the assembly definition using a single `.module` directive, which marks the official name of your .NET binary, `CILTypes.dll`:

```
.assembly CILTypes
{
 .ver 1:0:0:0
}
// The module of our single-file assembly.
.module CILTypes.dll
```

In addition to `.assembly` and `.module` are CIL directives that further qualify the overall structure of the .NET binary you are composing. Table 19-2 lists a few of the more common assembly-level directives.

Table 19-2. *Additional Assembly-Centric Directives*

Directive	Meaning in Life
`.mresources`	If your assembly makes use of internal resources (such as bitmaps or string tables), this directive is used to identify the name of the file that contains the resources to be embedded.
`.subsystem`	This CIL directive is used to establish the preferred UI that the assembly wishes to execute within. For example, a value of `2` signifies that the assembly should run within a Forms-based GUI, whereas a value of `3` denotes a console executable.

Defining Namespaces in CIL

Now that you have defined the look and feel of your assembly (and the required external references), you can create a .NET namespace (`MyNamespace`) using the `.namespace` directive:

```
// Our assembly has a single namespace.
.namespace MyNamespace {}
```

Like C#, CIL namespace definitions can be nested within further namespaces. We have no need to define a root namespace here; however, for the sake of argument, assume you wish to create a root namespace named `Intertech`:

```
.namespace Intertech
{
  .namespace MyNamespace {}
}
```

Like C#, CIL allows you to define a nested namespace as follows:

```
// Defining a nested namespace.
.namespace Intertech.MyNamespace{}
```

Defining Class Types in CIL

Empty namespaces are not very interesting, so let's now check out the process of defining a class type using CIL. Not surprisingly, the `.class` directive is used to define a new class type. However, this simple directive can be adorned with numerous additional attributes, to further qualify the nature of the type. To illustrate, add a public class to your namespace named `MyBaseClass`. As in C#, if you do not specify an explicit base class, your type will automatically be derived from `System.Object`, unless you compile the `*.il` code by specifying the `/noautoinherit` option of `ilasm.exe`.

```
.namespace MyNamespace
{
  // System.Object base class assumed.
  .class public MyBaseClass {}
}
```

When you are building a class type that derives from any class other than `System.Object`, you make use of the `extends` attribute. Whenever you need to reference a type defined within the same assembly, CIL demands that you also make use of the fully qualified name (however, if the base type is within the same assembly, you can omit the assembly's friendly name prefix). Therefore, the following attempt to extend `MyBaseClass` results in a compiler error:

```
// This will not compile!
.namespace MyNamespace
{
  .class public MyBaseClass {}

  .class public MyDerivedClass
    extends MyBaseClass {}
}
```

To correctly define the parent class of `MyDerivedClass`, you must specify the full name of `MyBaseClass` as follows:

```
// Better!
.namespace MyNamespace
{
  .class public MyBaseClass {}

  .class public MyDerivedClass
    extends MyNamespace.MyBaseClass {}
}
```

In addition to the `public` and `extends` attributes, a CIL class definition may take numerous additional qualifiers that control the type's visibility, field layout, and so on. Table 19-3 illustrates some (but not all) of the attributes that may be used in conjunction with the `.class` directive.

Table 19-3. *Various Attributes Used in Conjunction with the* `.class` *Directive*

Attributes	Meaning in Life
`public`, `private`, `nested assembly`, `nested famandassem`, `nested family`, `nested famorassem`, `nested public`, `nested private`	CIL defines various attributes that are used to specify the visibility of a given type. As you can see, raw CIL offers numerous possibilities other than those offered by C#.
`abstract`, `sealed`	These two attributes may be tacked onto a `.class` directive to define an abstract class or sealed class, respectively.
`auto`, `sequential`, `explicit`	These attributes are used to instruct the CLR how to lay out field data in memory. For class types, the default layout flag (`auto`) is appropriate.
`extends`, `implements`	These attributes allow you to define the base class of a type (via `extends`) or implement an interface on a type (via `implements`).

Defining and Implementing Interfaces in CIL

As odd as it may seem, interface types are defined in CIL using the `.class` directive. However, when the `.class` directive is adorned with the `interface` attribute, the type is realized as a CTS interface type. Once an interface has been defined, it may be bound to a class or structure type using the CIL `implements` attribute:

```
.namespace MyNamespace
{
  // An interface definition.
  .class public interface IMyInterface {}
  .class public MyBaseClass {}

  // MyDerivedClass now implements IAmAnInterface.
  .class public MyDerivedClass
    extends MyNamespace.MyBaseClass
    implements MyNamespace.IMyInterface {}
}
```

As you recall from Chapter 9, interfaces can function as the base interface to other interface types in order to build interface hierarchies. However, contrary to what you might be thinking, the `extends` attribute cannot be used to derive interface A from interface B. The `extends` attribute is used only to qualify a type's base class. When you wish to extend an interface, you will make use of the `implements` attribute yet again:

```
// Extending interfaces in terms of CIL.
.class public interface IMyInterface {}
.class public interface IMyOtherInterface
  implements MyNamespace.IMyInterface {}
```

Defining Structures in CIL

The `.class` directive can be used to define a CTS structure if the type extends `System.ValueType`. As well, the `.class` directive is qualified with the `sealed` attribute (given that structures can never be a base structure to other value types). If you attempt to do otherwise, `ilasm.exe` will issue a compiler error.

```
// A structure definition is always sealed.
.class public sealed MyStruct
  extends [mscorlib]System.ValueType{}
```

Do be aware that CIL provides a shorthand notation to define a structure type. If you use the value attribute, the new type will derive the type from [mscorlib]System.ValueType automatically. Therefore, you could define MyStruct as follows:

```
// Shorthand notation for declaring a structure.
.class public sealed value MyStruct{}
```

Defining Enums in CIL

.NET enumerations (as you recall) derive from System.Enum, which is a System.ValueType (and therefore must also be sealed). When you wish to define an enum in terms of CIL, simply extend [mscorlib]System.Enum:

```
// An enum.
.class public sealed MyEnum
  extends [mscorlib]System.Enum{}
```

Like a structure definition, enumerations can be defined with a shorthand notation using the enum attribute:

```
// Enum shorthand.
.class public sealed enum MyEnum{}
```

You'll see how to specify the name/value pairs of an enumeration in just a moment.

■ **Note** The other fundamental .NET type, the delegate, also has a specific CIL representation. See Chapter 11 for full details.

Defining Generics in CIL

Generic types also have a specific representation in the syntax of CIL. Recall from Chapter 10 that a given generic type or generic member may have one or more type parameters. For example, the List<T> type has a single type parameter, while Dictionary<TKey, TValue> has two. In terms of CIL, the number of type parameters is specified using a backward-leaning single tick, `, followed by a numerical value representing the number of type parameters. Like C#, the actual value of the type parameters is encased within angled brackets.

■ **Note** On most keyboards, the ` character can be found on the key above the Tab key (and to the left of the 1 key).

For example, assume you wish to create a List<T> type, where T is of type System.Int32. In CIL, you would author the following:

```
// In C#: List<int> myInts = new List<int>();
newobj instance void class [mscorlib]
  System.Collections.Generic.List`1<int32>::.ctor()
```

Notice that this generic class is defined as `List`1<int32>`, as `List<T>` has a single type parameter. However, if you needed to define a `Dictionary<string, int>`type, you would do so as the following:

```
// In C#: Dictionary<string, int> d = new Dictionary<string, int>();
newobj instance void class [mscorlib]
System.Collections.Generic.Dictionary`2<string,int32>::.ctor()
```

As another example, if you have a generic type that uses another generic type as a type parameter, you would author CIL code such as the following:

```
// In C#: List<List<int>> myInts = new List<List<int>>();
newobj instance void class [mscorlib]
 System.Collections.Generic.List`1<class
  [mscorlib]System.Collections.Generic.List`1<int32>>::.ctor()
```

Finally, when you are authoring a class, a structure, or an interface that is itself generic, you would make use of this same syntax at the point of type declaration. For example:

```
// A custom generic class with 1 type parameter.
.class public MyGenericClass`1<T>{}
```

Compiling the CILTypes.il file

Even though you have not yet added any members or implementation code to the types you have defined, you are able to compile this `*.il` file into a .NET DLL assembly (which you must do, as you have not specified a `Main()` method). Open up a command prompt and enter the following command to `ilasm.exe`:

```
ilasm /dll CilTypes.il
```

Once you have done so, you are able to open your binary into `ildasm.exe` (see Figure 19-5).

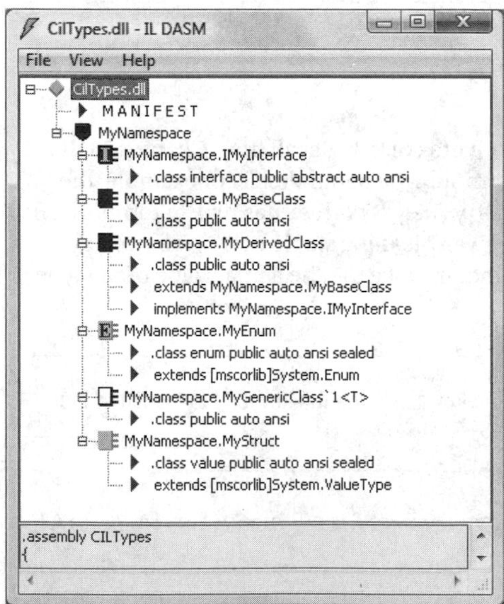

Figure 19-5. *The* `CILTypes.dll` *assembly*

Once you have confirmed the contents of your assembly, run peverify.exe against it. Notice that you are issued a number of errors, given that all your types are completely empty (see Figure 19-6).

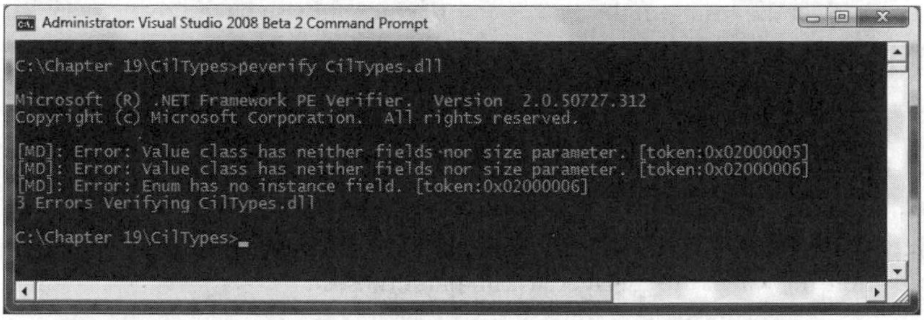

```
Administrator: Visual Studio 2008 Beta 2 Command Prompt
C:\Chapter 19\CilTypes>peverify CilTypes.dll

Microsoft (R) .NET Framework PE Verifier.  Version  2.0.50727.312
Copyright (c) Microsoft Corporation.  All rights reserved.

[MD]: Error: Value class has neither fields nor size parameter. [token:0x02000005]
[MD]: Error: Value class has neither fields nor size parameter. [token:0x02000006]
[MD]: Error: Enum has no instance field. [token:0x02000006]
3 Errors Verifying CilTypes.dll

C:\Chapter 19\CilTypes>
```

Figure 19-6. *Empty types yield verification errors!*

To understand how to populate a type with content, you first need to examine the fundamental data types of CIL.

.NET Base Class Library, C#, and CIL Data Type Mappings

Table 19-4 illustrates how a .NET base class type maps to the corresponding C# keyword, and how each C# keyword maps into raw CIL. As well, Table 19-4 documents the shorthand constant notations used for each CIL type. As you will see in just a moment, these constants are often referenced by numerous CIL opcodes.

Table 19-4. *Mapping .NET Base Class Types to C# Keywords, and C# Keywords to CIL*

.NET Base Class Type	C# Keyword	CIL Representation	CIL Constant Notation
System.SByte	sbyte	int8	I1
System.Byte	byte	unsigned int8	U1
System.Int16	short	int16	I2
System.UInt16	ushort	unsigned int16	U2
System.Int32	int	int32	I4
System.UInt32	uint	unsigned int32	U4
System.Int64	long	int64	I8
System.UInt64	ulong	unsigned int64	U8
System.Char	char	char	CHAR
System.Single	float	float32	R4
System.Double	double	float64	R8
System.Boolean	bool	bool	BOOLEAN
System.String	string	string	N/A
System.Object	object	object	N/A
System.Void	void	void	VOID

Defining Type Members in CIL

As you are already aware, .NET types may support various members. Enumerations have some set of name/value pairs. Structures and classes may have constructors, fields, methods, properties, static members, and so on. Over the course of this book's first 18 chapters, you have already seen partial CIL definitions for the items previously mentioned, but nevertheless, here is a quick recap of how various members map to CIL primitives.

Defining Field Data in CIL

Enumerations, structures, and classes can all support field data. In each case, the `.field` directive will be used. For example, let's breathe some life into the skeleton `MyEnum` enumeration and define three name/value pairs (note the values are specified within parentheses):

```
.class public sealed enum MyEnum
{
 .field public static literal valuetype
  MyNamespace.MyEnum A = int32(0)
 .field public static literal valuetype
  MyNamespace.MyEnum B = int32(1)
 .field public static literal valuetype
  MyNamespace.MyEnum C = int32(2)
}
```

Fields that reside within the scope of a .NET `System.Enum`-derived type are qualified using the `static` and `literal` attributes. As you would guess, these attributes set up the field data to be a fixed value accessible from the type itself (e.g., `MyEnum.NameOne`).

■ **Note** The values assigned to an enum value may also be in hexadecimal with an `0x` prefix.

Of course, when you wish to define a point of field data within a class or structure, you are not limited to a point of public static literal data. For example, you could update `MyBaseClass` to support two points of private, instance-level field data:

```
.class public MyBaseClass
{
  .field private string stringField
  .field private int32 intField
}
```

As in C#, class field data will automatically be initialized to an appropriate default value. If you wish to allow the object user to supply custom values at the time of creation for each of these points of private field data, you (of course) need to create custom constructors.

Defining Type Constructors in CIL

The CTS supports both instance-level and class-level (static) constructors. In terms of CIL, instance-level constructors are represented using the `.ctor` token, while a static-level constructor is expressed via `.cctor` (class constructor). Both of these CIL tokens must be qualified using the `rtspecialname` (return type special name) and `specialname` attributes. Simply put, these attributes are used to identify a specific CIL token that can be treated in unique ways by a given .NET language. For example, in C#, constructors do not define a return type; however, in terms of CIL, the return value of a constructor is indeed `void`:

```
.class public MyBaseClass
{
  .field private string stringField
  .field private int32 intField

  .method public hidebysig specialname rtspecialname
    instance void .ctor(string s, int32 i) cil managed
  {
    // TODO: Add implementation code...
  }
}
```

Note that the `.ctor` directive has been qualified with the `instance` attribute (as it is not a static constructor). The `cil managed` attributes denote that the scope of this method contains CIL code, rather than unmanaged code, which may be used during platform invocation requests.

Defining Properties in CIL

Properties and methods also have specific CIL representations. By way of an example, if `MyBaseClass` were updated to support a public property named `TheString`, you would author the following CIL (note again the use of the `specialname` attribute):

```
.class public MyBaseClass
{
...
  .method public hidebysig specialname
    instance string  get_TheString() cil managed
  {
    // TODO: Add implementation code...
  }

  .method public hidebysig specialname
    instance void  set_TheString(string 'value') cil managed
  {
    // TODO: Add implementation code...
  }

  .property instance string TheString()
  {
    .get instance string
      MyNamespace.MyBaseClass::get_TheString()
    .set instance void
      MyNamespace. MyBaseClass::set_TheString(string)
  }
}
```

Recall that in terms of CIL, a property maps to a pair of methods that take `get_` and `set_` prefixes. The `.property` directive makes use of the related `.get` and `.set` directives to map property syntax to the correct “specially named” methods.

■ **Note** Notice that the incoming parameter to the `set` method of a property is placed in single-tick quotation marks, which represents the name of the token to use on the right-hand side of the assignment operator within the method scope.

Defining Member Parameters

In a nutshell, specifying arguments in CIL is (more or less) identical to doing so in C#. For example, each argument is defined by specifying its data type followed by the parameter name. Furthermore, like C#, CIL provides a way to define input, output, and pass-by-reference parameters. As well, CIL allows you to define a parameter array argument (aka the C# `params` keyword) as well as optional parameters (which are not supported in C#, but are used in VB .NET).

To illustrate the process of defining parameters in raw CIL, assume you wish to build a method that takes an `int32` (by value), an `int32` (by reference), a `[mscorlib]System.Collection.ArrayList`, and a single output parameter (of type `int32`). In terms of C#, this method would look something like the following:

```
public static void MyMethod(int inputInt,
  ref int refInt, ArrayList ar, out int outputInt)
{
  outputInt = 0;  // Just to satisfy the C# compiler...
}
```

If you were to map this method into CIL terms, you would find that C# reference parameters are marked with an ampersand (&) suffixed to the parameter's underlying data type (`int32&`). Output parameters also make use of the `&` suffix, but they are further qualified using the CIL `[out]` token. Also notice that if the parameter is a reference type (in this case, the `[mscorlib]System.Collections.ArrayList` type), the `class` token is prefixed to the data type (not to be confused with the `.class` directive!):

```
.method public hidebysig static void  MyMethod(int32 inputInt,
  int32& refInt,
  class [mscorlib]System.Collections.ArrayList ar,
  [out] int32& outputInt) cil managed
{
  ...
}
```

Examining CIL Opcodes

The final aspect of CIL code you'll examine in this chapter has to do with the role of various operational codes (opcodes). Recall that an opcode is simply a CIL token used to build the implementation logic for a given member. The complete set of CIL opcodes (which is fairly large) can be grouped into the following broad categories:

- Opcodes that control program flow
- Opcodes that evaluate expressions
- Opcodes that access values in memory (via parameters, local variables, etc.)

To provide some insight to the world of member implementation via CIL, Table 19-5 defines some of the more useful opcodes that are directly related to member implementation logic, grouped by related functionality.

Table 19-5. *Various Implementation-Specific CIL Opcodes*

Opcodes	Meaning in Life
`add`, `sub`, `mul`, `div`, `rem`	These CIL opcodes allow you to add, subtract, multiply, and divide two values (`rem` returns the remainder of a division operation).
`and`, `or`, `not`, `xor`	These CIL opcodes allow you to perform binary operations on two values.
`ceq`, `cgt`, `clt`	These CIL opcodes allow you to compare two values on the stack in various manners, for example: `ceq`: Compare for equality `cgt`: Compare for greater than `clt`: Compare for less than
`box`, `unbox`	These CIL opcodes are used to convert between reference types and value types.
`ret`	This CIL opcode is used to exit a method and return a value to the caller (if necessary).
`beq`, `bgt`, `ble`, `blt`, `switch`	These CIL opcodes (in addition to many other related opcodes) are used to control branching logic within a method, for example: `beq`: Break to code label if equal `bgt`: Break to code label if greater than `ble`: Break to code label if less than or equal to `blt`: Break to code label if less than All of the branch-centric opcodes require that you specify a CIL code label to jump to if the result of the test is true.
`call`	This CIL opcode is used to call a member on a given type.
`nearer`, `newobj`	These CIL opcodes allow you to allocate a new array or new object type into memory (respectively).

The next broad category of CIL opcodes (a subset of which is shown in Table 19-6) are used to load (push) arguments onto the virtual execution stack. Note how these load-specific opcodes take an `ld` (load) prefix.

Table 19-6. *The Primary Stack-Centric Opcodes of CIL*

Opcode	Meaning in Life
`ldarg` (with numerous variations)	Loads a method's argument onto the stack. In addition to the general `ldarg` (which works in conjunction with a given index that identifies the argument), there are numerous other variations. For example, `ldarg` opcodes that have a numerical suffix (`ldarg_0`) hard-code which argument to load. As well, variations of the `ldarg` opcode allow you to hard-code the data type using the CIL constant notation shown in Table 19-4 (`ldarg_I4`, for an `int32`) as well as the data type and value (`ldarg_I4_5`, to load an `int32` with the value of `5`).
`ldc` (with numerous variations)	Loads a constant value onto the stack.
`ldfld` (with numerous variations)	Loads the value of an instance-level field onto the stack.
`ldloc` (with numerous variations)	Loads the value of a local variable onto the stack.
`ldobj`	Obtains all the values gathered by a heap-based object and places them on the stack.
`ldstr`	Loads a string value onto the stack.

In addition to the set of load-specific opcodes, CIL provides numerous opcodes that *explicitly* pop the topmost value off the stack. As shown over the first few examples in this chapter, popping a value off the stack typically involves storing the value into temporary local storage for further use (such as a parameter for an upcoming method invocation). Given this, note how many opcodes that pop the current value off the virtual execution stack take an `st` (store) prefix. Table 19-7 hits the highlights.

Table 19-7. *Various Pop-Centric Opcodes*

Opcode	Meaning in Life
`pop`	Removes the value currently on top of the evaluation stack, but does not bother to store the value
`starg`	Stores the value on top of the stack into the method argument at a specified index
`stloc` (with numerous variations)	Pops the current value from the top of the evaluation stack and stores it in a local variable list at a specified index
`stobj`	Copies a value of a specified type from the evaluation stack into a supplied memory address
`stsfld`	Replaces the value of a static field with a value from the evaluation stack

Do be aware that various CIL opcodes will *implicitly* pop values off the stack to perform the task at hand. For example, if you are attempting to subtract two numbers using the `sub` opcode, it should be clear that `sub` will have to pop off the next two available values before it can perform the calculation. Once the calculation is complete, the result of the value (surprise, surprise) is pushed onto the stack once again.

The .maxstack Directive

When you write method implementations using raw CIL, you need to be mindful of a special directive named `.maxstack`. As its name suggests, `.maxstack` establishes the maximum number of variables that may be pushed onto the stack at any given time during the execution of the method. The good news is that the `.maxstack` directive has a default value (`8`), which should be safe for a vast majority of methods you may be authoring. However, if you wish to be very explicit, you are able to manually calculate the number of local variables on the stack and define this value explicitly:

```
.method public hidebysig instance void
  Speak() cil managed
{
  // During the scope of this method, exactly
  // 1 value (the string literal) is on the stack.
  .maxstack  1
  ldstr "Hello there..."
  call void [mscorlib]System.Console::WriteLine(string)
  ret
}
```

Declaring Local Variables in CIL

Let's first check out how to declare a local variable. Assume you wish to build a method in CIL named `MyLocalVariables()` that takes no arguments and returns `void`. Within the method, you wish to define three local variables of type System.String, System.Int32, and System.Object. In C#, this member would appear as follows (recall that locally scoped variables do not receive a default value and should be set to an initial state before further use):

```
public static void MyLocalVariables()
{
  string myStr = "CIL code is fun!";
  int myInt = 33;
  object myObj = new object();
}
```

If you were to construct MyLocalVariables() directly in CIL, you could author the following:

```
.method public hidebysig static void
  MyLocalVariables() cil managed
{
  .maxstack  8
  // Define three local variables.
  .locals init ([0] string myStr, [1] int32 myInt, [2] object myObj)

  // Load a string onto the virtual execution stack.
  ldstr "CIL code is fun!"
  // Pop off current value and store in local variable [0].
  stloc.0

  // Load a constant of type "i4"
  // (shorthand for int32) set to the value 33.
  ldc.i4 33
  // Pop off current value and store in local variable [1].
  stloc.1

  // Create a new object and place on stack.
  newobj     instance void [mscorlib]System.Object::.ctor()
  // Pop off current value and store in local variable [2].
  stloc.2
  ret
}
```

As you can see, the first step taken to allocate local variables in raw CIL is to make use of the .locals directive, which is paired with the init attribute. Within the scope of the related parentheses, your goal is to associate a given numerical index to each variable (seen here as [0], [1], and [2]). As you can see, each index is identified by its data type and an optional variable name. Once the local variables have been defined, you load a value onto the stack (using the various load-centric opcodes) and store the value within the local variable (using the various storage-centric opcodes).

Mapping Parameters to Local Variables in CIL

You have already seen how to declare local variables in raw CIL using the .local init directive; however, you have yet to see exactly how to map incoming parameters to local methods. Consider the following static C# method:

```
public static int Add(int a, int b)
{
  return a + b;
}
```

This innocent-looking method has a lot to say in terms of CIL. First, the incoming arguments (a and b) must be pushed onto the virtual execution stack using the ldarg (load argument) opcode. Next, the add opcode will be used to pop the next two values off the stack and find the summation, and store the value on the stack yet again. Finally, this sum is popped off the stack and returned to the caller via the ret opcode. If you were to disassemble this C# method using ildasm.exe, you would find numerous additional tokens injected by csc.exe, but the crux of the CIL code is quite simple:

```
.method public hidebysig static int32  Add(int32 a,
     int32 b) cil managed
{
  .maxstack  2
  ldarg.0    // Load "a" onto the stack.
  ldarg.1    // Load "b" onto the stack.
  add        // Add both values.
  ret
}
```

The Hidden this Reference

Notice that the two incoming arguments (a and b) are referenced within the CIL code using their indexed position (index 0 and index 1), given that the virtual execution stack begins indexing at position 0.

One thing to be very mindful of when you are examining or authoring CIL code is that every nonstatic method that takes incoming arguments automatically receives an implicit additional parameter, which is a reference to the current object (think the C# this keyword). Given this, if the Add() method were defined as *non*static:

```
// No longer static!
public int Add(int a, int b)
{
  return a + b;
}
```

the incoming a and b arguments are loaded using ldarg.1 and ldarg.2 (rather than the expected ldarg.0 and ldarg.1 opcodes). Again, the reason is that slot 0 actually contains the implicit this reference. Consider the following pseudo-code:

```
// This is JUST pseudo-code!
.method public hidebysig static int32  AddTwoIntParams(
  MyClass_HiddenThisPointer this, int32 a, int32 b) cil managed
{
  ldarg.0   // Load MyClass_HiddenThisPointer onto the stack.
  ldarg.1   // Load "a" onto the stack.
  ldarg.2   // Load "b" onto the stack.
...
}
```

Representing Iteration Constructs in CIL

Iteration constructs in the C# programming language are represented using the for, foreach, while, and do keywords, each of which has a specific representation in CIL. Consider the classic for loop:

```
public static void CountToTen()
{
  for(int i = 0; i < 10; i++)
    ;
}
```

Now, as you may recall, the br opcodes (br, blt, and so on) are used to control a break in flow when some condition has been met. In this example, you have set up a condition in which the for loop should break out of its cycle when the local variable i is equal to or greater than the value of 10. With each pass, the value of 1 is added to i, at which point the test condition is yet again evaluated.

Also recall that when you make use of any of the CIL branching opcodes, you will need to define a specific code label (or two) that marks the location to jump to when the condition is indeed true. Given these points, ponder the following (augmented) CIL code generated via ildasm.exe (including the autogenerated code labels):

```
.method public hidebysig static void  CountToTen() cil managed
{
  .maxstack  2
  .locals init ([0] int32 i)  // Init the local integer "i".
  IL_0000:  ldc.i4.0          // Load this value onto the stack.
  IL_0001:  stloc.0           // Store this value at index "0".
  IL_0002:  br.s IL_0008      // Jump to IL_0008.
  IL_0004:  ldloc.0           // Load value of variable at index 0.
  IL_0005:  ldc.i4.1          // Load the value "1" on the stack.
  IL_0006:  add               // Add current value on the stack at index 0.
  IL_0007:  stloc.0
  IL_0008:  ldloc.0           // Load value at index "0".
  IL_0009:  ldc.i4.s   10     // Load value of "10" onto the stack.
  IL_000b:  blt.s IL_0004     // Less than?  If so, jump back to IL_0004
  IL_000d:  ret
}
```

In a nutshell, this CIL code begins by defining the local int32 and loading it onto the stack. At this point, you jump back and forth between code label IL_0008 and IL_0004, each time bumping the value of i by 1 and testing to see whether i is still less than the value 10. If so, you exit the method.

Source Code The CilTypes example is included under the Chapter 19 subdirectory.

Building a .NET Assembly with CIL

Now that you've taken a tour of the syntax and semantics of raw CIL, it's time to solidify your current understanding by building a .NET application using nothing but ilasm.exe and your text editor of choice. Specifically, your application will consist of a privately deployed, single-file *.dll that contains two class type definitions, and a console-based *.exe that interacts with these types.

Building CILCars.dll

The first order of business is to build the *.dll to be consumed by the client. Open a text editor and create a new *.il file named CILCars.il. This single-file assembly will make use of two external .NET binaries. Begin by updating your code file as follows:

```
// Reference mscorlib.dll and
// System.Windows.Forms.dll
.assembly extern mscorlib
{
  .publickeytoken = (B7 7A 5C 56 19 34 E0 89 )
  .ver 2:0:0:0
}
.assembly extern System.Windows.Forms
{
  .publickeytoken = (B7 7A 5C 56 19 34 E0 89 )
  .ver 2:0:0:0
}

// Define the single-file assembly.
.assembly CILCars
{
  .hash algorithm 0x00008004
  .ver 1:0:0:0
}
.module CILCars.dll
```

As mentioned, this assembly will contain two class types. The first type, CILCar, defines two points of field data and a custom constructor. The second type, CarInfoHelper, defines a single static method named DisplayCarInfo(), which takes CILCar as a parameter and returns void. Both types are in the CILCars namespace. In terms of CIL, CILCar can be implemented as follows:

```
// Implementation of CILCars.CILCar type.
.namespace CILCars
{
  .class public auto ansi beforefieldinit CILCar
    extends [mscorlib]System.Object
  {
    // The field data of the CILCar.
    .field public string petName
    .field public int32 currSpeed

    // The custom constructor simply allows the caller
    // to assign the field data.
    .method public hidebysig specialname rtspecialname
        instance void  .ctor(int32 c, string p) cil managed
    {
      .maxstack  8

      // Load first arg onto the stack and call base class ctor.
      ldarg.0  // "this" object, not the int32!
      call instance void [mscorlib]System.Object::.ctor()

      // Now load first and second args onto the stack.
      ldarg.0  // "this" object
      ldarg.1  // int32 arg

      // Store topmost stack (int 32) member in currSpeed field.
      stfld int32 CILCars.CILCar::currSpeed

      // Load string arg and store in petName field.
      ldarg.0  // "this" object
      ldarg.2  // string arg
```

```
      stfld string CILCars.CILCar::petName
      ret
    }
  }
}
```

Keeping in mind that the real first argument for any nonstatic member is the current object reference, the first block of CIL simply loads the object reference and calls the base class constructor. Next, you push the incoming constructor arguments onto the stack and store them into the type's field data using the `stfld` (store in field) opcode.

Now let's implement the second type in this namespace: `CILCarInfo`. The meat of the type is found within the static `Display()` method. In a nutshell, the role of this method is to take the incoming `CILCar` parameter, extract the values of its field data, and display it in a Windows Forms message box. Here is the complete implementation of `CILCarInfo`, with analysis to follow:

```
.class public auto ansi beforefieldinit CILCarInfo
  extends [mscorlib]System.Object
{
  .method public hidebysig static void
    Display(class CILCars.CILCar c) cil managed
  {
    .maxstack  8

    // We need a local string variable.
    .locals init ([0] string caption)

    // Load string and the incoming CILCar onto the stack.
    ldstr "{0}'s speed is:"
    ldarg.0

    // Now place the value of the CILCar's petName on the
    // stack and call the static String.Format() method.
    ldfld string CILCars.CILCar::petName
    call string [mscorlib]System.String::Format(string, object)
    stloc.0

    // Now load the value of the currSpeed field and get its string
    // representation (note call to ToString() ).
    ldarg.0
    ldflda int32 CILCars.CILCar::currSpeed
    call instance string [mscorlib]System.Int32::ToString()
    ldloc.0

    // Now call the MessageBox.Show() method with loaded values.
    call valuetype [System.Windows.Forms]
          System.Windows.Forms.DialogResult
          [System.Windows.Forms]
          System.Windows.Forms.MessageBox::Show(string, string)
    pop
    ret
  }
}
```

Although the amount of CIL code is a bit more than you see in the implementation of `CILCar`, things are still rather straightforward. First, given that you are defining a static method, you don't have to be concerned with the hidden object reference (thus, the `ldarg.0` opcode really does load the incoming `CILCar` argument).

The method begins by loading a string ("{0}'s speed is") onto the stack, followed by the CILCar argument. Once these two values are in place, you load the value of the petName field and call the static System.String.Format() method to substitute the curly bracket placeholder with the CILCar's pet name.

The same general procedure takes place when processing the currSpeed field, but note that you use the ldflda opcode, which loads the argument address onto the stack. At this point, you call System.Int32.ToString() to transform the value at said address into a string type. Finally, once both strings have been formatted as necessary, you call the MessageBox.Show() method.

At this point, you are able to compile your new *.dll using ilasm.exe with the following command:

```
ilasm /dll CILCars.il
```

and verify the contained CIL using peverify.exe:

```
peverify CILCars.dll
```

Building CILCarClient.exe

Now you can build a simple *.exe assembly that will

- Make a CILCar type.
- Pass the type into the static CILCarInfo.Display() method.

Create a new file named CarClient.il and define external references to mscorlib.dll and CILCars.dll (don't forget to place a copy of this .NET assembly in the client's application directory!). Next, define a single type (Program) that manipulates the CILCars.dll assembly. Here's the complete code:

```
// External assembly refs.
.assembly extern mscorlib
{
  .publickeytoken = (B7 7A 5C 56 19 34 E0 89 )
  .ver 2:0:0:0
}
.assembly extern CILCars
{
  .ver 1:0:0:0
}

// Our executable assembly.
.assembly CarClient
{
  .hash algorithm 0x00008004
  .ver 0:0:0:0
}
.module CarClient.exe

// Implementation of Program type
.namespace CarClient
{
  .class private auto ansi beforefieldinit Program
  extends [mscorlib]System.Object
  {
    .method private hidebysig static void
```

```
    Main(string[] args) cil managed
    {
      // Marks the entry point of the *.exe.
      .entrypoint
      .maxstack  8

      // Declare a local CILCar type and push
      // values on the stack for ctor call.
      .locals init ([0] class
      [CILCars]CILCars.CILCar myCilCar)
      ldc.i4 55
      ldstr "Junior"

      // Make new CilCar; store and load reference.
      newobj instance void
        [CILCars]CILCars.CILCar::.ctor(int32, string)
      stloc.0
      ldloc.0

      // Call Display() and pass in topmost value on stack.
      call void [CILCars]
         CILCars.CILCarInfo::Display(
             class [CILCars]CILCars.CILCar)
      ret
    }
  }
}
```

The one opcode that is important to point out is `.entrypoint`. Recall from the discussion earlier in this chapter that this opcode is used to mark which method of an `*.exe` functions as the entry point of the module. In fact, given that `.entrypoint` is how the CLR identifies the initial method to execute, this method can be called anything, although here we are using the standard method name of `Main()`. The remainder of the CIL code found in the `Main()` method is your basic pushing and popping of stack-based values.

Do note, however, that the creation of `CILCar` involves the use of the `.newobj` opcode. On a related note, recall that when you wish to invoke a member of a type using raw CIL, you make use of the double-colon syntax and, as always, make use of the fully qualified name of the type. With this, you can compile your new file with `ilasm.exe`, verify your assembly with `peverify.exe`, and execute your program. Issue the following commands within your command prompt:

```
ilasm CarClient.il
peverify CarClient.exe
CarClient.exe
```

Figure 19-7 shows the end result.

Figure 19-7. *Your* `CILCar` *in action*

That wraps up the CIL primer and the first goal of this chapter. At this point, I hope you feel confident that you can open a particular .NET assembly using `ildasm.exe` (or a similar tool) and gain a better understanding of what exactly is occurring behind the scenes.

■ **Source Code** The CilCars example is included under the Chapter 19 subdirectory.

Understanding Dynamic Assemblies

As you may have gathered, the process of building a complex .NET application in CIL would be quite the labor of love. On the one hand, CIL is an extremely expressive programming language that allows you to interact with all of the programming constructs allowed by the CTS. On the other hand, authoring raw CIL is tedious, error-prone, and painful. While it is true that knowledge is power, you may indeed wonder just how important it is to commit the laws of CIL syntax to memory. The answer is, "It depends." To be sure, most of your .NET programming endeavors will not require you to view, edit, or author CIL code. However, with the CIL primer behind you, you are now ready to investigate the world of dynamic assemblies (as opposed to static assemblies) and the role of the `System.Reflection.Emit` namespace.

The first question you may have is, "What exactly is the difference between static and dynamic assemblies?" By definition, *static assemblies* are .NET binaries loaded directly from disk storage, meaning they are located somewhere on your hard drive in a physical file (or possibly a set of files in the case of a multifile assembly) at the time the CLR requests them. As you might guess, every time you compile your C# source code, you end up with a static assembly.

A *dynamic assembly*, on the other hand, is created in memory on the fly using the types provided by the `System.Reflection.Emit` namespace. The `System.Reflection.Emit` namespace makes it possible to create an assembly and its modules, type definitions, and CIL implementation logic at *runtime*. Once you have done so, you are then free to save your in-memory binary to disk. This, of course, results in a new static assembly. To be sure, the process of building a dynamic assembly using the `System.Reflection.Emit` namespace does require some level of understanding regarding the nature of CIL opcodes.

Although creating dynamic assemblies is a fairly advanced (and uncommon) programming task, they can be useful under various circumstances:

- You are building a .NET programming tool that needs to generate assemblies on demand based on user input.
- You are building a program that needs to generate proxies to remote types on the fly based on the obtained metadata.
- You wish to load a static assembly and dynamically insert new types into the binary image.

Several aspects of the .NET runtime engine involve generating dynamic assemblies quietly in the background. For example, ASP.NET makes use of this technique to map markup and server-side script code into a runtime object model. LINQ also can generate code on the fly based on various query expressions. This being said, let's check out the types within `System.Reflection.Emit`.

Exploring the System.Reflection.Emit Namespace

Creating a dynamic assembly requires you to have some familiarity with CIL opcodes, but the types of the `System.Reflection.Emit` namespace hide the complexity of CIL as much as possible. For example, rather than directly specifying the necessary CIL directives and attributes to define a class type, you can simply make use of the TypeBuilder class. Likewise, if you wish to define a new instance-level constructor, you have no need to emit the specialname, rtspecialname, or .ctor tokens; rather, you can make use of the ConstructorBuilder. Table 19-8 documents the key members of the System.Reflection.Emit namespace.

Table 19-8. *Select Members of the* System.Reflection.Emit *Namespace*

Members	Meaning in Life
AssemblyBuilder	Used to create an assembly (*.dll or *.exe) at runtime. *.exes must call the ModuleBuilder.SetEntryPoint() method to set the method that is the entry point to the module. If no entry point is specified, a *.dll will be generated.
ModuleBuilder	Used to define the set of modules within the current assembly.
EnumBuilder	Used to create a .NET enumeration type.
TypeBuilder	May be used to create classes, interfaces, structures, and delegates within a module at runtime.
MethodBuilder LocalBuilder PropertyBuilder FieldBuilder ConstructorBuilder CustomAttributeBuilder ParameterBuilder EventBuilder	Used to create type members (such as methods, local variables, properties, constructors, and attributes) at runtime.
ILGenerator	Emits CIL opcodes into a given type member.
OpCodes	Provides numerous fields that map to CIL opcodes. This type is used in conjunction with the various members of System.Reflection.Emit.ILGenerator.

In general, the types of the System.Reflection.Emit namespace allow you to represent raw CIL tokens programmatically during the construction of your dynamic assembly. You will see many of these members in the example that follows; however, the ILGenerator type is worth checking out straightaway.

The Role of the System.Reflection.Emit.ILGenerator

As its name implies, the ILGenerator type's role is to inject CIL opcodes into a given type member. However, you cannot directly create ILGenerator objects, as this type has no public constructors, rather you receive an ILGenerator type by calling specific methods of the builder-centric types (such as the MethodBuilder and ConstructorBuilder types), for example:

```
// Obtain an ILGenerator from a ConstructorBuilder
// object named "myCtorBuilder".
ConstructorBuilder myCtorBuilder =
  new ConstructorBuilder(/* ...various args... */);
ILGenerator myCILGen = myCtorBuilder.GetILGenerator();
```

Once you have an ILGenerator in your hands, you are then able to emit the raw CIL opcodes using any number of methods. Table 19-9 documents some (but not all) methods of ILGenerator.

Table 19-9. *Various Methods of* `ILGenerator`

Method	Meaning in Life
`BeginCatchBlock()`	Begins a `catch` block
`BeginExceptionBlock()`	Begins an exception block for a nonfiltered exception
`BeginFinallyBlock()`	Begins a `finally` block
`BeginScope()`	Begins a lexical scope
`DeclareLocal()`	Declares a local variable
`DefineLabel()`	Declares a new label
`Emit()`	Is overloaded numerous times to allow you to emit CIL opcodes
`EmitCall()`	Pushes a `call` or `callvirt` opcode into the CIL stream
`EmitWriteLine()`	Emits a call to `Console.WriteLine()` with different types of values
`EndExceptionBlock()`	Ends an exception block
`EndScope()`	Ends a lexical scope
`ThrowException()`	Emits an instruction to throw an exception
`UsingNamespace()`	Specifies the namespace to be used in evaluating locals and watches for the current active lexical scope

The key method of `ILGenerator` is `Emit()`, which works in conjunction with the `System.Reflection.Emit.OpCodes` class type. As mentioned earlier in this chapter, this type exposes a good number of read-only fields that map to raw CIL opcodes. The full set of these members are all documented within online help, and you will see various examples in the pages that follow.

Emitting a Dynamic Assembly

To illustrate the process of defining a .NET assembly at runtime, let's walk through the process of creating a single-file dynamic assembly named `MyAssembly.dll`. Within this module is a class named `HelloWorld`. The `HelloWorld` type supports a default constructor and a custom constructor that is used to assign the value of a private member variable (`theMessage`) of type `string`. In addition, `HelloWorld` supports a public instance method named `SayHello()`, which prints a greeting to the standard I/O stream, and another instance method named `GetMsg()`, which returns the internal private string. In effect, you are going to programmatically generate the following class type:

```
// This class will be created at runtime
// using System.Reflection.Emit.
public class HelloWorld
{
  private string theMessage;
  HelloWorld() {}
  HelloWorld(string s) {theMessage = s;}

  public string GetMsg() {return theMessage;}
  public void SayHello()
  {
    System.Console.WriteLine("Hello from the HelloWorld class!");
  }
}
```

Assume you have created a new Visual Studio 2008 Console Application project workspace named DynamicAsmBuilder and import the `System.Reflection`, `System.Reflection.Emit`, and

System.Threading namespaces. Define a static method named CreateMyAsm(). This single method is in charge of the following:

- Defining the characteristics of the dynamic assembly (name, version, etc.)
- Implementing the HelloClass type
- Saving the in-memory assembly to a physical file

Also note that the CreateMyAsm() method takes as a single parameter a System.AppDomain type, which will be used to obtain access to the AssemblyBuilder type associated with the current application domain (see Chapter 17 for a discussion of .NET application domains). Here is the complete code, with analysis to follow:

```
// The caller sends in an AppDomain type.
public static void CreateMyAsm(AppDomain curAppDomain)
{
  // Establish general assembly characteristics.
  AssemblyName assemblyName = new AssemblyName();
  assemblyName.Name = "MyAssembly";
  assemblyName.Version = new Version("1.0.0.0");

  // Create new assembly within the current AppDomain.
  AssemblyBuilder assembly =
    curAppDomain.DefineDynamicAssembly(assemblyName,
    AssemblyBuilderAccess.Save);

  // Given that we are building a single-file
  // assembly, the name of the module is the same as the assembly.
  ModuleBuilder module =
    assembly.DefineDynamicModule("MyAssembly", "MyAssembly.dll");

  // Define a public class named "HelloWorld".
  TypeBuilder helloWorldClass = module.DefineType("MyAssembly.HelloWorld",
    TypeAttributes.Public);

  // Define a private String member variable named "theMessage".
  FieldBuilder msgField =
    helloWorldClass.DefineField("theMessage", Type.GetType("System.String"),
    FieldAttributes.Private);

  // Create the custom ctor.
  Type[] constructorArgs = new Type[1];
  constructorArgs[0] = typeof(string);
  ConstructorBuilder constructor =
    helloWorldClass.DefineConstructor(MethodAttributes.Public,
    CallingConventions.Standard,
    constructorArgs);
  ILGenerator constructorIL = constructor.GetILGenerator();
  constructorIL.Emit(OpCodes.Ldarg_0);
  Type objectClass = typeof(object);
  ConstructorInfo superConstructor =
    objectClass.GetConstructor(new Type[0]);
  constructorIL.Emit(OpCodes.Call, superConstructor);
  constructorIL.Emit(OpCodes.Ldarg_0);
  constructorIL.Emit(OpCodes.Ldarg_1);
  constructorIL.Emit(OpCodes.Stfld, msgField);
  constructorIL.Emit(OpCodes.Ret);
```

```
  // Create the default ctor.
  helloWorldClass.DefineDefaultConstructor(MethodAttributes.Public);

  // Now create the GetMsg() method.
  MethodBuilder getMsgMethod =
    helloWorldClass.DefineMethod("GetMsg", MethodAttributes.Public,
    typeof(string), null);
  ILGenerator methodIL = getMsgMethod.GetILGenerator();
  methodIL.Emit(OpCodes.Ldarg_0);
  methodIL.Emit(OpCodes.Ldfld, msgField);
  methodIL.Emit(OpCodes.Ret);

  // Create the SayHello method.
  MethodBuilder sayHiMethod =
    helloWorldClass.DefineMethod("SayHello",
    MethodAttributes.Public, null, null);
  methodIL = sayHiMethod.GetILGenerator();
  methodIL.EmitWriteLine("Hello from the HelloWorld class!");
  methodIL.Emit(OpCodes.Ret);

  // "Bake" the class HelloWorld.
  // (Baking is the formal term for emitting the type)
  helloWorldClass.CreateType();

  // (Optionally) save the assembly to file.
  assembly.Save("MyAssembly.dll");
}
```

Emitting the Assembly and Module Set

The method body begins by establishing the minimal set of characteristics about your assembly, using the AssemblyName and Version types (defined in the System.Reflection namespace). Next, you obtain an AssemblyBuilder type via the instance-level AppDomain.DefineDynamicAssembly() method (recall the caller will pass in an AppDomain reference into the CreateMyAsm() method):

```
// Establish general assembly characteristics
// and gain access to the AssemblyBuilder type.
public static void CreateMyAsm(AppDomain curAppDomain)
{
  AssemblyName assemblyName = new AssemblyName();
  assemblyName.Name = "MyAssembly";
  assemblyName.Version = new Version("1.0.0.0");

  // Create new assembly within the current AppDomain.
  AssemblyBuilder assembly =
    curAppDomain.DefineDynamicAssembly(assemblyName,
    AssemblyBuilderAccess.Save);
...
}
```

As you can see, when calling AppDomain.DefineDynamicAssembly(), you must specify the access mode of the assembly you wish to define, which can be any of the values shown in Table 19-10.

Table 19-10. *Values of the* `AssemblyBuilderAccess` *Enumeration*

Value	Meaning in Life
`ReflectionOnly`	Represents that a dynamic assembly that can only be reflected over
`Run`	Represents that a dynamic assembly can be executed in memory but not saved to disk
`RunAndSave`	Represents that a dynamic assembly can be executed in memory and saved to disk
`Save`	Represents that a dynamic assembly can be saved to disk but not executed in memory

The next task is to define the module set for your new assembly. Given that the assembly is a single file unit, you need to define only a single module. If you were to build a multifile assembly using the `DefineDynamicModule()` method, you would specify an optional second parameter that represents the name of a given module (e.g., `myMod.dotnetmodule`). However, when creating a single-file assembly, the name of the module will be identical to the name of the assembly itself. In any case, once the `DefineDynamicModule()` method has returned, you are provided with a reference to a valid `ModuleBuilder` type:

```
// The single-file assembly.
ModuleBuilder module =
  assembly.DefineDynamicModule("MyAssembly", "MyAssembly.dll");
```

The Role of the ModuleBuilder Type

`ModuleBuilder` is the key type used during the development of dynamic assemblies. As you would expect, `ModuleBuilder` supports a number of members that allow you to define the set of types contained within a given module (classes, interfaces, structures, etc.) as well as the set of embedded resources (string tables, images, etc.) contained within. Table 19-11 describes a few of the creation-centric methods. (Do note that each method will return to you a related type that represents the type you wish to construct.)

Table 19-11. *Select Members of the* `ModuleBuilder` *Type*

Method	Meaning in Life
`DefineEnum()`	Used to emit a .NET enum definition
`DefineResource()`	Defines a managed embedded resource to be stored in this module
`DefineType()`	Constructs a `TypeBuilder`, which allows you to define value types, interfaces, and class types (including delegates)

The key member of the `ModuleBuilder` class to be aware of is `DefineType()`. In addition to specifying the name of the type (via a simple string), you will also make use of the `System.Reflection.TypeAttributes` enum to describe the format of the type itself. Table 19-12 lists some (but not all) of the key members of the `TypeAttributes` enumeration.

Table 19-12. *Select Members of the* TypeAttributes *Enumeration*

Member	Meaning in Life
Abstract	Specifies that the type is abstract
Class	Specifies that the type is a class
Interface	Specifies that the type is an interface
NestedAssembly	Specifies that the class is nested with assembly visibility and is thus accessible only by methods within its assembly
NestedFamAndAssem	Specifies that the class is nested with assembly and family visibility, and is thus accessible only by methods lying in the intersection of its family and assembly
NestedFamily	Specifies that the class is nested with family visibility and is thus accessible only by methods within its own type and any subtypes
NestedFamORAssem	Specifies that the class is nested with family or assembly visibility, and is thus accessible only by methods lying in the union of its family and assembly
NestedPrivate	Specifies that the class is nested with private visibility
NestedPublic	Specifies that the class is nested with public visibility
NotPublic	Specifies that the class is not public
Public	Specifies that the class is public
Sealed	Specifies that the class is concrete and cannot be extended
Serializable	Specifies that the class can be serialized

Emitting the HelloClass Type and the String Member Variable

Now that you have a better understanding of the role of the ModuleBuilder.CreateType() method, let's examine how you can emit the public HelloWorld class type and the private string variable:

```
// Define a public class named "MyAssembly.HelloWorld".
TypeBuilder helloWorldClass = module.DefineType("MyAssembly.HelloWorld",
  TypeAttributes.Public);

// Define a private String member variable named "theMessage".
FieldBuilder msgField =
  helloWorldClass.DefineField("theMessage",
  typeof(string),
  FieldAttributes.Private);
```

Notice how the TypeBuilder.DefineField() method provides access to a FieldBuilder type. The TypeBuilder class also defines other methods that provide access to other "builder" types. For example, DefineConstructor() returns a ConstructorBuilder, DefineProperty() returns a PropertyBuilder, and so forth.

Emitting the Constructors

As mentioned earlier, the TypeBuilder.DefineConstructor() method can be used to define a constructor for the current type. However, when it comes to implementing the constructor of HelloClass, you need to inject raw CIL code into the constructor body, which is responsible for assigning the incoming parameter to the internal private string. To obtain an ILGenerator type, you call the GetILGenerator() method from the respective "builder" type you have reference to (in this case, the ConstructorBuilder type).

The Emit() method of the ILGenerator class is the entity in charge of placing CIL into a member implementation. Emit() itself makes frequent use of the OpCodes class type, which exposes the opcode set of CIL using read-only fields. For example, OpCodes.Ret signals the return of a method call. OpCodes.Stfld makes an assignment to a member variable. OpCodes.Call is used to call a given method (in this case, the base class constructor). That said, ponder the following constructor logic:

```
// Create the custom constructor taking
// a single System.String argument.
Type[] constructorArgs = new Type[1];
constructorArgs[0] = typeof(string);
ConstructorBuilder constructor =
  helloWorldClass.DefineConstructor(MethodAttributes.Public,
  CallingConventions.Standard, constructorArgs);

// Now emit the necessary CIL into the ctor.
ILGenerator constructorIL = constructor.GetILGenerator();
constructorIL.Emit(OpCodes.Ldarg_0);
Type objectClass = typeof(object);
ConstructorInfo superConstructor = objectClass.GetConstructor(new Type[0]);
constructorIL.Emit(OpCodes.Call, superConstructor);  // Call base class ctor.

// Load the object's "this" pointer on the stack.
constructorIL.Emit(OpCodes.Ldarg_0);

// Load incoming argument on virtual stack and store in msgField.
constructorIL.Emit(OpCodes.Ldarg_1);
constructorIL.Emit(OpCodes.Stfld, msgField);  // Assign msgField.
constructorIL.Emit(OpCodes.Ret);              // Return.
```

Now, as you are well aware, as soon as you define a custom constructor for a type, the default constructor is silently removed. To redefine the no-argument constructor, simply call the DefineDefaultConstructor() method of the TypeBuilder type as follows:

```
// Reinsert the default ctor.
helloWorldClass.DefineDefaultConstructor(MethodAttributes.Public);
```

This single call emits the standard CIL code used to define a default constructor:

```
.method public hidebysig specialname rtspecialname
  instance void  .ctor() cil managed
{
  .maxstack  1
  ldarg.0
  call instance void [mscorlib]System.Object::.ctor()
  ret
}
```

Emitting the SayHello() Method

Last but not least, let's examine the process of emitting the SayHello() method. The first task is to obtain a MethodBuilder type from the helloWorldClass variable. Once you do this, you define the method and obtain the underlying ILGenerator to inject the CIL instructions:

```
// Create the SayHello method.
MethodBuilder sayHiMethod =
  helloWorldClass.DefineMethod("SayHello",
  MethodAttributes.Public, null, null);
methodIL = sayHiMethod.GetILGenerator();

// Write a line to the Console.
methodIL.EmitWriteLine("Hello there!");
methodIL.Emit(OpCodes.Ret);
```

Here you have established a public method (`MethodAttributes.Public`) that takes no parameters and returns nothing (marked by the null entries contained in the `DefineMethod()` call). Also note the `EmitWriteLine()` call. This helper member of the `ILGenerator` class automatically writes a line to the standard output with minimal fuss and bother.

Using the Dynamically Generated Assembly

Now that you have the logic in place to create and save your assembly, all that's needed is a class to trigger the logic. To come full circle, assume your current project defines a second class named `AsmReader`. The logic in `Main()` obtains the current AppDomain via the `Thread.GetDoMain()` method that will be used to host the assembly you will dynamically create. Once you have a reference, you are able to call the `CreateMyAsm()` method.

To make things a bit more interesting, once the call to `CreateMyAsm()` returns, you will exercise some late binding (see Chapter 16) to load your newly created assembly into memory and interact with the members of the `HelloWorld` class. Update your `Main()` method as follows:

```
static void Main(string[] args)
{
  Console.WriteLine("***** The Amazing Dynamic Assembly Builder App *****");
  // Get the application domain for the current thread.
  AppDomain curAppDomain = Thread.GetDomain();

  // Create the dynamic assembly using our helper f(x).
  CreateMyAsm(curAppDomain);
  Console.WriteLine("-> Finished creating MyAssembly.dll.");

  // Now load the new assembly from file.
  Console.WriteLine("-> Loading MyAssembly.dll from file.");
  Assembly a = Assembly.Load("MyAssembly");

  // Get the HelloWorld type.
  Type hello = a.GetType("MyAssembly.HelloWorld");

  // Create HelloWorld object and call the correct ctor.
  Console.Write("-> Enter message to pass HelloWorld class: ");
  string msg = Console.ReadLine();
  object[] ctorArgs = new object[1];
  ctorArgs[0] = msg;
  object obj = Activator.CreateInstance(hello, ctorArgs);

  // Call SayHello and show returned string.
  Console.WriteLine("-> Calling SayHello() via late binding.");
  MethodInfo mi = hello.GetMethod("SayHello");
  mi.Invoke(obj, null);
```

```
    // Invoke method.
    mi = hello.GetMethod("GetMsg");
    Console.WriteLine(mi.Invoke(obj, null));
}
```

In effect, you have just created a .NET assembly that is able to create and execute .NET assemblies at runtime! That wraps up our examination of CIL and the role of dynamic assemblies. I hope this chapter has deepened your understanding of the .NET type system and the syntax and semantics of CIL.

■ **Note** Be sure to load your dynamically created assembly into `ildasm.exe` to connect the dots between raw CIL code and the functionality within the `System.Reflection.Emit` namespace.

■ **Source Code** The DynamicAsmBuilder project is included under the Chapter 19 subdirectory.

Summary

This chapter provided an overview of the syntax and semantics of CIL. Unlike higher-level managed languages such as C#, CIL does not simply define a set of keywords, but provides directives (used to define the structure of an assembly and its types), attributes (which further qualify a given directive), and opcodes (which are used to implement type members). You were introduced to the CIL compiler (`ilasm.exe`) and learned how to alter the contents of a .NET assembly with new CIL code and also the basic process of building a .NET assembly using raw CIL.

The latter half of this chapter introduced you to the `System.Reflection.Emit` namespace. Using these types, you are able to emit a .NET assembly on the fly to memory. As well, if you so choose, you may persist this in-memory image to a physical file. Recall that many types of `System.Reflection.Emit` will automatically generate the correct CIL directives and attributes using friendly types such as `ConstructorBuilder`, `TypeBuilder`, and so forth. The `ILGenerator` type can be used to inject the necessary CIL opcodes into a given member. While we do have a number of helper types that attempt to make the process of programming with the CIL opcode set more palatable, you must have an understanding of CIL when programming with dynamic assemblies.

PART 5

Introducing the .NET Base Class Libraries

CHAPTER 20

File I/O and Isolated Storage

When you are creating full-blown desktop applications, the ability to save information between user sessions is imperative. This chapter examines a number of I/O-related topics as seen through the eyes of the .NET Framework. The first order of business is to explore the core types defined in the System.IO namespace and come to understand how to programmatically modify a machine's directory and file structure. The next task is to explore various ways to read from and write to character-based, binary-based, string-based, and memory-based data stores.

Once you have learned to manipulate files and directories using the core I/O types, you will then be introduced to the topic of *isolated storage* (via the System.IO.IsolatedStorage namespace). This approach to persisting user and application data allows applications that are running under a restricted security environment to perform limited file I/O in a safe manner. To illustrate this API in action, you will examine a security-centric aspect of the .NET platform termed *Code Access Security* (CAS), which is commonly used in conjunction with isolated storage.

Exploring the System.IO Namespace

In the framework of .NET, the System.IO namespace is the region of the base class libraries devoted to file-based (and memory-based) input and output (I/O) services. Like any namespace, System.IO defines a set of classes, interfaces, enumerations, structures, and delegates, most of which are contained in mscorlib.dll. In addition to the types contained within mscorlib.dll, the System.dll assembly defines additional members of the System.IO namespace (given that all Visual Studio 2008 projects automatically set a reference to both assemblies, you should be ready to go).

Many of the types within the System.IO namespace focus on the programmatic manipulation of physical directories and files. However, additional types provide support to read data from and write data to string buffers as well as raw memory locations. To give you a road map of the functionality in System.IO, Table 20-1 outlines the core (nonabstract) classes.

Table 20-1. *Key Members of the* System.IO *Namespace*

Nonabstract I/O Class Type	Meaning in Life
BinaryReader, BinaryWriter	These types allow you to store and retrieve primitive data types (integers, Booleans, strings, and whatnot) as a binary value.
BufferedStream	This type provides temporary storage for a stream of bytes that may be committed to storage at a later time.
Directory, DirectoryInfo	These types are used to manipulate a machine's directory structure. The Directory type exposes functionality using *static members*. The DirectoryInfo type exposes similar functionality from a valid *object reference*.

Continued

Table 20-1. *Continued*

Nonabstract I/O Class Type	Meaning in Life
`DriveInfo`	This type provides detailed information regarding the drives used by a given machine.
`File`, `FileInfo`	These types are used to manipulate a machine's set of files. The `File` type exposes functionality using *static members*. The `FileInfo` type exposes similar functionality from a valid *object reference*.
`FileStream`	This type allows for random file access (e.g., seeking capabilities) with data represented as a stream of bytes.
`FileSystemWatcher`	This type allows you to monitor the modification of external files in a specified directory.
`MemoryStream`	This type provides random access to streamed data stored in memory rather than a physical file.
`Path`	This type performs operations on `System.String` types that contain file or directory path information in a platform-neutral manner.
`StreamWriter`, `StreamReader`	These types are used to store (and retrieve) textual information to (or from) a file. These types do not support random file access.
`StringWriter`, `StringReader`	Like the `StreamReader`/`StreamWriter` types, these classes also work with textual information. However, the underlying storage is a string buffer rather than a physical file.

In addition to these concrete class types, `System.IO` defines a number of enumerations, as well as a set of abstract classes (`Stream`, `TextReader`, `TextWriter`, and so forth), that define a shared polymorphic interface to all descendents. You will read about many of these types in this chapter.

The Directory(Info) and File(Info) Types

`System.IO` provides four types that allow you to manipulate individual files, as well as interact with a machine's directory structure. The first two types, `Directory` and `File`, expose creation, deletion, copying, and moving operations using various static members. The closely related `FileInfo` and `DirectoryInfo` types expose similar functionality as instance-level methods (and therefore must be allocated with the `new` keyword). In Figure 20-1, notice that the `Directory` and `File` types directly extend `System.Object`, while `DirectoryInfo` and `FileInfo` derive from the abstract `FileSystemInfo` type.

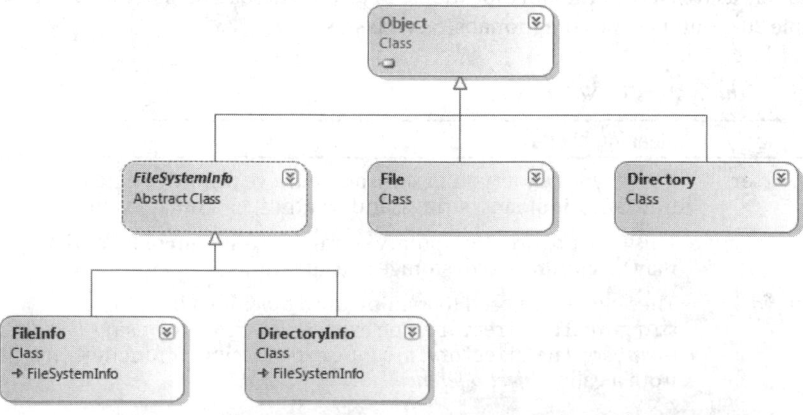

Figure 20-1. *The* `File`- *and* `Directory`-*centric types*

Generally speaking, FileInfo and DirectoryInfo are better choices for obtaining full details of a file or directory (e.g., time created, read/write capabilities, etc.), as their members tend to return strongly typed objects. In contrast, the Directory and File class members tend to return simple string values rather than strongly typed objects.

The Abstract FileSystemInfo Base Class

The DirectoryInfo and FileInfo types receive many behaviors from the abstract FileSystemInfo base class. For the most part, the members of the FileSystemInfo class are used to discover general characteristics (such as time of creation, various attributes, and so forth) about a given file or directory. Table 20-2 lists some core properties of interest.

Table 20-2. FileSystemInfo *Properties*

Property	Meaning in Life
Attributes	Gets or sets the attributes associated with the current file that are represented by the FileAttributes enumeration
CreationTime	Gets or sets the time of creation for the current file or directory
Exists	Can be used to determine whether a given file or directory exists
Extension	Retrieves a file's extension
FullName	Gets the full path of the directory or file
LastAccessTime	Gets or sets the time the current file or directory was last accessed
LastWriteTime	Gets or sets the time when the current file or directory was last written to
Name	Obtains the name of the current file or directory

FileSystemInfo also defines the Delete() method. This is implemented by derived types to delete a given file or directory from the hard drive. As well, Refresh() can be called prior to obtaining attribute information to ensure that the statistics regarding the current file (or directory) are not outdated.

Working with the DirectoryInfo Type

The first creatable I/O-centric type you will examine is the DirectoryInfo class. This class contains a set of members used for creating, moving, deleting, and enumerating over directories and subdirectories. In addition to the functionality provided by its base class (FileSystemInfo), DirectoryInfo offers the key members in Table 20-3.

Table 20-3. *Key Members of the* DirectoryInfo *Type*

Member	Meaning in Life
Create(), CreateSubdirectory()	Create a directory (or set of subdirectories), given a path name
Delete()	Deletes a directory and all its contents
GetDirectories()	Returns an array of strings that represent all subdirectories in the current directory
GetFiles()	Retrieves an array of FileInfo types that represent a set of files in the given directory

Continued

Table 20-3. *Continued*

Member	Meaning in Life
MoveTo()	Moves a directory and its contents to a new path
Parent	Retrieves the parent directory of the specified path
Root	Gets the root portion of a path

You begin working with the DirectoryInfo type by specifying a particular directory path as a constructor parameter. If you want to obtain access to the current working directory (i.e., the directory of the executing application), use the "." notation. Here are some examples:

```
// Bind to the current working directory.
DirectoryInfo dir1 = new DirectoryInfo(".");

// Bind to C:\Windows,
// using a verbatim string.
DirectoryInfo dir2 = new DirectoryInfo(@"C:\Windows");
```

In the second example, you are making the assumption that the path passed into the constructor (C:\Windows) already exists on the physical machine. However, if you attempt to interact with a nonexistent directory, a System.IO.DirectoryNotFoundException is thrown. Thus, if you specify a directory that is not yet created, you will need to call the Create() method before proceeding:

```
// Bind to a nonexistent directory, then create it.
DirectoryInfo dir3 = new DirectoryInfo(@"C:\MyCode\Testing");
dir3.Create();
```

Once you have created a DirectoryInfo object, you can investigate the underlying directory contents using any of the properties inherited from FileSystemInfo. To illustrate, create a new Console Application named DirectoryApp. Update your Program class with a new static method that creates a new DirectoryInfo object mapped to C:\Windows (adjust your path if need be) that displays a number of interesting statistics (see Figure 20-2 for output):

```
class Program
{
  static void Main(string[] args)
  {
    Console.WriteLine("***** Fun with Directory(Info) *****\n");
    ShowWindowsDirectoryInfo();
    Console.ReadLine();
  }

  static void ShowWindowsDirectoryInfo()
  {
    // Dump directory information.
    DirectoryInfo dir = new DirectoryInfo(@"C:\Windows");
    Console.WriteLine("***** Directory Info *****");
    Console.WriteLine("FullName: {0}", dir.FullName);
    Console.WriteLine("Name: {0}", dir.Name);
    Console.WriteLine("Parent: {0}", dir.Parent);
    Console.WriteLine("Creation: {0}", dir.CreationTime);
    Console.WriteLine("Attributes: {0}", dir.Attributes);
    Console.WriteLine("Root: {0}", dir.Root);
    Console.WriteLine("**************************\n");
  }
}
```

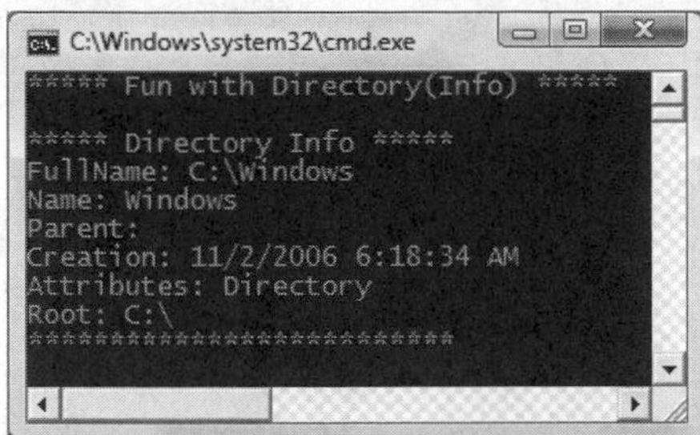

Figure 20-2. *Information about your Windows directory*

Enumerating Files with the DirectoryInfo Type

In addition to obtaining basic details of an existing directory, you can extend the current example to use some methods of the `DirectoryInfo` type. First, let's leverage the `GetFiles()` method to obtain information about all `*.jpg` files located under the C:\Windows\Web\Wallpaper directory.

Note If your machine does not have a C:\Windows\Web\Wallpaper directory, retrofit this code to read files of a directory on your machine (for example, to read all `*.bmp` files from the C:\Windows directory).

This method returns an array of `FileInfo` types, each of which exposes details of a particular file (full details of the `FileInfo` type are explored later in this chapter). Assume the following static method of the `Program` class, called from within `Main()`:

```
static void DisplayImageFiles()
{
  DirectoryInfo dir = new DirectoryInfo(@"C:\Windows\Web\Wallpaper");
  // Get all files with a *.jpg extension.
  FileInfo[] imageFiles = dir.GetFiles("*.jpg");

  // How many were found?
  Console.WriteLine("Found {0} *.jpg files\n", imageFiles.Length);

  // Now print out info for each file.
  foreach (FileInfo f in imageFiles)
  {
    Console.WriteLine("***************************");
    Console.WriteLine("File name: {0}", f.Name);
    Console.WriteLine("File size: {0}", f.Length);
    Console.WriteLine("Creation: {0}", f.CreationTime);
    Console.WriteLine("Attributes: {0}", f.Attributes);
    Console.WriteLine("***************************\n");
  }
}
```

Once you run the application, you see a listing something like that shown in Figure 20-3. (Your image names may vary!)

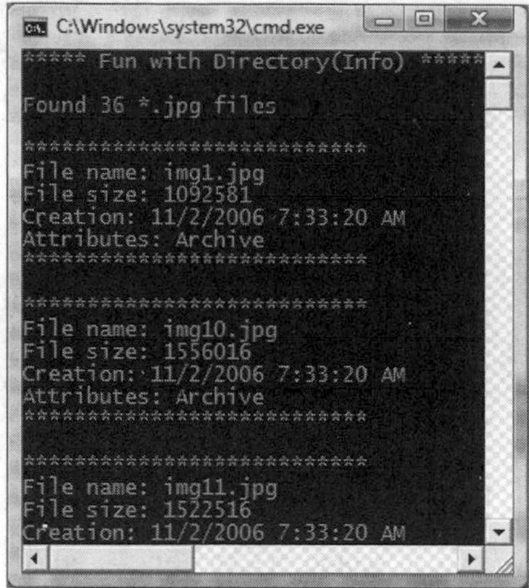

Figure 20-3. *Image file information*

Creating Subdirectories with the DirectoryInfo Type

You can programmatically extend a directory structure using the `DirectoryInfo.CreateSubdirectory()` method. This method can create a single subdirectory, as well as multiple nested subdirectories, in a single function call. To illustrate, here is a method that extends the directory structure of the application's install path with some custom subdirectories:

```
static void ModifyAppDirectory()
{
  DirectoryInfo dir = new DirectoryInfo(".");

  // Create \MyFolder off application directory.
  dir.CreateSubdirectory("MyFolder");

  // Create \MyFolder2\Data off application directory.
  dir.CreateSubdirectory(@"MyFolder2\Data");
}
```

If you call this method from within `Main()` and examine your Windows directory using Windows Explorer, you will see that the new subdirectories are present and accounted for (see Figure 20-4).

Although you are not required to capture the return value of the `CreateSubdirectory()` method, be aware that a `DirectoryInfo` type representing the newly created item is passed back on successful execution. Consider the following update:

```
static void ModifyAppDirectory()
{
  DirectoryInfo dir = new DirectoryInfo(".");

  // Create \MyFolder off initial directory.
  dir.CreateSubdirectory("MyFolder");

  // Capture returned DirectoryInfo object.
  DirectoryInfo myDataFolder = dir.CreateSubdirectory(@"MyFolder2\Data");

  // Prints path to ..\MyFolder2\Data.
  Console.WriteLine("New Folder is: {0}", myDataFolder);
}
```

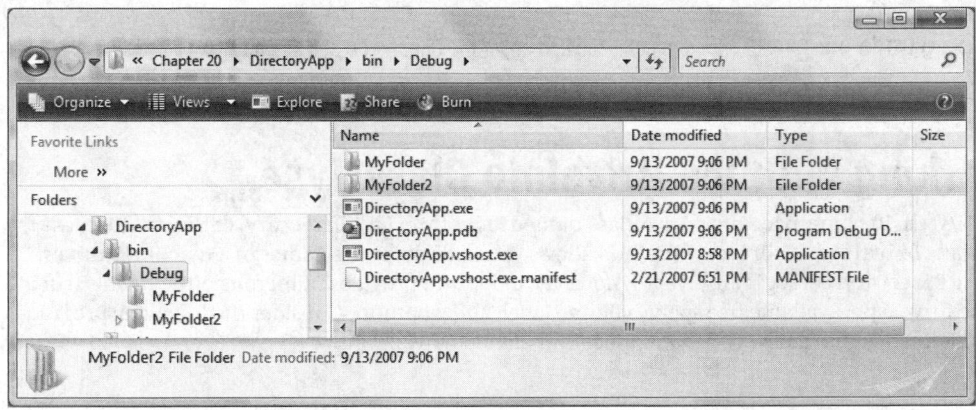

Figure 20-4. *Creating subdirectories*

Working with the Directory Type

Now that you have seen the `DirectoryInfo` type in action, you can learn about the `Directory` type. For the most part, the static members of `Directory` mimic the functionality provided by the instance-level members defined by `DirectoryInfo`. Recall, however, that the members of `Directory` typically return string types rather than strongly typed `FileInfo`/`DirectoryInfo` types.

To illustrate some functionality of the `Directory` type, this final helper function displays the names of all drives mapped to the current computer (via the `Directory.GetLogicalDrives()` method) and uses the static `Directory.Delete()` method to remove the \MyFolder and \MyFolder2\Data subdirectories previously created:

```
static void FunWithDirectoryType()
{
  // List all drives on current computer.
  string[] drives = Directory.GetLogicalDrives();
  Console.WriteLine("Here are your drives:");
  foreach (string s in drives)
    Console.WriteLine("--> {0} ", s);

  // Delete what was created.
  Console.WriteLine("Press Enter to delete directories");
  Console.ReadLine();
  try
  {
    Directory.Delete(string.Format(@"{0}\MyFolder",
      Environment.CurrentDirectory));

    // The second parameter specifies whether you
    // wish to destroy any subdirectories.
    Directory.Delete(string.Format(@"{0}\MyFolder2",
      Environment.CurrentDirectory), true);
  }
  catch (IOException e)
  {
    Console.WriteLine(e.Message);
  }
}
```

■ **Source Code** The DirectoryApp project is located under the Chapter 20 subdirectory.

Working with the DriveInfo Class Type

The System.IO namespace provides a class named DriveInfo. Like Directory.GetLogicalDrives(), the static DriveInfo.GetDrives() method allows you to discover the names of a machine's drives. Unlike Directory.GetLogicalDrives(), however, DriveInfo provides numerous other details (such as the drive type, available free space, volume label, and whatnot). Consider the following Program class defined within a new Console Application named DriveInfoApp:

```
class Program
{
  static void Main(string[] args)
  {
    Console.WriteLine("***** Fun with DriveInfo *****\n");

    // Get info regarding all drives.
    DriveInfo[] myDrives = DriveInfo.GetDrives();

    // Now print drive stats.
    foreach(DriveInfo d in myDrives)
    {
      Console.WriteLine("Name: {0}", d.Name);
      Console.WriteLine("Type: {0}", d.DriveType);

      // Check to see whether the drive is mounted.
      if (d.IsReady)
      {
        Console.WriteLine("Free space: {0}", d.TotalFreeSpace);
        Console.WriteLine("Format: {0}", d.DriveFormat);
        Console.WriteLine("Label: {0}", d.VolumeLabel);
        Console.WriteLine();
      }
    }
    Console.ReadLine();
  }
}
```

Figure 20-5 shows some possible output.

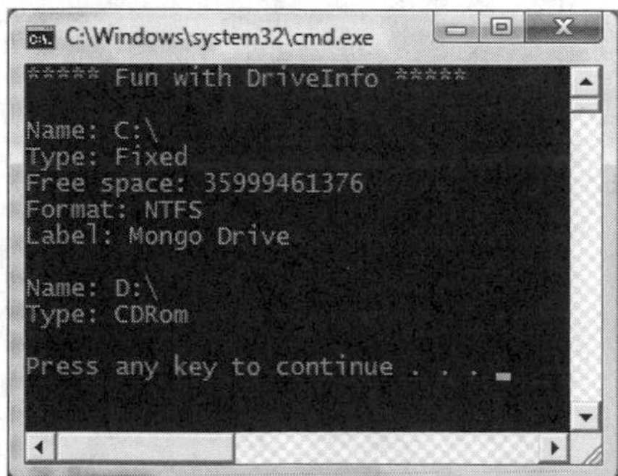

Figure 20-5. *Gather drive details via* DriveInfo.

At this point, you have investigated some core behaviors of the Directory, DirectoryInfo, and DriveInfo classes. Next, you'll learn how to create, open, close, and destroy the files that populate a given directory.

Source Code The DriveInfoApp project is located under the Chapter 20 subdirectory.

Working with the FileInfo Class

As shown in the previous DirectoryApp example, the FileInfo class allows you to obtain details regarding existing files on your hard drive (time created, size, file attributes, and so forth) and aids in the creation, copying, moving, and destruction of files. In addition to the set of functionality inherited by FileSystemInfo are some core members unique to the FileInfo class, which are described in Table 20-4.

Table 20-4. FileInfo *Core Members*

Member	Meaning in Life
AppendText()	Creates a StreamWriter type (described later) that appends text to a file
CopyTo()	Copies an existing file to a new file
Create()	Creates a new file and returns a FileStream type (described later) to interact with the newly created file
CreateText()	Creates a StreamWriter type that writes a new text file
Delete()	Deletes the file to which a FileInfo instance is bound
Directory	Gets an instance of the parent directory
DirectoryName	Gets the full path to the parent directory
Length	Gets the size of the current file or directory
MoveTo()	Moves a specified file to a new location, providing the option to specify a new file name
Name	Gets the name of the file
Open()	Opens a file with various read/write and sharing privileges
OpenRead()	Creates a read-only FileStream
OpenText()	Creates a StreamReader type (described later) that reads from an existing text file
OpenWrite()	Creates a write-only FileStream type

It is important to understand that a majority of the methods of the FileInfo class return a specific I/O-centric object (FileStream, StreamWriter, and so forth) that allows you to begin reading and writing data to (or reading from) the associated file in a variety of formats. You will check out these types in just a moment; however, before you see a working example, let's examine various ways to obtain a file handle using the FileInfo class type.

The FileInfo.Create() Method

The first way you can create a file handle is to make use of the FileInfo.Create() method:

```
static void Main(string[] args)
{
  // Make a new file on the C drive.
  FileInfo f = new FileInfo(@"C:\Test.dat");
  FileStream fs = f.Create();

  // Use the FileStream object...

  // Close down file stream.
  fs.Close();
}
```

Notice that the FileInfo.Create() method returns a FileStream type, which exposes synchronous and asynchronous write/read operations to/from the underlying file (more details in a moment). Be aware that the FileStream object returned by FileInfo.Create() grants full read/write access to all users.

Also notice that after we are done with the current FileStream object, we make sure to close down the handle to release the underlying unmanaged resources of the stream. Given that FileStream implements IDisposable, you can make use of the C# using scope to allow the compiler to generate the teardown logic (see Chapter 8 for details):

```
static void Main(string[] args)
{
  // Defining a 'using scope' for file I/O
  // types is ideal.
  FileInfo f = new FileInfo(@"C:\Test.dat");
  using (FileStream fs = f.Create())
  {
    // Use the FileStream object...
  }
}
```

The FileInfo.Open() Method

You can use the FileInfo.Open() method to open existing files as well as create new files with far more precision than FileInfo.Create(), given that Open() typically takes several parameters to qualify the overall structure of the file you are manipulating. Once the call to Open() completes, you are returned a FileStream object. Consider the following logic:

```
static void Main(string[] args)
{
  // Make a new file via FileInfo.Open().
  FileInfo f2 = new FileInfo(@"C:\Test2.dat");
  using(FileStream fs2 = f2.Open(FileMode.OpenOrCreate,
    FileAccess.ReadWrite, FileShare.None))
  {
    // Use the FileStream object...
  }
}
```

This version of the overloaded Open() method requires three parameters. The first parameter specifies the general flavor of the I/O request (e.g., make a new file, open an existing file, append to a file, etc.), which is specified using the FileMode enumeration (see Table 20-5 for details):

```
public enum FileMode
{
  CreateNew,
```

```
  Create,
  Open,
  OpenOrCreate,
  Truncate,
  Append
}
```

Table 20-5. *Members of the* `FileMode` *Enumeration*

Member	Meaning in Life
`CreateNew`	Informs the OS to make a new file. If it already exists, an `IOException` is thrown.
`Create`	Informs the OS to make a new file. If it already exists, it will be overwritten.
`Open`	Opens an existing file. If the file does not exist, a `FileNotFoundException` is thrown.
`OpenOrCreate`	Opens the file if it exists; otherwise, a new file is created.
`Truncate`	Opens a file and truncates the file to 0 bytes in size.
`Append`	Opens a file, moves to the end of the file, and begins write operations (this flag can only be used with a write-only stream). If the file does not exist, a new file is created.

The second parameter, a value from the `FileAccess` enumeration, is used to determine the read/write behavior of the underlying stream:

```
public enum FileAccess
{
  Read,
  Write,
  ReadWrite
}
```

Finally, you have the third parameter, `FileShare`, which specifies how the file is to be shared among other file handlers. Here are the core names:

```
public enum FileShare
{
  None,
  Read,
  Write,
  ReadWrite
}
```

The FileInfo.OpenRead() and FileInfo.OpenWrite() Methods

While the `FileInfo.Open()` method allows you to obtain a file handle in a very flexible manner, the `FileInfo` class also provides members named `OpenRead()` and `OpenWrite()`. As you might imagine, these methods return a properly configured read-only or write-only `FileStream` type, without the need to supply various enumeration values. Like `FileInfo.Create()` and `FileInfo.Open()`, `OpenRead()` and `OpenWrite()` return a `FileStream` object (do note that the following code assumes you have files named `Test3.dat` and `Test4.dat` on your C drive):

```
static void Main(string[] args)
{
  // Get a FileStream object with read-only permissions.
```

```
  FileInfo f3 = new FileInfo(@"C:\Test3.dat");
  using(FileStream readOnlyStream = f3.OpenRead())
  {
    // Use the FileStream object...
  }

  // Now get a FileStream object with write-only permissions.
  FileInfo f4 = new FileInfo(@"C:\Test4.dat");
  using(FileStream writeOnlyStream = f4.OpenWrite())
  {
    // Use the FileStream object...
  }
}
```

The FileInfo.OpenText() Method

Another open-centric member of the FileInfo type is OpenText(). Unlike Create(), Open(), OpenRead(), and OpenWrite(), the OpenText() method returns an instance of the StreamReader type, rather than a FileStream type. Assuming you have a file named boot.ini on your C drive, the following would be one manner to gain access to its contents:

```
static void Main(string[] args)
{
  // Get a StreamReader object.
  FileInfo f5 = new FileInfo(@"C:\boot.ini");
  using(StreamReader sreader = f5.OpenText())
  {
    // Use the StreamReader object...
  }
}
```

As you will see shortly, the StreamReader type provides a way to read character data from the underlying file.

The FileInfo.CreateText() and FileInfo.AppendText() Methods

The final two methods of interest at this point are CreateText() and AppendText(), both of which return a StreamWriter reference, as shown here:

```
static void Main(string[] args)
{
  FileInfo f6 = new FileInfo(@"C:\Test5.txt");
  using(StreamWriter swriter = f6.CreateText())
  {
    // Use the StreamWriter object...
  }

  FileInfo f7 = new FileInfo(@"C:\FinalTest.txt");
  using(StreamWriter swriterAppend = f7.AppendText())
  {
    // Use the StreamWriter object...
  }
}
```

As you would guess, the StreamWriter type provides a way to write character data to the underlying file.

Working with the File Type

The File type provides functionality almost identical to that of the FileInfo type, using a number of static members. Like FileInfo, File supplies AppendText(), Create(), CreateText(), Open(), OpenRead(), OpenWrite(), and OpenText() methods. In fact, in many cases, the File and FileInfo types may be used interchangeably. To illustrate, each of the previous FileStream examples can be simplified by using the File type instead:

```
static void Main(string[] args)
{
  // Obtain FileStream object via File.Create().
  using(FileStream fs = File.Create(@"C:\Test.dat"))
  {
  }

  // Obtain FileStream object via File.Open().
  using(FileStream fs2 = File.Open(@"C:\Test2.dat",
    FileMode.OpenOrCreate,
    FileAccess.ReadWrite, FileShare.None))
  {
  }

  // Get a FileStream object with read-only permissions.
  using(FileStream readOnlyStream = File.OpenRead(@"Test3.dat"))
  {
  }

  // Get a FileStream object with write-only permissions.
  using(FileStream writeOnlyStream = File.OpenWrite(@"Test4.dat"))
  {
  }

  // Get a StreamReader object.
  using(StreamReader sreader = File.OpenText(@"C:\boot.ini"))
  {
  }

  // Get some StreamWriters.
  using(StreamWriter swriter = File.CreateText(@"C:\Test3.txt"))
  {
  }

  using(StreamWriter swriterAppend = File.AppendText(@"C:\FinalTest.txt"))
  {
  }
}
```

Additional File-centric Members

The File type also supports a few unique members shown in Table 20-6, which can greatly simplify the processes of reading and writing textual data.

Table 20-6. *Methods of the* `File` *Type*

Method	Meaning in Life
`ReadAllBytes()`	Opens the specified file, returns the binary data as an array of bytes, and then closes the file
`ReadAllLines()`	Opens a specified file, returns the character data as an array of strings, and then closes the file
`ReadAllText()`	Opens a specified file, returns the character data as a `System.String`, and then closes the file
`WriteAllBytes()`	Opens the specified file, writes out the byte array, and then closes the file
`WriteAllLines()`	Opens a specified file, writes out an array of strings, and then closes the file
`WriteAllText()`	Opens a specified file, writes the character data, and then closes the file

Using these new methods of the `File` type, you are able to read and write batches of data in just a few lines of code. Even better, each of these new members automatically closes down the underlying file handle. For example, the following console program (named SimpleFileIO) will persist the string data into a new file on the C drive (and read it into memory) with minimal fuss:

```
using System;
using System.IO;

class Program
{
  static void Main(string[] args)
  {
    Console.WriteLine("***** Simple IO with the File Type *****\n");
    string[] myTasks = {
      "Fix bathroom sink", "Call Dave",
      "Call Mom and Dad", "Play Xbox 360"};

    // Write out all data to file on C drive.
    File.WriteAllLines(@"C:\tasks.txt", myTasks);

    // Read it all back and print out.
    foreach (string task in File.ReadAllLines(@"C:\tasks.txt"))
    {
      Console.WriteLine("TODO: {0}", task);
    }
    Console.ReadLine();
  }
}
```

Clearly, when you wish to quickly obtain a file handle, the `File` type will save you some keystrokes. However, one benefit of first creating a `FileInfo` object is that you are able to investigate the file using the members of the abstract `FileSystemInfo` base class.

■ **Source Code** The SimpleFileIO project is located under the Chapter 20 subdirectory.

The Abstract Stream Class

At this point, you have seen numerous ways to obtain `FileStream`, `StreamReader`, and `StreamWriter` objects, but you have yet to read data from, or write data to, a file using these types. To understand how to do so, you'll need to become familiar with the concept of a stream. In the world of I/O manipulation, a *stream* represents a chunk of data flowing between a source and a destination. Streams provide a common way to interact with *a sequence of bytes*, regardless of what kind of device (file, network connection, printer, etc.) is storing or displaying the bytes in question.

The abstract `System.IO.Stream` class defines a number of members that provide support for synchronous and asynchronous interactions with the storage medium (e.g., an underlying file or memory location). Figure 20-6 shows various descendents of the `Stream` type, seen through the eyes of the Visual Studio 2008 Object Browser.

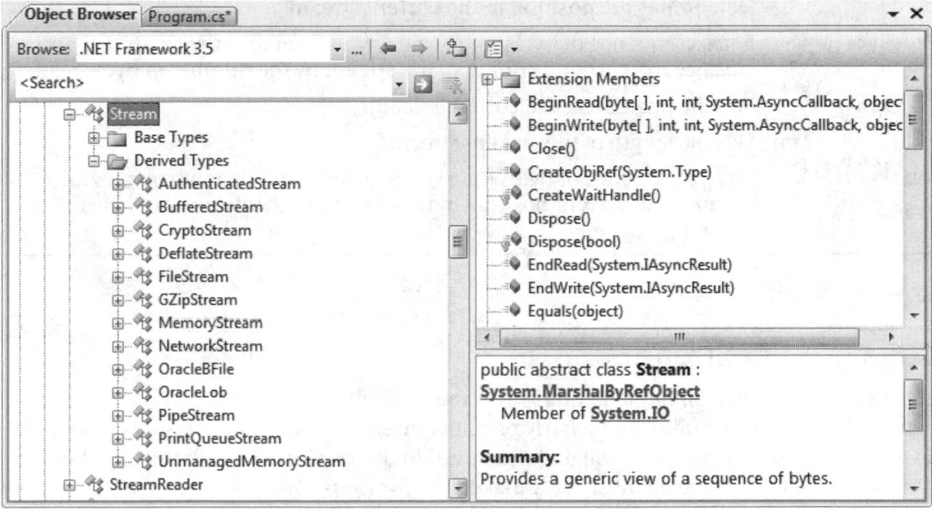

Figure 20-6. *Stream-derived types*

■ **Note** Be aware that the concept of a stream is not limited to files IO. To be sure, the .NET libraries provide stream access to networks, memory locations, and other stream-centric abstractions.

Again, `Stream` descendents represent data as a raw stream of bytes; therefore, working directly with raw streams can be quite cryptic. Some `Stream`-derived types support *seeking*, which refers to the process of obtaining and adjusting the current position in the stream. To begin understanding the functionality provided by the `Stream` class, take note of the core members described in Table 20-7.

Table 20-7. *Abstract Stream Members*

Member	Meaning in Life
`CanRead`, `CanWrite`	Determine whether the current stream supports reading, seeking, and/or `CanSeek` writing.
`Close()`	Closes the current stream and releases any resources (such as sockets and file handles) associated with the current stream. Internally, this method is aliased to the `Dispose()` method; therefore "closing a stream" is functionally equivalent to "disposing a stream."
`Flush()`	Updates the underlying data source or repository with the current state of the buffer and then clears the buffer. If a stream does not implement a buffer, this method does nothing.
`Length`	Returns the length of the stream, in bytes.
`Position`	Determines the position in the current stream.
`Read()`, `ReadByte()`	Read a sequence of bytes (or a single byte) from the current stream and advance the current position in the stream by the number of bytes read.
`Seek()`	Sets the position in the current stream.
`SetLength()`	Sets the length of the current stream.
`Write()`, `WriteByte()`	Write a sequence of bytes (or a single byte) to the current stream and advance the current position in this stream by the number of bytes written.

Working with FileStreams

The `FileStream` class provides an implementation for the abstract `Stream` members in a manner appropriate for file-based streaming. It is a fairly primitive stream; it can read or write only a single byte or an array of bytes. In reality, you will not often need to directly interact with the members of the `FileStream` type. Rather, you will most likely make use of various *stream wrappers*, which make it easier to work with textual data or .NET types. Nevertheless, for illustrative purposes, let's experiment with the synchronous read/write capabilities of the `FileStream` type.

Assume you have a new Console Application named FileStreamApp. Your goal is to write a simple text message to a new file named `myMessage.dat`. However, given that `FileStream` can operate only on raw bytes, you will be required to encode the `System.String` type into a corresponding byte array. Luckily, the `System.Text` namespace defines a type named `Encoding`, which provides members that encode and decode strings to (or from) an array of bytes (check out the .NET Framework 3.5 SDK documentation for full details of the `Encoding` type).

Once encoded, the byte array is persisted to file using the `FileStream.Write()` method. To read the bytes back into memory, you must reset the internal position of the stream (via the `Position` property) and call the `ReadByte()` method. Finally, you display the raw byte array and the decoded string to the console. Here is the complete `Main()` method:

```
// Don't forget to import the System.Text and System.IO namespaces.
static void Main(string[] args)
{
  Console.WriteLine("***** Fun with FileStreams *****\n");

  // Obtain a FileStream object.
  using(FileStream fStream = File.Open(@"C:\myMessage.dat",
    FileMode.Create))
  {
    // Encode a string as an array of bytes.
```

```
    string msg = "Hello!";
    byte[] msgAsByteArray = Encoding.Default.GetBytes(msg);

    // Write byte[] to file.
    fStream.Write(msgAsByteArray, 0, msgAsByteArray.Length);

    // Reset internal position of stream.
    fStream.Position = 0;

    // Read the types from file and display to console.
    Console.Write("Your message as an array of bytes: ");
    byte[] bytesFromFile = new byte[msgAsByteArray.Length];
    for (int i = 0; i < msgAsByteArray.Length; i++)
    {
      bytesFromFile[i] = (byte)fStream.ReadByte();
      Console.Write(bytesFromFile[i]);
    }

    // Display decoded messages.
    Console.Write("\nDecoded Message: ");
    Console.WriteLine(Encoding.Default.GetString(bytesFromFile));
  }
  Console.ReadLine();
}
```

While this example does indeed populate the file with data, it punctuates the major downfall of working directly with the `FileStream` type: it demands to operate on raw bytes. Other `Stream`-derived types operate in a similar manner. For example, if you wish to write a sequence of bytes to a region of memory, you can allocate a `MemoryStream`. Likewise, if you wish to push an array of bytes through a network connection, you can make use of the `NetworkStream` type.

As mentioned, the `System.IO` namespace thankfully provides a number of "reader" and "writer" types that encapsulate the details of working with `Stream`-derived types.

Source Code The FileStreamApp project is included under the Chapter 20 subdirectory.

Working with StreamWriters and StreamReaders

The `StreamWriter` and `StreamReader` classes are useful whenever you need to read or write character-based data (e.g., strings). Both of these types work by default with Unicode characters; however, you can change this by supplying a properly configured `System.Text.Encoding` object reference. To keep things simple, let's assume that the default Unicode encoding fits the bill.

`StreamReader` derives from an abstract type named `TextReader`, as does the related `StringReader` type (discussed later in this chapter). The `TextReader` base class provides a very limited set of functionality to each of these descendents, specifically the ability to read and peek into a character stream.

The `StreamWriter` type (as well as `StringWriter`, also examined later in this chapter) derives from an abstract base class named `TextWriter`. This class defines members that allow derived types to write textual data to a given character stream.

To aid in your understanding of the core writing capabilities of the `StreamWriter` and `StringWriter` classes, Table 20-8 describes the core members of the abstract `TextWriter` base class.

Table 20-8. *Core Members of* `TextWriter`

Member	Meaning in Life
`Close()`	This method closes the writer and frees any associated resources. In the process, the buffer is automatically flushed (again, this member is functionally equivalent to calling the `Dispose()` method).
`Flush()`	This method clears all buffers for the current writer and causes any buffered data to be written to the underlying device, but does not close the writer.
`NewLine`	This property indicates the newline constant for the derived writer class. The default line terminator for the Windows OS is a carriage return followed by a line feed (`\r\n`).
`Write()`	This overloaded method writes data to the text stream without a newline constant.
`WriteLine()`	This overloaded method writes data to the text stream with a newline constant.

■ **Note** The last two members of the `TextWriter` class probably look familiar to you. If you recall, the `System.Console` type has `Write()` and `WriteLine()` members that push textual data to the standard output device. In fact, the `Console.In` property wraps a `TextWriter`, and the `Console.Out` property wraps a `TextReader`.

The derived `StreamWriter` class provides an appropriate implementation for the `Write()`, `Close()`, and `Flush()` methods, and it defines the additional `AutoFlush` property. This property, when set to `true`, forces `StreamWriter` to flush all data every time you perform a write operation. Be aware that you can gain better performance by setting `AutoFlush` to `false`, provided you always call `Close()` when you are done writing with a `StreamWriter`.

Writing to a Text File

To see the `StreamWriter` type in action, create a new Console Application named StreamWriterReaderApp. The following `Main()` method creates a new file named `reminders.txt` using the `File.CreateText()` method. Using the obtained `StreamWriter` object, you add some textual data to the new file, as shown here:

```
static void Main(string[] args)
{
  Console.WriteLine("***** Fun with StreamWriter / StreamReader *****\n");

  // Get a StreamWriter and write string data.
  using(StreamWriter writer = File.CreateText("reminders.txt"))
  {
    writer.WriteLine("Don't forget Mother's Day this year...");
    writer.WriteLine("Don't forget Father's Day this year...");
    writer.WriteLine("Don't forget these numbers:");
    for(int i = 0; i < 10; i++)
      writer.Write(i + " ");

    // Insert a new line.
    writer.Write(writer.NewLine);
  }
```

```
  Console.WriteLine("Created file and wrote some thoughts...");
  Console.ReadLine();
}
```

Once you run this program, you can examine the contents of this new file (see Figure 20-7). You will find this file under the bin\Debug folder of your current application, given that you have not specified an absolute path at the time you called `CreateText()`.

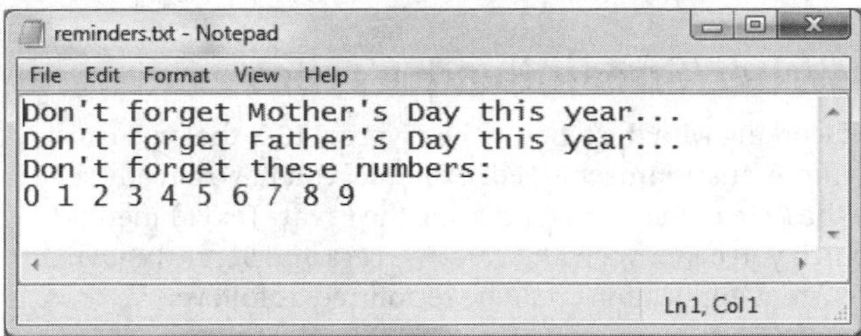

Figure 20-7. *The contents of your* `*.txt` *file*

Reading from a Text File

Now you need to understand how to programmatically read data from a file using the corresponding `StreamReader` type. As you recall, this class derives from the abstract `TextReader`, which offers the functionality described in Table 20-9.

Table 20-9. `TextReader` *Core Members*

Member	Meaning in Life
`Peek()`	Returns the next available character without actually changing the position of the reader. A value of `-1` indicates you are at the end of the stream.
`Read()`	Reads data from an input stream.
`ReadBlock()`	Reads a maximum of count characters from the current stream and writes the data to a buffer, beginning at index.
`ReadLine()`	Reads a line of characters from the current stream and returns the data as a string (a null string indicates EOF).
`ReadToEnd()`	Reads all characters from the current position to the end of the stream and returns them as a single string.

If you now extend the current `MyStreamWriterReader` class to use a `StreamReader`, you can read in the textual data from the `reminders.txt` file as shown here:

```
static void Main(string[] args)
{
  Console.WriteLine("***** Fun with StreamWriter / StreamReader *****\n");
...
  // Now read data from file.
  Console.WriteLine("Here are your thoughts:\n");
  using(StreamReader sr = File.OpenText("reminders.txt"))
  {
    string input = null;
    while ((input = sr.ReadLine()) != null)
    {
```

```
      Console.WriteLine (input);
    }
  }
  Console.ReadLine();
}
```

Once you run the program, you will see the character data within reminders.txt displayed to the console.

Directly Creating StreamWriter/StreamReader Types

One of the slightly confusing aspects of working with the types within System.IO is that you can often achieve an identical result using numerous approaches. For example, you have already seen that you can obtain a StreamWriter via the File or FileInfo type using the CreateText() method. In reality, there is yet another way in which you can work with StreamWriters and StreamReaders: create them directly. For example, the current application could be retrofitted as follows:

```
static void Main(string[] args)
{
  Console.WriteLine("***** Fun with StreamWriter / StreamReader *****\n");

  // Get a StreamWriter and write string data.
  using(StreamWriter writer = new StreamWriter("reminders.txt"))
  {
  ...
  }

  // Now read data from file.
  using(StreamReader sr = new StreamReader("reminders.txt"))
  {
    ...
  }
}
```

Although it can be a bit confusing to see so many seemingly identical approaches to file I/O, keep in mind that the end result is greater flexibility. In any case, now that you have seen how to move character data to and from a given file using the StreamWriter and StreamReader types, you will next examine the role of the StringWriter and StringReader classes.

■ **Source Code** The StreamWriterReaderApp project is included under the Chapter 20 subdirectory.

Working with StringWriters and StringReaders

Using the StringWriter and StringReader types, you can treat textual information as a stream of in-memory characters. This can prove helpful when you wish to append character-based information to an underlying buffer. To illustrate, the following Console Application (named StringReaderWriterApp) writes a block of string data to a StringWriter object rather than a file on the local hard drive:

```
static void Main(string[] args)
{
  Console.WriteLine("***** Fun with StringWriter / StringReader *****\n");
```

```
    // Create a StringWriter and emit character data to memory.
    using(StringWriter strWriter = new StringWriter())
    {
      strWriter.WriteLine("Don't forget Mother's Day this year...");
      // Get a copy of the contents (stored in a string) and pump
      // to console.
      Console.WriteLine("Contents of StringWriter:\n{0}", strWriter);
    }
    Console.ReadLine();
  }
```

Because StringWriter and StreamWriter both derive from the same base class (TextWriter), the writing logic is more or less identical. However, given that nature of StringWriter, be aware that this class allows you to extract a System.Text.StringBuilder object via the GetStringBuilder() method:

```
using (StringWriter strWriter = new StringWriter())
{
  strWriter.WriteLine("Don't forget Mother's Day this year...");
  Console.WriteLine("Contents of StringWriter:\n{0}", strWriter);

  // Get the internal StringBuilder.
  StringBuilder sb = strWriter.GetStringBuilder();
  sb.Insert(0, "Hey!! ");
  Console.WriteLine("-> {0}", sb.ToString());
  sb.Remove(0, "Hey!! ".Length);
  Console.WriteLine("-> {0}", sb.ToString());
}
```

When you wish to read from a stream of character data, make use of the corresponding StringReader type, which (as you would expect) functions identically to the related StreamReader class. In fact, the StringReader class does nothing more than override the inherited members to read from a block of character data, rather than a file, as shown here:

```
using (StringWriter strWriter = new StringWriter())
{
  strWriter.WriteLine("Don't forget Mother's Day this year...");
  Console.WriteLine("Contents of StringWriter:\n{0}", strWriter);

  // Read data from the StringWriter.
  using (StringReader strReader = new StringReader(strWriter.ToString()))
  {
    string input = null;
    while ((input = strReader.ReadLine()) != null)
    {
      Console.WriteLine(input);
    }
  }
}
```

Source Code The StringReaderWriterApp is included under the Chapter 20 subdirectory.

Working with BinaryWriters and BinaryReaders

The final writer/reader sets you will examine here are `BinaryReader` and `BinaryWriter`, both of which derive directly from `System.Object`. These types allow you to read and write discrete data types to an underlying stream in a compact binary format. The `BinaryWriter` class defines a highly overloaded `Write()` method to place a data type in the underlying stream. In addition to `Write()`, `BinaryWriter` provides additional members that allow you to get or set the `Stream`-derived type and offers support for random access to the data (see Table 20-10).

Table 20-10. `BinaryWriter` *Core Members*

Member	Meaning in Life
`BaseStream`	This read-only property provides access to the underlying stream used with the `BinaryWriter` object.
`Close()`	This method closes the binary stream.
`Flush()`	This method flushes the binary stream.
`Seek()`	This method sets the position in the current stream.
`Write()`	This method writes a value to the current stream.

The `BinaryReader` class complements the functionality offered by `BinaryWriter` with the members described in Table 20-11.

Table 20-11. `BinaryReader` *Core Members*

Member	Meaning in Life
`BaseStream`	This read-only property provides access to the underlying stream used with the `BinaryReader` object.
`Close()`	This method closes the binary reader.
`PeekChar()`	This method returns the next available character without actually advancing the position in the stream.
`Read()`	This method reads a given set of bytes or characters and stores them in the incoming array.
`Read`*`XXXX`*`()`	The `BinaryReader` class defines numerous read methods that grab the next type from the stream (`ReadBoolean()`, `ReadByte()`, `ReadInt32()`, and so forth).

The following example (a Console Application named BinaryWriterReader) writes a number of data types to a new `*.dat` file:

```
static void Main(string[] args)
{
  Console.WriteLine("***** Fun with Binary Writers / Readers *****\n");

  // Open a binary writer for a file.
  FileInfo f = new FileInfo("BinFile.dat");
  using(BinaryWriter bw = new BinaryWriter(f.OpenWrite()))
  {
    // Print out the type of BaseStream.
    // (System.IO.FileStream in this case).
    Console.WriteLine("Base stream is: {0}", bw.BaseStream);
```

```
    // Create some data to save in the file
    double aDouble = 1234.67;
    int anInt = 34567;
    string aString = "A, B, C";

    // Write the data
    bw.Write(aDouble);
    bw.Write(anInt);
    bw.Write(aString);
  }
  Console.ReadLine();
}
```

Notice how the FileStream object returned from FileInfo.OpenWrite() is passed to the constructor of the BinaryWriter type. Using this technique, it is very simple to "layer in" a stream before writing out the data. Do understand that the constructor of BinaryWriter takes any Stream-derived type (e.g., FileStream, MemoryStream, or BufferedStream). Thus, if you would rather write binary data to memory, simply supply a valid MemoryStream object.

To read the data out of the BinFile.dat file, the BinaryReader type provides a number of options. Here, you will call various read-centric members to pluck each chunk of data from the file stream:

```
static void Main(string[] args)
{
...
  FileInfo f = new FileInfo("BinFile.dat");
...
  // Read the binary data from the stream.
  using(BinaryReader br = new BinaryReader(f.OpenRead()))
  {
    Console.WriteLine(br.ReadDouble());
    Console.WriteLine(br.ReadInt32());
    Console.WriteLine(br.ReadString());
  }
  Console.ReadLine();
}
```

■ **Source Code** The BinaryWriterReader application is included under the Chapter 20 subdirectory.

Programmatically "Watching" Files

Now that you have a better handle on the use of various readers and writers, next you'll look at the role of the FileSystemWatcher class. This type can be quite helpful when you wish to programmatically monitor (or "watch") files on your system. Specifically, the FileSystemWatcher type can be instructed to monitor files for any of the actions specified by the System.IO.NotifyFilters enumeration (while many of these members are self-explanatory, check the .NET Framework 3.5 SDK documentation for further details):

```
public enum NotifyFilters
{
  Attributes, CreationTime,
  DirectoryName, FileName,
```

```
  LastAccess, LastWrite,
  Security, Size,
}
```

The first step you will need to take to work with the FileSystemWatcher type is to set the Path property to specify the name (and location) of the directory that contains the files to be monitored, as well as the Filter property that defines the file extensions of the files to be monitored.

At this point, you may choose to handle the Changed, Created, and Deleted events, all of which work in conjunction with the FileSystemEventHandler delegate. This delegate can call any method matching the following pattern:

```
// The FileSystemEventHandler delegate must point
// to methods matching the following signature.
void MyNotificationHandler(object source, FileSystemEventArgs e)
```

As well, the Renamed event may also be handled via the RenamedEventHandler delegate type, which can call methods matching the following signature:

```
// The RenamedEventHandler delegate must point
// to methods matching the following signature.
void MyNotificationHandler(object source, RenamedEventArgs e)
```

To illustrate the process of watching a file, assume you have created a new directory on your C drive named MyFolder that contains various *.txt files (named whatever you wish). The following Console Application (named MyDirectoryWatcher) will monitor the *.txt files within the MyFolder directory and print out messages in the event that the files are created, deleted, modified, or renamed:

```
static void Main(string[] args)
{
  Console.WriteLine("***** The Amazing File Watcher App *****\n");

  // Establish the path to the directory to watch.
  FileSystemWatcher watcher = new FileSystemWatcher();
  try
  {
    watcher.Path = @"C:\MyFolder";
  }
  catch(ArgumentException ex)
  {
    Console.WriteLine(ex.Message);
    return;
  }

  // Set up the things to be on the lookout for.
  watcher.NotifyFilter = NotifyFilters.LastAccess
    | NotifyFilters.LastWrite
    | NotifyFilters.FileName
    | NotifyFilters.DirectoryName;

  // Only watch text files.
  watcher.Filter = "*.txt";

  // Add event handlers.
  watcher.Changed += new FileSystemEventHandler(OnChanged);
  watcher.Created += new FileSystemEventHandler(OnChanged);
  watcher.Deleted += new FileSystemEventHandler(OnChanged);
  watcher.Renamed += new RenamedEventHandler(OnRenamed);
```

```
  // Begin watching the directory.
  watcher.EnableRaisingEvents = true;

  // Wait for the user to quit the program.
  Console.WriteLine(@"Press 'q' to quit app.");
  while(Console.Read()!='q');
}
```

The two event handlers simply print out the current file modification:

```
static void OnChanged(object source, FileSystemEventArgs e)
{
    // Specify what is done when a file is changed, created, or deleted.
    Console.WriteLine("File: {0} {1}!", e.FullPath, e.ChangeType);
}

static void OnRenamed(object source, RenamedEventArgs e)
{
    // Specify what is done when a file is renamed.
    Console.WriteLine("File: {0} renamed to\n{1}", e.OldFullPath, e.FullPath);
}
```

To test this program, run the application and open Windows Explorer. Try renaming your files, creating a `*.txt` file, deleting a `*.txt` file, and so forth. You will see various bits of information regarding the state of the text files within MyFolder (see Figure 20-8).

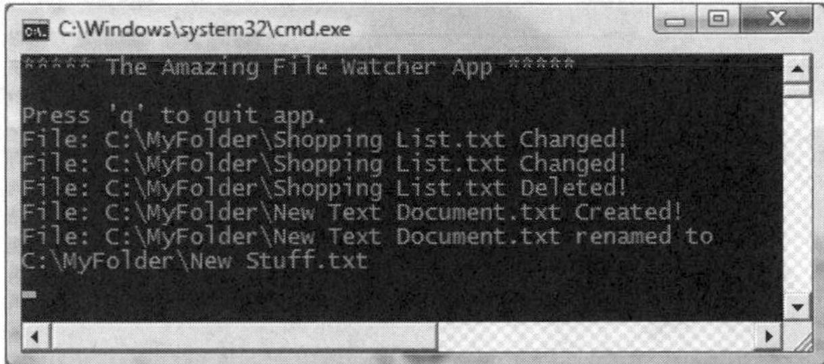

Figure 20-8. *Watching some text files*

■ **Source Code** The MyDirectoryWatcher application is included under the Chapter 20 subdirectory.

Performing Asynchronous File I/O

To conclude our examination of the `System.IO` namespace, let's see how to interact with `FileStream` types asynchronously. You have already seen the asynchronous support provided by the .NET Framework during the examination of multithreading (see Chapter 18). Because large file I/O operations can be a lengthy task, all types deriving from `System.IO.Stream` inherit a set of methods that enable asynchronous processing of the data. As you would expect, these methods work in conjunction with the `IAsyncResult` type:

```
public abstract class Stream :
  MarshalByRefObject, IDisposable
{
```

```
...
  public virtual IAsyncResult BeginRead(byte[] buffer, int offset,
    int count, AsyncCallback callback, object state);
  public virtual IAsyncResult BeginWrite(byte[] buffer, int offset,
    int count, AsyncCallback callback, object state);

  public virtual int EndRead(IAsyncResult asyncResult);
  public virtual void EndWrite(IAsyncResult asyncResult);
}
```

The process of working with the asynchronous behavior of Stream-derived types is identical to working with asynchronous delegates and asynchronous remote method invocations. While it's unlikely that asynchronous behaviors will greatly improve file access, other streams (e.g., socket based) are much more likely to benefit from asynchronous handling. In any case, the following Console Application (AsyncFileStream) illustrates one manner in which you can asynchronously interact with a FileStream type (be sure to import the System.Threading and System.IO namespaces):

```
class Program
{
  static void Main(string[] args)
  {
    Console.WriteLine("***** Fun with Async File I/O *****\n");

    Console.WriteLine("Main thread started. ThreadID = {0}",
      Thread.CurrentThread.GetHashCode());

    // Must use this ctor to get a FileStream with asynchronous
    // read or write access.
    FileStream fs = new FileStream("logfile.txt", FileMode.Append,
      FileAccess.Write, FileShare.None, 4096, true);

    string msg = "this is a test";
    byte[] buffer = Encoding.ASCII.GetBytes(msg);

    // Start the asynchronous write. WriteDone invoked when finished.
    // Note that the FileStream object is passed as state info to the
    // callback method.
    fs.BeginWrite(buffer, 0, buffer.Length,
      new AsyncCallback(WriteDone), fs);
  }

  private static void WriteDone(IAsyncResult ar)
  {
    Console.WriteLine("AsyncCallback method on ThreadID = {0}",
      Thread.CurrentThread.GetHashCode());

    Stream s = (Stream)ar.AsyncState;
    s.EndWrite(ar);
    s.Close();
  }
}
```

The only point of interest in this example (assuming you recall the process of working with delegates!) is that in order to enable the asynchronous behavior of the FileStream type, you must make use of a specific constructor (shown here). The final System.Boolean parameter (when set to true) informs the FileStream object to perform its work on a secondary thread of execution.

■ Source Code The AsyncFileStream application is included under the Chapter 20 subdirectory.

Understanding the Role of Isolated Storage

Each of the file I/O examples you have just examined make a very big assumption regarding the execution of the application: that it has been granted *full trust security privileges* by the CLR. As you would imagine, the act of reading from, or writing to, a machine's hard drive could be a potential security threat, based on the origin of the application. Recall that the .NET platform supports the ability to download assemblies from a variety of locations including external websites, from an intranet, or even dynamically in memory using an assembly created via the types of the `System.Reflection.Emit` namespace (examined in Chapter 19).

Furthermore, you may also recall from Chapter 15 that the `<codeBase>` element of a client `*.config` file allows you to declaratively specify such an arbitrary path for the CLR to find an external assembly; while the `Assembly.LoadFrom()` method (see Chapter 16) allows you to programmatically load assemblies located at an external URI.

It's a Matter of Trust

Given the fact that a .NET assembly can be loaded from a variety of locations beyond the current machine's local hard drive, the issue of trust becomes very important. By way of illustration, assume you have an application that executes code downloaded from a remote location. If this code library attempts to read files on the local computer, how can we ensure the library is not attempting to read sensitive information? Likewise, if we download a remote executable to run on a local machine, how can we make sure this assembly does not attempt to read sensitive data within the system registry, make calls to the underlying API of the operating system (for evil purposes), or other such potential security risks?

The answer, as far as the .NET platform is concerned, is to make use of a .NET-centric security mechanism known as Code Access Security. Using CAS, the CLR can deny or grant a number of security privileges to the executing assembly, including the following:

- Manipulation of a machine's directory/file structure
- Manipulation of network/web/database connections
- Creation of new application domains/dynamic assemblies
- Use of .NET reflection services
- Calls to unmanaged code using PInvoke

Focusing on the I/O-specific security concerns, assume that you are authoring an application that will be deployed to external users via some remote web-based URL. Based on how you configure the deployment script (and based on the security policy of the user's machine), it may run under a restricted security environment that will *prevent* access to the local file system. If your application must store user or application settings using the types of the `System.IO` namespace, the CLR will throw runtime security exceptions!

The types within the `System.IO.IsolatedStorage` namespace can be used to create an application that reads and writes data to a very specific location of a .NET-aware machine using *isolated storage*. This can be understood as a safe "sandbox" where the CLR will allow file I/O operations to occur, even if the application has been downloaded from an external URL or has in other ways been placed in a security sandbox by a system administrator.

Other Uses of the Isolated Storage API

Understand, however, that the isolated storage API is not limited to controlling read/write file operations on remotely downloaded code. This API also provides a simple way to persist per-user data in a manner that ensures other applications cannot indirectly (or directly) tamper with said data. For example, using isolated storage, it is possible to build a single application that saves data in isolated folders for each user logged on to a specific workstation.

Another benefit of using the isolated storage API is that your code base does not need to hard-code paths or directory names in the application. Rather, when using isolated storage, an application indirectly saves data to a unique data compartment that is associated with some aspect of the code's identity, such as its URL, strong name, or X509 digital signature (more information on code identity later in this chapter).

Thankfully, programming with the isolated storage API is very simple to those who understand basic file I/O operations. However, before we examine how to do so, allow me to provide an overview of the .NET Code Access Security model.

■ **Note** Complete coverage of CAS would easily entail an entire chapter (or two). Here I will explain the core operation of CAS in order to set the foundation for the role of the isolated storage API. Please consult the .NET Framework 3.5 SDK for further details of CAS if you are so inclined.

A Primer on Code Access Security

To address the security issues involved with downloading and executing remote .NET assemblies, the CLR will automatically determine the assembly's identity and assign it to one of many preconfigured code groups. Simply put, a *code group* is a collection of assemblies that all meet the same criteria (such as the point of origin).

The criterion used by the CLR to determine which code group an assembly belongs to is referred to as *evidence*. Beyond the point of origin, an assembly can be placed into a code group using other forms of evidence such as an assembly's strong name, an embedded X509 digital certificate, or some sort of custom criteria you have accounted for programmatically.

■ **Note** Strictly speaking, evidence comes in two flavors: assembly evidence and host evidence. While assembly evidence is compiled into the assembly, host evidence can only be specified programmatically using the AppDomain type.

Once an assembly's evidence has been evaluated to determine which code group it belongs to, the CLR will then consult the *permission set* (which, as you might guess, is simply a named collection of individual permissions) associated with the code group to determine what the assembly can and, more importantly, *cannot* do.

Collectively, code groups and their related permissions constitute a *security policy*, which can actually be partitioned at three major levels (enterprise, machine, and user). Using this stratified approach, it is possible for a system administrator to create unique policies for the company at large as well as at the machine/user level.

Once each of the security policies have been applied (enterprise, machine, and user), the assembly will execute under the .NET runtime. If the assembly attempts to execute code outside of its permission set, the CLR will throw a runtime security exception. Figure 20-9 illustrates how these building blocks of CAS (evidence, code groups/permission sets, and policies) intertwine from a high level.

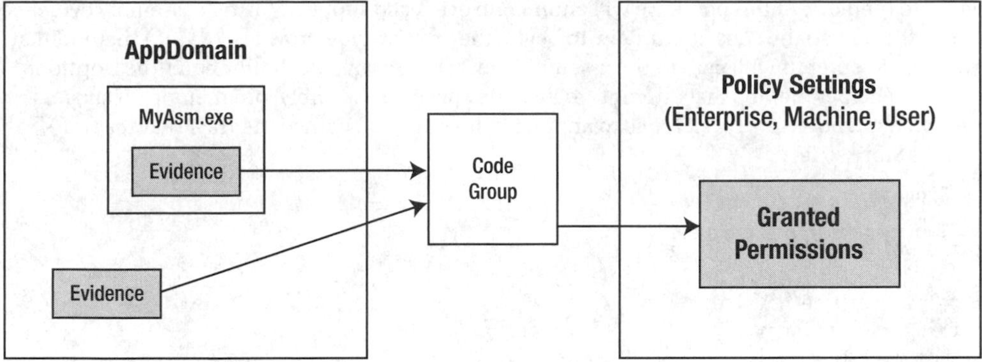

Figure 20-9. *The building blocks of CAS*

The act of evaluating evidence, placing assemblies into code groups, and mapping permission sets to the assembly in question happens transparently in the background whenever you run a .NET application. For the most part, the default CAS security settings and CLR/CAS interactions can be allowed to function in the background without any direct interaction on your part. However, it is worth your while to dig a bit deeper into the building blocks of CAS, beginning with the notion of assembly evidence.

The Role of Evidence

In order for the CLR to determine which code group to place an assembly into, the first step is to read the supplied evidence. As mentioned, evidence is simply information obtained from an assembly (or possible the hosting application domain) at the point it is loaded into memory. Table 20-12 documents the major types of evidence an assembly can present to the CLR.

Table 20-12. *Various Types of Assembly Evidence*

Host Evidence Type	Meaning in Life
Application directory	The installation directory of the assembly
Assembly hash code	The hash value of an assembly's contents
Publisher certificate	The Authenticode X509 digital certificate assigned to the assembly (if any)
Site	The source website where an assembly was loaded (does not apply to assemblies loaded from the local machine)
Assembly strong name	The strong name of an assembly (if any)
URL	The URL from which an assembly was loaded (HTTP, FTP, file, and so on)
Zone	The name of the zone where the assembly was loaded

While the reading of evidence happens automatically, it is possible to programmatically read evidence as well using the reflection APIs and the `Evidence` type within the `System.Security.Policy` namespace. To deepen your understanding of evidence, create a new Console Application named

MyEvidenceViewer. Once you have done so, be sure to import the `System.Reflection`, `System.Collections`, and `System.Security.Policy` namespaces.

We will now build a simple application that will prompt the user for the name of an assembly to load into memory. At this point, we will enumerate over each supplied form of assembly evidence and print the data to the console window. To begin, the `Program` type provides a `Main()` method that allows users to enter the full path to the assembly they wish to evaluate. If they enter the `L` option, we will call a helper method that attempts to load the specified assembly into memory. If successful, we will pass the `Assembly` reference to another helper method named `DisplayAsmEvidence()`. Here is the story so far:

```
class Program
{
  static void Main(string[] args)
  {
    bool isUserDone = false;
    string userOption = "";
    Assembly asm = null;

    Console.WriteLine("***** Evidence Viewer *****\n");
    do
    {
      Console.Write("L (load assembly) or Q (quit): ");
      userOption = Console.ReadLine();
      switch (userOption.ToLower())
      {
        case "l":
          asm = LoadAsm();
          if (asm != null)
          {
            DisplayAsmEvidence(asm);
          }
          break;

        case "q":
          isUserDone = true;
          break;

        default:
          Console.WriteLine("I have no idea what you want!");
          break;
      }
    } while (!isUserDone);
  }
}
```

The `LoadAsm()` method will simply call `Assembly.LoadFrom()` to set the private `Assembly` member variable:

```
private static Assembly LoadAsm()
{
  Console.Write("Enter path to assembly: ");
  try
  {
    return Assembly.LoadFrom(Console.ReadLine());
  }
  catch
  {
```

```
      Console.WriteLine("Load error...");
      return null;
    }
  }
```

Finally, the DisplayAsmEvidence() method will extract out the evidence of the loaded assembly via the Evidence property of the Assembly type. From here, we obtain an enumerator (via the GetHostEvidence() method of the Evidence type) and print out each flavor of presented evidence:

```
private static void DisplayAsmEvidence(Assembly asm)
{
  // Get evidence collection and underlying enumerator.
  Evidence e = asm.Evidence;
  IEnumerator itfEnum = e.GetHostEnumerator();

  // Now print out the evidence.
  while (itfEnum.MoveNext())
  {
    Console.WriteLine(" **** Press Enter to continue ****");
    Console.ReadLine();
    Console.WriteLine(itfEnum.Current);
  }
}
```

To test our application, my suggestion is to create a folder directly off your C drive named MyAsms. Into this folder, copy the strongly named CarLibrary.dll assembly (from Chapter 15), and run your program. Assuming you opt for the L command, specify the full path to your assembly and press Enter. Your application should now print out each flavor of evidence to the console, as shown in Figure 20-10 (note that the way our application was created, you will need to hit the Enter key to display each form of evidence).

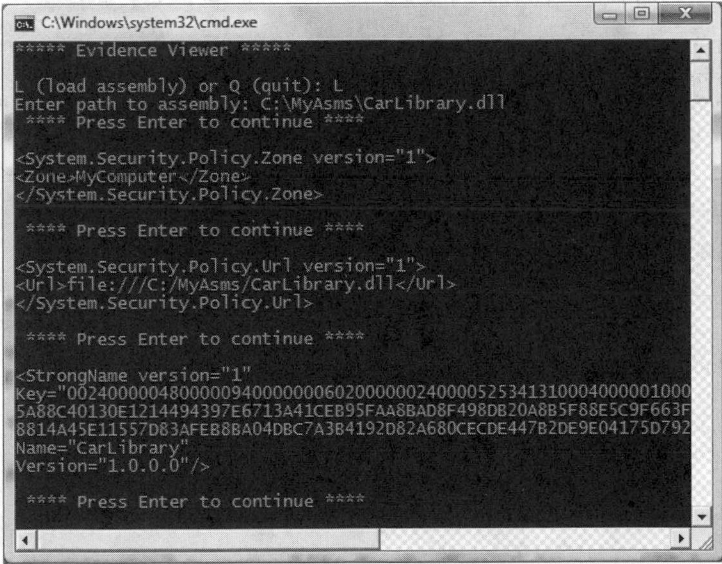

Figure 20-10. *Viewing the evidence of* CarLibrary.dll

Here you can see that `CarLibrary.dll` has been placed into the MyComputer zone, from the URL of `C:\MyAsms\CarLibrary.dll`, and has a specific strong name value. If you were to load assemblies from an entirely different location (such as a remote website), you would obviously see unique output. In any case, at this point simply understand that when an assembly is loaded into memory, the CLR will investigate the supplied evidence.

■ **Source Code** The MyEvidenceViewer project is included under the Chapter 20 subdirectory.

The Role of Code Groups

Using evidence, the CLR can then place the assembly into a code group. Each code group is mapped to a security zone that has a default out-of-the-box set of security settings the CLR will use to dictate exactly what the assembly can (or cannot) do. Table 20-13 documents some of the more common code groups to be aware of, including their default assigned permission set (examined in the next section).

Table 20-13. *Several Common Code Groups*

Default Code Group	Assigned Permission Set	Meaning in Life
My_Computer_Zone	Full Trust	Represents an assembly loaded directly from the local hard drive
LocalIntranet_Zone	LocalIntranet	Represents an assembly downloaded from a share point on the local intranet
Internet_Zone	Internet	Represents an assembly downloaded from the World Wide Web

The .NET Framework 3.5 SDK ships with a GUI administration tool that allows system administrators to view and tweak existing code groups or, if need be, define a brand new code group. For example, using this tool it is possible to inform the CLR that any external assembly downloaded from a particular URL (such as `http://www.intertech.com`) should execute within a customized security sandbox.

■ **Note** The .NET Framework 3.5 SDK also provides a command-line tool named `caspol.exe` that provides the same options.

This tool can be run by double-clicking the Microsoft .NET Framework Configuration applet located under the Administrative Tools folder of your machine's Control Panel. Once you launch this tool, you are able to configure CAS settings on three basic levels: the enterprise at large (e.g., all networked machines), the current machine, or on a per-user basis. (It is also possible to configure CAS on the application domain level as well, but this can only be done programmatically.) Figure 20-11 shows the expended nodes of the default "machine-level policy" settings for CAS on my current computer.

Again, notice that the All_Code code group (which represents all .NET assemblies) defines several zones to which an assembly can belong (My_Computer_Zone, etc.). If you were to right-click any of the nodes under the All_Code root, you would be able to activate a property page that describes further details. For example, Figure 20-12 shows the properties of the My_Computer_Zone code group, which again represents any assembly loaded directly from the local hard drive.

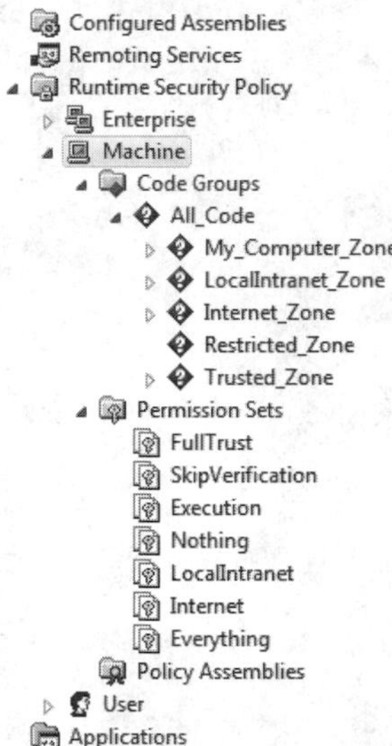

Figure 20-11. *The CAS-centric machine policy*

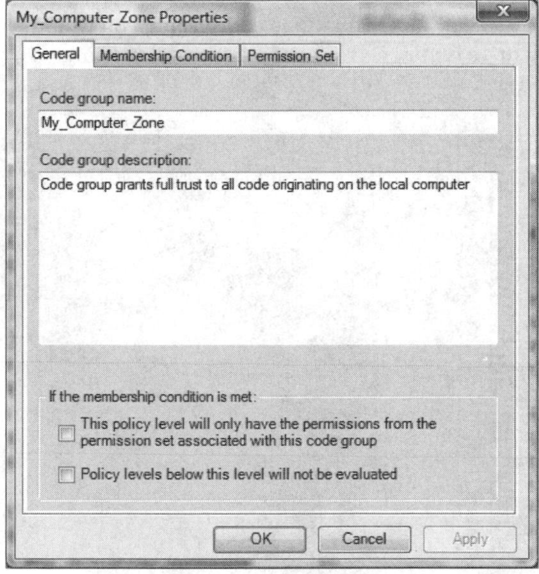

Figure 20-12. *Details of the My_Computer_Zone code group*

If you were to click the Membership Condition tab, you would be able to determine how the CLR figured out whether a given .NET assembly should be a member of this zone. In Figure 20-13, you can see the membership condition is the rather nondescript value Zone, meaning the location at which the assembly has been loaded.

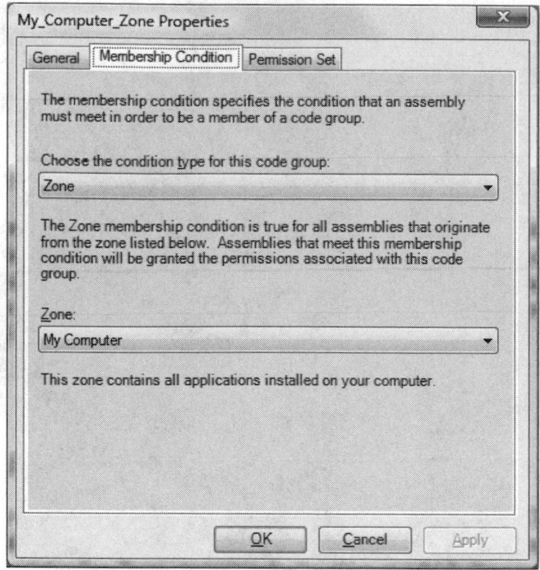

Figure 20-13. *The membership condition for the My_Computer_Zone code group*

If you were to click the Permission Set tab of the My_Computer_Zone code group, you would see that any assembly loaded from the local hard drive is assigned a set of security permissions given the name Full Trust (see Figure 20-14).

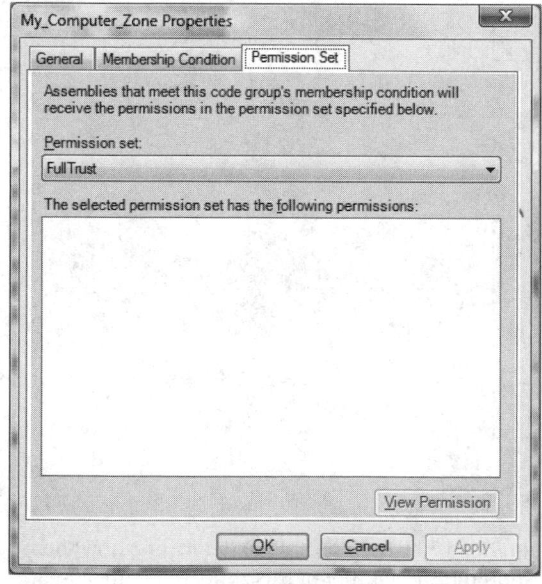

Figure 20-14. *Assemblies loaded from the local hard drive are granted Full Trust permissions by default.*

In contrast, the permission set granted to assemblies that are loaded from an external URL (outside of a company intranet) will be placed into the Internet_Zone code group, which runs under a much more restrictive set of privileges. As you can see in Figure 20-15, assemblies loaded into the Internet_Zone group are not given Full Trust permissions, but are rather assigned to a set of permissions named Internet.

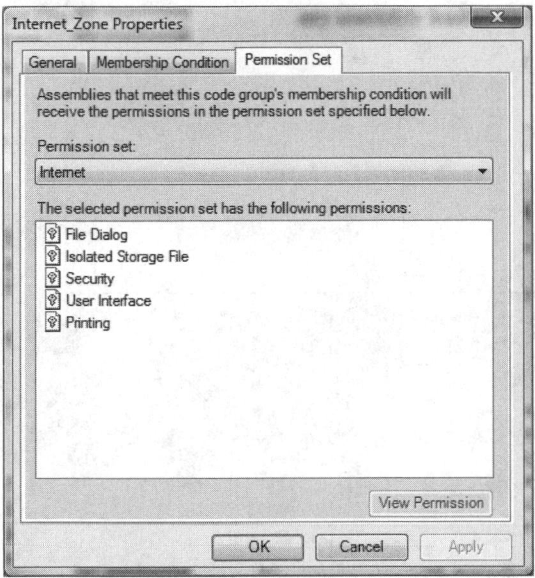

Figure 20-15. *Assemblies loaded from external URLs are not granted Full Trust permissions by default.*

The Role of Permission Sets

As you have seen, the CLR will place an assembly into a code group based on various criteria (origin of the load, strong name, etc.). The code group in turn has a set of permissions assigned to it that are given a friendly name such as Full Trust, Internet, and so forth. Each permission set (as the name implies) is a collection of individually configured permissions that control various security settings (access to the printer, access to the file system, use of the reflection API, etc.). Using the Microsoft .NET Framework Configuration utility, you are able to view the settings for any of the default permission sets simply by selecting the View Permissions link. Figure 20-16 shows the permissions for the Internet permission set, once the View Permissions link has been clicked.

Each of these icons (File Dialog, Isolated Storage File, Security, etc.) represents a specific permission in the set, all of which can be further configured by double-clicking a given item. For example, if you were to double-click the Security permission (which is sort of a catchall permission for common security settings), you could see that if an assembly is running under the Internet_Zone (thereby restricted by the Internet permission set), it is able to execute, but by default *cannot* perform a number of other basic details, such as make use of platform invocation services to call into the API of the operating system (see Figure 20-17).

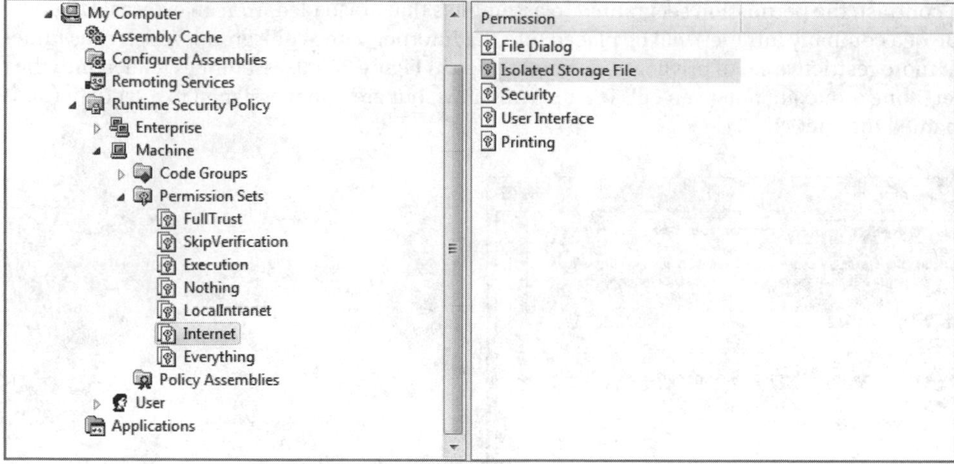

Figure 20-16. *Internet permission set*

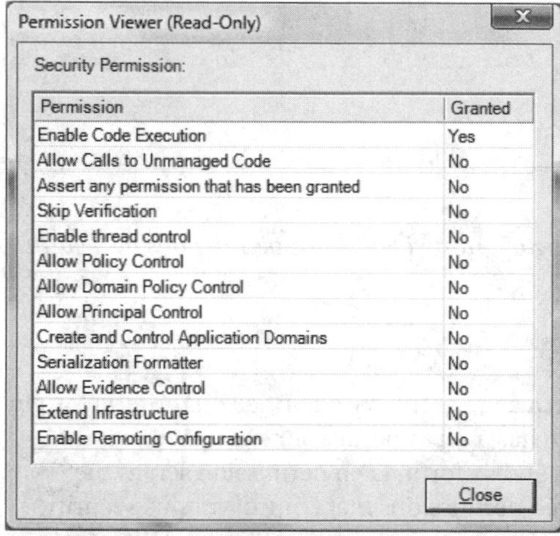

Figure 20-17. *Viewing individual permissions for a permisson set*

Observing CAS in Action

To illustrate a very simple example of CAS operations, we will change some default settings for the My_Computer code group and observe the results. Begin by right-clicking the My_Computer_Zone code group for your machine policy using the Microsoft .NET Framework Configuration applet to open the related property page. Next, click the Permission Set tab, and change the permission set from Full Trust to Internet (see Figure 20-18).

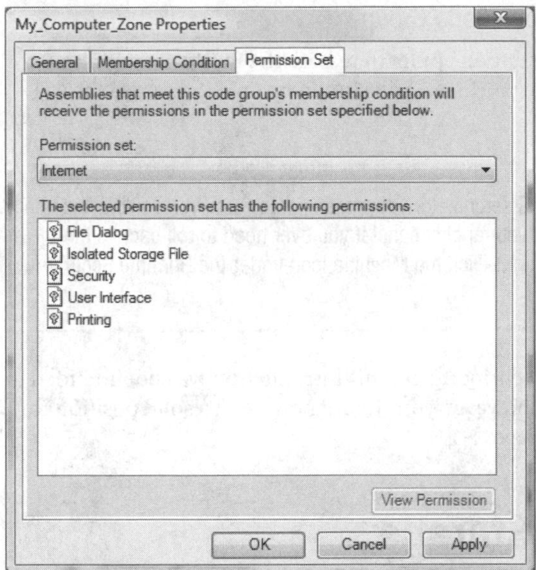

Figure 20-18. *Changing the permission set for the My_Computer_Zone code group*

Once you click the OK button, you have just changed the security policy for your local machine. Specifically for our purposes, any .NET executable that you load from your hard drive will no longer be able to access the local hard drive using the types of `System.IO`! To verify, attempt to run any of the IO-centric applications created in this chapter. To illustrate, use a command prompt to navigate to the directory containing the `DriveInfoApp.exe` application created earlier in this chapter. Now, attempt to run the program. When the runtime error dialog box is displayed, select the Close the Program option, and observe the output in the command window. As you can see from Figure 20-19, this application was denied access to the local hard drive, and the CLR threw a security exception.

Administrator: Visual Studio 2008 Beta 2 Command Prompt

```
C:\My Books\C# and the .NET Platform 4th ed\Code\Final Numbering\Chapter 20\DriveInfoApp\bin\
Debug>DriveInfoApp.exe
***** Fun with DriveInfo *****


Unhandled Exception: System.Security.SecurityException: Request for the permission of type 'S
ystem.Security.Permissions.SecurityPermission, mscorlib, Version=2.0.0.0, Culture=neutral, Pu
blicKeyToken=b77a5c561934e089' failed.
   at System.Security.CodeAccessSecurityEngine.Check(Object demand, StackCrawlMark& stackMark
, Boolean isPermSet)
   at System.Security.CodeAccessPermission.Demand()
   at System.IO.Directory.GetLogicalDrives()
   at System.IO.DriveInfo.GetDrives()
   at DriveInfoApp.Program.Main(String[] args)
The action that failed was:
Demand
The type of the first permission that failed was:
System.Security.Permissions.SecurityPermission
The first permission that failed was:
<IPermission class="System.Security.Permissions.SecurityPermission, mscorlib, Version=2.0.0.0
, Culture=neutral, PublicKeyToken=b77a5c561934e089"
version="1"
Flags="UnmanagedCode"/>
```

Figure 20-19. *Security breach! The My_Computer_Zone code group no longer allows IO operations!*

Restoring Full Trust to the My_Computer_Zone Code Group

Now, use the Microsoft .NET Framework Configuration applet to restore the Full Trust permission set to the My_Computer_Zone code group. Once you do so, you should be able to execute the `DriveInfoApp.exe` without error.

■Note Obviously, when you tinker with the default CAS settings for your machine account, you could accidentally establish settings that severely cripple the execution of your applications! If you ever need to roll back to the default out-of-the-box machine policy settings, simply right-click the Machine icon under the Runtime Security Policy folder and select the Reset menu option.

That wraps up our primer of Code Access Security. Again, this introduction was not intended to provide complete coverage of this very rich API; however, you should now be in a solid position to better understand the usefulness of isolated storage.

An Overview of Isolated Storage

As mentioned, one major reason for the isolated storage API is to provide a safe sandbox where applications can read/write data, regardless of which code group they are placed into and without the need to alter the default security policies. In addition, use of this technology is ideally under a number of circumstances such as the following:

- You need to save preferences for your application for each user or forms of per-user data (`DataSets`, XML files, etc.).
- You are deploying a ClickOnce application that functions in a sandbox and has no access to the (unrestrained) local file system.
- You have downloaded Windows Forms controls from a URL that integrate into a web application, and they must store settings on the client machine.
- You are deploying a XAML Browser Application, or XBAP (see Chapter 28), that needs to persist data on the user's machine.

Do be aware that if your application is using isolated storage, this does not mean that you would not also opt to store bits of data in a `*.config` file (such as connection strings) or place various application settings in the system registry. In fact, like any technology, isolated storage does have a few potential drawbacks. First and foremost, data placed into isolated storage is not automatically encrypted. Therefore, just like traditional IO, if you write out sensitive data (e.g., credit card information), you will need to manually encrypt (and decrypt) the information.

■Note Use of the .NET encryption APIs in not covered in this edition of the text. If you are interested in examining the details, look up the topic "Cryptographic Services" using the .NET Framework 3.5 SDK documentation.

As well, data placed into isolated storage, like any part of the file system, can be copied, moved, or deleted by the end user. However, as you will see, the types of the `System.IO.IsolatedStorage` namespace store data in a dynamically generated directory structure that is tucked away in a specific location of the hard drive. For this reason, it is true that most end users will have no direct encounters with their machine's isolated storage area.

Finally, be aware that a system administrator can limit the storage size of a machine's isolated storage quota. Thus, if your application is persisting vast amounts of data, and other applications on the machine are *also* persisting vast amounts of data, there is a chance that the storage area will meet its upper limit (it is always a good idea to make use of structured exception handling techniques to gracefully handle this possibility).

The Scope of Isolated Storage

By its very nature, isolated storage will also persist data using (at very least) the current user as a level of isolation. Therefore, if you have authored a program that saves data using isolated storage, the data is persisted based on the currently logged on user. If another user logs on to the same workstation and saves data using the same application, the data is persisted into a unique location for that particular user.

In addition to user-level partitioning, isolated storage can also be set up to further isolate data based on the assembly and/or application domain identity. If you configure isolation and the user + assembly level, the application will be able to use the same store regardless of which application domain is hosting the program. In this case, the most specific piece of available evidence (such as a strong name) will be used to create the store name. This would allow the end user to have multiple instances of the program running on a single machine, where each instance is "pointing" to the same store (see Figure 20-20).

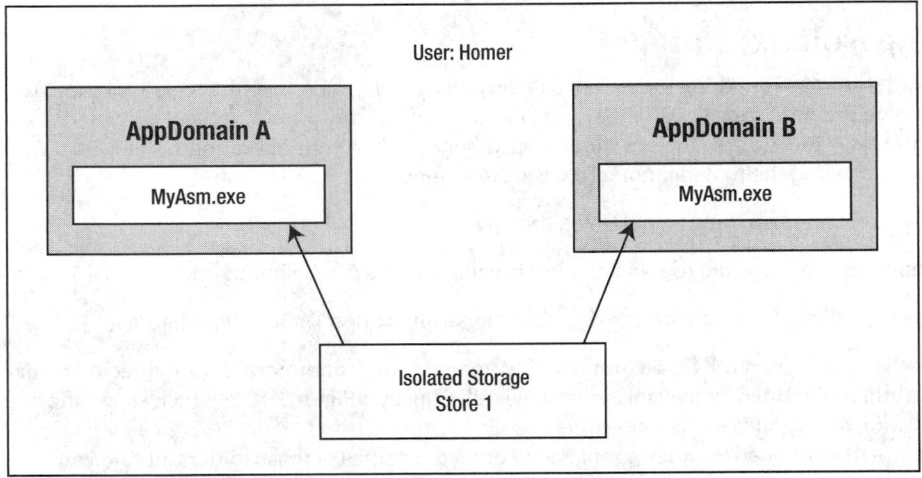

Figure 20-20. *User and assembly-level isolation*

On the other hand, if you configure a user + assembly + application domain isolation level, the application domain is also taken into consideration. In addition to the most specific form of assembly evidence, the most specific form of AppDomain evidence (typically Site) will be used to build the store. With this approach, even if the same assembly is used by unique AppDomains, the data is maintained in separate stores (see Figure 20-21).

Isolated storage can also be used to build roaming profiles. The roaming scope allows users to log on to unique workstations and obtain the same application data. In this case, the storage data is persisted to a network location and downloaded on demand when a user logs on to a given workstation. We will not be examining this aspect of isolated storage, so consult the .NET Framework 3.5 SDK documentation if you are interested.

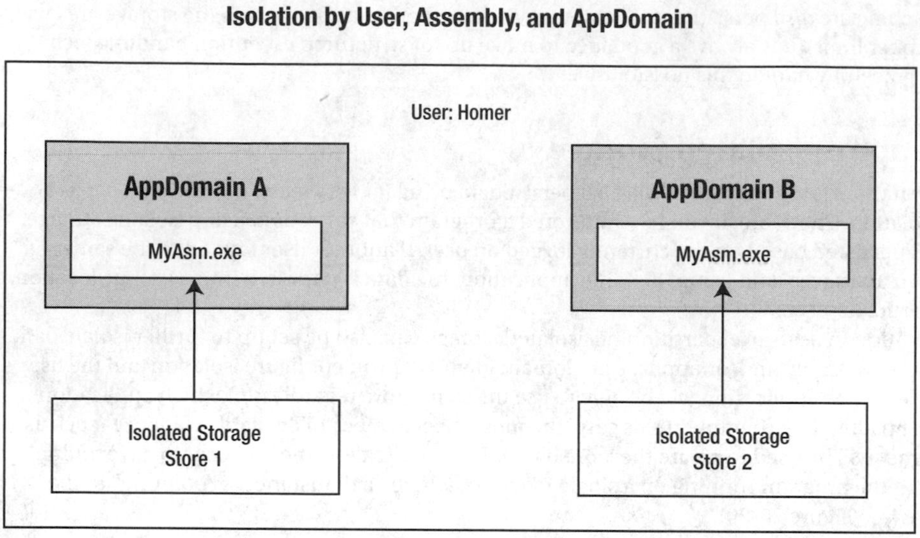

Isolation by User, Assembly, and AppDomain

User: Homer

AppDomain A

MyAsm.exe

AppDomain B

MyAsm.exe

Isolated Storage Store 1

Isolated Storage Store 2

Figure 20-21. *User, assembly, and application domain-level isolation*

Locating Isolated Storage

Again, isolated storage is nothing more than a dedicated part of a .NET machine's file system, so to this end it is no different from C:\Windows, C:\Program Files, or any other directory on your disk. However, the exact location of isolated storage will differ based on your operating system. On a Vista machine, you can find the root location of a given store under

C:\Users\<*user*>\App Data\Local\IsolatedStorage

On a Windows XP machine, the root location for isolated storage can be found under

C:\Documents and Settings\<*user*>\Local Settings\Application Data\IsolatedStorage

Beneath this root, you will find a number of (completely unpronounceable) subdirectories that are created and maintained by the isolated storage API. Consider Figure 20-22, which shows the storage location on my current Vista machine.

Again, you do not need to worry about deciphering the names of these folders, nor do you need to specify their names programmatically when creating stores for your users. These names are generated based on user identity and the required assembly and/or application domain evidence. When gathering evidence for assemblies and AppDomains, the CLR evaluates in this order (most specific to least):

- Publisher certificate
- Strong name
- URL
- Site
- Zone

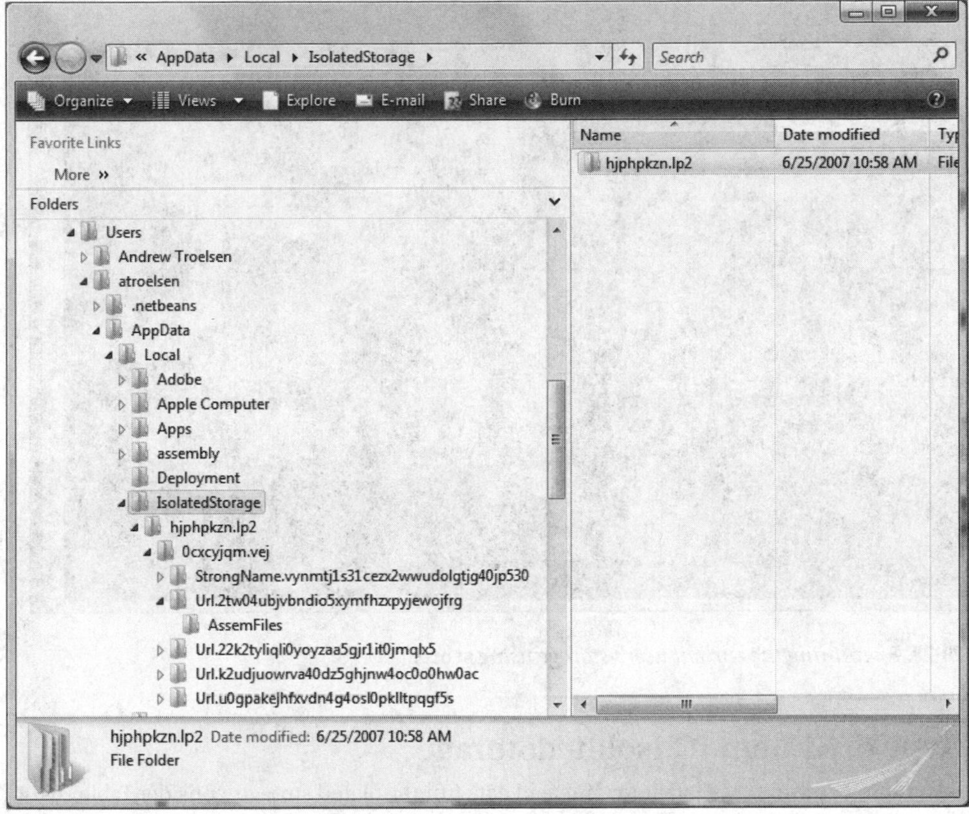

Figure 20-22. *Isolated storage on a Vista machine*

Interacting with Isolated Storage Using storeadm.exe

The .NET Framework 3.5 SDK ships with a command-line utility named `storeadm.exe`, which can be used to interact with the current storage system on a given .NET machine. Using this tool, you are able to view the current stores for the logged in user (via the `/list` option) and completely delete all storage for the current user (by specifying `/remove`). Consider Figure 20-23, which shows the output resulting from the `/list` option.

As you can glean from the previous figure output, this tool also displays the level of isolation (assembly, application domain) and the forms of evidence used to establish the store. What this tool does *not* display is the actual contents of the files placed in a given store. To do so, you will have to locate the generated store location using the Windows Explorer or read in the data programmatically.

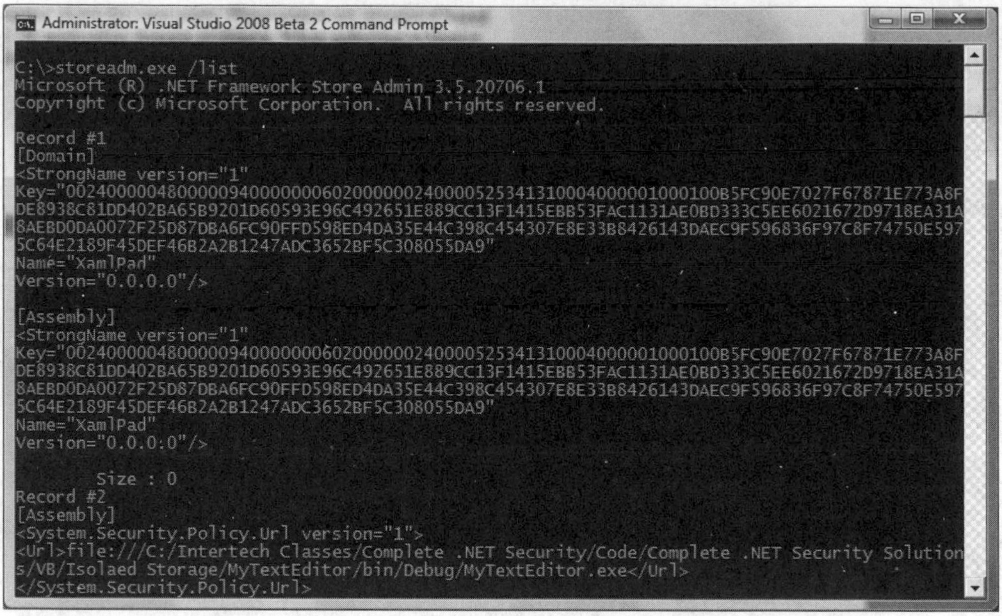

```
Administrator: Visual Studio 2008 Beta 2 Command Prompt

C:\>storeadm.exe /list
Microsoft (R) .NET Framework Store Admin 3.5.20706.1
Copyright (c) Microsoft Corporation.  All rights reserved.

Record #1
[Domain]
<StrongName version="1"
Key="0024000004800000940000000602000000240000525341310004000001000100B5FC90E7027F67871E773A8F
DE8938C81DD402BA65B9201D60593E96C492651E889CC13F1415EBB53FAC1131AE0BD333C5EE6021672D9718EA31A
8AEBD0DA0072F25D87DBA6FC90FFD598ED4DA35E44C398C454307E8E33B8426143DAEC9F596836F97C8F74750E597
5C64E2189F45DEF46B2A2B1247ADC3652BF5C308055DA9"
Name="XamlPad"
Version="0.0.0.0"/>

[Assembly]
<StrongName version="1"
Key="0024000004800000940000000602000000240000525341310004000001000100B5FC90E7027F67871E773A8F
DE8938C81DD402BA65B9201D60593E96C492651E889CC13F1415EBB53FAC1131AE0BD333C5EE6021672D9718EA31A
8AEBD0DA0072F25D87DBA6FC90FFD598ED4DA35E44C398C454307E8E33B8426143DAEC9F596836F97C8F74750E597
5C64E2189F45DEF46B2A2B1247ADC3652BF5C308055DA9"
Name="XamlPad"
Version="0.0.0:0"/>

        Size : 0
Record #2
[Assembly]
<System.Security.Policy.Url version="1">
<Url>file:///C:/Intertech Classes/Complete .NET Security/Code/Complete .NET Security Solution
s/VB/Isolaed Storage/MyTextEditor/bin/Debug/MyTextEditor.exe</Url>
</System.Security.Policy.Url>
```

Figure 20-23. *Examining the current user's storage using* `storeadm.exe`

The Type of System.IO.IsolatedStorage

Before examining how to write data into (and read data from) isolated storage, consider Table 20-14, which documents the core types of isolated storage. As you can see, this namespace is refreshingly small, given that the types are used in conjunction with the basic types of `System.IO`.

Table 20-14. *The Types of* `System.IO.IsolatedStorage`

System.IO.IsolatedStorage Type	Meaning in Life
`IsolatedStorage`	This type represents the abstract base class from which all isolated storage implementations must derive.
`IsolatedStorageScope`	This enum controls the level of isolation to make use of (assembly, application domain, roaming).
`IsolatedStorageException`	This type specifies the exception that is thrown when an operation in isolated storage fails.
`IsolatedStorageFile`	This type represents an isolated storage area containing files and directories.
`IsolatedStorageFileStream`	This type exposes a file within isolated storage.

Obtaining a Store Using IsolatedStorageFile

When you wish to store application data in isolated storage, the first step is to decide the level of isolation you which to establish. Recall that storage is always isolated by the current user; however, a store can also be established using assembly or application domain evidence (as well as via roaming profiles, which we will not examine here). To configure the correct isolation level, one option is to establish values using the IsolatedStorageScope enumeration and call IsolatedStorageFile.GetStore(). As a shorthand notation, however, you can call the static GetUserStoreForDomain() or GetUserStoreForAssembly() of the IsolatedStorageFile type. Consider the following examples:

```
static void GetAppDomainStorageForUser()
{
  // Open up isolated storage based on identity of
  // assembly and AppDomain (short hand).
  IsolatedStorageFile store =
    IsolatedStorageFile.GetUserStoreForDomain();

  // Or combine flags and use GetStore().
  IsolatedStorageFile store2 =
    IsolatedStorageFile.GetStore(IsolatedStorageScope.User |
    IsolatedStorageScope.Domain, null, null);
}

static void GetAssemblyStorageForUser()
{
  // Open up isolated storage based on identity of
  // assembly (short hand).
  IsolatedStorageFile store2 =
    IsolatedStorageFile.GetUserStoreForAssembly();

  // Or combine flags and use GetStore().
  IsolatedStorageFile store2 =
    IsolatedStorageFile.GetStore(IsolatedStorageScope.User |
    IsolatedStorageScope.Assembly, null, null);
}
```

Notice that regardless of the approach taken, the end result is you receive an IsolatedStorageFile object. Using this type, you are able to write data into the store, read data from a store, and create a custom directory structure within the current user's store. Table 20-15 documents some of the interesting members of IsolatedStorageFile.

Table 20-15. *Members of* IsolatedStorageFile

Member	Meaning in Life
CurrentSize, MaximumSize	These read-only properties allow you to view size characteristics of isolated storage.
Scope	This property shows the scope of isolation (user, assembly, AppDomain).
CreateDirectory()	This method creates a new directory in the store.
DeleteDirectory()	This method deletes a directory from the store.
DeleteFile()	This method deletes a file within a given directory.
GetDirectoryNames()	This method allows you to iterate over named directories.
GetEnumerator()	This method gets a scope-specific IEnumerator.
GetFiles()	This method gets files within a specific store.
GetStore()	This overloaded method obtains isolated storage corresponding to the given application domain and assembly evidence objects and isolated storage scope.

Continued

Table 20-15. *Continued*

Member	Meaning in Life
GetUserStoreForAssembly()	This method obtains isolated storage corresponding to the calling code's assembly identity.
GetUserStoreForDomain()	This method obtains isolated storage corresponding to the application domain identity and assembly identity.
Remove()	This method removes stores.

Writing Data to Storage

Once you have obtained a store, your next task is to create an instance of the IsolatedStorageFileStream type, which represents the file in the store you will be using to persist your data. Like other IO streams, this type can be configured using the System.IO.FileMode enumeration examined earlier in this chapter. To illustrate, create a new Console Application project named SimpleIsoStorage and be sure you import the System.IO and System.IO.IsolatedStorage namespaces. Now, update Main() to call the following helper method of the Program type:

```
static void WriteTextToIsoStorage()
{
  // Open up isolated storage based on identity of
  // user + assembly evidence.
  using (IsolatedStorageFile store =
    IsolatedStorageFile.GetUserStoreForAssembly())
  {
    // Now create an IsolatedStorageFileStream type.
    using (IsolatedStorageFileStream isStream
      = new IsolatedStorageFileStream("MyData.txt",
        FileMode.OpenOrCreate, store))
    {
      // Layer this stream into a StreamWriter
      // and write out some text.
      using (StreamWriter sw = new StreamWriter(isStream))
      {
        sw.WriteLine("This is my data.");
        sw.WriteLine("Cool, huh?");
      }
    }
  }
}
```

Here, we begin by obtaining a store for the user based on the identity of the executing assembly (SimpleIsoStorage.exe) by calling IsolatedStorageFile.GetUserStoreForAssembly(). Next, we create a new IsolatedStorageFileStream object, specifying a new file to be named MyData.txt that will be created (or opened if it currently exists) in the store we just obtained. Finally, we layer the IsolatedStorageFileStream object into a System.IO.StreamWriter and pump out a few lines of text.

If you execute this application, you will then be able to dig into your isolated storage location of your computer and (after a bit of hunting) discover the MyData.txt file (see Figure 20-24). If you were to open this file in notepad.exe, you would of course see the two lines of textual data.

Of course, you can layer into an IsolatedStorageFileStream object a Stream-derived type. For example, if you would rather write out data in a binary format, simply make use of the BinaryWriter rather than StreamWriter.

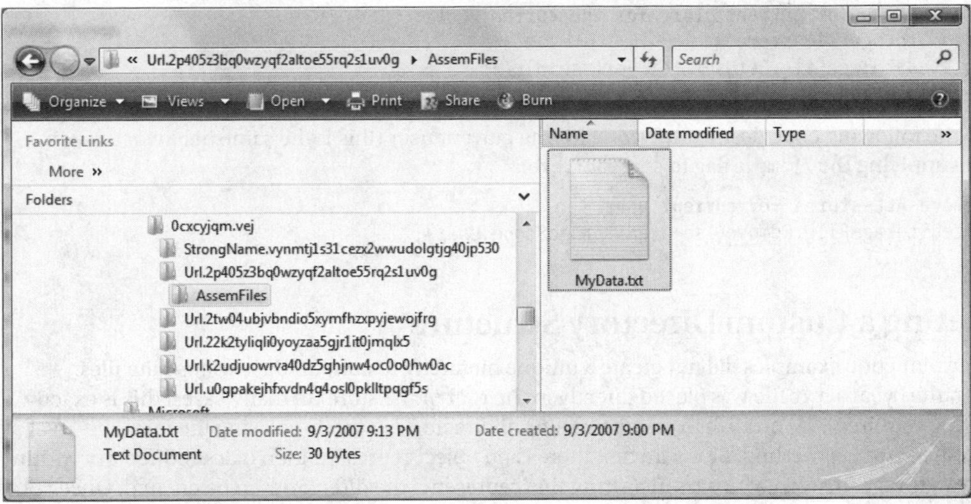

Figure 20-24. *Our text file placed in isolated storage*

Reading Data from Storage

Reading data from a user's store is also very simple. Consider the following new method (which I am assuming you will also call from `Main()` after the call to the `WriteTextToIsoStorage()` method) that will read the data within the `MyData.txt` file and display it to the console window:

```
private static void ReadTextFromIsoStorage()
{
  using (IsolatedStorageFile store =
    IsolatedStorageFile.GetUserStoreForAssembly())
  {
    using (IsolatedStorageFileStream isStream
      = new IsolatedStorageFileStream("MyData.txt", FileMode.Open,
        FileAccess.Read, store))
    {
      // Layer into StreamReader.
      using (StreamReader sr = new StreamReader(isStream))
      {
        string allTheData = sr.ReadToEnd();
        Console.WriteLine(allTheData);
      }
    }
  }
}
```

Deleting User Data from Storage

The `IsolatedStorageFile` type supplies two mechanisms for deleting user stores. The instance-level `Remove()` deletes the store that calls it. The static method `IsolatedStorageFile.Remove()` method takes the `IsolatedStorageScope.User` value and deletes all stores for the user running the code. For example, the following code deletes the active store and destroys all contents:

```
// Remove data for current store for the current user.
IsolatedStorageFile store =
  IsolatedStorageFile.GetUserStoreForAssembly();
store.Remove();
```

while the following code destroys *all stores* for the current user (this is the same behavior as seen when supplying the `/remove` flag to `storeadm.exe`):

```
// Remove ALL stores for current user.
IsolatedStorageFile.Remove(IsolatedStorageScope.User);
```

Creating a Custom Directory Structure

The current code examples did not create a unique hierarchy to contain the various data files. Rather, the `MyData.txt` file was placed directly in the root of the store (in many cases, this is exactly what you required). If you wish to create unique subdirectories, you do so using the instance-level `CreateDirectory()` method. Be aware that there is no object representation of a subdirectory within isolated storage. Instead, you pass in a string that represents the directories to be created. Once you do, `CreateDirectory()` returns an `IsolatedStorageFile` type that represents the access to the most nested directory. Consider the following code:

```
private static void CreateStorageDirectories()
{
  // Forward slashes and backwards slashes are acceptable.
  using (IsolatedStorageFile store =
    IsolatedStorageFile.GetUserStoreForAssembly())
  {
    store.CreateDirectory(@"MyDir\XmlData");
    store.CreateDirectory("MyDir\\BinaryData");
    store.CreateDirectory("MyDir/TextData");
  }
}
```

If you call this method from within `Main()`, you will now be able to find the directory structure shown in Figure 20-25 under your isolated storage area.

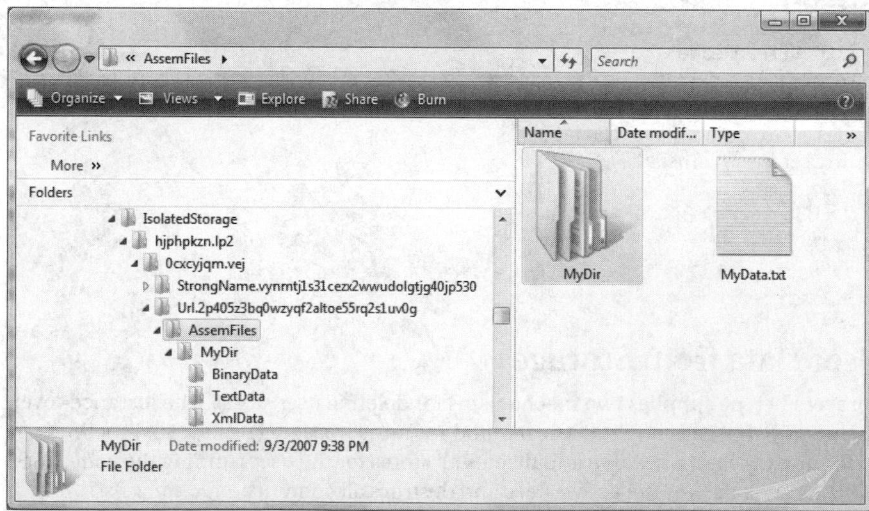

Figure 20-25. *Establishing a directory structure for a given store*

Source Code The SimpleIsoStorage project is included under the Chapter 20 subdirectory.

Isolated Storage in Action: ClickOnce Deployment

At this point, isolated storage might seem like little more than a unique approach to persisting application data on a per-user level (which is very useful in its own right). However, recall that one of the problems this API solves is how to allow applications that do not run under the umbrella of Full Trust security to persist data in a safe manner.

To close this chapter, assume you have a Windows Forms application (named FileOrIsoStorageWinApp) that defines a `Form` containing two buttons. Chapter 27 examines the details of the Windows Forms API; however, if you are following along, handle the `Click` event for each `Button` type.

The first button will attempt to save data to the local hard drive using standard file IO techniques (be sure to import the `System.IO` and `System.IO.IsolatedStorage` namespaces in your code file):

```
private void btnFileIO_Click(object sender, EventArgs e)
{
  using (StreamWriter sw = new StreamWriter(@"C:\MyData.txt"))
  {
    sw.WriteLine("This is my data.");
    sw.WriteLine("Cool, huh?");
  }
}
```

The second button will write the same data to a file in isolated storage. The implementation of this `Click` event handler is identical to the `WriteTextToIsoStorage()` method you created in the previous project; however, here it is again for your convenience:

```
private void btnIsoStorage_Click(object sender, EventArgs e)
{
  // Open up isolated storage based on identity of
  // user + assembly evidence.
  using (IsolatedStorageFile store =
    IsolatedStorageFile.GetUserStoreForAssembly())
  {
    // Now create an IsolatedStorageFileStream type.
    using (IsolatedStorageFileStream isStream
       = new IsolatedStorageFileStream("MyData.txt",
         FileMode.OpenOrCreate, store))
    {
      // Layer this stream into a StreamWriter
      // and write out some text.
      using (StreamWriter sw = new StreamWriter(isStream))
      {
        sw.WriteLine("This is my data.");
        sw.WriteLine("Cool, huh?");
      }
    }
  }
}
```

The IsolatedStorageFilePermission Attribute

Now, before we test our application, add the following `using` directive in the C# file defining your initial `Form`-derived type:

```
using System.Security.Permissions;
```

This namespace defines a number of security-centric attributes that can be applied to your application to inform the security subsystem which security settings a given assembly requires to operate correctly (among other details). Here, we wish to inform the CLR that our application requires, at minimum, assembly-level store isolation permissions. This can be achieved by adding the following assembly-level attribute to the code file of your `Form`-derived type:

```
[assembly: IsolatedStorageFilePermission(SecurityAction.RequestMinimum,
 UsageAllowed = IsolatedStorageContainment.AssemblyIsolationByUser)]
```

Now, when you compile and run this application directly within Visual Studio 2008 (via Ctrl+F5), you will see that clicking either button results in the creation of a new file with blobs of textual data. This is because the application has loaded from My_Computer_Zone, which as you recall grants Full Trust privileges to the assembly.

Constraining the Security Zone

Let's deploy this application in such a way as to load it into Internet_Zone using a more restrictive permission set. To do so, we will deploy our application using ClickOnce deployment. As you might know, ClickOnce is a way to deploy an executable application to an end user's machine via a remote web server. The remote application is hosted within an IIS virtual directory, which can be downloaded and installed to a local machine simply by using a web browser to point to the URL.

■ **Note** Full coverage of ClickOnce is beyond the scope of this chapter. If you have never deployed an application in this manner, simply follow the instructions I provide next (and consult the .NET Framework 3.5 SDK documentation for further details if you so choose).

To begin, open your project's Properties page by double-clicking the Properties icon of Solution Explorer. Once you have done so, click the Security tab. By default, ClickOnce applications are deployed with Full Trust, and therefore they have all the security privileges as a local application installed using traditional means.

Here, we want to build a deployment script that will force our program to run under the Internet zone, which as you recall does not allow access to the hard drive using standard file IO operations. To do so, click the Enable Click Once Security Settings check box, select the This is a partial trust application radio button, and select Internet from the zone drop-down list box. Last but not least, click the Calculate Permissions button at the bottom of the Security configuration page. This will calculate the final permission set required by your application (see Figure 20-26).

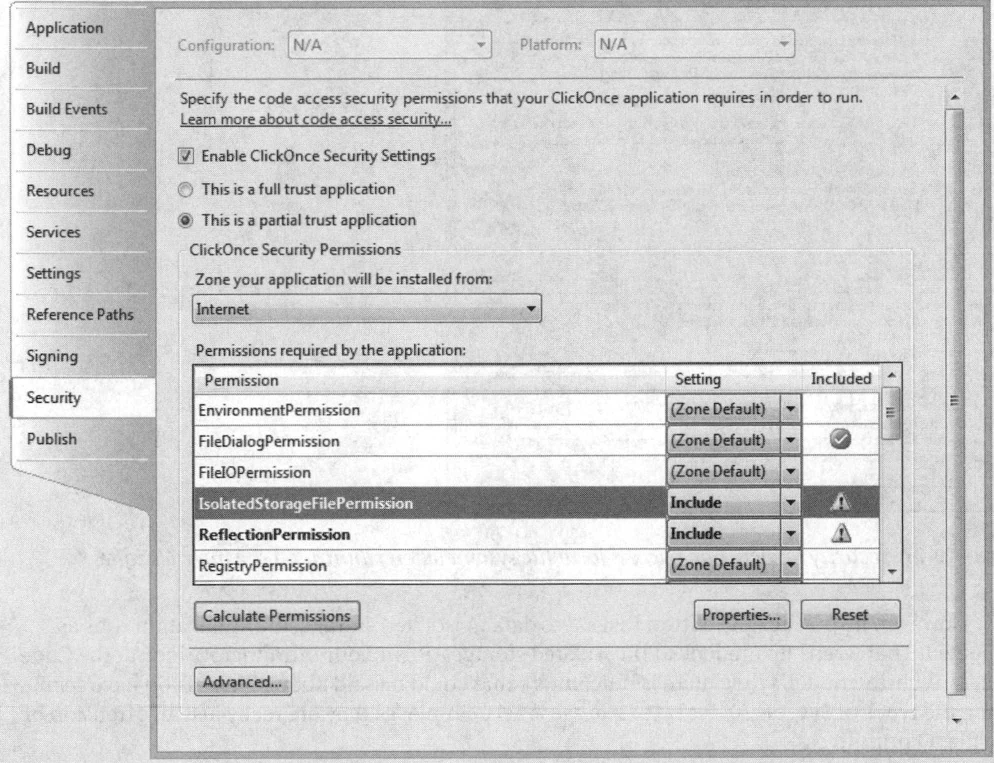

Figure 20-26. *Constraining our application's security zone*

Publishing the Application to a Web Server

Now, click the Publish tab of the Properties editor. Click the Publish Wizard button on the lower part of this page, and on the first page of this wizard, enter the following URL to specify a new IIS virtual directory on your local machine to host this application:

```
http://localhost/MyIsolatedStorageApp/
```

The remaining options of the tool may be left at their defaults. Once you click the Finish button, your web browser will load the autogenerated `publish.htm` file. This is what end users will see when navigating to the remote web server that contains the application they wish to download and install locally (and yes, this web page can be customized to your heart's content; you'll find this file and related content under your project's bin\Debug folder). Click the Install button and run the `setup.exe` application (and accept each security prompt). After a moment or two, the application will install to an area of the user's machine named the ClickOnce cache and the program should launch.

Viewing the Results

Given that we have configured this application to run under restricted security, if you click the button that attempts to save data using the `System.IO` types, you will find the security exception shown in Figure 20-27.

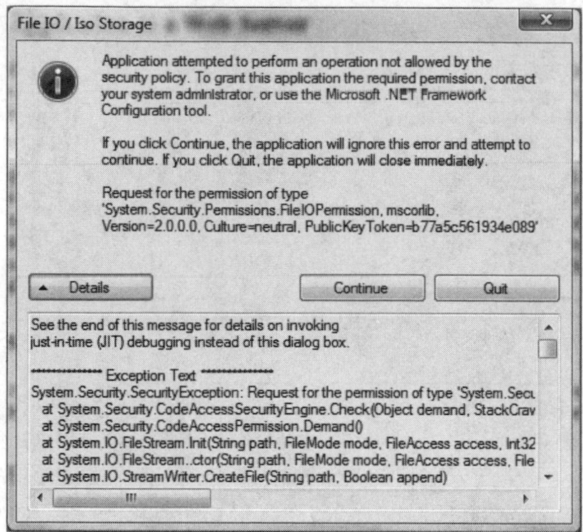

Figure 20-27. *Security breach! Can't access local file system when running in the Internet zone.*

However, if you click the button that saves data to isolated storage, the application runs as expected. That wraps up our look at the isolated storage API and our introductory look at the Code Access Security model. While there is much more that could be said about CAS, as you have seen, using the types of `System.IO.IsolatedStorage` is very simple, as they are really just an extension of the file IO primitives.

■ **Source Code** The FileOrIsoStorageWinApp project is included under the Chapter 20 subdirectory.

Summary

This chapter began by examining the use of the `Directory(Info)` and `File(Info)` types. As you learned, these classes allow you to manipulate a physical file or directory on your hard drive. Next, you examined a number of types derived from the abstract `Stream` class, specifically `FileStream`. Given that `Stream`-derived types operate on a raw stream of bytes, the `System.IO` namespace provides numerous reader/writer types (`StreamWriter`, `StringWriter`, `BinaryWriter`, etc.) that simplify the process. Along the way, you also checked out the functionality provided by `DriveType`, and you learned how to monitor files using the `FileSystemWatcher` type and how to interact with streams in an asynchronous manner.

The second part of this chapter introduced you to the topic of isolated storage. As explained, this API allows a program to read and write data in a safe sandbox, even if the application has been loaded in a constrained security environment. While the programming model is very straightforward (if you have a grasp of basic file IO), the surrounding topics add some level of complexity. Given this, you also were given a whirlwind tour of Code Access Security.

Here, you learned that assemblies present evidence to the CLR at the time they are loaded into an application domain. At this point, they are assigned a code group that has a default set of permissions. The interesting aspect of CAS as it relates to file IO is that if an application is not granted Full Trust, use of the traditional IO operations result in a security exception. However, using isolated storage, your programs can persist data on a per-user level in a safe manner.

CHAPTER 21

■ ■ ■

Introducing Object Serialization

In Chapter 20, you learned about the functionality provided by the System.IO namespace and the role of isolated storage (using the types of System.IO.IsolatedStorage). As shown, these namespaces provide numerous readers and writers that can be used to persist data to a given location (in a given format). This chapter examines the related topic of *object serialization*. Using object serialization, you are able to persist and retrieve the state of an object to (or from) any System.IO.Stream-derived type (including the IsolatedStorageFileStream type).

The ability to serialize types is critical when attempting to copy an object to a remote machine via various remoting technologies such as the .NET remoting layer, XML web services, and Windows Communication Foundation. Understand, however, that serialization is quite useful in its own right and will likely play a role in many of your .NET applications (distributed or not). Over the course of this chapter, you will be exposed to numerous aspects of the .NET serialization scheme, including a set of attributes (and interfaces) that allow you to customize the process.

Understanding Object Serialization

The term *serialization* describes the process of persisting (and possibly transferring) the state of an object into a stream (file stream, memory stream, etc.). The persisted data sequence contains all necessary information needed to reconstruct (or *deserialize*) the state of the object for use later. Using this technology, it is trivial to save vast amounts of data (in various formats) with minimal fuss and bother. In fact, in many cases, saving application data using serialization services results in less code than making use of the readers/writers found within the System.IO namespace.

For example, assume you have created a GUI-based desktop application and wish to provide a way for end users to save their preferences (window color, font size, etc.). To do so, you might define a class named UserPrefs that encapsulates 20 or so pieces of field data. Now, if you were to make use of a System.IO.BinaryWriter type, you would need to *manually* save each field of the UserPrefs object. Likewise, when you wished to load the data from a file back into memory, you would need to make use of a System.IO.BinaryReader and (once again) *manually* read in each value to reconfigure a new UserPrefs object.

While this is certainly doable, you would save yourself a good amount of time simply by marking the UserPrefs class with the [Serializable] attribute:

```
[Serializable]
public class UserPrefs
{
  // Various points of data...
}
```

By doing so, the entire state of the object can be persisted out using a few lines of code. Without getting hung up on the details for the time being, consider the following `Main()` method:

```
static void Main(string[] args)
{
  // Assume UserPrefs defines the following properties.
  UserPrefs userData= new UserPrefs();
  userData.WindowColor = "Yellow";
  userData.FontSize = "50";

  // The BinaryFormatter persists state data in a binary format.
  BinaryFormatter binFormat = new BinaryFormatter();

  // Store object in a local file.
  using(Stream fStream = new FileStream("user.dat",
    FileMode.Create, FileAccess.Write, FileShare.None))
  {
    binFormat.Serialize(fStream, userData);
  }
  Console.ReadLine();
}
```

While it is quite simple to persist objects using .NET object serialization, the processes used behind the scenes are quite sophisticated. For example, when an object is persisted to a stream, all associated data (base class data, contained objects, etc.) are automatically serialized as well. Therefore, if you are attempting to persist a derived class, all data up the chain of inheritance comes along for the ride. As you will see, a set of interrelated objects is represented using an object graph.

.NET serialization services also allow you to persist an object graph in a variety of formats. The previous code example made use of the `BinaryFormatter` type; therefore, the state of the `UserPrefs` object was persisted as a compact binary format. You are also able to persist an object graph into SOAP or XML format using other types. These formats can be quite helpful when you wish to ensure that your persisted objects travel well across operating systems, languages, and architectures.

Finally, understand that an object graph can be persisted into *any* `System.IO.Stream`-derived type. In the previous example, you persisted a `UserPrefs` object into a local file via the `FileStream` type. However, if you would rather store an object to a specific region of memory, you could make use of a `MemoryStream` type instead. All that matters is the fact that the sequence of data correctly represents the state of objects within the graph.

The Role of Object Graphs

As mentioned, when an object is serialized, the CLR will account for all related objects to ensure the data is persisted correctly. This set of related objects is referred to as an *object graph*. Object graphs provide a simple way to document how a set of objects refer to each other and do not necessarily map to classic OO relationships (such as the "is-a" or "has-a" relationship), although they do model this paradigm quite well.

Each object in an object graph is assigned a unique numerical value. Keep in mind that the numbers assigned to the members in an object graph are arbitrary and have no real meaning to the outside world. Once all objects have been assigned a numerical value, the object graph can record each object's set of dependencies.

As a simple example, assume you have created a set of classes that model some automobiles (of course). You have a base class named `Car`, which "has-a" `Radio`. Another class named `JamesBondCar` extends the `Car` base type. Figure 21-1 shows a possible object graph that models these relationships.

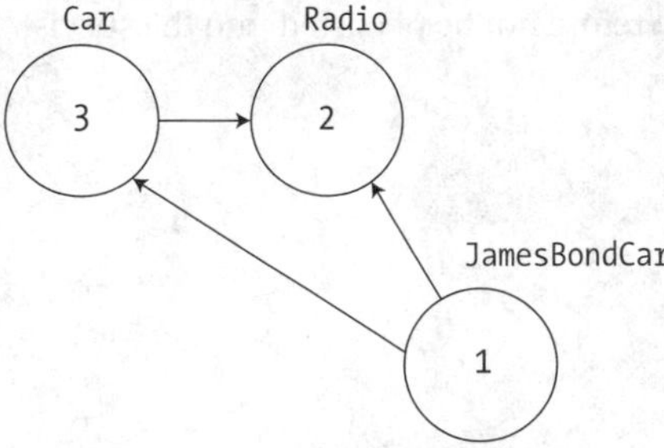

Figure 21-1. *A simple object graph*

When reading object graphs, you can use the phrase "depends on" or "refers to" when connecting the arrows. Thus, in Figure 21-1 you can see that the `Car` class refers to the `Radio` class (given the "has-a" relationship). `JamesBondCar` refers to `Car` (given the "is-a" relationship) as well as `Radio` (as it inherits this protected member variable).

Of course, the CLR does not paint pictures in memory to represent a graph of related objects. Rather, the relationship documented in the previous diagram is represented by a mathematical formula that looks something like this:

```
[Car 3, ref 2], [Radio 2], [JamesBondCar 1, ref 3, ref 2]
```

If you parse this formula, you can again see that object 3 (the `Car`) has a dependency on object 2 (the `Radio`). Object 2, the `Radio`, is a lone wolf and requires nobody. Finally, object 1 (the `JamesBondCar`) has a dependency on object 3 as well as object 2. In any case, when you serialize or deserialize an instance of `JamesBondCar`, the object graph ensures that the `Radio` and `Car` types also participate in the process.

The beautiful thing about the serialization process is that the graph representing the relationships among your objects is established automatically behind the scenes. As you will see later in this chapter, however, if you do wish to become more involved in the construction of a given object graph, it is possible to do so by customizing the serialization process via attributes and interfaces.

■ **Note** Strictly speaking, the `XmlSerializer` type (described later in this chapter) does not persist state using object graphs; however, this type will still serialize and deserialize related objects in a predictable manner.

Configuring Objects for Serialization

To make an object available to .NET serialization services, all you need to do is decorate each related class (or structure) with the `[Serializable]` attribute. If you determine that a given type has some member data that should not (or perhaps cannot) participate in the serialization scheme, you can mark such fields with the `[NonSerialized]` attribute. This can be helpful if you have member variables in a serializable class that do not need to be "remembered" (e.g., fixed values, random values, transient data, etc.) and you wish to reduce the size of the persisted data.

Defining Serializable Types

To get the ball rolling, create a new Console Application named SimpleSerialize. Insert a new class named `Radio`, which has been marked `[Serializable]`, excluding a single member variable (radioID) that has been marked [NonSerialized] and will therefore not be persisted into the specified data stream:

```
[Serializable]
public class Radio
{
  public bool hasTweeters;
  public bool hasSubWoofers;
  public double[] stationPresets;

  [NonSerialized]
  public string radioID = "XF-552RR6";
}
```

Next, insert two additional class types to represent the JamesBondCar and Car base classes, both of which are also marked [Serializable] and define the following pieces of field data:

```
[Serializable]
public class Car
{
  public Radio theRadio = new Radio();
  public bool isHatchBack;
}

[Serializable]
public class JamesBondCar : Car
{
  public bool canFly;
  public bool canSubmerge;
}
```

Be aware that the [Serializable] attribute cannot be inherited from a parent class. Therefore, if you derive a class from a type marked [Serializable], the child class must be marked [Serializable] as well, or it cannot be persisted. In fact, all objects in an object graph must be marked with the [Serializable] attribute. If you attempt to serialize a nonserializable object using the BinaryFormatter or SoapFormatter, you will receive a SerializationException at runtime.

■ **Note** Because the XmlSerializer type does not make use of object graphs, you are not technically required to mark types with the [Serializable] attribute in order to persist an object's state as XML. However, to ensure that your types can be persisted in all possible formats, you will typically always want to mark types that will be persisted with the serialization attributes.

Public Fields, Private Fields, and Public Properties

Notice that in each of these classes, I have defined the field data as public, just to simplify the example. Of course, private data exposed using public properties would be preferable from an OO point of view. Also, for the sake of simplicity, I have not defined any custom constructors on these types, and therefore all unassigned field data will receive the expected default values.

OO design principles aside, you may wonder how the various formatters expect a type's field data to be defined in order to be serialized into a stream. The answer is, it depends. If you are persisting an object's state using the BinaryFormatter or SoapFormatter it makes absolutely no difference. These types are programmed to serialize *all* serializable fields of a type, regardless of whether they are public fields, private fields, or private fields exposed through public properties. Do recall, however, that if you have points of data that you do not want to be persisted into the object graph, you can selectively mark public or private fields as [NonSerialized], as done with the string field of the Radio type.

The situation is quite different if you make use of the XmlSerializer type, however. This type will *only* serialize public data fields or private data exposed by public properties. Private data not exposed from properties will be ignored. For example, consider the following serializable Person type:

```
[Serializable]
public class Person
{
  // A public field.
  public bool isAlive = true;

  // A private field.
  private int personAge = 21;

  // Public property/private data.
  private string fName = string.Empty;
  public string FirstName
  {
    get { return fName; }
    set { fName = value; }
  }
}
```

When processed by the BinaryFormatter or SoapFormatter, you would indeed find that the isAlive, personAge, and fName fields are each saved into the selected stream. However, the XmlSerializer would *not* save the value of personAge, as this piece of private data is not encapsulated by a type property. If you wished to persist the age of the person with the XmlSerializer, you would need to define the field publicly or encapsulate the private member using a public property.

Choosing a Serialization Formatter

Once you have configured your types to participate in the .NET serialization scheme by applying the necessary attributes, your next step is to choose which format (binary, SOAP, or XML) should be used when persisting your object's state. Each possibility is represented by the following classes:

- BinaryFormatter
- SoapFormatter
- XmlSerializer

The BinaryFormatter type serializes your object's state to a stream using a compact binary format. This type is defined within the System.Runtime.Serialization.Formatters.Binary namespace that is part of mscorlib.dll. Therefore, if you wish to gain access to this type, simply specify the following C# using directive:

```
// Gain access to the BinaryFormatter in mscorlib.dll.
using System.Runtime.Serialization.Formatters.Binary;
```

The SoapFormatter type persists an object's state as a SOAP message. This type is defined within the System.Runtime.Serialization.Formatters.Soap namespace that is defined within a *separate assembly*. Thus, to format your object graph into a SOAP message, you must first set a reference to System.Runtime.Serialization.Formatters.Soap.dll using the Visual Studio 2008 Add Reference dialog box and then specify the following C# using directive:

```
// Must reference System.Runtime.Serialization.Formatters.Soap.dll.
using System.Runtime.Serialization.Formatters.Soap;
```

Finally, if you wish to persist a tree of objects as an XML document, you have the XmlSerializer type. To use this type, you will need to specify that you are using the System.Xml.Serialization namespace and set a reference to the assembly System.Xml.dll. As luck would have it, all Visual Studio 2008 project templates automatically reference System.Xml.dll, therefore you will simply need to use the following namespace:

```
// Defined within System.Xml.dll.
using System.Xml.Serialization;
```

The IFormatter and IRemotingFormatter Interfaces

Regardless of which formatter you choose to make use of, be aware that each of them derives directly from System.Object, so they do *not* share a common set of members from a serialization-centric base class. However, the BinaryFormatter and SoapFormatter types do support common members through the implementation of the IFormatter and IRemotingFormatter interfaces (strange as it may seem, the XmlSerializer implements neither).

System.Runtime.Serialization.IFormatter defines the core Serialize() and Deserialize() methods, which do the grunt work to move your object graphs into and out of a specific stream. Beyond these members, IFormatter defines a few properties that are used behind the scenes by the implementing type:

```
public interface IFormatter
{
  SerializationBinder Binder { get; set; }
  StreamingContext Context { get; set; }
  ISurrogateSelector SurrogateSelector { get; set; }
  object Deserialize(System.IO.Stream serializationStream);
  void Serialize(System.IO.Stream serializationStream, object graph);
}
```

The System.Runtime.Remoting.Messaging.IRemotingFormatter interface (which is leveraged internally by the .NET remoting layer) overloads the Serialize() and Deserialize() members into a manner more appropriate for distributed persistence. Note that IRemotingFormatter derives from the more general IFormatter interface:

```
public interface IRemotingFormatter  : IFormatter
{
  object Deserialize(Stream serializationStream, HeaderHandler handler);
  void Serialize(Stream serializationStream, object graph,
    Header[] headers);
}
```

Although you may not need to directly interact with these interfaces for most of your serialization endeavors, recall that interface-based polymorphism allows you to hold an instance of BinaryFormatter or SoapFormatter using an IFormatter reference. Therefore, if you wish to build a method that can serialize an object graph using either of these classes, you could write the following:

```
static void SerializeObjectGraph(IFormatter itfFormat,
  Stream destStream, object graph)
{
  itfFormat.Serialize(destStream, graph);
}
```

Type Fidelity Among the Formatters

The most obvious difference among the three formatters is how the object graph is persisted to the stream (binary, SOAP, or XML). You should be aware of a few more subtle points of distinction, specifically how the formatters contend with *type fidelity*. When you make use of the BinaryFormatter type, it will persist not only the field data of the objects in the object graph, but also each type's fully qualified name and the full name of the defining assembly (name, version, public key token, and culture). These extra points of data make the BinaryFormatter an ideal choice when you wish to transport objects by value (e.g., as a full copy) across machine boundaries for .NET-centric applications.

The SoapFormatter persists traces of the assembly of origin through the use of an XML namespace. For example, recall the Person type earlier in this chapter. If this type were persisted as a SOAP message, you would find that the opening element of Person is qualified by the generated xmlns. Consider this partial definition, taking note of the a1 XML namespace:

```
<a1:Person id="ref-1" xmlns:a1=
  "http://schemas.microsoft.com/clr/nsassem/SimpleSerialize/MyApp%2C%20
  Version%3D1.0.0.0%2C%20Culture%3Dneutral%2C%20PublicKeyToken%3Dnull">
  <isAlive>true</isAlive>
  <personAge>21</personAge>
  <fName id="ref-3"></fName>
</a1:Person>
```

However, the XmlSerializer, does *not* attempt to preserve full type fidelity and therefore does not record the type's fully qualified name or assembly of origin. While this may seem like a limitation at first glance, the reason has to do with the open-ended nature of XML data representation. Here is a possible XML representation of the Person type:

```
<?xml version="1.0"?>
<Person xmlns:xsi="http://www.w3.org/2001/XMLSchema-instance"
        xmlns:xsd="http://www.w3.org/2001/XMLSchema">
  <isAlive>true</isAlive>
  <PersonAge>21</PersonAge>
  <FirstName />
</Person>
```

If you wish to persist an object's state in a manner that can be used by any operating system (Windows XP, Mac OS X, and various Linux distributions), application framework (.NET, J2EE, COM, etc.), or programming language, you do not want to maintain full type fidelity, as you cannot assume all possible recipients can understand .NET-specific data types. Given this, SoapFormatter and XmlSerializer are ideal choices when you wish to ensure as broad a reach as possible for the persisted tree of objects.

Serializing Objects Using the BinaryFormatter

To illustrate how easy it is to persist an instance of the JamesBondCar to a physical file, let's first make use of the BinaryFormatter type. Again, the two key methods of the BinaryFormatter type to be aware of are Serialize() and Deserialize():

- Serialize(): Persists an object graph to a specified stream as a sequence of bytes
- Deserialize(): Converts a persisted sequence of bytes to an object graph

Assume you have created an instance of JamesBondCar, modified some state data, and want to persist your spy mobile into a *.dat file. The first task is to create the *.dat file itself. This can be achieved by creating an instance of the System.IO.FileStream type (see Chapter 20). At this point, simply create an instance of the BinaryFormatter and pass in the FileStream and object graph to persist. Consider the following Main() method:

```
// Be sure to import the System.Runtime.Serialization.Formatters.Binary
// and System.IO namespaces.
static void Main(string[] args)
{
  Console.WriteLine("***** Fun with Object Serialization *****\n");

  // Make a JamesBondCar and set state.
  JamesBondCar jbc = new JamesBondCar();
  jbc.canFly = true;
  jbc.canSubmerge = false;
  jbc.theRadio.stationPresets = new double[]{89.3, 105.1, 97.1};
  jbc.theRadio.hasTweeters = true;

  // Now save the car to a specific file in a binary format.
  SaveAsBinaryFormat(jbc, "CarData.dat");
  Console.ReadLine();
}
```

The SaveAsBinaryFormat() method is implemented as so:

```
static void SaveAsBinaryFormat(object objGraph, string fileName)
{
  // Save object to a file named CarData.dat in binary.
  BinaryFormatter binFormat = new BinaryFormatter();

  using(Stream fStream = new FileStream(fileName,
        FileMode.Create, FileAccess.Write, FileShare.None))
  {
    binFormat.Serialize(fStream, objGraph);
  }
  Console.WriteLine("=> Saved car in binary format!");
}
```

As you can see, the BinaryFormatter.Serialize() method is the member responsible for composing the object graph and moving the byte sequence to some Stream-derived type. In this case, the stream happens to be a physical file. Again, you could also serialize your object types to any Stream-derived type such as a memory location, network stream, and so forth. Once you run your program, you can view the contents of the CarData.dat file that represents this instance of the JamesBondCar by navigating to the \bin\Debug folder of the current project. Figure 21-2 shows this file opened within Visual Studio 2008.

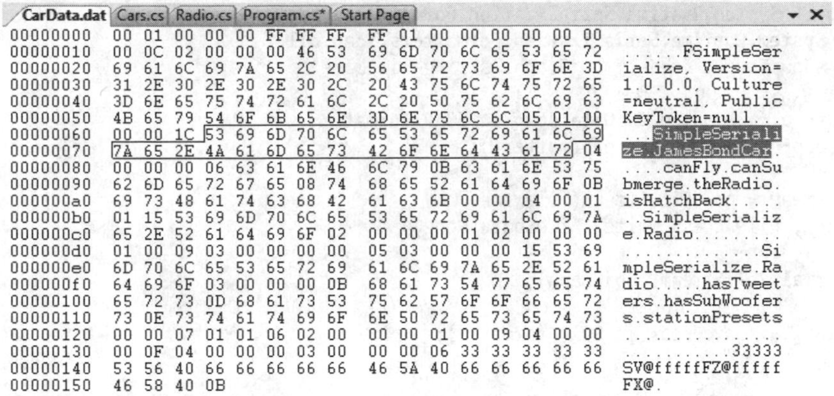

```
CarData.dat | Cars.cs | Radio.cs | Program.cs* | Start Page
00000000  00 01 00 00 00 FF FF FF  FF 01 00 00 00 00 00 00  ................
00000010  00 0C 02 00 00 00 46 53  69 6D 70 6C 65 53 65 72  ......FSimpleSer
00000020  69 61 6C 69 7A 65 2C 20  56 65 72 73 69 6F 6E 3D  ialize, Version=
00000030  31 2E 30 2E 30 2E 30 2C  20 43 75 6C 74 75 72 65  1.0.0.0, Culture
00000040  3D 6E 65 75 74 72 61 6C  2C 20 50 75 62 6C 69 63  =neutral, Public
00000050  4B 65 79 54 6F 6B 65 6E  3D 6E 75 6C 6C 05 01 00  KeyToken=null...
00000060  00 00 1C 53 69 6D 70 6C  65 53 65 72 69 61 6C 69  ...SimpleSeriali
00000070  7A 65 2E 4A 61 6D 65 73  42 6F 6E 64 43 61 72 04  ze.JamesBondCar.
00000080  00 00 00 06 63 61 6E 46  6C 79 0B 63 61 6E 53 75  ....canFly.canSu
00000090  62 6D 65 72 67 65 08 74  68 65 52 61 64 69 6F 0B  bmerge.theRadio.
000000a0  69 73 48 61 74 63 68 42  61 63 6B 00 00 04 00 01  isHatchBack.....
000000b0  01 15 53 69 6D 70 6C 65  53 65 72 69 61 6C 69 7A  ..SimpleSerializ
000000c0  65 2E 52 61 64 69 6F 02  00 00 00 01 02 00 00 00  e.Radio.........
000000d0  01 00 09 03 00 00 00 00  05 03 00 00 00 15 53 69  ..............Si
000000e0  6D 70 6C 65 53 65 72 69  61 6C 69 7A 65 2E 52 61  mpleSerialize.Ra
000000f0  64 69 6F 03 00 00 00 0B  68 61 73 54 77 65 65 74  dio.....hasTweet
00000100  65 72 73 0D 68 61 73 53  75 62 57 6F 6F 66 65 72  ers.hasSubWoofer
00000110  73 0E 73 74 61 74 69 6F  6E 50 72 65 73 65 74 73  s.stationPresets
00000120  00 00 07 01 01 06 02 00  00 00 01 00 09 04 00 00  ................
00000130  00 0F 04 00 00 00 03 00  00 00 06 33 33 33 33 33  ...........33333
00000140  53 56 40 66 66 66 66 66  46 5A 40 66 66 66 66 66  SV@fffffFZ@fffff
00000150  46 58 40 0B                                       FX@.
```


Figure 21-2. `JamesBondCar` *serialized using a* `BinaryFormatter`

Deserializing Objects Using the BinaryFormatter

Now suppose you want to read the persisted `JamesBondCar` from the binary file back into an object variable. Once you have programmatically opened `CarData.dat` (via the `File.OpenRead()` method), simply call the `Deserialize()` method of the `BinaryFormatter`. Be aware that `Deserialize()` returns a generic `System.Object` type, so you need to impose an explicit cast, as shown here:

```
static void LoadFromBinaryFile(string fileName)
{
  BinaryFormatter binFormat = new BinaryFormatter();

  // Read the JamesBondCar from the binary file.
  using(Stream fStream = File.OpenRead(fileName))
  {
    JamesBondCar carFromDisk =
      (JamesBondCar)binFormat.Deserialize(fStream);
    Console.WriteLine("Can this car fly? : {0}", carFromDisk.canFly);
  }
}
```

Notice that when you call `Deserialize()`, you pass the `Stream`-derived type that represents the location of the persisted object graph. Once you cast the object back into the correct type, you will find the state data has been retained from the point at which you saved the object.

Serializing Objects Using the SoapFormatter

Your next choice of formatter is the `SoapFormatter` type. The `SoapFormatter` will persist an object graph into a SOAP message, which makes this formatter a solid choice when you wish to distribute objects remotely across diverse environments. If you are unfamiliar with the Simple Object Access Protocol (SOAP) specification, in a nutshell, SOAP defines a standard process in which methods may be invoked in a platform- and OS-neutral manner.

Assuming you have set a reference to the `System.Runtime.Serialization.Formatters.Soap.dll` assembly (and imported the `System.Runtime.Serialization.Formatters.Soap` namespace), you could persist and retrieve a `JamesBondCar` as a SOAP message simply by replacing each occurrence of `BinaryFormatter` with `SoapFormatter`. Consider the following new method of the `Program` class, which serializes an object to a local file:

```
// Be sure to import System.Runtime.Serialization.Formatters.Soap
// and reference System.Runtime.Serialization.Formatters.Soap.dll.
static void SaveAsSoapFormat (object objGraph, string fileName)
{
  // Save object to a file named CarData.soap in SOAP format.
  SoapFormatter soapFormat = new SoapFormatter();

  using(Stream fStream = new FileStream(fileName,
    FileMode.Create, FileAccess.Write, FileShare.None))
  {
    soapFormat.Serialize(fStream, objGraph);
  }
  Console.WriteLine("=> Saved car in SOAP format!");
}
```

As before, simply use `Serialize()` and `Deserialize()` to move the object graph into and out of the stream. If you call this method from `Main()` and run the application, you can open the resulting `*.soap` file. Here you can locate the XML elements that mark the stateful values of the current `JamesBondCar` as well as the relationship between the objects in the graph via the `#ref` tokens (see Figure 21-3).

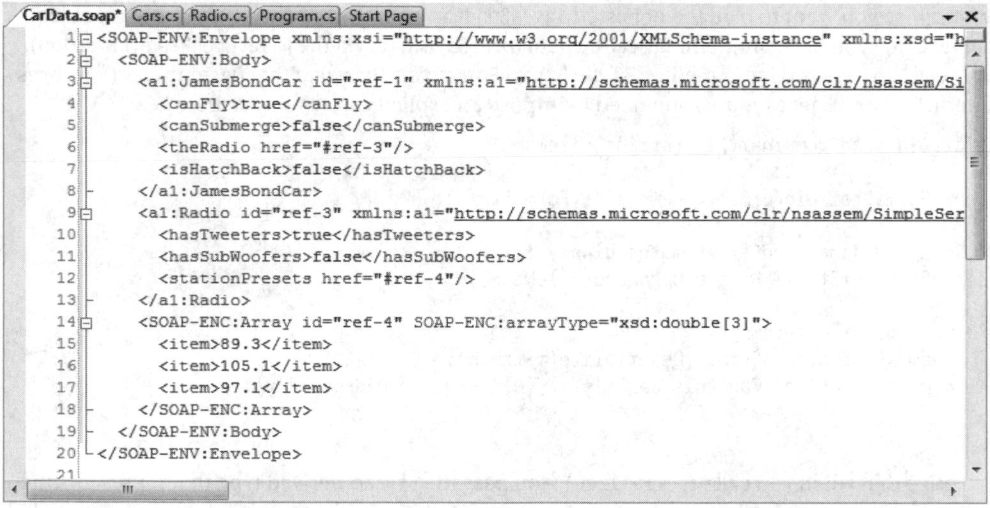

CarData.soap* | Cars.cs | Radio.cs | Program.cs | Start Page

```
<SOAP-ENV:Envelope xmlns:xsi="http://www.w3.org/2001/XMLSchema-instance" xmlns:xsd="h
  <SOAP-ENV:Body>
    <a1:JamesBondCar id="ref-1" xmlns:a1="http://schemas.microsoft.com/clr/nsassem/Si
      <canFly>true</canFly>
      <canSubmerge>false</canSubmerge>
      <theRadio href="#ref-3"/>
      <isHatchBack>false</isHatchBack>
    </a1:JamesBondCar>
    <a1:Radio id="ref-3" xmlns:a1="http://schemas.microsoft.com/clr/nsassem/SimpleSer
      <hasTweeters>true</hasTweeters>
      <hasSubWoofers>false</hasSubWoofers>
      <stationPresets href="#ref-4"/>
    </a1:Radio>
    <SOAP-ENC:Array id="ref-4" SOAP-ENC:arrayType="xsd:double[3]">
      <item>89.3</item>
      <item>105.1</item>
      <item>97.1</item>
    </SOAP-ENC:Array>
  </SOAP-ENV:Body>
</SOAP-ENV:Envelope>
```

Figure 21-3. `JamesBondCar` *serialized using a* `SoapFormatter`

Serializing Objects Using the XmlSerializer

In addition to the SOAP and binary formatters, the `System.Xml.dll` assembly provides a third formatter, `System.Xml.Serialization.XmlSerializer`, which can be used to persist the *public* state of a given object as pure XML, as opposed to XML data wrapped within a SOAP message. Working with this type is a bit different from working with the `SoapFormatter` or `BinaryFormatter` type. Consider the following code, which assumes you have imported the `System.Xml.Serialization` namespace:

```
static void SaveAsXmlFormat(object objGraph, string fileName)
{
  // Save object to a file named CarData.xml in XML format.
```

```
  XmlSerializer xmlFormat = new XmlSerializer(typeof(JamesBondCar),
    new Type[] { typeof(Radio), typeof(Car) });

  using(Stream fStream = new FileStream(fileName,
    FileMode.Create, FileAccess.Write, FileShare.None))
  {
    xmlFormat.Serialize(fStream, objGraph);
  }
  Console.WriteLine("=> Saved car in XML format!");
}
```

The key difference is that the `XmlSerializer` type requires you to specify type information that represents each subelement nested within the root. The first constructor argument of the `XmlSerializer` defines the root element of the XML file, while the second argument is an array of `System.Type` types that hold metadata regarding the subelements. If you were to look within the newly generated XML file (assuming you indeed call this new method from within `Main()`), you would find the XML data shown in Figure 21-4.

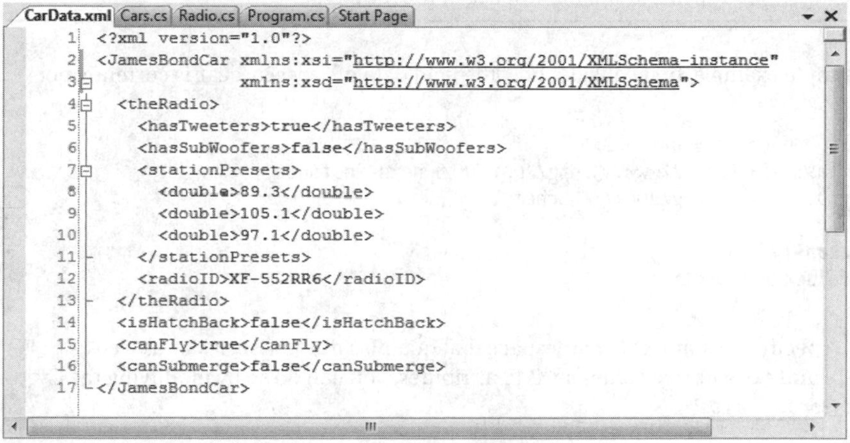

CarData.xml | Cars.cs | Radio.cs | Program.cs | Start Page

```
<?xml version="1.0"?>
<JamesBondCar xmlns:xsi="http://www.w3.org/2001/XMLSchema-instance"
              xmlns:xsd="http://www.w3.org/2001/XMLSchema">
  <theRadio>
    <hasTweeters>true</hasTweeters>
    <hasSubWoofers>false</hasSubWoofers>
    <stationPresets>
      <double>89.3</double>
      <double>105.1</double>
      <double>97.1</double>
    </stationPresets>
    <radioID>XF-552RR6</radioID>
  </theRadio>
  <isHatchBack>false</isHatchBack>
  <canFly>true</canFly>
  <canSubmerge>false</canSubmerge>
</JamesBondCar>
```

Figure 21-4. `JamesBondCar` *serialized using an* `XmlSerializer`

Note The `XmlSerializer` demands that all serialized types in the object graph support a default constructor (so be sure to add it back if you define custom constructors). If this is not the case, you will receive an `InvalidOperationException` at runtime.

Controlling the Generated XML Data

If you have a background in XML technologies, you are well aware that it is often critical to ensure the data within an XML document conforms to a set of rules that establish the *validity* of the data. Understand that a "valid" XML document does not have to do with the syntactic well-being of the XML elements (e.g., all opening elements must have a closing element). Rather, valid documents conform to agreed-upon formatting rules (e.g., field `X` must be expressed as an attribute and not a subelement), which are typically defined by an XML schema or document-type definition (DTD) file.

By default, all public data of a [Serializable] type is formatted as elements rather than XML attributes. If you wish to control how the XmlSerializer generates the resulting XML document, you may decorate your [Serializable] types with any number of additional attributes from the System.Xml.Serialization namespace. Table 21-1 documents some (but not all) of the attributes that influence how XML data is encoded to a stream.

Table 21-1. *Select Attributes of the* System.Xml.Serialization *Namespace*

Attribute	Meaning in Life
XmlAttributeAttribute	The member will be serialized as an XML attribute.
XmlElementAttribute	The field or property will be serialized as an XML element.
XmlEnumAttribute	The element name of an enumeration member.
XmlRootAttribute	This attribute controls how the root element will be constructed (namespace and element name).
XmlTextAttribute	The property or field should be serialized as XML text.
XmlTypeAttribute	The name and namespace of the XML type.

By way of a simple example, first consider how the field data of JamesBondCar is currently persisted as XML:

```
<?xml version="1.0" encoding="utf-8"?>
<JamesBondCar xmlns:xsi="http://www.w3.org/2001/XMLSchema-instance"
  xmlns:xsd="http://www.w3.org/2001/XMLSchema">
...
  <canFly>true</canFly>
  <canSubmerge>false</canSubmerge>
</JamesBondCar>
```

If you wish to specify a custom XML namespace that qualifies the JamesBondCar as well as encodes the canFly and canSubmerge values as XML attributes, you can do so by modifying the C# definition of JamesBondCar as so:

```
[Serializable,
XmlRoot(Namespace = "http://www.intertech.com")]
public class JamesBondCar : Car
{
  [XmlAttribute]
  public bool canFly;
  [XmlAttribute]
  public bool canSubmerge;
}
```

This yields the following XML document (note the opening <JamesBondCar> element):

```
<?xml version="1.0"""?>
<JamesBondCar xmlns:xsi="http://www.w3.org/2001/XMLSchema-instance"
   xmlns:xsd="http://www.w3.org/2001/XMLSchema"
   canFly="true" canSubmerge="false"
   xmlns="http://www.intertechtraining.com">
...
</JamesBondCar>
```

Of course, numerous other attributes can be used to control how the XmlSerializer generates the resulting XML document. For full details, look up the System.Xml.Serialization namespace using the .NET Framework 3.5 SDK documentation.

Serializing Collections of Objects

Now that you have seen how to persist a single object to a stream, let's examine how to save a set of objects. As you may have noticed, the `Serialize()` method of the `IFormatter` interface does not provide a way to specify an arbitrary number of objects as input (only a single `System.Object`). On a related note, the return value of `Deserialize()` is, again, a single `System.Object` (the same basic limitation holds true for the `XmlSerializer`):

```
public interface IFormatter
{
...
  object Deserialize(System.IO.Stream serializationStream);
  void Serialize(System.IO.Stream serializationStream, object graph);
}
```

Recall that the `System.Object` in fact represents a complete tree of objects. Given this, if you pass in an object that has been marked as `[Serializable]` and contains other `[Serializable]` objects, the entire set of objects is persisted in a single method call. As luck would have it, most of the types found within the `System.Collections` and `System.Collections.Generic` namespaces have already been marked as `[Serializable]`. Therefore, if you wish to persist a set of objects, simply add the set to the container (such as an `ArrayList` or a `List<T>`) and serialize the object to your stream of choice.

Assume you have updated the `JamesBondCar` class with a two-argument constructor to set a few pieces of state data (note that you add back the default constructor as required by the `XmlSerializer`):

```
[Serializable,
 XmlRoot(Namespace = "http://www.intertech.com")]
public class JamesBondCar : Car
{
  public JamesBondCar(bool skyWorthy, bool seaWorthy)
  {
    canFly = skyWorthy;
    canSubmerge = seaWorthy;
  }
  // The XmlSerializer demands a default constructor!
  public JamesBondCar(){}
...
}
```

With this, you are now able to persist any number of `JamesBondCar`s as so:

```
static void SaveListOfCars()
{
  // Now persist a List<T> of JamesBondCars.
  List<JamesBondCar> myCars = new List<JamesBondCar>();
  myCars.Add(new JamesBondCar(true, true));
  myCars.Add(new JamesBondCar(true, false));
  myCars.Add(new JamesBondCar(false, true));
  myCars.Add(new JamesBondCar(false, false));

  using(Stream fStream = new FileStream("CarCollection.xml",
    FileMode.Create, FileAccess.Write, FileShare.None))
  {
    XmlSerializer xmlFormat = new XmlSerializer(typeof(List<JamesBondCar>),
      new Type[] { typeof(JamesBondCar), typeof(Car), typeof(Radio) });
    xmlFormat.Serialize(fStream, myCars);
```

```
  }
  Console.WriteLine("=> Saved list of cars!");
}
```

Here, because you made use of the `XmlSerializer`, you are required to specify type information for each of the subobjects within the root object (which in this case is the `List<JamesBondCar>`). Had you made use of the `BinaryFormatter` or `SoapFormatter` type, the logic would be even more straightforward, for example:

```
static void  SaveListOfCarsAsBinary()
{
  // Save ArrayList object (myCars) as binary.
  List<JamesBondCar> myCars = new List<JamesBondCar>();

  BinaryFormatter binFormat = new BinaryFormatter();
  using(Stream fStream = new FileStream("AllMyCars.dat",
    FileMode.Create, FileAccess.Write, FileShare.None))
  {
    binFormat.Serialize(fStream, myCars);
  }
  Console.WriteLine("=> Saved list of cars in binary!");
}
```

■ **Source Code** The SimpleSerialize application is located under the Chapter 21 subdirectory.

Customizing the Serialization Process

In a majority of cases, the default serialization scheme provided by the .NET platform will be exactly what you require. Simply apply the `[Serializable]` attribute to your related types and pass the tree of objects to your formatter of choice for processing. In some cases, however, you may wish to become more involved with how a tree is constructed and handled during the serialization process. For example, maybe you have a business rule that says all field data must be persisted using a particular format, or perhaps you wish to add additional bits of data to the stream that do not directly map to fields in the object being persisted (timestamps, unique identifiers, or whatnot).

When you wish to become more involved with the process of object serialization, the `System.Runtime.Serialization` namespace provides several types that allow you to do so. Table 21-2 describes some of the core types to be aware of.

Table 21-2. `System.Runtime.Serialization` *Namespace Core Types*

Type	Meaning in Life
`ISerializable`	This interface can be implemented on a `[Serializable]` type to control its serialization and deserialization.
`ObjectIDGenerator`	This type generates IDs for members in an object graph.
`[OnDeserialized]`	This attribute allows you to specify a method that will be called immediately after the object has been deserialized.
`[OnDeserializing]`	This attribute allows you to specify a method that will be called before the deserialization process.

Type	Meaning in Life
[OnSerialized]	This attribute allows you to specify a method that will be called immediately after the object has been serialized.
[OnSerializing]	This attribute allows you to specify a method that will be called before the serialization process.
[OptionalField]	This attribute allows you to define a field on a type that can be missing from the specified stream.
SerializationInfo	In essence, this class is a "property bag" that maintains name/value pairs representing the state of an object during the serialization process.

A Deeper Look at Object Serialization

Before we examine various ways in which you can customize the serialization process, it will be helpful to take a deeper look at what takes place behind the scenes. When the BinaryFormatter serializes an object graph, it is in charge of transmitting the following information into the specified stream:

- The fully qualified name of the objects in the graph (e.g., MyApp.JamesBondCar)
- The name of the assembly defining the object graph (e.g., MyApp.exe)
- An instance of the SerializationInfo class that contains all stateful data maintained by the members in the object graph

During the deserialization process, the BinaryFormatter uses this same information to build an identical copy of the object, using the information extracted from the underlying stream. The process used by the SoapFormatter is quite similar.

■Note Recall that the XmlSerializer does not persist a type's fully qualified name or the name of the defining assembly in order to keep the state of the object as mobile as possible. This type is concerned only with persisting exposed public data.

Beyond moving the required data into and out of a stream, formatters also analyze the members in the object graph for the following pieces of infrastructure:

- A check is made to determine whether the object is marked with the [Serializable] attribute. If the object is not, a SerializationException is thrown.
- If the object is marked [Serializable], a check is made to determine if the object implements the ISerializable interface. If this is the case, GetObjectData() is called on the object.
- If the object does not implement ISerializable, the default serialization process is used, serializing all fields not marked as [NonSerialized].

In addition to determining if the type supports ISerializable, formatters are also responsible for discovering if the types in question support members that have been adorned with the [OnSerializing], [OnSerialized], [OnDeserializing], or [OnDeserialized] attribute. We'll examine the role of these attributes in just a bit, but first let's look at the role of ISerializable.

Customizing Serialization Using ISerializable

Objects that are marked [Serializable] have the option of implementing the ISerializable interface. By doing so, you are able to "get involved" with the serialization process and perform any pre- or post-data formatting.

■ **Note** Since the release of .NET 2.0, the preferred way to customize the serialization process is to use the serialization attributes (described next). However, knowledge of ISerializable is important for the purpose of maintaining existing systems.

The ISerializable interface is quite simple, given that it defines only a single method, GetObjectData():

```
// When you wish to tweak the serialization process,
// implement ISerializable.
public interface ISerializable
{
  void GetObjectData(SerializationInfo info,
    StreamingContext context);
}
```

The GetObjectData() method is called automatically by a given formatter during the serialization process. The implementation of this method populates the incoming SerializationInfo parameter with a series of name/value pairs that (typically) map to the field data of the object being persisted. SerializationInfo defines numerous variations on the overloaded AddValue() method, in addition to a small set of properties that allow the type to get and set the type's name, defining assembly, and member count. Here is a partial snapshot:

```
public sealed class SerializationInfo : object
{
  public SerializationInfo(Type type, IFormatterConverter converter);
  public string AssemblyName { get; set; }
  public string FullTypeName { get; set; }
  public int MemberCount { get; }
  public void AddValue(string name, short value);
  public void AddValue(string name, UInt16 value);
  public void AddValue(string name, int value);
...
}
```

Types that implement the ISerializable interface must also define a special constructor taking the following signature:

```
// You must supply a custom constructor with this signature
// to allow the runtime engine to set the state of your object.
[Serializable]
class SomeClass : ISerializable
{
  protected SomeClass (SerializationInfo si, StreamingContext ctx) {...}
  ...
}
```

Notice that the visibility of this constructor is set as *protected*. This is permissible given that the formatter will have access to this member regardless of its visibility. These special constructors tend to be marked as protected (or private for that matter) to ensure that the casual object user would never create an object in this manner. As you can see, the first parameter of this constructor is an instance of the SerializationInfo type (seen previously).

The second parameter of this special constructor is a StreamingContext type, which contains information regarding the source or destination of the bits. The most informative member of this type is the State property, which represents a value from the StreamingContextStates enumeration. The values of this enumeration represent the basic composition of the current stream.

To be honest, unless you are implementing some low-level custom remoting services, you will seldom need to deal with this enumeration directly. Nevertheless, here are the possible names of the StreamingContextStates enum (consult the .NET Framework 3.5 SDK documentation for full details):

```
public enum StreamingContextStates
{
  CrossProcess,
  CrossMachine,
  File,
  Persistence,
  Remoting,
  Other,
  Clone,
  CrossAppDomain,
  All
}
```

To illustrate customizing the serialization process using ISerializable, assume you have a new Console Application project (named CustomSerialization) that defines a class type containing two points of string data. Furthermore, assume that you must ensure the string objects are serialized to the stream in all uppercase and deserialized from the stream in all lowercase. To account for such rules, you could implement ISerializable as so (be sure to import the System.Runtime.Serialization namespace):

```
[Serializable]
class StringData : ISerializable
{
  public string dataItemOne = "First data block";
  public string dataItemTwo= "More data";

  public StringData(){}
  protected StringData(SerializationInfo si, StreamingContext ctx)
  {
    // Rehydrate member variables from stream.
    dataItemOne = si.GetString("First_Item").ToLower();
    dataItemTwo = si.GetString("dataItemTwo").ToLower();
  }

  void ISerializable.GetObjectData(SerializationInfo info, StreamingContext ctx)
  {
    // Fill up the SerializationInfo object with the formatted data.
    info.AddValue("First_Item", dataItemOne.ToUpper());
    info.AddValue("dataItemTwo", dataItemTwo.ToUpper());
  }
}
```

Notice that when you are filling the SerializationInfo type from within the GetObjectData() method, you are *not* required to name the data points identically to the type's internal member variables. This can obviously be helpful if you need to further decouple the type's data from the persisted format. Do be aware, however, that you will need to obtain the values from within the special protected constructor using the same names assigned within GetObjectData().

To test your customization, assume you have persisted an instance of MyStringData using a SoapFormatter:

```
static void Main(string[] args)
{
  Console.WriteLine("***** Fun with Custom Serialization *****");

  // Recall that this type implements ISerializable.
  StringData myData = new StringData();

  // Save to a local file in SOAP format.
  SoapFormatter soapFormat = new SoapFormatter();
  using(Stream fStream = new FileStream("MyData.soap",
    FileMode.Create, FileAccess.Write, FileShare.None))
  {
    soapFormat.Serialize(fStream, myData);
  }
  Console.ReadLine();
}
```

When you view the resulting *.soap file, you will note that the string fields have indeed been persisted in uppercase (see Figure 21-5).

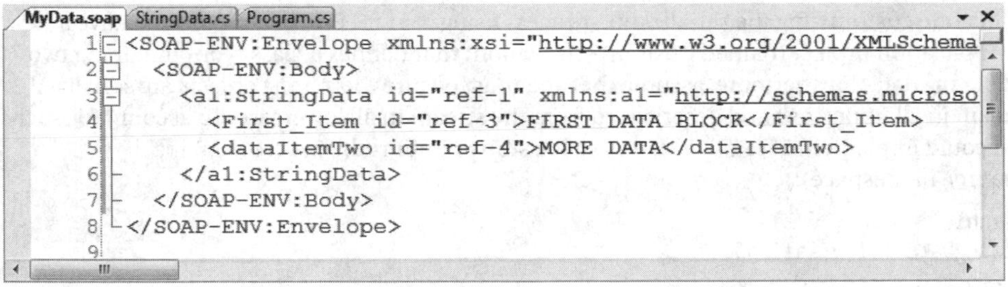

```
MyData.soap | StringData.cs | Program.cs
<SOAP-ENV:Envelope xmlns:xsi="http://www.w3.org/2001/XMLSchema
  <SOAP-ENV:Body>
    <a1:StringData id="ref-1" xmlns:a1="http://schemas.microso
      <First_Item id="ref-3">FIRST DATA BLOCK</First_Item>
      <dataItemTwo id="ref-4">MORE DATA</dataItemTwo>
    </a1:StringData>
  </SOAP-ENV:Body>
</SOAP-ENV:Envelope>
```

Figure 21-5. *Customizing our serialization via* ISerializable

Customizing Serialization Using Attributes

Although implementing the ISerializable interface is one possible way to customize the serialization process, since the release of .NET 2.0 the preferred way to customize the serialization process is to define methods that are attributed with any of the new serialization-centric attributes: [OnSerializing], [OnSerialized], [OnDeserializing], or [OnDeserialized]. Using these attributes is less cumbersome than implementing ISerializable, given that you do not need to manually interact with an incoming SerializationInfo parameter. Instead, you are able to directly modify your state data while the formatter is operating on the type.

■ **Note** These serialization attributes are defined within the System.Runtime.Serialization namespace.

When applying these attributes, the methods must be defined to receive a StreamingContext parameter and return nothing (otherwise, you will receive a runtime exception). Do note that you are not required to account for each of the serialization-centric attributes, and you can simply contend with the stages of serialization you are interested in intercepting. To illustrate, here is a new

[Serializable] type that has the same requirements as StringData, this time accounted for using the [OnSerializing] and [OnDeserialized] attributes:

```
[Serializable]
class MoreData
{
  public string dataItemOne = "First data block";
  public string dataItemTwo= "More data";

  [OnSerializing]
  private void OnSerializing(StreamingContext context)
  {
    // Called during the serialization process.
    dataItemOne = dataItemOne.ToUpper();
    dataItemTwo = dataItemTwo.ToUpper();
  }

  [OnDeserialized]
  private void OnDeserialized(StreamingContext context)
  {
    // Called once the deserialization process is complete.
    dataItemOne = dataItemOne.ToLower();
    dataItemTwo = dataItemTwo.ToLower();
  }
}
```

If you were to serialize this new type, you would again find that the data has been persisted as uppercase and deserialized as lowercase.

Source Code The CustomSerialization project is included under the Chapter 21 subdirectory.

With this example behind us, you have now been exposed to the core details regarding object serialization services, including various ways to customize the process. As you have seen, the serialization and deserialization process makes it very simple to persist large amounts of data, and it can be less labor-intensive than working with the various reader/writer classes of the System.IO namespace. If you wish to dig deeper into this aspect of the .NET platform, be sure to look up the BinaryFormatter, SoapFormatter, and XmlSerializer using the .NET Framework 3.5 SDK documentation.

Summary

This chapter introduced the topic of object serialization services. As you have seen, the .NET platform makes use of an object graph to correctly account for the full set of related objects that are to be persisted to a stream. As long as each member in the object graph has been marked with the [Serializable] attribute, the data is persisted using your format of choice (binary, SOAP, or XML).

You also learned that it is possible to customize the out-of-the-box serialization process using two possible approaches. First, you learned how to implement the ISerializable interface (and support a special private constructor) to become more involved with how formatters persist the supplied data. Next, you came to know a set of .NET attributes that simplify the process of custom serialization. Just apply the [OnSerializing], [OnSerialized], [OnDeserializing], or [OnDeserialized] attribute on members taking a StreamingContext parameter, and the formatters will invoke them accordingly.

CHAPTER 22

ADO.NET Part I: The Connected Layer

As you would expect, the .NET platform defines a number of namespaces that allow you to interact with machine local and remote relational databases. Collectively speaking, these namespaces are known as *ADO.NET*. In this chapter, once I frame the overall role of ADO.NET, I'll move on to discuss the topic of ADO.NET data providers. The .NET platform supports numerous data providers, each of which is optimized to communicate with a specific database management system (Microsoft SQL Server, Oracle, MySQL, etc.).

After you understand the common functionality provided by various data providers, you will then examine the data provider factory pattern. As you will see, using types within the `System.Data.Common` namespace (and a related `App.config` file), you are able to build a single code base that can dynamically pick and choose the underlying data provider without the need to recompile or redeploy the application's code base.

Perhaps most importantly, this chapter will give you the chance to build a custom data access library assembly (`AutoLotDAL.dll`) that will encapsulate various database operations performed on a custom database named AutoLot. This library will be expanded upon in Chapter 23 and leveraged over many of this text's remaining chapters. We wrap things up by examining how to communicate with Microsoft SQL Server in an asynchronous manner using the types within the `System.Data.SqlClient` namespace and introduce the topic of database transactions.

A High-Level Definition of ADO.NET

If you have a background in Microsoft's previous COM-based data access model (Active Data Objects, or ADO), understand that ADO.NET has very little to do with ADO beyond the letters "A," "D," and "O." While it is true that there is some relationship between the two systems (e.g., each has the concept of connection and command objects), some familiar ADO types (e.g., the `Recordset`) no longer exist. Furthermore, there are a number of new ADO.NET types that have no direct equivalent under classic ADO (e.g., the data adapter).

Unlike classic ADO, which was primarily designed for tightly coupled client/server systems, ADO.NET was built with the disconnected world in mind, using `DataSets`. This type represents a local copy of any number of related data tables, each of which contain a collection of rows and column. Using the `DataSet`, the calling assembly (such as a web page or desktop executable) is able to manipulate and update a `DataSet`'s contents while disconnected from the data source, and send any modified data back for processing using a related data adapter.

Another major difference between classic ADO and ADO.NET is that ADO.NET has deep support for XML data representation. In fact, the data obtained from a data store is serialized (by default) as XML. Given that XML is often transported between layers using standard HTTP, ADO.NET is not limited by firewall constraints.

Perhaps the most fundamental difference between classic ADO and ADO.NET is that ADO.NET is a managed library of code, therefore it plays by the same rules as any managed library. The types that make up ADO.NET use the CLR memory management protocol, adhere to the same type system (classes, interfaces, enums, structures, and delegates), and can be accessed by any .NET language.

From a programmatic point of view, the bulk of ADO.NET is represented by a core assembly named `System.Data.dll`. Within this binary, you will find a good number of namespaces (see Figure 22-1), many of which represent the types of a particular ADO.NET data provider (defined shortly).

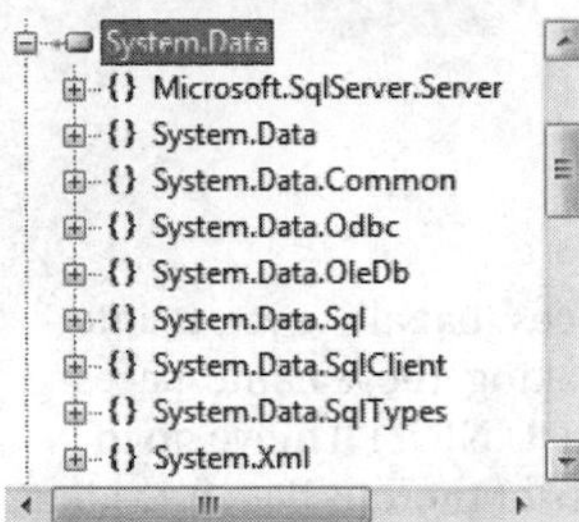

Figure 22-1. `System.Data.dll` *is the core ADO.NET assembly.*

As it turns out, most Visual Studio 2008 project templates automatically reference this key data access library. However, you will need to update your code files to import the namespaces you wish to use; for example:

```
using System;

// Bring in some ADO.NET namespaces!
using System.Data;
using System.Data.SqlClient;

namespace MyApp
{
  class Program
  {
    static void Main(string[] args)
    {
    }
  }
}
```

Do understand that there are other ADO.NET-centric assemblies beyond `System.Data.dll` (such as `System.Data.OracleClient.dll`) that you may need to manually reference in your current project using the Add Reference dialog box.

■ **Note** With the release of .NET 3.5, ADO.NET has received many additional assemblies/namespaces that facilitate ADO.NET/LINQ integration. Chapter 24 will examine LINQ-centric aspects of ADO.NET.

The Two Faces of ADO.NET

The ADO.NET libraries can be used in two conceptually unique manners: connected or disconnected. When you are making use of the *connected layer*, your code base will explicitly connect to and disconnect from the underlying data store. When you are using ADO.NET in this manner, you typically interact with the data store using connection objects, command objects, and data reader objects.

The disconnected layer, which is the subject of Chapter 23, allows you to manipulate a set of `DataTable` objects (contained within a `DataSet`) that functions as a client-side copy of the external data. When you obtain a `DataSet` using a related data adapter object, the connection is automatically opened and closed on your behalf. As you would guess, this approach helps quickly free up connections for other callers and goes a long way to increasing the scalability of your systems.

Once a caller receives a `DataSet`, it is able to traverse and manipulate the contents without incurring the cost of network traffic. As well, if the caller wishes to submit the changes back to the data store, the data adapter (in conjunction with a set of SQL statements) is used once again to update the data source, at which point the connection is closed immediately.

Understanding ADO.NET Data Providers

Unlike classic ADO, ADO.NET does not provide a single set of types that communicate with multiple database management systems (DBMSs). Rather, ADO.NET supports multiple *data providers*, each of which is optimized to interact with a specific DBMS. The first benefit of this approach is that a specific data provider can be programmed to access any unique features of a particular DBMS. Another benefit is that a specific data provider is able to directly connect to the underlying engine of the DBMS in question without an intermediate mapping layer standing between the tiers.

Simply put, a *data provider* is a set of types defined in a given namespace that understand how to communicate with a specific data source. Regardless of which data provider you make use of, each defines a set of class types that provide core functionality. Table 22-1 documents some of the core common objects, their base class (all defined in the `System.Data.Common` namespace), and the data-centric interfaces (each defined in the `System.Data` namespace) they implement.

Table 22-1. *Core Objects of an ADO.NET Data Provider*

Object	Base Class	Implemented Interfaces	Meaning in Life
`Connection`	`DbConnection`	`IDbConnection`	Provides the ability to connect to and disconnect from the data store. Connection objects also provide access to a related transaction object.
`Command`	`DbCommand`	`IDbCommand`	Represents a SQL query or a stored procedure. Command objects also provide access to the provider's data reader object.
`DataReader`	`DbDataReader`	`IDataReader`, `IDataRecord`	Provides forward-only, read-only access to data using a server-side cursor.

Continued

Table 22-1. *Continued*

Object	Base Class	Implemented Interfaces	Meaning in Life
DataAdapter	DbDataAdapter	IDataAdapter, IDbDataAdapter	Transfers DataSets between the caller and the data store. Data adapters contain a connection and a set of four internal command objects used to select, insert, update, and delete information from the data store.
Parameter	DbParameter	IDataParameter, IDbDataParameter	Represents a named parameter within a parameterized query.
Transaction	DbTransaction	IDbTransaction	Encapsulates a database transaction.

Although the specific names of these core objects will differ among data providers (e.g., SqlConnection versus OracleConnection versus OdbcConnection versus MySqlConnection), each object derives from the same base class (DbConnection in the case of connection objects) that implements identical interfaces (such as IDbConnection). Given this, you are correct to assume that once you learn how to work with one data provider, the remaining providers are quite straightforward.

■ **Note** Understand that under ADO.NET, when speaking of a "connection object," one is really referring to a specific DbConnection-derived type; there is no class literally named "Connection". The same idea holds true for a "command object," "data adapter object," and so forth. As a naming convention, the objects in a specific data provider are prefixed with the name of the related DBMS (for example, SqlConnection, OracleConnection, SqlDataReader, etc.).

Figure 22-2 illustrates the big picture behind ADO.NET data providers. Note that in the diagram, the "Client Assembly" can literally be any type of .NET application: console program, Windows Forms application, ASP.NET web page, WCF service, a .NET code library, and so on.

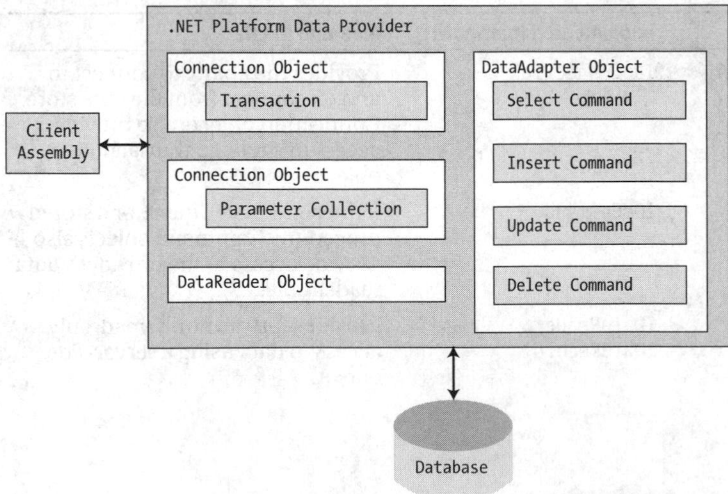

Figure 22-2. *ADO.NET data providers provide access to a given DBMS.*

Now, to be sure, a data provider will supply you with other types beyond the objects shown in Figure 22-2. However, these core objects define a common baseline across all data providers.

The Microsoft-Supplied ADO.NET Data Providers

Microsoft's .NET distribution ships with numerous data providers, including a provider for Oracle, SQL Server, and OLE DB/ODBC-style connectivity. Table 22-2 documents the namespace and containing assembly for each Microsoft ADO.NET data provider.

Table 22-2. *Microsoft ADO.NET Data Providers*

Data Provider	Namespace	Assembly
OLE DB	`System.Data.OleDb`	`System.Data.dll`
Microsoft SQL Server	`System.Data.SqlClient`	`System.Data.dll`
Microsoft SQL Server Mobile	`System.Data.SqlServerCe`	`System.Data.SqlServerCe.dll`
ODBC	`System.Data.Odbc`	`System.Data.dll`
Oracle	`System.Data.OracleClient`	`System.Data.OracleClient.dll`

■Note There is no specific data provider that maps directly to the Jet engine (and therefore Microsoft Access). If you wish to interact with an Access data file, you can do so using the OLE DB or ODBC data provider.

The OLE DB data provider, which is composed of the types defined in the `System.Data.OleDb` namespace, allows you to access data located in any data store that supports the classic COM-based OLE DB protocol. Using this provider, you may communicate with any OLE DB–compliant database simply by tweaking the `Provider` segment of your connection string.

Be aware, however, that the OLE DB provider interacts with various COM objects behind the scenes, which can affect the performance of your application. By and large, the OLE DB data provider is only useful if you are interacting with a DBMS that does not define a specific .NET data provider. However, given the fact that these days any DBMS worth its salt should have a custom ADO.NET data provider for download, `System.Data.OleDb` should be considered a legacy namespace that has little use in the .NET 3.5 world (this is even more the case with the advent of the data provider factory model introduced under .NET 2.0).

■Note There is one case in which using the types of `System.Data.OleDb` is necessary; specifically if you need to communicate with Microsoft SQL Server version 6.5 or earlier. The `System.Data.SqlClient` namespace can only communicate with Microsoft SQL Server version 7.0 or higher.

The Microsoft SQL Server data provider offers direct access to Microsoft SQL Server data stores, and *only* SQL Server data stores (version 7.0 and greater). The `System.Data.SqlClient` namespace contains the types used by the SQL Server provider and offers the same basic functionality as the OLE DB provider. The key difference is that the SQL Server provider bypasses the OLE DB layer and thus gives numerous performance benefits. As well, the Microsoft SQL Server data provider allows you to gain access to the unique features of this particular DBMS.

The remaining Microsoft-supplied providers (`System.Data.OracleClient`, `System.Data.Odbc`, and `System.Data.SqlClientCe`) provide access to Oracle databases, interactivity with ODBC connections, and the SQL Server Mobile edition DBMS (commonly used by handheld devices, such as a

Pocket PC). The ODBC types defined within the `System.Data.Odbc` namespace are typically only useful if you need to communicate with a given DBMS for which there is no custom .NET data provider (in that ODBC is a widespread model that provides access to a number of data stores).

Obtaining Third-Party ADO.NET Data Providers

In addition to the data providers that ship from Microsoft, numerous third-party data providers exist for various open source and commercial databases. While you will most likely be able to obtain an ADO.NET data provider directly from the database vendor, you should be aware of the following site (please note that this URL is subject to change): `http://www.sqlsummit.com/DataProv.htm`.

This website is one of many sites that documents each known ADO.NET data provider and provides links for more information and downloads. Here you will find numerous ADO.NET providers, including SQLite, DB2, MySQL, PostgreSQL, and Sybase (among others).

Given the large number of ADO.NET data providers, the examples in this chapter will make use of the Microsoft SQL Server data provider (`System.Data.SqlClient.dll`). Recall that this provider allows you to communicate with Microsoft SQL Server version 7.0 and higher, including SQL Server 2005 Express Edition. If you intend to use ADO.NET to interact with another DBMS, you should have no problem doing so once you understand the material presented in the pages that follow.

Additional ADO.NET Namespaces

In addition to the .NET namespaces that define the types of a specific data provider, the .NET base class libraries provide a number of additional ADO.NET-centric namespaces, some of which are shown in Table 22-3.

Table 22-3. *Select Additional ADO.NET-Centric Namespaces*

Namespace	Meaning in Life
`Microsoft.SqlServer.Server`	This namespace provides types that facilitate CLR and SQL Server 2005 integration services.
`System.Data`	This namespace defines the core ADO.NET types used by all data providers, including common interfaces and numerous types that represent the disconnected layer (`DataSet`, `DataTable`, etc.).
`System.Data.Common`	This namespace contains types shared between all ADO.NET data providers, including the common abstract base classes.
`System.Data.Sql`	This namespace contains types that allow you to discover Microsoft SQL Server instances installed on the current local network.
`System.Data.SqlTypes`	This namespace contains native data types used by Microsoft SQL Server. Although you are always free to use the corresponding CLR data types, the `SqlTypes` are optimized to work with SQL Server.

Do understand that this chapter will not examine each and every type within each and every ADO.NET namespace (that task would require a large book in and of itself). However, it is quite important for you to understand the types within the `System.Data` namespace.

The Types of the System.Data Namespace

Of all the ADO.NET namespaces, `System.Data` is the lowest common denominator. You simply cannot build ADO.NET applications without specifying this namespace in your data access applications. This namespace contains types that are shared among all ADO.NET data providers, regardless of the underlying data store. In addition to a number of database-centric exceptions (`NoNullAllowedException`, `RowNotInTableException`, `MissingPrimaryKeyException`, and the like), `System.Data` contains types that represent various database primitives (tables, rows, columns, constraints, etc.), as well as the common interfaces implemented by data provider objects. Table 22-4 lists some of the core types to be aware of.

Table 22-4. *Core Members of the* `System.Data` *Namespace*

Type	Meaning in Life
`Constraint`	Represents a constraint for a given `DataColumn` object
`DataColumn`	Represents a single column within a `DataTable` object
`DataRelation`	Represents a parent/child relationship between two `DataTable` objects
`DataRow`	Represents a single row within a `DataTable` object
`DataSet`	Represents an in-memory cache of data consisting of any number of interrelated `DataTable` objects
`DataTable`	Represents a tabular block of in-memory data
`DataTableReader`	Allows you to treat a `DataTable` as a fire-hose cursor (forward only, read-only data access)
`DataView`	Represents a customized view of a `DataTable` for sorting, filtering, searching, editing, and navigation
`IDataAdapter`	Defines the core behavior of a data adapter object
`IDataParameter`	Defines the core behavior of a parameter object
`IDataReader`	Defines the core behavior of a data reader object
`IDbCommand`	Defines the core behavior of a command object
`IDbDataAdapter`	Extends `IDataAdapter` to provide additional functionality of a data adapter object
`IDbTransaction`	Defines the core behavior of a transaction object

A vast majority of the classes within `System.Data` are used when programming against the disconnected layer of ADO.NET. In the next chapter, you will get to know the details of the `DataSet` and its related cohorts (`DataTable`, `DataRelation`, `DataRow`, etc.) and how to use them (and a related data adapter) to represent and manipulate client side copies of remote data.

However, your next task is to examine the core interfaces of `System.Data` at a high level, to better understand the common functionality offered by any data provider. You will learn specific details throughout this chapter, so for the time being let's simply focus on the overall behavior of each interface type.

The Role of the IDbConnection Interface

First up is the `IDbConnection` type, which is implemented by a data provider's *connection object*. This interface defines a set of members used to configure a connection to a specific data store, and it also allows you to obtain the data provider's transaction object. Here is the formal definition of `IDbConnection`:

```
public interface IDbConnection : IDisposable
{
  string ConnectionString { get; set; }
  int ConnectionTimeout { get; }
  string Database { get; }
  ConnectionState State { get; }
  IDbTransaction BeginTransaction();
  IDbTransaction BeginTransaction(IsolationLevel il);
  void ChangeDatabase(string databaseName);
  void Close();
  IDbCommand CreateCommand();
  void Open();
}
```

■ **Note** Like many other types in the .NET base class libraries, the `Close()` method is functionally equivalent to calling the `Dispose()` method directly or indirectly within a C# using scope (see Chapter 8).

The Role of the IDbTransaction Interface

As you can see, the overloaded `BeginTransaction()` method defined by `IDbConnection` provides access to the provider's *transaction object*. Using the members defined by `IDbTransaction`, you are able to programmatically interact with a transactional session and the underlying data store:

```
public interface IDbTransaction : IDisposable
{
  IDbConnection Connection { get; }
  IsolationLevel IsolationLevel { get; }
  void Commit();
  void Rollback();
}
```

The Role of the IDbCommand Interface

Next, we have the `IDbCommand` interface, which will be implemented by a data provider's *command object*. Like other data access object models, command objects allow programmatic manipulation of SQL statements, stored procedures, and parameterized queries. In addition, command objects provide access to the data provider's data reader type via the overloaded `ExecuteReader()` method:

```
public interface IDbCommand : IDisposable
{
  string CommandText { get; set; }
  int CommandTimeout { get; set; }
  CommandType CommandType { get; set; }
  IDbConnection Connection { get; set; }
  IDataParameterCollection Parameters { get; }
  IDbTransaction Transaction { get; set; }
  UpdateRowSource UpdatedRowSource { get; set; }
  void Cancel();
  IDbDataParameter CreateParameter();
  int ExecuteNonQuery();
  IDataReader ExecuteReader();
  IDataReader ExecuteReader(CommandBehavior behavior);
```

```
  object ExecuteScalar();
  void Prepare();
}
```

The Role of the IDbDataParameter and IDataParameter Interfaces

Notice that the Parameters property of IDbCommand returns a strongly typed collection that implements IDataParameterCollection. This interface provides access to a set of IDbDataParameter-compliant class types (e.g., parameter objects):

```
public interface IDbDataParameter : IDataParameter
{
  byte Precision { get; set; }
  byte Scale { get; set; }
  int Size { get; set; }
}
```

IDbDataParameter extends the IDataParameter interface to obtain the following additional behaviors:

```
public interface IDataParameter
{
  DbType DbType { get; set; }
  ParameterDirection Direction { get; set; }
  bool IsNullable { get; }
  string ParameterName { get; set; }
  string SourceColumn { get; set; }
  DataRowVersion SourceVersion { get; set; }
  object Value { get; set; }
}
```

As you will see, the functionality of the IDbDataParameter and IDataParameter interfaces allows you to represent parameters within a SQL command (including stored procedures) via specific ADO.NET parameter objects rather than hard-coded string literals.

The Role of the IDbDataAdapter and IDataAdapter Interfaces

Data adapters are used to push and pull DataSets to and from a given data store. Given this, the IDbDataAdapter interface defines a set of properties that are used to maintain the SQL statements for the related select, insert, update, and delete operations:

```
public interface IDbDataAdapter : IDataAdapter
{
  IDbCommand DeleteCommand { get; set; }
  IDbCommand InsertCommand { get; set; }
  IDbCommand SelectCommand { get; set; }
  IDbCommand UpdateCommand { get; set; }
}
```

In addition to these four properties, an ADO.NET data adapter also picks up the behavior defined in the base interface, IDataAdapter. This interface defines the key function of a data adapter type: the ability to transfer DataSets between the caller and underlying data store using the Fill() and Update() methods. As well, the IDataAdapter interface allows you to map database column names to more user-friendly display names via the TableMappings property:

```
public interface IDataAdapter
{
  MissingMappingAction MissingMappingAction { get; set; }
  MissingSchemaAction MissingSchemaAction { get; set; }
  ITableMappingCollection TableMappings { get; }
  int Fill(System.Data.DataSet dataSet);
  DataTable[] FillSchema(DataSet dataSet, SchemaType schemaType);
  IDataParameter[] GetFillParameters();
  int Update(DataSet dataSet);
}
```

The Role of the IDataReader and IDataRecord Interfaces

The next key interface to be aware of is `IDataReader`, which represents the common behaviors supported by a given data reader object. When you obtain an `IDataReader`-compatible type from an ADO.NET data provider, you are able to iterate over the result set in a forward-only, read-only manner.

```
public interface IDataReader : IDisposable, IDataRecord
{
  int Depth { get; }
  bool IsClosed { get; }
  int RecordsAffected { get; }
  void Close();
  DataTable GetSchemaTable();
  bool NextResult();
  bool Read();
}
```

Finally, as you can see, `IDataReader` extends `IDataRecord`, which defines a good number of members that allow you to extract a strongly typed value from the stream, rather than casting the generic `System.Object` retrieved from the data reader's overloaded indexer method. Here is a partial listing of the various `Get`*`XXX`*`()` methods defined by `IDataRecord` (see the .NET Framework 3.5 SDK documentation for a complete listing):

```
public interface IDataRecord
{
  int FieldCount { get; }
  object this[ string name ] { get; }
  object this[ int i ] { get; }
  bool GetBoolean(int i);
  byte GetByte(int i);
  char GetChar(int i);
  DateTime GetDateTime(int i);
  Decimal GetDecimal(int i);
  float GetFloat(int i);
  short GetInt16(int i);
  int GetInt32(int i);
  long GetInt64(int i);
...
  bool IsDBNull(int i);
}
```

■ **Note** The `IDataReader.IsDBNull()` method can be used to programmatically discover if a specified field is set to `null` before obtaining a value from the data reader (to avoid triggering a runtime exception). Also recall that C# supports nullable data types (see Chapter 4), which are ideal for interacting with data columns that could be empty.

Abstracting Data Providers Using Interfaces

At this point, you should have a better idea of the common functionality found among all .NET data providers. Recall that even though the exact names of the implementing types will differ among data providers, you are able to program against these types in a similar manner—that's the beauty of interface-based polymorphism. For example, if you define a method that takes an `IDbConnection` parameter, you can pass in any ADO.NET connection object:

```
public static void OpenConnection(IDbConnection cn)
{
  // Open the incoming connection for the caller.
  cn.Open();
}
```

■ **Note** Interfaces are not strictly required; the same end result could be achieved using abstract base classes (such as `DbConnection`) as parameters or return values.

The same holds true for member return values. For example, consider the following simple C# Console Application project (named MyConnectionFactory), which allows you to obtain a specific connection object based on the value of a custom enumeration. For diagnostic purposes, we will simply print out the underlying connection object via reflection services:

```
// Need these to get definitions of common interfaces,
// and various connection objects for our test.
using System;
using System.Data;
using System.Data.SqlClient;
using System.Data.Odbc;
using System.Data.OleDb;

// Need to reference System.Data.OracleClient.dll to nab this namespace!
using System.Data.OracleClient;

namespace MyConnectionFactory
{
  // A list of possible providers.
  enum DataProvider
  { SqlServer, OleDb, Odbc, Oracle, None }

  class Program
  {
    static void Main(string[] args)
    {
      Console.WriteLine("**** Very Simple Connection Factory *****\n");
```

```
    // Get a specific connection.
    IDbConnection myCn = GetConnection(DataProvider.SqlServer);
    Console.WriteLine("Your connection is a {0}", myCn.GetType().Name);

    // Open, use and close connection...

    Console.ReadLine();
  }

  // This method returns a specific connection object
  // based on the value of a DataProvider enum.
  static IDbConnection GetConnection(DataProvider dp)
  {
    IDbConnection conn = null;
    switch (dp)
    {
      case DataProvider.SqlServer:
        conn = new SqlConnection();
        break;
      case DataProvider.OleDb:
        conn = new OleDbConnection();
        break;
      case DataProvider.Odbc:
        conn = new OdbcConnection();
        break;
      case DataProvider.Oracle:
        conn = new OracleConnection();
        break;
    }
    return conn;
  }
 }
}
```

The benefit of working with the general interfaces of `System.Data` (or for that matter, the abstract base classes of `System.Data.Common`) is that you have a much better chance of building a flexible code base that can evolve over time. For example, perhaps today you are building an application targeting Microsoft SQL Server, but what if your company switches to Oracle months down the road? If you build a solution that hard-codes the MS SQL Server–specific types of `System.Data.SqlClient`, you will obviously need to edit, recompile, and redeploy the assembly should the back-end database management system change.

Increasing Flexibility Using Application Configuration Files

To further increase the flexibility of your ADO.NET applications, you could incorporate a client-side `*.config` file that makes use of custom key/value pairs within the `<appSettings>` element. Recall from Chapter 15 that custom data stored within a `*.config` file can be programmatically obtained using types within the `System.Configuration` namespace. For example, assume you have specified a data provider value within a configuration file as follows:

```
<configuration>
  <appSettings>
   <!-- This key value maps to one of our enum values-->
   <add key="provider" value="SqlServer"/>
  </appSettings>
</configuration>
```

With this, you could update `Main()` to programmatically obtain the underlying data provider. By doing so, you have essentially build a *connection object factory* that allows you to change the provider without requiring you to recompile your code base (simply change the `*.config` file). Here are the relevant updates to `Main()`:

■Note To use the `ConfigurationManager` type, be sure to set a reference to the `System.Configuration.dll` assembly and import the `System.Configuration` namespace.

```
static void Main(string[] args)
{
  Console.WriteLine("**** Very Simple Connection Factory *****\n");

  // Read the provider key.
  string dataProvString = ConfigurationManager.AppSettings["provider"];

  // Transform string to enum.
  DataProvider dp = DataProvider.None;
  if(Enum.IsDefined(typeof(DataProvider), dataProvString))
    dp = (DataProvider)Enum.Parse(typeof(DataProvider), dataProvString);
  else
    Console.WriteLine("Sorry, no provider exists!");

  // Get a specific connection.
  IDbConnection myCn = GetConnection(dp);
  if(myCn != null)
    Console.WriteLine("Your connection is a {0}", myCn.GetType().Name);

  // Open, use, and close connection...

  Console.ReadLine();
}
```

At this point we have authored some ADO.NET code that allows us to specify the underlying connection dynamically. One obvious problem, however, is that this abstraction is only used within the `MyConnectionFactory.exe` application. If we were to rework this example within a .NET code library (for example, `MyConnectionFactory.dll`), you would be able to build any number of clients that could obtain various connection objects using layers of abstraction.

However, obtaining a connection object is only one aspect of working with ADO.NET. To make a worthwhile data provider factory library, you would also have to account for command objects, data readers, data adapters, transaction objects, and other data-centric types. While building such a code library would not necessarily be difficult, it would require a good amount of code and a considerable amount of time.

Thankfully, since the release of .NET 2.0, the kind folks in Redmond have built this very functionality directly within the .NET base class libraries. We will examine this formal API in just a moment, but first we need to create custom database for use throughout this chapter, as well as many chapters to come.

■Source Code The MyConnectionFactory project is included under the Chapter 22 subdirectory.

Creating the AutoLot Database

As we work through this chapter, we will execute queries against a simple SQL Server test database named AutoLot. In keeping with the automotive theme used throughout this text, this database will contain three interrelated tables (Inventory, Orders, and Customers) that contain various bits of data representing order information for a fictional automobile sales company.

The assumption in this text is that you have a copy of Microsoft SQL Server (7.0 or higher) or a copy of Microsoft SQL Server 2005 Express Edition (`http://msdn.microsoft.com/vstudio/express/sql`). This lightweight database server is perfect for our needs, in that (a) it is free, (b) it provides a GUI front end (the SQL Server Management Tool) to create and administer your databases, and (c) it integrates with Visual Studio 2008/Visual C# Express Edition.

To illustrate the last point, the remainder of this section will walk you through the construction of the AutoLot database using Visual Studio 2008. If you are using Visual C# Express, you can perform similar operations to what is explained here, using the Database Explorer window (which can be loaded from the View ➤ Other Windows menu option).

■Note Do be aware that the AutoLot database will be used throughout the remainder of this text.

Creating the Inventory Table

To begin building our testing database, launch Visual Studio 2008 and open the Server Explorer perspective using the View menu of the IDE. Next, right-click the Data Connections node and select the Create New SQL Server Database menu option. Within the resulting dialog box, connect to the SQL Server installation on your local machine and specify AutoLot as the database name (Windows Authentication should be fine—see Figure 22-3).

Figure 22-3. *Creating a new SQL Server 2005 Express database using Visual Studio 2008*

■ **Note** Rather than specifying the name of your machine (such as INTERUBER in Figure 22-3), you can simply enter **(local)\SQLEXPRESS** in the Server name text box.

At this point, the AutoLot database is completely devoid of any database objects (tables, stored procedures, etc.). To insert the Inventory table, simply right-click the Tables node and select Add New Table (see Figure 22-4).

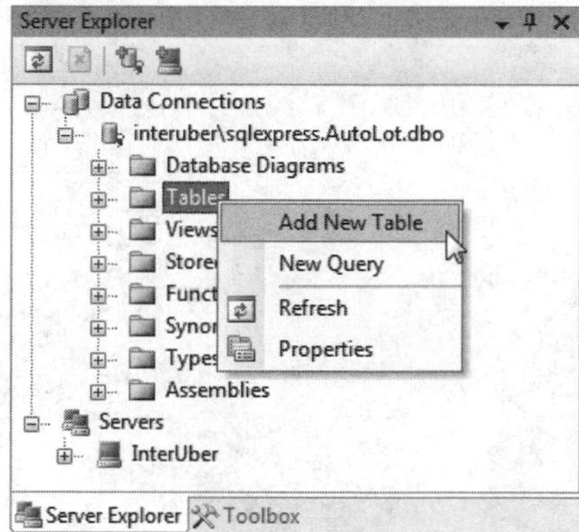

Figure 22-4. *Adding the Inventory table*

Using the table editor, add four data columns (CarID, Make, Color, and PetName). Ensure that the CarID column has been set to the Primary Key (via right-clicking the CarID row and selecting Set Primary Key). Figure 22-5 shows the final table settings.

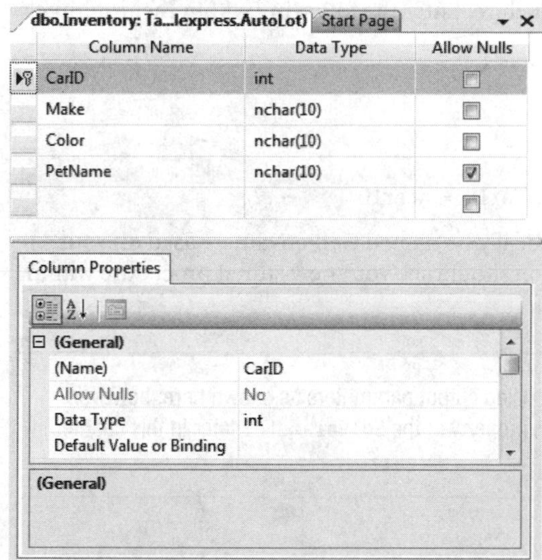

Figure 22-5. *Designing the Inventory table*

Save (and then close) your new table and be sure you name this new database object as Inventory. At this point, you should see the Inventory table under the Tables node of the Server Explorer. Right-click the Inventory table icon and select Show Table Data. Enter a handful of new automobiles of your choosing (to make it interesting, be sure to have some cars that have identical colors and makes). Figure 22-6 shows one possible list of inventory.

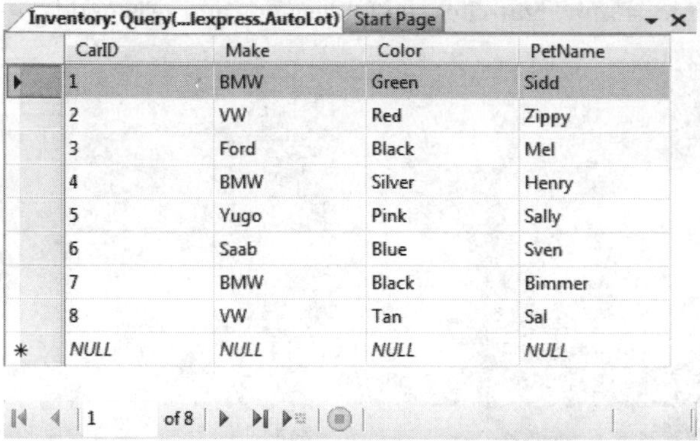

Inventory: Query(...lexpress.AutoLot) Start Page

	CarID	Make	Color	PetName
▶	1	BMW	Green	Sidd
	2	VW	Red	Zippy
	3	Ford	Black	Mel
	4	BMW	Silver	Henry
	5	Yugo	Pink	Sally
	6	Saab	Blue	Sven
	7	BMW	Black	Bimmer
	8	VW	Tan	Sal
*	NULL	NULL	NULL	NULL

1 of 8

Figure 22-6. *Populating the Inventory table*

Authoring the GetPetName() Stored Procedure

Later in this chapter in the section "Executing a Stored Procedure," we will examine how to make use of ADO.NET to invoke stored procedures. As you may already know, stored procedures are routines stored within a particular database that operate often on table data to yield a return value. We will add a single stored procedure that will return an automobile's pet name based on the supplied CarID value. To do so, simply right-click the Stored Procedures node of the AutoLot database within the Server Explorer and select Add New Stored Procedure. Enter the following within the resulting editor:

```
CREATE PROCEDURE GetPetName
@carID int,
@petName char(10) output
AS
SELECT @petName = PetName from Inventory where CarID = @carID
```

When you save your procedure, it will automatically be named GetPetName, based on your `CREATE PROCEDURE` statement. Once you are done, you should see your new stored procedure within the Server Explorer (see Figure 22-7).

■ **Note** Stored procedures are not required to return data using output parameters as shown here; however, doing so will set the stage for talking about the `Direction` property of the `SqlParameter` later in this chapter in the section "Executing a Stored Procedure."

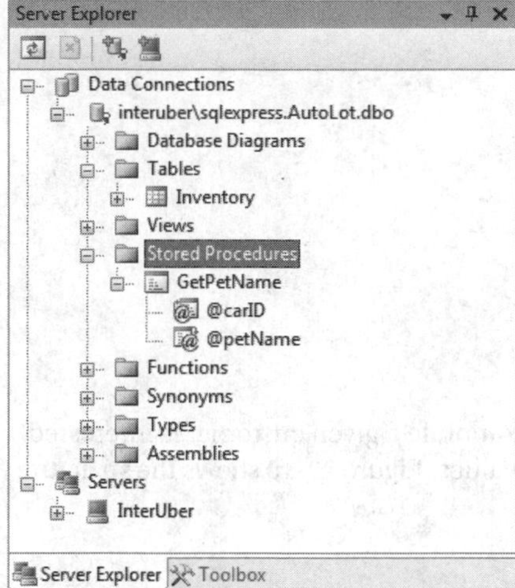

Figure 22-7. *The* `GetPetName` *stored procedure*

Creating the Customers and Orders Tables

Our testing database will have two additional tables. The Customers table (as the name suggests) will contain a list of customers, which will be represented by three columns (CustID [which should be set as the primary key], FirstName, and LastName). Taking the same steps you took to create the Inventory table, create the Customers table using the following schema (see Figure 22-8).

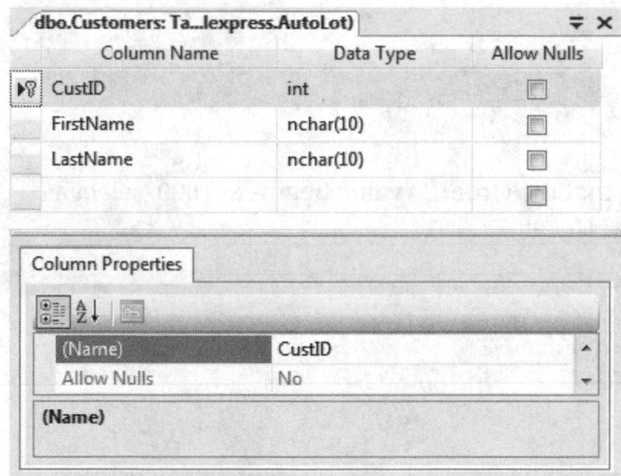

Figure 22-8. *Designing the Customers table*

Once you have saved your table, add a handful of customer records (see Figure 22-9).

Customers: Query(...lexpress.AutoLot) | Start Page

CustID	FirstName	LastName
1	Dave	Brenner
2	Matt	Walton
3	Pat	Walton
4	Jim	White
NULL	NULL	NULL

1 of 4

Figure 22-9. *Populating the Customers table*

Our final table, Orders, will be used to represent the automobile a given customer is interested in purchasing by mapping OrderID values to CarID/CustID values. Figure 22-10 shows the structure of our final table (again note that OrderID is the primary key).

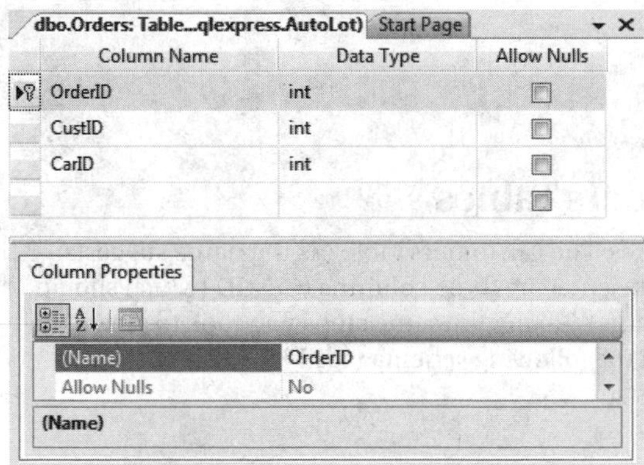
dbo.Orders: Table...qlexpress.AutoLot) | Start Page

Column Name	Data Type	Allow Nulls
OrderID	int	☐
CustID	int	☐
CarID	int	☐
		☐

Figure 22-10. *Designing the Orders table*

Now, add data to your Orders table. Assuming that the OrderID value begins at 1000, select a unique CarID for each CustID value (see Figure 22-11).

Orders: Query(my...lexpress.AutoLot)

OrderID	CustID	CarID
1000	1	2
1001	2	4
1003	4	7
1010	3	8
NULL	NULL	NULL

1 of 4

Figure 22-11. *Populating the Orders table*

Given the entries used in this text, we can see that Dave Brenner (CustID = 1) is interested in the red Volkswagen (CarID = 2), while Pat Walton (CustID = 3) has her eye on the tan Volkswagen (CarID = 8).

Visually Creating Table Relationships

The final task is to establish parent/child table relationships between the Customers, Orders, and Inventory tables. Doing so using Visual Studio 2008 is quite simple, as we can elect to insert a new database diagram by right-clicking the Database Diagrams node of the AutoLot database in the Server Explorer. Once you do so, be sure to select each of the tables from the resulting dialog box before clicking the Add button.

To establish the relationships between the tables, begin by clicking the CarID key of the Inventory table and (while holding down the mouse button) drag to the CarID field of the Orders table. Once you release the mouse, accept all defaults from the resulting dialog boxes.

Now, repeat the same process to map the CustID key of the Customers table to the CustID field of the Orders table. Once you are finished, you should find the class dialog box shown in Figure 22-12 (note that I enabled the display of the table relationships by right-clicking the designer and selecting Show Relationship Labels).

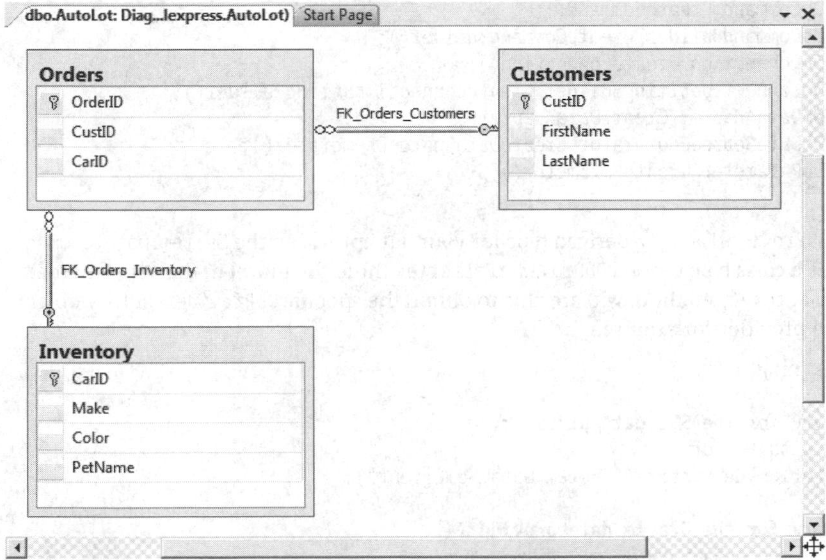

Figure 22-12. *The interconnected Orders, Inventory, and Customers tables*

With this, the AutoLot database is complete! While it is a far cry from a real-world corporate database, it will most certainly serve our purposes over the remainder of this book. Now that we have a database to test with, let's dive into the details of the ADO.NET data provider factory model.

The ADO.NET Data Provider Factory Model

The .NET data provider factory pattern allows us to build a single code base using generalized data access types. Furthermore, using application configuration files (and the `<connectionStrings>` subelement), we are able to obtain providers and connection strings declaratively without the need to recompile or redeploy the assembly.

To understand the data provider factory implementation, recall from Table 22-1 that the objects within a data provider each derive from the same base classes defined within the `System.Data.Common` namespace:

- `DbCommand`: Abstract base class for all command objects
- `DbConnection`: Abstract base class for all connection objects
- `DbDataAdapter`: Abstract base class for all data adapter objects
- `DbDataReader`: Abstract base class for all data reader objects
- `DbParameter`: Abstract base class for all parameter objects
- `DbTransaction`: Abstract base class for all transaction objects

In addition, each of the Microsoft-supplied data providers contains a class type deriving from `System.Data.Common.DbProviderFactory`. This base class defines a number of methods that retrieve provider-specific data objects. Here is a snapshot of the relevant members of `DbProviderFactory`:

```
public abstract class DbProviderFactory
{
...
  public virtual DbCommand CreateCommand();
  public virtual DbCommandBuilder CreateCommandBuilder();
  public virtual DbConnection CreateConnection();
  public virtual DbConnectionStringBuilder CreateConnectionStringBuilder();
  public virtual DbDataAdapter CreateDataAdapter();
  public virtual DbDataSourceEnumerator CreateDataSourceEnumerator();
  public virtual DbParameter CreateParameter();
}
```

To obtain the `DbProviderFactory`-derived type for your data provider, the `System.Data.Common` namespace provides a class type named `DbProviderFactories` (note the plural in this type's name). Using the static `GetFactory()` method, you are able to obtain the specific `DbProviderFactory` object of the specified data provider, for example:

```
static void Main(string[] args)
{
  // Get the factory for the SQL data provider.
  DbProviderFactory sqlFactory =
    DbProviderFactories.GetFactory("System.Data.SqlClient");
...
  // Get the factory for the Oracle data provider.
  DbProviderFactory oracleFactory =
    DbProviderFactories.GetFactory("System.Data.OracleClient");
...
}
```

Of course, rather than obtaining a factory using a hard-coded string literal, you could read in this information from a client-side `*.config` file (much like the previous MyConnectionFactory example). You will do so in just a bit. However, in any case, once you have obtained the factory for your data provider, you are able to obtain the associated provider-specific data objects (connections, commands, data readers, etc.).

Registered Data Provider Factories

Before you build a full example of working with ADO.NET data provider factories, it is important to note that the `DbProviderFactories` type is able to fetch factories for only a subset of all possible data providers. The list of valid provider factories is recorded within the `<DbProviderFactories>` element within the `machine.config` file for your .NET 3.5 installation (note that the value of the `invariant` attribute is identical to the value passed into the `DbProviderFactories.GetFactory()` method):

```
<system.data>
  <DbProviderFactories>
    <add name="Odbc Data Provider" invariant="System.Data.Odbc"
      description=".Net Framework Data Provider for Odbc"
      type="System.Data.Odbc.OdbcFactory,
      System.Data, Version=2.0.0.0, Culture=neutral,
      PublicKeyToken=b77a5c561934e089" />
    <add name="OleDb Data Provider" invariant="System.Data.OleDb"
      description=".Net Framework Data Provider for OleDb"
      type="System.Data.OleDb.OleDbFactory,
      System.Data, Version=2.0.0.0, Culture=neutral,
      PublicKeyToken=b77a5c561934e089" />
    <add name="OracleClient Data Provider" invariant="System.Data.OracleClient"
      description=".Net Framework Data Provider for Oracle"
      type="System.Data.OracleClient.OracleClientFactory, System.Data.OracleClient,
      Version=2.0.0.0, Culture=neutral, PublicKeyToken=b77a5c561934e089" />
    <add name="SqlClient Data Provider" invariant="System.Data.SqlClient"
      description=".Net Framework Data Provider for SqlServer"
      type="System.Data.SqlClient.SqlClientFactory, System.Data,
      Version=2.0.0.0, Culture=neutral, PublicKeyToken=b77a5c561934e089" />
  </DbProviderFactories>
</system.data>
```

■ **Note** If you wish to leverage a similar data provider factory pattern for DMBSs not accounted for in the machine.config file, it is technically possible to add new invariant values that point to shared assemblies in the GAC. However, you must ensure that the data provider is ADO.NET 2.0 compliant and works with the data provider factory model.

A Complete Data Provider Factory Example

For a complete example, let's create a new C# Console Application (named DataProviderFactory) that prints out the automobile inventory of the AutoLot database. For this initial example, we will hard-code the data access logic directly within the DataProviderFactory.exe assembly (just to keep things simple for the time being). However, once we begin to dig into the details of the ADO.NET programming model, we will isolate our data logic to a specific .NET code library that will be used throughout the remainder of this text.

First, add a reference to the System.Configuration.dll assembly and import the System.Configuration namespace. Next, insert an App.config file to the current project and define an empty <appSettings> element. Add a new key named provider that maps to the namespace name of the data provider you wish to obtain (System.Data.SqlClient). As well, define a connection string that represents a connection to the AutoLot database:

```
<?xml version="1.0" encoding="utf-8" ?>
<configuration>
 <appSettings>
  <!-- Which provider? -->
  <add key="provider" value="System.Data.SqlClient" />
  <!-- Which connection string? -->
  <add key="cnStr" value=
  "Data Source=(local)\SQLEXPRESS;Initial Catalog=AutoLot;Integrated Security=True"
```

```
  />
 </appSettings>
</configuration>
```

Note We will examine connection strings in more detail in just a bit. However, be aware that if you select your AutoLot database icon within the Server Explorer, you can copy and paste the correct connection string from the Connection String property of the Visual Studio 2008 Properties Window.

Now that you have a proper `*.config` file, you can read in the `provider` and `cnStr` values using the `ConfigurationManager.AppSettings()` method. The `provider` value will be passed to `DbProviderFactories.GetFactory()` to obtain the data provider–specific factory type. The `cnStr` value will be used to set the `ConnectionString` property of the `DbConnection`-derived type. Assuming you have imported the `System.Data` and `System.Data.Common` namespaces, update your `Main()` method as follows:

```
static void Main(string[] args)
{
  Console.WriteLine("***** Fun with Data Provider Factories *****\n");

  // Get Connection string/provider from *.config.
  string dp =
    ConfigurationManager.AppSettings["provider"];
  string cnStr =
    ConfigurationManager.AppSettings["cnStr"];

  // Get the factory provider.
  DbProviderFactory df = DbProviderFactories.GetFactory(dp);

  // Now make connection object.
  DbConnection cn = df.CreateConnection();
  Console.WriteLine("Your connection object is a: {0}", cn.GetType().FullName);
  cn.ConnectionString = cnStr;
  cn.Open();

  // Make command object.
  DbCommand cmd = df.CreateCommand();
  Console.WriteLine("Your command object is a: {0}", cmd.GetType().FullName);
  cmd.Connection = cn;
  cmd.CommandText = "Select * From Inventory";

  // Print out data with data reader.
  // Because we specified CommandBehavior.CloseConnection, we
  // don't need to explicitly call Close() on the connection.
  DbDataReader dr =
    cmd.ExecuteReader(CommandBehavior.CloseConnection);
  Console.WriteLine("Your data reader object is a: {0}", dr.GetType().FullName);

  Console.WriteLine("\n***** Current Inventory *****");
  while (dr.Read())
    Console.WriteLine("-> Car #{0} is a {1}.",
      dr["CarID"], dr["Make"].ToString().Trim());
  dr.Close();
  Console.ReadLine();
}
```

■ **Note** When you specify `CommandBehavior.CloseConnection` as a parameter to `ExecuteReader()`, the connection will automatically be closed when you close the data reader object.

Notice that for diagnostic purposes, you are printing out the fully qualified name of the underlying connection, command, and data reader using reflection services. If you run this application, you will find that the Microsoft SQL Server provider has been used to read data from the Inventory table of the AutoLot database (see Figure 22-13).

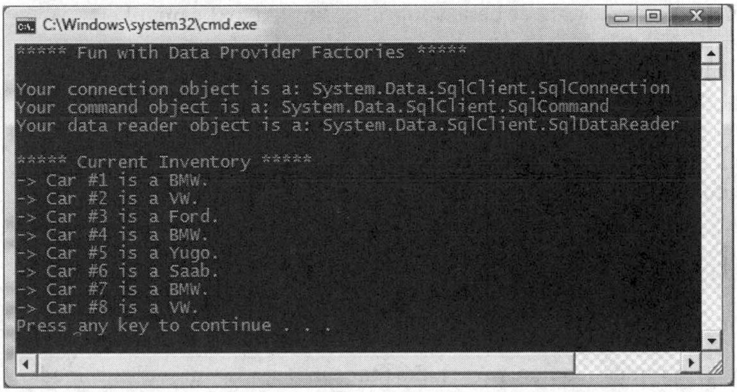

```
C:\Windows\system32\cmd.exe
***** Fun with Data Provider Factories *****

Your connection object is a: System.Data.SqlClient.SqlConnection
Your command object is a: System.Data.SqlClient.SqlCommand
Your data reader object is a: System.Data.SqlClient.SqlDataReader

***** Current Inventory *****
-> Car #1 is a BMW.
-> Car #2 is a VW.
-> Car #3 is a Ford.
-> Car #4 is a BMW.
-> Car #5 is a Yugo.
-> Car #6 is a Saab.
-> Car #7 is a BMW.
-> Car #8 is a VW.
Press any key to continue . . .
```

Figure 22-13. *Obtaining the SQL Server data provider factory*

Now, if you change the `*.config` file to specify `System.Data.OleDb` as the data provider (and update your connection string with a `Provider` segment) as follows:

```
<configuration>
 <appSettings>
  <!-- Which provider? -->
  <add key="provider" value="System.Data.OleDb" />
  <!-- Which connection string? -->
  <add key="cnStr" value=
  "Provider=SQLOLEDB;Data Source=(local)\SQLEXPRESS;
  Integrated Security=SSPI;Initial Catalog=AutoLot"/>
 </appSettings>
</configuration>
```

you will find the `System.Data.OleDb` types are used behind the scenes (see Figure 22-14).

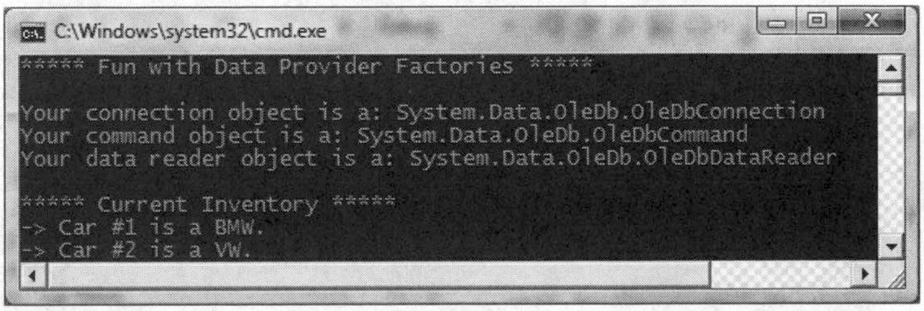

```
C:\Windows\system32\cmd.exe
***** Fun with Data Provider Factories *****

Your connection object is a: System.Data.OleDb.OleDbConnection
Your command object is a: System.Data.OleDb.OleDbCommand
Your data reader object is a: System.Data.OleDb.OleDbDataReader

***** Current Inventory *****
-> Car #1 is a BMW.
-> Car #2 is a VW.
```

Figure 22-14. *Obtaining the OLE DB data provider factory*

Of course, based on your experience with ADO.NET, you may be a bit unsure exactly what the connection, command, and data reader objects are actually doing. Don't sweat the details for the time being (quite a few pages remain in this chapter, after all!). At this point, just understand that with the ADO.NET data provider factory model, it is possible to build a single code base that can consume various data providers in a declarative manner.

A Potential Drawback with the Provide Factory Model

Although this is a very powerful model, you must make sure that the code base does indeed make use only of types and methods that are common to all providers via the members of the abstract base classes. Therefore, when authoring your code base, you will be limited to the members exposed by `DbConnection`, `DbCommand`, and the other types of the `System.Data.Common` namespace.

Given this, you may find that this "generalized" approach will prevent you from directly accessing some of the bells and whistles of a particular DBMS. If you must be able to invoke specific members of the underlying provider (`SqlConnection` for example), you can do so via an explicit cast. When doing so, however, your code base will become a bit harder to maintain (and less flexible) given that you must add a number of runtime checks.

The <connectionStrings> Element

Currently our connection string data is within the `<appSettings>` element of our `*.config` file. Application configuration files may define an element named `<connectionStrings>`. Within this element, you are able to define any number of name/value pairs that can be programmatically read into memory using the `ConfigurationManager.ConnectionStrings` indexer. One advantage of this approach (rather than using the `<appSettings>` element and the `ConfigurationManager.AppSettings` indexer) is that you can define multiple connection strings for a single application in a consistent manner.

To illustrate, update your current `App.config` file as follows (note that each connection string is documented using the `name` and `connectionString` attributes rather than the `key` and `value` attributes as found in `<appSettings>`):

```
<configuration>
 <appSettings>
  <!-- Which provider? -->
  <add key="provider" value="System.Data.SqlClient" />
 </appSettings>

 <!-- Here are the connection strings -->
 <connectionStrings>
  <add name ="AutoLotSqlProvider"  connectionString =
  "Data Source=(local)\SQLEXPRESS;
   Integrated Security=SSPI;Initial Catalog=AutoLot"/>
  <add name ="AutoLotOleDbProvider"  connectionString =
  "Provider=SQLOLEDB;Data Source=(local)\SQLEXPRESS;
  Integrated Security=SSPI;Initial Catalog=AutoLot"/>
 </connectionStrings>
</configuration>
```

With this, you can now update your `Main()` method as follows:

```
static void Main(string[] args)
{
  Console.WriteLine("***** Fun with Data Provider Factories *****\n");
  string dp =
    ConfigurationManager.AppSettings["provider"];
```

```
  string cnStr =
    ConfigurationManager.ConnectionStrings["AutoLotSqlProvider"].ConnectionString;
...
}
```

At this point, you have an application that is able to display the results of the Inventory table of the AutoLot database using a neutral code base. As you have seen, by offloading the provider name and connection string to an external `*.config` file, the data provider factory model will dynamically load the correct provider in the background. With this first example behind us, we can now dive into the details of working with the connected layer of ADO.NET.

■ Note Now that you understand the role of ADO.NET data provider factories, the remaining examples in this book will make explicit use of the types within the `System.Data.SqlClient` namespace just to keep focused on the task at hand. If you are using a different database management system (such as Oracle), you will need to update your code base accordingly.

■ Source Code The DataProviderFactory project is included under the Chapter 22 subdirectory.

Understanding the Connected Layer of ADO.NET

Recall that the *connected layer* of ADO.NET allows you to interact with a database using the connection, command, and data reader objects of your data provider. Although you have already made use of these objects in the previous DataProviderFactory application, let's walk through the process once again in detail using an expanded example. When you wish to connect to a database and read the records using a data reader object, you need to perform the following steps:

1. Allocate, configure, and open your connection object.
2. Allocate and configure a command object, specifying the connection object as a constructor argument or via the `Connection` property.
3. Call `ExecuteReader()` on the configured command object.
4. Process each record using the `Read()` method of the data reader.

To get the ball rolling, create a brand-new Console Application named AutoLotDataReader and import the `System.Data` and `System.Data.SqlClient` namespaces. The goal is to open a connection (via the `SqlConnection` object) and submit a SQL query (via the `SqlCommand` object) to obtain all records within the Inventory table. At this point, you will use a `SqlDataReader` to print out the results using the type indexer. Here is the complete code within `Main()`, with analysis to follow:

```
class Program
{
  static void Main(string[] args)
  {
    Console.WriteLine("***** Fun with Data Readers *****\n");

    // Create an open a connection.
    SqlConnection cn = new SqlConnection();
    cn.ConnectionString =
      @"Data Source=(local)\SQLEXPRESS;Integrated Security=SSPI;" +
```

```
        "Initial Catalog=AutoLot";
      cn.Open();

      // Create a SQL command object.
      string strSQL = "Select * From Inventory";
      SqlCommand myCommand = new SqlCommand(strSQL, cn);

      // Obtain a data reader a la ExecuteReader().
      SqlDataReader myDataReader;
      myDataReader = myCommand.ExecuteReader(CommandBehavior.CloseConnection);

      // Loop over the results.
      while (myDataReader.Read())
      {
        Console.WriteLine("-> Make: {0}, PetName: {1}, Color: {2}.",
          myDataReader["Make"].ToString().Trim(),
          myDataReader["PetName"].ToString().Trim(),
          myDataReader["Color"].ToString().Trim());
      }

      // Because we specified CommandBehavior.CloseConnection, we
      // don't need to explicitly call Close() on the connection.
      myDataReader.Close();
      Console.ReadLine();
    }
  }
```

Working with Connection Objects

The first step to take when working with a data provider is to establish a session with the data source using the connection object (which, as you recall, derives from DbConnection). .NET connection objects are provided with a formatted *connection string*, which contains a number of name/value pairs separated by semicolons. This information is used to identify the name of the machine you wish to connect to, required security settings, the name of the database on that machine, and other data provider–specific information.

As you can infer from the preceding code, the Initial Catalog name refers to the database you are attempting to establish a session with. The Data Source name identifies the name of the machine that maintains the database. Here, (local) allows you to define a single token to specify the current local machine (regardless of the literal name of said machine) while the \SQLEXPRESS token informs the SQL server provider you are connecting to the default SQL Server Express edition installation (if you created AutoLot on a full version of SQL Server 2005 or earlier, simply specify Data Source=(local)).

Beyond this you are able to supply any number of tokens that represent security credentials. Here, we are setting the Integrated Security to SSPI (which is the equivalent to true), which uses the current Windows account credentials for user authentication.

■ **Note** Look up the ConnectionString property of your data provider's connection object in the .NET Framework 3.5 SDK documentation to learn about each name/value pair for your specific DBMS. As you will quickly notice, a single segment (such as Integrated Security) can be set to multiple, redundant values (e.g., SSPI, true, and yes behave identically for the Integrated Security value). Furthermore, you may find multiple terms for the same task (for example, Initial Catalog and Database are interchangeable).

Once your construction string has been established, a call to Open() establishes your connection with the DBMS. In addition to the ConnectionString, Open(), and Close() members, a connection object provides a number of members that let you configure additional settings regarding your connection, such as timeout settings and transactional information. Table 22-5 lists some (but not all) members of the DbConnection base class.

Table 22-5. *Members of the* DbConnection *Type*

Member	Meaning in Life
BeginTransaction()	This method is used to begin a database transaction.
ChangeDatabase()	This method changes the database on an open connection.
ConnectionTimeout	This read-only property returns the amount of time to wait while establishing a connection before terminating and generating an error (the default value is 15 seconds). If you wish to change the default, specify a "Connect Timeout" segment in the connection string (e.g., Connect Timeout=30).
Database	This property gets the name of the database maintained by the connection object.
DataSource	This property gets the location of the database maintained by the connection object.
GetSchema()	This method returns a DataSet that contains schema information from the data source.
State	This property sets the current state of the connection, represented by the ConnectionState enumeration.

As you can see, the properties of the DbConnection type are typically read-only in nature and are only useful when you wish to obtain the characteristics of a connection at runtime. When you wish to override default settings, you must alter the construction string itself. For example, the connection string sets the connection timeout setting from 15 seconds to 30 seconds:

```
static void Main(string[] args)
{
  Console.WriteLine("***** Fun with Data Readers *****\n");

  SqlConnection cn = new SqlConnection();
  cn.ConnectionString =
    @"Data Source=(local)\SQLEXPRESS;" +
    "Integrated Security=SSPI;Initial Catalog=AutoLot;Connect Timeout=30";
  cn.Open();

  // New helper function (see below).
  ShowConnectionStatus(cn);
...
}
```

In the preceding code, notice you have now passed your connection object as a parameter to a new static helper method in the Program class named ShowConnectionStatus(), implemented as follows (be sure to import the System.Data.Common namespace to get the definition of DbConnection):

```
static void ShowConnectionStatus(DbConnection cn)
{
  // Show various stats about current connection object.
  Console.WriteLine("***** Info about your connection *****");
  Console.WriteLine("Database location: {0}", cn.DataSource);
```

```
  Console.WriteLine("Database name: {0}", cn.Database);
  Console.WriteLine("Timeout: {0}", cn.ConnectionTimeout);
  Console.WriteLine("Connection state: {0}\n", cn.State.ToString());
}
```

While most of these properties are self-explanatory, the `State` property is worth special mention. Although this property may be assigned any value of the `ConnectionState` enumeration:

```
public enum ConnectionState
{
  Broken, Closed,
  Connecting, Executing,
  Fetching, Open
}
```

the only valid `ConnectionState` values are `ConnectionState.Open` and `ConnectionState.Closed` (the remaining members of this enum are reserved for future use). Also, understand that it is always safe to close a connection whose connection state is currently `ConnectionState.Closed`.

Working with ConnectionStringBuilder Objects

Working with connection strings programmatically can be a bit cumbersome, given that they are often represented as string literals, which are difficult to maintain and error-prone at best. The Microsoft-supplied ADO.NET data providers support *connection string builder objects*, which allow you to establish the name/value pairs using strongly typed properties. Consider the following update to the current `Main()` method:

```
static void Main(string[] args)
{
  Console.WriteLine("***** Fun with Data Readers *****\n");

  // Create a connection string via the builder object.
  SqlConnectionStringBuilder cnStrBuilder =
    new SqlConnectionStringBuilder();
  cnStrBuilder.InitialCatalog = "AutoLot";
  cnStrBuilder.DataSource = @"(local)\SQLEXPRESS";
  cnStrBuilder.ConnectTimeout = 30;
  cnStrBuilder.IntegratedSecurity = true;

  SqlConnection cn = new SqlConnection();
  cn.ConnectionString = cnStrBuilder.ConnectionString;
  cn.Open();

  ShowConnectionStatus(cn);
...
}
```

In this iteration, you create an instance of `SqlConnectionStringBuilder`, set the properties accordingly, and obtain the internal string via the `ConnectionString` property. Also note that you make use of the default constructor of the type. If you so choose, you can also create an instance of your data provider's connection string builder object by passing in an existing connection string as a starting point (which can be helpful when you are reading these values dynamically from an `App.config` file). Once you have hydrated the object with the initial string data, you can change specific name/value pairs using the related properties, for example:

```
static void Main(string[] args)
{
  Console.WriteLine("***** Fun with Data Readers *****\n");

  // Assume you really obtained the cnStr value from a *.config file.
  string cnStr = @"Data Source=(local)\SQLEXPRESS;" +
                 "Integrated Security=SSPI;Initial Catalog=AutoLot";

  SqlConnectionStringBuilder cnStrBuilder =
    new SqlConnectionStringBuilder(cnStr);

  // Change timeout value.
  cnStrBuilder.ConnectTimeout = 5;
...
}
```

Working with Command Objects

Now that you better understand the role of the connection object, the next order of business is to check out how to submit SQL queries to the database in question. The SqlCommand type (which derives from DbCommand) is an OO representation of a SQL query, table name, or stored procedure. The type of command is specified using the CommandType property, which may take any value from the CommandType enum:

```
public enum CommandType
{
  StoredProcedure,
  TableDirect,
  Text  // Default value.
}
```

When creating a command object, you may establish the SQL query as a constructor parameter or directly via the CommandText property. Also when you are creating a command object, you need to specify the connection to be used. Again, you may do so as a constructor parameter or via the Connection property:

```
static void Main(string[] args)
{
...
  SqlConnection cn = new SqlConnection();
...
  // Create command object via ctor args.
  string strSQL = "Select * From Inventory";
  SqlCommand myCommand = new SqlCommand(strSQL, cn);

  // Create another command object via properties.
  SqlCommand testCommand = new SqlCommand();
  testCommand.Connection = cn;
  testCommand.CommandText = strSQL;
...
}
```

Realize that at this point, you have not literally submitted the SQL query to the AutoLot database, but rather prepared the state of the command object for future use. Table 22-6 highlights some additional members of the DbCommand type.

Table 22-6. *Members of the* DbCommand *Type*

Member	Meaning in Life
CommandTimeout	Gets or sets the time to wait while executing the command before terminating the attempt and generating an error. The default is 30 seconds.
Connection	Gets or sets the DbConnection used by this instance of the DbCommand.
Parameters	Gets the collection of DbParameter types used for a parameterized query.
Cancel()	Cancels the execution of a command.
ExecuteReader()	Returns the data provider's DbDataReader object, which provides forward-only, read-only access to the underlying data.
ExecuteNonQuery()	Issues the command text to the data store where no results are expected or desired.
ExecuteScalar()	A lightweight version of the ExecuteNonQuery() method, designed specifically for singleton queries (such as obtaining a record count).
ExecuteXmlReader()	Microsoft SQL Server (2000 and higher) is capable of returning result sets as XML. As you might suspect, this method returns a System.Xml.XmlReader that allows you to process the incoming stream of XML.
Prepare()	Creates a prepared (or compiled) version of the command on the data source. As you may know, a *prepared query* executes slightly faster and is useful when you wish to execute the same query multiple times.

Note As illustrated later in this chapter, the SqlCommand object defines additional members that facilitate asynchronous database interactions.

Working with Data Readers

Once you have established the active connection and SQL command, the next step is to submit the query to the data source. As you might guess, you have a number of ways to do so. The DbDataReader type (which implements IDataReader) is the simplest and fastest way to obtain information from a data store. Recall that data readers represent a read-only, forward-only stream of data returned one record at a time. Given this, it should stand to reason that data readers are useful only when submitting SQL selection statements to the underlying data store.

Data readers are useful when you need to iterate over large amounts of data very quickly and have no need to maintain an in-memory representation. For example, if you request 20,000 records from a table to store in a text file, it would be rather memory-intensive to hold this information in a DataSet. A better approach is to create a data reader that spins over each record as rapidly as possible. Be aware, however, that data reader objects (unlike data adapter objects, which you'll examine later) maintain an open connection to their data source until you explicitly close the session.

Data reader objects are obtained from the command object via a call to ExecuteReader(). When invoking this method, you may optionally instruct the reader to automatically close down the related connection object by specifying CommandBehavior.CloseConnection.

The following use of the data reader leverages the Read() method to determine when you have reached the end of your records (via a false return value). For each incoming record, you are making use of the type indexer to print out the make, pet name, and color of each automobile. Also note that you call Close() as soon as you are finished processing the records, to free up the connection object:

```
static void Main(string[] args)
{
...
  // Obtain a data reader via ExecuteReader().
  SqlDataReader myDataReader;
  myDataReader = myCommand.ExecuteReader(CommandBehavior.CloseConnection);

  // Loop over the results.
  while (myDataReader.Read())
  {
    Console.WriteLine("-> Make: {0}, PetName: {1}, Color: {2}.",
      myDataReader["Make"].ToString().Trim(),
      myDataReader["PetName"].ToString().Trim(),
      myDataReader["Color"].ToString().Trim());
  }
  myDataReader.Close();
  Console.ReadLine();
}
```

■ **Note** The trimming of the string data shown here is only used to remove trailing blank spaces in the database entries; it is not directly related to ADO.NET! Whether this is necessary or not depends on the column definitions and the data placed in the table and isn't always required.

The indexer of a data reader object has been overloaded to take either a string (representing the name of the column) or an int (representing the column's ordinal position). Thus, you could clean up the current reader logic (and avoid hard-coded string names) with the following update (note the use of the FieldCount property):

```
while (myDataReader.Read())
{
  Console.WriteLine("***** Record *****");
  for (int i = 0; i < myDataReader.FieldCount; i++)
  {
    Console.WriteLine("{0} = {1} ",
      myDataReader.GetName(i),
      myDataReader.GetValue(i).ToString().Trim());
  }
  Console.WriteLine();
}
```

If you compile and run your project, you should be presented with a list of all automobiles in the Inventory table of the AutoLot database (see Figure 22-15).

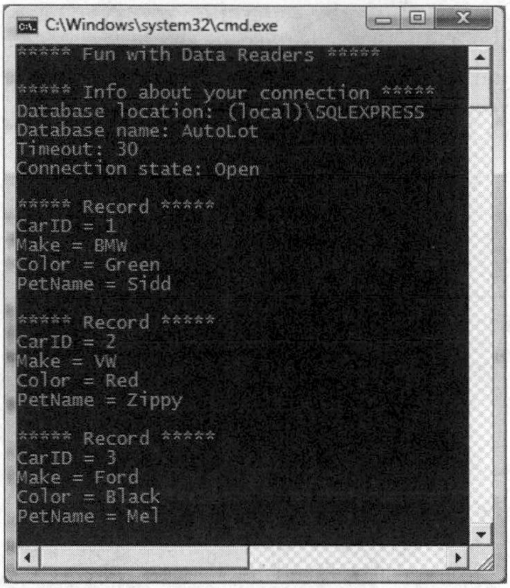

```
C:\Windows\system32\cmd.exe
***** Fun with Data Readers *****

***** Info about your connection *****
Database location: (local)\SQLEXPRESS
Database name: AutoLot
Timeout: 30
Connection state: Open

***** Record *****
CarID = 1
Make = BMW
Color = Green
PetName = Sidd

***** Record *****
CarID = 2
Make = VW
Color = Red
PetName = Zippy

***** Record *****
CarID = 3
Make = Ford
Color = Black
PetName = Mel
```

Figure 22-15. *Fun with data reader objects*

Obtaining Multiple Result Sets Using a Data Reader

Data reader objects are able to obtain multiple result sets using a single command object. For example, if you are interested in obtaining all rows from the Inventory table as well as all rows from the Customers table, you are able to specify both SQL select statements using a semicolon delimiter:

```
string strSQL = "Select * From Inventory;Select * from Customers";
```

Once you obtain the data reader, you are able to iterate over each result set via the `NextResult()` method. Do be aware that you are always returned the first result set automatically. Thus, if you wish to read over the rows of each table, you will be able to build the following iteration construct:

```
do
{
  while (myDataReader.Read())
  {
    Console.WriteLine("***** Record *****");
    for (int i = 0; i < myDataReader.FieldCount; i++)
    {
      Console.WriteLine("{0} = {1}",
        myDataReader.GetName(i),
        myDataReader.GetValue(i).ToString().Trim());
    }
    Console.WriteLine();
  }
} while (myDataReader.NextResult());
```

So, at this point, you should be more aware of the functionality data reader objects bring to the table. Always remember that a data reader can only process SQL `Select` statements and cannot be used to modify an existing database table via `Insert`, `Update`, or `Delete` requests. To understand how to modify an existing database requires a further investigation of command objects.

Source Code The AutoLotDataReader project is included under the Chapter 22 subdirectory.

Building a Reusable Data Access Library

As you have just seen, the `ExecuteReader()` method extracts a data reader object that allows you to examine the results of a SQL `Select` statement using a forward-only, read-only flow of information. However, when you wish to submit SQL statements that result in the modification of a given table, you will call the `ExecuteNonQuery()` method of your command object. This single method will perform inserts, updates, and deletes based on the format of your command text.

Note Technically speaking, a *nonquery* is a SQL statement that does not return a result set. Thus, `Select` statements are queries, while `Insert`, `Update`, and `Delete` statements are not. Given this, `ExecuteNonQuery()` returns an `int` that represents the number of rows affected, not a new set of records.

To illustrate how to modify an existing database using nothing more than a call to `ExecuteNonQuery()`, your next goal is to build a custom data access library that will encapsulate the process of operating upon the AutoLot database. In a production-level environment, your ADO.NET logic will almost always be isolated to a .NET `*.dll` assembly for one simple reason: code reuse! The first examples of this chapter have not done so just to keep focused on the task at hand; however, as you might imagine, it is would be a waste of time to author the *same* connection logic, the *same* data reading logic, and the *same* command logic for every application that needs to interact with the AutoLot database.

By isolating data access logic to a .NET code library, multiple applications using any sort of front end (console based, desktop based, web based, etc.) can reference the library at hand in a language-independent manner. Thus, if you author your data library using C#, other .NET programmers would be able to build a UI in his or her language of choice (VB, C++/CLI, etc.).

In this chapter, our data library (`AutoLotDAL.dll`) will contain a single namespace (`AutoLotConnectedLayer`) that interacts with AutoLot using the connected types of ADO.NET. The next chapter will add a new namespace (`AutoLotDisconnectionLayer`) to this same `*.dll` that contains types to communicate with AutoLot using the disconnected layer. This library will then be used by numerous applications over the remainder of the text.

To begin, create a new C# Class Library project named AutoLotDAL (short for AutoLot Data Access Layer) and rename your initial C# code file to `AutoLotConnDAL.cs`. Next, rename your namespace scope to `AutoLotConnectedLayer` and change the name of your initial class to `InventoryDAL`, as this class will define various members to interact with the Inventory table of the AutoLot database. Finally, import the following .NET namespaces:

```
using System;
using System.Collections.Generic;
using System.Text;

// We will make use of the SQL server
// provider; however, it would also be
// permissible to make use of the ADO.NET
// factory pattern for greater flexibility.
using System.Data;
using System.Data.SqlClient;
```

```
namespace AutoLotConnectedLayer
{
  public class InventoryDAL
  {
  }
}
```

■ **Note** Recall from Chapter 8 that when objects make use of types managing raw resources (such as a database connection), it is a good practice to implement `IDisposable` and author a proper finalizer. In a production environment, classes such as `InventoryDAL` would do the same; however, I'll avoid doing so to stay focused on the particulars of ADO.NET.

Adding the Connection Logic

The first task we must attend to is to define some methods that allow the caller to connect to and disconnect from the data source using a valid connection string. Because our `AutoLotDAL.dll` assembly will be hard-coded to make use of the types of `System.Data.SqlClient`, define a private member variable of `SqlConnection` that is allocated at the time the `InventoryDAL` object is created. As well, define a method named `OpenConnection()` and another named `CloseConnection()` that interact with this member variable as follows:

```
public class InventoryDAL
{
  // This member will be used by all methods.
  private SqlConnection sqlCn = new SqlConnection();

  public void OpenConnection(string connectionString)
  {
    sqlCn.ConnectionString = connectionString;
    sqlCn.Open();
  }

  public void CloseConnection()
  {
    sqlCn.Close();
  }
}
```

For the sake of brevity, our `InventoryDAL` type will not test for possible exceptions nor will it throw custom exceptions under various circumstances (such as a malformed connection string). If you were to build an industrial-strength data access library, you would most certainly want to make use of structured exception handling techniques to account for any runtime anomalies.

Adding the Insertion Logic

Inserting a new record into the Inventory table is as simple as formatting the SQL `Insert` statement (based on user input) and calling the `ExecuteNonQuery()` using your command object. To illustrate, add a public method to your `InventoryDAL` type named `InsertAuto()` that takes four parameters which map to the four columns of the Inventory table (CarID, Color, Make, and PetName). Using the arguments, format a string type to insert the new record. Finally, using your `SqlConnection` object, execute the SQL statement:

```
public void InsertAuto(int id, string color, string make, string petName)
{
  // Format and execute SQL statement.
  string sql = string.Format("Insert Into Inventory" +
    "(CarID, Make, Color, PetName) Values" +
    "('{0}', '{1}', '{2}', '{3}')", id, make, color, petName);

  // Execute using our connection.
  using(SqlCommand cmd = new SqlCommand(sql, this.sqlCn))
  {
    cmd.ExecuteNonQuery();
  }
}
```

■Note As you may know, building a SQL statement using string concatenation can be risky from a security point of view (think SQL injection attacks). The preferred way to build command text is using a parameterized query, which I describe shortly.

Adding the Deletion Logic

Deleting an existing record is just as simple as inserting a new record. Unlike the code listing for `InsertAuto()`, I will show one important `try/catch` scope that handles the possibility of attempting to delete a car that is currently on order for an individual in the Customers table. Add the following method to the `InventoryDAL` class type:

```
public void DeleteCar(int id)
{
  // Get ID of car to delete, then do so.
  string sql = string.Format("Delete from Inventory where CarID = '{0}'",
    id);
  using(SqlCommand cmd = new SqlCommand(sql, this.sqlCn))
  {
    try
    {
      cmd.ExecuteNonQuery();
    }
    catch(SqlException ex)
    {
      Exception error = new Exception("Sorry! That car is on order!", ex);
      throw error;
    }
  }
}
```

Adding the Updating Logic

When it comes to the act of updating an existing record in the Inventory table, the first obvious question is what exactly do we wish to allow the caller to change? The car's color? The pet name or make? All of the above? Of course one way to allow the caller complete flexibility is to simply define a method that takes a `string` type to represent any sort of SQL statement, but that is risky at best. Ideally, we would have a set of methods that allow the caller to update a record in a variety of manners. However, for our simple data access library, we will define a single method that allows the caller to update the pet name of a given automobile:

```
public void UpdateCarPetName(int id, string newPetName)
{
  // Get ID of car to modify and new pet name.
  string sql =
    string.Format("Update Inventory Set PetName = '{0}' Where CarID = '{1}'",
    newPetName, id);
  using(SqlCommand cmd = new SqlCommand(sql, this.sqlCn))
  {
    cmd.ExecuteNonQuery();
  }
}
```

Adding the Selection Logic

The next method to add is a selection method. As seen earlier in this chapter, a data provider's data reader object allows for a selection of records using a read-only, forward-only server-side cursor. As you call the `Read()` method, you are able to process each record in a fitting manner. While this is all well and good, we need to contend with the issue of how to return these records to the calling tier of our application.

One approach would be to populate and return a multidimensional array (or other such object, like a generic `List<T>`) with the data obtained by the `Read()` method. Another approach (which we will opt for in the current example) is to return a `System.Data.DataTable` object, which is actually part of the disconnected layer of ADO.NET.

Full coverage of the `DataTable` type can be found in the next chapter; however, for the time being, simply understand that a `DataTable` is a class type that represents a tabular block of data (like a grid on a spreadsheet). To do so, the `DataTable` type maintains a collection of rows and columns. While these collections can be filled programmatically, the `DataTable` type provides a method named `Load()`, which will automatically populate these collections using a data reader object! Consider the following:

```
public DataTable GetAllInventory()
{
  // This will hold the records.
  DataTable inv = new DataTable();

  // Prep command object.
  string sql = "Select * From Inventory";
  using(SqlCommand cmd = new SqlCommand(sql, this.sqlCn))
  {
    SqlDataReader dr = cmd.ExecuteReader();
    // Fill the DataTable with data from the reader and clean up.
    inv.Load(dr);
    dr.Close();
  }
  return inv;
}
```

Working with Parameterized Command Objects

Currently, the insert, update, and delete logic for the `InventoryDAL` type uses hard-coded string literals for each SQL query. As you may know, a *parameterized query* can be used to treat SQL parameters as objects, rather than a simple blob of text. Treating SQL queries in a more object-oriented manner not only helps reduce the number of typos (given strongly typed properties), but parameterized queries typically execute much faster than a literal SQL string, in that they are parsed exactly once (rather than each time the SQL string is assigned to the `CommandText` property). Furthermore, parameterized queries also help protect against SQL injection attacks (a well-known data access security issue).

To support parameterized queries, ADO.NET command objects maintain a collection of individual parameter objects. By default, this collection is empty, but you are free to insert any number of parameter objects that map to a "placeholder parameter" in the SQL query. When you wish to associate a parameter within a SQL query to a member in the command object's parameters collection, prefix the SQL text parameter with the `@` symbol (at least when using Microsoft SQL Server; not all DBMSs support this notation).

Specifying Parameters Using the DbParameter Type

Before you build a parameterized query, let's get to know the `DbParameter` type (which is the base class to a provider's specific parameter object). This class maintains a number of properties that allow you to configure the name, size, and data type of the parameter, as well as other characteristics such as the parameter's direction of travel. Table 22-7 describes some key properties of the `DbParameter` type.

Table 22-7. *Key Members of the* `DbParameter` *Type*

Property	Meaning in Life
`DbType`	Gets or sets the native data type from the data source, represented as a CLR data type
`Direction`	Gets or sets whether the parameter is input-only, output-only, bidirectional, or a return value parameter
`IsNullable`	Gets or sets whether the parameter accepts null values
`ParameterName`	Gets or sets the name of the `DbParameter`
`Size`	Gets or sets the maximum parameter size of the data (only truly useful for textual data)
`Value`	Gets or sets the value of the parameter

To illustrate how to populate a command object's collection of `DBParameter`-compatible objects, let's rework the previous `InsertAuto()` method to make use of parameter objects (a similar reworking could also be performed for your remaining SQL-centric methods; however, it is not necessary for this example):

```
public void InsertAuto(int id, string color, string make, string petName)
{
  // Note the "placeholders" in the SQL query.
  string sql = string.Format("Insert Into Inventory" +
      "(CarID, Make, Color, PetName) Values" +
      "(@CarID, @Make, @Color, @PetName)");

  // This command will have internal parameters.
  using(SqlCommand cmd = new SqlCommand(sql, this.sqlCn))
  {
    // Fill params collection.
    SqlParameter param = new SqlParameter();
    param.ParameterName = "@CarID";
```

```
    param.Value = id;
    param.SqlDbType = SqlDbType.Int;
    cmd.Parameters.Add(param);

    param = new SqlParameter();
    param.ParameterName = "@Make";
    param.Value = make;
    param.SqlDbType = SqlDbType.Char;
    param.Size = 10;
    cmd.Parameters.Add(param);

    param = new SqlParameter();
    param.ParameterName = "@Color";
    param.Value = color;
    param.SqlDbType = SqlDbType.Char;
    param.Size = 10;
    cmd.Parameters.Add(param);

    param = new SqlParameter();
    param.ParameterName = "@PetName";
    param.Value = petName;
    param.SqlDbType = SqlDbType.Char;
    param.Size = 10;
    cmd.Parameters.Add(param);

    cmd.ExecuteNonQuery();
  }
}
```

Again, notice that our SQL query consists of four embedded placeholder symbols, each of which is prefixed with the @ token. Using the `SqlParameter` type, we are able to map each placeholder using the `ParameterName` property and specify various details (its value, data type, size, etc.) in a strongly typed matter. Once each parameter object is hydrated, it is added to the command object's collection via a call to `Add()`.

■ **Note** Here, I made use of various properties to establish a parameter object. Do know, however, that parameter objects support a number of overloaded constructors that allow you to set the values of various properties (which will result in a more compact code base). Also be aware that Visual Studio 2008 provides numerous graphical designers that will generate a good deal of this grungy parameter-centric code on your behalf (see Chapter 23).

While building a parameterized query often requires a larger amount of code, the end result is a more convenient way to tweak SQL statements programmatically as well as better overall performance. While you are free to make use of this technique whenever a SQL query is involved, parameterized queries are most helpful when you wish to trigger a stored procedure.

Executing a Stored Procedure

Recall that a *stored procedure* is a named block of SQL code stored in the database. Stored procedures can be constructed to return a set of rows or scalar data types and may take any number of optional parameters. The end result is a unit of work that behaves like a typical function, with the obvious difference of being located on a data store rather than a binary business object. Currently our AutoLot database defines a single stored procedure named `GetPetName`, which was formatted as follows:

```
CREATE PROCEDURE GetPetName
@carID int,
@petName char(10) output
AS
SELECT @petName = PetName from Inventory where CarID = @carID
```

Now, consider the following final method of the `InventoryDAL` type, which invokes our stored procedure:

```
public string LookUpPetName(int carID)
{
  string carPetName = string.Empty;

  // Establish name of stored proc.
  using (SqlCommand cmd = new SqlCommand("GetPetName", this.sqlCn))
  {
    cmd.CommandType = CommandType.StoredProcedure;

    // Input param.
    SqlParameter param = new SqlParameter();
    param.ParameterName = "@carID";
    param.SqlDbType = SqlDbType.Int;
    param.Value = carID;
    param.Direction = ParameterDirection.Input;
    cmd.Parameters.Add(param);

    // Output param.
    param = new SqlParameter();
    param.ParameterName = "@petName";
    param.SqlDbType = SqlDbType.Char;
    param.Size = 10;
    param.Direction = ParameterDirection.Output;
    cmd.Parameters.Add(param);

    // Execute the stored proc.
    cmd.ExecuteNonQuery();

    // Return output param.
    carPetName = ((string)cmd.Parameters["@petName"].Value).Trim();
  }
  return carPetName;
}
```

The first important aspect of invoking a stored procedure is to recall that a command object can represent a SQL statement (the default) *or* the name of a stored procedure. When you wish to inform a command object that it will be invoking a stored procedure, you pass in the name of the procedure (as a constructor argument or via the `CommandText` property) and must set the `CommandType` property to the value `CommandType.StoredProcedure` (if you fail to do so, you will receive a runtime exception, as the command object is expecting a SQL statement by default):

```
SqlCommand cmd = new SqlCommand("GetPetName", this.sqlCn);
cmd.CommandType = CommandType.StoredProcedure;
```

Next, notice that the `Direction` property of a parameter object allows you to specify the direction of travel for each parameter passed to the stored procedure (e.g., input parameters and the output parameter). As before, each parameter object is added to the command object's parameters collection:

```
// Input param.
SqlParameter param = new SqlParameter();
param.ParameterName = "@carID";
param.SqlDbType = SqlDbType.Int;
param.Value = carID;
param.Direction = ParameterDirection.Input;
cmd.Parameters.Add(param);
```

Finally, once the stored procedure completes via a call to ExecuteNonQuery(), you are able to obtain the value of the output parameter by investigating the command object's parameter collection and casting accordingly:

```
// Return output param.
carPetName = (string)cmd.Parameters["@petName"].Value;
```

■ **Source Code** The AutoLotDAL project is included under the Chapter 22 subdirectory.

Creating a Console UI–Based Front End

At this point, our first iteration of the AutoLotDAL.dll data access library is complete. Using this assembly, we can build any sort of front end to display and edit our data (console based, Windows Forms based, Windows Presentation Foundation applications, or an HTML-based web application). Given that we have not yet examined how to build graphical user interfaces, we will test our data library from a new Console Application named AutoLotCUIClient. Once you create your new project, be sure to add a reference to your AutoLotDAL.dll assembly as well as System.Configuration.dll and update your using statements as follows:

```
using AutoLotConnectedLayer;
using System.Configuration;
using System.Data;
```

Next, insert a new App.config file into your project that contains a <connectionString> element used to connect to your instance of the AutoLot database, for example:

```
<configuration>
  <connectionStrings>
    <add name ="AutoLotSqlProvider" connectionString =
    "Data Source=(local)\SQLEXPRESS;" +
    "Integrated Security=SSPI;Initial Catalog=AutoLot"/>
  </connectionStrings>
</configuration>
```

Implementing the Main() Method

The Main() method is responsible for prompting the user for a specific course of action and executing that request via a switch statement. This program will allow the user to enter the following commands:

- I: Inserts a new record into the Inventory table
- U: Updates an existing record in the Inventory table
- D: Deletes an existing record from the Inventory table

- L: Displays the current inventory using a data reader
- S: Shows these options to the user
- P: Look up pet name from car ID
- Q: Quits the program

Each possible option is handled by a unique static method within the Program class. Here is the complete implementation of Main(). Notice that each method invoked from the do/while loop (with the exception of the ShowInstructions() method) takes an InventoryDAL object as its sole parameter:

```
static void Main(string[] args)
{
  Console.WriteLine("***** The AutoLot Console UI *****\n");

  // Get connection string from App.config.
  string cnStr =
    ConfigurationManager.ConnectionStrings["AutoLotSqlProvider"].ConnectionString;
  bool userDone = false;
  string userCommand = "";

  // Create our InventoryDAL object.
  InventoryDAL invDAL = new InventoryDAL();
  invDAL.OpenConnection(cnStr);

  // Keep asking for input until user presses the Q key.
  try
  {
    ShowInstructions();
    do
    {
      Console.Write("Please enter your command: ");
      userCommand = Console.ReadLine();
      Console.WriteLine();
      switch (userCommand.ToUpper())
      {
      case "I":
        InsertNewCar(invDAL);
        break;
      case "U":
        UpdateCarPetName(invDAL);
        break;
      case "D":
        DeleteCar(invDAL);
        break;
      case "L":
        ListInventory(invDAL);
        break;
      case "S":
        ShowInstructions();
        break;
      case "P":
        LookUpPetName(invDAL);
        break;
      case "Q":
        userDone = true;
        break;
      default:
```

```
          Console.WriteLine("Bad data!  Try again");
          break;
        }
      } while (!userDone);
    }
    catch (Exception ex)
    {
      Console.WriteLine(ex.Message);
    }
    finally
    {
      invDAL.CloseConnection();
    }
  }
```

Implementing the ShowInstructions() Method

The ShowInstructions() method does what you would expect:

```
private static void ShowInstructions()
{
  Console.WriteLine("I: Inserts a new car.");
  Console.WriteLine("U: Updated an existing car.");
  Console.WriteLine("D: Deletes an existing car.");
  Console.WriteLine("L: List current inventory.");
  Console.WriteLine("S: Show these instructions.");
  Console.WriteLine("P: Look up pet name.");
  Console.WriteLine("Q: Quits program.");
}
```

Implementing the ListInventory() Method

The ListInventory() method obtains the DataTable returned from the GetAllInventory() method of the InventoryDAL object. After this point, we call a (yet to be created) function named DisplayTable():

```
private static void ListInventory(InventoryDAL invDAL)
{
  // Get the list of inventory.
  DataTable dt = invDAL.GetAllInventory();
  DisplayTable(dt);
}
```

The DisplayTable() helper method displays the table data using the Rows and Columns properties of the incoming DataTable (again, full details of the DataTable object appear in the next chapter, so don't fret over the details):

```
private static void DisplayTable(DataTable dt)
{
  // Print out the column names.
  for (int curCol = 0; curCol < dt.Columns.Count; curCol++)
  {
    Console.Write(dt.Columns[curCol].ColumnName.Trim() + "\t");
  }
  Console.WriteLine("\n----------------------------------");
```

```
  // Print the DataTable.
  for (int curRow = 0; curRow < dt.Rows.Count; curRow++)
  {
    for (int curCol = 0; curCol < dt.Columns.Count; curCol++)
    {
      Console.Write(dt.Rows[curRow][curCol].ToString().Trim() + "\t");
    }
    Console.WriteLine();
  }
}
```

Implementing the DeleteCar() Method

Deleting an existing automobile is as simple as asking the user for the ID of the car to blow out of the data table and passing this to the `DeleteCar()` method of the `InventoryDAL` type:

```
private static void DeleteCar(InventoryDAL invDAL)
{
  // Get ID of car to delete.
  Console.Write("Enter ID of Car to delete: ");
  int id = int.Parse(Console.ReadLine());

  // Just in case we have a primary key
  // violation!
  try
  {
    invDAL.DeleteCar(id);
  }
  catch(Exception ex)
  {
    Console.WriteLine(ex.Message);
  }
}
```

Implementing the InsertNewCar() Method

Inserting a new record into the Inventory table is simply a matter of asking the user for the new bits of data (via `Console.ReadLine()` calls) and passing this data into the `InsertAuto()` method of `InventoryDAL`:

```
private static void InsertNewCar(InventoryDAL invDAL)
{
  // First get the user data.
  int newCarID;
  string newCarColor, newCarMake, newCarPetName;

  Console.Write("Enter Car ID: ");
  newCarID = int.Parse(Console.ReadLine());
  Console.Write("Enter Car Color: ");
  newCarColor = Console.ReadLine();
  Console.Write("Enter Car Make: ");
  newCarMake = Console.ReadLine();
  Console.Write("Enter Pet Name: ");
  newCarPetName = Console.ReadLine();
```

```
  // Now pass to data access library.
  invDAL.InsertAuto(newCarID, newCarColor, newCarMake, newCarPetName);
}
```

Implementing the UpdateCarPetName() Method

The implementation of UpdateCarPetName() is very similar:

```
private static void UpdateCarPetName(InventoryDAL invDAL)
{
  // First get the user data.
  int carID;
  string newCarPetName;

  Console.Write("Enter Car ID: ");
  carID = int.Parse(Console.ReadLine());
  Console.Write("Enter New Pet Name: ");
  newCarPetName = Console.ReadLine();

  // Now pass to data access library.
  invDAL.UpdateCarPetName(carID, newCarPetName);
}
```

Invoking Our Stored Procedure

Obtaining the pet name of a given automobile is also very similar to the previous methods, given that the data access library has encapsulated all of the lower-level ADO.NET calls:

```
private static void LookUpPetName(InventoryDAL invDAL)
{
  // Get ID of car to look up.
  Console.Write("Enter ID of Car to look up: ");
  int id = int.Parse(Console.ReadLine());
  Console.WriteLine("Petname of {0} is {1}.",
    id, invDAL.LookUpPetName(id));
}
```

With this, our console-based front end is finished. Figure 22-16 shows a test run.

■ **Source Code** The AutoLotCUIClient application is included under the Chapter 22 subdirectory.

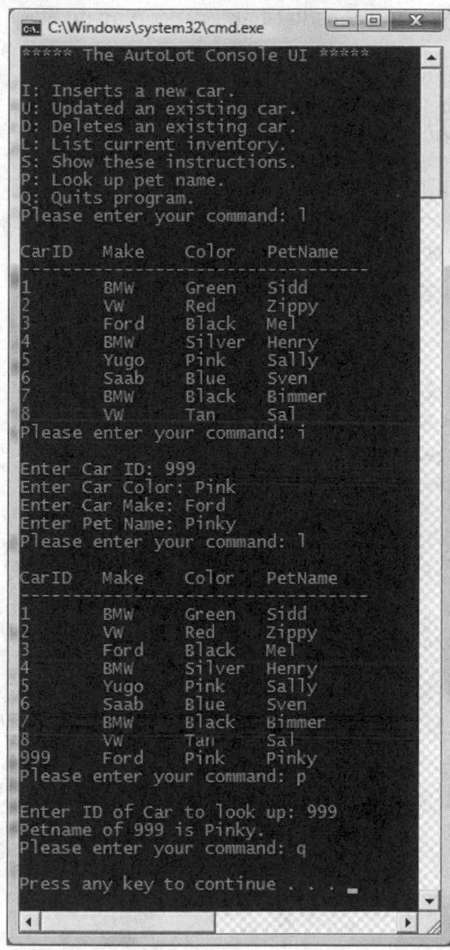

Figure 22-16. *Inserting, updating, and deleting records via command objects*

Asynchronous Data Access Using SqlCommand

Currently, all of our data access logic is happening on a single thread of execution. However, allow me to point out that since the release of .NET 2.0, the SQL data provider has been enhanced to support asynchronous database interactions via the following new members of `SqlCommand`:

- `BeginExecuteReader()/EndExecuteReader()`
- `BeginExecuteNonQuery()/EndExecuteNonQuery()`
- `BeginExecuteXmlReader()/EndExecuteXmlReader()`

Given your work in Chapter 18, the naming convention of these method pairs may ring a bell. Recall that the .NET asynchronous delegate pattern makes use of a "begin" method to execute a task on a secondary thread, whereas the "end" method can be used to obtain the result of the asynchronous invocation using the members of `IAsyncResult` and the optional `AsyncCallback` delegate. Because the process of working with asynchronous commands is modeled after the standard delegate patterns, a simple example should suffice (so be sure to consult Chapter 18 for full details of asynchronous delegates).

Assume you wish to select the records from the Inventory table on a secondary thread of execution using a data reader object. Here is a completely new Console Application (which does not make use of our `InventoryDAL.dll` assembly) named AsyncCmdObjectApp:

Note When you wish to enable access data in an asynchronous manner, you must update your connection string with `Asynchronous Processing=true` (the default value is in fact, `false`).

```
static void Main(string[] args)
{
  Console.WriteLine("***** Fun with ASNYC Data Readers *****\n");

  // Create and open a connection that is async-aware.
  SqlConnection cn = new SqlConnection();
  cn.ConnectionString =
    @"Data Source=(local)\SQLEXPRESS;Integrated Security=SSPI;" +
    "Initial Catalog=AutoLot;Asynchronous Processing=true";
  cn.Open();

  // Create a SQL command object that waits for approx 2 seconds.
  string strSQL = "WaitFor Delay '00:00:02';Select * From Inventory";
  SqlCommand myCommand = new SqlCommand(strSQL, cn);

  // Execute the reader on a second thread.
  IAsyncResult itfAsynch;
  itfAsynch = myCommand.BeginExecuteReader(CommandBehavior.CloseConnection);

  // Do something while other thread works.
  while (!itfAsynch.IsCompleted)
  {
    Console.WriteLine("Working on main thread...");
    Thread.Sleep(1000);
  }
  Console.WriteLine();

  // All done! Get reader and loop over results.
  SqlDataReader myDataReader = myCommand.EndExecuteReader(itfAsynch);
  while (myDataReader.Read())
  {
    Console.WriteLine("-> Make: {0}, PetName: {1}, Color: {2}.",
      myDataReader["Make"].ToString().Trim(),
      myDataReader["PetName"].ToString().Trim(),
      myDataReader["Color"].ToString().Trim());
  }
  myDataReader.Close();
}
```

The first point of interest is the fact that you need to enable asynchronous activity using the new `Asynchronous Processing` segment of the connection string. Also note that you have padded into the command text of your `SqlCommand` object a `WaitFor Delay` segment simply to simulate a long-running database interaction.

Beyond these points, notice that the call to `BeginExecuteDataReader()` returns the expected `IAsyncResult`-compatible type, which is used to synchronize the calling thread (via the `IsCompleted` property) as well as obtain the `SqlDataReader` once the query has finished executing.

■ **Source Code** The AsyncCmdObjectApp application is included under the Chapter 22 subdirectory.

Understanding Database Transactions

To wrap up our examination of the connected layer of ADO.NET, we will take a look at the concept of a database transaction. Simply put, a *transaction* is a set of database operations that must either *all* work or *all* fail as a collective whole. As you would imagine, transactions are quite important to ensure that table data is safe, valid, and consistent.

Transactions are very important when a database operation involves interacting with multiple tables or multiple stored procedures (or a combination of database atoms). The classic transaction example involves the process of transferring monetary funds between two bank accounts. For example, if you were to transfer $500.00 from your savings account into your checking account, the following steps should occur in a transactional manner:

- The bank should remove $500.00 from your savings account.
- The bank should then add $500.00 from to your checking account.

It would be a very bad thing indeed if the money was removed from the savings account, yet was not transferred to the checking account (due to some error on the bank's part), as you are now out $500.00! However, if these steps were wrapped up into a database transaction, the DBMS would ensure that all related steps occur as a single unit. If any part of the transaction fails, the entire operation is "rolled back" to the original state. On the other hand, if all steps succeed, the transaction is "committed."

■ **Note** You may have heard of the acronym ACID when examining transactional literature. This represents the four key properties of a prim-and-proper transaction, specifically Atomic (all or nothing), Consistent (data remains stable throughout the transaction), Isolated (transactions do not step on each other's feet) and Durable (transactions are saved and logged).

As it turns out, the .NET platform supports transactions in a variety of ways. Most importantly for this chapter is the transaction object of your ADO.NET data provider (`SqlTransaction` in the case of `System.Data.SqlClient`). In addition, the .NET base class libraries provide transactional supports within numerous APIs, including the following:

- `System.EnterpriseServices`: This namespace provides types that allow you to integrate with the COM+ runtime layer, including its support for distributed transactions.
- `System.Transactions`: This namespace contains classes that allow you to write your own transactional applications and resource managers for a variety of services (MSMQ, ADO.NET, COM+, etc.).
- *Windows Communication Foundation*: The WCF API provides services to facilitate transactions.
- *Windows Workflow Foundations*: The WF API provides transactional support for workflow activities.

In addition to the baked-in transactional support found within the .NET base class libraries, it is also possible to make use of the SQL language itself of your database management system. For example, you could author a stored procedure that makes use of the `BEGIN TRANSACTION`, `ROLLBACK`, and `COMMIT` statements.

Key Members of an ADO.NET Transaction Object

While transactional-aware types exist throughout the base class libraries, we will focus on transaction objects found within an ADO.NET data provider, all of which derive from `DBTransaction` and implement the `IDbTransaction` interface. Recall from the beginning of this chapter that `IDbTransaction` defines a handful of members:

```
public interface IDbTransaction : IDisposable
{
  IDbConnection Connection { get; }
  IsolationLevel IsolationLevel { get; }
  void Commit();
  void Rollback();
}
```

Notice first of all that the `Connection` property, which will return to you a reference to the connection object that initiated the current transaction (as you'll see, you obtain a transaction object from a given connection object). The `Commit()` method is called when each of your database operations have succeeded. By doing so, each of the pending changes will be persisted in the data store. Conversely, the `Rollback()` method can be called in the event of a runtime exception, which will inform the DMBS to disregard any pending changes, leaving the original data intact.

■**Note** The `IsolationLevel` property of a transaction object allows you to specify how aggressively a transaction should be guarded against the activities of other parallel transactions. By default, transactions are isolated completely until committed. Consult the .NET Framework 3.5 SDK documentation for full details regarding the values of the `IsolationLevel` enumeration.

Beyond the members defined by the `IDbTransaction` interface, the `SqlTransaction` type defines an additional member named `Save()`, which allows you to define *save points*. This concept allows you to roll back a failed transaction up until a named point, rather than rolling back the entire transaction. Essentially, when you call `Save()` using a `SqlTransaction` object, you are able to specify a friendly string moniker. When calling `Rollback()`, you are able to specify this same moniker as an argument to effectively do a "partial rollback." When calling `Rollback()` with no arguments, all of the pending changes will indeed be rolled back.

Adding a Transaction Method to InventoryDAL

To illustrate the use of the ADO.NET transactions, begin by using the Server Explorer of Visual Studio 2008 to add a new table named CreditRisks to the AutoLot database, which has the same exact columns (CustID [which is the primary key], FirstName, and LastName) as the Customers table created earlier in this chapter. As suggested by the name, CreditRisks is where the undesirable customers are banished if they fail a credit check.

■**Note** We will be using this new transactional functionality in Chapter 26 when we examine the Windows Workflow Foundation API, so be sure to add the CreditRisks table to the AutoLot database as just described.

Much like the savings-to-checking money transfer example described previously, the act of moving a risky customer from the Customers table into the CreditRisks table should occur under the watchful eye of a transactional scope (after all, we will want to remember the ID and names of those who are not creditworthy). Specifically, we need to ensure that *either* we successfully delete the current credit risks from the Customers table and add them to the CreditRisks table *or* neither of these database operations occurs.

To illustrate how to programmatically work with ADO.NET transactions, open the AutoLotDAL Code Library project you created earlier in this chapter. Add a new public method named `ProcessCreditRisk()` to the `InventoryDAL` class that will deal with a perceived a credit risk as follows:

```
// A new member of the InventoryDAL class.
public void ProcessCreditRisk(bool throwEx, int custID)
{
  // First, look up current name based on customer ID.
  string fName = string.Empty;
  string lName = string.Empty;
  SqlCommand cmdSelect = new SqlCommand(
    string.Format("Select * from Customers where CustID = {0}", custID), sqlCn);
  using (SqlDataReader dr = cmdSelect.ExecuteReader())
  {
    while (dr.Read())
    {
      fName = (string)dr["FirstName"];
      lName = (string)dr["LastName"];
    }
  }

  // Create command objects that represent each step of the operation.
  SqlCommand cmdRemove = new SqlCommand(
    string.Format("Delete from Customers where CustID = {0}", custID), sqlCn);

  SqlCommand cmdInsert = new SqlCommand(string.Format("Insert Into CreditRisks" +
                   "(CustID, FirstName, LastName) Values" +
                   "({0}, '{1}', '{2}')", custID, fName, lName), sqlCn);

  // We will get this from the connection object.
  SqlTransaction tx = null;
  try
  {
    tx = sqlCn.BeginTransaction();

    // Enlist the commands into this transaction.
    cmdInsert.Transaction = tx;
    cmdRemove.Transaction = tx;

    // Execute the commands.
    cmdInsert.ExecuteNonQuery();
    cmdRemove.ExecuteNonQuery();

    // Simulate error.
    if (throwEx)
    {
      throw new ApplicationException("Sorry!  Database error! Tx failed...");
    }
```

```
    // Commit it!
    tx.Commit();
  }
  catch (Exception ex)
  {
    Console.WriteLine(ex.Message);
    // Any error will roll back transaction.
    tx.Rollback();
  }
}
```

Here, we are using an incoming bool parameter to represent whether we will throw an arbitrary exception when attempting to process the offending customer. This will allow us to easily simulate an unforeseen circumstance that will cause the database transaction to fail. Obviously, this is only done here for illustrative purposes; a true database transaction method would certainly not want to allow the caller to force the logic to fail on a whim!

Once we obtain the customer's first and last name based on the incoming custID parameter, note that we are using two SqlCommand objects that represent each step in the transaction we will be kicking off, and we obtain a valid SqlTransaction object from the connection object via BeginTransaction(). Next, and most importantly, we must *enlist each command object* by assigning the Transaction property to the transaction object we have just obtained. If you fail to do so, the Insert/Delete logic will not be under a transactional context.

After we call ExecuteNonQuery() on each command, we will throw an exception if (and only if) the value of the bool parameter is true. In this case, all pending database operations are rolled back. If we do not throw an exception, both steps will be committed to the database tables once we call Commit(). Compile your modified AutoLotDAL project to ensure you do not have any typos.

Testing Our Database Transaction

While you could update your previous AutoLotCUIClient application with a new option to invoke the ProcessCreditRisk() method, let's create a new Console Application named AdoNetTransaction to do so. Set a reference to your AutoLotDAL.dll assembly, and import the AutoLotConnectedLayer namespace.

Next, open your Customers table for data entry by right-clicking the table icon from the Server Explorer and selecting Show Table Data. Add a new customer who will be the victim of a low credit score, for example:

- *CustID*: 333
- *FirstName*: Homer
- *LastName*: Simpson

Now, update your Main() method as follows:

```
static void Main(string[] args)
{
  Console.WriteLine("***** Simple Transaction Example *****\n");

  // A simple way to allow the tx to succeed or not.
  bool throwEx = true;
  string userAnswer = string.Empty;

  Console.Write("Do you want to throw an exception (Y or N): ");
  userAnswer = Console.ReadLine();
  if (userAnswer.ToLower() == "n")
```

```
  {
    throwEx = false;
  }

  InventoryDAL dal = new InventoryDAL();
  dal.OpenConnection(@"Data Source=(local)\SQLEXPRESS;Integrated Security=SSPI;" +
    "Initial Catalog=AutoLot");

  // Process customer 333.
  dal.ProcessCreditRisk(throwEx, 333);
  Console.ReadLine();
}
```

If you were to run your program and elect to throw an exception, you would find that Homer is *not* removed from the Customers table, as the entire transaction has been rolled back. However, if you did not throw an exception, you would find that Customer ID 333 is no longer in the Customers table and has been placed in the CreditRisks table (see Figure 22-17).

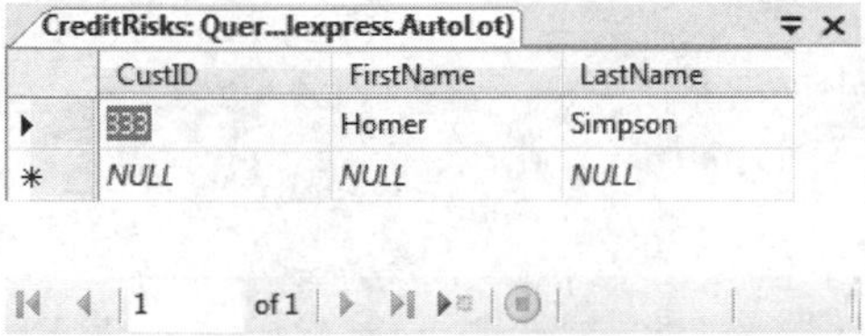

CreditRisks: Quer...lexpress.AutoLot)

	CustID	FirstName	LastName
▶	333	Homer	Simpson
*	*NULL*	*NULL*	*NULL*

1 of 1

Figure 22-17. *The result of our database transaction*

■ **Source Code** The AdoNetTransaction project is included under the Chapter 22 subdirectory.

Summary

ADO.NET is the native data access technology of the .NET platform, which can be used in two distinct manners: connected or disconnected. In this chapter, you examined the connected layer and came to understand the role of data providers, which are essentially concrete implementations of several abstract base classes (in the `System.Data.Common`) namespace and interface types (in the `System.Data` namespace). As you have seen, it is possible to build a provider-neutral code base using the ADO.NET data provider factory model.

Using connection objects, transaction objects, command objects, and data reader objects of the connected layer, you are able to select, update, insert, and delete records. Also recall that command objects support an internal parameter collection, which can be used to add some type safety to your SQL queries and are quite helpful when triggering stored procedures.

CHAPTER 23

ADO.NET Part II: The Disconnected Layer

This chapter picks up where the previous one left off and digs deeper into the .NET database APIs. Here, you will be introduced to the *disconnected layer* of ADO.NET. When you use this facet of ADO.NET, you are able to model database data in memory within the calling tier using numerous members of the `System.Data` namespace (most notably, `DataSet`, `DataTable`, `DataRow`, `DataColumn`, `DataView`, and `DataRelation`). By doing so, you are able to provide the illusion that the calling tier is continuously connected to an external data source, while in reality it is simply operating on a local copy of relational data.

While it is completely possible to use this "disconnected" aspect of ADO.NET without ever making a literal connection to a relational database, you will most often obtain populated `DataSet` objects using the data adapter object of your data provider. As you will see, data adapter objects function as a bridge between the client tier and a relational database. Using these objects, you are able to obtain `DataSet` objects, manipulate their contents, and send modified rows back for processing. The end result is a highly scalable data-centric .NET application.

To showcase the usefulness of the disconnected layer, you will be updating the `AutoLotDAL.dll` data library created in Chapter 22 with new namespaces that make use of disconnected types. As well, you will come to understand the role of data binding and various UI elements within the Windows Forms API that allow you to display and update client-side local data. We wrap things up by examining the role of strongly typed `DataSet` objects and see how they can be used to expose data using a more object-oriented model.

Understanding the Disconnected Layer of ADO.NET

As you saw in the previous chapter, working with the connected layer allows you to interact with a database using the primary connection, command, and data reader objects. With this handful of types, you are able to select, insert, update, and delete records to your heart's content (as well as invoke stored procedures). However, you have seen only half of the ADO.NET story. Recall that the ADO.NET object model can be used in a disconnected manner.

Using the disconnected types, it is possible to model relational data via an in-memory object model. Far beyond simply modeling a tabular block of rows and columns, the types within `System.Data` allow you to represent table relationships, column constraints, primary keys, views, and other database primitives. Furthermore, once you have modeled the data, you are able to apply filters, submit in-memory queries, and persist (or load) your data in XML and binary formats. You can do all of this without ever making a literal connection to a DBMS (hence the term *disconnected layer*).

While you could indeed use the disconnected types without ever connecting to a database, you will most often still make use of connection and command objects. In addition, you will leverage a specific object, the *data adapter* (which extends the abstract `DbDataAdapter`), to fetch and update data. Unlike the connected layer, data obtained via a data adapter is not processed using data reader objects. Rather, data adapter objects make use of DataSet objects to move data between the caller and data source. The DataSet type is a container for any number of DataTable objects, each of which contains a collection of DataRow and DataColumn objects.

The data adapter object of your data provider handles the database connection automatically. In an attempt to increase scalability, data adapters keep the connection open for the shortest amount of time possible. Once the caller receives the DataSet object, the calling tier is completely disconnected from the database and left with a local copy of the remote data. The caller is free to insert, delete, or update rows from a given DataTable, but the physical database is not updated until the caller explicitly passes the DataSet to the data adapter for updating. In a nutshell, DataSets allow the clients to pretend they are indeed always connected, when in fact they are operating on an in-memory database (see Figure 23-1).

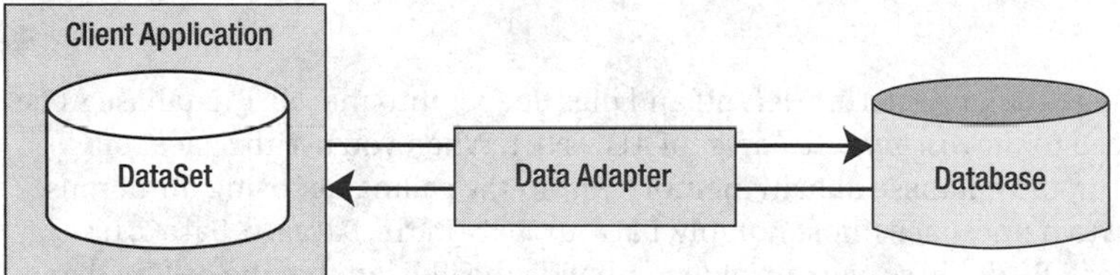

Figure 23-1. *Data adapter objects move* DataSet*s to and from the client tier.*

Given that the centerpiece of the disconnected layer is the DataSet type, the first task of this chapter is to learn how to manipulate a DataSet manually. Once you understand how to do so, you will have no problem manipulating the contents of a DataSet retrieved from a data adapter object.

Understanding the Role of the DataSet

As said, a DataSet is an in-memory representation of relational data. More specifically, a DataSet is a class type that maintains three internal strongly typed collections (see Figure 23-2).

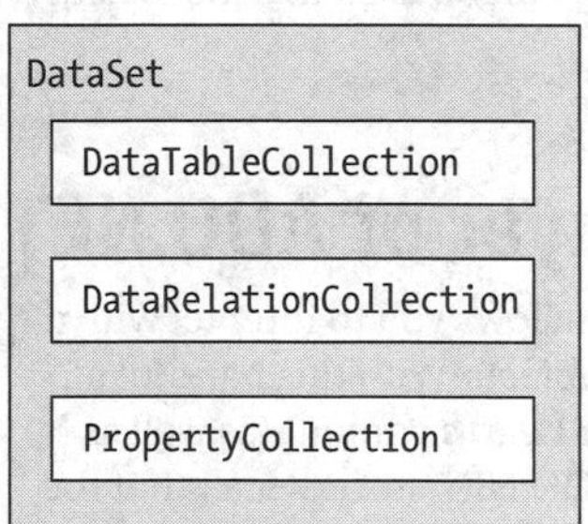

Figure 23-2. *The anatomy of a* DataSet

The Tables property of the DataSet allows you to access the DataTableCollection that contains the individual DataTables. Another important collection used by the DataSet is the DataRelationCollection. Given that a DataSet is a disconnected version of a database schema, it can be used to programmatically represent the parent/child relationships between its tables. For example, a relation can be created between two tables to model a foreign key constraint using the DataRelation type. This object can then be added to the DataRelationCollection through the

Relations property. At this point, you can navigate between the connected tables as you search for data. You will see how this is done a bit later in the chapter.

The ExtendedProperties property provides access to the PropertyCollection object, which allows you to associate any extra information to the DataSet as name/value pairs. This information can literally be anything at all, even if it has no bearing on the data itself. For example, you can associate your company's name to a DataSet, which can then function as in-memory metadata. Other examples of extended properties might include time stamps, an encrypted password that must be supplied to access the contents of the DataSet, a number representing a data refresh rate, and so forth.

Note The DataTable class also supports extended properties via the ExtendedProperties property.

Key Properties of the DataSet

Before exploring too many other programmatic details, let's take a look at some core members of the DataSet. Beyond the Tables, Relations, and ExtendedProperties properties, Table 23-1 describes some additional properties of interest.

Table 23-1. *Properties of the Mighty* DataSet

Property	Meaning in Life
CaseSensitive	Indicates whether string comparisons in DataTable objects are case sensitive (or not).
DataSetName	Represents the friendly name of this DataSet. Typically this value is established as a constructor parameter.
EnforceConstraints	Gets or sets a value indicating whether constraint rules are followed when attempting any update operation.
HasErrors	Gets a value indicating whether there are errors in any of the rows in any of the DataTables of the DataSet.
RemotingFormat	Allows you to define how the DataSet should serialize its content (binary or XML).

Key Methods of the DataSet

The methods of the DataSet work in conjunction with some of the functionality provided by the aforementioned properties. In addition to interacting with XML streams, the DataSet provides methods that allow you to copy the contents of your DataSet, navigate between the internal tables, and establish the beginning and ending points of a batch of updates. Table 23-2 describes some core methods.

Table 23-2. *Methods of the Mighty* DataSet

Methods	Meaning in Life
AcceptChanges()	Commits all the changes made to this DataSet since it was loaded or the last time AcceptChanges() was called.
Clear()	Completely clears the DataSet data by removing every row in each DataTable.

Continued

Table 23-2. *Continued*

Methods	Meaning in Life
Clone()	Clones the structure of the DataSet, including all DataTables, as well as all relations and any constraints.
Copy()	Copies both the structure and data for this DataSet.
GetChanges()	Returns a copy of the DataSet containing all changes made to it since it was last loaded or since AcceptChanges() was called.
GetChildRelations()	Returns the collection of child relations that belong to a specified table.
GetParentRelations()	Gets the collection of parent relations that belong to a specified table.
HasChanges()	Gets a value indicating whether the DataSet has changes, including new, deleted, or modified rows.
Merge()	Merges this DataSet with a specified DataSet.
ReadXml() ReadXmlSchema()	Allow you to read XML data from a valid stream (file based, memory based, or network based) into the DataSet.
RejectChanges()	Rolls back all the changes made to this DataSet since it was created or the last time AcceptChanges() was called.
WriteXml() WriteXmlSchema()	Allow you to write out the contents of a DataSet into a valid stream.

Building a DataSet

Now that you have a better understanding of the role of the DataSet (and some idea of what you can do with one), create a new Console Application named SimpleDataSet. Within the Main() method, define a new DataSet object that contains three extended properties representing your company name, a unique identifier (represented as a System.Guid type), and a time stamp (don't forget to import the System.Data namespace):

```
static void Main(string[] args)
{
  Console.WriteLine("***** Fun with DataSets *****\n");

  // Create the DataSet object and add a few properties.
  DataSet carsInventoryDS = new DataSet("Car Inventory");

  carsInventoryDS.ExtendedProperties["TimeStamp"] = DateTime.Now;
  carsInventoryDS.ExtendedProperties["DataSetID"] = Guid.NewGuid();
  carsInventoryDS.ExtendedProperties["Company"] = "Intertech Training";
  Console.ReadLine();
}
```

If you are unfamiliar with the concept of a globally unique identifier (GUID), simply understand that it is a statically unique 128-bit number. While GUIDs are used throughout the COM framework to identify numerous COM-atoms (classes, interfaces, applications, etc.), the System.Guid type is still very helpful under .NET when you need to quickly generate a unique identifier.

In any case, a DataSet object is not terribly interesting until you insert any number of DataTables. Therefore, the next task is to examine the internal composition of the DataTable, beginning with the DataColumn type.

Working with DataColumns

The DataColumn type represents a single column within a DataTable. Collectively speaking, the set of all DataColumn types bound to a given DataTable represents the foundation of a table's *schema* information. For example, if you were to model the Inventory table of the AutoLot database (see Chapter 22), you would create four DataColumns, one for each column (CarID, Make, Color, and PetName). Once you have created your DataColumn objects, they are typically added into the columns collection of the DataTable type (via the Columns property).

Based on your background, you may know that a given column in a database table can be assigned a set of constraints (e.g., configured as a primary key, assigned a default value, configured to contain read-only information, etc.). Also, every column in a table must map to an underlying data type. For example, the Inventory table's schema requires that the CarID column map to an integer, while Make, Color, and PetName map to an array of characters. The DataColumn class has numerous properties that allow you to configure these very things. Table 23-3 provides a rundown of some core properties.

Table 23-3. *Properties of the* DataColumn

Properties	Meaning in Life
AllowDBNull	This property is used to indicate if a row can specify null values in this column. The default value is true.
AutoIncrement AutoIncrementSeed AutoIncrementStep	These properties are used to configure the autoincrement behavior for a given column. This can be helpful when you wish to ensure unique values in a given DataColumn (such as a primary key). By default, a DataColumn does not support autoincrement behavior.
Caption	This property gets or sets the caption to be displayed for this column. This allows you to define a user-friendly version of a literal database column name.
ColumnMapping	This property determines how a DataColumn is represented when a DataSet is saved as an XML document using the DataSet.WriteXml() method.
ColumnName	This property gets or sets the name of the column in the Columns collection (meaning how it is represented internally by the DataTable). If you do not set the ColumnName explicitly, the default values are Column with (*n*+1) numerical suffixes (i.e., Column1, Column2, Column3, etc.).
DataType	This property defines the data type (Boolean, string, float, etc.) stored in the column.
DefaultValue	This property gets or sets the default value assigned to this column when inserting new rows. This is used if not otherwise specified.
Expression	This property gets or sets the expression used to filter rows, calculate a column's value, or create an aggregate column.
Ordinal	This property gets the numerical position of the column in the Columns collection maintained by the DataTable.
ReadOnly	This property determines if this column can be modified once a row has been added to the table. The default is false.
Table	This property gets the DataTable that contains this DataColumn.
Unique	This property gets or sets a value indicating whether the values in each row of the column must be unique or if repeating values are permissible. If a column is assigned a primary key constraint, the Unique property should be set to true.

Building a DataColumn

To continue with the SimpleDataSet project (and illustrate the use of the DataColumn), assume you wish to model the columns of the Inventory table. Given that the CarID column will be the table's primary key, you will configure the DataColumn object as read-only, unique, and non-null (using the ReadOnly, Unique, and AllowDBNull properties). Update the Main() method to build four DataColumn objects:

```
static void Main(string[] args)
{
...
  // Create data columns that map to the
  // 'real' columns in the Inventory table
  // of the AutoLot database.
  DataColumn carIDColumn = new DataColumn("CarID", typeof(int));
  carIDColumn.Caption = "Car ID";
  carIDColumn.ReadOnly = true;
  carIDColumn.AllowDBNull = false;
  carIDColumn.Unique = true;

  DataColumn carMakeColumn = new DataColumn("Make", typeof(string));
  DataColumn carColorColumn = new DataColumn("Color", typeof(string));
  DataColumn carPetNameColumn = new DataColumn("PetName", typeof(string));
  carPetNameColumn.Caption = "Pet Name";
  Console.ReadLine();
}
```

Notice that when configuring the carIDColumn object, you have assigned a value to the Caption property. This property is very helpful in that it allows you to define a string value for display purposes, which can be distinct from the literal column name (column names in a literal database table are typically better suited for programming purposes [e.g., au_fname] than display purposes [e.g., Author First Name]).

Enabling Autoincrementing Fields

One aspect of the DataColumn you may choose to configure is its ability to *autoincrement*. Simply put, an autoincrementing column is used to ensure that when a new row is added to a given table, the value of this column is assigned automatically, based on the current step of the increase. This can be helpful when you wish to ensure that a column has no repeating values (such as a primary key).

This behavior is controlled using the AutoIncrement, AutoIncrementSeed, and AutoIncrementStep properties. The seed value is used to mark the starting value of the column, whereas the step value identifies the number to add to the seed when incrementing. Consider the following update to the construction of the carIDColumn DataColumn:

```
static void Main(string[] args)
{
...
  DataColumn carIDColumn = new DataColumn("CarID", typeof(int));
  carIDColumn.ReadOnly = true;
  carIDColumn.Caption = "Car ID";
  carIDColumn.AllowDBNull = false;
  carIDColumn.Unique = true;
  carIDColumn.AutoIncrement = true;
```

```
  carIDColumn.AutoIncrementSeed = 0;
  carIDColumn.AutoIncrementStep = 1;
...
}
```

Here, the carIDColumn object has been configured to ensure that as rows are added to the respective table, the value for this column is incremented by 1. Because the seed has been set at 0, this column would be numbered 0, 1, 2, 3, and so forth.

Adding DataColumn Objects to a DataTable

The DataColumn type does not typically exist as a stand-alone entity, but is instead inserted into a related DataTable. To illustrate, create a new DataTable type (fully detailed in just a moment) and insert each DataColumn object in the columns collection using the Columns property:

```
static void Main(string[] args)
{
...
  // Now add DataColumns to a DataTable.
  DataTable inventoryTable = new DataTable("Inventory");
  inventoryTable.Columns.AddRange(new DataColumn[]
    { carIDColumn, carMakeColumn, carColorColumn, carPetNameColumn });
  Console.ReadLine();
}
```

At this point, the DataTable object contains four DataColumn objects that represent the schema of the in-memory Inventory table. However, the table is currently devoid of data, and the table is currently outside of the table collection maintained by the DataSet. We will deal with both of these shortcomings, beginning with populating the table with data via DataRow objects.

Working with DataRows

As you have seen, a collection of DataColumn objects represents the schema of a DataTable. In contrast, a collection of DataRow types represents the actual data in the table. Thus, if you have 20 listings in the Inventory table of the AutoLot database, you can represent these records using 20 DataRow types. Using the members of the DataRow class, you are able to insert, remove, evaluate, and manipulate the values in the table. Table 23-4 documents some (but not all) of the members of the DataRow type.

Table 23-4. *Key Members of the* DataRow *Type*

Members	Meaning in Life
HasErrors GetColumnsInError() GetColumnError() ClearErrors() RowError	The HasErrors property returns a Boolean value indicating if there are errors. If so, the GetColumnsInError() method can be used to obtain the offending members, and GetColumnError() can be used to obtain the error description, while the ClearErrors() method removes each error listing for the row. The RowError property allows you to configure a textual description of the error for a given row.
ItemArray	This property gets or sets all of the values for this row using an array of objects.
RowState	This property is used to pinpoint the current "state" of the DataRow using values of the RowState enumeration.

Continued

Table 23-4. *Continued*

Members	Meaning in Life
`Table`	This property is used to obtain a reference to the `DataTable` containing this `DataRow`.
`AcceptChanges()` `RejectChanges()`	These methods commit or reject all changes made to this row since the last time `AcceptChanges()` was called.

`BeginEdit()`
`EndEdit()`
`CancelEdit()`
	These methods begin, end, or cancel an edit operation on a `DataRow` object.

`Delete()`	This method marks this row to be removed when the `AcceptChanges()` method is called.
`IsNull()`	This method gets a value indicating whether the specified column contains a null value.

Working with a `DataRow` is a bit different from working with a `DataColumn`, because you cannot create a direct instance of this type, as there is no public constructor:

```
// Error!  No public constructor!
DataRow r = new DataRow();
```

Rather, you obtain a `DataRow` reference from a given `DataTable`. For example, assume you wish to insert two rows in the Inventory table. The `DataTable.NewRow()` method allows you to obtain the next slot in the table, at which point you can fill each column with new data via the type indexer. When doing so, you can specify either the string name assigned to the `DataColumn` or its ordinal position:

```
static void Main(string[] args)
{
...
  // Now add some rows to the Inventory Table.
  DataRow carRow = inventoryTable.NewRow();
  carRow["Make"] = "BMW";
  carRow["Color"] = "Black";
  carRow["PetName"] = "Hamlet";
  inventoryTable.Rows.Add(carRow);

  carRow = inventoryTable.NewRow();
  // Column 0 is the autoincremented ID field,
  // so start at 1.
  carRow[1] = "Saab";
  carRow[2] = "Red";
  carRow[3] = "Sea Breeze";
  inventoryTable.Rows.Add(carRow);
  Console.ReadLine();
}
```

■ **Note** If you pass the `DataRow`'s indexer method an invalid column name or ordinal position, you will receive a runtime exception.

At this point, you have a single DataTable containing two rows. Of course, you can repeat this general process to create a number of DataTables to define the schema and data content. Before you insert the inventoryTable object into your DataSet object, let's check out the all-important RowState property.

Understanding the RowState Property

The RowState property is useful when you need to programmatically identify the set of all rows in a table that have changed from their original value, have been newly inserted, and so forth. This property may be assigned any value from the DataRowState enumeration, as shown in Table 23-5.

Table 23-5. *Values of the* DataRowState *Enumeration*

Value	Meaning in Life
Added	The row has been added to a DataRowCollection, and AcceptChanges() has not been called.
Deleted	The row has been marked for deletion via the Delete() method of the DataRow.
Detached	The row has been created but is not part of any DataRowCollection. A DataRow is in this state immediately after it has been created and before it is added to a collection, or if it has been removed from a collection.
Modified	The row has been modified, and AcceptChanges() has not been called.
Unchanged	The row has not changed since AcceptChanges() was last called.

While you are programmatically manipulating the rows of a given DataTable, the RowState property is set automatically. By way of example, add a new method to your Program class, which operates on a local DataRow object, printing out its row state along the way:

```
private static void ManipulateDataRowState()
{
  // Create a temp DataTable for testing.
  DataTable temp = new DataTable("Temp");
  temp.Columns.Add(new DataColumn("TempColumn", typeof(int)));

  // RowState = Detached.
  DataRow row = temp.NewRow();
  Console.WriteLine("After calling NewRow(): {0}", row.RowState);

  // RowState = Added.
  temp.Rows.Add(row);
  Console.WriteLine("After calling Rows.Add(): {0}", row.RowState);

  // RowState = Added.
  row["TempColumn"] = 10;
  Console.WriteLine("After first assignment: {0}", row.RowState);

  // RowState = Unchanged.
  temp.AcceptChanges();
  Console.WriteLine("After calling AcceptChanges: {0}", row.RowState);

  // RowState = Modified.
  row["TempColumn"] = 11;
  Console.WriteLine("After first assignment: {0}", row.RowState);
```

```
  // RowState = Deleted.
  temp.Rows[0].Delete();
  Console.WriteLine("After calling Delete: {0}", row.RowState);
}
```

As you can see, the ADO.NET DataRow is smart enough to remember its current state of affairs. Given this, the owning DataTable is able to identify which rows have been modified. This is a key feature of the DataSet, as when it comes time to send updated information to the data store, only the modified data is submitted.

Understanding the DataRowVersion Property

Beyond maintaining the current state of a row via the RowState property, a DataRow object maintains three possible versions of the data it contains via the DataRowVersion property. When a DataRow object is first constructed, it contains only a single copy of data, represented as the "current version." However, as you programmatically manipulate a DataRow object (via various method calls), additional versions of the data spring to life. Specifically, the DataRowVersion can be set to any value of the related DataRowVersion enumeration (see Table 23-6).

Table 23-6. *Values of the* DataRowVersion *Enumeration*

Value	Meaning in Life
Current	Represents the current value of a row, even after changes have been made.
Default	The default version of DataRowState. For a DataRowState value of Added, Modified, or Deleted, the default version is Current. For a DataRowState value of Detached, the version is Proposed.
Original	Represents the value first inserted into a DataRow, or the value the last time AcceptChanges() was called.
Proposed	The value of a row currently being edited due to a call to BeginEdit().

As suggested in Table 23-6, the value of the DataRowVersion property is dependent on the value of the DataRowState property in a good number of cases. As mentioned, the DataRowVersion property will be changed behind the scenes when you invoke various methods on the DataRow (or, in some cases, the DataTable) object. Here is a breakdown of the methods that can affect the value of a row's DataRowVersion property:

- If you call the DataRow.BeginEdit() method and change the row's value, the Current and Proposed values become available.
- If you call the DataRow.CancelEdit() method, the Proposed value is deleted.
- After you call DataRow.EndEdit(), the Proposed value becomes the Current value.
- After you call the DataRow.AcceptChanges() method, the Original value becomes identical to the Current value. The same transformation occurs when you call DataTable.AcceptChanges().
- After you call DataRow.RejectChanges(), the Proposed value is discarded, and the version becomes Current.

Yes, this is a bit convoluted—especially due to the fact that a DataRow may or may not have all versions at any given time (you'll receive runtime exceptions if you attempt to obtain a row version that is not currently tracked). Regardless of the complexity, given that the DataRow maintains three copies of data, it becomes very simple to build a front end that allows an end user to alter values, change his or her mind and "roll back" values, or commit values permanently. You'll see various examples of manipulating these methods over the remainder of this chapter.

Working with DataTables

The DataTable type defines a good number of members, many of which are identical in name and functionality to those of the DataSet. Table 23-7 describes some core members of the DataTable type beyond Rows and Columns.

Table 23-7. *Key Members of the* DataTable *Type*

Member	Meaning in Life
CaseSensitive	Indicates whether string comparisons within the table are case sensitive (or not). The default value is false.
ChildRelations	Returns the collection of child relations for this DataTable (if any).
Constraints	Gets the collection of constraints maintained by the table.
Copy()	A method that copies the schema and data of a given DataTable into a new instance.
DataSet	Gets the DataSet that contains this table (if any).
DefaultView	Gets a customized view of the table that may include a filtered view or a cursor position.
MinimumCapacity	Gets or sets the initial number of rows in this table (the default is 25).
ParentRelations	Gets the collection of parent relations for this DataTable.
PrimaryKey	Gets or sets an array of columns that function as primary keys for the data table.
RemotingFormat	Allows you to define how the DataSet should serialize its content (binary or XML) for the .NET remoting layer.
TableName	Gets or sets the name of the table. This same property may also be specified as a constructor parameter.

To continue with our current example, let's set the PrimaryKey property of the DataTable to the carIDColumn DataColumn object. Be aware that the PrimaryKey property is assigned a collection of DataColumn objects, to account for a multicolumned key. In our case, however, we need to specify only the CarID column (being the first ordinal position in the table):

```
static void Main(string[] args)
{
...
  // Mark the primary key of this table.
  inventoryTable.PrimaryKey = new DataColumn[] { inventoryTable.Columns[0] };
...
}
```

Inserting DataTables into DataSets

At this point, our DataTable object is complete. The final step is to insert the DataTable into the carsInventoryDS DataSet object using the Tables collection. Assume that you have updated Main() to do so, and pass the DataSet object into a new (yet to be written) helper method named PrintDataSet():

```
static void Main(string[] args)
{
...
  // Finally, add our table to the DataSet.
  carsInventoryDS.Tables.Add(inventoryTable);

  // Now print the DataSet.
  PrintDataSet(carsInventoryDS);
  Console.ReadLine();
}
```

The PrintDataSet() method simply iterates over the DataSet metadata (via the ExtendedProperties collection) and each DataTable in the DataSet, printing out the column names and row values using the type indexers:

```
static void PrintDataSet(DataSet ds)
{
  // Print out any name and extended properties.
  Console.WriteLine("DataSet is named: {0}", ds.DataSetName);
  foreach (System.Collections.DictionaryEntry de in ds.ExtendedProperties)
  {
    Console.WriteLine("Key = {0}, Value = {1}", de.Key, de.Value);
  }
  Console.WriteLine();

  foreach (DataTable dt in ds.Tables)
  {
    Console.WriteLine("=> {0} Table:", dt.TableName);

    // Print out the column names.
    for (int curCol = 0; curCol < dt.Columns.Count; curCol++)
    {
      Console.Write(dt.Columns[curCol].ColumnName + "\t");
    }
    Console.WriteLine("\n----------------------------------");

    // Print the DataTable.
    for (int curRow = 0; curRow < dt.Rows.Count; curRow++)
    {
      for (int curCol = 0; curCol < dt.Columns.Count; curCol++)
      {
        Console.Write(dt.Rows[curRow][curCol].ToString() + "\t");
      }
      Console.WriteLine();
    }
  }
}
```

Figure 23-3 shows the program's output.

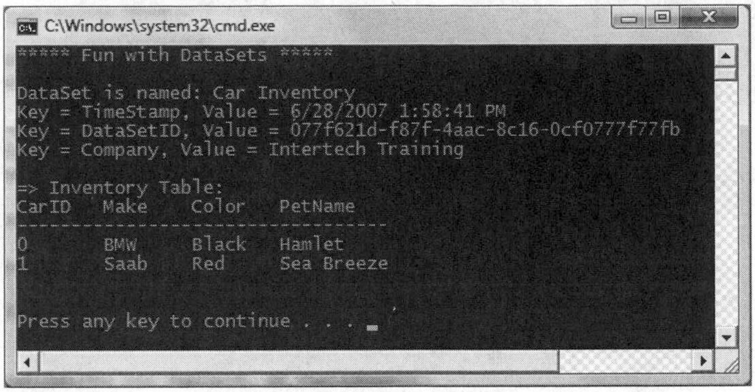

Figure 23-3. *Contents of the example's* DataSet *object*

Processing DataTable Data Using DataTableReader Objects

Given your work in the previous chapter, you are sure to notice that the manner in which you process data using the connected layer (e.g., data reader objects) and the disconnected layer (e.g., DataSet objects) is quite different. Working with a data reader typically involves establishing a while loop, calling the Read() method, and using an indexer to pluck out the name/value pairs. On the other hand, DataSet processing typically involves a series of iteration constructs to drill into the data within the tables, rows, and columns.

Since the release of .NET 2.0, DataTables were provided with a method named CreateDataReader(). This method allows you to obtain the data within a DataTable using a data reader–like navigation scheme (forward-only, read-only). The major benefit of this approach is that you now use a single model to process data, regardless of which "layer" of ADO.NET you use to obtain it. Assume you have authored the following helper function named PrintTable(), implemented as so:

```
static void PrintTable(DataTable dt)
{
  // Get the DataTableReader type.
  DataTableReader dtReader = dt.CreateDataReader();

  // The DataTableReader works just like the DataReader.
  while (dtReader.Read())
  {
    for (int i = 0; i < dtReader.FieldCount; i++)
    {
      Console.Write("{0}\t", dtReader.GetValue(i).ToString().Trim());
    }
    Console.WriteLine();
  }
  dtReader.Close();
}
```

Notice that the DataTableReader works identically to the data reader object of your data provider. Using a DataTableReader can be an ideal choice when you wish to quickly pump out the data within a DataTable without needing to traverse the internal row and column collections. Now, assume you have updated the previous PrintDataSet() method to invoke PrintTable(), rather than drilling into the Rows and Columns collections:

```
static void PrintDataSet(DataSet ds)
{
  // Print out any name and extended properties.
  Console.WriteLine("DataSet is named: {0}", ds.DataSetName);
  foreach (System.Collections.DictionaryEntry de in ds.ExtendedProperties)
  {
    Console.WriteLine("Key = {0}, Value = {1}", de.Key, de.Value);
  }
  Console.WriteLine();

  foreach (DataTable dt in ds.Tables)
  {
    Console.WriteLine("=> {0} Table:", dt.TableName);

    // Print out the column names.
    for (int curCol = 0; curCol < dt.Columns.Count; curCol++)
    {
      Console.Write(dt.Columns[curCol].ColumnName.Trim() + "\t");
    }
    Console.WriteLine("\n----------------------------------");

    // Call our new helper method.
    PrintTable(dt);
  }
}
```

When you run the application, the output is identical to that of Figure 23-3. The only difference is how you are internally accessing the DataTable's contents.

Serializing DataTable/DataSet Objects As XML

DataSets and DataTables both support the WriteXml() and ReadXml() methods. WriteXml() allows you to persist the object's content to a local file (as well as into any System.IO.Stream-derived type) as an XML document. ReadXml() allows you to hydrate the state of a DataSet (or DataTable) from a given XML document. In addition, DataSets and DataTables both support WriteXmlSchema() and ReadXmlSchema() to save or load an *.xsd file.

To test this out for yourself, update your Main() method to call the following final helper function (notice you will pass in a DataSet as the sole parameter):

```
static void DataSetAsXml(DataSet carsInventoryDS)
{
  // Save this DataSet as XML.
  carsInventoryDS.WriteXml("carsDataSet.xml");
  carsInventoryDS.WriteXmlSchema("carsDataSet.xsd");

  // Clear out DataSet.
  carsInventoryDS.Clear();

  // Load DataSet from XML file.
  carsInventoryDS.ReadXml("carsDataSet.xml");
}
```

If you open the carsDataSet.xml file (which will be located under the \bin\Debug folder of your project), you will find that each column in the table has been encoded as an XML element:

```
<?xml version="1.0" standalone="yes"?>
<Car_x0020_Inventory>
  <Inventory>
    <CarID>0</CarID>
    <Make>BMW</Make>
    <Color>Black</Color>
    <PetName>Hamlet</PetName>
  </Inventory>
  <Inventory>
    <CarID>1</CarID>
    <Make>Saab</Make>
    <Color>Red</Color>
    <PetName>Sea Breeze</PetName>
  </Inventory>
</Car_x0020_Inventory>
```

Serializing DataTable/DataSet Objects in a Binary Format

It is also possible to persist the contents of a `DataSet` (or an individual `DataTable`) as a compact binary format. This can be especially helpful when a `DataSet` object needs to be passed across a machine boundary (in the case of a distributed application); one drawback of XML data representation is that its very descriptive nature can result in a good deal of overhead.

In order to persist `DataTables` or `DataSets` in a binary format, simply set the `RemotingFormat` property to `SerializationFormat.Binary`. After this point, you can make use of the `BinaryFormatter` type (see Chapter 21) as expected. Consider the following final method of the SimpleDataSet project (don't forget to import the `System.IO` and `System.Runtime.Serialization.Formatters.Binary` namespaces):

```
static void DataSetAsBinary(DataSet carsInventoryDS)
{
  // Set binary serialization flag.
  carsInventoryDS.RemotingFormat = SerializationFormat.Binary;

  // Save this DataSet as binary.
  FileStream fs = new FileStream("BinaryCars.bin", FileMode.Create);
  BinaryFormatter bFormat = new BinaryFormatter();
  bFormat.Serialize(fs, carsInventoryDS);
  fs.Close();

  // Clear out DataSet.
  carsInventoryDS.Clear();

  // Load DataSet from binary file.
  fs = new FileStream("BinaryCars.bin", FileMode.Open);
  DataSet data = (DataSet)bFormat.Deserialize(fs);
}
```

Figure 23-4 shows the contents of the `BinaryCars.bin` file.

Source Code The SimpleDataSet application is included under the Chapter 23 subdirectory.

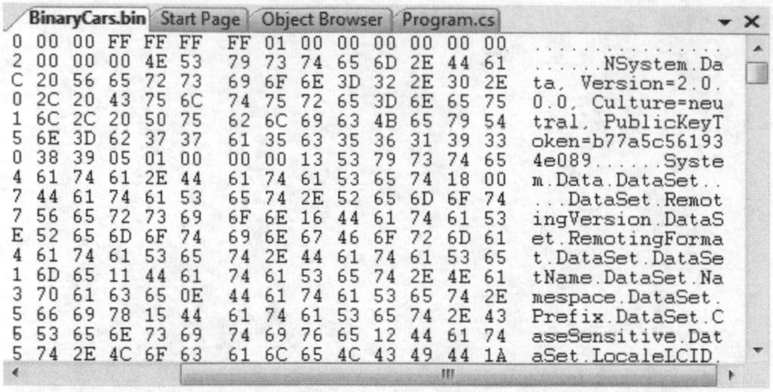

BinaryCars.bin | Start Page | Object Browser | Program.cs

```
0 00 00 FF FF FF  FF 01 00 00 00 00 00 00   ................
2 00 00 00 4E 53  79 73 74 65 6D 2E 44 61   ......NSystem.Da
C 20 56 65 72 73  69 6F 6E 3D 32 2E 30 2E   ta, Version=2.0.
0 2C 20 43 75 6C  74 75 72 65 3D 6E 65 75   0.0, Culture=neu
1 6C 2C 20 50 75  62 6C 69 63 4B 65 79 54   tral, PublicKeyT
5 6E 3D 62 37 37  61 35 63 35 36 31 39 33   oken=b77a5c56193
0 38 39 05 01 00  00 00 13 53 79 73 74 65   4e089......Syste
4 61 74 61 2E 44  61 74 61 53 65 74 18 00   m.Data.DataSet..
7 44 61 74 61 53  65 74 2E 52 65 6D 6F 74   ...DataSet.Remot
7 56 65 72 73 69  6F 6E 16 44 61 74 61 53   ingVersion.DataS
E 52 65 6D 6F 74  69 6E 67 46 6F 72 6D 61   et.RemotingForma
4 61 74 61 53 65  74 2E 44 61 74 61 53 65   t.DataSet.DataSe
1 6D 65 11 44 61  74 61 53 65 74 2E 4E 61   tName.DataSet.Na
3 70 61 63 65 0E  44 61 74 61 53 65 74 2E   mespace.DataSet.
5 66 69 78 15 44  61 74 61 53 65 74 2E 43   Prefix.DataSet.C
5 53 65 6E 73 69  74 69 76 65 12 44 61 74   aseSensitive.Dat
5 74 2E 4C 6F 63  61 6C 65 4C 43 49 44 1A   aSet.LocaleLCID.
```


Figure 23-4. *Serializing a* `DataSet` *in a binary format*

Binding DataTable Objects to User Interfaces

At this point in the chapter, you have examined how to manually create, hydrate, and iterate over the contents of a `DataSet` object using the inherit object model of ADO.NET. While understanding how to do so is quite important, the .NET platform ships with numerous APIs that have the ability to "bind" data to user interface elements automatically.

For example, the original GUI toolkit of .NET, Windows Forms, supplies a control named `DataGridView` that has the built-in ability to display the contents of a `DataSet` or `DataTable` object using just a few lines of code. ASP.NET (.NET's web development API) and the Windows Presentation Foundation API (the new, supercharged GUI API introduced with .NET 3.0) also support the notion of data binding in one form or another.

To continue our investigation of the disconnected layer of ADO.NET, our next task is to build a Windows Forms application that will display the contents of a `DataTable` object within its user interface. Along the way, we will also examine how to filter and change table data, and we'll come to know the role of the `DataView` object. To begin, create a brand-new Windows Forms project workspace named WindowsFormsDataTableViewer, as shown in Figure 23-5.

■ **Note** The current example assumes you have some experience using Windows Forms to build graphical user interfaces. If this is not the case, you may wish to simply open the solution and follow along, or return to this section once you have read Chapter 27, where you will formally investigate the Windows Forms API.

Rename your initial `Form1.cs` file to the more fitting `MainForm.cs`. Next, using the Visual Studio 2008 Toolbox drag a `DataGridView` control (renamed to `carInventoryGridView` via the `Name` property of the Properties window) onto the designer surface. Notice that when you do, you activate a context menu that allows you to connect to a physical data source. For the time being, completely ignore this aspect of the designer, as you will be binding your `DataTable` object programmatically. Finally, add a descriptive `Label` to your designer for information purposes. Figure 23-6 shows one possible look and feel.

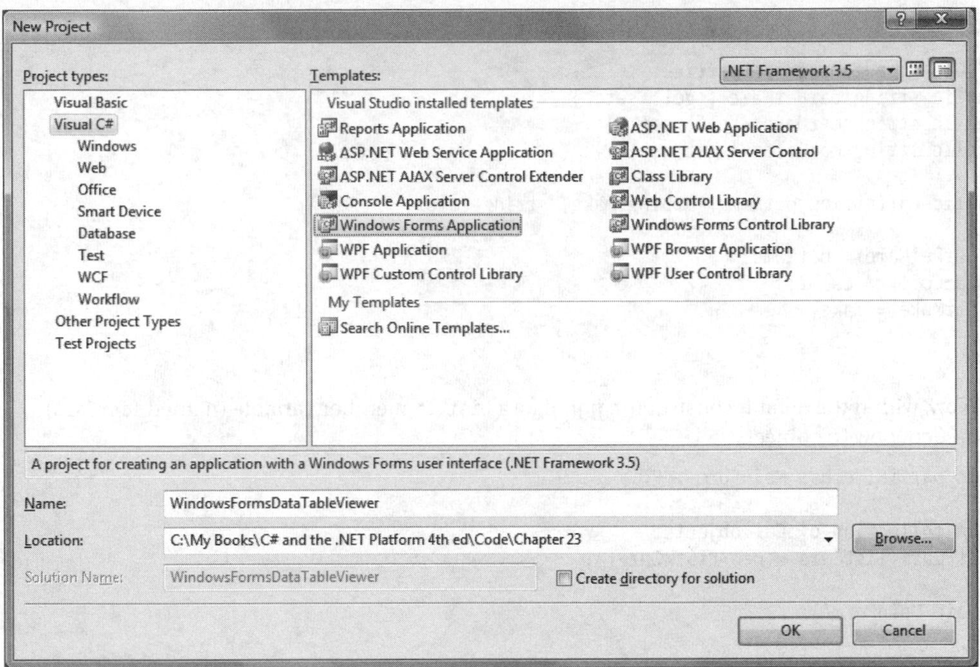

Figure 23-5. *Creating a Windows Forms application*

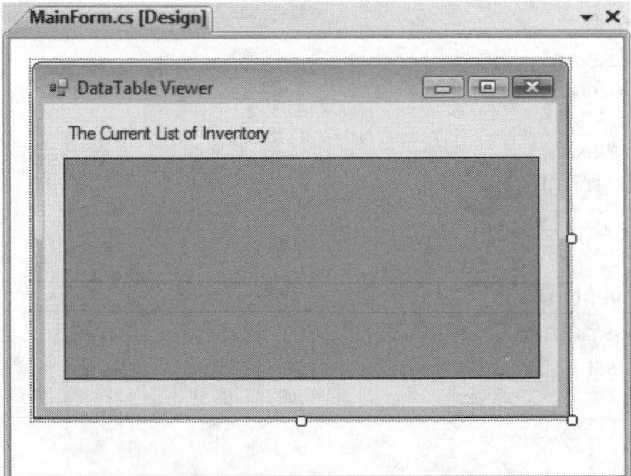

Figure 23-6. *The initial UI*

Hydrating a DataTable from a Generic List<T>

Similar to the previous SimpleDataSet example, the WindowsFormsDataTableViewer application will construct a `DataTable` that contains a set of `DataColumns` representing various columns and rows of data. This time, however, you will fill the rows using your generic `List<T>` member variable. First, insert a new C# class into your project (named `Car`), defined as follows:

```
class Car
{
  // Use C# automatic properties.
  public string carPetName { get; set; }
  public string carMake { get; set; }
  public string carColor { get; set; }

  public Car(string petName, string make, string color)
  {
    carPetName = petName;
    carColor = color;
    carMake = make;
  }
}
```

Now, within the default constructor, populate a `List<T>` member variable (named `listCars`) with a set of new `Car` objects:

```
public partial class MainForm : Form
{
  // A collection of Car objects.
  List<Car> listCars = new List<Car>();

  public MainForm()
  {
    InitializeComponent();

    // Fill the list with some cars.
    listCars.Add(new Car("Chucky", "BMW", "Green"));
    listCars.Add(new Car("Tiny", "Yugo", "White"));
    listCars.Add(new Car("Ami", "Jeep", "Tan"));
    listCars.Add(new Car("Pain Inducer", "Caravan", "Pink"));
    listCars.Add(new Car("Fred", "BMW", "Pea Soup Green"));
    listCars.Add(new Car("Sidd", "BMW", "Black"));
    listCars.Add(new Car("Mel", "Firebird", "Red"));
    listCars.Add(new Car("Sarah", "Colt", "Black"));
  }
}
```

Next, add a new member variable named `inventoryTable` of type `DataTable` to your `MainForm` class type. Add a new helper function to your class named `CreateDataTable()`, and call this method within the default constructor of the `MainForm` class:

```
void CreateDataTable()
{
  // Create table schema.
  DataColumn carMakeColumn = new DataColumn("Make", typeof(string));
  DataColumn carColorColumn = new DataColumn("Color", typeof(string));
  DataColumn carPetNameColumn = new DataColumn("PetName", typeof(string));
  carPetNameColumn.Caption = "Pet Name";
  inventoryTable.Columns.AddRange(new DataColumn[] { carMakeColumn,
    carColorColumn, carPetNameColumn });

  // Iterate over the array list to make rows.
  foreach (Car c in listCars)
  {
    DataRow newRow = inventoryTable.NewRow();
    newRow["Make"] = c.carMake;
```

```
        newRow["Color"] = c.carColor;
        newRow["PetName"] = c.carPetName;
        inventoryTable.Rows.Add(newRow);
    }

    // Bind the DataTable to the carInventoryGridView.
    carInventoryGridView.DataSource = inventoryTable;
}
```

The method implementation begins by creating the schema of the DataTable by creating three DataColumn objects (for simplicity, I did not bother to add the autoincrementing CarID field), after which point they are added to the DataTable member variable. The row data is mapped from the List<T> field into the DataTable using a foreach iteration construct and the native ADO.NET object model.

However, notice that the final code statement within the CreateDataTable() method assigns the inventoryTable to the DataSource property. This single property is all you need to set to bind a DataTable to a DataGridView object. Under the hood, this GUI control is reading the row and column collections internally, much like you did with the PrintDataSet() method of the SimpleDataSet example. At this point, you should be able to run your application and see the DataTable within the DataGridView control, as shown in Figure 23-7.

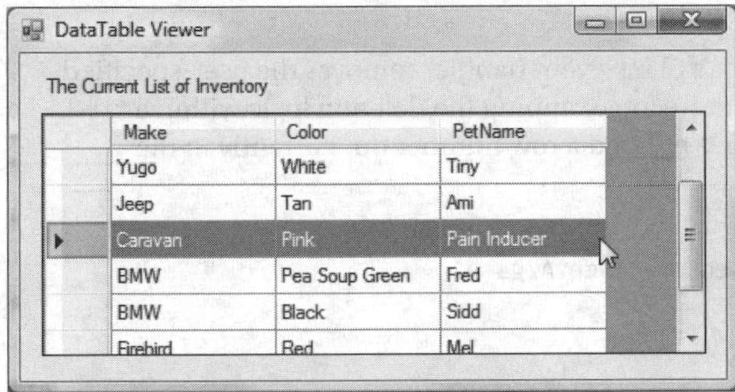

Figure 23-7. *Binding a* DataTable *to a Windows Forms* DataGridView

Programmatically Deleting Rows

Now, assume you wish to update your graphical interface to allow the user to delete a row from the DataTable that is bound to the DataGridView. One approach is to call the Delete() method of the DataRow object that represents the row to terminate. Simply specify the index (or DataRow object) representing the row to remove. To allow the user to specify which row to delete, add a TextBox (named txtRowToRemove) and a Button control (named btnRemoveRow) to the current designer, as shown in Figure 23-8.

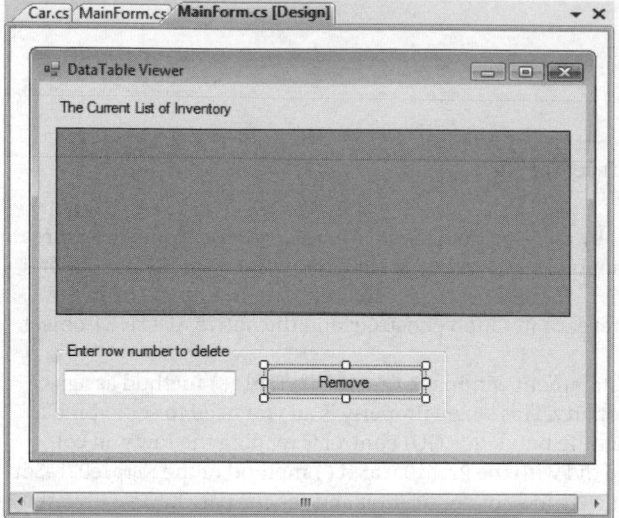

Figure 23-8. *Updating the UI to enable removal of rows from the underlying* `DataTable`

The following logic behind the new `Button`'s `Click` event handler removes the user-specified row from your in-memory `DataTable`. Note that we are wrapping the deletion logic within a `try` scope, to account for the possibility the user has entered a row number not currently in the `DataGridView`:

```
// Remove this row from the DataRowCollection.
private void btnRemoveRow_Click (object sender, EventArgs e)
{
  try
  {
    inventoryTable.Rows[(int.Parse(txtRowToRemove.Text))].Delete();
    inventoryTable.AcceptChanges();
  }
  catch(Exception ex)
  {
    MessageBox.Show(ex.Message);
  }
}
```

The `Delete()` method might have been better named `MarkedAsDeletable()`, as the row is not literally removed until the `DataTable.AcceptChanges()` method is called. In effect, the `Delete()` method simply sets a flag that says, "I am ready to die when my table tells me to." Also understand that if a row has been marked for deletion, a `DataTable` may reject the delete operation via `RejectChanges()`. We have no need to do so for this example; however, we could update our code base as follows:

```
// Mark a row as deleted, but reject the changes.
private void btnRemoveRow_Click (object sender, EventArgs e)
{
  ...
  inventoryTable.Rows[(int.Parse(txtRemove.Text))].Delete();

  // Do more work
  ...
```

```
  // Restore previous RowState value.
  inventoryTable.RejectChanges();
  ...
}
```

You should now be able to run your application and specify a row to delete from the DataTable, based on a given row of the DataGridView (note the internal row collection is zero based). As you remove DataRow objects from the DataTable, you will notice that the grid's UI is updated immediately, as it is bound to the state of the object. Recall, however, that the row is still literally in the DataTable, but the grid chooses not to display it because of the RowState value.

Selecting Rows Based on Filter Criteria

Many data-centric applications require the need to view a small subset of a DataTable's data, as specified by some sort of filtering criteria. For example, what if you wish to see only a certain make of automobile from the in-memory DataTable (such as only BMWs)? The Select() method of the DataTable class provides this very functionality. Using the Select() method, you are able to specify a search criteria that supports a syntax intentionally designed to model a normal SQL query. This method will return an array of DataRow objects that represent each entry that matches the criteria.

To illustrate, update your UI once again, this time allowing users to specify a string that represents the make of the automobile they are interested in viewing (see Figure 23-9) using a new TextBox (named txtMakeToView) and a new Button (named btnDisplayMakes).

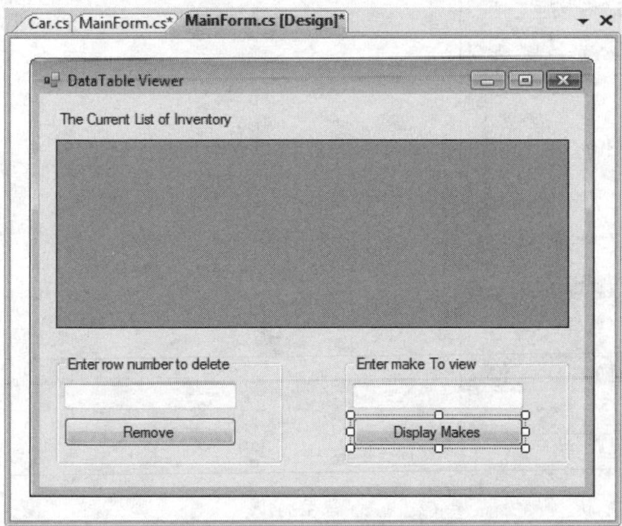

Figure 23-9. *Updating the UI to enable row filtering*

The Select() method has been overloaded a number of times to provide different selection semantics. At its most basic level, the parameter sent to Select() is a string that contains some conditional operation. To begin, observe the following logic for the Click event handler of your new button:

```
private void btnDisplayMakes_Click(object sender, EventArgs e)
{
  // Build a filter based on user input.
  string filterStr = string.Format("Make= '{0}'", txtMakeToView.Text);
```

```
    // Find all rows matching the filter.
    DataRow[] makes = inventoryTable.Select(filterStr);

    // Show what we got!
    if (makes.Length == 0)
      MessageBox.Show("Sorry, no cars...", "Selection error!");
    else
    {
      string strMake = null;
      for (int i = 0; i < makes.Length; i++)
      {
        DataRow temp = makes[i];
        strMake += temp["PetName"] + "\n";
      }
      // Now show all matches in a message box.
      MessageBox.Show(strMake,
        string.Format("{0} type(s):", txtMakeToView.Text));
    }
}
```

Here, you first build a simple filter based on the value in the associated `TextBox`. If you specify BMW, your filter is `Make = 'BMW'`. When you send this filter to the `Select()` method, you get back an array of `DataRow` types that represent each row that matches the filter (see Figure 23-10).

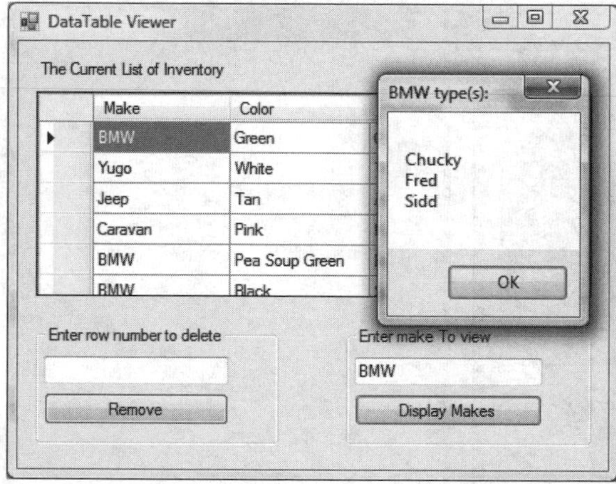

Figure 23-10. *Displaying filtered data*

Again, filtering logic is based on standard SQL syntax. To illustrate, assume you wish to obtain the results of the previous `Select()` invocation alphabetically based on pet name. In terms of SQL, this translates into a sort based on the PetName column. Luckily, the `Select()` method has been overloaded to send in a sort criterion, as shown here:

```
// Sort by PetName.
makes = inventoryTable.Select(filterStr, "PetName");
```

If you want the results in descending order, call `Select()` as so:

```
// Return results in descending order.
makes = inventoryTable.Select(filterStr, "PetName DESC");
```

In general, the sort string contains the column name followed by ASC (ascending, which is the default) or DESC (descending). If need be, multiple columns can be separated by commas. Finally, understand that a filter string can be composed of any number of relational operators. For example, what if you want to find all cars with an ID greater than 5? Here is a helper function that does this very thing:

```
private void ShowCarsWithIdGreaterThanFive()
{
  // Now show the pet names of all cars with ID greater than 5.
  DataRow[] properIDs;
  string newFilterStr = "ID > 5";
  properIDs = inventoryTable.Select(newFilterStr);
  string strIDs = null;
  for(int i = 0; i < properIDs.Length; i++)
  {
    DataRow temp = properIDs[i];
    strIDs += temp["PetName"]
          + " is ID " + temp["ID"] + "\n";
  }
  MessageBox.Show(strIDs, "Pet names of cars where ID > 5");
}
```

Updating Rows

The final aspect of the DataTable you should be aware of is the process of updating an existing row with new values. One approach is to first obtain the row(s) that match a given filter criterion using the Select() method. Once you have the DataRow(s) in question, modify them accordingly. For example, assume you have a new Button on your form-derived type named btnChangeBeemersToYugos that (when clicked) searches the DataTable for all rows where Make is equal to BMW. Once you identify these items, you change the Make from BMW to Yugo:

```
// Find the rows you want to edit with a filter.
private void btnChangeBeemersToYugos_Click(object sender, EventArgs e)
{
  // Make sure user has not lost his or her mind.
  if (DialogResult.Yes ==
    MessageBox.Show("Are you sure?? BMWs are much nicer than Yugos!",
      "Please Confirm!", MessageBoxButtons.YesNo))
  {
    // Build a filter.
    string filterStr = "Make='BMW'";
    string strMake = string.Empty;

    // Find all rows matching the filter.
    DataRow[] makes = inventoryTable.Select(filterStr);

    // Change all Beemers to Yugos!
    for (int i = 0; i < makes.Length; i++)
    {
      makes[i]["Make"] = "Yugo";
    }
  }
}
```

The DataRow class also provides the BeginEdit(), EndEdit(), and CancelEdit() methods, which allow you to edit the content of a row while temporarily suspending any associated validation rules.

In the previous logic, each row was validated with each assignment. (Also, if you handle any events from the DataRow, they fire with each modification.) When you call BeginEdit() on a given DataRow, the row is placed in edit mode. At this point you can make your changes as necessary and call either EndEdit() to commit these changes or CancelEdit() to roll back the changes to the original version, for example:

```
private void UpdateSomeRow()
{
  // Assume you have obtained a row to edit.
  // Now place this row in edit mode.
  rowToUpdate.BeginEdit();

  // Send the row to a helper function, which returns a Boolean.
  if( ChangeValuesForThisRow( rowToUpdate) )
    rowToUpdate.EndEdit();      // OK!
  else
    rowToUpdate.CancelEdit();  // Forget it.
}
```

Although you are free to manually call these methods on a given DataRow, these members are automatically called when you edit a DataGridView widget that has been bound to a DataTable. For example, when you select a row to edit from a DataGridView, that row is automatically placed in edit mode. When you shift focus to a new row, EndEdit() is called automatically.

Working with the DataView Type

In database nomenclature, a *view object* is an alternative representation of a table (or set of tables). For example, using Microsoft SQL Server, you could create a view for your Inventory table that returns a new table containing automobiles only of a given color. In ADO.NET, the DataView type allows you to programmatically extract a subset of data from the DataTable into a stand-alone object.

One great advantage of holding multiple views of the same table is that you can bind these views to various GUI widgets (such as the DataGridView). For example, one DataGridView might be bound to a DataView showing all autos in the Inventory, while another might be configured to display only green automobiles.

To illustrate, update the current UI with an additional DataGridView type named dataGridColtsView and a descriptive Label. Next, define a member variable named coltsOnlyView of type DataView:

```
public partial class MainForm : Form
{
  // View of the DataTable.
  DataView coltsOnlyView;
...
}
```

Now, create a new helper function named CreateDataView(), and call this method within the form's default constructor directly after the DataTable has been fully constructed, as shown here:

```
public MainForm()
{
...
  // Make a data table.
  CreateDataTable();

  // Make a view.
  CreateDataView();
}
```

Here is the implementation of this new helper function. Notice that the constructor of each DataView has been passed the DataTable that will be used to build the custom set of data rows.

```
private void CreateDataView()
{
  // Set the table that is used to construct this view.
  coltsOnlyView = new DataView(inventoryTable);

  // Now configure the views using a filter.
  coltsOnlyView.RowFilter = "Make = 'Colt'";

  // Bind to the new grid.
  dataGridColtsView.DataSource = coltsOnlyView;
}
```

As you can see, the DataView class supports a property named RowFilter, which contains the string representing the filtering criteria used to extract matching rows. Once you have your view established, set the grid's DataSource property accordingly. Figure 23-11 shows the completed application in action.

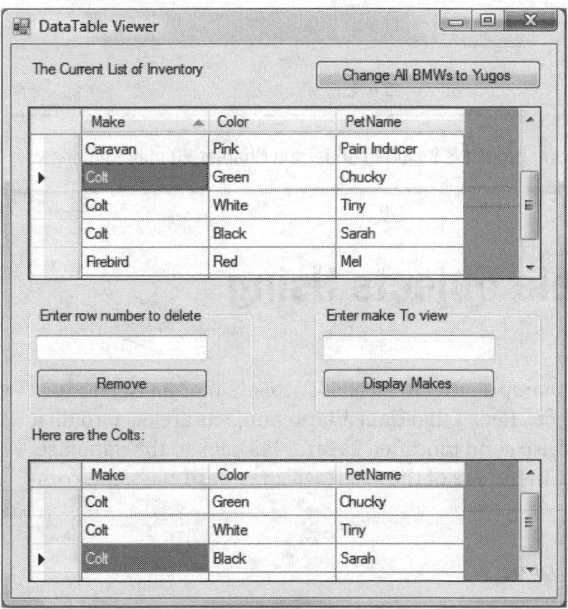

Figure 23-11. *Displaying a unique view of our data*

One Final UI Enhancement: Rendering Row Numbers

Before wrapping up this section, let's add one small enhancement to the current application. Currently, the grids on this window do not provide any sort of visual cue to the end user about which row number he or she is editing (or possibly deleting). If you wish to display row numbers on a DataGridView, your first step is to handle the RowPostPaint event on the grid itself. This event will fire after all of the data in the grid's cells have been rendered in the UI, and it gives you a chance to finalize the graphical look and feel of the rows before they are presented to the user.

Once you have handled this event, you are able to take the incoming DataGridViewRowPostPaintEventArgs parameter to obtain a Graphics object. As you will see in Chapter 27, the Graphics type is part of the GDI+ API, which is the native Windows Forms 2D rendering toolkit. Using this Graphics object, you are able invoke various methods (such as DrawString(), which is appropriate for this example) to render content. Again, Chapter 27 will examine GDI+; however, here is an implementation of the RowPostPaint event that will paint the numbers of each row on the carInventoryGridView object (you could, of course, handle the same event on the dataGridColtsView object for a similar effect):

```
void carInventoryGridView_RowPostPaint(object sender,
  DataGridViewRowPostPaintEventArgs e)
{
  // Paint row numbers using a solid brush, in the
  // native font on the current row style.
  using (SolidBrush b = new SolidBrush(Color.Black))
  {
    e.Graphics.DrawString((e.RowIndex).ToString(),
      e.InheritedRowStyle.Font, b,
      e.RowBounds.Location.X + 15,
      e.RowBounds.Location.Y + 4);
  }
}
```

■ **Source Code** The WindowsFormsDataTableViewer project is included under the Chapter 23 subdirectory.

Filling DataSet/DataTable Objects Using Data Adapters

Now that you understand the ins and outs of manipulating ADO.NET DataSets manually, let's turn our attention to the topic of data adapter objects. Recall that data adapter objects are used to fill a DataSet with DataTable objects, and they can also send modified DataTables back to the database for processing. Table 23-8 documents the core members of the DbDataAdapter base class, the common parent to every data adapter object.

Table 23-8. *Core Members of the* DbDataAdapter *Class*

Members	Meaning in Life
Fill()	Fills a given table in the DataSet with some number of records based on the command object–specified SelectCommand.
SelectCommand InsertCommand UpdateCommand DeleteCommand	Establish SQL commands that will be issued to the data store when the Fill() and Update() methods are called.
Update()	Updates a DataTable using command objects within the InsertCommand, UpdateCommand, or DeleteCommand property. The exact command that is executed is based on the RowState value for a given DataRow in a given DataTable (of a given DataSet).

First of all, notice that a data adapter defines four properties (SelectCommand, InsertCommand, UpdateCommand, and DeleteCommand), each of which operates upon discrete command objects. When you create the data adapter object for your particular data provider (e.g., SqlDataAdapter), you are able to pass in a string type that represents the command text used by the SelectCommand's command object. However, the remaining three command objects (used by the InsertCommand, UpdateCommand, and DeleteCommand properties) must be configured manually.

Assuming each of the four command objects has been properly configured, you are then able to call the Fill() method to obtain a DataSet (or a single DataTable, if you wish). To do so, the data adapter will use whichever command object is found via the SelectCommand property. In a similar manner, when you wish to pass a modified DataSet (or DataTable) object back to the database for processing, you can call the Update() method, which will make use of any of the remaining command objects based on the state of each row in the DataTable (more details in just a bit).

One of the strangest aspects of working with a data adapter object is the fact that you are never required to open or close a connection to the database. Rather, the underlying connection to the database is managed on your behalf. However, you will still need to supply the data adapter with a valid connection object or a connection string (which will be used to build a connection object internally) to inform the data adapter exactly which database you wish to communicate with.

A Simple Data Adapter Example

Before we add new functionality to the AutoLotDAL.dll assembly created in Chapter 22, let's begin with a very simple example that fills a DataSet with a single table using an ADO.NET data adapter object. Create a new Console Application named FillDataSetWithSqlDataAdapter, and import the System.Data and System.Data.SqlClient namespaces into your initial C# code file.

Now, update your Main() method as follows (for reasons of simplicity, feel free to make use of a hard-coded connection string, as shown here):

```
static void Main(string[] args)
{
  Console.WriteLine("***** Fun with Data Adapters *****\n");

  // Hard-coded connection string.
  string cnStr = "Integrated Security = SSPI;Initial Catalog=AutoLot;" +
    @"Data Source=(local)\SQLEXPRESS";

  // Caller creates the DataSet object.
  DataSet ds = new DataSet("AutoLot");

  // Inform adapter of the Select command text and connection.
  SqlDataAdapter dAdapt =
    new SqlDataAdapter("Select * From Inventory", cnStr);

  // Fill our DataSet with a new table, named Inventory.
  dAdapt.Fill(ds, "Inventory");

  // Display contents of DataSet.
  PrintDataSet(ds);
  Console.ReadLine();
}
```

Notice that the data adapter has been constructed by specifying a string literal that will map to the SQL Select statement. This value will be used to build a command object internally, which can be later obtained via the SelectCommand property.

Next, notice that it is the job of the caller to create an instance of the DataSet type, which is passed into the Fill() method. Optionally, the Fill() method can be passed as a second argument a string name that will be used to set the TableName property of the new DataTable (if you do not specify a table name, the data adapter will simply name the table Table). While in most cases the name you assign a DataTable will be identical to the name of the physical table in the relational database, this is not required.

■Note The Fill() method returns an integer that represents the number of rows returned by the SQL query.

Finally, notice that nowhere in the Main() method are you explicitly opening or closing the connection to the database. The Fill() method of a given data adapter has been preprogrammed to open and then close the underlying connection before returning from the Fill() method. Therefore, when you pass the DataSet to the PrintDataSet() method (implemented earlier in this chapter), you are operating on a local copy of disconnected data, incurring no round-trips to fetch the data.

Mapping Database Names to Friendly Names

As mentioned earlier, database administrators tend to create table and column names that can be less than friendly to end users (e.g., au_id, au_fname, au_lname, etc.). The good news is that data adapter objects maintain an internal strongly typed collection (named DataTableMappingCollection) of System.Data.Common.DataTableMapping types. This collection can be accessed via the TableMappings property of your data adapter object.

If you so choose, you may manipulate this collection to inform a DataTable which "display names" it should use when asked to print its contents. For example, assume that you wish to map the table name Inventory to Current Inventory for display purposes. Furthermore, say you wish to display the CarID column name as Car ID (note the extra space) and the PetName column name as Name of Car. To do so, add the following code before calling the Fill() method of your data adapter object (and be sure to import the System.Data.Common namespace to gain the definition of the DataTableMapping type):

```
static void Main(string[] args)
{
...
  // Now map DB column names to user-friendly names.
  DataTableMapping custMap =
    dAdapt.TableMappings.Add("Inventory", "Current Inventory");
  custMap.ColumnMappings.Add("CarID", "Car ID");
  custMap.ColumnMappings.Add("PetName", "Name of Car");
  dAdapt.Fill(myDS, "Inventory");
...
}
```

If you were to run this program once again, you would find that the PrintDataSet() method now displays the "friendly names" of the DataTable and DataRow objects, rather than the names established by the database schema. Figure 23-12 shows the output of the current example.

■Source Code The FillDataSetWithSqlDataAdapter project is included under the Chapter 23 subdirectory.

```
***** Fun with Data Adapters *****

DataSet is named: AutoLot

=> Current Inventory Table:
Car ID  Make    Color   Name of Car
-----------------------------------
1       BMW     Green   Sidd
2       VW      Red     Zippy
3       Ford    Black   Mel
4       BMW     Silver  Henry
5       Yugo    Pink    Sally
6       Saab    Blue    Sven
7       BMW     Black   Bimmer
8       VW      Tan     Sal
999     Ford    Pink    Pinky

Press any key to continue . . .
```

Figure 23-12. `DataTable` *objects with custom mappings*

Revisiting AutoLotDAL.dll

To illustrate the process of using a data adapter to push modifications in a `DataTable` back to the database for processing, we will now update the `AutoLotDAL.dll` assembly created back in Chapter 22 to include a new namespace (named `AutoLotDisconnectedLayer`). This namespace will contain a new class, `InventoryDALDisLayer`, that will make use of a data adapter to interact with a `DataTable`.

Defining the Initial Class Type

Open the AutoLotDAL project in Visual Studio 2008, insert a new class type named `InventoryDALDisLayer` using the Project ➤ Add New Item menu option, and ensure you have a *public* class type in your new code file. Unlike the connection-centric `InventoryDAL` type, this new class will not need to provide custom open/close methods, as the data adapter will handle the details automatically.

To begin, add a custom constructor that sets a private `string` variable representing the connection string. As well, define a private `SqlDataAdapter` member variable, which will be configured by calling a (yet to be created) helper method called `ConfigureAdapter()`, which takes a `SqlDataAdapter` output parameter:

```
public class InventoryDALDisLayer
{
  // Field data.
  private string cnString = string.Empty;
  private SqlDataAdapter dAdapt = null;

  public InventoryDALDisLayer(string connectionString)
  {
    cnString = connectionString;

    // Configure the SqlDataAdapter.
    ConfigureAdapter(out dAdapt);
  }
}
```

Configuring the Data Adapter Using the SqlCommandBuilder

When you are using a data adapter to modify tables in a DataSet, the first order of business is to assign the UpdateCommand, DeleteCommand, and InsertCommand properties with valid command objects (until you do so, these properties return null references). By "valid" command objects, I am referring to the set of command objects used in conjunction with the table you are attempting to update (the Inventory table in our example).

To fill up our adapter with the necessary data can entail a good amount of code, especially if we make use of parameterized queries. Recall from Chapter 22 that a parameterized query allows us to build a SQL statement using a set of parameter objects. Thus, if we were to take the long road, we could implement ConfigureAdapter() to manually create three new SqlCommand objects, each of which contains a set of SqlParameter objects. After this point, we could set each object to the UpdateCommand, DeleteCommand, and InsertCommand properties of the adapter.

Thankfully, Visual Studio 2008 provides a number of designer tools to take care of this mundane and tedious code on our behalf. You'll see some of these shortcuts in action at the conclusion of this chapter. Rather than forcing you to author the numerous code statements to fully configure a data adapter, let's take a massive shortcut by implementing ConfigureAdapter() as so:

```
private void ConfigureAdapter(out SqlDataAdapter dAdapt)
{
  // Create the adapter and set up the SelectCommand.
  dAdapt = new SqlDataAdapter("Select * From Inventory", cnString);

  // Obtain the remaining command objects dynamically at runtime
  // using the SqlCommandBuilder.
  SqlCommandBuilder builder = new SqlCommandBuilder(dAdapt);
}
```

To help simplify the construction of data adapter objects, each of the Microsoft-supplied ADO.NET data providers provides a *command builder* type. The SqlCommandBuilder automatically generates the values contained within the SqlDataAdapter's InsertCommand, UpdateCommand, and DeleteCommand properties based on the initial SelectCommand. Clearly, the benefit is that you have no need to build all the SqlCommand and SqlParameter types by hand.

An obvious question at this point is how a command builder is able to build these SQL command objects on the fly. The short answer is metadata. At runtime, when you call the Update() method of a data adapter, the related command builder will read the database's schema data to autogenerate the underlying insert, delete, and update command objects.

Obviously, doing so requires additional round-trips to the remote database, and therefore it will certainly hurt performance if you use the SqlCommandBuilder numerous times in a single application. Here, we are minimizing the negative effect by calling our ConfigureAdapter() method at the time the InventoryDALDisLayer object is constructed, and retaining the configured SqlDataAdapter for use throughout the object's lifetime.

In the previous code, notice that we made no use of the command builder object (SqlCommandBuilder in this case) beyond passing in the data adapter object as a constructor parameter. As odd as this may seem, this is all we are required to do (at a minimum). Under the hood, this type will configure the data adapter with the remaining command objects.

Now, while you may love the idea of getting something for nothing, do understand that command builders come with some critical restrictions. Specifically, a command builder is only able to autogenerate SQL commands for use by a data adapter if all of the following conditions are true:

- The SQL Select command interacts with only a single table (e.g., no joins).
- The single table has been attributed with a primary key.
- The table must have a column(s) representing the primary key that is included in your SQL Select statement.

Based on the way we constructed our AutoLot database, these restrictions pose no problem. However, in a more industrial-strength database, you will need to consider if this type is at all useful (if not, remember that Visual Studio 2008 will autogenerate a good deal of the required code, as you'll see at the end of this chapter).

Implementing GetAllInventory()

Now that our data adapter is ready to go, the first method of our new class type will simply use the `Fill()` method of the `SqlDataAdapter` object to fetch a `DataTable` representing all records in the Inventory table of the AutoLot database:

```
public DataTable GetAllInventory()
{
  DataTable inv = new DataTable("Inventory");
  dAdapt.Fill(inv);
  return inv;
}
```

Implementing UpdateInventory()

The `UpdateInventory()` method is very simple:

```
public void UpdateInventory(DataTable modifiedTable)
{
  dAdapt.Update(modifiedTable);
}
```

Here, the data adapter object will examine the `RowState` value of each row of the incoming `DataTable`. Based on this value (`RowState.Added`, `RowState.Deleted`, or `RowState.Modified`), the correct command object will be leveraged behind the scenes.

Source Code The AutoLotDAL (Part 2) project is included under the Chapter 23 subdirectory.

Building a Windows Forms Front End

At this point we can build a front end to test our new `InventoryDALDisLayer` object, which will be a Windows Forms application named WindowsFormsInventoryUI. Once you have created the project, set a reference to your updated `AutoLotDAL.dll` assembly and import the following namespace:

```
using AutoLotDisconnectedLayer;
```

The design of the form consists of a single `Label`, `DataGridView` (named `inventoryGrid`), and `Button` type (named `btnUpdateInventory`), which has been configured to handle the `Click` event. Here is the definition of the form (which does not contain error-handling logic for simplicity; feel free to add `try`/`catch` logic if you so choose):

```
public partial class MainForm : Form
{
  InventoryDALDisLayer dal = null;
  public MainForm()
  {
    InitializeComponent();
```

```
    // Assume we have an App.config file
    // storing the connection string.
    string cnStr =
      ConfigurationManager.ConnectionStrings["AutoLotSqlProvider"].ConnectionString;

    // Create our data access object.
    dal = new InventoryDALDisLayer(cnStr);

    // Fill up our grid!
    inventoryGrid.DataSource = dal.GetAllInventory();
  }

  private void btnUpdateInventory_Click(object sender, EventArgs e)
  {
    // Get modified data from the grid.
    DataTable changedDT = (DataTable)inventoryGrid.DataSource;

    // Commit our changes.
    dal.UpdateInventory(changedDT);
  }
}
```

Notice that in this example, I am assuming you have added an App.config file to store the connection string data, within a <connectionStrings> section. To make use of the ConnectionStrings indexer of the ConfigurationManager type, be sure to set a reference to the System.Configuration.dll assembly. Once we create the InventoryDALDisLayer object, we bind the DataTable returned from GetAllInventory() to the DataGridView object. When the end user clicks the Update button, we extract out the modified DataTable from the grid (via the DataSource property) and pass it into our UpdateInventory() method.

That's it! Once you run this application, add a set of new rows to the grid and update/delete a few others. Assuming you click the Button control, you will see your changes have persisted into the AutoLot database.

Source Code The updated WindowsFormsInventoryUI project is included under the Chapter 23 subdirectory.

Navigating Multitabled DataSet Objects

So far, all of this chapter's examples have operated on a single DataTable object. However, the power of the disconnected layer really comes to light when a DataSet object contains numerous interrelated DataTables. In this case, you are able to insert any number of DataRelation objects into the DataSet's DataRelation collection to account for the interdependencies of the tables. Using these objects, the client tier is able to navigate between the table data without incurring network round-trips.

Note Rather than updating AutoLotDAL.dll yet again in order to account for the Customers and Orders tables, this example isolates all of the data access logic within a new Windows Forms project. However, intermixing UI and data logic in a production-level application is certainly not recommended. The final examples of this chapter leverage various database design tools to decouple the UI and data logic code.

Begin this example by creating a new Windows Forms application named MultitabledDataSetApp. The GUI is simple enough. In Figure 23-13 you can see three `DataGridView` widgets that hold the data retrieved from the Inventory, Orders, and Customers tables of the AutoLot database. In addition, the initial `Button` (named `btnUpdateDatabase`) submits any and all changes entered within the grids back to the database for processing via data adapter objects.

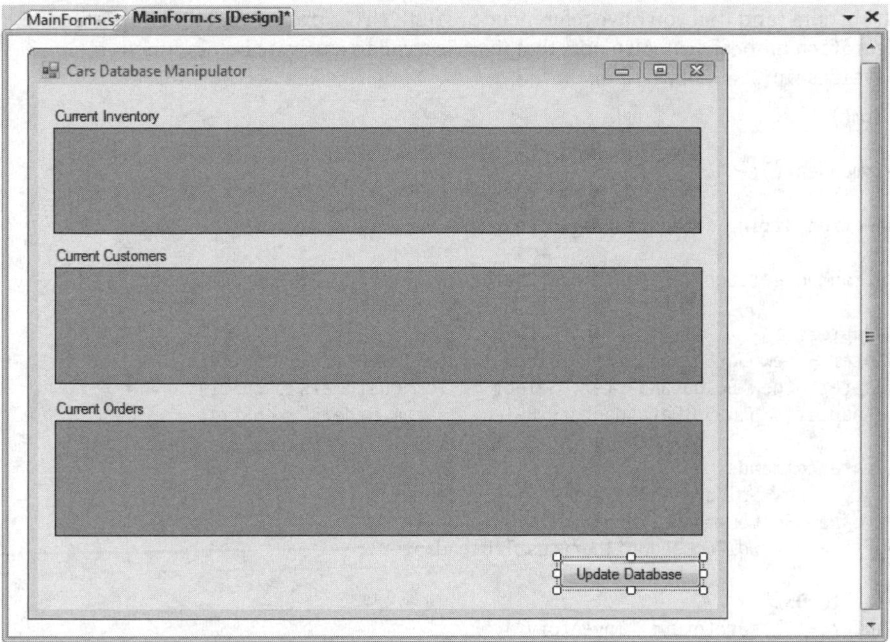

Figure 23-13. *The initial UI will display data from each table of the AutoLot database.*

Prepping the Data Adapters

To keep the data access code as simple as possible, the `MainForm` will make use of command builder objects to autogenerate the SQL commands for each of the three `SqlDataAdapters` (one for each table). Here is the initial update to the `Form`-derived type:

```
public partial class MainForm : Form
{
  // Form wide DataSet.
  private DataSet autoLotDS = new DataSet("AutoLot");

  // Make use of command builders to simplify data adapter configuration.
  private SqlCommandBuilder sqlCBInventory;
  private SqlCommandBuilder sqlCBCustomers;
  private SqlCommandBuilder sqlCBOrders;

  // Our data adapters (for each table).
  private SqlDataAdapter invTableAdapter;
  private SqlDataAdapter custTableAdapter;
  private SqlDataAdapter ordersTableAdapter;
```

```
  // Form wide connection string.
  private string cnStr = string.Empty;
...
}
```

The constructor does the grunge work of creating your data-centric member variables and filling the DataSet. Here, I am assuming you have authored an App.config file that contains the correct connection string data (and that you have referenced System.Configuration.dll and imported the System.Configuration namespace). Also note that there is a call to a private helper function, BuildTableRelationship(), as shown here:

```
public MainForm()
{
  InitializeComponent();

  // Get connection string from *.config file.
  cnStr =
    ConfigurationManager.ConnectionStrings["AutoLotSqlProvider"].ConnectionString;

  // Create adapters.
  invTableAdapter = new SqlDataAdapter("Select * from Inventory", cnStr);
  custTableAdapter = new SqlDataAdapter("Select * from Customers", cnStr);
  ordersTableAdapter = new SqlDataAdapter("Select * from Orders", cnStr);

  // Autogenerate commands.
  sqlCBInventory = new SqlCommandBuilder(invTableAdapter);
  sqlCBOrders = new SqlCommandBuilder(ordersTableAdapter);
  sqlCBCustomers = new SqlCommandBuilder(custTableAdapter);

  // Add tables to DS.
  invTableAdapter.Fill(autoLotDS, "Inventory");
  custTableAdapter.Fill(autoLotDS, "Customers");
  ordersTableAdapter.Fill(autoLotDS, "Orders");

  // Build relations between tables.
  BuildTableRelationship();

  // Bind to grids
  dataGridViewInventory.DataSource = autoLotDS.Tables["Inventory"];
  dataGridViewCustomers.DataSource = autoLotDS.Tables["Customers"];
  dataGridViewOrders.DataSource = autoLotDS.Tables["Orders"];
}
```

Building the Table Relationships

The BuildTableRelationship() helper function does the grunt work to add two DataRelation objects into the autoLotDS object. Recall from Chapter 22 that the AutoLot database expresses a number of parent/child relationships, accounted for with the following code:

```
private void BuildTableRelationship()
{
  // Create CustomerOrder data relation object.
  DataRelation dr = new DataRelation("CustomerOrder",
    autoLotDS.Tables["Customers"].Columns["CustID"],
    autoLotDS.Tables["Orders"].Columns["CustID"]);
  autoLotDS.Relations.Add(dr);
```

```
  // Create InventoryOrder data relation object.
  dr = new DataRelation("InventoryOrder",
    autoLotDS.Tables["Inventory"].Columns["CarID"],
    autoLotDS.Tables["Orders"].Columns["CarID"]);
  autoLotDS.Relations.Add(dr);
}
```

Note that when creating a DataRelation object, you establish a friendly string moniker with the first parameter (you'll see the usefulness of doing so in just a minute) as well as the keys used to build the relationship itself. Notice that the parent table (the second constructor parameter) is specified before the child table (the third constructor parameter).

Updating the Database Tables

Now that the DataSet has been filled and disconnected from the data source, you can manipulate each DataTable locally. To do so, simply insert, update, or delete values from any of the three DataGridViews. When you are ready to submit the data back for processing, click the Update button. The code behind the related Click event should be clear at this point:

```
private void btnUpdateDatabase_Click(object sender, EventArgs e)
{
  try
  {
    invTableAdapter.Update(carsDS, "Inventory");
    custTableAdapter.Update(carsDS, "Customers");
    ordersTableAdapter.Update(carsDS, "Orders");
  }
  catch (Exception ex)
  {
    MessageBox.Show(ex.Message);
  }
}
```

Now run your application and perform various updates. When you rerun the application, you should find that your grids are populated with the recent changes.

Navigating Between Related Tables

To illustrate how a DataRelation allows you to move between related tables programmatically, extend your UI to include a new Button type (named btnGetOrderInfo), a related TextBox (named txtCustID), and a descriptive Label (I grouped these controls within a GroupBox simply for visual appeal). Figure 23-14 shows one possible UI of the application.

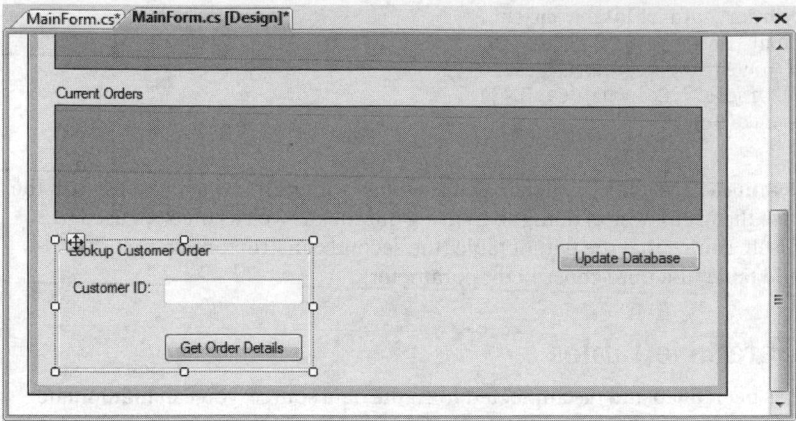

Figure 23-14. *The updated UI allows the user to look up customer order information.*

Using this updated UI, the end user is able to enter the ID of a customer and retrieve all the relevant information about that customer's order (name, order ID, car order, etc.), which will be formatted into a `string` type that is eventually displayed within a message box. Ponder the code behind the new `Button`'s `Click` event handler:

```
private void btnGetOrderInfo_Click(object sender, System.EventArgs e)
{
  string strOrderInfo = string.Empty;
  DataRow[] drsCust = null;
  DataRow[] drsOrder = null;

  // Get the customer ID in the text box.
  int custID = int.Parse(this.txtCustID.Text);

  // Now based on custID, get the correct row in Customers table.
  drsCust = autoLotDS.Tables["Customers"].Select(
    string.Format("CustID = {0}", custID));
  strOrderInfo += string.Format("Customer {0}: {1} {2}\n",
    drsCust[0]["CustID"].ToString(),
    drsCust[0]["FirstName"].ToString().Trim(),
    drsCust[0]["LastName"].ToString().Trim());

  // Navigate from Customers table to Orders table.
  drsOrder = drsCust[0].GetChildRows(autoLotDS.Relations["CustomerOrder"]);

  // Get order number.
  foreach (DataRow r in drsOrder)
    strOrderInfo += string.Format("Order Number: {0}\n", r["OrderID"]);

  // Now navigate from Orders table to Inventory table.
  DataRow[] drsInv =
    drsOrder[0].GetParentRows(autoLotDS.Relations["InventoryOrder"]);

  // Get car info.
  foreach (DataRow r in drsInv)
  {
    strOrderInfo += string.Format("Make: {0}\n", r["Make"]);
```

```
    strOrderInfo += string.Format("Color: {0}\n", r["Color"]);
    strOrderInfo += string.Format("Pet Name: {0}\n", r["PetName"]);
  }
  MessageBox.Show(strOrderInfo, "Order Details");
}
```

Let's break down this code step by step. First, you obtain the correct customer ID from the text box and use it to select the correct row in the Customers table, via the `Select()` method. Given that `Select()` returns an *array* of `DataRow` objects, you must use double indexing to ensure you fetch the data for the first (and only) member of this array:

```
// Get the customer ID in the text box.
int custID = int.Parse(this.txtCustID.Text);

// Now based on custID, get the correct row in Customers table.
drsCust = autoLotDS.Tables["Customers"].Select(
  string.Format("CustID = {0}", custID));
strOrderInfo += string.Format("Customer {0}: {1} {2}\n",
  drsCust[0]["CustID"].ToString(),
  drsCust[0]["FirstName"].ToString().Trim(),
  drsCust[0]["LastName"].ToString().Trim());
```

Next, you navigate from the Customers table to the Orders table, using the CustomerOrder data relation. Notice that the `DataRow.GetChildRows()` method allows you to grab rows from your child table. Once you do, you can read information out of the table:

```
// Navigate from Customers table to Orders table.
drsOrder = drsCust[0].GetChildRows(autoLotDS.Relations["CustomerOrder"]);

// Get order number.
foreach (DataRow r in drsOrder)
  strOrderInfo += string.Format("Order Number: {0}\n", r["OrderID"]);
```

The final step is to navigate from the Orders table to its parent table (Inventory), using the `GetParentRows()` method. At this point, you can read information from the Inventory table using the Make, PetName, and Color columns, as shown here:

```
// Now navigate from Orders table to Inventory table.
DataRow[] drsInv =
  drsOrder[0].GetParentRows(autoLotDS.Relations["InventoryOrder"]);

// Get car info.
foreach (DataRow r in drsInv)
{
  strOrderInfo += string.Format("Make: {0}\n", r["Make"]);
  strOrderInfo += string.Format("Color: {0}\n", r["Color"]);
  strOrderInfo += string.Format("Pet Name: {0}\n", r["PetName"]);
}
```

Figure 23-15 shows one possible output when specifying a customer ID with the value of 2 (Matt Walton in my copy of the AutoLot database).

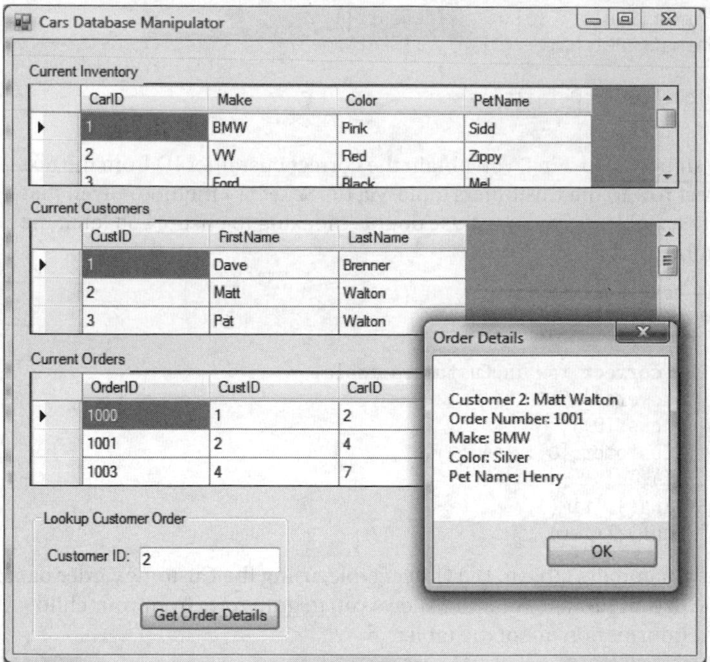

Figure 23-15. *Navigating data relations*

Hopefully, this last example has you convinced of the usefulness of the `DataSet` type. Given that a `DataSet` is completely disconnected from the underlying data source, you can work with an in-memory copy of data and navigate around each table to make any necessary updates, deletes, or inserts. Once you've finished, you can submit your changes to the data store for processing. The end result is a very scalable and robust application.

■ **Source Code** The MultitabledDataSetApp project is included under the Chapter 23 subdirectory.

The Data Access Tools of Visual Studio 2008

All of the ADO.NET examples in this text thus far have involved a fair amount of elbow grease, in that we were authoring all data access logic by hand. While we did offload a good amount of said code to a .NET code library (`AutoLotDAL.dll`) for reuse in later chapters of the book, we were still required to manually create the various objects of our data provider before interacting with the relational database.

To wrap up our examination of the disconnected layer of ADO.NET, we will now take a look at a number of services provided by Visual Studio 2008 that can assist you in authoring data access logic. As you might suspect, this IDE supports a number of visual designers and code generation tools (aka wizards) that can produce a good deal of starter code.

■ **Note** Don't get lulled into the belief that you will never be required to author ADO.NET logic by hand, or that the wizard-generated code will always fit the bill 100 percent for your current project. While these tools can save you a significant amount of time, the more you know about the ADO.NET programming model, the better, as this enables you to customize and tweak the generated code as required.

Visually Designing the DataGridView

The first data access shortcut can be found via the `DataGridView` designer. While we have used this widget in previous examples for display and editing purposes, we have not used the associated wizard that will generate data access code on our behalf. To begin, create a brand-new Windows Forms application project named VisualDataGridViewApp. Add a descriptive `Label` control and an instance of the `DataGridView` control. When you do, note that an inline editor opens to the right of the UI widget. From the Choose Data Source drop-down box, select the Add Project Data Source link (see Figure 23-16).

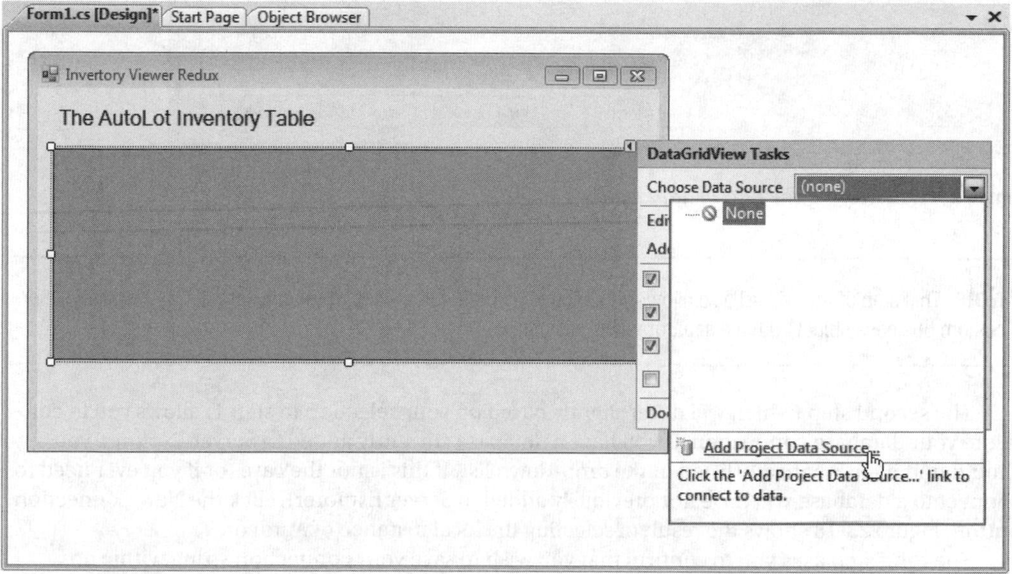

Figure 23-16. *The* `DataGridView` *editor*

The Data Source Configuration Wizard launches. This tool will guide you through a series of steps that allow you to select and configure a data source, which will then be bound to the `DataGridView` using a custom data adapter type. The first step of the wizard simply asks you to identify the type of data source you wish to interact with. Select Database (see Figure 23-17) and click the Next button.

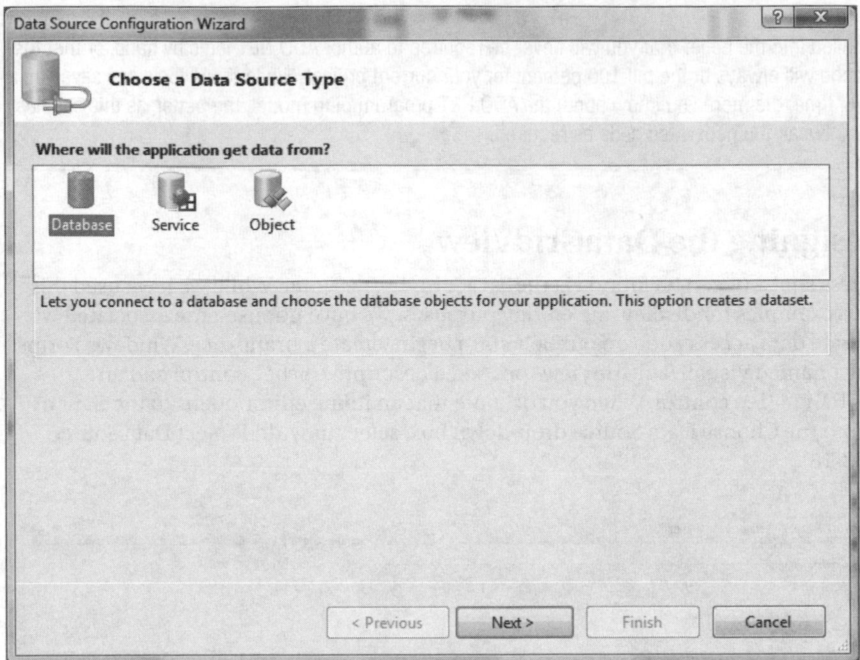

Figure 23-17. *Selecting the type of data source*

Note This step of the wizard also allows you to connect data that comes from an external XML web service or a custom business object within a separate .NET assembly.

The second step (which will differ slightly based on your selection in step 1) allows you to configure your database connection. If you have a database currently added to Server Explorer, you should find it automatically listed in the drop-down list. If this is not the case (or if you ever need to connect to a database you have not previously added to Server Explorer), click the New Connection button. Figure 23-18 shows the result of selecting the local instance of AutoLot.

The third step asks you to confirm that you wish to save your connection string within an external `App.config` file, and if so, the name to use within the `<connectionStrings>` element. Keep the default settings for this step of the wizard and click the Next button.

The final step of the wizard is where you are able to select the database objects that will be accounted for by the autogenerated `DataSet` and related data adapters. While you could select each of the data objects of the AutoLot database, here you will only concern yourself with the Inventory table. Given this, change the suggested name of the `DataSet` to InventoryDataSet (see Figure 23-19), check the Inventory table, and click the Finish button.

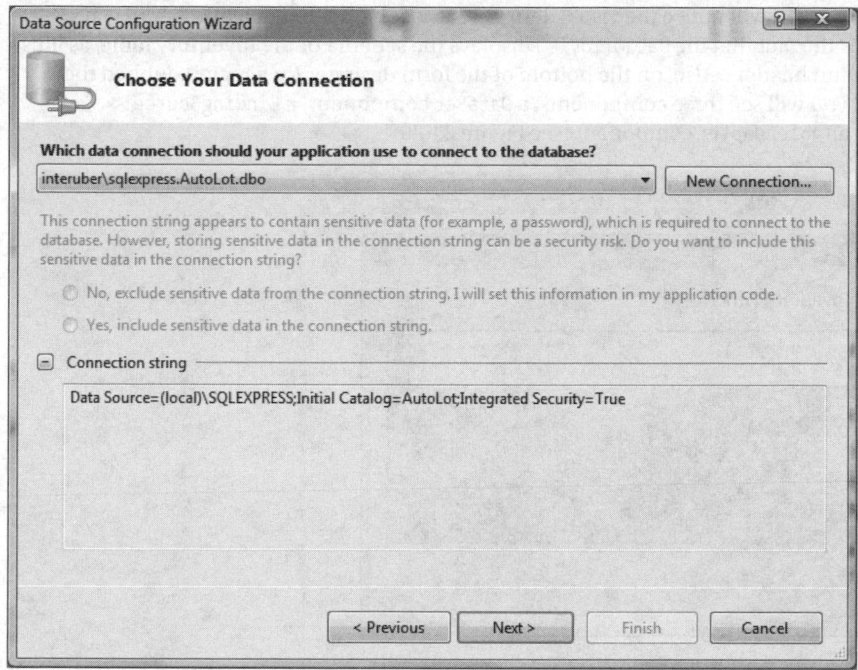

Figure 23-18. *Selecting the AutoLot database*

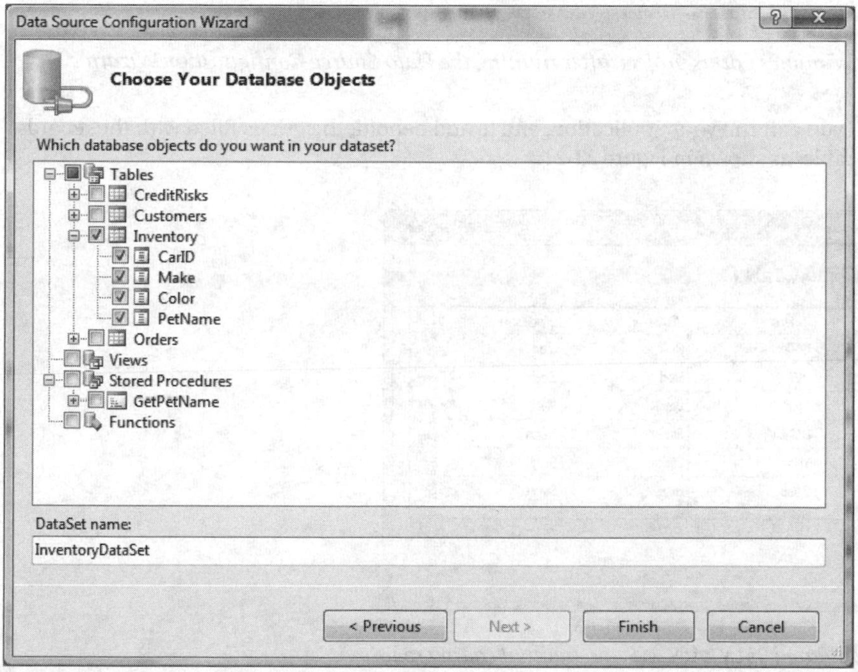

Figure 23-19. *Selecting the Inventory table*

Once you do so, you will notice the visual designer has been updated in a number of ways. Most noticeable is the fact that the DataGridView displays the schema of the Inventory table, as illustrated by the column headers. Also, on the bottom of the form designer (in a region dubbed the *component tray*), you will see three components: a DataSet component, a BindingSource component, and a TableAdapter component (see Figure 23-20).

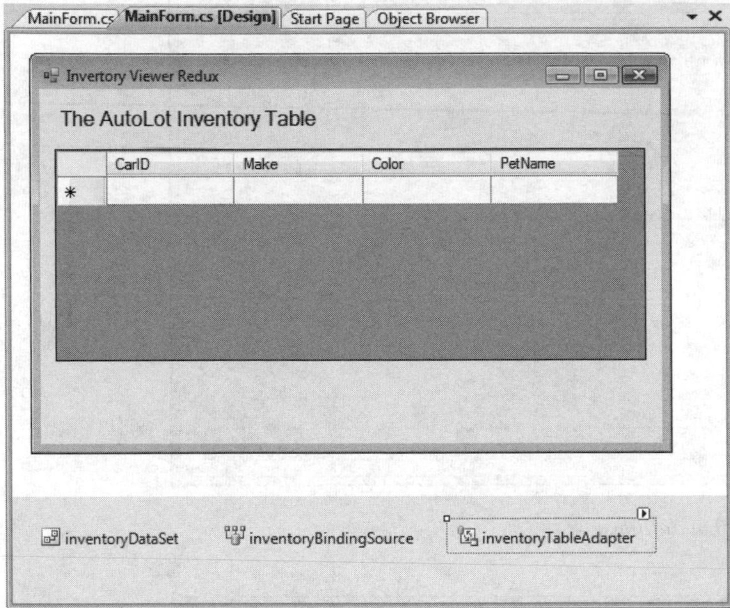

Figure 23-20. *Our Windows Forms project, after running the Data Source Configuration Wizard*

At this point you can run your application, and lo and behold, the grid is filled with the records of the Inventory table, as shown in Figure 23-21.

Invertory Viewer Redux

The AutoLot Inventory Table

CarID	Make	Color	PetName
1	BMW	Pink	Sidd
2	VW	Red	Zippy
3	Ford	Black	Mel
4	BMW	Silver	Henry
5	Yugo	Pink	Sally
6	Saab	Blue	Sven

Figure 23-21. *A populated* DataGridView*—no manual coding required!*

The App.config File and the Settings.Settings File

If you examine your Solution Explorer, you will find your project now contains an App.config file. If you open this file, you will notice the name attribute of the <connectionStrings> element used in previous examples:

```
<?xml version="1.0" encoding="utf-8" ?>
<configuration>
  <configSections>
  </configSections>
  <connectionStrings>
    <add name="VisualDataGridViewApp.Properties.Settings.AutoLotConnectionString"
      connectionString=
      "Data Source=(local)\SQLEXPRESS;
      Initial Catalog=AutoLot;Integrated Security=True"
      providerName="System.Data.SqlClient" />
  </connectionStrings>
</configuration>
```

Specifically, the lengthy "VisualDataGridViewApp.Properties.Settings. AutoLotConnectionString" value has been set as the name of the connection string. Even stranger is the fact that if you scan all of the generated code, you will not find any reference to the ConfigurationManager type to read the value from the <connectionStrings> element. However, you will find that the autogenerated data adapter object (which you will examine in more detail in just a moment) is constructed in part by calling the following private helper function:

```
private void InitConnection()
{
  this._connection = new global::System.Data.SqlClient.SqlConnection();
  this._connection.ConnectionString = global::
    VisualDataGridViewApp.Properties.Settings.Default.AutoLotConnectionString;
}
```

As you can see, the ConnectionString property is set via a call to Settings.Default. As it turns out, every Visual Studio 2008 project type maintains a set of application-wide settings that are burned into your assembly as metadata when you compile the application. The short answer is that if you open your compiled application using reflector.exe (see Chapter 2), you can view this internal type (see Figure 23-22).

Given the previous point, it would be possible to deploy your application *without* shipping the *.config file, as the embedded value will be used by default if a client-side *.config file is not present.

Note The Visual Studio 2008 settings programming model is really quite interesting; however, full coverage is outside of the scope of this chapter (and this edition of the text, for that matter). If you are interested in learning more, look up the topic "Managing Application Settings" in the .NET Framework 3.5 SDK documentation.

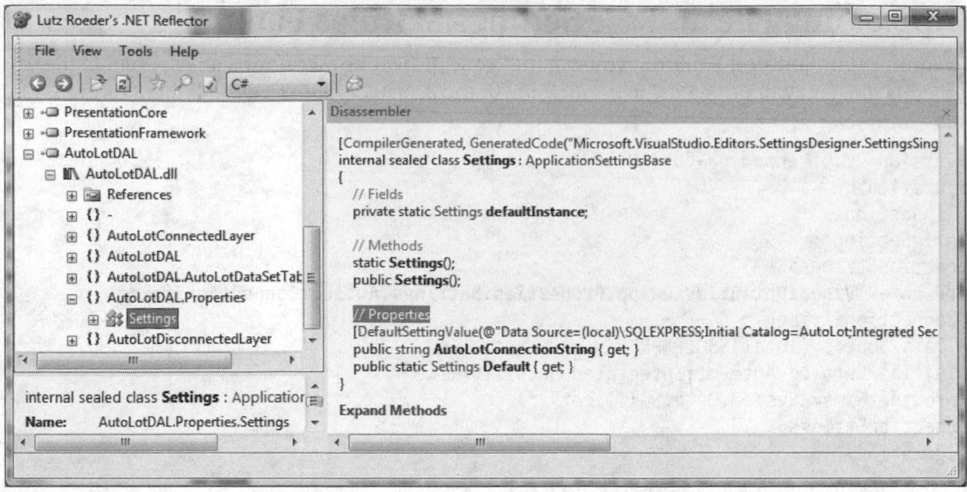

Figure 23-22. *The* `Settings` *object contains an embedded connection string value.*

Examining the Generated DataSet

Now let's take a look at some of the core aspects of this generated code. First of all, insert a new class diagram type into your project by selecting the project icon in Solution Explorer and clicking the View Class Diagram button. Notice that the wizard has created a new `DataSet` type based on your input, which in this case is named `InventoryDataSet`. As you can see, this class defines a handful of members, the most important of which is a property named `Inventory` (see Figure 23-23).

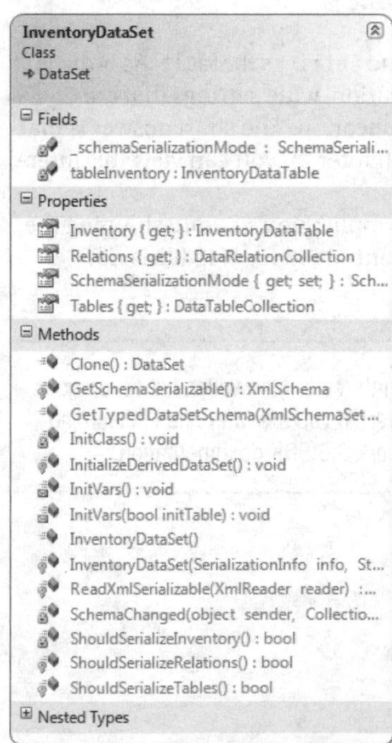

Figure 23-23. *The Data Source Configuration Wizard created a strongly typed* `DataSet`.

If you double-click the InventoryDataSet.xsd file within Solution Explorer, you will load the Visual Studio 2008 Dataset Designer (more details on this designer in just a bit). If you right-click anywhere within this designer and select the View Code option, you will notice a fairly empty partial class definition:

```
public partial class InventoryDataSet {
  partial class InventoryDataTable
  {
  }
}
```

The real action is taking place within the designer-maintained file, InventoryDataSet.Designer.cs. If you open this file using Solution Explorer, you will notice that InventoryDataSet is actually extending the DataSet class type. When you (or a wizard) create a class extending DataSet, you are building what is termed a *strongly typed* DataSet. One benefit of using strongly typed DataSet objects is that they contain a number of properties that map directly to the database tables names. Thus, rather than having to drill into the collection of tables using the Tables property, you can simply use the Inventory property. Consider the following partial code, commented for clarity:

```
// This is all designer-generated code!
public partial class InventoryDataSet : global::System.Data.DataSet
{
  // A member variable of type InventoryDataTable.
  private InventoryDataTable tableInventory;

  // Each constructor calls a helper method named InitClass().
  public InventoryDataSet()
  {
  ...
    this.InitClass();
  }

  // InitClass() preps the DataSet and adds the InventoryDataTable
  // to the Tables collection.
  private void InitClass()
  {
    this.DataSetName = "InventoryDataSet";
    this.Prefix = "";
    this.Namespace = "http://tempuri.org/InventoryDataSet.xsd";
    this.EnforceConstraints = true;
    this.SchemaSerializationMode =
      global::System.Data.SchemaSerializationMode.IncludeSchema;
    this.tableInventory = new InventoryDataTable();
    base.Tables.Add(this.tableInventory);
  }

  // The read-only Inventory property returns
  // the InventoryDataTable member variable.
  public InventoryDataTable Inventory
  {
    get { return this.tableInventory; }
  }
}
```

In addition to wrapping the details of maintaining a DataTable object, the designer-generated strongly typed DataSet could contain similar logic to expose any DataRelation objects (which we do not currently have) that represent the connections between each of the tables.

Examining the Generated DataTable and DataRow

In a similar fashion, the wizard created a *strongly typed* `DataTable` class and a *strongly typed* `DataRow` class, both of which have been nested within the `InventoryDataSet` class. The `InventoryDataTable` class (which is the same type as the member variable of the strongly typed `DataSet` we just examined) defines a set of properties that are based on the column names of the physical Inventory table (`CarIDColumn`, `ColorColumn`, `MakeColumn`, and `PetNameColumn`) as well as a custom indexer and a `Count` property to obtain the current number of records.

More interestingly, this strongly typed `DataTable` class defines a set of methods (see Figure 23-24) that allow you to insert, locate, and delete rows within the table using strongly typed members (an attractive alternative to manually navigating the `Rows` and `Columns` indexers).

Figure 23-24. *The custom* `DataTable` *type*

■ **Note** The strongly typed `DataTable` also defines a handful of events you can handle to monitor changes to your table data.

The custom `DataRow` type is far less exotic than the generated `DataSet` or `DataTable`. As shown in Figure 23-25, this class extends `DataRow` and exposes properties that map directly to the schema of the Inventory table (also be aware that the columns are appropriately typed).

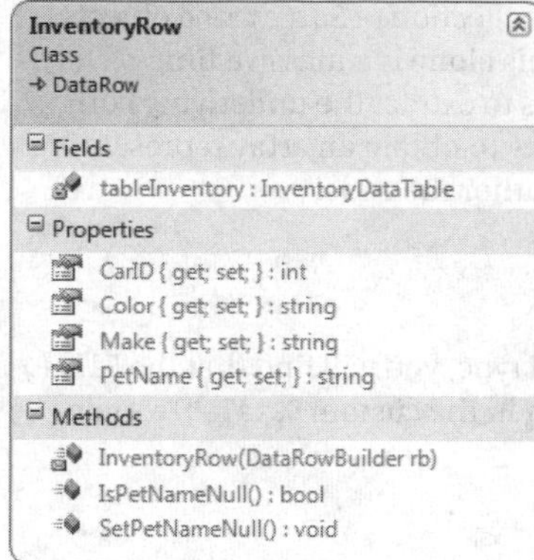

Figure 23-25. *The custom* `DataRow` *type*

Examining the Generated Data Adapter

Having some strong typing for our disconnected types is a solid benefit of using the Data Source Configuration Wizard, given that adding strongly typed classes by hand would be tedious (but entirely possible). This same wizard was kind enough to generate a custom data adapter object that is able to fill and update the `InventoryDataSet` and `InventoryDataTable` class types (see Figure 23-26).

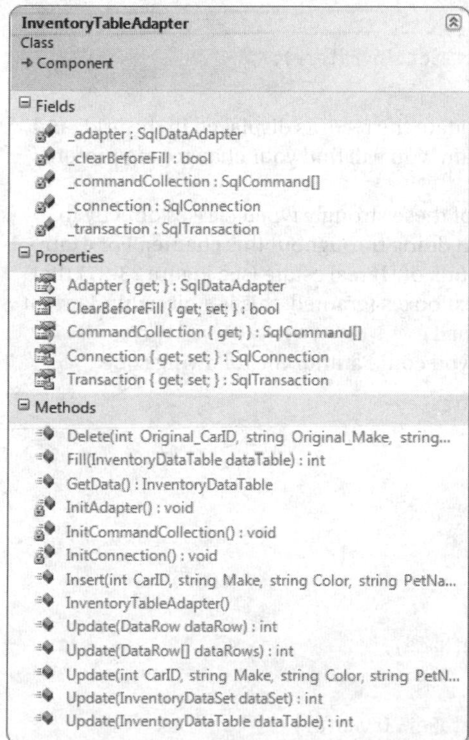

Figure 23-26. *A customized data adapter that operates on the strongly typed types*

The autogenerated InventoryTableAdapter type maintains a collection of SqlCommand objects, each of which has a fully populated set of SqlParameter objects (this alone is a massive time-saver). Furthermore, this custom data adapter provides a set of properties to extract the underlying connection, transaction, and data adapter objects, as well as a property to obtain an array representing each command type. The obvious benefit is you did not have to author the code!

Using the Generated Types in Code

If you were to examine the Load event handler of the form-derived type, you will find that the Fill() method of the custom data adapter is called upon startup, passing in the custom DataTable maintained by the custom DataSet:

```
private void MainForm_Load(object sender, EventArgs e)
{
  this.inventoryTableAdapter.Fill(this.inventoryDataSet.Inventory);
}
```

You can use this same custom data adapter object to update changes to the grid. Update the UI of your form with a single Button control (named btnUpdateInventory). Handle the Click event, and author the following code within the event handler:

```
private void btnUpdateInventory_Click(object sender, EventArgs e)
{
  // This will push any changes within the Inventory table back to
  // the database for processing.
  this.inventoryTableAdapter.Update(this.inventoryDataSet.Inventory);

  // Get fresh copy for grid.
  this.inventoryTableAdapter.Fill(this.inventoryDataSet.Inventory);
}
```

Run your application once again; add, delete, or update the records displayed in the grid; and click the Update button. When you run the program again, you will find your changes are present and accounted for.

Understand that you are able to make use of each of these strongly typed classes directly in your code, in (more or less) the same way you have been doing throughout this chapter. For example, assume you have updated your form with a new chunk of UI real estate (see Figure 23-27) that allows the user to enter a new record using a series of text boxes (granted, this is a bit redundant for this example, as the DataGridView will do so on your behalf).

Within the Click event handler of the new Button, you could author the following code:

```
private void btnAddRow_Click(object sender, EventArgs e)
{
  // Get data from widgets
  int id = int.Parse(txtCarID.Text);
  string make = txtMake.Text;
  string color = txtColor.Text;
  string petName = txtPetName.Text;

  // Use custom adapter to add row.
  inventoryTableAdapter.Insert(id, make, color, petName);

  // Refill table data.
  this.inventoryTableAdapter.Fill(this.inventoryDataSet.Inventory);
}
```

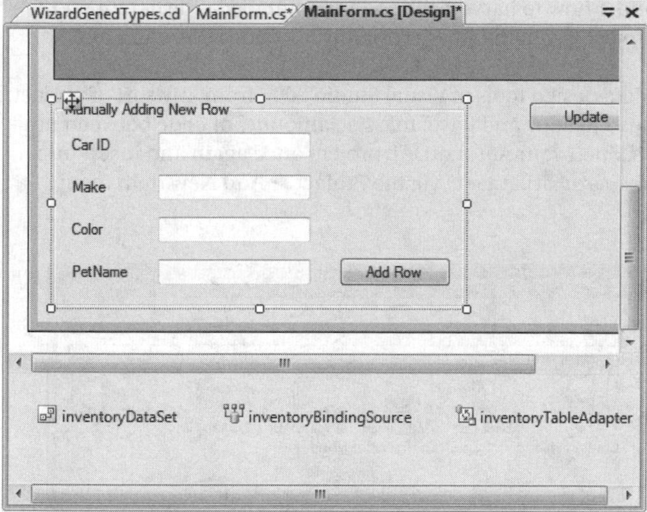

Figure 23-27. *A simple update to the form type*

Or, if you so choose, you can manually add a new row:

```
private void btnAddRow_Click(object sender, EventArgs e)
{
  // Get new Row.
  InventoryDataSet.InventoryRow newRow =
    inventoryDataSet.Inventory.NewInventoryRow();
  newRow.CarID = int.Parse(txtCarID.Text);
  newRow.Make = txtMake.Text;
  newRow.Color = txtColor.Text;
  newRow.PetName = txtPetName.Text;
  inventoryDataSet.Inventory.AddInventoryRow(newRow);

  // Use custom adapter to add row.
  inventoryTableAdapter.Update(inventoryDataSet.Inventory);

  // Refill table data.
  this.inventoryTableAdapter.Fill(this.inventoryDataSet.Inventory);
}
```

■ **Source Code** The VisualDataGridViewApp project is included under the Chapter 23 subdirectory.

Decoupling Autogenerated Code from the UI Layer

To close, allow me to point out that while the Data Source Configuration Wizard launched by the `DataGridView` has done a fantastic job of authoring a ton of grungy code on our behalf, the previous example hard-coded the data access logic directly within the user interface layer—a major design faux pas. Ideally, this sort of code belongs in our `AutoLotDAL.dll` assembly (or some other data access library). However, you may wonder how to harvest the code generated via the DataGridView's associated wizard in a Class Library project, given that there certainly is no form designer by default.

Thankfully, you can activate the data design tools of Visual Studio 2008 from any sort of project (UI based or otherwise) without the need to copy and paste massive amounts of code between projects. To illustrate some of your options, open your AutoLotDAL project once again and insert into your project a new DataSet type (named AutoLotDataSet) via the Project ➤ Add New Item menu option (see Figure 23-28).

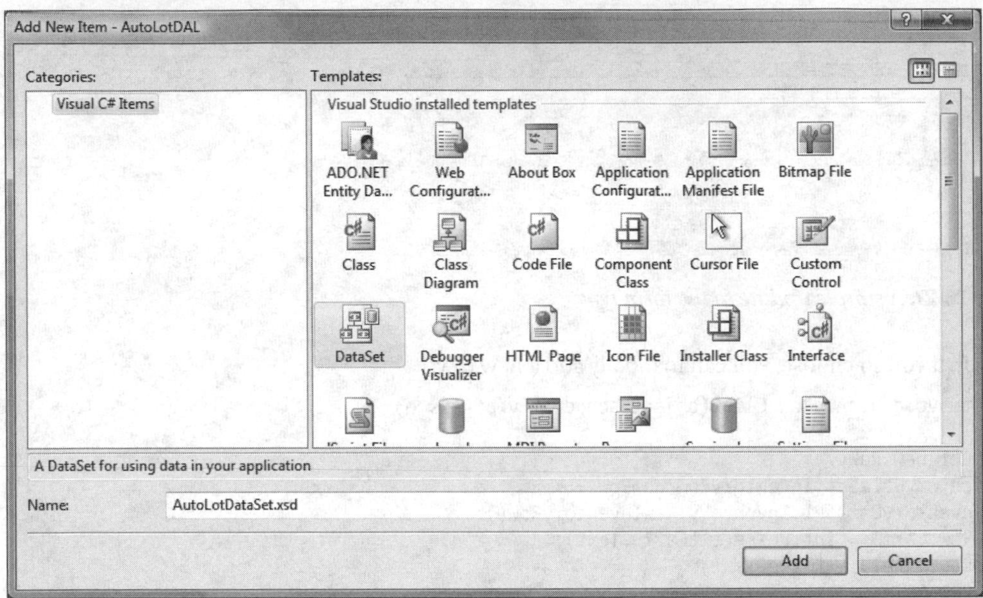

Figure 23-28. *Inserting a new* DataSet

This will open a blank Dataset Designer surface. At this point, use Server Explorer to connect to a given database (you should already have a connection to AutoLot), and drag and drop each database object (here, I did not bother to drag over the CreditRisk table) you wish to generate onto the surface. In Figure 23-29, you can see each of the custom aspects of AutoLot are now accounted for.

If you look at the generated code, you will find a new batch of strongly typed DataSets, DataTables, and DataRows, and a custom data adapter object for each table. Because the AutoLotDataSet type contains code to fill and update all of the tables of the AutoLot database, the amount of code autogenerated is more than an eye-popping 3,000 lines! However, much of this is grungy infrastructure you can remain blissfully unaware of. As you can see in Figure 23-30, the AutoLotDataSet type is constructed in a way that is very close to the previous InventoryDataSet type.

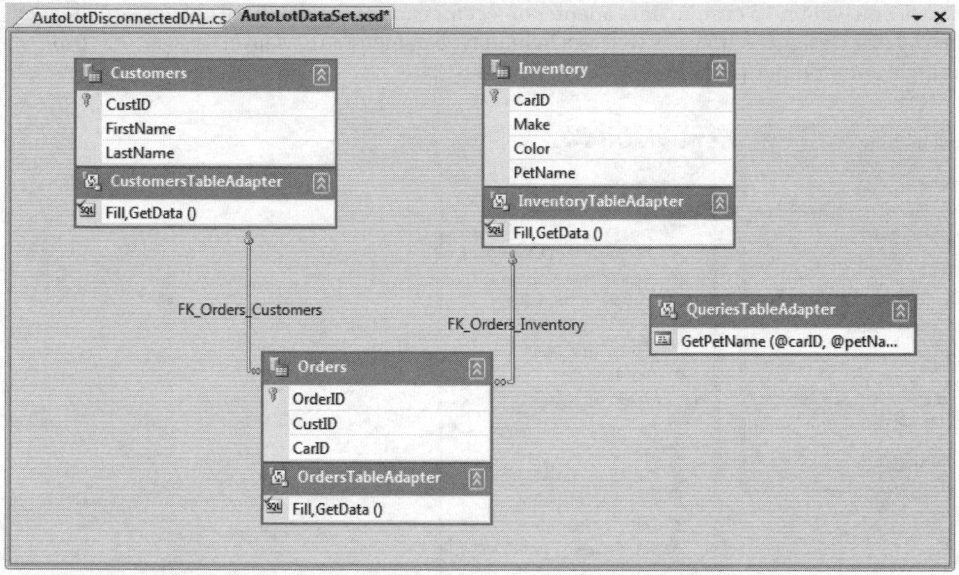

Figure 23-29. *Our custom strongly typed types, this time within a Class Library project*

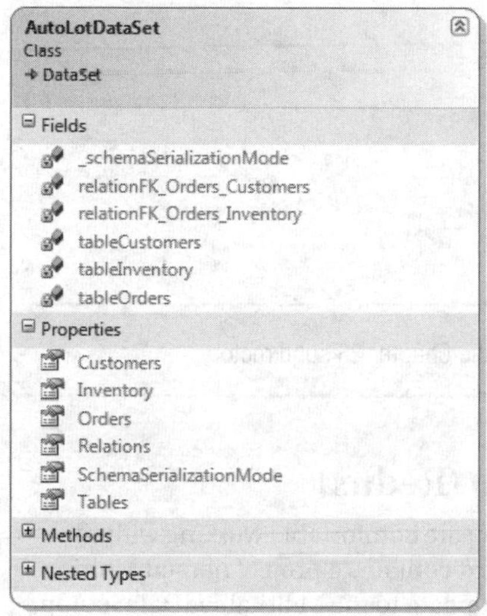

Figure 23-30. *The* `AutoLotDataSet`

As well, you will find a custom data adapter object for each of the database objects you dragged onto the Dataset Designer surface as well as a helpful type named `TableAdapterManager` that provides a single entry point to each object (see Figure 23-31).

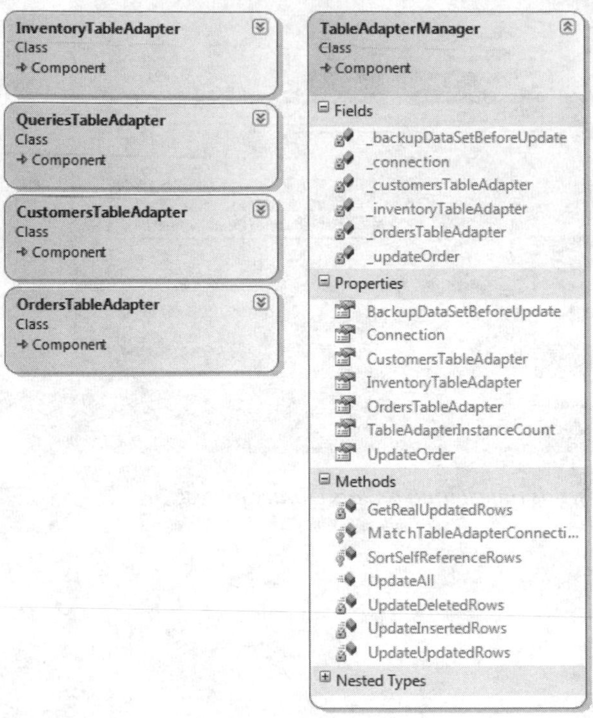

Figure 23-31. *The autogenerated data adapter objects*

Source Code The AutoLotDAL (Part 3) project is included under the Chapter 23 subdirectory.

A UI Front End: MultitabledDataSetApp (Redux)

Using these autogenerated types is quite simple, provided you are comfortable working with the disconnected layer. The downloadable source code for this text contains a project named MultitabledDataSetApp-Redux, which, as the name implies, is an update to the MultitabledDataSetApp project you created earlier in this chapter.

Recall that the original example made use of a loosely typed `DataSet` and a batch of `SqlDataAdapter` types to move the table data to and fro. This updated version makes use of the third iteration of `AutoLotDAL.dll` and the wizard-generated types. While I won't bother to list all of the code here (as it is more or less the same as the first iteration of this project), here are the highlights:

- You no longer need to manually author an `App.config` file or use the `ConfigurationManager` to obtain the connection string, as this is handled via the `Settings` object.
- You are now making use of the strongly typed classes within the `AutoLotDAL` and `AutoLotDAL.AutoLotDataSetTableAdapters` namespaces.

- You are no longer required to manually create or configure the relationships between your tables, as the Dataset Designer has done so automatically.

Regarding the last bullet point, be aware that the names the Dataset Designer gave the table relationships are *different* from the names we gave to them in the first iteration of this project. Therefore, the `btnGetOrderInfo_Click()` method must be updated to use the correct relationship names (which can be seen on the designer surface of the Dataset Designer), for example:

```
private void btnGetOrderInfo_Click(object sender, System.EventArgs e)
{
...
  // Need to update relationship name!
  drsOrder = drsCust[0].GetChildRows(autoLotDS.Relations["FK_Orders_Customers"]);
...
  // Need to update relationship name!
  DataRow[] drsInv =
       drsOrder[0].GetParentRows(autoLotDS.Relations["FK_Orders_Inventory"]);
...
}
```

Source Code The MultitabledDataSetApp-Redux project is included under the Chapter 23 subdirectory.

Summary

This chapter dove into the details of the disconnected layer of ADO.NET. As you have seen, the centerpiece of the disconnected layer is the `DataSet`. This type is an in-memory representation of any number of tables and any number of optional interrelationships, constraints, and expressions. The beauty of establishing relations on your local tables is that you are able to programmatically navigate between them while disconnected from the remote data store.

You also examined the role of the data adapter type in this chapter. Using this type (and the related `SelectCommand`, `InsertCommand`, `UpdateCommand`, and `DeleteCommand` properties), the adapter can resolve changes in the `DataSet` with the original data store. As well, you learned how to navigate the object model of a `DataSet` using the brute-force manual approach, as well as via strongly typed objects, typically generated by the Dataset Designer tools of Visual Studio 2008.

CHAPTER 24

■ ■ ■

Programming with the LINQ APIs

Now that you have spent the previous two chapters examining the ADO.NET programming model, we are in a position to return to the topic of Language Integrated Query (LINQ). Here, you will begin by examining the role of *LINQ to ADO.NET*. This particular term is used to describe two related facets of the LINQ programming model, specifically LINQ to DataSet and LINQ to SQL. As you would expect, these APIs allow you to apply LINQ queries to relational databases and ADO.NET `DataSet` objects.

The remainder of this chapter will examine the role of LINQ to XML. This aspect of LINQ not only allows you to extract data from an XML document using the expected set of query operators, but also enables you to load, save, and generate XML documents in an extremely straightforward manner (much more so than working with the types packaged in the `System.Xml.dll` assembly).

Note This chapter assumes you are already comfortable with the LINQ programming model as described in Chapter 14.

The Role of LINQ to ADO.NET

As explained in Chapter 14, LINQ is a programming model that allows programmers to build strongly typed query expressions that can be applied to a wide variety of data stores (arrays, collections, databases, XML documents). While it is true that you always use the same query operators regardless of the target of your LINQ query, the LINQ to ADO.NET API provides some additional types and infrastructure to enable LINQ/database integration.

As mentioned, LINQ to ADO.NET is a blanket term that describes two database-centric aspects of LINQ. First we have LINQ to DataSet. This API is essentially a set of extensions to the standard ADO.NET DataSet programming model that allows `DataSets`, `DataTables`, and `DataRows` to be a natural target for a LINQ query expression. Beyond using the types of `System.Core.dll`, LINQ to DataSet requires your projects to make use of auxiliary types within the `System.Data.DataSetExtensions.dll` assembly.

The second component of LINQ to ADO.NET is LINQ to SQL. This API allows you to interact with a relational database by abstracting away the underlying ADO.NET data types (connections, commands, data adapters, etc.) through the use of *entity classes*. Through these entity classes, you are able to represent relational data using an intuitive object model and manipulate the data using LINQ queries. The LINQ to SQL functionality is contained within the `System.Data.Linq.dll` assembly.

■Note As of .NET 3.5, LINQ to SQL does not support a data provider factory model (see Chapter 22). Therefore, when using this API, your data must be contained within Microsoft SQL Server. The LINQ to DataSet API, however, is agnostic in nature, as the `DataSet` being manipulated can come from any relational database.

Programming with LINQ to DataSet

Recall from the previous chapter that the `DataSet` type is the centerpiece of the disconnected layer and is used to represent a cached copy of interrelated `DataTable` objects and (optionally) the relationships between them. On a related note, you may also recall that the data within a `DataSet` can be manipulated in three distinct manners:

- Indexers
- Data table readers
- Strongly typed data members

When you make use of the various indexers of the `DataSet` and `DataTable` type, you are able to interact with the contained data in a fairly straightforward but very loosely typed manner. Recall that this approach requires you to treat the data as a tabular block of cells. For example:

```
static void PrintDataWithIndxers(DataTable dt)
{
  // Print the DataTable.
  for (int curRow = 0; curRow < dt.Rows.Count; curRow++)
  {
    for (int curCol = 0; curCol < dt.Columns.Count; curCol++)
    {
      Console.Write(dt.Rows[curRow][curCol].ToString() + "\t");
    }
    Console.WriteLine();
  }
}
```

The `CreateDataReader()` method of the `DataTable` type offers a second approach, where we are able to treat the data in the `DataSet` as a linear set of rows to be processed in a sequential manner:

```
static void PrintDataWithDataTableReader(DataTable dt)
{
  // Get the DataTableReader type.
  DataTableReader dtReader = dt.CreateDataReader();
  while (dtReader.Read())
  {
    for (int i = 0; i < dtReader.FieldCount; i++)
    {
      Console.Write("{0}\t", dtReader.GetValue(i));
    }
    Console.WriteLine();
  }
  dtReader.Close();
}
```

Finally, using a strongly typed `DataSet` yields a code base that allows you to interact with data in the object using properties that map to the actual column names in the relational database.

Recall from Chapter 23 that we used strongly typed objects to allow us to author code such as the following:

```
static void AddRowWithTypedDataSet()
{
  InventoryTableAdapter invDA = new InventoryTableAdapter();
  AutoLotDataSet.InventoryDataTable inv = invDA.GetData();
  inv.AddInventoryRow(999, "Ford", "Yellow", "Sal");
  invDA.Update(inv);
}
```

While all of these approaches have their place, LINQ to DataSet provides yet another option to manipulate the contained data using LINQ query expressions. Out of the box, the ADO.NET `DataSet` (and related types such as `DataTable` and `DataView`) do not have the necessary infrastructure to be a direct target for a LINQ query. For example, the following method would result in a compile-time error:

```
static void LinqOverDataTable()
{
  // Get a DataTable of data.
  InventoryDALDisLayer dal = new InventoryDALDisLayer(
    @"Data Source=(local)\SQLEXPRESS;" +
     "Initial Catalog=AutoLot;Integrated Security=True");
  DataTable data = dal.GetAllInventory();

  // Get cars with CarID > 5?
  var moreData = from c in data where (int)c["CarID"] > 5 select c;
}
```

If you were to compile the `LinqOverDataTable()` method, the compiler would inform you that the `DataTable` type does provide a "query pattern implementation." Similar to the process of applying LINQ queries to objects that do not implement `IEnumerable<T>` (such as the `ArrayList`), ADO.NET objects must be transformed into a compatible type. To understand how to do so requires examining the types of `System.Data.DataSetExtensions.dll`.

The Role of the DataSet Extensions

The `System.Data.DataSetExtensions.dll` assembly extends the `System.Data` namespace with a handful of new members (see Figure 24-1).

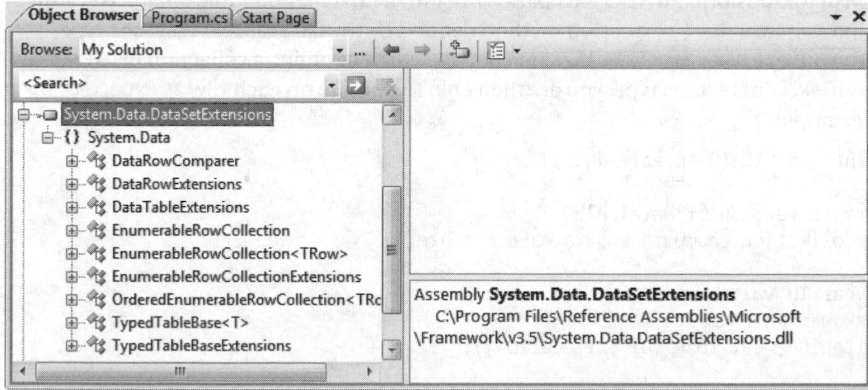

Figure 24-1. *The* `System.Data.DataSetExtensions.dll` *assembly*

Far and away the two most useful members are `DataTableExtensions` and `DataRowExtensions`. As their names imply, these types extend the functionality of `DataTable` and `DataRow` using a set of extension methods. The other key type is `TypedTableBaseExtensions`, which defines extension methods that can be applied to strongly typed `DataSet` objects to make the internal `DataTable` objects LINQ aware. All of the remaining members within the `System.Data.DataSetExtensions.dll` assembly are pure infrastructure and not intended to be used directly in your code base.

Obtaining a LINQ-Compatible DataTable

To illustrate using the DataSet extensions, assume you have a new C# Console Application named LinqOverDataSet. Be aware that when you create projects that target .NET 3.5, you will automatically be given a reference to `System.Core.dll` and `System.Data.DataSetExtensions.dll`; however, for this example, add an additional assembly reference to the `AutoLotDAL.dll` assembly you created in Chapter 23, and update your initial code file with the following logic:

```
using System.Data;
using AutoLotDisconnectedLayer;

namespace LinqOverDataSet
{
  class Program
  {
    static void Main(string[] args)
    {
      Console.WriteLine("***** LINQ over DataSet *****\n");
      // Get a DataTable containing the current Inventory
      // of the AutoLot database.
      InventoryDALDisLayer dal = new InventoryDALDisLayer(
        @"Data Source=(local)\SQLEXPRESS;Initial Catalog=AutoLot;" +
         "Integrated Security=True");
      DataTable data = dal.GetAllInventory();

      // Invoke the methods that follow here!

      Console.ReadLine();
    }
  }
}
```

When you wish to transform an ADO.NET `DataTable` into a LINQ-compatible object, you simply need to call the `AsEnumerable()` extension method defined by the `DataTableExtensions` type. This will return to you an `EnumerableRowCollection` object, which contains a collection of `DataRows`. Using the `EnumerableRowCollection` type, you are then able to operate on each row as expected. By way of a simple example:

```
static void PrintAllCarIDs(DataTable data)
{
  // Get enumerable version of DataTable.
  EnumerableRowCollection enumData = data.AsEnumerable();

  // Print the car ID values.
  foreach (DataRow r in enumData)
    Console.WriteLine("Car ID = {0}", r["CarID"]);
}
```

Because `EnumerableRowCollection` implements `IEnumerable<T>`, it would also be permissible to capture the return value using either of these code statements:

```
// Store return value as IEnumerable<T>.
IEnumerable<DataRow> enumData = data.AsEnumerable();

// Store return value implicitly.
var enumData = data.AsEnumerable();
```

At this point, we have not actually applied a LINQ query; however, the point is that the enumData object is now able to be the target of a LINQ query expression. Do notice that the EnumerableRowCollection does indeed contain a collection of DataRow objects, as we are applying a type indexer against each subobject to print out the value of the CarID column.

In most cases, you will not need to declare a variable of type EnumerableRowCollection to hold the return value of AsEnumerable(). Rather, you can invoke this method from within the query expression itself. Here is a more interesting method, which obtains a projection of CarID/Makes from all entries in the DataTable where the CarID is greater than the value of 5:

```
static void ApplyLinqQuery(DataTable data)
{
  // Project a new result set containing
  // the ID/color for rows with a CarID > 5
  var cars = from car in data.AsEnumerable()
             where
               (int)car["CarID"] > 5
             select new
             {
               ID = (int)car["CarID"],
               Color = (string)car["Color"]
             };

  Console.WriteLine("Cars with ID greater than 5:");
  foreach (var item in cars)
  {
    Console.WriteLine("-> CarID = {0} is {1}", item.ID, item.Color);
  }
}
```

The Role of the DataRowExtensions.Field<T>() Extension Method

One undesirable aspect of the current LINQ query expression is that we are making use of numerous casting operations and DataRow indexers to gather the result set, which could result in runtime exceptions if we attempt to cast to an incompatible data type. To inject some strong typing into our query, we can make use of the Field<T>() extension method of the DataRow type. By doing so, we increase the type safety of our query, as the compatibility of data types is checked at compile time. Consider the following update:

```
var cars = from car in data.AsEnumerable()
  where
    car.Field<int>("CarID") > 5
  select new
  {
    ID = car.Field<int>("CarID"),
    Color = car.Field<string>("Color")
  };
```

Notice in this case we are able to invoke Field<T>() and specify a type parameter to represent the underlying data type of the column. As an argument to this method, we pass in the column name itself. Given the additional compile-time checking, consider it a best practice to make use of `Field<T>()` when processing the roles of a `EnumerableRowCollection`, rather than the `DataRow` indexer.

Beyond the fact that we call the `AsEnumerable()` method, the overall format of the LINQ query is identical to what you have already seen in Chapter 14. Given this point, I won't bother to repeat the details of the various LINQ operators here. If you wish to see additional examples, look up the topic "LINQ to DataSet Examples" using the .NET Framework 3.5 SDK documentation.

Hydrating New DataTables from LINQ Queries

It is also possible to easily populate the data of a new `DataTable` based on the results of a LINQ query, provided that you are *not* using projections. When you have a result set where the underlying type can be represented as `IEnumerable<T>`, you can call the `CopyToDataTable<T>()` extension method on the result. For example:

```
static void BuildDataTableFromQuery(DataTable data)
{
  var cars = from car in data.AsEnumerable()
             where
               car.Field<int>("CarID") > 5
             select car;

  // Use this result set to build a new DataTable.
  DataTable newTable = cars.CopyToDataTable();

  // Print the DataTable.
  for (int curRow = 0; curRow < newTable.Rows.Count; curRow++)
  {
    for (int curCol = 0; curCol < newTable.Columns.Count; curCol++)
    {
      Console.Write(newTable.Rows[curRow][curCol].ToString().Trim() + "\t");
    }
    Console.WriteLine();
  }
}
```

■ **Note** It is also possible to transform a LINQ query to a `DataView` type, via the `AsDataView<T>()` extension method.

This approach can be very helpful when you wish to use the result of a LINQ query as the source of a data binding operation. For example, the `DataGridView` of Windows Forms (as well as the `GridView` of ASP.NET) each support a property named `DataSource`. You could bind a LINQ result to the grid as follows:

```
// Assume myDataGrid is a GUI-based grid object.
myDataGrid.DataSource = (from car in data.AsEnumerable()
             where
               car.Field<int>("CarID") > 5
             select car).CopyToDataTable();
```

Now that you have seen the role of LINQ to DataSet, let's turn our attention to LINQ to SQL.

■ **Source Code** The LinqOverDataSet example can be found under the Chapter 24 subdirectory.

Programming with LINQ to SQL

LINQ to SQL is an API that allows you to apply well-formed LINQ query expressions to data held within relational databases. LINQ to SQL provides a number of types (within the `System.Data.Linq.dll` assembly) that facilitate the communication between your code base and the physical database engine.

The major goal of LINQ to SQL is to provide consistency between relational databases and the programming logic used to interact with them. For example, rather than representing database queries using a big clunky string, we can use strongly typed LINQ queries. As well, rather than having to treat relational data as a stream of records, we are able to interact with the data using standard object-oriented programming techniques. Given the fact that LINQ to SQL allows us to integrate data access directly within our C# code base, the need to manually build dozens of custom classes and data access libraries that hide ADO.NET grunge from view is greatly minimized.

When programming with LINQ to SQL, you see no trace of common ADO.NET types such as `SqlConnection`, `SqlCommand`, or `SqlDataAdapter`. Using LINQ query expressions, entity classes (defined shortly) and the `DataContext` type, you are able to perform all the expected database CRUD (create, remove, update, and delete), as well as define transactional contexts, create new database entities (or entire databases), invoke stored procedures, and perform other database-centric activities.

Furthermore, the LINQ to SQL types (again, such as `DataContext`) have been developed to integrate with standard ADO.NET data types. For example, one of the overloaded constructors of `DataContext` takes as an input an `IDbConnection`-comparable object, which as you may recall is a common interface supported by all ADO.NET connection objects. In this way, existing ADO.NET data access libraries can integrate with C# 2008 LINQ query expressions (and vice versa). In reality, as far as Microsoft is concerned, LINQ to SQL is simply a new member of the ADO.NET family.

The Role of Entity Classes

When you wish to make use of LINQ to SQL within your applications, the first step is to define *entity classes*. In a nutshell, entity classes are types that represent the relational data you wish to interact with. Programmatically speaking, entity classes are class definitions that are annotated with various LINQ to SQL attributes (such as `[Table]` and `[Column]`) that map to a physical table in a specific database. A majority of the LINQ to SQL attributes are defined with the `System.Data.Linq.Mapping` namespace (see Figure 24-2).

As you will see in just a bit, the .NET Framework 3.5 SDK (as well as Visual Studio 2008) ships with tools that automate the construction of the entity types required by your application. Until that point, our first LINQ to SQL example will illustrate how to build entity classes by hand.

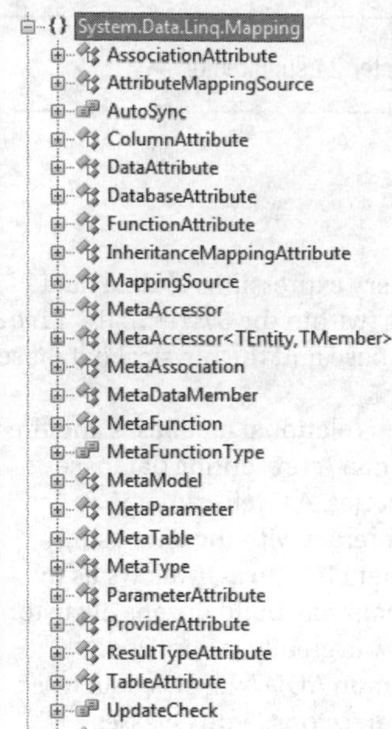

Figure 24-2. *The* `System.Data.Linq.Mapping` *namespace defines numerous LINQ to SQL attributes.*

The Role of the DataContext Type

Once you have defined your entity classes, you are then able to pass your query expressions to the relational database using a `DataContext` type. This LINQ to SQL–specific class type is in charge of translating your LINQ query expressions into proper SQL queries as well as communicating with the specified database. In some ways, the `DataContext` looks and feels like an ADO.NET connection object, in that it requires a connection string. However, unlike a typically connection object, the `DataContext` type has numerous members that will map the results of your query expressions back into the entity classes you define.

Furthermore, the `DataContext` type defines a factory pattern to obtain instances of the entity classes used within your code base. Once you obtain an entity instance, you are free to change its state in any way you desire (adding records, updating records, etc.) and submit the modified object back for processing. In this way, the `DataContext` is similar to an ADO.NET data adapter type.

A Simple LINQ to SQL Example

Before we dive into too many details, let's see a simple example of using LINQ to SQL to interact with the Inventory table of the AutoLot database created in Chapter 22. In this example, we will not be making use of our `AutoLotDAL.dll` library, but will instead author all the code by hand. Create a new Console Application named SimpleLinqToSqlApp and reference the `System.Data.Linq.dll` assembly.

Next, insert a new C# class file named `Inventory.cs`. This file will define our entity class, which requires decorating the type with various LINQ-centric attributes; therefore, be sure to specify you are using the `System.Data.Linq.Mapping` and `System.Data.Linq` namespaces. With this detail out of the way, here is the definition of the `Inventory` type:

```
[Table]
public class Inventory
{
```

```
  [Column]
  public string Make;
  [Column]
  public string Color;
  [Column]
  public string PetName;

  // Identify the primary key.
  [Column(IsPrimaryKey = true)]
  public int CarID;

  public override string ToString()
  {
    return string.Format("ID = {0}; Make = {1}; Color = {2}; PetName = {3}",
      CarID, Make.Trim(), Color.Trim(), PetName.Trim());
  }
}
```

First of all notice that our entity class has been adorned with the [Table] attribute, while each public field has been marked with [Column]. In both cases, the names are a direct mapping to the physical database table. However, this is not a strict requirement, as the TableAttribute and ColumnAttribute types both support a Name property that allows you to decouple your programmatic representation of the data table from the physical table itself. Also notice that the CarID field has been further qualified by setting the IsPrimaryKey property of the ColumnAttribute type using named property syntax.

Here, for simplicity, each field has been declared publicly. If you require stronger encapsulation, you could most certainly define private fields wrapped by public properties (or automatic properties if you so choose). If you do so, it will be the *property*, not the fields, that will be marked with the [Column] attribute.

It is also worth pointing out that an entity class can contain any number of members that do not map to the data table it represents. As far as the LINQ runtime is concerned, only items marked with LINQ to SQL attributes will be used during the data exchange. For example, this Inventory class definition provides a custom implementation of ToString() to allow the application to quickly display its state.

Now that we have an entity class, we can make use of the DataContext type to submit (and translate) our LINQ query expressions to the specified database. Ponder the following Main() method, which will display the result of all items in the Inventory table maintained by the AutoLot database:

```
class Program
{
  const string cnStr =
    @"Data Source=(local)\SQLEXPRESS;Initial Catalog=AutoLot;" +
     "Integrated Security=True";

  static void Main(string[] args)
  {
    Console.WriteLine("***** LINQ to SQL Sample App *****\n");

    // Create a DataContext object.
    DataContext db = new DataContext(cnStr);

    // Now create a Table<> type.
    Table<Inventory> invTable = db.GetTable<Inventory>();
```

```
    // Show all data using a LINQ query.
    Console.WriteLine("-> Contents of Inventory Table from AutoLot database:\n");
    foreach (var car in from c in invTable select c)
      Console.WriteLine(car.ToString());
    Console.ReadLine();
  }
}
```

Notice that when you create a DataContext type, you will feed in a proper connection string, which is represented here as a simple string constant. Of course, you are free to store this in an application configuration file and/or make use of the SqlConnectionStringBuilder type to treat this string type in a more object-oriented manner.

Next up, we obtain an instance of our Inventory entity class by calling the generic GetTable<T>() method of the DataContext type, specifying the entity class as the type parameter when doing so. Finally, we build a LINQ query expression and apply it to the invTable object. As you would expect, the end result is a display of each item in the Inventory table.

Building a Strongly Typed DataContext

While our first example is strongly typed as far as the database query is concerned, we do have a bit of a disconnect between the DataContext and the Inventory entity class it is maintaining. To remedy this situation, it is typically preferable to create a class that extends the DataContext type that defines member variables for each table it operates upon. Insert a new class called AutoLotDatabase, specify you are using the System.Core and System.Data.Linq namespaces, and implement the type as follows:

```
class AutoLotDatabase : DataContext
{
  public Table<Inventory> Inventory;

  public AutoLotDatabase(string connectionString)
    : base(connectionString){}
}
```

With this new class type, we are now able to simplify the code within Main() quite a bit:

```
static void Main(string[] args)
{
  Console.WriteLine("***** LINQ to SQL Sample App *****\n");

  // Create an AutoLotDatabase object.
  AutoLotDatabase db = new AutoLotDatabase(cnStr);

  // Note we can now use the Inventory field of AutoLotDatabase.
  Console.WriteLine("-> Contents of Inventory Table from AutoLot database:\n");
  foreach (var car in from c in db.Inventory select c)
    Console.WriteLine(car.ToString());
  Console.ReadLine();
}
```

One aspect of building a strongly typed data context that may surprise you is that the DataContext-derived type (AutoLotDatabase in this example) does not directly create the Table<T> member variables and has no trace of the expected GetTable() method call. At runtime, however, when you iterate over your LINQ result set, the DataContext will create the Table<T> type transparently in the background.

Of course, any LINQ query can be used to obtain a given result set. Assume we have authored the following helper method that is called from `Main()` before exiting (note this method expects us to pass in an `AutoLotDatabase` instance):

```
static void ShowOnlyBimmers(AutoLotDatabase db)
{
  Console.WriteLine("***** Only BMWs *****\n");

  // Get the BMWs.
  var bimmers = from s in db.Inventory
    where s.Make == "BMW"
    orderby s.CarID
    select s;

  foreach (var c in bimmers)
    Console.WriteLine(c.ToString());
}
```

Figure 24-3 shows the output of this first LINQ to SQL example.

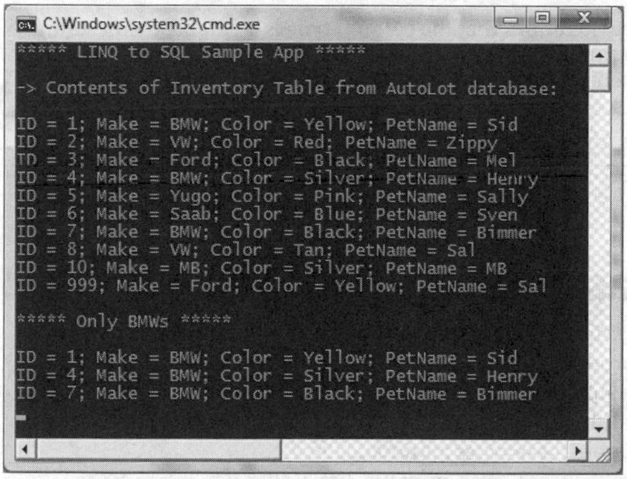

```
C:\Windows\system32\cmd.exe
***** LINQ to SQL Sample App *****

-> Contents of Inventory Table from AutoLot database:

ID = 1; Make = BMW; Color = Yellow; PetName = Sid
ID = 2; Make = VW; Color = Red; PetName = Zippy
ID = 3; Make = Ford; Color = Black; PetName = Mel
ID = 4; Make = BMW; Color = Silver; PetName = Henry
ID = 5; Make = Yugo; Color = Pink; PetName = Sally
ID = 6; Make = Saab; Color = Blue; PetName = Sven
ID = 7; Make = BMW; Color = Black; PetName = Bimmer
ID = 8; Make = VW; Color = Tan; PetName = Sal
ID = 10; Make = MB; Color = Silver; PetName = MB
ID = 999; Make = Ford; Color = Yellow; PetName = Sal

***** Only BMWs *****

ID = 1; Make = BMW; Color = Yellow; PetName = Sid
ID = 4; Make = BMW; Color = Silver; PetName = Henry
ID = 7; Make = BMW; Color = Black; PetName = Bimmer
```

Figure 24-3. *A first look at LINQ to SQL*

Source Code The SimpleLinqToSqlApp example can be found under the Chapter 24 subdirectory.

The [Table] and [Column] Attributes: Further Details

As you have seen, entity classes are adorned with various attributes that are used by LINQ to SQL to translate queries for your objects into SQL queries against the database. At absolute minimum, you will make use of the `[Table]` and `[Column]` attributes; however, additional attributes exist to mark the methods that perform SQL insert, update, and delete commands. As well, each of the LINQ to SQL attributes defines a set of properties that further qualify to the LINQ to SQL runtime engine how to process the annotated item.

The `[Table]` attribute is very simple, given that it only defines a single property of interest: `Name`. As mentioned, this allows you to decouple the name of the entity class from the physical table.

If you do not set the Name property at the time you apply the [Table] attribute, LINQ to SQL assumes the entity class and database table names are one and the same.

The [Column] attribute provides a bit more meat than [Table]. Beyond the IsPrimaryKey property, ColumnAttribute defines additional members that allow you to fully qualify the details of each field in the entity class and how it maps to a particular column in the physical database table. Table 24-1 documents the additional properties of interest.

Table 24-1. *Select Properties of the* [Column] *Attribute*

ColumnAttribute Property	Meaning in Life
CanBeNull	This property indicates that the column can contain null values.
DbType	LINQ to SQL will automatically infer the data types to pass to the database engine based on declaration of your field data. Given this, it is typically only necessary to set DbType directly if you are dynamically creating databases using the CreateDatabase() method of the DataContext type.
IsDbGenerated	This property establishes that a field's value is autogenerated by the database.
IsVersion	This property identifies that the column type is a database timestamp or a version number. Version numbers are incremented and timestamp columns are updated every time the associated row is updated.
UpdateCheck	This property controls how LINQ to SQL should handle database conflicts via optimistic concurrency.

Generating Entity Classes Using SqlMetal.exe

Our first LINQ to SQL example was fairly simplistic, partially due to the fact that our DataContext was operating on a single data table. A production-level LINQ to SQL application may instead be operating on multiple interrelated data tables, each of which could define dozens of columns. In these cases, it would be very tedious to author each and every required entity class by hand. Thankfully, we do have two approaches to generate these types automatically.

The first option is to make use of the sqlmetal.exe command-line utility, which can be executed using a Visual Studio 2008 command prompt. This tool automates the creation of entity classes by generating an appropriate C# class type from the database metadata. While this tool has numerous command-line options, Table 24-2 documents the major flags of interest.

Table 24-2. *Options of the* sqlmetal.exe *Command*

sqlmetal.exe Command-Line Option	Meaning in Life
/server	Specifies the server hosting the database
/database	Specifies the name of the database to read metadata from
/user	Specifies user ID to log in to the server
/password	Specifies password to log in to the server
/views	Informs sqlmetal.exe to generate code based on existing database views
/functions	Informs sqlmetal.exe to extract database functions
/sprocs	Informs sqlmetal.exe to extract stored procedures

sqlmetal.exe Command-Line Option	Meaning in Life
/code	Informs sqlmetal.exe to output results as C# code (or as VB, if you set the /language flag)
/language	Specifies the language used to defined the generated types
/namespace	Specifies the namespace to define the generated types

By way of an example, the following command set will generate entity classes for each table within the AutoLot database, expose the GetPetName stored procedure, and wrap all generated C# code within a namespace named AutoLotDatabase (of course, this would be entered on a single line within a Visual Studio 2008 command prompt):

```
sqlmetal /server:(local)\SQLEXPRESS /database:AutoLot /namespace:AutoLotDatabase
      /code:autoLotDB.cs /sprocs
```

Once you have executed the command, create a new Console Application named LinqWithSqlMetalGenedCode, reference the System.Data.Linq.dll assembly, and include the autoLotDB.cs file into your project using the Project ➤ Add Existing Item menu option. As well, insert a new class diagram into your project (via Project ➤ Add New Item) and expand each of the generated classes (see Figure 24-4).

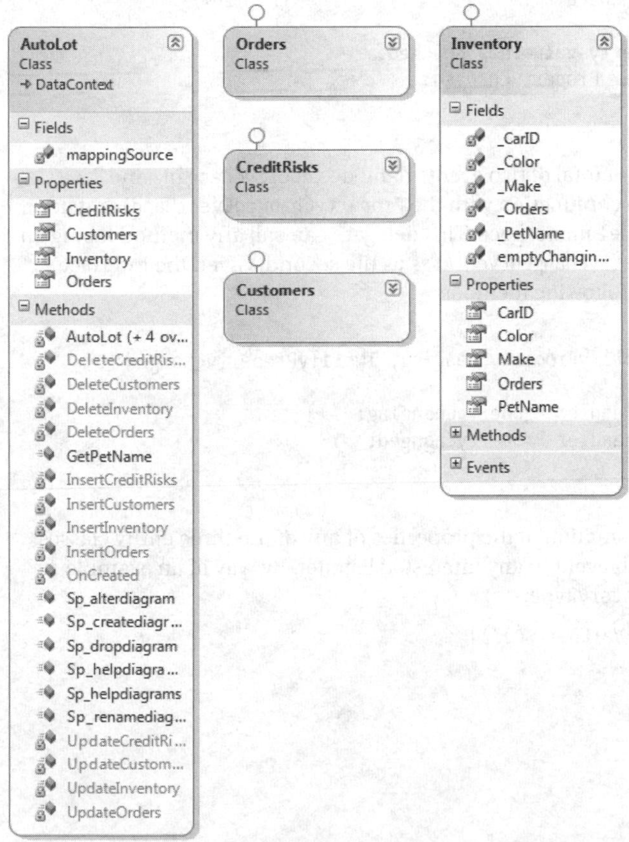

Figure 24-4. *The* sqlmetal.exe*-generated entity classes*

Notice that you have a new type extending DataContext that contains properties for each data table in the specified database (as well, notice that the GetPetName() stored procedure is represented by a public method of the same name). Before we program against these new types, let's examine this autogenerated code in a bit more detail.

Examining the Generated Entity Classes

As you can see, sqlmetal.exe defined a separate entity class for each table in the AutoLot database (Inventory, Customers, Orders, CreditRisks), with each column encapsulated by a type property. In addition, notice that each entity class implements two interfaces (INotifyPropertyChanging and INotifyPropertyChanged), each of which defines a single event:

```
namespace System.Data.Linq
{
  public interface INotifyPropertyChanging
  {
    // This event fires when a property is being changed.
    event PropertyChangedEventHandler PropertyChanging;
  }
}

namespace System.ComponentModel
{
  public interface INotifyPropertyChanged
  {
    // This event fires when a property value has changed.
    event PropertyChangedEventHandler PropertyChanged;
  }
}
```

Collectively, these interfaces define a total of two events named PropertyChanging and PropertyChanged, both of which work in conjunction with the PropertyChangedEventHandler delegate defined in the System.ComponentModel namespace. This delegate can call any method taking an object as the first parameter and a PropertyChangedEventArgs as the second. Given the interface contract, each entity class supports the following members:

```
[Table(Name="Inventory")]
public partial class Inventory : INotifyPropertyChanging, INotifyPropertyChanged
{
  public event PropertyChangedEventHandler PropertyChanging;
  public event PropertyChangedEventHandler PropertyChanged;
...
}
```

If you were to examine the implementation of the properties of any of the three entity classes, you will note that the set scope fires each event to any interested listener. By way of an example, here is the PetName property of the Inventory type:

```
[Column(Storage="_PetName", DbType="VarChar(50)")]
public string PetName
{
  get
  {
    return this._PetName;
  }
  set
  {
```

```
      if ((this._PetName != value))
      {
        this.OnPetNameChanging(value);
        this.SendPropertyChanging();
        this._PetName = value;
        this.SendPropertyChanged("PetName");
        this.OnPetNameChanged();
      }
    }
  }
```

Notice that the set scope invokes the OnPetNameChanging() and OnPetNameChanged() methods on the entity class type to actually fire the events themselves. However, these members are defined as *partial methods*, which you may recall from Chapter 13 perform a type of lightweight event handling, allowing interested callers to provide an implementation if they so choose (if not, they are removed from the type definition at compile time):

```
partial void OnPetNameChanging(string value);
partial void OnPetNameChanged();
```

Defining Relationships Using Entity Classes

Beyond simply defining properties with backing fields to represent data table columns, the sqlmetal.exe utility will also model the relationships between interrelated tables using the EntitySet<T> type. Recall from Chapter 22 that the AutoLot database defined three interrelated tables, connected by primary and foreign keys. Rather than forcing us to author SQL-centric join syntax to navigate between these tables, LINQ to SQL allows us to navigate using the object-centric C# dot operator.

To account for this sort of table relationship, the parent entity class may encode the child table as property references. This property is marked with the [Association] attribute to establish an *association relationship* made by matching column values between tables. For example, consider the (partial) generated code for the Customer type, which can have any number of orders:

```
[Table(Name="Customers")]
public partial class Customers :
  INotifyPropertyChanging, INotifyPropertyChanged
{
  private EntitySet<Orders> _Orders;

  [Association(Name="FK_Orders_Customers", Storage="_Orders",
   OtherKey="CustID", DeleteRule="NO ACTION")]
  public EntitySet<Orders> Orders
  {
      get { return this._Orders; }
      set { this._Orders.Assign(value); }
  }
...
}
```

Here, the Orders property is understood by the LINQ to SQL runtime engine as the member that allows navigation *from* the Customers table *to* the Orders table via the column defined by the OtherKey named property. The EntitySet<T> member variable is used to represent the one-to-many nature of this particular relationship.

The Strongly Typed DataContext

The final aspect of the sqlmetal.exe-generated code to be aware of is the DataContext-derived type. Like the AutoLotDatabase class we authored in the previous example, each table is represented by a Table<T>-compatible property. As well, this class has a series of constructors, one of which takes an object implementing IDbConnection, which represents an ADO.NET connection object (remember, LINQ to SQL and ADO.NET types can be intermixed within a single application).

As well, this DataContext-derived class is how we are able to interact with the stored procedures defined by the database. Given the fact that we supplied the /sprocs flag as part of our sqlmetal.exe command set, we find a method named GetPetName():

```
[Function(Name="dbo.GetPetName")]
[return: Parameter(DbType="Int")]
public int GetPetName([Parameter(DbType="Int")] System.Nullable<int> carID,
                      [Parameter(DbType="Char(10)")] ref string petName)
{
  IExecuteResult result = this.ExecuteMethodCall(this,
    ((MethodInfo)(MethodInfo.GetCurrentMethod())), carID, petName);
  petName = ((string)(result.GetParameterValue(1)));
  return ((int)(result.ReturnValue));
}
```

Notice that the GetPetName() method is marked with the [Function] attributes and [return:] attribute qualifier, while each parameter is marked with the [Parameter] attribute. The implementation makes use of the inherited ExecuteMethodCall() method (and a bit of reflection services) to take care of the details of invoking the stored proc and returning the result to the caller.

Programming Against the Generated Types

Now that you have a better idea regarding the code authored by sqlmetal.exe, consider the following implementation of the Program type, which invokes our stored procedure:

```
class Program
{
  const string cnStr =
    @"Data Source=(local)\SQLEXPRESS;Initial Catalog=AutoLot;" +
     "Integrated Security=True";

  static void Main(string[] args)
  {
    Console.WriteLine("***** More Fun with LINQ to SQL *****\n");
    AutoLot carsDB = new AutoLot(cnStr);
    InvokeStoredProc(carsDB);
    Console.ReadLine();
  }

  private static void InvokeStoredProc(AutoLot carsDB)
  {
    int carID = 0;
    string petName = "";
    Console.Write("Enter ID: ");
    carID = int.Parse(Console.ReadLine());

    // Invoke stored proc and print out the petname.
    carsDB.GetPetName(carID, ref petName);
```

```
      Console.WriteLine("Car ID {0} has the petname: {1}",
        carID, petName);
    }
  }
```

Notice that LINQ to SQL completely hides the underlying stored procedure logic from view. Here, we have no need to manually create a SqlCommand object, fill the parameters collection, or call ExecuteNonQuery(). Instead, we simply invoke the GetPetName() method of our DataContext-derived type. Do note, however, that output parameters are represented as reference parameters, and therefore must be called using the C# ref keyword.

Now assume we have a second helper function (also called from within Main()) named PrintOrderForCustomer(). This method will print out some order details for the specified customer as well as the first and last name of the customer:

```
static void PrintOrderForCustomer(AutoLot carsDB)
{
  int custID = 0;
  Console.Write("Enter customer ID: ");
  custID = int.Parse(Console.ReadLine());

  var customerOrders =
    from cust in carsDB.Customers
    from o in cust.Orders
    where cust.CustID == custID
    select new { cust, o };

  Console.WriteLine("***** Order Info for Customer ID: {0}. *****", custID);
  foreach (var q in customerOrders)
  {
    Console.WriteLine("{0} {1} is order ID # {2}.",
      q.cust.FirstName.Trim(),
      q.cust.LastName.Trim(),
      q.o.OrderID);
    Console.WriteLine("{0} bought Car ID # {1}.",
      q.cust.FirstName.Trim(), q.o.CarID);
  }
}
```

Figure 24-5 shows the output when querying about the customer assigned the ID of 1.

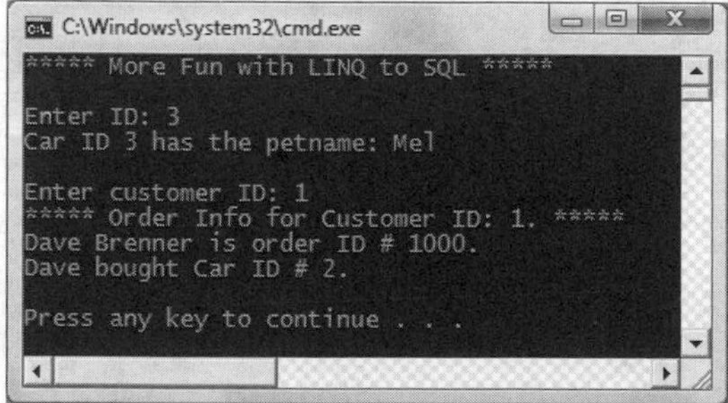

Figure 24-5. *Printing our order details for a specified customer*

Again, the benefit of LINQ to SQL is that we are able to interact with relational databases using a consistent, object-based model. Just to shed some more light on our LINQ query expression, add the following code statement at the end of your `PrintOrderForCustomer()` method:

```
Console.WriteLine("\ncustomerOrders as a string: {0}", customerOrders);
```

When you run your program once again, you may be surprised to find that the stringified value of your query expression reveals the underlying SQL query:

```
SELECT [t0].[FirstName], [t0].[LastName], [t0].[CustID],
       [t1].[OrderID], [t1].[CarID], [t1].[CustID] AS [CustID2]
FROM [Customers] AS [t0], [Orders] AS [t1]
WHERE ([t0].[CustID] = @p0) AND ([t1].[CustID] = [t0].[CustID])
```

■ **Source Code** The LinqWithSqlMetalGenedCode example can be found under the Chapter 24 subdirectory.

Building Entity Classes Using Visual Studio 2008

To wrap up our look at LINQ to SQL, create a new Console Application named LinqToSqlCrud and reference the `System.Data.Linq.dll` assembly. This time, rather than running `sqlmetal.exe` to generate our entity classes, we will allow Visual Studio 2008 to do the grunt work. To do so, select Project ➤ Add New Item, and add a new LINQ to SQL Classes item named AutoLotObjects (see Figure 24-6).

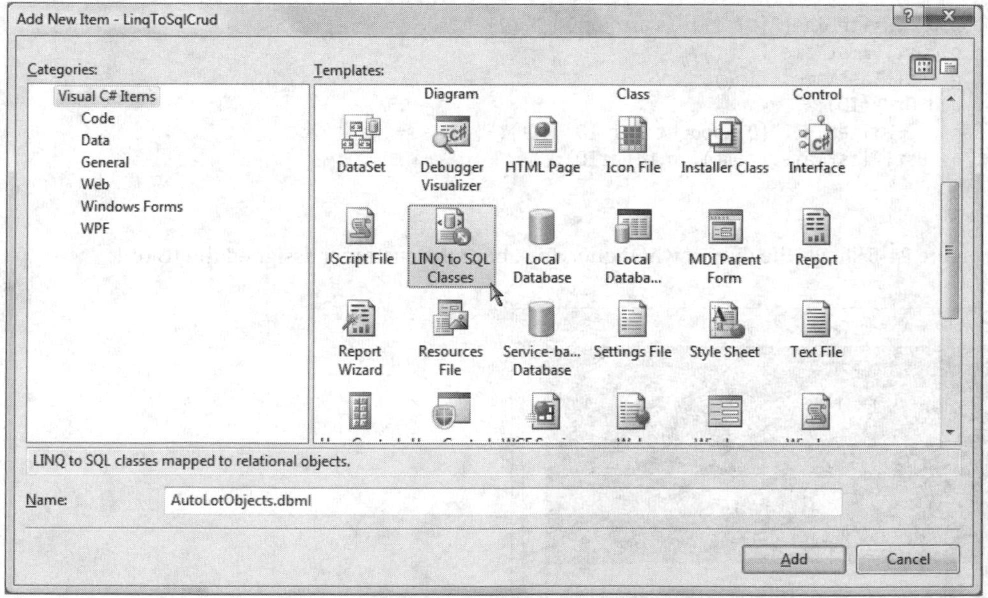

Figure 24-6. *The LINQ to SQL Classes item performs the same duties as* `sqlmetal.exe`.

Open the Server Explorer, and ensure you have an active connection to the AutoLot database (if not, right-click the Data Connections icon and select Add Connection). At this point, select each table and drag it onto the LINQ to SQL designer surface. Once you are done, your screen should resemble Figure 24-7.

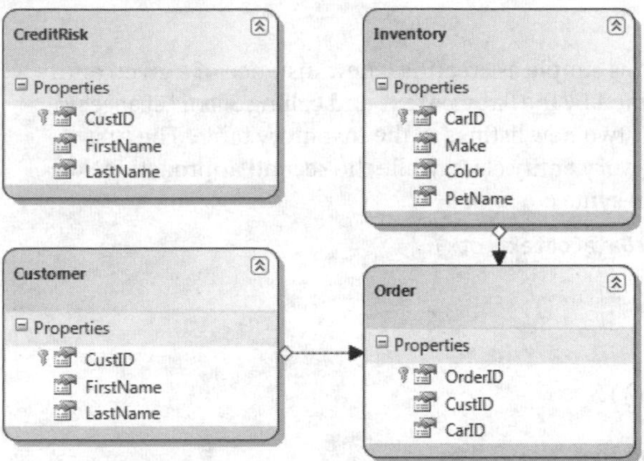

Figure 24-7. *Creating entity classes using the LINQ to SQL designer*

Once you perform your initial compile, go to the Solution Explorer and open the related `*.cs` file (see Figure 24-8). As you look over the generated C# code, you'll quickly notice it is the same overall code generated by the `sqlmetal.exe` command-line utility. Also note that the visual LINQ to SQL designer added an `app.config` file to your project to store the necessary connection string data.

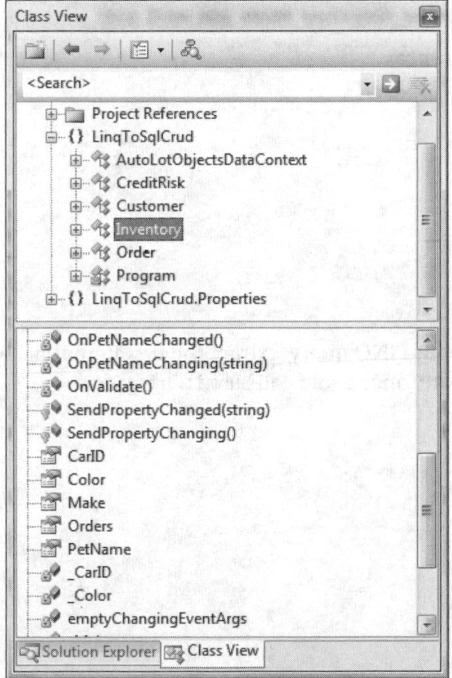

Figure 24-8. *The generated namespace with the contained types*

Now that all the generated types are accounted for, here is a Program class that illustrates inserting, updating, and deleting data on the Inventory table.

Inserting New Items

Adding new items to a relational database is as simple as creating a new instance of a given entity class, adding into the Table<T> type maintained by the DataContext and calling SubmitChanges(). The following InsertNewCars() method adds two new listings to the Inventory table. The first approach directly sets each field of the Inventory entity class, while the second approach makes use of the more compact object initialization syntax:

```
static void InsertNewCars(AutoLotObjectsDataContext ctx)
{
  Console.WriteLine("***** Adding 2 Cars *****");
  int newCarID = 0;
  Console.Write("Enter ID for Betty: ");
  newCarID = int.Parse(Console.ReadLine());

  // Add a new row using "longhand" notation.
  Inventory newCar = new Inventory();
  newCar.Make = "Yugo";
  newCar.Color = "Pink";
  newCar.PetName = "Betty";
  newCar.CarID = newCarID;
  ctx.Inventories.InsertOnSubmit(newCar);
  ctx.SubmitChanges();

  Console.Write("Enter ID for Henry: ");
  newCarID = int.Parse(Console.ReadLine());

  // Add another row using "shorthand" object init syntax.
  newCar = new Inventory { Make = "BMW", Color = "Silver",
    PetName = "Henry", CarID = newCarID };

  ctx.Inventories.InsertOnSubmit(newCar);
  ctx.SubmitChanges();
}
```

Updating Existing Items

Updating an item is also very straightforward. Based on your LINQ query, extract the first item that meets the search criteria. Once you update the object's state, once again call SubmitChanges().

```
static void UpdateCar(AutoLotObjectsDataContext ctx)
{
  Console.WriteLine("***** Updating color of 'Betty' *****");

  // Update Betty's color to light pink.
  var betty = (from c in ctx.Inventories
               where c.PetName == "Betty"
               select c).First();
  betty.Color = "Green";
  ctx.SubmitChanges();
}
```

Deleting Existing Items

And finally, if you wish to delete an item from the relational database table, simply build a LINQ query to locate the item you are no longer interested in, and remove it from the correct Table<T> member variable of the DataContext using the DeleteOnSubmit() method. Once you have done so, again call SubmitChanges():

```
static void DeleteCar(AutoLotObjectsDataContext ctx)
{
  int carToDelete = 0;
  Console.Write("Enter ID of car to delete: ");
  carToDelete = int.Parse(Console.ReadLine());

  // Remove specified car.
  ctx.Inventories.DeleteOnSubmit((from c in ctx.Inventories
                        where c.CarID == carToDelete
                        select c).First());
  ctx.SubmitChanges();
}
```

At this point you can call each method from within Main() to verify the output:

```
static void Main(string[] args)
{
  Console.WriteLine("***** CRUD with LINQ to SQL *****\n");
  const string cnStr =
    @"Data Source=(local)\SQLEXPRESS;Initial Catalog=AutoLot;" +
     "Integrated Security=True";

  AutoLotObjectsDataContext ctx = new AutoLotObjectsDataContext(cnStr);
  InsertNewCars(ctx);
  UpdateCar(ctx);
  DeleteCar(ctx);
  Console.ReadLine();
}
```

That wraps up our look at LINQ to SQL. Obviously, there is much more to the story than you have seen here; however, hopefully at this point you feel you are better equipped to dive into further details as you see fit.

■ Source Code The LinqToSqlCrud example can be found under the Chapter 24 subdirectory.

Manipulating XML Documents Using LINQ to XML

The final section of this chapter is to introduce you to the role of LINQ to XML, which as you recall allows you to apply LINQ query expressions against XML documents. Although this edition of this book does not provide a chapter solely dedicated to programming with .NET's XML APIs, by now you have probably picked up on the fact of how deeply XML data representation has been integrated into the .NET Framework.

Application and web-based configuration files store data as XML. ADO.NET DataSets can easily save out (or load in) data as XML. Windows Presentation Foundation makes use of an XML-based grammar (XAML) to represent desktop UIs and Windows Communication Foundation (as well as the original .NET remoting APIs) also store numerous settings as the well-formatted string we call XML.

Although XML is indeed everywhere, programming with XML has historically been very tedious, very verbose, and very complex if one is not well versed in a great number of XML technologies (XPath, XQuery, XSLT, DOM, SAX, etc.). Since the inception of the .NET platform, Microsoft has provided a specific assembly devoted to programming with XML documents named `System.Xml.dll`. Within this binary are a number of namespaces and types to various XML programming techniques, as well as a few .NET-specific XML APIs such as the `XmlReader`/`XmlWriter` models.

LINQ to XML As a Better DOM

Just as LINQ to SQL intends to integrate relational database manipulation directly within .NET programming languages, LINQ to XML aspires to the same goals for XML data processing. Not only can you use LINQ to XML as a vehicle to obtain subsets of data from an existing XML document via LINQ queries, this same API can be used to create, modify, and parse XML data. To this end, LINQ to XML can be thought of as a "better DOM" programming model. As well, just as LINQ to SQL can interoperate with ADO.NET types, LINQ to XML can also interoperate with many members of the `System.Xml.dll` assemblies.

The System.Xml.XLinq Namespace

Somewhat surprisingly, the core LINQ to XML assembly (`System.Xml.Linq.dll`) defines a very small number of types in three distinct namespaces, specifically `System.Xml.Linq`, `System.Xml.Schema`, and `System.Xml.XPath` (see Figure 24-9).

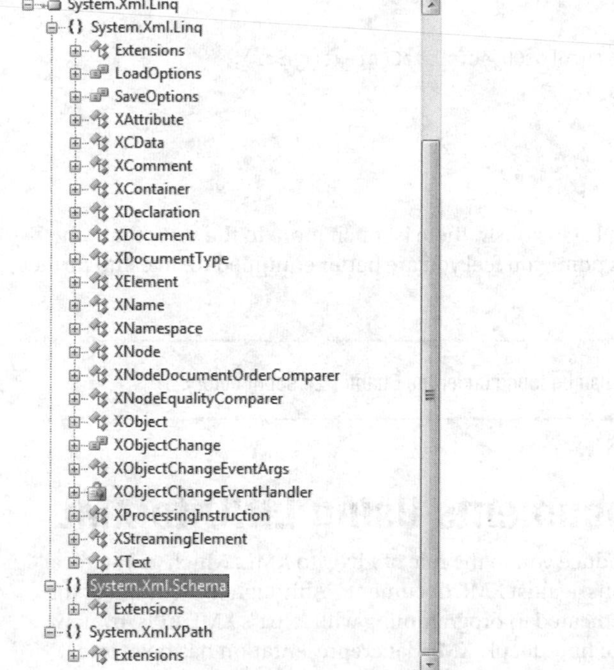

Figure 24-9. *The namespaces of* `System.Xml.Linq.dll`

The core namespace, System.Xml.Linq, contains a very manageable set of types that represents various aspects of an XML document (its elements and their attributes, XML namespaces, XML comments, and processing instructions, etc.). Table 24-3 documents the core members of System.Xml.Linq.

Table 24-3. *Select Members of the* System.Xml.Linq *Namespace*

Member of System.Xml.Linq	Meaning in Life
XAttribute	Represents an XML attribute on a given XML element
XComment	Represents an XML comment
XDeclaration	Represents the opening declaration of an XML document
XDocument	Represents the entirety of an XML document
XElement	Represents a given element within an XML document
XName/XNamespace	Provide a very simple manner to define and reference XML namespaces

To begin our investigation of these (and other) types, create a new Console Application named LinqToXmlBasics and import the System.Xml.Linq namespace in your initial code file.

Programmatically Creating XML Documents

Unlike the original .NET XML programming model (à la System.Xml.dll), manipulating an XML document using LINQ can be achieved in a *functional manner*. Thus, rather than building a document in memory using the very verbose DOM API, LINQ to XML allows you to do go "DOM free" if you so choose.

Not only does this greatly reduce the amount of required code, but the programming model maps almost directly to the format of well-formed XML data. To illustrate, add a method to your Program class named CreateFunctionalXmlElement(), implemented as follows:

```
static void CreateFunctionalXmlElement()
{
  // A "functional" approach to build an
  // XML element in memory.
  XElement inventory =
    new XElement("Inventory",
      new XElement("Car", new XAttribute("ID", "1"),
        new XElement("Color", "Green"),
        new XElement("Make", "BMW"),
        new XElement("PetName", "Stan")
      )
    );
  // Call ToString() on our XElement.
  Console.WriteLine(inventory);
}
```

Here, notice that the constructor of the inventory XElement object is in fact a tree of additional XElements and XAttributes. Also note that by mindfully indenting our code statements, our code base has a similar look and feel to the XML document itself. If we call our method from within Main(), we find the output shown in Figure 24-10.

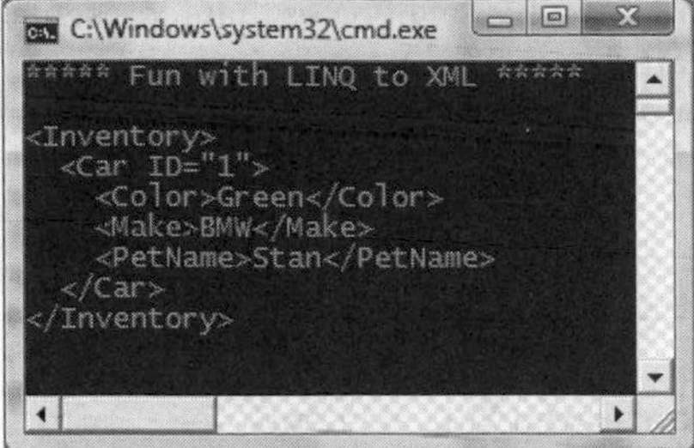

Figure 24-10. *A functional approach to XML document creation*

To create an entire XML document in memory (with comments, processing instructions, opening declarations, etc.), you can load the object tree into the constructor of an `XDocument` type. Consider the following `CreateFunctionalXmlDoc()` method, which first creates an in-memory document and then saves it to a local file:

```
static void CreateFunctionalXmlDoc()
{
  XDocument inventoryDoc =
    new XDocument(
      new XDeclaration("1.0", "utf-8", "yes"),
      new XComment("Current Inventory of AutoLot"),
        new XElement("Inventory",
          new XElement("Car", new XAttribute("ID", "1"),
            new XElement("Color", "Green"),
            new XElement("Make", "BMW"),
            new XElement("PetName", "Stan")
          ),
          new XElement("Car", new XAttribute("ID", "2"),
            new XElement("Color", "Pink"),
            new XElement("Make", "Yugo"),
            new XElement("PetName", "Melvin")
          )
        )
      );
  // Display the document and save to disk.
  Console.WriteLine(inventoryDoc);
  inventoryDoc.Save("SimpleInventory.xml");
}
```

Figure 24-11 shows the `SimpleInventory.xml` file opened within Visual Studio 2008.

As you can see, the `XElement` and `XDocument` types each define a constructor that takes an `XName` as the first parameter and a parameter array of objects as the second. The `XName` type is used in LINQ to SQL to represent (obviously) the name of the item you are creating, while the parameter array of objects can consist of any number of additional LINQ to XML types (`XComment`, `XProcessingInstruction`, `XElement`, `XAttribute`, etc.), as well as simple strings (for element content) or an object implementing `IEnumerable`.

SimpleInventory.xml | Object Browser | Program.cs

```
<?xml version="1.0" encoding="utf-8" standalone="yes"?>
<!--Current Inventory of AutoLot-->
<Inventory>
  <Car ID="1">
    <Color>Green</Color>
    <Make>BMW</Make>
    <PetName>Stan</PetName>
  </Car>
  <Car ID="2">
    <Color>Pink</Color>
    <Make>Yugo</Make>
    <PetName>Melvin</PetName>
  </Car>
</Inventory>
```

Figure 24-11. *The persisted XML document*

Generating Documents from LINQ Queries

As far as that last point is concerned, assume we have an anonymous array of anonymous types that represent a simple `Car` class. We could now create an array of these objects and build a LINQ query that will select each name/value pair to dynamically build a new `XElement`:

```
static void CreateXmlDocFromArray()
{
  // Create an anonymous array of anonymous types.
  var data = new [] {
    new { PetName = "Melvin", ID = 10 },
    new { PetName = "Pat", ID = 11 },
    new { PetName = "Danny", ID = 12 },
    new { PetName = "Clunker", ID = 13 }
  };

  // Now enumerate over the array to build
  // an XElement.
  XElement vehicles =
    new XElement("Inventory",
      from c in data
      select new XElement("Car",
       new XAttribute("ID", c.ID),
       new XElement("PetName", c.PetName)
      )
    );
  Console.WriteLine(vehicles);
}
```

Loading and Parsing XML Content

The `XElement` and `XDocument` types both support `Load()` and `Parse()` methods, which allow you to hydrate an XML object model from string data or external files. Consider the following method, which illustrates both approaches:

```
static void LoadExistingXml()
{
  // Build an XElement from string.
  string myElement =
    @"<Car ID ='3'>
      <Color>Yellow</Color>
      <Make>Yugo</Make>
    </Car>";
  XElement newElement = XElement.Parse(myElement);
  Console.WriteLine(newElement);
  Console.WriteLine();

  // Load the SimpleInventory.xml file.
  XDocument myDoc = XDocument.Load("SimpleInventory.xml");
  Console.WriteLine(myDoc);
}
```

■ **Source Code** The LinqToXmlBasics example can be found under the Chapter 24 subdirectory.

Navigating an In-Memory Document

So, that this point you have seen various ways in which LINQ to XML can be used to create, save, parse, and load XML data. The next aspect of LINQ to XML we need to examine is how to navigate a given document to locate specific elements/attributes. While the LINQ to XML object model provides a number of methods that can be used to programmatically navigate a document, not too surprisingly LINQ query expressions can also be used for this very purpose.

Since you have already seen numerous examples of building query expressions, the next example will be short and sweet. First, create a new Console Application named NavigationWithLinqToXml and import the `System.Xml.Linq` namespace. Next, add a new XML document into your current project named `Inventory.xml`, which supports a small set of entries within the root `<Inventory>` element. Here is one possibility:

```
<?xml version="1.0" encoding="utf-8"?>
<Inventory>
  <Car carID ="0">
    <Make>Ford</Make>
    <Color>Blue</Color>
    <PetName>Chuck</PetName>
  </Car>
  <Car carID ="1">
    <Make>VW</Make>
    <Color>Silver</Color>
    <PetName>Mary</PetName>
  </Car>
  <Car carID ="2">
    <Make>Yugo</Make>
    <Color>Pink</Color>
    <PetName>Gipper</PetName>
  </Car>
  <Car carID ="55">
    <Make>Ford</Make>
    <Color>Yellow</Color>
```

```
    <PetName>Max</PetName>
  </Car>
  <Car carID ="98">
    <Make>BMW</Make>
    <Color>Black</Color>
    <PetName>Zippy</PetName>
  </Car>
</Inventory>
```

Now, select this file within the Solution Explorer and use the Properties window to set the Copy to Output Directory property to Copy Always (to ensure a copy of the file ends up in your Bin folder). Finally, update your `Main()` method to load this file into memory using `XElement.Load()`. The local `doc` variable will be passed into various helper methods to modify the data in various manners:

```
static void Main(string[] args)
{
  Console.WriteLine("***** Fun with LINQ to XML *****\n");

  // Load the Inventory.xml document into memory.
  XElement doc = XElement.Load("Inventory.xml");

  // We will author each of these next...
  PrintAllPetNames(doc);
  Console.WriteLine();
  GetAllFords(doc);
  Console.ReadLine();
}
```

The `PrintAllPetNames()` method illustrates the use of the `XElement.Descendants()` method, which allows you to directly specify a given subelement you wish to navigate to in order to apply a LINQ query expression. Here we are selecting each `PetName` value and printing out the contents to the console:

```
static void PrintAllPetNames(XElement doc)
{
  var petNames = from pn in doc.Descendants("PetName")
                 select pn.Value;

  foreach (var name in petNames)
    Console.WriteLine("Name: {0}", name);
}
```

The `GetAllFords()` method is very similar in nature. Given the incoming `XElement`, we define a `where` operator and select the all `XElements` where the `Make` element is equal to the value `"Ford"`:

```
static void GetAllFords(XElement doc)
{
  var fords = from c in doc.Descendants("Make")
              where c.Value == "Ford"
              select c;

  foreach (var f in fords)
    Console.WriteLine("Name: {0}", f);
}
```

Figure 24-12 shows the output of this program.

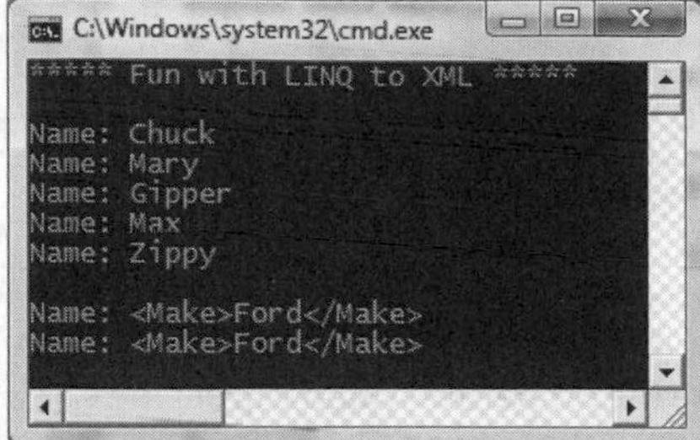

Figure 24-12. *LINQ to XML in action*

Modifying Data in an XML Document

Finally, as you would hope, LINQ to XML provides numerous ways to insert, delete, copy, and update XML content. Adding new XElements to an existing XElement (or XDocument) is no harder than calling the Add() method, which adds the data to the end of the element/document. As an alternative, you can call AddFirst() to add the item to the top of the element/document or AddAfterThis()/AddBeforeThis() to insert data at a specific location.

Updating or deleting content is also very straightforward. After constructing a LINQ query statement to identify the item (or items) you wish to tinker with, simply call ReplaceContent() (for updating) or Remove()/RemoveContent() (for deletion of data). By way of a simple example, consider the following code, which adds a set of new <Car> elements to the incoming XElement parameter:

```
static void AddNewElements(XElement doc)
{
  // Add 5 new purple Fords to the incoming document.
  for (int i = 0; i < 5; i++)
  {
    // Create a new XElement
    XElement newCar =
      new XElement("Car", new XAttribute("ID", i + 1000),
        new XElement("Color", "Green"),
        new XElement("Make", "Ford"),
        new XElement("PetName", "")
    );

    // Add to doc.
    doc.Add(newCar);
  }
  // Show the updates.
  Console.WriteLine(doc);
}
```

That wraps up our look at the major LINQ APIs that ship with .NET 3.5, and this chapter as well! Over the remainder of this book, you will find various LINQ queries where appropriate; however, be aware that each of the APIs examined here (LINQ to DataSet, LINQ to SQL, and LINQ to XML) are extensively documented in the .NET Framework 3.5 SDK documentation.

Source Code The NavigationWithLinqToXml to XML example can be found under the Chapter 24 subdirectory.

Summary

This chapter extended your understanding of LINQ by introducing three LINQ-centric APIs. We began by examining how to transform an ADO.NET DataSet into a LINQ-compatible container using the AsEnumerable() extension method. Once you have extracted an IEnumerable<T> type, you are able to apply any flavor of LINQ query.

Closely related to LINQ to DataSet is the LINQ to SQL API. This aspect of LINQ not only allows you to apply query expressions to data held within relational databases, it also provides infrastructure that essentially encapsulates all trace of the underlying ADO.NET data types. As you have seen, the DataContext type can be used to perform all of the expected database operations, including invoking stored procedures.

We wrapped up by examining LINQ to XML. Similar to LINQ to SQL, this API can be used either to apply LINQ queries to data within an XML document or to build XML documents in a functional manner. The end result is an extreme simplification of how the .NET platform supports the manipulation of XML documents.

CHAPTER 25

Introducing Windows Communication Foundation

.NET 3.0 introduced an API specifically for the process of building distributed systems named Windows Communication Foundation (WCF). Unlike other distributed APIs you may have used in the past (DCOM, .NET remoting, XML web services, etc.), WCF provides a single, unified, and extendable programming object model that can be used to interact with a number of previously diverse distributed technologies.

This chapter begins by framing the need for WCF and examining the problems it intends to solve by way of a quick review of previous distributed computing APIs. After we look at the services provided by WCF, we'll turn to examine the .NET assemblies (and core types) that represent this programming model. Over the remainder of this chapter, we'll build several WCF services, hosts, and clients using various WCF development tools.

Note This chapter will provide you with a firm foundation in WCF development. However, if you require a comprehensive treatment of the subject, check out *Pro WCF: Practical Microsoft SOA Implementation* by Chris Peiris and Dennis Mulder (Apress, 2007).

A Potpourri of Distributed Computing APIs

The Windows operating system has historically provided a number of APIs for building distributed systems. While it is true that most people consider a "distributed system" to involve at the very least two networked computers, this term in the broader sense can simply refer to two executables that need to exchange data, even if they happen to be running on the same physical machine. Using this definition, selecting a distributed API for your current programming task typically involves asking the following pivotal question:

> *Will this system be used exclusively "in house," or will external users require access to the application's functionality?*

If you are building a distributed system for in-house use, you have a far greater chance of ensuring that each connected computer is running the same operating system, using the same programming framework (.NET, COM, J2EE, etc.), and you will be able to leverage your existing security system for purposes of authentication, authorization, and so forth. In this situation, you may be willing to select a particular distributed API that will tie you to a specific operating system/programming framework for the purposes of performance.

In contrast, if you are building a system that must be reached by those outside of your walls, you have a whole other set of issues to contend with. First of all, you will most likely *not* be able to dictate to external users which operating system they make use of, which programming framework they use to build their software, or how they configure their security settings.

Furthermore, if you happen to work for a larger company or in a university setting that makes use of numerous operating systems and programming technologies, an in-house application suddenly faces the same challenges as an outward-facing application. In either of these cases, you need to limit yourself to a more flexible distributed API to ensure the furthest "reach" of your application.

Based on the answer to this key distributed computing question, the next task is to pinpoint exactly which API (or set of APIs) to make use of. By way of a painless overview, the following sections present a quick recap of some of the major distributed APIs historically used by Windows software developers. Once you finish this brief history lesson, you will easily be able to see the usefulness of Windows Communication Foundation.

■ **Note** Just to make sure we are all on the same page here, I feel compelled to point out that WCF (and the technologies it encompasses) has nothing to do with building an HTML-based web application. While it is true that web applications can be considered "distributed" in that two machines are typically involved in the exchange, WCF is about establishing connections to machines to share the functionality of remote components—not for displaying HTML in a web browser. Chapter 31 will begin your examination of building websites with the .NET platform.

The Role of DCOM

Prior to the release of the .NET platform, Distributed Component Object Model (DCOM) was the remoting API of choice for Microsoft-centric development endeavors. Using DCOM, it was possible to build distributed systems using COM objects, the system registry, and a good amount of elbow grease. One benefit of DCOM was that it allowed for *location transparency* of components. Simply put, this allowed client software to be programmed in such a way that the physical locations of the remote objects were not hard-coded. Regardless of whether the remote object was on the same machine or a secondary networked machine, the code base could remain neutral, as the actual location was recorded externally in the system registry.

While DCOM did enjoy some degree of success, for all practical purposes it was a Windows-centric API. Even though DCOM was ported to a few other operating systems, DCOM alone did not provide a fabric to build comprehensive solutions involving multiple operating systems (Windows, Unix, Mac) or promote sharing of data between diverse architectures (COM, J2EE, CORBA, etc.).

■ **Note** There were some attempts to port DCOM to run on various flavors of Unix/Linux, but the end result was lackluster and eventually became a technology footnote.

By and large, DCOM was best suited for in-house application development, as exposing COM types outside company walls entailed a set of additional complications (firewalls and so forth). With the release of the .NET platform, DCOM quickly became a legacy programming model, and unless you are maintaining legacy DCOM systems, you can consider it a deprecated technology.

The Role of COM+/Enterprise Services

DCOM alone did little more than define a way to establish a communication channel between two pieces of COM-based software. To fill in the missing pieces required for building a feature-rich distributed computing solution, Microsoft eventually released Microsoft Transaction Server (MTS), which was subsequently renamed to COM+ at a later release.

Despite its name, COM+ is not only used by COM programmers—it is completely accessible to .NET professionals. Since the first release of the .NET platform, the base class libraries provided a namespace named `System.EnterpriseServices`. Here, .NET programmers could build managed libraries that could be installed into the COM+ runtime in order to access the same set of services as a traditional COM+-aware COM server. In either case, once a COM+-aware library was installed into the COM+ runtime, it was termed a *serviced component*.

COM+ provides a number of features that serviced components can leverage, including transaction management, object lifetime management, pooling services, a role-based security system, a loosely coupled event model, and so on. This was a major benefit at the time, given that most distributed systems require the same set of services. Rather than forcing developers to code them by hand, COM+ provided an out-of-the-box solution.

One of the very compelling aspects of COM+ was the fact that all of these settings could be configured in a declarative manner using administrative tools. Thus, if you wished to ensure an object was monitored under a transactional context or belonged to a particular security role, you simply needed to select the correct check boxes.

While COM+/Enterprise Services is still in use today, this technology is a Windows-only solution that is best suited for in-house application development or as a back-end service indirectly manipulated by more agonistic front ends (e.g., a public website that makes calls on serviced components [aka COM+ objects] in the background).

■ **Note** WCF does not currently provide a way to build serviced components. However, it does provide a manner for WCF services to communicate with existing COM+ objects. If you need to build serviced components using C#, you will need to make direct use of the `System.EnterpriseServices` namespace. Consult the .NET Framework 3.5 SDK documentation for details.

The Role of MSMQ

The Microsoft Message Queuing (MSMQ) API allows developers to build distributed systems that need to ensure reliable delivery of message data on the network. As we all know too well, in any distributed system there is the risk that a network server is down, a database is offline, or connections are lost for mysterious reasons. Furthermore, a number of applications need to be constructed in such a way that they hold message data for delivery at a later time (known as *queuing data*).

At first, MSMQ was packaged as a set of low-level C-based APIs and COM objects. As well, using the `System.Messaging` namespace, .NET programmers could hook into MSMQ and build software that communicated with intermittently connected applications in a dependable fashion. Last but not least, the COM+ layer incorporated MSMQ functionality into the runtime (in a simplified format) using a technology termed Queued Components (QC).

Regardless of which programming model you used to interact with the MSMQ runtime, the end result ensured that applications could deliver messages in a reliable and timely fashion. Like COM+, MSMQ is still certainly part of the fabric of building distributed software on the Windows operating system.

The Role of .NET Remoting

As mentioned, with the release of the .NET platform, DCOM quickly became a legacy distributed API. In its place, the .NET base class libraries shipped with the .NET remoting layer, represented by the `System.Runtime.Remoting` namespaces. This API allows multiple computers to distribute objects, provided they are all running the applications under the .NET platform.

The .NET remoting APIs provided a number of very useful features. Most important was the use of XML-based configuration files to declaratively define the underlying plumbing used by the client and the server software. Using `*.config` files, it was very simple to radically alter the functionality of your distributed system simply by changing the content of the configuration files and restarting the application.

As well, given the fact that this API is useable only by .NET applications, you can gain various performance benefits, as data can be encoded in a compact binary format, and you can make use of the Common Type System (CTS) when defining parameters and return values. While it is possible to make use of .NET remoting to build distributed systems that span multiple operating systems (via Mono, briefly mentioned in Chapter 1 and detailed in Appendix B), interoperability between other programming architectures (such as J2EE) was still not directly possible.

■ **Note** Previous editions of this text included an entire chapter devoted to the topic of the .NET remoting APIs. With the release of WCF, however, I have decided not to include this chapter in this edition. The chapter on .NET remoting APIs (titled "The .NET Remoting Layer") can be obtained free of charge from the Apress website (`http://www.apress.com`) by those who have purchased this text.

The Role of XML Web Services

Each of the previous distributed APIs provided little (if any) support to allow external callers to access the supplied functionality in an *agnostic manner*. When you need to expose the services of remote objects to *any* operating system and *any* programming model, XML web services provide the most straightforward way of doing so.

Unlike a traditional browser-based web application, a web service is simply a way to expose the functionality of remote components via standard web protocols. Since the initial release of .NET, programmers have been provided with superior support for building and consuming XML web services via the `System.Web.Services` namespace. In fact, in many cases, building a feature-complete web service is no more complicated than applying the `[WebMethod]` attribute to each public method you wish to provide access to. Furthermore, Visual Studio 2008 allows you to connect to a remote web service with the click of a button (or two).

Web services allow developers to build .NET assemblies containing types that can be accessed via simple HTTP. Furthermore, a web service encodes its data as simple XML. Given the fact that web services are based on open industry standards (HTTP, XML, SOAP, etc.) rather than proprietary type systems and proprietary wire formats (as is the case with DCOM or .NET remoting), they allow for a high degree of interoperability and data exchange. Figure 25-1 illustrates the agnostic nature of XML web services.

Of course, no distributed API is perfect. One potential drawback of web services is the fact that they can suffer from some performance issues (given the use of HTTP and XML data representation), and they may not be an ideal solution for in-house applications where a TCP-based protocol and binary formatting of data could be used without penalty.

A .NET Web Service Example

For many years now, .NET programmers have created web services using the ASP.NET Web Service project template of Visual Studio, which can be accessed using the File ➤ New ➤ Web Site dialog box. This particular project template creates a commonly used directory structure and a handful of initial files to represent the web service itself. While this project template is very helpful to get you up and running, you are able to build a .NET XML web service using a simple text editor and test it immediately using the ASP.NET development web server, `WebDev.WebServer.exe` (Chapter 31 examines this utility in more detail).

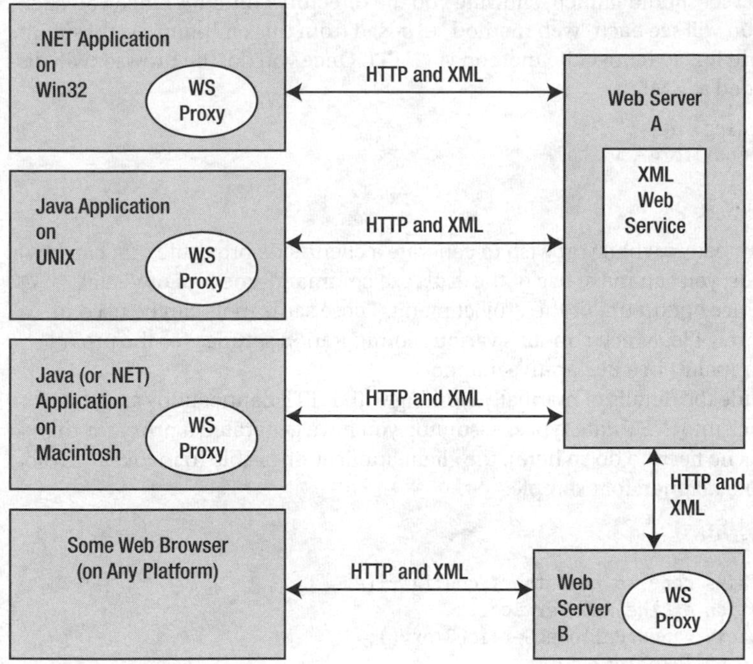

Figure 25-1. *XML web services allow for a very high degree of interoperability.*

By way of a quick example, assume you have authored the following programming logic in a new file named `HelloWebService.asmx` (`*.asmx` is the default file extension for a .NET XML web service file). Once you have done so, save it into C:\HelloWebService.

```
<%@ WebService Language="C#" Class="HelloWebService" %>
using System;
using System.Web.Services;

public class HelloWebService
{
  [WebMethod]
  public string HelloWorld()
  {
    return "Hello World";
  }
}
```

While this simple service is hardly doing anything terribly useful, notice that the file opens with the `WebService` directive, which is used to specify which .NET programming language is used in the file, and the name of the class type representing the service. Beyond this, the only point of interest is that the `HelloWorld()` method has been decorated with the `[WebMethod]` attribute. In many cases, this is all you need to do to expose a method to external callers via HTTP. Finally, notice that you do not need to do anything special to encode the return value into XML, as this is done automatically by the runtime.

If you wish to test this web service, simply open up a Visual Studio 2008 command prompt and enter the following command (if you'd like to see each option you can use with this development web server, simply enter the -? argument):

```
webdev.webserver /port:8080 /path:"C:\HelloWebService"
```

At this point, your browser should launch, showing you the directory contents. Once you click the `HelloWorld.asmx` file, you will see each "web method" exposed from this endpoint. At this point, you can click the HelloWorld link to invoke the method via HTTP. Once you do, the browser will display the return value encoded as XML:

```
<?xml version="1.0" encoding="utf-8" ?>
<string xmlns="http://tempuri.org/">
  Hello World
</string>
```

Simple stuff, huh? Even better, when you wish to generate a client-side proxy file that can be used to invoke web methods, you can make use of the `wsdl.exe` command-line tool or Visual Studio's Add Service Reference option under the Project menu. These same tools can be used to generate a client-side `*.config` file, which contains various configuration settings for the proxy (such as the web service endpoint) in a declarative manner.

This proxy code will hide the details of manually working with HTTP connections and the translation of XML data back into .NET data types. Assuming you have generated a proxy for this simple web service (there is no need to do so here), the client application is able to invoke the web method in a painfully simple manner, for example:

```
static void Main(string[] args)
{
  // The proxy type contains code to read the *.config file
  // to resolve the location of the web service.
  HelloWebServiceProxy proxy = new HelloWebServiceProxy();
  Console.WriteLine(proxy.HelloWorld());
}
```

■ **Note** Previous editions of this text included an entire chapter devoted to the topic of .NET XML web services. With the release of WCF, however, I have decided not to include this chapter in this edition. This chapter on .NET XML web services (titled "Understanding XML Web Services") can be obtained free of charge from the Apress website (`http://www.apress.com`) by those who have purchased this text.

While it is still perfectly possible to build this "traditional" flavor of XML web service under .NET 3.5, most new service projects will benefit from instead making use of the WCF templates. As you will see, you have many HTTP-based bindings to choose from, which allow you to essentially build a web service without selecting a specific "web service" project template.

■ **Source Code** The HelloWorldWebService project is located under the Chapter 25 subdirectory.

Web Service Standards

A major problem that web services faced early on was the fact that all of the big industry players (Microsoft, IBM, and Sun Microsystems) created web service implementations that were not 100 percent compatible with other web service implementations. Obviously, this was an issue, given that the whole point of web services was to achieve a very high degree of interoperability across platforms and operating systems!

In order to ensure the interoperability of web services, groups such as the World Wide Web Consortium (W3C; `http://www.w3.org`) and the Web Services Interoperability Organization (WS-I; `http://www.ws-i.org`) began to author several specifications that laid out the details of how a software vendor (again, such as IBM, Microsoft, or Sun Microsystems) should build web service–centric software libraries to ensure compatibility.

Collectively all of these specifications are given the blanket name WS-* and cover the issues of security, attachments, the description of web services (via the Web Service Description Language, or WSDL), policies, SOAP formats, and a slew of other important details.

As you may know, Microsoft's implementation of most of these standards (for both managed and unmanaged code) is embodied in the Web Services Enhancements (WSE) 3.0 toolkit, which can be downloaded free of charge from the supporting website: `http://msdn2.microsoft.com/en-us/webservices`.

When you are building WCF service applications, you will not need to make direct use of the assemblies that are part of the WSE 3.0 toolkit. Rather, if you build a WCF service that makes use of an HTTP-based binding, these same WS-* specifications will be given to you out of the box (exactly which ones will be based on the binding you choose).

Named Pipes, Sockets, and P2P

As if choosing among DCOM, .NET remoting, web services, COM+, and MSMQ was not challenging enough, the list of distributed APIs continues. Programmers can also make use of additional interprocess communication APIs such as named pipes, sockets, and peer-to-peer (P2P) services. These lower-level APIs typically provide better performance (especially for machines on the same LAN); however, using these APIs becomes more complex (if not impossible) for outward-facing applications.

If you are building a distributed system involving a set of applications running on the same physical machine, you can make use of the named pipes API via the `System.IO.Pipes` namespace (which is new to .NET 3.5). This approach can provide the absolute fastest way to push data between applications on the same machine.

As well, if you are building an application that requires absolute control over how network access is obtained and maintained, sockets and P2P functionality can be achieved under the .NET platform using the `System.Net.Sockets` and `System.Net.PeerToPeer` namespaces, respectively.

The Role of WCF

As I am sure you already figured out from the previous few pages, the wide array of distributed technologies makes it very difficult to pick the right tool for the job. This is further complicated by the fact that several of these technologies overlap in the services they provide (most notably in the areas of transactions and security).

Even when a .NET developer has selected what appear to be the "correct" technologies for the task at hand, building, maintaining, and configuring such an application is complex at best. Each API has its own programming model, its own unique set of configuration utilities, and so forth.

Because of this, prior to .NET 3.0, it was very difficult to "plug and play" distributed APIs without authoring a considerable amount of custom infrastructure. For example, if you build your system using the .NET remoting APIs, and you later decide that XML web services are a more appropriate solution, you need to reengineer your code base.

WCF is a distributed computing toolkit introduced with .NET 3.0 that integrates these previous independent distributed technologies into a streamlined API represented primarily via the `System.ServiceModel` namespace. Using WCF, you are able to expose services to callers using a wide variety of techniques. For example, if you are building an in-house application where all connected machines are Windows based, you can make use of various TCP protocols to ensure the fastest possible performance. This same service can also be exposed using the XML web service–based protocol to allow external callers to leverage its functionality regardless of the programming language or operating system.

Given the fact that WCF allows you to pick the correct protocol for the job (using a common programming model), you will find that it becomes quite easy to plug and play the underlying plumbing of your distributed application. In most cases, you can do so without being required to recompile or redeploy the client/service software, as the grungy details are often relegated to application configuration files (much like the older .NET remoting APIs).

An Overview of WCF Features

Interoperability and integration of diverse APIs are only two (very important) aspects of WCF. In addition, WCF provides a rich software fabric that complements the remoting technologies it exposes. Consider the following list of major WCF features:

- Support for strongly typed *as well as* untyped messages. This approach allows .NET applications to share custom types efficiently, while software created using other platforms (such as J2EE) can consume streams of loosely typed XML.
- Support for several *bindings* (raw HTTP, TCP, MSMQ, and named pipes) to allow you to choose the most appropriate plumbing to transport message data to and fro.
- Support for the latest and greatest web service specifications (WS-*).
- A fully integrated security model encompassing both native Win32/.NET security protocols and numerous neutral security techniques built upon web service standards.
- Support for sessionlike state management techniques, as well as support for one-way stateless messages.

As impressive as this list of features may be, it really only scratches the surface of the functionality WCF provides. WCF also offers tracing and logging facilities, performance counters, a publish and subscribe event model, and transactional support, among other features.

An Overview of Service-Oriented Architecture

Yet another benefit of WCF is that it is based on the design principles established by *service-oriented architecture* (SOA). To be sure, SOA is a major buzzword in the industry, and like most buzzwords, SOA can be defined in numerous ways. Simply put, SOA is a way to design a distributed system where several autonomous *services* work in conjunction by passing *messages* across boundaries (either networked machines or simply two processes on the same machine) using well-defined *interfaces*.

In the world of WCF, these "well-defined interfaces" are typically created using actual CLR interface types (see Chapter 9). In a more general sense, however, the interface of a service simply describes the set of members that may be invoked by external callers.

When WCF was designed, the WCF team did so by observing four tenets of SOA design principles. While these tenets are typically honored automatically simply by building a WCF application, understanding these four cardinal design rules of SOA can help put WCF in further perspective. The sections that follow provide a brief overview of each tenet.

Tenet 1: Boundaries Are Explicit

This tenet reiterates the fact that the functionality of a WCF service is expressed using well-defined interfaces (e.g., descriptions of each member, its parameters, and its return values). The only way that an external caller is able to communicate with a WCF service is via the interface, and the external caller remains blissfully unaware of the underlying implementation details.

Tenet 2: Services Are Autonomous

When speaking of services as "autonomous" entities, we are referring to the fact that a given WCF service is (as much as possible) an island unto itself. An autonomous service should be independent with regard to version issues, deployment issues, and installation issues. To help promote this tenet, we yet again fall back on a key aspect of interface-based programming. Once an interface is in production, it should never be changed (or you will risk breaking existing clients). When you need to extend the functionality of your WCF service, simply author new interfaces that model the desired functionality.

Tenet 3: Services Communicate via Contract, Not Implementation

The third tenet is yet another byproduct of interface-based programming in that the implementation details of a WCF service (which language it was written in, how it gets its work accomplished, etc.) are of no concern to the external caller. WCF clients interact with services solely through their exposed public interfaces. Furthermore, if the members of a service interface expose custom complex types, they need to be fully detailed as a *data contract* to ensure all callers can map the content into a particular data structure.

Tenet 4: Service Compatibility Is Based on Policy

Because CLR interfaces provide strongly typed contracts for all WCF clients (and may also be used to generate a related WSDL document based on your choice of binding), it is important to point out that interfaces/WSDL alone is not expressive enough to detail aspects of what the service is capable of doing. Given this, SOA allows us to define "policies" that further qualify the semantics of the service (e.g., the expected security requirements used to talk to the service). Using these policies, we are able to basically separate the low-level syntactic description of our service (the exposed interfaces) from the semantic details of how they work and how they need to be invoked.

WCF: The Bottom Line

Hopefully this little history lesson has illustrated that WCF is the preferred approach for building distributed applications under .NET 3.0 and higher. Whether you are attempting to build an in-house application using TCP protocols, are moving data between programs on the same machine using named pipes, or are exposing data to the world at large using web service protocols, WCF is the recommended API to do so.

This is not to say you cannot use the original .NET distributed-centric namespaces (`System.Runtime.Remoting`, `System.Messaging`, `System.EnterpriseServices`, `System.Web.Services`, etc.) in new development efforts. In fact, in some cases (specifically if you need to build COM+ objects), you will be required to do so. In any case, if you have used these APIs in previous projects, you will find learning WCF straightforward. Like the technologies that preceded it, WCF makes considerable use of XML-based configuration files, .NET attributes, and proxy generation utilities.

With this introductory foundation behind us, we can now turn to the topic of actually building WCF applications. Again, do understand that full coverage of WCF would require a entire book, as each of the supported services (MSMQ, COM+, P2P, named pipes, etc.) could easily be a chapter unto itself. Here, you will learn the overall process of building WCF programs using both TCP- and HTTP-based (e.g., web service) protocols. This should put you in a good position for future study as you see fit.

Investigating the Core WCF Assemblies

As you would expect, the programming fabric of WCF is represented by a set of .NET assemblies installed into the GAC. Table 25-1 describes the overall role of the core WCF assemblies you will need to make use of in just about any WCF application.

Table 25-1. *Core WCF Assemblies*

Assembly	Meaning in Life
`System.Runtime.Serialization.dll`	Defines namespaces and types that can be used for serializing and deserializing objects within the WCF framework
`System.ServiceModel.dll`	The core assembly that contains the types used to build any sort of WCF application

These two assemblies define a number of new namespaces and types. While you should consult the .NET Framework 3.5 SDK documentation for complete details, Table 25-2 documents the roles of some of the important namespaces to be aware of.

Table 25-2. *Core WCF Namespaces*

Namespace	Meaning in Life
`System.Runtime.Serialization`	Defines numerous types used to control how data is serialized and deserialized within the WCF framework
`System.ServiceModel`	The primary WCF namespace that defines binding and hosting types, as well as basic security and transactional types
`System.ServiceModel.Configuration`	Defines numerous types that provide programmatic access to WCF configuration files
`System.ServiceModel.Description`	Defines types that provide an object model to the addresses, bindings, and contracts defined within WCF configuration files
`System.ServiceModel.MsmqIntegration`	Contains types to integrate with the MSMQ service
`System.ServiceModel.Security`	Defines numerous types to control aspects of the WCF security layers

A BRIEF WORD REGARDING CARDSPACE

In addition to `System.ServiceModel.dll` and `System.Runtime.Serialization.dll`, WCF provides a third WCF assembly named `System.IdentityModel.dll`. Here you will find a number of additional namespaces and types that support the WCF CardSpace API. This technology allows you to establish and manage digital identities within a WCF application. Essentially, the CardSpace API provides a unified programming model to account for various security-related details for WCF applications, such as caller identity, user authentication/authorization services, and whatnot.

We will not examine CardSpace further in this edition of the text, so be sure to consult the .NET Framework 3.5 SDK documentation if you are interested in learning more.

The Visual Studio WCF Project Templates

As will be explained in more detail later in this chapter, a WCF application is typically represented by three interrelated assemblies, one of which is a `*.dll` that contains the types that external callers can communicate with (in other words, the WCF service itself). When you wish to build a WCF service, it is perfectly permissible to select a standard Class Library project template (see Chapter 15) as a starting point and manually reference the WCF assemblies.

Alternatively, you can create a new WCF service by selecting the WCF Service Library project template of Visual Studio 2008 (see Figure 25-2). This project type automatically sets references to the required WCF assemblies; however, it also generates a good deal of "starter code," which you will more likely than not simply delete.

Figure 25-2. *The Visual Studio 2008 WCF Service Library project template*

One benefit of selecting the WCF Service Library project template is that it also supplies you with an `App.config` file, which may seem strange since we are building a .NET `*.dll`, not a .NET `*.exe`. This file, however, is very useful in that when you debug or run your WCF Service Library project, the Visual Studio IDE will automatically launch the WCF Test Client application. This program (`WcfTestClient.exe`) will read the settings in the `App.config` file in order to host your service for testing purposes. You'll learn more about the WCF Test Client later in this chapter.

■ **Note** The `App.config` file of the WCF Service Library project is also useful in that it shows you the bare-bones settings used to configure a WCF host application. In fact, you can copy and paste much of this code into your host's actual configuration file.

In addition to the basic WCF Service Library template, the WCF project category of the New Project dialog box defines two WCF library projects that integrate Windows Workflow Foundation functionality into a WCF service as well as a template to build an RSS library (all of which are also seen in Figure 25-2). The next chapter will introduce you to the Windows Workflow Foundation, so I'll ignore these particular WCF project templates for the time being (and I'll leave it to the interested reader to dig into the RSS feed project template).

The WCF Service Website Project Template

Truth be told, there is yet another Visual Studio 2008 WCF-centric project template that you will find in the New Web Site dialog box, activated via the File ➤ New ➤ Web Site menu option (see Figure 25-3).

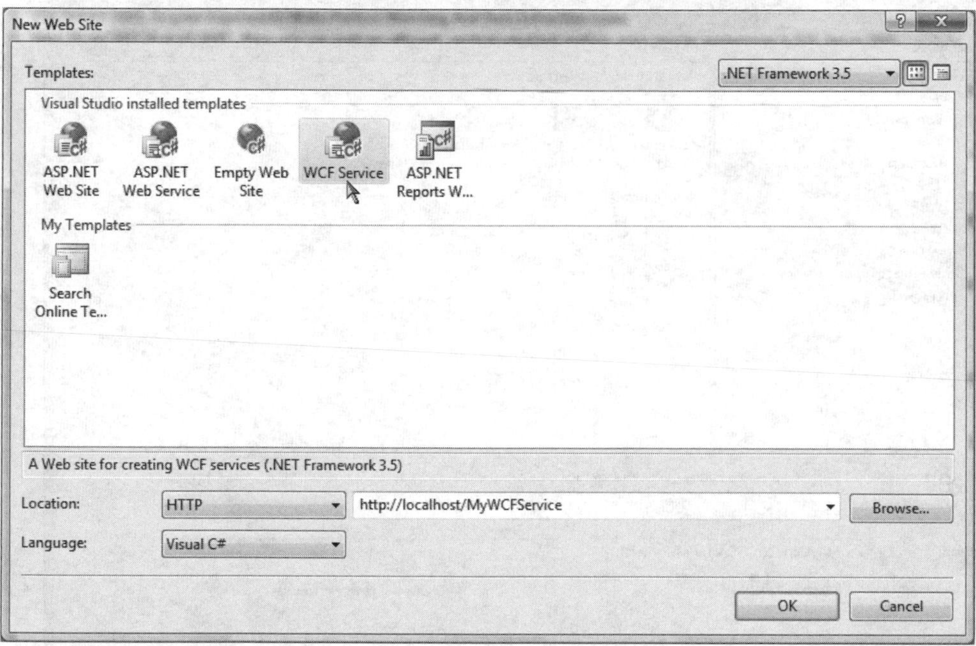

Figure 25-3. *The Visual Studio 2008 web-based WCF Service project template*

This WCF Service project template is useful when you know from the outset that your WCF service will make use of web service–based protocols rather than, for example, named pipes. This option can automatically create a new Internet Information Services (IIS) virtual directory to contain your WCF program files, create a proper `Web.config` file to expose the service via HTTP, and author the necessary `*.svc` file (more about `*.svc` files later in this chapter). In this light, the web-based WCF Service project is simply a time-saver, as the IDE will automatically set up the required IIS infrastructure.

In contrast, if you build a new WCF service using the WCF Service Library option, you have the ability to host the service in a variety of ways (custom host, Windows service, manually built IIS virtual directory, etc.). This option is more appropriate when you wish to build a custom host for your WCF service.

The Basic Composition of a WCF Application

When you are building a WCF distributed system, you will typically do so by creating three interrelated assemblies:

- *The WCF Service assembly*: This `*.dll` contains the classes and interfaces that represent the overall functionality you are exposing to external callers.
- *The WCF Service host*: This software module is the entity that hosts your WCF service assembly.
- *The WCF client*: This is the application that accesses the service's functionality through an intervening proxy.

As mentioned, the WCF service assembly is a .NET class library that contains a number of WCF contracts and their implementations. The one key difference is that the interface contracts are adorned with various attributes that control data type representation, how the WCF runtime interacts with the exposed types, and so forth.

The second assembly, the WCF host, can literally be any .NET executable. As you will see in this chapter, WCF was set up in such a way that services can be easily exposed from any type of application (Windows Forms, a Windows service, WPF applications, etc.). When you are building a custom host, you will make use of the `ServiceHost` type and a related `*.config` file, which contains details regarding the server-side plumbing you wish to make use of. However, if you are using IIS as the host for your WCF service, there is no need to programmatically build a custom host, as IIS will make use of the `ServiceHost` type behind the scenes.

■ **Note** It is also possible to host a WCF service using the Vista-specific Windows Activation Service (WAS). Consult the .NET Framework 3.5 SDK documentation for details.

The final assembly represents the client that is making calls into the WCF service. As you might expect, this client could be any type of .NET application. Similar to the host, client applications also typically make use of a client-side `*.config` file that defines the client-side plumbing.

Figure 25-4 illustrates (from a very high level) the relationship between these three interrelated WCF assemblies. As you would assume, behind the scenes are several lower-level details used to represent the required plumbing (factories, channels, listeners, etc.). These low-level details are most often hidden from view; however, they can be extended or customized if required. Thankfully, in most cases, the default plumbing will fit the bill.

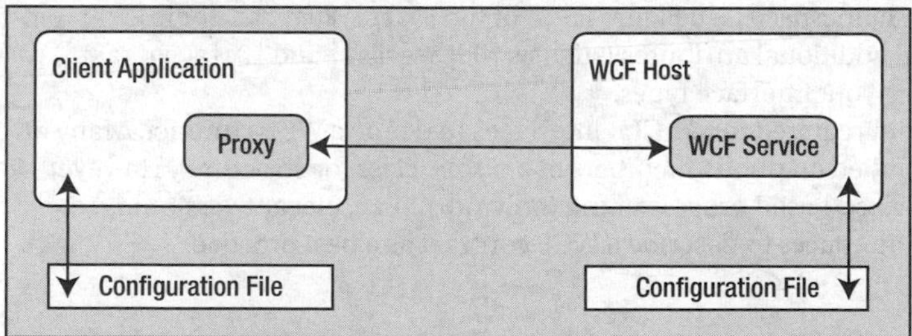

Figure 25-4. *A high-level look at a typical WCF application*

It is also worth pointing out that the use of a server-side or client-side `*.config` file is technically optional. If you wish, you can hard-code the host (as well as the client) to specify the necessary plumbing (endpoints, binding, addresses, etc.). The obvious problem with this approach is that if you need to change the plumbing details, you will be required to recode, recompile, and redeploy a number of assemblies. Using a `*.config` file keeps your code base much more flexible, as changing the plumbing is as simple as updating the file's content and restarting the application.

The ABCs of WCF

Hosts and clients communicate with each other by agreeing on the ABCs, a friendly mnemonic for remembering the core building blocks of a WCF application, specifically *address*, *binding*, and *contract*.

- *Address*: The location of the service. In code, this is represented with a `System.Uri` type; however, the value is typically stored in `*.config` files.
- *Binding*: WCF ships with a number of different bindings that specify network protocols, encoding mechanisms, and the transport layer.
- *Contract*: A description of each method exposed from the WCF service.

Do understand that the ABC abbreviation does not imply that a developer must define the address first, followed by binding, and ending with the contract. In many cases, a WCF developer begins by defining a contract for the service, followed by establishing an address and bindings (but any order will do, so long as each aspect is accounted for). Before we build our first WCF application, here is a more detailed walk-through of the ABCs.

Understanding WCF Contracts

The notion of a *contract* is the key to building a WCF service. While not mandatory, the vast majority of your WCF applications will begin by defining a set of .NET interface types that are used to represent the set of members a given WCF type will support. Specifically, interfaces that represent a WCF contract are termed *service contracts*. The classes (or structures) that implement them are termed *service types*.

WCF service contracts are adorned with various attributes, the most common of which are defined in the `System.ServiceModel` namespace. When the members of a service contract contain only simple data types (such as numerical data, Booleans, and string data) you can build a complete WCF service using nothing more than the `[ServiceContract]` and `[OperationContract]` attributes.

However, if your members expose custom types, you will need to make use of types in the `System.Runtime.Serialization` namespace (see Figure 25-5) of the `System.Runtime.Serialization.dll` assembly. Here you will find additional attributes (such as `[DataMember]` and `[DataContract]`) to fine-tune the process of defining your interface types.

Strictly speaking, you are not required to use CLR interfaces to define a WCF contract. Many of these same attributes can be applied on public members of a public class (or structure). However, given the many benefits of interface-based programming (polymorphism, elegant versioning, etc.), it is safe to consider using CLR interfaces to describe a WCF contract as a best practice.

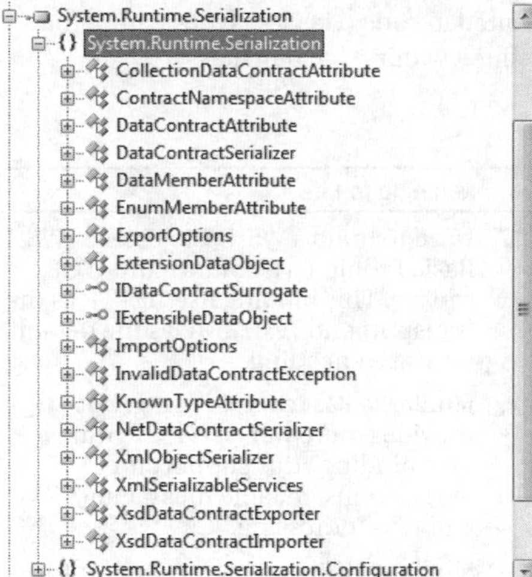

Figure 25-5. `System.Runtime.Serialization` *defines a number of attributes used when building WCF data contracts.*

Understanding WCF Bindings

Once a contract (or a set of contracts) has been defined and implemented within your service library, the next logical step is to build a hosting agent for the WCF service itself. As mentioned, you have a variety of possible hosts to choose from, all of which must specify the *bindings* used by remote callers to gain access to the service type's functionality.

Choosing a set of bindings is one area that makes WCF development quite different from .NET remoting and/or XML web service development in that WCF ships with a number of binding choices, each of which is tailored to a specific need. If none of the out-of-the-box bindings fits the bill, it is possible to create your own by extending the `CustomBinding` type (something we will not do in this chapter). Simply put, a WCF binding can specify the following characteristics:

- The contracts implemented by the service
- The transport layer used to move data (HTTP, MSMQ, named pipes, TCP)
- The channels used by the transport (one-way, request-reply, duplex)
- The encoding mechanism used to deal with the data itself (XML, binary, etc.)
- Any supported web service protocols (if permitted by the binding) such as WS-Security, WS-Transactions, WS-Reliability, and so on

Let's take a look at our choices.

HTTP-Based Bindings

The `BasicHttpBinding`, `WSHttpBinding`, `WSDualHttpBinding`, and `WSFederationHttpBinding` options are geared toward exposing contract types via XML web service protocols. Clearly, if you require the furthest reach possible for your service (multiple operating systems and multiple programming architectures), these are the bindings to focus on, because all of these binding types encode data based on XML representation and use HTTP on the wire.

In Table 25-3, note that a WCF binding can be represented in code (via class types within the System.ServiceModel namespace) or as XML attributes defined within *.config files.

Table 25-3. *The HTTP-Centric WCF Bindings*

Binding Class	Binding Element	Meaning in Life
BasicHttpBinding	<basicHttpBinding>	Used to build a WS-Basic Profile (WS-I Basic Profile 1.1)–conformant WCF service. This binding uses HTTP as the transport and Text/XML as the default message encoding.
WSHttpBinding	<wsHttpBinding>	Similar to BasicHttpBinding, but provides more web service features. This binding adds support for transactions, reliable messaging, and WS-Addressing.
WSDualHttpBinding	<wsDualHttpBinding>	Similar to WSHttpBinding, but for use with duplex contracts (e.g., the service and client can send messages back and forth). This binding supports only SOAP security and requires reliable messaging.
WSFederationHttpBinding	<wsFederationHttpBinding>	A secure and interoperable binding that supports the WS-Federation protocol, enabling organizations that are in a federation to efficiently authenticate and authorize users.

As the name suggests, BasicHttpBinding is the simplest of all web service–centric protocols. Specifically, this binding will ensure that your WCF service conforms to a specification named WS-I Basic Profile 1.1 defined by WS-I. The main reason to use this binding is to maintain backward compatibility with applications that were previously built to communicate with ASP.NET web services (which have been part of the .NET libraries since version 1.0).

The WSHttpBinding protocol not only incorporates support for a subset of the WS-* specification (transactions, security, and reliable sessions), but also supports the ability to handle binary data encoding using Message Transmission Optimization Mechanism (MTOM).

The main benefit of WSDualHttpBinding is that it adds the ability to allow the caller and sender to communicate using *duplex messaging*, which is just a fancy way of saying they can engage in a two-way conversation. When selecting WSDualHttpBinding, you can hook into the WCF publish/subscribe event model.

Finally, WSFederationHttpBinding is the web service–based protocol you may wish to consider when security is of the utmost importance. This binding supports the WS-Trust, WS-Security, and WS-SecureConversation specifications, which are represented by the WCF CardSpace APIs.

TCP-Based Bindings

If you are building a distributed application involving machines that are configured with the .NET 3.0/3.5 libraries (in other words, all machines are running Windows XP, Windows Server 2003, or Windows Vista), you can gain performance benefits bypassing web service bindings and opting for a TCP binding, which ensures all data is encoded in a compact binary format rather than XML. Again, when using the bindings shown in Table 25-4, the client and host must be .NET applications.

Table 25-4. *The TCP-Centric WCF Bindings*

Binding Class	Binding Element	Meaning in Life
`NetNamedPipeBinding`	`<netNamedPipeBinding>`	A secure, reliable, optimized binding for on-the-same-machine communication between .NET applications
`NetPeerTcpBinding`	`<netPeerTcpBinding>`	Provides a secure binding for P2P network applications
`NetTcpBinding`	`<netTcpBinding>`	A secure and optimized binding suitable for cross-machine communication between .NET applications

The `NetTcpBinding` class uses TCP to move binary data between the client and WCF service. As mentioned, this will result in higher performance than the web service protocols, but you are limited to an in-house Windows solution. On the plus side, `NetTcpBinding` does support transactions, reliable sessions, and secure communications.

Like `NetTcpBinding`, `NetNamedPipeBinding` supports transactions, reliable sessions, and secure communications, but it has no ability to make cross-machine calls. If you are looking for the fastest way to push data between WCF applications on the same machine (e.g., cross-application domain communications), `NetNamedPipeBinding` is the binding choice of champions. As far as `NetPeerTcpBinding` is concerned, consult the .NET Framework 3.5 documentation for details regarding P2P networking.

MSMQ-Based Bindings

Finally, if you are attempting to integrate with a Microsoft MSMQ server, the `NetMsmqBinding` and `MsmqIntegrationBinding` bindings are of immediate interest. We will not examine the details of using MSMQ bindings in this chapter, but Table 25-5 documents the basic role of each.

Table 25-5. *The MSMQ-Centric WCF Bindings*

Binding Class	Binding Element	Meaning in Life
`MsmqIntegrationBinding`	`<msmqIntegrationBinding>`	This binding can be used to enable WCF applications to send and receive messages to and from existing MSMQ applications that use COM, native C++, or the types defined in the `System.Messaging` namespace.
`NetMsmqBinding`	`<netMsmqBinding>`	This queued binding is suitable for cross-machine communication between .NET applications.

A BRIEF NOTE ON COMMUNICATING WITH COM+ OBJECTS

Notice that there is not a specific binding to interact with COM+ objects. Communicating with COM+ components via WCF is entirely possible; however, doing so involves exposing the COM+ types through an XML web service binding via the `ComSvcConfig.exe` command-line tool that ships with the .NET Framework 3.5 SDK or by using the `SvcConfigEditor.exe` utility (which we will examine later in this chapter).

Understanding WCF Addresses

Once the contracts and bindings have been established, the final piece of the puzzle is to specify an *address* for the WCF service. This is obviously quite important, in that remote callers will be unable to communicate with the remote types if they cannot locate them! Like most aspects of WCF, an address can be hard-coded in an assembly (via the `System.Uri` type) or offloaded to a `*.config` file.

In either case, the exact format of the WCF address will differ based on your choice of binding (HTTP based, named pipes, TCP based, or MSMQ based). From a high level, WCF addresses can specify the following bits of information:

- `Scheme`: The transport protocol (HTTP, etc.).
- `MachineName`: Fully qualified domain of the machine.
- `Port`: This is optional in many cases. For example, the default for HTTP bindings is port 80.
- `Path`: The path to the WCF service.

This information can be represented by the following generalized template (the `Port` value is optional, as some bindings make no use of them):

```
scheme://<MachineName>[:Port]/Path
```

When you are using a web service–based binding (`basicHttpBinding`, `wsHttpBinding`, `wsDualHttpBinding`, or `wsFederationHttpBinding`), the address breaks down as so (recall that if you do not specify a port number, HTTP-based protocols will default to port 80):

```
http://localhost:8080/MyWCFService
```

Note If you wish to make use of Secure Sockets Layer (SSL), simply replace `http` with `https`.

If you are making use of TCP-centric bindings (such as `NetTcpBinding` or `NetPeerTcpBinding`), the URI takes the following format:

```
net.tcp://localhost:8080/MyWCFService
```

The MSMQ-centric bindings (`NetMsmqBinding` and `MsmqIntegrationBinding`) are a bit unique in their URI format, given that MSMQ can make use of public or private queues (which are available only on the local machine) and port numbers have no meaning within an MSMQ-centric URI. Consider the following URI, which describes a private queue named `MyPrivateQ`:

```
net.msmq://localhost/private$/MyPrivateQ
```

Last but not least, the address format used for the named-pipe binding, `NetNamedPipeBinding`, breaks down as so (recall that named pipes allow for interprocess communication for applications on the same physical machine):

```
net.pipe://localhost/MyWCFService
```

While a single WCF service might expose only a single address (based on a single binding), it is possible to configure a collection of unique addresses (with different bindings). This can be done within a `*.config` file by defining multiple `<endpoint>` elements. Here, you can specify any number of ABCs for the same service. This approach can be helpful when you want to allow callers to select which protocol they would like to use when communicating with the service.

Building a WCF Service

Now that you have a better understanding about the building blocks of a WCF application, let's create our first sample application to see how the ABCs are accounted for in code. Our first step is to define our WCF service library consisting of the contracts and their implementations.

This first example will not use the Visual Studio WCF project templates, in order to keep focused on the specific steps involved in making a WCF service. To begin, create a new C# Class Library project named MagicEightBallServiceLib. Once you have done so, rename your initial file from `Class1.cs` to `MagicEightBallService.cs` and add a reference to the `System.ServiceModel.dll` assembly. In the initial code file, specify that you are using the `System.ServiceModel` namespace. At this point, your C# file should look like so:

```
using System;
using System.Collections.Generic;
using System.Linq;
using System.Text;

// The key WCF namespace.
using System.ServiceModel;

namespace MagicEightBallServiceLib
{
  public class MagicEightBallService
  {
  }
}
```

Our class type will implement a single WCF service contract represented by a strongly typed CLR interface named `IEightBall`. As you most likely know, the Magic 8-Ball is a toy that allows you to view one of a handful of fixed answers to a question you may ask. Our interface will define a single method that allows the caller to pose a question to the Magic 8-Ball to obtain a random answer.

WCF service interfaces are adorned with the `[ServiceContract]` attribute, while each interface member is decorated with the `[OperationContract]` attribute (more details regarding these two attributes in just a moment). Here is the definition of the `IEightBall` interface:

```
[ServiceContract]
public interface IEightBall
{
  // Ask a question, receive an answer!
  [OperationContract]
  string ObtainAnswerToQuestion(string userQuestion);
}
```

■Note It is permissible to define a service contract interface that contains methods not adorned with the `[OperationContract]` attribute. However, such members will not be exposed through the WCF runtime.

As you know from your study of the interface type (see Chapter 9), interfaces are quite useless until they are implemented by a class or structure, in order to flesh out their functionality. Like a real Magic 8-Ball, the implementation of our service type (`MagicEightBallService`) will randomly return a canned answer from an array of strings. Also, our default constructor will display an information message that will be (eventually) displayed within the host's console window (for diagnostic purposes):

```
public class MagicEightBallService : IEightBall
{
  // Just for display purposes on the host.
  public MagicEightBallService()
  {
    Console.WriteLine("The 8-Ball awaits your question...");
  }

  public string ObtainAnswerToQuestion(string userQuestion)
  {
    string[] answers = { "Future Uncertain", "Yes", "No",
      "Hazy", "Ask again later", "Definitely" };

    // Return a random response.
    Random r = new Random();
    return string.Format("{0}? {1}.",
      userQuestion, answers[r.Next(answers.Length)]);
  }
}
```

At this point, our WCF service library is complete. However, before we construct a host for this service, let's examine some additional details of the [ServiceContract] and [OperationContract] attributes.

The [ServiceContract] Attribute

In order for a CLR interface to participate in the services provided by WCF, it must be adorned with the [ServiceContract] attribute. Like many other .NET attributes, the ServiceContractAttribute type supports a number of properties to further qualify its intension. Two properties, Name and Namespace, can be set to control the name of the service type and the name of the XML namespace defining the service type. If you are using a web service–specific binding, these values are used to define the <portType> elements of the related WSDL document.

Here, we have not bothered to assign a Name value, given that the default name of the service type is directly based on the C# class name. However, the default name for the underlying XML namespace is simply http://tempuri.org (which really should be changed for all of your WCF services).

When you are building a WCF service that will send and receive custom data types (which we are currently not doing), it is important to establish a meaningful value to the underlying XML namespace, as this will make sure that your custom types are unique. As you may know from your experience building XML web services, XML namespaces provide a way to wrap your custom types in a unique container to ensure that your types do not clash with types in another organization.

For this reason, we can update our interface definition with a more fitting definition, which, much like the process of defining an XML namespace in a .NET Web Service project, is typically the URI of the service's point of origin, for example:

```
[ServiceContract(Namespace = "http://Intertech.com")]
public interface IEightBall
{
  ...
}
```

Beyond Namespace and Name, the [ServiceContract] attribute can be configured with the additional properties shown in Table 25-6. Be aware that some of these settings will be ignored depending on your selection of binding.

Table 25-6. *Various Named Properties of the* `[ServiceContract]` *Attribute*

Property	Meaning in Life
`CallbackContract`	Establishes if this service contract requires callback functionality for two-way message exchange.
`ConfigurationName`	The name used to locate the service element in an application configuration file. The default is the name of the service implementation class.
`ProtectionLevel`	Allows you to specify the degree to which the contract binding requires encryption, digital signatures, or both for endpoints that expose the contract.
`SessionMode`	Used to establish if sessions are allowed, not allowed, or required by this service contract.

The [OperationContract] Attribute

Methods that you wish to be used within the WCF framework must be attributed with the `[OperationContract]` attribute, which may also be configured with various named properties. Using the properties shown in Table 25-7, you are able to declare that a given method is intended to be one-way in nature, supports asynchronous invocation, requires encrypted message data, and so forth (again, many of these values may be ignored based on your binding selection).

Table 25-7. *Various Named Properties of the* `[OperationContract]` *Attribute*

Property	Meaning in Life
`Action`	Gets or sets the WS-Addressing action of the request message.
`AsyncPattern`	Indicates if the operation is implemented asynchronously using a `Begin`/`End` method pair on the service. This allows the service to offload processing to another server-side thread; this has nothing to do with the client calling the method asynchronously!
`IsInitiating`	Specifies if this operation can be the initial operation in a session.
`IsOneWay`	Indicates if the operation consists of only a single input message (and no associated output).
`IsTerminating`	Specifies if the WCF runtime should attempt to terminate the current session after the operation completes.

For this initial example, we don't need to configure the `ObtainAnswerToQuestion()` method with additional traits, so the `[OperationContract]` attribute can be used as currently defined.

Service Types As Operational Contracts

Finally, recall that the use of interfaces is not required when building WCF service types. It is in fact possible to apply the `[ServiceContract]` and `[OperationContract]` attributes directly on the service type itself:

```
// This is only for illustrative purposes
// and not used for the current example.
[ServiceContract(Namespace = "http://Intertech.com")]
public class ServiceTypeAsContract
{
  [OperationContract]
  void SomeMethod() { }
```

```
  [OperationContract]
  void AnotherMethod() { }
}
```

Although this approach is possible, there are many benefits to explicitly defining an interface type to represent the service contract. The most obvious benefit is that a given interface can be applied to multiple service types (authored in a variety of languages and architectures) to achieve a high degree of polymorphism. Another benefit is that a service contract interface can be used as the basis of new contracts (via interface inheritance), without having to carry any implementation baggage.

In any case, at this point our first WCF service library is complete. Compile your project to ensure you do not have any typos.

■ Source Code The MagicEightBallServiceLib project is located under the Chapter 25 subdirectory.

Hosting the WCF Service

We are now ready to define a host. Although a production-level service would be hosted from a Windows service or an IIS virtual directory, our first host will be a simple console named MagicEightBallServiceHost.

Once you have created this new Console Application project, add a reference to the `System.ServiceModel.dll` and `MagicEightBallServiceLib.dll` assemblies, and update your initial code file by importing the `System.ServiceModel` and `MagicEightBallServiceLib` namespaces:

```
using System;
using System.Collections.Generic;
using System.Linq;
using System.Text;

using System.ServiceModel;
using MagicEightBallServiceLib;

namespace MagicEightBallServiceHost
{
  class Program
  {
    static void Main(string[] args)
    {
      Console.WriteLine("***** Console Based WCF Host *****");
      Console.ReadLine();
    }
  }
}
```

The first step you must take when building a host for a WCF service type is to decide whether you want to define the necessary hosting logic completely in code or to relegate several low-level details to an application configuration file. As mentioned, the benefit of `*.config` files is that the host is able to change the underlying plumbing without requiring you to recompile and redeploy the executable. However, always remember this is strictly optional, as you can hard-code the hosting logic using the types within the `System.ServiceModel.dll` assembly.

This console-based host will indeed make use of an application configuration file, so insert a new Application Configuration File into your current project using the Project ➤ Add New Item menu option.

Establishing the ABCs Within an App.config File

When you are building a host for a WCF service type, you will follow a very predictable set of steps—some via configuration and some via code:

1. Define the *endpoint* for the WCF service being hosted within the host's configuration file.
2. Programmatically make use of the ServiceHost type to expose the service types available from this endpoint.
3. Ensure the host remains running to service incoming client requests. Obviously, this step is not required if you are hosting your service types using a Windows service or IIS.

In the world of WCF, the term "endpoint" simply represents the address, binding, and contract rolled together in a nice tidy package. In XML, an endpoint is expressed using the <endpoint> element and the address, binding, and contract elements. Update your *.config file to specify a single endpoint (reachable via port 8080) exposed by this host:

```
<?xml version="1.0" encoding="utf-8" ?>
<configuration>
  <system.serviceModel>
    <services>
      <service name="MagicEightBallServiceLib.MagicEightBallService">
        <endpoint address ="http://localhost:8080/MagicEightBallService"
                  binding="basicHttpBinding"
                  contract="MagicEightBallServiceLib.IEightBall"/>
      </service>
    </services>
  </system.serviceModel>
</configuration>
```

Notice that the <system.serviceModel> element is the root for all of a host's WCF settings. Each service exposed by the host is represented by a <service> element, wrapped within the <services> base element. Here, our single <service> element makes use of the (optional) name attribute to specify the friendly name of the service type.

The nested <endpoint> element handles the task of defining the address, the binding model (basicHttpBinding in this example), and the fully qualified name of the interface type defining the WCF service contract (IEightBall). Because we are using an HTTP-based binding, we make use of the http:// scheme, specifying an arbitrary port ID.

Coding Against the ServiceHost Type

With the current configuration file in place, the actual programming logic required to complete the host is painfully simple. When our executable starts up, we will create an instance of the ServiceHost type. At runtime, this object will automatically read the data within the scope of the <system.serviceModel> element of the host's *.config file to determine the correct address, binding, and contract, and create the necessary plumbing:

```
static void Main(string[] args)
{
  Console.WriteLine("***** Console Based WCF Host *****");
```

```
    using (ServiceHost serviceHost = new ServiceHost(typeof(MagicEightBallService)))
    {
      // Open the host and start listening for incoming messages.
      serviceHost.Open();

      // Keep the service running until the Enter key is pressed.
      Console.WriteLine("The service is ready.");
      Console.WriteLine("Press the Enter key to terminate service.");
      Console.ReadLine();
    }
  }
```

If you now run this application, you will find that the host is alive in memory, ready to take incoming requests from remote clients (see Figure 25-6).

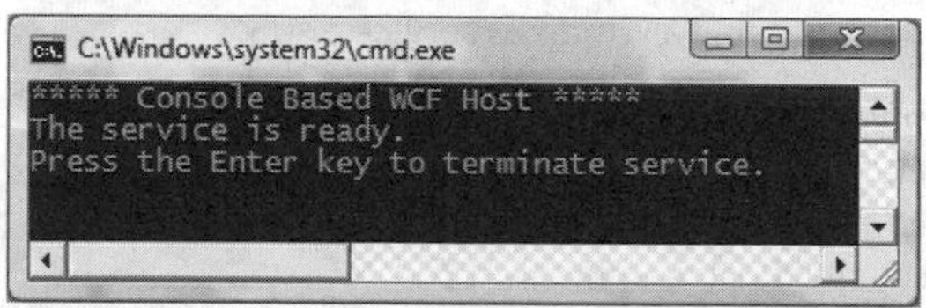

Figure 25-6. *Our host, ready for external calls via basic HTTP binding*

Host Coding Options

Currently, we are creating our `ServiceHost` using a constructor that simply requires the service's type information. However, it is also possible to pass in an array of `System.Uri` types as a constructor argument to represent the collection of addresses this service is accessible from. Currently, the address is found via the `*.config` file; however, if we were to update the `using` scope as so:

```
using (ServiceHost serviceHost = new ServiceHost(typeof(MagicEightBallService),
  new Uri[]{new Uri("http://localhost:8080/MagicEightBallService")}))
{
  ...
}
```

we would be able to define our endpoint as so:

```
<endpoint address =""
          binding="basicHttpBinding"
          contract="MagicEightBallServiceLib.IEightBall"/>
```

Of course, too much hard-coding within a host's code base decreases flexibility, so for the purposes of this current host example, I'll assume you are creating the service host simply by supplying the type information as we did before:

```
using (ServiceHost serviceHost = new ServiceHost(typeof(MagicEightBallService)))
{
  ...
}
```

One of the (slightly frustrating) aspects of authoring host `*.config` files is that you have a number of ways to construct the XML descriptors, based on the amount of hard-coding you have in the code base (as you have just seen in the case of the optional `Uri` array). To show yet another way to author `*.config` files, consider the following reworking:

```
<?xml version="1.0" encoding="utf-8" ?>
<configuration>
  <system.serviceModel>
    <services>
      <service name="MagicEightBallServiceLib.MagicEightBallService">

        <!-- Address obtained from <baseAddresses> -->
        <endpoint address =""
                  binding="basicHttpBinding"
                  contract="MagicEightBallServiceLib.IEightBall"/>

        <!-- List all of the base addresses in a dedicated section-->
        <host>
          <baseAddresses>
            <add baseAddress ="http://localhost:8080/MagicEightBallService"/>
          </baseAddresses>
        </host>
      </service>
    </services>
  </system.serviceModel>
</configuration>
```

In this case, the address attribute of the `<endpoint>` element is still empty, and regardless of the fact that we are not specifying an array of `Uri` objects in code when creating the `ServiceHost`, the application runs as before as the value is pulled from the `baseAddresses` scope. The benefit of storing the base address in a `<host>`'s `<baseAddresses>` region is that other parts of a `*.config` file (such as MEX, described shortly) also need to know the address of the service's endpoint. Thus, rather than having to copy and pass address values within a single `*.config` file, we can isolate the single value as shown here.

■ **Note** In a later example, I'll introduce you to a graphical configuration tool that allows you to author configuration files in a less tedious manner.

In any case, before we build a client application to communicate with our service, let's dig a bit deeper into the role of the `ServiceHost` class type and `<service.serviceModel>` element as well as the role of metadata exchange (MEX) services.

Details of the ServiceHost Type

The `ServiceHost` class type is used to configure and expose a WCF service from the hosting executable. However, be aware that you will only make direct use of this type when building a custom `*.exe` to host your services. If you are using IIS (or the Vista-specific WAS) to expose a service, the `ServiceHost` object is created automatically on your behalf.

As you have seen, this type requires a complete service description, which is obtained dynamically through the configuration settings of the host's `*.config` file. While this happens automatically upon object creation, it is possible to manually configure the state of your `ServiceHost` object using a number of members. In addition to `Open()` and `Close()` (which communicate with your service in a synchronous manner), Table 25-8 illustrates some further members of interest.

Table 25-8. *Select Members of the* `ServiceHost` *Type*

Members	Meaning in Life
`Authorization`	This property gets the authorization level for the service being hosted.
`AddServiceEndpoint()`	This method allows you to programmatically register an endpoint to the host.
`BaseAddresses`	This property obtains the list of registered base addresses for the current service.
`BeginOpen()` `BeginClose()`	These methods allow you to asynchronously open and close a `ServiceHost` object, using the standard asynchronous .NET delegate syntax.
`CloseTimeout`	This property allows you to set and get the time allowed for the service to close down.
`Credentials`	This property obtains the security credentials used by the current service.
`EndOpen()` `EndClose()`	These methods are the asynchronous counterparts to `BeginOpen()` and `BeginClose()`.
`OpenTimeout`	This property allows you to set and get the time allowed for the service to start up.
`State`	This property gets a value that indicates the current state of the communication object, represented by the `CommunicationState` enum (opened, closed, created, etc.).

To illustrate some additional aspects of `ServiceHost`, update your `Program` class with a new static method that prints out various aspects of the current host:

```
static void DisplayHostInfo(ServiceHost host)
{
  Console.WriteLine();
  Console.WriteLine("***** Host Info *****");

  Console.WriteLine("Name: {0}",
    host.Description.ConfigurationName);
  Console.WriteLine("Port: {0}",
    host.BaseAddresses[0].Port);
  Console.WriteLine("LocalPath: {0}",
    host.BaseAddresses[0].LocalPath);
  Console.WriteLine("Uri: {0}",
    host.BaseAddresses[0].AbsoluteUri);
  Console.WriteLine("Scheme: {0}",
    host.BaseAddresses[0].Scheme);
  Console.WriteLine("**********************");
  Console.WriteLine();
}
```

Assuming you call this new method from within `Main()` after opening your host:

```
using (ServiceHost serviceHost = new ServiceHost(typeof(MagicEightBallService)))
{
  // Open the host and start listening for incoming messages.
  serviceHost.Open();
  DisplayHostInfo(serviceHost);
...
}
```

you will see the statistics shown in Figure 25-7.

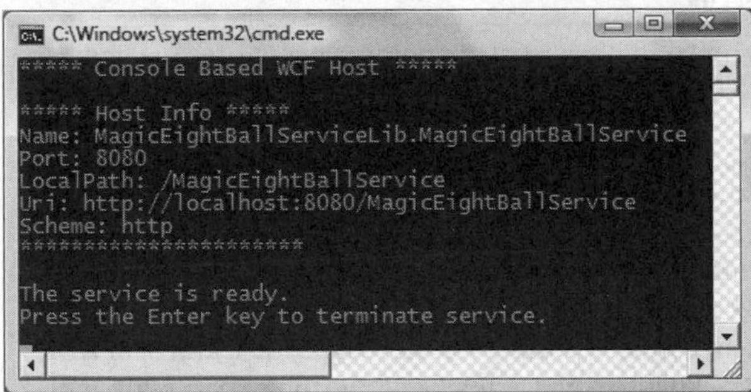

Figure 25-7. *Details of our host*

Details of the <system.serviceModel> Element

Like any XML element, <system.serviceModel> can define a set of subelements, each of which can be qualified via numerous attributes. While you should consult the .NET Framework 3.5 SDK documentation for full details regarding the set of possible attributes, here is a skeleton that lists the valid subelements:

```
<system.serviceModel>
  <behaviors>
  </behaviors>
  <client>
  </client>
  <commonBehaviors>
  </commonBehaviors>
  <diagnostics>
  </diagnostics>
  <serviceHostingEnvironment>
  </serviceHostingEnvironment>
  <comContracts>
  </comContracts>
  <services>
  </services>
  <bindings>
  </bindings>
</system.serviceModel>
```

You'll see more exotic configuration files as you move through the chapter; however, the crux of each subelement can be discovered in Table 25-9.

Table 25-9. *Subelements of* <service.serviceModel>

Subelement	Meaning in Life
behaviors	WCF supports various endpoint and service behaviors. In a nutshell, a *behavior* allows you to further qualify the functionality of a host or client.
bindings	This element allows you to fine-tune each of the WCF-supplied bindings (basicHttpBinding, netMsmqBinding, etc.) as well as specify any custom bindings used by the host.

Continued

Table 25-9. *Continued*

Subelement	Meaning in Life
client	This element contains a list of endpoints a client uses to connect to a service. Obviously, this is not terribly useful in a host's *.config file.
comContracts	This element defines COM contracts enabled for WCF and COM interoperability.
commonBehaviors	This element can only be set within a machine.config file. It can be used to define all of the behaviors used by each WCF service on a given machine.
diagnostics	This element contains settings for the diagnostic features of WCF. The user can enable/disable tracing, performance counters, and the WMI provider, and can add custom message filters.
serviceHostingEnvironment	This element specifies if this operation can be the initial operation in a session.
services	This element contains a collection of WCF services exposed from the host.

Enabling Metadata Exchange

Recall that WCF client applications communicate with the WCF service via an intervening proxy type. While you could most certainly author the proxy code completely by hand, doing so would be tedious and error-prone. Ideally, a tool could be used to generate the necessary grunge code (including the client-side *.config file). Thankfully, the .NET Framework 3.5 SDK provides a command-line tool (svcutil.exe) for this very purpose. As well, Visual Studio 2008 provides similar functionality via the Project ➤ Add Service Reference menu option.

However, in order for these tools to generate the necessary proxy code/*.config file, they must be able to discover the format of the WCF service interfaces and any defined data contracts (the method names, type of parameters, etc.).

Metadata exchange (MEX) is a WCF *service behavior* that can be specified to fine-tune how the WCF runtime handles your service. Simply put, each <behavior> element can define a set of activities a given service can subscribe to. WCF provides numerous behaviors out of the box, and it is possible to build your own.

The MEX behavior (which is disabled by default) will intercept any metadata requests sent via HTTP GET. If you want to allow svcutil.exe or Visual Studio 2008 to automate the creation of the required client-side proxy *.config file, you must enable MEX.

Enabling MEX is a matter of tweaking the host's *.config file with the proper settings (or authoring the corresponding C# code). First, you must add a new <endpoint> just for MEX. Second, you need to define a WCF behavior to allow HTTP GET access. Third, you need to associate this behavior by name to your service via the behaviorConfiguration attribute on the opening <service> element. Finally, you need to add a <host> element to define the base address of this service (MEX will look here to figure out the locations of the types to describe).

■ **Note** This final step can be bypassed if you pass in a System.Uri object to represent the base address as a parameter to the ServiceHost constructor.

Consider the following updated host *.config file, which creates a custom <behavior> element (named EightBallMEXBehavior) that is associated to our service via the behaviorConfiguration attribute within the <service> definition:

```
<?xml version="1.0" encoding="utf-8" ?>
<configuration>
  <system.serviceModel>
    <services>
      <service name="MagicEightBallServiceLib.MagicEightBallService"
               behaviorConfiguration = "EightBallServiceMEXBehavior">
        <endpoint address =""
                  binding="basicHttpBinding"
                  contract="MagicEightBallServiceLib.IEightBall"/>

        <!-- Enable the MEX endpoint -->
        <endpoint address="mex"
                  binding="mexHttpBinding"
                  contract="IMetadataExchange" />

        <!-- Need to add this so MEX knows the address of our service -->
        <host>
          <baseAddresses>
            <add baseAddress ="http://localhost:8080/MagicEightBallService"/>
          </baseAddresses>
        </host>
      </service>
    </services>

    <!-- A behavior definition for MEX -->
    <behaviors>
      <serviceBehaviors>
        <behavior name="EightBallServiceMEXBehavior" >
          <serviceMetadata httpGetEnabled="true" />
        </behavior>
      </serviceBehaviors>
    </behaviors>
  </system.serviceModel>
</configuration>
```

You are now able to restart the service and view its metadata description using the web browser of your choice. To do so, while the host is still running simply enter the address as the URL:

```
http://localhost:8080/MagicEightBallService
```

Once you are at the homepage for your WCF service (see Figure 25-7), you are provided with basic details regarding how to interact with this service programmatically as well as a way to view the WSDL contract by clicking the hyperlink at the top of the page. Recall that Web Service Description Language (WSDL) is a grammar that describes the structure of web services at a given endpoint.

Source Code The MagicEightBallServiceHost project is located under the Chapter 25 subdirectory.

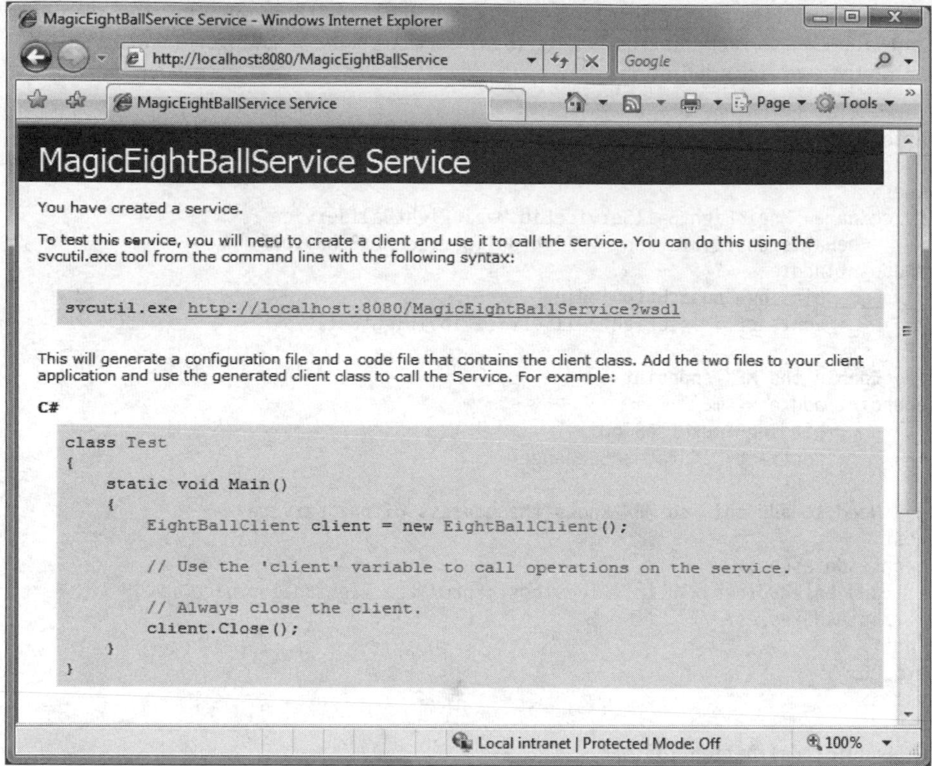

Figure 25-8. *Ready to view metadata, via MEX*

Building the WCF Client Application

Now that our host is in place, the final task is to build a piece of software to communicate with this WCF service type. While we could take the long road and build the necessary infrastructure by hand (a feasible but labor-intensive task), the .NET Framework 3.5 SDK provides several approaches to quickly generate a client-side proxy. To begin, create a new Console Application named MagicEightBallServiceClient.

Generating Proxy Code Using svcutil.exe

The first way you can build a client-side proxy is to make use of the svcutil.exe command-line tool. Using svcutil.exe, you can generate a new C# language file that represents the proxy code itself as well as a client-side configuration file. To do so, simply specify the service's endpoint as the first parameter. The /out: flag is used to define the name of the *.cs file containing the proxy, while the /config: option specifies the name of the generated client-side *.config file.

Assuming your service is currently running, the following command set passed into svcutil.exe will generate two new files in the working directory (which should, of course, be entered as a single line within a Visual Studio 2008 command prompt):

```
svcutil http://localhost:8080/MagicEightBallService
  /out:myProxy.cs /config:app.config
```

If you open the myProxy.cs file, you will find a client-side representation of the IEightBall interface, as well as a new class named EightBallClient, which is the proxy class itself. This class derives from the generic class, System.ServiceModel.ClientBase<T>, where T is the registered service interface.

In addition to a number of custom constructors, each method adorned with the [OperationContract] attribute will be implemented to delegate to the parent class's Channels property to invoke the correct external method. Here is a partial snapshot of the proxy type:

```
[System.Diagnostics.DebuggerStepThroughAttribute()]
[System.CodeDom.Compiler.GeneratedCodeAttribute("System.ServiceModel", "3.0.0.0")]
public partial class EightBallClient :
  System.ServiceModel.ClientBase<IEightBall>, IEightBall
{
...
  public string ObtainAnswerToQuestion(string userQuestion)
  {
    return base.Channel.ObtainAnswerToQuestion(userQuestion);
  }
}
```

When you create an instance of the proxy type, the base class will establish a connection to the endpoint using the settings specified in the client-side application configuration file. Much like the server-side configuration file, the generated client-side App.config file contains an <endpoint> element and details regarding the basicHttpBinding used to communicate with the service.

In addition, you will find the following <client> element, which (once again) establishes the ABCs from the client's perspective:

```
<client>
  <endpoint
   address="http://localhost:8080/MagicEightBallService"
   binding="basicHttpBinding" bindingConfiguration="BasicHttpBinding_IEightBall"
   contract="ServiceReference.IEightBall" name="BasicHttpBinding_IEightBall" />
</client>
```

At this point, you could include these two files into a client project (and reference the System.ServiceModel.dll assembly) and use the proxy type to communicate with the remote WCF service. However, rather than doing so, let's see how Visual Studio can help to further automate the creation of client-side proxy files.

Generating Proxy Code Using Visual Studio 2008

Like any good command-line tool, svcutil.exe provides a great number of options that can be used to control how the client proxy is generated. If you do not require these advanced options, you are able to generate the same two files using the Visual Studio 2008 IDE. Simply select the Add Service Reference option from the Project menu.

Once you activate this menu option, you will be prompted to enter the service URI. At this point click the Go button to see the service description (see Figure 25-9).

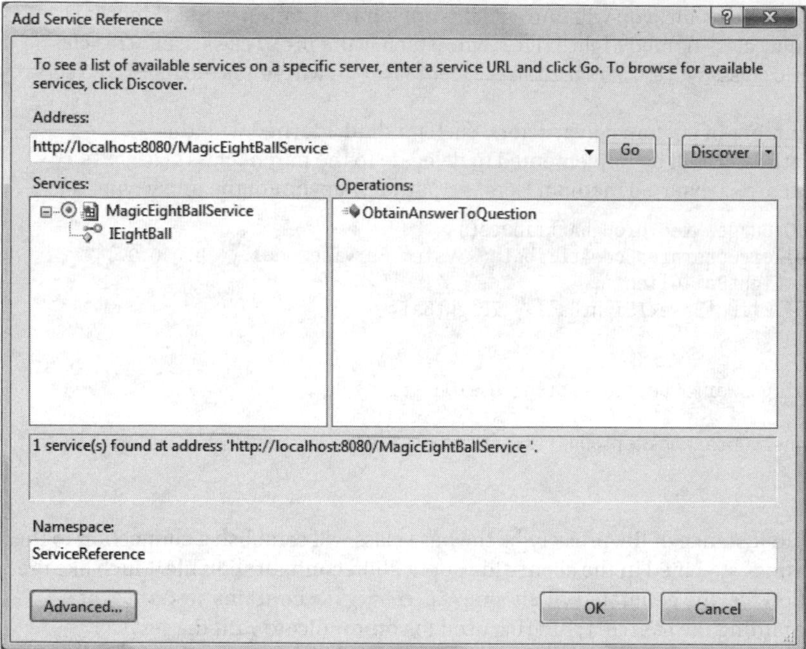

Figure 25-9. *Generating the proxy files using Visual Studio 2008*

Beyond creating and inserting the proxy files into your current project, this tool is kind enough to reference the WCF assemblies automatically on your behalf. As a naming convention, the proxy class is defined within a namespace called ServiceReference, which is nested in the client's namespace (to avoid possible name clashes). Here, then, is the complete client code:

```
// Location of the proxy.
using MagicEightBallServiceClient.ServiceReference;

namespace MagicEightBallServiceClient
{
  class Program
  {
    static void Main(string[] args)
    {
      Console.WriteLine("***** Ask the Magic 8 Ball *****\n");

      using (EightBallClient ball = new EightBallClient())
      {
        Console.Write("Your question: ");
        string question = Console.ReadLine();
        string answer =
          ball.ObtainAnswerToQuestion(question);
        Console.WriteLine("8-Ball says: {0}", answer);
      }
      Console.ReadLine();
    }
  }
}
```

Now, assuming your WCF host is currently running, you can execute the client. Figure 25-10 shows one possible response (apologies to Grace Wong at Apress).

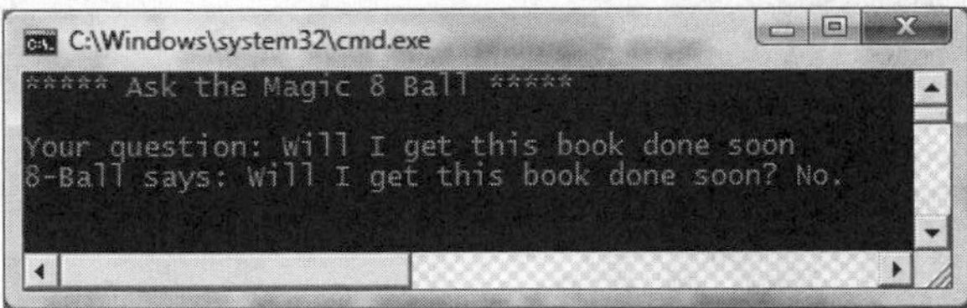

Figure 25-10. *The completed WCF client host*

Source Code The MagicEightBallServiceClient project is located under the Chapter 25 subdirectory.

Configuring a TCP-Based Binding

At this point, the host and client applications are both configured to make use of the simplest of the HTTP-based bindings, basicHttpBinding. Recall that the benefit of offloading settings to configuration files is that we can change the underlying plumbing in a declarative manner.

To illustrate, let's try a little experiment. Create a new folder on your C drive (or wherever you happen to be saving your code) named EightBallTCP, and within this new folder create two subdirectories named Host and Client.

Next, using Windows Explorer, navigate to the \bin\Debug folder of the host project and copy MagicEightBallServiceHost.exe, MagicEightBallServiceHost.exe.config, and MagicEightBallServiceLib.dll to the C:\EightBallTCP\Host folder. Open the *.config file for editing using a simple text editor, and modify the existing contents as follows:

```
<?xml version="1.0" encoding="utf-8" ?>
<configuration>
  <system.serviceModel>
    <services>
      <service name="MagicEightBallServiceLib.MagicEightBallService">
        <endpoint address =""
                  binding="netTcpBinding"
                  contract="MagicEightBallServiceLib.IEightBall"/>
        <host>
          <baseAddresses>
            <add baseAddress ="net.tcp://localhost:8080/MagicEightBallService"/>
          </baseAddresses>
        </host>
      </service>
    </services>
  </system.serviceModel>
</configuration>
```

Essentially, this host's *.config file has stripped out all the MEX settings (as we already built the proxy) and established that it is using the netTcpBinding binding type. Now run the application by double-clicking the *.exe. If all is well, you should find the host output shown in Figure 25-11.

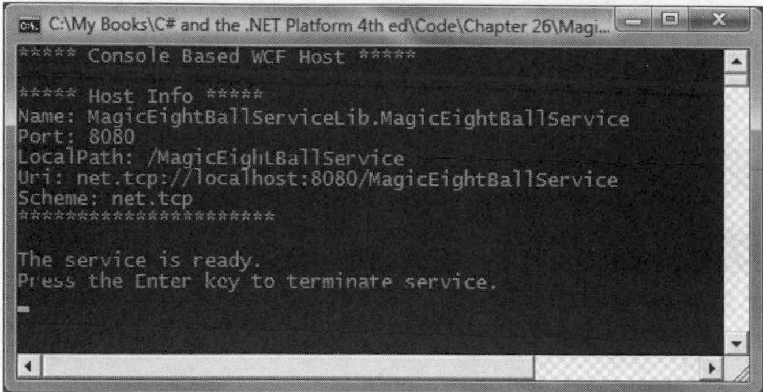

Figure 25-11. *Hosting the WCF service using TCP bindings*

To complete the test, copy the `MagicEightBallServiceClient.exe` and `MagicEightBallServiceClient.exe.config` files from the \bin\Debug folder of the client application into the C:\EightBallTCP\Client folder. Update the client configuration file as so:

```
<?xml version="1.0" encoding="utf-8" ?>
<configuration>
  <system.serviceModel>
    <client>
      <endpoint address="net.tcp://localhost:8080/MagicEightBallService"
                binding="netTcpBinding"
                contract="ServiceReference.IEightBall"
                name="netTcpBinding_IEightBall" />
    </client>
  </system.serviceModel>
</configuration>
```

This client-side configuration file is a massive simplification from what the Visual Studio proxy generator authored. Notice how we have completely removed the existing `<bindings>` element. Originally, the `*.config` file contained a `<bindings>` element with a `<basicHttpBinding>` subelement that supplied numerous details of the client's binding settings (timeouts, etc.).

In reality, we never needed that detail for our example, as we automatically obtain the default values of the underlying `BasicHttpBinding` object. If we needed to, we could of course update the existing `<bindings>` element to define details of the `<netTcpBinding>` subelement, but doing so is not required if we are happy with the default values of the `NetTcpBinding` object.

In any case, you should now be able to run your client application, and assuming the host is still running in the background, you are able to move data between your assemblies using TCP.

■ **Source Code** The MagicEightBallTCP project is located under the Chapter 25 subdirectory.

Using the WCF Service Library Project Template

Before we build a more exotic WCF service that communicates with our AutoLot database created in Chapter 22, the next example will illustrate a number of important topics, including the benefits of the WCF Service Library project template, the WCF Test Client, the WCF configuration editor, hosting WCF services within a Windows service, and asynchronous client calls. To stay focused on these new concepts, this WCF service will also be intentionally simple.

Building a Simple Math Service

To begin, create a brand-new WCF Service Library project named MathServiceLibrary, being sure to select the correct option under the WCF node of the New Project dialog box (see Figure 25-2 if you need a nudge). Now change the name of the initial `IService1.cs` file to `IBasicMath.cs`. Once you have done so, *delete* all of the example code within the `MathServiceLibrary` namespace and replace it with the following:

```
namespace MathServiceLibrary
{
  [ServiceContract(Namespace="www.Intertech.com")]
  public interface IBasicMath
  {
    [OperationContract]
    int Add(int x, int y);
  }
}
```

Next, change the name of the `Service1.cs` file to `MathService.cs`, and (once again) delete all the example code within the `MathServiceLibrary` namespace and implement your service contract as so:

```
namespace MathServiceLibrary
{
  public class MathService : IBasicMath
  {
    public int Add(int x, int y)
    {
      // To simulate a lengthy request.
      System.Threading.Thread.Sleep(5000);
      return x + y;
    }
  }
}
```

Finally, open the supplied `App.config` file and replace all occurrences of `IService1` with `IBasicMath`, and all occurrences of `Service1` with `MathService`. As well, take a moment to notice that this `*.config` file has already been enabled to support MEX, and by default it is making use of the `wsHttpBinding` protocol.

Testing the WCF Service with WcfTestClient.exe

One benefit of using the WCF Service Library project is that when you debug or run your library, it will read the settings in the `*.config` file and use them to load the WCF Test Client application (`WcfTestClient.exe`). This GUI-based application allows you to test each member of your service interface as you build the WCF service, rather than having to manually build a host/client as you did previously simply for testing purposes.

Figure 25-12 shows the testing environment for `MathService`. Notice that when you double-click an interface method, you are able to specify input parameters and invoke the member.

While this utility works out of the box when you have created a WCF Service Library project, be aware that you can use this tool to test any WCF service when you start it at the command line by specifying a MEX endpoint. For example, if you were to start the `MagicEightBallServiceHost.exe` application, you would be able to specify the following command within a Visual Studio 2008 command prompt:

```
wcftestclient http://localhost:8080/MagicEightBallService
```

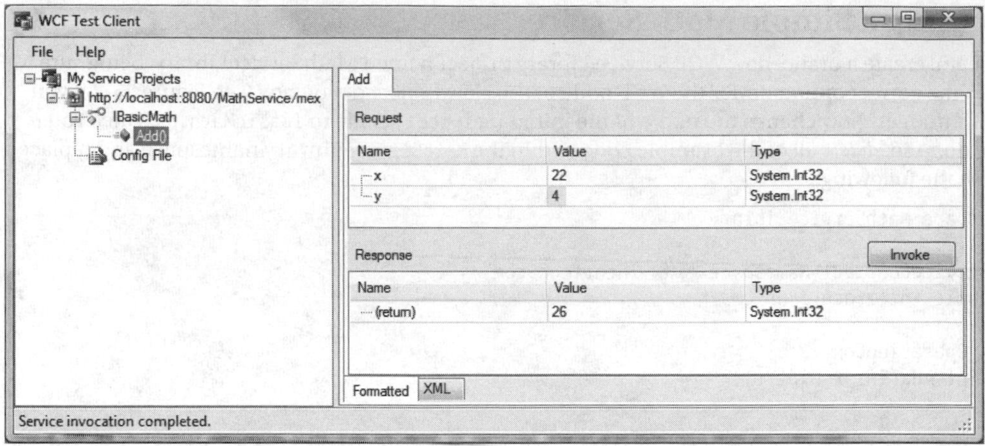

Figure 25-12. *Testing the WCF service using* `WcfTestClient.exe`

Once you do, you will be able to invoke `ObtainAnswerToQuestion()` in a similar manner.

Altering Configuration Files Using SvcConfigEditor.exe

Another benefit of making use of the WCF Service Library project is that you are able to right-click on the `App.config` file within the Solution Explorer to activate the GUI-based Service Configuration Editor, `SvcConfigEditor.exe` (see Figure 29-13). This same technique can be used from a client application that has referenced a WCF service.

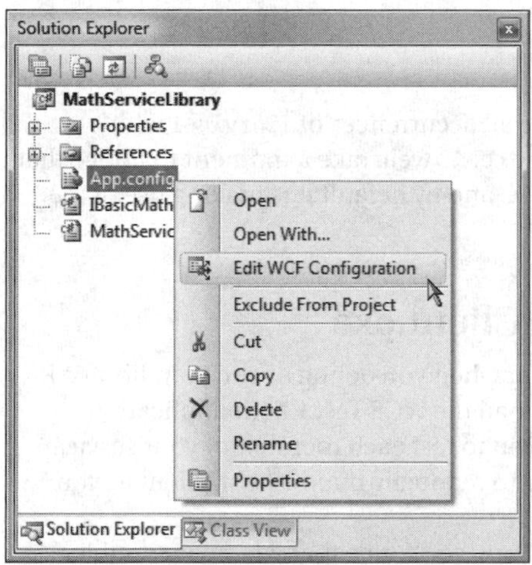

Figure 25-13. *GUI-based* `*.config` *file editing starts here.*

Once you activate this tool, you are able to change the XML-based data using a friendly user interface. There are many obvious benefits of using a tool such as this to maintain your `*.config` files. First and foremost, you can rest assured that the generated markup conforms to the expected format and is typo-free. Next, it is a great way to *see* the valid values that could be assigned to a given attribute. Last but not least, you no longer need to manually author tedious XML data.

Figure 25-14 shows the overall look and feel of the Service Configuration Editor. Truth be told, an entire chapter could be written describing all of the interesting options `SvcConfigEditor.exe` supports (COM+ integration, creation of new `*.config` files, etc.). Be sure to take time to investigate this tool, and be aware that you can access a fairly detailed help system by pressing F1.

■ **Note** The `SvcConfigEditor.exe` utility can edit (or create) configuration files even if you do not select an initial WCF Service Library project. Using a Visual Studio 2008 command window, launch the tool and make use of the File ➤ Open menu option to load an existing `*.config` file for editing.

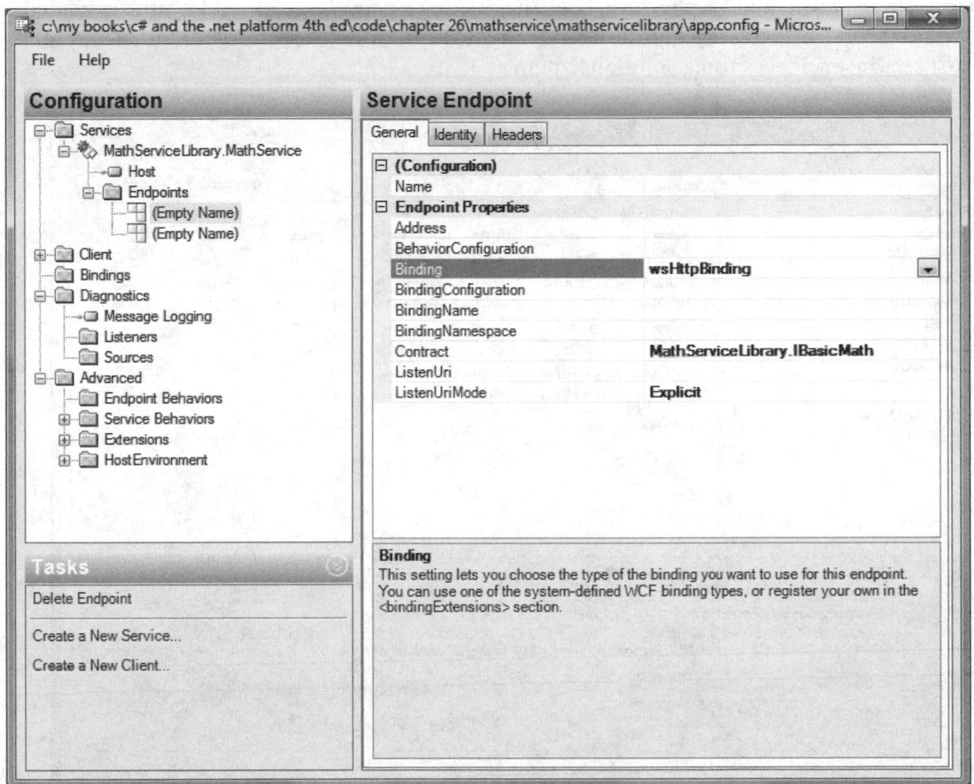

Figure 25-14. *Working with the WCF Service Configuration Editor*

We have no need to further configure our WCF `MathService`, so at this point we can move on to the task of building a custom host.

Hosting the WCF Service As a Windows Service

As you might agree, hosting a WCF service from within a console application (or within a GUI desktop application, for that matter) is not an ideal choice for a production-level server, given that the host must remain running visibly in the background to service clients. Even if you were to minimize the hosting application to the Windows taskbar, it would still be far too easy to accidentally shut down the host, thereby terminating the connection with any client applications.

■ **Note** While it is true that a desktop Windows application does not *have* to show a main window, a typical `*.exe` does require user interaction to load the executable. A Windows service (described next) can be configured to run even if no users are currently logged on to the workstation.

If you are building an in-house WCF application, another alternative is to host your WCF service library from within a dedicated Windows service. One benefit of doing so is that a Windows service can be configured to automatically start when the target machine boots up. Another benefit is that Windows services run invisibly in the background (unlike our console application) and do not require user interactivity.

To illustrate how to build such a host, begin by creating a new Windows service project named MathWindowsServiceHost (see Figure 25-15). Once you have done so, rename your initial `Service1.cs` file to `MathWinService.cs` using Solution Explorer.

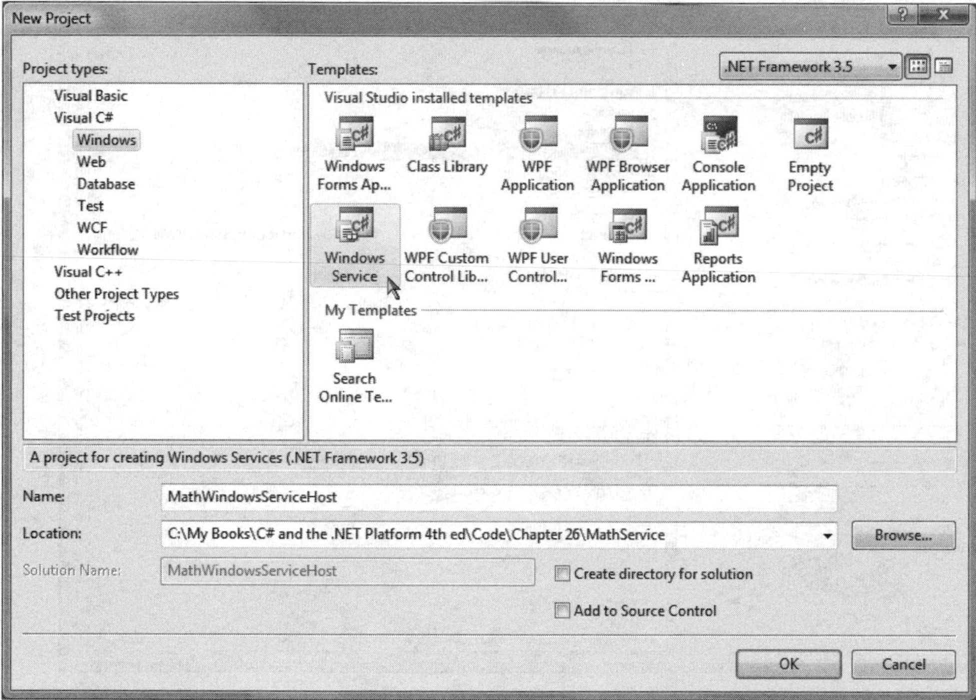

Figure 25-15. *Creating a Windows service to host our WCF service*

Specifying the ABCs in Code

Now, assuming you have set a reference to your `MathServiceLibrary.dll` and `System.ServiceModel.dll` assemblies, all you need to do is make use of the `ServiceHost` type within the `OnStart()` and `OnStop()` methods of your Windows service type. Open the code file for your service host class (by right-clicking the designer and selecting View Code), and add the following logic:

```
// Be sure to import these namespaces:
using MathServiceLibrary;
using System.ServiceModel;
```

```
public partial class MathWinService: ServiceBase
{
  // A member variable of type ServiceHost.
  private ServiceHost myHost;

  public MathWinService()
  {
    InitializeComponent();
  }

  protected override void OnStart(string[] args)
  {
    // Just to be really safe.
    if (myHost != null)
    {
      myHost.Close();
      myHost = null;
    }

    // Create the host.
    myHost = new ServiceHost(typeof(MathService));

    // The ABCs in code!
    Uri address = new Uri("http://localhost:8080/MathServiceLibrary");
    WSHttpBinding binding = new WSHttpBinding();
    Type contract = typeof(IBasicMath);

    // Add this endpoint.
    myHost.AddServiceEndpoint(contract, binding, address);

    // Open the host.
    myHost.Open();
  }

  protected override void OnStop()
  {
    // Shut down the host.
    if(myHost != null)
      myHost.Close();
  }
}
```

While nothing is preventing you from using a configuration file when building a Windows service host for a WCF service, here (for a change of pace) notice that you are programmatically establishing the endpoint using the `Uri`, `WSHttpBinding`, and `Type` classes, rather than making use of a `*.config` file. Once you have created each aspect of the ABCs, you inform the host programmatically by calling `AddServiceEndpoint()`.

Enabling MEX

While we could enable MEX programmatically as well, we will opt for a configuration file. Insert a new `App.config` file into your Windows service project that contains the following MEX settings:

```
<?xml version="1.0" encoding="utf-8" ?>
<configuration>
  <system.serviceModel>
    <services>
```

```
      <service name="MathServiceLibrary.MathService"
               behaviorConfiguration = "MathServiceMEXBehavior">

      <!-- Enable the MEX endpoint -->
      <endpoint address="mex"
                binding="mexHttpBinding"
                contract="IMetadataExchange" />

      <!-- Need to add this so MEX knows the address of our service -->
      <host>
        <baseAddresses>
          <add baseAddress ="http://localhost:8080/MathService"/>
        </baseAddresses>
      </host>
    </service>
  </services>

    <!-- A behavior definition for MEX -->
    <behaviors>
      <serviceBehaviors>
        <behavior name="MathServiceMEXBehavior" >
          <serviceMetadata httpGetEnabled="true" />
        </behavior>
      </serviceBehaviors>
    </behaviors>
  </system.serviceModel>
</configuration>
```

Creating a Windows Service Installer

In order to register your Windows service with the operating system, you need to add an installer to your project that will contain the necessary code to allow you to register the service. To do so, simply right-click the Windows service designer surface and select Add Installer (see Figure 25-16).

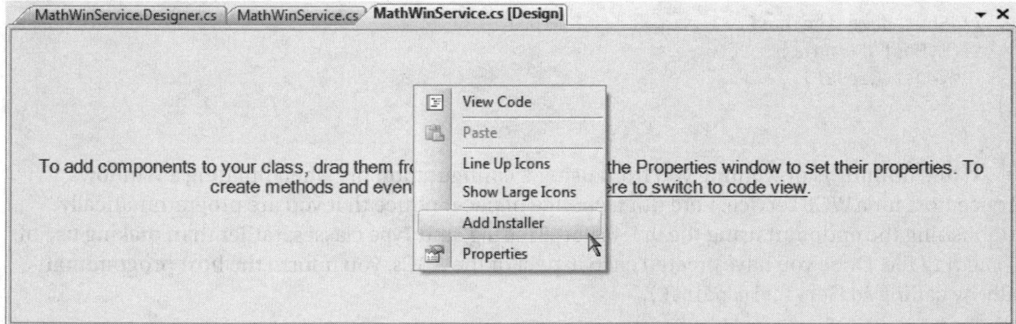

Figure 25-16. *Adding an installer for the Windows service*

Once you have done so, you will see two components have been added to a new designer surface. The first component (named `serviceProcessInstaller1` by default) represents a type that is able to install a new Windows service on the target machine. Select this type on the designer and use the Properties window to set the `Account` property to `LocalSystem`.

The second component (named `serviceInstaller1`) represents a type that will install your particular Windows service. Again, using the Properties window, change the `ServiceName` property to Math Order Service (as you might have guessed, this represents the friendly display name of the registered Windows service), set the `StartType` property to `Automatic`, and add a friendly description of your Windows service via the `Description` property. At this point you can compile your application.

Installing the Windows Service

A Windows service can be installed on the host machine using a traditional setup program (such as an `*.msi` installer) or via the `installutil.exe` command-line tool. Using a Visual Studio 2008 command prompt, change into the \bin\Debug folder of your MathWindowsServiceHost project. Now, enter the following command:

```
installutil MathWindowsServiceHost.exe
```

Assuming the installation succeeded, you can now open the Services applet located under the Administrative Tools folder of your Control Panel. You should see the friendly name of your Windows service listed alphabetically. Once you locate it, you can start the service on your local machine (see Figure 25-17).

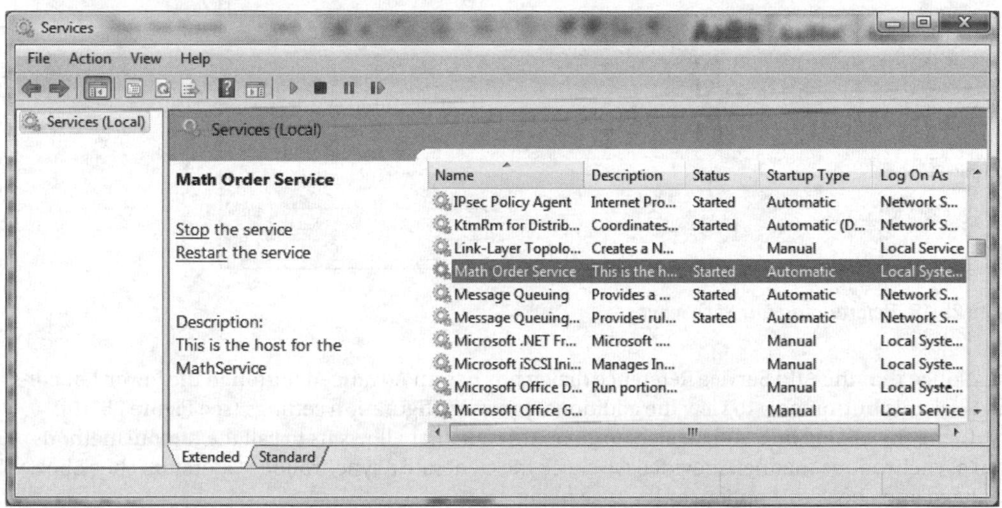

Figure 25-17. *Viewing our Windows service, which is hosting our WCF service*

Now that the service is alive and kicking, the last step is to build a client application to consume its services.

Source Code The MathWindowsServiceHost project is located under the Chapter 25 subdirectory.

Invoking a Service Asynchronously

Create a new Console Application named MathClient and set a Service Reference to your running WCF service that is current hosted by the Windows service running in the background using the Add Service Reference option of Visual Studio. Don't click the OK button yet, however (see Figure 25-18).

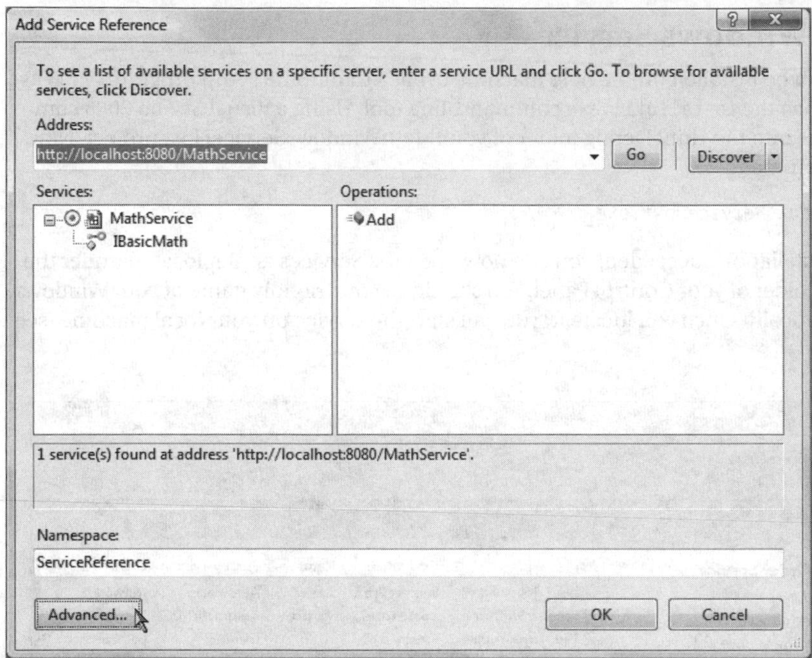

Figure 25-18. *Referencing our* `MathService`

Notice that the Add Service Reference dialog box has an Advanced button in the lower-left corner. Click this button now to view the additional proxy configuration settings (see Figure 25-19).

Using this dialog box, we can elect to generate code that allows us to call the remote methods in an asynchronous manner, provided we check the Generate Asynchronous Operators check box. Go ahead and check this option for the time being.

The other option on this dialog box you should be aware of is the Add Web Reference button. If you have a background in building XML web services in Visual Studio 2005 or earlier, you may recall that you had an Add Web Reference option rather than an Add Service Reference option. If you click this particular button, you will be able to receive proxy code that will allow you to communicate with a traditional web service described within an `*.asmx` file.

The remaining options of this dialog box are used to control the generation of data contracts, which we will examine a bit later in this chapter. In any case, be sure you did indeed check the Generate Asynchronous Operators check box and click OK on each dialog box to return to the Visual Studio IDE.

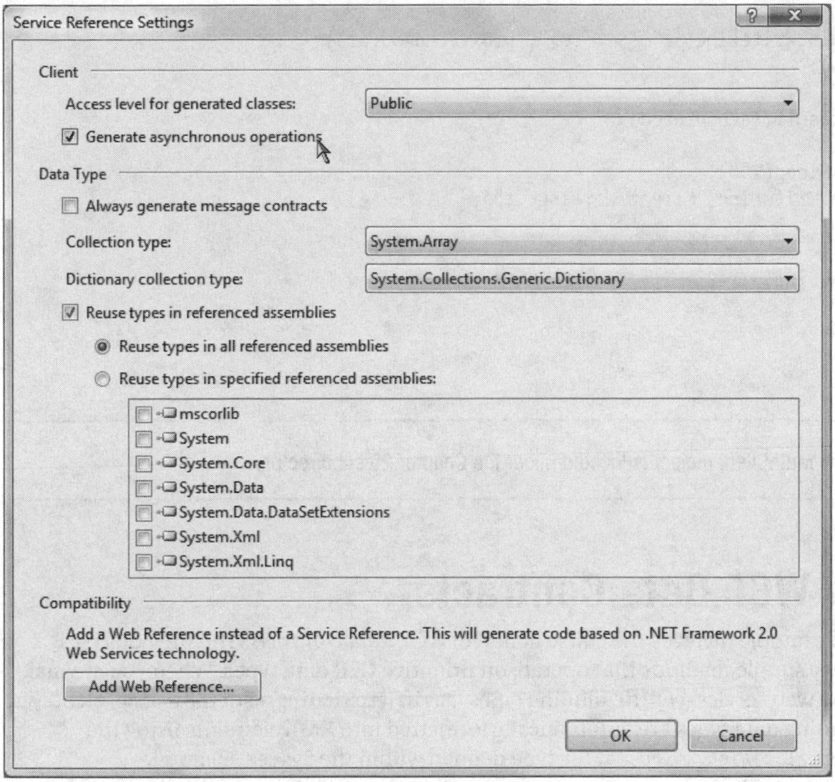

Figure 25-19. *Advanced client-side proxy configuration options*

At this point, the proxy code will contain additional methods that allow you to invoke each member of the service contract using the expected Begin/End asynchronous invocation pattern described in Chapter 18. Here is a simple implementation that makes use of a lambda expression rather than a strongly typed AsyncCallback delegate.

```
using System;
using MathClient.ServiceReference;
using System.Threading;

namespace MathClient
{
  class Program
  {
    static void Main(string[] args)
    {
      Console.WriteLine("***** The Async Math Client *****\n");

      using (BasicMathClient proxy = new BasicMathClient())
      {
        proxy.Open();

        // Add numbers in an async manner, using a lambda expression.
        IAsyncResult result = proxy.BeginAdd(2, 3,
          ar =>
```

```
        {
          Console.WriteLine("2 + 5 = {0}", proxy.EndAdd(ar));
        }, null);

      while (!result.IsCompleted)
      {
        Thread.Sleep(200);
        Console.WriteLine("Client working...");
      }
    }
    Console.ReadLine();
  }
 }
}
```

Source Code The MathClient project is located under the Chapter 25 subdirectory.

Designing WCF Data Contracts

This chapter's final example involves the construction of WCF *data contracts*. The previous WCF services defined very simple methods that operate on primitive CLR data types. When you are making use of any of the web service–centric binding types (`basicHttpBinding`, `wsHttpBinding`, etc.), incoming and outgoing data types are automatically formatted into XML elements using the `System.Runtime.Serialization.XmlFormatter` type defined within the `System.Runtime.Serialization.dll` assembly. On a related note, if you make use of a TCP-based binding (such as `netTcpBinding`), the parameters and return values of simple data types are transmitted using a compact binary format.

Note The WCF runtime will also automatically encode any type marked with the `[Serializable]` attribute.

However, when you define service contracts that make use of custom types as parameters or return values, these types must be defined using a data contract. Simply put, a data contract is a type adorned with the `[DataContract]` attribute. Each field you expect to be used as part of the proposed contract is likewise marked with the `[DataMember]` attribute.

Note If a data contract contains fields not marked with the `[DataMember]` attribute, it will not be serialized by the WCF runtime.

To illustrate the construction of data contracts, let's create a brand-new WCF service that interacts with the AutoLot database created back in Chapter 22. As well, this final WCF service will be created using the web-based WCF Service template. Recall that this type of WCF service will automatically be placed into an IIS virtual directory, and it will function in a similar fashion to a traditional .NET XML web service. Once you understand the composition of such a WCF service, you should have little problem porting an existing WCF service into a new IIS virtual directory.

■ **Note** This example assumes you are somewhat comfortable with the structure of an IIS virtual directory (and IIS itself). If this is not the case, Chapter 31 will examine the details.

Using the Web-Centric WCF Service Project Template

Using the File ➤ New ➤ Web Site menu option, create a new WCF service named AutoLotWCFService, exposed from the following URI: `http://localhost/AutoLotWCFService` (see Figure 25-20). Be sure the Location drop-down list has HTTP as the active selection.

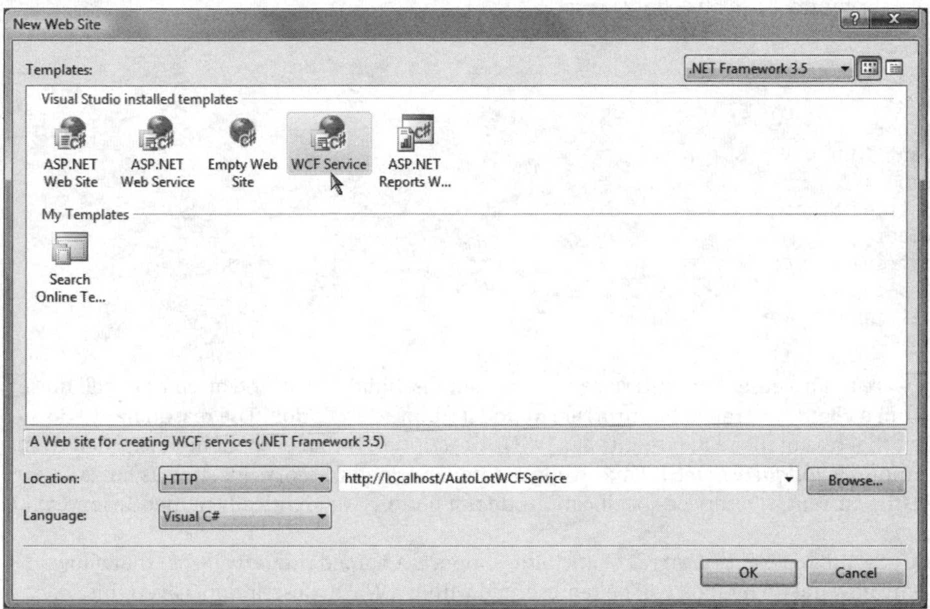

Figure 25-20. *Creating a web-centric WCF service*

Once you have done so, set a reference to the `AutoLotDAL.dll` assembly you created in Chapter 22 (via the Website ➤ Add Reference menu option). Much like a WCF Service Library project, you have been given some example starter code (located under the App_Code folder), which you will obviously want to delete. To begin, rename the initial `IService.cs` file to `IAutoLotService.cs`, and define the initial service contract within your newly named file:

```
[ServiceContract]
public interface IAutoLotService
{
  [OperationContract]
  void InsertCar(int id, string make, string color, string petname);

  [OperationContract]
  void InsertCar(InventoryRecord car);

  [OperationContract]
  InventoryRecord[] GetInventory();
}
```

This interface defines three methods, one of which returns an array of the (yet-to-be-created) InventoryRecord type. You may recall that the GetInventory() method of InventoryDAL simply returned a DataTable object, which might make you question why our service's GetInventory() method does not do the same.

While it would work to return a DataTable from a WCF service method, recall that WCF was built to honor the use of SOA principles, one of which is to program against contracts, not implementations. Therefore, rather than returning the .NET-specific DataTable type to an external caller, we will return a custom data contract (InventoryRecord) that will be correctly expressed in the contained WSDL document in an agnostic manner.

Also note that this interface defines an overloaded method named InsertCar(). The first version takes four incoming parameters, while the second version takes an InventoryRecord type as input. This data contract can be defined as so:

```
[DataContract]
public class InventoryRecord
{
  [DataMember]
  public int ID;
  [DataMember]
  public string Make;
  [DataMember]
  public string Color;
  [DataMember]
  public string PetName;
}
```

If you were to implement this interface as it now stands, build a host, and attempt to call these methods from a client, you might be surprised to find a runtime exception. The reason has to do with the fact that one of the requirements of a WSDL description is that each method exposed from a given endpoint is *uniquely named*. Thus, while method overloading works just fine as far as C# is concerned, the current web service specifications do not permit two identically named InsertCar() methods.

Thankfully, the [OperationContract] attribute supports a named property (Name) that allows you to specify how the C# method will be represented within a WSDL description. Given this, update the second version of InsertCar() as so:

```
public interface IAutoLotService
{
...
  [OperationContract(Name = "InsertCarWithDetails")]
  void InsertCar(InventoryRecord car);
}
```

Implementing the Service Contract

The AutoLotService type implements this interface as follows (be sure to import the AutoLotConnectedLayer and System.Data namespaces in this code file):

```
using AutoLotConnectedLayer;
using System.Data;

public class AutoLotService : IAutoLotService
{
  private const string ConnString =
    @"Data Source=(local)\SQLEXPRESS;Initial Catalog=AutoLot"+
     ";Integrated Security=True";
```

```
    public void InsertCar(int id, string make, string color, string petname)
    {
      InventoryDAL d = new InventoryDAL();
      d.OpenConnection(ConnString);
      d.InsertAuto(id, color, make, petname);
      d.CloseConnection();
    }

    public void InsertCar(InventoryRecord car)
    {
      InventoryDAL d = new InventoryDAL();
      d.OpenConnection(ConnString);
      d.InsertAuto(car.ID, car.Color, car.Make, car.PetName);
      d.CloseConnection();
    }

    public InventoryRecord[] GetInventory()
    {
      // First, get the DataTable from the database.
      InventoryDAL d = new InventoryDAL();
      d.OpenConnection(ConnString);
      DataTable dt = d.GetAllInventory();
      d.CloseConnection();

      // Now make a List<T> to contain the records.
      List<InventoryRecord> records = new List<InventoryRecord>();

      // Copy the data table into List<> of custom contracts.
      DataTableReader reader = dt.CreateDataReader();
      while (reader.Read())
      {
        InventoryRecord r = new InventoryRecord();
        r.ID = (int)reader["CarID"];
        r.Color = ((string)reader["Color"]).Trim();
        r.Make = ((string)reader["Make"]).Trim();
        r.PetName = ((string)reader["PetName"]).Trim();
        records.Add(r);
      }

      // Transform List<T> to array of InventoryRecord types.
      return (InventoryRecord[])records.ToArray();
    }
  }
```

Not too much to say here. For simplicity, we are hard-coding the connection string value (which you may need to adjust based on your machine settings) rather than storing it in our `Web.config` file. Given that our data access library does all the real work of communicating with the AutoLot database, all we need to do is pass the incoming parameters to the `InsertAuto()` method of the `InventoryDAL` class type. The only other point of interest is the act of mapping the `DataTable` object's values into a generic list of `InventoryRecord` types (using a `DataTableReader` to do so) and then transforming the `List<T>` into an array of `InventoryRecord` types.

The Role of the *.svc File

When you create a web-centric WCF service, you will find your project contains a specific file with a `*.svc` file extension. This particular file is required for any WCF service hosted by IIS; it describes the name and location of the service implementation within the install point. Because we have changed the names of our starter files and WCF types, we must now update the contents of the Service.svc file as so:

```
<%@ ServiceHost Language="C#" Debug="true"
  Service="AutoLotService" CodeBehind="~/App_Code/AutoLotService.cs" %>
```

Updating the Web.config File

Before we can take this service out for a test drive, the final task is to update the <system.serviceModel> section of the Web.config file. As described in more detail during our examination of ASP.NET later in this book, the Web.config file serves a similar purpose to an executable's *.config file; however, it also controls a number of web-specific settings. For this example, all we need to do is update the WCF-specific section of the file as follows:

```
<system.serviceModel>
  <services>
    <service name="AutoLotService" behaviorConfiguration="ServiceBehavior">
      <endpoint address="" binding="wsHttpBinding" contract="IAutoLotService"/>

      <endpoint address="mex" binding="mexHttpBinding"
                contract="IMetadataExchange"/>
    </service>
  </services>
  <behaviors>
    <serviceBehaviors>
      <behavior name="ServiceBehavior">
        <serviceMetadata httpGetEnabled="true"/>
        <serviceDebug includeExceptionDetailInFaults="false"/>
      </behavior>
    </serviceBehaviors>
  </behaviors>
</system.serviceModel>
```

Testing the Service

Now you are free to build any sort of client to test your service, including passing in the endpoint of the *.svc file to the WcfTestClient.exe application:

```
WcfTestClient http://localhost/AutoLotWCFService/Service.svc
```

Consider Figure 25-21, which illustrates the result of invoking GetInventory().

■ **Source Code** The AutoLotService project is located under the Chapter 25 subdirectory.

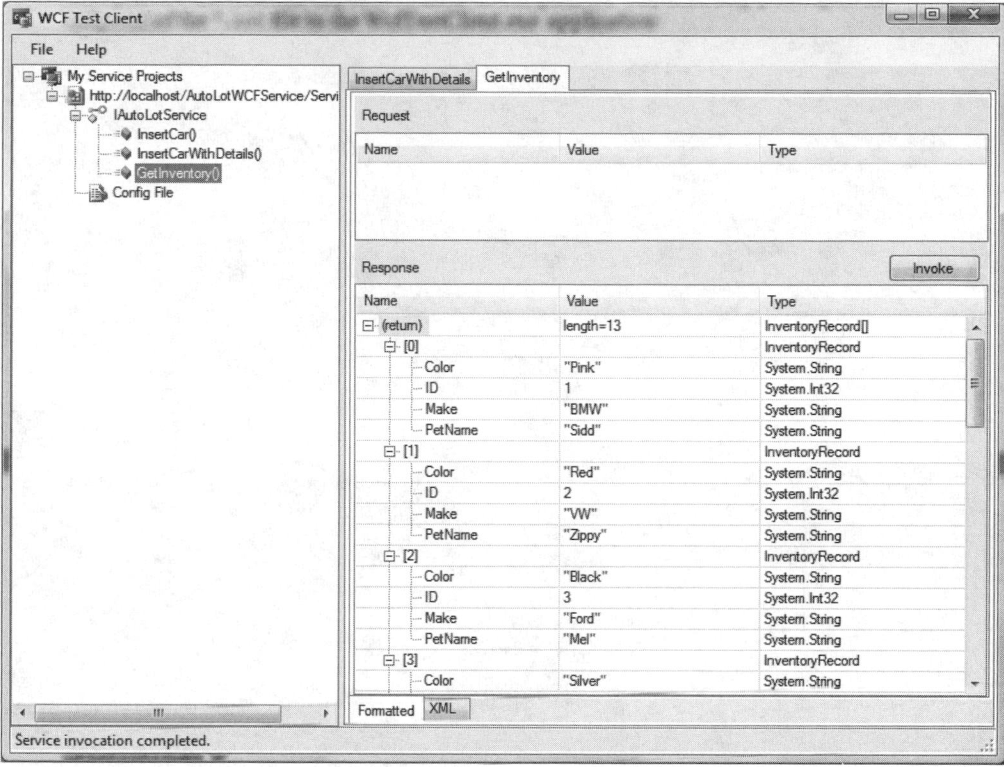

Figure 25-21. *Creating a web-centric WCF service*

If you wish to build a custom client application, simply use the Add Service Reference dialog box as you did for the MagicEightBallServiceClient and MathClient project examples earlier in this chapter.

Summary

This chapter introduced you to the Windows Communication Foundation (WCF) API, which has been part of the base class libraries since .NET 3.0. As explained, the major motivation behind WCF is to provide a unified object model that exposes a number of (previously unrelated) distributed computing APIs under a single umbrella. Furthermore, as you saw at the onset of this chapter, a WCF service is represented by specified addresses, bindings, and contracts (easily remembered by the friendly abbreviation ABC).

As you have seen, a typical WCF application involves the use of three interrelated assemblies. The first assembly defines the service contracts and service types that represent the services functionality. This assembly is then hosted by a custom executable, an IIS virtual directory, or a Windows service. Finally, the client assembly makes use of a generated code file defining a proxy type (and settings within the application configuration file) to communicate with the remote type.

The chapter also examined using a number of WCF programming tools such as `SvcConfigEditor.exe` (which allows you to modify `*.config` files), the `WcfTestClient.exe` application (to quickly test a WCF service), and various Visual Studio 2008 WCF project templates.

Summary

CHAPTER 26

Introducing Windows Workflow Foundation

.NET 3.0 shipped with a particular programming framework named Windows Workflow Foundation (WF). This API allows you to model, configure, monitor, and execute the *workflows* (which, for the time being, can simply be regarded as a collection of related tasks) used internally by a given application. The out-of-the-box solution provided by WF is a huge benefit when building software, as we are no longer required to manually develop complex infrastructure to support workflow-enabled applications.

This chapter begins by defining the role of *business processes* and describes how they relate to the WF API. As well, you will be exposed to the concept of a WF "activity," the two major flavors of workflows (sequential and state machine), and various WF assemblies, project templates, and programming tools. Once we've covered the basics, we'll build several example programs that illustrate how to leverage the WF programming model to establish business processes that execute under the watchful eye of the WF runtime engine.

Note The entirety of WF cannot be covered in a single introductory chapter. If you require a deeper treatment of the topic than presented here, check out *Pro WF: Windows Workflow in .NET 3.0* by Bruce Bukovics (Apress, 2007).

Defining a Business Process

Any real-world application must be able to model various business processes. Simply put, a *business process* is a conceptual grouping of tasks that logically work as a collective whole. For example, assume you are building an application that allows a user to purchase an automobile online. Once the user submits the order, a large number of activities are set in motion. We might begin by performing a credit check. If the user passes our credit verification, we might start a database transaction in order to remove the entry from an Inventory table, add a new entry to an Orders table, and update the customer account information. After the database transaction has completed, we still might need to send a confirmation e-mail to the buyer, and then invoke a remote XML web service to place the order at the dealership. Collectively, all of these tasks could represent a single business process.

Historically speaking, modeling a business process was yet another detail that programmers had to account for, often by authoring custom code to ensure that a business process was not only modeled correctly, but also executed correctly within the application itself. For example, you may need to author code to account for points of failure, tracing, and logging support (to see what a given business process is up to); persistence support (to save the state of long-running processes);

and whatnot. As you may know firsthand, building this sort of infrastructure from scratch entails a great deal of time and manual labor.

Assuming that a development team did, in fact, build a custom business process framework for their applications, their work was not yet complete. Simply put, a raw C# code base cannot be easily explained to nonprogrammers on the team who *also* need to understand the business process. The truth of the matter is that subject matter experts (SMEs), managers, salespeople, and members of a graphical design team often do not speak the language of code. Given this, we were required to make use of other modeling tools (such as Microsoft Visio) to graphically represent our processes using skill set–neutral terms. The obvious problem here is we now have two entities to keep in sync: If we change the code, we need to update the diagram. If we change the diagram, we need to update the code.

Furthermore, when building a sophisticated software application using the *100% code approach*, the code base has very little trace of the internal "flow" of the application. For example, a typical .NET program might be composed of hundreds of custom types (not to mention the numerous types used by the base class libraries). While programmers may have a feel for which objects are making calls on other objects, the code itself is a far cry from a living document that explains the overall sequence of activity. While the development team may build external documentation and workflow charts, again we run into the problem of multiple representations of the same process.

The Role of WF

Since the release of .NET 3.0, we were provided with the Windows Workflow Foundation API. In essence, WF allows programmers to declaratively design business processes using a prefabricated set of *activities*. Thus, rather than building a custom set of assemblies to represent a given business activity and the necessary infrastructure, we can make use of the WF designers of Visual Studio 2008 to create our business process at design time. In this respect, WF allows us to build the skeleton of a business process, which can be fleshed out through code.

When programming with the WF API, a single entity can then be used to represent the overall business process as well as the code that defines it. Since a single WF document is used to represent the code driving the process in addition to being a friendly visual representation of the process, we no longer need to worry about multiple documents falling out of sync. Better yet, this WF document will clearly illustrate the process itself.

The Building Blocks of WF

As you build a workflow-enabled application, you will undoubtedly notice that it "feels different" from building a typical .NET application. For example, up until this point in the text, every code example began by creating a new project workspace (most often a Console Application project) and involved authoring code to represent the program at large. A WF application also consists of custom code; however, in addition, you are building *directly into the assembly* the business process itself. Consider Figure 26-1, which illustrates the initial workflow diagram generated by Visual Studio 2008 when selecting a new Sequential Workflow Console Application project workspace.

Using this designer (and the various WF-centric tools integrated into Visual Studio) you are able to model your process and eventually author code to execute it under the appropriate circumstances. You'll examine these tools in more detail a bit later in this chapter.

Understand that WF is far more than a pretty designer that allows you to model the activities of a business process. As you are building your WF diagram, the designer tools are authoring code to represent the skeleton of your process. Thus, the first thing to be aware of is that a visual WF diagram is executable code, not just simply a Visio-like static image. As such, WF is represented by a set of .NET assemblies, namespaces, and types, just like any other .NET technology.

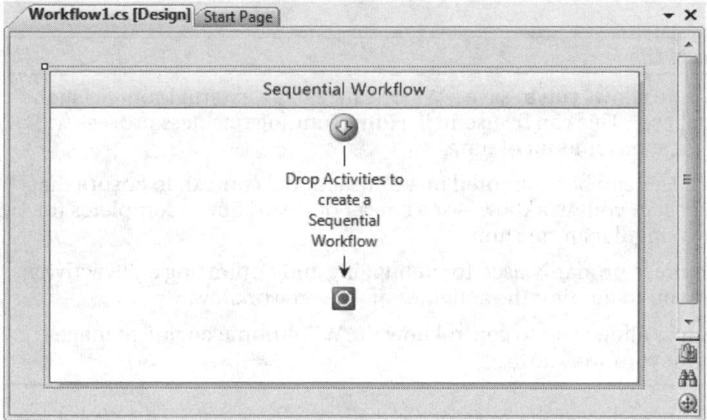

Figure 26-1. *An empty sequential workflow diagram designer*

The WF Runtime

Given the fact that a WF diagram equates to real types and custom code, the next thing to understand is that the WF API also consists of a runtime engine to load, execute, unload, and in other ways manipulate a workflow process. The WF runtime engine can be hosted within any .NET application domain; however, be aware that a single application domain can only have one running instance of the WF engine.

Recall from Chapter 17 that an AppDomain is a partition within a Win32 process that plays host to a .NET application and any external code libraries. As such, the WF engine can be embedded within a simple console program, a GUI desktop application (Windows Forms or Windows Presentation Foundation [WPF]), or exposed from a WCF service or XML web service.

If you are modeling a business process that needs to be used by a wide variety of systems, you also have the option of authoring your WF within a C# Class Library project. In this way, new applications can simply reference your `*.dll` to reuse a predefined collection of business processes. This is obviously helpful in that you would not want to have to re-create the same WF multiple times.

In any case, at this point understand that the WF API provides a full-blown object model that allows you to programmatically interact with the runtime engine as well as the workflows you have designed.

The Core Services of WF

In addition to designer tools, activities, and a runtime engine, WF provides a set of out-of-the-box services that complete the overall framework of a workflow-enabled application. Using these services we can "inherit" a good deal of commonly required WF infrastructure, rather than having to commit time and resources to build this infrastructure by hand. Table 26-1 documents the intrinsic services baked into the WF API.

Collectively, the four intrinsic services seen in Table 26-1 are termed the *core services*. The WF APIs provide default implementations of each of these services, two of which are mandatory (scheduling and transactions), while tracking and persistence services are optional and not registered with the runtime by default. While the .NET base class libraries do provide types that support each core service, you are able to exchange them with your own custom implementations. Thus, if you wish to customize the way in which a long-running workflow should be persisted, you can do so. As well, if you wish to extend the basic functionality of a service with new functionality, it is possible to do so.

Table 26-1. *Intrinsic Services of WF*

Services	Meaning in Life
Persistence services	This feature allows you to save a WF instance to an external source (such as a database). This can be useful if a long-running business process will be idle for some amount of time.
Transaction services	WF instances can be monitored in a transactional context, to ensure that each aspect of your workflow—or a subset of a workflow—completes (or fails) as a singular atomic unit.
Tracking services	This feature is primarily used for debugging and optimizing a WF activity; it allows you to monitor the activities of a given workflow.
Scheduling services	This feature allows you to control how the WF runtime engine manages threads for your workflows.

When you create an instance of the WF runtime engine in order to execute one of your workflows, you have the option of calling the `AddService()` method to plug in tracking or persistence service objects (such as `SqlWorkflowPersistanceService` and `SqlTrackingService`) as well as any customized service you may have designed. At this point you are able to execute a given WF instance and allow these auxiliary services to further monitor its lifetime.

In this introductory chapter, we will not build custom implementations of the core services, nor will we dive too deeply into the default functionality of them. Here, we will focus on the building blocks of a workflow-enabled application, and we will examine numerous WF activities. Be sure to check out the .NET Framework 3.5 SDK documentation for further details of the core services.

A First Look at WF Activities

Recall that the purpose of WF is to allow you to model a business process in a declarative manner, which is then executed by the WF runtime engine. In the vernacular of WF, a business process is composed of any number of *activities*. Simply put, a WF activity is an atomic "step" in the overall process. When you create a new WF-enabled application using Visual Studio 2008, you will find a Windows Workflow area of the Toolbox that contains iconic representations of the built-in activities (see Figure 26-2).

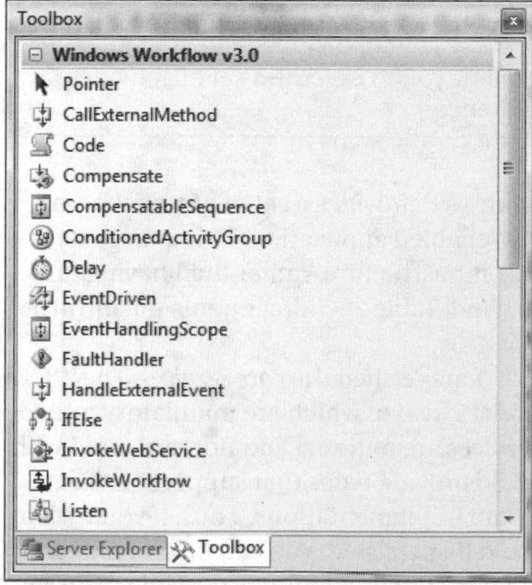

Figure 26-2. *The Windows Workflow Toolbox*

Note Visual Studio 2008 divides the Activities Toolbox into .NET 3.0 and .NET 3.5 activity categories. The activities under the Windows Workflow v3.5 node allow you to interact with Windows Communication Foundation (WCF) services.

.NET 3.5 provides numerous out-of-the-box activities that you can use to model your business process, each of which maps to real types within the `System.Workflow.Activities` namespace and therefore can be represented by, and driven from, code. You'll make use of several of these baked-in activities over the course of this chapter. Table 26-2 describes the high-level functionality of some useful activities, grouped by related functionality.

Table 26-2. *A Sampling of Intrinsic WF Activities*

Activities	Meaning in Life
`CodeActivity`	This activity represents a unit of custom code to execute within the workflow.
`IfElseActivity`, `WhileActivity`	These activities provide basic looping and decision support within a workflow.
`InvokeWebServiceActivity`, `WebServiceInputActivity`, `WebServiceOutputActivity`, `WebServiceFaultActivity`	These activities allow your workflow to interact with XML web services.
`SendActivity`, `ReceiveActivity`	These activities allow you to interact with Windows Communication Foundation services. Be aware that these two activities are .NET 3.5 specific.
`ConditionedActivity`, `GroupActivity`	These activities allow you to define a group of related activities that execute when a given condition is true.
`DelayActivity`, `SuspendActivity`, `TerminateActivity`	These activities allow you to define wait periods as well as pause or terminate a course of action within a workflow.
`EventDrivenActivity`, `EventHandlingScopeActivity`	These activities allow you to associate CLR events to a given activity within the workflow.
`ThrowActivity`, `FaultHandlerActivity`	These activities allow you to raise and handle exceptions within a workflow.
`ParallelActivity`, `SequenceActivity`	These activities allow you to execute a set of activities in parallel or in sequence.

While the current number of intrinsic activities is impressive and provides a solid foundation for many WF-enabled applications, you are also able to create custom activities that seamlessly integrate into the Visual Studio IDE and the WF runtime engine.

Sequential and State Machine Workflows

The WF API provides support for modeling two flavors of business process workflows: sequential workflows and state machine workflows. Ultimately, both categories are constructed by piecing together any number of related activities; however, exactly *how* they execute is what sets them apart.

The most straightforward workflow type is *sequential*. As its name implies, a sequential workflow allows you to model a business process where each activity executes in sequence until the final activity completes. This is not to say that a sequential workflow is necessarily linear or predictable in nature—it is entirely possible to build a sequential workflow that contains various branching and looping activities, as well as a set of activities that execute in parallel on separate threads.

The key aspect of a sequential workflow is that it has a crystal-clear beginning and ending point. Within the Visual Studio 2008 workflow designer, the path of execution begins at the top of the WF diagram and proceeds downward to the end point. Figure 26-3 shows a simple sequential workflow that models a partial business process for verifying a given automobile is in stock.

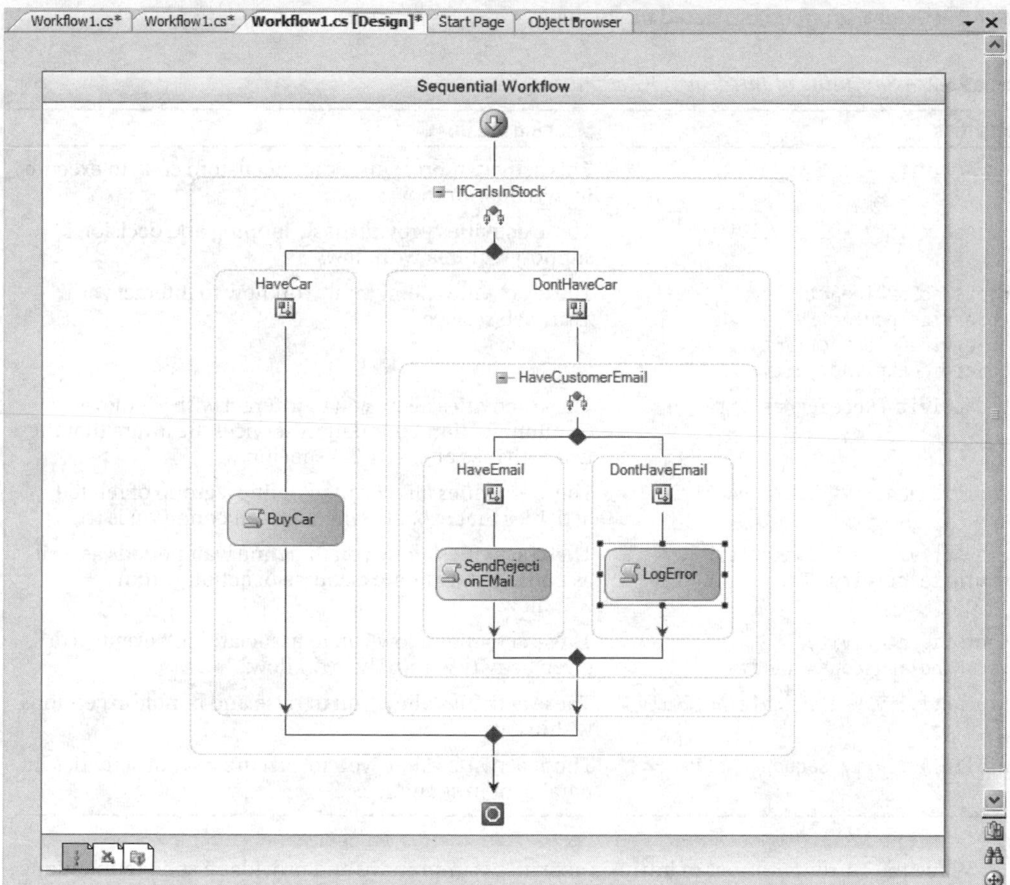

Figure 26-3. *Sequential workflows have a clear starting point and ending point.*

Sequential workflows work well when the workflow models interactions with various system-level entities, and when there is no requirement for backtracking in the process. For example, the business process modeled in Figure 26-3 has two possible outcomes: the car is in stock or it isn't. If the car is indeed in stock, the order is processed using some block of custom code (whatever that may be). If the car isn't in stock, we send a notification e-mail, provided that we have the client's e-mail address at our disposal.

In contrast to sequential workflows, *state machine workflows* do not model activities using a simple linear path. Instead, the workflow defines a number of *request states* and a set of related *events* that trigger transitions between these states. Figure 26-4 illustrates a simple state machine WF diagram that represents the processing of an order. Don't worry about the details of what each activity is doing behind the scenes, but do notice that each request state in the workflow can flow across various states based on some internal event.

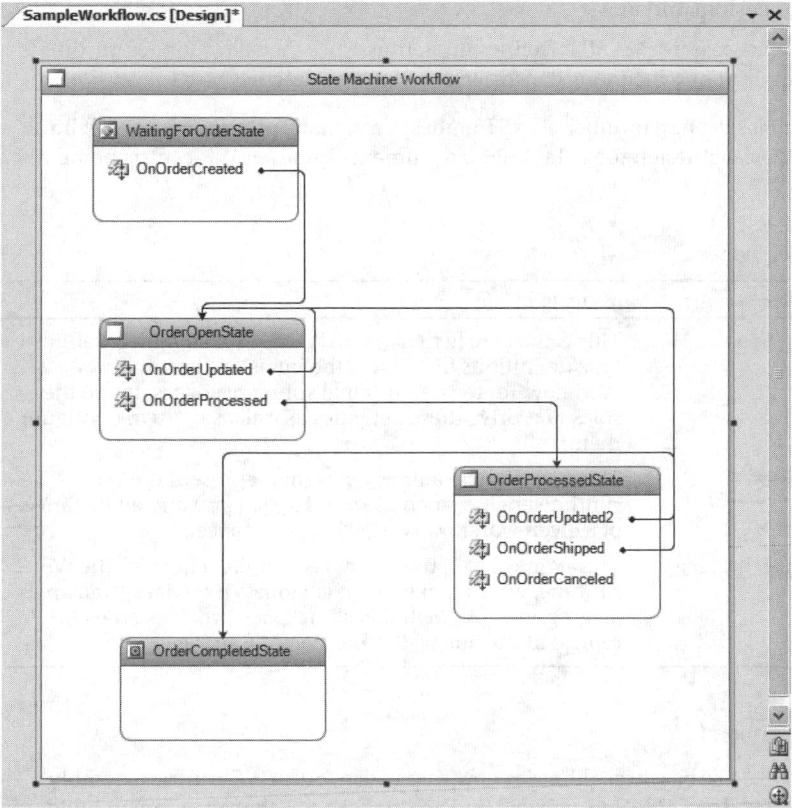

Figure 26-4. *State machine workflows do not follow a fixed, linear path.*

State machine workflows can be very helpful when you need to model a business process that can be in various states of completion, typically due to the fact that human interaction is involved to move between states. Here, we have a request state that is waiting for an order to be created. Once that occurs, an event forces the flow of activity to the order open state, which may trigger an order processed state (or loop back to the previous open state), and so forth.

■ **Note** In this introductory chapter, I don't dig into the details of building state machine workflows. Consult the .NET Framework 3.5 SDK documentation for further information if you are interested.

WF Assemblies, Namespaces, and Projects

From a programmer's point of view, WF is represented by three core assemblies:

- `System.Workflow.Activities.dll`: Defines the intrinsic activities and the rules that drive them
- `System.Workflow.Runtime.dll`: Defines types that represent the WF runtime engine and instances of your custom workflows
- `System.Workflow.ComponentModel.dll`: Defines numerous types that allow for design-time support of WF applications, including construction of custom designer hosts

While these assemblies define a number of .NET namespaces, many of them are used behind the scenes by various WF visual design tools. Table 26-3 documents some key WF-centric namespaces to be aware of.

Table 26-3. *Core WF Namespaces*

Namespace	Meaning in Life
`System.Workflow.Activities`	This is the core activity-centric namespace, which defines type definitions for each of the items on the Windows Workflow Toolbox. Additional subnamespaces define the rules that drive these activities as well as types to configure them.
`System.Workflow.Runtime`	This namespace defines types that represent the WF runtime engine (such as `WorkflowRuntime`) and an instance of a given workflow (via `WorkflowInstance`).
`System.Workflow.Runtime.Hosting`	This namespace provides types to build a host for the WF runtime, which make use of custom WF services (tracking, logging, etc.). As well, this namespace provides types to represent the out-of-the-box core WF services.

.NET 3.5 WF Support

With the release of .NET 3.5, the base class libraries now ship with a fourth WF-centric assembly named `System.WorkflowServices.dll`. Here you will find additional types that allow you to build WF-enabled applications that integrate with the Windows Communications Foundation APIs. The most important aspect of this assembly is that it augments the `System.Workflow.Activities` namespace with new types to support WCF integration.

■ **Note** When you build any WF-aware Visual Studio 2008 project, the IDE will automatically set references to each of the Windows Workflow Foundation assemblies.

Visual Studio Workflow Project Templates

As you would expect, the Visual Studio 2008 IDE provides a good number of WF project templates. First and foremost, when you select the File ➤ New ➤ Project dialog box, you will find a Workflow node under the C# programming category (see Figure 26-5). Here you will find projects that allow you to build sequential and state machine workflows contained within a simple console or custom `*.dll` assembly.

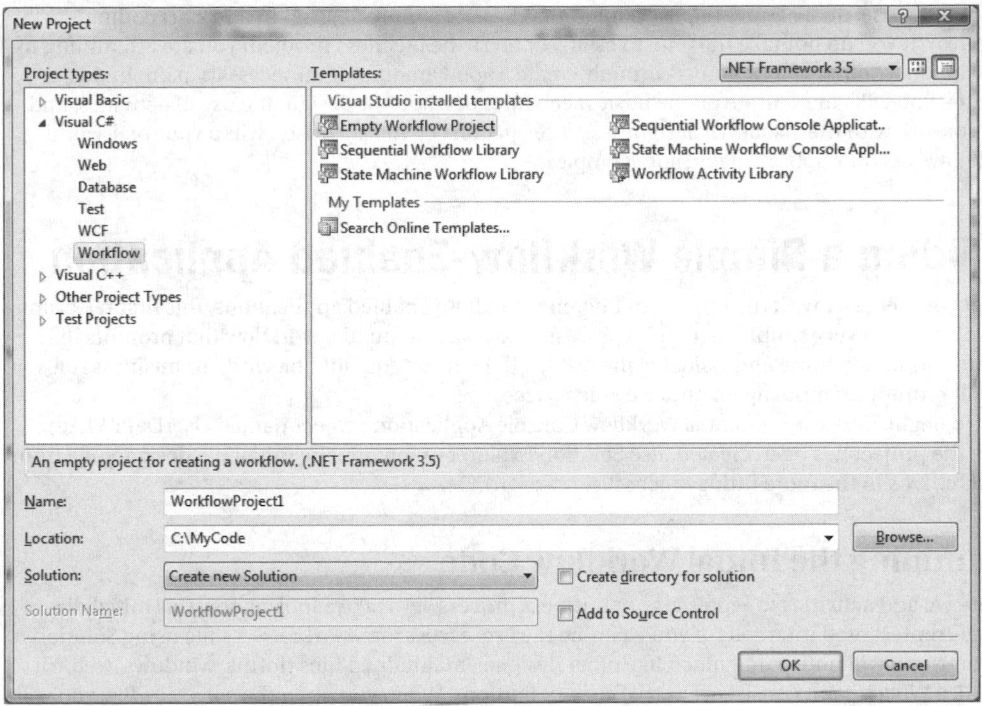

Figure 26-5. *The core WF project templates*

In addition, you may recall from Chapter 26 that the Windows Communication Foundation (WCF) node of the New Project dialog box also provides a set of WF templates. Here you will find two project templates (Sequential Workflow Service Library and State Machine Workflow Service Library), which allow you to build a WCF service that internally makes use of workflows. We will not make use of this group of WF project templates in this chapter; however, do remember that when you are building WCF services, you can elect to integrate WF functionality when creating a new project.

Getting into the Flow of Workflow

Before we dive into our first code example, allow me to point out a few final thoughts regarding the "workflow mind-set." When programming with the WF API, you must keep in mind that you are ultimately attempting to model a *business process*; therefore, the first step is to investigate the business process itself, including all the substeps within the process and each of the possible outcomes. For example, assume you are modeling the process of registering for a training class online. When a request comes in, what should you do if the salesperson is out of the office? What if the class is currently full? What if the class has been canceled or moved to a new date? How can you determine if the trainer is available, is not on vacation, is not teaching a class that same week, or whatnot?

Depending on your current background, the process of gathering these requirements may be a very new task, as figuring out a business process may be "someone else's problem." However, in small companies, the act of determining the necessary business processes may fall on the shoulders of the developers themselves. Larger organizations typically have business analysts who take on the role of discovering (and often modeling) the business processes.

In any case, do be aware that working with WF is not simply a "jump in and start coding" endeavor. If you do not take the time to clearly analyze the business problem you are attempting to solve before coding, you will most certainly create a good amount of unnecessary pain. In this chapter, you will concentrate on the basic mechanics of workflow design, the use of activities, and how to work with the visual WF designers. However, don't be too surprised when your real-world workflows become substantially more complex.

Building a Simple Workflow-Enabled Application

To get your feet wet with the process of building workflow-enabled applications, this first WF example will model a very simple sequential process. The goal is to build a workflow that prompts the user for his or her name and validates the results. If the results do not jibe with our business rules, we will prompt for input again until we reach success.

To begin, create a Sequential Workflow Console Application project named UserDataWFApp. Once the project has been created, use Solution Explorer to rename the initial WF designer file from `Workflow1.cs` to the more fitting `ProcessUsernameWorkflow.cs`.

Examining the Initial Workflow Code

Before we add activities to represent our business process, let's take a look at how this initial diagram is represented internally. If you examine the `ProcessUsernameWorkflow.cs` file using Solution Explorer, you will notice that much like other designer-maintained files (forms, windows, web pages), a WF diagram consists of partial class definitions. When you open the core `*.cs` file, you will find a class type that extends the `SequentialWorkflowActivity` type and a default constructor that makes a call to the `InitializeComponent()` method:

```
public sealed partial class ProcessUsernameWorkflow : SequentialWorkflowActivity
{
  public ProcessUsernameWorkflow()
  {
    InitializeComponent();
  }
}
```

■ **Note** One of the tenets of WF development is that workflows are singular, atomic entities. Given this fact, notice that the workflow class type is explicitly sealed, thereby preventing it from functioning as a parent class for derived types.

If you now open the related `*.Designer.cs` file, you will find that `InitializeComponent()` has set the `Name` property accordingly:

```
partial class ProcessUsernameWorkflow
{
  [System.Diagnostics.DebuggerNonUserCode]
  private void InitializeComponent()
  {
    this.Name = "ProcessUsernameWorkflow";
  }
}
```

As you make use of the Windows Workflow Toolbox to drag various activities onto the designer surface and configure them using the Properties window (or the inline smart tags), the `*.Designer.cs` file will be updated automatically. Like other IDE-maintained files, you can typically ignore the code within this file completely and keep focused on authoring code within the primary `*.cs` file.

Adding a Code Activity

The first activity you will add in the sequence is a Code activity. To do so, drag a Code activity component from the Windows Workflow Toolbox and drop it onto the line connecting the starting and ending points of the workflow. Next, use the Properties window to rename this activity as ShowInstructionsActivity. At this point, your designer should look like Figure 26-6.

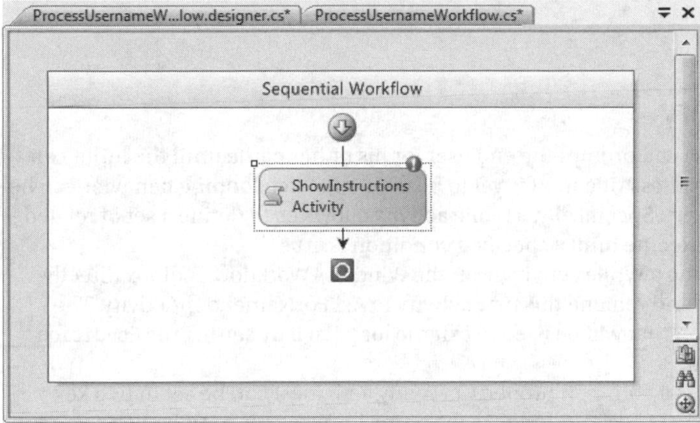

Figure 26-6. *A (not quite ready for prime time) Code activity*

As you can see, the designer is currently reporting an error, which you can view by clicking the red exclamation point on top of the Code activity. The error informs you that the `ExecuteCode` value has not been set, which is a mandatory step for all Code activity types. Not too surprisingly, `ExecuteCode` establishes the name of the method to execute when this task is encountered by the WF runtime engine.

Using the Properties window, set the value of `ExecuteCode` to a method named `ShowInstructions`. Once you press the Enter key, the IDE will update the primary `*.cs` code file with the following stub code:

```
public sealed partial class ProcessUsernameWorkflow : SequentialWorkflowActivity
{
  public ProcessUsernameWorkflow()
  {
    InitializeComponent();
  }

  private void ShowInstructions(object sender, EventArgs e)
  {

  }
}
```

Truth be told, ExecuteCode is an event of the CodeActivity class type. When the WF engine encounters this phase of the sequential workflow, the ExecuteCode event will fire and be handled by the ShowInstructions() method. Implement this method with a handful of Console.WriteLine() statements that display some basic instructions to the end user:

```
private void ShowInstructions(object sender, EventArgs e)
{
  ConsoleColor previousColor = Console.ForegroundColor;
  Console.ForegroundColor = ConsoleColor.Yellow;
  Console.WriteLine("*******************************************");
  Console.WriteLine("***** Welcome to the first WF Example *****");
  Console.WriteLine("*******************************************\n");
  Console.WriteLine("I will now ask for your name and validate the data...\n");
  Console.ForegroundColor = previousColor;
}
```

Adding a While Activity

Recall that our sequential process will prompt the end user for his or her name until the input can be validated against a custom business rule (that is yet to be defined). Such looping behavior can be represented using the While activity. Specifically, a While activity allows us to define a set of related activities that will continuously execute until a specified condition is true.

To illustrate, begin by dragging a While activity from the Windows Workflow Toolbox directly below the previous Code activity and rename this new activity to AskForNameLoopActivity. The next step is to define the condition that will be used to exit the loop itself by setting the Condition value from the Properties window.

The Condition value (which is a common property of many activities) can be set in two key ways. First of all, you can establish a *code condition*. As the name implies, this option allows you to specify a method in your class that will be called by the activity in order to determine if it should proceed. To inform the activity of this fact, the method specified will eventually need to return a Boolean value (true to repeat, false to exit).

The second way the Condition value can be set is by establishing a *declarative rule condition*. This option can be useful in that you are able to specify a single code statement that evaluates to true or false; however, this statement is not hard-coded in your assembly, but is instead offloaded to a *.rules file. One benefit of this approach is that it makes it possible to modify rules in a declarative manner.

Our condition will be based on some custom code that we have yet to author; however, the first step is to select the Code Condition option from the Condition value, and then specify the name of the method that will perform the test. Again using the Properties window, name this method GetAndValidateUserName (see Figure 26-7).

As soon as you specify the name of the code condition used to test the While activity, the IDE will generate a method stub where the second parameter is of type ConditionalEventArgs. This type contains a property named Result, which can be set to true or false based on the success or failure of the condition you are modeling.

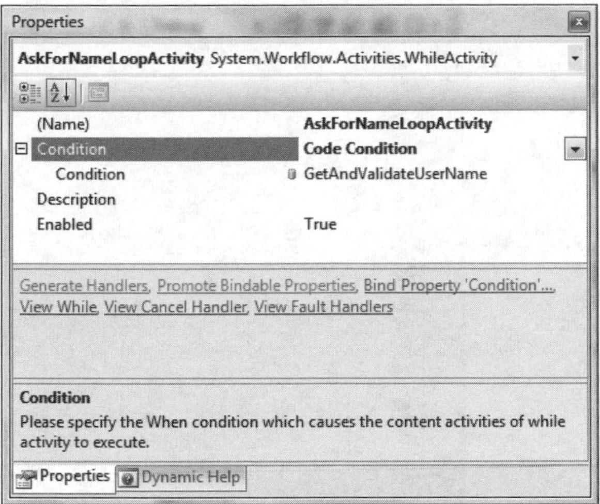

Figure 26-7. *The configured While activity*

Add a new automatic property of type `string` named `UserName` to your `ProcessUsernameWorkflow` class. Within the scope of the `GetAndValidateUserName()` method, ask the user to enter his or her name, and if the name consists of fewer than ten characters, set the `Result` property accordingly. Here are the updates in question:

```
public sealed partial class ProcessUsernameWorkflow : SequentialWorkflowActivity
{
  // Use C# automatic property.
  public string UserName { get; set; }

  private void GetAndValidateUserName(object sender, ConditionalEventArgs e)
  {
    Console.Write("Please enter name, which must be less than 10 chars: ");
    UserName = Console.ReadLine();

    // See if name is correct length, and set the result.
    e.Result = (UserName.Length >= 10);
  }
...
}
```

The final task to complete the While activity involves adding at least a single activity within the scope of the While logic. Here we will add a new Code activity named NameNotValidActivity, which has been connected to a method named `NameNotValid` via the `ExecuteCode` value. Figure 26-8 shows the final workflow diagram. The implementation of `NameNotValid()` is intentionally simple:

```
private void NameNotValid(object sender, EventArgs e)
{
  Console.WriteLine("Sorry, try again...");
}
```

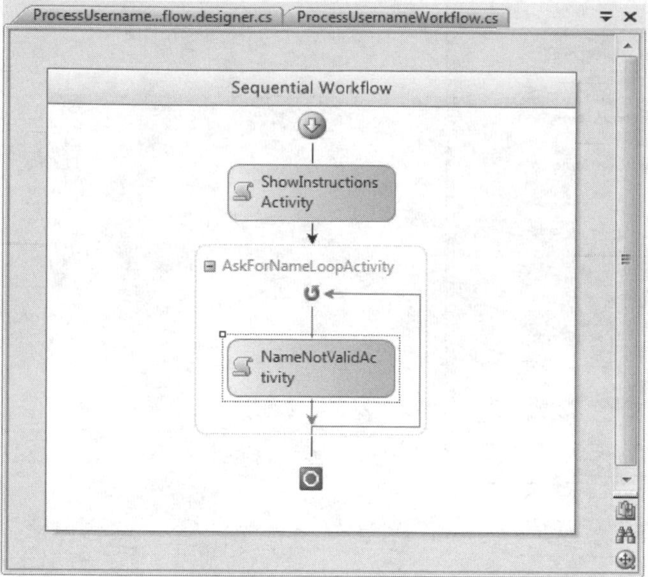

Figure 26-8. *The final workflow design*

At this point, you may compile and run this workflow-enabled application. When you execute the program, purposely enter more than ten characters a few times. You will notice that the runtime engine forces the user to reenter data until the business rule (a name of fewer than ten characters) is honored. Figure 26-9 shows one possible output.

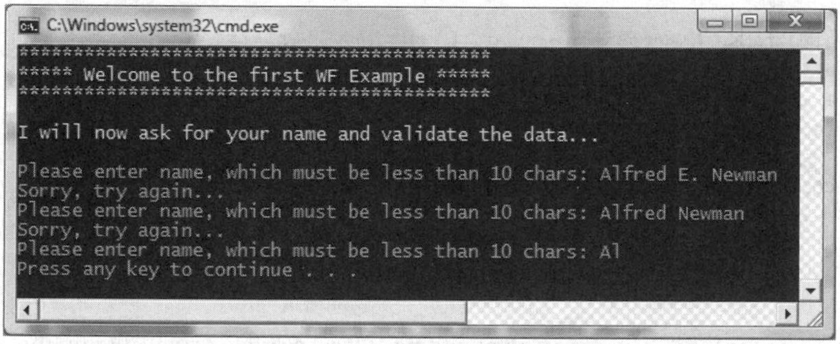

```
C:\Windows\system32\cmd.exe
*********************************************
***** Welcome to the first WF Example *****
*********************************************

I will now ask for your name and validate the data...

Please enter name, which must be less than 10 chars: Alfred E. Newman
Sorry, try again...
Please enter name, which must be less than 10 chars: Alfred Newman
Sorry, try again...
Please enter name, which must be less than 10 chars: Al
Press any key to continue . . .
```

Figure 26-9. *The workflow-enabled application in action*

Examining the WF Engine Hosting Code

While our first example executes as expected, we have yet to examine the code that actually instructs the WF runtime engine to execute the tasks that represent the current workflow. To understand this aspect of WF, open the `Program.cs` file that was created when you defined your initial project. Within the `Main()` method, you will find code that makes use of two primary types, `WorkflowRuntime` and `WorkflowInstance`.

As the names suggest, the WorkflowRuntime type represents the WF runtime engine itself, while WorkflowInstance is used to represent an instance of a given (pardon the redundancy) workflow instance. Here is the Main() method in question, annotated with my various code comments:

```
static void Main(string[] args)
{
  // Ensure the runtime shuts down when we are finished.
  using(WorkflowRuntime workflowRuntime = new WorkflowRuntime())
  {
    AutoResetEvent waitHandle = new AutoResetEvent(false);

    // Handle events that capture when the engine completes
    // the workflow process and if the engine shuts down with an error.
    workflowRuntime.WorkflowCompleted
      += delegate(object sender, WorkflowCompletedEventArgs e)
    {
      waitHandle.Set();
    };

    workflowRuntime.WorkflowTerminated
      += delegate(object sender, WorkflowTerminatedEventArgs e)
    {
      Console.WriteLine(e.Exception.Message);
      waitHandle.Set();
    };

    // Now, create a WF instance that represents our type.
    WorkflowInstance instance =
    workflowRuntime.CreateWorkflow(typeof(UserDataWFApp.ProcessUsernameWorkflow));
    instance.Start();

    waitHandle.WaitOne();
  }
}
```

First of all, notice that the WorkflowCompleted and WorkflowTerminated events of WorkflowRuntime are handled using C# anonymous method syntax. The WorkflowCompleted event fires when the WF engine has completed executing a workflow instance, while WorkflowTerminated fires if the engine terminates with an error.

Strictly speaking, you are not required to handle these events, although the IDE-generated code does so in order to inform the waiting thread these events have occurred using the AutoResetEvent type. This is especially important for a console-based application, as the WF engine is operating on a secondary thread of execution. If the workflow logic did not make use of some sort of wait handle, the main thread might terminate before the WF instance was able to perform its work.

The next point of interest regarding the code within Main() is the creation of the WorkflowInstance type. Notice that the WorkflowRuntime type exposes a method named CreateWorkflow(), which expects type information representing the workflow to be created. At this point, we simply call Start() from the returned object reference. This is all that is required to fire up the WF runtime engine and begin the processing of our custom workflow.

Adding Custom Startup Parameters

Before we move on to a more interesting workflow example, allow me to address how to define application-wide parameters. If you examine the signature of the designer-generated methods used by our Code activities (ShowInstructions() and NameNotValid() specifically), you may have noticed that they are called via WF events that are making use of the System.EventHandler delegate (given the incoming parameters of type object and System.EventArgs).

Because this .NET delegate demands the registered event handler and takes System.Object and System.EventArgs as arguments, you may wonder how to pass in *custom* parameters to be used by a Code activity. In fact, you may be wondering how to define custom arguments that can be used by any activity within the current workflow instance.

As it turns out, the WF engine supports the use of custom parameters using a generic Dictionary<string, object> type. The name/value pairs added to the Dictionary object must then be associated to (identically named) properties on your workflow instance. Once you've done this, you can pass these arguments into the WF runtime engine when you start your workflow instance. Using this approach, you are able to get and set custom parameters throughout a particular workflow instance.

■ **Note** The names defined within a Dictionary object must map to public properties, *not* public member variables! If you attempt to do so, you will generate a runtime exception.

To try this out firsthand, begin by updating the code within Main() to define a Dictionary<string, object> containing two data items. The first item is a string that represents the error message to display if the name is too long; the second item is a numeric value that will be used to specify the maximum length of the user name. To register these parameters with the WF runtime engine, pass in your Dictionary object as a second parameter to the CreateWorkflow() method. Here are the relevant updates:

```
using (WorkflowRuntime workflowRuntime = new WorkflowRuntime())
{
...
  // Define two parameters for use by our workflow.
  // Remember!  These must be mapped to identically named
  // properties in our workflow class type.
  Dictionary<string, object> parameters = new Dictionary<string, object>();
  parameters.Add("ErrorMessage", "Ack!  Your name is too long!");
  parameters.Add("NameLength", 5);

  // Now, create a WF instance that represents our type
  // and pass in parameters.
  WorkflowInstance instance =
    workflowRuntime.CreateWorkflow(
    typeof(UserDataWFApp.ProcessUsernameWorkflow), parameters);
  instance.Start();
  waitHandle.WaitOne();
}
```

■ **Note** In the preceding code, the values assigned to the ErrorMessage and NameLength dictionary items are hard-coded. A more dynamic approach is to read these values from a related *.config file, or perhaps from incoming command-line arguments.

If you try running your program at this point, you will encounter a runtime exception, as you have yet to associate these incoming values to public properties on your workflow type. Once you have done so, however, the runtime will invoke them upon workflow creation. After this point, you can use these properties to get and set the underlying data values. Here are the relevant updates to the `ProcessUsernameWorkflow` class type:

```
public sealed partial class ProcessUsernameWorkflow : SequentialWorkflowActivity
{
...
  // These properties map to the names within the Dictionary object.
  public string ErrorMessage { get; set; }
  public int NameLength { get; set; }

  private void GetAndValidateUserName(object sender, ConditionalEventArgs e)
  {
    Console.Write("Please enter name, which much be less than {0} chars: ",
      NameLength);
    UserName = Console.ReadLine();

    // See if name is correct length, and set the result.
    e.Result = (UserName.Length >= NameLength);
  }

  private void NameNotValid(object sender, EventArgs e)
  {
    Console.WriteLine(ErrorMessage);
  }
...
}
```

Beyond the fact that you have added two new automatic properties, notice that the `GetAndValidateUserName()` method is now checking for the length specified by the `NameLength` property, while the error message prints out the value found within the `ErrorMessage` property. In both cases, these values are determined via the `Dictionary` object passed in at the time the workflow instance was created. Figure 26-10 shows some possible output for this modified example.

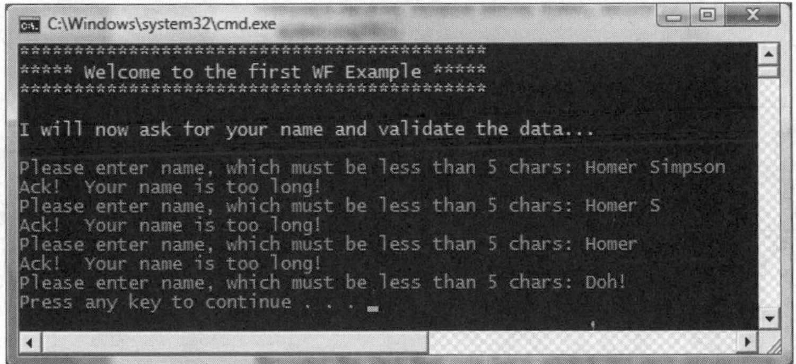

Figure 26-10. *The workflow in action, now with custom parameters*

■ Source Code The UserDataWFApp example is included under the Chapter 26 subdirectory.

Invoking Web Services Within Workflows

WF provides several activities that allow you to interact with XML web services during the lifetime of your workflow-enabled application. When you wish to simply call an existing web service, you can make use of the InvokeWebService activity.

Note Given that WCF is the preferred API to build services, this edition of the text does not cover the construction of XML web services in any great detail (Chapter 25 broached the topic in passing); therefore the web service we will be calling here is intentionally simple.

Creating the MathWebService

The first task is to build an XML web service that can be utilized by a workflow-enabled application. To do so, create a brand-new XML web service project by accessing the File ➤ New Web Site menu option. Select the ASP.NET Web Service icon and be sure to select the HTTP location option in order to create this web service within a new IIS virtual directory mapped to http://localhost/MathWebService (see Figure 26-11).

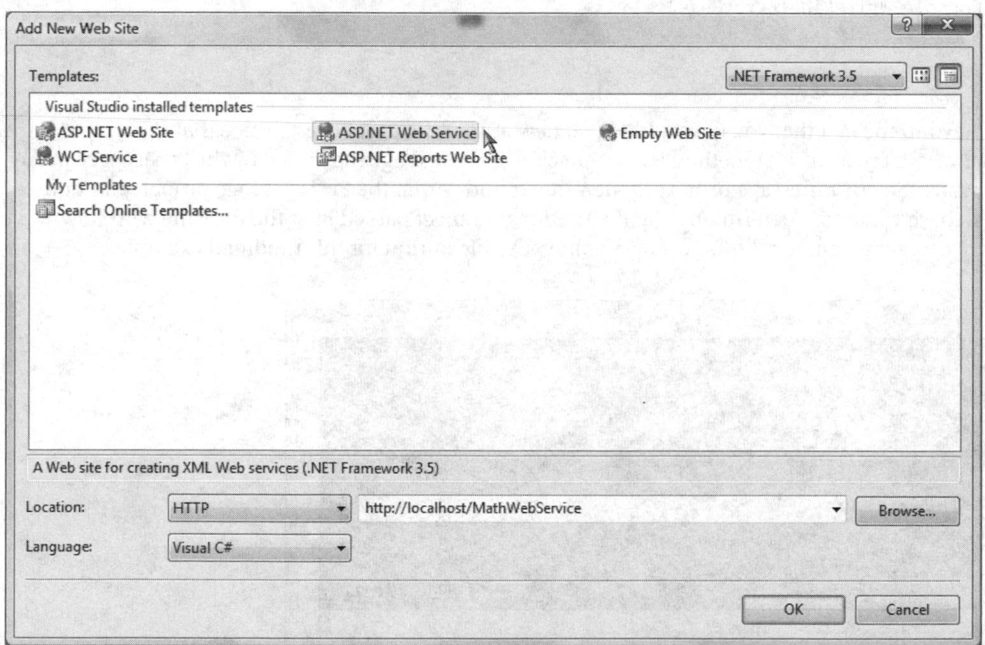

Figure 26-11. *Adding an XML web service project to the WF application*

This XML web service will allow external callers to perform basic mathematical operations on two integers using the following [WebMethod]-adorned public members:

```
[WebService(Namespace = "http://intertech.com/")]
[WebServiceBinding(ConformsTo = WsiProfiles.BasicProfile1_1)]
public class MathService : System.Web.Services.WebService
{
  [WebMethod]
```

```
  public int Add(int x, int y)
  { return x + y; }
  [WebMethod]
  public int Subtract(int x, int y)
  { return x - y; }
  [WebMethod]
  public int Multiply(int x, int y)
  { return x * y; }
  [WebMethod]
  public int Divide(int x, int y)
  {
    if (y == 0)
      return 0;
    else
      return x / y;
  }
}
```

Notice that we have accounted for a division by zero error by simply returning `0` if the `y` value is in fact zero. Also notice that we have renamed this service to `MathService`, and therefore we must also update the `Class` attribute in the `*.asmx` file as so:

```
<%@ WebService Language="C#" CodeBehind="~/App_Code/Service.cs"
    Class="MathService" %>
```

At this point you can test your XML web service by running (Ctrl+F5) or debugging (F5) the project. When you do so, you will find a web-based testing front end that allows you to invoke each web method (see Figure 26-12).

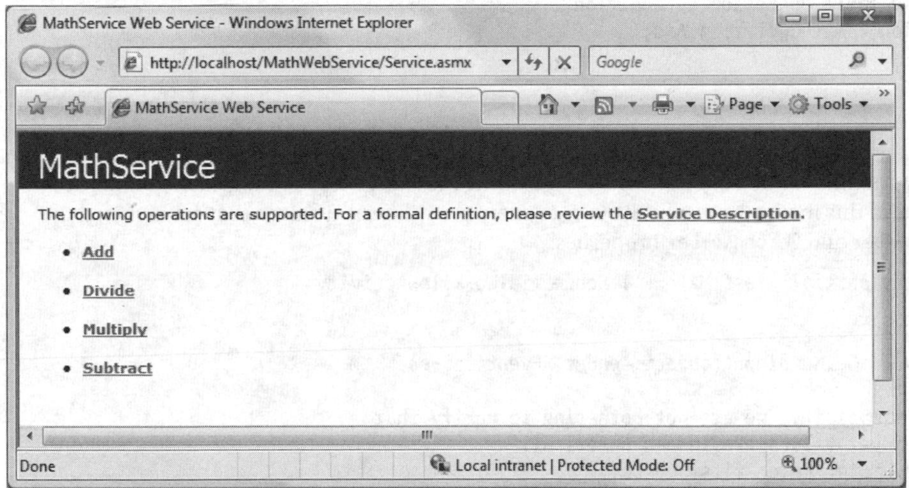

Figure 26-12. *Testing our MathWebService*

At this point you can close down the web service project.

Source Code The MathWebService example is included under the Chapter 26 subdirectory.

Building the WF Web Service Consumer

Now create a new Sequential Workflow Console Application project named WFMathClient and rename your initial C# file to MathWF.cs. This application will ask the user for data to process and which operation they wish to perform (addition, subtraction, etc.). To begin, open your code file and define a new enum type named MathOperation:

```
public enum MathOperation
{
  Add, Subtract, Multiply, Divide
}
```

Next, define four automatic properties in your class, two of which represent the numerical data to process, one of which represents the result of the operation, and one of which represents the mathematical operation itself (note the default constructor of MathWF sets the value of the Operation property to MathOperation.Add):

```
public sealed partial class MathWF : SequentialWorkflowActivity
{
  // Properties.
  public int FirstNumber { get; set; }
  public int SecondNumber { get; set; }
  public int Result { get; set; }
  public MathOperation Operation { get; set; }

  public MathWF()
  {
    InitializeComponent();

    // Set default Operation to addition.
    Operation = MathOperation.Add;
  }
...
}
```

Now, using the WF designer, add a new Code activity named GetNumericalInput that is mapped to a method named GetNumbInput(), by setting the ExecuteCode value via the Properties window. Within this method, prompt the user to enter two numerical values that are assigned to your FirstNumber and SecondNumber properties:

```
public sealed partial class MathWF : SequentialWorkflowActivity
{
...
  private void GetNumbInput(object sender, EventArgs e)
  {
    // For simplicity, we are not bothering to verify that
    // the input values are indeed numerical.
    Console.Write("Enter first number: ");
    FirstNumber = int.Parse(Console.ReadLine());

    Console.Write("Enter second number: ");
    SecondNumber = int.Parse(Console.ReadLine());
  }
}
```

Add a second Code activity named GetMathOpInput mapped to a method named GetOpInput() in order to ask the user how he or she wishes to process the numerical data. To do so, we will assume the user will specify the letters A, S, M, or D, and based on this character value, set the `MathOperation` property to the correct enumeration value. Here is one possible implementation:

```
private void GetOpInput(object sender, EventArgs e)
{
  Console.WriteLine("Do you wish to A[dd], S[ubtract],");
  Console.Write("Do you wish to M[ultiply] or D[ivide]: ");
  string option = Console.ReadLine();

  switch (option.ToUpper())
  {
    case "A":
      Operation = MathOperation.Add;
      break;
    case "S":
      Operation = MathOperation.Subtract;
      break;
    case "M":
      Operation = MathOperation.Multiply;
      break;
    case "D":
      Operation = MathOperation.Divide;
      break;
    default:
      numericalOp = MathOperation.Add;
      break;
  }
}
```

At this point we have the necessary data. Now let's check out how to pass it to our XML web service for processing.

Configuring the IfElse Activity

Given that fact that our numerical data can be processed in four unique manners, we will use an IfElse activity to determine which web method of the service to invoke. When you drag an IfElse activity onto your designer, you will automatically be given two branches. To add additional branches to an IfElse activity, right-click the IfElse activity icon and select the Add Branch menu option. Figure 26-13 shows the current WF designer (note that each branch and the entire IfElse activity have been given proper names).

Each branch of an IfElse activity can contain any number of internal activities that represent what should take place if the decision logic results in moving the flow of the application down a given path. Before we add these subactivities, however, we first need to add the logic that allows the WF engine to determine which branch to take by setting the `Condition` value to each IfElseBranch activity.

Recall that the `Condition` event can be configured to establish a code condition or a declarative rule condition. The first example project in this chapter already illustrated how to create a code condition, so in this example we will opt for rule conditions. Starting with the AddBranch, set the `Condition` value to Declarative Rule Condition using the Visual Studio Properties window. Next, click the ellipsis button for the ConditionName subnode, and click the New button from the resulting dialog box. Here, you are able to author a code expression that will determine the truth or falsity of the current branch. For this first branch, the expression is as follows:

```
this.Operation == MathOperation.Add
```

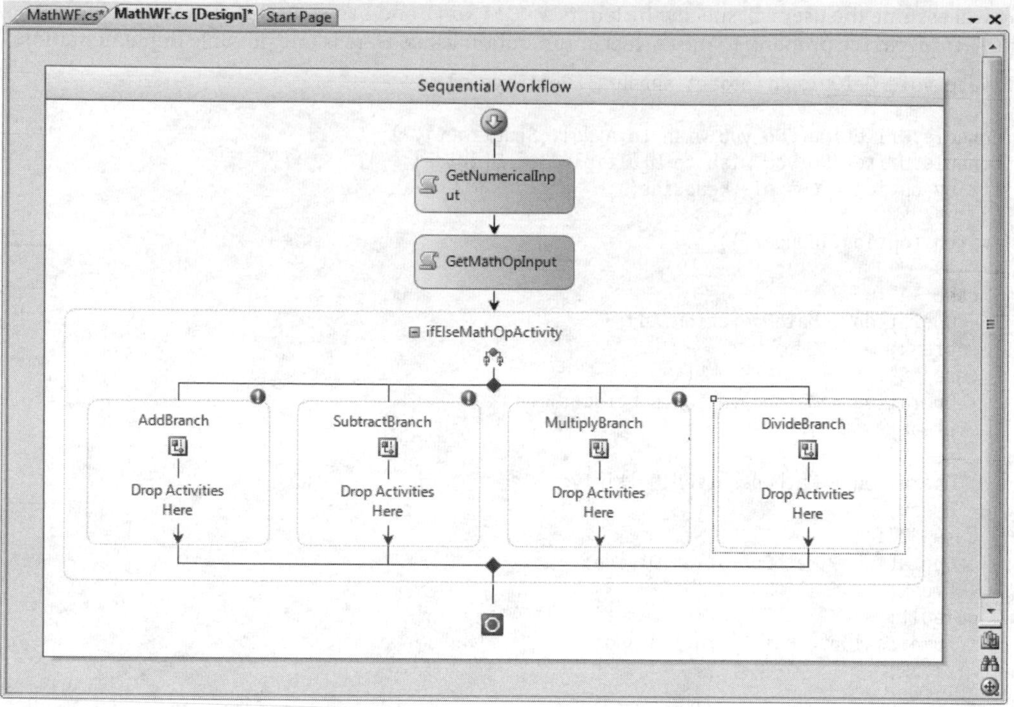

Figure 26-13. *A multibranching IfElse activity*

You'll notice that this dialog box supports IntelliSense, which is always a welcome addition (see Figure 26-14).

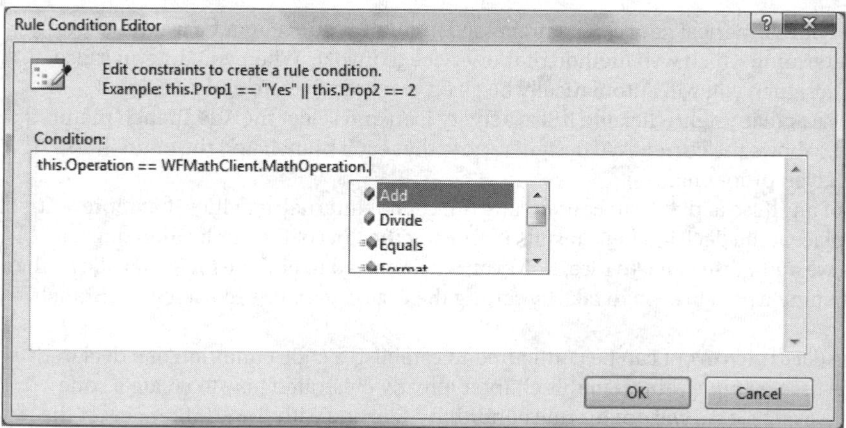

Figure 26-14. *Defining a declarative rule condition*

Once you have set each rule, you will now notice that a new file with a `*.rules` extension has been added to your project (see Figure 26-15).

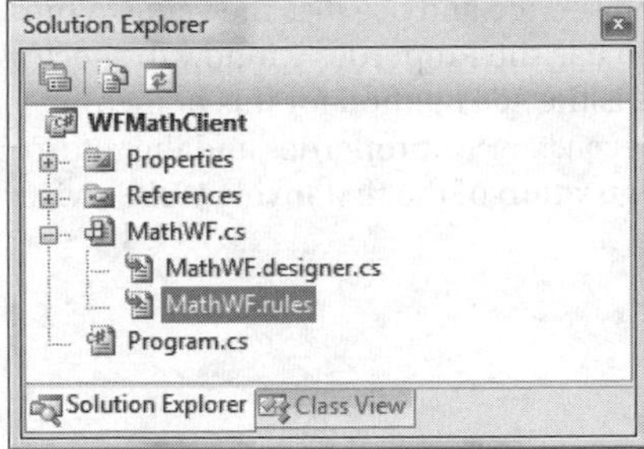

Figure 26-15. `*.rules` *files hold each declarative rule you have established for a WF.*

If you were to open this file, you would find a number of `<RuleExpressionCondition>` elements that describe the conditions you have established.

Configuring the InvokeWebService Activities

The final tasks are to pass the incoming data to the correct web method and print out the result. Drag an InvokeWebService activity into the leftmost branch. Doing so will automatically open the Add Web Reference dialog box, where you can specify the URL of the web service (which for this example is `http://localhost/MathWebService/Service.asmx`) and click the Add Reference button (see Figure 26-16).

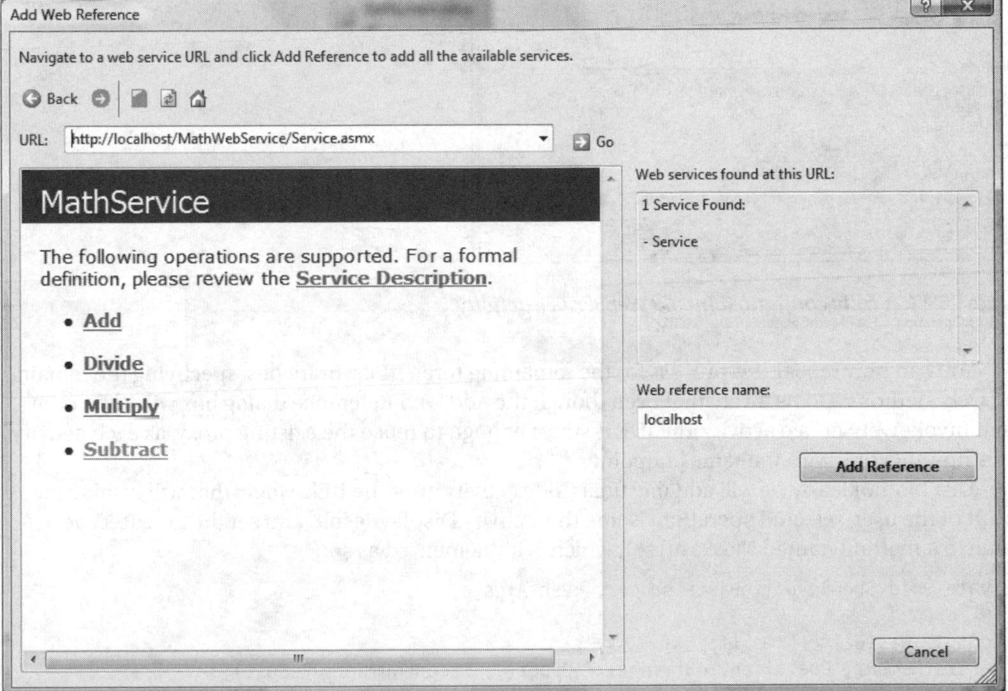

Figure 26-16. *Referencing our XML web service*

When you do so, the IDE will generate a proxy to your web service and use it as the value to the InvokeWebService's `ProxyClass` property. At this point, you can use the Properties window to specify the web method to invoke via the `MethodName` property (which is the `Add` method for this branch), and map the two input parameters to your `FirstNumber` and `SecondNumber` properties and the return value to the `Result` property. Figure 26-17 shows the full configuration of the first InvokeWebService activity.

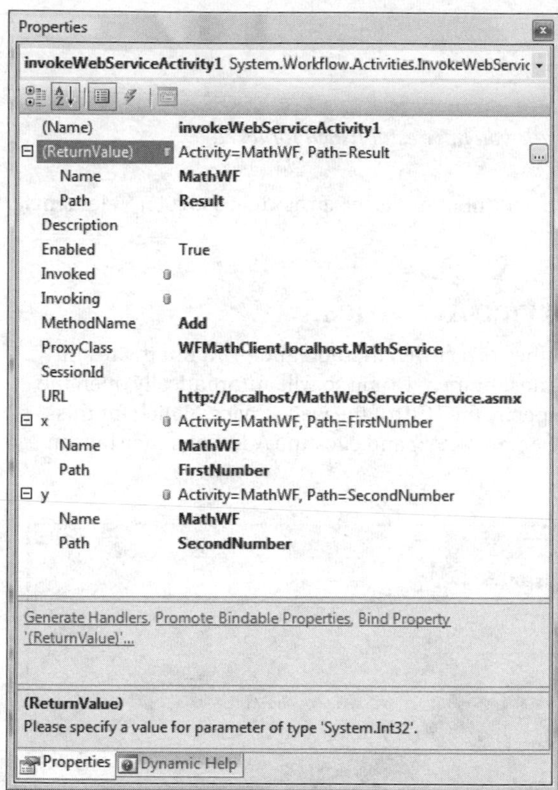

Figure 26-17. *A fully configured InvokeWebService activity*

You can now repeat this process for the remaining three IfElse branches, specifying the remaining web methods. Do be aware that even though the Add Web Reference dialog box will appear for each InvokeWebService activity, the IDE is smart enough to reuse the existing proxy, as each activity is communicating with the same endpoint.

Last but not least, we will add one final Code activity after the IfElse logic that will display the result of the user-selected operation. Name this activity DisplayResult, and set the `ExecuteCode` value to a method named `ShowResult()`, which is implemented as so:

```
private void ShowResult(object sender, EventArgs e)
{
  Console.WriteLine("{0} {1} {2} = {3}",
    FirstNumber, Operation.ToString().ToUpper(), SecondNumber, Result);
}
```

For simplicity, we are using the textual value of the `Operation` property to represent the selected mathematical operator, rather than adding additional code to map `MathOperation.Add` to a + sign and `MathOperation.Subtract` to a - sign, and so on. In any case, Figure 26-18 shows the final design of our workflow; Figure 26-19 shows one possible output.

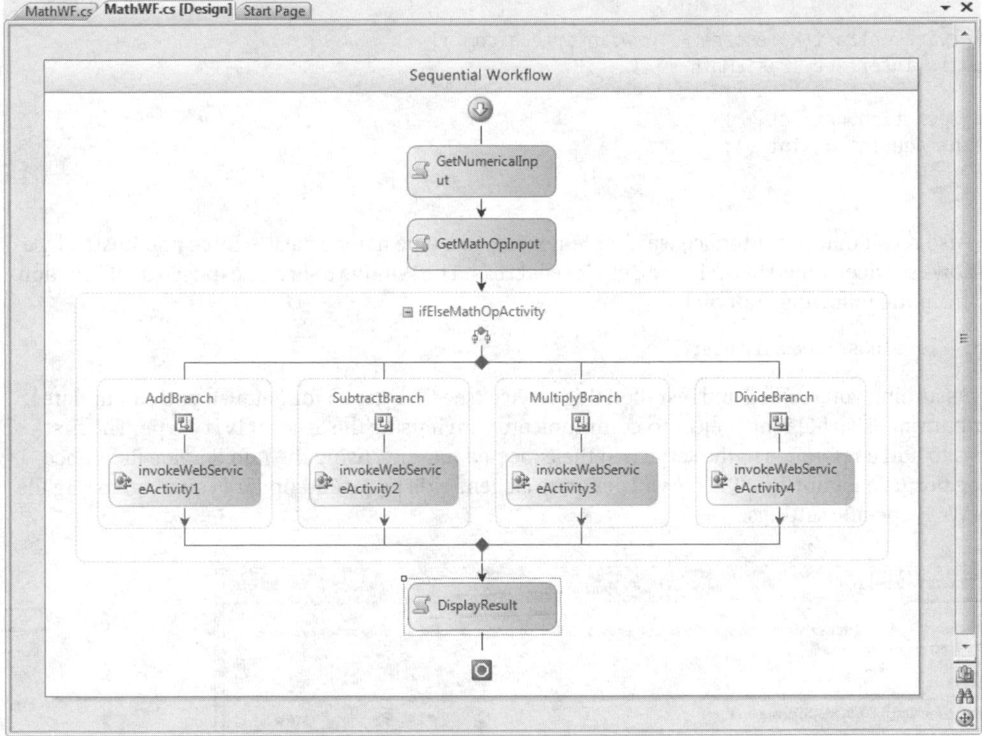

Figure 26-18. *The completed web service–centric workflow*

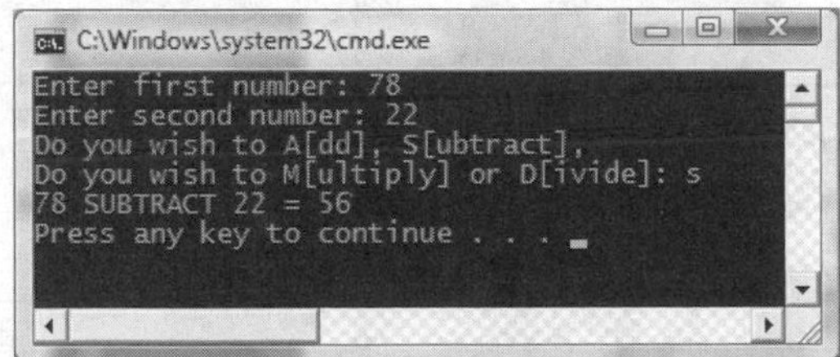

Figure 26-19. *Communicating with XML web services from a WF application*

Communicating with WCF Services Using SendActivity

To complete this example, let's examine how a workflow-enabled application can communicate with WCF services. The .NET 3.5–centric `SendActivity` and `ReceiveActivity` types allow you to build workflow-enabled applications that communicate with WCF services. As the name implies, the `SendActivity` type can be used to make calls on WCF service operations, while `ReceiveActivity` provides a way for the WCF service to make calls back on the WF (in the case of a duplex calling contract).

Recall that in Chapter 25 we defined a WCF service contract that also manipulated two numbers via an addition operation, using the following service interface:

```
namespace MathServiceLibrary
{
  [ServiceContract(Namespace = "www.intertech.com")]
  public interface IBasicMath
  {
    [OperationContract]
    int Add(int x, int y);
  }
}
```

Also recall that this interface was implemented on a type named `MathService` and hosted by a Windows service named `MathWindowsServiceHost.exe`. The Windows service exposed said functionality from the following endpoint:

```
http://localhost:8080/MathService
```

Assuming you created and installed this service (see Chapter 25 for details), you can update your current `WFMathClient` project to communicate with it using the `SendActivity` type. The first step is to add a reference to the service in the expected manner, using the Add Service Reference dialog box (see Figure 26-20). This will generate a client-side proxy and update your `App.config` file with WCF-specific settings.

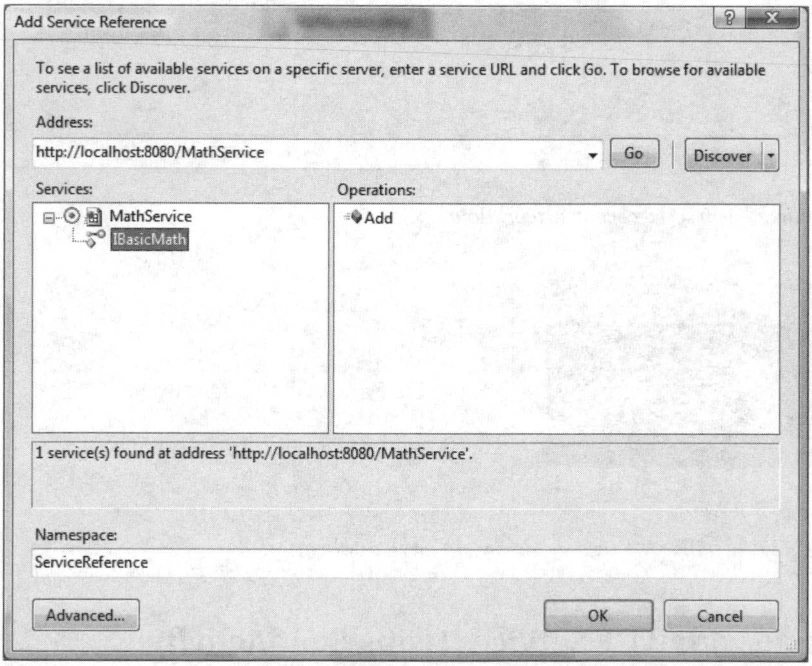

Figure 26-20. *Referencing the WCF MathService*

Now, drag a SendActivity type onto your WF designer surface (named `WCFSendAddActivity`), directly after the final Code activity. Using the Properties window, click the ellipsis button of the `ServiceOperationInfo` property and from the resulting dialog box click Import. This will present you with a secondary dialog box where you are able to associate a SendActivity type with a metadata description for a given WCF service contract. Select the only contract available at this endpoint, IBasicMath (see Figure 26-21).

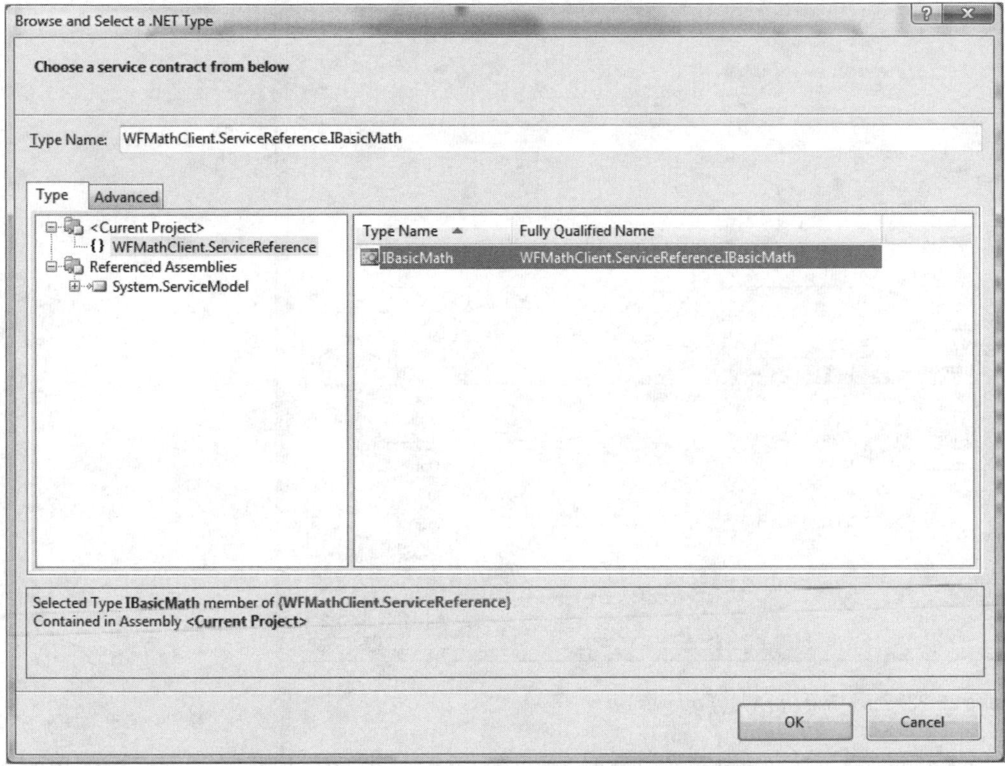

Figure 26-21. *Associating a service method to a SendActivity type*

Once you do so, you will then be able to pick which operation on the selected contract the SendActivity should invoke. In our case, the only option is the Add() method (see Figure 26-22).

We have a few additional configuration steps to take before the SendActivity is ready to pass the values maintained by the FirstNumber and SecondNumber properties to the MathService for processing. Specifically, we need to inform the SendActivity which binding will be used during the invocation by setting a value to the ChannelToken property (recall that a single WCF service can be configured in such a way that it is exposed from several bindings). If you open the updated App.config file and locate the <client> section, you will find that the name of the generated binding is WSHttpBinding_IBasicMath:

```
<client>
  <endpoint address="http://localhost:8080/MathServiceLibrary"
            binding="wsHttpBinding"
            bindingConfiguration="WSHttpBinding_IBasicMath"
            contract="WFMathClient.ServiceReference.IBasicMath"
            name="WSHttpBinding_IBasicMath"
  >
    <identity>
      <servicePrincipalName value="host/InterUber.intertech-inc.com" />
    </identity>
  </endpoint>
</client>
```

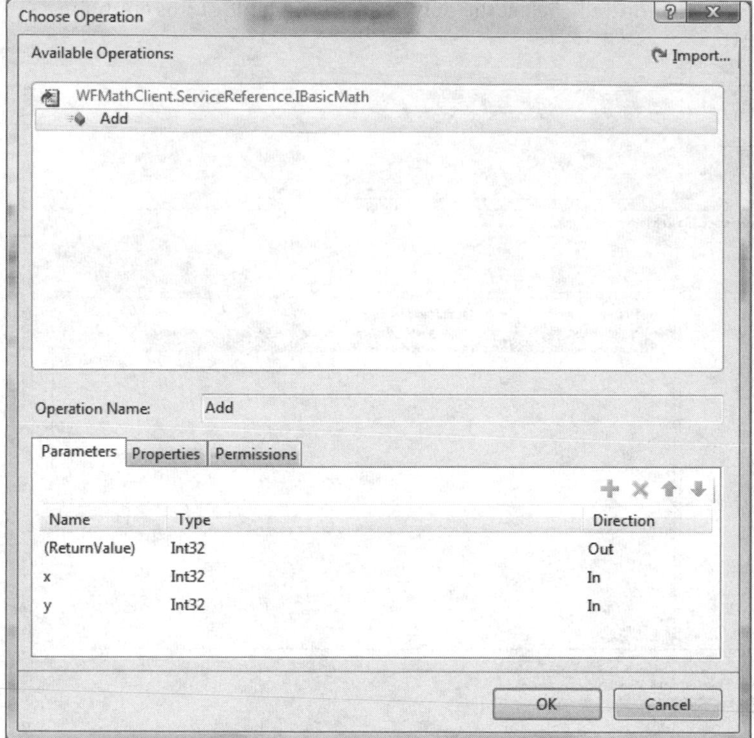

Figure 26-22. *Selecting the* `Add()` *operation*

Copy this value to your clipboard and paste it into the `ChannelToken` property using the IDE's Properties window. Once you have done so, you will notice that the `ChannelToken` property has two subnodes named `EndpointName` and `OwnerActivityName`. Because the MathService exposes only a single endpoint, copy the same value set to `ChannelToken` (`WSHttpBinding_IBasicMath`) to the `EndpointName`, and select the name of your workflow instance (`WCFSendAddActivity`) as the owner.

Last but not least, we need to connect the `x` and `y` parameters of the `Add()` method to our `FirstNumber` and `SecondNumber` properties, and the return value to our `Result` property. The process of doing so is identical to configuring the `InvokeWebService` activity (click the ellipsis buttons to pick the property name). Figure 26-23 shows the fully configured `SendActivity`.

To view the result, place a final Code activity on your workflow designer and assign the `ExecuteCode` value to a method named `WCFResult()`, which is implemented like so:

```
private void WCFResult(object sender, EventArgs e)
{
  Console.WriteLine("***** WCF Service Addition *****");
  Console.WriteLine("{0} + {1} = {2}",
    FirstNumber, SecondNumber, Result);
}
```

Figure 26-24 shows the final output.

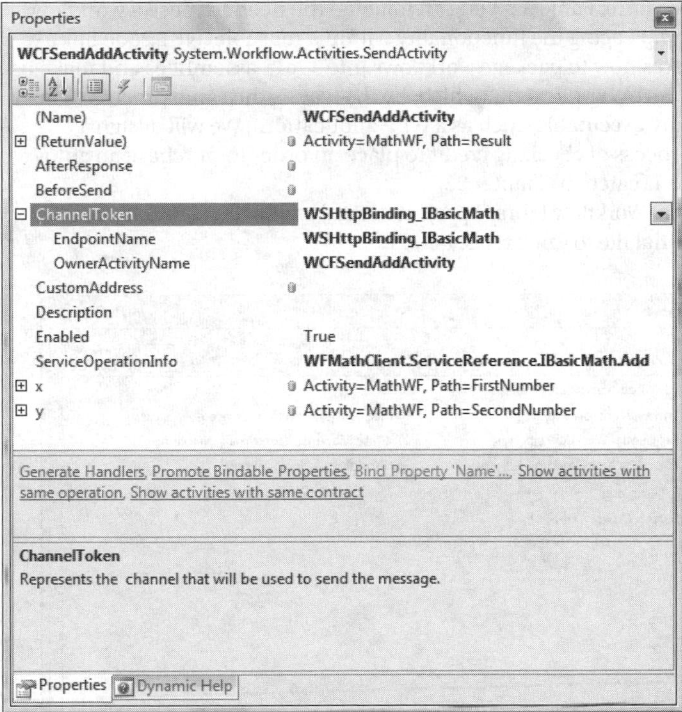

Figure 26-23. *The fully configured SendActivity*

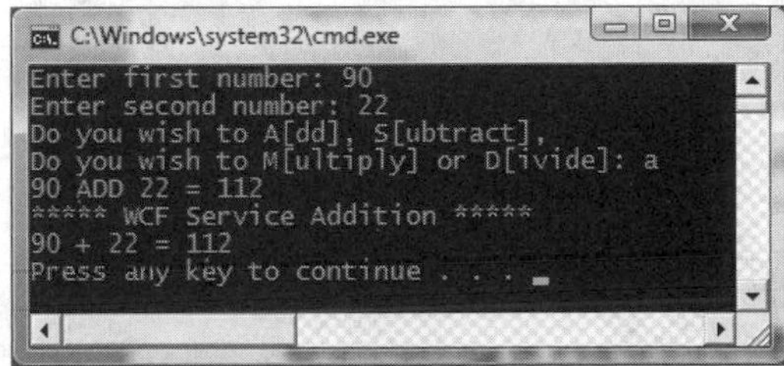

Figure 26-24. *Communicating with a WCF service*

Source Code The WFMathClient example is included under the Chapter 26 subdirectory.

Building a Reusable WF Code Library

These first examples allowed you to play around with various WF activities at design time, interact with the workflow runtime engine (by passing custom parameters), and get into the overall WF mind-set using console-based WF hosts. While this is great from a learning point of view, I bet you can easily envision building workflow-enabled Windows Forms applications, WPF applications, or

ASP.NET web applications. Furthermore, I am sure you can imagine the need to reuse a workflow across numerous applications by packaging the functionality within a reusable .NET code library.

The next WF example illustrates how to package workflows into `*.dll` assemblies and make use of them from a hosting Windows Forms application (which, by the way, is the same process as hosting an external workflow within any executable, such as a WPF application). We will design a workflow that models the basic process of checking credit to place an order to purchase an automobile from the AutoLot database created in Chapter 22.

Begin by selecting a Sequential Workflow Library project named CreditCheckWFLib (see Figure 26-25) and rename your initial file to `CreditCheckWF.cs`.

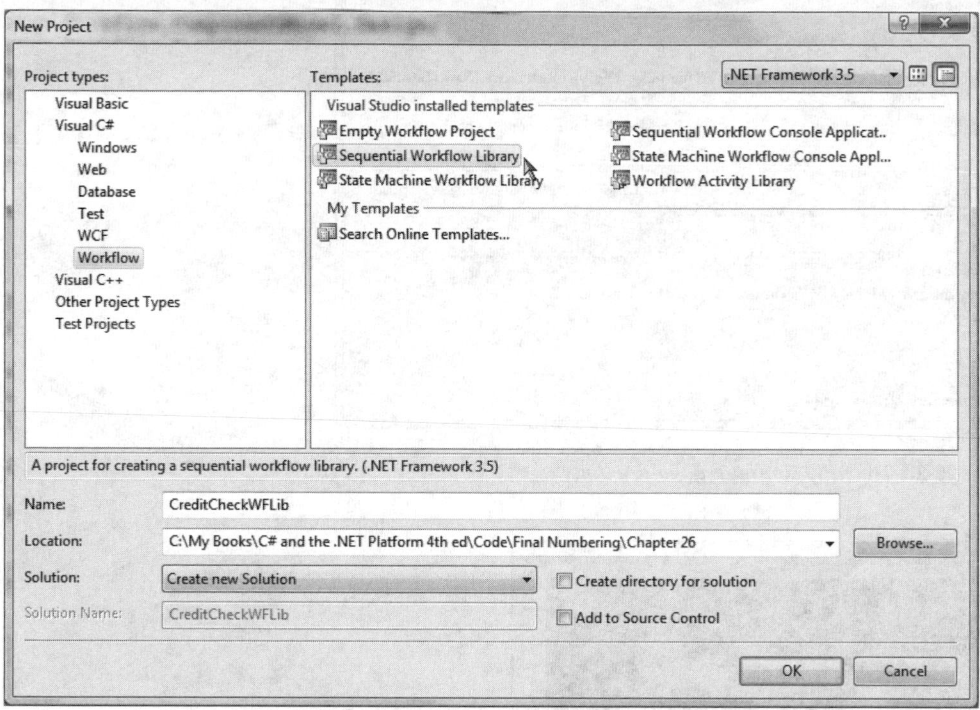

Figure 26-25. *Creating a Sequential Workflow Library project*

At this point, you will be provided with an initial workflow designer. Be aware that a single workflow code library can contain multiple workflows, each of which can be inserted using the Project ➤ Add New Item dialog box. In any case, add a reference to your `AutoLotDAL.dll` assembly created in Chapter 22, and update your initial code file to import the `AutoLotConnectedLayer` namespace:

```
// Add the following import.
using AutoLotConnectedLayer;

namespace CreditCheckWFLib
{
  ...
}
```

Next, add an automatic property to represent the customer's ID:

```
public sealed partial class CreditCheckWF : SequentialWorkflowActivity
{
  // ID of customer to run credit check against.
  public int ID { get; set; }
  ...
}
```

When we build the client application at a later step, this property will be set using an incoming `Dictionary<string, object>` object passed to the workflow runtime.

Performing a Credit Check

Modify your class with an addition automatic property (`CreditOK`), which represents if the customer has passed our "rigorous" credit validation process:

```
public sealed partial class CreditCheckWF : SequentialWorkflowActivity
{
  // We will use this to determine if the credit check
  // has passed or failed.
  public bool CreditOK { get; set; }
  ...
}
```

Now place a Code activity onto your WF designer named `ValidateCreditActivity` and set the `ExecuteCode` value to a new method named `ValidateCredit`. Obviously, a production-level credit check could involve a good number of subactivities, database lookups, and so forth. Here, we will generate a random number to represent the chance the caller passes our credit test:

```
private void ValidateCredit(object sender, EventArgs e)
{
  // Pretend that we have preformed some exotic
  // credit validation here...
  Random r = new Random();
  int value = r.Next(500);
  if (value > 300)
    CreditOK = true;
  else
    CreditOK = false;
}
```

Next, add an IfElse activity named `CreditCheckPassedActivity` with two branches named `CreditCheckOK` and `CreditCheckFailed`. Configure the left branch to be evaluated using a new declarative rule condition using the following conditional expression:

```
this.CreditOK == true
```

If the user *fails* the credit check, our goal is to remove them from the Customers table and add them to the CreditRisks table. Given that Chapter 22 already accounted for this possibility using the `ProcessCreditRisk()` method of the `InventoryDAL` type, add a new `CodeActivity` type within the `CreditCheckFailed` branch named `ProcessCreditRiskActivity` mapped to a method named `ProcessCreditRisk()`. Implement this method as so:

Note Recall that we added a `bool` parameter to the `InventoryDAL.ProcessCreditRisk()` method to force the transaction to fail for testing purposes. Be sure to pass the value `false` as the first parameter.

```
private void ProcessCreditRisk(object sender, EventArgs e)
{
  // Ideally we would store the connection string externally.
  InventoryDAL dal = new InventoryDAL();
  dal.OpenConnection(@"Data Source=(local)\SQLEXPRESS;Integrated Security=SSPI;" +
    "Initial Catalog=AutoLot");
  try
  {
    dal.ProcessCreditRisk(false, ID);
  }
  finally
  {
    dal.CloseConnection();
  }
}
```

If the credit check succeeds, we will simply display an informational message box to inform the caller that the credit check succeeded. In a real workflow, the next steps might involve placing an order, sending out an order verification e-mail, and so on. Assuming you have referenced the System.Windows.Forms.dll assembly, place a Code activity in the leftmost branch of your IfElse activity named PurchaseCarActivity, which is mapped to a method name PurchaseCar() implemented as so:

```
private void PurchaseCar(object sender, EventArgs e)
{
  // Here, we will opt for simplicity. However, we could easily update
  // AutoLotDAL.dll with a new method to place a new order within the Orders table.
  System.Windows.Forms.MessageBox.Show("Your credit has been approved!");
}
```

To complete your workflow, add a final CodeActivity to the rightmost branch directly after the ProcessCreditRiskActitity. Name this new activity ShowDenyMessageActivity, which is mapped to the following method:

```
private void CreditDenied(object sender, EventArgs e)
{
  System.Windows.Forms.MessageBox.Show("You are a CREDIT RISK!",
    "Order Denied!");
}
```

At this point, your workflow looks something like Figure 26-26.

Source Code The CreditCheckWFLib example is included under the Chapter 26 subdirectory.

Creating a Windows Forms Client Application

Now that you have authored a reusable .NET code library that contains a custom workflow, you are able to build any sort of .NET application to make use of it. Although we have not yet examined the details of building GUIs using the Windows Forms API, here we will build a very crude UI just to test our workflow logic (Chapter 27 will begin your investigation of GUI-based .NET applications). To begin, create a new Windows Forms Application project named CreditCheckApp (see Figure 26-27).

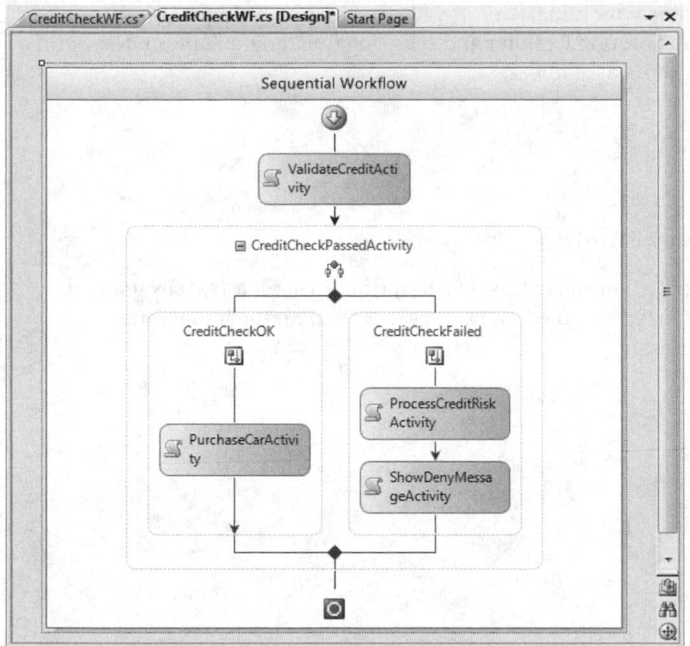

Figure 26-26. *The completed Sequential Workflow Library project*

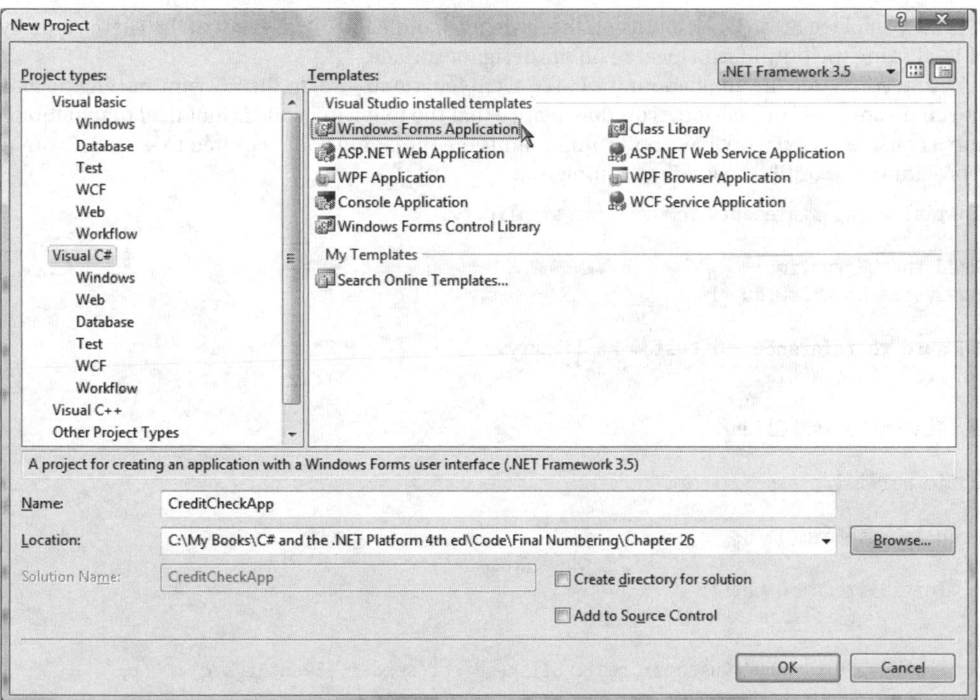

Figure 26-27. *Building a Windows Forms Application project to test our workflow library*

Once you have done so, rename your initial `Form1.cs` file to the more fitting `MainForm.cs` by right-clicking the Form1.cs icon in Solution Explorer and selecting the Rename option. Next, add a reference to each of the following .NET assemblies:

- `CreditCheckWFLib.dll`
- `System.Workflow.Runtime.dll`
- `System.Workflow.Activities.dll`
- `System.Workflow.ComponentModel.dll`

The user interface of our application will consist of a descriptive `Label`, a `TextBox` (named `txtCustomerID`), and a single `Button` type (named `btnExecuteWorkflow`) on the initial form. Figure 26-28 shows one possible design.

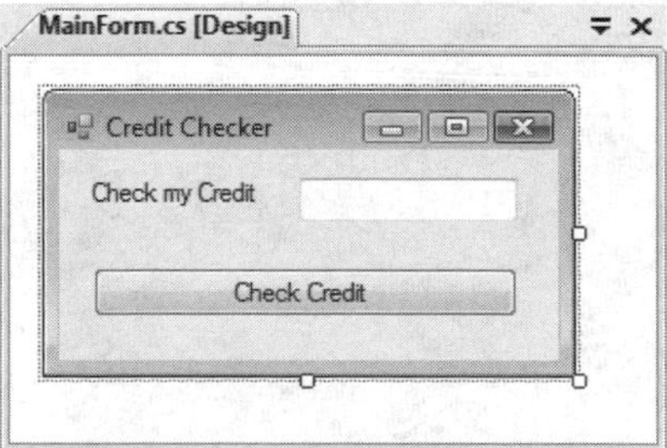

Figure 26-28. *A simple UI to test our workflow library*

Once you place these UI elements on the designer, handle the `Click` event of the `Button` type by double-clicking the button icon located on the designer surface.

Within your code file, implement the `Click` event handler to fire up the WF runtime engine and create an instance of your custom workflow. Notice that the following code is identical to that found within a console-based workflow application (minus the threading code required to keep the console program alive until the workflow completes):

```
// Initial using statements removed for simplicity.
...
// Need the WF runtime!
using System.Workflow.Runtime;

// Be sure to reference our custom WF library.
using CreditCheckWFLib;

namespace WinFormsWFClient
{
  public partial class MainForm : Form
  {
    public MainForm()
    {
      InitializeComponent();
    }

    private void btnCheckCustomerCredit_Click(object sender, EventArgs e)
    {
      // Create the WF runtime.
      WorkflowRuntime wfRuntime = new WorkflowRuntime();
```

```
      // Get ID in the TextBox to pass to the workflow.
      Dictionary<string, object> args = new
        Dictionary<string, object>();
      args.Add("ID", int.Parse(txtCustomerID.Text));

      // Get an instance of our WF.
      WorkflowInstance myWorkflow =
        wfRuntime.CreateWorkflow(typeof(CreditCheckWF), args);

      // Start it up!
      myWorkflow.Start();
    }
  }
}
```

When you run your application, enter a customer ID value, ensuring that the customer ID you enter does not current have a reference in the Orders table (to ensure that the item will be successfully deleted from the Customers table).

As you test credit ratings, you should eventually find that a risky customer has been deleted from the Customers table and placed into the CreditRisk table. In fact, for testing purposes, you may wish to add a dummy entry into the Customers table and attempt to verify credit for a fixed individual.

■ **Source Code** The WinFormsWFClient example is included under the Chapter 26 subdirectory.

A Brief Word Regarding Custom Activities

At this point, you have seen how to configure a handful of common WF activities within different types of projects. While these built-in activities certainly are a firm starting point for many WF applications, they do not account for every possible circumstance. Thankfully, the WF community has been creating new custom activities, many of which are freely downloadable, and others of which are offered through third parties at various price points.

■ **Note** If you are interested in examining some additional workflow activities, a good starting point is `http://wf.netfx3.com`. Here, you can download a good number of additional activities that extend those that ship with the product.

Despite the number of auxiliary activities that can be obtained from the online WF community, it is also entirely possible (and in some cases necessary) to build a custom activity from scratch. As you might guess, Visual Studio 2008 provides a Workflow Activity Library project template for this very purpose. If you select this project type, you will be given a designer surface to create your custom activity, using an identical approach to building a workflow itself (add new activities, connect them to code, etc.).

Much like the process of building a custom Windows Forms control, a custom activity can be adorned with numerous .NET attributes that control how the component should integrate within the IDE—for example, which bitmap image to display on the toolbar, which configuration dialogs (if any) to display when a property is configured within the Properties window, and so forth.

If you are interested in learning more about building custom activities, the .NET Framework 3.5 SDK documentation provides a number of interesting examples, including the construction of a "Send E-mail Activity." For more details, simply browse the Custom Activities samples found under the WF Samples node of the provided documentation (see Figure 26-29).

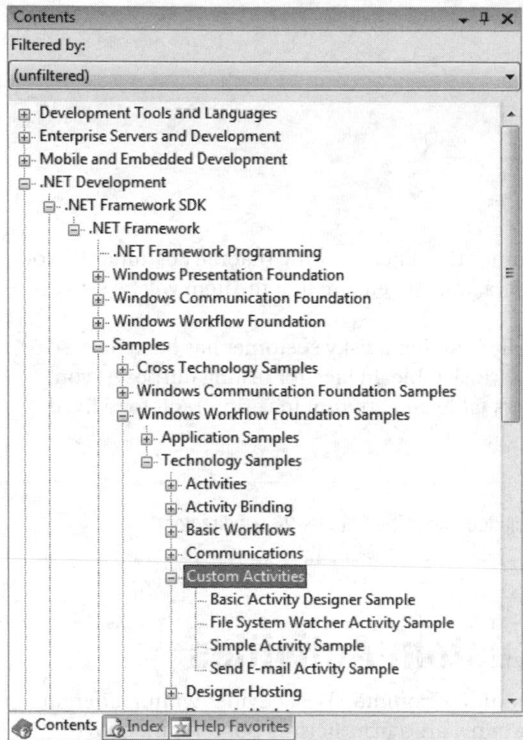

Figure 26-29. *The .NET Framework 3.5 SDK documentation provides numerous workflow examples.*

Summary

Windows Workflow Foundation (WF) is an API that was released with .NET 3.0. In essence, WF allows you to model an application's internal business processes directly within the application itself. Beyond simply modeling the overall workflow, however, WF provides a complete runtime engine and several services that round out this API's overall functionality (transaction services, persistence and tracking services, etc.). While this introductory chapter did not examine these services in any great detail, do remember that a production-level WF application will most certainly make use of these facilities.

When building a workflow-enabled application, Visual Studio 2008 provides several designer tools, including a workflow designer, configuration using the Properties window, and (most important) the Windows Workflow Toolbox. Here, you will find numerous built-in *activities* that constitute the overall composition of a particular workflow. Once you have modeled your workflow, you are then able to execute the workflow instance using the `WorkflowRuntime` type, using your host of choice.

PART 6

Desktop User Interfaces

CHAPTER 27

Programming with Windows Forms

Since the release of the .NET platform (circa 2001), the base class libraries have included a particular API named Windows Forms (represented by the `System.Windows.Forms.dll` assembly). As you may know, the Windows Forms toolkit provides the types necessary to build desktop graphical user interfaces (GUIs), create custom controls, manage resources (string tables, icons, etc.), and perform other GUI-centric programming tasks. In addition, a separate API named GDI+ (bundled within the `System.Drawing.dll` assembly) provides additional types that allow programmers to generate 2D graphics, interact with networked printers, and manipulate image data.

The Windows Forms (and GDI+) APIs are still alive and well with the release of .NET 3.5, and will exist within the base class library for quite some time (arguably forever, in fact). However, since the release of .NET 3.0, Microsoft shipped a brand new GUI toolkit called Windows Presentation Foundation (WPF). As you will see beginning in the next chapter, WPF provides a massive amount of horsepower that can be used to build bleeding-edge user interfaces.

The point of this chapter, however, is to provide a tour of the traditional Windows Forms API for one simple reason: many GUI applications simply might not require the horsepower offered by WPF. In fact, for many UI applications, WPF can be overkill. Furthermore, there are many existing Windows Forms applications scattered throughout the .NET universe that will need to be maintained.

Given these points, in this chapter you will come to understand the Windows Forms programming model, work with the integrated designers of Visual Studio 2008, experiment with numerous Windows Forms controls, and receive an overview of graphics programming using GDI+. To pull this information together in a cohesive whole, we wrap things up by creating a (semicapable) painting application.

Note Earlier editions of this text included three (fairly lengthy) chapters dedicated to the Windows Forms API. Given that WPF is poised to become the preferred toolkit for .NET GUI development, this edition has consolidated Windows Forms/GDI+ coverage to this single chapter. However, those who have purchased this book can download the previous Windows Forms/GDI+ chapters in PDF format from the Apress website for free.

The Windows Forms Namespaces

The Windows Forms API consists of hundreds of types (classes, interfaces, structures, enums, and delegates) that are organized within various namespaces of the `System.Windows.Forms.dll` assembly. Figure 27-1 shows these namespaces displayed through the Visual Studio 2008 object browser.

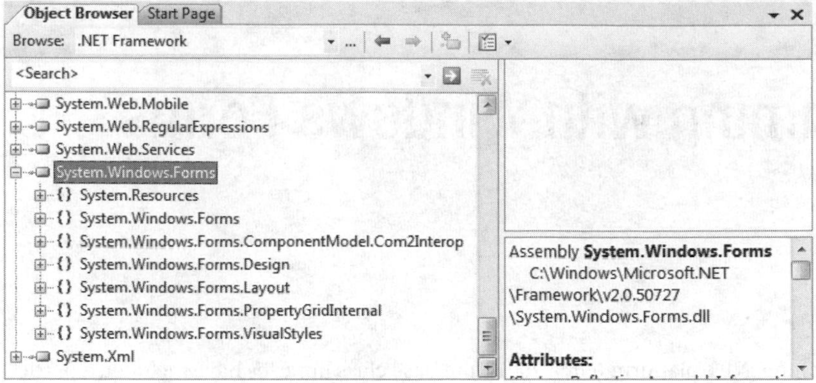

Figure 27-1. *The Windows Forms namespaces of* `System.Windows.Forms.dll`

By far and away, the most important namespace is `System.Windows.Forms`. From a high level, the types within the `System.Windows.Forms` namespace can be grouped into the following broad categories:

- *Core infrastructure*: These are types that represent the core operations of a Windows Forms program (`Form`, `Application`, etc.) and various types to facilitate interoperability with legacy ActiveX controls.
- *Controls*: These are types used to create rich UIs (`Button`, `MenuStrip`, `ProgressBar`, `DataGridView`, etc.), all of which derive from the `Control` base class. Controls are configurable at design time and are visible (by default) at runtime.
- *Components*: These are types that do not derive from the `Control` base class but still provide visual features to a Windows Forms program (`ToolTip`, `ErrorProvider`, etc.). Many components (such as the `Timer` and `BackgroundWorker`) are not visible at runtime, but can be configured visually at design time.
- *Common dialog boxes*: Windows Forms provides a number of canned dialog boxes for common operations (`OpenFileDialog`, `PrintDialog`, `ColorDialog`, etc.). As you would hope, you can certainly build your own custom dialog boxes if the standard dialog boxes do not suit your needs.

Given that the total number of types within `System.Windows.Forms` is well over 100 strong, it would be redundant (not to mention a terrible waste of paper) to list every member of the Windows Forms family. As you work through this chapter, you will gain a firm foundation upon which to build. However, be sure to check out the .NET Framework 3.5 SDK documentation for further details.

Building a Simple Windows Forms Application (IDE-Free)

As you would expect, modern .NET IDEs (such as Visual Studio 2008, C# 2008 Express, or SharpDevelop) provide numerous form designers, visual editors, and integrated code generation tools (aka wizards) to facilitate the construction of a Windows Forms application. While these tools are extremely useful, they can also hinder the process of learning Windows Forms, as these same tools tend to generate a good deal of boilerplate code that can obscure the core object model.

Given this, our first Windows Forms example will be created using a no-frills text editor and the C# command-line compiler (see Chapter 2 for the details of working with `csc.exe`).

To begin, create a folder named SimpleWinFormsApp (I'd suggest creating this directly off your C drive), open a Visual Studio 2008 command prompt, and using your text editor of choice, create a file named `SimpleWFApp.cs`. Author the following code within your new file, and save it in the SimpleWinFormsApp folder.

```
// The minimum required namespaces.
using System;
using System.Windows.Forms;

namespace SimpleWFApp
{
  // This is our application object.
  class Program
  {
    static void Main()
    {
      Application.Run(new MainWindow());
    }
  }

  // This is our main window.
  class MainWindow : Form {}
}
```

This code represents the absolute simplest Windows Forms application. At bare minimum, we need a class type that extends the `Form` base class and a `Main()` method to call the static `Application.Run()` method (more details on `Form` and `Application` later in this chapter). You can compile this application using the following command set (recall from Chapter 2 that the default response file [`csc.rsp`] automatically references numerous .NET assemblies, including `System.Windows.Forms.dll` and `System.Drawing.dll`):

```
csc /target:winexe *.cs
```

■ **Note** Technically speaking, you can build a Windows application at the command line using the `/target:exe` option; however, if you do, you will find that a command window will be looming in the background (and it will stay there until you shut down the main window). When you specify `/target:winexe`, your executable runs as a native Windows Forms application (without the looming command window).

If you were to run your application, you would find you have a resizable, minimizable, maximizable, and closable topmost window (see Figure 27-2).

Figure 27-2. *A very simple Windows Forms application*

Granted, our current application is not terribly exciting, but it does illustrate how simple a Windows Forms application can be. To spruce things up a bit, let's add a custom constructor to our `MainWindow` type, which allows the caller to set various properties on the window to be displayed. For example:

```
// This is our main window.
class MainWindow : Form
{
  public MainWindow(string title, int height, int width)
  {
    // Set various properties from our parent classes.
    Text = title;
    Width = width;
    Height = height;

    // Inherited method to center the form on the screen.
    CenterToScreen();
  }
}
```

We can now update the call to `Application.Run()` as follows:

```
static void Main()
{
  Application.Run(new MainWindow("My Window", 200, 300));
}
```

While this is a step in the right direction, any window worth its salt will require various user interface elements (menu systems, status bars, buttons, etc.) to allow for input. To understand how a `Form`-derived type can contain such elements, you must understand the role of the `Controls` property and the underlying controls collection.

Populating the Controls Collection

The `System.Windows.Forms.Control` base class (which is the inheritance chain of the `Form` type) defines a property named `Controls`. This property wraps a custom collection nested in the `Control` class named `ControlsCollection`. This collection (as the name suggests) references each UI element maintained by the derived type. Like other containers, this type supports a number of methods to insert, remove, and find a given UI widget (see Table 27-1).

Table 27-1. `ControlCollection` *Members*

Member	Meaning in Life
`Add()` `AddRange()`	Used to insert a new `Control`-derived type (or array of types) in the collection
`Clear()`	Removes all entries in the collection
`Count`	Returns the number of items in the collection
`GetEnumerator()`	Returns the `IEnumerator` interface for this collection
`Remove()` `RemoveAt()`	Used to remove a control from the collection

When you wish to populate the UI of a `Form`-derived type, you will typically follow a very predictable series of steps:

- Define a member variable of a given UI element within the Form derived class.
- Configure the look and feel of the UI element.
- Add the UI element to the form's ControlsCollection container via a call to Controls.Add().

Assume you wish to update your MainWindow class to support a File ➤ Exit menu system. Here are the relevant updates, with code analysis to follow:

```
class MainWindow : Form
{
  //  Members for a simple menu system.
  private MenuStrip mnuMainMenu = new MenuStrip();
  private ToolStripMenuItem mnuFile = new ToolStripMenuItem();
  private ToolStripMenuItem mnuFileExit = new ToolStripMenuItem();

  public MainWindow(string title, int height, int width)
  {
    ...
    // Method to create our menu system.
    BuildMenuSystem();
  }

  private void BuildMenuSystem()
  {
    // Add the File menu item to the main menu.
    mnuFile.Text = "&File";
    mnuMainMenu.Items.Add(mnuFile);

    // Now add the Exit menu to the File menu.
    mnuFileExit.Text = "E&xit";
    mnuFile.DropDownItems.Add(mnuFileExit);
    mnuFileExit.Click += new System.EventHandler(this.mnuFileExit_Click);

    // Finally, set the menu for this Form.
    Controls.Add(this.mnuMainMenu);
    MainMenuStrip = this.mnuMainMenu;
  }

  // Handler for the File | Exit event.
  private void mnuFileExit_Click(object sender, EventArgs e)
  {
    Application.Exit();
  }
}
```

First off, notice that the MainWindow type now maintains three new member variables. The MenuStrip type represents the entirety of the menu system, where a given ToolStripMenuItem represents any given topmost menu item (e.g., File) or submenu item (e.g., Exit) supported by the host.

Note If you have programmed with earlier versions of Windows Forms (1.0 or 1.1), you may recall that the MainMenu type was used to hold any number of MenuItem objects. The MenuStrip control (introduced with .NET 2.0) is similar to MainMenu; however, MenuStrip is able to contain controls beyond "normal menu items" (combo boxes, text boxes, etc.).

The menu system is configured within our BuildMenuSystem() helper function. Notice that the text of each ToolStripMenuItem is controlled via the Text property, each of which has been assigned a string literal containing an embedded ampersand symbol. As you may already know, this syntax sets the Alt key shortcut, thus selecting Alt+F will activate the File menu, while selecting Alt+X will activate the Exit menu. Also notice that the File ToolStripMenuItem object (mnuFile) adds subitems via the DropDownItems property. The MenuStrip object itself adds a topmost menu item via the Items property.

Once the menu system has been established, it is then added to the controls collection (via the Controls property), after which we assign our MenuStrip object to the inherited MainMenuStrip property. While this step may seem redundant, having a specific property such as MainMenuStrip makes it possible to dynamically establish which menu system to show a user, perhaps due to user preferences or security settings.

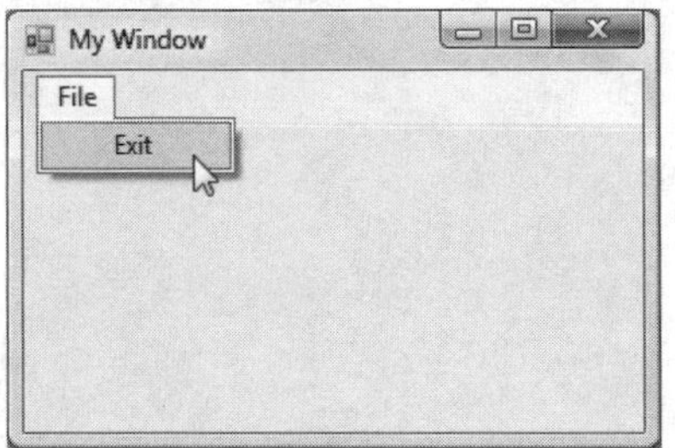

Figure 27-3. *A simple window, with a simple menu system*

The only other point of interest is the fact that we are handling the Click event of the File ➤ Exit menu, in order to capture when the user selects this submenu. The Click event works in conjunction with a standard delegate type named System.EventHandler. This event can only call methods that take a System.Object as the first parameter and a System.EventArgs as the second. Here, our delegate target (mnuFileExit_Click) has been implemented to terminate the entire Windows application using the static Application.Exit() method.

Once this application has been recompiled and executed, you will now find your simple window sports a custom menu system (see Figure 27-3).

The Role of System.EventArgs and System.EventHandler

System.EventHandler is one of many delegate types used within the Windows Forms (and ASP.NET) APIs during the event-handling process. As you have seen, this delegate can only point to methods where the first argument is of type System.Object, which is a reference to the type that sent the event. For example, if we were to update the implementation of the mnuFileExit_Click() method as follows:

```
private void mnuFileExit_Click(object sender, EventArgs e)
{
  MessageBox.Show(string.Format("{0} sent this event", sender.ToString()));
  Application.Exit();
}
```

we would be able to verify that the mnuFileExit type sent the event, as the string

```
"E&xit sent this event"
```

is displayed within the message box. You may be wondering what purpose the second argument, System.EventArgs, serves. In reality, the System.EventArgs type brings little to the table, as it simply extends Object and provides practically nothing by way of addition functionality:

```
public class EventArgs
{
  public static readonly EventArgs Empty;
  static EventArgs();
  public EventArgs();
}
```

This type is, however, very useful in the overall scheme of .NET event handling, in that it is the parent to many (very useful) derived types. For example, the `MouseEventArgs` type extends `EventArgs` to provide details regarding the current state of the mouse. `KeyEventArgs` also extends `EventArgs` to provide details of the state of the keyboard (such as which key was pressed), `PaintEventArgs` extends `EventArgs` to yield graphically relevant data, and so forth. You will see numerous `EventArgs` descendents (and the delegates that make use of them) not when working with Windows Forms, but with the WPF and ASP.NET APIs as well.

In any case, while we could most certainly continue to build more and more functionality into our `MainWindow` (status bars, dialog boxes, etc.) using a simple text editor, we will eventually end up with hand cramps, as we have to manually author all the grungy control configuration logic. Thankfully, Visual Studio 2008 provides numerous integrated designers that take care of these details on our behalf. As we use these tools during the remainder of this chapter, always remember that they are authoring everyday C# code. There is nothing "magical" about them whatsoever.

■ **Source Code** The SimpleWinFormsApp project can be found under the Chapter 27 subdirectory.

The Visual Studio Windows Forms Project Template

When you wish to leverage the Windows Forms designer tools of Visual Studio 2008, your first step is to select the Windows Application project template via the File ➤ New Project menu option. To get comfortable with the core Windows Forms designer tools, create a new application named SimpleVSWinFormsApp (see Figure 27-4).

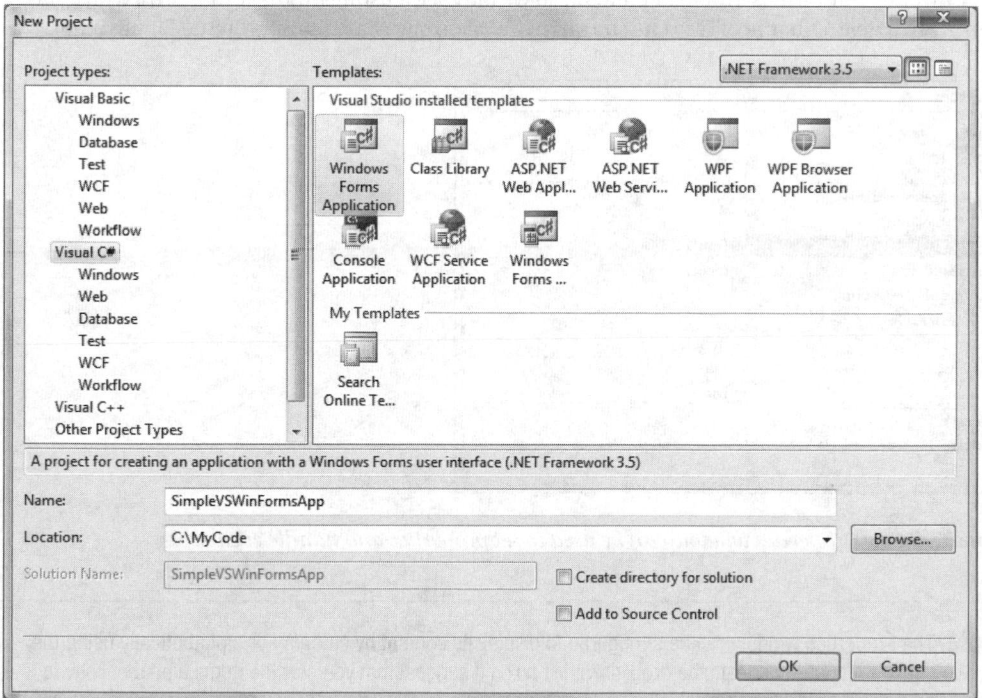

Figure 27-4. *The Visual Studio Windows Forms project template*

The Visual Designer Surface

Before we begin to build more interesting Windows applications, this first example will re-create the previous example while leveraging the designer tools. First of all, once you create a new Windows Forms project, you will notice that Visual Studio 2008 presents a designer surface to which you can drag and drop any number of controls. This same designer can be used to configure the initial size of the window, simply by resizing the form itself via the supplied grab handles (see Figure 27-5).

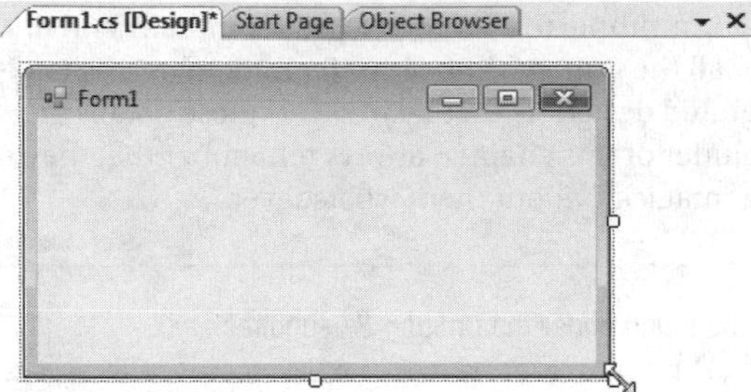

Figure 27-5. *The visual Forms designer*

When you wish to configure the look and feel of your window (as well as any control placed on a form), you will do so using the Properties window. As you will see over the course of this chapter, this window can be used to assign values to properties as well as establish event handlers for a given widget. When you have a collection of controls on the designer surface, they can be selected for configuration using the drop-down list box mounted on the top of the Properties window.

Currently our form is devoid of content, so we only see a listing for the initial `Form`, which has been given a default name of `Form1` as shown in the read-only `(Name)` property (see Figure 27-6).

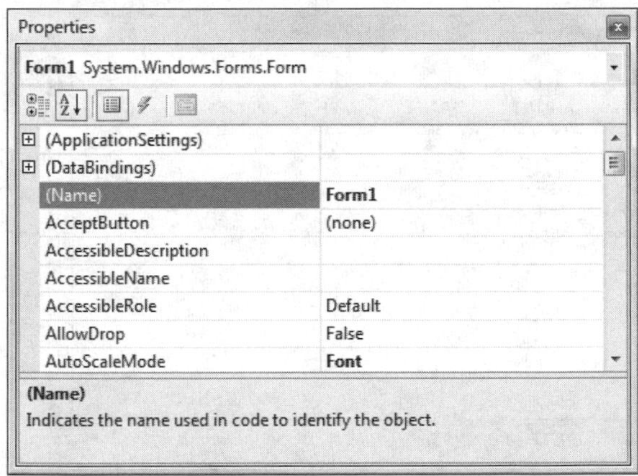

Figure 27-6. *The Properties window can be used to set properties and handle events.*

■ **Note** The Properties window can be configured to display its content by category or alphabetically using the first two buttons mounted beneath the drop-down list box. I'd suggest that you sort the items alphabetically to quickly find a given property or event.

The next designer element to be aware of is the Solution Explorer window. While all Visual Studio projects support this window, when you are building Windows Forms applications, it is especially helpful in that you can (1) quickly change the name of the file and related class for any window and (2) view the file that contains the designer-maintained code (more information on this tidbit in just a moment). For now, simply right-click the `Form1.cs` icon and select the Rename option. Name this initial window to the more fitting `MainWindow.cs`. Figure 27-7 shows the end result.

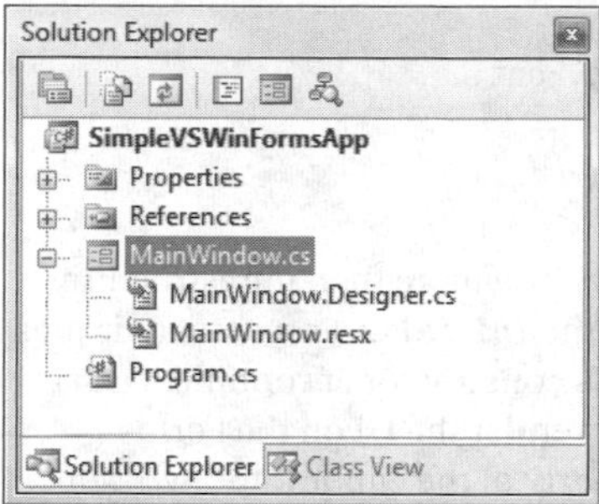

Figure 27-7. *The Solution Explorer window allows you to rename your* `Form`*-derived type and the related files.*

Dissecting the Initial Form

Before we build our menu system, let's examine exactly what Visual Studio 2008 has created by default. First, right-click the `MainWindow.cs` icon from the Solution Explorer window and select View Code. Notice that the form has been defined as a partial type, which as you may recall from Chapter 5 allows a single type to be defined within multiple code files. Also note the form's constructor is making a call to a method named `InitializeComponent()` and the fact that your type "is-a" `Form`.

```
namespace SimpleVSWinFormsApp
{
  public partial class MainWindow : Form
  {
    public MainWindow()
    {
      InitializeComponent();
    }
  }
}
```

As you may be expecting, `InitializeComponent()` is defined in a separate file that completes the partial class definition. As a naming convention, this file always ends in `.Designer.cs`, preceded by the name of the related C# file containing the `Form`-derived type. Using the Solution Explorer window, open your `MainWindow.Designer.cs` file. Now, ponder the following code (stripped of the code comments for simplicity):

```
partial class MainWindow
{
  private System.ComponentModel.IContainer components = null;

  protected override void Dispose(bool disposing)
  {
    if (disposing && (components != null))
```

```
    {
      components.Dispose();
    }
    base.Dispose(disposing);
  }

  private void InitializeComponent()
  {
    this.components = new System.ComponentModel.Container();
    this.AutoScaleMode = System.Windows.Forms.AutoScaleMode.Font;
    this.Text = "Form1";
  }
}
```

The IContainer member variable and Dispose() methods are little more than infrastructure used by the Visual Studio designer tools. However, do notice that the InitializeComponent() is present and accounted for. Not only is this method invoked by a form's constructor at runtime, Visual Studio makes use of this same method at design time to correctly render the UI on the Forms designer. To illustrate, change the value assigned to the Text property of the window to "My Main Window". Once you activate the designer, you will find the form's caption updates accordingly.

As well, when you are making use of the visual design tools (such as the Properties window), the IDE will update InitializeComponent() automatically. To illustrate this aspect of the Windows Forms designer tools, ensure the Forms designer is the active window within the IDE and find the Opacity property listed in the Properties window. Change this value to 0.8 (80%), which will give your window a slightly transparent look and feel the next time you compile and run your program. Once you have made this change, examine the implementation of InitializeComponent() once again:

```
private void InitializeComponent()
{
  this.SuspendLayout();
  //
  // MainWindow
  //
  this.AutoScaleDimensions = new System.Drawing.SizeF(6F, 13F);
  this.AutoScaleMode = System.Windows.Forms.AutoScaleMode.Font;
  this.ClientSize = new System.Drawing.Size(284, 264);
  this.Name = "MainWindow";
  this.Opacity = 0.8;
  this.Text = "My Main Window";
  this.ResumeLayout(false);
}
```

For all practical purposes, when you are building a Windows Forms application using Visual Studio, you can (and typically should) ignore the *.Designer.cs files and allow the IDE to maintain them on your behalf. If you were to author syntactically (or logically) incorrect code within InitializeComponent(), you might break the designer. As well, Visual Studio often reformats this method at design time. Thus, if you were to add custom code to InitializeComponent(), the IDE may delete it! In any case, simply remember that each window of a Windows Forms application is composed using partial classes.

Dissecting the Program Class

Beyond providing implementation code for an initial Form-derived type, Windows Application project types also provide a static class (named Program) that defines your program's entry point—Main():

```
static class Program
{
  [STAThread]
  static void Main()
  {
    Application.EnableVisualStyles();
    Application.SetCompatibleTextRenderingDefault(false);
    Application.Run(new MainWindow());
  }
}
```

As expected, the `Main()` method invokes `Application.Run()`, as well as a few other calls on the `Application` type to establish some basic rendering options. Last but not least, note that the `Main()` method has been adorned with the `[STAThread]` attribute. This informs the runtime that if this thread happens to create any classic COM objects (including legacy ActiveX UI controls) during its lifetime, they are to be placed in a COM-maintained area termed the *single-threaded apartment*. In a nutshell, this ensures that the COM objects are thread-safe, even if the author of a given COM object did not explicitly include code to ensure this is the case.

Visually Building a Menu System

To wrap up our look at the Windows Forms visual designer tools and move on to some more illustrative examples, activate the Forms designer window, locate the Toolbox window of Visual Studio 2008, and find the `MenuStrip` control within the Menus & Toolbars node (see Figure 27-8).

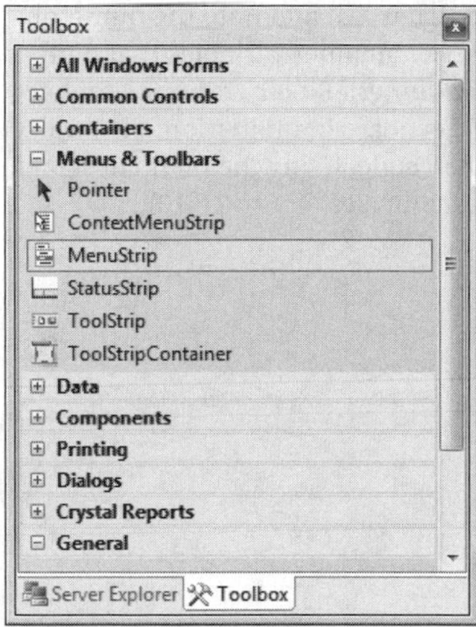

Figure 27-8. *The Toolbox window displays the Windows Forms controls that may be added to your designer surface.*

Drag a `MenuStrip` control onto the top of your Forms designer. Notice that Visual Studio responds by activating the menu editor. If you look closely at this editor, you will notice a (very) small triangle on the top-right of the control. If you click this icon, you will open a context-sensitive inline editor that allows you to make numerous property settings at once (be aware that many Windows Forms controls have similar inline editors). Just to see an example, click the Insert Standard Items option, as shown in Figure 27-9.

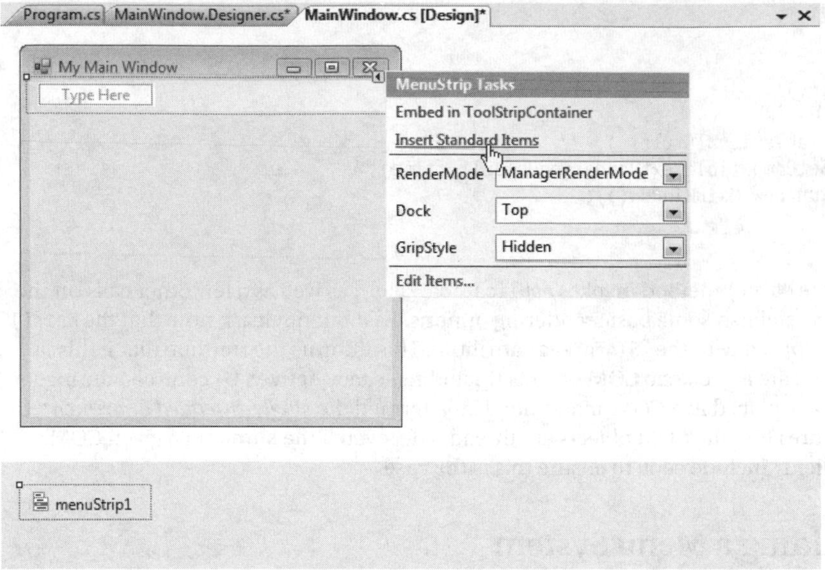

Figure 27-9. *The inline menu editor*

As you can see, Visual Studio was kind enough to establish an entire menu system on your behalf. Now, open your designer-maintained file (`MainWindow.Designer.cs`) and note the numerous lines of code added to `InitializeComponent()`, as well as several new member variables that represent your menu system (as you may agree, designer tools are *good things*). Finally, flip back to the designer and undo the previous operation by clicking the Ctrl+Z keyboard combination. This will bring you back to the initial menu editor and remove the generated code. Using the menu designer, simply type in a topmost **File** menu item followed by an **Exit** submenu (see Figure 27-10).

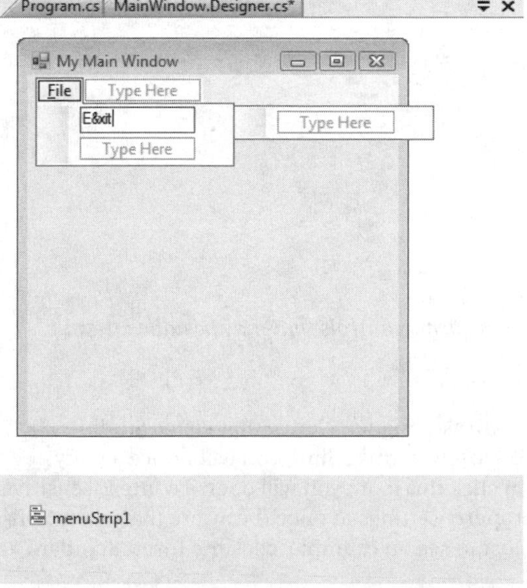

Figure 27-10. *Manually building our menu system*

If you take a look at `InitializeComponent()`, you will find the same sort of code you authored by hand in the first example of this chapter. To complete this exercise, flip back to the Forms designer and click the lightning bolt button mounted on the Properties window. This will show you all of the events you can handle for the selected control. Be sure you have selected the Exit menu (named `exitToolStripMenuItem` by default) and locate the `Click` event (see Figure 27-11).

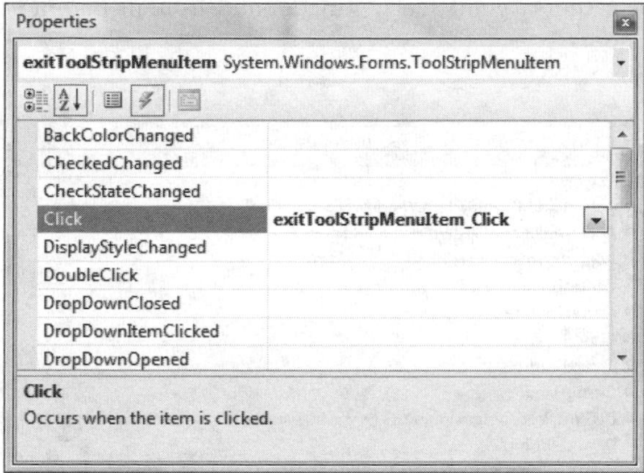

Figure 27-11. *Establishing events with the IDE*

At this point you can enter in the name of the method to be called when the item is clicked, or if you are feeling lazy at this point, simply double-click the event listed in the Properties window. This will let the IDE pick the name of the event handler on your behalf (which follows the pattern *NameOfControl_NameOfEvent()*).In either case, the IDE will create stub code, to which you can fill in the implementation details. For example:

```
public partial class MainWindow : Form
{
  public MainWindow()
  {
    InitializeComponent();
    CenterToScreen();
  }
  private void exitToolStripMenuItem_Click(object sender, EventArgs e)
  {
    Application.Exit();
  }
}
```

And if you are interested, take a quick peek at `InitializeComponent()`. As you can see, the necessary event riggings have also been accounted for:

```
this.exitToolStripMenuItem.Click +=
  new System.EventHandler(this.exitToolStripMenuItem_Click);
```

Hopefully, you now feel more comfortable moving around the IDE when building Windows Forms applications. While there are obviously many additional shortcuts, editors, and integrated code wizards, this information is more than enough to press onward.

The Anatomy of a Form

Now that you have examined how to build simple Windows Forms applications with (and without) the aid of Visual Studio, let's examine the `Form` type in greater detail. In the world of Windows Forms, the `Form` type represents any window in the application, including topmost main windows, child windows of a multiple document interface (MDI) application, as well as modal and modaless dialog boxes. As shown in Figure 27-12, the `Form` type gathers a good deal of functionality from its parent classes and the numerous interfaces it implements.

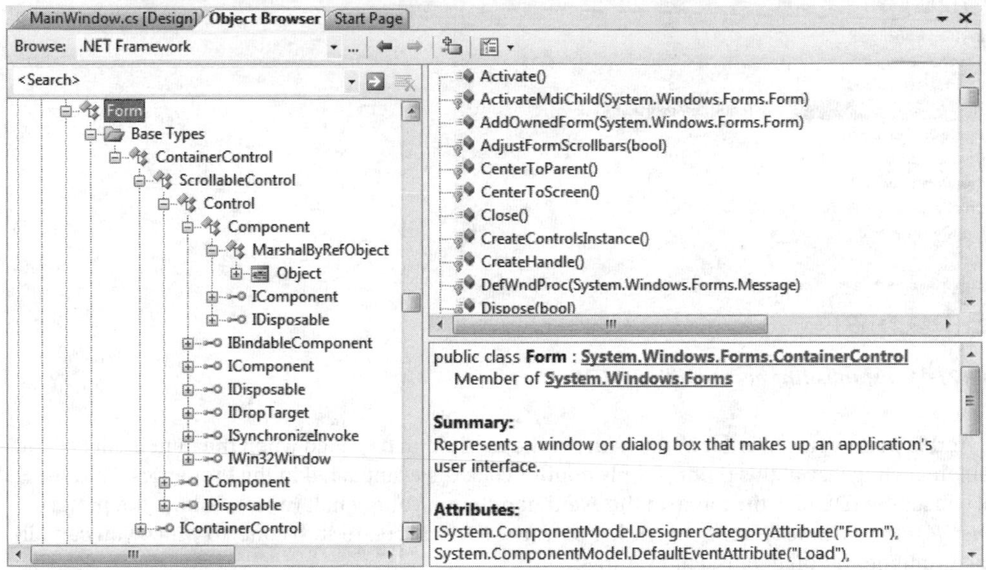

Figure 27-12. *The inheritance chain of* `System.Windows.Forms.Form`

Table 27-2 offers a high-level look at each parent class in the `Form`'s inheritance chain.

Table 27-2. *Base Classes in the* `Form` *Inheritance Chain*

Parent Class	Meaning in Life
`System.Object`	Like any class in .NET, a `Form` "is-a" `object`.
`System.MarshalByRefObject`	Types deriving from this class are accessed remotely via a *reference to* (not a local copy of) the remote type.
`System.ComponentModel.Component`	This class provides a default implementation of the `IComponent` interface. In the .NET universe, a component is a type that supports design-time editing, but is not necessarily visible at runtime.
`System.Windows.Forms.Control`	This class defines common UI members for all Windows Forms UI controls, including the `Form` type itself.
`System.Windows.Forms.ScrollableControl`	This class defines support for horizontal and vertical scrollbars, as well as members, which allow you to manage the viewport shown within the scrollable region.

Parent Class	Meaning in Life
`System.Windows.Forms.ContainerControl`	This class provides focus-management functionality for controls that can function as a container for other controls.
`System.Windows.Forms.Form`	This class represents any custom form, MDI child, or dialog box.

Although the complete derivation of a `Form` type involves numerous base classes and interfaces, do understand that you are *not* required to learn the role of each and every member from each and every parent class or implemented interface to be a proficient Windows Forms developer. In fact, the majority of the members (specifically, properties and events) you will use on a daily basis are easily set using the Visual Studio 2008 Properties window. This being said, it is important that you understand the functionality provided by the `Control` and `Form` parent classes.

The Functionality of the Control Class

The `System.Windows.Forms.Control` class establishes the common behaviors required by any GUI type. The core members of `Control` allow you to configure the size and position of a control, capture keyboard and mouse input, get or set the focus/visibility of a member, and so forth. Table 27-3 defines some properties of interest, grouped by related functionality.

Table 27-3. *Core Properties of the Control Type*

Property	Meaning in Life

`BackColor`
`ForeColor`
`BackgroundImage`
`Font`
`Cursor`
	These properties define the core UI of the control (colors, font for text, mouse cursor to display when the mouse is over the widget, etc.).

`Anchor`
`Dock`
`AutoSize`
	These properties control how the control should be positioned within the container.

`Top`
`Left`
`Bottom`
`Right`
`Bounds`
`ClientRectangle`
`Height`
`Width`
	These properties specify the current dimensions of the control.

`Enabled`
`Focused`
`Visible`
	These properties each return a Boolean that specifies the state of the current control.

`ModifierKeys`	This static property checks the current state of the modifier keys (Shift, Ctrl, and Alt) and returns the state in a `Keys` type.
`MouseButtons`	This static property checks the current state of the mouse buttons (left, right, and middle mouse buttons) and returns this state in a `MouseButtons` type.
`TabIndex` `TabStop`	These properties are used to configure the tab order of the control.

Continued

Table 27-3. *Continued*

Property	Meaning in Life
Opacity	This property determines the opacity of the control (0.0 is completely transparent; 1.0 is completely opaque).
Text	This property indicates the string data associated with this control.
Controls	This property allows you to access a strongly typed collection (ControlsCollection) that contains any child controls within the current control.

As you would guess, the Control class also defines a number of events that allow you to intercept mouse, keyboard, painting, and drag-and-drop activities (among other things). Table 27-4 lists some events of interest, grouped by related functionality.

Table 27-4. *Events of the Control Type*

Event	Meaning in Life
Click DoubleClick MouseEnter MouseLeave MouseDown MouseUp MouseMove MouseHover MouseWheel	Various events that allow you to interact with the mouse
KeyPress KeyUp KeyDown	Various events that allow you to interact with the keyboard
DragDrop DragEnter DragLeave DragOver	Various events used to monitor drag-and-drop activity
Paint	An event that allows you to interact with the graphical rendering services of GDI+

Finally, the Control base class also defines a number of methods that allow you to interact with any Control-derived type. As you examine the methods of the Control type, you will notice that a good number of them have an On prefix followed by the name of a specific event (OnMouseMove, OnKeyUp, OnPaint, etc.). Each of these On-prefixed virtual methods is the default event handler for its respective event. If you override any of these virtual members, you gain the ability to perform any necessary pre- or postprocessing of the event before (or after) invoking your parent's default implementation:

```
public partial class MainWindow : Form
{
  protected override void OnMouseDown(MouseEventArgs e)
  {
    // Add custom code for MouseDown event.

    // Call parent implementation when finished.
    base.OnMouseDown(e);
  }
}
```

While this can be helpful in some circumstances (especially if you are building a custom control that derives from a standard control), you will often handle events using the standard C# event syntax (in fact, this is the default behavior of the Visual Studio designers). When you handle events in this manner, the framework will call your custom event handler once the parent's implementation has completed. For example, here is how you can manually handle the MouseDown event:

```
public partial class MainWindow : Form
{
  public MainWindow()
  {
    MouseDown += new MouseEventHandler(MainWindow_MouseDown);
  }

  private void MainWindow_MouseDown(object sender, MouseEventArgs e)
  {
    // Add code for MouseDown event.
  }
}
```

Beyond these On*XXX*() methods, here are a few other methods to be aware of:

- Hide(): Hides the control and sets the Visible property to false
- Show(): Shows the control and sets the Visible property to true
- Invalidate(): Forces the control to redraw itself by sending a Paint event (more information on graphical rendering in the section "Rendering Graphical Data Using GDI+" later in this chapter).

The Functionality of the Form Class

The Form class is typically (but not necessarily) the direct base class for your custom Form types. In addition to the large set of members inherited from the Control, ScrollableControl, and ContainerControl classes, the Form type adds additional functionality in particular to main windows, MDI child windows, and dialog boxes. Let's start with the core properties in Table 27-5.

Table 27-5. *Properties of the* Form *Type*

Property	Meaning in Life
AcceptButton	Gets or sets the button on the form that is clicked when the user presses the Enter key.
ActiveMDIChild IsMDIChildIsMDIContainer	Used within the context of an MDI application.
CancelButton	Gets or sets the button control that will be clicked when the user presses the Esc key.
ControlBox	Gets or sets a value indicating whether the form has a control box.
FormBorderStyle	Gets or sets the border style of the form. Used in conjunction with the FormBorderStyle enumeration.
Menu	Gets or sets the menu to dock on the form.
MaximizeBox MinimizeBox	Used to determine whether this form will enable the maximize and minimize boxes.
ShowInTaskbar	Determines whether this form will be seen on the Windows taskbar.

Continued

Table 27-5. *Continued*

Property	Meaning in Life
`StartPosition`	Gets or sets the starting position of the form at runtime, as specified by the `FormStartPosition` enumeration.
`WindowState`	Configures how the form is to be displayed on startup. Used in conjunction with the `FormWindowState` enumeration.

In addition to numerous `On`-prefixed default event handlers, Table 27-6 gives a list of some core methods defined by the `Form` type.

Table 27-6. *Key Methods of the* `Form` *Type*

Method	Meaning in Life
`Activate()`	Activates a given form and gives it focus
`Close()`	Closes a form
`CenterToScreen()`	Places the form in the dead-center of the screen
`LayoutMDI()`	Arranges each child form (as specified by the `LayoutMDI` enumeration) within the parent form
`ShowDialog()`	Displays a form as a modal dialog box

Finally, the `Form` class defines a number of events, many of which fire during the form's lifetime. Table 27-7 hits the highlights.

Table 27-7. *Select Events of the* `Form` *Type*

Event	Meaning in Life
`Activated`	Occurs whenever the form is *activated,* meaning the form has been given the current focus on the desktop
`Closed`, `Closing`	Used to determine when the form is about to close or has closed
`Deactivate`	Occurs whenever the form is *deactivated,* meaning the form has lost current focus on the desktop
`Load`	Occurs after the form has been allocated into memory, but is not yet visible on the screen
`MDIChildActive`	Sent when a child window is activated

The Life Cycle of a Form Type

If you have programmed user interfaces using GUI toolkits such as Java Swing, Mac OS X Cocoa, or the raw Win32 API, you are aware that "window types" have a number of events that fire during their lifetime. The same holds true for Windows Forms. As you have seen, the life of a form begins when the type constructor is called prior to being passed into the `Application.Run()` method.

Once the object has been allocated on the managed heap, the framework fires the `Load` event. Within a `Load` event handler, you are free to configure the look and feel of the `Form`, prepare any contained child controls (such as `ListBoxes`, `TreeViews`, and whatnot), or simply allocate resources used during the `Form`'s operation (database connections, proxies to remote objects, and whatnot).

Once the `Load` event has fired, the next event to fire is `Activated`. This event fires when the form receives focus as the active window on the desktop. The logical counterpart to the `Activated` event is (of course) Deactivate, which fires when the form loses focus as the active window. As you can guess, the Activated and Deactivate events can fire numerous times over the life of a given Form type as the user navigates between active applications.

When the user has chosen to close the form in question, two close-centric events fire: Closing and Closed. The Closing event is fired first and is an ideal place to prompt the end user with the much hated (but useful) "Are you *sure* you wish to close this application?" message. This conformational step is quite helpful to ensure the user has a chance to save any application-centric data before terminating the program.

The Closing event works in conjunction with the CancelEventHandler delegate defined in the System.ComponentModel namespace. If you set the CancelEventArgs.Cancel property to true, you prevent the window from being destroyed and instruct it to return to normal operation. If you set CancelEventArgs.Cancel to false, the Closed event fires, and the Windows Forms application exits, which unloads the AppDomain and terminates the process.

To solidify the sequence of events that take place during a form's lifetime, assume you have a new Windows Forms project named FormLifeTime and have renamed the initial form to MainWindow.cs (via Solution Explorer). Now, within your form's constructor, handle the Load, Activated, Deactivate, Closing, and Closed events (recall from Chapter 11 that the IDE will autogenerate the correct delegate and event handler when you press the Tab key twice after typing +=):

```
public MainWindow()
{
  InitializeComponent();

  // Handle various lifetime events.
  Closing += new CancelEventHandler(MainWindow_Closing);
  Load += new EventHandler(MainWindow_Load);
  Closed += new EventHandler(MainWindow_Closed);
  Activated += new EventHandler(MainWindow_Activated);
  Deactivate += new EventHandler(MainWindow_Deactivate);
}
```

■Note The reason we are handling these events manually is that the Properties window (for some strange reason) does not list the Closing or Closed events. However, the Load, Activated, and Deactivate events can be handled using this design-time tool.

Within the Load, Closed, Activated, and Deactivate event handlers, you are going to update the value of a new Form-level string member variable (named lifeTimeInfo) with a simple message that displays the name of the event that has just been intercepted. As well, notice that within the Closed event handler, you will display the value of this string within a message box:

```
private void MainWindow_Load(object sender, System.EventArgs e)
{
  lifeTimeInfo += "Load event\n";
}

private void MainWindow_Activated(object sender, System.EventArgs e)
{
  lifeTimeInfo += "Activate event\n";
}

private void MainWindow_Deactivate(object sender, System.EventArgs e)
{
```

```
  lifeTimeInfo += "Deactivate event\n";
}

private void MainWindow_Closed(object sender, System.EventArgs e)
{
  lifeTimeInfo += "Closed event\n";
  MessageBox.Show(lifeTimeInfo);
}
```

Within the `Closing` event handler, you will prompt the user to ensure he or she wishes to terminate the application using the incoming `CancelEventArgs`. In the following code, notice that the `MessageBox.Show()` method returns a `DialogResult` type that contains a value representing which button has been selected by the end user. Here, we have crafted a message box that displays Yes and No buttons; therefore, we are interested in discovering whether the return value from `Show()` is `DialogResult.No`.

```
private void MainWindow_Closing(object sender, CancelEventArgs e)
{
  lifeTimeInfo += "Closing event\n";

  // Show a message box with Yes and No buttons.
  DialogResult dr = MessageBox.Show("Do you REALLY want to close this app?",
    "Closing event!", MessageBoxButtons.YesNo);

  // Which button was clicked?
  if (dr == DialogResult.No)
    e.Cancel = true;
  else
    e.Cancel = false;
}
```

Now run your application and shift the form into and out of focus a few times (to trigger the `Activated` and `Deactivate` events). Once you finally shut down the application, you will see a message box that looks something like Figure 27-13.

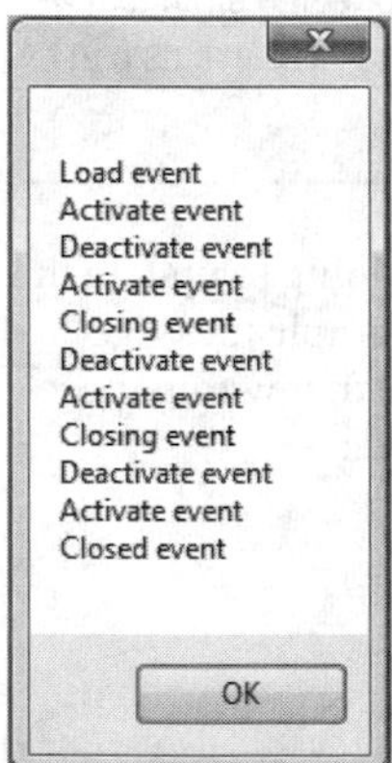

Figure 27-13. *The life and times of a* `Form`*-derived type*

Source Code The FormLifeTime project can be found under the Chapter 27 subdirectory.

Responding to Mouse Activity

Recall that the Control parent class defines a set of events that allow you to monitor mouse activity in a variety of manners. To check this out firsthand, create a new Windows Application project named MouseEventsApp, rename the initial form to MainWindow.cs (via Solution Explorer), and handle the MouseMove event using the Properties window. This will generate the following event handler:

```
public partial class MainWindow : Form
{
  public MainWindow()
  {
    InitializeComponent();
  }

  // Generated via the Properties window.
  private void MainWindow_MouseMove(object sender, MouseEventArgs e)
  {
  }
}
```

The MouseMove event works in conjunction with the System.Windows.Forms.MouseEventHandler delegate. This delegate can only call methods where the first parameter is a System.Object, while the second is of type MouseEventArgs. This type contains various members that provide detailed information regarding the state of the event when mouse-centric events occur:

```
public class MouseEventArgs : EventArgs
{
  private readonly MouseButtons button;
  private readonly int clicks;
  private readonly int delta;
  private readonly int x;
  private readonly int y;

  public MouseEventArgs(MouseButtons button, int clicks, int x,
    int y, int delta);

  public MouseButtons Button { get; }
  public int Clicks { get; }
  public int Delta { get; }
  public Point Location { get; }
  public int X { get; }
  public int Y { get; }
}
```

While I'd bet most of the public properties are rather self-explanatory, Table 27-8 provides the details.

Table 27-8. *Properties of the* MouseEventArgs *Type*

Property	Meaning in Life
Button	Gets which mouse button was pressed, as defined by the MouseButtons enumeration
Clicks	Gets the number of times the mouse button was pressed and released
Delta	Gets a signed count of the number of detents the mouse wheel has rotated

Continued

Table 27-8. *Continued*

Property	Meaning in Life
Location	Returns a Point that contains the current X and Y values
X	Gets the *x*-coordinate of a mouse click
Y	Gets the *y*-coordinate of a mouse click

Let's implement our MouseMove handler to display the current X and Y position of the mouse on the Form's caption using the Location property:

```
private void MainWindow_MouseMove(object sender, MouseEventArgs e)
{
  Text = string.Format("Mouse Position: {0}", e.Location);
}
```

When you run the application and move the mouse over the window, you will find the position displayed on the title area of your MainWindow type (see Figure 27-14).

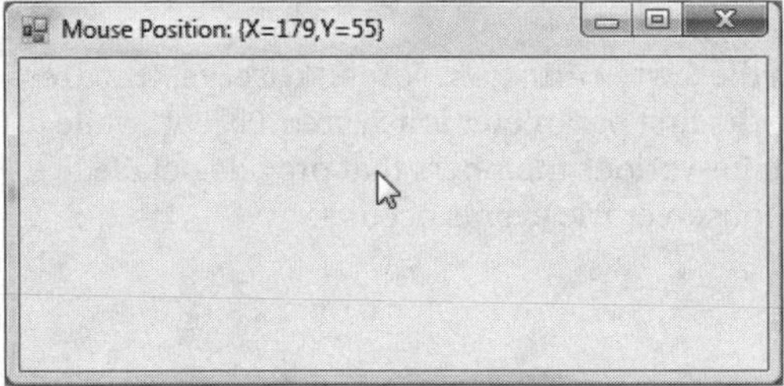

Figure 27-14. *Intercepting mouse movement*

Determining Which Mouse Button Was Clicked

Another common mouse-centric detail to attend to is determining which button has been clicked when a MouseUp, MouseDown, MouseClick, or MouseDoubleClick event occurs. When you wish to determine exactly which button was clicked (such as left, right, or middle), you need to examine the Button property of the MouseEventArgs class. The value of the Button property is constrained by the related MouseButtons enumeration:

```
public enum MouseButtons
{
  Left,
  Middle,
  None,
  Right,
  XButton1,
  XButton2
}
```

To illustrate, handle the MouseUp event on your MainWindow type using the Properties window. The following MouseUp event handler displays which mouse button was clicked inside a message box:

```
private void MainWindow_MouseUp (object sender, MouseEventArgs e)
{
  // Which mouse button was clicked?
```

```
  if(e.Button == MouseButtons.Left)
    MessageBox.Show("Left click!");
  if(e.Button == MouseButtons.Right)
    MessageBox.Show("Right click!");
  if (e.Button == MouseButtons.Middle)
    MessageBox.Show("Middle click!");
}
```

Source Code The MouseEventApp project is included under the Chapter 27 subdirectory.

Responding to Keyboard Activity

Windows applications typically define numerous input controls (such as the TextBox) where the user can enter information via the keyword. When you capture keyboard input in this manner, there is no need to explicitly handle keyboard events, as you can simply extract the textual data from the control using various properties (such as the Text property of the TextBox type).

However, if you need to monitor keyboard input for more exotic purposes (such as filtering keystrokes on a control, or capturing keypresses on the form itself), the base class libraries provide the KeyUp and KeyDown events. These events work in conjunction with the KeyEventHandler delegate, which can point to any method taking an object as the first parameter and KeyEventArgs as the second. This type is defined as follows:

```
public class KeyEventArgs : EventArgs
{
  private bool handled;
  private readonly Keys keyData;
  private bool suppressKeyPress;

  public KeyEventArgs(Keys keyData);

  public virtual bool Alt { get; }
  public bool Control { get; }
  public bool Handled { get; set; }
  public Keys KeyCode { get; }
  public Keys KeyData { get; }
  public int KeyValue { get; }
  public Keys Modifiers { get; }
  public virtual bool Shift { get; }
  public bool SuppressKeyPress { get; set; }
}
```

Table 27-9 documents some of the more interesting properties supported by KeyEventArgs.

Table 27-9. *Properties of the* KeyEventArgs *Type*

Property	Meaning in Life
Alt	Gets a value indicating whether the Alt key was pressed
Control	Gets a value indicating whether the Ctrl key was pressed
Handled	Gets or sets a value indicating whether the event was fully handled in your handler

Continued

Table 27-9. *Continued*

Property	Meaning in Life
KeyCode	Gets the keyboard code for a KeyDown or KeyUp event
Modifiers	Indicates which modifier keys (Ctrl, Shift, and/or Alt) were pressed
Shift	Gets a value indicating whether the Shift key was pressed

To illustrate, assume you have a new Windows Application named KeyboardEventApp, which handles the KeyUp event as follows.

```
public partial class MainWindow : Form
{
  public MainWindow()
  {
    InitializeComponent();
  }

  private void MainWindow_KeyUp(object sender, KeyEventArgs e)
  {
    Text = string.Format("Key Pressed: {0} Modifiers: {1}",
      e.KeyCode.ToString(), e.Modifiers.ToString());
  }
}
```

Now compile and run your program. You should be able to determine not only which mouse button was clicked, but also which keyboard key was pressed. For example, Figure 27-15 shows the result of pressing the P, Ctrl, and Shift keys simultaneously.

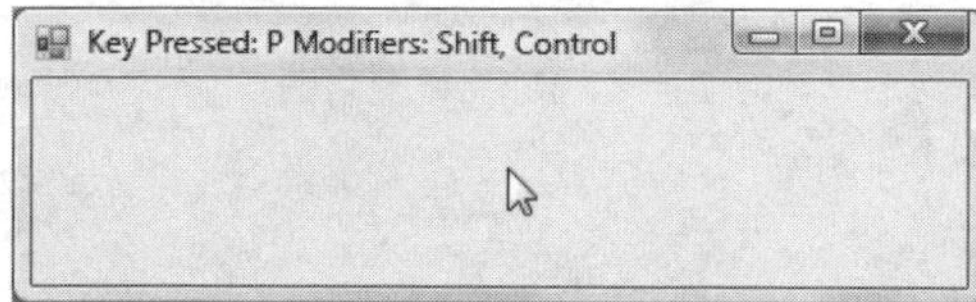

Figure 27-15. *Intercepting keyboard activity*

■ **Source Code** The KeyboardEventApp project is included under the Chapter 27 subdirectory.

Designing Dialog Boxes

Within a graphical user interface program, dialog boxes tend to be the primary way to capture user input for use within the application itself. Unlike other GUI APIs you may have used in the past, there is no "Dialog" base class. Rather, dialog boxes under Windows Forms are simply types deriving from the Form class.

In addition, many dialog boxes are intended to be nonsizable; therefore, you will typically want to set the `FormBorderStyle` property to `FormBorderStyle.FixedDialog`. As well, dialog boxes typically set the `MinimizeBox` and `MaximizeBox` properties to `false`. In this way, the dialog box is configured to be a fixed constant. Finally, if you set the `ShowInTaskbar` property to `false`, you will prevent the form from being visible in the Windows taskbar.

To illustrate building and manipulating dialog boxes, create a new Windows Application project named CarOrderApp. Rename the initial `Form1.cs` file to `MainWindow.cs` using Solution Explorer, and using the Forms designer, create a simple File ➤ Exit menu as well as a Tool ➤ Order Automobile . . . menu item. Once you have done so, handle the `Click` event for the Exit and Order Automobile submenus via the Properties window. Figure 27-16 shows the initial design of the main window.

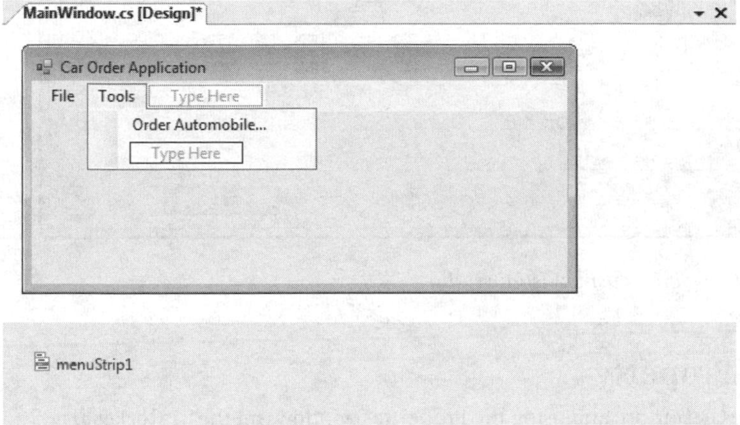

Figure 27-16. *Menu system of the main window*

Implement the File ➤ Exit menu handler to simply terminate the application via a call to `Application.Exit()`:

```
private void exitToolStripMenuItem_Click(object sender, EventArgs e)
{
  Application.Exit();
}
```

Now, using the Project menu of Visual Studio, select the Add Windows Forms menu option. Name your new form `OrderAutoDialog.cs` (see Figure 27-17).

For this example, design a dialog box that has the expected OK and Cancel button (named `btnOK` and `btnCancel`, respectively) as well as three `TextBox` controls named `txtMake`, `txtColor`, and `txtPrice`. Now, using the Properties window, finalize the design of your dialog box as follows:

- Set the `FormBorderStyle` property to `FixedDialog`.
- Set the `MinimizeBox` and `MaximizeBox` properties to `false`.
- Set the `StartPosition` property to `CenterParent`.
- Set the `ShowInTaskbar` property to `false`.

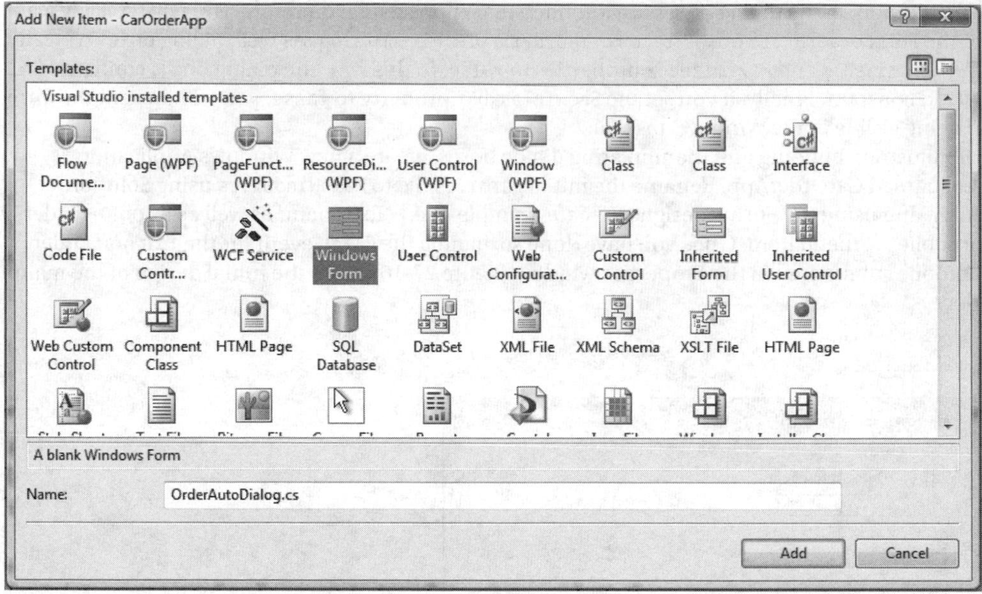

Figure 27-17. *Inserting new dialog boxes using Visual Studio*

The DialogResult Property

Last but not least, select the OK button, and using the Properties window, set the `DialogResult` property to `OK`. In a similar way, set the `DialogResult` property of the Cancel button to (you guessed it) `Cancel`. As you will see in just a moment, the `DialogResult` property is quite useful in that the launching form can quickly determine which button the user has clicked to take the appropriate course of action. The `DialogResult` property can be set to any value from the related `DialogResult` enumeration:

```
public enum DialogResult
{
  Abort, Cancel, Ignore, No,
  None, OK, Retry, Yes
}
```

Figure 27-18 shows one possible design of our dialog box, with a few descriptive `Label` controls to boot.

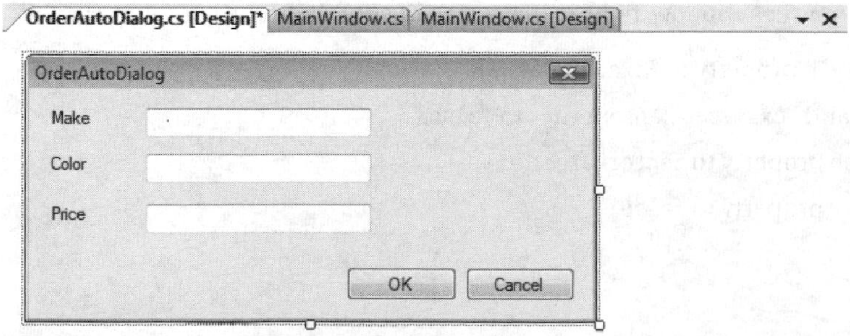

Figure 27-18. *The* `OrderAutoDialog` *type*

Configuring the Tab Order

Now that you have created a somewhat interesting dialog box, let's formalize the issue of tab order. As you may know, when a form contains multiple GUI widgets, users expect to be able to shift focus using the Tab key. Configuring the tab order for your set of controls requires that you understand two key properties: `TabStop` and `TabIndex`.

The `TabStop` property can be set to `true` or `false`, based on whether or not you wish this GUI item to be reachable using the Tab key. Assuming the `TabStop` property has been set to `true` for a given widget, the `TabOrder` property is then set to establish its order of activation in the tabbing sequence (which is zero based). Consider this example:

```
// Configure tabbing properties.
txtMake.TabIndex = 0;
txtMake.TabStop = true;
```

The Tab Order Wizard

While you could set the `TabStop` and `TabIndex` manually using the Properties window, the Visual Studio 2008 IDE supplies a Tab Order Wizard, which you access by choosing View ➤ Tab Order (be aware that you will not find this menu option unless the Forms designer is active). Once activated, your design-time form displays the current `TabIndex` value for each widget. To change these values, click each item in the order you choose (see Figure 27-19).

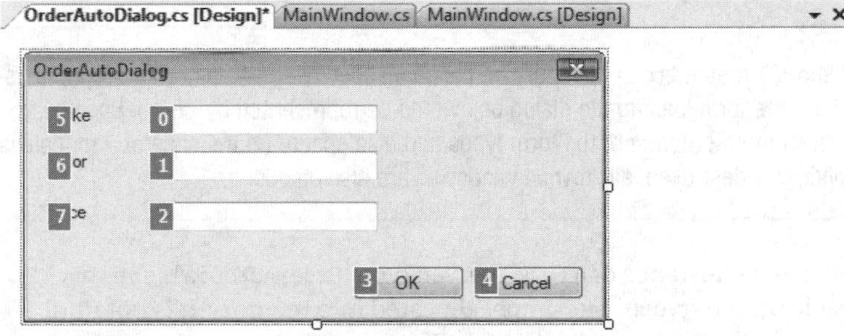

Figure 27-19. *The Tab Order Wizard*

To exit the Tab Order Wizard, simply press the Esc key.

Setting the Form's Default Input Button

Many user-input forms (especially dialog boxes) have a particular `Button` that will automatically respond to the user pressing the Enter key. For the current form, if you wish to ensure that when the user presses the Enter key, the `Click` event handler for `btnOK` is invoked, simply set the form's `AcceptButton` property as follows (this same setting can be established using the Properties window):

```
// When the Enter key is pressed, it is as if
// the user clicked the btnOK button.
this.AcceptButton = btnOK;
```

■ Note Some forms require the ability to simulate clicking the form's Cancel button when the user presses the Esc key. This can be done by assigning the `CancelButton` property of the `Form` to the `Button` object representing the clicking of the Cancel button.

Displaying Dialog Boxes

When you wish to display a dialog box, you must first decide whether you wish to launch the dialog box in a modal or modaless fashion. As you may know, modal dialog boxes must be dismissed by the user before he or she is able to return to the window that launched the dialog box in the first place (for example, most About boxes are modal in nature). To show a modal dialog box, simply call `ShowDialog()` off your dialog box object. On the other hand, a modaless dialog box can be displayed by calling `Show()`, which allows the user to switch focus between the dialog box and the main window (for example, a Find/Replace dialog box).

For our example, update the Tools ➤ Order Automobile . . . menu handler of the `MainWindow` type to show the `OrderAutoDialog` object in a modal manner. Consider the following initial code:

```
private void orderAutomobileToolStripMenuItem_Click(object sender, EventArgs e)
{
  // Create your dialog object.
  OrderAutoDialog dlg = new OrderAutoDialog();

  // Show as modal dialog box, and figure out which button
  // was clicked using the DialogResult return value.
  if (dlg.ShowDialog() == DialogResult.OK)
  {
    // They clicked OK, so do something...
  }
}
```

■ Note The `ShowDialog()` and `Show()` methods can optionally be called by specifying an object that represents the owner of the dialog box (which for the form loading the dialog box would be represented by `this`). Specifying the owner of a dialog box will establish the z-ordering of the form types and also ensure (in the case of a modaless dialog box) that when the main window is destroyed, all "owned windows" are also disposed.

Be aware that when you create an instance of a `Form`-derived type (`OrderAutoDialog` in this case), the dialog box is *not* visible on the screen, but simply allocated into memory. It is not until you call `Show()` or `ShowDialog()` that the form is indeed visible. Next, notice that `ShowDialog()` returns you the `DialogResult` value that has been assigned to the button (the `Show()` method simply returns `void`).

Once `ShowDialog()` returns, the form is no longer visible on the screen, but is still in memory. Therefore, we are able to extract the values in each `TextBox`. However, if you were to attempt to compile the following code:

```
private void orderAutomobileToolStripMenuItem_Click(object sender, EventArgs e)
{
  // Create your dialog object.
  OrderAutoDialog dlg = new OrderAutoDialog();

  // Show as modal dialog box, and figure out which button
  // was clicked using the DialogResult return value.
  if (dlg.ShowDialog() == DialogResult.OK)
  {
    // Get values in each text box? Compiler errors!
    string orderInfo = string.Format("Make: {0}, Color: {1}, Cost: {2}",
      dlg.txtMake.Text, dlg.txtColor.Text, dlg.txtPrice.Text);
    MessageBox.Show(orderInfo, "Information about your order!");
  }
}
```

you will receive compiler errors. The reason is that Visual Studio 2008 declares the controls you add to the Forms designer as *private* member variables of the class! If you were to open the `OrderAutoDialog.Designer.cs` file, you could verify this very fact. While a prim-and-proper dialog box might preserve encapsulation by adding public properties to get and set the values within these text boxes, let's take a shortcut and simply redefine them using the `public` keyword:

```
partial class OrderAutoDialog
{
...
  // Form member variables are defined within the designer-maintained file.
  public System.Windows.Forms.TextBox txtMake;
  public System.Windows.Forms.TextBox txtColor;
  public System.Windows.Forms.TextBox txtPrice;
}
```

At this point, you can compile and run your application. Once you launch your dialog box, you should be able to see the input data displayed within a message box (provided you click the OK button).

■ **Note** Rather than directly editing the `*.Designer.cs` file to define the access modifier of a control, you can select the control you wish to tweak on the designer and use the `Modifiers` property of the Properties window to do so.

Understanding Form Inheritance

Up until this point in the chapter, each one of your custom windows/dialog boxes has derived directly from `System.Windows.Forms.Form`. However, one intriguing aspect of Windows Forms development is the fact that `Form` types can function as the base class to derived `Forms`. For example, assume you have created a .NET code library that contains each of your company's core dialog boxes. Later, you decide that your About box is a bit on the bland side, and therefore wish to add a 3D image of your company logo. Rather than having to re-create the entire About box, you can simply extend the basic About box, thereby inheriting the core look and feel:

```
// ThreeDAboutBox "is-a" AboutBox
public class ThreeDAboutBox : AboutBox
{
  // Add code to render company logo...
}
```

To see form inheritance in action, insert a new form into your project using the Project ➤ Add Form menu option. This time, however, pick the Inherited Form icon, and name your new form `ImageOrderAutoDialog.cs` (see Figure 27-20).

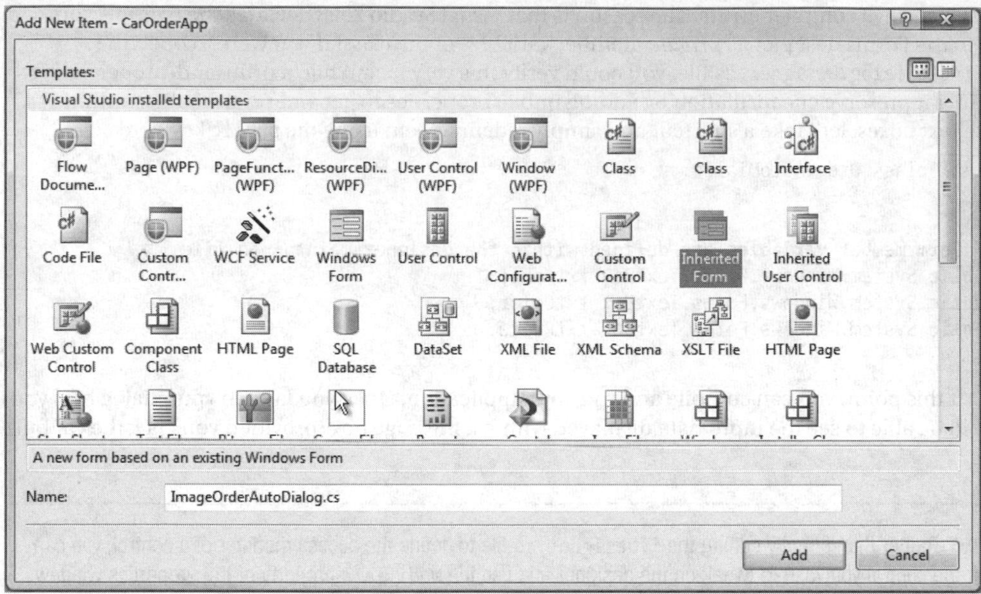

Figure 27-20. *Adding a derived form to your project*

This option will bring up the Inheritance Picker dialog box, which will show you each of the forms in your current project. Notice that the Browse button allows you to pick a form in an external .NET assembly. Here, simply pick your `OrderAutoDialog` type (see Figure 27-21).

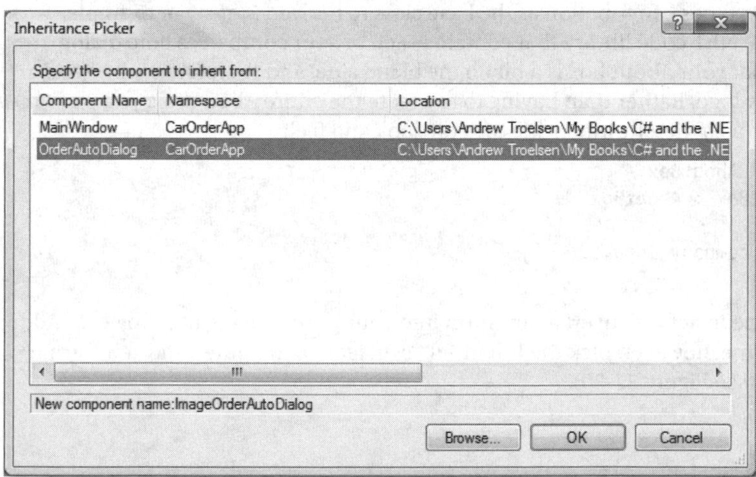

Figure 27-21. *The Inheritance Picker dialog box*

■ **Note** You must compile your project at least one time to see the forms of your project in the Inheritance Picker dialog box, as this tool is reading assembly metadata to show you your options.

Once you click the OK button, you will find that the visual designer tools show each of the base controls on your parents, each of which has a small arrow icon mounted on the upper-left of the control (symbolizing inheritance). To complete our derived dialog box, locate the `PictureBox` control from the Common Controls section of the Toolbox, and add one to your derived form. Next, using the `Image` property, select an image file of your choosing. Figure 27-22 shows one possible UI, using the logo for the company I work with, Intertech Training.

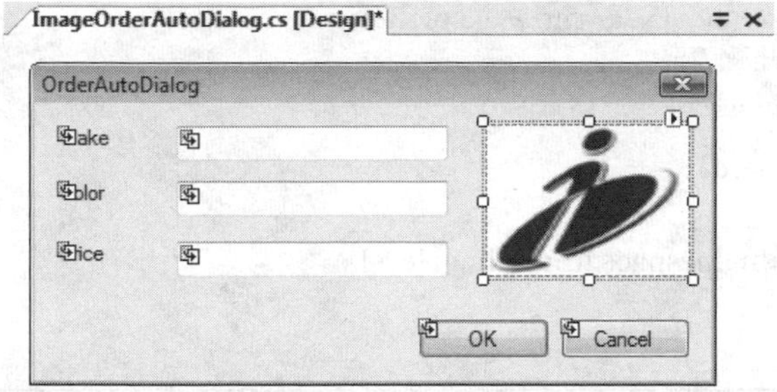

Figure 27-22. *The* `ImageOrderAutoDialog` *type*

With this, you can now update the Tools ➤ Order Automobile . . . `Click` event handler to create an instance of your derived type, rather than the `OrderAutoDialog` base class:

```
private void orderAutomobileToolStripMenuItem_Click(object sender, EventArgs e)
{
  // Create the derived dialog object.
  ImageOrderAutoDialog dlg = new ImageOrderAutoDialog();
...
}
```

Source Code The CarOrderApp project is included under the Chapter 27 subdirectory.

Rendering Graphical Data Using GDI+

Many GUI applications require the ability to dynamically generate graphical data for display on the surface of a window. For example, perhaps you have selected a set of records from a relational database and wish to render a pie chart (or bar chart) that visually shows items in stock. Or, perhaps you are interested in re-creating some old-school video game using the .NET platform. Regardless of your goal, when you need to graphically render data within a Windows Forms application, GDI+ is the API to do so. This technology is bundled within the `System.Drawing.dll` assembly, which defines a number of namespaces (see Figure 27-23).

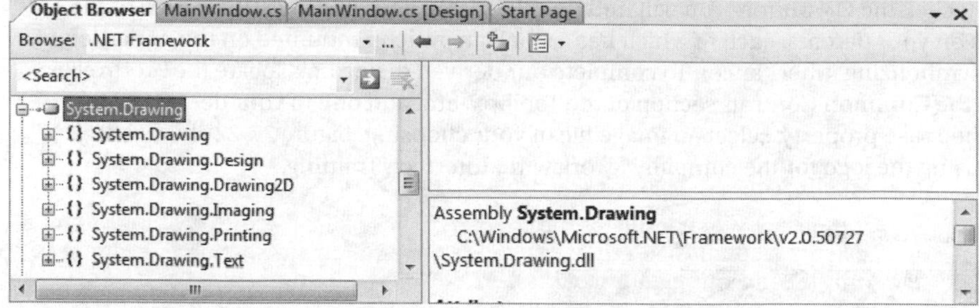

Figure 27-23. *The namespaces of* `System.Drawing.dll`

Table 27-10 documents the role of each GDI+ namespace from a high level.

Table 27-10. *Core GDI+ Namespaces*

Namespace	Meaning in Life
`System.Drawing`	This is the core GDI+ namespace that defines numerous types for basic rendering (fonts, pens, basic brushes, etc.) as well as the almighty `Graphics` type.
`System.Drawing.Drawing2D`	This namespace provides types used for more advanced 2D/vector graphics functionality (e.g., gradient brushes, pen caps, geometric transforms, etc.).
`System.Drawing.Imaging`	This namespace defines types that allow you to manipulate graphical images (e.g., change the palette, extract image metadata, manipulate metafiles, etc.).
`System.Drawing.Printing`	This namespace defines types that allow you to render images to the printed page, interact with the printer itself, and format the overall appearance of a given print job.
`System.Drawing.Text`	This namespace allows you to manipulate collections of fonts.

The System.Drawing Namespace

The vast majority of the types you'll use when programming GDI+ applications are found within the `System.Drawing` namespace. As you would expect, there are classes that represent images, brushes, pens, and fonts. Furthermore, `System.Drawing` defines a number of related utility types such as `Color`, `Point`, and `Rectangle`. Table 27-11 lists some (but not all) of the core types.

Table 27-11. *Core Types of the* `System.Drawing` *Namespace*

Type	Meaning in Life
`Bitmap`	This type encapsulates image data (`*.bmp` or otherwise).

`Brush`
`Brushes`
`SolidBrush`
`SystemBrushes`
`TextureBrush`
	Brush objects are used to fill the interiors of graphical shapes such as rectangles, ellipses, and polygons.

Type	Meaning in Life
BufferedGraphics	This type provides a graphics buffer for double buffering, which is used to reduce or eliminate flicker caused by redrawing a display surface.
Color SystemColors	The Color and SystemColors types define a number of static read-only properties used to obtain specific colors for the construction of various pens/brushes.
Font FontFamily	The Font type encapsulates the characteristics of a given font (i.e., type name, bold, italic, point size, etc.). FontFamily provides an abstraction for a group of fonts having a similar design but with certain variations in style.
Graphics	This core class represents a valid drawing surface, as well as a number of methods to render text, images, and geometric patterns.
Icon SystemIcons	These classes represent custom icons, as well as the set of standard system-supplied icons.
Image ImageAnimator	Image is an abstract base class that provides functionality for the Bitmap, Icon, and Cursor types. ImageAnimator provides a way to iterate over a number of Image-derived types at some specified interval.
Pen Pens SystemPens	Pens are objects used to draw lines and curves. The Pens type defines a number of static properties that return a new Pen of a given color.
Point PointF	These structures represent an (*x*, *y*) coordinate mapping to an underlying integer or float, respectively.
Rectangle RectangleF	These structures represent a rectangular dimension (again mapping to an underlying integer or float).
Size SizeF	These structures represent a given height/width (again mapping to an underlying integer or float).
StringFormat	This type is used to encapsulate various features of textual layout (i.e., alignment, line spacing, etc.).
Region	This type describes the interior of a geometric image composed of rectangles and paths.

The Role of the Graphics Type

The System.Drawing.Graphics class is the gateway to GDI+ rendering functionality. This class not only represents the surface you wish to draw upon (such as a form's surface, a control's surface, or a region of memory), but also defines dozens of members that allow you to render text, images (icons, bitmaps, etc.), and numerous geometric patterns. Table 27-12 gives a partial list of members.

Table 27-12. *Members of the* Graphics *Class*

Method	Meaning in Life
FromHdc() FromHwnd() FromImage()	These static methods provide a way to obtain a valid Graphics object from a given image (e.g., icon, bitmap, etc.) or GUI widget.
Clear()	This method fills a Graphics object with a specified color, erasing the current drawing surface in the process.

Continued

Table 27-12. *Continued*

Method	Meaning in Life
DrawArc() DrawBeziers() DrawCurve() DrawEllipse() DrawIcon() DrawLine() DrawLines() DrawPie() DrawPath() DrawRectangle() DrawRectangles() DrawString()	These methods are used to render a given image or geometric pattern. All DrawXXX() methods require the use of GDI+ Pen objects.
FillEllipse() FillPie() FillPolygon() FillRectangle() FillPath()	These methods are used to fill the interior of a given geometric shape. All FillXXX() methods require the use of GDI+ Brush objects.

Now, despite what you may be assuming, the Graphics class is not directly creatable via the new keyword, as there are no publicly defined constructors. How, then, do you obtain a valid Graphics object? Glad you asked.

Obtaining a Graphics Object via the Paint Event

The most common way to obtain a Graphics object is to handle the Paint event on the window you are attempting to render upon using the Visual Studio 2008 Properties window. This event is defined in terms of the PaintEventHandler delegate, which can point to any method taking a System.Object as the first parameter and a PaintEventArgs as the second.

The PaintEventArgs parameter contains the Graphics object you require to render onto the Form's surface. To illustrate, create a new Windows Application project named PaintEventApp. Using Solution Explorer, rename your initial Form.cs file to MainWindow.cs and then handle the Paint event using the Properties window. This will result in the following stub code:

```
public partial class MainWindow : Form
{
  public MainWindow()
  {
    InitializeComponent();
  }

  private void MainWindow_Paint(object sender, PaintEventArgs e)
  {

  }
}
```

Now that you have handled the Paint event, you may wonder when it will fire. Whenever a window becomes "dirty," the Paint event will fire. A window is considered "dirty" whenever it is resized, uncovered by another window (partially or completely), or minimized and then restored. In all these cases, the .NET platform ensures that when your Form needs to be redrawn, the Paint event handler is called automatically. Consider the following implementation of MainWindow_Paint():

```
private void MainWindow_Paint(object sender, PaintEventArgs e)
{
  // Get the graphics object for this Form.
  Graphics g = e.Graphics;

  // Draw a circle.
  g.FillEllipse(Brushes.Blue, 10, 20, 150, 80);

  // Draw a string in a custom font.
  g.DrawString("Hello GDI+", new Font("Times New Roman", 30),
             Brushes.Red, 200, 200);

  // Draw a line with a custom pen.
  using (Pen p = new Pen(Color.YellowGreen, 10))
  {
    g.DrawLine(p, 80, 4, 200, 200);
  }
}
```

Once we obtain the Graphics object from the incoming PaintEventArgs parameter, we call FillEllipse(). Notice that this method (as well as any Fill-prefixed method) requires a Brush-derived type as the first parameter. While we could create any number of interesting brush objects from the System.Drawing.Drawing2D namespace (HatchBrush, LinearGradientBrush, etc.), the Brushes utility class provides handy access to a variety of solid-colored brush types.

Next, we make a call to DrawString(), which requires a string to render as its first parameter. Given this, GDI+ provides the Font type, which represents not only the name of the font to use when rendering the textual data, but also related characteristics such as the point size (30 in this case). Also notice that DrawString() requires a Brush type as well, given that as far as GDI+ is concerned, "Hello GDI+" is simply a collection of geometric patterns to fill on the screen. Finally, DrawLine() is called to render a line using a custom Pen type, 10 pixels wide. Figure 27-24 shows the output of this rendering logic.

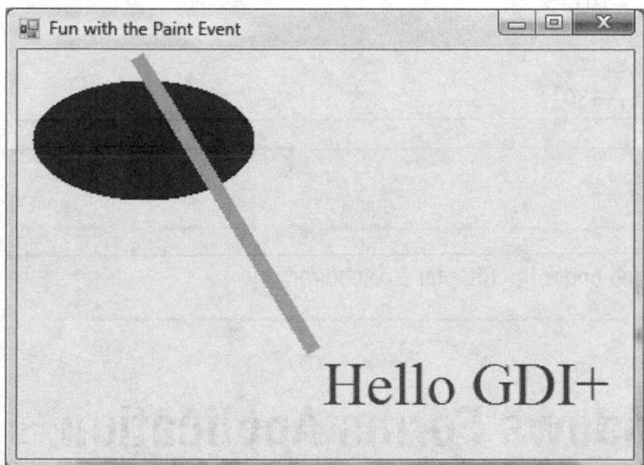

Figure 27-24. *A simple GDI+ rendering operation*

Note Notice in the preceding code, we are explicitly disposing of the Pen object. As a rule, when you directly create a GDI+ type that implements IDisposable, call the Dispose() method as soon as you are done with the object. By doing so, you are able to release the underlying resources as soon as possible. If you do not do so, the resources will eventually be freed by the garbage collector in a nondeterministic manner.

Invalidating the Form's Client Area

During the flow of a Windows Forms application, you may need to explicitly fire the Paint event in your code, rather than waiting for the window to become "naturally dirty" by the actions of the end user. For example, you may be building a program that allows the user to select from a number of predefined images using a custom dialog box. Once the dialog box is dismissed, you need to draw the newly selected image onto the form's client area. Obviously, if you waited for the window to become "naturally dirty," the user would not see the change take place until the window was resized or uncovered by another window. To force a window to repaint itself programmatically, simply call the inherited Invalidate() method:

```
public partial class MainForm: Form
{
...
  private void MainForm_Paint(object sender, PaintEventArgs e)
  {
    Graphics g = e.Graphics;
    // Render the correct image here.
  }

  private void GetImageFromDialog()
  {
    // Show dialog box and get new image.
    // Repaint the entire client area.
    Invalidate();
  }
}
```

The Invalidate() method has been overloaded a number of times to allow you to specify a specific rectangular region to repaint, rather than repainting the entire client area (which is the default). If you wish to only update the extreme upper-left rectangle of the client area, you could write the following:

```
// Repaint a given rectangular area of the Form.
private void UpdateUpperArea()
{
  Rectangle myRect = new Rectangle(0, 0, 75, 150);
  Invalidate(myRect);
}
```

Source Code The PaintEventApp project is included under the Chapter 27 subdirectory.

Building a Complete Windows Forms Application

To conclude our introductory look at the Windows Forms and GDI+ APIs, let's wrap up this chapter by building a complete GUI application that illustrates several of the techniques discussed in this chapter working as a cohesive unit. The program we will create is a rudimentary painting program that allows users to select between two shape types (a circle or rectangle for simplicity) using the color of their choice, to render data to the form. Furthermore, we will allow end users to save their pictures to a local file on their hard drive for later use via object serialization services.

Building the Main Menu System

Begin by creating a new Windows Forms application named MyPaintProgram and rename your initial `Form1.cs` file to `MainWindow.cs`. Now design a menu system on this initial window that supports a topmost File menu that provides Save . . ., Load . . ., and Exit submenus (see Figure 27-25).

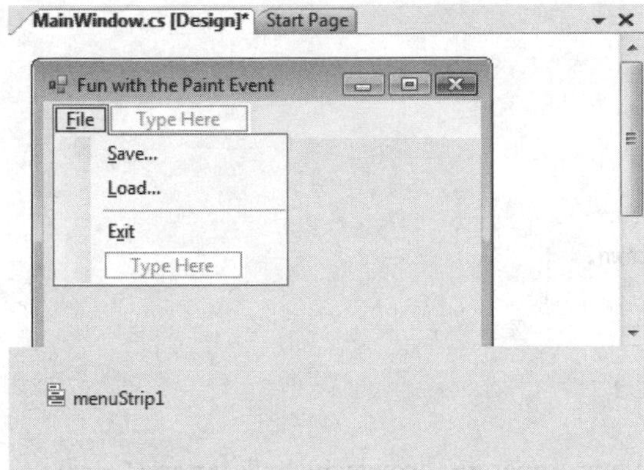

Figure 27-25. *The File menu system*

Next, create a second topmost Tools menu that provides options to select a shape and color to use for rendering as well as an option to clear the form of all graphical data (see Figure 27-26).

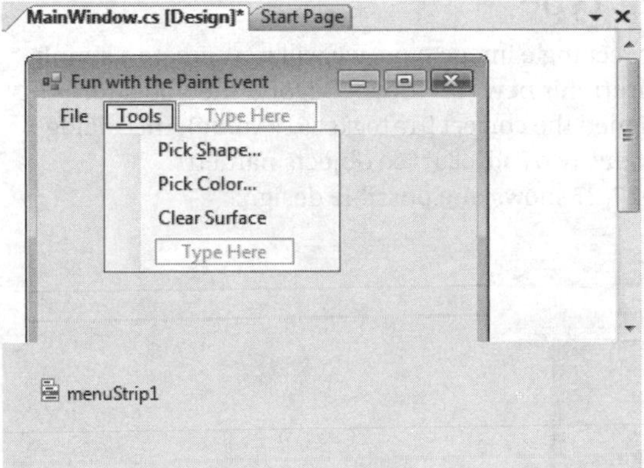

Figure 27-26. *The Tools menu system*

Finally, handle the `Click` event for each one of these subitems. We will implement each handler as we progress through the example; however, we can finish up the File ➤ Exit menu handler simply by calling `Application.Exit()`:

```
private void exitToolStripMenuItem_Click(object sender, EventArgs e)
{
  Application.Exit();
}
```

Defining the ShapeData Type

Recall that our application will allow end users to select from two predefined shapes in a given color. Because we will provide a way to allow users to save their graphical data to a file, we will want to define a custom class type that encapsulates each of these details; for simplicity, we will do so using C# automatic properties (see Chapter 13). Add a new class to your project named ShapeData.cs. Implement this type as follows:

```
[Serializable]
class ShapeData
{
  // The upper left of the shape to be drawn.
  public Point UpperLeftPoint { get; set; }

  // The current color of the shape to be drawn.
  public Color Color { get; set; }

  // The type of shape.
  public SelectedShape ShapeType { get; set; }
}
```

Here, ShapeData is making use of three automatic properties, two of which (Point and Color) are defined in the System.Drawing namespace, so be sure to import this namespace within your code file. Also notice that this type has been adorned with the [Serializable] attribute. In a later step, we will configure our MainWindow type to maintain a list of ShapeData types that will be persisted using object serialization services (see Chapter 21).

Defining the ShapePickerDialog Type

To allow the user to choose between the circle or rectangle image type, we will now create a simple custom dialog box named ShapePickerDialog (insert this new Form now). Beyond the obligatory OK and Cancel buttons (each of which has been assigned the correct DialogResult value), this dialog box will make use of a single GroupBox that maintains two RadioButton objects named radioButtonCircle and radioButtonRect. Figure 27-27 shows one possible design.

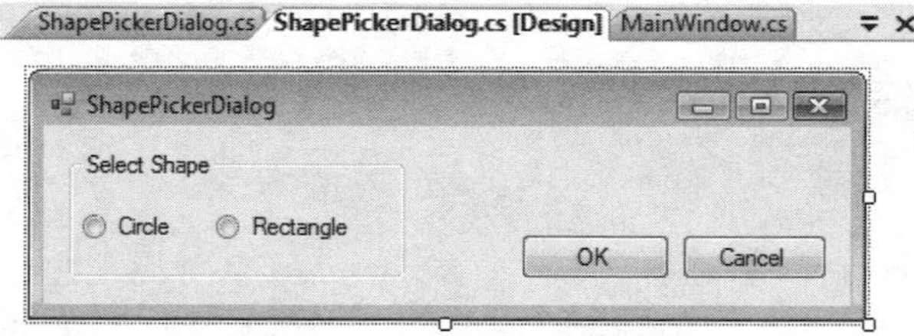

Figure 27-27. *The* ShapePickerDialog *type*

Now, open the code window for your dialog box by right-clicking the Forms designer and selecting the View Code menu option. Within the MyPaintProgram namespace, define an enumeration (named SelectedShape) that defines names for each possible shape:

```
public enum SelectedShape
{
  Circle, Rectangle
}
```

Now, update your current ShapePickerDialog class type as follows:

- Add an automatic property of type SelectedShape. The caller will be able to use this property to determine which shape to render.
- Handle the Click event for the OK button using the Properties window.
- Implement this event handler to determine whether the circle radio button has been selected (via the Checked property). If so, set your currentShape variable to SelectedShape.Circle; otherwise, set this member variable to SelectedShape.Rectangle.

Here is the complete code:

```
public partial class ShapePickerDialog : Form
{
  public SelectedShape SelectedShape { get; set; }

  public ShapePickerDialog()
  {
    InitializeComponent();
  }

  private void btnOK_Click(object sender, EventArgs e)
  {
    if (radioButtonCircle.Checked)
      SelectedShape = SelectedShape.Circle;
    else
      SelectedShape = SelectedShape.Rectangle;
  }
}
```

That wraps up the infrastructure of our program. Now we simply need to implement the Click event handlers for the remaining menu items on the main window.

Adding Infrastructure to the MainWindow Type

Returning to the construction of the main window, add three new member variables to this Form that allow you to keep track of the selected shape (via a SelectedShape enum type), the selected color (represented by a System.Drawing.Color type), as well as each of the rendered images held in a generic List<T>:

```
public partial class MainWindow : Form
{
  // Current shape / color to draw.
  private SelectedShape currentShape;
  private Color currentColor = Color.DarkBlue;

  // This maintains each ShapeData.
  private List<ShapeData> shapes = new List<ShapeData>();
...
}
```

Next, handle the MouseDown and Paint events for this Form-derived type using the Properties window. We will implement them in a later step; however, for the time being, you should find that the IDE has generated the following stub code:

```
private void MainWindow_Paint(object sender, PaintEventArgs e)
{
}
```

```
private void MainWindow_MouseClick(object sender, MouseEventArgs e)
{
}
```

Implementing the Tools Menu Functionality

To allow users to set the currentShape member variable, implement the Click handler for the Tools ➤ Pick Shape . . . menu option to launch your custom dialog box, and based on their selection, assign this member variable accordingly:

```
private void pickShapeToolStripMenuItem_Click(object sender, EventArgs e)
{
  // Load our dialog box and set the correct shape type.
  ShapePickerDialog dlg = new ShapePickerDialog();
  if (DialogResult.OK == dlg.ShowDialog())
  {
    currentShape = dlg.SelectedShape;
  }
}
```

To allow users to set the currentColor member variable, implement the Click event handler for the Tools ➤ Pick Color . . . menu to make use of the System.Windows.Forms.ColorDialog type:

```
private void pickColorToolStripMenuItem_Click(object sender, EventArgs e)
{
  ColorDialog dlg = new ColorDialog();

  if (dlg.ShowDialog() == DialogResult.OK)
  {
    currentColor = dlg.Color;
  }
}
```

If you were to run your program as it now stands and select the Tools ➤ Pick Color menu option, you would get the dialog box shown in Figure 27-28.

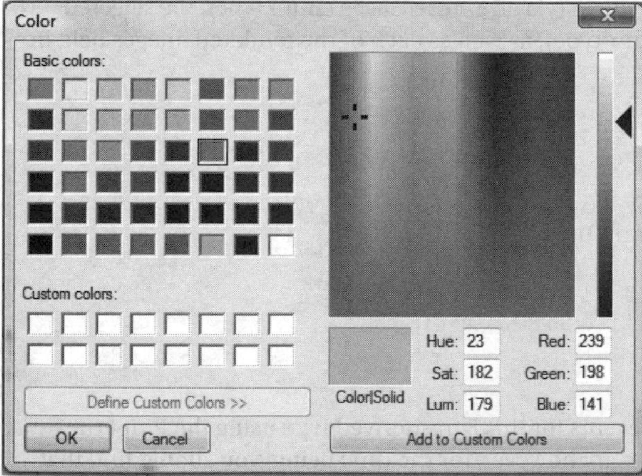

Figure 27-28. *The stock* ColorDialog *type*

Finally, implement the Tools ➤ Clear Surface menu handler to empty the contents of the List<T> member variable and programmatically fire the Paint event via a call to Invalidate():

```
private void clearSurfaceToolStripMenuItem_Click(object sender, EventArgs e)
{
  shapes.Clear();

  // This will fire the paint event.
  Invalidate();
}
```

Capturing and Rendering the Graphical Output

Given that a call to Invalidate() will fire the Paint event, we will obviously need to author code within our Paint event handler. Our goal is to loop through each item in the (currently empty) List<T> member variable and render a circle or square at the current mouse location. The first step is to implement the MouseDown event handler to insert a new ShapeData type into our generic List<T> type, based on the user-selected color, shape type, and current location of the mouse:

```
private void MainWindow_MouseClick(object sender, MouseEventArgs e)
{
  // Make a ShapeData type based on current user
  // selections.
  ShapeData sd = new ShapeData();
  sd.ShapeType = currentShape;
  sd.Color = currentColor;
  sd.UpperLeftPoint = new Point(e.X, e.Y);

  // Add to the List<T> and force the form to repaint itself.
  shapes.Add(sd);
  Invalidate();
}
```

With this, we can now implement our Paint event handler as follows:

```
private void MainWindow_Paint(object sender, PaintEventArgs e)
{
  // Get the Graphics type for this window.
  Graphics g = e.Graphics;

  // Render each shape in the selected color.
  foreach (ShapeData s in shapes)
  {
    // Render a rectangle or circle 20 x 20 pixels in size
    // using the correct color.
    if (s.ShapeType == SelectedShape.Rectangle)
      g.FillRectangle(new SolidBrush(s.Color),
                      s.UpperLeftPoint.X,
                      s.UpperLeftPoint.Y, 20, 20);
    else
      g.FillEllipse(new SolidBrush(s.Color),
                    s.UpperLeftPoint.X,
                    s.UpperLeftPoint.Y, 20, 20);
  }
}
```

If you were to run your application at this point, you should now be able to render any number of shapes in a variety of colors (see Figure 27-29).

Figure 27-29. `MyPaintProgram` *in action*

Implementing the Serialization Logic

The final aspect of our project involves implementing `Click` event handlers for the File ➤ Save . . . and File ➤ Load . . . menu items. Given that `ShapeData` has been marked with the `[Serialization]` attribute (and given that `List<T>` itself is serializable), we can very quickly save out the current graphical data using the Windows Forms `SaveFileDialog` type. First, update your `using` directives to specify you are using the `System.Runtime.Serialization.Formatters.Binary` and `System.IO` namespaces.

```
// For the binary formatter.
using System.Runtime.Serialization.Formatters.Binary;
using System.IO;
```

With this, update your File ➤ Save . . . handler as follows:

```
private void saveToolStripMenuItem_Click(object sender, EventArgs e)
{
  using (SaveFileDialog saveDlg = new SaveFileDialog())
  {
    // Configure the look and feel of the save dialog box.
    saveDlg.InitialDirectory = ".";
    saveDlg.Filter = "Shape files (*.shapes)|*.shapes";
    saveDlg.RestoreDirectory = true;
    saveDlg.FileName = "MyShapes";

    // If they click the OK button, open the new
    // file and serialize the List<T>.
    if (saveDlg.ShowDialog() == DialogResult.OK)
    {
      Stream myStream = saveDlg.OpenFile();
      if ((myStream != null))
      {
        // Save the shapes!
        BinaryFormatter myBinaryFormat = new BinaryFormatter();
        myBinaryFormat.Serialize(myStream, shapes);
        myStream.Close();
```

```
        }
      }
    }
}
```

The File ➤ Load event handler simply opens the selected file and deserializes the data back into the List<T> member variable with the help of the Windows Forms OpenFileDialog type:

```
private void loadToolStripMenuItem_Click(object sender, EventArgs e)
{
  using (OpenFileDialog openDlg = new OpenFileDialog())
  {
    openDlg.InitialDirectory = ".";
    openDlg.Filter = "Shape files (*.shapes)|*.shapes";
    openDlg.RestoreDirectory = true;
    openDlg.FileName = "MyShapes";

    if (openDlg.ShowDialog() == DialogResult.OK)
    {
      Stream myStream = openDlg.OpenFile();
      if ((myStream != null))
      {
        // Get the shapes!
        BinaryFormatter myBinaryFormat = new BinaryFormatter();
        shapes = (List<ShapeData>)myBinaryFormat.Deserialize(myStream);
        myStream.Close();
        Invalidate();
      }
    }
  }
}
```

Given your work in Chapter 21, I'd guess the overall serialization logic looks familiar. It is worth pointing out that the SaveFileDialog and OpenFileDialog types both support a Filter property that is assigned a rather cryptic string value. This filter controls a number of settings for the save/open dialog boxes such as the file extension (*.shapes). The FileName property is used to control what the default name of the file to be created should be, which in this example is MyShapes.

At this point, your painting application is complete. You should now be able to save and load your current graphical data to any number of *.shapes files. If you are interested in enhancing this Windows Forms program, you may wish to account for additional shapes, or allow the user to control the size of the shape to draw or perhaps select the format used to save the data (binary, XML, SOAP).

Summary

The purpose of this chapter was to examine the process of building traditional desktop applications using the Windows Forms and GDI+ APIs, which have been part of the .NET Framework since version 1.0. At minimum, a Windows Forms application consists of a type-extending Form and a Main() method that interacts with the Application type.

When you wish to populate your forms with UI elements (menu systems, GUI input controls, etc.), you do so by inserting new objects into the inherited Controls collection. This chapter also illustrated how to capture mouse, keyboard, and rendering events. Along the way, you were introduced to the Graphics type and numerous ways to generate graphical data at runtime.

As mentioned during the overview of this chapter, the Windows Forms API has been (in some ways) superseded by the WPF API introduced with the release of .NET 3.0 (which you will begin to examine in the next chapter). While it is true that WPF will eventually become the toolkit of choice for supercharged UI front ends, the Windows Forms API is still the simplest (and in many cases, most direct) way to author standard business applications, in-house applications, and simple configuration utilities. For these reasons, Windows Forms will be part of the .NET base class libraries for years to come.

CHAPTER 28

Introducing Windows Presentation Foundation and XAML

In the previous chapter, you were introduced to the functionality contained within the `System.Windows.Forms.dll` and `System.Drawing.dll` assemblies. As explained, the Windows Forms API is the original GUI toolkit of the .NET platform, which provides numerous types that can be used to build sophisticated desktop user interfaces. While it is true that Windows Forms/GDI+ is still entirely supported under .NET 3.5, Microsoft shipped a brand-new desktop API termed Windows Presentation Foundation (WPF) beginning with the release of .NET 3.0.

This initial WPF chapter begins by examining the motivation behind this new UI framework and provides a brief overview of the various types of WPF applications supported by the API. After this point we will examine the core WPF programming model and come to know the role of the `Application` and `Window` types as well as the key WFP assemblies and namespaces.

The latter part of this chapter will introduce you to a brand-new XML-based grammar: Extensible Application Markup Language (XAML). As you will see, XAML provides WPF developers with a way to partition UI definitions from the logic that drives them. Here, you will be exposed to several critical XAML topics including attached property syntax, type converters, markup extensions, and understanding how to parse XAML at runtime. This chapter wraps up by examining the various WPF-specific tools that ship with the Visual Studio 2008 IDE and examines the role of Microsoft Expression Blend.

The Motivation Behind WPF

Over the years, Microsoft has developed numerous graphical user interface toolkits (raw C/C++/Win32 API development, VB6, MFC, etc.) to build desktop executables. Each of these APIs provided a code base to represent the basic aspects of a GUI application, including main windows, dialog boxes, controls, menu systems, and other necessities. With the initial release of the .NET platform, the Windows Forms API (see Chapter 27) quickly became the preferred model for UI development, given its simple yet very powerful object model.

While many full-featured desktop applications have been successfully created using Windows Forms, the fact of the matter is that this programming model is rather *asymmetrical.* Simply put, `System.Windows.Forms.dll` and `System.Drawing.dll` do not provide direct support for many additional technologies required to build a full-fledged desktop application. To illustrate this point, consider the ad hoc nature of GUI development prior to the release of WPF (e.g., .NET 2.0; see Table 28-1).

Table 28-1. *.NET 2.0 Solutions to Desired Functionalities*

Desired Functionality	.NET 2.0 Solution
Building forms with controls	Windows Forms
2D graphics support	GDI+ (`System.Drawing.dll`)
3D graphics support	DirectX APIs
Support for streaming video	Windows Media Player APIs
Support for flow-style documents	Programmatic manipulation of PDF files

As you can see, a Windows Forms developer must pull in types from a number of different APIs and object models. While it is true that making use of these diverse APIs may look similar syntactically (it is just C# code, after all), you may also agree that each technology requires a radically different mind-set. For example, the skills required to create a 3D rendered animation using DirectX are completely different from those used to bind data to a grid. To be sure, it is very difficult for a Windows Forms programmer to master the diverse nature of each API.

Unifying Diverse APIs

WPF (introduced with .NET 3.0) was purposely created to merge these previous unrelated programming tasks into a single unified object model. Thus, if you need to author a 3D animation, you have no need to manually program against the DirectX API (although you could), as 3D functionality is baked directly into WPF. To see how well things have cleaned up, consider Table 28-2, which illustrates the desktop development model ushered in as of .NET 3.0.

Table 28-2. *.NET 3.0 Solutions to Desired Functionalities*

Desired Functionality	.NET 3.0 and Higher Solution
Building forms with controls	WPF
2D graphics support	WPF
3D graphics support	WPF
Support for streaming video	WPF
Support for flow-style documents	WPF

Providing a Separation of Concerns via XAML

Perhaps one of the most compelling benefits is that WPF provides a way to cleanly separate the look and feel of a Windows application from the programming logic that drives it. Using XAML, it is possible to define the UI of an application via *markup*. This markup (ideally created by those with an artistic mind-set using dedicated tools) can then be connected to a managed code base to provide the guts of the program's functionality.

■ **Note** XAML is not limited to WPF applications! Any application can use XAML to describe a tree of .NET objects, even if they have nothing to do with a visible user interface. For example, it is possible to build custom activities for a Windows Workflow Foundation application using XAML.

As you dig into WPF, you may be surprised how much flexibility "desktop markup" provides. XAML allows you to define not only simple UI elements (buttons, grids, list boxes, etc.) in markup, but also graphical renderings, animations, data binding logic, and multimedia functionality (such as video playback). For example, defining a circular button control that animates a company logo requires just a few lines of markup. Even better, WPF elements can be modified through styles and templates, which allow you to change the overall look and feel of an application with minimum fuss and bother, independent of the core application processing code.

Given all these points, the need to build custom controls greatly diminishes under WPF. Unlike Windows Forms development, the only compelling reason to build a custom WPF control library is if you need to change the *behaviors* of a control (e.g., add custom methods, properties, or events; subclass an existing control to override virtual members; etc.). If you simply need to change the *look and feel* of a control (again, such as a circular animated button), you can do so entirely through markup.

■ **Note** Other valid reasons to build custom WPF controls include achieving binary reuse (via a WPF control library), as well as building controls that expose custom design-time functionality and integration with the Visual Studio 2008 IDE.

Providing an Optimized Rendering Model

Also be aware of the fact that WPF is optimized to take advantage of the new video driver model supported under the Windows Vista operating system. While WPF applications can be developed on and deployed to Windows XP machines (as well as Windows Server 2003 machines), the same application running on Vista will perform much better, especially when making use of animations/ multimedia services. This is due to the fact that the display services of WPF are rendered via the DirectX engine, allowing for efficient hardware and software rendering.

■ **Note** Allow me to reiterate this key point: WPF is not limited to Windows Vista! Although the Vista operating system has the .NET 3.0 libraries (which include WPF) installed out of the box, you can build and execute WPF applications on XP and Windows Server 2003 once you install the .NET Framework 3.5 SDK (for programmers) or .NET 3.5 runtime (for end users).

WPF applications also tend to behave better under Vista. If one graphics-intensive application crashes, it will not take down the entire operating system (à la the blue screen of death); rather, the misbehaving application in question will simply terminate. As you may know, the most common cause of the infamous blue screen of death is misbehaving video drivers.

Additional WPF-Centric Bells and Whistles

To recap the story thus far, Windows Presentation Foundation (WPF) is a new API to build desktop applications that integrates various desktop APIs into a single object model and provides a clean separation of concerns via XAML. In addition to these major points, WPF applications also benefit from various other bells and whistles, many of which are explained over the next several chapters. Here is a quick rundown of the core services:

- A number of layout managers (far more than Windows Forms) to provide extremely flexible control over placement and reposition of content
- Use of an enhanced data-binding engine to bind content to UI elements in a variety of ways
- A built-in style engine, which allows you to define "themes" for a WPF application
- Use of vector graphics, which allows content to be automatically resized to fit the size and resolution of the screen hosting the application
- Support for 2D and 3D graphics, animations, and video and audio playback
- A rich typography API, such as support for XML Paper Specification (XPS) documents, fixed documents (WYSIWYG), flow documents, and document annotations (e.g., a Sticky Notes API)
- Support for interoperating with legacy GUI models (e.g., Windows Forms, ActiveX, and Win32 HWNDs)

The Various Flavors of WPF Applications

The WPF API can be used to build a variety of GUI-centric applications, which basically differ in their navigational structure and deployment models. The sections that follow present a high-level walk through each option.

Traditional Desktop Applications

The first (and most familiar) option is a traditional executable assembly that runs on a local machine. For example, you could use WPF to build a text editor, painting program, or multimedia program such as a digital music player, photo viewer, and so forth. Like any other desktop applications, these `*.exe` files can be installed using traditional means (setup programs, Windows Installer packages, etc.) or via ClickOnce technology to allow desktop applications to be distributed and installed via a remote web server.

In this light, WPF is simply a new API to build traditional desktop applications. Programmatically speaking, this type of WPF application will make use (at a minimum) of the `Window` and `Application` types, in addition to the expected set of dialog boxes, toolbars, status bars, menu systems, and other UI elements.

Navigation-Based WPF Applications

WPF applications can optionally choose to make use of a navigation-based structure, which makes a traditional desktop application take on the basic behavior of a web browser application. Using this model, you can build a desktop `*.exe` that provides a "forward" and "back" button that allows the end user to move back and forth between various UI displays called *pages*. The application itself maintains a list of each page and provides the necessary infrastructure to navigate between them, pass data across pages (similar to a web-based application variable), and maintain a history list. By way of a concrete example, consider Vista's Windows Explorer (see Figure 28-1), which makes use of such functionality. Notice the navigational buttons (and history list) mounted on the upper-left corner of the window.

Regardless of the fact that a WPF desktop application can take on a weblike navigational scheme, understand that this is simply a UI design issue. The application itself is still little more than a local executable assembly running on a desktop machine, and it has nothing to do with a web application beyond a slightly similar look and feel. Programmatically speaking, this navigational structure is represented using types such as `Page`, `NavigationWindow`, and `Frame`.

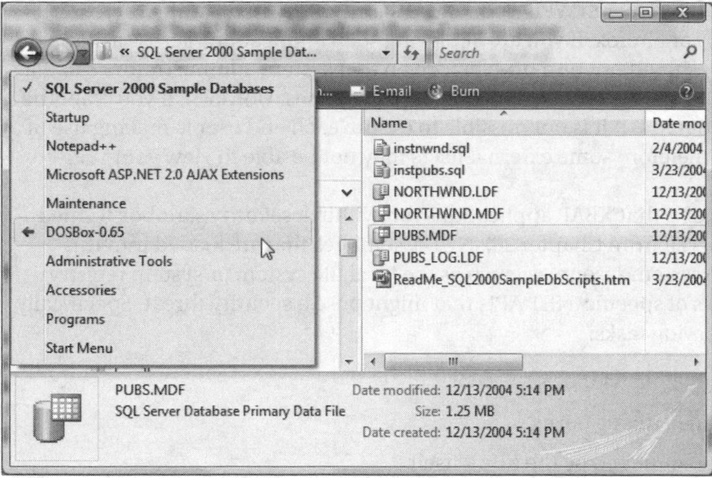

Figure 28-1. *A navigation-based desktop program*

XBAP Applications

WPF also allows you to build applications that can be hosted *within* a web browser. This flavor of WPF application is termed an XAML browser application, or XBAP. Under this model, the end user navigates to a given URL, at which point the XBAP application (which takes an `*.xbap` file extension) is transparently downloaded and installed to the local machine. Unlike a traditional ClickOnce installation for an executable application, however, the XBAP program is hosted directly within the browser and adopts the browser's intrinsic navigational system. Figure 28-2 illustrates an XBAP program in action (specifically, the ExpenseIt WPF sample program that ships with the .NET Framework 3.5 SDK).

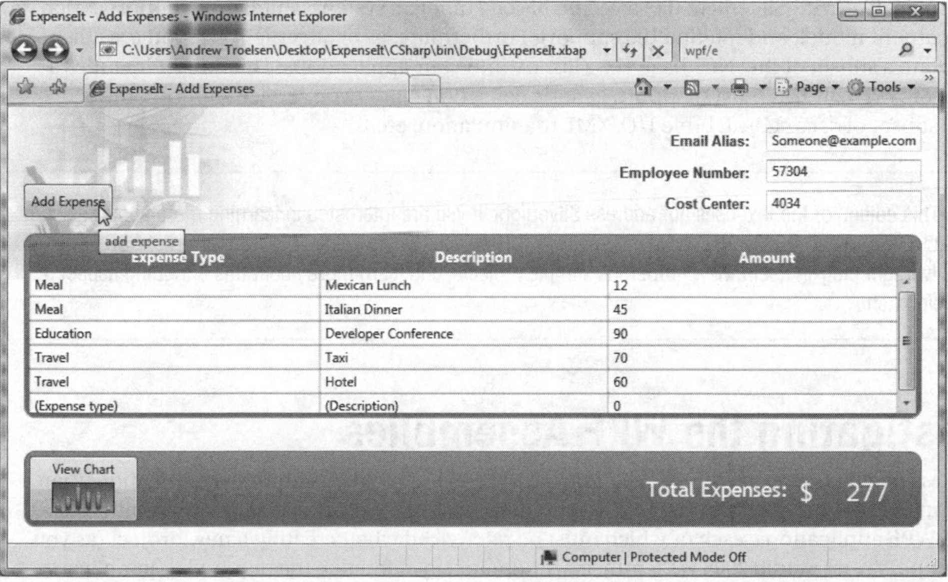

Figure 28-2. *XBAP programs are downloaded to a local machine and hosted within a web browser.*

One possible downside to this flavor of WPF is that XBAPs must be hosted within Microsoft Internet Explorer 6.0 (or higher) or Firefox. If you are deploying such applications across a company intranet, browser compatibility should not be a problem, given that system administrators can play dictator regarding which browser should be installed on users' machines. However, if you want the outside world to make use of your XBAP, it is not possible to ensure each end user is making use of Internet Explorer/Firefox, and therefore some external users may not be able to view your WPF XBAP application.

Another issue to be aware of is that XBAP applications run within a security sandbox termed the *Internet zone*. As you may recall from Chapter 20, .NET assemblies that are loaded into this sandbox have limited access to system resources (such as the local file system or system registry) and cannot freely use all aspects of specific .NET APIs that might pose a security threat. Specifically, XBAPs cannot perform the following tasks:

- Create and display stand-alone windows
- Display application-defined dialog boxes
- Display a Save dialog box launched by the XBAP itself
- Access the file system (use of isolated storage is permitted)
- Make use of legacy UI models (Windows Forms, ActiveX) or call unmanaged code

At first glance, the inability to create secondary windows (or dialog boxes) may seem very limiting. In reality, an XBAP can show users multiple user interfaces by using the page-navigation model mentioned previously.

Silverlight Applications

WPF and XAML also provide the foundation for a *cross-platform* WPF-centric plug-in termed Silverlight. Using the Silverlight SDK, it is possible to build browser-based applications that can be hosted by Mac OS X as well as Microsoft Windows (additional operating systems are supposedly also in the works).

With Silverlight, you are able to build extremely feature-rich (and interactive) web applications. For example, like WPF, Silverlight has a vector-based graphical system, animation support, a rich text document model, and multimedia support. Furthermore, as of Silverlight 1.1, you are able to incorporate a subset of the .NET base class library into your applications. This subset includes a number of WPF controls, LINQ support, generic collection types, web service support, and a healthy subset of `mscorlib.dll` (file I/O, XML manipulation, etc.).

■ **Note** This edition of the text does not address Silverlight. If you are interested in learning more about this API, check out `http://www.microsoft.com/silverlight`. Here you can download the free Silverlight SDK (including the Silverlight plug-in itself), view numerous sample projects, and learn more about this intriguing aspect of WPF development.

Investigating the WPF Assemblies

Regardless of which type of WPF application you wish to build, WPF is ultimately little more than a collection of types bundled within .NET assemblies. Table 28-3 describes the core assemblies used to build WPF applications, each of which must be referenced when creating a new project (as you would hope, Visual Studio 2008 WPF projects automatically reference the required assemblies).

Table 28-3. *Core WPF Assemblies*

Assembly	Meaning in Life
`PresentationCore.dll`	This assembly defines numerous types that constitute the foundation of the WPF GUI layer. For example, this assembly contains support for the WPF Ink API (for programming against stylus input for Pocket PCs and Tablet PCs), several animation primitives (via the `System.Windows.Media.Animation` namespace), and numerous graphical rendering types (via `System.Windows.Media`).
`PresentationFoundation.dll`	Here you will find the WPF control set, additional animation and multimedia types, data binding support, types that allow for programmatic access to XAML, and other WPF services.
`WindowsBase.dll`	This assembly defines the core (and in many cases lower-level) types that constitute the infrastructure of the WPF API. Here you will find types representing WPF threading types, security types, various type converters, and other basic programming primitives (`Point`, `Vector`, `Rect`, etc.).

Collectively, these three assemblies define a number of new namespaces and hundreds of new .NET classes, interfaces, structures, enumerations, and delegates. While you should consult the .NET Framework 3.5 SDK documentation for complete details, Table 28-4 documents the role of some (but certainly not all) of the core namespaces you should be aware of.

Table 28-4. *Core WPF Namespaces*

Namespace	Meaning in Life
`System.Windows`	This is the root namespace of WPF. Here you will find core types (such as `Application` and `Window`) that are required by any WPF desktop project.
`System.Windows.Controls`	Here you will find all of the expected WPF widgets, including types to build menu systems, tool tips, and numerous layout managers.
`System.Windows.Markup`	This namespace defines a number of types that allow XAML markup (and the equivalent binary format, BAML) to be parsed and processed programmatically.
`System.Windows.Media`	This is the root namespace to several media-centric namespaces. Within these namespaces you will find types to work with animations, 3D rendering, text rendering, and other multimedia primitives.
`System.Windows.Navigation`	This namespace provides types to account for the navigation logic employed by XAML browser applications (XBAPs) as well as standard desktop applications that require a navigational page model.
`System.Windows.Shapes`	This namespace defines various 2D graphic types (`Rectangle`, `Polygon`, etc.) used by various aspects of the WPF framework.

To begin our journey into the WPF programming model, we'll examine two members of the `System.Windows` namespace that are commonplace to any traditional desktop development effort: `Application` and `Window`.

The Role of the Application Class

The `System.Windows.Application` class type represents a global instance of a running WPF application. Like its Windows Forms counterpart, this type supplies a `Run()` method (to start the application), a series of events that you are able to handle in order to interact with the application's lifetime (such as `Startup` and `Exit`), and a number of members that are specific to XAML browser applications (such as events that fire as a user navigates between pages). Table 28-5 details some of the key members to be aware of.

Table 28-5. *Key Properties of the* `Application` *Type*

Property	Meaning in Life
`Current`	This static property allows you to gain access to the running `Application` object from anywhere in your code. This can be very helpful when a window or dialog box needs to gain access to the `Application` object that created it.
`MainWindow`	This property allows you to programmatically get or set the main window of the application.
`Properties`	This property allows you to establish and obtain data that is accessible throughout all aspects of a WPF application (windows, dialog boxes, etc.). In many ways, this looks and feels very much like establishing application variables for an ASP.NET web application.
`StartupUri`	This property gets or sets a URI that specifies a window or page to open automatically when the application starts.
`Windows`	This property returns a `WindowCollection` type, which provides access to each window created from the thread that created the `Application` object. This can be very helpful when you wish to iterate over each open window of an application and alter its state (such as minimizing all windows).

Unlike its Windows Forms counterpart, however, the WPF `Application` type does not expose its functionality exclusively through static members. Rather, WPF programs define a class that extends this type to represent the entry point to the executable. For example:

```
// Define the global application object
// for this WPF program.
class MyApp : Application
{
  [STAThread]
  static void Main()
  {
    // Handle events, run the application,
    // launch the main window, etc.
  }
}
```

You'll build a complete `Application`-derived type in an upcoming example. Until then, let's check out the core functionality of the `Window` type and learn about a number of key WPF base classes in the process.

The Role of the Window Class

The `System.Windows.Window` type represents a single window owned by the `Application`-derived type, including any dialog boxes displayed by the main window. As you might expect, the `Window` type has a series of parent classes, each of which brings more functionality to the table. Consider

Figure 28-3, which shows the inheritance chain (and implemented interfaces) for the `System.Windows.Window` type as seen through the Visual Studio 2008 object browser.

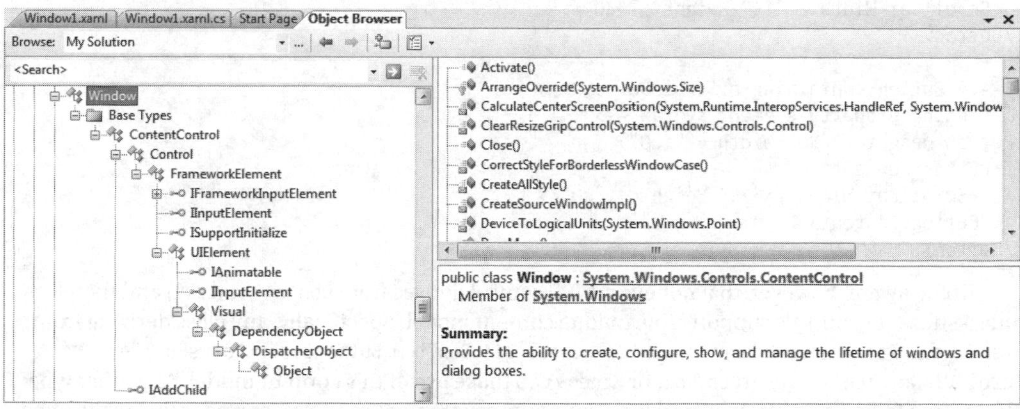

Figure 28-3. *The hierarchy of the* `Window` *type*

You'll come to understand the functionality provided by many of these base classes as you progress through this chapter and the chapters to come. However, to whet your appetite, the following sections present a breakdown of the functionality provided by each base class (consult the .NET Framework 3.5 SDK documentation for full details).

The Role of System.Windows.Controls.ContentControl

The direct parent of `Window` is `ContentControl`. This base class provides derived types with the ability to host *content*, which simply put refers to a collection of objects placed within the control's surface area. Under the WPF content model, a content control has the ability to contain a great number of UI elements beyond simple string data. For example, it is entirely possible to define a `Button` that contains an embedded `ScrollBar` as content. The `ContentControl` base class provides a key property named (not surprisingly) `Content` for this purpose.

If the value you wish to assign to the `Content` property can be represented as a simple string literal, you may set the `Content` property *explicitly* as an attribute within the element's opening definition:

```
<!-- Setting the Content value explicitly -->
<Button Height="80" Width="100" Content="ClickMe"/>
```

Alternatively, you are able to *implicitly* set the `Context` property by specifying a value within the scope of the content control's element definition. Consider the following functionally equivalent XAML description of the previous button:

```
<!-- Setting the Content value implicitly -->
<Button Height="80" Width="100">
  ClickMe
</Button>
```

However, if the value you wish to assign to the `Content` property cannot be represented as a simple array of characters, you are unable to assign the `Content` property using an attribute in the control's opening definition. For these cases, you must establish content either implicitly or by using *property-element syntax*. Consider the following functionally equivalent XAML definition, which sets the `Content` property to a `ScrollBar` type (you'll find more information on XAML later in this chapter, so don't sweat the details just yet):

```
<!-- A Button containing a ScrollBar
     as implicit content -->
<Button Height = "80" Width = "100">
  <ScrollBar Width = "75" Height = "40"/>
</Button>

<!-- A Button containing a ScrollBar
     using property-element syntax -->
<Button Height = "80" Width = "100">
  <Button.Content>
    <ScrollBar Width = "75" Height = "40"/>
  </Button.Content>
</Button>
```

Do be aware, however, that not every WPF control derives from `ContentControl`, and therefore only a subset of controls supports this unique content model. Specifically, any class deriving from `Frame`, `GroupItem`, `HeaderedContentControl`, `Label`, `ListBoxItem`, `ButtonBase`, `StatusBarItem`, `ScrollViewer`, `ToolTip`, `UserControl`, or `Window` can make use of this content model. Any other type attempting to do so results in a markup/compile-time error. For example, consider this malformed `ScrollBar` type:

```
<!-- Error!  ScrollBars don't derive from ContentControl! -->
<ScrollBar Height = "80" Width = "100">
  <Button Width = "75" Height = "40"/>
</ScrollBar >
```

Another important point regarding this new content model is that controls deriving from `ContentControl` (including the `Window` type itself) can assign only a *single* value to the `Content` property. Therefore, the following XAML `Button` definition is also illegal, as the `Content` property has been implicitly set twice:

```
<!-- Try to add a TextBox and an Ellipse to a Button?  Error! -->
<Button Height = "200" Width = "200">
  <Ellipse Fill = "Green" Height = "80" Width = "80"/>
  <TextBox Width = "50" Height = "40"/>
</Button >
```

At first glance, this fact might appear to be extremely limiting (imagine how nonfunctional a dialog box would be with only a single button!). Thankfully, it is indeed possible to add numerous elements to a `ContentControl`-derived type using panels. To do so, each bit of content must first be arranged into one of the WPF panel types, after which point the panel becomes the single value assigned to the `Content` property. You will learn more about the WPF content model as well as the various panel types (and the controls they contain) in Chapter 29.

■ **Note** The `System.Windows.ContentControl` class also provides the `HasContent` property to determine if the value of `Content` is currently `null`.

The Role of System.Windows.Controls.Control

Unlike `ContentControl`, all WPF controls share the `Control` base class as a common parent. This base class provides numerous core members that account for basic UI functionality. For example, `Control` defines properties to establish the control's size, opacity, tab order logic, the display cursor, background color, and so forth. Furthermore, this parent class provides support for *templating services*. As explained in Chapter 30, WPF controls can dynamically change their appearance using templates, styles, and themes. Table 28-6 documents some key members of the `Control` type, grouped by related functionality.

Table 28-6. *Key Members of the* `Control` *Type*

Members	Meaning in Life
`Background`, `Foreground`, `BorderBrush`, `BorderThickness`, `Padding`, `HorizontalContentAlignment`, `VerticalContentAlignment`	These properties allow you to set basic settings regarding how the control will be rendered and positioned.
`FontFamily`, `FontSize`, `FontStretch`, `FontWeight`	These properties control various font-centric settings.
`IsTabStop`, `TabIndex`	These properties are used to establish tab order among controls on a window.
`MouseDoubleClick`, `PreviewMouseDoubleClick`	These events handle the act of double-clicking a widget.
`Template`	This property allows you to get and set the control's template, which can be used to change the rendering output of the widget.

The Role of System.Windows.FrameworkElement

This base class provides a number of lower-level members that are used throughout the WPF framework, such as support for storyboarding (used within animations) and support for data binding, as well as the ability to name a member (via the `Name` property), obtain any resources defined by the derived type, and establish the overall dimensions of the derived type. Table 28-7 hits the highlights.

Table 28-7. *Key Members of the* `FrameworkElement` *Type*

Members	Meaning in Life
`ActualHeight`, `ActualWidth`, `MaxHeight`, `MaxWidth`, `MinHeight`, `MinWidth`, `Height`, `Width`	Control the size of the derived type (not surprisingly)
`ContextMenu`	Gets or sets the pop-up menu associated with the derived type
`Cursor`	Gets or sets the mouse cursor associated with the derived type
`HorizontalAlignment`, `VerticalAlignment`	Control how the type is positioned within a container (such as a panel or list box)
`Name`	Allows to you assign a name to the type, in order to access its functionality in a code file
`Resources`	Provides access to any resources defined by the type (see Chapter 30 for an examination of the WPF resource system)
`ToolTip`	Gets or sets the tool tip associated with the derived type

The Role of System.Windows.UIElement

Of all the types within a Window's inheritance chain, the UIElement base class provides the greatest amount of functionality. The key task of UIElement is to provide the derived type with numerous events to allow the derived type to receive focus and process input requests. For example, this class provides numerous events to account for drag-and-drop operations, mouse movement, keyboard input, and stylus input (for Pocket PCs and Tablet PCs).

Chapter 29 digs into the WPF event model in detail; however, many of the core events will look quite familiar (MouseMove, KeyUp, MouseDown, MouseEnter, MouseLeave, etc.). In addition to defining dozens of events, this parent class provides a number of properties to account for control focus, enabled state, visibility, and hit testing logic, as shown in Table 28-8.

Table 28-8. *Key Members of the* UIElement *Type*

Members	Meaning in Life
Focusable, IsFocused	These properties allow you to set focus on a given derived type.
IsEnabled	These properties allow you to control whether a given derived type is enabled or disabled.
IsMouseDirectlyOver, IsMouseOver	These properties provide a simple way to perform hit-testing logic.
IsVisible, Visibility, Visible	These properties allow you to work with the visibility setting of a derived type.
RenderTransform	This property allows you to establish a transformation that will be used to render the derived type.

The Role of System.Windows.Media.Visual

The Visual class type provides core rendering support in WPF, which includes hit testing of rendered data, coordinate transformation, and bounding box calculations. In fact, this type is the connection point between the managed WPF assembly stack and the unmanaged milcore.dll binary that communicates with the DirectX subsystem.

As examined in Chapter 30, WPF provides three possible manners in which you can render graphical data, each of which differs in terms of functionality and performance. Use of the Visual type (and its children, such as DrawingVisual) provides the most lightweight way to render graphical data, but it also entails the greatest amount of manual code to account for all the required services. Again, more details to come in Chapter 30.

The Role of System.Windows.DependencyObject

WPF supports a particular flavor of .NET properties termed *dependency properties*. Simply put, this approach allows a type to compute the value of a property based on the value of other properties (hence the term "dependency"). In order for a type to participate in this new property scheme, it will need to derive from the DependencyObject base class. In addition, DependencyObject allows derived types to support *attached properties*, which are a form of dependency property very useful when programming against the WPF data-binding model as well as when laying out UI elements within various WPF panel types.

The DependencyObject base class provides two key methods to all derived types: GetValue() and SetValue(). Using these members, you are able to establish the property itself. Other bits of infrastructure allow you to "register" who can use the dependent/attached property in question.

While dependency properties are a key aspect of WPF development, much of the time their details are hidden from view. Chapter 29 dives further into the details of the "new" property type.

The Role of System.Windows.Threading.DispatcherObject

The final base class of the Window type (beyond System.Object, which I assume needs no further explanation at this point in the text) is DispatcherObject. This type provides one property of interest, Dispatcher, which returns the associated System.Windows.Threading.Dispatcher object. The Dispatcher type is the entry point to the event queue of the WPF application, and it provides the basic constructs for dealing with concurrency and threading. By and large, this is a lower-level class that can be ignored by the majority of your WPF applications.

Building a (XAML-Free) WPF Application

Given all of the functionality provided by the parent classes of the Window type, it is possible to represent a window in your application by either directly creating a Window type or using this class as the parent to a strongly typed descendent. Let's examine both approaches in the following code example. Although most WPF applications will make use of XAML, doing so is entirely optional. Anything that can be expressed in XAML can be expressed in code and (for the most part) vice versa. If you wish, it is possible to build a complete WPF project using the underlying object model and procedural code.

To illustrate, let's create a minimal but complete application *without* the use of XAML using the Application and Window types directly. Consider the following C# code file (SimpleWPFApp.cs), which creates a main window of modest functionality:

```
// A simple WPF application, written without XAML.
using System;
using System.Windows;
using System.Windows.Controls;

namespace SimpleWPFApp
{
  // In this first example, we are defining a single class type to
  // represent the application itself and the main window.
  class MyWPFApp : Application
  {
    [STAThread]
    static void Main()
    {
      // Handle the Startup and Exit events, and then run the application.
      MyWPFApp app = new MyWPFApp();
      app.Startup += AppStartUp;
      app.Exit += AppExit;
      app.Run();  // Fires the Startup event.
    }

    static void AppExit(object sender, ExitEventArgs e)
    {
      MessageBox.Show("App has exited");
    }

    static void AppStartUp(object sender, StartupEventArgs e)
    {
      // Create a Window object and set some basic properties.
```

```
      Window mainWindow = new Window();
      mainWindow.Title = "My First WPF App!";
      mainWindow.Height = 200;
      mainWindow.Width = 300;
      mainWindow.WindowStartupLocation = WindowStartupLocation.CenterScreen;
      mainWindow.Show();
    }
  }
}
```

■ **Note** The `Main()` method of a WPF application must be attributed with the `[STAThread]` attribute, which ensures any legacy COM objects used by your application are thread-safe. If you do not annotate `Main()` in this way, you will trigger a runtime exception!

Note that the `MyWPFApp` class extends the `System.Windows.Application` type. Within this type's `Main()` method, we create an instance of our application object and handle the `Startup` and `Exit` events using method group conversion syntax. Recall from Chapter 11 that this shorthand notation removes the need to manually specify the underlying delegates used by a particular event.

However, if you wish, you can specify the underlying delegates directly by name. In the following modified `Main()` method, notice that the `Startup` event works in conjunction with the `StartupEventHandler` delegate, which can only point to methods taking an `Object` as the first parameter and a `StartupEventArgs` as the second. The `Exit` event, on the other hand, works with the `ExitEventHandler` delegate, which demands that the method pointed to take an `ExitEventArgs` type as the second parameter:

```
[STAThread]
static void Main()
{
  // This time, specify the underlying delegates.
  MyWPFApp app = new MyWPFApp();
  app.Startup += new StartupEventHandler(AppStartUp);
  app.Exit += new ExitEventHandler(AppExit);
  app.Run();  // Fires the Startup event.
}
```

The `AppStartUp()` method has been configured to create a `Window` type, establish some very basic property settings, and call `Show()` to display the window on the screen in a modal-less fashion (like Windows Forms, the `ShowDialog()` method can be used to launch a modal dialog). The `AppExit()` method simply makes use of the WPF `MessageBox` type to display a diagnostic message when the application is being terminated.

To compile this C# code into an executable WPF application, assume that you have created a C# response file named `build.rsp` that references each of the WPF assemblies. Note that the path to each assembly should be defined on a single line (see Chapter 2 for more information on response files and working with the command-line compiler):

```
# build.rsp
#
/target:winexe
/out:SimpleWPFApp.exe
/r:"C:\Program Files\Reference Assemblies\Microsoft\Framework\v3.0\WindowsBase.dll"
/r:"C:\Program Files\Reference Assemblies\Microsoft\Framework
     \v3.0\PresentationCore.dll"
```

```
/r:"C:\Program Files\Reference Assemblies\Microsoft\Framework
      \v3.0\PresentationFramework.dll"
*.cs
```

You can now compile this WPF program at the command prompt as follows:

```
csc @build.rsp
```

Once you run the program, you will find a very simple main window that can be minimized, maximized, and closed. To spice things up a bit, we need to add some user interface elements. Before we do, however, let's refactor our code base to account for a strongly typed and well-encapsulated Window-derived class.

Extending the Window Class Type

Currently, our Application-derived class directly creates an instance of the Window type upon application startup. Ideally, we would create a class deriving from Window in order to encapsulate its functionality. Assume we have created the following class definition within our current SimpleWPFApp namespace:

```
class MainWindow : Window
{
  public MainWindow(string windowTitle, int height, int width)
  {
    this.Title = windowTitle;
    this.WindowStartupLocation = WindowStartupLocation.CenterScreen;
    this.Height = height;
    this.Width = width;
    this.Show();
  }
}
```

We can now update our Startup event handler to simply directly create an instance of MainWindow:

```
static void AppStartUp(object sender, StartupEventArgs e)
{
  // Create a MainWindow object.
  MainWindow wnd = new MainWindow("My better WPF App!", 200, 300);
}
```

Once the program is recompiled and executed, the output is identical. The obvious benefit is that we now have a strongly typed class to build upon.

■ **Note** When you create a Window (or Window-derived) object, it will automatically be added to the internal windows collection of the Application type (via some constructor logic found in the Window class itself). Given this fact, a window will be alive in memory until it is terminated or is explicitly removed from the collection via the Application.Windows property.

Creating a Simple User Interface

Adding UI elements into a Window-derived type is similar (but not identical) to adding UI elements into a System.Windows.Forms.Form-derived type:

1. Define a member variable to represent the required widget.
2. Configure the variable's look and feel upon the creation of your Window type.
3. Add the widget to the Window's client area via a call to AddChild().

Although the process might feel familiar to Windows Forms development, one obvious difference is that the UI controls used by WPF are defined within the System.Windows.Controls namespace rather than System.Windows.Forms (thankfully, in many cases, they are identically named and feel quite similar to their Windows Forms counterparts).

A more drastic change from Windows Forms is the fact that a Window-derived type can contain only a *single child element* (due to the WPF content model). When a window needs to contain multiple UI elements (which will be the case for practically any window), you will need to make use of a layout manager such as DockPanel, Grid, Canvas, or StackPanel to control their positioning.

For this example, we will add single Button type to the Window-derived type. When we click this button, we terminate the application by gaining access to the global application object (via the Application.Current property) in order to call the Shutdown() method. Ponder the following update to the MainWindow class:

```
class MainWindow : Window
{
  // Our UI element.
  private Button btnExitApp = new Button();

  public MainWindow(string windowTitle, int height, int width)
  {
    // Configure button and set the child control.
    btnExitApp.Click += new RoutedEventHandler(btnExitApp_Clicked);
    btnExitApp.Content = "Exit Application";
    btnExitApp.Height = 25;
    btnExitApp.Width = 100;

    // Set the content of this window to a single button.
    this.AddChild(btnExitApp);

    // Configure the window.
    this.Title = windowTitle;
    this.WindowStartupLocation = WindowStartupLocation.CenterScreen;
    this.Height = height;
    this.Width = width;
    this.Show();
  }

  private void btnExitApp_Clicked(object sender, RoutedEventArgs e)
  {
    // Get a handle to the current application and shut it down.
    Application.Current.Shutdown();
  }
}
```

Given your work with Windows Forms in Chapter 27, the code within the window's constructor should not look too threatening. Do notice, however, that the Click event of the WPF button works in conjunction with a delegate named RoutedEventHandler, which obviously begs the question, what is a routed event? You'll examine the details of the WPF event model in the next chapter; for the time being, simply understand that targets of the RoutedEventHandler delegate must supply an object as the first parameter and a RoutedEventArgs as the second.

In any case, once you recompile and run this application, you will find the customized window shown in Figure 28-4. Notice that our button is automatically placed in the dead center of the window's client area, which is the default behavior when content is not placed within a WPF panel type.

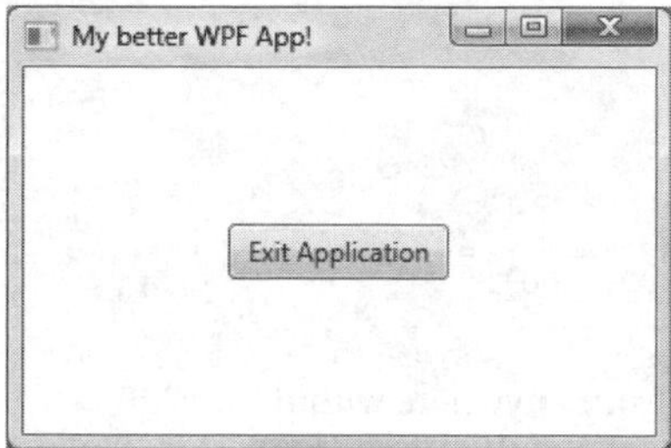

Figure 28-4. *A somewhat interesting WPF application*

Source Code The SimpleWPFApp project is included under the Chapter 28 subdirectory.

Additional Details of the Application Type

Now that you have created a simple WPF program using a 100-percent pure code approach, let's illustrate some additional details of the `Application` type, beginning with the construction of application-wide data. To do so, we will extend the previous SimpleWPFApp application with new functionality.

Application-wide Data and Processing Command-Line Arguments

Recall that the `Application` type defines a property named `Properties`, which allows you to define a collection of name/value pairs via a type indexer. Because this indexer has been defined to operate on type `System.Object`, you are able to store any sort of item within this collection (including your custom classes), to be retrieved at a later time using a friendly moniker. Using this approach, it is simple to share data across all windows in a WPF application.

To illustrate, we will update the current `Startup` event handler to check the incoming command-line arguments for a value named `/GODMODE` (a common cheat code for many PC video games). If we find such a token, we will establish a `bool` value set to `true` within the properties collection of the same name (otherwise we will set the value to `false`).

Sounds simple enough, but one question you may have is, how are we going to pass the incoming command-line arguments (typically obtained from the `Main()` method) to our `Startup` event handler? One approach is to call the static `Environment.GetCommandLineArgs()` method. However, these same arguments are automatically added to the incoming `StartupEventArgs` parameter and can be accessed via the `Args` property. This being said, here is our first update:

```
static void AppStartUp(object sender, StartupEventArgs e)
{
  // Check the incoming command-line arguments and see if they
  // specified a flag for /GODMODE.
  Application.Current.Properties["GodMode"] = false;
```

```
  foreach(string arg in e.Args)
  {
    if (arg.ToLower() == "/godmode")
    {
      Application.Current.Properties["GodMode"] = true;
      break;
    }
  }

  // Create a MainWindow object.
  MainWindow wnd = new MainWindow("My better WPF App!", 200, 300);
}
```

Now recall that this new name/value pair can be accessed from anywhere within the WPF application. All we are required to do is obtain an access point to the global application object (via `Application.Current`) and investigate the collection. For example, we could update the `Click` event handler of the `Button` type of the main window like so:

```
private void btnExitApp_Clicked(object sender, RoutedEventArgs e)
{
  // Did user enable /godmode?
  if((bool)Application.Current.Properties["GodMode"])
    MessageBox.Show("Cheater!");

  // Get a handle to the current application and shut it down.
  Application.Current.Shutdown();
}
```

With this, if the end user launches our program as follows:

```
SimpleWPFApp.exe /godmode
```

he or she will see our shameful message box displayed when terminating the application.

Iterating over the Application's Windows Collection

Another interesting property exposed by `Application` is `Windows`, which provides access to a collection representing each window loaded into memory for the current WPF application. Recall that as you create new `Window` types, they are automatically added into the global application object's `Windows` collection. We have no need to update our current example to illustrate this; however, here is an example method that will minimize each window of the application (perhaps in response to a given keyboard gesture or menu option triggered by the end user):

```
static void MinimizeAllWindows()
{
  foreach (Window wnd in Application.Current.Windows)
  {
    wnd.WindowState = WindowState.Minimized;
  }
}
```

Additional Events of the Application Type

Like many types within the .NET base class libraries, `Application` also defines a set of events that you can intercept. You have already seen the `Startup` and `Exit` events in action. You should also be aware of `Activated` and `Deactivated`. At first glance these events can seem a bit confusing, given that the `Window` type supplied identically named methods. Unlike their UI counterparts, however, the `Activated` and `Deactivated` events fire whenever *any* window maintained by the application object received or lost focus (in contrast to the same events of the `Window` type, which are unique to that `Window` object).

Our current example has no need to handle these two events, but if you need to do so, be aware that each event works in conjunction with the `System.EventHandler` delegate, and therefore the event handler will take an `Object` as the first parameter and `System.EventArgs` as the second (see Chapter 27 for a refresher on the `EventHandler` delegate).

■ **Note** A majority of the remaining events of the `Application` type are specific to a navigation-based WPF application. Using these events, you are able to intercept the process of moving between `Page` objects of your program.

Additional Details of the Window Type

The `Window` type, as you saw earlier in this chapter, gains a ton of functionality from its set of parent classes and implemented interfaces. Over the chapters to come, you'll glean more and more information about what these base classes bring to the table; however, it is important to revisit the `Window` type itself and come to understand some core services you'll need to use on a day-to-day basis, beginning with the set of events that are fired over its lifetime.

The Lifetime of a Window Object

Like the `System.Windows.Forms.Form` type, `System.Windows.Window` has a set of events that will fire over the course of its lifetime. When you handle some (or all) of these events, you will have a convenient manner in which you can perform custom logic as your `Window` goes about its business. First of all, because a window is a class type, the very first step in its initialization entails a call to a specified constructor. After that point, the first WPF-centric event that fires is `SourceInitialized`, which is only useful if your `Window` is making use of various interoperability services (e.g., using legacy ActiveX controls in a WPF application). Even then, the need to intercept this event is limited, so consult the .NET Framework 3.5 documentation if you require more information.

The first immediately useful event that fires after the `Window`'s constructor is `Activate`, which works in conjunction with the `System.EventHandler` delegate. This event is fired when a window receives focus and thus becomes the foreground window. The counterpart to this event is `Deactivate` (which also works with the `System.EventHandler` delegate), which fires when a window loses focus.

Here is an update to our existing `Window`-derived type that adds an informative message to a private `string` variable (you'll see the usefulness of this string variable in just a bit) when the `Activate` and `Deactivate` events occur:

```
class MainWindow : Window
{
  private Button btnExitApp = new Button();

  // This string will document which events fire, and when.
  private string lifeTimeData = String.Empty;

  protected void MainWindow_Activated(object sender, EventArgs e)
  {
```

```
    lifeTimeData += "Activate Event Fired!\n";
  }
  protected void MainWindow_Deactivated(object sender, EventArgs e)
  {
    lifeTimeData += "Deactivated Event Fired!\n";
  }

  public MainWindow(string windowTitle, int height, int width)
  {
    // Rig up events.
    this.Activated += MainWindow_Activated;
    this.Deactivated += MainWindow_Deactivated;
    ...
  }
}
```

■ **Note** Recall that you can handle application-level activation/deactivation for all windows with the `Application.Activated` and `Application.Deactivated` events.

Once the `Activated` event fires, the next event to do so is `Loaded` (which works with the `RoutedEventHandler` delegate), which signifies that the window has been for all practical purposes fully laid out and rendered, and is ready to respond to user input.

■ **Note** While the `Activated` event can fire many times as a window gains or loses focus, the `Loaded` event will fire only one time during the window's lifetime.

Assume that our `MainWindow` type has handled this event and defines the following event handler:

```
protected void MainWindow_Loaded(object sender, RoutedEventArgs e)
{
  lifeTimeData += "Loaded Event Fired!\n";
}
```

■ **Note** Should the need arise (which can be the case with custom WPF controls), you can capture the exact moment when a window's content has been loaded by handling the `ContentRendered` event.

Handling the Closing of a Window Object

End users can shut down a window using numerous built-in system-level techniques (e.g., clicking the "X" close button on the window's frame) or by indirectly calling the `Close()` method in response to some user interaction element (e.g., File ➤ Exit). In either case, WPF provides two events that you can intercept to determine if the user is truly ready to shut down the window and remove it from memory. The first event to fire is `Closing`, which works in conjunction with the `CancelEventHandler` delegate.

This delegate expects target methods to take System.ComponentModel.CancelEventArgs as the second parameter. CancelEventArgs provides the Cancel property, which when set to false will prevent the window from actually closing (this is handy when you have asked the user if he really wants to close the window, or perhaps needs to save his work).

If the user did indeed wish to close the window, CancelEventArgs.Cancel can be set to true, which will then cause the Closed event to fire (which works with the System.EventHandler delegate), which is the point at which the window is about to be closed for good. Assuming the MainWindow type has handled these two events, consider the final event handlers:

```
protected void MainWindow_Closing(object sender,
  System.ComponentModel.CancelEventArgs e)
{
  lifeTimeData += "Closing Event Fired!\n";

  // See if the user really wants to shut down this window.
  string msg = "Do you want to close without saving?";
  MessageBoxResult result = MessageBox.Show(msg,
    "My App", MessageBoxButton.YesNo, MessageBoxImage.Warning);
   if (result == MessageBoxResult.No)
  {
    // If user doesn't want to close, cancel closure.
    e.Cancel = true;
  }
}

protected void MainWindow_Closed(object sender, EventArgs e)
{
  lifeTimeData += "Closing Event Fired!\n";
  MessageBox.Show(lifeTimeData);
}
```

When you compile and run your application, shift the window into and out of focus a few times. Also attempt to close the window once or twice. When you do indeed close the window for good, you will see a message box pop up that displays the events that fired during the window's lifetime (Figure 28-5 shows one possible test run).

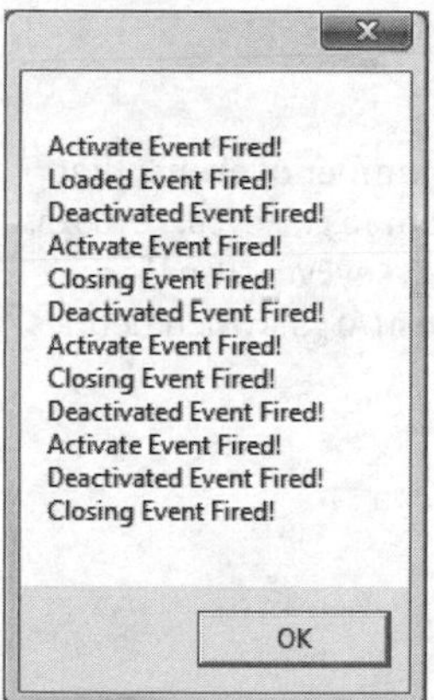

Figure 28-5. *The life and times of a* System.Windows.Window

Handling Window-Level Mouse Events

Much like Windows Forms, the WPF API provides a number of events you can capture in order to interact with the mouse. Specifically, the `UIElement` base class defines a number of mouse-centric events such as `MouseMove`, `MouseUp`, `MouseDown`, `MouseEnter`, `MouseLeave`, and so forth.

Consider, for example, the act of handling the `MouseMove` event. This event works in conjunction with the `System.Windows.Input.MouseEventHandler` delegate, which expects its target to take a `System.Windows.Input.MouseEventArgs` type as the second parameter. Using `MouseEventArgs` (like a Windows Forms application) you are able to extract out the (*x*, *y*) position of the mouse and other relevant details. Consider the following partial definition:

```
public class MouseEventArgs : InputEventArgs
{
...
  public Point GetPosition(IInputElement relativeTo);
  public MouseButtonState LeftButton { get; }
  public MouseButtonState MiddleButton { get; }
  public MouseDevice MouseDevice { get; }
  public MouseButtonState RightButton { get; }
  public StylusDevice StylusDevice { get; }
  public MouseButtonState XButton1 { get; }
  public MouseButtonState XButton2 { get; }
}
```

The `GetPosition()` method allows you to get the (*x*, *y*) value relative to a UI element on the window. If you are interested in capturing the position relative to the activated window, simply pass in `this`. Here is an event handler for `MouseMove` that will display the location of the mouse in the window's title area (notice we are translating the returned `Point` type into a string value via `ToString()`):

```
protected void MainWindow_MouseMove(object sender,
  System.Windows.Input.MouseEventArgs e)
{
  // Set the title of the window to the current X,Y of the mouse.
  this.Title = e.GetPosition(this).ToString();
}
```

Handling Window-Level Keyboard Events

Processing keyboard input is also very straightforward. `UIElement` defines a number of events that you can capture to intercept keypresses from the keyboard on the active element (e.g., `KeyUp`, `KeyDown`, etc.). The `KeyUp` and `KeyDown` events both work with the `System.Windows.Input.KeyEventHandler` delegate, which expects the target's second event handler to be of type `KeyEventArgs`, which defines several public properties of interest:

```
public class KeyEventArgs : KeyboardEventArgs
{
...
  public bool IsDown { get; }
  public bool IsRepeat { get; }
  public bool IsToggled { get; }
  public bool IsUp { get; }
  public Key Key { get; }
  public KeyStates KeyStates { get; }
  public Key SystemKey { get; }
}
```

To illustrate handling the KeyUp event, the following event handler will display the previously pressed key on the window's title:

```
protected void MainWindow_KeyUp(object sender, System.Windows.Input.KeyEventArgs e)
{
  // Display keypress.
  this.Title = e.Key.ToString();
}
```

At this point in the chapter, WPF might look like nothing more than a new GUI model that is providing (more or less) the same services as System.Windows.Forms.dll. If this were in fact the case, you might question the usefulness of yet another UI toolkit. To truly see what makes WPF so unique requires an understanding of a new XML-based grammar, XAML.

Source Code The SimpleWPFAppRevisited project is included under the Chapter 28 subdirectory.

Building a (XAML-Centric) WPF Application

Extensible Application Markup Language, or XAML, is an XML-based grammar that allows you to define the state (and, to some extent, the functionality) of a tree of .NET objects through markup. While XAML is frequently used when building UIs with WPF, in reality it can be used to describe any tree of *nonabstract* .NET types (including your own custom types defined in a custom .NET assembly), provided each supports a default constructor. As you will see, the markup found within a *.xaml file is transformed into a full-blown object model that maps directly to the types within a related .NET namespace.

Because XAML is an XML-based grammar, we gain all the benefits and drawbacks XML affords us. On the plus side, XAML files are very self-describing (as any XML document should be). By and large, each element in an XAML file represents a type name (such as Button, Window, or Application) within a given .NET namespace. Attributes within the scope of an opening element map to properties (Height, Width, etc.) and events (Startup, Click, etc.) of the specified type.

Given the fact that XAML is simply a declarative way to define the state of an object, it is possible to define a WPF widget via markup or procedural code. For example, the following XAML:

```
<!-- Defining a WPF Button in XAML -->
<Button Name = "btnClickMe" Height = "40" Width = "100" Content = "Click Me" />
```

can be represented programmatically as follows:

```
// Defining the same WPF Button in C# code.
Button btnClickMe = new Button();
btnClickMe.Height = 40;
btnClickMe.Width = 100;
btnClickMe.Content = "Click Me";
```

On the downside, XAML can be verbose and is (like any XML document) case sensitive, thus complex XAML definitions can result in a good deal of markup. Most developers will not need to manually author a complete XAML description of their WPF applications. Rather, the majority of this task will (thankfully) be relegated to development tools such as Visual Studio 2008, Microsoft Expression Blend, or any number of third-party products. Once the tools generate the basic markup, you can go in and fine-tune the XAML definitions by hand if necessary.

While tools can generate a good deal of XAML on your behalf, it is important for you to understand the basic workings of XAML syntax and how this markup is eventually transformed into a valid .NET assembly. To illustrate XAML in action, in our next example we'll build a WPF application using nothing more than a pair of *.xaml files.

Defining MainWindow in XAML

Our first Window-derived class (MainWindow) was defined in C# as a class type that extends the System.Windows.Window base class. This class contains a single Button type that calls a registered event handler when clicked. Defining this same Window type in the grammar of XAML can be achieved as so (assume this markup has been defined in a file named MainWindow.xaml):

```
<!-- Here is our Window definition -->
<Window x:Class="SimpleXamlApp.MainWindow"
  xmlns="http://schemas.microsoft.com/winfx/2006/xaml/presentation"
  xmlns:x="http://schemas.microsoft.com/winfx/2006/xaml"
  Title="My Xaml App" Height="200" Width="300"
  WindowStartupLocation ="CenterScreen">

  <!--Set the content of this window -->
  <Button Width="133" Height="24" Name="btnExitApp" Click ="btnExitApp_Clicked">
    Exit Application
  </Button>

  <!--The implementation of our button's Click event handler! -->
  <x:Code>
  <![CDATA[
  private void btnExitApp_Clicked(object sender, RoutedEventArgs e)
  {
    // Get a handle to the current app and shut it down.
    Application.Current.Shutdown();
  }
  ]]>
  </x:Code>
</Window>
```

First of all, notice that the root element, <Window>, defines the name of the derived type via the Class attribute. The x prefix is used to denote that this attribute is defined within the XAML-centric XML namespace, http://schemas.microsoft.com/winfx/2006/xaml (more details on these XML namespaces later in this chapter). Within the scope of the opening <Window> element we have specified values for the Title, Height, Width, and WindowsStartupLocation attributes, which as you can see are a direct mapping to properties of the same name supported by the System.Windows.Window type.

Next up, notice that within the scope of the window's definition, we have authored markup to describe the look and feel of the Button instance, which will be used to implicitly set the Content property of the window. Beyond setting up the variable name and its overall dimensions, we have also handled the Click event of the Button type by assigning the method to delegate to when the Click event occurs.

The final aspect of this XAML file is the <Code> element, which allows us to author event handlers and other methods of this class directly within an *.xaml file. As a safety measure, the code itself is wrapped within a CDATA scope, to prevent XML parsers from attempting to directly interpret the data (although this is not strictly required for the current example).

It is important to point out that authoring functionality within a <Code> element is not recommended. Although this "single-file approach" isolates all the action to one location, inline code does not provide us with a clear separation of concerns between UI markup and programming logic. In most WPF applications, "real code" will be found within an associated C# code file (which we will do eventually).

Defining the Application Object in XAML

Remember that XAML can be used to define in markup any nonabstract .NET class that supports a default constructor. Given this, we could most certainly define our application object in markup as well. Consider the following content within a new file, `MyApp.xaml`:

```
<!-- The Main() method seems to be missing!
     However, the StartupUri attribute is the
     functional equivalent -->
<Application x:Class="SimpleXamlApp.MyApp"
  xmlns="http://schemas.microsoft.com/winfx/2006/xaml/presentation"
  xmlns:x="http://schemas.microsoft.com/winfx/2006/xaml"
  StartupUri="MainWindow.xaml">
</Application>
```

Here, you might agree, the mapping between the `Application`-derived C# class type and its XAML description is not as clear-cut as was the case for our `MainWindow`'s XAML definition. Specifically, there does not seem to be any trace of a `Main()` method. Given that any .NET executable must have a program entry point, you are correct to assume it is generated at compile time, based in part on the `StartupUrl` property. The assigned `*.xaml` file will be used to determine which `Window`-derived class to create when this application starts up.

Although the `Main()` method is automatically created at compile time, we are free to use the `<Code>` element to establish our `Exit` event handler if we so choose, as follows (notice this method is no longer static, as it will be translated into an instance-level member in the `MyApp` class):

```
<Application x:Class="SimpleXamlApp.MyApp"
  xmlns="http://schemas.microsoft.com/winfx/2006/xaml/presentation"
  xmlns:x="http://schemas.microsoft.com/winfx/2006/xaml"
  StartupUri="MainWindow.xaml" Exit ="AppExit">
  <x:Code>
  <![CDATA[
  private void AppExit(object sender, ExitEventArgs e)
  {
    MessageBox.Show("App has exited");
  }
  ]]>
  </x:Code>
</Application>
```

Processing the XAML Files via msbuild.exe

At this point, we are ready to transform our markup into a valid .NET assembly. When doing so, we cannot make direct use of the C# compiler and a response file. To date, the C# compiler does not have a direct understanding of XAML markup. However, the `msbuild.exe` command-line utility does understand how to transform XAML into C# code and compile this code on the fly when it is informed of the correct `*.targets` files.

`msbuild.exe` is a tool that allows you to define complex build scripts via (surprise, surprise) an XML grammar. One interesting aspect of these XML definitions is that they are the same format as Visual Studio `*.csproj` files. Given this, we are able to define a single file for automated command-line builds as well as a Visual Studio 2008 project. Consider the following minimalist build file, `SimpleXamlApp.csproj`:

```
<Project DefaultTargets="Build"
  xmlns="http://schemas.microsoft.com/developer/msbuild/2003">
  <PropertyGroup>
    <RootNamespace>SimpleXamlApp</RootNamespace>
    <AssemblyName>SimpleXamlApp</AssemblyName>
    <OutputType>winexe</OutputType>
  </PropertyGroup>
  <ItemGroup>
    <Reference Include="System" />
    <Reference Include="WindowsBase" />
    <Reference Include="PresentationCore" />
    <Reference Include="PresentationFramework" />
  </ItemGroup>
  <ItemGroup>
    <ApplicationDefinition Include="MyApp.xaml" />
    <Page Include="MainWindow.xaml" />
  </ItemGroup>
  <Import Project="$(MSBuildBinPath)\Microsoft.CSharp.targets" />
  <Import Project="$(MSBuildBinPath)\Microsoft.WinFX.targets" />
</Project>
```

Here, the `<PropertyGroup>` element is used to specify some basic aspects of the build, such as the root namespace, the name of the resulting assembly, and the output type (the equivalent of the `/target:winexe` option of `csc.exe`).

The first `<ItemGroup>` specifies the set of external assemblies to reference with the current build, which as you can see are the core WPF assemblies examined earlier in this chapter. The second `<ItemGroup>` is much more interesting. Notice that the `<ApplicationDefinition>` element's `Include` attribute is assigned to the `*.xaml` file that defines our application object. The `<Page>`'s `Include` element can be used to list each of the remaining `*.xaml` files that define the windows (and pages, which are often used when building XAML browser applications) processed by the application object.

However, the "magic" of this `*.csproj` file is the final `<Import>` subelements. Notice that our build script is referencing two `*.targets` files, each of which contains numerous other instructions used during the build process. The `Microsoft.WinFX.targets` file contains the necessary build settings to transform the XAML definitions into equivalent C# code files, while `Microsoft.CSharp.Targets` contains data to interact with the C# compiler itself.

■ **Note** A full examination of the `msbuild.exe` utility is beyond the scope of this text. If you'd like to learn more, perform a search for the topic "MSBuild" in the .NET Framework 3.5 SDK documentation.

At this point, we can pass our `SimpleXamlApp.csproj` file into `msbuild.exe` for processing:

```
msbuild SimpleXamlApp.csproj
```

Once the build has completed, you should be able to find your assembly within the generated \bin\Debug folder. At this point, you can launch your WPF application as expected. As you may agree, it is quite bizarre to generate valid .NET assemblies by authoring a few lines of markup. However, to be sure, if you open `SimpleXamlApp.exe` in `ildasm.exe`, you can see that (somehow) your XAML has been transmogrified into an executable application (see Figure 28-6).

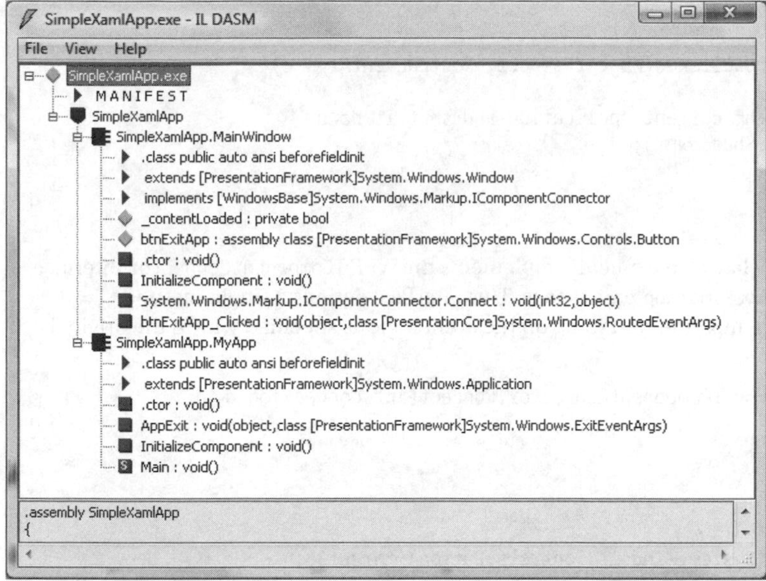

Figure 28-6. *Transforming markup into a .NET assembly? Interesting . . .*

Transforming Markup into a .NET Assembly

To understand exactly how our markup was transformed into a .NET assembly, we need to dig a bit deeper into the `msbuild.exe` process and examine a number of compiler-generated files, including a particular binary resource embedded within the assembly at compile time.

Mapping XAML to C# Code

As mentioned, the `*.targets` files specified in an MSBuild script define numerous instructions to translate XAML elements into C# code for compilation. When `msbuild.exe` processed our `*.csproj` file, it produced two files with the form `*.g.cs` (where g denotes auto*generated*), which were saved into the \obj\Debug directory. Based on the names of our `*.xaml` file names, the C# files in question are `MainWindow.g.cs` and `MyApp.g.cs`.

If you open the `MainWindow.g.cs` file, you will find your class extends the `Window` base class and contains the `btnExitApp_Clicked()` method as expected. Also, this class defines a member variable of type `System.Windows.Controls.Button`. Strangely enough, there does *not* appear to be any code that establishes the property settings for the `Button` or `Window` type (`Height`, `Width`, `Title`, etc.). This part of the mystery will become clear in just a moment.

Finally, note that this class defines a private member variable of type `bool` (named `_contentLoaded`), which was not directly accounted for in the XAML markup. Here is a partial definition of the generated `MainWindow` type:

```
public partial class MainWindow :
  System.Windows.Window, System.Windows.Markup.IComponentConnector
{
  internal System.Windows.Controls.Button btnExitApp;

  // This member variable will be explained soon enough.
```

```
  private bool _contentLoaded;

  private void btnExitApp_Clicked(object sender, RoutedEventArgs e)
  {
    // Get a handle to the current application and shut it down.
    Application.Current.Shutdown();
  }
...
}
```

This Windows-derived class also explicitly implements the WPF IComponentConnector interface defined in the System.Windows.Markup namespace. This interface defines a single method, Connect(), which has been implemented to rig up the event logic as specified within the original MainWindow.xaml file:

```
void System.Windows.Markup.IComponentConnector.Connect(int connectionId,
object target)
{
  switch (connectionId)
  {
  case 1:
    this.btnExitApp = ((System.Windows.Controls.Button)(target));
    this.btnExitApp.Click += new
      System.Windows.RoutedEventHandler(this.btnExitApp_Clicked);
    return;
  }
  this._contentLoaded = true;
}
```

Finally, the MainWindow class also implements a method named InitializeComponent(). This method ultimately resolves the location of an embedded resource within the assembly, given the name of the original *.xaml file. Once the resource is located, it is loaded into the current application object via a call to Application.LoadComponent(). Finally, the private bool member variable (mentioned previously) is set to true, to ensure the requested resource is loaded exactly once during the lifetime of this application:

```
public void InitializeComponent() {
  if (_contentLoaded) {
    return;
  }
  _contentLoaded = true;
  System.Uri resourceLocater = new
    System.Uri("/SimpleXamlApp;component/mainwindow.xaml",
    System.UriKind.RelativeOrAbsolute);
  System.Windows.Application.LoadComponent(this, resourceLocater);
}
```

At this point, the question becomes, *what exactly is this embedded resource?*

The Role of BAML

When msbuild.exe processed our *.csproj file, it generated a file with a *.baml file extension, which is named based on the initial MainWindow.xaml file. As you might have guessed from the name, Binary Application Markup Language (BAML) is a binary representation of XAML. This *.baml file is embedded as a resource (via a generated *.g.resources file) into the compiled assembly. Using BAML, WPF assemblies contain within them their complete XAML definition (in a much more compact format). You can verify this for yourself by opening your assembly using `reflector.exe`, as shown in Figure 28-7.

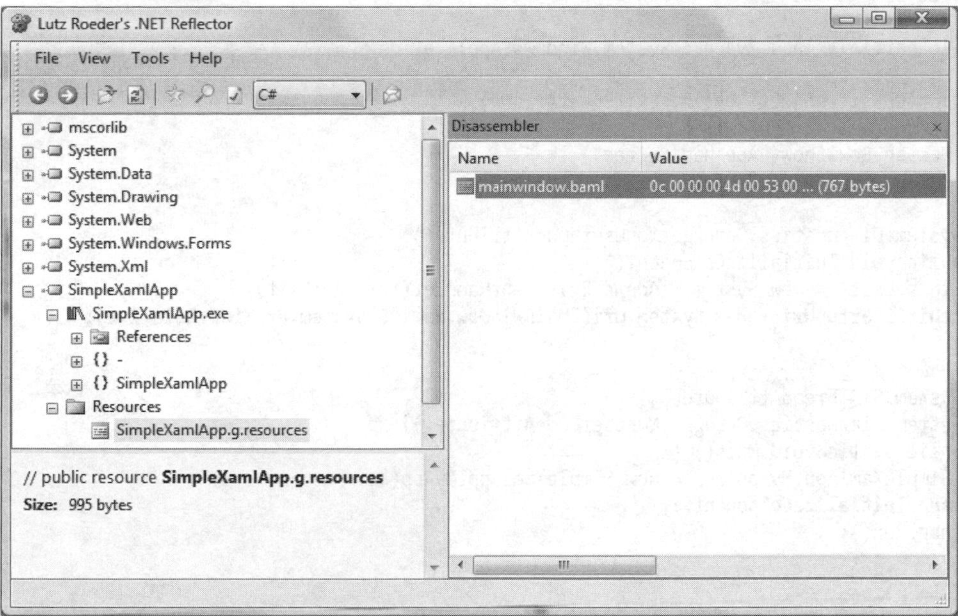

Figure 28-7. *Viewing the embedded* `*.baml` *resource via Lutz Roeder's .NET Reflector*

The call to `Application.LoadComponent()` reads the embedded BAML resource and populates the tree of defined objects with their correct state (again, such as the window's `Height` and `Width` properties). In fact, if you open the `*.baml` or `*.g.resources` file via Visual Studio, you can see traces of the initial XAML attributes. As an example, Figure 28-8 highlights the `StartupLocation.CenterScreen` property.

```
MainWindow.baml | UIElement Class | Window1.xaml | Window1.xaml.cs | Start Page | Object Browser
000001b0  00 00 00 03 00 00 00 14  36 01 78 2C 68 74 74 70  ........6.x,http
000001c0  3A 2F 2F 73 63 68 65 6D  61 73 2E 6D 69 63 72 6F  ://schemas.micro
000001d0  73 6F 66 74 2E 63 6F 6D  2F 77 69 6E 66 78 2F 32  soft.com/winfx/2
000001e0  30 30 36 2F 78 61 6D 6C  02 00 01 00 02 00 35 04  006/xaml......5.
000001f0  00 00 00 03 00 00 00 1F  0C 00 00 1D FD 00 05 54  ...............T
00000200  69 74 6C 65 24 11 00 00  0B 4D 79 20 58 61 6D 6C  itle$....My Xaml
00000210  20 41 70 70 99 FD 35 05  00 00 00 03 00 00 00 24   App..5........$
00000220  09 D1 FF 03 32 30 30 A4  FE 36 17 00 00 00 24 09  ....200..6....$.
00000230  C7 FF 03 33 30 30 A4 FE  36 24 00 00 00 1F 1C 01  ...300..6$......
00000240  00 1D FD 00 15 57 69 6E  64 6F 77 53 74 61 72 74  .....WindowStart
00000250  75 70 4C 6F 63 61 74 69  6F 6E 24 12 01 00 0C 43  upLocation$....C
00000260  65 6E 74 65 72 53 63 72  65 65 6E 3D FF 35 06 00  enterScreen=.5..
00000270  00 00 03 00 00 00 2E F2  FF 35 09 00 00 00 04 00  .........5......
00000280  00 00 03 C9 FF 00 2D 01  00 00 00 35 00 00 00 00  ......-....5....
00000290  00 00 00 00 24 10 CA FF  0A 62 74 6E 45 78 69 74  ....$....btnExit
000002a0  41 70 70 99 FD 35 09 00  00 00 23 00 00 00 24 09  App..5....#...$.
000002b0  C7 FF 03 31 33 33 A4 FE  36 0B 00 00 00 24 08 D1  ...133..6....$..
000002c0  FF 02 32 34 A4 FE 36 17  00 00 00 2E F2 FF 36 51  ..24..6.......6Q
000002d0  00 00 00 10 12 10 45 78  69 74 20 41 70 70 6C 69  ......Exit Appli
```

Figure 28-8. *Behold the BAML!*

The final piece of the autogenerated code puzzle occurs in the `MyApp.g.cs` file. Here we see our `Application`-derived class with a proper `Main()` entry point method. The implementation of this method calls `InitializeComponent()` on the `Application`-derived type, which in turn sets the

StartupUri property, allowing each of the objects to establish its correct property settings based on the binary XAML definition.

```
namespace SimpleXamlApp
{
  public partial class MyApp : System.Windows.Application
  {
    void AppExit(object sender, ExitEventArgs e)
    {
      MessageBox.Show("App has exited");
    }

    [System.Diagnostics.DebuggerNonUserCodeAttribute()]
    public void InitializeComponent() {
      this.Exit += new System.Windows.ExitEventHandler(this.AppExit);
      this.StartupUri = new System.Uri("MainWindow.xaml", System.UriKind.Relative);
    }

    [System.STAThreadAttribute()]
    [System.Diagnostics.DebuggerNonUserCodeAttribute()]
    public static void Main() {
      SimpleXamlApp.MyApp app = new SimpleXamlApp.MyApp();
      app.InitializeComponent();
      app.Run();
    }
  }
}
```

XAML-to-Assembly Process Summary

Whew! So, at this point we have created a full-blown .NET assembly using nothing but three XML documents (one of which was used by the msbuild.exe utility). As you have seen, msbuild.exe leverages auxiliary settings defined within the *.targets file to process the XAML files (and generate the *.baml) for the build process. While these gory details happen behind the scenes, Figure 28-9 illustrates the overall picture regarding the compile-time processing of *.xaml files.

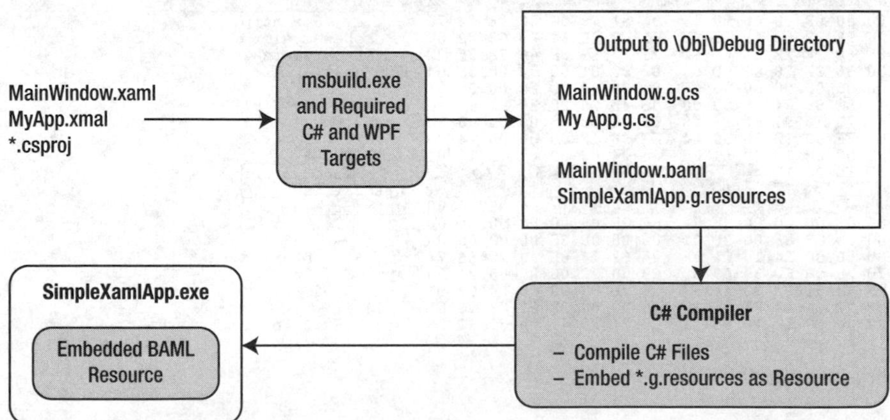

Figure 28-9. *The XAML-to-assembly compile-time process*

It is also important to point out that once the compiler has processed all of your *.xaml files in order to build the related C# code and binary resource, they are technically no longer required (and would never need to be shipped along with your executable). However, as shown at the end of this chapter, it is possible to dynamically create a Window object by reading a *.xaml file programmatically. In this case, the physical *.xaml file would indeed need to be shipped with the application itself.

Source Code The SimpleXamlApp project can be found under the Chapter 28 subdirectory.

Separation of Concerns Using Code-Behind Files

Before we truly begin digging into the details of XAML, we have one final aspect of the basic programming model to address: the separation of concerns. Recall that one of the major motivations for WPF was to separate UI content from programming logic, which our current examples have not done.

Rather than directly embedding our event handlers (and other custom methods) within the scope of the XAML <Code> element, it is preferable to define a separate C# file to define the implementation logic, leaving the *.xaml files to contain nothing but UI markup content. Assume the following code-behind file, MainWindow.xaml.cs (by convention, the name of a C# code-behind file takes the form *.xaml.cs):

```
// MainWindow.xaml.cs
using System;
using System.Windows;
using System.Windows.Controls;

namespace SimpleXamlApp
{
  public partial class MainWindow : Window
  {
    public MainWindow()
    {
      // Remember!  This method is defined
      // within the generated MainWindow.g.cs file.
      InitializeComponent();
    }

    private void btnExitApp_Clicked(object sender, RoutedEventArgs e)
    {
      // Get a handle to the current application and shut it down.
      Application.Current.Shutdown();
    }
  }
}
```

Here, we have defined a partial class (to contain the event handling logic) that will be merged with the partial class definition of the same type in the *.g.cs file. Given that InitializeComponent() is defined within the MainWindow.g.cs file, our window's constructor makes a call in order to load and process the embedded BAML resource.

If desired, we could also build a code-behind file for our Application-derived type. Because most of the action takes place in the MyApp.g.cs file, the code within MyApp.xaml.cs is little more than the following:

```
// MyApp.xaml.cs
using System;
using System.Windows;
using System.Windows.Controls;

namespace SimpleXamlApp
{
  public partial class MyApp : Application
  {
    private void AppExit(object sender, ExitEventArgs e)
    {
      MessageBox.Show("App has exited");
    }
  }
}
```

Before we recompile our files using msbuild.exe, we need to update our *.csproj file to account for the new C# files to include in the compilation process, via the <Compile> elements (shown in bold):

```
<Project DefaultTargets="Build" xmlns=
  "http://schemas.microsoft.com/developer/msbuild/2003">
  <PropertyGroup>
    <RootNamespace>SimpleXamlApp</RootNamespace>
    <AssemblyName>SimpleXamlApp</AssemblyName>
    <OutputType>winexe</OutputType>
  </PropertyGroup>
  <ItemGroup>
    <Reference Include="System" />
    <Reference Include="WindowsBase" />
    <Reference Include="PresentationCore" />
    <Reference Include="PresentationFramework" />
  </ItemGroup>
  <ItemGroup>
    <ApplicationDefinition Include="MyApp.xaml" />
      <Compile Include = "MainWindow.xaml.cs" />
      <Compile Include = "MyApp.xaml.cs" />
      <Page Include="MainWindow.xaml" />
  </ItemGroup>
  <Import Project="$(MSBuildBinPath)\Microsoft.CSharp.targets" />
  <Import Project="$(MSBuildBinPath)\Microsoft.WinFX.targets" />
</Project>
```

Once we pass our build script into msbuild.exe, we find once again the same executable assembly. However, as far as development is concerned, we now have a clean partition of presentation (XAML) from programming logic (C#). Given that this is the preferred method for WPF development, you'll be happy to know that WPF applications created using Visual Studio 2008 always make use of the code-behind model just presented.

Source Code The CodeBehindXamlApp project can be found under the Chapter 28 subdirectory.

The Syntax of XAML

As mentioned earlier in this chapter, the chances of you needing to manually author reams of XAML markup in your WPF applications will be slim to none, as this task will be done on your behalf using dedicated tools (Visual Studio 2008, Microsoft Expression Blend, etc.). Nevertheless, the more you understand about the syntax of a well-formed `*.xaml` file, the better equipped you will be to tweak and modify autogenerated markup, and the deeper your understanding of WPF itself. This being said, let's dig into the core syntax of XAML (subsequent chapters will provide additional XAML syntax examples where required).

Experimenting with XAML Using XamlPad

When you are investigating XAML, you will certainly want to author content and quickly see the end result. To facilitate such exploration, the Microsoft Windows SDK ships with a utility named `xamlpad.exe`.

Note Strangely enough, neither the .NET Framework 3.5 SDK nor Visual Studio 2008 ship with `xamlpad.exe`. While you could download the Windows SDK to obtain this tool, the final example program in this chapter will have you create a slimmed-down version of `xamlpad.exe` using C#.

If you have downloaded the Windows SDK to obtain a copy of `xamlpad.exe`, you can launch this tool via the Start ➤ All Programs ➤ Microsoft Windows SDK ➤ Tools menu option. Figure 28-10 shows the initial launch of `xamlpad.exe`, with the Visual Tree Explorer option activated (via the related toolbar button).

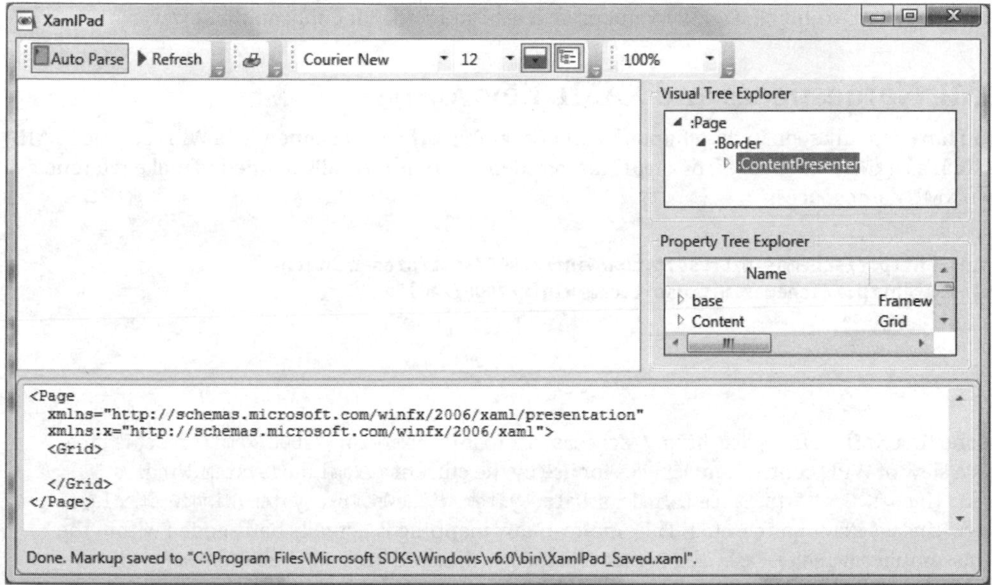

Figure 28-10. *XamlPad provides real-time display of XAML markup.*

Using XamlPad, you are able to author XAML markup in the pane mounted at the bottom of the window and view the output above. When you first start this tool, you will find little more than an empty <Page> declaration, which is used to contain markup for an XBAP application:

```
<Page
  xmlns="http://schemas.microsoft.com/winfx/2006/xaml/presentation"
  xmlns:x="http://schemas.microsoft.com/winfx/2006/xaml">
  <Grid>
    <!-- Add your XAML here! -->
  </Grid>
</Page>
```

Although XamlPad does not allow you to view markup for a <Window> element directly within the XamlPad view window, you are free to change <Page> to <Window> and press the F5 key to launch a stand-alone window to display your content. Furthermore, be aware that the markup you enter in a <Page> or <Window> element is identical.

■ **Note** XamlPad does not allow you author any markup that entails code compilation. This includes defining a Class attribute (for specifying a code file), using <Code> elements, or using any XMAL keywords that also entail code compilation (such as FieldModifier or ClassModifier). Any attempt to do so will result in a markup error.

As you are authoring markup with XamlPad, you will notice a lack of IntelliSense. However, clicking the Show Visual Tree button opens a UI that mimics the Visual Studio Properties window to help you visualize the structure of your XAML markup. Sadly, the Visual Tree window cannot (currently) be used to change the XAML itself; it is a read-only view of the XAML markup.

Also be aware that XamlPad currently has no way in which you can save individual *.xaml files; markup is automatically saved to XamlPad_Saved.xaml and will be displayed the next time you load the tool (feel free to copy the markup and paste it into your current application, however).

XAML Namespaces and XAML Keywords

As you have already seen in this chapter's earlier examples, the root element of a WPF-centric XAML file (such as a <Window>, <Page>, or <Application> definition) is typically defined to make reference to two XML namespaces:

```
<Page
  xmlns="http://schemas.microsoft.com/winfx/2006/xaml/presentation"
  xmlns:x="http://schemas.microsoft.com/winfx/2006/xaml">
  <Grid>

  </Grid>
</Page>
```

The first XML namespace, http://schemas.microsoft.com/winfx/2006/xaml/presentation, maps a slew of WPF-centric namespaces for use by the current *.xaml file (System.Windows, System.Windows.Controls, System.Windows.Data, System.Windows.Ink, System.Windows.Media, System.Windows.Navigation, etc.). This one-to-many mapping is actually hard-coded within the WPF assemblies (WindowsBase.dll, PresentationCore.dll, and PresentationFramework.dll) using the assembly-level [XmlnsDefinition] attribute. If you load these WPF assemblies into reflector.exe, you can view these mappings firsthand (see Figure 28-11).

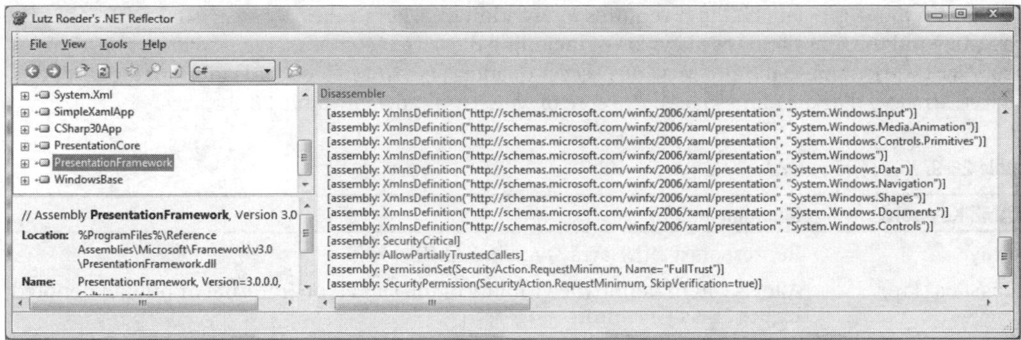

Figure 28-11. *The* `http://schemas.microsoft.com/winfx/2006/xaml/presentation` *namespace maps to the core WPF namespaces.*

The second XML namespace, `http://schemas.microsoft.com/winfx/2006/xaml`, is used to include XAML-specific keywords as well as a subset of types within the `System.Windows.Markup` namespace. A well-formed XML document must define a root element that designates a single XML namespace as the primary namespace, which typically is the namespace that contains the most commonly used items. If a root element requires the inclusion of additional secondary namespaces (as seen here), they must be defined using a unique prefix (to resolve any possible name clashes). As a convention, the prefix is simply `x`; however, this can be any unique token you require, such as `XamlSpecificStuff`:

```
<Page
  xmlns="http://schemas.microsoft.com/winfx/2006/xaml/presentation"
  xmlns:XamlSpecificStuff="http://schemas.microsoft.com/winfx/2006/xaml">
  <Grid>

  </Grid>
</Page>
```

The obvious downside of defining wordy XML namespace prefixes is you would be required to type `XamlSpecificStuff` each time your XAML file needs to refer to one of the types defined in the namespace in question. For example, one of the items within `http://schemas.microsoft.com/winfx/2006/xaml` is the XAML keyword `Code`, which as you have seen allows you to embed C# code within an XAML document. Another XAML keyword is `Class`, which allows you to define the name of the generated C# class type.

If we were to change the definition of the MyApp XAML definition created earlier in this chapter to make use of this more verbose XML namespace prefix, we would now be required to author the following:

```
<Application XamlSpecificStuff:Class="SimpleXamlApp.MyApp"
  xmlns="http://schemas.microsoft.com/winfx/2006/xaml/presentation"
  xmlns:XamlSpecificStuff ="http://schemas.microsoft.com/winfx/2006/xaml"
  StartupUri="MainWindow.xaml" Exit ="AppExit">
  < XamlSpecificStuff:Code>
  <![CDATA[
  private void AppExit(object sender, ExitEventArgs e)
  {
    MessageBox.Show("App has exited");
  }
  ]]>
  </XamlSpecificStuff:Code>
</Application>
```

Given that XamlSpecificStuff requires many additional keystrokes, let's just stick with x. In any case, beyond the Class and Code keywords, including the http://schemas.microsoft.com/winfx/2006/xaml XML namespace also provides access to additional XAML keywords (and members of the System.Windows.Markup namespace), the core of which are shown in Table 28-9.

Table 28-9. *XAML Keywords*

XAML Keyword	Meaning in Life
Array	Represents a .NET array type in XAML.
ClassModifier	Allows you to define the visibility of the class type (internal or public) denoted by the Class keyword.
DynamicResource	Allows you to make reference to a WPF resource that should be monitored for changes.
FieldModifier	Allows you to define the visibility of a type member (internal, public, private, or protected) for any named subelement of the root (e.g., a <Button> within a <Window> element). A "named element" is defined using the Name XAML keyword.
Key	Allows you to establish a key value for an XAML item that will be placed into a dictionary element.
Name	Allows you to specify the generated C# name of a given XAML element.
Null	Represents a null reference.
Static	Allows you to make reference to a static member of a type.
StaticResource	Allows you to make reference to a WPF resource that should not be monitored for changes.
Type	The XAML equivalent of the C# typeof operator (it will yield a System.Type based on the supplied name).
TypeArguments	Allows you to establish an element as a generic type with a specific type parameter (e.g., List<int> vs. List<bool>).

You will see many of these keywords in action where required; however, by way of a simple example, consider the following XAML <Window> definition that makes use of the ClassModifier and FieldModifier keywords, as well as Name and Class (remember that xamlpad.exe will not allow you to make use of any XAML keyword that entails code compilation, such as Code, FieldModifier, or ClassModifier):

```
<!-- This class will now be internal.
     If using a code file, the partial class must
     also be defined as internal! -->
<Window x:Class="MyWPFApp.MainWindow" x:ClassModifier ="internal"
    xmlns="http://schemas.microsoft.com/winfx/2006/xaml/presentation"
    xmlns:x="http://schemas.microsoft.com/winfx/2006/xaml">

  <!-- This button will be public in the *.g.cs file -->
  <Button x:Name ="myButton" x:FieldModifier ="public">
    OK
  </Button>
</Window>
```

By default, all C#/XAML type definitions are public, while members default to internal. However, based on our XAML definition, the resulting autogenerated file contains an internal class type with a public Button type:

```
internal partial class MainWindow : System.Windows.Window,
  System.Windows.Markup.IComponentConnector
{
  public System.Windows.Controls.Button myButton;
  ...
}
```

XAML Elements and XAML Attributes

Once you have established your root element and any required XML namespaces, your next task is to populate the root with a *child element*. As mentioned, in a real-world WPF application, the child will be one of the panel types, which contains in turn any number of additional UI elements that describe the user interface. The next chapter examines these panel types in detail, so for the time being assume that our `<Window>` type will contain a single `Button` element.

As you have already seen over the course of this chapter, XAML elements map to a class or structure type within a given .NET namespace, while the attributes within the opening element tag map to properties or events of the type (you cannot reference the methods of a type via an XAML attribute). Thus, when you author code such as the following:

```
<Window x:Class="MyWPFApp.MainWindow" x:ClassModifier ="internal"
  xmlns="http://schemas.microsoft.com/winfx/2006/xaml/presentation"
  xmlns:x="http://schemas.microsoft.com/winfx/2006/xaml">

  <!-- This assumes you have a method named myButton_Click in
       your code file! -->
  <Button x:Name ="myButton" x:FieldModifier ="public"
          Height ="50" Width ="100" Click ="myButton_Click">
    OK
  </Button>
</Window>
```

you have effectively authored a `Button` that could be expressed in code as so:

```
Button myButton = new Button();
myButton.Height = 50;
myButton.Width = 100;
myButton.Content = "OK";
myButton.Click += new RoutedEventHandler(myButton_Click);
```

Given your work thus far in the chapter, this mapping may seem straightforward; however, consider the assignment of the button's content. Recall that many WPF controls derive from `ContentControl`. By doing so, they are able to contain any number of internal items (such as a `Button` with a `ScrollBar`). Here, the `Content` property was implicitly set due to the fact that we placed the text `"OK"` within the opening and closing element. If we wish, we could explicitly set the `Content` property as follows:

```
<Button x:Name ="myButton"
  Height ="50" Width ="100" Content = "OK">
</Button>
```

At this point, the act of setting the `Content` property implicitly or explicitly may seem to be nothing more than a personal preference. The story becomes more interesting when you consider how you would use XAML to assign a `Button`'s content to be an object other than a simple string (a graphical rendering, a `ScrollBar` or `TextBox`, etc.). As mentioned earlier in this chapter, the solution is to use property-element syntax.

Understanding XAML Property-Element Syntax

Property-element syntax allows you to assign complex objects to a property. Here is an XAML description for the "scrollbar in a button" scenario that sets the Content property using property-element syntax:

```
<Button x:Name ="myButton" Height ="100" Width ="100">
  <Button.Content>
    <ScrollBar Height = "50" Width = "20"/>
  </Button.Content>
</Button>
```

Notice that in this case, we have made use of a nested element named <Button.Content> to define the ScrollBar type. Property-element syntax always breaks down to the pattern <TypeName.PropertyName>; obviously the type in this case is <Button> while the property is Content. Figure 28-12 shows the output as seen in xamlpad.exe.

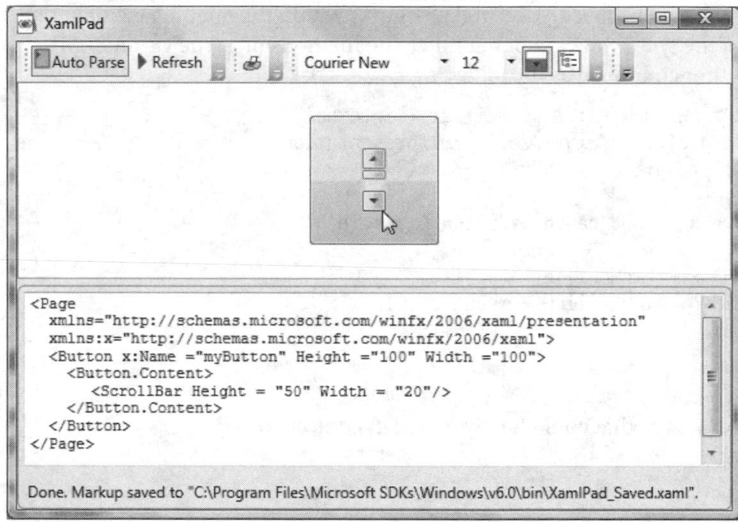

Figure 28-12. *Property-element syntax allows you to assign complex objects to properties.*

Also recall that the child element of a ContentControl-derived type will automatically be used to set the Content property, therefore the following definition is also legal:

```
<Button x:Name ="myButton" Height ="100" Width ="100">
  <ScrollBar Height = "50" Width = "20"/>
</Button>
```

Property-element syntax is not limited to setting the Content property. Rather, this XAML syntax can be used whenever you need to set a complex object to a type property. Consider, for example, the Background property of the Button type. This property can be set on any Brush type found within the WPF APIs. If you need a solid color brush type, the following markup is all that is required, as the string value assigned to properties requiring a Brush-derived type (such as Background) is converted into a brush type automatically:

```
<!-- Here, "Green" maps to Brushes.Green -->
<Button x:Name ="myButton" Height ="100" Width ="100" Background ="Green">
  <Button.Content>
```

```
    <ScrollBar Height = "50" Width = "20"/>
  </Button.Content>
</Button>
```

However, if you need a more elaborate brush (such as a LinearGradientBrush), name/value syntax will not suffice. Considering that LinearGradientBrush is a full-blown class type, we must make use of property-element syntax to pass in startup values to the type:

```
<Button x:Name ="myButton" Height ="100" Width ="100">
  <Button.Content>
    <ScrollBar Height = "50" Width = "20"/>
  </Button.Content>
  <Button.Background>
    <LinearGradientBrush StartPoint="0,0" EndPoint="1,1">
      <GradientStop Color="Blue" Offset="0" />
      <GradientStop Color="Yellow" Offset="0.25" />
      <GradientStop Color="Green" Offset="0.75" />
      <GradientStop Color ="Red" Offset="0.50" />
    </LinearGradientBrush>
  </Button.Background>
</Button>
```

Don't concern yourself with the configuration of the LinearGradientBrush type for the time being (Chapter 30 addresses WPF's graphical rendering services). Simply notice that we have used property-element syntax to establish the Content and Background property of the Button type. Figure 28-13 shows the rendering of this rather fancy button.

Figure 28-13. *A very fancy button type*

While property-element syntax is most often used to assign complex objects (such as LinearGradientBrush) to property values, it is permissible to make use of simple string values as well:

```
<Button x:Name ="myButton" Height ="100" Width ="100">
  <Button.Content>
    <ScrollBar Height = "50" Width = "20"/>
  </Button.Content>
  <Button.Background>
    Pink
  </Button.Background>
</Button>
```

In this case, you have really gained nothing. Rather, you have just complicated the process, as you could simply have typed the following:

```
<Button x:Name ="myButton" Height ="100" Width ="100" Background = "Pink">
  <Button.Content>
    <ScrollBar Height = "50" Width = "20"/>
  </Button.Content>
</Button>
```

Understanding XAML Attached Properties

In addition to property-element syntax, XAML defines syntax used to define an *attached property*. While attached properties have many uses, one purpose of an attached property is to allow different child elements to specify unique values for a property that is actually defined in a parent element. The most common use of attached property syntax is to position UI elements within one of the WPF panel types (Grid, DockPanel, etc.). The next chapter dives into these panels in some detail. For the time being, here is an example of attached-property syntax:

```
<Page
  xmlns="http://schemas.microsoft.com/winfx/2006/xaml/presentation"
  xmlns:x="http://schemas.microsoft.com/w1nfx/2006/xaml">
  <DockPanel LastChildFill ="True">
    <!-- Dock items to the panel using attached properties -->
    <Label DockPanel.Dock ="Top" Name="lblInstruction"
           FontSize="15">Enter Car Information</Label>
    <Label DockPanel.Dock ="Left" Name="lblMake">Make</Label>
    <Label DockPanel.Dock ="Right" Name="lblColor">Color</Label>
    <Label DockPanel.Dock ="Bottom" Name="lblPetName">Pet Name</Label>
    <Button Name="btnOK">OK</Button>
  </DockPanel>
</Page>
```

Here, we have defined a DockPanel type that contains four Label types docked within the container. Notice the format of this particular attached property syntax is <ParentType.ParentProperty> (e.g., DockPanel.Dock). Note that the Button type does not specify a docking area; however, it will take over the remaining area in the DockPanel, giving the assignment of the LastChildFill property in the opening <DockPanel> definition.

There are a few items to be aware of regarding attached properties. First and foremost, this is not an all-purpose syntax that can be applied to *any* element of *any* parent. For example, the following XAML cannot be parsed without error:

```
<!-- Set Height property on Button via attached property? -->
<Button x:Name ="myButton" Width ="100">
  <Button.Content>
    <ScrollBar Button.Height = "100" Height = "50" Width = "20"/>
  </Button.Content>
  <Button.Background>
    Pink
  </Button.Background>
</Button>
```

In reality, attached properties are a specialized form of a WPF-specific concept termed a *dependency property*. In a nutshell, dependency properties allow the value of a field to be computed based on multiple inputs. Dependency properties, and therefore attached properties, need to "register" which properties can be set by which objects (which has not been done for the ScrollBar/Button scenario just shown).

WPF uses the dependency property mechanism under the hood for several technologies such as data binding, styles and themes, and animation services. As well, a dependency property can be implemented to provide self-contained validation, default values, and a callback mechanism, and it provides a way to establish property values based on runtime information.

The odd thing about dependency properties is the fact that *setting* a dependency property value looks no different from setting a "normal" .NET property. Therefore, in most cases, you will be blissfully unaware that you have set a dependency property value.

However, the manner in which dependency properties are implemented behind the scenes is quite different indeed. For the vast majority of your WPF applications, you will *not* need to author custom dependency properties. The only time this may become a common task is when you are in the position of building custom WFP controls, which again is not a common activity in the first place given the advent of XAML. You will explore dependency properties in a bit more detail in Chapter 29.

Understanding XAML Type Converters

For all practical purposes, when you are assigning values to attributes (e.g., `Background = "Pink"`) or implicitly setting content within the scope of an opening and closing element (e.g., `<Button>OK</Button>`), you can simply assume the values to be string data. However, if you think this through, it clearly could not be the case. Consider, for example, the definition of the `Background` property of the `Button` type (which we inherited from the `Control` base class):

```
// The System.Windows.Controls.Control.Background property.
public Brush Background
{
  ...
}
```

As you can see, this property is wrapping a `Brush` type, not a `System.String`! This begs the question, what is transforming `"Pink"` into (in this case) a `SolidColorBrush` object with RGB values that equal the color pink? Here's another example. Consider the following XAML definition of a purple ellipse of a given size:

```
<Ellipse Fill = "Purple" Width = "100.5" Height = "87.4">
</Ellipse>
```

If you were to look at the definition of the `Width` and `Height` properties of the `Ellipse` type, you would find they are prototyped to operate on `doubles`, not `strings`.

Behind the scenes, XAML parsers make use of various *type converters* to transform this string data into the correct underlying object. For example, the value `"Pink"`, when assigned to a property prototyped to operate on brush types, makes use of the `ColorConverter` and `BrushConverter` types. Numerous other converters exist as well: `SizeConverter` (used to set the `Width` and `Height` properties of the previous `Ellipse`), `RectConverter`, `VectorConverter`, and so on.

Regardless of their names, all type converters derive from the `System.ComponentModel.TypeConverter` base class. This type defines a number of virtual methods such as `CanConvertTo()`, `ConvertTo()`, `CanConvertFrom()`, and `ConvertFrom()`, which can be overridden by a derived type to account for the underlying translation.

For the most part, you do not need to know *which* type converter is mapping your XAML string data to the correct underlying object. At the very least, simply understand that they are used transparently in the background to simplify XAML definitions.

■ Note Although XAML itself is a relativity new technology, the concept of type converters has existed since the release of the .NET platform. Windows Forms and GDI+ make use of various converters behind the scenes. For example, the GDI+ `System.Drawing` namespace defines a type converter named `FontConverter`, which can map the string `"Wingdings"` into a `Font` object using the Wingdings font face.

Understanding XAML Markup Extensions

Type converters are interesting constructs in that there is no physical evidence that you are interacting with them at the level of XAML. Rather, type converters are used internally behind the scenes when an `*.xaml` file is processed. In contrast, XAML also supports *markup extensions.* Like a type converter, markup extensions allow you to transform a simple markup value into a runtime object. The difference, however, is that markup extensions have a very specific XAML syntax.

Given that type converters and markup extensions appear to serve an identical purpose, you might wonder why we have two approaches to generate type definitions. Simply put, markup extensions allow for a greater level of flexibility than type converters and provide a way to cleanly extend the grammar of XAML with new functionality.

Using markup extensions, you could assign the value of a property to the return value of a static property on another type, declare an array of data via markup, or obtain type information. In fact, a subset of XAML keywords (such as `Array`, `Null`, `Static`, and `Type`) are markup extensions in disguise. Like type converters, a markup extension is represented internally as a class that derives from `MarkupExtension` (as a naming convention, all types that subclass `MarkupExtension` take an `Extension` suffix).

To see a markup extension in action, assume you wish to set the `Content` property for a set of `Labels` to display information regarding the machine your application is executing on using static members of `System.Environment`. Here is the complete markup, with a discussion to follow:

```
<Page
  xmlns="http://schemas.microsoft.com/winfx/2006/xaml/presentation"
  xmlns:x="http://schemas.microsoft.com/winfx/2006/xaml"
  xmlns:CorLib="clr-namespace:System;assembly=mscorlib">

  <StackPanel>
    <Label Content ="{x:Static CorLib:Environment.MachineName}"/>
    <Label Content ="{x:Static CorLib:Environment.OSVersion}"/>
    <Label Content ="{x:Static CorLib:Environment.ProcessorCount}"/>
  </StackPanel>
</Page>
```

First of all, notice that the `<Page>` definition has a new XML namespace declaration, which we have given the namespace prefix of `CorLib` (the name of this prefix, like any XML namespace prefix, is arbitrary). The value assigned to this XML namespace is unique, however, as we are making use of a registered token named `clr-namespace` (which allows us to point to a .NET namespace that contains the type definition) and another token named `assembly` (which represents the friendly name of the assembly containing the namespace).

With this XML namespace established, notice how each of the `Label` types can invoke a static member of the `Environment` type via the `Static` markup extension. As you can see, markup extensions are always sandwiched between curly brackets. In its simplest form, the markup extension takes two values: the name of the markup extension (`Static` in this case) followed by the value to assign it (such as `CorLib:System.Environment.OSVersion`).

```
<!-- Using the 'Static' markup extension to set the Content property to
     the value of a static property. -->
<Label Content ="{x:Static CorLib:Environment.OSVersion}"/>
```

Here is another example. Assume you wish to obtain the fully qualified name of various types to assign the `Content` property to another set of `Label` types. In this case, you can make use of the baked-in `Type` markup extension:

```
<Page
  xmlns="http://schemas.microsoft.com/winfx/2006/xaml/presentation"
  xmlns:x="http://schemas.microsoft.com/winfx/2006/xaml"
  xmlns:CorLib="clr-namespace:System;assembly=mscorlib">
```

```
  <StackPanel>
    <Label Content ="{x:Static CorLib:Environment.MachineName}"/>
    <Label Content ="{x:Static CorLib:Environment.OSVersion}"/>
    <Label Content ="{x:Static CorLib:Environment.ProcessorCount}"/>

    <Label Content ="{x:Type Label}" />
    <Label Content ="{x:Type Page}" />
    <Label Content ="{x:Type CorLib:Boolean}" />
    <Label Content ="{x:Type x:TypeExtension}" />
  </StackPanel>
</Page>
```

Here you are obtaining the fully qualified names of the WPF `Label` type, the `Button` type, as well as the `Boolean` data type within `mscorlib.dll` and, just for good measure, the fully qualified name of the `Type` markup extension itself. If you were to view this page within `xamlpad.exe`, you would find something like Figure 28-14.

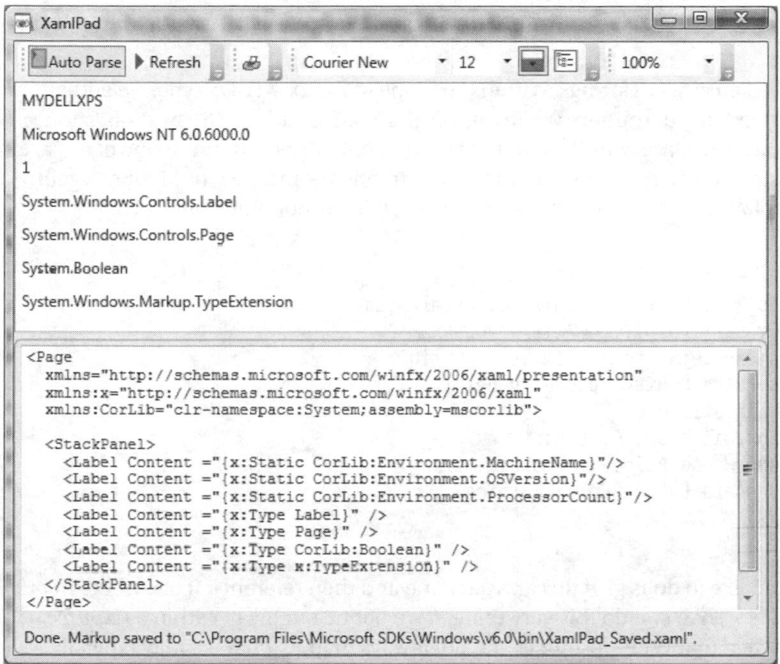

Figure 28-14. *Using markup extensions to set properties to values of static members and obtain type information*

A Preview of Resources and Data Binding

To wrap up our introductory look at the syntax of XAML, this final example will not only illustrate using the `Array` markup extension (represented by the `ArrayExtension` class type), but also show some simple declarative data binding and preview the concept of WPF resources. The `Array` markup extension allows you to assign an array of data to a given property. When using XAML to define such an array, we do so by making use of the `Type` markup extension to establish what kind of array we are creating (array of strings, array of bitmaps, etc.). Consider the following `<Page>` definition:

```
<Page
  xmlns="http://schemas.microsoft.com/winfx/2006/xaml/presentation"
  xmlns:x="http://schemas.microsoft.com/winfx/2006/xaml"
  xmlns:CorLib="clr-namespace:System;assembly=mscorlib">

  <StackPanel>
    <Label Content ="{x:Array Type = CorLib:String}"/>
  </StackPanel>
</Page>
```

If you view the rendered markup using xamlpad.exe, you will see the value System.String[] print out in the view pane. Using the expected curly bracket syntax, we have no way to populate the array with data. To do so, we must create our array using subelements that match the specified type of the array. Consider the following partial XAML definition:

```
<x:Array Type="CorLib:String">
  <CorLib:String>Sun Kil Moon</CorLib:String>
  <CorLib:String>Red House Painters</CorLib:String>
  <CorLib:String>Besnard Lakes</CorLib:String>
</x:Array>
```

Here, we have created an array of strings. Within the scope of the <x:Array> type, we add in three textual values and close the definition. While this is valid XAML markup, the next question is, where we can place our array declaration? If we were to place it directly within the scope of a <Page> element, we have just set the Content property of the <Page> implicitly and we would (once again) see System.String[] display in the view port of xamlpad.exe (which is not quite what we are aiming for).

```
<Page
  xmlns="http://schemas.microsoft.com/winfx/2006/xaml/presentation"
  xmlns:x="http://schemas.microsoft.com/winfx/2006/xaml"
  xmlns:CorLib="clr-namespace:System;assembly=mscorlib">
  <!-- Humm, we just set the Content property here! -->
    <x:Array Type="CorLib:String">
      <CorLib:String>Sun Kil Moon</CorLib:String>
      <CorLib:String>Red House Painters</CorLib:String>
      <CorLib:String>Besnard Lakes</CorLib:String>
    </x:Array>
</Page>
```

What we really would like to do is give this array a name and then reference it elsewhere in our markup (e.g., to fill a ListBox). We can do this very thing, *if* we define our array within a *resource element.* Now, let me be clear that WPF "resources" do not always map to what we may typically think (string tables, icons, bitmaps, etc.). While they certainly could, WPF resources can be used to represent any custom blob of markup, such as our array of strings (more information on WPF resources can be found in Chapter 30).

Consider the final <Page> definition that adds a string array resource named "GoodMusic" to a <StackPanel> via the Key markup extension. Once we have done so, we then set the ItemsSource property of the ListBox type to our array using the StaticResource markup extension (notice we are referencing the same key at this time):

```
<Page
  xmlns="http://schemas.microsoft.com/winfx/2006/xaml/presentation"
  xmlns:x="http://schemas.microsoft.com/winfx/2006/xaml"
  xmlns:CorLib="clr-namespace:System;assembly=mscorlib">

  <StackPanel>
    <StackPanel.Resources>
```

```
    <x:Array Type="CorLib:String" x:Key = "GoodMusic">
      <CorLib:String>Sun Kil Moon</CorLib:String>
      <CorLib:String>Red House Painters</CorLib:String>
      <CorLib:String>Besnard Lakes</CorLib:String>
    </x:Array>
  </StackPanel.Resources>

  <Label Content ="Really good music"/>
  <ListBox Width = "200" ItemsSource ="{StaticResource GoodMusic}"/>
 </StackPanel>
</Page>
```

As you can see, we are nesting within the scope of the `<StackPanel>` a nested `<StackPanel.Resources>` element as the home for our array of strings. The `StaticResource` markup extensions represent any resource that is not expected to change after the initial binding (hence the notion of "static"). If you are working with a resource that may change after the first bind (such as a given system color), you can use the alternative markup extension, `DynamicResource`. In any case, Figure 28-15 shows how `xamlpad.exe` looks now.

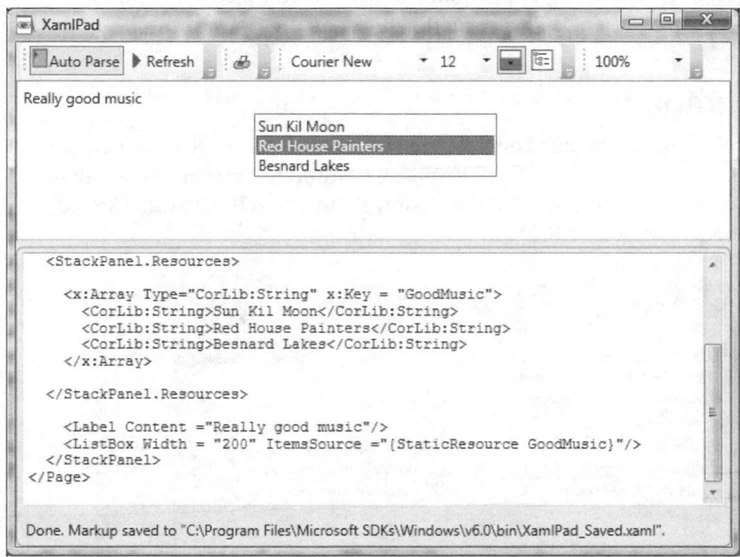

Figure 28-15. *Markup extensions, static resources, and simple data binding*

■ **Note** The reason that the `Key` and `StaticResource` markup extensions have not been qualified with an `x` prefix (unlike the other markup extensions examined here) is because they are defined within the root `http://schemas.microsoft.com/winfx/2006/xaml/presentation` XML namespace (as they are WPF-centric).

So! At this point you have seen numerous examples that showcase each of the core aspects of XAML syntax. As you might agree, XAML is very interesting in that it allows us to describe a tree of .NET objects in a declarative manner. While this is extremely helpful when configuring graphical user interfaces, do remember that XAML can describe *any* type from *any* assembly provided it is a nonabstract type containing a default constructor.

■ **Note** XAML can also be processed at runtime. You'll see an example of doing so later in this chapter.

That wraps up our introductory look at WPF and the core syntax of XAML. The next chapter builds on this information by exploring the role of WPF layout managers and the controls they contain. Before moving on, however, allow me to mention the role of the Visual Studio 2008 WPF project templates and Microsoft Expression Blend.

Building WPF Applications Using Visual Studio 2008

Over the course of this chapter you created examples using no-frills text editors, the command-line compiler, and `xamlpad.exe`. The reason for doing so, of course, was to focus on the core syntax of WPF applications without getting distracted by the bells and whistles of a graphical designer. However, now that you have seen how to build WPF applications in the raw, let's examine how Visual Studio 2008 can simplify the construction of WPF applications.

The WPF Project Templates

The New Project dialog box of Visual Studio 2008 defines a set of WPF-centric project workspaces, all of which are contained under the Window node of the Visual C# root. As you can see in Figure 28-16, you can choose from a WPF Application, WPF User Control Library, WPF Custom Control Library, and WPF Browser Application (e.g., XBAP).

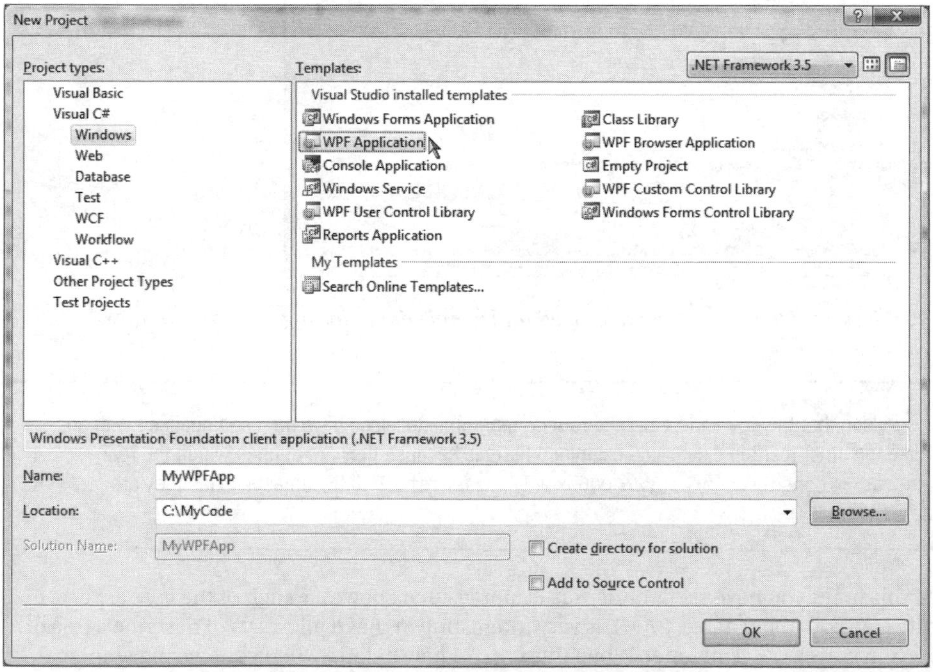

New Project

Project types:
Visual Basic
Visual C#
Windows
Web
Database
Test
WCF
Workflow
Visual C++
Other Project Types
Test Projects

Templates: .NET Framework 3.5
Visual Studio installed templates
Windows Forms Application
WPF Application
Console Application
Windows Service
WPF User Control Library
Reports Application
Class Library
WPF Browser Application
Empty Project
WPF Custom Control Library
Windows Forms Control Library
My Templates
Search Online Templates...

Windows Presentation Foundation client application (.NET Framework 3.5)

Name: MyWPFApp
Location: C:\MyCode
Browse...
Solution Name: MyWPFApp
Create directory for solution
Add to Source Control
OK
Cancel

Figure 28-16. *The WPF project templates of Visual Studio 2008*

When you wish to build a WPF desktop application, you'll want to select the WPF Application project workspace type. Beyond setting references to each of the WPF assemblies (PresentationCore.dll, PresentationFoundation.dll, and WindowsBase.dll), you will also be provided with initial Window- and Application-derived types, making use of code files and an XAML definition (see Figure 28-17).

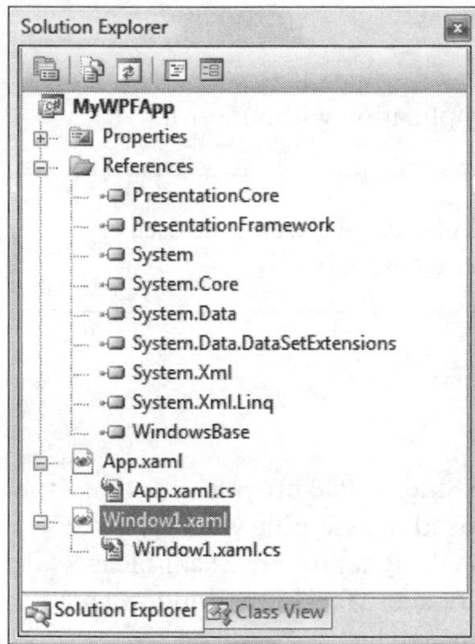

Figure 28-17. *The initial files of a WPF Application project type*

Changing the Name of the Initial Window

For a production-level project, you will most certainly wish to rename your initial Window-derived type (and the file that defines it) from the default name of Window1 to a more fitting description. However, given all of the moving parts required by a WPF application, doing so is a bit more complex than meets the eye. Here is a walk-through of the process.

First, if you right-click the name of your initial Window1.xaml file and select the Rename menu option, you will be pleased to find that the related Windows1.xaml.cs is also renamed according to your selection (e.g., MainWindow.xaml). However, the name of the class type within the *.xaml.cs file will still be named Window1. If you right-click the class name within the *.xaml.cs file and select the Refactor ➤ Rename option, you will be able to supply a fitting name (MainWindow). At this point, if you attempt to run your program, you will generate a runtime exception!

The first reason for this is that the Class attribute of the opening <Window> element is still referring to the original Window1 class name, which must be updated to match your new class name:

```
<Window x:
    Class="MyWPFApplication.MainWindow"
    xmlns="http://schemas.microsoft.com/winfx/2006/xaml/presentation"
    xmlns:x="http://schemas.microsoft.com/winfx/2006/xaml"
    Title="Window1" Height="300" Width="300">
    <Grid>

    </Grid>
</Window>
```

In addition, the StartupUri property in the <Application> declaration must also be updated to specify the name of the renamed XAML file containing the initial Window type (MainWindow.xaml):

```
<Application x:Class="MyWPFApp.App"
    xmlns="http://schemas.microsoft.com/winfx/2006/xaml/presentation"
    xmlns:x="http://schemas.microsoft.com/winfx/2006/xaml"
    StartupUri="MainWindow.xaml"
  >
    <Application.Resources>

    </Application.Resources>
</Application>
```

At this point, you should be able to compile and run your applIcation without error.

Note When you insert new `Window` types into a WPF project, the name of your initial file will be used to correctly name the files and type definitions, so no additional configuration is required.

The WPF Designer

Similar to a Windows Forms application (see Chapter 27), Visual Studio 2008 provides a Toolbox that contains numerous WPF controls, a visual designer that can be used to assemble your UI, and a Properties window to set the properties of a selected control. The designer for an `*.xaml` file is divided into two panes. By default, the upper pane displays the look and feel of the window you are creating, while the bottom pane displays the XAML definition (see Figure 28-18).

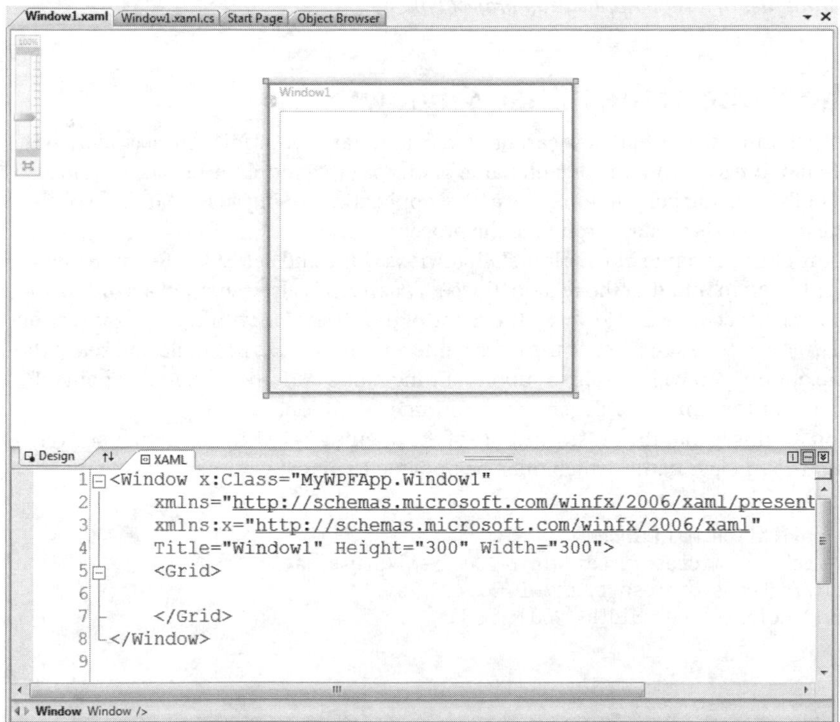

Figure 28-18. *The WPF designer*

■ Note You can reposition the display panes of the visual designer using the buttons embedded within the splitter window—for example, the Swap Panes button (indicated by the up/down arrows), the Horizontal and Vertical split buttons, and so on. Take a moment to find a configuration you are comfortable with.

When you author XAML markup in the XAML pane, you will find the expected IntelliSense. For example, if you type a `Button` declaration in the scope of the initial `<Grid>` type, you will see a list of the properties and events supported by the type. Furthermore, when you select a property member, you will see a list of possible values, as shown in Figure 28-19.

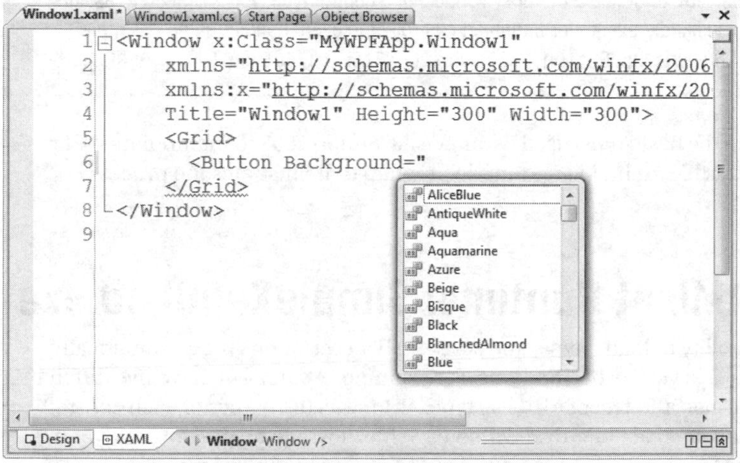
Window1.xaml*
Window1.xaml.cs
Start Page
Object Browser
<Window x:Class="MyWPFApp.Window1"
xmlns="http://schemas.microsoft.com/winfx/2006
xmlns:x="http://schemas.microsoft.com/winfx/20
Title="Window1" Height="300" Width="300">
<Grid>
<Button Background="
</Grid>
</Window>
AliceBlue
AntiqueWhite
Aqua
Aquamarine
Azure
Beige
Bisque
Black
BlanchedAlmond
Blue
Design
XAML
Window Window />

Figure 28-19. *XAML IntelliSense*

Unlike Windows Forms, handling events within a WPF application is *not* done by clicking the lightning bolt button of the Properties window (in fact, this button does not exist when building a WPF application!). When you wish to handle events for a WPF widget, you could author all of the code manually using the expected C# syntax; however, if you type an event name in the XAML editor, you will activate the New Event Handler pop-up menu (see Figure 28-20).

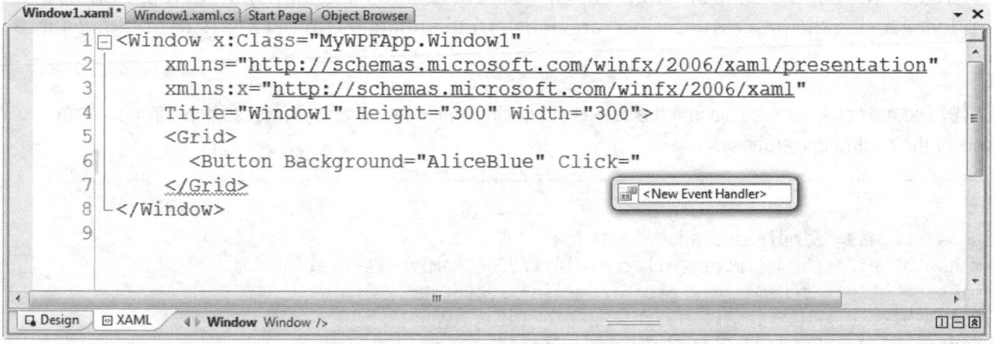
Window1.xaml*
Window1.xaml.cs
Start Page
Object Browser
<Window x:Class="MyWPFApp.Window1"
xmlns="http://schemas.microsoft.com/winfx/2006/xaml/presentation"
xmlns:x="http://schemas.microsoft.com/winfx/2006/xaml"
Title="Window1" Height="300" Width="300">
<Grid>
<Button Background="AliceBlue" Click="
</Grid>
</Window>
<New Event Handler>
Design
XAML
Window Window />

Figure 28-20. *Handling events using the visual designer*

If you manually enter an event name (encased in quotation marks, as required by XAML), you can specify any method name you wish. If you would rather simply have the IDE generate a default name (which takes the form *NameOfControl_NameOfEvent*), you can double-click the <New Event Handler> pop-up menu item. In either case, the IDE responds by adding the correct event handler in your code file:

```
private void Button_Click(object sender, RoutedEventArgs e)
{
}
```

■ **Note** Recall that if you wish the IDE to define a member variable of a control type, you will need to assign a value to the `Name` property. If you handle events for unnamed controls, the event handler name is simply *TypeOfControl_NameOfEvent[_Number]* (e.g., `Button_Click`, `Button_Click_1`, `Button_Click_2`, etc.).

Now that you have seen the basic tools used within Visual Studio 2008 to manipulate WPF applications, let's leverage this IDE to build an example program that illustrates the process of parsing XAML at runtime.

Processing XAML at Runtime: SimpleXamlPad.exe

The WPF API supports the ability to load, parse, and save XAML descriptions programmatically. Doing so can be quite useful in a variety of situations. For example, assume you have five different XAML files that describe the look and feel of a `Window` type. As long as the names of each control (and any necessary event handlers) are identical within each file, it would be possible to dynamically apply "skins" to the window (perhaps based on a startup argument passed into the application).

Interacting with XAML at runtime revolves around the `XamlReader` and `XamlWriter` types, both of which are defined within the `System.Windows.Markup` namespace. To illustrate how to programmatically hydrate a `Window` object from an external `*.xaml` file, we will create a WPF Application project (named SimpleXamlPad) that mimics the basic functionality of the `xamlpad.exe` application examined earlier in this chapter.

While our application will certainly not be as feature-rich as `xamlpad.exe`, it will provide the ability to enter XAML definitions, view the results, and save the XAML to an external file. Once you have created the SimpleXamlPad project using Visual Studio 2008, rename your initial window to `MainWindow` (using the process described previously) and update the initial XAML definition as so:

■ **Note** The next chapter will dive into the details of working with controls and panels, so don't fret over the details of the control declarations.

```
<Window x:Class="SimpleXamlPad.MainWindow"
  xmlns="http://schemas.microsoft.com/winfx/2006/xaml/presentation"
  xmlns:x="http://schemas.microsoft.com/winfx/2006/xaml"
  Title="Simple XAMl Viewer" Height="338" Width="1041"
  Loaded="Window_Loaded" Closed="Window_Closed"
  WindowStartupLocation="CenterScreen">
  <DockPanel LastChildFill="True" >
```

```
    <!-- This button will launch a window with defined XAML -->
    <Button DockPanel.Dock="Top" Name = "btnViewXaml" Width="100" Height="40"
           Content ="View Xaml" Click="btnViewXaml_Click" />

    <!-- This will be the area to type within -->
    <TextBox AcceptsReturn ="True" Name ="txtXamlData"
             FontSize ="14" Background="Black" Foreground="Yellow"
             BorderBrush ="Blue" VerticalScrollBarVisibility="Auto"
             AcceptsTab="True">
      </TextBox>
    </DockPanel>
</Window>
```

First of all, notice that we have replaced the initial <Grid> with a <DockPanel> type that contains a Button (named btnViewXaml) and a TextBox (named txtXamlData), and that the Click event of the Button type has been handled. Also notice that the Loaded and Closed events of the Window itself have been handled within the opening <Window> element. If you have used the designer to handle your events, you should find the following code in your MainWindow.xaml.cs file:

```
public partial class MainWindow : Window
{
  public MainWindow()
  {
    InitializeComponent();
  }

  private void btnViewXaml_Click(object sender, RoutedEventArgs e)
  {
  }

  private void Window_Closed(object sender, EventArgs e)
  {
  }

  private void Window_Loaded(object sender, RoutedEventArgs e)
  {
  }
}
```

Before continuing, be sure to import the following namespaces into your MainWindow.xaml.cs file:

```
using System.IO;
using System.Windows.Markup;
```

Implementing the Loaded Event

The Loaded event of our main window is in charge of determining if there is currently a file named YourXaml.xaml in the folder containing the application. If this file does exist, you will read in the data and place it into the TextBox on the main window. If not, you will fill the TextBox with an initial default XAML description of an empty window (this description is the exact same markup as an initial window definition, except that we are using a <StackPanel>, rather than a <Grid>, to set the Window's Content property [implicitly]).

■Note The string we are building to represent the XML namespaces is a bit nasty to type, given the escape characters required for the embedded quotations (type carefully).

```
private void Window_Loaded(object sender, RoutedEventArgs e)
{
  // When the main window of the app loads,
  // place some basic XAML text into the text block.
  if (File.Exists(System.Environment.CurrentDirectory + "\\YourXaml.xaml"))
  {
    txtXamlData.Text = File.ReadAllText("YourXaml.xaml");
  }
  else
  {
    txtXamlData.Text =
    "<Window xmlns=\"http://schemas.microsoft.com"
    +"/winfx/2006/xaml/presentation\"\n"
    +"xmlns:x=\"http://schemas.microsoft.com/winfx/2006/xaml\""
    +" Height =\"400\" Width =\"500\" WindowStartupLocation=\"CenterScreen\">\n"
    +"<StackPanel>\n"
    +"</StackPanel>\n"
    +"</Window>";
  }
}
```

Using this approach, the `SimpleXamlPad.exe` application will be able to load the XAML entered in a previous session, or supply a default block of markup if necessary. At this point, you should be able to run your program and find the display shown in Figure 28-21 within the `TextBox` type.

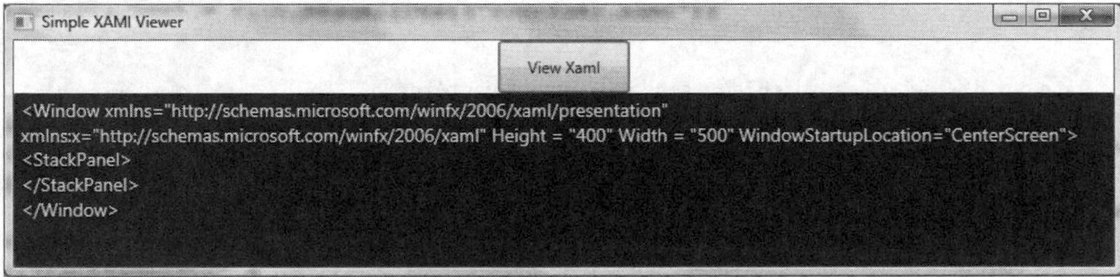

Figure 28-21. *The first run of* `SimpleXamlPad.exe`

Implementing the Button's Click Event

When you click the `Button` type, you will first save the current data in the `TextBox` into the `YourXaml.xaml` file. At this point, you will read in the persisted data via `File.Open()` to obtain a `Stream`-derived type. This is necessary, as the `XamlReader.Load()` method requires a `Stream`-derived type (rather than a simple `System.String`) to represent the XAML to be parsed.

Once you have loaded the XAML description of the `<Window>` you wish to construct, create an instance of `System.Windows.Window` based on the in-memory XAML, and display the `Window` as a modal dialog:

```
private void btnViewXaml_Click(object sender, RoutedEventArgs e)
{
  // Write out the data in the text block to a local *.xaml file.
  File.WriteAllText("YourXaml.xaml", txtXamlData.Text);

  // This is the window that will be dynamically XAML-ed.
  Window myWindow = null;

  // Open local *.xaml file.
  try
  {
    using (Stream sr = File.Open("YourXaml.xaml", FileMode.Open))
    {
      // Connect the XAML to the Window object.
      myWindow = (Window)XamlReader.Load(sr);
      myWindow.ShowDialog();
    }
  }
  catch (Exception ex)
  { MessageBox.Show(ex.Message); }
}
```

Note that we are wrapping much of our logic within a `try/catch` block. In this way, if the `YourXaml.xaml` file contains ill-formed markup, we can see the error of our ways within the resulting message box.

Implementing the Closed Event

Finally, the `Closed` event of our `Window` type will ensure that the latest and greatest data in the `TextBox` is persisted to the `YourXaml.xaml` file:

```
private void Window_Closed(object sender, EventArgs e)
{
  // Write out the data in the text block to a local *.xaml file.
  File.WriteAllText("YourXaml.xaml", txtXamlData.Text);
}
```

Testing the Application

Now fire up your program and enter some XAML into your text area. Do be aware that (like `xamlpad.exe`) this program does not allow you to specify any code generation–centric XAML attributes (such as `Class` or any event handlers). As a test, enter the following XAML within your `<StackPanel>` scope:

```
<StackPanel>
  <Rectangle Fill = "Green" Height = "40" Width = "200" />
  <Button Content = "OK!" Height = "40" Width = "100" />
  <Label Content ="{x:Type Label}" />
</StackPanel>
```

Once you click the button, you will see a window appear that renders your XAML definitions (or possibly you'll see a parsing error in message box—watch your typing!). Figure 28-22 shows possible output.

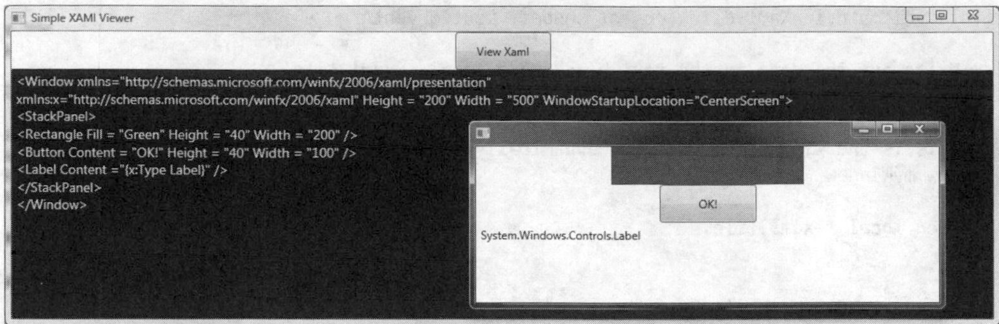

Figure 28-22. `SimpleXamlPad.exe` *in action*

Great! I am sure you can think of many possible enhancements to this application, but to do so you need to be aware of how to work with WPF controls and the panels that contain them. Before examining the WPF control model in the next chapter, we will close this chapter by quickly examining the Microsoft Expression Blend application.

Source Code The SimpleXamlPad project can be found under the Chapter 28 subdirectory.

The Role of Microsoft Expression Blend

While learning new technologies such as XAML and WPF is exciting to most developers, few of us are thrilled by the thought of authoring thousands of lines of markup to describe windows, 3D images, animations, and other such things. Even with the assistance of Visual Studio 2008, generating a feature-rich XAML description of complex entities is tedious and error-prone. Visual Studio 2008 is much better equipped to author procedural code and *tweak* XAML definitions generated by a tool that is dedicated to the automation of XAML descriptions.

Recall that one of the biggest benefits of WPF is the separation of concerns. However, WPF does not simply use separation of concerns at the file level (e.g., C# code files and XAML files). In fact, a WPF application honors the separation of concerns at the level of the tools we use to build our applications. This is important, as a professional WPF application will typically require you to make use of the services of a talented graphic artist to give the application the proper look and feel. As you can imagine, nontechnical individuals would rather *not* use Visual Studio 2008 to author XAML.

To address these problems, Microsoft has created a new family of products that fall under the Expression umbrella. Full details of each member of the Expression family can be found at `http://www.microsoft.com/expression`, but in a nutshell, Expression Blend is a tool geared toward building feature-rich WPF front ends.

Benefits of Expression Blend

The first major benefit of Expression Blend is that the manner in which a graphic artist would author the UI feels similar (but certainly not identical to) to other multimedia applications such as Adobe Photoshop or Macromedia Director. For example, Expression Blend supports tools to build story frames for animations, color blending utilities, layout and graphical transformation tools, and so forth. In addition, Expression Blend provides features that lean a bit closer to the world of code, including support to establish data bindings and event triggers. Regardless, a graphic artist can build extremely rich UIs without ever seeing a single line of XAML or procedural C# code. Figure 28-23 shows a screen shot of Expression Blend in action.

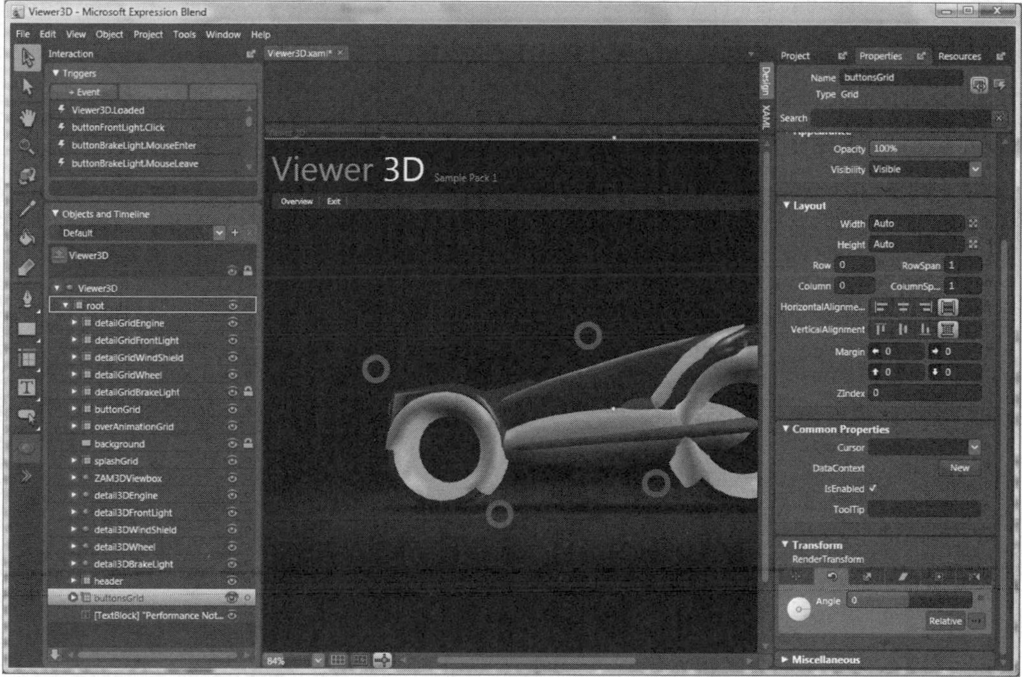

Figure 28-23. *Expression Blend generates XAML transparently in the background.*

The next major benefit of Expression Blend is that it makes use of the *same* exact project workspace as Visual Studio 2008! Therefore, once a graphic artist renders the UI, a C# professional is able to open the same project and author code, add event handlers, tweak XAML, and so forth. Likewise, graphic artists can open existing Visual Studio 2008 WPF project into Expression Blend to spruce up a lackluster front end. The short answer is, WPF is a highly collaborative endeavor between related code files *and* development tools.

While it is true that use of a tool like Expression Blend is more or less mandatory when using WPF to generate bleeding-edge media-rich applications, this edition of the text will not cover the details of doing so. To be sure, the purpose of this book is to examine the underlying programming model of WPF, not to dive into the details of art theory. However, if you are interested in learning more, you are able to download evaluation copies of the members of the Microsoft Expression family from the supporting website. At the very least I suggest downloading a trial copy of Expression Blend just to see what this tool is capable of.

Summary

Windows Presentation Foundation (WPF) is a user interface toolkit introduced since the release of .NET 3.0. The major goal of WPF is to integrate and unify a number of previously unrelated desktop technologies (2D graphics, 3D graphics, window and control development, etc.) into a single unified programming model. Beyond this point, WPF programs typically make use of Extendable

Application Markup Language (XAML), which allows you to declare the look and feel of your WPF elements via markup.

As you have seen in this chapter, XAML allows you to describe trees of .NET objects using a declarative syntax. During this chapter's investigation of XAML, you were exposed to several new bits of syntax including property-element syntax and attached properties, as well as the role of type converters and XAML markup extensions. The chapter wrapped up with an examination of how you can programmatically interact with XAML definitions using the `XamlReader` and `XamlWriter` types, you took a tour of the WPF-specific features of Visual Studio 2008, and you briefly looked at the role of Microsoft Expression Blend.

CHAPTER 29

Programming with WPF Controls

The previous chapter provided a foundation on the WPF programming model, including an examination of the Window and Application types as well as several details regarding the Extendable Application Markup Language (XAML). Here, you will build upon your current understanding by digging into the WPF control set. We begin this chapter with a survey of the intrinsic WPF controls, followed by an examination of two important control-related WPF topics: dependency properties and routed events.

Once you have been exposed to the core programming model, the remainder of this chapter will illustrate several interesting ways to use WPF controls within your applications. For example, you will learn how to organize controls within various WPF containers (Canvas, Grid, StackPanel, WrapPanel, etc.) and how to construct a main window complete with a menu system, status bar, and toolbar. This chapter concludes by examining how to make use of *control commands* (which can be used to tack on built-in behaviors to UI elements and input commands) and introduces you to the WPF *data-binding* model.

Note Many of the control XAML definitions have been included in the code download as "loose XAML files." To view the rendered output, you can copy and paste the markup within a given *.xaml file into your SimpleXamlPad.exe application you created in Chapter 28. As an alternative, you can change the <Window> and </Window> elements to <Page> and </Page> and double-click the file to view them within Internet Explorer.

A Survey of the WPF Control Library

Unless you are very new to the concept of building graphical user interfaces, the intrinsic set of WPF controls should not raise any eyebrows, regardless of which GUI toolkit you have used in the past (MFC, Java AWT/Swing, Windows Forms, VB 6.0, Mac OS X [Cocoa], GTK+/GTK#, etc.). Table 29-1 provides a road map of the core WPF controls, grouped by related functionality.

Table 29-1. *The Core WPF Controls*

WPF Control Category	Example Members	Meaning in Life
Core user input controls	Button, RadioButton, ComboBox, CheckBox, Expander, ListBox Slider, ToggleButton, TreeView, ContextMenu, ScrollBar, Slider, TabControl, TextBox, RepeatButton, RichTextBox, Label	As expected, WPF provides a whole family of controls that can be used to build the crux of a user interface.
Window frame adornment controls	Menu, ToolBar, StatusBar, ToolTip, ProgressBar	These UI elements are used to decorate the frame of a Window object with input devices (such as the Menu) and user informational elements (StatusBar, ToolTip, etc.).
Media controls	Image, MediaElement, SoundPlayerAction	These provide support for audio/video playback and image display.
Layout controls	Border, Canvas, DockPanel, Grid, GridView, GroupBox, Panel, StackPanel, Viewbox, WrapPanel	WPF provides numerous controls that allow you to group and organize other controls for the purpose of layout management.

Beyond the GUI types in Table 29-1, WPF defines additional controls for advanced document processing (DocumentViewer, FlowDocumentReader, etc.) as well as types to support the Ink API (useful for tablet PC development) and various canned dialog boxes (PasswordBox, PrintDialog, FileDialog, OpenFileDialog, and SaveFileDialog).

■ **Note** The FileDialog, OpenFileDialog, and SaveFileDialog types are defined within the Microsoft.Win32 namespace of the PresentationFramework.dll assembly.

If you are coming to WPF from a Windows Forms background, you may notice that the current offering of intrinsic controls is somewhat less than that of Windows Forms (for example, WPF does not have "spin button" controls). The good news is that many of these missing controls can be expressed in XAML quite quickly and can even be modeled as a user control or custom control for reuse between projects.

■ **Note** This edition of the text does not cover the construction of custom WPF user controls or WPF control libraries. If you are interested in learning how to do so, consult the .NET Framework 3.5 SDK documentation.

WPF Controls and Visual Studio 2008

When you create a new WPF Application project using Visual Studio 2008 (see the previous chapter), you will see a majority of controls exposed from the Toolbox (grouped by related category), as shown in Figure 29-1.

Like a Windows Forms project, these controls can be dragged onto the visual designer and configured with the Properties window. Furthermore, recall from Chapter 28 that if you handle events using the XAML editor, the IDE will autogenerate an appropriate event handler in your code file.

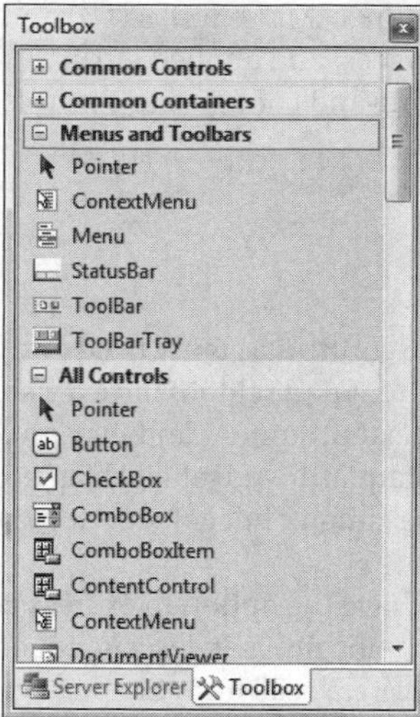

Figure 29-1. *The Visual Studio 2008 Toolbox exposes the intrinsic WPF controls.*

The Details Are in the Documentation

Now, despite what you may be thinking, the intent of this chapter is *not* to walk through each and every member of each and every WPF control. Rather, you will receive an overview of the core controls with emphasis on the underlying programming model (dependency properties, routed events, commands, etc.) and key services common to most WPF controls.

To round out your understanding of the particular functionality of a given control, be sure to consult the .NET Framework 3.5 SDK documentation—specifically, the "Control Library" section of the help system, located under .NET Framework Development ➤ Windows Presentation Foundation ➤ Controls (see Figure 29-2).

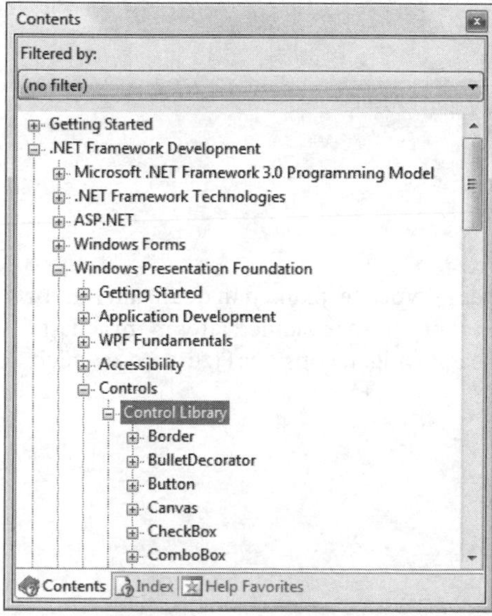

Figure 29-2. *Full details of each WPF control is just a keypress away (F1).*

Here you will find full details of each control, various code samples (in XAML as well as C#) and information regarding a control's inheritance chain, implemented interfaces, and applied attributes. With this disclaimer aside, let's begin with a quick review of declaring and configuring controls in XAML, and using them within a related C# code file.

Declaring Controls in XAML

Over the course of many years, developers have been conditioned to see controls as fairly fixed and predictable entities. For example, `Label` widgets always have textual content and seldom have a visible border (although they could). `Buttons` are gray rectangles that have textual content and may on occasion have an embedded image. When a project demanded that a "standard" widget (such as a `Button`) needed to be customized (such as a `Button` control rendered as a circular image), developers were often forced to build a customized control through code.

WPF radically changes the way we look at controls. Not only do we have the option to express a control's look and feel through markup, but also many WPF controls (specifically, any descendant of `ContentControl`) have been designed to contain any sort of *content* you desire. Recall from Chapter 28 that the `Content` property may be set explicitly (as an attribute within an element's opening tag) or implicitly by specifying nested content as the child element of the root.

Assume you have a new Visual Studio 2008 WPF Application project named ControlReview. Rather than assuming that "all `Buttons` are gray rectangles that have text and maybe an image," we can describe via XAML the following implicit content for a `Button` type (assume this is declared within the `<Grid>` element of your initial `<Window>`):

```
<!-- A custom button with built-in selections! -->
<Button Name="btnPurchaseOptions" Height="100" Width = "300">
  <StackPanel>
    <Label Name="lblInstructions" Foreground = "DarkGreen"
           Content = "Select Your Options and Press to Commit"/>
    <StackPanel Orientation = "Horizontal">
      <Expander Name="colorExpander" Header = "Color">
        <!-- Assume items are placed here... -->
      </Expander>
      <Expander Name="MakeExpander" Header = "Make">
        <!-- Assume items are placed here... -->
      </Expander>
      <Expander Name="paymentExpander" Header = "Payment Plan">
        <!-- Assume items are placed here... -->
      </Expander>
    </StackPanel>
  </StackPanel>
</Button>
```

Notice that this `<Button>` type contains three `<Expander>` types (explained in detail later in this chapter), which are arranged within a set of `<StackPanel>` types (also explained later in this chapter). Without getting too hung up on the functionality of each widget, consider Figure 29-3, which shows the rendered output.

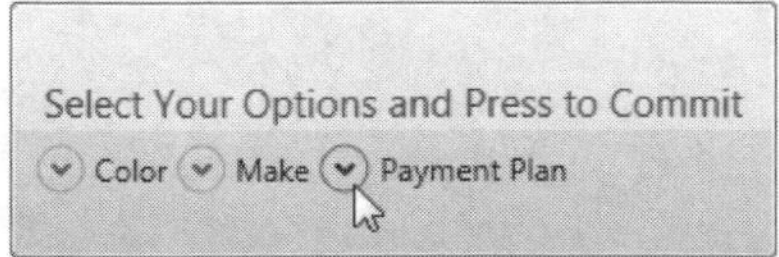

Figure 29-3. *A customized* `Button` *declared via XAML*

By way of a simple compare and contrast, consider how this same control would be built using Windows Forms. Under this API, you could achieve this control only by building a custom Button-derived type that manually handled the rendering of the graphical content, updated the internal controls collection, overrode various event handlers, and so forth.

Given the birth of desktop markup, the only compelling reasons to build custom WPF controls are if you need a widget that supports custom behaviors (events, overriding of virtual methods, support for additional interface types, etc.) or must support customized design-time configuration utilities. If you are only concerned with generating a customized rendering, XAML fits the bill.

Interacting with Controls in Code Files

Recall from the previous chapter that the properties of a WPF type can be set using attributes within an element's opening tag (or alternatively using property-element syntax). In the majority of cases, attributes of an XAML element directly map to the properties and events of the control's class representation within the `System.Windows.Controls` namespace. As such, you always have the option to define a control completely in markup or completely in code, or to use a mix of the two.

Note You can only gain direct access to a control within a related code file if it has been declared using the `Name` attribute in the opening element of the XAML definition.

Given that the previous XAML markup contains types that have been assigned a `Name` attribute, you can directly access the type in your code file as well as handle any declared events. For example, we could change the value of the `Label`'s `FontSize` property as follows:

```
public partial class MainWindow : System.Windows.Window
{
  public MainWindow()
  {
    InitializeComponent();

    // Change FontSize of Label.
    lblInstructions.FontSize = 14;
  }
}
```

This is possible because controls that are given a `Name` attribute in the XAML definition result in a member variable in the autogenerated `*.g.cs` file (see Chapter 28):

```
public partial class MainWindow : System.Windows.Window,
  System.Windows.Markup.IComponentConnector
{
  // Member variables defined based on the XAML markup.
  internal System.Windows.Controls.Button btnPurchaseOptions;
  internal System.Windows.Controls.Label lblInstructions;
  internal System.Windows.Controls.Expander colorExpander;
  internal System.Windows.Controls.Expander MakeExpander;
  internal System.Windows.Controls.Expander paymentExpander;
...
}
```

When you wish to handle events for a given control, you are able to assign a method name to a given event in your XAML definition as follows:

```
<Button Name="btnPurchaseOptions"
  Click="btnPurchaseOptions_Click"
  Height="100" Width = "300">
...
</Button>
```

The related code file would contain a definition of this method, whose format will be based on the underlying delegate (recall again that the Visual Studio 2008 IDE will update your code file automatically):

```
private void btnPurchaseOptions_Click(object sender, RoutedEventArgs e)
{
  MessageBox.Show("Button has been clicked");
}
```

On a related note, you are free to handle your events entirely in code. For example, if the previous `Click` event XAML definition were deleted, you could update your `Window`'s constructor as follows:

```
public MainWindow()
{
  InitializeComponent();

  // Change FontSize of Label.
  lblInstructions.FontSize = 14;

  // Handle Click event for button.
  btnPurchaseOptions.Click +=
    new RoutedEventHandler(btnPurchaseOptions_Click);
}
```

Now that the basic control model is fresh in your mind, the next task is to examine the details of two important (but somewhat challenging) aspects of the WPF control model: dependency properties and routed events. While the details of these concepts are typically hidden from view during your day-to-day WPF programming tasks, the more you understand these lower-level details, the better prepared you will be to dive into more advanced WPF programming tasks in the future.

■ Source Code The ControlReview project is included under the Chapter 29 subdirectory.

Understanding the Role of Dependency Properties

As you would assume, the Windows Presentation Foundation APIs make use of each member of the .NET type system (classes, structures, interfaces, delegates, enumerations) and each possible type member (properties, methods, events, constant data/read-only fields, etc.) within its implementation. However, WPF introduces a new programming mechanism termed a *dependency property*.

■ Note Dependency properties are a WPF-specific programming construct. To date, no .NET programming language has a native syntax to define this particular flavor of a property. However, the C# "propdp" code snippet will generate the skeleton of a new dependency property (see Chapter 2 for coverage of code snippets).

Like a "normal" .NET property (often termed a *CLR property* in the WPF literature), dependency properties can be set declaratively using XAML or programmatically within a code file. Furthermore, dependency properties (like CLR properties) exist to encapsulate data fields and can be configured as read-only, write-only, or read-write, and so forth.

To make matters more interesting, in most cases you will be blissfully unaware that you have actually set a dependency property as opposed to a CLR property! For example, the `Height` and `Width` members WPF controls inherit from `FrameworkElement`, as well as the `Content` member inherited from `ControlContent`, are all dependency properties:

```
<!-- You just set three dependency properties! -->
<Button Name = "btnMyButton" Height = "50" Width = "100" Content = "OK"/>
```

Given all of these similarities, you may wonder exactly why WPF has introduced a new term for a familiar concept. The answer lies in how a dependency property is implemented under the hood. Once implemented, dependency properties provide a number of powerful features that are used by various WPF technologies including data binding, animation services, themes and styles, and so forth. In a nutshell, dependency properties provide the following benefits above and beyond the simple data encapsulation found with a CLR property:

- Dependency properties can inherit their values from a parent element's XAML definition.
- Dependency properties support the ability to have values set by external types (recall from Chapter 28 that attached properties do this very thing, as attached properties are based on dependency properties).
- Dependency properties allow WPF to compute a value based on multiple external values.
- Dependency properties provide the infrastructure for callback notifications and triggers (used quite often when building animations, styles, and themes).
- Dependency properties allow for static storage of their data (which helps conserve memory consumption).

One key difference of a dependency property is that it allows WPF to compute a value based on values from multiple property inputs. The other properties in question could include OS system properties (including systemwide user preferences), values based on data binding and animation/storyboard logic, resources and styles, or values known through parent/child relationships with other XAML elements.

Another major difference is that dependency properties can be configured to monitor changes of the property value to force external actions to occur. For example, changing the value of a dependency property might cause WPF to change the layout of controls on a `Window`, rebind to external data sources, or move through the steps of a custom animation.

Examining an Existing Dependency Property

To be completely honest, the chances that you will need to manually build a dependency property for your WPF projects are quite slim. In reality, the only time you will typically need to do so is if you are building a custom WPF control, where you have subclassed an existing control to modify its behaviors. In this case, if you are creating a property that needs to work with the WPF data-binding engine, theme engine, or animation engine, or if the property must broadcast when it has changed, a dependency property is the correct course of action. In all other cases, a normal CLR property will do.

While this is true, it is helpful to understand the basic composition of a dependency property, as it will make some of the more "mysterious" features of WPF less so and deepen your understanding of underlying WPF programming model. To illustrate the internal composition of a dependency property, consider the following C# code, which approximates the implementation of the Height property of the FrameworkElement class type:

```
public class FrameworkElement : UIElement, IFrameworkInputElement,
  IInputElement, ISupportInitialize, IHaveResources
{
...
  // Notice this is a static field of type DependencyProperty
  public static readonly DependencyProperty HeightProperty;

  // The static DependencyProperty field is created and "registered"
  // in the static constructor.
  static FrameworkElement()
  {
    HeightProperty = DependencyProperty.Register(
      "Height",
      typeof(double),
      typeof(FrameworkElement),
      new FrameworkPropertyMetadata((double) 1.0 / (double) 0.0,
        FrameworkPropertyMetadataOptions.AffectsMeasure,
        new PropertyChangedCallback(FrameworkElement.OnTransformDirty)),
      new ValidateValueCallback(FrameworkElement.IsWidthHeightValid));
  }

  // Note that the Height property still has get/set blocks.
  // However, the implemention is using the inherited
  // GetValue()/SetValue() methods.
  public double Height
  {
    get { return (double) base.GetValue(HeightProperty); }
    set { base.SetValue(HeightProperty, value); }
  }
}
```

As you can see, dependency properties require quite a bit of additional logic from a typical CLR property! Here is a breakdown of what is happening: First and foremost, dependency properties are represented using the System.Windows.DependencyProperty class type and are almost always declared as public, static read-only fields. Recall that one benefit of dependency properties is that they are not directly tied to an object instance (which helps memory consumption), hence the use of static data.

Registering Dependency Property

Given that dependency properties are declared as static, they are assigned an initial value within the static constructor of the type. However, unlike a simple numerical field, the DependencyProperty object is created indirectly by capturing the return value of the static DependencyProperty.Register() method. This method has been overloaded a number of times; however, in this example, Register() is invoked as follows:

```
HeightProperty = DependencyProperty.Register(
  "Height",
  typeof(double),
  typeof(FrameworkElement),
  new FrameworkPropertyMetadata((double) 1.0 / (double) 0.0,
    FrameworkPropertyMetadataOptions.AffectsMeasure,
    new PropertyChangedCallback(FrameworkElement.OnTransformDirty)),
  new ValidateValueCallback(FrameworkElement.IsWidthHeightValid));
```

The first argument to Register() is the name of the "normal" CLR property on the class that makes use of the DependencyProperty field (Height in this case), while the second argument is the type information of the underlying data type it is bound to (a double).

The third argument specifies the type information of the class that this property belongs to (FrameworkElement in this case). While this might seem redundant (after all, the HeightProperty field is already defined within the FrameworkElement class), this is a very clever aspect of WPF in that it allows one type to "attach" properties to another type (even if the class definition has been sealed!).

Note Recall that C# 2008 extension methods (see Chapter 13) also allow you to add new members to sealed types. Extension methods would be the most direct way of adding new functionality to types that do not need to participate in WPF-centric services (e.g., animation).

The final arguments passed to Register() are what really give dependency properties their own flavor. Here we are able to provide a FrameworkPropertyMetadata object that describes all of the details regarding how WPF should handle this property with respect to callback notifications (if the property needs to notify others when the value changes), how the value will be validated, and various options (represented by the FrameworkPropertyMetadataOptions enum) that control what is effected by the property in question (does it work with data binding, can it be inherited, etc.).

Defining a Wrapper Property for a DependencyProperty Field

Once the details of configuring the DependencyProperty object have been established within a static constructor, the final task is to wrap the field within a typical CLR property (Height in this case). Notice, however, that the "get" and "set" scopes do not simply return or set a class-level double-member variable, but do so indirectly using the GetValue() and SetValue() methods from the System.Windows.DependencyObject base class:

```
public double Height
{
  get { return (double) base.GetValue(HeightProperty); }
  set { base.SetValue(HeightProperty, value); }
}
```

Note Strictly speaking, you do not need to build a wrapper property for a DependencyProperty field, if the field is public, as you can access it statically when calling the inherited GetValue()/SetValue() public methods. In practice, most dependency properties do have a friendly wrapper, as it is very XAML-friendly.

Now that you have seen the details of how a dependency property is assembled under the hood, be aware that it would be entirely possible to use a normal CLR property that supported the same services as a WPF dependency property (notifications, static memory allocation, etc.). However, to do so would require a good deal of boilerplate code that you would need to author by hand and replicate in numerous places. Using the intrinsic DependencyProperty type (and additional bits of infrastructure), we are provided with an out-of-the-box implementation of the same services.

Because a dependency property is built using various WPF-centric types, it would certainly be possible for you to build your own dependency properties, which will not be necessary for the examples in this text. However, the following code summarizes the core pieces of a dependency property declaration (note here we are registering the property at the time we declare the static read-only DependencyProperty type):

```
public class MyOwnerClass : DependencyObject
{
  // Using a DependencyProperty as the backing store for MyProperty.
  // This enables animation, styling, binding, etc...
  public static readonly DependencyProperty MyPropertyProperty =
    DependencyProperty.Register("MyProperty", typeof(int),
    typeof(OwnerClass), new UIPropertyMetadata(0));

  // XAML-friendly wrapper for the
  // static read-only field. This is necessary,
  // as we can't call methods (GetValue/SetValue)
  // in XAML.
  public int MyProperty
  {
    // GetValue/SetValue come from the
    // DependencyObject base class.
    get { return (int)GetValue(MyPropertyProperty); }
    set { SetValue(MyPropertyProperty, value); }
  }
}
```

If you are interested in learning further details regarding this WPF programming construct, check out the topic "Custom Dependency Properties" within the .NET Framework 3.5 SDK documentation.

Understanding Routed Events

Properties are not the only .NET programming construct to be given a facelift to work well within the WPF API. The standard CLR event model has also been refined just a bit to ensure that events can be processed in a manner that is fitting for XAML's description of a tree of objects. Assume you have a new WPF Application project named WPFControlEvents. Now, update the initial XAML description of the initial window by adding the following <Button> type within the initial <Grid>:

```
<Button Name="btnClickMe" Height="75" Width = "250" Click ="btnClickMe_Clicked">
  <StackPanel Orientation ="Horizontal">
    <Label Height="50" FontSize ="20">Fancy Button!</Label>
    <Canvas Height ="50" Width ="100" >
    <Ellipse Name = "outerEllipse" Fill ="Green" Height ="25"
             Width ="50" Cursor="Hand" Canvas.Left="25" Canvas.Top="12"/>
    <Ellipse Name = "innerEllipse" Fill ="Yellow" Height = "15" Width ="36"
             Canvas.Top="17" Canvas.Left="32"/>
    </Canvas>
  </StackPanel>
</Button>
```

Notice in the <Button>'s opening definition we have handled the Click event by specifying the name of a method to be called when the event is raised. The Click event works with the RoutedEventHandler delegate, which expects an event handler that takes an object as the first parameter and a System.Windows.RoutedEventArgs as the second:

```
public void btnClickMe_Clicked(object sender, RoutedEventArgs e)
{
  // Do something when button is clicked.
  MessageBox.Show("Clicked the button");
}
```

Figure 29-4 shows the expected output when clicking the current control (for display purposes, I changed the initial `<Grid>` type to a `<StackPanel>`, which explains why the `Button` is mounted on the top-center of this `Window`, rather than positioned in the center).

Figure 29-4. *Handling events for a composite* `Button` *type*

Now, consider the current composition of our `Button`. It contains numerous nested elements to fully represent its user interface (`Canvas`, `Ellipse`, `Label`, etc.). Imagine how tedious WPF event handling would be if we were forced to handle a `Click` event for each and every one of these subelements. After all, the end user could click anywhere within the scope of the button's boundaries (on the `Label`, on the green area of the oval, on the surface of the button, etc.). Not only would the creation of separate event handlers for each aspect of the `Button` be labor intensive, we would end up with some mighty nasty code to maintain down the road.

Under the Windows Forms event model, a custom control such as this would require us to handle the `Click` event for each item on the button. Thankfully, WPF *routed events* take care of this automatically. Simply put, the routed events model automatically propagates an event up (or down) a tree of objects, looking for an appropriate handler.

Specifically speaking, a routed event can make use of three "routing strategies." If an event is moving from the point of origin up to other defining scopes within the object tree, the event is said to be a *bubbling event*. Conversely, if an event is moving from its point of origin down into related subelements, the event is said to be a *tunneling event*. Finally, if an event is raised and handled only by the originating element (which is what could be described as a normal CLR event), it is said to be a *direct event*.

■ Note Like dependency properties, routed events are a WPF-specific construct implemented using WPF-specific helper types. Thus, there is no special C# syntax you need to learn to handle routed events.

The Role of Routed Bubbling Events

In the current example, if the user clicks the inner yellow oval, the `Click` event bubbles out to the next level of scope (the `Canvas`), and then to the `StackPanel`, and finally to the `Button` where the `Click` event handler is handled. In a similar way, if the user clicks the `Label`, the event is bubbled to the `StackPanel` and then finally to the `Button` type.

Given this routed bubbling event pattern, we have no need to worry about registering specific Click event handlers for all members of a composite control. However, if you wished to perform custom clicking logic for multiple elements within the same object tree, you can do so. By way of illustration, assume you need to handle the clicking of the outerEllipse control in a unique manner. First, handle the MouseDown event for this subelement (graphically rendered types such as the Ellipse do not support a "click" event; however, they can monitor mouse button activity via MouseDown, MouseUp, etc.):

```
<Button Name="btnClickMe" Height="75" Width = "250" Click ="btnClickMe_Clicked">
  <StackPanel Orientation ="Horizontal">
    <Label Height="50" FontSize ="20">Fancy Button!</Label>
    <Canvas Height ="50" Width ="100" >
    <Ellipse Name = "outerEllipse" Fill ="Green"
             Height ="25" MouseDown ="outerEllipse_MouseDown"
             Width ="50" Cursor="Hand" Canvas.Left="25" Canvas.Top="12"/>
    <Ellipse Name = "innerEllipse" Fill ="Yellow" Height = "15" Width ="36"
             Canvas.Top="17" Canvas.Left="32"/>
    </Canvas>
  </StackPanel>
</Button>
```

Then implement an appropriate event handler, which for illustrative purposes will simply change the Title property of the main window:

```
public void outerEllipse_MouseDown(object sender, RoutedEventArgs e)
{
  // Change title of window.
  this.Title = "You clicked the outer ellipse!";
}
```

With this, we now can take different courses of action depending on where the end user has clicked (which boils down to the outer ellipse and everywhere else within the button's scope).

■ **Note** Routed bubbling events always move from the point of origin to the *next defining scope*. Thus, in this example, if we were to click the innerEllipse object, the event would be bubbled to the Canvas, *not* to the outerEllipse, as they are both Ellipse types within the scope of Canvas.

Continuing or Halting Bubbling

Currently, if the user clicks the outerEllipse object, it will trigger the registered MouseDown event handler for this Ellipse type, at which the bubbling logic stops (therefore, we would not see the Button's Click event handler execute). Most of the time, this is the effect you desire; however, if you wish to inform WPF to continue bubbling up the object tree, you can set the Handled property of the RountedEventArgs type to false:

```
public void outerEllipse_MouseDown(object sender, RoutedEventArgs e)
{
  // Change title of window.
  this.Title = "You clicked the outer ellipse!";

  // Keep bubbling!
  e.Handled = false;
}
```

In this case, we would find that the title of the window is changed, followed by the launching of the MessageBox displayed within the Click event handler of the Button type. In a nutshell, routed bubbling events make it possible to allow a complex group of content to act either as a single logical element (e.g., a Button) or as discrete items (e.g., an Ellipse within the Button).

The Role of Routed Tunneling Events

Strictly speaking, routed events can be *bubbling* (as just described) or *tunneling* in nature. Tunneling events (which all begin with the Preview suffix—e.g., PreviewMouseDown) drill down from the originating element into the inner scopes of the object tree. By and large, each bubbling event in the WPF base class libraries is paired with a related tunneling event that fires *before* the bubbling counterpart. For example, before the bubbling MouseDown event fires, the tunneling PreviewMouseDown event fires first.

Handling a tunneling event looks just like the processing of handling any other events; simply assign the event handler name in XAML (or, if needed, using the corresponding C# event-handling syntax in your code file) and implement the handler in the code file. Just to illustrate the interplay of tunneling and bubbling events, begin by handling the PreviewMouseDown event for the outerEllipse object:

```
<Ellipse Name = "outerEllipse" Fill ="Green" Height ="25"
  MouseDown ="outerEllipse_MouseDown"
  PreviewMouseDown ="outerEllipse_PreviewMouseDown"
  Width ="50" Cursor="Hand" Canvas.Left="25" Canvas.Top="12"/>
```

Next, retrofit the current C# class definition by updating each event handler (for all types) to append data to and eventually display the value within a new string member variable. This will allow us to observe the flow of events firing in the background:

```
public partial class MainWindow : System.Windows.Window
{
  // This is used to hold data on the mouse-related
  // activity.
  string mouseActivity = string.Empty;

  public MainWindow()
  {
    InitializeComponent();
  }

  public void btnClickMe_Clicked(object sender, RoutedEventArgs e)
  {
    // Show the final string.
    mouseActivity += "Button Click event fired!\n";
    MessageBox.Show(mouseActivity);

    // Clear string for next test.
    mouseActivity = string.Empty;
  }

  public void outerEllipse_MouseDown(object sender, RoutedEventArgs e)
  {
    // Add data to string.
    mouseActivity += "MouseDown event fired!\n";
```

```
    // Keep bubbling!
    e.Handled = false;
  }

  public void outerEllipse_PreviewMouseDown(object sender, RoutedEventArgs e)
  {
    // Add data to string.
    mouseActivity = "PreviewMouseDown event fired!\n";

    // Keep bubbling!
    e.Handled = false;
  }
}
```

When you run the program and do not click within the bounds of the outer ellipse, you will simply see the message "Button Click event fired!" displayed within the message box. However, if you do click within the outer ellipse image, the message box shown in Figure 29-5 will display.

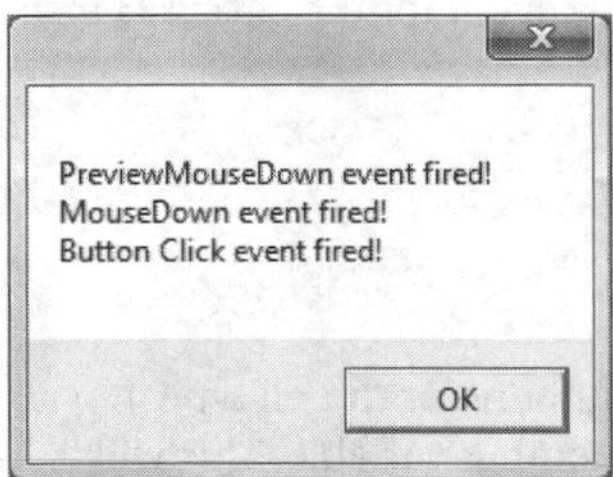

Figure 29-5. *Tunneling first, bubbling second*

So you may be wondering why in the world WPF events typically tend to come in pairs (one tunneling and one bubbling)? The answer is that by previewing events, you have the power to perform any special logic (data validation, disable bubbling action, etc.) before the bubbling counterpart fires. In a vast majority of cases, you will *not need* to handle the `Preview` prefixed tunneling events and simply have to worry about the (non–`Preview`-prefixed) bubbling events.

Much like the task of manually authoring a dependency property, the need to handle tunneling events is typically only necessary when subclassing an existing WPF control. On a related note, if you are building a custom WPF control, be aware that you can create custom routed events (which may be bubbling or tunneling) using a mechanism similar to that of building a custom dependency property. If you are interested, check out the topic "How to: Create a Custom Routed Event" within the .NET Framework 3.5 SDK documentation.

■ **Source Code** The WPFControlEvents project is included under the Chapter 29 subdirectory.

Working with Button Types

Now that you have examined the details of dependency properties and routed events, you are in a good position to better understand the WPF controls themselves, beginning with button types. Instinctively, we all know the role of button types. They are UI elements that can be pressed via the mouse or via the keyboard (with the Enter key or spacebar) if they have the current focus. In WPF, the ButtonBase class serves as a parent for three core derived types: Button, RepeatButton, and ToggleButton.

The ButtonBase Type

Like any parent class, ButtonBase provides a polymorphic interface for derived types (in addition to the members inherited from its base class ContentControl). For example, it is ButtonBase that defines the Click event. As well, this parent class defines the IsPressed property, which allows you to take a course of action when the derived type has been pressed, but not yet released. In addition, Table 29-2 describes some other members of interest for the ButtonBase abstract base class.

Table 29-2. *Select Members of the* ButtonBase *Type*

ButtonBase Member	Meaning in Life
ClickMode	This property allows you to establish when the Click event should fire, based on values from the ClickMode enumeration.
Command	As explained later in this chapter, many UI elements can have an associated "command" that can be attached to a UI element by assigning the Command property.
CommandParameter	This property allows you to pass parameters to the item specified by the Command property.
CommandTarget	This property allows you to establish the recipient of the command set by the Command property.

Beyond the command-centric members (examined at the conclusion of this chapter), the most interesting member would be ClickMode, which allows you to specify three different modes of clicking a button. This property can be assigned any value from the related System.Windows.Controls.ClickMode enumeration:

```
public enum ClickMode
{
  Release,
  Press,
  Hover
}
```

For example, assume you have the following XAML description for a Button type using the ClickMode.Hover value for the ClickMode property:

```
<Button Name = "bntHoverClick" ClickMode = "Hover" Click ="btnHoverClick_Click"/>
```

With this, the Click event will fire as soon as the mouse cursor is anywhere within the bounds of the Button type. While this may not be the most helpful course of action for a typical push button, hover mode can be useful when building custom styles, templates, or animations.

The Button Type

The first derived type, Button, provides two properties of immediate interest, IsCancel and IsDefault, which are very helpful when building dialog boxes containing OK and Cancel buttons. When IsCancel is set to true, the button will be artificially clicked when the user presses the Esc key. If IsDefault is set to true, the button will be artificially clicked when the user presses the Enter key. Consider the following XAML description of two Button types:

```
<!-- Assume these are defined within a <StackPanel> of a Window type -->
<Button Name ="btnOK" IsDefault = "true" Click ="btnOK_Click" Content = "OK"/>
<Button Name ="btnCancel" IsCancel= "true"
        Click ="btnCancel_Click" Content = "Cancel"/>
```

If you were to implement each of the declared event handlers in a related code file, you will be able to run the application and verify the correct handler is invoked when the Enter key or Esc key is pressed. This would be the case even if another UI element of the window (such as a text entry area) has the current focus.

The ToggleButton Type

The ToggleButton type (defined in the System.Windows.Controls.Primitives namespace) has by default a UI identical to the Button type; however, it has the unique ability to hold its pressed state when clicked. To account for this, ToggleButton provides an IsChecked property, which toggles between true and false when the end user clicks the UI element. Furthermore, ToggleButton provides two events (Checked and Unchecked) that can be handled to intercept this state change. Here is an XAML description of a simple toggle that handles each event on two unique event handlers:

```
<!-- A Yes/No toggle button -->
<ToggleButton Name ="toggleOnOffButton"
  Checked ="toggleOnOffButton_Checked"
  Unchecked ="toggleOnOffButton_Unchecked">
  Off!
</ToggleButton >
```

The event handlers simply update the Content property with a fitting textual message:

```
protected void toggleOnOffButton_Checked(object sender, RoutedEventArgs e)
{
  toggleOnOffButton.Content = "On!";
}

protected void toggleOnOffButton_Unchecked(object sender, RoutedEventArgs e)
{
  toggleOnOffButton.Content = "Off!";
}
```

If you wish to consolidate your code-behind file to use a single handler for each event, you could update your XAML definition so that the Checked and Unchecked events both point to a single handler (say, toggleOnOffButtonPressed), and then use the IsChecked property to flip between the message:

```
protected void toggleOnOffButtonPressed(object sender, RoutedEventArgs e)
{
  if (toggleOnOffButton.IsChecked == false )
    toggleOnOffButton.Content = "Off!";
  else
    toggleOnOffButton.Content = "On!";
}
```

Finally, be aware that ToggleButton also supports tri-state functionality (via the IsThreeState property and Indeterminate event), allowing you to test if the widget is checked, unchecked, or neither. While it might seem odd for a button to monitor itself in this manner, it makes perfect sense for types that derive from ToggleButton, such as the CheckBox type examined in just a moment.

Note As a general rule, types defined in the `System.Windows.Controls.Primitives` namespace (including the `ToggleButton`) are not assumed to be very useful out of the box without additional customizations.

The RepeatButton Type

The final `ButtonBase`-derived type to discuss is the `RepeatButton` type, also defined within `System.Windows.Controls.Primitives`. This type also has a default look and feel to a standard `Button`; however, it supports the ability to continuously fire its `Click` event when the end user has the widget in a pressed state. The frequency in which it will fire the `Click` event is dependent upon the values you assign to the `Delay` and `Interval` properties (both of which are recorded in milliseconds).

In reality, the `RepeatButton` type (like the `ToggleButton` type) is not that useful on its own. However, the exposed behavior is useful when constructing customized user interfaces. To illustrate, consider the fact that unlike Windows Forms, the initial release of WPF does not supply a spin button control, which allows the user to adjust a numerical value using up and down arrows. Composing a spin button widget can be done quite simply in XAML given the functionality of `RepeatButton`.

To illustrate, create a new Visual Studio WPF Application project named CustomSpinButtonApp. Replace the initial `<Grid>` definition with a `<StackPanel>` containing the following markup:

```
<Window x:Class="CustomSpinButtonApp.MainWindow"
  xmlns="http://schemas.microsoft.com/winfx/2006/xaml/presentation"
  xmlns:x="http://schemas.microsoft.com/winfx/2006/xaml"
  Title="CustomSpinButtonApp" Height="300" Width="300">
  <StackPanel>
    <!-- The 'Up' button -->
    <RepeatButton Height ="25" Width = "25" Name ="repeatAddValueButton"
      Delay ="200" Interval ="1" Click ="repeatAddValueButton_Click"
      Content = "+"/>

    <!-- Displays the current value -->
    <Label Name ="lblCurrentValue" Background ="LightGray"
           Height ="30" Width = "25"VerticalContentAlignment="Center"
           HorizontalContentAlignment="Center" FontSize="15"/>

    <!-- The 'Down' button -->
    <RepeatButton Height ="25" Width = "25" Name ="repeatRemoveValueButton"
      Delay ="200" Interval ="1"
      Click ="repeatRemoveValueButton_Click" Content = "-"/>
  </StackPanel>
</Window>
```

Notice how each `RepeatButton` type handles the `Click` event with a unique event handler. With this, we can author the following C# logic to increase or decrease the value displayed within the `<Label>` (feel free to add extra logic to trap maximum and minimum values if you so choose):

```
public partial class MainWindow : System.Windows.Window
{
  private int currValue = 0;

  public MainWindow()
  {
    InitializeComponent();
    lblCurrentValue.Content = currValue;
```

```
  }
  protected void repeatAddValueButton_Click(object sender, RoutedEventArgs e)
  {
    // Add 1 to the current value and show in label.
    currValue++;
    lblCurrentValue.Content = currValue;
  }

  protected void repeatRemoveValueButton_Click(object sender, RoutedEventArgs e)
  {
    // Subtract 1 from the current value and show in label.
    currValue--;
    lblCurrentValue.Content = currValue;
  }
}
```

As you can see, when the user clicks either RepeatButton, we increment or decrement the private currValue accordingly, and set the Content property of the Label type. Figure 29-6 shows our custom spin button UI in action.

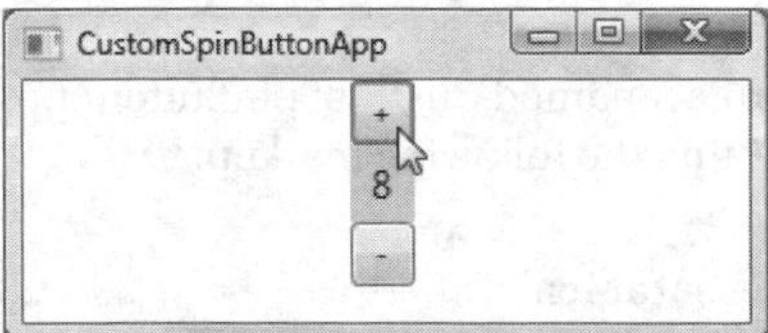

Figure 29-6. *Building a spin button using* RepeatButton *as a starting point*

Source Code The CustomSpinButtonApp project is included under the Chapter 29 subdirectory.

Working with CheckBoxes and RadioButtons

As mentioned previously, CheckBox "is-a" ToggleButton, which "is-a" ButtonBase, which may seem very odd given that the UI of a button looks very different from that of a check box. However, a CheckBox type, like a Button, can be clicked, responds to mouse and keyboard input, and follows the WPF content model. Given all of these similarities, it turns out that the CheckBox type simply overrides various virtual members of ToggleButton to establish a check box look and feel (recall that a major motivator of WPF is to decouple the display of a control from its functionality). Consider the following <CheckBox> declarations, which yield the output shown in Figure 29-7:

```
<StackPanel>
  <!-- CheckBox types -->
  <CheckBox Name ="checkInfo" >Send me more information</CheckBox>
  <CheckBox Name ="checkPhoneContact" >Contact me over the phone</CheckBox>
</StackPanel>
```

Send me more information
Contact me over the phone

Figure 29-7. *Simple* CheckBox *types*

RadioButton is another type that "is-a" ToggleButton. Unlike the CheckBox type, however, it has the innate ability to ensure all RadioButtons in the same container (such as a StackPanel, Grid, or whatnot) are mutually exclusive without any additional work on your part. Consider the following:

```
<StackPanel>
  <!-- RadioButton types for music selection -->
  <Label FontSize = "15" Content = "Select Your Music Media"/>
  <RadioButton>CD Player</RadioButton>
  <RadioButton>MP3 Player</RadioButton>
  <RadioButton>8-Track</RadioButton>

  <!-- RadioButton types for color selection -->
  <Label FontSize = "15" Content = "Select Your Color Choice"/>
  <RadioButton>Red</RadioButton>
  <RadioButton>Green</RadioButton>
  <RadioButton>Blue</RadioButton>
</StackPanel>
```

If you were to test this XAML, you would find that you can only select one of the six options, which is probably not what is intended, as there seem to be two separate groups within the mix (radio options and color options).

Establishing Logical Groupings

When you wish to have a single container with multiple RadioButton types, which behave as distinct physical groupings, you can do so setting the GroupName property on the opening element of the RadioButton type:

```
<StackPanel>
  <!-- The Music group  -->
  <Label FontSize = "15" Content = "Select Your Music Media"/>
  <RadioButton GroupName = "Music" >CD Player</RadioButton>
  <RadioButton GroupName = "Music" >MP3 Player</RadioButton>
  <RadioButton GroupName = "Music" >8-Track</RadioButton>

  <!–The Color group (optional for this example, see Note below) -->
  <Label FontSize = "15" Content = "Select Your Color Choice"/>
  <RadioButton GroupName = "Color">Red</RadioButton>
  <RadioButton GroupName = "Color">Green</RadioButton>
  <RadioButton GroupName = "Color">Blue</RadioButton>
</StackPanel>
```

With this, we will now be able to set each logical grouping independently, even though they are in the same physical container.

■ **Note** By default, all RadioButtons in a container that do not have a GroupName value work as a single physical group. Therefore, in the previous example, the color-centric buttons would have been mutually exclusive, even with the GroupName omitted, given the presence of the Music group.

Framing Related Elements in GroupBoxes

When you design a collection of radio buttons or check boxes, it is common to surround them with a visual container to denote that they behave as a group. The most common way to do so is using a GroupBox control. As the Header property is prototyped to operate on a System.Object, you are able to assign any object to function as the header (a simple string, a colored rectangle, a button, etc.). Consider the following two GroupBox declarations, which frame the previous RadioButtons in various manners:

```
<StackPanel>
  <GroupBox Header = "Select Your Music Media" BorderBrush ="Black">
    <StackPanel>
      <RadioButton GroupName = "Music" >CD Player</RadioButton>
      <RadioButton GroupName = "Music" >MP3 Player</RadioButton>
      <RadioButton GroupName = "Music" >8-Track</RadioButton>
    </StackPanel>
  </GroupBox>

  <GroupBox BorderBrush ="Black">
    <GroupBox.Header>
      <Label Background = "Blue" Foreground = "White"
             FontSize = "15" Content = "Select your color choice"/>
    </GroupBox.Header>
    <StackPanel>
      <RadioButton>Red</RadioButton>
      <RadioButton>Green</RadioButton>
      <RadioButton>Blue</RadioButton>
    </StackPanel>
  </GroupBox>
</StackPanel>
```

The output can be seen in Figure 29-8.

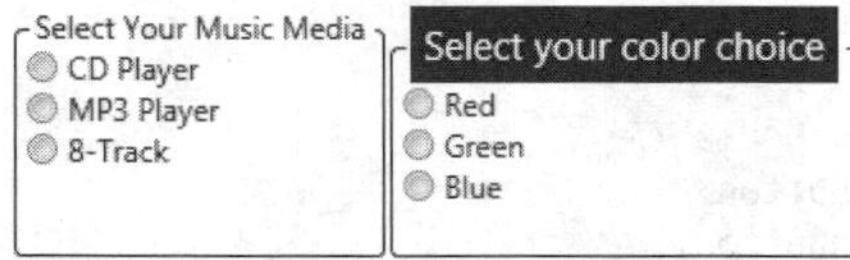

Figure 29-8. GroupBox *types framing* RadioButton *types*

Framing Related Elements in Expanders

In addition to the customary group box, WPF ships with a new UI element that can group a collection of UI elements that can be hidden or shown via a toggle. This element, the Expander type, allows you to define the direction elements will be displayed (up, down, left, or right) using the ExpandDirection property. Consider the following XAML (which basically just changes <GroupBox> to <Expander>):

```
<StackPanel>
  <Expander Header = "Select Your Music Media" BorderBrush ="Black">
    <StackPanel>
      <RadioButton GroupName = "Music" >CD Player</RadioButton>
      <RadioButton GroupName = "Music" >MP3 Player</RadioButton>
      <RadioButton GroupName = "Music" >8-Track</RadioButton>
    </StackPanel>
  </Expander>

  <Expander BorderBrush ="Black">
    <Expander.Header>
      <Label Background = "Blue" Foreground = "White"
```

```
            FontSize = "15" Content = "Select your color choice"/>
    </Expander.Header>
    <StackPanel>
      <RadioButton>Red</RadioButton>
      <RadioButton>Green</RadioButton>
      <RadioButton>Blue</RadioButton>
    </StackPanel>
  </Expander >
</StackPanel>
```

Figure 29-9 shows each Expander in the collapsed state.

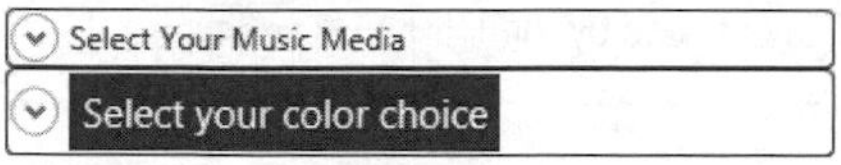

Figure 29-9. *Collapsed* Expanders

Figure 29-10 shows each Expander (pardon the redundancy) expanded.

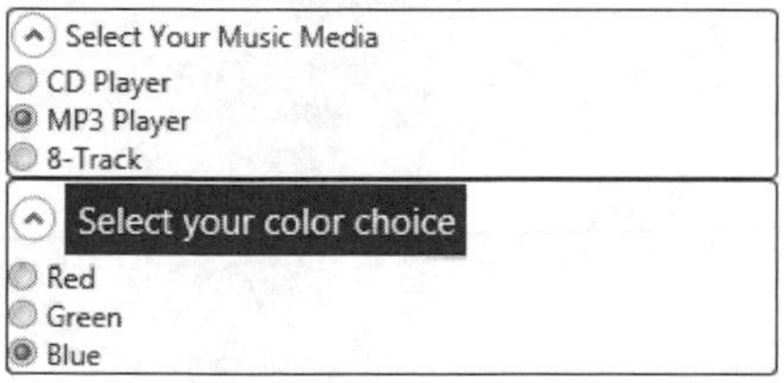

Figure 29-10. *Expanded* Expanders

Source Code The CheckRadioGroup.xaml file is included under the Chapter 29 subdirectory.

Working with the ListBox and ComboBox Types

As you would hope, WPF provides types that contain a group of selectable items, such as ListBox and ComboBox, both of which derive from the ItemsControl abstract base class. Most importantly, this parent class defines a property named Items, which returns a strongly typed ItemCollection object that holds onto the subitems. As it turns out, the ItemCollection type has been constructed to operate on System.Object types, and therefore it can contain anything whatsoever. If you wish to fill an ItemsControl-derived type with simply textual data via markup, you can do so using a set of <ListBoxItem> types. For example, consider the following XAML:

```
<!-- Simple list box -->
<ListBox Name = "lstVideoGameConsoles">
  <ListBoxItem>Microsoft XBox 360</ListBoxItem>
  <ListBoxItem>Sony Playstation 3</ListBoxItem>
  <ListBoxItem>Nintendo Wii</ListBoxItem>
  <ListBoxItem>Sony PSP</ListBoxItem>
  <ListBoxItem>Nintendo DS</ListBoxItem>
</ListBox>
```

```
<!-- Simple combo box -->
<ComboBox Name = "comboVideoGameConsoles">
  <ListBoxItem>Microsoft XBox 360</ListBoxItem>
  <ListBoxItem>Sony Playstation 3</ListBoxItem>
  <ListBoxItem>Nintendo Wii</ListBoxItem>
  <ListBoxItem>Sony PSP</ListBoxItem>
  <ListBoxItem>Nintendo DS</ListBoxItem>
</ComboBox>
```

Note ComboBox types can also be populated using <ComboBoxItem> elements, rather than <ListBoxItem>. By doing so, you gain access to the IsHighlighted property, which is not used by the ListBoxItem type.

Not surprisingly, we find the rendering shown in Figure 29-11.

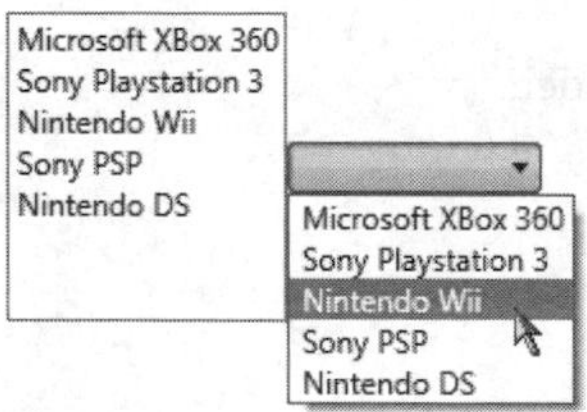

Figure 29-11. *A simple* ListBox *and* ComboBox

Filling List Controls Programmatically

Oftentimes, the data contained within a list control is not known until runtime; for example, you may need to fill items in a list box based on values returned from a database read, invoking a WCF service, or reading an external file. When you need to populate a ListBox or ComboBox control programmatically, simply use the members of the ItemCollection type to do so (Add(), Remove(), etc.). Assume you have a new Visual Studio 2008 WPF Application project named ListControls. The previous XAML declaration of the lstVideoGameConsole type could be defined in XAML as follows:

```
<Window x:Class="ListControls.MainWindow"
  xmlns="http://schemas.microsoft.com/winfx/2006/xaml/presentation"
  xmlns:x="http://schemas.microsoft.com/winfx/2006/xaml"
  Title="ListControls" Height="300" Width="300" >
  <StackPanel>
    <!-- This is filled via code -->
    <ListBox Name = "lstVideoGameConsoles">
    </ListBox>
  </StackPanel>
</Window>
```

and populated in a related code file as follows:

```
public partial class MainWindow : System.Windows.Window
{
  public MainWindow()
  {
    InitializeComponent();
```

```
    FillListBox();
  }

  private void FillListBox()
  {
    // Add items to the list box.
    lstVideoGameConsoles.Items.Add("Microsoft XBox 360");
    lstVideoGameConsoles.Items.Add("Sony Playstation 3");
    lstVideoGameConsoles.Items.Add("Nintendo Wii");
    lstVideoGameConsoles.Items.Add("Sony PSP");
    lstVideoGameConsoles.Items.Add("Nintendo DS");
  }
}
```

One thing that might strike you as odd is that in the XAML description of the ListBox, we made use of <ListBoxItem> types to populate the items; however, here we have made use of string types when calling the Add() method. The short explanation is that when using XAML, <ListBoxItem> types are more convenient in that they are defined within the http://schemas.microsoft.com/winfx/2006/xaml/presentation XML namespace, and therefore we have a direct reference to them.

Under the hood, ToString() is called on each <ListBoxItem> type, so the end result is identical. If you truly wanted to use a System.String to fill the ListBox (or ComboBox) type in XAML, you would need to define a new XML namespace to bring in mscorlib.dll (see Chapter 28 for more details):

```
<StackPanel xmlns:CorLib = "clr-namespace:System;assembly=mscorlib">
  <ListBox Name = "lstVideoGameConsoles">
    <CorLib:String>Microsoft XBox 360</CorLib:String>
    <CorLib:String>Sony Playstation 3</CorLib:String>
    <CorLib:String>Nintendo Wii</CorLib:String>
    <CorLib:String>Sony PSP</CorLib:String>
    <CorLib:String>Nintendo DS</CorLib:String>
  </ListBox>
</StackPanel>
```

Conversely, if you really wanted to, you could programmatically populate an ItemsControl-derived type using strongly typed ListBoxItem objects; however, you really gain nothing for the current example and have in fact created additional work for yourself (as the ListBoxItem does not have a constructor to set the Content property!).

Adding Arbitrary Content

Because ListBox and ComboBox both have ContentControl in their inheritance chain, they can contain data well beyond a simple string. Consider the following ComboBox, which contains various <StackPanels> containing 2D graphical objects and a descriptive label:

```
<StackPanel>
  <!-- A ListBox with content! -->
  <ListBox Name = "lstColors">
    <StackPanel Orientation ="Horizontal">
      <Ellipse Fill ="Yellow" Height ="50" Width ="50"/>
      <Label FontSize ="20" HorizontalAlignment="Center"
             VerticalAlignment="Center">Yellow</Label>
    </StackPanel>
    <StackPanel Orientation ="Horizontal">
      <Ellipse Fill ="Blue" Height ="50" Width ="50"/>
      <Label FontSize ="20" HorizontalAlignment="Center"
             VerticalAlignment="Center">Blue</Label>
    </StackPanel>
```

```
    <StackPanel Orientation ="Horizontal">
      <Ellipse Fill ="Green" Height ="50" Width ="50"/>
      <Label FontSize ="20" HorizontalAlignment="Center"
             VerticalAlignment="Center">Green</Label>
    </StackPanel>
  </ListBox>
</StackPanel>
```

Figure 29-12 shows the output of our current list types.

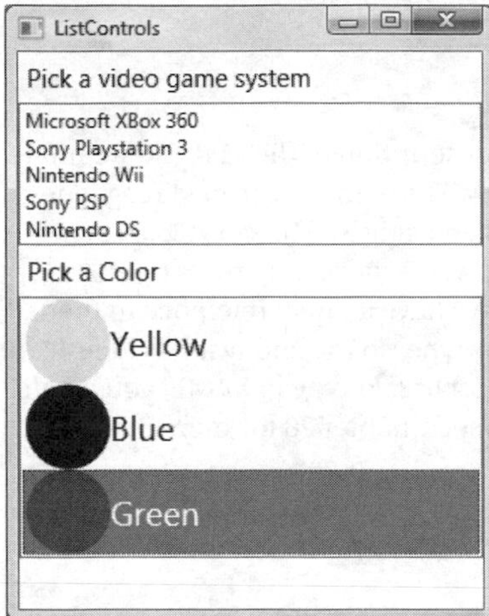

Figure 29-12. `ItemsControl`*-derived types can contain any sort of content you desire.*

Determining the Current Selection

Once you have populated a `ListBox` or `ComboBox` type, the next obvious issue is how to determine at runtime which item the user has selected. As it turns out, you have three ways to do so. If you are interested in finding the numerical index of the item selected, you can use the `SelectedIndex` property (which is zero based; a value of `-1` represents no selection). If you wish to obtain the object within the list that has been selected, the `SelectedItem` property fits the bill. Finally, the `SelectedValue` allows you to obtain the value of the selected object (typically obtained via a call to `ToString()`).

Sounds simple enough, right? Well, to test how each property behaves, assume you have defined two new `Button` types for the current window, both of which handle the `Click` event:

```
<!-- Buttons to get the selected items -->
<Button Name ="btnGetGameSystem" Click ="btnGetGameSystem_Click">
  Get Video Game System
</Button>
<Button Name ="btnGetColor" Click ="btnGetColor_Click">
  Get Color
</Button>
```

The `Click` handler for `btnGetGameSystem` will obtain the values of the `SelectedIndex`, `SelectedItem`, and `SelectedValue` properties of the `lstVideoGameConsoles` object and display them in a message box:

```
protected void btnGetGameSystem_Click(object sender, RoutedEventArgs args)
{
  string data = string.Empty;
  data += string.Format("SelectedIndex = {0}\n",
    lstVideoGameConsoles.SelectedIndex);
  data += string.Format("SelectedItem = {0}\n",
    lstVideoGameConsoles.SelectedItem);
  data += string.Format("SelectedValue = {0}\n",
    lstVideoGameConsoles.SelectedValue);
  MessageBox.Show(data, "Your Game Info");
}
```

If you were to select "Nintendo Wii" from the list of game consoles and click the related button, you would find the message box shown in Figure 29-13.

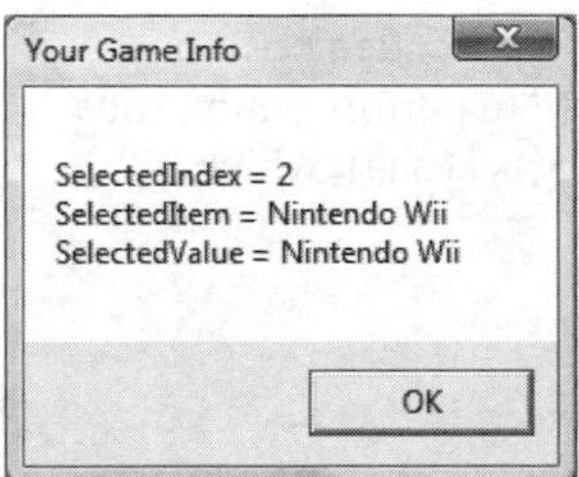

Figure 29-13. *Finding a selected string*

However, what about obtaining the selected color?

Determining the Current Selection for Nested Content

Assume the `Click` event handler for the `btnGetColor` `Button` has implemented `btnGetColor_Click()` to print out the current selection, index, and value of the `lstColors` `ListBox` object. Now, if you were to select the first item in the `lstColors` list box (and click the related button), you may be surprised to find the output shown in Figure 29-14.

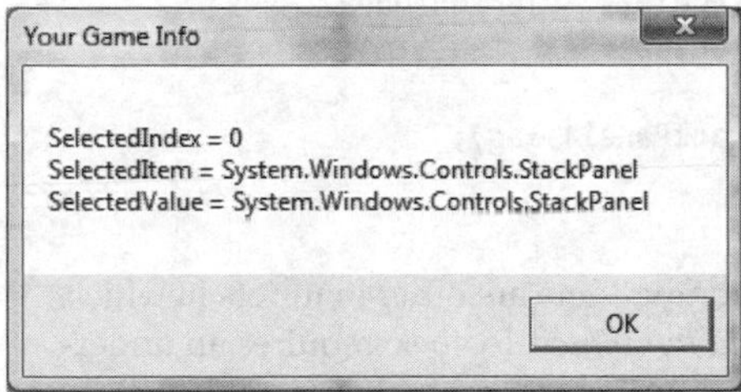

Figure 29-14. *Finding a selected . . .* `StackPanel`*?*

The reason for this output is the fact that the `lstColors` object is maintaining three `StackPanel` objects, each of which contains nested content. Therefore, `SelectedItem` and `SelectedValue` are simply calling `ToString()` on the `StackPanel` type, which returns its fully qualified name.

While you would be able to simply figure out which item was selected using the numerical value returned from `SelectedIndex`, another approach is to drill into the `StackPanel`'s child collection to grab the Content value of the Label using the StackPanel's internally maintained Children collection as follows:

```
protected void btnGetColor_Clicked(object sender, RoutedEventArgs args)
{
  // Get the Content value in the selected Label in the StackPanel.
  StackPanel selectedStack =
    (StackPanel)lstColors.Items[lstColors.SelectedIndex];
  string color = ((Label)(selectedStack.Children[1])).Content.ToString();

  string data = string.Empty;
  data += string.Format("SelectedIndex = {0}\n", lstColors.SelectedIndex);
  data += string.Format("Color = {0}", color);
  MessageBox.Show(data, "Your Game Info");
}
```

While this does the trick, this solution is very fragile in that we have hard-coded positions within the StackPanel (the second child, being the Label) and are required to perform numerous casting operations. Another alternative is to set the Tag property of each StackPanel, which is defined in the FrameworkElement base class:

```
<ListBox Name = "lstColors">
  <StackPanel Orientation ="Horizontal" Tag ="Yellow">
...
  </StackPanel>
  <StackPanel Orientation ="Horizontal" Tag ="Blue">
...
  </StackPanel>
  <StackPanel Orientation ="Horizontal" Tag ="Green">
...
  </StackPanel>
</ListBox>
```

Using this approach, our code cleans up considerably, as we can pluck out the value assigned to Tag programmatically as follows:

```
protected void btnGetColor_Clicked(object sender, RoutedEventArgs args)
{
  string data = string.Empty;
  data += string.Format("SelectedIndex = {0}\n", lstColors.SelectedIndex);
  data += string.Format("SelectedItem = {0}\n", lstColors.SelectedItem);
  data += string.Format("SelectedValue = {0}",
    (lstColors.Items[lstColors.SelectedIndex] as StackPanel).Tag);
  MessageBox.Show(data, "Your Color Info");
}
```

While this approach is a bit cleaner than our first attempt, there are other manners in which you can capture values from a complex control using *data templates*. To do so requires an understanding of the WPF data-binding engine, which you will examine at the conclusion of this chapter.

Source Code The ListControls project is included under the Chapter 29 subdirectory.

Working with Text Areas

WPF ships with a number of UI elements that allow you to gather textual-based user input. The most primitive types would be TextBox and PasswordBox, which we will examine here using a new Visual Studio 2008 WPF Application named TextControls.

Working with the TextBox Type

Like other TextBox types you have used in the past, the WPF TextBox type can be configured to hold a single line of text (the default setting) or multiple lines of text if the AcceptReturn property is set to true. Information within a TextBox will always be treated as character data, and therefore the "content" is always a string type that can be set and retrieved using the Text property:

```
<TextBox Name ="txtData" Text = "Hello!" BorderBrush ="Blue" Width ="100"/>
```

One aspect of the WPF TextBox type that is very unique is that it has the built-in ability to check the spelling of the data entered within it by setting the SpellCheck.IsEnabled property to true. When you do so, you will notice that like Microsoft Office, misspelled words are underlined in a red squiggle. Even better, there is an underlying programming model that gives you access to the spell-checker engine, which allows you to get a list of suggestions for misspelled words.

Update your current window XAML definition to make use of a Label, TextBox, and Button as follows (notice this TextBox supports multiple lines of text and has enabled spell checking):

```
<Window x:Class="TextControls.MainWindow"
    xmlns="http://schemas.microsoft.com/winfx/2006/xaml/presentation"
    xmlns:x="http://schemas.microsoft.com/winfx/2006/xaml"
    Title="TextControls" Height="204" Width="292" >
  <StackPanel>
    <Label FontSize ="15">Is this word spelled correctly?</Label>
    <TextBox  SpellCheck.IsEnabled ="True" AcceptsReturn ="True"
      Name ="txtData"  FontSize ="12"
      BorderBrush ="Blue" Height ="100">
    </TextBox>
    <Button Name ="btnOK" Content ="Get Selections"
            Width = "100" Click ="btnOK_Click"/>
  </StackPanel>
</Window>
```

With just this much functionality, you will already notice that when you type misspelled words into your TextBox, errors are marked as such. To complete our simple spell checker, update the Click event handler for the Button type as follows:

```
protected void btnOK_Click(object sender, RoutedEventArgs args)
{
  string spellingHints = string.Empty;

  // Try to get a spelling error at the current caret location.
  SpellingError error = txtData.GetSpellingError(txtData.CaretIndex);
  if (error != null)
  {
    // Build a string of spelling suggestions.
    foreach (string s in error.Suggestions)
    {
      spellingHints += string.Format("{0}\n", s);
```

```
    }

    // Show suggestions.
    MessageBox.Show(spellingHints, "Try these instead");
  }
}
```

The code is quite simple. We simply figure the current location of the caret in the text box using the `CaretIndex` property in order to extract a `SpellingError` object. If there is an error at said location (meaning the value is not `null`), we loop over the list of suggestions via the aptly named `Suggestions` property. Finally, we display the possibilities using a simple `MessageBox.Show()` request. Figure 29-15 shows a possible test run when the caret is within the misspelled word "auromatically."

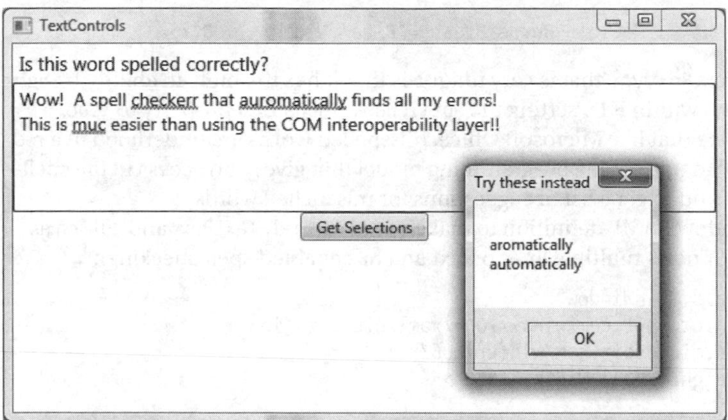

Figure 29-15. *A custom spell checker!*

Working with the PasswordBox Type

The `PasswordBox` type, not surprisingly, allows you to define a safe place to enter sensitive text data. By default, the password character is a circle type; however, this can be changed using the `PasswordChar` property. To obtain the value entered by the end user, simply check the `Password` property. Let's update our current spell-checking application by requiring the correct password to see the list of spelling suggestions. First, update your existing <StackPanel> with a nested <StackPanel> that places the `PasswordBox` horizontally alongside the existing <Button>:

```
<StackPanel>
  <Label FontSize ="15">Is this word spelled correctly?</Label>
  <TextBox SpellCheck.IsEnabled ="True" AcceptsReturn ="True"
           Name ="txtFavoriteColor"  FontSize ="14"
           BorderBrush ="Blue" Height ="100">
  </TextBox>
  <StackPanel Orientation ="Horizontal">
    <PasswordBox Name ="pwdText" BorderBrush ="Black" Width ="100"></PasswordBox>
    <Button Name ="btnOK" Content ="Get Selections"
            Width = "100" Click ="btnOK_Click"/>
  </StackPanel>
</StackPanel>
```

Now update your current Button Click event handler to make a call to a helper function named CheckPassword(), which tests against a hard-coded string. Be sure to only allow the suggestions to be presented if the check is successful. Here are the relevant updates:

```
public partial class MainWindow : System.Windows.Window
{
...
  protected void btnOK_Click(object sender, RoutedEventArgs args)
  {
    if (CheckPassword())
    {
      // Same spell-checking logic as before...
    }
    else
      MessageBox.Show("Security error!!");
  }

  private bool CheckPassword()
  {
    if (pwdText.Password == "Chucky")
      return true;
    else
      return false;
  }
}
```

Beyond TextBox and PasswordBox, do be aware that if you are building an application that has a text area that can contain any type of content (graphical renderings, text, etc.), WPF also provides the RichTextBox. Furthermore, if you require the horsepower to build an extremely text-intensive application, WPF provides an entire document presentation API represented primarily within the System.Windows.Documents namespace.

Here you will find types that allow you to build *flow documents*, which allow you to programmatically represent (in XAML or C# code) paragraphs, sections of related text blocks, sticky notes, annotations, tables, and other rich document-centric types. This edition of the text does not cover the RichTextBox or the flow document API, however; be sure to consult the .NET Framework 3.5 SDK documentation for further details if you are so inclined.

Source Code The TextControls project is included under the Chapter 29 subdirectory.

That wraps up our initial look at the WPF control set. You'll see how to build menu systems, status bars, and toolbars later in this chapter. The next task, however, is to learn how to arrange UI elements within a Window type using any number of panel types.

Controlling Content Layout Using Panels

A real-world WPF application invariability contains a good number of UI elements (user input controls, graphical content, menu systems, status bars, etc.) that need to be well organized within the containing window. As well, once the UI widgets have been placed in their new home, you will want to make sure they behave as intended when the end user resizes the window or possibly a portion of the window (as in the case of a splitter window). To ensure your WPF controls retain their position within the hosting window, we are provided with a good number of *panel* types.

As you may recall from the previous chapter, when you place content within a window that does not make use of panels, it is positioned dead center within the container. Consider the following simple window declaration containing a single Button type. Regardless of how you resize the window, the UI widget is always equidistant on all four sizes of the client area.

```
<!-- This button is in the center of the window at all times-->
<Window x:Class="MyWPFApp.MainWindow"
  xmlns="http://schemas.microsoft.com/winfx/2006/xaml/presentation"
  xmlns:x="http://schemas.microsoft.com/winfx/2006/xaml"
  Title="Fun with Panels!" Height="285" Width="325">
  <Button Name="btnOK" Height = "100" Width="80">OK</Button>
</Window>
```

Also recall that if you attempt to place multiple elements directly within the scope of a <Window>, you will receive markup and/or compile-time errors. The reason for these errors is that a window (or any descendant of ContentControl for that matter) can assign only a single object to its Content property:

```
<!-- Error! Content property is implicitly set more than once!-->
<Window x:Class="MyWPFApp.MainWindow"
  xmlns="http://schemas.microsoft.com/winfx/2006/xaml/presentation"
  xmlns:x="http://schemas.microsoft.com/winfx/2006/xaml"
  Title="Fun with Panels!" Height="285" Width="325">

  <!-- Ack! Two direct child elements of the <Window>!
  <Label Name="lblInstructions"
    Width="328" Height="27" FontSize="15">Enter Car Information</Label>
  <Button Name="btnOK" Height = "100" Width="80">OK</Button>
</Window>
```

Obviously a window that can only contain a single item is of little use. When a window needs to contain multiple elements, they must be arranged within any number of panels. The panel will contain all of the UI elements that represent the window, after which the panel itself is used as the object assigned to the Content property.

The Core Panel Types of WPF

The System.Windows.Controls namespace System.Windows.Controls namespace provides numerous panel types, each of which controls how subelements are positioned. Using panels, you can establish how the widgets behave when the end user resizes the window, if they remain exactly where placed at design time, if they reflow horizontally left to right or vertically top to bottom, and so forth.

To build complex user interfaces, panel controls can be intermixed (e.g., a DockPanel that contains a StackPanel) to provide for a great deal of flexibility and control. Furthermore, the panel types can work in conjunction with other document-centric controls (such as the ViewBox, TextBlock, TextFlow, and Paragraph types) to further customize how content is arranged within a given panel. Table 29-3 documents the role of some commonly used WPF panel controls.

Table 29-3. *Core WPF Panel Controls*

Panel Control	Meaning in Life
Canvas	Provides a "classic" mode of content placement. Items stay exactly where you put them at design time.
DockPanel	Locks content to a specified side of the panel (Top, Bottom, Left, or Right).
Grid	Arranges content within a series of cells, maintained within a tabular grid.

Panel Control	Meaning in Life
`StackPanel`	Stacks content in a vertical or horizontal manner, as dictated by the `Orientation` property.
`WrapPanel`	Positions content from left to right, breaking the content to the next line at the edge of the containing box. Subsequent ordering happens sequentially from top to bottom or from right to left, depending on the value of the `Orientation` property.

To illustrate the use of these commonly used panel types, in the next sections we'll build the UI shown in Figure 29-16 within various panels and observe how the positioning changes when the window is resized.

Figure 29-16. *Our target UI layout*

Positioning Content Within Canvas Panels

Far and away, the simplest panel is `Canvas`. Most likely, `Canvas` is the panel you will feel most at home with, as it emulates the default layout of a Windows Forms application. Simply put, a `Canvas` panel allows for absolute positioning of UI content. If the end user resizes the window to an area that is smaller than the layout maintained by the `Canvas` panel, the internal content will not be visible until the container is stretched to a size equal to or larger than the `Canvas` area.

To add content to a `Canvas`, define the required subelements within the scope of the opening `<Canvas>` and closing `</Canvas>` tags and specify the location where rendering should occur (note that the content position can be relative to the left/right or top/bottom of the `Canvas`, but not both). If you wish to have the `Canvas` stretch over the entire surface of the container, simply omit the `Height` and `Width` properties. Consider the following XAML markup, which defines the layout shown in Figure 29-16:

```
<Window
  xmlns="http://schemas.microsoft.com/winfx/2006/xaml/presentation"
  xmlns:x="http://schemas.microsoft.com/winfx/2006/xaml"
  Title="Fun with Panels!" Height="285" Width="325">

  <Canvas Background="LightSteelBlue">
    <Button Canvas.Left="212" Canvas.Top="203" Name="btnOK" Width="80">OK</Button>
    <Label Canvas.Left="17" Canvas.Top="14" Name="lblInstructions"
           Width="328" Height="27" FontSize="15">Enter Car Information</Label>
    <Label Canvas.Left="17" Canvas.Top="60" Name="lblMake">Make</Label>
```

```
    <TextBox Canvas.Left="94" Canvas.Top="60" Name="txtMake"
             Width="193" Height="25"/>
    <Label Canvas.Left="17" Canvas.Top="109" Name="lblColor">Color</Label>
    <TextBox Canvas.Left="94" Canvas.Top="107" Name="txtColor"
             Width="193" Height="25"/>
    <Label Canvas.Left="17" Canvas.Top="155" Name="lblPetName">Pet Name</Label>
    <TextBox Canvas.Left="94" Canvas.Top="153" Name="txtPetName"
             Width="193" Height="25"/>
  </Canvas>

</Window>
```

In this example, each item within the <Canvas> scope is qualified by a `Canvas.Left` and `Canvas.Top` value, which control the content's top-left positioning within the panel, using attached property syntax (see Chapter 28). As you may have gathered, vertical positioning is controlled using the `Top` or `Bottom` property, while horizontal positioning is established using `Left` or `Right`.

Given that each widget has been placed within the <Canvas> element, we find that as the window is resized, widgets are covered up if the container's surface area is smaller than the content (see Figure 29-17).

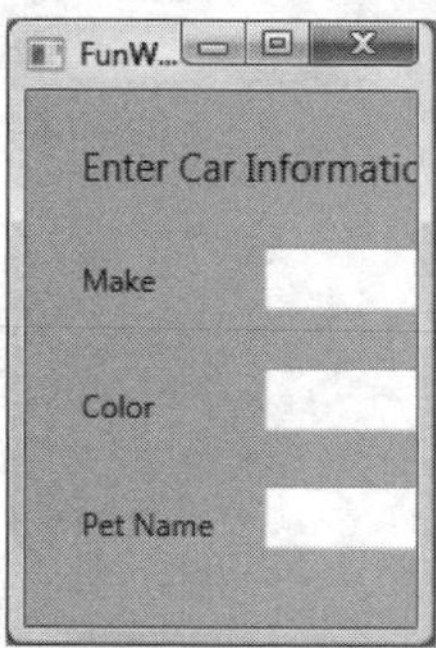

Figure 29-17. *Content in a* `Canvas` *panel allows for absolute positioning.*

The order you declare content within a `Canvas` is not used to calculate placement, as this is based on the control's size and the `Canvas.Top`, `Canvas.Bottom`, `Canvas.Left`, and `Canvas.Right` properties. Given this, the following markup (which groups together like-minded controls) results in an identical rendering:

```
<Canvas Background="LightSteelBlue">
  <TextBox Canvas.Left="94" Canvas.Top="153" Name="txtColor"
           Width="193" Height="25"/>
  <TextBox Canvas.Left="94" Canvas.Top="60" Name="txtPetName"
           Width="193" Height="25"/>
  <TextBox Canvas.Left="94" Canvas.Top="107" Name="txtMake"
           Width="193" Height="25"/>

  <Label Canvas.Left="17" Canvas.Top="14" Name="lblInstructions"
   Width="328" Height="27" FontSize="15">Enter Car Information</Label>
  <Label Canvas.Left="17" Canvas.Top="109" Name="lblColor">Color</Label>
  <Label Canvas.Left="17" Canvas.Top="155" Name="lblMake">Pet Name</Label>
  <Label Canvas.Left="17" Canvas.Top="60" Name="lblPetName">Make</Label>

  <Button Canvas.Left="212" Canvas.Top="203" Name="btnOK" Width="80">OK</Button>
</Canvas>
```

Note If subelements within a Canvas do not define a specific location using attached property syntax, they automatically attach to the extreme upper-left corner of the Canvas.

Although using the Canvas type may seem like a preferable way to arrange content (because it feels so familiar), it does suffer from some limitations. First of all, items within a Canvas do not dynamically resize themselves when applying styles or templates (e.g., their font sizes are unaffected). The other obvious limitation is that the Canvas will not attempt to keep elements visible when the end user resizes the window to a smaller surface.

Perhaps the best use of the Canvas type is to position graphical content. For example, if you were building a custom image using XAML, you certainly would want the lines, shapes, and text to remain in the same location, rather than having them dynamically repositioned as the user resizes the window! You'll revisit the Canvas in the next chapter when we examine WPF's graphical rendering services.

Source Code The SimpleCanvas.xaml file can be found under the Chapter 29 subdirectory.

Positioning Content Within WrapPanel Panels

A WrapPanel allows you to define content that will flow across the panel as the window is resized. When positioning elements in a WrapPanel, you do not specify top, bottom, left, and right docking values as you typically do with the Canvas. However, each subelement is free to define a Height and Width value (among other property values) to control its overall size in the container.

Because content within a WrapPanel does not "dock" to a given side of the panel, the order in which you declare the elements is critical (content is rendered from the first element to the last). Consider the following XAML snippet:

```
<WrapPanel Background="LightSteelBlue">
  <Label Name="lblInstruction" Width="328"
         Height="27" FontSize="15">Enter Car Information</Label>
  <Label Name="lblMake">Make</Label>
  <TextBox Name="txtMake" Width="193" Height="25"/>
  <Label Name="lblColor">Color</Label>
  <TextBox Name="txtColor" Width="193" Height="25"/>
  <Label Name="lblPetName">Pet Name</Label>
  <TextBox Name="txtPetName" Width="193" Height="25"/>
  <Button Name="btnOK" Width="80">OK</Button>
</WrapPanel>
```

When you view this markup, the content will look out of sorts as you resize the width, as it is flowing left to right across the window (see Figure 29-18).

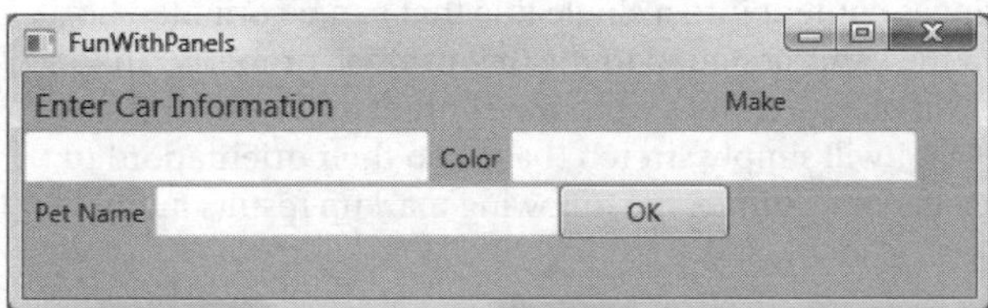

Figure 29-18. *Content in a* WrapPanel *behaves much like a vanilla-flavored HTML page.*

By default, content within a `WrapPanel` flows left to right. However, if you change the value of the `Orientation` property to `Vertical`, you can have content wrap in a top-to-bottom manner:

```
<WrapPanel Background="LightSteelBlue" Orientation ="Vertical">
```

A `WrapPanel` (as well as some other panel types) may be declared by specifying `ItemWidth` and `ItemHeight` values, which control the default size of each item. If a subelement does provide its own `Height` and/or `Width` value, it will be positioned relative to the size established by the panel. Consider the following markup:

```
<WrapPanel Background="LightSteelBlue" ItemWidth ="200" ItemHeight ="30">
  <Label Name="lblInstruction"
        FontSize="15">Enter Car Information</Label>
  <Label Name="lblMake">Make</Label>
  <TextBox Name="txtMake"/>
  <Label Name="lblColor">Color</Label>
  <TextBox Name="txtColor"/>
  <Label Name="lblPetName">Pet Name</Label>
  <TextBox Name="txtPetName"/>
  <Button Name="btnOK" Width ="80">OK</Button>
</WrapPanel>
```

When rendered, we find the output shown in Figure 29-19 (notice the size and position of the `Button` widget).

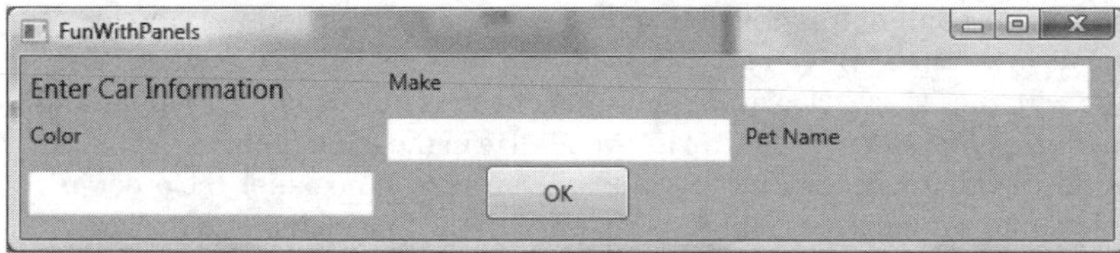

Figure 29-19. *A* `WrapPanel` *can establish the width and height of a given item.*

As you might agree after looking at Figure 29-19, a `WrapPanel` is not typically the best choice for arranging content directly in a window, as the elements can become scrambled as the user resizes the window. In most cases, a `WrapPanel` will be a subelement to another panel type, to allow a small area of the window to wrap its content when resized.

Source Code The `SimpleWrapPanel.xaml` file can be found under the Chapter 29 subdirectory.

Positioning Content Within StackPanel Panels

Like a `WrapPanel`, a `StackPanel` control arranges content into a single line that can be oriented horizontally or vertically (the default), based on the value assigned to the `Orientation` property. The difference, however, is that the `StackPanel` will *not* attempt to wrap the content as the user resizes the window. Rather, the items in the `StackPanel` will simply stretch (based on their orientation) to accommodate the size of the `StackPanel` itself. For example, the following markup results in the output shown in Figure 29-20:

```
<StackPanel Background="LightSteelBlue">
  <Label Name="lblInstruction"
         FontSize="15">Enter Car Information</Label>
  <Label Name="lblMake">Make</Label>
  <TextBox Name="txtMake"/>
  <Label Name="lblColor">Color</Label>
  <TextBox Name="txtColor"/>
  <Label Name="lblPetName">Pet Name</Label>
  <TextBox Name="txtPetName"/>
  <Button Name="btnOK">OK</Button>
</StackPanel>
```

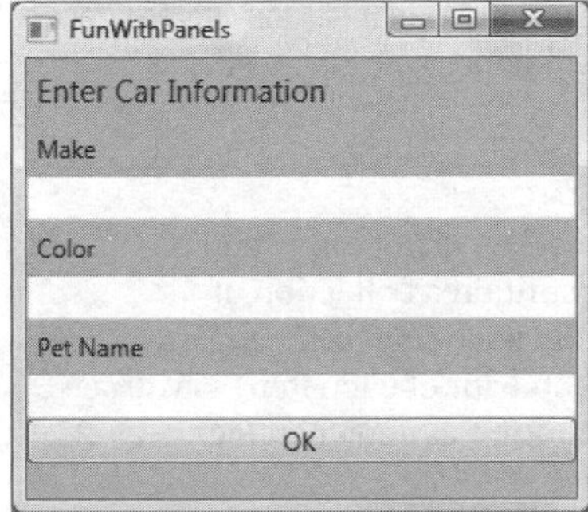

Figure 29-20. *Vertical stacking of content*

If we assign the `Orientation` property to `Horizontal` as follows, the rendered output will match that of Figure 29-21:

```
<StackPanel Background="LightSteelBlue" Orientation ="Horizontal">
```

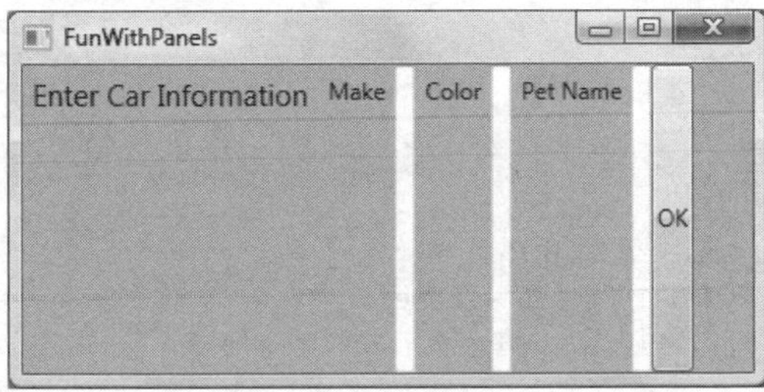

Figure 29-21. *Horizontal stacking of content*

Again, like the `WrapPanel`, you will seldom want to use a `StackPanel` to directly arrange content within a window. Rather, a `StackPanel` is better suited as a subpanel to a master panel.

Source Code The `SimpleStackPanel.xaml` file can be found under the Chapter 29 subdirectory.

Positioning Content Within Grid Panels

Of all the panels provided with the WPF APIs, Grid is far and away the most flexible. Like an HTML table, the Grid can be carved up into a set of cells, each one of which provides content. When defining a Grid, you perform three steps:

1. Define and configure each column.
2. Define and configure each row.
3. Assign content to each cell of the grid using attached property syntax.

■ **Note** If you do not define any rows or columns, the <Grid> defaults to a single cell that fills the entire surface of the window. Furthermore, if you do not assign a cell value for a subelement within a <Grid>, it automatically attaches to column 0, row 0.

The first two steps (defining the columns and rows) are achieved by using the <Grid.ColumnDefinitions> and <Grid.RowDefinitions> elements, which contain a collection of <ColumnDefinition> and <RowDefinition> elements, respectively. Because each cell within a grid is indeed a true .NET type, you can configure the look and feel and behavior of each item as you see fit. Here is a rather simple <Grid> definition that arranges our UI content as shown in Figure 29-22:

```
<Grid ShowGridLines ="True" Background ="AliceBlue">
  <!-- Define the rows/columns -->
  <Grid.ColumnDefinitions>
    <ColumnDefinition/>
    <ColumnDefinition/>
  </Grid.ColumnDefinitions>
  <Grid.RowDefinitions>
    <RowDefinition/>
    <RowDefinition/>
  </Grid.RowDefinitions>

  <!-- Now add the elements to the grid's cells-->
  <Label Name="lblInstruction" Grid.Column ="0" Grid.Row ="0"
         FontSize="15">Enter Car Information</Label>
  <Button Name="btnOK"  Height ="30" Grid.Column ="0" Grid.Row ="0" >OK</Button>
  <Label Name="lblMake" Grid.Column ="1" Grid.Row ="0">Make</Label>
  <TextBox Name="txtMake" Grid.Column ="1" Grid.Row ="0" Width="193" Height="25"/>
  <Label Name="lblColor" Grid.Column ="0" Grid.Row ="1" >Color</Label>
  <TextBox Name="txtColor" Width="193" Height="25" Grid.Column ="0" Grid.Row ="1" />

  <!-- Just to keep things interesting, add some color to the pet name cell -->
  <Rectangle Fill ="LightGreen" Grid.Column ="1" Grid.Row ="1" />
  <Label Name="lblPetName" Grid.Column ="1" Grid.Row ="1" >Pet Name</Label>
  <TextBox Name="txtPetName" Grid.Column ="1" Grid.Row ="1"
           Width="193" Height="25"/>
</Grid>
```

Notice that each element (including a light green Rectangle element, thrown in for good measure) connects itself to a cell in the grid using the Grid.Row and Grid.Column attached properties. By default, the ordering of cells in a grid begins at the upper left, which is specified via Grid.Column="0" Grid.Row="0". Given that our grid defines a total of four cells, the bottom-right cell can be identified via Grid.Column="1" Grid.Row="1".

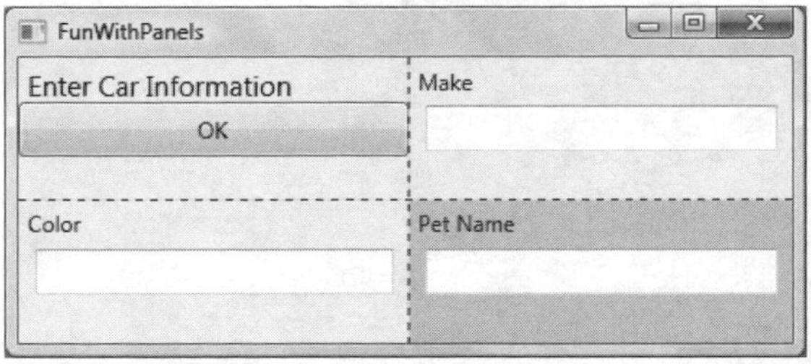

Figure 29-22. *The* `Grid` *panel in action*

■ **Source Code** The `SimpleGrid.xaml` file can be found under the Chapter 29 subdirectory.

Grids with GridSplitter Types

`Grid` types can also support splitters. As you most likely know, splitters allow the end user to resize rows or columns of a grid type. As this is done, the content within each resizable cell will reshape itself based on how the items have been contained. Adding splitters to a `Grid` is very easy to do; simply define the `<GridSplitter>` type, using attached property syntax to establish which row or column it affects. Do be aware that you must assign a `Width` or `Height` value (depending on vertical or horizontal splitting) in order to be visible on the screen. Consider the following simple `Grid` type with a splitter on the first column (`Grid.Column = "0"`):

```
<Window
  xmlns="http://schemas.microsoft.com/winfx/2006/xaml/presentation"
  xmlns:x="http://schemas.microsoft.com/winfx/2006/xaml"
  Title="FunWithPanels" Height="191" Width="436">
  <Grid Background ="AliceBlue">
    <!-- Define columns -->
    <Grid.ColumnDefinitions>
      <ColumnDefinition Width ="Auto"/>
      <ColumnDefinition/>
    </Grid.ColumnDefinitions>

    <!-- Add this label to cell 0 -->
    <Label Name="lblLeft" Background ="GreenYellow"
             Grid.Column="0" Content ="Left!"/>

    <!-- Define the splitter -->
    <GridSplitter Grid.Column ="0" Width ="5"/>

    <!-- Add this label to cell 1 -->
    <Label Name="lblRight" Grid.Column ="1" Content ="Right!"/>
  </Grid>
</Window>
```

First and foremost, notice that the column that will support the splitter has a `Width` property of `Auto`. Next, notice that the `<GridSplitter>` makes use of attached property syntax to establish which column it is working with. If you were to view this output, you would find a 5-pixel splitter that allows you to resize each `Label` (because we have not specified `Height` or `Width` properties for either `Label`, they fill up the entire cell). See Figure 29-23.

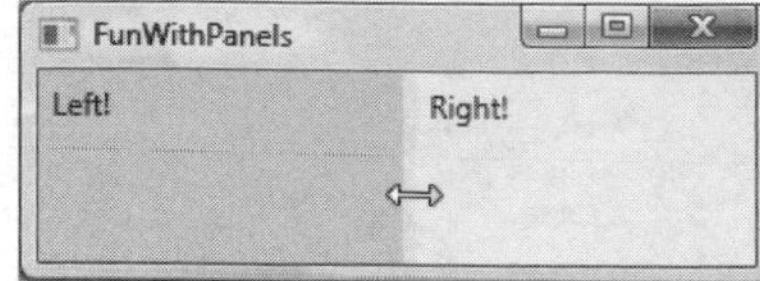

Figure 29-23. `Grid` *types containing splitters*

■ Source Code The `GridWithSplitter.xaml` file can be found under the Chapter 29 subdirectory.

Positioning Content Within DockPanel Panels

`DockPanel` is typically used as a master panel that contains any number of additional panels for grouping of related content. `DockPanels` make use of attached property syntax as seen with the `Canvas` type, to control where their upper-left corner (the default) will attach itself within the panel. Here is a very simple `DockPanel` definition, which results in the output shown in Figure 29-24:

```
<DockPanel LastChildFill ="True">
  <!-- Dock items to the panel -->
  <Label DockPanel.Dock ="Top" Name="lblInstruction"
         FontSize="15">Enter Car Information</Label>
  <Label DockPanel.Dock ="Left" Name="lblMake">Make</Label>
  <Label DockPanel.Dock ="Right" Name="lblColor">Color</Label>
  <Label DockPanel.Dock ="Bottom" Name="lblPetName">Pet Name</Label>
  <Button Name="btnOK">OK</Button>
</DockPanel>
```

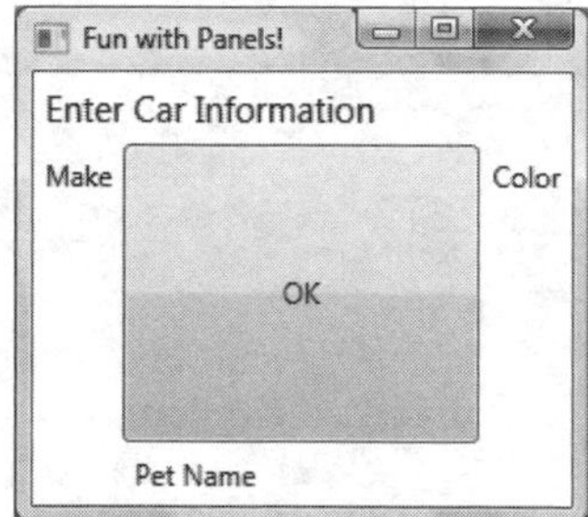

Figure 29-24. *A simple* `DockPanel`

■ Note If you add multiple elements to the same side of a `DockPanel`, they will be stacked along the specified edge in the order that they are declared.

The benefit of using `DockPanel` types is that as the user resizes the window, each element remains “connected” to the specified side of the panel (via `DockPanel.Dock`). Also notice that the opening `<DockPanel>` element sets the `LastChildFill` attribute to `true`. Given that the `Button` type has not specified any `DockPanel.Dock` value, it will therefore be stretched within the remaining space.

Source Code The `SimpleDockPanel.xaml` file can be found under the Chapter 29 subdirectory.

Enabling Scrolling for Panel Types

It is worth pointing out the WPF supplies a `<ScrollViewer>` type, which provides automatic scrolling behaviors for nested panel types:

```
<ScrollViewer>
  <StackPanel>
    <Button Content ="First" Background = "Green" Height ="40"/>
    <Button Content ="Second" Background = "Red" Height ="40"/>
    <Button Content ="Third" Background = "Pink" Height ="40"/>
    <Button Content ="Fourth" Background = "Yellow" Height ="40"/>
    <Button Content ="Fifth" Background = "Blue" Height ="40"/>
  </StackPanel>
</ScrollViewer>
```

The result of the previous XAML definition is shown in Figure 29-25.

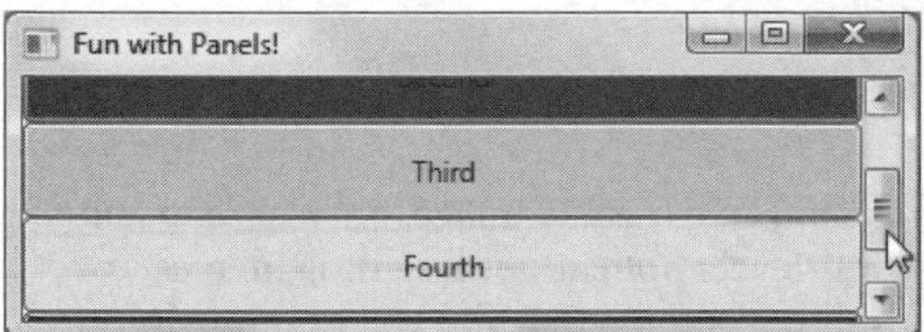

Figure 29-25. *Working with the* `ScrollViewer` *type*

Source Code The `ScrollViewer.xaml` file can be found under the Chapter 29 subdirectory.

As you would expect, each panel provides numerous members that allow you to fine-tune content placement. On a related note, WPF controls all support two properties of interest (`Padding` and `Margin`) that allow the control itself to inform the panel how it wishes to be treated. Specifically, the `Padding` property controls how much extra space should surround the interior control, while `Margin` controls the extra space around the exterior of a control.

This wraps up our look at the major panel types of WPF, and the various ways they position their content. Next, we will see an example using nested panels to create a layout system for a main window. To do so, we will enhance the functionality of the TextControls project (e.g., the spell-checker app) to support a main menu, a status bar, and a toolbar.

Building a Window's Frame Using Nested Panels

This updated version of the application (which we will assume is a new Visual Studio 2008 WPF Application project named MySpellChecker) will be extended and finalized over the pages to come, so for the time being, you will construct the core layout and base functionality.

Our goal is to construct a layout where the main window has a topmost menu system, a toolbar, and a status bar mounted on the bottom of the window. The status bar will contain a pane to hold text prompts that are displayed when the user selects a menu item (or toolbar button), while the menu system and toolbar will offer UI triggers to close the application and display spelling suggestions in an Expander widget. Figure 29-26 shows the initial layout we are shooting for, displaying spelling suggestions for "XAML."

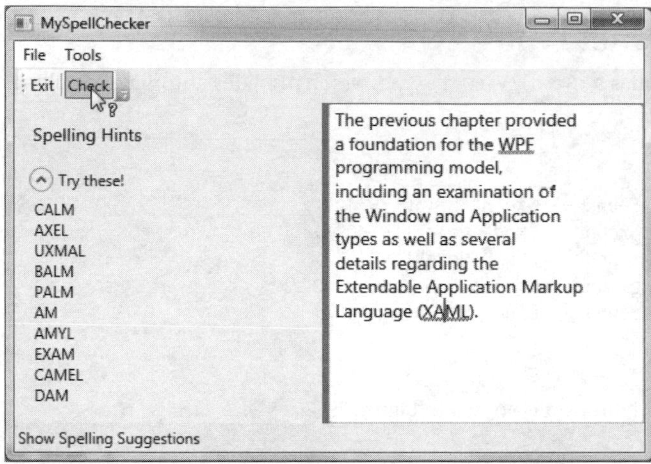

Figure 29-26. *Using nested panels to establish a window's UI*

Notice that our two toolbar buttons are not supporting an expected image, but a simple text value. While this would not be sufficient for a production-level application, assigning images to toolbar buttons typically involves using embedded resources, a topic that you will examine in Chapter 30 (so text data will do for now). Also note that as the mouse button is placed over the Check button, the mouse cursor changes and the single pane of the status bar displays a useful UI message.

To begin building this UI, update the initial XAML definition for your Window type to make use of a <DockPanel> child element, rather than the default <Grid>:

```
<Window x:Class="MySpellChecker.MainWindow"
  xmlns="http://schemas.microsoft.com/winfx/2006/xaml/presentation"
  xmlns:x="http://schemas.microsoft.com/winfx/2006/xaml"
  Title="MySpellChecker" Height="331" Width="508"
  WindowStartupLocation ="CenterScreen" >

  <!-- This panel establishes the content for the window -->
  <DockPanel>
  </DockPanel>

</Window>
```

Building the Menu System

Menu systems in WPF are represented by the Menu type, which maintains a collection of MenuItem objects. When building a menu system in XAML, each MenuItem may handle various events, most notably Click, which occurs when the end user selects a subitem. In our example, we will build two topmost menu items (File and Tools), which expose Exit and Spelling Hints subitems (respectively). In addition to handling the Click event for each subitem, we will also handle the MouseEnter and MouseExit events, which will be used to set the status bar text in a later step. Add the following markup within your <DockPanel> scope:

```
<!--Doc menu system on the top-->
<Menu DockPanel.Dock ="Top"
      HorizontalAlignment="Left" Background="White" BorderBrush ="Black">
  <MenuItem Header="_File" Click ="FileExit_Click" >
    <Separator/>
    <MenuItem Header ="_Exit" MouseEnter ="MouseEnterExitArea"
             MouseLeave ="MouseLeaveArea" Click ="FileExit_Click"/>
    </MenuItem>
    <MenuItem Header="_Tools">
      <MenuItem Header ="_Spelling Hints" MouseEnter ="MouseEnterToolsHintsArea"
               MouseLeave ="MouseLeaveArea" Click ="ToolsSpellingHints_Click"/>
  </MenuItem>
</Menu>
```

Notice that we have docked the menu system to the top of the DockPanel. As well, the <Separator> element has been used to insert a thin horizontal line in the menu system, directly before the Exit option. Also notice that the Header values for each MenuItem contain an embedded underbar token (for example, _Exit). This is used to establish which letter will be underlined when the end user presses the Alt key (for keyboard shortcuts).

The complete the menu system definition, we now need to implement the various event handlers. First, we have the File ➤ Exit handler, FileExit_Click(), which will simply terminate the application via Application.Current.Shutdown(). The MouseEnter and MouseExit event handlers for each subitem will eventually update our status bar; however, for now, we will simply provide shells. Finally, the ToolsSpellingHints_Click() handler for the Tools ➤ Spelling Hints menu item will also be a shell for the time being. Here are the current updates to your code-behind file:

```
public partial class MainWindow : System.Windows.Window
{
  public MainWindow()
  {
    InitializeComponent();
  }

  protected void FileExit_Click(object sender, RoutedEventArgs args)
  {
    // Terminate the application.
    Application.Current.Shutdown();
  }

  protected void ToolsSpellingHints_Click(object sender, RoutedEventArgs args)
  {
  }
  protected void MouseEnterExitArea(object sender, RoutedEventArgs args)
  {
  }
  protected void MouseEnterToolsHintsArea(object sender, RoutedEventArgs args)
  {
  }
  protected void MouseLeaveArea(object sender, RoutedEventArgs args)
  {
  }
}
```

Building the ToolBar Type

Toolbars (represented by the ToolBar type in WPF) typically provide an alternative manner to activate a menu option. Add the following markup directly after the closing scope of your <Menu> definition:

```
<!-- Put Toolbar under the Menu -->
<ToolBar DockPanel.Dock ="Top" >
  <Button Content ="Exit" MouseEnter ="MouseEnterExitArea"
          MouseLeave ="MouseLeaveArea" Click ="FileExit_Click"/>
  <Separator/>
  <Button Content ="Check" MouseEnter ="MouseEnterToolsHintsArea"
          MouseLeave ="MouseLeaveArea" Click ="ToolsSpellingHints_Click"
          Cursor="Help" />
</ToolBar>
```

Our <ToolBar> type consists of two Button types, which just so happen to handle the same events and are handled by the same methods in our code file. Using this technique, we are able to double-up our handlers to serve both menu items and toolbar buttons. Although this toolbar is making use of the typical push buttons, do know that the ToolBar type "is-a" ContentControl, and therefore you are free to embed any types into its surface (drop-down lists, images, graphics, etc.). The only other point of interest is that the Check button supports a custom mouse cursor via the Cursor property.

■ Note The ToolBar type may optionally be wrapped within a <ToolBarTray> element, which controls layout, docking, and drag-and-drop operations for a set of ToolBar objects. Consult the .NET Framework 3.5 SDK documentation for details.

Building the StatusBar Type

The StatusBar type will be docked to the lower portion of the <DockPanel> and contain a single <TextBlock> type, which up until this point in the chapter we have not made use of. Like a TextBox, a TextBlock can be used to hold text. In addition, TextBlock types honor the use of numerous textual annotations such as bold text, underlined text, line breaks, and so forth. While our StatusBar does not technically need this support, another benefit of a TextBlock type is that it is optimized for small blurbs of text, such as UI prompts in a status bar pane. Add the following markup directly after the previous ToolBar definition:

```
<!-- Put a StatusBar at the bottom -->
<StatusBar DockPanel.Dock ="Bottom" Background="Beige" >
  <StatusBarItem>
    <TextBlock Name="statBarText">Ready</TextBlock>
  </StatusBarItem>
</StatusBar>
```

At this point, your Visual Studio designer should look something like Figure 29-27.

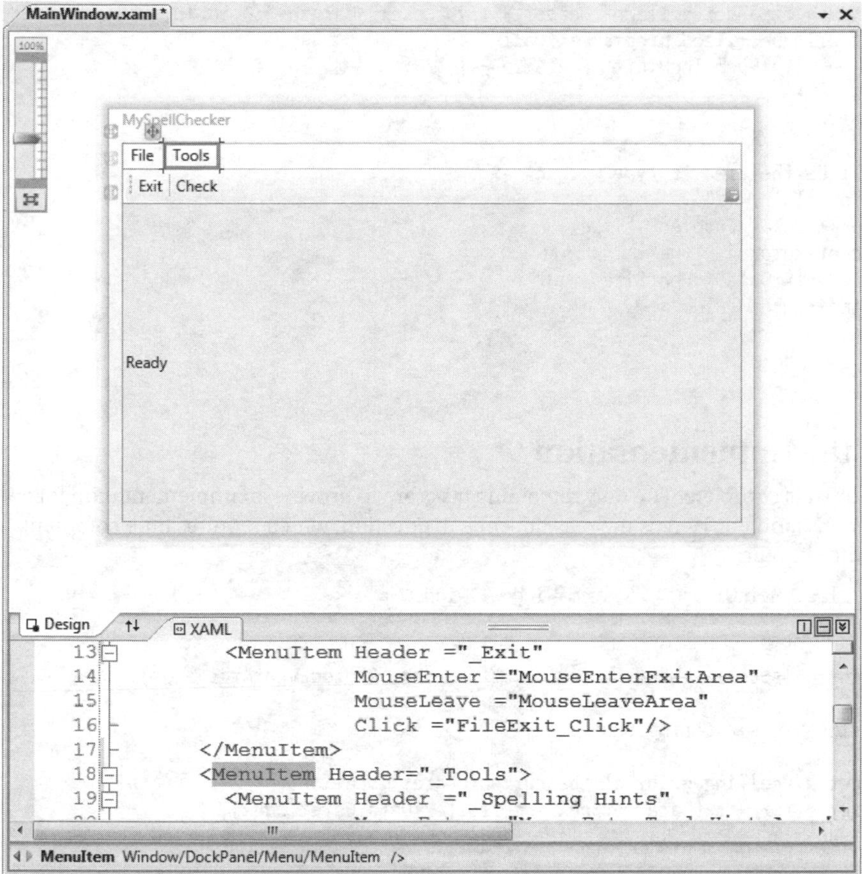

Figure 29-27. *The current user interface of our spell-checker application*

Finalizing the UI Design

The final aspect of our UI design is to define a splittable Grid type that defines two columns. On the left will be the Expander type that will display a list of spelling suggestions, wrapped within a <StackPanel>. On the right will be a TextBox type that supports multiple lines and has enabled spell checking. The entire <Grid> will be mounted to the left of the parent <DockPanel>. Add the following XAML markup to complete the definition of our Window's UI:

```
<Grid DockPanel.Dock ="Left" Background ="AliceBlue">
  <!-- Define the rows and columns -->
  <Grid.ColumnDefinitions>
    <ColumnDefinition />
    <ColumnDefinition />
  </Grid.ColumnDefinitions>
  <GridSplitter Grid.Column ="0" Width ="5" Background ="Gray" />
  <StackPanel Grid.Column="0" VerticalAlignment ="Stretch" >
    <Label Name="lblSpellingInstructions" FontSize="14" Margin="10,10,0,0">
      Spelling Hints
    </Label>
```

```
    <Expander Name="expanderSpelling" Header ="Try these!" Margin="10,10,10,10">
      <!-- This will be filled programmatically -->
      <Label Name ="lblSpellingHints" FontSize ="12"/>
    </Expander>
  </StackPanel>

  <!-- This will be the area to type within -->
  <TextBox  Grid.Column ="1"
            SpellCheck.IsEnabled ="True"
            AcceptsReturn ="True"
            Name ="txtData"  FontSize ="14"
            BorderBrush ="Blue">
  </TextBox>
</Grid>
```

Finalizing the Implementation

At this point, your UI is complete. The only remaining tasks are to provide an implementation for the remaining event handlers. Here is the relevant code in question, which requires little comment by this point in the chapter:

```
public partial class MainWindow : System.Windows.Window
{
...
  protected void ToolsSpellingHints_Click(object sender, RoutedEventArgs args)
  {
    string spellingHints = string.Empty;

    // Try to get a spelling error at the current caret location.
    SpellingError error = txtData.GetSpellingError(txtData.CaretIndex);
    if (error != null)
    {
      // Build a string of spelling suggestions.
      foreach (string s in error.Suggestions)
      {
        spellingHints += string.Format("{0}\n", s);
      }

      // Show suggestions on Label within Expander.
      lblSpellingHints.Content = spellingHints;

      // Expand the expander.
      expanderSpelling.IsExpanded = true;
    }
  }
  protected void MouseEnterExitArea(object sender, RoutedEventArgs args)
  {
    statBarText.Text = "Exit the Application";
  }
  protected void MouseEnterToolsHintsArea(object sender, RoutedEventArgs args)
  {
    statBarText.Text = "Show Spelling Suggestions";
  }
  protected void MouseLeaveArea(object sender, RoutedEventArgs args)
  {
```

```
    statBarText.Text = "Ready";
  }
}
```

So there you have it! With just a few lines of procedural code (and a healthy dose of XAML), we have the beginnings of a functioning word processor. To add just a bit more pizzazz requires an understanding of *control commands*.

Understanding WPF Control Commands

The next major discussion of this chapter is to examine the topic of *control commands*. Windows Presentation Foundation provides support for what might be considered "control-agnostic events" via control commands. As you know, a typical .NET event is defined within a specific base class and can only be used by that class or a derivative thereof. Furthermore, normal .NET events are tightly coupled to the class in which they are defined.

In contrast, WPF control commands are event-like entities that are independent from a specific control and in many cases can be successfully applied to numerous (and seemingly unrelated) control types. By way of a few examples, WPF supports Copy, Paste, and Cut commands, which can be applied to a wide variety of UI elements (menu items, toolbar buttons, custom buttons) as well as keyboard shortcuts (Ctrl+C, Ctrl+V, etc.).

While other UI toolkits (such as Windows Forms) provided standard events for such purposes, the end result was typically redundant and hard to maintain code. Under the WPF model, commands can be used as an alternative. The end result typically yields a smaller and more flexible code base.

The Intrinsic Control Command Objects

WPF ships with numerous built-in control commands, all of which can be configured with associated keyboard shortcuts (or other input gestures). Programmatically speaking, a WPF control command is any object that supports a property (often called `Command`) that returns an object implementing the `ICommand` interface, shown here:

```
public interface ICommand
{
  // Occurs when changes occur that affect whether
  // or not the command should execute.
  event EventHandler CanExecuteChanged;

  // Defines the method that determines whether the command
  // can execute in its current state.
  bool CanExecute(object parameter);

  // Defines the method to be called when the command is invoked.
  void Execute(object parameter);
}
```

While you could provide your own implementation of this interface to account for a control command, the chances that you will need to are slim, given functionality provided by the five WPF command objects out of the box. These static classes define numerous properties that expose objects that implement `ICommand`, most commonly the `RoutedUICommand` type, which adds support for the WPF routed event model.

Table 29-4 documents some core properties exposed by each of the intrinsic command objects (be sure to consult the .NET Framework 3.5 SDK documentation for complete details).

Table 29-4. *The Intrinsic WPF Control Command Objects*

WPF Control Command Object	Example Control Command Properties	Meaning in Life
ApplicationCommands	Close, Copy, Cut, Delete, Find, Open, Paste, Save, SaveAll, Redo, Undo	Defines properties that represent application-level commands
ComponentsCommands	MoveDown, MoveFocusBack, MoveLeft, MoveRight, ScrollToEnd, ScrollToHome	Defines properties that map to common commands performed by UI elements
MediaCommands	BoostBase, ChannelUp, ChannelDown, FastForward, NextTrack, Play, Rewind, Select, Stop	Defines properties that allow various media-centric controls to issue common commands
NavigationCommands	BrowseBack, BrowseForward, Favorites, LastPage, NextPage, Zoom	Defines numerous properties that are used for the applications that utilize the WPF navigation model
EditingCommands	AlignCenter, CorrectSpellingError, DecreaseFontSize, EnterLineBreak, EnterParagraphBreak, MoveDownByLine, MoveRightByWord	Defines numerous properties typically used when programming with objects exposed by the WPF document API

Connecting Commands to the Command Property

If you wish to connect any of these command properties to a UI element that supports the Command property (such as a Button or MenuItem), you have very little work to do. To see how to do so, update the current menu system to support a new topmost menu item named Edit and three subitems to account for copying, pasting, and cutting of textual data:

```
<Menu DockPanel.Dock ="Top"
  HorizontalAlignment="Left" Background="White" BorderBrush ="Black">
<MenuItem Header="_File" Click ="FileExit_Click" >
  <Separator/>
  <MenuItem Header ="_Exit" MouseEnter ="MouseEnterExitArea"
     MouseLeave ="MouseLeaveArea" Click ="FileExit_Click"/>
</MenuItem>

  <!-- New menu item with commands! -->
  <MenuItem Header="_Edit">
    <MenuItem Command ="ApplicationCommands.Copy"/>
    <MenuItem Command ="ApplicationCommands.Cut"/>
    <MenuItem Command ="ApplicationCommands.Paste"/>
  </MenuItem>

<MenuItem Header="_Tools">
  <MenuItem Header ="_Spelling Hints" MouseEnter ="MouseEnterToolsHintsArea"
   MouseLeave ="MouseLeaveArea" Click ="ToolsSpellingHints_Click"/>
  </MenuItem>
</Menu>
```

Notice that each subitem has a value assigned to the Command property. By doing so, the menu items automatically receive the correct name and shortcut key (for example, Ctrl+C for a cut operation) in the menu item UI and the application is now "copy, cut, and paste" aware with no procedural code. Thus, if you were to run the application and select some of your text, you will be able to use your new menu items out of the box, as shown in Figure 29-28.

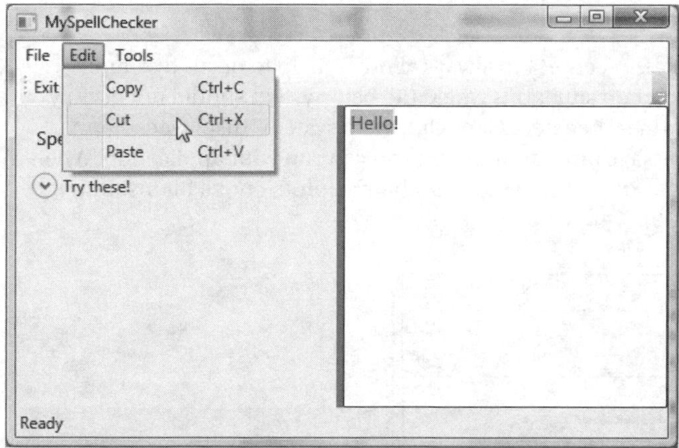

Figure 29-28. *Command objects provide a good deal of canned functionality for free.*

Connection Commands to Arbitrary UI Elements

If you wish to connect a command to a UI element that does not support the Command property, doing so requires you to drop down to procedural code. Doing so is certainly not complex, but it does involve a bit more logic than you see in XAML. For example, what if you wished to have the entire window respond to the F1 key, so that when the end user presses this key, he or she would activate an associated help system?

Assume your code file for the main window defines a new method named SetF1CommandBinding(), which is called within the constructor after the call to InitializeComponent(). This new method will programmatically create a new CommandBinding object, which is configured to operate with the ApplicationCommands.Help option, which is automatically F1-aware:

```
private void SetF1CommandBinding()
{
  CommandBinding helpBinding = new CommandBinding(ApplicationCommands.Help);
  helpBinding.CanExecute += CanHelpExecute;
  helpBinding.Executed += HelpExecuted;
  CommandBindings.Add(helpBinding);
}
```

Most CommandBinding objects will want to handle the CanExecute event (which allows you to specify whether the command occurs or not based on the operation of your program) and the Executed event (which is where you can author the content that should occur once the command occurs). Add the following event handlers to your Window-derived type (take note of the format of each method as required by the associated delegates):

```
private void CanHelpExecute(object sender, CanExecuteRoutedEventArgs e)
{
  // Here, you can set CanExecute to false if you wish to prevent the
  // command from executing if you desire.
```

```
  e.CanExecute = true;
}

private void HelpExecuted(object sender, ExecutedRoutedEventArgs e)
{
  MessageBox.Show("Dude, it is not that difficult. Just type something!",
                  "Help!");
}
```

Here, we have implemented `CanHelpExecute()` to always allow F1 help to occur by simply returning `true`. However, if you have certain situations where the help system should not display, you can account for this and return `false` when necessary. Our "help system" displayed within `HelpExecute()` is little more than a message box. At this point, you can run your application. When you press the F1 key on your keyboard, you will see your (less than helpful, if not a bit insulting) user guidance system (see Figure 29-29).

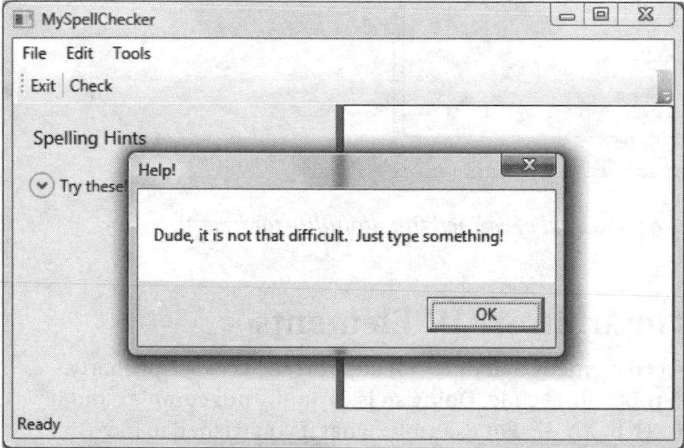

Figure 29-29. *Our custom help system*

Source Code The MySpellChecker project can be found under the Chapter 29 subdirectory.

Understanding the WPF Data-Binding Model

Controls are often the target of various data-binding operations. Simply put, *data binding* is the act of connecting control properties to data values that may change over the course of your application's lifetime. By doing so, a user interface element can display the state of a variable in your code; for example:

- Checking a `CheckBox` control based on a Boolean property of a given object
- Displaying data in `TextBox` types from a relational database table
- A `Label` connected to an integer representing the number of files in a folder

When using the intrinsic WPF data-binding engine, you must be aware of the distinction between the *source* and the *destination* of the binding operation. As you might expect, the source of a data-binding operation is the data itself (a Boolean property, relational data, etc.), while the destination (or target) is the UI control property that will use the data content (a `CheckBox`, `TextBox`, and so on).

■ **Note** The target property of a data-binding operation must be a dependency property of the UI control.

Truth be told, using the WPF data-binding infrastructure is always optional. If a developer were to roll his or her own data-binding logic, the connection between a source and destination typically would involve handling various events and authoring procedural code to connect the source and destination. For example, if you had a `ScrollBar` on a window that needed to display its value on a `Label` type, you might handle the `ScrollBar`'s `ValueChange` event and update the `Label`'s content accordingly.

However, using WPF data binding, you can connect the source and destination directly in XAML (or using C# code in your code file) without the need to handle various events or hard-code the connections between the source/destination. As well, based on how you set up your data-binding logic, you can ensure that the source and destination stay in sync if either of their values change.

A First Look at Data Binding

To begin examining WPF's data-binding capabilities, assume you have a new WPF Application project (named SimpleDataBinding) that defines the following markup for a `Window` type:

```
<Window x:Class="SimpleDataBinding.MainWindow"
  xmlns="http://schemas.microsoft.com/winfx/2006/xaml/presentation"
  xmlns:x="http://schemas.microsoft.com/winfx/2006/xaml"
  Title="Simple Data Binding" Height="152" Width="300"
  WindowStartupLocation="CenterScreen">

  <StackPanel Width="250">
    <Label Content="Move the scroll bar to see the current value"/>

    <!-- The scrollbar's value is the source of this data bind -->
    <ScrollBar Orientation="Horizontal" Height="30" Name="mySB"
            Maximum = "100" LargeChange="1" SmallChange="1"/>

    <!-- The label's content value is the target of the data bind -->
    <Label Height="30" BorderBrush="Blue" BorderThickness="2"
          Content = "{Binding ElementName=mySB, Path=Value}"
    />
  </StackPanel>
</Window>
```

Notice that the `<ScrollBar>` type (which we have named `mySB`) has been configured with a range between 0 and 100. As you reposition the thumb of the scrollbar (or click the left or right arrow), the `Label` will be automatically updated with the current value. The "glue" that makes this happen is the `{Binding}` markup extension that has been assigned to the `Label`'s `Content` property. Here, the `ElementName` value represents the source of the data-binding operation (the `ScrollBar` object), while the `Path` value represents (in this case) the property of the element to obtain.

Note `ElementName` and `Path` may seem oddly named, as you might expect to find more intuitive names such as "Source" and "Destination." However, as you will see later in this chapter, XML documents can be the source of a data-binding operation (typically using XPath). In this case, the names `ElementName` and `Path` fit the bill.

As an alternative format, it is possible to break out the values specified by the `{Binding}` markup extension by explicitly setting the `DataContext` property to the source of the binding operation as follows:

```
<!-- Breaking object/value apart via DataContext -->
<Label Height="30" BorderBrush="Blue" BorderThickness="2"
  DataContext = "{Binding ElementName=mySB}"
  Content = "{Binding Path=Value}"
/>
```

In either case, if you were to run this application, you would be pleased to find this `Label` updating without the need to write any procedural C# code (see Figure 29-30).

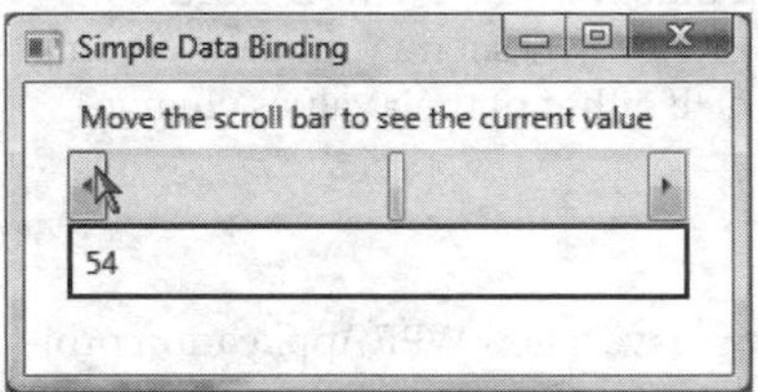

Figure 29-30. *Binding the* `ScrollBar` *value to a* `Label`

The DataContext Property

In the current example, you have seen two approaches to establish the source and destination of a data-binding operation, both of which resulted in the same output. Given this point, you might wonder when you would want to explicitly set the `DataContext` property. This property can be very helpful in that it is a dependency property, and therefore its value can be inherited by subelements. In this way, you can easily set the same data source to a family of controls, rather than having to repeat a bunch of redundant `"{Binding ElementName=X, Path=Y}"` XAML values to multiple controls. Consider the following updated XAML definition for our current `<StackPanel>`:

```
<!-- Note the StackPanel sets the DataContext property -->
<StackPanel Width="250" DataContext = "{Binding ElementName=mySB}">
  <Label Content="Move the scroll bar to see the current value"/>

  <ScrollBar Orientation="Horizontal" Height="30" Name="mySB"
             Maximum = "100" LargeChange="1" SmallChange="1"/>

  <!-- Now both UI elements use the scrollbar's value in unique ways. -->
  <Label Height="30" BorderBrush="Blue" BorderThickness="2"
         Content = "{Binding Path=Value}"/>

  <Button Content="Click" Height="200"
          FontSize = "{Binding Path=Value}"/>
</StackPanel>
```

Here, the DataContext property has been set on the <StackPanel> directly. Therefore, as we move the thumb, not only will we see the current value on the Label, but we will also find the font size of the Button grow and shrink accordingly based on the same value. Figure 29-31 shows one possible output.

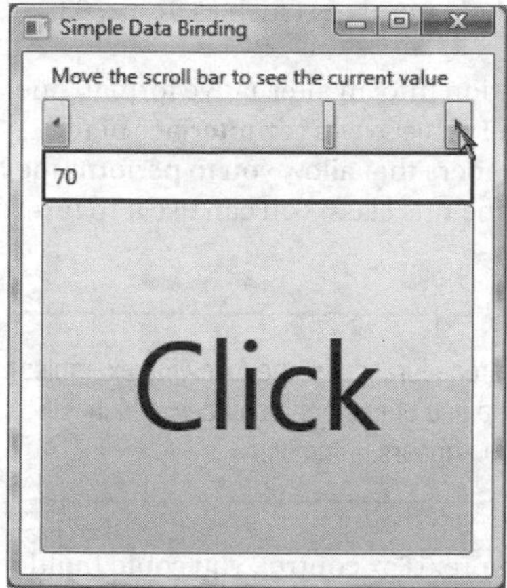

Figure 29-31. *Binding the* ScrollBar *value to a* Label *and a* Button

The Mode Property

When establishing a data-binding operation, you are able to choose among various modes of operation by setting a value to the Mode property at the time you establish the Path value. By default, the Mode property is set to the value OneWay, which specifies that changes in the target do not affect the source. In our example, changing the Content property of the Label does not set the position of the ScrollBar's thumb.

If you wish to keep changes between the source and the target in sync, you can set the Mode property to TwoWay. Thus, changing the value of the Label's content changes the value of the scrollbar's thumb position. Of course, the end user would be unable to change the content of the Label, as the content is presented in a read-only manner (we could of course change the value programmatically).

To illustrate the use of the TwoWay mode, assume we have replaced the Label displaying the current scrollbar value with the following TextBox (note the value of the Text property). In this case, when you type a new value into the text area, the thumb position (and font of the Button type) automatically update when you tab off the TextBox object:

```
<TextBox Height="30" BorderBrush="Blue"
        BorderThickness="2" Text = "{Binding Path=Value}"/>
```

■ Note You may also set the Mode property to OneTime. This option sets the target when initialized but does not track further changes.

Data Conversion Using IValueConverter

The `ScrollBar` type uses a `double` to represent the value of the thumb, rather than an expected whole number (e.g., an integer). Therefore, as you drag the thumb, you will find various floating-point numbers displayed within the `TextBox` (such as 61.0576923076923), which would be rather unintuitive to the end user, who is most likely expecting to see whole numbers (such as 61, 62, 63, and so on).

When you wish to convert the value of a data-binding operation into an alternative format, one way to do so is to create a custom class type that implements the `IValueConverter` interface of the `System.Windows.Data` namespace. This interface defines two members that allow you to perform the conversion to and from the target and destination. Once you define this class, you can use it to further qualify the processing of your data-binding operation.

■ Note While any data-binding operation can be achieved entirely using procedural code, the following examples will make use of XAML to convert between data types. Doing so involves the use of custom resources, which will be fully examined in Chapter 30. Therefore, don't fret if some of the markup appears unfamiliar.

Assuming that you wish to display whole numbers within the `TextBox` control, you could build the following class type (be sure you import the `System.Windows.Data` namespace in the defining file):

```
class MyDoubleConverter : IValueConverter
{
  public object Convert(object value, Type targetType, object parameter,
                        System.Globalization.CultureInfo culture)
  {
    // Convert the double to an int.
    double v = (double)value;
    return (int)v;
  }

  public object ConvertBack(object value, Type targetType, object parameter,
                            System.Globalization.CultureInfo culture)
  {
    // Return the incoming value directly.
    // This will be used for 2-way bindings.
    // In our example, when the user tabs
    // off the TextBlock.
    return value;
  }
}
```

The `Convert()` method will be called when the value is transferred from the source (the `ScrollBar`) to the destination (the `Text` property of the `TextBox`). While we receive a number of incoming arguments, for this conversion we only need to manipulate the incoming `object`, which is the value of the current `double`. Using this type, we simply cast the type into an integer and return the new number.

The `ConvertBack()` method will be called when the value is passed from the destination to the source (if you have enabled a two-way binding mode). Here, we simply return the value straightaway. By doing so, we are able to type a floating-point value into the `TextBox` (such as 99.9) and have it automatically convert to a whole number value (99) when the user tabs off the control. This "free" conversion happens due to the fact that the `Convert()` method is called once again after a call to

ConvertBack(). If you were to simply return null from ConvertBack(), your binding would appear to be out of sync, as the text box would still be displaying a floating-point number!

With this class in place, consider the following XAML updates, which will leverage our custom converter class to display data in the TextBox:

```
<Window x:Class="SimpleDataBinding.MainWindow"
    xmlns="http://schemas.microsoft.com/winfx/2006/xaml/presentation"
    xmlns:x="http://schemas.microsoft.com/winfx/2006/xaml"

    <!-- Need to define a CLR namespace to gain access to our type -->
    xmlns:myConverters ="clr-namespace:SimpleDataBinding"

    Title="Simple Data Binding" Height="334" Width="288"
    WindowStartupLocation="CenterScreen">

  <!-- Resource dictionaries allow us to define objects that can
       be obtained by their key. More details in Chapter 30. -->
  <Window.Resources>
    <myConverters:MyDoubleConverter x:Key="DoubleConverter"/>
  </Window.Resources>

  <!-- The panel is setting the data context to the scrollbar object -->
    <StackPanel Width="250" DataContext = "{Binding ElementName=mySB}">

      <Label Content="Move the scroll bar to see the current value"/>

      <ScrollBar Orientation="Horizontal" Height="30" Name="mySB"
      Maximum = "100" LargeChange="1" SmallChange="1"/>

    <!-- Notice that the {Binding} extension now sets the Converter property. -->
    <TextBox Height="30" BorderBrush="Blue" BorderThickness="2" Name="txtThumbValue"
    Text = "{Binding Path=Value, Converter={StaticResource DoubleConverter}}"/>

    <Button Content="Click" Height="200"
    FontSize = "{Binding Path=Value}"/>

  </StackPanel>
</Window>
```

Once we define a custom XML namespace that maps to our project's root namespace (see Chapter 28), we add to the Window's resource dictionary an instance of our MyDoubleConverter type, which we can obtain later in the XAML file by the key name DoubleConverter. The Text property of the TextBox has been modified to make use of our MyDoubleConverter type, assigning the Converter property to yet another markup extension named StaticResource. Again, full details of the WPF resource system can be found in Chapter 30. In any case, if you were to run your application, you would find that only whole numbers will be displayed in the TextBox.

Converting Between Diverse Data Types

An implementation of the IValueConverter interface can be used to convert between any data types, even if they do not seem related on the surface. In reality, you are able to use the current value of the ScrollBar's thumb to return any object type to connect to a dependency property. Consider the following ColorConverter type, which uses the value of the thumb to return a new green SolidColorBrush (with a green value between 155 and 255):

```
class MyColorConverter : IValueConverter
{
  public object Convert(object value, Type targetType, object parameter,
    System.Globalization.CultureInfo culture)
  {
    // Use value of thumb to build a varied green brush.
    double d = (double)value;
    byte v = (byte)d;

    Color color = new Color();
    color.A = 255;
    color.G = (byte) (155 + v);
    return new SolidColorBrush(color);
  }

  public object ConvertBack(object value, Type targetType, object parameter,
    System.Globalization.CultureInfo culture)
  {
    return value;
  }
}
```

If we were to add a new member to our resource dictionary as follows:

```
<Window.Resources>
  <myConverters:MyDoubleConverter x:Key="DoubleConverter"/>
  <myConverters:MyColorConverter x:Key="ColorConverter"/>
</Window.Resources>
```

we could then use the key name to set the `Background` property of our `Button` type as follows:

```
<Button Content="Click" Height="200"
  FontSize = "{Binding Path=Value}"
  Background= "{Binding Path=Value, Converter={StaticResource ColorConverter}}"/>
```

Sure enough, if you run your application once again, you'll find the color of the `Button` change based on the scrollbar's position. To wrap up our look at WPF data binding, let's check out how to map custom objects and XML document data to our UI layer.

■ **Source Code** The SimpleDataBinding project can be found under the Chapter 29 subdirectory.

Binding to Custom Objects

The next flavor of data binding we will examine is how to connect the properties of custom objects to your UI layer. Begin by creating a new WPF Application project named CarViewerApp and, using the steps outlined in Chapter 28, change the name of your initial `Window1` type to `MainWindow`. Next, handle the `Loaded` event of `MainWindow`, and update the `<Grid>` definition to contain two rows and two columns:

```
<Window x:Class="CarViewerApp.MainWindow"
  xmlns="http://schemas.microsoft.com/winfx/2006/xaml/presentation"
  xmlns:x="http://schemas.microsoft.com/winfx/2006/xaml"
  Title="Car Viewer Application" Height="294" Width="502"
  ResizeMode="NoResize" WindowStartupLocation="CenterScreen"
  Loaded="Window_Loaded"
```

```
  >
<Grid>
  <Grid.ColumnDefinitions>
    <ColumnDefinition Width="200"/>
    <ColumnDefinition Width="*"/>
  </Grid.ColumnDefinitions>
  <Grid.RowDefinitions>
    <RowDefinition Height="Auto"/>
    <RowDefinition Height="*"/>
  </Grid.RowDefinitions>
</Grid>
</Window>
```

The first row of the <Grid> will consist of a menu system containing a File menu with two submenus (Add New Car and Exit). Notice that we are handling the Click event of each submenu, and that we are assigning an "input gesture" to the Exit menu to allow the item to be activated when the user presses the Alt+F4 keystroke. Finally, notice the value of Grid.ColumnSpan has been set to 2, allowing the menu system to be positioned within each cell of the first row.

```
<!-- Menu Bar -->
<DockPanel
  Grid.Column="0"
  Grid.ColumnSpan="2"
  Grid.Row="0">
  <Menu DockPanel.Dock ="Top" HorizontalAlignment="Left" Background="White">
    <MenuItem Header="File">
      <MenuItem Header="New Car" Click="AddNewCarWizard"/>
      <Separator />
      <MenuItem Header="Exit" InputGestureText="Alt-F4"
      Click="ExitApplication"/>
    </MenuItem>
  </Menu>
</DockPanel>
```

The remaining left portion of the <Grid> consists of a <DockPanel> containing a ListBox, while the right portion of the <Grid> contains a single TextBlock. The ListBox type will eventually become the destination for a data-binding operation involving a collection of custom objects, so set the ItemsSource property to the {Binding} markup extension (the source of the binding will be specified in code in just a bit). As the user selects one of the items in the ListBox, we will capture the SelectionChanged event in order to update the content within the TextBlock. Here is the definition of these remaining types:

```
<!-- Left pane of grid -->
<ListBox Grid.Column="0"
  Grid.Row="2" Name="allCars" SelectionChanged="ListItemSelected"
  Background="LightBlue" ItemsSource="{Binding}">
</ListBox>

<!-- Right pane of grid -->
<TextBlock Name="txtCarStats" Background="LightYellow"
  Grid.Column="1" Grid.Row="2"/>
```

At this point, the UI of your window should look like what you see in Figure 29-32.

Before we implement the data-binding logic, finalize the File ➤ Exit menu handler as follows:

```
private void ExitApplication(object sender, RoutedEventArgs e)
{
  Application.Current.Shutdown();
}
```

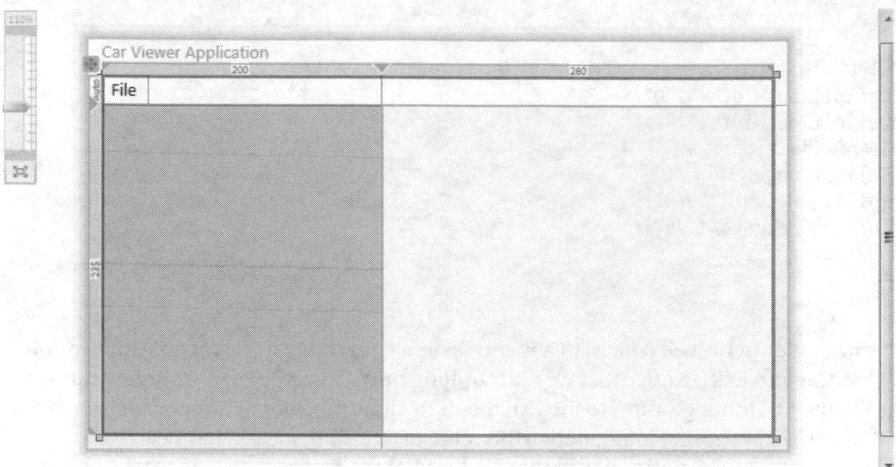

Figure 29-32. *The UI of our main window*

Working with the ObservableCollection<T> Type

.NET 3.0 introduced a new collection type within the `System.Collections.ObjectModel` namespace named `ObservableCollection<T>`. The benefit of working with this type is that when its contents are updated, it will send notifications to interested listeners, such as the destination of a data-binding operation. Insert a new C# file into your application that defines a class named `CarList` that extends `ObservableCollection<T>`, where `T` is of type `Car`. This iteration of the `Car` type makes use of C# automatic properties to establish some basic state data (which can be set using a custom constructor), and provides a fitting implementation of `ToString()`:

```
using System;
using System.Collections.ObjectModel;

namespace CarViewerApp
{
  public class CarList : ObservableCollection<Car>
  {
    public CarList()
    {
      // Add a few entries to the list.
      Add(new Car(40, "BMW", "Black", "Sidd"));
      Add(new Car(55, "VW", "Black", "Mary"));
      Add(new Car(100, "Ford", "Tan", "Mel"));
      Add(new Car(0, "Yugo", "Green", "Clunker"));
    }
  }

  public class Car
  {
    public int Speed { get; set; }
    public string Make { get; set; }
    public string Color { get; set; }
    public string PetName { get; set; }
```

```
    public Car(int speed, string make, string color, string name)
    {
      Speed = speed; Make = make; Color = color; PetName = name;
    }
    public Car(){}

    public override string ToString()
    {
      return string.Format("{0} the {1} {2} is going {3} MPH",
        PetName, Color, Make, Speed);
    }
  }
}
```

Now, open the code file for your `MainWindow` class and define a member variable of type `CarList` named `myCars`. Within the `Loaded` event handler of your `Window` type, set the `DataContext` property of the `allCars` `ListBox` to the `myCars` object (recall we did not set this value via XAML with the `{Binding}` extension, therefore for a change of pace, we will do so using procedural code):

```
private void Window_Loaded(object sender, RoutedEventArgs e)
{
  // Set the data context.
  allCars.DataContext = myCars;
}
```

At this point, you should be able to run your application and see the `ListBox` containing the `ToString()` values for each `Car` in the custom `ObservableCollection<T>`, as shown in Figure 29-33.

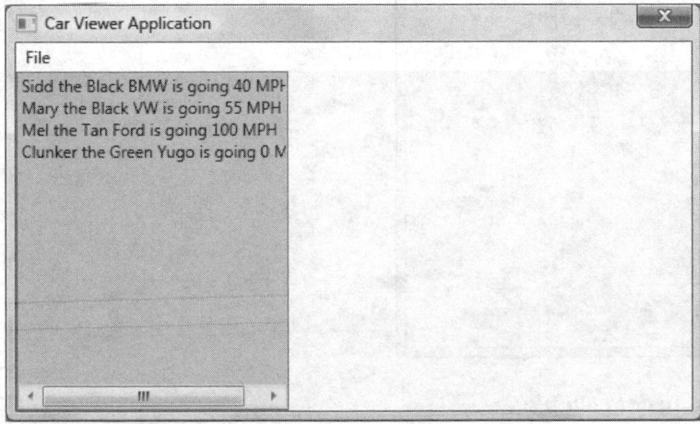

Figure 29-33. *The initial data-binding operation*

Creating a Custom Data Template

Currently, `ListBox` is displaying each item in the `CarList` object; however, because we have not specified a binding path, each list entry is simply the result of calling `ToString()` on the subobjects. As we have already examined how to establish simple binding paths, this time we will construct a custom *data template*. Simply put, a data template can be used to inform the destination of a data-binding operation how to display the data connected to it. Our template will fill each item in the `ListBox` with a `<StackPanel>` that consists of an `Ellipse` object and a `TextBlock` that has been bound to the `PetName` property of each item in the `CarList` type. Here is the modified markup of the `ListBox` type.

```
<ListBox Grid.Column="0"
  Grid.Row="2" Name="allCars" SelectionChanged="ListItemSelected"
   Background="LightBlue" ItemsSource="{Binding}">
  <ListBox.ItemTemplate>
    <DataTemplate>
      <StackPanel Orientation="Horizontal">
        <Ellipse Height="10" Width="10" Fill="Blue"/>
        <TextBlock FontStyle="Italic" FontSize="14" Text="{Binding Path=PetName}"/>
      </StackPanel>
    </DataTemplate>
  </ListBox.ItemTemplate>
</ListBox>
```

Here we connect our `<DataTemplate>` to the `ListBox` using the `<ListBox.ItemTemplate>` element. Before we see the result of this data template, implement the `SelectionChanged` handler of your `ListBox` to display the `ToString()` of the current selection within the rightmost `TextBlock`:

```
private void ListItemSelected(object sender, SelectionChangedEventArgs e)
{
  // Get correct car from the ObservableCollection based
  // on the selected item in the list box. Then call toString().
  txtCarStats.Text = myCars[allCars.SelectedIndex].ToString();
}
```

With this update, you should now see a more stylized display of our data, as shown Figure 29-34.

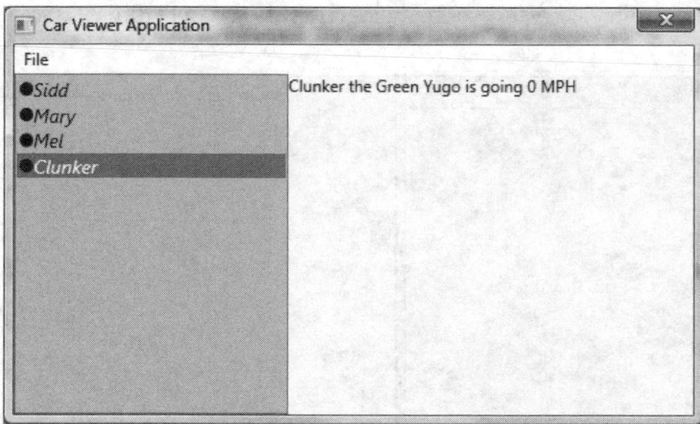

Figure 29-34. *Data binding with a custom data template*

Binding UI Elements to XML Documents

The next task is to build a custom dialog box that will use data binding to display the content of an external XML file within a stylized `ListView` object. First, insert the `Inventory.xml` file you created in Chapter 24 during the NavigationWithLinqToXml project using the Project ➤ Add Existing Item menu option. Select this item within the Solution Explorer, and using the Properties window, set the Copy to Output Directory option to Copy Always. This will ensure that when you compile your application, the `Inventory.xml` file will be copied to your \bin\Debug folder.

Building a Custom Dialog

Insert a new WPF Window type into your project (named AddNewCarDialog) using the Project ➤ Add Window menu option of Visual Studio 2008. This new Window will display the content of the Inventory.xml file within a customized ListView type, via data binding. The first step is to author the XAML to define the look and feel of this new window. Here is the full markup, with analysis to follow:

```
<Window x:Class="CarViewerApp.AddNewCarDialog"
  xmlns="http://schemas.microsoft.com/winfx/2006/xaml/presentation"
  xmlns:x="http://schemas.microsoft.com/winfx/2006/xaml"
  Title="AddNewCarDialog" Height="234" Width="529"
  ResizeMode="NoResize" WindowStartupLocation="CenterScreen" >
 <Grid>
  <Grid.RowDefinitions>
    <RowDefinition Height="144" />
    <RowDefinition Height="51" />
  </Grid.RowDefinitions>

  <!-- Use the XmlDataProvider-->
  <Grid.Resources>
    <XmlDataProvider x:Key="CarsXmlDoc"
     Source="Inventory.xml"/>
  </Grid.Resources>

  <!-- Now, build a grid of data, mapping attributes/elements to columns
       using XPath expressions -->
  <ListView Name="lstCars" Grid.Row="0"ItemsSource=
   "{Binding Source={StaticResource CarsXmlDoc}, XPath=/Inventory/Car}"
  >
    <ListView.View>
      <GridView>
        <GridViewColumn Width="100" Header="ID"
                        DisplayMemberBinding="{Binding XPath=@carID}"/>
        <GridViewColumn Width="100" Header="Make"
                        DisplayMemberBinding="{Binding XPath=Make}"/>
        <GridViewColumn Width="100" Header="Color"
                        DisplayMemberBinding="{Binding XPath=Color}"/>
        <GridViewColumn Width="150" Header="Pet Name"
                        DisplayMemberBinding="{Binding XPath=PetName}"/>
      </GridView>
    </ListView.View>
  </ListView>

  <WrapPanel Grid.Row="1">
    <Label Content="Select a Row to Add to your car collection" Margin="10" />
    <Button Name="btnOK" Content="OK" Width="80" Height="25"
            Margin="10" IsDefault="True" TabIndex="1" Click="btnOK_Click"/>
    <Button Name="btnCancel" Content="Cancel" Width="80" Height="25"
            Margin="10" IsCancel="True" TabIndex="2"/>
  </WrapPanel>
 </Grid>
</Window>
```

Starting at the top, notice that the opening <Window> element has been defined by specifying a value of NoResize to the ResizeMode attribute, given that most dialog boxes do not allow the user to alter the size of the window's dimensions.

Beyond carving up our <Grid> into two rows of a given size, the next point of interest is that we are placing into the grid's resource dictionary a new object of type XmlDataProvider. This type can be connected to an external *.xml file (or an XML data island within the XAML file) via the Source attribute. As we have configured the Inventory.xml file to be located within the application directory of our current project, we have no need to worry about hard-coding a fixed path.

The real bulk of this markup takes place within the definition of the ListView type. First of all, notice that the ItemsSource attribute has been assigned to the CarsXmlDoc resource, which is qualified using the XPath attribute. Based on your experience, you may know that XPath is an XML technology that allows you to navigate within an XML document using a query-like syntax. Here we are saying that our initial data-binding path begins with the <Car> element of the <Inventory> root.

To inform the ListView type to display a grid-like front end, we next make use of the <ListView.View> element to define a <GridView> consisting of four <GridViewColumns>. Each of these types specifies a Header value (for display purposes) and most importantly a DisplayMemberBinding data-binding value. Given that the <ListView> itself has already specified the initial path within the XML document to be the <Car> subelement of <Inventory>, each of the XPath bindings for the column types use this as a starting point.

The first <GridViewColumn> is displaying the ID attribute of the <Car> element using an XPath-specific syntax for plucking our attribute values (@caID). The remaining columns simply further qualify the path within the XML document by appending the next subelement using the XPath qualifier of the {Binding} markup extension.

Last but not least, the final row of the <Grid> contains a <WrapPanel> that contains two Buttons (and a descriptive Label) to complete the UI. The only points of interest here would be that we are handling the Click event of the OK button and the use of the IsDefault and IsCancel properties. These establish which button on a window should respond to the Click event when the Enter key or Esc key is pressed.

Finally, note that these Button types specify a TabIndex value and a Margin value, the latter of which allows you to define spacing around each item in the <WrapPanel>.

Assigning the DialogResult Value

Before we display this new dialog box, we need to implement the Click handler for the OK button. Similar to Windows Forms (see Chapter 27), WPF dialog boxes can inform the caller which button has been clicked via the DialogResult property. However, *unlike* the DialogResult property found in Windows Forms, in the WPF model, this property operates on a nullable Boolean value, rather than a strongly typed enumeration. Thus, if you wish to inform the caller the user wishes to employ the data in the dialog box for use within the program (typically indicated by clicking an OK, a Yes, or an Accept button), set the inherited DialogResult property to true in the Click handler of said button:

```
private void btnOK_Click(object sender, RoutedEventArgs e)
{
  DialogResult = true;
}
```

As the default value of DialogResult is false, we have no need to do anything if the user clicks the Cancel button.

Obtaining the Current Selection

Finally, add a custom read-only property to your AddNewCarDialog named SelectedCar, which returns a new Car object to the caller based on the values of the selected row of the grid:

```
public Car SelectedCar
{
  get
```

```
  {
    // Cast selected item on grid to an XmlElement.
    System.Xml.XmlElement carRow =
      (System.Xml.XmlElement)lstCars.SelectedItem;

    // Make sure the user selected something!
    if (carRow == null)
    {
      return null;
    }
    else
    {
      // Generate a random speed.
      Random r = new Random();
      int speed = r.Next(100);

      // Return new Car based on the data in selected XmlElement/speed.
      return new Car(speed, carRow["Make"].InnerText,
        carRow["Color"].InnerText, carRow["PetName"].InnerText);
    }
  }
}
```

Notice we cast the return value of the `SelectedItem` property (which is of type `System.Object`) into an `XmlElement` type. This is possible because our `ListView` is indeed connected to the `Inventory.xml` file via our data-binding operation. Once we nab the current `XmlElement`, we are able to access the `Make`, `Color`, and `PetName` elements (using the type indexer) and extract out the values by calling `InnerText`.

■ **Note** If you have never worked with the types of the `System.Xml` namespace, simply know that the `InnerText` property obtains the value between the opening and closing elements of an XML node. For example, the inner text of `<Make>Ford</Make>` would be `Ford`.

Displaying a Custom Dialog Box

Now that our dialog box is complete, we are able to launch it from the `Click` handler of the File ➤ Add New Car menu option:

```
private void AddNewCarWizard(object sender, RoutedEventArgs e)
{
  AddNewCarDialog dlg = new AddNewCarDialog();
  if (true == dlg.ShowDialog())
  {
    if (dlg.SelectedCar != null)
    {
      myCars.Add(dlg.SelectedCar);
    }
  }
}
```

Like Windows Forms, a WPF dialog box may be shown as a modal dialog box (by calling `ShowDialog()`) or as a modaless dialog (by calling `Show()`). If the return value of `ShowDialog()` is `true`, we ask the dialog box for the new `Car` object and add it to our `ObservableCollection<T>`. Because this collection type sends out notifications when its contents are altered, you will find your `ListBox` will automatically refresh itself as you insert new items. Figure 29-35 shows the UI of our custom dialog box.

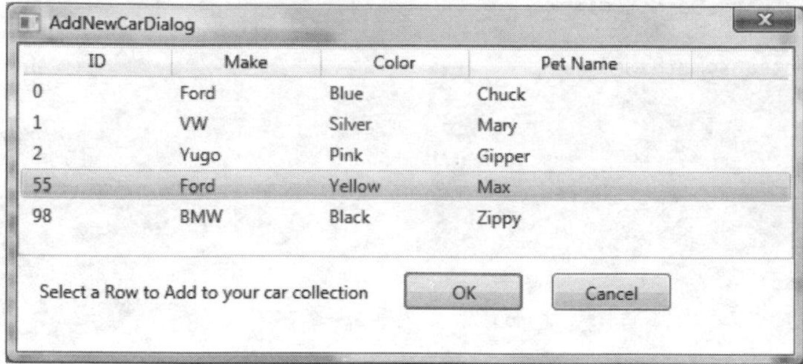

Figure 29-35. *A custom grid of data, bound to an XML document*

■ **Source Code** The CarViewerApp project can be found under the Chapter 29 subdirectory.

That wraps up our look at the WPF data-binding engine and the core controls found within this UI API. In the next chapter, you will complete your investigation of Windows Presentation Foundation by examining the role of graphical rendering, resource management, and the construction of custom themes.

Summary

This chapter examined several aspects of WPF controls, beginning with a discussion of dependency properties and routed events. These WPF mechanisms are very important for several aspects of WPF programming including data binding, animation services, and a slew of other features. Over the course of this chapter, you have had a chance to configure and tweak several controls and learned to arrange your UI content in various panel types.

More importantly, you examined the use of WPF commands. Recall that these control-agnostic events can be attached to a UI element or an input gesture to automatically inherit out-of-the-box services (such as clipboard operations). You also dove into the mechanics of the WPF data-binding engine and learned how to bind property values, custom objects, and XML documents to your UI layer. At this time, you also learned how to build WPF dialog boxes and discovered the role of the `IValueConverter` and `ObservableCollection<T>` types.

CHAPTER 30

WPF 2D Graphical Rendering, Resources, and Themes

The purpose of this chapter is to examine three ultimately independent, yet interrelated topics, which will enable you to build more sophisticated Windows Presentation Foundation (WPF) applications than shown in the previous two chapters. The first order of business is to investigate the WPF 2D graphical programming APIs. Here you will examine numerous ways to render 2D geometric images (via shapes, drawings, and visuals) and work with graphical primitives such as brushes and pens. Along the way, you will also be introduced to the topic of WPF animation services and the types of the `System.Windows.Media.Animation` namespace.

Once you understand the basic 2D graphical rendering/animation primitives of WPF, we will then move on to an examination of how WPF allows you to define, embed, and reference application resources. Generally speaking, the term "application resources" refers to string tables, image files, icons, and other non-code-based entities used by an application. While this is still true under WPF, a "resource" can also represent custom graphical and UI objects you wish to embed into an assembly for later use.

The final topic of this chapter closes the gap between these two seemingly unrelated topics by examining how to define styles and templates for your control types. As you will see, creating styles and templates almost always involves making extensive use of WPF's graphical rendering/animation services and packaging them into your assembly as application resources.

Note You may recall from Chapter 28 that WPF provides comprehensive support for 3D graphics programming, which is beyond the scope of this text. If you require details regarding this aspect of WPF, check out *Pro WPF in C# 2008: Windows Presentation Foundation with .NET 3.5, Second Edition* by Matthew MacDonald (Apress, 2008).

The Philosophy of WPF Graphical Rendering Services

WPF makes use of a particular flavor of graphical rendering that goes by the term *retained mode graphics*. Simply put, this means that as you are using XAML or procedural code to generate graphical renderings, it is the responsibility of WPF to persist these visual items and ensure they are correctly redrawn and refreshed in an optimal manner. Thus, when you render graphical data, it is always present regardless of whether the end user hides the image by resizing the window, minimizing the window, covering the window with another, and so forth.

In stark contrast, previous Microsoft graphical rendering APIs (including GDI+) were *immediate mode* graphics systems. Under this model, it is up to the programmer to ensure that rendered visuals are correctly "remembered" and updated during the life of the application. For example, recall from Chapter 27 that under GDI+, rendering a rectangle involves handling the `Paint` event (or overriding the virtual `OnPaint()` method), obtaining a `Graphics` object to draw the rectangle and, most important, adding the infrastructure to ensure that the image is persisted when the user resizes the window (e.g., create member variables to represent the position of the rectangle, call `Invalidate()` throughout your program, etc.). This conceptual shift from immediate mode to retained mode graphics is indeed a good thing, as programmers have much less grungy graphics code to author and maintain.

However, this point is not to suggest that the WPF graphics API is *completely* different from earlier rendering toolkits. For example, like GDI+, WPF supports various brush types and pen types, the ability to render graphics at runtime through code, techniques for hit-testing support, and so forth. So to this end, if you currently have a background in GDI+ (or C/C++-based GDI), you already know a good deal about how to perform basic renderings under WPF.

WPF Graphical Rendering Options

Like other aspects of WPF development, you have a number of choices regarding *how* you will perform your graphical rendering, above and beyond the decision to do so via XAML or procedural C# code. Specifically, WPF provides three distinct ways to render graphical data:

- `System.Windows.Shapes`: This namespace defines a number of types used to render 2D geometric objects (rectangles, ellipses, polygons, etc.). While these types are very simple to use, they do come with a good deal of overhead.
- `System.Windows.Media.Drawing`: This abstract base class defines a more lightweight set of services for a number of derived types (`GeometryDrawing`, `ImageDrawing`, etc.).
- `System.Windows.Media.Visual`: This abstract base class provides the most lightweight approach to render graphical data; however, it also requires authoring a fair amount of procedural code.

The motivation behind offering a number of different ways to do the exact same thing (e.g., render graphical data) has to do with memory usage and ultimately application performance. Given that WPF is such a graphically intensive system, it is not unreasonable for an application to render hundreds of different images upon a window's surface, and your choice of implementation (shapes, drawings, or visuals) could have a huge impact.

To set the stage for the sections to come, let's begin with a brief overview of each option, from the "heaviest" to the "lightest." If you wish to try out each option firsthand, create a new WPF Windows Application named WPFGraphicsOptions, change the name of your initial `Window` type to `MainWindow`, and replace the window's initial XAML `<Grid>` definition with a `<StackPanel>` type:

```
<Window x:Class="WPFGraphicsOptions.MainWindow"
  xmlns="http://schemas.microsoft.com/winfx/2006/xaml/presentation"
  xmlns:x="http://schemas.microsoft.com/winfx/2006/xaml"
  Title="WPFGraphicsOptions" Height="300" Width="300" >
  <StackPanel>

  </StackPanel>
</Window>
```

Use of the Shape-Derived Types

The members of the `System.Windows.Shapes` namespace (`Ellipse`, `Line`, `Path`, `Polygon`, `Polyline`, and `Rectangle`) are the absolute simplest way to render a 2D image and are appropriate when you need to render infrequently used images (such as a region of a stylized button) or you need a graphical image that can support user interaction. Using these types typically entails selecting a "brush" for the interior fill and a "pen" for the border outline (you'll examine WPF's brush and pen options later in this chapter). To illustrate the basic use of shape types, if you add the following to your `<StackPanel>`, you will find a simple light blue rectangle with a blue outline:

```
<!-- Draw a rectangle using Shape types -->
<Rectangle Height="55" Width="105" Stroke="Blue"
  StrokeThickness="5" Fill="LightBlue"/>
```

While these types are ridiculously simple to use, they are a bit on the bloated side due to the fact that their parent class, `Sysem.Windows.Shapes.Shape`, attempts to be all things to all people (if you will). `Shape` inherits a ton of services from its long list of parents in the inheritance chain: `Shape` is-a `FrameworkElement`, which is-a `UIElement`, which is-a `Visual`, which is-a `DependencyObject`, `DispatcherObject`, and `Object`!

Collectively, these base classes provide the derived types with support for styles and temples, data binding support, resource management, the ability to send numerous events, the ability to monitor keyboard and mouse input, complex layout management, and animation services. Figure 30-1 illustrates the inheritance of the `Shape` type, as seen through the eyes of the Visual Studio object browser.

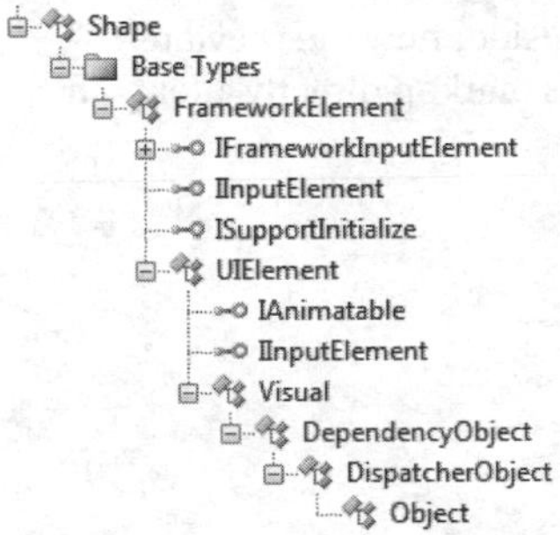

Figure 30-1. `Shape`*-derived types gain a ton of functionality from their parent types.*

While each parent adds various bits of functionality, `UIElement` is a key culprit. For example, `UIElement` defines over *80 events* to handle numerous forms of input (mouse, keyboard, and stylus for Tablet PCs). `FrameworkElement` is the other suspect, in that this type provides members for changing the mouse cursor, various events representing object lifetime, context menus support, and so on. Given this, the `Shape`-derived types can be as interactive as other UI elements such as `Buttons`, `ProgressBars`, and other widgets.

The bottom line is that while the `Shape`-derived types are very simple to use and quite powerful, this very fact makes them the heaviest option for rendering 2D graphics. Again, using these types is just fine for "occasional rendering" (the definition of which can be more of a gut feel than a hard science) or when you honestly do need a graphical rendering that is responsive to user interaction. However, if you are designing a more graphically intensive application, you will likely find some performance gains by using the `Drawing`-derived types.

Use of the Drawing-Derived Types

The `System.Windows.Media.Drawing` abstract base class represents the bare bones of a two-dimensional surface. The derived types (such as `GeometryDrawing`, `ImageDrawing`, and `VideoDrawing`) are more lightweight than the `Shape`-derived types in that neither `UIElement` nor `FrameworkElement` is in the inheritance chain. Given this, Drawing-derived types do not have intrinsic support for handling input events (although it is possible to programmatically perform hit-testing logic); however, they can be animated due to the fact that Animatable is in the family (see Figure 30-2).

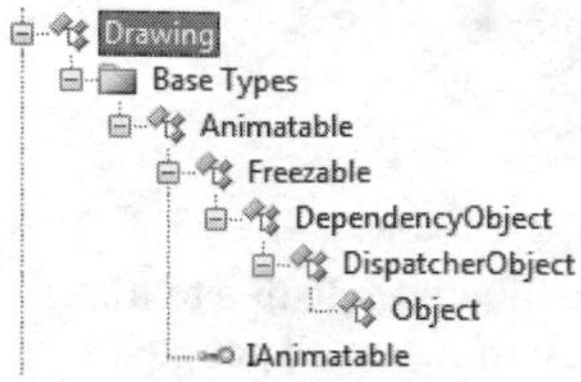

Drawing
Base Types
Animatable
Freezable
DependencyObject
DispatcherObject
Object
IAnimatable

Figure 30-2. Drawing-*derived types are significantly more lightweight than* Shape-*derived types.*

Another key difference between Drawing-derived types and Shape-derived types is that Drawing-derived types have no ability to render themselves, as they do not derive from UIElement! Rather, derived types must be placed within a hosting object (such as DrawingImage, DrawingBrush, or DrawingVisual) to display their content. This decoupling of composition from display makes the Drawing-derived types much more lightweight than the Shape-derived types, while still retaining key services.

Without getting too hung up on the details for the time being, consider how the previous Rectangle could be rendered using the drawing-centric types (add this markup directly after your previous <Rectangle> if you are following along):

```
<!-- Draw a rectangle using Drawing types -->
<Image Height="55" Width="105">
  <Image.Source>
    <DrawingImage>
      <DrawingImage.Drawing>
        <GeometryDrawing Brush="LightBlue">
          <GeometryDrawing.Pen>
           <Pen Brush="Blue" Thickness="5"/>
          </GeometryDrawing.Pen>
          <GeometryDrawing.Geometry>
            <RectangleGeometry Rect="0,0,100,50"/>
          </GeometryDrawing.Geometry>
        </GeometryDrawing>
      </DrawingImage.Drawing>
    </DrawingImage>
  </Image.Source>
</Image>
```

While the output is identical to the previous <Rectangle>, it is clearly more verbose. What we have here is the classic "more code for better performance" dilemma. Thankfully, when you make use of XAML graphical design tools (such as Microsoft Expression Blend or Microsoft Expression Design), the underlying markup is rendered behind the scenes (see Chapter 28 for details of the Microsoft Expression product family).

Use of the Visual-Derived Types

The abstract System.Windows.Media.Visual class type provides a minimal and complete set of services to render a derived type (rendering, hit testing, transformation), but it does not provide support for addition nonvisual services, which can lead to code bloat (input events, layout services, styles, and data binding). Given this, the Visual-derived types (DrawingVisual, Viewport3DVisual, and

ContainerVisual) are the most lightweight of all graphical rendering options and offer the best performance. Notice the simple inheritance chain of the Visual type, as shown in Figure 30-3.

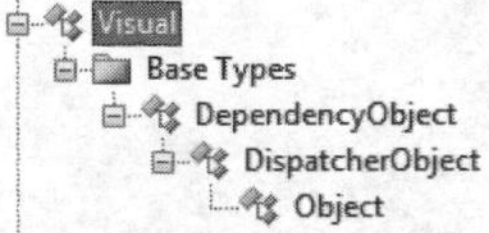

Figure 30-3. *The* Visual *type provides basic hit testing, coordinate transformation, and bounding box calculations.*

Because the Visual type exposes the lowest level of functionality, it has limited support for direct XAML definitions (unless you use a Visual within a type that *can* be expressed in XAML). Using these types feels a bit closer to making use of GDI/GDI+ rendering APIs, in that they are often manipulated through procedural code. When doing so, you are manually populating the object graph representing your window with custom Visual-derived types. Furthermore, you are required to override various virtual methods that will be called by the WPF graphics system to figure out how many items you are rendering, and the Visual item itself to be rendered.

To illustrate how you can use the Visual-derived types to render 2D data, open the code file for your main window type and comment out the entire definition (so you can restore it shortly, with minimal effort):

```
/*
public partial class MainWindow : System.Windows.Window
{
  public MainWindow()
  {
    InitializeComponent();
  }
}
*/
```

Now create the following Window-derived type that renders a rectangle directly on the surface of the window, bypassing any content defined in the XAML markup (your previous XAML descriptions will be ignored and not displayed):

```
public partial class MainWindow : System.Windows.Window
{
  // Our single drawing visual.
  private DrawingVisual rectVisual = new DrawingVisual();
  private const int NumberOfVisualItems = 1;

  public MainWindow()
  {
    InitializeComponent();

    // Helper function to create the rectangle.
    CreateRectVisual();
  }

  private void CreateRectVisual()
  {
    using (DrawingContext drawCtx = rectVisual.RenderOpen())
    {
      // The top, left, bottom, and right position of the rectangle.
```

```
      Rect rect = new Rect(50, 50, 105, 55);
      drawCtx.DrawRectangle(Brushes.AliceBlue, new Pen(Brushes.Blue, 5), rect);
    }

    // Register our visual with the object tree,
    // to ensure it supports routed events, hit testing, etc.
    AddVisualChild(rectVisual);
    AddLogicalChild(rectVisual);
  }

  // Necessary overrides. The WPF graphics system
  // will call these to figure out how many items to
  // render and what to render.
  protected override int VisualChildrenCount
  {
    get { return NumberOfVisualItems; }
  }

  protected override Visual GetVisualChild(int index)
  {
    // Collection is zero based, so subtract 1.
    if (index != (NumberOfVisualItems - 1))
      throw new ArgumentOutOfRangeException("index", "Don't have that visual!");
    return rectVisual;
  }
}
```

Notice that the DrawingVisual type (rectVisual) provides the RenderOpen() method, which will return a DrawingContext object. Similar to GDI+'s Graphics object, DrawingContext has numerous methods that can be used to render a variety of items (DrawRectangle(), DrawEllipse(), etc.). Once you have constructed your rectangle, you make calls to two inherited methods (AddVisualChild() and AddLogicalChild()) which, while technically optional, ensure your custom Visual-derived type integrates into the window's tree of objects.

Last but not least, you are required to override the virtual VisualChildrenCount read-only property and GetVisualChild() method. These members are called by the WPF graphics engine to determine exactly what to render (a single DrawingVisual in this example).

As you can see, as soon as you move into the realm of working with Visual-derived types, you are knee-deep in procedural code and therefore have a great deal of control and power (and the associated complexity that follows).

Building a Custom Visual Rendering Agent

Your current custom Visual rendering operation was set up in such a way that the window's content (e.g., the <StackPanel>) was blown away and therefore not rendered, in favor of the hard-coded DrawingVisual. Just to dig a bit deeper into the Visual programming layer, what if you wished to use XAML descriptions for a majority of your window's rendering and dip into the Visual layer for just a small portion of the overall UI?

One approach to do so is to define a custom class deriving from FrameworkElement and override the virtual OnRender() method. This method (which is in fact what the Shape-derived types use to render their output) can contain the same sort of code found in our previous CreateRectVisual() helper method. Once you have defined this custom class, you can then refer to your custom class type from within a window's XAML description.

To illustrate, to your current project add a new class named MyCustomRenderer, which extends the FrameworkElement base class (be sure to import the System.Windows and System.Windows.Media namespaces into your new file). Now, implement your type as so:

```
public class MyCustomRenderer : FrameworkElement
{
  // Default size for our rectangle.
  double rectWidth = 105, rectHeight = 55;

  // Allow user to override the defaults.
  public double RectHeight
  {
    set { rectHeight = value; }
    get { return rectHeight; }
  }
  public double RectWidth
  {
    set { rectWidth = value; }
    get { return rectWidth; }
  }

  protected override void OnRender(DrawingContext drawCtx)
  {
    // Do parent rendering first.
    base.OnRender(drawCtx);

    // Add our custom rendering.
    Rect rect = new Rect();
    rect.Width = rectWidth;
    rect.Height = rectHeight;
    drawCtx.DrawRectangle(Brushes.LightBlue, new Pen(Brushes.Blue, 5), rect);
  }
}
```

Most of the action of our custom type takes place in the OnRender() implementation. Notice that we have set the size of the local Rect variable based on our rectHeight and rectWidth members which, while not necessary, allow the creator to define the overall size of the image.

Gaining access to this type in XAML is simply a matter of defining a custom XML namespace that maps to the name of our type and using this prefix to create our type. Here are the relevant updates to the <StackPanel> type (recall from Chapter 28 that XML namespaces that map to your own .NET namespaces must be defined using the clr-namespace token):

```
<StackPanel xmlns:custom = "clr-namespace:WPFGraphicsOptions">
  ...
  <custom:MyCustomRenderer RectHeight ="100" RectWidth ="100"/>
</StackPanel>
```

Before you run your application, be sure to *uncomment* your original main window definition and *comment* out your custom window definition. Once you do, you can run your application and see three rectangular renderings, using each of the WPF 2D graphics programming techniques (see Figure 30-4).

Source Code The WPFGraphicsOptions project can be found under the Chapter 30 subdirectory.

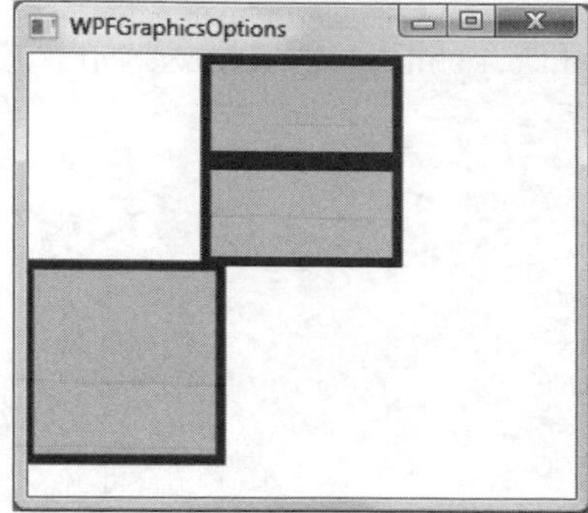

Figure 30-4. *Three rectangles, three approaches*

Picking Your Poison

At this point you have seen three different approaches to interacting with the WPF 2D graphical rendering services (shapes, drawings, and visuals). By and large, the need to render graphics using the `Visual`-derived types is only necessary if you are building custom controls, or you need a great deal of control over the rendering process. This is a good thing, as working with `Visual` and friends entails a healthy amount of effort compared to simple XAML descriptions. Given this, I will not dive into the `Visual` rending APIs beyond this point in the chapter (do feel free to consult the .NET Framework 3.5 SDK documentation for further details if you are interested).

Using the `Drawing`-derived types is a perfect middle-of-the-road approach, as these types still support core non-UI services (such as hit testing, etc.) at a lower cost than the `Shape` types. While this approach does entail more markup than required by the `Shape` types, you end up with an application using less overhead. We will examine more details of the `Drawing`-derived types a bit later in this chapter.

That being said, however, the `Shape` types are still a perfectly valid approach when you need to render a handful of 2D images within a given window. Recall that if you truly do need 2D shapes that are just about as capable as traditional UI elements, the `Shape` types are a perfect choice, given that the required infrastructure is already in place.

■ **Note** Always remember that your choice of rendering services can affect your application's performance. Thankfully, we are provided with a collection of various WPF profiling utilities to monitor your current application. Look up the topic "Performance Profiling Tools for WPF" within the .NET Framework 3.5 SDK documentation for further details.

Exploring the Shape-Derived Types

To continue exploring 2D graphical rendering, let's start by digging into the details of the members of the `System.Windows.Shapes` namespace. Recall these types provide the most straightforward, yet most bloated, way to render a two-dimensional image. This namespace (defined in the `PresentationFramework.dll` assembly) is quite small and consists of only six sealed types that extend the abstract `Shape` base class: `Ellipse`, `Line`, `Path`, `Polygon`, `Polyline`, and `Rectangle`.

Because the Shape base class is-a FrameworkElement, you are able to assign derived types as content using XAML or procedural C# code without the additional complexities of working with drawing geometries:

```
<Window x:Class="SomeShapes.MainWindow"
  xmlns="http://schemas.microsoft.com/winfx/2006/xaml/presentation"
  xmlns:x="http://schemas.microsoft.com/winfx/2006/xaml"
  Height="300" Width="300" >

  <!-- A window with a circle as content -->
  <Ellipse Height = "100" Width = "100" Fill = "Black" />
</Window>
```

Like any other UI element, if you are building a window that requires multiple contained widgets, you will need to define your 2D types within a panel type, as described in Chapter 29.

The Functionality of the Shape Base Class

While most of Shape's functionality comes from its long list of parent classes, this type does define some specific properties (most of which are dependency properties) that are common to the child types, some of the more interesting of which are shown in Table 30-1.

Table 30-1. *Key Properties of the* Shape *Base Class*

Properties	Meaning in Life
Fill	Allows you to specify a brush type to render the interior part of a derived type.
GeometryTransform	Allows you to apply a transformation to the rendering of the derived type.
Stretch	Describes how to fill a shape within its allocated space. This is controlled using the corresponding System.Windows.Media.Stretch enumeration.
Stroke, StrokeDashArray, StrokeEndLineCap, StrokeThickness	These (and other) stroke-centric properties control how lines are configured when drawing the border of a shape.

Also recall that Shape-derived types have support for hit testing, themes and styles, tool tips, and numerous services.

Working with Rectangles, Ellipses, and Lines

To check out some of the derived types firsthand, create a new Visual Studio WPF Windows Application named FunWithSystemWindowsShapes. Declaring Rectangle, Ellipse, and Line types in XAML is quite straightforward and requires little comment. One interesting feature of the Rectangle type is that it defines RadiusX and RadiusY properties to allow you to render curved corners if you require. Line represents its starting and end points using the X1, X2, Y1, and Y2 properties (given that "height" and "width" make little sense when describing a line). Without belaboring the point, consider the following <StackPanel>:

```
<StackPanel>
  <!-- A line that monitors the mouse entering its area -->
  <Line Name ="SimpleLine" X1 ="0" X2 ="50" Y1 ="0" Y2 ="50"
    Stroke ="DarkOliveGreen" StrokeThickness ="5"
    ToolTip ="This is a line!" MouseEnter ="SimpleLine_MouseEnter"/>
```

```
  <!-- A rectangle with curved corners -->
  <Rectangle RadiusX ="20" RadiusY ="50"
             Fill ="DarkBlue" Width ="150" Height ="50"/>
</StackPanel>
```

The MouseEnter event of the SimpleLine object simply updates the Title property of the window with the location of the mouse cursor at the time it entered the Line object:

```
protected void SimpleLine_MouseEnter(object sender, MouseEventArgs args)
{
  this.Title = String.Format("Mouse entered at: {0}",
    args.GetPosition(SimpleLine));
}
```

Working with Polylines, Polygons, and Paths

The Polyline type allows you define a collection of (*x*, *y*) coordinates (via the Points property) to draw a series of connected line segments that do not require connecting ends. The Polygon type is similar; however, it is programmed in such a way that it will always close the starting and ending points. Consider the following additions to the current <StackPanel>:

```
<!-- Polyline types do not have connecting ends -->
<Polyline Stroke ="Red" StrokeThickness ="20" StrokeLineJoin ="Round"
  Points ="10,10  40,40  10,90  300,50"/>

<!-- A Polygon always closes the end points-->
<Polygon Fill ="AliceBlue" StrokeThickness ="5" Stroke ="Green"
  Points ="40,10 70,80 10,50" />
```

Figure 30-5 shows the rendered output for each of these Shape-derived types.

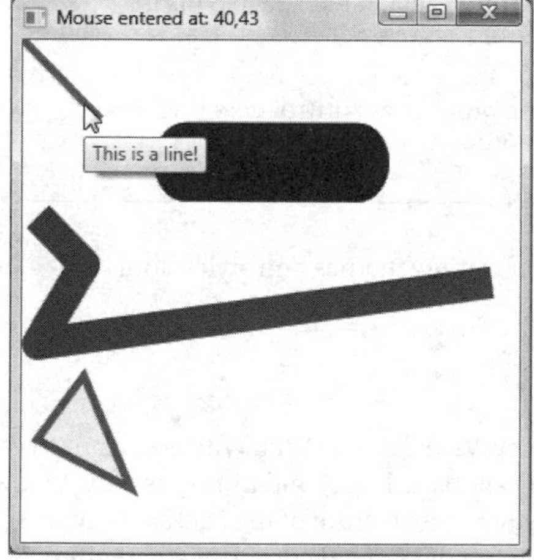

Figure 30-5. *Rendered* Shape-*derived types*

The final type, Path (not examined here), can be considered the superset of Rectangle, Ellipse, Polyline, and Polygon in that Path can render any of these types. In fact, all 2D types could be rendered using nothing but Path (however, doing so would require additional work).

Source Code The FunWithSystemWindowsShapes project can be found under the Chapter 30 subdirectory.

Working with WPF Brushes

Each of the WPF graphical rendering options (shape types, drawing types, and visual types) makes extensive use of *brushes*, which allow you to control how the interior of a 2D surface is filled. WPF provides six different brush types, all of which extend `System.Windows.Media.Brush`. While `Brush` is abstract, the descendents described in Table 30-2 can be used to fill a region with just about any conceivable option.

Table 30-2. *WPF* `Brush`*-Derived Types*

Brush Type	Meaning in Life
`DrawingBrush`	Paints an area with a `Drawing`-derived object (`GeometryDrawing`, `ImageDrawing`, or `VideoDrawing`)
`ImageBrush`	Paints an area with an image (represented by an `ImageSource` object)
`LinearGradientBrush`	A brush used to paint an area with a linear gradient
`RadialGradientBrush`	A brush used to paint an area with a radial gradient
`SolidColorBrush`	A brush consisting of a single color, set with the `Color` property
`VisualBrush`	Paints an area with a `Visual`-derived object (`DrawingVisual`, `Viewport3DVisual`, and `ContainerVisual`)

The `DrawingBrush` and `VisualBrush` types allow you to build a brush based on the `Drawing`- or `Visual`-derived types examined at the beginning of this chapter. The remaining brush types are quite straightforward to make use of and are very close in functionality to similar types found within GDI+. The following sections present a quick overview of `SolidColorBrush`, `LinearGradientBrush`, `RadialGradientBrush`, and `ImageBrush`.

Note Given that these examples will not respond to any events, you can enter each of the following examples directly into the custom XAML viewer you created in Chapter 28, rather than creating new Visual Studio 2008 WPF Application project workspaces.

Building Brushes with Solid Colors

The `SolidColorBrush` type provides the `Color` property to establish a solid colored brush type. The `Color` property takes a `System.Windows.Media.Color` type, which contains various properties (such as `A`, `R`, `G`, and `B`) to establish the color itself. While the capability to have solid colors is useful, ironically you typically will not need to directly create a `SolidColorBrush` explicitly, given that XAML supports a type converter that maps known color names (e.g., `"Blue"`) to a `SolidColorBrush` object behind the scenes. Consider the following approaches to fill an `Ellipse` with a solid color:

```
<StackPanel>
  <!-- Solid brush using type converter -->
  <Ellipse Fill ="DarkRed" Height ="50" Width ="50"/>
```

```
  <!-- Using the SolidColorBrush type -->
  <Ellipse Height ="50" Width ="50">
    <Ellipse.Fill>
      <SolidColorBrush Color ="DarkGoldenrod"/>
    </Ellipse.Fill>
  </Ellipse>

  <!-- Using the SolidColorBrush and Color type -->
  <Ellipse Height ="50" Width ="50">
    <Ellipse.Fill>
      <SolidColorBrush>
        <SolidColorBrush.Color>
          <Color A ="40" R ="100" G ="87" B ="98"/>
        </SolidColorBrush.Color>
      </SolidColorBrush>
    </Ellipse.Fill>
  </Ellipse>
</StackPanel>
```

The output is what you would expect (three circles of various solid colors); however, the approach you take to define the color scheme will be based on the level of flexibility you require. For example, if you do need to change the value of the `Opacity` property (to control transparency), you will need to declare a `<SolidColorBrush>` element to gain direct access to its members. In all other cases, you are able to make use of a simple string value assigned to the `Fill` property.

■ **Note** The WPF graphics API provides a helper class named `Brushes`, which defines properties for dozens of predefined colors. This is very useful when you need a solid colored brush in procedural code.

Working with Gradient Brushes

The two gradient brush types (`LinearGradientBrush` and `RadialGradientBrush`) allow you to fill an area by transitioning between two (or more) colors. The distinction is that while a `LinearGradientBrush` always transitions between colors using a straight line (which could, of course, be rotated into any position using a graphical transformation or by setting the starting and ending point), a `RadialGradientBrush` transitions from a specified starting point outward within an elliptical boundary. Consider the following:

```
<!-- A rectangle with a linear fill -->
<Rectangle RadiusX ="15" RadiusY ="15" Height ="40" Width ="100">
  <Rectangle.Fill>
    <LinearGradientBrush StartPoint="0,0.5" EndPoint="1,0.5">
      <GradientStop Color="LimeGreen" Offset="0.0" />
      <GradientStop Color="Orange" Offset="0.25" />
      <GradientStop Color="Yellow" Offset="0.75" />
      <GradientStop Color="Blue" Offset="1.0" />
    </LinearGradientBrush>
  </Rectangle.Fill>
</Rectangle>

<!-- An ellipse with a radial fill -->
<Ellipse  Height ="75" Width ="75">
  <Ellipse.Fill>
    <RadialGradientBrush GradientOrigin="0.5,0.5"
      Center="0.5,0.5" RadiusX="0.5" RadiusY="0.5">
```

```
      <GradientStop Color="Yellow" Offset="0" />
      <GradientStop Color="Red" Offset="0.25" />
      <GradientStop Color="Blue" Offset="0.75" />
      <GradientStop Color="LimeGreen" Offset="1" />
    </RadialGradientBrush>
  </Ellipse.Fill>
</Ellipse>
```

Notice how both brush types maintain a list of `<GradientStop>` types (which can be of any number) that specify a color and offset value, which specifies where in the image the next color will peak to blend with the previous color.

The ImageBrush Type

The final brush type we will examine here is `ImageBrush`, which as the name suggests allows you to load an external image file (or better yet, to load an embedded image resource) as the basis of a brush type. To assign an external file to an `ImageBrush`, one approach requires you to set the `ImageSource` property to a valid `BitmapImage` object. Consider the following simple definition, which assumes you have a `*.jpg` file, `Gooseberry0007.JPG`, located in the same location as this `*.xaml` file:

```
<!-- A large rectangle built using an image brush-->
<Rectangle Height ="100" Width ="300">
  <Rectangle.Fill>
    <ImageBrush>
      <ImageBrush.ImageSource>
        <BitmapImage  UriSource ="Gooseberry0007.JPG"/>
      </ImageBrush.ImageSource>
    </ImageBrush>
  </Rectangle.Fill>
</Rectangle>
```

Figure 30-6 shows each of our brush types in action.

Figure 30-6. *Numerous brushes at work*

■ **Source Code** The `FunWithBrushes.xaml` file can be found under the Chapter 30 subdirectory.

Working with WPF Pens

In comparison to brushes, the topic of pens is trivial, as the Pen type is really nothing more than a Brush in disguise. Specifically, Pen represents a brush type that has a specified thickness, represented by a double value. Given this point, you could create a Pen that has a Thickness property value so large that it appears to be, in fact, a brush! However, in most cases you will build a Pen of more modest thickness to represent how to render the outline of a 2D image.

In many cases, you will not directly need to create a Pen type, as this will be done indirectly when you assign a value to properties such as StrokeThickness. However, building a custom Pen type is very handy when working with Drawing-derived types (described next). Before we see a customized pen doing something useful, consider the following example:

```
<Pen Thickness="10" LineJoin="Round" EndLineCap="Triangle" StartLineCap="Round" />
```

This particular Pen type has set the LineJoin property, which controls how to render the connection point between two lines (e.g., the corners). EndLineCap, as the name suggests, controls how to render the endpoint of a line stroke (a triangle in this case), while StartLineCap controls the same setting at the line's point of origin.

A Pen can also be configured to make use of a *dash style*, which affects how the pen draws the line itself. The default setting is to use a solid color (as dictated by a given brush); however, the DashStyle property may be assigned to any custom DashStyle object. While creating a custom DashStyle object gives you complete control over how a Pen should render its data, the DashStyles helper class defines a number of static members that provide common default styles. Because these are *static members of a class* rather than values from an enumeration, we must make use of the XAML {x:Static} markup extension:

```
<Pen Thickness="10" LineJoin="Round" EndLineCap="Triangle"
  StartLineCap="Round" DashStyle = "{x:Static DashStyles.DashDotDot}" />
```

Now that you have a better idea of the Pen type, let's make use of some of them within various Drawing-derived types.

Exploring the Drawing-Derived Types

Recall that while the Shape types allow you to generate any sort of interactive two-dimensional surface, they entail quite a bit of overhead due to their rich inheritance chain. As an alternative, WPF provides a sophisticated drawing and geometry programming interface, which renders more lightweight 2D images. The entry point into this API is the abstract System.Windows.Media.Drawing class, which on its own does little more than define a bounding rectangle to hold the rendering. WPF provides five types that extend Drawing, each of which represents a particular flavor of drawing content, as described in Table 30-3.

Table 30-3. *WPF* Drawing*-Derived Types*

Type	Meaning in Life
DrawingGroup	Used to combine a collection of separate Drawing-derived types into a single composite rendering.
GeometryDrawing	Used to render 2D shapes.
GlyphRunDrawing	Used to render textual data using WPF graphical rendering services.
ImageDrawing	Used to render an image file into a bounding rectangle.
VideoDrawing	Used to play (not "draw") an audio file or video file. This type can only be fully exploited using procedural code. If you wish to play videos via XAML, the MediaPlayer type is a better choice.

While each of these types is useful in its own right, GeometryDrawing is the type of interest when you wish to render 2D images, and it is the one we will focus on during this section. In a nutshell, the GeometryDrawing type represents a *geometric type* detailing the structure of the 2D image, a Brush-derived type to fill its interior, and a Pen to draw its border.

The Role of Geometry Types

The geometric structure described by a GeometryDrawing type is actually one of the WPF geometry-centric class types, or possibly a collection of geometry-centric types that work together as a single unit. Each of these geometries can be expressed in XAML or via C# code. All of the geometries derive from the System.Windows.Media.Geometry base class, which defines a number of useful members common to all derived types, some of which appear in Table 30-4.

Table 30-4. *Select Members of the* System.Windows.Media.Geometry *Type*

Member	Meaning in Life
Bounds	A property used to establish the current bounding rectangle.
FillContains()	Allows you to determine if a given Point (or other Geometry type) is within the bounds of a particular Geometry-derived type. Obviously, this is useful for hit-testing calculations.
GetArea()	Returns a double that represents the entire area a Geometry-derived type occupies.
GetRenderBounds()	Returns a Rect that contains the smallest possible rectangle that could be used to render the Geometry-derived type.
Transform	Allows you to assign a Transform object to the geometry to alter the rendering.

WPF provides a good number of Geometry-derived types out of the box, and these can be grouped into two simple categories: basic shapes and paths. The first batch of geometric types, RectangleGeometry, EllipseGeometry, LineGeometry, and PathGeometry, are used to render basic shapes. As luck would have it, these four types mimic the functionality of the System.Windows.Media.Shapes types you have already examined (and in many cases they have identical members).

For many of your rendering operations, the basic shape types will do just fine. Do be aware, however, that if you require more exotic geometries, WPF supplies numerous auxiliary types that work in conjunction with the PathGeometry type. In a nutshell, PathGeometry maintains a collection of "path segments," which can be any of the following: ArchSegment, BezierSegment, LineSegment, PolyBezierSegment, PolyLineSegment, PolyQuadraticBezierSegment, and QuadraticBezierSegment.

Dissecting a Simple Drawing Geometry

Let's take a closer look at the <GeometryDrawing> type created at the beginning of this chapter:

```
<GeometryDrawing Brush ="LightBlue">
  <GeometryDrawing.Pen>
    <Pen Brush ="Blue" Thickness ="5"/>
  </GeometryDrawing.Pen>
  <GeometryDrawing.Geometry>
    <RectangleGeometry Rect="0,0,100,50"/>
  </GeometryDrawing.Geometry>
</GeometryDrawing>
```

Recall that a <GeometryDrawing> consists of a brush, pen, and any of the WPF geometry types. Here, we have indirectly defined a light blue SolidColorBrush using the Brush property in the open element. The Pen type is declared using property-element syntax, to define a blue brush with a specific thickness. Here, we are making use of a <RectangleGeometry> as the value assigned to the Geometry property of the <GeometryDrawing> type.

If you attempt to author this XAML directly within a <Page> scope using xamlpad.exe (or within any ContentControl-derived type), you will generate a markup error that essentially tells you that <GeometryDrawing> does not extend the UIElement base class and therefore cannot be used as a value to the Content property.

This brings up an interesting aspect of working with the Drawing-derived types: they do not have any user interface in and of themselves! Types such as <GeometryDrawing> simply describe how a 2D element *would* look if placed into a suitable container. WPF provides three different hosting objects for Drawing objects: DrawingImage, DrawingBrush, and DrawingVisual.

Containing Drawing Types in a DrawingImage

The DrawingImage type allows you to plug your drawing geometry into a WPF <Image> control. Thus, if you wish to render the previous <GeometryDrawing>, you would need to wrap it as so:

```
<Image>
  <Image.Source>
    <DrawingImage>
      <DrawingImage.Drawing>
        <GeometryDrawing Brush ="LightBlue">
          ...
        </GeometryDrawing>
      </DrawingImage.Drawing>
    </DrawingImage>
  </Image.Source>
</Image>
```

Notice how the Source property of the Image type is assigned a Drawing-derived type.

Containing Drawing Types in a DrawingBrush

If you instead wrap a <GeometryDrawing> using a DrawingBrush type, you have essentially created a complex custom brush, given that DrawingBrush is actually one of the Brush-derived types (more information on brushes in the next section). You could then use it anywhere a Brush type is required, such as the Background property of the <Window> type:

```
<Window x:Class="FunWithDrawingAndGeometries.MainWindow"
  xmlns="http://schemas.microsoft.com/winfx/2006/xaml/presentation"
  xmlns:x="http://schemas.microsoft.com/winfx/2006/xaml"
  Title="FunWithDrawingAndGeometries" Height="190" Width="224">

  <!-- Set the background of this window to a custom DrawingBrush -->
  <Window.Background>
    <DrawingBrush>
      <DrawingBrush.Drawing>
        <GeometryDrawing Brush ="LightBlue">
          <GeometryDrawing.Pen>
            <Pen Brush ="Blue" Thickness ="5"/>
          </GeometryDrawing.Pen>
```

```
          <GeometryDrawing.Geometry>
            <RectangleGeometry Rect="0,0,100,50"/>
          </GeometryDrawing.Geometry>
        </GeometryDrawing>
      </DrawingBrush.Drawing>
    </DrawingBrush>
  </Window.Background>
</Window>
```

A More Complex Drawing Geometry

A DrawingImage object can be composed of multiple individual Drawing objects, placed in a <DrawingGroup> in order to build much more elaborate 2D images. Consider the following Image type, which uses a <DrawingImage> as its source:

```
<Image>
  <Image.Source>
    <DrawingImage>
      <DrawingImage.Drawing>
        <!-- A group of various geometries -->
        <DrawingGroup>
          <GeometryDrawing>
            <GeometryDrawing.Geometry>
              <GeometryGroup>
                <RectangleGeometry Rect="0,0,20,20" />
                <RectangleGeometry Rect="160,120,20,20" />
                <EllipseGeometry Center="75,75" RadiusX="50" RadiusY="50" />
                <LineGeometry StartPoint="75,75" EndPoint="180,0" />
              </GeometryGroup>
            </GeometryDrawing.Geometry>
            <!-- A custom pen to draw the borders -->
            <GeometryDrawing.Pen>
             <Pen Thickness="10" LineJoin="Round"
                      EndLineCap="Triangle" StartLineCap="Round">
               <Pen.Brush>
                 <LinearGradientBrush>
                   <GradientStop Offset="0.0" Color="Red" />
                   <GradientStop Offset="1.0" Color="Green" />
                 </LinearGradientBrush>
                </Pen.Brush>
              </Pen>
            </GeometryDrawing.Pen>
          </GeometryDrawing>
        </DrawingGroup>
      </DrawingImage.Drawing>
    </DrawingImage>
  </Image.Source>
</Image>
```

The <DrawingImage> is composed of a <DrawingGroup> that contains a <GeometryGroup> to build an image consisting of two rectangles, an ellipse, and a line. The borders of our images are rendered using a custom pen type, which is in turn composed of a custom LinearGradientBrush. The end result can be seen in Figure 30-7.

Figure 30-7. *An image consisting of a* DrawingGroup

If we were to update our Pen type to make use of a DashStyle such as DashStyles.DashDotDot (seen previously)

```
<Pen Thickness="10" LineJoin="Round"
  EndLineCap="Triangle" StartLineCap="Round"
  DashStyle = "{x:Static DashStyles.DashDotDot}" >
  <Pen.Brush>
    <LinearGradientBrush>
        <GradientStop Offset="0.0" Color="Red" />
        <GradientStop Offset="1.0" Color="Green" />
      </LinearGradientBrush>
  </Pen.Brush>
</Pen>
```

we would now find the rendering shown in Figure 30-8.

Figure 30-8. *A* Pen *with a* DashStyle *setting of dash-dot-dot*

■ Source Code The FunWithDrawingGeometries.xaml file can be found under the Chapter 30 subdirectory.

The Role of UI Transformations

Before moving on to the topic of animation services, allow me to wrap up our look at 2D graphic rendering by examining the topic of *transformations*. WPF ships with numerous types that extend the `Transform` abstract base class, which can be applied to any `FrameworkElement` (e.g., descendents of `Shape` as well as UI elements such as `Buttons`, `TextBoxes`, etc.). Using these types, you are able to render a `FrameworkElement` at a given angle, skew the image across a surface, and expand or shrink the image in a variety of ways.

Transform-Derived Types

Table 30-5 documents many of the key out-of-the-box `Transform` types.

Table 30-5. *Key Descendents of the* `System.Windows.Media.Transform` *Type*

Type	Meaning in Life
`MatrixTransform`	Creates an arbitrary matrix transformation that is used to manipulate objects or coordinate systems in a 2D plane
`RotateTransform`	Rotates an object clockwise about a specified point in a 2D (*x*, *y*) coordinate system
`ScaleTransform`	Scales an object in the 2D (*x*, *y*) coordinate system
`SkewTransform`	Skews an object in the 2D (*x*, *y*) coordinate system
`TransformGroup`	Represents a composite `Transform` composed of other `Transform` objects

Once you create a `Transform`-derived object, you can apply it to two properties provided by the `FrameworkElement` base class. The `LayoutTransform` property is helpful in that the transformation occurs before elements are rendered into a panel. The `RenderTransform` property, on the other hand, occurs after the items are in their container, and therefore it is quite possible that elements can be transformed in such a way that they overlap each other. As well, types that extend `UIElement` can also assign a value to the `RenderTransformOrigin` property, which simply specifies an (*x*, *y*) position to begin the transformation.

Applying Transformations

Assume we have a `<Grid>` containing a single row with four columns. Within each cell, we will rotate, skew, and scale various `UIElements`, for example:

```
<!-- A Rectangle with a rotate transformation -->
<Rectangle Height ="100" Width ="40" Fill ="Red" Grid.Row="0" Grid.Column="0">
  <Rectangle.LayoutTransform>
    <RotateTransform Angle ="45"/>
  </Rectangle.LayoutTransform>
</Rectangle>

<!-- A Button with a skew transformation -->
<Button Content ="Click Me!" Grid.Row="0" Grid.Column="1" Width="95" Height="40">
  <Button.RenderTransform>
    <SkewTransform AngleX ="20" AngleY ="20"/>
  </Button.RenderTransform>
</Button>
```

```
<!-- An Ellipse that has been scaled by 20% -->
<Ellipse Fill ="Blue" Grid.Row="0" Grid.Column="2" Width="5" Height="5">
  <Ellipse.RenderTransform>
    <ScaleTransform ScaleX ="20" ScaleY ="20"/>
  </Ellipse.RenderTransform>
</Ellipse>

<!-- A Button that has been skewed, rotated, and skewed again -->
<Button Content ="Me Too!" Grid.Row="0" Grid.Column="3" Width="50" Height="40">
  <Button.RenderTransform>
    <TransformGroup>
    <SkewTransform AngleX ="20" AngleY ="20"/>
    <RotateTransform Angle ="45"/>
    <SkewTransform AngleX ="5" AngleY ="20"/>
    </TransformGroup>
  </Button.RenderTransform>
</Button>
```

Our first type, the `<Rectangle>`, makes use of the `RotateTransform` type that renders the UI item at a 45-degree angle via the `Angle` property. The first `<Button>` type uses a `SkewTransform` object, which slants the rendering of the widget based on (at minimum) the `AngleX` and `AngleY` properties. The `<ScaleTransform>` type used by the `<Ellipse>` grows the height and width of the circle quite a bit. Notice, for example, that the `Height` and `Width` properties of the `<Ellipse>` are set to 5, while the rendered output is much larger. Last but not least, the final `<Button>` type makes use of the `<TransformGroup>` type to apply a skew and a rotation. Figure 30-9 shows the rendered output.

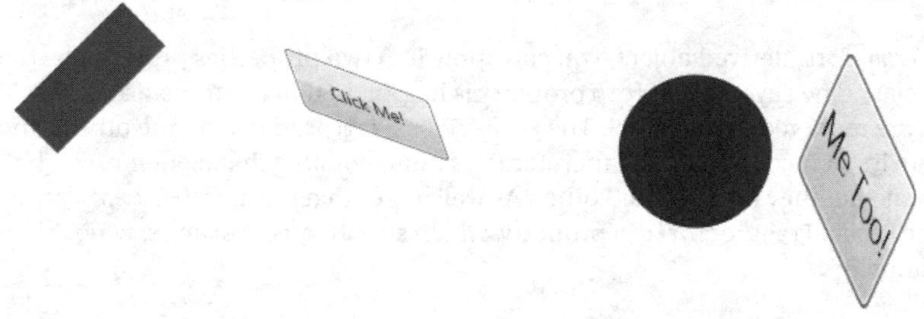

Figure 30-9. *Applying transformations*

■ **Source Code** The `FunWithTransformations.xaml` file can be found under the Chapter 30 subdirectory.

Understanding WPF's Animation Services

In addition to providing a full-fledged API to support 2D (and 3D) graphical rendering, WPF supplies a programming interface to support animation services. The term "animation" may bring to mind visions of spinning company logos, a sequence of rotating image resources (to provide the illusion of movement), text bouncing across the screen, or specific types of programs such as video games or multimedia applications.

While WPF's animation APIs could certainly be used for such purposes, animation can be used anytime you wish to give an application additional flair. For example, you could build an animation for a button on a screen that magnifies slightly in size when the mouse cursor hovers within its boundaries (and shrinks back once the mouse cursor moves beyond the boundaries). Perhaps you wish to animate a window so that it closes using a particular visual appearance (such as slowly fading into transparency). The short answer is that WPF's animation support can be used within any sort of application (business application, multimedia programs/video games, etc.) whenever you wish to provide a more engaging user experience.

Like many other aspects of WPF, the notion of building animations is nothing new in and of itself. However, unlike other APIs you may have used in the past (including GDI+), developers are not required to author the necessary infrastructure by hand. Under WPF, we have no need to create the background threads (or timers) used to advance the animation sequence, define custom types to represent the animation, or bother with numerous mathematical calculations.

Like other aspects of WPF, we are able to build an animation entirely using XAML, entirely using C# code, or a combination of the two. Furthermore, Microsoft Expression Blend (mentioned a few times within these WPF-centric chapters) can be used to design an animation using integrated tools and wizards without seeing a bit of C# or XAML in the foreground. This approach is ideal for graphic artists, who may not feel comfortable viewing such details.

The Role of Animation-Suffixed Types

To understand WPF's animation support, we must begin by examining the core animation types within the `System.Windows.Media.Animation` namespace of `PresentationCore.dll`. Here you will find a number of class types that all take the `Animation` suffix (`ByteAnimation`, `ColorAnimation`, `DoubleAnimation`, `In32Animation`, etc.). Obviously, these types are *not* used to somehow provide an animation sequence directly to a variable to a particular data type (after all, how exactly could we animate the value "9" using an `Int32Animation`?). Rather, these `Animation`-suffixed types can be connected to any *dependency property* of a given type that matches the underlying types.

■ Note Allow me to repeat this key point: `Animation`-suffixed types can only work in conjunction with dependency properties, not normal CLR properties (see Chapter 29). If you attempt to apply animation objects to CLR properties, you will receive a compile-time error.

For example, consider the `Label` type's `Height` and `Width` properties, both of which are dependency properties wrapping a `double`. If you wish to define an animation that would increase the height of a label over a time span, you could connect a `DoubleAnimation` object to the `Height` property and allow WPF to take care of the details of performing the actual animation itself. By way of another example, if you wish to transition the color of a brush type from green to yellow, you could do so using the `ColorAnimation` type.

Regardless of which `Animation`-suffixed type you wish to make use of, they all define a handful of key properties that control the starting and ending values used to perform the animation:

- `To`: This property represents the animation's ending value.
- `From`: This property represents the animation's starting value.
- `By`: This property represents the total amount by which the animation changes its starting value.

Despite the fact that all `Animation`-suffixed types support the `To`, `From`, and `By` properties, they do not receive them via virtual members of a base class. The reason for this is that the underlying types wrapped by these properties vary greatly (integers, colors, `Thickness` objects, etc.), and representing all possibilities using a `System.Object` would cause numerous boxing/unboxing penalties for stack-based data.

You might also wonder why .NET generics were not used to define a single animation class with a single type parameter (e.g., `Animate<T>`). Again, given that there are so many underlying data types (colors, vectors, ints, strings, etc.) used by animated dependency properties, it would not be as clean a solution as you might expect (not to mention XAML has only limited support for generic types).

The Role of the Timeline Base Class

Although a single base class was not used to define virtual `To`, `From`, and `By` properties, the `Animation`-suffixed types do share a common base class: `System.Windows.Media.Timeline`. This type provides a number of additional properties that control the pacing of the animation, as described in Table 30-6.

Table 30-6. *Key Members of the* `Timeline` *Base Class*

Properties	Meaning in Life
`AccelerationRatio`, `DecelerationRatio`, `SpeedRatio`	These properties can be used to control the overall pacing of the animation sequence.
`AutoReverse`	This property gets or sets a value that indicates whether the timeline plays in reverse after it completes a forward iteration.
`BeginTime`	This property gets or sets the time at which this timeline should begin. The default value is 0, which begins the animation immediately.
`Duration`	This property allows you to set a duration of time to play the timeline.
`FillBehavior`, `RepeatBehavior`	These properties are used to control what should happen once the timeline has completed (e.g., repeat the animation, do nothing, etc.).

Authoring an Animation in C# Code

Our first look at WPF's animation services will make use of the `DoubleAnimation` type to control various properties of various `Label` types on a main window. Create a new WPF Windows Application named AnimatedLabel, and design a `<Grid>` consisting of two rows and two columns. Into the first column place a `Button` type in each cell and handle the `Click` event for each widget. In the second column, place a `Label` type into each cell (named `lblHeight` and `lblTransparency`). Figure 30-10 shows one possible UI.

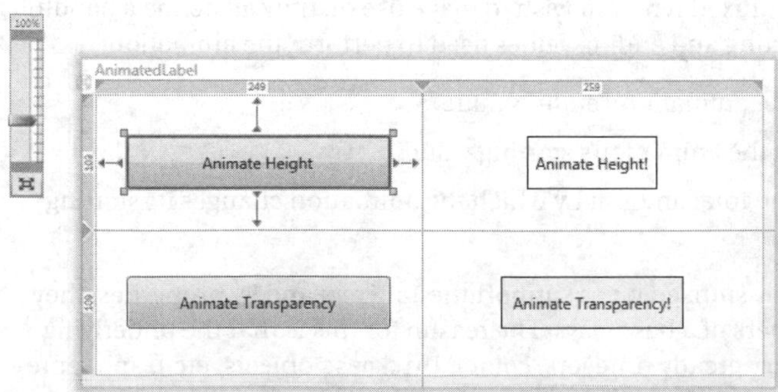

Figure 30-10. *The initial UI of the AnimatedLabel application*

Now, within each Click event handler, author the following code:

```
public partial class MainWindow : System.Windows.Window
{
  public MainWindow()
  {
    InitializeComponent();
  }

  protected void btnAnimatelblMessage_Click(object sender, RoutedEventArgs args)
  {
    // This will grow the height of the label.
    DoubleAnimation dblAnim = new DoubleAnimation();
    dblAnim.From = 40;
    dblAnim.To = 60;
    lblHeight.BeginAnimation(Label.HeightProperty, dblAnim);
  }

  protected void btnAnimatelblTransparency_Click(object sender,
    RoutedEventArgs args)
  {
    // This will change the opacity of the label.
    DoubleAnimation dblAnim = new DoubleAnimation();
    dblAnim.From = 1.0;
    dblAnim.To = 0.0;
    lblTransparency.BeginAnimation(Label.OpacityProperty, dblAnim);
  }
}
```

Notice in each Click event handler we set the From and To values of the DoubleAnimation type to represent the beginning and ending value. After this point, we call BeginAnimation() on the correct Label object, passing in the correct dependency property field of the related widget (again, the Label) followed by the Animation-suffixed object used to perform the animation.

■ **Note** Recall from our examination of dependency properties in Chapter 29 that public read-only static fields of type DependencyObject are used to represent a given dependency property exposed by the (optional) CLR property wrapper.

If you now run your application and click each button, you will find that the lblHeight label will grow in size, while the lblTransparency button will slowly fade from view.

Controlling the Pacing of an Animation

By default, an animation will take approximately one second to transition between the values assigned to the From and To properties. For example, if you were to modify the Click event handler that grows the Height of the Label from 40 to 200 (a larger increase than what we currently have in place), it would still take approximately one second to do so.

If you wish to define a custom amount of time for an animation's transition, you may do so via the Duration property, which can be set to an instance of a Duration object. Typically, the time span is established by passing a TimeSpan object to the Duration's constructor. Consider the following update to the current Click handlers, which will grow the label's height over four seconds and fade the other label from view over the course of ten seconds:

```
protected void btnAnimatelblMessage_Click(object sender, RoutedEventArgs args)
{
  // Take 4 seconds to complete the animation.
  DoubleAnimation dblAnim = new DoubleAnimation();
  dblAnim.From = 40;
  dblAnim.To = 200;

  dblAnim.Duration = new Duration(TimeSpan.FromSeconds(4));
  lblHeight.BeginAnimation(Label.HeightProperty, dblAnim);
}

protected void btnAnimatelblTransparency_Click(object sender, RoutedEventArgs args)
{
  // This will change the opacity of the label
  DoubleAnimation dblAnim = new DoubleAnimation();
  dblAnim.From = 1.0;
  dblAnim.To = 0.0;
  dblAnim.Duration = new Duration(TimeSpan.FromSeconds(10));
  lblTransparency.BeginAnimation(Label.OpacityProperty, dblAnim);
}
```

■ **Note** The `BeginTime` property of an `Animation`-suffixed type also takes a `TimeSpan` object. Recall this property can be set to establish a wait time before starting an animation sequence.

Reversing and Looping an Animation

You can also tell `Animation`-suffixed types to play an animation in reverse at the completion of the animation sequence by setting the `AutoReverse` property to `true`. For example, the following update to our `Click` event handler will cause the `Label` to grow from 40 to 100 pixels in height, after which it will "shrink" from 100 back to 40 (over the course of eight seconds, four seconds each "direction"):

```
// Reverse when done.
dblAnim.AutoReverse = true;
```

If you wish to have an animation repeat some number of times (or to never stop once activated), you can do so using the `RepeatBehavior` property, which is common to all `Animation`-suffixed types. The `RepeatBehavior` property is set to an object of the same name. If you pass in a simple numerical value to the constructor, you can specify a hard-coded number of times to repeat. On the other hand, if you pass in a `TimeSpan` object to the constructor, you can establish an amount of time the animation should repeat. Finally, if you wish an animation to loop ad infinitum, you can simply specify `RepeatBehavior.Forever`. Consider the following ways we could change the height of our `Label` object:

```
// Loop forever.
dblAnim.RepeatBehavior = RepeatBehavior.Forever;

// Loop three times.
dblAnim.RepeatBehavior = new RepeatBehavior(3);

// Loop for 30 seconds.
dblAnim.RepeatBehavior = new RepeatBehavior(TimeSpan.FromSeconds(30));
```

Source Code The AnimatedLabel project can be found under the Chapter 30 subdirectory.

Authoring an Animation in XAML

When you need to dynamically interact with the state of an animation, your best approach is to do so in procedural code, as we have just done. However, if you have a "fixed" animation that is predefined and will not require runtime interaction, you can author your entire animation sequence in XAML. For the most part, this process is identical to what you have already seen; however, the various Animation-suffixed types are wrapped within *storyboard* types. The storyboard types in turn are associated to an *event trigger*.

Let's walk through a complete example of an animation defined in terms of XAML, followed by a detailed breakdown. Our goal is to represent the eternally growing and shrinking Label of the previous example using XAML. Consider the following markup, which will be examined in the next several sections:

```
<Label Content = "Interesting...">
  <Label.Triggers>
    <EventTrigger RoutedEvent = "Label.Loaded">
      <EventTrigger.Actions>
        <BeginStoryboard>
          <Storyboard TargetProperty = "Height">
            <DoubleAnimation From ="40" To = "200" Duration = "0:0:4"
                             RepeatBehavior = "Forever"/>
          </Storyboard>
        </BeginStoryboard>
      </EventTrigger.Actions>
    </EventTrigger>
  </Label.Triggers>
</Label>
```

The Role of Storyboards

Working from the innermost element outward, we first encounter the <DoubleAnimation> type, which is making use of the same properties we set in procedural code (To, From, Duration, and RepeatBehavior). As mentioned, Animation-suffixed types are placed within a <Storyboard> type, which is used to map the animation to a given property on the parent type via the TargetProperty property (which again in this case is Height).

The reason for this level of indirection is that XAML does not support a syntax to invoke methods on objects, such as the necessary BeginAnimation() method of the Label. Essentially a <Storyboard> and the <BeginStoryboard> parent are the XAML-centric version of specifying the following procedural code:

```
// This necessary animation logic is represented with storyboards in XAML.
lblHeight.BeginAnimation(Label.HeightProperty, dblAnim);
```

The Use of <EventTrigger>

Once the <Storyboard> has been defined, we next need to define an event trigger to contain it. WPF supports three different types of triggers that allow you to define a set of actions that will occur when a given routed event is raised.

The first type of trigger observes conditions for dependency properties on a type. When defining triggers for dependency properties, you will do so by defining the trigger using `<Trigger>` elements. The second type of trigger accounts for "normal" .NET property types and is defined within a `<DataTrigger>` element. This flavor of trigger can be helpful for data binding operations. We will look at the `<Trigger>` element later in this chapter during our examination of styles and themes.

The final type of trigger relevant for the current example is an *event trigger* (defined within an `<EventTrigger>` element), which is used when building WPF animations. Here, our `<EventTrigger>` is connected to the `Loaded` event of the `Label`. When this event fires, the action to take is to execute the `<DoubleAnimation>` sequence on the `Label`'s `Height` property.

■ **Source Code** The `AnimationInXaml.xaml` file can be found under the Chapter 30 subdirectory.

The Role of Animation Key Frames

The final aspect of the WPF animation system we will examine is the use of *key frames*. The `System.Windows.Media.Animation` namespace also contains a number of members that end with the `AnimationUsingKeyFrames` suffix (`ByteAnimationUsingKeyFrames`, `ColorAnimationUsingKeyFrames`, `DoubleAnimationUsingKeyFrames`, `In32AnimationUsingKeyFrames`, etc.). Each of these types provides a `Duration` property, which controls how long the entire animation sequence should take. However, it is up to the key frames themselves to inform the animation system when they are up for duty.

Unlike the `Animation`-suffixed types, which can only move between a starting point and an ending point, the *key frame* counterparts allow us to create a collection of specific values for an animation that should take place at specific times. For example, the `AnimationUsingKeyFrames`-suffixed types could allow us to create an animation that bounces a circle around window, causes a custom image to move around the outline of a geometric shape, or cycles the colors within a text box over a time slice.

Within the scope of an `AnimationUsingKeyFrames`-suffixed element, you may add a collection of three different key frame types, each of which controls that frame of movement of the animated item:

- `LinearXXXKeyFrame`: The linear key frame types are used to move an item between points on a straight line.
- `SplineXXXKeyFrame`: The spline key frame types are used to move an item along a Bezier curve, using the `KeySpline` property.
- `DiscreteXXXKeyFrame`: The discrete key frame types do not provide a transition between key frames. For example, this can be useful when "animating" string data that grows in size or a border that "animates" between various colors.

Following a similar pattern, the exact name of the subelements will be based on the type of item you are animating (doubles, colors, bools, etc.). Here, `XXX` is obviously being used as a placeholder. The real names of any of these three key frame types would be along the lines of `LinearDoubleKeyFrame`, `SplineDoubleKeyFrame`, and `DiscreteDoubleKeyFrame`.

Animation Using Discrete Key Frames

To illustrate the use of a discrete key frame type, assume you wish to build a `Button` type that animates its content in such a way that over the course of three seconds, the value "OK!" appears one character at a time. Also assume that this behavior should happen as soon as the button has loaded into memory, and it should repeat continuously. To see this behavior firsthand, author the following XAML within the `SimpleXamlApp.exe` program you created in Chapter 28:

```
<Window xmlns="http://schemas.microsoft.com/winfx/2006/xaml/presentation"
  xmlns:x="http://schemas.microsoft.com/winfx/2006/xaml">
  <Grid>
    <Button Name="myButton" Height="40"
     FontSize="16pt" FontFamily="Verdana" Width = "100">
     <Button.Triggers>
       <EventTrigger RoutedEvent="Button.Loaded">
         <BeginStoryboard>
           <Storyboard>
             <StringAnimationUsingKeyFrames RepeatBehavior = "Forever"
               Storyboard.TargetName="myButton" Storyboard.TargetProperty="Content"
               Duration="0:0:3" FillBehavior="HoldEnd">
               <DiscreteStringKeyFrame Value="" KeyTime="0:0:0" />
               <DiscreteStringKeyFrame Value="O" KeyTime="0:0:1" />
               <DiscreteStringKeyFrame Value="OK" KeyTime="0:0:1.5" />
               <DiscreteStringKeyFrame Value="OK!" KeyTime="0:0:2" />
             </StringAnimationUsingKeyFrames>
           </Storyboard>
         </BeginStoryboard>
       </EventTrigger>
     </Button.Triggers>
    </Button>
  </Grid>
</Window>
```

Notice first of all that we have defined an event trigger for our button to ensure that our storyboard executes when the button has loaded. The StringAnimationUsingKeyFrames type is in charge of changing the content of our button, via the Storyboard.TargetName and Storyboard.TargetProperty values. Within the scope of our <StringAnimationUsingKeyFrames> element, we have defined three DiscreteStringKeyFrame types, which change the button's content over the course of two seconds (note that the duration established by StringAnimationUsingKeyFrames is a total of three seconds, so we will see a slight pause between the final "!" and looping "O").

Source Code The AnimatedButtonWithDiscreteKeyFrames.xaml file can be found under the Chapter 30 subdirectory.

Animation Using Linear Key Frames

To see the use of a linear key frame at work, consider the following XAML, which spins a Button in a complete circle using the center of the button as the point of origin. Once the 360-degree rotation has completed, the button will then flip itself upside down (and then right side up again). Assume this XAML markup is defined within a <Grid> type:

```
<!-- This button will rotate in a circle, then flip, when clicked -->
<Button Name="myAnimatedButton" Width="120" Height = "40"
  RenderTransformOrigin="0.5,0.5" Content = "OK">

<Button.RenderTransform>
  <RotateTransform Angle="0"/>
</Button.RenderTransform>

<!-- The animation is triggered when the button is clicked -->
<Button.Triggers>
  <EventTrigger RoutedEvent="Button.Click">
```

```
    <BeginStoryboard>
      <Storyboard>
        <DoubleAnimationUsingKeyFrames
          Storyboard.TargetName="myAnimatedButton"
          Storyboard.TargetProperty=
            "(Button.RenderTransform).(RotateTransform.Angle)"
          Duration="0:0:2" FillBehavior="Stop">
            <DoubleAnimationUsingKeyFrames.KeyFrames>
              <LinearDoubleKeyFrame Value="360" KeyTime="0:0:1" />
              <DiscreteDoubleKeyFrame Value="180" KeyTime="0:0:1.5" />
            </DoubleAnimationUsingKeyFrames.KeyFrames>
          </DoubleAnimationUsingKeyFrames>
        </Storyboard>
      </BeginStoryboard>
    </EventTrigger>
  </Button.Triggers>
</Button>
```

This Button's definition begins by specifying a value to the RenderTransformOrigin property, which ensures the rotation occurs using the dead center of the button as the turning point. Next, we establish the initial starting value for the rendering transformation, using the nested <Button.RenderTransform> scope (note the starting angle is zero). Finally, we define an event trigger to ensure our storyboard will execute when the end user clicks the Button widget.

With these initial settings complete, we create a <Storyboard> scope that makes use of the DoubleAnimationUsingKeyFrames type. Notice that the target of this storyboard is our Button instance (myAnimatedButton) and the property we are targeting on this object is ultimately the Angle property. However, notice the new bit of XAML syntax that we must use when assigning a dependency property to a property value:

```
<DoubleAnimationUsingKeyFrames
  Storyboard.TargetName="myAnimatedButton"
  Storyboard.TargetProperty="(Button.RenderTransform).(RotateTransform.Angle)"
  Duration="0:0:2" FillBehavior="Stop">
```

As you can see, we must wrap dependency properties within parentheses; therefore, the single bold line of code allows us to say in effect, "I am animating the Angle property of the RotateTransform object exposed by the button." This point aside, the total time allowed for this animation is set to two seconds.

Within the scope of our DoubleAnimationUsingKeyFrames type, we add two key frame types. The first (LinearDoubleKeyFrame) will rotate the button 360 degrees over a one-second time period. Approximately half a second later, the DiscreteDoubleKeyFrame flips the button 180 degrees (turning the button upside down). Finally, once the animation expires (again, half a second later, given our Duration property of the DoubleAnimationUsingKeyFrames type), the button flips right side up again, as the DoubleAnimationUsingKeyFrames type has a FillBehavior value of Stop (which returns the item to the initial state).

■Source Code The SpinButtonWithLinearKeyFrames.xaml file can be found under the Chapter 30 subdirectory.

That wraps up our look at the basic animation services (and 2D rendering techniques) that are baked into WPF. Both of these topics could easily require a book of their own to cover all of the bells and whistles. Nevertheless, at this time you should be in a solid position for further exploration. Next up, we will turn our attention to how to package application resources.

Understanding the WPF Resource System

Our next task is to examine the seemingly unrelated topic of embedding and accessing application resources. WPF supports two flavors of resources, the first of which is *binary resources*, which represents what most programmers consider a "resource" in the traditional sense of the word (bitmap files, icons, string tables, etc.).

The second flavor of resources, termed *object resources* or *logical resources*, represents any type of .NET object that is named and embedded within an assembly. As you will see, logical resources are extremely helpful when working with graphical data of any sort, given that you can define commonly used graphic primitives (brushes, pens, animations, etc.) within a resources dictionary.

Working with Binary Resources

As mentioned, binary resources are the auxiliary bits used by a .NET application, such as string tables, icons, and image files (e.g., company logos, images for an animation, etc.). If you are creating a WPF application using Visual Studio, you are able to instruct the compiler to embed an external resource into the assembly simply by specifying the Resource build option. To illustrate, create a new WPF Windows Application named FunWithResources. Update your initial XAML definition for the main window with a three-column `<Grid>`, where the first cell contains an `Image` widget:

```
<Window x:Class="FunWithResources.MainWindow"
  xmlns="http://schemas.microsoft.com/winfx/2006/xaml/presentation"
  xmlns:x="http://schemas.microsoft.com/winfx/2006/xaml"
  Title="FunWithResources" Height="207" Width="612"
  WindowStartupLocation="CenterScreen">
  <Grid>
    <Grid.ColumnDefinitions>
      <ColumnDefinition/>
      <ColumnDefinition/>
      <ColumnDefinition/>
    </Grid.ColumnDefinitions>
    <Image Grid.Column ="0" Name ="companyLogo"/>
  </Grid>
</Window>
```

The first goal is to embed an image file into our application as a binary resource, which will be used to set the `Source` property of the `companyLogo Image` control. Using your image file of choice, add it into your current project using the Project ➤ Add Existing Item menu option of Visual Studio (here, I am assuming a file named `IntertechBlue.gif`).

The Resource Build Action

Once you have added an external image file to your application, you should now see it listed within Solution Explorer. When selected, the Properties can now be used to instruct the compiler how to process these external files using the Build Action option (see Figure 30-11).

If you select the default setting, Resource, the compiler will embed the data into the .NET assembly, and therefore these external files do not need to be shipped with the completed application. Assuming you have set the Build Action of your image file to Resources, you can update the XAML definition of the `Image` control as so (notice you refer to the name of the binary resource by name):

```
<Image Grid.Column ="0" Name ="companyLogo" Source ="IntertechBlue.gif"/>
```

When you now compile and run your program, you should see your image file stretched within the first cell of your `<Grid>`.

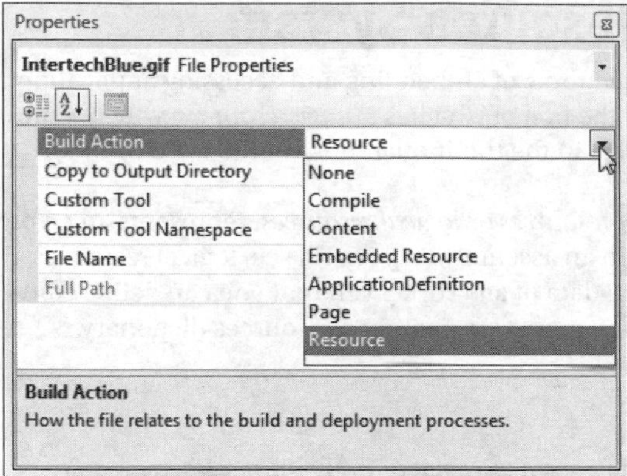

Figure 30-11. *Options for packaging binary resources*

■Note Be careful that your WPF applications use the Resource option to embed resources, which is a WPF-aware option. The tempting-sounding Embedded Resource option is used for Windows Forms application.

If you load your compiled application into `reflector.exe` (see Chapter 2), you can view the embedded resource directly, as shown in Figure 30-12.

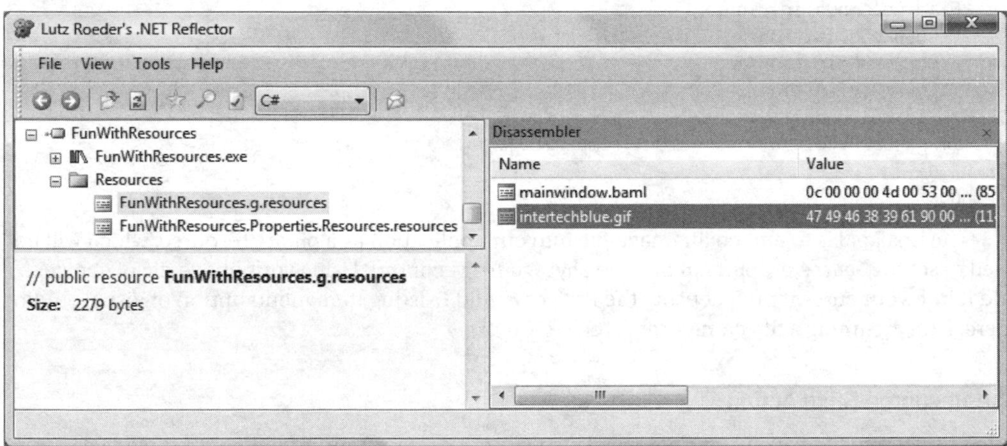

Figure 30-12. *An embedded binary resource*

The Content Build Action

It is also possible to set the Build Action of a related external file to Content, rather than Resource. When you do so, your assembly is compiled in such a way that it is aware of the relative location of the external file, but does not actually contain the binary data. This setting can be helpful when you deploy an application that contains a subfolder (or two) containing external resources that need to be replaced from time to time, or when the location of external resources is on a network share point.

In these cases, the WPF resource management system defines a number of additional URI formats (including a syntax to load resources embedded in an external assembly) beyond a simple file name. If you are interested in examining the various URI formats that can be used with local resources not compiled into the current assembly, look up the topic "Pack URIs in WPF" within the .NET Framework 3.5 SDK documentation.

The Role of Object (a.k.a. Logical) Resources

WPF resources really come into their own when you embed custom .NET objects into an assembly for use within your application. At first glance, this may seem like a very odd thing to do. However, by doing so you can define commonly used graphical elements (brushes, pens, etc.) for use by multiple areas of your program. This technique is often used when creating custom themes and styles for your WPF applications, which we will examine next.

Defining and Applying Styles for WPF Controls

When you are building the UI of a WPF application, it is not uncommon for a family of widgets to all have a shared look and feel. For example, you may wish to ensure that all button types have the same height, width, background color, and font size for their string content. While you could do so by setting each button's individual properties to identical values, this approach certainly makes it difficult to implement changes down the road, as you would need to reset the same set of properties on multiple objects for every change.

Thankfully, WPF offers numerous ways to change the look and feel of UI elements (styles, templates, skins, etc.) with minimal fuss and bother. As you will see, building such styles entails the use of each topic presented thus far in this chapter (2D graphics, animations, and resources). To get the ball rolling, let's begin by examining the use of styles.

Working with Inline Styles

The first way in which you can change the look and feel of a WPF widget is through *styles*. A style is a kindred spirit to a web-based style sheet, in that styles do not have a UI of their own, but simply establish a number of property settings that other UI elements can adopt. Any descendent of `Control` has the ability to support styles (via the `Style` property), including, of course, the `Window` itself. When you wish to author a style, one possible approach is to make use of property-element syntax that allows you to assign a style "inline."

To illustrate, update your current `<Grid>` definition of the FunWithResources project to define a `Button` within the remaining two cells. Now, consider the following markup, which establishes a custom style for a button named `btnClickMe` (but not the second button, `btnClickMeToo`):

```
<Window x:Class="FunWithResources.MainWindow"
  xmlns="http://schemas.microsoft.com/winfx/2006/xaml/presentation"
  xmlns:x="http://schemas.microsoft.com/winfx/2006/xaml"
  Title="FunWithResources" Height="207" Width="612"
  WindowStartupLocation="CenterScreen">
  <Grid>
  <Grid.ColumnDefinitions>
    <ColumnDefinition/>
    <ColumnDefinition/>
    <ColumnDefinition/>
  </Grid.ColumnDefinitions>
  <Image Grid.Column ="0" Name ="companyLogo" Source ="IntertechBlue.gif"/>
```

```
    <!-- This button has an inline style! -->
    <Button Grid.Column ="1" Name="btnClickMe" Height="80"
     Width = "100" Content ="Click Me">
      <Button.Style>
        <Style>
          <Setter Property ="Button.FontSize" Value ="20"/>
          <Setter Property ="Button.Background">
            <Setter.Value>
              <LinearGradientBrush StartPoint="0,0" EndPoint="1,1">
                <GradientStop Color="Green" Offset="0" />
                <GradientStop Color="Yellow" Offset="0.25" />
                <GradientStop Color="Pink" Offset="0.75" />
                <GradientStop Color ="Red" Offset="1" />
              </LinearGradientBrush>
            </Setter.Value>
          </Setter>
        </Style>
      </Button.Style>
    </Button>

    <!-- No style for this button! -->
    <Button Grid.Column ="2" Name="btnClickMeToo"
     Height="80" Width = "100" Content ="Me Too"/>
    </Grid>
  </Window>
```

As you can see, a WPF style is defined using the `<Style>` element. Within this scope, we define any number of `<Setter>` elements, which are used to establish the name/value pairs of the properties we wish to set. Here we have established a `FontSize` property of the `Button` to be 20, and the `Background` property of the `Button` type via a `LinearGradientBrush` type that is composed of four interconnected colors.

■ **Note** If necessary, you can programmatically establish a style in your code file. Simply set the `Style` property on the control-derived type.

While this approach to building a style is syntactically correct, one obvious limitation is that inline styles are bound to a specific instance of a UI type (`btnClickMe` in our example), not each button within the scope. In Figure 30-13, notice that the second `Button` type, `btnClickMeToo`, is unaffected by the style assigned to `btnClickMe`.

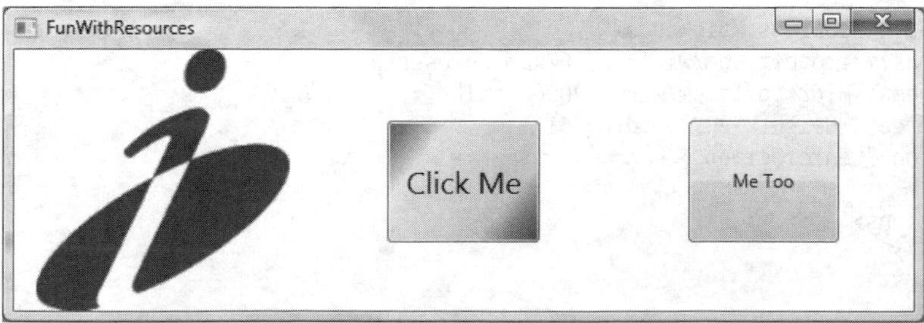

Figure 30-13. *Inline styles are bound to the control that defined them.*

Working with Named Styles

To define a style that can be used by multiple UI elements of the same type (e.g., all Buttons, all ListBoxes, etc.), you may define the style within a container's *resource dictionary*, thereby defining an object (a.k.a. logical) resource. For example, you could add a named style to the <Window>'s resource dictionary and identify it by name through the Key property. That way, the same theme can be referenced everywhere in your XAML document. Consider the following update:

```
<Window x:Class="FunWithResources.MainWindow"
  xmlns="http://schemas.microsoft.com/winfx/2006/xaml/presentation"
  xmlns:x="http://schemas.microsoft.com/winfx/2006/xaml"
  Title="FunWithResources" Height="207"
  Width="612" WindowStartupLocation="CenterScreen">

  <!-- Add a logical resource to the window's resource dictionary -->
  <Window.Resources>
    <Style x:Key ="MyFunkyStyle">
      <Setter Property ="Button.FontSize" Value ="20"/>
      <Setter Property ="Button.Background">
        <Setter.Value>
          <LinearGradientBrush StartPoint="0,0" EndPoint="1,1">
            <GradientStop Color="Green" Offset="0" />
            <GradientStop Color="Yellow" Offset="0.25" />
            <GradientStop Color="Pink" Offset="0.75" />
            <GradientStop Color ="Red" Offset="1" />
          </LinearGradientBrush>
        </Setter.Value>
      </Setter>
    </Style>
  </Window.Resources>
  <Grid>
  <Grid.ColumnDefinitions>
    <ColumnDefinition/>
    <ColumnDefinition/>
    <ColumnDefinition/>
  </Grid.ColumnDefinitions>
  <Image Grid.Column ="0" Name ="companyLogo" Source ="IntertechBlue.gif"/>

  <!-- Both buttons now use the same style -->
  <Button Grid.Column ="1" Name="btnClickMe" Height="80" Width = "100"
          Style ="{StaticResource MyFunkyStyle}" Content = "Click Me"/>
  <Button Grid.Column ="2" Name="btnClickMeToo" Height="80" Width = "100"
          Style ="{StaticResource MyFunkyStyle}" Content = "Me Too"/>
  </Grid>
</Window>
```

This time, note that the style has been defined within the scope of a <Window.Resources> element and has been assigned the name MyFunkyStyle via the Key attribute. Beyond these points, the style declaration itself is identical to the previous style we created inline. Also notice that when we want to apply a style (as we do within the <Button> definitions), we do so using the StaticResource markup extension (see Chapter 28). With this update, each button takes on the same look and feel, as shown in Figure 30-14.

Figure 30-14. *Named styles can be used by multiple UI elements in the same scope.*

Overriding Style Settings

It is important to point out that when a UI element adopts a particular style (either an inline style or a named style) it has the freedom to "override" a property setting. For example, assume you want the second Button type to make use of the Background setting established by MyFunkyStyle, but you prefer a smaller font. To do so, simply assign a new value to the property you wish to change within the opening XAML element:

```
<Button Grid.Column ="2" Name="btnClickMeToo" Height="80" Width = "100"
  Style ="{StaticResource MyFunkyStyle}" FontSize = "10" Content = "Me Too"/>
```

Subclassing Existing Styles

It is also possible to build new styles using an existing style, via the BasedOn property, provided the style you are extending has been given a specific name via the Key property. For example, the following NewFunkyStyle style (which is added as a new child element of the <Window.Resources> scope) gathers the font size and background color of MyFunkyStyle, but rotates the UI element 20 degrees:

```
<Style x:Key ="NewFunkyStyle" BasedOn = "{StaticResource MyFunkyStyle}">
  <Setter Property = "Button.Foreground" Value = "Blue"/>
  <Setter Property = "Button.RenderTransform">
    <Setter.Value>
      <RotateTransform Angle = "20"/>
    </Setter.Value>
  </Setter>
</Style>
```

Figure 30-15 shows the new style in action when applied to each button.

Figure 30-15. *Using a derived style*

Widening Styles

Moving a style into a resource dictionary is a step in the right direction to be sure. However, what if you want to use the same style for multiple UI elements? Currently, MyFunkyStyle can only be applied to button widgets, given that the style explicitly references the Button type using property-element syntax.

One of the very interesting aspects of WPF styles is that the values assigned within a <Setter> scope honor the concept of inheritance. Thus, if we set properties on the common parent of all UI elements (System.Windows.Controls.Control) within our style, we can effectively define a style that is common to all WPF controls. For example, the following style update:

```
<Window.Resources>
  <Style x:Key ="MyFunkyStyle">
    <Setter Property ="Control.FontSize" Value ="20"/>
    <Setter Property ="Control.Background">
      <Setter.Value>
        <LinearGradientBrush StartPoint="0,0" EndPoint="1,1">
          <GradientStop Color="Green" Offset="0" />
          <GradientStop Color="Yellow" Offset="0.25" />
          <GradientStop Color="Pink" Offset="0.75" />
          <GradientStop Color ="Red" Offset="1" />
        </LinearGradientBrush>
      </Setter.Value>
    </Setter>
  </Style>
...
</Window.Resources>
```

allows us to apply MyFunkyStyle to TextBox types as well as Button types (or to any item extending Control, for that matter). Assume the following new UI element added within a new column of the current <Grid>:

```
<TextBox Grid.Column ="3" Name="txtAndMe" Height="40" Width = "100"
                  Style ="{StaticResource MyFunkyStyle}" Text = "And me!"/>
```

■ Note When you are building a style that is making use of a base class type, you needn't be concerned if you assign a value to a dependency property not supported by derived types. If the derived type does not support a given dependency property, it is ignored.

Narrowing Styles

If you wish to define a style that can be applied *only* to certain types of UI elements (e.g., only Buttons and nothing else), you can do so by setting the TargetType property on the style's opening element. This property expects a metadata description of the target widget, so you will make use of the x:Type markup extension (see Chapter 28). By way of illustration, we could update MyFunkyStyle as follows. With this update, it would now be a markup error for the previous TextBox to attempt to apply this style.

```
<Style x:Key ="MyFunkyStyle" TargetType = "{x:Type Button}">
...
</Style>
```

Assigning Styles Implicitly

WPF styles also support the ability to be implicitly set to all UI widgets within a given XAML scope. When you build a named style, assigning a Key property is technically optional, *if* you have narrowed the application of your style using the TargetType property:

```
<Style TargetType = "{x:Type Button}">
...
</Style>
```

By doing so, all Button types within scope will implicitly take on the MyFunkyStyle style, even though they are not making use of the StaticResource markup extension:

```
<Button Grid.Column ="1" Name="btnClickMe"
        Height="80" Width = "100" Content = "Click Me"/>

<Button Grid.Column ="2" Name="btnClickMeToo"
        Height="80" Width = "100" Content = "Me Too"/>
```

Be aware that when you define a style using the TargetType property that does *not* have a Key value established, the style is applied only to identically named types. Therefore, if we were to update the current style to the following:

```
<Style TargetType = "{x:Type Control}">
  ...
</Style>
```

neither the Button nor the TextBox type would adopt the style! Again, the reason is that this iteration of our style is targeting the Control base class. Always remember that the notion of a style representing a class or a derivative thereof works only for named styles.

■ **Source Code** The FunWithResources project can be found under the Chapter 30 subdirectory.

Defining Styles with Triggers

The next aspect of WPF styles to examine here is the notion of *triggers*, which allow you to define certain <Setter> elements in such a way that they will only be applied if a given condition is true. For example, perhaps you want to increase the size of a font when the mouse is over a button. Or maybe you want to make sure that the text box with the current focus is highlighted with a given color. Triggers are very useful for these sorts of situations, in that they allow you to take specific actions when a property changes without the need to author explicit C# code in a code-behind file.

The following XAML markup defines three TextBox types, all of which have their Style property set to the TextBoxStyle style. While all text boxes will have a shared look and feel (height, width, etc.), only the text box that has the current focus will receive a yellow background.

```
<Window
    xmlns="http://schemas.microsoft.com/winfx/2006/xaml/presentation"
    xmlns:x="http://schemas.microsoft.com/winfx/2006/xaml">

  <Window.Resources>
    <Style x:Key ="TextBoxStyle" TargetType = "{x:Type TextBox}">
      <Setter Property = "Foreground" Value = "Black"/>
      <Setter Property = "Background" Value = "LightGray"/>
      <Setter Property = "Height" Value = "30"/>
      <Setter Property = "Width" Value = "100"/>
```

```
    <!-- The following setter will only be applied when the text box is
         in focus. -->
     <Style.Triggers>
       <Trigger Property = "IsFocused" Value = "True">
         <Setter Property = "Background" Value = "Yellow"/>
       </Trigger>
     </Style.Triggers>
   </Style>
 </Window.Resources>

 <StackPanel>
   <TextBox Name = "txtOne" Style = "{StaticResource TextBoxStyle}" />
   <TextBox Name = "txtTwo" Style = "{StaticResource TextBoxStyle}" />
   <TextBox Name = "txtThree" Style = "{StaticResource TextBoxStyle}" />
  </StackPanel>
</Window>
```

If you type the previous XAML into the SimpleXamlPad.exe application, you will now find that as you tab between your TextBox objects, the currently selected widget has a bright yellow background, while the others receive the default assigned background color of gray. Triggers are also very smart, in that when the trigger's condition is *not true*, the widget automatically receives the default value assignment. Therefore, as soon as a TextBox loses focus, it also automatically becomes the default assigned color without any work on your part.

Triggers can also be designed in such a way that the defined <Setter> elements will be applied when *multiple conditions* are true (similar to building an if statement for multiple conditions). Let's say that we want to set the background of a text box to yellow only if it has the active focus and the mouse is hovering within its boundaries. To do so, we can make use of the <MultiTrigger> element to define each condition:

```
<Window.Resources>
  <Style x:Key ="TextBoxStyle" TargetType = "{x:Type TextBox}">
    <Setter Property = "Foreground" Value = "Black"/>
    <Setter Property = "Background" Value = "LightGray"/>
    <Setter Property = "Height" Value = "30"/>
    <Setter Property = "Width" Value = "100"/>
    <!-- The following setter will only be applied when the text box is
           in focus and the mouse is over the text box. -->
     <Style.Triggers>
       <MultiTrigger>
       <MultiTrigger.Conditions>
         <Condition Property = "IsFocused" Value = "True"/>
         <Condition Property = "IsMouseOver" Value = "True"/>
       </MultiTrigger.Conditions>
       <Setter Property = "Background" Value = "Yellow"/>
     </MultiTrigger>
    </Style.Triggers>
  </Style>
</Window.Resources>
```

■ **Source Code** The StyleWithTriggers.xaml file can be found under the Chapter 30 subdirectory.

Assigning Styles Programmatically

To conclude our examination of styles, let's now build a simple application that illustrates how you can assign styles to UI elements in code using a new Visual Studio WPF Windows Application project named StylesAtRuntime.

Our goal is to define three different styles for a `Button` type within the resource dictionary of the `<Window>` element. The first style, `TiltStyle`, rotates the button 10 degrees. The second style, `GreenStyle`, simply sets the `Background`, `Foreground`, and `FontSize` properties to preset values. The final style, `MouseOverStyle`, is based on `GreenStyle`, but adds a trigger condition that will increase the font size and text of the button widget. Here are the XAML descriptions for each style:

```
<Window.Resources>
  <!-- This style tilts buttons at a 10-degree angle -->
  <Style x:Key ="TiltStyle" TargetType = "{x:Type Button}">
    <Setter Property = "RenderTransform">
      <Setter.Value>
        <RotateTransform Angle = "10"/>
      </Setter.Value>
    </Setter>
  </Style>

  <!-- This style gives buttons a springtime feel -->
  <Style x:Key ="GreenStyle" TargetType = "{x:Type Button}">
    <Setter Property = "Background" Value ="Green"/>
    <Setter Property = "Foreground" Value ="Yellow"/>
    <Setter Property ="FontSize" Value ="15" />
  </Style>

  <!-- This style increases the size of a button when
       the mouse is over it -->
  <Style x:Key ="MouseOverStyle"  BasedOn ="{StaticResource GreenStyle}"
         TargetType = "{x:Type Button}">
    <Style.Triggers>
      <Trigger Property ="IsMouseOver" Value ="True">
        <Setter Property ="FontSize" Value ="20" />
        <Setter Property ="Foreground" Value ="Black" />
      </Trigger>
    </Style.Triggers>
  </Style>
</Window.Resources>
```

The `Window` object will maintain a `Grid` that maps out locations for a `TextBlock`, `ListBox`, and `Button`. This `ListBox` will contain the names of each theme and will handle the `SelectionChanged` event. Here is the relevant XAML for the UI:

```
<Grid>
  <Grid.ColumnDefinitions>
    <ColumnDefinition />
    <ColumnDefinition />
  </Grid.ColumnDefinitions>
  <StackPanel Grid.Column="0">
    <TextBlock TextWrapping ="Wrap" FontSize ="20"
      Padding="5,5,5,5">
        Please select a style for the button on the left.
    </TextBlock>
    <ListBox Name ="lstStyles" Height ="60" Background = "Yellow"
      SelectionChanged ="comboStyles_Changed" />
```

```
    </StackPanel>
  <Button Name="btnMouseOverStyle" Grid.Column="1"
    Height="40" Width="100">My Button</Button>
</Grid>
```

The final task it to fill the `ListBox` and handle the `SelectionChanged` event in the related code file. Notice in the following code how we are able to extract the current resource by name, using the inherited `FindResource()` method:

```
public partial class MainWindow : Window
{
  public MainWindow()
  {
    InitializeComponent();

    // Add items to our list box.
    lstStyles.Items.Add("TiltStyle");
    lstStyles.Items.Add("GreenStyle");
    lstStyles.Items.Add("MouseOverStyle");
  }

  protected void comboStyles_Changed(object sender, RoutedEventArgs args)
  {
    // Get the selected style name from the list box.
    System.Windows.Style currStyle = (System.Windows.Style)
      FindResource(lstStyles.SelectedValue);

    // Set the style of the button type.
    this.btnMouseOverStyle.Style = currStyle;
  }
}
```

Once we have done so, we can compile the application. As you click each list item, you can watch the button take on a new identity (see Figure 30-16).

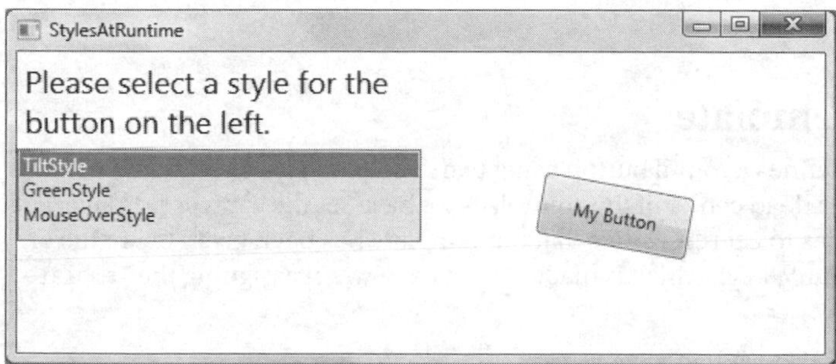

Figure 30-16. *Setting styles programmatically*

■ **Source Code** The StylesAtRuntime project can be found under the Chapter 30 subdirectory.

Altering a Control's UI Using Templates

Styles are a great (and simple) way to change the basic look of a WPF control, by establishing a default set of values for a widget's property set. However, even though styles allow us to change various UI settings, the overall look and feel of the widget remains intact. Regardless of how we style a Button using various properties, it is basically still the same rectangular widget we have come to know over the years. However, what if you wish to completely replace the look and feel of the Button type (such as a hexagonal 3D image) while still having it behave as a Button? What if you wish to use the functionality of the WPF progress bar, but you would rather have it render its UI as a pie chart to show the completion percentage? Rather than building a custom control by hand (as we would have to do with many other GUI toolkits), WPF provides *control templates*.

Templates provide a clear separation between the *UI* of a control (i.e., the look and feel) and the *behavior* of the control (i.e., its set of events and methods). Using templates, you are free to completely change the rendered output of a WPF widget. Programmatically speaking, control templates are represented by the ControlTemplate base class, which can be expressed in XAML using the identically named <ControlTemplate> element. Once you have established your template, you can then attach it to WPF pages, windows, or controls using the Template property.

One interesting aspect of building a control template is that you have full control over how the widget's content is positioned within the template using the <ContentPresenter> element. Using this element, you are able to specify the location and UI of the content for a given control template. More important, if you do not define a <ContentPresenter> element within a template, the control that adopts it will not render *any* content, even if it defines it:

```
<!-- If the applied template does not have a <ContentPresenter>,
     it will not display 'OK' -->
<Button Name ="myButton" Template ="{StaticResource roundButtonTemplate}">
  Click!
</Button>
```

Beyond this point, when you are defining a control template, you may not be too surprised by the fact that it feels similar to the process of building a style. For example, templates are typically stored within a resource dictionary, can support triggers, and so on. Given this, you are already quite well equipped to build templates. Let's see some in action using a new WPF Windows Application project named ControlTemplates.

Building a Custom Template

Here is a simple template that defines a round button using two <Ellipse> types contained within a <Grid>. The content will be in the dead center of the control, as we have set the HorizontalAlignment and VerticalAlignment properties to Center. Notice that our template has been given the name of roundButtonTemplate (via a resource key), which is made reference to when assigning the Template property of the Button:

```
<Window x:Class="ControlTemplates.MainWindow"
  xmlns="http://schemas.microsoft.com/winfx/2006/xaml/presentation"
  xmlns:x="http://schemas.microsoft.com/winfx/2006/xaml"
  Title="Fun with Control Templates" Height="162" Width="281" >
  <Grid>
    <Grid.Resources>
      <!-- A simple template for a round button for items in this grid -->
        <ControlTemplate x:Key ="roundButtonTemplate" TargetType ="{x:Type Button}">
        <Grid>
          <Ellipse Name ="OuterRing" Width ="75" Height ="75" Fill ="DarkGreen"/>
          <Ellipse Name ="InnerRing" Width ="60" Height ="60" Fill ="MintCream"/>
          <ContentPresenter HorizontalAlignment="Center"
```

```
                                    VerticalAlignment="Center"/>
        </Grid>
      </ControlTemplate>
    </Grid.Resources>

    <!-- Applying our template to a Button -->
    <Button Name ="myButton" Foreground ="Black" FontSize ="20" FontWeight ="Bold"
            Template ="{StaticResource roundButtonTemplate}"
            Click ="myButton_Click"> Click!
    </Button>
  </Grid>
</Window>
```

Also notice that our Button type is handling the Click event (assume the Click event handler simply displays an informative message via the MessageBox.Show() method). This is significant, as the Button—despite the fact that it no longer looks anything like a traditional "gray rectangle"—is still a System.Windows.Controls.Button type and has all of the same properties, methods, and events as the canned UI look and feel. Figure 30-17 shows our custom button type in action.

Figure 30-17. *A simple template for the* Button *type*

Adding Triggers to Templates

Currently, our control template allows a Button type to render itself in a circular fashion. However, if you actually click the button, you will notice that the Click event does fire (as the MessageBox.Show() method will display your string data); however, there is no visual sign of the button being pressed. The reason is that the default push-button animation has been gutted and replaced by our custom UI! If you wish to put back (or replace) this notion of push-button animation, you will need to add your own custom triggers.

Here is an update to our current template that handles two triggers. The first trigger will monitor if the mouse is over the button. If so, we will change the background color of the outer ellipse (a simple visual effect). The second trigger will monitor if the mouse is clicked over the surface of the button. If this is the case, we will increase the Height and Width values of the outer ellipse to provide visual feedback to the user:

```
<Grid.Resources>
  <!-- A simple template for a round button-->
  <ControlTemplate x:Key ="roundButtonTemplate" TargetType ="{x:Type Button}">
    <Grid>
      <Ellipse Name ="OuterRing" Width ="75" Height ="75" Fill ="DarkGreen"/>
      <Ellipse Name ="InnerRing" Width ="60" Height ="60" Fill ="MintCream"/>
      <ContentPresenter HorizontalAlignment="Center"
                        VerticalAlignment="Center"/>
    </Grid>
    <!-- Triggers to give the 'push' effect -->
    <ControlTemplate.Triggers>
```

```
      <Trigger Property ="IsMouseOver" Value ="True">
        <Setter TargetName ="OuterRing" Property ="Fill" Value ="MediumSeaGreen"/>
      </Trigger>
      <Trigger Property ="IsPressed" Value ="True">
        <Setter TargetName ="OuterRing" Property ="Height" Value ="90"/>
        <Setter TargetName ="OuterRing" Property ="Width" Value ="90"/>
      </Trigger>
    </ControlTemplate.Triggers>
  </ControlTemplate>
</Grid.Resources>
```

Figure 30-18 shows the effect of the `IsMouseOver` trigger, and Figure 30-19 shows the result of the `IsPressed` trigger.

Figure 30-18. *The* `IsMouseOver` *trigger in action*

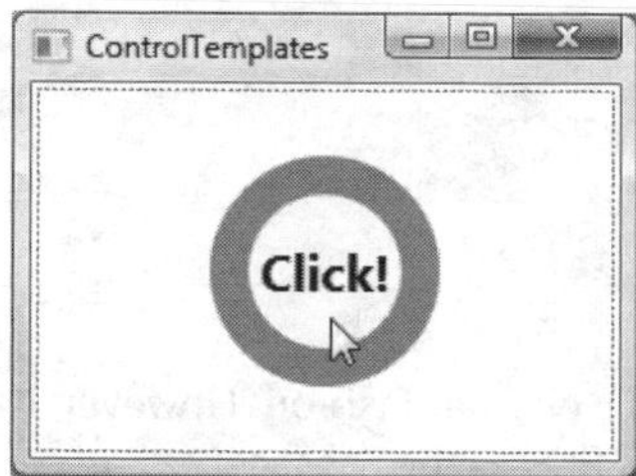

Figure 30-19. *The* `IsPressed` *trigger in action*

Incorporating Templates into Styles

Currently, our template simply defines the look and feel of the `Button` type. The process of establishing the basic properties of the widget (content, font size, font weight, etc.) is the responsibility of the `Button` itself:

```
<!-- Currently the Button must set basic property values, not the template -->
<Button Name ="myButton" Foreground ="Black" FontSize ="20" FontWeight ="Bold"
  Template ="{StaticResource roundButtonTemplate}" Click ="myButton_Click">
```

It would be ideal to establish these values *in the template*. By doing so, we can effectively create a default look and feel. As you may have already realized, this is a job for WPF styles. When you build a style (to account for basic property settings), you can define a template *within the style*! Here is our updated grid resource, with analysis to follow:

```
<Grid.Resources>
  <!-- Our style defines basic settings for the Button here -->
  <Style x:Key ="roundButtonTemplate" TargetType ="{x:Type Button}">
```

```
    <Setter Property ="Foreground" Value ="Black"/>
    <Setter Property ="FontSize" Value ="20"/>
    <Setter Property ="FontWeight" Value ="Bold"/>

    <!-- Here is our template! -->
    <Setter Property ="Template">
      <Setter.Value>
        <!-- A simple template for a round button-->
        <ControlTemplate TargetType ="{x:Type Button}">
          <Grid>
           <Ellipse Name ="OuterRing" Width ="75" Height ="75" Fill ="DarkGreen"/>
           <Ellipse Name ="InnerRing" Width ="60" Height ="60" Fill ="MintCream"/>
           <ContentPresenter HorizontalAlignment="Center"
                             VerticalAlignment="Center"/>
          </Grid>

          <!-- A trigger to give the 'push' effect -->
          <ControlTemplate.Triggers>
            <Trigger Property ="IsMouseOver" Value ="True">
              <Setter TargetName ="OuterRing"
               Property ="Fill" Value ="MediumSeaGreen"/>
            </Trigger>
            <Trigger Property ="IsPressed" Value ="True">
              <Setter TargetName ="OuterRing" Property ="Height" Value ="90"/>
              <Setter TargetName ="OuterRing" Property ="Width" Value ="90"/>
            </Trigger>
          </ControlTemplate.Triggers>
        </ControlTemplate>
      </Setter.Value>
    </Setter>
  </Style>
</Grid.Resources>
```

First of all, notice that the <Style> has now been given the resource key value, rather than the <ControlTemplate>. Next, notice that the style is setting the same basic properties we were setting in the Button type's declaration (Foreground, FontSize, and FontWeight). The <ControlTemplate> element is defined using a normal style <Setter> element by tweaking the Template property. With this update, we can now create our custom button types by setting the Style property as so:

```
<!-- Applying our style/template to a Button -->
<Button Name ="myButton"
  Style ="{StaticResource roundButtonTemplate}"
  Click ="myButton_Click">
  Click!
</Button>
```

While the rendering and behavior of the button is identical, the benefit of nesting templates within styles is that you are able to provide a canned set of values for common properties. Recall, of course, that you are free to change these defaults on a widget-by-widget value:

```
<!-- Get style, but change foreground color -->
<Button Name =" myButton"
  Style ="{StaticResource roundButtonTemplate}"
  Click ="myButton_Click" Foreground ="Red">
  Click!
</Button>
```

■ **Source Code** The ControlTemplates project can be found under the Chapter 30 subdirectory.

That wraps up our look at the styling and template mechanism of WPF. As you have seen, templates are typically composed on numerous graphical types and are ultimately bundled into your application as binary resources.

For that matter, this concludes our examination of WPF itself for this edition of the text. Over the last three chapters, you have learned quite a bit about the underlying WPF programming model, the syntax of XAML, control manipulation, and the generation of graphical content. While there is certainly much more to WPF than examined here, you should be in a solid position for further exploration as you see fit.

Summary

Given that fact that Windows Presentation Foundation (WPF) is such a graphically intensive GUI API, it comes as no surprise that we are provided with a number of ways to render graphical output. This chapter began by examining each of three ways a WPF application can do so (shapes, drawings and visuals), and along the way discussed various rendering primitives such as brushes, pens, and transformations.

Next, you covered the role of WPF animation services, from the perspective of procedural C# code as well as XAML declarations. Here you learned various details regarding timelines, storyboards, and key frames. You were exposed to the WPF resource management APIs and came to see that WPF resources can entail items other than the expected set of string tables, icons, and bitmap types, but can also represent custom objects that can be held in a resource dictionary.

The chapter wrapped up by pulling together all of these topics into a cohesive unit and exploring the role of WPF styles and templates. As shown, WPF makes it very simple to stylize the look and feel of a control using graphical primitives, animation services, and a collection of embedded resources.

PART 7

Building Web Applications with ASP.NET

CHAPTER 31

Building ASP.NET Web Pages

Until now, all of the example applications in this text have focused on console-based and desktop GUI-based front ends. In the next three chapters, you'll explore how the .NET platform facilitates the construction of browser-based presentation layers using a technology named ASP.NET. To begin, you'll quickly review a number of key web-centric concepts (HTTP, HTML, client-side scripting, and server-side scripting) and examine the role of Microsoft's commercial web server (IIS) as well as the ASP.NET development web server, `WebDev.WebServer.exe`.

With this web primer out of the way, the remainder of this chapter concentrates on the structure of ASP.NET web pages (including the single-page and code-behind model) and examines the composition of a `Page`-derived type. This chapter also introduces the role of the `Web.config` file, which will be used in the web-centric chapters to come.

The Role of HTTP

Web applications are very different animals from traditional desktop applications (to say the least). The first obvious difference is that a production-level web application will always involve at least two networked machines (of course, during development it is entirely possible to have a single machine play the role of both the browser-based client and the web server itself). Given the nature of web applications, the networked machines in question must agree upon a particular wire protocol to determine how to send and receive data. The wire protocol that connects the computers in question is the Hypertext Transfer Protocol (HTTP).

The HTTP Request/Response Cycle

When a client machine launches a web browser (such as Opera, Mozilla Firefox, or Microsoft Internet Explorer), an HTTP request is made to access a particular resource (typically a web page) on the remote server machine. HTTP is a text-based protocol that is built upon a standard request/response paradigm. For example, if you navigate to `http://www.intertech.com`, the browser software leverages a web technology termed *Domain Name Service* (DNS) that converts the registered URL into a four-part, 32-bit numerical value, termed an *IP address*. At this point, the browser opens a socket connection (typically via port 80 for a nonsecure connection) and sends the HTTP request for processing to the target site.

The web server receives the incoming HTTP request and may choose to process out any client-supplied input values (such as values within a text box, check box selections, etc.) in order to format a proper HTTP response. Web programmers may leverage any number of technologies (CGI, ASP, ASP.NET, JSP, etc.) to dynamically generate the content to be emitted into the HTTP response. At this point, the client-side browser renders the HTML sent from the web server. Figure 31-1 illustrates the basic HTTP request/response cycle.

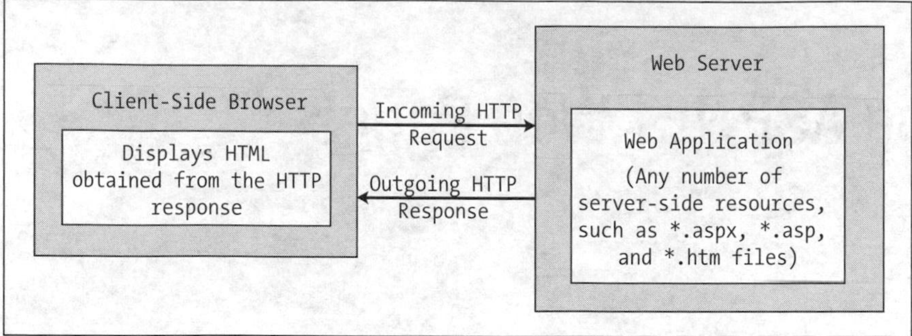

Figure 31-1. *The HTTP request/response cycle*

HTTP Is a Stateless Protocol

Another aspect of web development that is markedly different from traditional desktop programming is the fact that HTTP is essentially a *stateless* wire protocol. As soon as the web server emits a response to the client, everything about the previous interaction is forgotten. This is certainly not the case for a traditional desktop application, where the state of the executable is most often alive and kicking until the user shuts down the application in question.

Given this point, as a web developer, it is up to you take specific steps to "remember" information (such as items in a shopping cart, credit card numbers, home and work addresses, etc.) about the users who are currently logged on to your site. As you will see in Chapter 33, ASP.NET provides numerous ways to handle state, many of which are commonplace to any web platform (session variables, cookies, and application variables) as well as some .NET-particular techniques such as the ASP.NET profile management API.

Understanding Web Applications and Web Servers

A *web application* can be understood as a collection of files (`*.htm`, `*.asp`, `*.aspx`, image files, XML-based file data, etc.) and related components (such as a .NET code library or legacy COM server) stored within a particular set of directories on a given web server. As shown in Chapter 33, ASP.NET web applications have a specific life cycle and provide numerous events (such as initial startup or final shutdown) that you can hook into to perform specialized processing during your website's operation.

A *web server* is a software product in charge of hosting your web applications, and it typically provides a number of related services such as integrated security, File Transfer Protocol (FTP) support, mail exchange services, and so forth. Internet Information Services (IIS) is Microsoft's enterprise-level web server product, and as you would guess, it has intrinsic support for classic ASP as well as ASP.NET web applications.

When you build production-ready ASP.NET web applications, you will often need to interact with IIS. Be aware, however, that IIS is *not* automatically selected as an installation option when you install the Windows operating system (also be aware that not all versions of Windows can support IIS, such as Windows XP Home). Thus, depending on the configuration of your development machine, you may wish to install IIS before proceeding through this chapter. To do so, simply access the Add/Remove Program applet from the Control Panel folder and select Add/Remove Windows Components. Consult the Windows help system if you require further details.

■Note Ideally, your development machine will have IIS installed *before* you install Visual Studio 2008. If you install IIS *after* you install Visual Studio 2008, none of your ASP.NET web applications will execute correctly (you will simply get back a blank page). Luckily, you can reconfigure IIS to host .NET applications by running the `aspnet_regiis.exe` command-line tool and specifying the `/i` option.

Assuming you have IIS properly installed on your workstation, you can interact with IIS from the Administrative Tools folder (located in the Control Panel folder) by double-clicking the Internet Information Services applet. For the purposes of this chapter, you are concerned only with the Default Web Site node (see Figure 31-2).

Figure 31-2. *The IIS applet*

The Role of IIS Virtual Directories

A single IIS installation is able to host numerous web applications, each of which resides in a *virtual directory*. Each virtual directory is mapped to a physical directory on the hard drive. Therefore, if you create a new virtual directory named CarsRUs, the outside world can navigate to this site using a URL such as `http://www.CarsRUs.com` (assuming your site's IP address has been registered with the world at large). Under the hood, this virtual directory maps to a physical root directory on the web server, such as C:\inetpub\wwwroot\AspNetCarsSite, which contains the content of the CarsRUs web application.

As you will see later in this chapter, when you create ASP.NET web applications using Visual Studio 2008, you have the option of having the IDE generate a new virtual directory for the current website automatically. If required, you are certainly able to manually create a virtual directory by hand by right-clicking the Default Web Site node of IIS and selecting New ➤ Virtual Directory (or on Vista, simply Add Virtual Directory) from the context menu.

When you select the option to create a new virtual directory, you will be prompted for the name and physical folder that will contain the web content. To illustrate working with IIS (and to set us up for our first web example), create a new directory on your hard drive that will hold yet-to-be-generated web content. For this discussion I'll assume this directory to be C:\CodeTests\CarsWebSite. Now, right-click the Default Web Site node of IIS to create a new virtual directory named Cars that maps to this new directory. Figure 31-3 shows the end result.

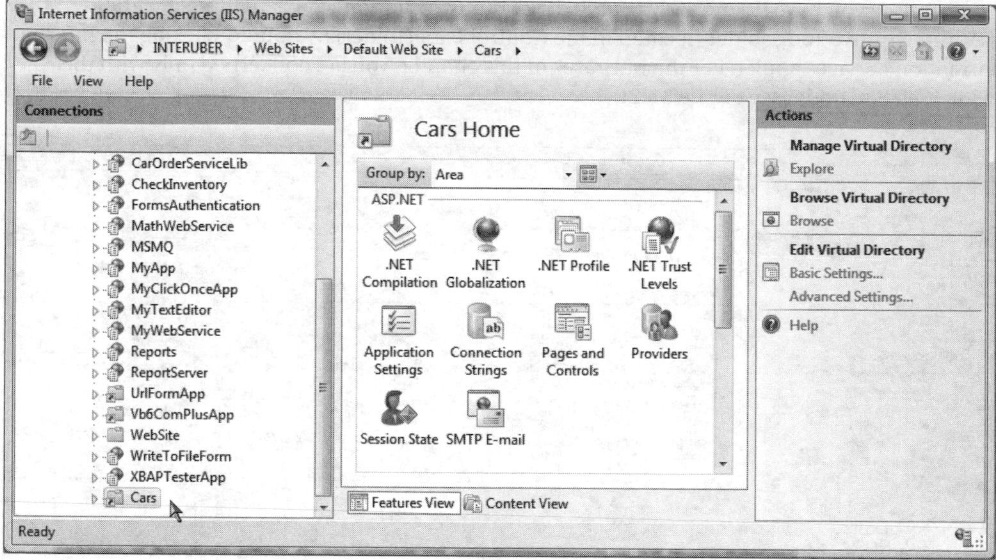

Figure 31-3. *The Cars virtual directory*

We will add some content to this website in just a moment.

The ASP.NET Development Server

Prior to .NET 2.0, ASP.NET developers were required to make use of IIS virtual directories during the development and testing of their web content. In many cases, this tight dependency on IIS made team development more complex than necessary (not to mention that many network administrators frowned upon installing IIS on every developer's machine). Thankfully, we now have the option to use a lightweight web server named `WebDev.WebServer.exe`. This utility allows developers to host an ASP.NET web application outside the bounds of IIS. Using this tool, you can build and test your web pages from any directory on your machine. This is quite helpful for team development scenarios and for building ASP.NET web programs on versions of Windows that do not support IIS installations (such as Windows XP Home).

■ **Note** `WebDev.WebServer.exe` cannot be used to test or host classic (COM-based) ASP web applications. This web server can host only ASP.NET web applications and/or .NET-based XML web services.

When building a website with Visual Studio 2008, you have the option of using `WebDev.WebServer.exe` to host your pages (as you will see a bit later in this chapter). However, you are also able to manually interact with this tool from a Visual Studio 2008 command prompt. If you enter the following command:

```
WebDev.WebServer.exe -?
```

you will be presented with a message box that describes the valid command-line options. In a nutshell, you will need to specify an unused port (via the /port: option), the root directory of the web application (via the /path: option), and an optional virtual path using the /vpath: option (if you do not supply a /vpath: option, the default is simply /). Consider the following usage, which opens an arbitrary port to view content in the C:\CodeTests\CarsWebSite directory created previously:

```
WebDev.WebServer.exe /port:12345 /path:"C:\CodeTests\CarsWebSite"
```

Once you have entered this command, you can launch your web browser of choice to request pages. Thus, if the CarsWebSite folder had a file named Default.aspx, you could enter the following URL:

```
http://localhost:12345/CarsWebSite/Default.aspx
```

Many of the examples in this chapter and the next will make use of WebDev.WebServer.exe via Visual Studio 2008, rather than hosting web content under an IIS virtual directory. While this approach can simplify the development of your web application, do be aware that this web server is *not* intended to host production-level web applications. It is intended purely for development and testing purposes. Once a web application is ready for prime time, your site will need to be copied to an IIS virtual directory.

■ Note The Mono project (see Appendix B) provides a free ASP.NET plug-in for the Apache web server. This makes it possible to build and host ASP.NET web applications on operating systems other than Microsoft Windows. If you are interested, check out http://www.mono-project.com/ASP.NET for details.

The Role of HTML

Now that you have configured a directory to host your web application, and you have chosen a web server to serve as the host, you need to create the content itself. Recall that "web application" is simply the term given to the set of files that constitute the functionality of the site. To be sure, a vast number of these files will contain tokens defined by Hypertext Markup Language (HTML). HTML is a standard markup language used to describe how literal text, images, external links, and various HTML-based UI widgets are to be rendered within the client-side browser.

This particular aspect of web development is one of the major reasons why many programmers dislike building web-based programs. While it is true that modern IDEs (including Visual Studio 2008) and web development platforms (such as ASP.NET) generate much of the HTML automatically, you will do well to have a working knowledge of HTML as you work with ASP.NET.

■ Note Recall from Chapter 2 that Microsoft has released a number of free IDEs under the Express family of products (such as Visual C# Express). If you are interested in web development, you may wish to also download Visual Web Developer Express. This free IDE is geared exclusively at the construction of ASP.NET web applications.

While this section will most certainly not cover all aspects of HTML (by any means), let's check out some basics and build a simple web application using HTML, classic (COM-based) ASP, and IIS. This will serve as a road map for those of you coming to ASP.NET from a traditional desktop application development background.

■ **Note** If you are already comfortable with the overall process of web page development, feel free to skip ahead to the section "Problems with Classic ASP."

HTML Document Structure

An HTML file consists of a set of tags that describe the look and feel of a given web page. As you would expect, the basic structure of an HTML document tends to remain the same. For example, `*.htm` files (or, equivalently, `*.html` files) open and close with `<html>` and `</html>` tags, typically define a `<body>` section, and so forth. Keep in mind that traditional HTML is *not* case sensitive. Therefore, in the eyes of the hosting browser, `<HTML>`, `<html>`, and `<HtmL>` are identical.

To illustrate some HTML basics, open Visual Studio 2008, create an empty HTML file using the File ➤ New ➤ File menu selection, and save this file under your C:\CodeTests\CarsWebSite directory as `default.htm`. As you can see, the initial markup is rather uneventful:

```
<!DOCTYPE html PUBLIC "-//W3C//DTD XHTML 1.0 Transitional//EN"
"http://www.w3.org/TR/xhtml1/DTD/xhtml1-transitional.dtd">
<html xmlns="http://www.w3.org/1999/xhtml" >
<head>
  <title>Untitled Page</title>
</head>
<body>

</body>
</html>
```

First of all, notice that this HTML file opens with a `DOCTYPE` processing instruction. This informs the IDE that the contained HTML tags should be validated against the XHTML standard. As suggested, traditional HTML was very "loose" in its syntax. For example, it was permissible to define an opening element (such as `<br>`, for a line break) that did not have a corresponding closing break (`</br>` in this case), was not case sensitive, and so forth. The XHTML standard is a W3C specification that adds some much-needed rigor to the HTML markup language.

■ **Note** By default, Visual Studio 2008 validates all HTML documents against the XHTML 1.0 Transitional validation scheme. Simply put, HTML *validation schemes* are used to ensure the markup is in sync with specific standards. If you wish to specify an alternative validation scheme, activate the Tools ➤ Options dialog box, and then select the Validation node under HTML. If you would rather not see validation errors, simply uncheck the Show Errors check box.

The `<html>` and `</html>` tags are used to mark the beginning and end of your document. Notice that the opening `<html>` tag is further qualified with an `xmlns` (XML namespace) attribute that qualifies the various tags that may appear within this document (again, by default these tags are based on the XHTML standard). Web browsers use these particular tags to understand where to begin applying the rendering formats specified in the body of the document. The `<body>` scope is where the vast majority of the actual content is defined. To spruce things up just a bit, update the title of your page as follows:

```
<head>
  <title>This Is the Cars Web site</title>
</head>
```

Not surprisingly, the `<title>` tags are used to specify the text string that should be placed in the title bar of the calling web browser.

HTML Form Development

The real meat of most `*.htm` files occurs within the scope of the `<form>` elements. An *HTML form* is simply a named group of related UI elements used to gather user input, which is then transmitted to the web application via an HTTP request. Do not confuse an HTML form with the entire display area shown by a given browser. In reality, an HTML form is more of a *logical grouping* of widgets placed in the `<form>` and `</form>` tag set:

```
<html xmlns="http://www.w3.org/1999/xhtml" >
<head>
  <title>This Is the Cars Web site</title>
</head>
<body>
  <form id="defaultPage">
    <!-- Insert web UI content here ->
  </form>
</body>
</html>
```

This form has been assigned the ID and name of `"defaultPage"`. Typically, the opening `<form>` tag supplies an `action` attribute that specifies the URL to which to submit the form data, as well as the method of transmitting that data itself (POST or GET). You will examine this aspect of the `<form>` tag in just a bit. For the time being, let's look at the sorts of items that can be placed in an HTML form (beyond simple literal text). Visual Studio 2008 provides an HTML tab on the Toolbox that allows you to select each HTML-based UI widget, as shown in Figure 31-4.

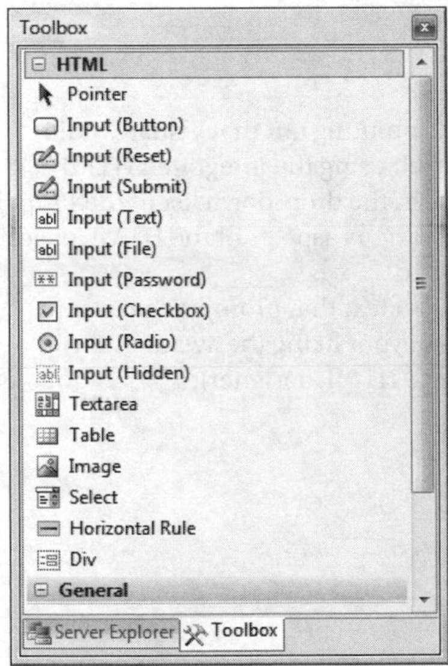

Figure 31-4. *The HTML tab of the Toolbox*

Similar to the process of building a Windows Forms or WPF application, these HTML controls can be dragged onto the HTML designer surface. By default, the bottom pane of the HTML editor will display the HTML visual layout, while the upper pane will show the related markup. Another benefit of this editor is that as you select markup or an HTML UI element, the corresponding representation is highlighted. This makes it very simple to see the scope of your changes (see Figure 31-5).

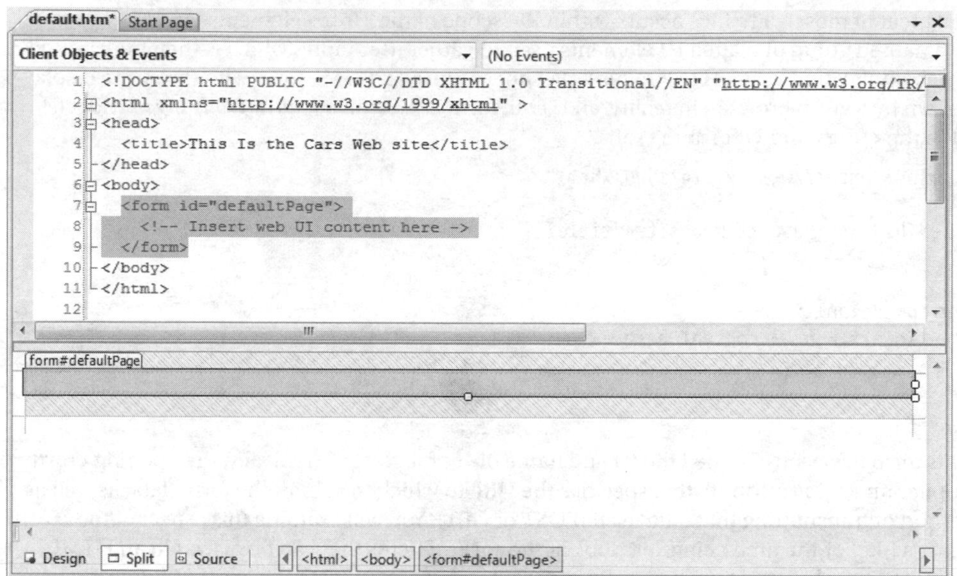

Figure 31-5. *The Visual Studio 2008 HTML editor displays markup and UI layout.*

Building an HTML-Based User Interface

Before you add the HTML widgets to the HTML `<form>`, it is worth pointing out that Visual Studio 2008 allows you to edit the overall look and feel of the `*.htm` file itself using the integrated HTML designer and the Properties window. If you select DOCUMENT from the drop-down list of the Properties window, as shown in Figure 31-6, you are able to configure various aspects of the HTML page, such as the background color, background image, title, and so forth.

Update the `<body>` of the `default.htm` file to display some literal text that prompts the user to enter a username and password, and choose a background color of your liking (be aware that you can enter and format literal textual content by typing directly in the HTML designer):

```
<html xmlns="http://www.w3.org/1999/xhtml" >
<head>
  <title>This is the Cars Web site</title>
</head>
<body bgcolor="NavajoWhite">
  <!-- Prompt for user input-->
  <h1 align="center"> The Cars Login Page</h1>
  <p align="center"> <br/>
    Please enter your <i>user name</i> and <i>password</i>.
  </p>
  <form id="defaultPage">
  </form>
</body>
</html>
```

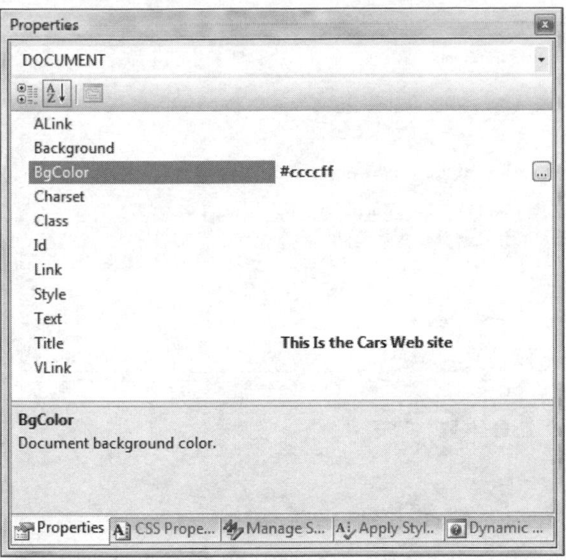

Figure 31-6. *Editing an HTML document via the Visual Studio 2008 Properties window*

Now let's build the HTML form itself. In general, each HTML widget is described using a `name` attribute (used to identify the item programmatically) and a `type` attribute (used to specify which UI element you are interested in placing in the `<form>` declaration). Depending on which UI widget you manipulate, you will find additional attributes specific to that particular item that can be modified using the Properties window.

The UI you will build here will contain two text fields (one of which is a `Password` widget) and two button types (one to submit the form data and the other to reset the form data to the default values):

```
<!-- Build a form to get user info -->
<form id="defaultPage">
  <p align="center">
    User Name:
    <input id="txtUserName" type="text" name="txtUserName"/></p>
  <p align="center">
    Password:
    <input name="txtPassword" type="password" id="txtPassword"/></p>
  <p align="center">
    <input name="btnSubmit" type="submit" value="Submit" id="btnSubmit"/>
    <input name="btnReset" type="reset" value="Reset" id="btnReset"/>
  </p>
</form>
```

Notice that you have assigned relevant names and IDs to each widget (`txtUserName`, `txtPassword`, `btnSubmit`, and `btnReset`). Of greater importance, note that each input item has an extra attribute named `type` that marks these buttons as UI items that automatically clear all fields to their initial values (`type="reset"`), mask the input as a password (`type="password"`), or send the form data to the recipient (`type="submit"`). Figure 31-7 displays the page thus far.

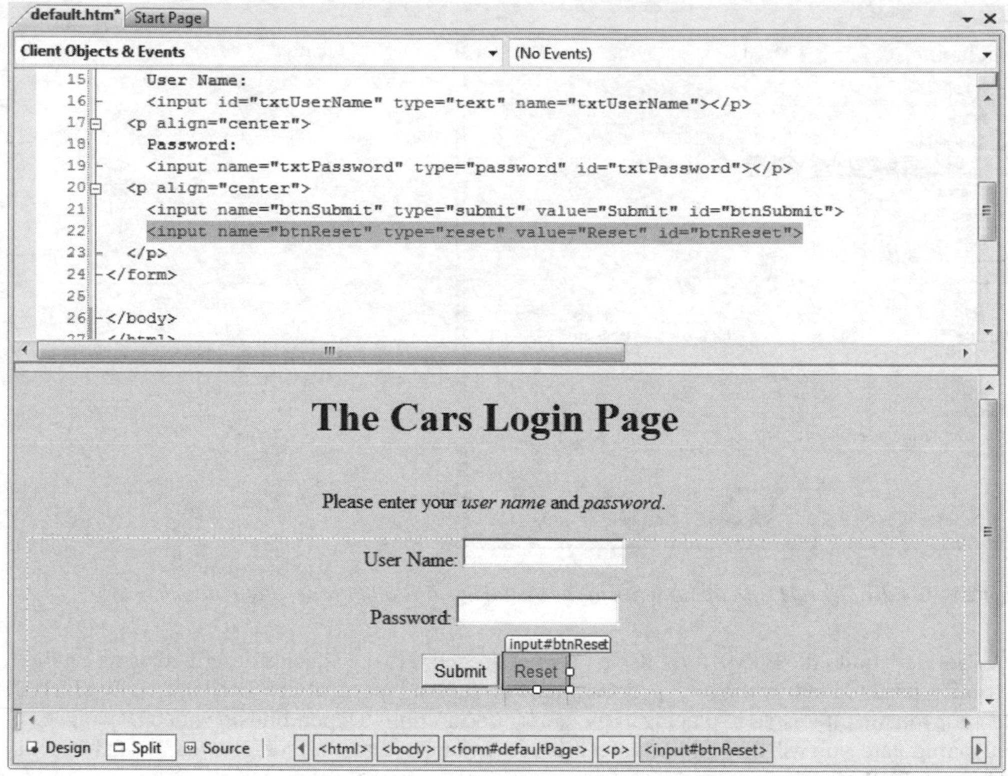

Figure 31-7. *The initial crack at the* `default.htm` *page*

The Role of Client-Side Scripting

In addition to HTML UI elements, a given `*.htm` file may contain blocks of script code that will be emitted into the response stream and processed by the requesting browser. There are two major reasons why client-side scripting is used:

- To validate user input in the browser before posting back to the web server
- To interact with the Document Object Model (DOM) of the target browser

Regarding the first point, understand that the inherent evil of a web application is the need to make frequent round-trips (termed *postbacks*) to the server machine to update the HTML rendered into the browser. While postbacks are unavoidable, you should always be mindful of ways to minimize travel across the wire. One technique that saves round-trips is to use client-side scripting to validate user input before submitting the form data to the web server. If an error is found (such as not supplying data within a required field), you can alert the user to the error without incurring the cost of posting back to the web server (after all, nothing is more annoying to users than posting back on a slow connection, only to receive instructions to address input errors!).

■ **Note** Do be aware that even when performing client-side validation (for improved response time), validation should *also* occur on the web server itself. This will help ensure that the data has not been tampered with as it was sent across the wire. As explained in the following chapter, the ASP.NET validation controls will automatically perform client- and server-side validation.

In addition to validating user input, client-side scripts can also be used to interact with the underlying object model (the DOM) of the web browser itself. Most commercial browsers expose a set of objects that can be leveraged to control how the browser should behave. One major annoyance is the fact that different browsers tend to expose similar, but not identical, object models. Thus, if you emit a block of client-side script code that interacts with the DOM, it may not work identically on all browsers.

■ **Note** ASP.NET provides the `HttpRequest.Browser` property, which allows you to determine at runtime the capacities of the browser that sent the current request.

There are many scripting languages that can be used to author client-side script code. Two of the more popular ones are VBScript and JavaScript. VBScript is a subset of the Visual Basic 6.0 programming language. Be aware that Microsoft Internet Explorer is the only web browser that has built-in support for client-side VBScript support (other browsers may or may not provide optional plug-ins). Thus, if you wish your HTML pages to work correctly in any commercial web browser, do *not* use VBScript for your client-side scripting logic.

The other popular scripting language is JavaScript. Be very aware that JavaScript is in no way, shape, or form a subset of the Java language. While JavaScript and Java have a somewhat similar syntax, JavaScript is not a full-fledged OOP language, and thus it is far less powerful than Java. The good news is that all modern-day web browsers support JavaScript, which makes it a natural candidate for client-side scripting logic.

■ **Note** To further confuse the issue, recall that JScript .NET is a managed language that can be used to build valid .NET assemblies using a scriptlike syntax.

A Client-Side Scripting Example

To illustrate the role of client-side scripting, let's first examine how to intercept events sent from client-side HTML GUI widgets. Assume you have added an additional HTML button (`btnHelp`) to your `default.htm` page that allows the user to view help information. To capture the `Click` event for this button, select `btnHelp` from the upper-left drop-down list of the HTML form designer and select the `onclick` event from the right drop-down list. This will add an `onclick` attribute to the definition of the new `Button` type:

```
<input id="btnHelp" type="button" value="Help" language="javascript"
onclick="return btnHelp_onclick()" />
```

Visual Studio 2008 will also create an empty JavaScript function that will be called when the user clicks the button. Within this stub, simply make use of the `alert()` method to display a client-side message box:

```
<script language="javascript" type="text/javascript">
// <![CDATA[
function btnHelp_onclick() {
  alert("Dude, it is not that hard. Click the Submit button!");
}
// ]]>
</script>
```

Note that the scripting block has been wrapped within a CDATA section. The reason for this is simple. If your page ends up on a browser that does not support JavaScript, the code will be treated as a comment block and ignored. Of course, your page may be less functional, but the upside is that your page will not blow up when rendered by the browser.

Validating the default.htm Form Data

Now, let's update the default.htm page to support some client-side validation logic. The goal is to ensure that when the user clicks the Submit button, you call a JavaScript function that checks each text box for empty values. If this is the case, you pop up an alert that instructs the user to enter the required data. First, handle an onclick event for the Submit button:

```
<input name="btnSubmit" type="submit" value="Submit" id="btnSubmit"
 language="javascript" onclick="return btnSubmit_onclick()">
```

Implement this handler like so:

```
function btnSubmit_onclick(){
  // If they forget either item, pop up a message box.
  if((defaultPage.txtUserName.value == "") ||
    (defaultPage.txtPassword.value == ""))
  {
    alert("You must supply a user name and password!");
    return false;
  }
  return true;
}
```

At this point, save your work. You can open your browser of choice, navigate to the default.htm page hosted by your Cars virtual directory, and test out your client-side script logic:

```
http://localhost/Cars/default.htm
```

If you click the Help or Submit button, you should find the correct message box launched by your browser of choice. Do notice that if you enter some random data into your text boxes, you will not see the validation error displayed when you do click the Submit button.

Submitting the Form Data (GET and POST)

Now that you have a simple HTML page, you need to examine how to transmit the form data back to the web server for processing. When you build an HTML form, you typically supply an action attribute on the opening <form> tag to specify the recipient of the incoming form data. Possible receivers include mail servers, other HTML files, an Active Server Pages (ASP) file, and so forth. For this example, you'll use a classic ASP file named ClassicAspPage.asp. Update your default.htm file by specifying the following attribute in the opening <form> tag:

```
<form name="defaultPage" id="defaultPage"
 action="http://localhost/Cars/ClassicAspPage.asp" method="GET">
...
</form>
```

These extra attributes ensure that when the Submit button for this form is clicked, the form data is sent to the ClassicAspPage.asp at the specified URL. When you specify method="GET" as the mode of transmission, the form data is appended to the query string as a set of name/value pairs separated by ampersands:

```
http://localhost/Cars/ClassicAspPage.asp?txtUserName=
Andrew&txtPassword=Foo$&btnSubmit=Submit
```

The other method of transmitting form data to the web server is to specify method="POST":

```
<form name="defaultPage" id="defaultPage"
  action="http://localhost/Cars/ClassicAspPage.asp" method = "POST">
...
</form>
```

In this case, the form data is not appended to the query string, but instead is written to a separate line within the HTTP header. Using POST, the form data is not directly visible to the outside world. More important, POST data does not have a character-length limitation (many browsers have a limit for GET queries). For the time being, make use of HTTP GET to send the form data to the receiving *.asp page.

Building a Classic ASP Page

A classic ASP page is a hodgepodge of HTML and server-side script code. If you have never worked with classic ASP, understand that the goal of ASP is to dynamically build HTML on the fly using a *server-side* script using a small set of COM objects and a bit of elbow grease. For example, you may have a server-side VBScript (or JavaScript) block that reads a table from a data source using classic ADO and returns the rows as a generic HTML table.

For this example, the ASP page uses the intrinsic ASP Request COM object to read the values of the incoming form data (appended to the query string) and echo them back to the caller (not terribly exciting, but it illustrates the basic operation of the request/response cycle). The server-side script logic will make use of VBScript (as denoted by the language directive).

To do so, create a new HTML file using Visual Studio 2008 and save this file under the name ClassicAspPage.asp into the folder to which your virtual directory has been mapped (e.g., C:\CodeTests\CarsWebSite). Implement this page as follows:

```
<%@ language="VBScript" %>
<html>
<head>
  <title>The Cars Page</title>
</head>
  <body>
    <h1 align="center">Here is what you sent me:</h1>
    <P align="center"> <b>User Name: </b>
    <%= Request.QueryString("txtUserName") %> <br>
    <b>Password: </b>
    <%= Request.QueryString("txtPassword") %> <br>
    </P>
  </body>
</html>
```

Here, you use the classic ASP Request COM object to call the QueryString() method to examine the values contained in each HTML widget submitted via method="GET". The <%= ...%> notation is a shorthand way of saying, "Insert the following directly into the outbound HTTP response." To gain a finer level of flexibility, you could interact with the ASP Response COM object within a full server-side script block (denoted by the <%, %> notation). You have no need to do so here; however, the following is a simple example:

```
<%
  Dim pwd
  pwd = Request.QueryString("txtPassword")
  Response.Write(pwd)
%>
```

Obviously, the Request and Response objects of classic ASP provide a number of additional members beyond those shown here. Furthermore, classic ASP also defines a small number of additional COM objects (Session, Server, Application, etc.) that you can use while constructing your web application.

■ **Note** Under ASP.NET, these COM objects are officially dead. However, you will see that the System.Web.UI.Page base class defines identically named properties that expose objects with similar functionality.

At this point be sure to save each of your web files. To test the ASP logic, simply load the default.htm page from a browser and submit the form data. Once the script is processed on the web server, you are returned a brand-new (dynamically generated) HTML display, as you see in Figure 31-8.

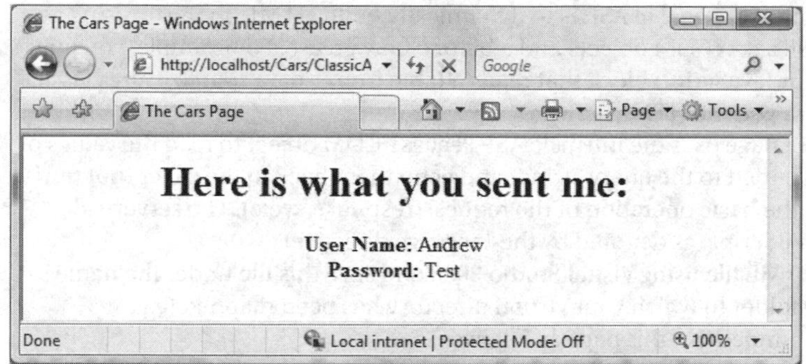

Figure 31-8. *The dynamically generated HTML*

Currently, your default.htm file specifies HTTP GET as the method of sending the form data to the target *.asp file. Using this approach, the values contained in the various GUI widgets are appended to the end of the query string. It is important to note that the ASP Request.QueryString() method is *only* able to extract data submitted via the GET method.

If you would rather submit form data to the web resource using HTTP POST, you can use the Request.Form collection to read the values on the server, for example:

```
<body>
  <h1 align="center">Here is what you sent me:</h1>
  <P align="center">
    <b>User Name: </b>
    <%= Request.Form("txtUserName") %> <br>
```

```
    <b>Password: </b>
    <%= Request.Form("txtPassword") %> <br>
  </P>
</body>
```

That wraps up our web-centric primer. Hopefully, if you're new to web development you now have a better understanding of the basic building blocks of a web-based application. However, before we check out how the ASP.NET web platform improves upon the current state of affairs, let's take a brief moment to critique classic ASP and understand its core limitations.

Source Code The ClassicAspCars project is included under the Chapter 31 subdirectory.

Problems with Classic ASP

While many successful websites have been created using classic ASP, this architecture is not without its downsides. Perhaps the biggest downside of classic ASP is the same thing that makes it a powerful platform: server-side scripting languages. Scripting languages such as VBScript and JavaScript are interpreted, typeless entities that do not lend themselves to robust OO programming techniques.

Another problem with classic ASP is the fact that an `*.asp` page does not yield very modularized code. Given that ASP is a blend of HTML and script in a *single* page, most ASP web applications are a confused mix of two different programming techniques. While it is true that classic ASP allows you to partition reusable code into distinct include files, the underlying object model does not support true separation of concerns. In an ideal world, a web framework would allow the presentation logic (i.e., HTML tags) to exist independently from the business logic (i.e., functional code).

A final issue to consider here is the fact that classic ASP demands a good deal of boilerplate, redundant script code that tends to repeat between projects. Almost all web applications need to validate user input, repopulate the state of HTML widgets before emitting the HTTP response, generate an HTML table of data, and so forth.

Major Benefits of ASP.NET 1.x

The first release of ASP.NET (version 1.x) did a fantastic job of addressing each of the limitations found with classic ASP. In a nutshell, the .NET platform brought about the following techniques to the Microsoft web development paradigm:

- ASP.NET provides a model termed *code-behind*, which allows you to separate presentation logic from business logic.
- ASP.NET pages are coded using .NET programming languages, rather than interpreted scripting languages. The code files are compiled into valid .NET assemblies (which translates into much faster execution).
- Web controls allow programmers to build the GUI of a web application in a manner similar to building a Windows Forms/WPF application.
- ASP.NET web controls automatically maintain their state during postbacks using a hidden form field named `__VIEWSTATE`.
- ASP.NET web applications are completely object-oriented and make use of the Common Type System (CTS).
- ASP.NET web applications can be easily configured using standard IIS settings *or* using a web application configuration file (`Web.config`).

Major Enhancements of ASP.NET

While ASP.NET 1.x was a major step in the right direction, ASP.NET 2.0 provided additional bells and whistles. Consider this partial list:

- Introduction of the `WebDev.WebServer.exe` testing web server
- A large number of additional web controls (navigation controls, security controls, new data controls, new UI controls, etc.)
- The introduction of *master pages*, which allow you to attach a common UI frame to a set of related pages
- Support for *themes*, which offer a declarative manner to change the look and feel of the entire web application
- Support for *Web Parts*, which can be used to allow end users to customize the look and feel of a web page
- Introduction of a web-based configuration and management utility that maintains your `Web.config` files

Major .NET 3.5 Web Enhancements

As you would expect, .NET 3.5 further increases the scope of the ASP.NET programming model. Perhaps most important, we now have

- New controls to support Silverlight development (recall that this is a WPF-based API for designing rich media content for a website)
- Integrated support for Ajax-style development, which essentially allows for "micro-postbacks" to refresh part of a web page as quickly as possible

Given that this book is not focused exclusively on web development, be sure to consult the .NET Framework 3.5 documentation for details of topics not covered here. The truth of the matter is that if I were to truly do justice to every aspect of ASP.NET, this book would easily double in size. Rest assured that by the time you complete this section of the text, you will have a solid ASP.NET foundation to build upon as you see fit.

■ Note If you require a comprehensive examination of ASP.NET, I suggest picking up a copy of *Pro ASP.NET 3.5 in C# 2008, Second Edition* by Matthew MacDonald (Apress, 2007).

The ASP.NET Namespaces

As of .NET 3.5, there are well over 30 web-centric namespaces in the base class libraries. From a high level, these namespaces can be grouped into several major categories:

- Core functionality (e.g., types that allow you to interact with the HTTP request and response, Web Form infrastructure, theme and profiling support, Web Parts, security, etc.)
- Web Form and HTML controls
- Mobile web development
- Silverlight development

- Ajax development
- XML web services

Table 31-1 describes several of the core ASP.NET namespaces.

Table 31-1. *The Core ASP.NET Web-Centric Namespaces*

Namespaces	Meaning in Life
`System.Web`	Defines types that enable browser/web server communication (such as request and response capabilities, cookie manipulation, and file transfer)
`System.Web.Caching`	Defines types that facilitate caching support for a web application
`System.Web.Hosting`	Defines types that allow you to build custom hosts for the ASP.NET runtime
`System.Web.Management`	Defines types for managing and monitoring the health of an ASP.NET web application
`System.Web.Profile`	Defines types that are used to implement ASP.NET user profiles
`System.Web.Security`	Defines types that allow you to programmatically secure your site
`System.Web.SessionState`	Defines types that allow you to maintain stateful information on a per-user basis (e.g., session state variables)
`System.Web.UI`, `System.Web.UI.WebControls`, `System.Web.UI.HtmlControls`	Define a number of types that allow you to build a GUI front end for your web application

The ASP.NET Web Page Code Model

ASP.NET web pages can be constructed using one of two approaches. You are free to create a single `*.aspx` file that contains a blend of server-side code and HTML (much like classic ASP). Using the single-file page model, server-side code is placed within a `<script>` scope, but the code itself is *not* script code proper (e.g., VBScript/JScript). Rather, the code statements within a `<script>` block are written in your .NET language of choice (C#, Visual Basic, etc.).

If you are building a page that contains very little code (but a good deal of HTML), a single-file page model may be easier to work with, as you can see the code and the markup in one unified `*.aspx` file. In addition, placing your procedural code and HTML markup into a single `*.aspx` file provides a few other advantages:

- Pages written using the single-file model are slightly easier to deploy or to send to another developer.
- Because there is no dependency between files, a single-file page is easier to rename.
- Managing files in a source code control system is slightly easier, as all the action is taking place in a single file.

The default approach taken by Visual Studio 2008 (when creating a new website solution) is to make use of a technique known as code-behind, which allows you to separate your programming code from your HTML presentation logic using two distinct files. This model works quite well when your pages contain a significant amount of code or when multiple developers are working on the same website. The code-behind model offers several benefits as well:

- Because code-behind pages offer a clean separation of HTML markup and code, it is possible to have designers working on the markup while programmers author the C# code.
- Code is not exposed to page designers or others who are working only with the page markup (as you might guess, HTML folks are not always interested in viewing reams of C# code).
- Code files can be used across multiple `*.aspx` files.

Regardless of which approach you take, do know that there is *no* difference in terms of performance. In fact, many ASP.NET web applications will benefit by building sites that make use of both approaches.

Building a Data-Centric Single-File Test Page

First up, let's examine the single-file page model. Our goal is to build an `*.aspx` file that displays the Inventory table of the AutoLot database (created in Chapter 22). While you could build this page using nothing but Notepad, Visual Studio 2008 can simplify matters via IntelliSense, code completion, and a visual page designer.

To begin, open Visual Studio 2008 and create a new Web Form using the File ➤ New ➤ File menu option (see Figure 31-9). Once you have done so, save this file (with the name `Default.aspx`) under a new directory on your hard drive named C:\CodeTests\SinglePageModel.

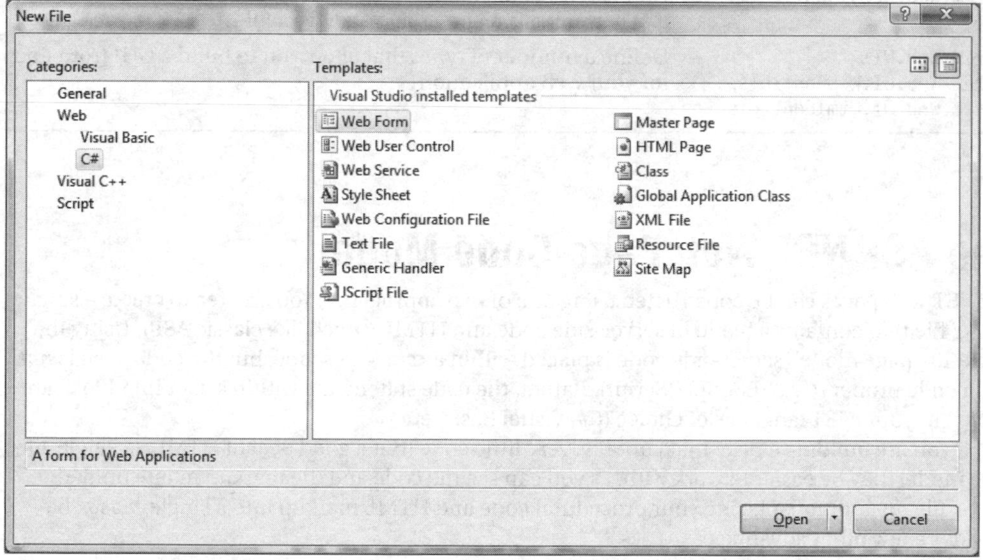

Figure 31-9. *Creating a new* `*.aspx` *file*

Manually Referencing AutoLotDAL.dll

Next, use Windows Explorer to create a subdirectory under the SinglePageModel folder named "bin". The specially named bin subdirectory is a registered name with the ASP.NET runtime engine. Into the \bin folder of a website's root, you are able to deploy any private assemblies used by the web application. For this example, place a copy of `AutoLotDAL.dll` (see Chapter 22) into the C:\CodeTests\SinglePageModel\bin folder.

Note As shown later in this chapter, when you use Visual Studio 2008 to create a full-blown ASP.NET web application, the IDE will maintain the \bin folder on your behalf.

Designing the UI

Now, using the Visual Studio 2008 Toolbox, select the Standard tab and drag and drop a `Button`, `Label`, and `GridView` control onto the page designer (the `GridView` widget can be found under the Data tab of the Toolbox). Feel free to make use of the Properties window (or the HTML IntelliSense) to set various UI properties and give each web widget a proper name via the ID property. Figure 31-10 shows one possible design. (I kept the example's look and feel intentionally bland to minimize the amount of generated control markup, but feel free to spruce things up to your liking.)

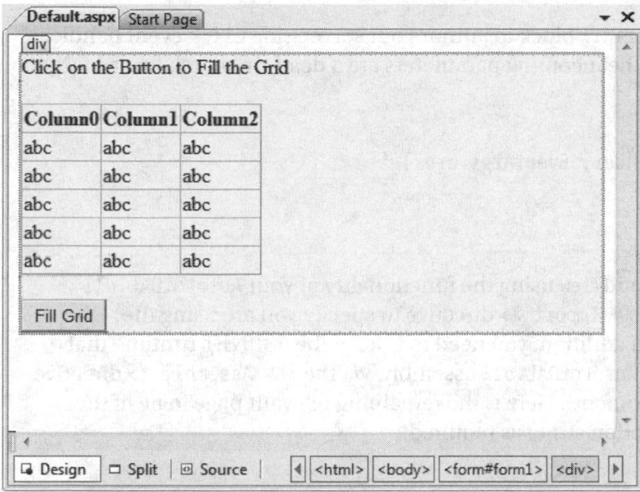

Figure 31-10. *The* `Default.aspx` *UI*

Now, locate the `<form>` section of your page. Notice how each web control has been defined using an `<asp:>` tag. Before the closing tag, you will find a series of name/value pairs that correspond to the settings you made in the Properties window:

```
<form id="form1" runat="server">
<div>
  <asp:Label ID="lblInfo" runat="server"
    Text="Click on the Button to Fill the Grid">
  </asp:Label>
  <br />
  <br />
  <asp:GridView ID="carsGridView" runat="server">
  </asp:GridView>
  <br />
  <asp:Button ID="btnFillData" runat="server" Text="Fill Grid" />
</div>
</form>
```

You will dig into the full details of ASP.NET web controls later in Chapter 32. Until then, understand that web controls are objects processed on the web server that emit back their HTML representation into the outgoing HTTP response automatically (that's right—you don't author the HTML!). Beyond this major benefit, ASP.NET web controls mimic a desktoplike programming model, given that the names of the properties, methods, and events typically echo a Windows Forms/WPF equivalent.

Adding the Data Access Logic

Handle the Click event for the Button type using either the Visual Studio Properties window (via the lightning bolt icon) or using the drop-down boxes mounted at the top of the designer window. Once you do, you will find your Button's definition has been updated with an OnClick attribute that is assigned to the name of your Click event handler:

```
<asp:Button ID="btnFillData" runat="server"
    Text="Fill Grid" OnClick="btnFillData_Click"/>
```

As well, you receive an empty <script> block to author your server-side Click event handler. Add the following code, noticing that the incoming parameters are a dead-on match for the target of the System.EventHandler delegate:

```
<script runat="server">
  void btnFillData_Click(object sender, EventArgs args)
  {
  }
</script>
```

The next step is to populate the GridView using the functionality of your AutoLotDAL.dll assembly. To do so, you must use the <%@ Import %> directive to specify you are using the AutoLotConnectedLayer namespace. In addition, you need to inform the ASP.NET runtime that this single-file page is referencing the AutoLotDAL.dll assembly, via the <%@ Assembly %> directive (more details on directives in just a moment). Here is the remaining relevant page logic of the Default.aspx file (modify your connection string as required):

```
<%@ Page Language="C#" %>
<%@ Import Namespace = "AutoLotConnectedLayer" %>
<%@ Assembly Name ="AutoLotDAL" %>

<!DOCTYPE html PUBLIC "-//W3C//DTD XHTML 1.0 Transitional//EN"
  "http://www.w3.org/TR/xhtml1/DTD/xhtml1-transitional.dtd">

<script runat="server">
  void btnFillData_Click(object sender, EventArgs args)
  {
    InventoryDAL dal = new InventoryDAL();
    dal.OpenConnection(@"Data Source=(local)\SQLEXPRESS;" +
      "Initial Catalog=AutoLot;Integrated Security=True");
    carsGridView.DataSource = dal.GetAllInventory();
    carsGridView.DataBind();
    dal.CloseConnection();
  }
</script>
<html xmlns="http://www.w3.org/1999/xhtml" >
...
</html>
```

Before we dive into the details behind the format of this *.aspx file, let's try a test run. First, save your *.aspx file. If you wish to make use of WebDev.WebServer.exe manually, open a .NET command prompt and run the WebDev.WebServer.exe utility, making sure you specify the path where you saved your Default.aspx file, for example (here I specified an arbitrary port of 12345):

```
webdev.webserver.exe /port:12345 /path:"C:\CodeTests\SinglePageModel"
```

Now, using your browser of choice, enter the following URL:

```
http://localhost:12345/
```

When the page is served, you will initially see your Label and Button types. However, when you click the button, a postback occurs to the web server, at which point the web controls render back their corresponding HTML tags.

As a shortcut, you can indirectly launch WebDev.WebServer.exe from Visual Studio 2008. Simply right-click the page you wish to browse and select the View In Browser menu option. In either case, Figure 31-11 shows the output once you click the Fill Grid button.

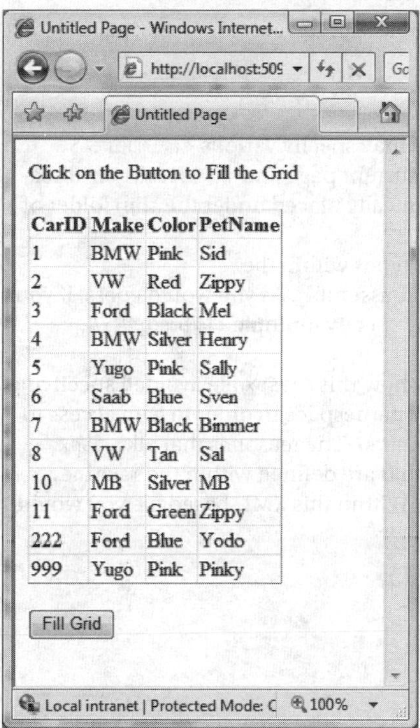

Figure 31-11. *Web-based data access*

That was simple, yes? Of course, as they say, the devil is in the details, so let's dig a bit deeper into the composition of this *.aspx file, beginning by examining the role of the *page directive*.

Understanding the Role of ASP.NET Directives

The first thing to be aware of is that a given *.aspx file will typically open with a set of directives. ASP.NET directives are always denoted with <%@ ... %> markers and may be qualified with various attributes to inform the ASP.NET runtime how to process the attribute in question.

Every *.aspx file must have at minimum a <%@Page%> directive that is used to define the managed language used within the page (via the language attribute). Also, the <%@Page%> directive may define the name of the related code-behind file (if any), enable tracing support, and so forth. Table 31-2 documents some of the more interesting <%@Page%>-centric attributes.

Table 31-2. *Select Attributes of the <%@Page%> Directive*

Attribute	Meaning in Life
CodePage	Specifies the name of the related code-behind file
CompilerOptions	Allows you to define any command-line flags (represented as a single string) passed into the compiler when this page is processed
EnableTheming	Establishes whether the controls on the *.aspx page support ASP.NET themes
EnableViewState	Indicates whether view state is maintained across page requests (more details on this property in Chapter 33)
Inherits	Defines a class in the code-behind page the *.aspx file derives from, which can be any class derived from System.Web.UI.Page
MasterPageFile	Sets the master page used in conjunction with the current *.aspx page
Trace	Indicates whether tracing is enabled

In addition to the <%@Page%> directive, a given *.aspx file may specify various <%@Import%> directives to explicitly state the namespaces required by the current page and <%@Assembly%> directives to specify the external code libraries used by the site (typically placed under the \bin folder of the website).

In this example, we specified we were making use of the types within the AutoLotConnectedLayer namespace within the AutoLotDAL.dll assembly. As you would guess, if you need to make use of additional .NET namespaces, you simply specify multiple <%@Import%>/<%@Assembly%> directives.

Given your current knowledge of .NET, you may wonder how this *.aspx file avoided specifying additional <%@Import%> directives to gain access to the System namespace in order to gain access to the System.Object and System.EventHandler types (among others). The reason is that all *.aspx pages automatically have access to a set of key namespaces that are defined within the machine.config file under your installation path of the .NET platform. Within this XML-based file you would find a number of autoimported namespaces:

```
<pages>
  <namespaces>
    <add namespace="System"/>
    <add namespace="System.Collections"/>
    <add namespace="System.Collections.Specialized"/>
    <add namespace="System.Configuration"/>
    <add namespace="System.Text"/>
    <add namespace="System.Text.RegularExpressions"/>
    <add namespace="System.Web"/>
    <add namespace="System.Web.Caching"/>
    <add namespace="System.Web.SessionState"/>
    <add namespace="System.Web.Security"/>
    <add namespace="System.Web.Profile"/>
    <add namespace="System.Web.UI"/>
    <add namespace="System.Web.UI.WebControls"/>
    <add namespace="System.Web.UI.WebControls.WebParts"/>
    <add namespace="System.Web.UI.HtmlControls"/>
...
```

```
  </namespaces>
</pages>
```

To be sure, ASP.NET does define a number of other directives that may appear in an *.aspx file above and beyond <%@Page%>, <%@Import%>, and <%@Assembly%>; however, I'll reserve commenting on those for the time being.

Analyzing the Script Block

Under the single-file page model, an *.aspx file may contain server-side scripting logic that executes on the web server. Given this, it is *critical* that all of your server-side code blocks are defined to execute at the server, using the runat="server" attribute. If the runat="server" attribute is not supplied, the runtime assumes you have authored a block of *client-side* script to be emitted into the outgoing HTTP response:

```
<script runat="server">
  void btnFillData_Click(object sender, EventArgs args)
  {
    InventoryDAL dal = new InventoryDAL();
    dal.OpenConnection(@"Data Source=(local)\SQLEXPRESS;" +
        "Initial Catalog=AutoLot;Integrated Security=True");
    carsGridView.DataSource = dal.GetAllInventory();
    carsGridView.DataBind();
    dal.CloseConnection();
  }
</script>
```

The signature of this helper method should look strangely familiar. Recall from our examination of Windows Forms (or WPF for that matter) that a given control event handler must match the pattern defined by a related .NET delegate. And, just like Windows Forms, when you wish to handle a server-side button click, the delegate in question is System.EventHandler which, as you recall, can only call methods that take System.Object as the first parameter and System.EventArgs as the second.

Looking at the ASP.NET Control Declarations

The final point of interest for this first example is the declaration of the Button, Label, and GridView Web Form controls. Like classic ASP and raw HTML, ASP.NET web widgets are scoped within <form> elements. This time, however, the opening <form> element is marked with the runat="server" attribute. This again is critical, as this tag informs the ASP.NET runtime that before the HTML is emitted into the response stream, the contained ASP.NET widgets have a chance to render their HTML appearance:

```
<form id="form1" runat="server">
<div>
  <asp:Label ID="lblInfo" runat="server"
    Text="Click on the Button to Fill the Grid">
  </asp:Label>
  <br />
  <br />
  <asp:GridView ID="carsGridView" runat="server">
  </asp:GridView>
  <br />
  <asp:Button ID="btnFillData" runat="server" Text="Fill Grid" />
</div>
</form>
```

Note that the ASP.NET web controls are declared with `<asp>` and `</asp>` tags, and they are also marked with the `runat="server"` attribute. Within the opening tag, you will specify the name of the Web Form control and any number of name/value pairs that will be used at runtime to render the correct HTML.

Source Code The SinglePageModel example is included under the Chapter 31 subdirectory.

Working with the Code-behind Page Model

To illustrate the code-behind page model, let's re-create the previous example using the Visual Studio 2008 Web Site template. (Do know that Visual Studio 2008 is not required to build pages using code-behind; however, this is the out-of-the-box behavior for new websites.) Activate the File ➤ New ➤ Web Site menu option, and select the ASP.NET Web Site template, as shown in Figure 31-12.

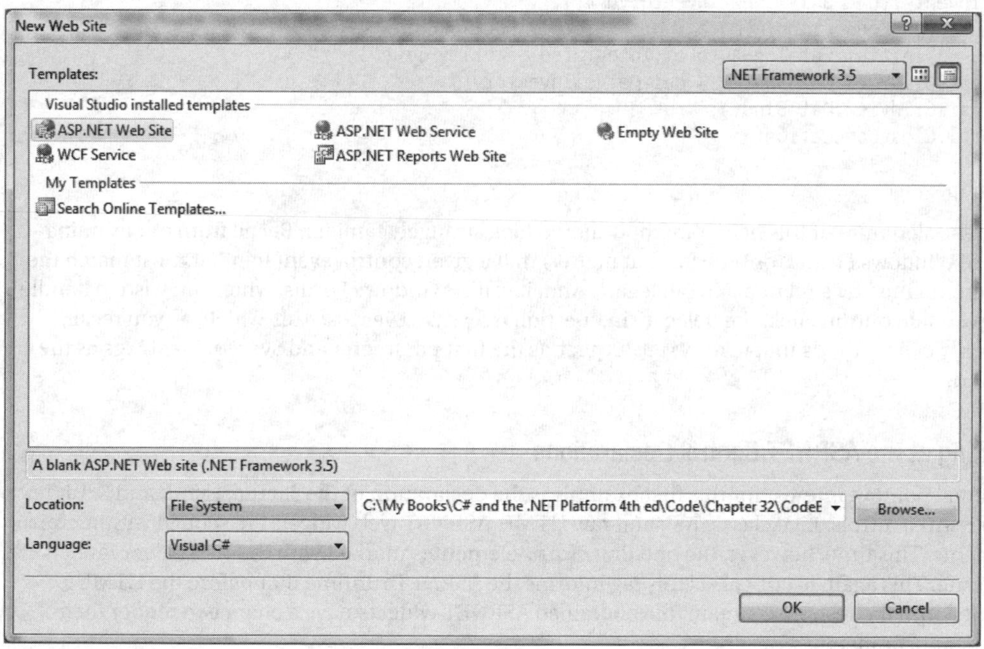

Figure 31-12. *The Visual Studio 2008 ASP.NET Web Site template*

Notice in Figure 31-12 that you are able to select the location of your new site. If you select File System, your content files will be placed within a local directory and pages will be served via `WebDev.WebServer.exe`. If you select FTP or HTTP, your site will be hosted within a new virtual directory maintained by IIS. For this example, it makes no difference which option you select, but for simplicity I suggest selecting the File System option and specifying a new folder named C:\CodeBehindPageModel.

Once again, make use of the designer to build a UI consisting of a `Label`, `Button`, and `GridView`, and make use of the Properties window to build a UI of your liking.

Note When you wish to open an existing website into Visual Studio 2008, select the File ➤ Open ➤ Web Site menu option and select the folder (or IIS virtual directory) containing the web content.

Note that the <%@Page%> directive has been updated with a few new attributes:

```
<%@ Page Language="C#" AutoEventWireup="true"
         CodeFile="Default.aspx.cs" Inherits="_Default" %>
```

The `CodeFile` attribute is used to specify the related external file that contains this page's coding logic. By default, these code-behind files are named by adding the suffix `.cs` to the name of the `*.aspx` file (`Default.aspx.cs` in this example). If you examine Solution Explorer, you will see this code-behind file is visible via a subnode on the Web Form icon (see Figure 31-13).

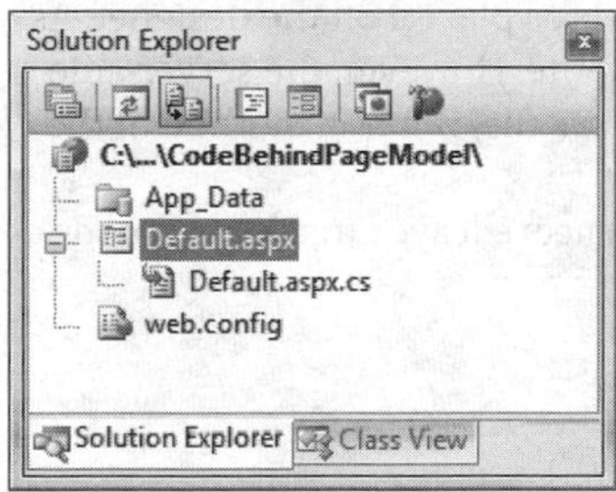

Figure 31-13. *The associated code-behind file for a given* `*.aspx` *file*

If you were to open your code-behind file, you would find a partial class deriving from `System.Web.UI.Page` with support for handling the `Load` event. Notice that the name of this class (`_Default`) is identical to the `Inherits` attribute within the <%@Page%> directive:

```
public partial class _Default : System.Web.UI.Page
{
  protected void Page_Load(object sender, EventArgs e)
  {

  }
}
```

Referencing the AutoLotDAL.dll Assembly

As previously mentioned, when creating web application projects using Visual Studio 2008, you do not need to manually build a \bin subdirectory and copy private assemblies by hand. For this example, activate the Add Reference dialog box using the Website menu option and reference `AutoLotDAL.dll`. When you do so, you will see the new \bin folder within Solution Explorer, as shown in Figure 31-14.

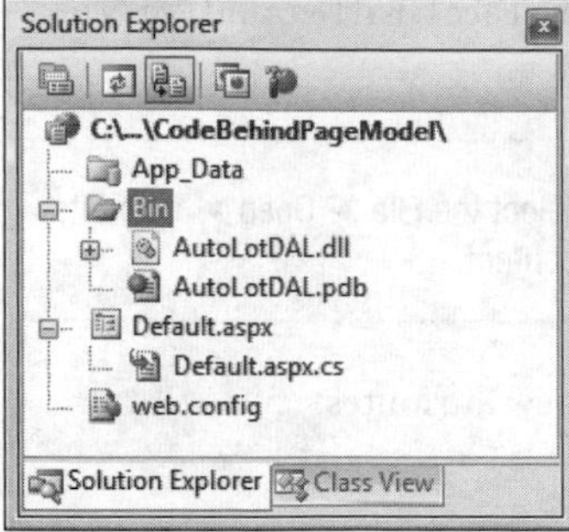

Figure 31-14. *Visual Studio typically maintains "special" ASP.NET folders*

Updating the Code File

Handle the `Click` event for the `Button` type by double-clicking the `Button` placed on the designer. As before, the `Button` definition has been updated with an `OnClick` attribute. However, the server-side event handler is no longer placed within a `<script>` scope of the `*.aspx` file, but as a method of the `_Default` class type.

To complete this example, add a `using` statement for `AutoLotConnectedLayer` inside your code-behind file and implement the handler using the previous logic:

```
using AutoLotConnectedLayer;

public partial class _Default : System.Web.UI.Page
{
  protected void Page_Load(object sender, EventArgs e)
  {

  }
  protected void btnFillData_Click(object sender, EventArgs e)
  {
    InventoryDAL dal = new InventoryDAL();
    dal.OpenConnection(@"Data Source=(local)\SQLEXPRESS;" +
      "Initial Catalog=AutoLot;Integrated Security=True");
    carsGridView.DataSource = dal.GetAllInventory();
    carsGridView.DataBind();
    dal.CloseConnection();
  }
}
```

If you selected the File System option, `WebDev.WebServer.exe` starts up automatically when you run your web application (if you selected IIS, this obviously does not occur). In either case, the default browser should now display the page's content.

Debugging and Tracing ASP.NET Pages

By and large, when you are building ASP.NET web projects, you can use the same debugging techniques as you would with any other sort of Visual Studio 2008 project type. Thus, you can set breakpoints in your code-behind file (as well as embedded "script" blocks in an `*.aspx` file), start a debug session (via the F5 key, by default), and step through your code.

However, to debug your ASP.NET web applications, your site must contain a properly configured `Web.config` file. The conclusion of this chapter will introduce you to `Web.config` files, but in a nutshell these XML files have the same general purpose as an executable assembly's `App.config` file. By default, all Visual Studio 2008 web projects will automatically have a `Web.config` file. However, debugging support is initially disabled (as this will degrade performance). When you start a debugging session, the IDE will prompt you for permissions to enable debugging. Once you have opted to do so, the `<compilation>` element of the `Web.config` file is updated like so:

```
<compilation debug="true"/>
```

On a related note, you are also able to enable *tracing support* for an `*.aspx` file by setting the `Trace` attribute to `true` within the `<%@Page%>` directive (it is also possible to enable tracing for your entire site by modifying the `Web.config` file):

```
<%@ Page Language="C#" AutoEventWireup="true"
      CodeFile="Default.aspx.cs" Inherits="_Default" Trace="true" %>
```

Once you do, the emitted HTML contains numerous details regarding the previous HTTP request/response (server variables, session and application variables, request/response, etc.). To insert your own trace messages into the mix, you can use the `Trace` property of the `System.Web.UI.Page` type. Anytime you wish to log a custom message (from a script block or C# source code file), simply call the `Write()` method:

```
protected void btnFillData_Click(object sender, EventArgs e)
{
  Trace.Write("My Category", "Filling the grid!");
...
}
```

If you run your project once again and post back to the web server, you will find your custom category and custom message are present and accounted for. In Figure 31-15, take note of the highlighted message, which displays the trace information.

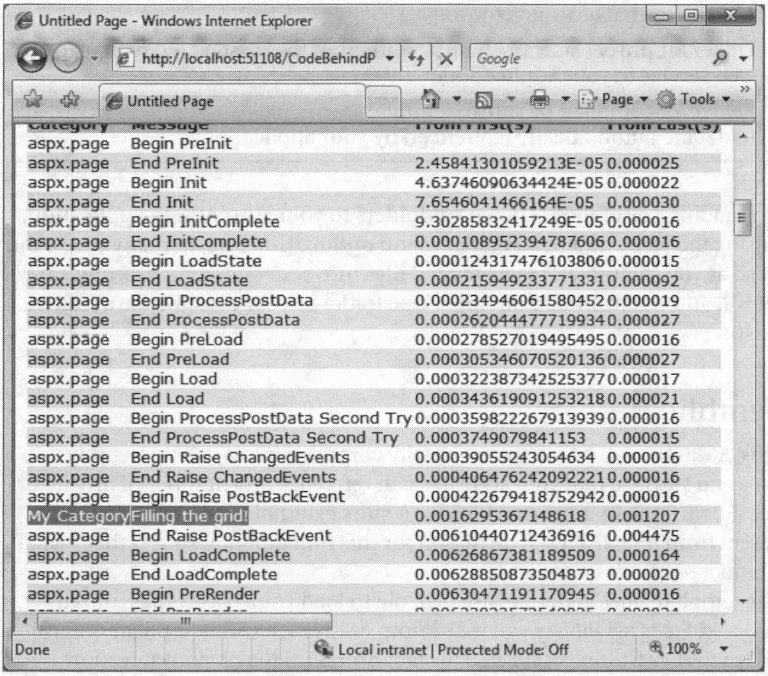

Figure 31-15. *Logging custom trace messages*

Source Code The CodeBehindPageModel example is included under the Chapter 31 subdirectory.

Details of an ASP.NET Website Directory Structure

By default, new Visual Studio 2008 web applications will be provided with an initial web page, a `Web.config` file, and a particular folder named App_Data (which is empty by default). ASP.NET websites may contain any number of specifically named subdirectories, each of which has a special meaning to the ASP.NET runtime. Table 31-3 documents these "special subdirectories."

Table 31-3. *Special ASP.NET Subdirectories*

Subfolder	Meaning in Life
App_Browsers	Folder for browser definition files that are used to identify individual browsers and determine their capabilities.
App_Code	Folder for source code for components or classes that you want to compile as part of your application. ASP.NET compiles the code in this folder when pages are requested. Code in the App_Code folder is automatically accessible by your application.
App_Data	Folder for storing Access `*.mdb` files, SQL Express `*.mdf` files, XML files, or other data stores.
App_GlobalResources	Folder for `*.resx` files that are accessed programmatically from application code.
App_LocalResources	Folder for `*.resx` files that are bound to a specific page.
App_Themes	Folder that contains a collection of files that define the appearance of ASP.NET web pages and controls.
App_WebReferences	Folder for proxy classes, schemas, and other files associated with using a web service in your application.
Bin	Folder for compiled private assemblies (`*.dll` files). Assemblies in the Bin folder are automatically referenced by your application.

If you are interested in adding any of these known subfolders to your current web application, you may do so explicitly using the Web Site ➤ Add Folder menu option. However, in many cases, the IDE will automatically do so as you "naturally" insert related files into your site (e.g., inserting a new class file into your project will automatically add an App_Code folder to your directory structure if one does not currently exist).

Referencing Assemblies

As described in a few pages, ASP.NET web pages are eventually compiled into a .NET assembly. Given this, it should come as no surprise that your websites can reference any number of private or shared assemblies. Under ASP.NET, the manner in which your site's externally required assemblies are recorded is quite different from ASP.NET 1.x. The reason for this fundamental shift is that Visual Studio 2008 treats websites in a *projectless manner*.

Although the Web Site template does generate an `*.sln` file to load your `*.aspx` files into the IDE, there is no longer a related `*.csproj` file. As you may know, ASP.NET 1.x Web Application projects recorded all external assemblies within `*.csproj`. This fact brings up the obvious question, where are the external assemblies recorded under ASP.NET?

As you have seen, when you reference a private assembly, Visual Studio 2008 will automatically create a \bin directory within your directory structure to store a local copy of the binary. When your code base makes use of types within these code libraries, they are automatically loaded on demand.

If you reference a shared assembly, Visual Studio 2008 will automatically insert a `Web.config` file into your current web solution (if one is not currently in place) and record the external reference within the `<assemblies>` element. For example, if you again activate the Web Site ➤ Add Reference menu option and this time select a shared assembly (such as `System.Data.OracleClient.dll`), you will find that your `Web.config` file has been updated as follows:

```
<assemblies>
  <add assembly="System.Data.OracleClient, Version=2.0.0.0,
      Culture=neutral, PublicKeyToken=B77A5C561934E089"/>
</assemblies>
```

As you can see, each assembly is described using the same information required for a dynamic load via the `Assembly.Load()` method (see Chapter 16).

The Role of the App_Code Folder

The App_Code folder is used to store source code files that are not directly tied to a specific web page (such as a code-behind file) but are to be compiled for use by your website. Code within the App_Code folder will be automatically compiled on the fly on an as-needed basis. After this point, the assembly is accessible to any other code in the website. To this end, the App_Code folder is much like the Bin folder, except that you can store source code in it instead of compiled code. The major benefit of this approach is that it is possible to define custom types for your web application without having to compile them independently.

A single App_Code folder can contain code files from multiple languages. At runtime, the appropriate compiler kicks in to generate the assembly in question. If you would rather partition your code, however, you can define multiple subdirectories that are used to hold any number of managed code files (`*.vb`, `*.cs`, etc.).

For example, assume you have added an App_Code folder to the root directory of a website application that has two subfolders (MyCSharpCode and MyVbNetCode) that contain language-specific files. Once you do, you are able to update your `Web.config` file to specify these subdirectories using a `<codeSubDirectories>` element nested within the `<configuration>` element:

```
<compilation debug="true" strict="false" explicit="true">
  <codeSubDirectories>
    <add directoryName="MyCSharpCode" />
    <add directoryName="MyVbNetCode" />
  </codeSubDirectories>
</compilation>
```

■ Note The App_Code directory will also be used to contain files that are not language files, but are useful nonetheless (`*.xsd` files, `*.wsdl` files, etc.).

Beyond Bin and App_Code, the App_Data and App_Themes folders are two additional “special subdirectories” that you should be familiar with, both of which will be detailed in the next several chapters. As always, consult the .NET Framework 3.5 SDK documentation for full details of the remaining ASP.NET subdirectories if you require further information.

The ASP.NET Page Compilation Cycle

Regardless of which page model you make use of (single-file or code-behind), your *.aspx files (and any related code-behind file) are compiled on the fly into a valid .NET assembly. This assembly is then hosted by the ASP.NET worker process (aspnet_wp.exe) within its own application domain boundary (see Chapter 17 for details on AppDomains). The manner in which your website's assembly is compiled under ASP.NET, however, is quite different.

Compilation Cycle for Single-File Pages

If you are making use of the single-file page model, the HTML markup, server side <script> blocks, and web control definitions are dynamically compiled into a class type deriving from System.Web.UI.Page. The name of this class is based on the name of the *.aspx file and takes an _aspx suffix (e.g., a page named MyPage.aspx becomes a class type named MyPage_aspx). Figure 31-16 illustrates the basic process.

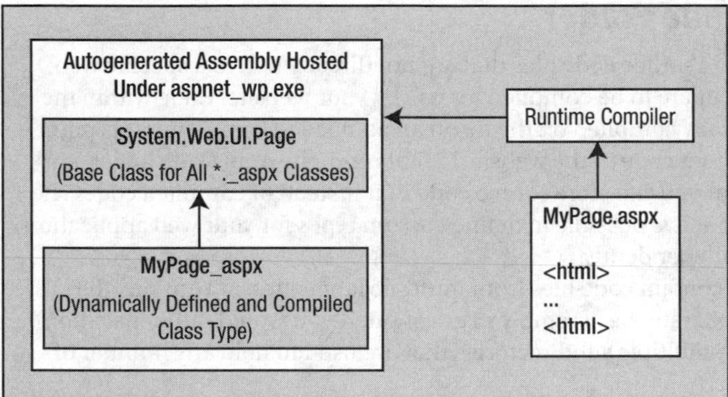

Figure 31-16. *The compilation model for single-file pages*

This dynamically compiled assembly is deployed to a runtime-defined subdirectory under the C:\WINDOWS\Microsoft.NET\Framework\v2.0.50727\Temporary ASP.NET Files root directory. The path beneath this root will differ based on a number of factors (hash codes, etc.), but if you are determined, eventually you will find the *.dll (and supporting files) in question. Figure 31-17 shows the generated assembly for the SinglePageModel example shown earlier in this chapter.

■ **Note** Because these autogenerated assemblies are true-blue .NET binaries, if you were to open your web applications–related *.dll using ildasm.exe or reflector.exe you would indeed find CIL code, metadata, and an assembly-level manifest.

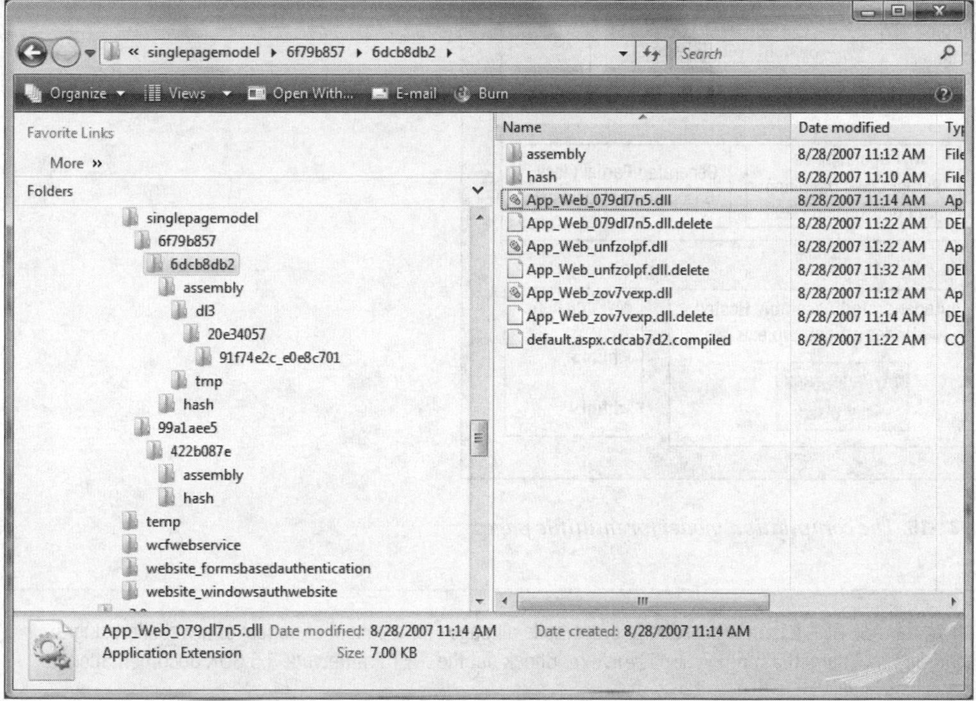

Figure 31-17. *The ASP.NET autogenerated assembly*

Compilation Cycle for Multifile Pages

The compilation process of a page making use of the code-behind model is similar to that of the single-file model. However, the type deriving from `System.Web.UI.Page` is composed of three (yes, *three*) files rather than the expected two.

Looking back at the previous CodeBehindPageModel example, recall that the `Default.aspx` file was connected to a partial class named `_Default` within the code-behind file. If you have a background in ASP.NET 1.x, you may wonder what happened to the member variable declarations for the various web controls as well as the code within `InitializeComponent()`, such as event-handling logic. Under ASP.NET, these details are accounted for by a third aspect of the partial class generated in memory. In reality, this is not a literal file, but an in-memory representation of the partial class. Consider Figure 31-18.

In this model, the web controls declared in the `*.aspx` file are used to build the additional partial class that defines each UI member variable and the configuration logic that used to be found within the `InitializeComponent()` method of ASP.NET 1.x (we just never directly see it). This partial class is combined at compile time with the code-behind file to result in the *base class* of the generated `_aspx` class type (in the single-file page compilation model, the generated `_aspx` file derived directly from `System.Web.UI.Page`).

In either case, once the assembly has been created upon the initial HTTP request, it will be reused for all subsequent requests, and thus will not have to be recompiled. Understanding this factoid should help explain why the first request of an `*.aspx` page takes the longest, and subsequent hits to the same page are extremely efficient.

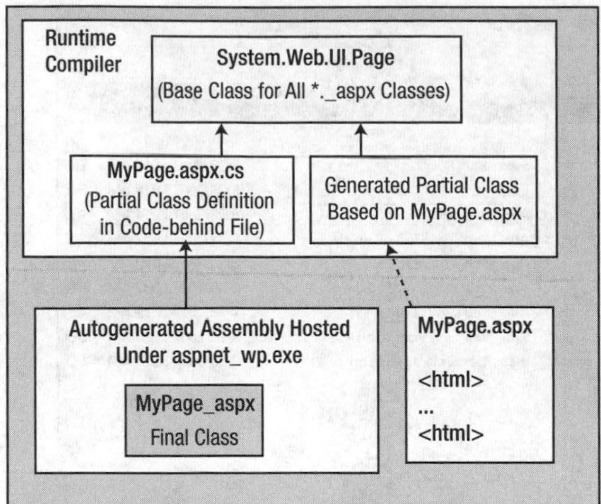

Figure 31-18. *The compilation model for multifile pages*

■ **Note** Under ASP.NET, it is now possible to precompile all pages (or a subset of pages) of a website using a command-line tool named `aspnet_compiler.exe`. Check out the .NET Framework 3.5 SDK documentation for details.

The Inheritance Chain of the Page Type

As you have just seen, the final generated class that represents your `*.aspx` file eventually derives from `System.Web.UI.Page`. Like any base class, this type provides a polymorphic interface to all derived types. However, the `Page` type is not the only member in your inheritance hierarchy. If you were to locate the `Page` type (within the `System.Web.dll` assembly) using the Visual Studio 2008 object browser, you would find that `Page` "is-a" `TemplateControl`, which "is-a" `Control`, which "is-a" `Object` (see Figure 31-19).

As you would guess, each of these base classes brings a good deal of functionality to each and every `*.aspx` file. For the majority of your projects, you will make use of the members defined within the `Page` and `Control` parent classes. By and large, the functionality gained from the `System.Web.UI.TemplateControl` class is only of interest if you are building custom Web Form controls or interacting with the rendering process.

The first parent class of interest is `Page` itself. Here you will find numerous properties that enable you to interact with various web primitives such as application and session variables, the HTTP request/response, theme support, and so forth. Table 31-4 describes some (but by no means all) of the core properties.

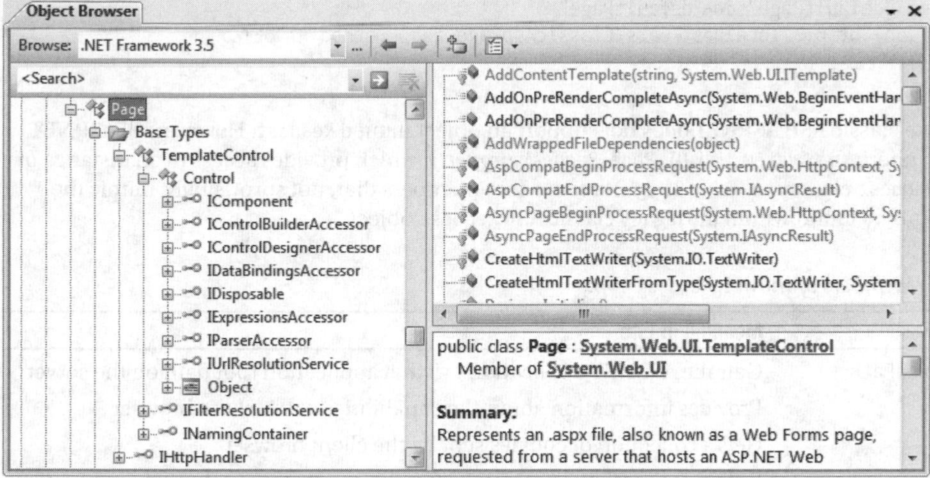

Figure 31-19. *The derivation of an ASP.NET page*

Table 31-4. *Select Properties of the* `Page` *Type*

Property	Meaning in Life
`Application`	Allows you to interact with application variables for the current website
`Cache`	Allows you to interact with the cache object for the current website
`ClientTarget`	Allows you to specify how this page should render itself based on the requesting browser
`IsPostBack`	Gets a value indicating whether the page is being loaded in response to a client postback or whether it is being loaded and accessed for the first time
`MasterPageFile`	Establishes the master page for the current page
`Request`	Provides access to the current HTTP request
`Response`	Allows you to interact with the outgoing HTTP response
`Server`	Provides access to the `HttpServerUtility` object, which contains various server-side helper functions
`Session`	Allows you to interact with the session data for the current caller
`Theme`	Gets or sets the name of the theme used for the current page
`Trace`	Provides access to a `TraceContext` object, which allows you to log custom messages during debugging sessions

Interacting with the Incoming HTTP Request

As you saw earlier in this chapter, the basic flow of a web session begins with a client logging on to a site, filling in user information, and clicking a Submit button to post back the HTML form data to a given web page for processing. In most cases, the opening tag of the `form` statement specifies an `action` attribute and a `method` attribute that indicates the file on the web server that will be sent the data in the various HTML widgets, as well as the method of sending this data (GET or POST):

```
<form name="defaultPage" id="defaultPage"
      action="http://localhost/Cars/ClassicAspPage.asp" method = "GET">
...
</form>
```

Unlike classic ASP, ASP.NET does not support an object named `Request`. However, all ASP.NET pages do inherit the `System.Web.UI.Page.Request` *property*, which provides access to an instance of the `HttpRequest` class type. Table 31-5 lists some core members that, not surprisingly, mimic the same members found within the legacy classic ASP `Request` object.

Table 31-5. *Members of the* `HttpRequest` *Type*

Member	Meaning in Life
`ApplicationPath`	Gets the ASP.NET application's virtual application root path on the server
`Browser`	Provides information about the capabilities of the client browser
`Cookies`	Gets a collection of cookies sent by the client browser
`FilePath`	Indicates the virtual path of the current request
`Form`	Gets a collection of HTTP form variables
`Headers`	Gets a collection of HTTP headers
`HttpMethod`	Indicates the HTTP data transfer method used by the client (GET, POST)
`IsSecureConnection`	Indicates whether the HTTP connection is secure (i.e., HTTPS)
`QueryString`	Gets the collection of HTTP query string variables
`RawUrl`	Gets the current request's raw URL
`RequestType`	Indicates the HTTP data transfer method used by the client (GET, POST)
`ServerVariables`	Gets a collection of web server variables
`UserHostAddress`	Gets the IP host address of the remote client
`UserHostName`	Gets the DNS name of the remote client

In addition to these properties, the `HttpRequest` type has a number of useful methods, including the following:

- `MapPath()`: Maps the virtual path in the requested URL to a physical path on the server for the current request.
- `SaveAs()`: Saves details of the current HTTP request to a file on the web server (which can prove helpful for debugging purposes).
- `ValidateInput()`: If the validation feature is enabled via the `Validate` attribute of the page directive, this method can be called to check all user input data (including cookie data) against a predefined list of potentially dangerous input data.

Obtaining Brower Statistics

The first interesting aspect of the `HttpRequest` type is the `Browser` property, which provides access to an underlying `HttpBrowserCapabilities` object. `HttpBrowserCapabilities` in turn exposes numerous members that allow you to programmatically investigate statistics regarding the browser that sent the incoming HTTP request.

Create a new ASP.NET website named `FunWithPageMembers` (again, elect to use the File System option). Your first task is to build a UI that allows users to click a `Button` web control (named btnGetBrowserStats) to view various statistics about the calling browser. These statistics will be generated dynamically and attached to a Label type (named lblOutput). The Click event handler is as follows:

```
protected void btnGetBrowserStats_Click(object sender, EventArgs e)
{
  string theInfo = "";
  theInfo += string.Format("<li>Is the client AOL? {0}</li>",
    Request.Browser.AOL);
  theInfo += string.Format("<li>Does the client support ActiveX? {0}</li>",
    Request.Browser.ActiveXControls);
  theInfo += string.Format("<li>Is the client a Beta? {0}</li>",
    Request.Browser.Beta);
  theInfo += string.Format("<li>Does the client support Java Applets? {0}</li>",
    Request.Browser.JavaApplets);
  theInfo += string.Format("<li>Does the client support Cookies? {0}</li>",
    Request.Browser.Cookies);
  theInfo += string.Format("<li>Does the client support VBScript? {0}</li>",
    Request.Browser.VBScript);
  lblOutput.Text = theInfo;
}
```

Here you are testing for a number of browser capabilities. As you would guess, it is (very) helpful to discover a browser's support for ActiveX controls, Java applets, and client-side VBScript code. If the calling browser does not support a given web technology, your *.aspx page would be able to take an alternative course of action.

Access to Incoming Form Data

Other aspects of the HttpResponse type are the Form and QueryString properties. These two properties allow you to examine the incoming form data using name/value pairs, and they function identically to classic ASP. Recall from our earlier discussion of classic ASP that if the data is submitted using HTTP GET, the form data is accessed using the QueryString property, whereas data submitted via HTTP POST is obtained using the Form property.

While you could most certainly make use of the HttpRequest.Form and HttpRequest.QueryString properties to access client-supplied form data on the web server, these old-school techniques are (for the most part) unnecessary. Given that ASP.NET supplies you with server-side web controls, you are able to treat HTML UI elements as true objects. Therefore, rather than obtaining the value within a text box as follows:

```
protected void btnGetFormData_Click(object sender, System.EventArgs e)
{
  // Get value for a widget with ID txtFirstName.
  string firstName = Request.Form("txtFirstName");

  // Use this value in your page...
}
```

you can simply ask the server-side widget directly via the Text property for use in your program:

```
protected void btnGetFormData_Click(object sender, System.EventArgs e)
{
  // Get value for a widget with ID txtFirstName.
  string firstName = txtFirstName.Text;

  // Use this value in your page...
}
```

Not only does this approach lend itself to solid OO principles, but also you do not need to concern yourself with how the form data was submitted (GET or POST) before obtaining the values. Furthermore, working with the widget directly is much more type-safe, given that typing errors are discovered at compile time rather than runtime. Of course, this is not to say that you will *never* need to make use of the `Form` or `QueryString` property in ASP.NET; rather, the need to do so has greatly diminished and is usually optional.

The IsPostBack Property

Another very important member of `HttpRequest` is the `IsPostBack` property. Recall that "postback" refers to the act of returning to a particular web page while still in session with the server. Given this definition, understand that the `IsPostBack` property will return `true` if the current HTTP request has been sent by a currently logged-on user and `false` if this is the user's first interaction with the page.

Typically, the need to determine whether the current HTTP request is indeed a postback is most helpful when you wish to execute a block of code only the first time the user accesses a given page. For example, you may wish to populate an ADO.NET `DataSet` when the user first accesses an `*.aspx` file and cache the object for later use. When the caller returns to the page, you can avoid the need to hit the database unnecessarily (of course, some pages may require that the `DataSet` always be updated upon each request, but that is another issue). Assuming your `*.aspx` file has handled the page's `Load` event (described in detail later in this chapter), you could programmatically test for postback conditions as follows:

```
protected void Page_Load(object sender, System.EventArgs e)
{
  // Fill DataSet only the very first time
  // the user comes to this page.
  if (!IsPostBack)
  {
    // Populate DataSet and cache it!
  }
  // Use cached DataSet.
}
```

Interacting with the Outgoing HTTP Response

Now that you have a better understanding of how the `Page` type allows you to interact with the incoming HTTP request, the next step is to see how to interact with the outgoing HTTP response. In ASP.NET, the `Response` property of the `Page` class provides access to an instance of the `HttpResponse` type. This type defines a number of properties that allow you to format the HTTP response sent back to the client browser. Table 31-6 lists some core properties.

Table 31-6. *Properties of the* `HttpResponse` *Type*

Property	Meaning in Life
`Cache`	Returns the caching semantics of the web page (e.g., expiration time, privacy, vary clauses)
`ContentEncoding`	Gets or sets the HTTP character set of the output stream
`ContentType`	Gets or sets the HTTP MIME type of the output stream
`Cookies`	Gets the `HttpCookie` collection sent by the current request
`IsClientConnected`	Gets a value indicating whether the client is still connected to the server

Property	Meaning in Life
Output	Enables custom output to the outgoing HTTP content body
OutputStream	Enables binary output to the outgoing HTTP content body
StatusCode	Gets or sets the HTTP status code of output returned to the client
StatusDescription	Gets or sets the HTTP status string of output returned to the client
SuppressContent	Gets or sets a value indicating that HTTP content will not be sent to the client

Also, consider the partial list of methods supported by the HttpResponse type described in Table 31-7.

Table 31-7. *Methods of the* HttpResponse *Type*

Method	Meaning in Life
AddCacheDependency()	Adds an object to the application catch (see Chapter 33)
Clear()	Clears all headers and content output from the buffer stream
End()	Sends all currently buffered output to the client, and then closes the socket connection
Flush()	Sends all currently buffered output to the client
Redirect()	Redirects a client to a new URL
Write()	Writes values to an HTTP output content stream
WriteFile()	Writes a file directly to an HTTP content output stream

Emitting HTML Content

Perhaps the most well-known aspect of the HttpResponse type is the ability to write content directly to the HTTP output stream. The HttpResponse.Write() method allows you to pass in any HTML tags and/or text literals. The HttpResponse.WriteFile() method takes this functionality one step further, in that you can specify the name of a physical file on the web server whose contents should be rendered to the output stream (this is quite helpful to quickly emit the contents of an existing *.htm file).

To illustrate, assume you have added another Button type to your current *.aspx file that implements the server-side Click event handler like so:

```
protected void btnHttpResponse_Click(object sender, EventArgs e)
{
  Response.Write("<b>My name is:</b><br>");
  Response.Write(this.ToString());
  Response.Write("<br><br><b>Here was your last request:</b><br>");
  Response.WriteFile("MyHTMLPage.htm");
}
```

The role of this helper function (which you can assume is called by some server-side event handler) is quite simple. The only point of interest is the fact that the HttpResponse.WriteFile() method is now emitting the contents of a server-side *.htm file within the root directory of the website.

Again, while you can always take this old-school approach and render HTML tags and content using the Write() method, this approach is far less common under ASP.NET than with classic ASP.

The reason is (once again) due to the advent of server-side web controls. Thus, if you wish to render a block of textual data to the browser, your task is as simple as assigning a string to the Text property of a Label widget.

Redirecting Users

Another aspect of the HttpResponse type is the ability to redirect the user to a new URL:

```
protected void btnSomeTraining_Click(object sender, EventArgs e)
{
  Response.Redirect("http://www.intertech.com");
}
```

If this event handler is invoked via a client-side postback, the user will automatically be redirected to the specified URL.

■Note The HttpResponse.Redirect() method will always entail a trip back to the client browser. If you simply wish to transfer control to an *.aspx file in the same virtual directory, the HttpServerUtility.Transfer() method (accessed via the inherited Server property) is more efficient.

So much for investigating the functionality of System.Web.UI.Page. We will examine the role of the System.Web.UI.Control base class in the next chapter. Next up, let's examine the life and times of a Page-derived object.

■Source Code The FunWithPageMembers files are included under the Chapter 31 subdirectory.

The Life Cycle of an ASP.NET Web Page

Every ASP.NET web page has a fixed life cycle. When the ASP.NET runtime receives an incoming request for a given *.aspx file, the associated System.Web.UI.Page-derived type is allocated into memory using the type's default constructor. After this point, the framework will automatically fire a series of events. By default, the Load event is automatically accounted for, where you can add your custom code:

```
public partial class Default : System.Web.UI.Page
{
  protected void Page_Load(object sender, EventArgs e)
  {
    Response.Write("Load event fired!");
  }
}
```

Beyond the Load event, a given Page is able to intercept any of the core events in Table 31-8, which are listed in the order in which they are encountered (consult the .NET Framework 3.5 SDK documentation for details on all possible events that may fire during a page's lifetime).

Table 31-8. *Select Events of the* Page *Type*

Event	Meaning in Life
PreInit	The framework uses this event to allocate any web controls, apply themes, establish the master page, and set user profiles. You may intercept this event to customize the process.
Init	The framework uses this event to set the properties of web controls to their previous values via postback or view state data.
Load	When this event fires, the page and its controls are fully initialized, and their previous values are restored. At this point, it is safe to interact with each web widget.
"Event that triggered the postback"	There is of course, no event of this name. This "event" simply refers to whichever event caused the browser to perform the postback to the web server (such as a Button click).
PreRender	All control data binding and UI configuration has occurred and the controls are ready to render their data into the outbound HTTP response.
Unload	The page and its controls have finished the rendering process, and the page object is about to be destroyed. At this point, it is a runtime error to interact with the outgoing HTTP response. You may, however, capture this event to perform any page-level cleanup (close file or database connections, perform any form of logging activity, dispose of objects, etc.).

When a C# programmer needs to handle events beyond Load, you might be surprised to find that there is no IDE support to do so! Rather, you must manually author a method in your code file taking the name Page_*NameOfEvent*. For example, here is how you can handle the Unload event:

```
public partial class Default : System.Web.UI.Page
{
  protected void Page_Load(object sender, EventArgs e)
  {
    Response.Write("Load event fired!");
  }

  protected void Page_Unload(object sender, EventArgs e)
  {
    // No longer possible to emit data to the HTTP
    // response, so we will write to a local file.
    System.IO.File.WriteAllText(@"C:\MyLog.txt", "Page unloading!");
  }
}
```

■ **Note** Each event of the Page type works in conjunction with the System.EventHandler delegate; therefore, the subroutines that handle these events always take an Object as the first parameter and an EventArgs as the second parameter.

The Role of the AutoEventWireup Attribute

When you wish to handle events for your page, you will need to update your <script> block or code-behind file with an appropriate event handler. However, if you examine the <%@Page%> directive, you will notice a specific attribute named AutoEventWireUp, which by default is set to true:

```
<%@ Page Language="C#" AutoEventWireup="true"
  CodeFile="Default.aspx.cs" Inherits="_Default" %>
```

With this default behavior, each page-level event handler will automatically be handled if you enter the appropriately named method. However, if you disable AutoPageWireUp by setting this attribute to false:

```
<%@ Page Language="C#" AutoEventWireup="false"
  CodeFile="Default.aspx.cs" Inherits="_Default" %>
```

the page-level events will no longer be captured. As its name suggests, this attribute (when enabled) will generate the necessary event riggings within the autogenerated partial class described earlier in this chapter. Even if you disable AutoEventWireup, you can still process page-level events by making use of C# event-handling logic, for example:

```
public _Default()
{
  // Explicitly hook into the Load and Unload events.
  this.Load += new EventHandler(Page_Load);
  this.Unload += new EventHandler(Page_Unload);
}
```

As you might suspect, by and large you will simply leave AutoEventWireup enabled.

The Error Event

Another event that may occur during your page's life cycle is Error. This event will be fired if a method on the Page-derived type triggered an exception that was not explicitly handled. Assume that you have handled the Click event for a given Button on your page, and within the event handler (which I named btnGetFile_Click), you attempt to write out the contents of a local file to the HTTP response.

Also assume you have *failed* to test for the presence of this file via standard structured exception handling. If you have rigged up the page's Error event in the default constructor, you have one final chance to deal with the problem on this page before the end user finds an ugly error. Consider the following code:

```
public partial class _Default : System.Web.UI.Page
{
  void Page_Error(object sender, EventArgs e)
  {
    Response.Clear();
    Response.Write("I am sorry...I can't find a required file.<br>");
    Response.Write(string.Format("The error was: <b>{0}</b>",
        Server.GetLastError().Message));
    Server.ClearError();
  }

  protected void Page_Load(object sender, EventArgs e)
  {
    Response.Write("Load event fired!");
  }

  protected void Page_Unload(object sender, EventArgs e)
  {
    // No longer possible to emit data to the HTTP
    // response at this point, so we will write to a local file.
    System.IO.File.WriteAllText(@"C:\MyLog.txt", "Page unloading!");
  }
```

```
  protected void btnPostback_Click(object sender, EventArgs e)
  {
    // Nothing happens here, this is just to ensure a
    // postback to the page.
  }
  protected void btnTriggerError_Click(object sender, EventArgs e)
  {
    System.IO.File.ReadAllText(@"C:\IDontExist.txt");
  }
}
```

Notice that your `Error` event handler begins by clearing out any content currently within the HTTP response and emits a generic error message. If you wish to gain access to the specific `System.Exception` object, you may do so using the `HttpServerUtility.GetLastError()` method exposed by the inherited `Server` property.

Finally, note that before exiting this generic error handler, you are explicitly calling the `HttpServerUtility.ClearError()` method via the `Server` property. This is required, as it informs the runtime that you have dealt with the issue at hand and require no further processing. If you forget to do so, the end user will be presented with the runtime's error page. Figure 31-20 shows the result of this error-trapping logic.

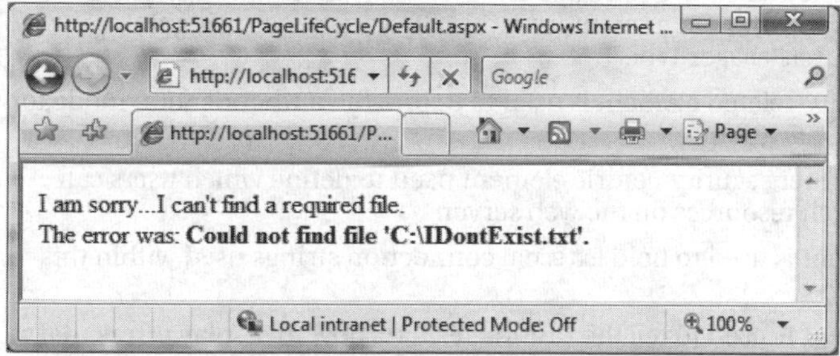

Figure 31-20. *Page-level error handling*

At this point, you should feel confident with the composition of an ASP.NET `Page` type. Now that you have such a foundation, you can turn your attention to the role of ASP.NET web controls, themes, and master pages, all of which are the subject of the next chapter. To wrap up this chapter, however, let's examine the role of the `Web.config` file.

Source Code The PageLifeCycle files are included under the Chapter 31 subdirectory.

The Role of the Web.config File

By default, all C# ASP.NET web applications created with Visual Studio 2008 are automatically provided with a `Web.config` file. However, if you ever need to manually insert a `Web.config` file into your site (e.g., when you are working with the single-page model and have not created a web solution), you may do so using the using the Web Site ➤ Add New Item menu option. In either case, within this scope of a `Web.config` file you are able to add settings that control how your web application will function at runtime.

■ **Note** It is not mandatory for your web applications to include a `Web.config` file. If you do not have such a file, your website will be granted the default web-centric settings recorded in the `machine.config` file for your .NET installation.

Recall during your examination of .NET assemblies (in Chapter 15) that you learned client applications can leverage an XML-based configuration file to instruct the CLR how it should handle binding requests, assembly probing, and other runtime details. The same holds true for ASP.NET web applications, with the notable exception that web-centric configuration files are always named `Web.config` (unlike `*.exe` configuration files, which are named based on the related client executable).

The default structure of a `Web.config` file is rather verbose with the release of .NET 3.5, but the essentials settings break down as follows. Table 31-9 outlines some of the more interesting sub-elements that can be found within a `Web.config` file.

Table 31-9. *Select Elements of a* `Web.config` *File*

Element	Meaning in Life
`<appSettings>`	This element is used to establish custom name/value pairs that can be programmatically read in memory for use by your pages using the `ConfigurationManager` type.
`<authentication>`	This security-related element is used to define the authentication mode for this web application.
`<authorization>`	This is another security-centric element used to define which users can access which resources on the web server.
`<connectionStrings>`	This element is used to hold external connection strings used within this website.
`<customErrors>`	This element is used to tell the runtime exactly how to display errors that occur during the functioning of the web application.
`<globalization>`	This element is used to configure the globalization settings for this web application.
`<namespaces>`	This element documents all of the namespaces to include if your web application has been precompiled using the new `aspnet_compiler.exe` command-line tool.
`<sessionState>`	This element is used to control how and where session state data will be stored by the .NET runtime.
`<trace>`	This element is used to enable (or disable) tracing support for this web application.

A `Web.config` file may contain additional subelements above and beyond the set presented in Table 31-9. The vast majority of these items are security related, while the remaining items are useful only during advanced ASP.NET scenarios such as creating with custom HTTP headers or custom HTTP modules (topics that are not covered here).

If you wish to see the complete set of elements (and the related attributes) that can appear in a `Web.config` file, you may do so using the .NET Framework 3.5 SDK documentation. Simply search for the topic "ASP.NET Configuration Settings" as shown in Figure 31-21, and dive in.

You will come to know various aspects of the `Web.config` file over the remainder of this text.

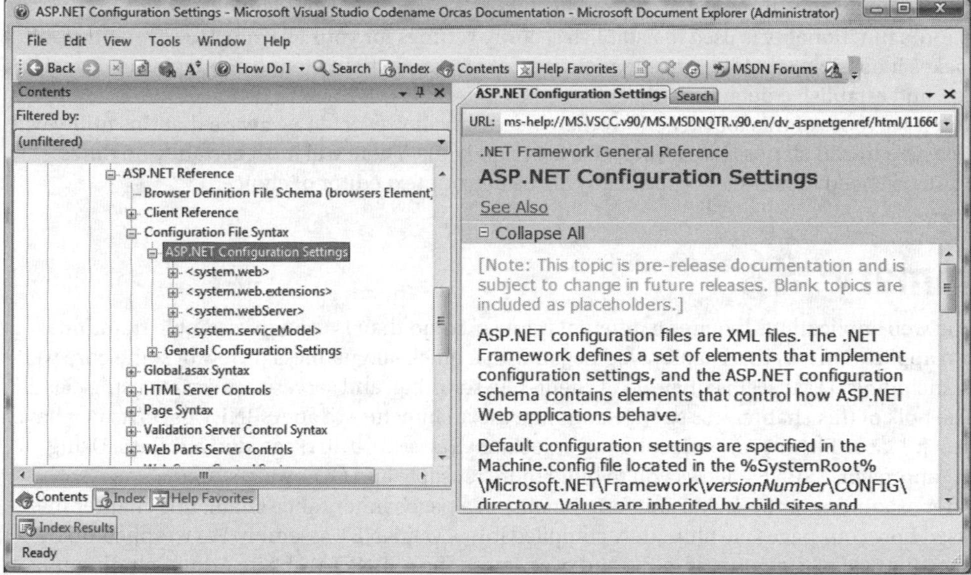

Figure 31-21. *Documentation details of a* `Web.config` *file*

The ASP.NET Website Administration Utility

Although you are always free to modify the content of a `Web.config` file directly using Visual Studio 2008, ASP.NET web projects can make use of a handy web-based editor that will allow you to graphically edit numerous elements and attributes of your project's `Web.config` file. To launch this tool, shown in Figure 31-22, simply activate the Web Site ➤ ASP.NET Configuration menu option.

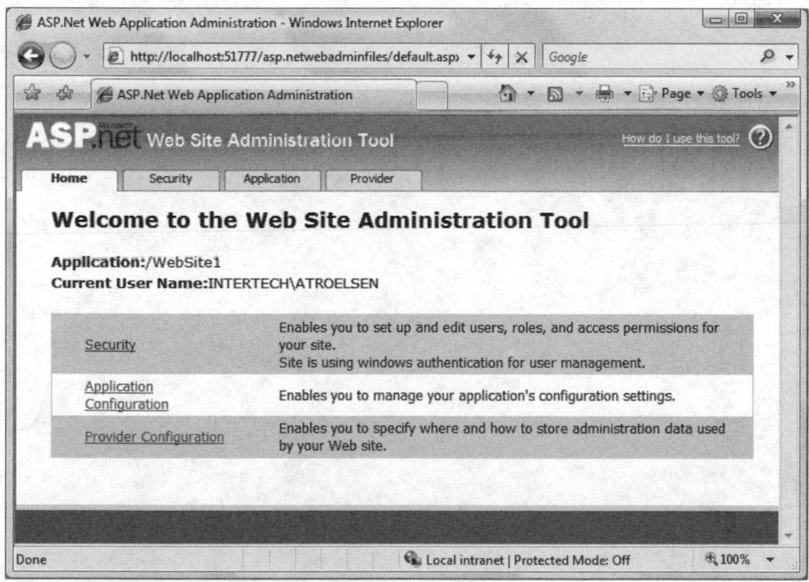

Figure 31-22. *The ASP.NET Web Site Administration tool*

If you were to click the tabs located on the top of the page, you would quickly notice that most of this tool's functionality is used to establish security settings for your website. However, this tool also makes it possible to add settings to your `<appSettings>` element, define debugging and tracing settings, and establish a default error page.

You'll see more of this tool in action where necessary; however, do be aware that this utility will *not* allow you to add all possible settings to a `Web.config` file. There will most certainly be times when you will need to manually update this file using your text editor of choice.

Summary

Building web applications requires a different frame of mind than is used to assemble traditional desktop applications. In this chapter, you began with a quick and painless review of some core web topics, including HTML, HTTP, the role of client-side scripting, and server-side scripts using classic ASP. The bulk of this chapter was spent examining the architecture of an ASP.NET page. As you have seen, each `*.aspx` file in your project has an associated `System.Web.UI.Page`-derived class. Using this OO approach, ASP.NET allows you to build more reusable and OO-aware systems.

After examining some of the core functionality of a page's inheritance chain, this chapter then discussed how your pages are ultimately compiled into a valid .NET assembly. We wrapped up by exploring the role of the `Web.config` file and overviewed the ASP.NET Web Site Administration tool.

CHAPTER 32

ASP.NET Web Controls, Themes, and Master Pages

The previous chapter concentrated on the composition and behavior of ASP.NET Page objects. This chapter will dive into the details of the *web controls* that make up a page's user interface. After examining the overall nature of an ASP.NET web control, you will come to understand how to make use of several UI elements including the validation controls and data-centric controls.

The latter half of this chapter will examine the role of *master pages* and show how they provide a simplified manner to define a common UI skeleton that will be replicated across the pages in your website. I wrap up by showing you how to apply *themes* to your pages in order to define a consistent look and feel for your page's controls. As you will see, the ASP.NET theme engine provides a server-side alternative to traditional client-side style sheets.

Understanding the Nature of Web Controls

A major benefit of ASP.NET is the ability to assemble the UI of your pages using the types defined in the System.Web.UI.WebControls namespace. As you have seen, these controls (which go by the names *server controls*, *web controls*, or *Web Form controls*) are extremely helpful in that they automatically generate the necessary HTML for the requesting browser and expose a set of events that may be processed on the web server. Furthermore, because each ASP.NET control has a corresponding class in the System.Web.UI.WebControls namespace, it can be manipulated in an object-oriented manner.

When you configure the properties of a web control using the Visual Studio 2008 Properties window, your edits are recorded in the opening control declaration of a given element in the *.aspx file as a series of name/value pairs. Thus, if you add a new TextBox to the designer of a given *.aspx file and change the ID, BorderStyle, BorderWidth, BackColor, and Text properties, the opening <asp:TextBox> tag is modified accordingly (note that the Text value becomes the inner text of the TextBox scope):

```
<asp:TextBox ID="txtNameTextBox" runat="server"
  BackColor="#C0FFC0" BorderStyle="Dotted"BorderWidth="5px">
  Enter Your Name
</asp:TextBox>
```

Given that the HTML declaration of a web control eventually becomes a member variable from the System.Web.UI.WebControls namespace (via the dynamic compilation cycle examined in Chapter 31), you are able to interact with the members of this type within a server-side <script> block or the page's code-behind file. For example, if you handled the Click event for a given Button type, you could change the background color of the TextBox as follows:

```
partial class _Default : System.Web.UI.Page
{
  protected void btnChangeTextBoxColor_Click(object sender, System.EventArgs e)
  {
    // Change color of text box object in code.
    this.txtNameTextBox.BackColor = Drawing.Color.DarkBlue;
  }
}
```

All ASP.NET web controls ultimately derive from a common base class named System.Web.UI.WebControls.WebControl. WebControl in turn derives from System.Web.UI.Control (which derives from System.Object). Control and WebControl each define a number of properties common to all server-side controls. Before we examine the inherited functionality, let's formalize what it means to handle a server-side event.

Understanding Server-Side Event Handling

Given the current state of the World Wide Web, it is impossible to avoid the fundamental nature of browser/web server interaction. Whenever these two entities communicate, there is always an underlying, stateless, HTTP request-and-response cycle. While ASP.NET server controls do a great deal to shield you from the details of the raw HTTP protocol, always remember that treating the Web as an event-driven entity is just a magnificent smoke-and-mirrors show provided by the CLR, and it is not identical to the event-driven model of a Windows-based UI.

For example, although the System.Windows.Forms, System.Windows.Controls, and System.Web.UI.WebControls namespaces define types with the same simple names (Button, TextBox, Label, and so on), they do not expose an identical set of events. For example, there is no way to handle a server-side MouseMove event when the user moves the cursor over a Web Form Button type. Obviously, this is a good thing. (Who wants to post back to the server each time the user mouse moves in the browser?)

The bottom line is that a given ASP.NET web control will expose a limited set of events, all of which ultimately result in a postback to the web server. Any necessary client-side event processing will require you to author blurbs of *client-side* JavaScript/VBScript script code to be processed by the requesting browser's scripting engine. Given that ASP.NET is primarily a server-side technology, I will not be addressing the topic of authoring client-side scripts in this text.

■ Note Handling an event for a given web control using Visual Studio 2008 can be done in an identical manner to doing so for a Windows Forms control. Simply select the widget from the designer and click the "lightning bolt" icon on the Properties window.

The AutoPostBack Property

It is also worth pointing out that many of the ASP.NET web controls support a property named AutoPostBack (most notably, the CheckBox, RadioButton, and TextBox controls, as well as any widget that derives from the abstract ListControl type). By default, this property is set to false, which disables the automatic processing of server-side events (even if you have indeed rigged up the event in the code-behind file). In most cases, this is the exact behavior you require, given that UI elements such as check boxes typically don't require postback functionality (as the page object can obtain the state of the widget within a more natural Button Click event handler).

However, if you wish to cause any of these widgets to post back to a server-side event handler, simply set the value of AutoPostBack to true. This technique can be helpful if you wish to have the state of one widget automatically populate another value within another widget on the same page. To illustrate, assume you have a web page that contains a single TextBox (named txtAutoPostback) and a single ListBox control (named lstTextBoxData). Here is the relevant markup:

```
<form id="form1" runat="server">
  <asp:TextBox ID="txtAutoPostback" runat="server"></asp:TextBox>
  <br/>
  <asp:ListBox ID="lstTextBoxData" runat="server"></asp:ListBox>
</form>
```

Now, handle the TextChanged event of the TextBox, and within the server-side event handler, populate the ListBox with the current value in the TextBox:

```
partial class _Default : System.Web.UI.Page
{
  protected void txtAutoPostback_TextChanged(object sender, System.EventArgs e)
  {
    lstTextBoxData.Items.Add(txtAutoPostback.Text);
  }
}
```

If you run the application as is, you will find that as you type in the TextBox, nothing happens. Furthermore, if you type in the TextBox and tab to the next control, nothing happens. The reason is that the AutoPostBack property of the TextBox is set to false by default. However, if you set this property to true:

```
<asp:TextBox ID="txtAutoPostback"
  runat="server" AutoPostBack="true">
</asp:TextBox>
```

you will find that when you tab away from the TextBox (or press the Enter key), the ListBox is automatically populated with the current value in the TextBox. To be sure, beyond the need to populate the items of one widget based on the value of another widget, you will typically not need to alter the state of a widget's AutoPostBack property (and even then, sometimes this can be accomplished purely in client script, removing the need for server interaction at all).

The System.Web.UI.Control Type

The System.Web.UI.Control base class defines various properties, methods, and events that allow the ability to interact with core (typically non-GUI) aspects of a web control. Table 32-1 documents some, but not all, members of interest.

Table 32-1. *Select Members of* System.Web.UI.Control

Member	Meaning in Life
Controls	This property gets a ControlCollection object that represents the child controls within the current control.
DataBind()	This method binds a data source to the invoked server control and all its child controls.
EnableTheming	This property establishes whether the control supports theme functionality.
HasControls()	This method determines whether the server control contains any child controls.
ID	This property gets or sets the programmatic identifier assigned to the server control.

Continued

Table 32-1. *Continued*

Member	Meaning in Life
`Page`	This property gets a reference to the `Page` instance that contains the server control.
`Parent`	This property gets a reference to the server control's parent control in the page control hierarchy.
`SkinID`	This property gets or sets the "skin" to apply to the control. Under ASP.NET, it is now possible to establish a control's overall look and feel on the fly via skins.
`Visible`	This property gets or sets a value that indicates whether a server control is rendered as a UI element on the page.

Enumerating Contained Controls

The first aspect of `System.Web.UI.Control` we will examine is the fact that all web controls (including `Page` itself) inherit a custom controls collection (accessed via the `Controls` property). Much like in a Windows Forms application, the `Controls` property provides access to a strongly typed collection of `WebControl`-derived types. Like any .NET collection, you have the ability to add, insert, and remove items dynamically at runtime.

While it is technically possible to add web controls directly to a `Page`-derived type, it is easier (and more robust) to make use of a `Panel` widget. The `Panel` class represents a container of widgets that may or may not be visible to the end user (based on the value of its `Visible` and `BorderStyle` properties).

To illustrate, create a new website named DynamicCtrls. Using the Visual Studio 2008 page designer, add a `Panel` type (named `myPanel`) that contains a `TextBox`, `Button`, and `HyperLink` widget named whatever you choose (be aware that the designer requires that you drag internal items within the UI of the `Panel` type). Once you have done so, the `<form>` element of your `*.aspx` file will have been updated as follows:

```
<asp:Panel ID="myPanel" runat="server" Height="50px" Width="125px">
  <asp:TextBox ID="TextBox1" runat="server"></asp:TextBox><br/>
  <asp:Button ID="Button1" runat="server" Text="Button"/><br/>
  <asp:HyperLink ID="HyperLink1" runat="server">HyperLink
  </asp:HyperLink>
</asp:Panel>
```

Next, place a `Label` widget outside the scope of the `Panel` (named `lblControlInfo`) to hold the rendered output. Assume in the `Page_Load()` event you wish to obtain a list of all the controls contained within the `Panel` and assign the results to the `Label` type (named `lblControlInfo`):

```
public partial class _Default : System.Web.UI.Page
{
  private void ListControlsInPanel()
  {
    string theInfo = "";
    theInfo = string.Format("Has controls? {0} <br/>", myPanel.HasControls());
    foreach (Control c in myPanel.Controls)
    {
      if (!object.ReferenceEquals(c.GetType(),
        typeof(System.Web.UI.LiteralControl)))
      {
        theInfo += "***************************<br/>";
        theInfo += string.Format("Control Name? {0} <br/>", c.ToString());
        theInfo += string.Format("ID? {0} <br>", c.ID);
```

```
        theInfo += string.Format("Control Visible? {0} <br/>", c.Visible);
        theInfo += string.Format("ViewState? {0} <br/>", c.EnableViewState);
      }
    }
    lblControlInfo.Text = theInfo;
  }

  protected void Page_Load(object sender, System.EventArgs e)
  {
    ListControlsInPanel();
  }
}
```

Here, you iterate over each WebControl maintained on the Panel and perform a check to see whether the current type is of type System.Web.UI.LiteralControl. This type is used to represent literal HTML tags and content (such as <br>, text literals, etc.). If you do not do this sanity check, you might be surprised to find a total of seven types in the scope of the Panel (given the *.aspx declaration seen previously). Assuming the type is not literal HTML content, you then print out some various statistics about the widget. Figure 32-1 shows the output.

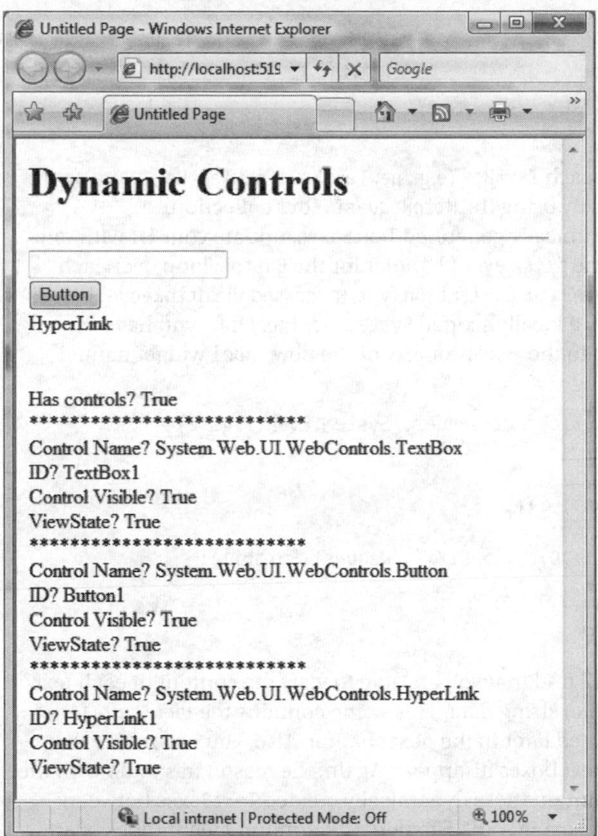

Figure 32-1. *Enumerating contained widgets*

Dynamically Adding (and Removing) Controls

Now, what if you wish to modify the contents of a Panel at runtime? Let's update the current page to support an additional Button (named btnAddWidgets) that dynamically adds three new TextBox types to the Panel, and another Button (named btnRemovePanelItems) that clears the Panel widget of all controls. The Click event handlers for each are shown here:

```
protected void btnRemovePanelItems_Click(object sender, System.EventArgs e)
{
  myPanel.Controls.Clear();
  ListControlsInPanel();
}

protected void btnAddWidgets_Click(object sender, System.EventArgs e)
{
  for (int i = 0; i < 3; i++)
  {
    // Assign a name so we can get
    // the text value out later
    // using the incoming form data.
    TextBox t = new TextBox();
    t.ID = string.Format("newTextBox{0}", i);
    myPanel.Controls.Add(t);
    ListControlsInPanel();
  }
}
```

Notice that you assign a unique ID to each TextBox (e.g., newTextBox1, newTextBox2, and so on) to obtain its contained text programmatically using the HttpRequest.Form collection.

To obtain the values within these dynamically generated TextBoxes, update your UI with one additional Button and Label type. Within the Click event handler for the Button, loop over each item contained within the HttpRequest.NameValueCollection type (accessed via HttpRequest.Form) and concatenate the textual information to a locally scoped System.String. Once you have exhausted the collection, assign this string to the Text property of the new Label widget named lblTextBoxText:

```
protected void btnGetTextBoxValues_Click(object sender, System.EventArgs e)
{
  string textBoxValues = "";
  for (int i = 0; i < Request.Form.Count; i++)
  {
    textBoxValues += string.Format("<li>{0}</li><br/>", Request.Form[i]);
  }
  lblTextBoxText.Text = textBoxValues;
}
```

When you run the application, you will find that you are able to view the content of each text box, including some rather long (unreadable) string data. This string contains the *view state* for each widget on the page and will be examined later in the next chapter. Also, you will notice that once the request has been processed, the text boxes disappear. Again, the reason has to do with the stateless nature of HTTP. If you wish to maintain these dynamically created TextBoxes between postbacks, you need to persist these objects using ASP.NET state programming techniques (also examined in the next chapter).

Source Code The DynamicCtrls project is included under the Chapter 32 subdirectory.

The System.Web.UI.WebControls.WebControl Type

As you can tell, the `Control` type provides a number of non–GUI-related behaviors (the controls collection, autopostback support, etc.). On the other hand, the `WebControl` base class provides a graphical polymorphic interface to all web widgets, as suggested in Table 32-2.

Table 32-2. *Select Properties of the* `WebControl` *Base Class*

Property	Meaning in Life
`BackColor`	Gets or sets the background color of the web control
`BorderColor`	Gets or sets the border color of the web control
`BorderStyle`	Gets or sets the border style of the web control
`BorderWidth`	Gets or sets the border width of the web control
`Enabled`	Gets or sets a value indicating whether the web control is enabled
`CssClass`	Allows you to assign a class defined within a Cascading Style Sheet to a web widget
`Font`	Gets font information for the web control
`ForeColor`	Gets or sets the foreground color (typically the color of the text) of the web control
`Height`, `Width`	Get or set the height and width of the web control
`TabIndex`	Gets or sets the tab index of the web control
`ToolTip`	Gets or sets the tool tip for the web control to be displayed when the cursor is over the control

Almost all of these properties are self-explanatory, so rather than drill through the use of all these properties, let's shift gears a bit and check out a number of ASP.NET Web Form controls in action.

Major Categories of ASP.NET Web Controls

The types in `System.Web.UI.WebControls` can be broken down into several major categories:

- Simple controls
- Feature-rich controls
- Data-centric controls
- Input validation controls
- Web part controls
- Security controls

The *simple controls* are so named because they are ASP.NET web controls that map to standard HTML widgets (buttons, lists, hyperlinks, image holders, tables, etc.). Next, we have a small set of controls named the *rich controls* for which there is no direct HTML equivalent (such as the `Calendar`, `TreeView`, `Menu`, `Wizard`, etc.). The *data-centric controls* are widgets that are typically populated via a given data connection. The best (and most exotic) example of such a control would be the ASP.NET `GridView`. Other members of this category include "repeater" controls and the lightweight `DataList`.

The *validation controls* are server-side widgets that automatically emit client-side JavaScript, for the purpose of form field validation. Finally, the base class libraries ship with a number of security-centric controls. These UI elements encapsulate the details of logging into a site, providing password-retrieval services and managing user roles. The full set of ASP.NET web controls can be seen using the Visual Studio 2008 Toolbox. In Figure 32-2, notice that related controls are grouped together under a specifically named tab.

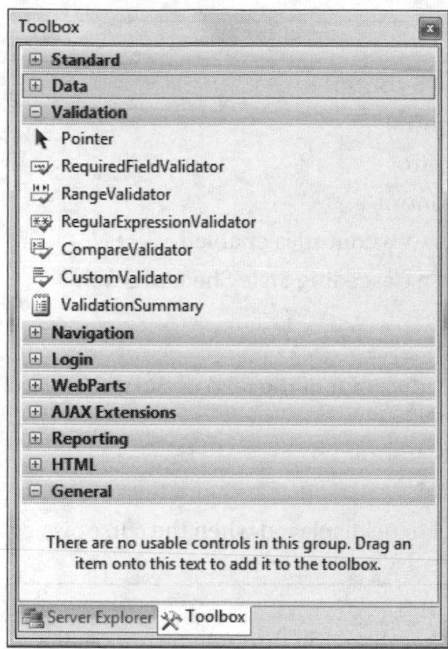

Figure 32-2. *The ASP.NET web controls*

A Brief Word Regarding System.Web.UI.HtmlControls

Truth be told, there are two distinct web control toolkits that ship with ASP.NET. In addition to the ASP.NET web controls (within the `System.Web.UI.WebControls` namespace), the base class libraries also provide the `System.Web.UI.HtmlControls` widgets.

The HTML controls are a collection of types that allow you to make use of traditional HTML controls on a web forms page. However, unlike raw HTML tags, HTML controls are object-oriented entities that can be configured to run on the server and thus support server-side event handling. Unlike ASP.NET web controls, HTML controls are quite simplistic in nature and offer little functionality beyond standard HTML tags (`HtmlButton`, `HtmlInputControl`, `HtmlTable`, etc.). As you would expect, Visual Studio 2008 provides a specific section of the Toolbox to contain the HTML control types (see Figure 32-3).

The HTML controls provide a public interface that mimics standard HTML attributes. For example, to obtain the information within an input area, you make use of the `Value` property, rather than the web control–centric `Text` property. Given that the HTML controls are not as feature-rich as the ASP.NET web controls, I won't make further mention of them in this text. If you wish to investigate these types, consult the .NET Framework 3.5 SDK documentation for further details.

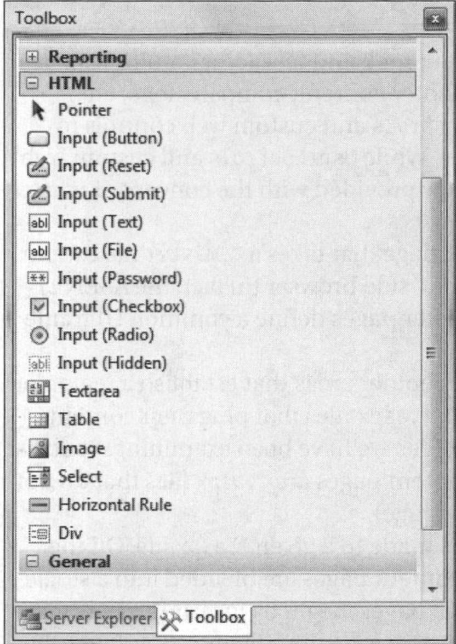

Figure 32-3. *The HTML controls*

■Note The HTML controls can be useful if your team has a clear division between those who build HTML UIs and .NET developers. HTML folks can make use of their web editor of choice using familiar markup tags and pass the HTML files to the development team. At this point, developers can configure these HTML controls to run as server controls (by right-clicking an HTML widget within Visual Studio 2008). This will allow developers to handle server-side events and work with the HTML widget programmatically.

Building a Feature-Rich ASP.NET Website

Given that many of the "simple" controls look and feel so close to their Windows Forms counterparts, I won't bother to enumerate the details of the basic widgets (`Buttons`, `Labels`, `TextBoxes`, etc.). Rather, let's build a new website that illustrates working with several of the more exotic controls as well as the ASP.NET master page model and enhanced data binding engine. Specifically, this next example will illustrate the following techniques:

- Working with master pages
- Working with the `Menu` control
- Working with the `GridView` control
- Working with the `Wizard` control

To begin, create a new ASP.NET Web Application project named AspNetCarsSite.

Working with Master Pages

As I am sure you are aware, many websites provide a consistent look and feel across multiple pages (a common menu navigation system, common header and footer content, company logo, etc.). Under ASP.NET 1.*x*, developers made extensive use of `UserControls` and custom web controls to define web content that was to be used across multiple pages. While `UserControls` and custom web controls are still a very valid option under ASP.NET, we are now provided with the concept of *master pages*, which complements these existing technologies.

Simply put, a master page is little more than an ASP.NET page that takes a `*.master` file extension. On their own, master pages are not viewable from a client-side browser (in fact, the ASP.NET runtime will not serve this flavor of web content). Rather, master pages define a common UI frame shared by all pages (or a subset of pages) in your site.

As well, a `*.master` page will define various content placeholder areas that establish a region of UI real estate other `*.aspx` files may plug into. As you will see, `*.aspx` files that plug their content into a master file look and feel a bit different from the `*.aspx` files we have been examining. Specifically, this flavor of an `*.aspx` file is termed a *content page*. Content pages are `*.aspx` files that do not define an HTML `<form>` element (that is the job of the master page).

However, as far as the end user is concerned, a request is made to a given `*.aspx` file. On the web server, the related `*.master` file and any related `*.aspx` content pages are blended into a single unified page. To illustrate the use of master pages and content pages, begin by inserting a new master page into your website via the Web Site ➤ Add New Item menu selection (Figure 32-4 shows the resulting dialog box).

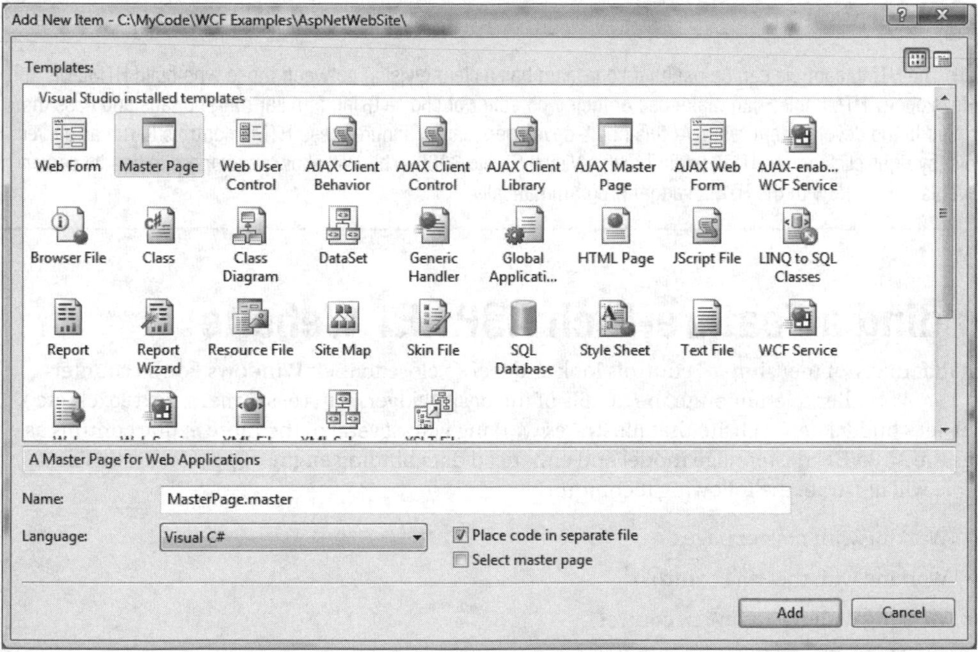

Figure 32-4. *Inserting a new* `*.master` *file*

The initial markup of the MasterPage.master file looks like the following:

```
<%@ Master Language="C#" AutoEventWireup="true"
  CodeFile="MasterPage.master.cs" Inherits="MasterPage" %>

<!DOCTYPE html PUBLIC "-//W3C//DTD XHTML 1.0 Transitional//EN"
  "http://www.w3.org/TR/xhtml1/DTD/xhtml1-transitional.dtd">

<html xmlns="http://www.w3.org/1999/xhtml">
<head runat="server">
  <title>Untitled Page</title>
  <asp:ContentPlaceHolder id="head" runat="server">
  </asp:ContentPlaceHolder>
</head>
<body>
  <form id="form1" runat="server">
  <div>
    <asp:ContentPlaceHolder id="ContentPlaceHolder1" runat="server">
    </asp:ContentPlaceHolder>
  </div>
  </form>
</body>
</html>
```

The first point of interest is the new <%@Master%> directive. For the most part, this directive supports the same attributes as the <%@Page%> directive described in the previous chapter. Like Page types, a master page derives from a specific base class, which in this case is MasterPage. If you were to open up your related code file, you would find the following class definition:

```
public partial class MasterPage : System.Web.UI.MasterPage
{
  protected void Page_Load(object sender, EventArgs e)
  {
  }
}
```

The other point of interest within the markup of the master is the <asp:ContentPlaceHolder> type. This region of a master page represents the area of the master that the UI widgets of the related *.aspx content file may plug into, not the content defined by the master page itself. If you flip to the designer surface of the *.master page, you will find that each <asp:ContentPlaceHolder> element is accounted for, as shown in Figure 32-5.

If you do intend to blend an *.aspx file within this region, the scope within the <asp:ContentPlaceHolder> and </asp:ContentPlaceHolder> tags will be empty. However, if you so choose, you are able to populate this area with various web controls that function as a default UI to use in the event that a given *.aspx file in the site does not supply specific content. For this example, assume that each *.aspx page in your site will indeed supply custom content, and therefore our <asp:ContentPlaceHolder> elements will be empty.

■ **Note** A *.master page may define as many content placeholders as necessary. As well, a single *.master page may nest additional *.master pages.

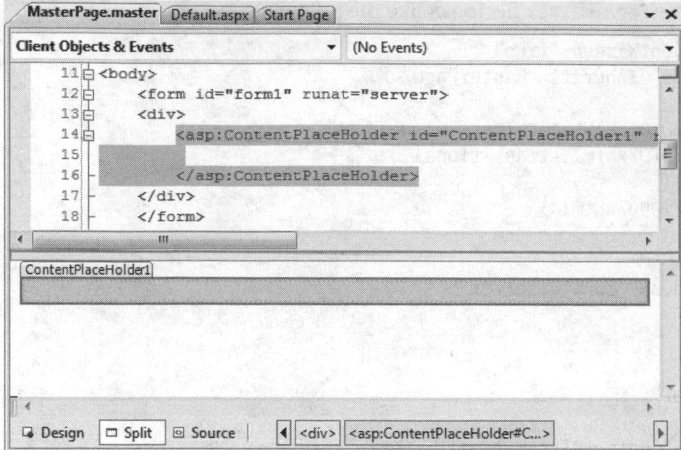

Figure 32-5. *The design-time view of a* `*.master` *file's* `<asp:ContentPlaceHolder>` *tags*

As you would hope, you are able to build a common UI of a `*.master` file using the same Visual Studio 2008 designers used to build `*.aspx` files. For this site, you will add a descriptive `Label` (to serve as a common welcome message), an `AdRotator` control (which will randomly display one of two images), and a `Menu` control (to allow the user to navigate to other areas of the site). Figure 32-6 shows one possible UI of the master page that we will be constructing (again notice that the content placeholder is empty).

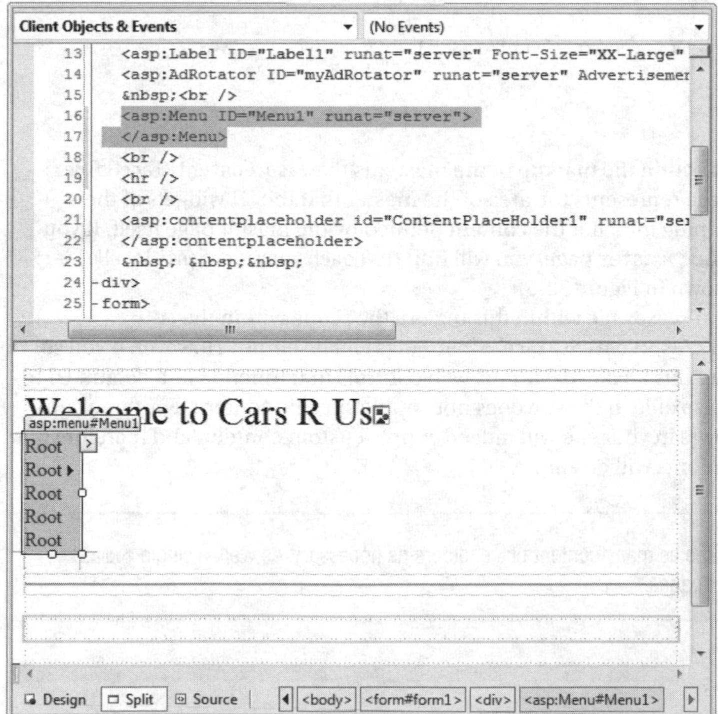

Figure 32-6. *The* `*.master` *file's shared UI*

Working with the Menu Control and *.sitemap Files

ASP.NET ships with several web controls that allow you to handle site navigation: SiteMapPath, TreeView, and Menu. As you would expect, these web widgets can be configured in multiple ways. For example, each of these controls can dynamically generate its nodes via an external XML file (or an XML-based *.sitemap file), programmatically in code, or through markup using the designers of Visual Studio 2008. Our menu system will be dynamically populated using a *.sitemap file. The benefit of this approach is that we can define the overall structure of our website in an external file, and then bind it to a Menu (or TreeView) widget on the fly. This way, if the navigational structure of our website changes, we simply need to modify the *.sitemap file and reload the page. To begin, insert a new Web.sitemap file into your project using the Web Site ➤ Add New Item menu option, to bring up the dialog box shown in Figure 32-7.

Figure 32-7. *Inserting a new* Web.sitemap *file*

As you can see, the initial Web.sitemap file defines a topmost item with two subnodes:

```
<?xml version="1.0" encoding="utf-8" ?>
<siteMap xmlns="http://schemas.microsoft.com/AspNet/SiteMap-File-1.0" >
  <siteMapNode url="" title=""  description="">
    <siteMapNode url="" title=""  description="" />
    <siteMapNode url="" title=""  description="" />
  </siteMapNode>
</siteMap>
```

If we were to bind this structure to a Menu control, we would find a topmost menu item with two submenus. Therefore, when you wish to define subitems, simply define new <siteMapNode> elements within the scope of an existing <siteMapNode>. In any case, the goal is to define the overall structure of your website within a Web.sitemap file using various <siteMapNode> elements. Each one of these elements can define a title and URL attribute. The URL attribute represents which *.aspx file to navigate to when the user clicks a given menu item (or node of a TreeView). Our site contains three subelements, which are set up as follows:

- *Home*: Default.aspx
- *Build a Car*: BuildCar.aspx
- *View Inventory*: Inventory.aspx

Our menu system has a single topmost "Welcome" item with three subelements. Therefore, we can update the Web.sitemap file as follows. (Be aware that each url value must be unique! If not, you receive a runtime error.)

```
<?xml version="1.0" encoding="utf-8" ?>
<siteMap xmlns="http://schemas.microsoft.com/AspNet/SiteMap-File-1.0" >
  <siteMapNode url="" title="Welcome!"  description="">
    <siteMapNode url="~/Default.aspx" title="Home"
      description="The Home Page" />
    <siteMapNode url="~/BuildCar.aspx" title="Build a car"
      description="Create your dream car" />
    <siteMapNode url="~/Inventory.aspx" title="View Inventory"
      description="See what is in stock" />
  </siteMapNode>
</siteMap>
```

■ Note The ~/ prefix before each page in the url attribute is a notation that represents the root of the website.

Now, despite what you may be thinking, you do not associate a Web.sitemap file directly to a Menu or TreeView control using a given property. Rather, the *.master or *.aspx file that contains the UI widget that will display the Web.sitemap file must contain a SiteMapDataSource component. This type will automatically load the Web.sitemap file into its object model when the page is requested. The Menu and TreeView types then set their DataSourceID property to point to the SiteMapDataSource instance. The reason for this level of indirection is that it makes it possible for us to build a custom provider to fetch the website's structure from another source (such as a table in a database, an existing XML file, etc.). Figure 32-8 illustrates the interplay between a Web.sitemap, SiteMapDataSource, and various UI elements.

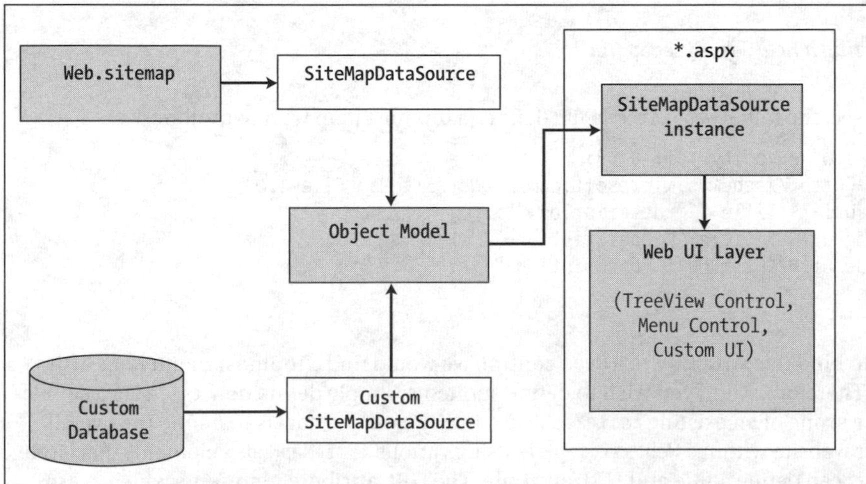

Figure 32-8. *The ASP.NET sitemap navigation model*

To add a new SiteMapDataSource to your *.master file and automatically set the DataSourceID property, you can make use of the Visual Studio 2008 designer. Activate the inline editor of the Menu widget and select New Data Source, as shown in Figure 32-9.

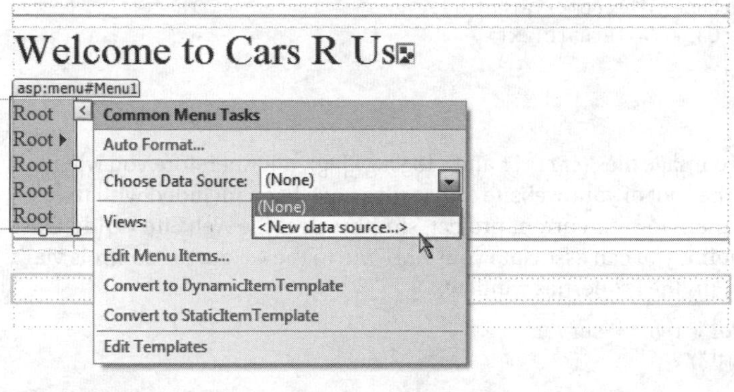

Figure 32-9. *Adding a new* SiteMapDataSource

From the resulting dialog box, select the SiteMap icon. This will set the DataSourceID property of the Menu item as well as add a new SiteMapDataSource component to your page. This is all you need to do to configure your Menu widget to navigate to the additional pages on your site. If you wish to perform additional processing when the user selects a given menu item, you may do so by handling the MenuItemClick event. There is no need to do so for this example, but be aware that you are able to determine which menu item was selected using the incoming MenuEventArgs parameter.

Establishing Bread Crumbs with the SiteMapPath Type

Before moving on to the AdRotator control, add a SiteMapPath type onto your *.master file, beneath the content placeholder element. This widget will automatically adjust its content based on the current selection of the menu system. As you may know, this can provide a helpful visual cue for the end user (formally, this UI technique is termed *bread crumbs*). Once you complete this example, you will notice that when you select the Welcome ➤ Build a Car menu item, the SiteMapPath widget updates accordingly automatically.

Working with the AdRotator

The role of the ASP.NET AdRotator widget is to randomly display a given image at some position in the browser. When you first place an AdRotator widget on the designer, it is displayed as an empty placeholder. Functionally, this control cannot do its magic until you assign the AdvertisementFile property to point to the source file that describes each image. For this example, the data source will be a simple XML file named Ads.xml.

Once you have inserted this new XML file to your site, specify a unique <Ad> element for each image you wish to display. At minimum, each <Ad> element specifies the image to display (ImageUrl), the URL to navigate to if the image is selected (TargetUrl), mouseover text (AlternateText), and the weight of the ad (Impressions):

```
<Advertisements>
  <Ad>
    <ImageUrl>SlugBug.jpg</ImageUrl>
    <TargetUrl>http://www.Cars.com</TargetUrl>
```

```
    <AlternateText>Your new Car?</AlternateText>
    <Impressions>80</Impressions>
  </Ad>
  <Ad>
    <ImageUrl>car.gif</ImageUrl>
    <TargetUrl>http://www.CarSuperSite.com</TargetUrl>
    <AlternateText>Like this Car?</AlternateText>
    <Impressions>80</Impressions>
  </Ad>
</Advertisements>
```

Here you have specified two image files (car.gif and slugbug.jpg), and therefore you will need to ensure that these files are in the root of your website (these files have been included with this book's code download). To add them to your current project, simply select the Web Site ➤ Add Existing Item menu option. At this point, you can associate your XML file to the AdRotator controls via the AdvertisementFile property (in the Properties window):

```
<asp:AdRotator ID="myAdRotator" runat="server"
  AdvertisementFile="~/Ads.xml"/>
```

Later when you run this application and post back to the page, you will be randomly presented with one of two image files. Figure 32-10 illustrates the final design-time UI of the master page.

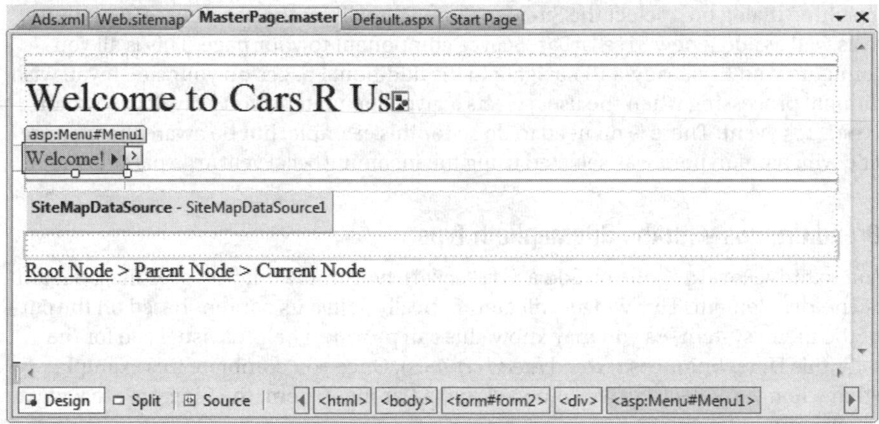

Figure 32-10. *The final design of the master page*

Defining the Default.aspx Content Page

Now that you have a master page established, you can begin designing the individual *.aspx pages that will define the UI content to merge within the <asp:ContentPlaceHolder> tag of the master page. When you created this new website, Visual Studio 2008 automatically provided you with an initial *.aspx file, but as the file now stands, it cannot be merged within the master page.

The reason is that it is the *.master file that defines the <form> section of the final HTML page. Therefore, the existing <form> area within the *.aspx file will need to be replaced with an <asp:content> scope. While you could update the markup of your initial *.aspx file by hand, go ahead and delete Default.aspx from your project. When you wish to automatically insert a new content page to your project, simply right-click anywhere on the designer surface of the *.master file, and select the Add Content Page menu option. This will generate a new *.aspx file with the following initial markup:

```
<%@ Page Language="C#" MasterPageFile="~/MasterPage.master"
  AutoEventWireup="true" CodeFile="Default.aspx.cs"
  Inherits="_Default" Title="Untitled Page" %>

<asp:Content ID="Content1"
  ContentPlaceHolderID="head" Runat="Server">
</asp:Content>
<asp:Content ID="Content2"
  ContentPlaceHolderID="ContentPlaceHolder1" Runat="Server">
</asp:Content>
```

First, notice that the <%@Page%> directive has been updated with a new `MasterPageFile` attribute that is assigned to your `*.master` file. Also note that rather than having a `<form>` element, we have an `<asp:Content>` scope (currently empty) that has set the `ContentPlaceHolderID` value identical to the `<asp:ContentPlaceHolder>` component in the master file.

Given these associations, the content page understands where to "plug in" its content, while the master's content is displayed in a read-only nature on the content page. There is no need to build a complex UI for your `Default.aspx` content area, so for this example, simply add some literal text that provides some basic site instructions, as you see in Figure 32-11 (also notice on the upper right of the content page that there is a link to switch to the related master file).

Figure 32-11. *Authoring the first content page*

Now, if you run your project, you will find that the UI content of the `*.master` and `Default.aspx` files have been merged into a single stream of HTML. As you can see from Figure 32-12, the end user is unaware that the master page even exists. Also, as you refresh the page (via the F5 key), you should see the AdRotator randomly displaying one of two images.

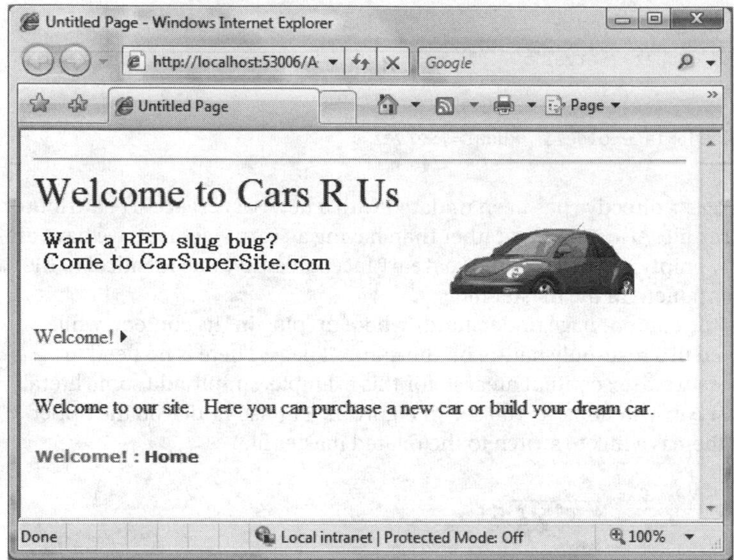

Figure 32-12. *At runtime, master files and content pages render back a single form.*

■ **Note** Do be aware that a Page object's master page can be assigned programmatically within the PreInit event of a Page derived type, using the Master property.

Designing the Inventory Content Page

To insert the Inventory.aspx content page into your current project, open the *.master page in the IDE, select Web Site ➤ Add Content Page (if a *.master file is not the active item in the designer, this menu option is not present), and rename this file to Inventory.aspx. The role of the Inventory content page is to display the contents of the Inventory table of the AutoLot database within a GridView control.

Although this control behaves in many ways identically to the legacy ASP.NET 1.*x* DataGrid, GridView has intrinsic support for the latest data binding engine of ASP.NET. Under the new model, it is now possible to represent connection string data and SQL Select, Insert, Update, and Delete statements (or alternatively stored procedures) *in markup*. Therefore, rather than authoring all of the necessary ADO.NET code by hand, you can make use of the new SqlDataSource type. Using the visual designers, you are able to declaratively create the necessary markup and then assign the DataSourceID property of the GridView to the SqlDataSource component.

■ **Note** Despite the name, the SqlDataSource provider can be configured to communicate with any ADO.NET data provider (ODBC, Oracle, etc.) that ships with the Microsoft .NET platform; it is not limited to Microsoft SQL Server. You may set the target DBMS with via the Provider property.

With a few simple mouse clicks, you can configure the GridView to automatically select, update, and delete records of the underlying data store. While this zero-code mindset greatly simplifies the amount of boilerplate code, understand that this simplicity comes with a loss of control and may not be the best approach for an enterprise-level application. This model can be wonderful for low-trafficked pages, prototyping a website, or smaller in-house applications.

To illustrate how to work with the GridView (and the new data binding engine) in a declarative manner, begin by updating the Inventory.aspx content page with a descriptive label. Next, open the Server Explorer tool (via the View menu) and make sure you have added a data connection to the AutoLot database created during our examination of ADO.NET (see Chapter 22 for a walkthrough of the process of adding a data connection). Now, select the Inventory icon and drag it onto the content area of the Inventory.aspx file. Once you have done so, the IDE responds by performing the following steps:

1. Your web.config file was updated with a new <connectionStrings> element.
2. A SqlDataSource component was configured with the necessary Select, Insert, Update, and Delete logic.
3. The DataSourceID property of the GridView has been set to the new SqlDataSource component.

■ **Note** As an alternative, you can configure a GridView widget using the inline editor. Select New Data Source from the Choose Data Source drop-down box. This will activate a wizard that walks you through a series of steps to connect this component to the required data source.

If you examine the opening declaration of the GridView control, you will see that the DataSourceID property has been set to the SqlDataSource you just defined:

```
<asp:GridView ID="GridView1" runat="server" AutoGenerateColumns="False"
  CellPadding="4" DataKeyNames="CarID" DataSourceID="SqlDataSource1"
  ForeColor="#333333" GridLines="None">
...
</asp:GridView>
```

The SqlDataSource type is where a majority of the action is taking place. In the markup that follows, notice that this type has recorded the necessary SQL statements (with parameterized queries no less) to interact with the Inventory table of the AutoLot database. As well, using the $ syntax of the ConnectionString property, this component will automatically read the <connectionString> value from web.config:

```
<asp:SqlDataSource ID="SqlDataSource1" runat="server"
 ConnectionString="<%$ ConnectionStrings:CarsConnectionString1 %>"
  DeleteCommand="DELETE FROM [Inventory] WHERE [CarID] = @CarID"
  InsertCommand="INSERT INTO [Inventory] ([CarID], [Make], [Color], [PetName])
    VALUES (@CarID, @Make, @Color, @PetName)"
  ProviderName="<%$ ConnectionStrings:CarsConnectionString1.ProviderName %>"
  SelectCommand="SELECT [CarID], [Make], [Color], [PetName] FROM [Inventory]"
  UpdateCommand="UPDATE [Inventory] SET [Make] = @Make,
    [Color] = @Color, [PetName] = @PetName WHERE [CarID] = @CarID">
  <DeleteParameters>
    <asp:Parameter Name="CarID" Type="Int32" />
  </DeleteParameters>
  <UpdateParameters>
    <asp:Parameter Name="Make" Type="String" />
    <asp:Parameter Name="Color" Type="String" />
```

```
    <asp:Parameter Name="PetName" Type="String" />
    <asp:Parameter Name="CarID" Type="Int32" />
  </UpdateParameters>
  <InsertParameters>
    <asp:Parameter Name="CarID" Type="Int32" />
    <asp:Parameter Name="Make" Type="String" />
    <asp:Parameter Name="Color" Type="String" />
    <asp:Parameter Name="PetName" Type="String" />
  </InsertParameters>
</asp:SqlDataSource>
```

At this point, you are able to run your web program, click the View Inventory menu item, and view your data, as shown in Figure 32-13. Also notice that the "bread crumbs" provided by the `SiteMapPath` widget have updated automatically.

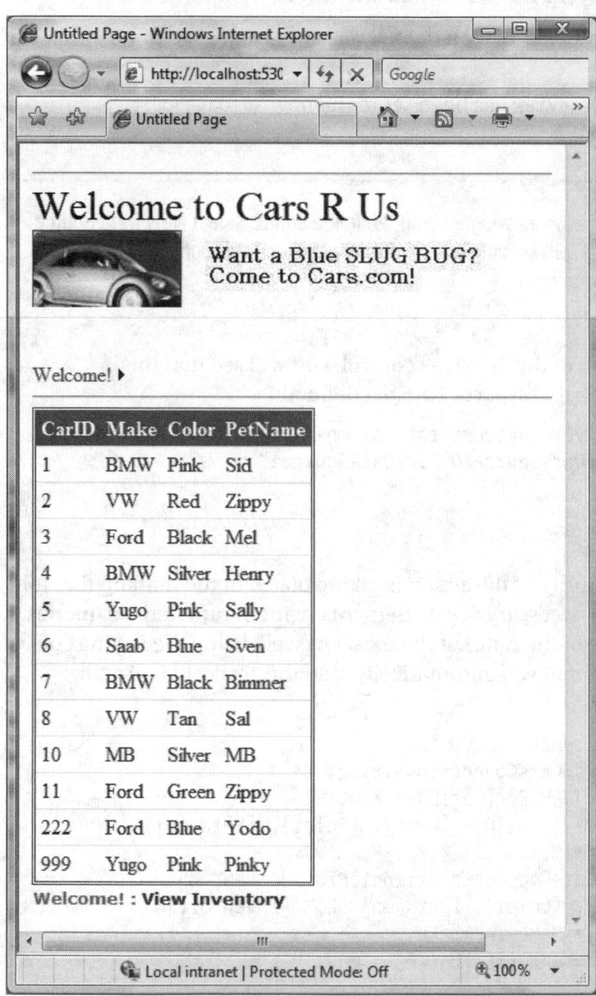

Figure 32-13. *The "zero-code" model of the* `SqlDataSource` *component*

Enabling Sorting and Paging

The `GridView` control can easily be configured for sorting (via column name hyperlinks) and paging (via numeric or next/previous hyperlinks). To do so, activate the inline editor and check the appropriate options, as shown in Figure 32-14.

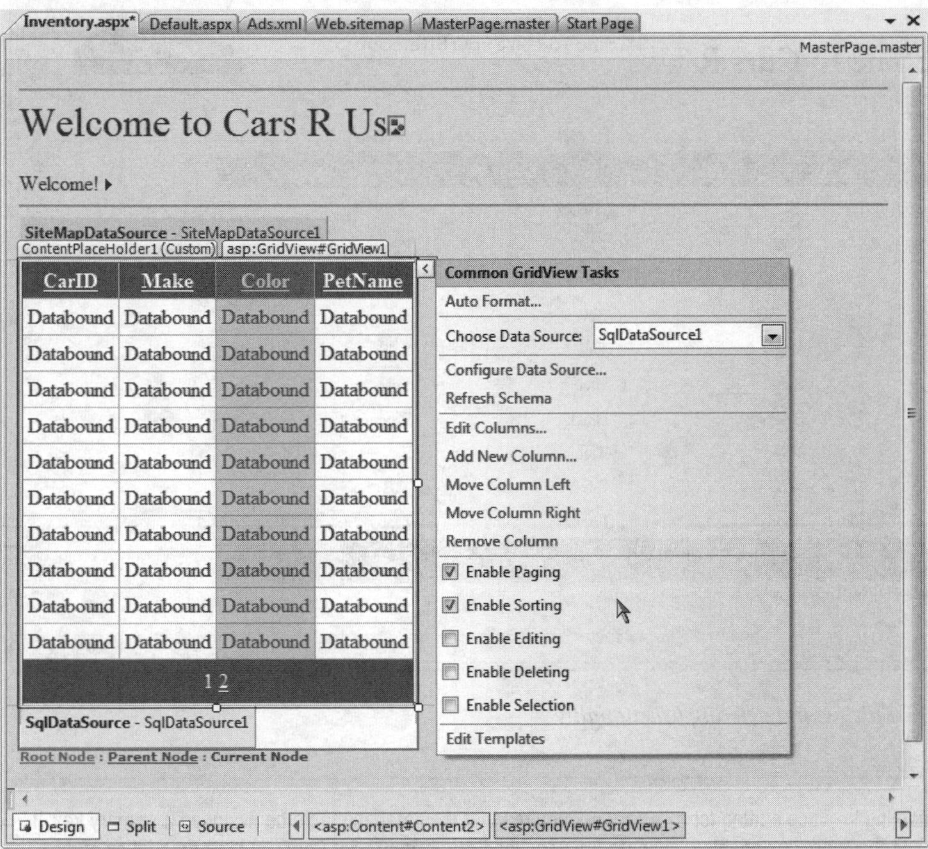

Figure 32-14. *Enabling sorting and paging*

When you run your page again, you will be able to sort your data by clicking the column names and scrolling through your data via the paging links (provided you have enough records in the Inventory table!).

Enabling In-Place Editing

The final detail of this page is to enable the `GridView` control's support for in-place activation. Given that your `SqlDataSource` already has the necessary `Delete` and `Update` logic, all you need to do is check the Enable Deleting and Enable Editing check boxes of the `GridView` (see Figure 32-14 for a reference point). Sure enough, when you navigate back to the `Inventory.aspx` page, you are able to edit and delete records, as shown in Figure 32-15, and update the underlying Inventory table of the AutoLot database.

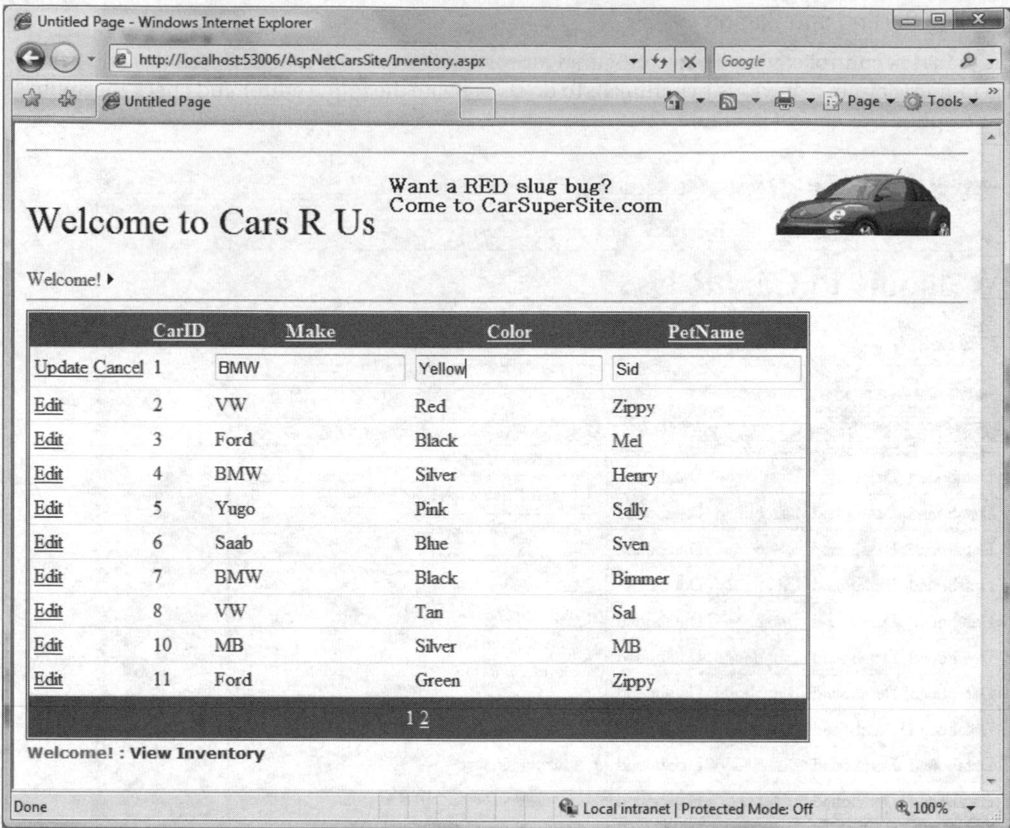

Figure 32-15. *Editing and deleting functionality*

■ **Note** Enabling in-place editing for a `GridView` requires that the database table be assigned a primary key. If you do not see these options enabled, chances are very good you forgot to set CarID as the primary key of the Inventory table within the AutoLot database.

Designing the Build-a-Car Content Page

The final task for this example is to design the `BuildCar.aspx` content page. Insert this file into the current project (via the Web Site ➤ Add Content Page menu option). This new page will make use of the ASP.NET `Wizard` web control, which provides a simple way to walk the end user through a series of related steps. Here, the steps in question will simulate the act of building an automobile for purchase.

Place a descriptive `Label` and `Wizard` control onto the content area. Next, activate the inline editor for the `Wizard` and click the Add/Remove WizardSteps link. Add a total of four steps, as shown in Figure 32-16.

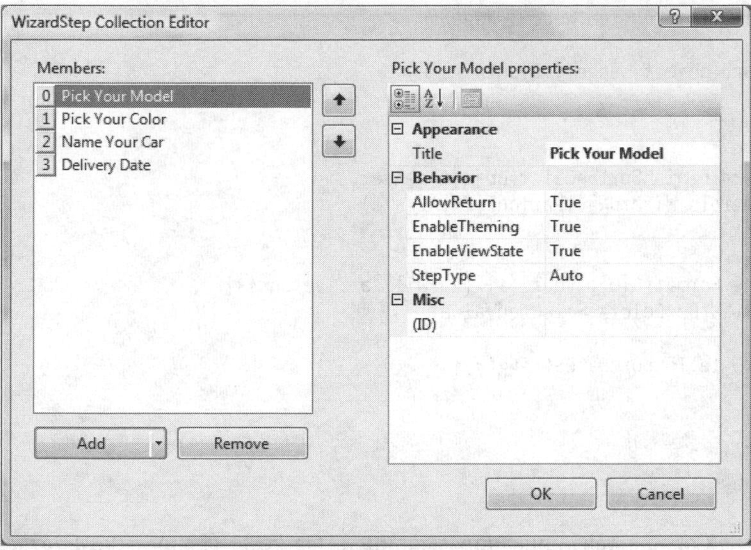

Figure 32-16. *Configurng our wizard*

Once you have defined these steps, you will notice that the Wizard defines an empty content area where you can now drag and drop controls for the currently selected step. For this example, update each step with the following UI elements (be sure to provide a descent ID value for each item using the Properties window):

- *Pick Your Model*: A TextBox control
- *Pick Your Color*: A ListBox control
- *Name Your Car*: A TextBox control
- *Delivery Date*: A Calendar control

The ListBox control is the only UI element of the Wizard that requires additional steps. Select this item on the designer (making sure you first select the Pick Your Color link) and fill this widget with a set of colors using the Items property of the Properties window. Once you do, you will find markup much like the following within the scope of the Wizard definition:

```
<asp:ListBox ID="ListBoxColors" runat="server" Width="237px">
  <asp:ListItem>Purple</asp:ListItem>
  <asp:ListItem>Green</asp:ListItem>
  <asp:ListItem>Red</asp:ListItem>
  <asp:ListItem>Yellow</asp:ListItem>
  <asp:ListItem>Pea Soup Green</asp:ListItem>
  <asp:ListItem>Black</asp:ListItem>
  <asp:ListItem>Lime Green</asp:ListItem>
</asp:ListBox>
```

Now that you have defined each of the steps, you can handle the FinishButtonClick event for the autogenerated Finish button. Within the server-side event handler, obtain the selections from each UI element and build a description string that is assigned to the Text property of an additional Label type named lblOrder:

```
public partial class Default2 : System.Web.UI.Page
{
  protected void Page_Load(object sender, EventArgs e)
  {
  }

  protected void carWizard_FinishButtonClick(object sender,
    System.Web.UI.WebControls.WizardNavigationEventArgs e)
  {
    // Get each value.
    string order = string.Format("{0}, your {1} {2} will arrive on {3}.",
    txtCarPetName.Text, ListBoxColors.SelectedValue,
    txtCarModel.Text,
    carCalendar.SelectedDate.ToShortDateString());

    // Assign to label
    lblOrder.Text = order;
  }
}
```

At this point your AspNetCarsSite web application is complete! Figure 32-17 shows the `Wizard` in action.

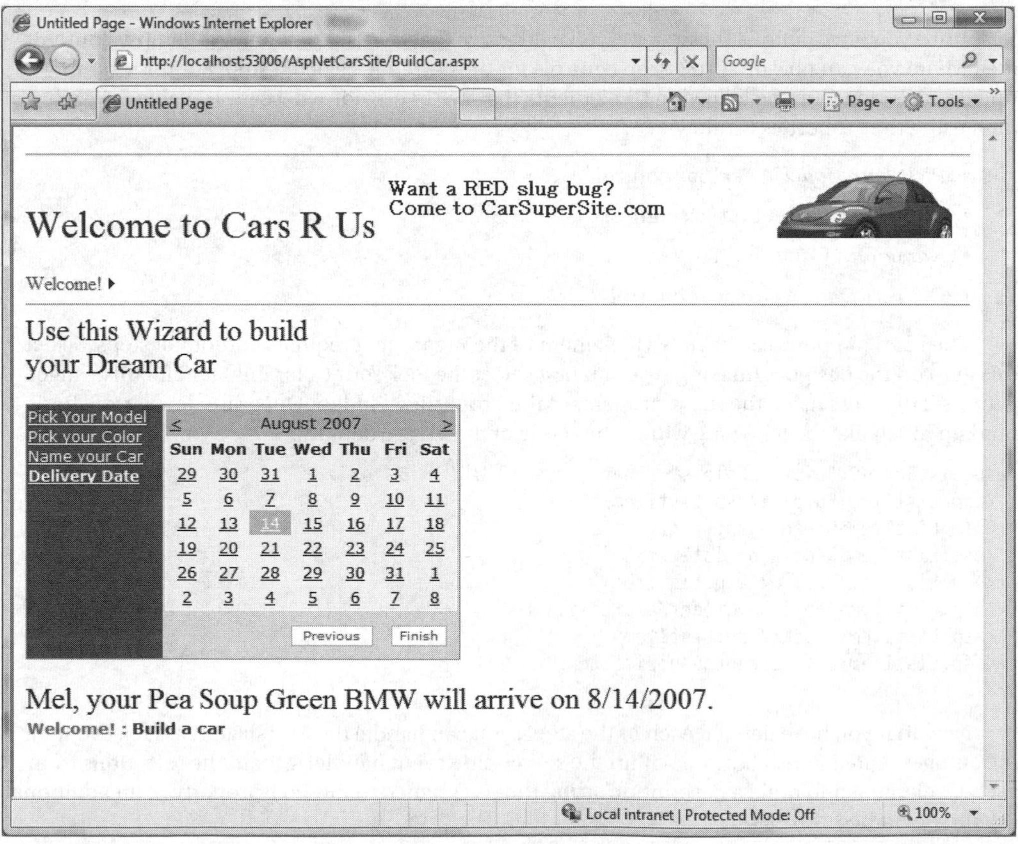

Figure 32-17. *The* `Wizard` *widget in action*

That wraps up our examination of various ASP.NET UI-centric web controls. Next up, let's look at the validation controls.

Source Code The AspNetCarsSite project is included under the Chapter 32 subdirectory.

The Role of the Validation Controls

The next set of Web Form controls we will examine are known collectively as *validation controls*. Unlike the other Web Form controls we've examined, validation controls are not used to emit HTML for rendering purposes, but are used to emit client-side JavaScript (and possibly related server-side code) for the purpose of form validation. As illustrated at the beginning of this chapter, client-side form validation is quite useful in that you can ensure that various constraints are in place before posting back to the web server, thereby avoiding expensive round-trips. Table 32-3 gives a rundown of the ASP.NET validation controls.

Table 32-3. *ASP.NET Validation Controls*

Control	Meaning in Life
`CompareValidator`	Validates that the value of an input control is equal to a given value of another input control or a fixed constant.
`CustomValidator`	Allows you to build a custom validation function that validates a given control.
`RangeValidator`	Determines that a given value is in a predetermined range.
`RegularExpressionValidator`	Checks whether the value of the associated input control matches the pattern of a regular expression.
`RequiredFieldValidator`	Ensures that a given input control contains a value (i.e., is not empty).
`ValidationSummary`	Displays a summary of all validation errors of a page in a list, bulleted list, or single-paragraph format. The errors can be displayed inline and/or in a pop-up message box.

All of the validation controls ultimately derive from a common base class named `System.Web.UI.WebControls.BaseValidator`, and therefore they have a set of common features. Table 32-4 documents the key members.

Table 32-4. *Common Properties of the ASP.NET Validators*

Member	Meaning in Life
`ControlToValidate`	Gets or sets the input control to validate
`Display`	Gets or sets the display behavior of the error message in a validation control
`EnableClientScript`	Gets or sets a value indicating whether client-side validation is enabled
`ErrorMessage`	Gets or sets the text for the error message
`ForeColor`	Gets or sets the color of the message displayed when validation fails

To illustrate working with these validation controls, create a new Web Site project named ValidatorCtrls. To begin, place four (well-named) `TextBox` types (with four corresponding and descriptive `Labels`) onto your page. Next, place a `RequiredFieldValidator`, `RangeValidator`, `RegularExpressionValidator`, and `CompareValidator` type adjacent to each respective field. Finally, add a single `Button` and final `Label` (see Figure 32-18).

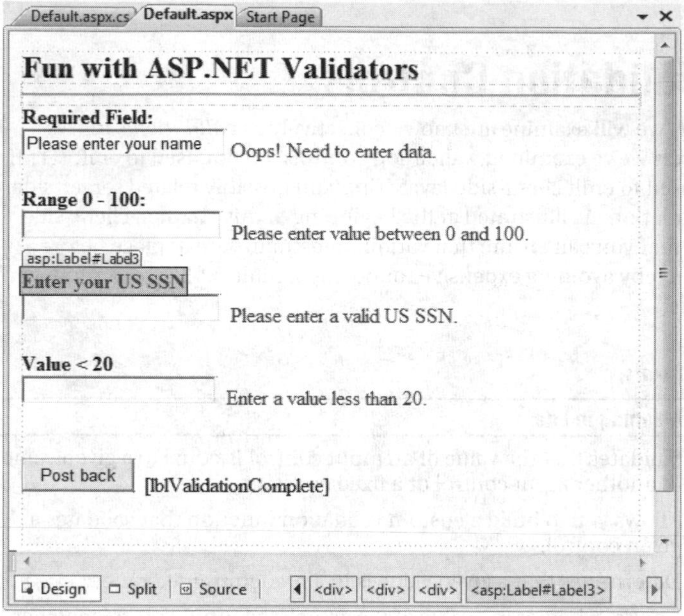

Figure 32-18. *Various validators*

Now that you have a UI, let's walk through the process of configuring each member.

The RequiredFieldValidator

Configuring the `RequiredFieldValidator` is straightforward. Simply set the `ErrorMessage` and `ControlToValidate` properties accordingly using the Visual Studio 2008 Properties window. Here would be the resulting markup to ensure the `txtRequiredField` text box is not empty:

```
<asp:RequiredFieldValidator ID="RequiredFieldValidator1"
  runat="server" ControlToValidate="txtRequiredField"
  ErrorMessage="Oops!  Need to enter data.">
</asp:RequiredFieldValidator>
```

The `RequiredFieldValidator` supports an `InitialValue` property. You can use this property to ensure that the user enters any value other than the initial value in the related `TextBox`. For example, when the user first posts to a page, you may wish to configure a `TextBox` to contain the value "Please enter your name". Now, if you did not set the `InitialValue` property of the `RequiredFieldValidator`, the runtime would assume that the string "Please enter your name" is valid. Thus, to ensure a required `TextBox` is valid only when the user enters anything other than "Please enter your name", configure your widgets as follows:

```
<asp:RequiredFieldValidator ID="RequiredFieldValidator1"
  runat="server" ControlToValidate="txtRequiredField"
  ErrorMessage="Oops!  Need to enter data."
  InitialValue="Please enter your name">
</asp:RequiredFieldValidator>
```

The RegularExpressionValidator

The `RegularExpressionValidator` can be used when you wish to apply a pattern against the characters entered within a given input field. To ensure that a given `TextBox` contains a valid US Social Security number, you could define the widget as follows:

```
<asp:RegularExpressionValidator ID="RegularExpressionValidator1"
  runat="server" ControlToValidate="txtRegExp"
  ErrorMessage="Please enter a valid US SSN."
  ValidationExpression="\d{3}-\d{2}-\d{4}">
</asp:RegularExpressionValidator>
```

Notice how the `RegularExpressionValidator` defines a `ValidationExpression` property. If you have never worked with regular expressions before, all you need to be aware of for this example is that they are used to match a given string pattern. Here, the expression `"\d{3}-\d{2}-\d{4}"` is capturing a standard US Social Security number of the form *xxx-xx-xxxx* (where *x* is any digit).

This particular regular expression is fairly self-explanatory; however, assume you wish to test for a valid Japanese phone number. The correct expression now becomes much more complex: `"(0\d{1,4}-|\(0\d{1,4}\)?)?\d{1,4}-\d{4}"`. The good news is that when you select the `ValidationExpression` property using the Properties window, you can pick from a predefined set of common regular expressions by clicking the ellipse button.

Note If you are interested in regular expressions, you will be happy to know that the .NET platform supplies two namespaces (`System.Text.RegularExpressions` and `System.Web.RegularExpressions`) devoted to the programmatic manipulation of such patterns.

The RangeValidator

In addition to a `MinimumValue` and `MaximumValue` property, `RangeValidators` have a property named `Type`. Because you are interested in testing the user-supplied input against a range of whole numbers, you need to specify `Integer` (which is *not* the default!):

```
<asp:RangeValidator ID="RangeValidator1"
  runat="server" ControlToValidate="txtRange"
  ErrorMessage="Please enter value between 0 and 100."
  MaximumValue="100" MinimumValue="0" Type="Integer">
</asp:RangeValidator>
```

The `RangeValidator` can also be used to test whether a given value is between a currency value, date, floating-point number, or string data (the default setting).

The CompareValidator

Finally, notice that the `CompareValidator` supports an `Operator` property:

```
<asp:CompareValidator ID="CompareValidator1" runat="server"
  ControlToValidate="txtComparison"
  ErrorMessage="Enter a value less than 20." Operator="LessThan"
  ValueToCompare="20">
</asp:CompareValidator>
```

Given that the role of this validator is to compare the value in the text box against another value using a binary operator, it should be no surprise that the `Operator` property may be set to values such as `LessThan`, `GreaterThan`, `Equal`, and `NotEqual`. Also note that the `ValueToCompare` is used to establish a value to compare against.

■ Note The `CompareValidator` can also be configured to compare a value within another Web Form control (rather than a hard-coded value) using the `ControlToValidate` property.

To finish up the code for this page, handle the `Click` event for the `Button` type and inform the user he or she has succeeded in the validation logic:

```
public partial class _Default : System.Web.UI.Page
{
  protected void Page_Load(object sender, EventArgs e)
  {

  }
  protected void btnPostback_Click(object sender, EventArgs e)
  {
    lblValidationComplete.Text = "You passed validation!";
  }
}
```

Now, navigate to this page using your browser of choice. At this point, you should not see any noticeable changes. However, when you attempt to click the Submit button after entering bogus data, your error message is suddenly visible. Once you enter valid data, the error messages are removed and postback occurs.

If you look at the HTML rendered by the browser, you see that the validation controls generate a client-side JavaScript function that makes use of a specific library of JavaScript functions (contained in the `WebUIValidation.js` file) that is automatically downloaded to the user's machine. Once the validation has occurred, the form data is posted back to the server, where the ASP.NET runtime will perform the *same* validation tests on the web server (just to ensure that no along-the-wire tampering has taken place).

On a related note, if the HTTP request was sent by a browser that does not support client-side JavaScript, all validation will occur on the server. In this way, you can program against the validation controls without being concerned with the target browser; the returned HTML page redirects the error processing back to the web server.

Creating Validation Summaries

The next validation-centric topic we will examine here is the use of the `ValidationSummary` widget. Currently, each of your validators displays its error message at the exact place in which it was positioned at design time. In many cases, this may be exactly what you are looking for. However, on a complex form with numerous input widgets, you may not want to have random blobs of red text pop up. Using the `ValidationSummary` type, you can instruct all of your validation types to display their error messages at a specific location on the page.

The first step is to simply place a ValidationSummary on your *.aspx file. You may optionally set the HeaderText property of this type as well as the DisplayMode, which by default will list all error messages as a bulleted list.

```
<asp:ValidationSummary id="ValidationSummary1"
  runat="server" Width="353px"
  HeaderText="Here are the things you must correct.">
</asp:ValidationSummary>
```

Next, you need to set the Display property to None for each of the individual validators (e.g., RequiredFieldValidator, RangeValidator, etc.) on the page. This will ensure that you do not see duplicate error messages for a given validation failure (one in the summary pane and another at the validator's location). Figure 32-19 shows the summary pane in action.

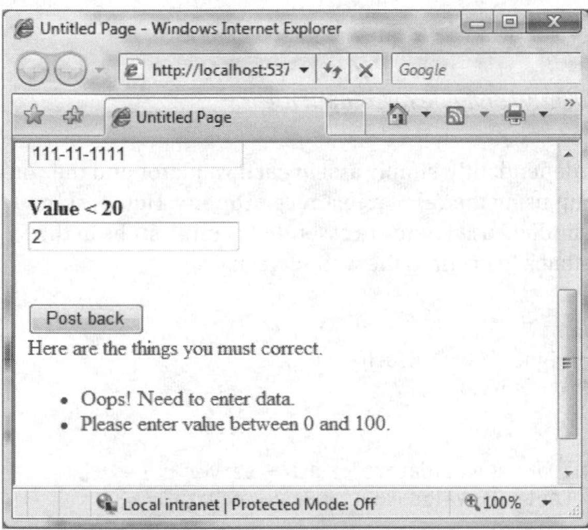

Figure 32-19. *Using a validation summary*

Last but not least, if you would rather have the error messages displayed using a client-side MessageBox, set the ShowMessageBox property to true and the ShowSummary property to false.

Defining Validation Groups

It is also possible to define *groups* for validators to belong to. This can be very helpful when you have regions of a page that work as a collective whole. For example, you may have one group of controls in a Panel object to allow the user to enter his or her mailing address and another Panel containing UI elements to gather credit card information. Using groups, you can configure each group of controls to be validated independently.

Insert a new page into your current project named ValidationGroups.aspx that defines two Panels. The first Panel object expects a TextBox to contain some form of user input (via a RequiredFieldValidator), while the second Panel expects a US SSN value (via a RegularExpressionValidator). Figure 32-20 shows one possible UI.

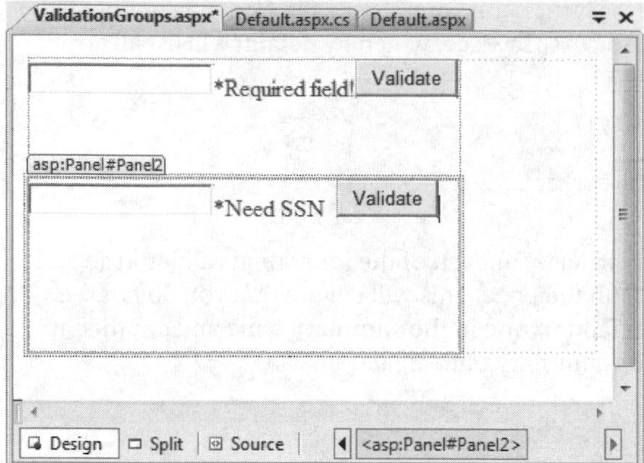

Figure 32-20. *These* `Panel` *objects will independently configure their input areas.*

To ensure that the validators function independently, simply assign each validator and the control being validated to a uniquely named group using the `ValidationGroup` property. Here is some possible markup (note that the `Click` event handlers used here are essentially empty stubs in the code file, and they are only used to allow postback to occur to the web server):

```
<form id="form1" runat="server">

  <asp:Panel ID="Panel1" runat="server" Height="83px" Width="296px">
    <asp:TextBox ID="txtRequiredData" runat="server"
         ValidationGroup="FirstGroup">
    </asp:TextBox>
    <asp:RequiredFieldValidator ID="RequiredFieldValidator1" runat="server"
         ErrorMessage="*Required field!" ControlToValidate="txtRequiredData"
         ValidationGroup="FirstGroup">
    </asp:RequiredFieldValidator>
    <asp:Button ID="bntValidateRequired" runat="server"
         OnClick="bntValidateRequired_Click"
         Text="Validate" ValidationGroup="FirstGroup" />
  </asp:Panel>

  <asp:Panel ID="Panel2" runat="server" Height="119px" Width="295px">
    <asp:TextBox ID="txtSSN" runat="server"
         ValidationGroup="SecondGroup">
    </asp:TextBox>
    <asp:RegularExpressionValidator ID="RegularExpressionValidator1"
         runat="server" ControlToValidate="txtSSN"
         ErrorMessage="*Need SSN" ValidationExpression="\d{3}-\d{2}-\d{4}"
         ValidationGroup="SecondGroup">
    </asp:RegularExpressionValidator> 
    <asp:Button ID="btnValidateSSN" runat="server"
         OnClick="btnValidateSSN_Click" Text="Validate"
         ValidationGroup="SecondGroup" />
  </asp:Panel>

</form>
```

Now, right-click this page's designer and select the View In Browser menu option to verify each panel's widgets operate in a mutually exclusive manner.

■ **Source Code** The ValidatorCtrls project is included under the Chapter 32 subdirectory.

Working with Themes

At this point, you have had the chance to work with numerous ASP.NET web controls. As you have seen, each control exposes a set of properties (many of which are inherited by `System.Web.UI.WebControls.WebControl`) that allow you to establish a given UI look and feel (background color, font size, border style, and whatnot). Of course, on a multipaged website, it is quite common for the site as a whole to define a common look and feel for various types of widgets. For example, all `TextBoxes` might be configured to support a given font, all `Buttons` have a custom image, and all `Calendars` have a light blue border.

Obviously it would be very labor intensive (and error prone) to establish the *same* property settings for every widget on *every* page within your website. Even if you were able to manually update the properties of each UI widget on each page, imagine how painful it would be when you now need to change the background color for each `TextBox` yet again. Clearly there must be a better way to apply sitewide UI settings.

One approach that can be taken to simplify applying a common UI look and feel is to define *style sheets*. If you have a background in web development, you are aware that style sheets define a common set of UI-centric settings that are applied on the browser. As you would hope, ASP.NET web controls can be assigned a given style by assigning the `CssStyle` property.

However, ASP.NET ships with an alternative technology to define a common UI termed *themes*. Unlike a style sheet, themes are applied on the web server (rather than the browser) and can be done so programmatically or declaratively. Given that a theme is applied on the web server, it has access to all the server-side resources on the website. Furthermore, themes are defined by authoring the same markup you would find within any `*.aspx` file (as you may agree, the syntax of a style sheet is a bit on the terse side).

Recall from Chapter 31 that ASP.NET web applications may define any number of "special" subdirectories, one of which is App_Theme. This single subdirectory may be further partitioned with additional subdirectories, each of which represents a possible theme on your site. For example, consider Figure 32-21, which illustrates a single App_Theme folder containing three subdirectories, each of which has a set of files that make up the theme itself.

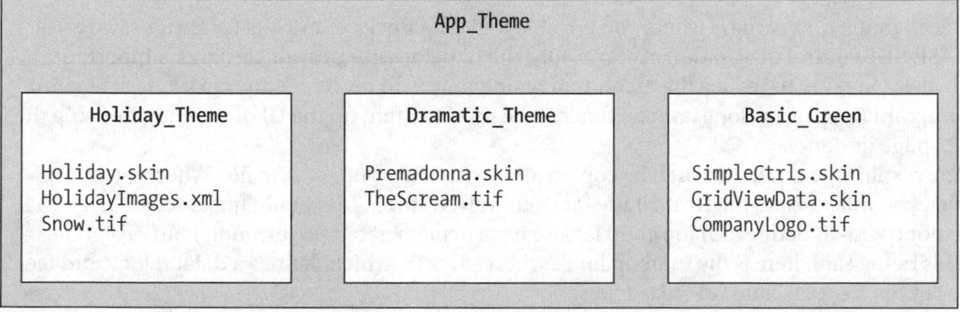

Figure 32-21. *A single App_Theme folder may define numerous themes.*

Understanding *.skin Files

The one file that every theme subdirectory is sure to have is a `*.skin` file. These files define the look and feel for various web controls. To illustrate, create a new website named FunWithThemes. Next, insert a new `*.skin` file (using the Web Site ➤ Add New Item menu option) named `BasicGreen.skin`, as shown in Figure 32-22.

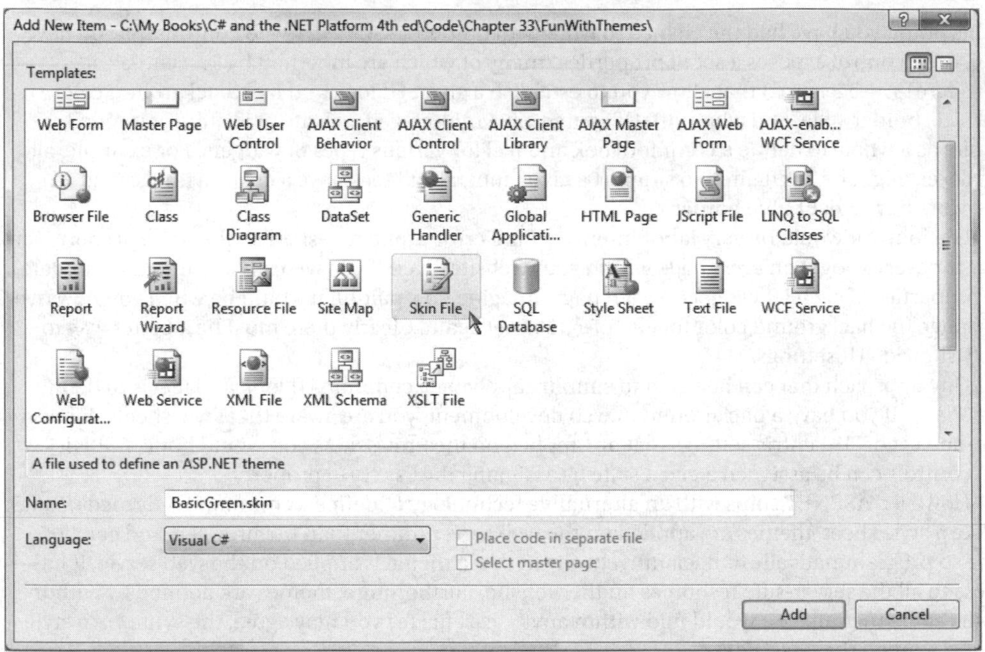

Figure 32-22. *Inserting* `*.skin` *files*

Visual Studio 2008 will prompt you to confirm this file can be added into an App_Theme folder (which is exactly what we want). If you were now to look in your Solution Explorer, you would indeed find your App_Theme folder has a subfolder named BasicGreen containing your new `BasicGreen.skin` file.

Recall that a `*.skin` file is where you are able to define the look and feel for various widgets using ASP.NET control declaration syntax. Sadly, the IDE does not provide designer support for `*.skin` files. One way to reduce the amount of typing time is to insert a temporary `*.aspx` file into your program (`temp.aspx`, for example) that can be used to build up the UI of the widgets using the VS 2005 page designer.

The resulting markup can then be copied and pasted into your `*.skin` file. When you do so, however, you *must* delete the `ID` attribute for each web control! This should make sense, given that we are not trying to define a UI look and feel for a particular `Button` (for example) but *all* `Buttons`.

This being said, here is the markup for `BasicGreen.skin`, which defines a default look and feel for the `Button`, `TextBox`, and `Calendar` types:

```
<asp:Button runat="server" BackColor="#80FF80"/>
<asp:TextBox runat="server" BackColor="#80FF80"/>
<asp:Calendar runat="server" BackColor="#80FF80"/>
```

Notice that each widget still has the `runat="server"` attribute (which is mandatory), and none of the widgets have been assigned an `ID` attribute.

Now, let's define a second theme named CrazyOrange. Using the Solution Explorer, right-click your App_Theme folder and add a new theme named CrazyOrange. This will create a new subdirectory under your site's App_Theme folder. Next, right-click the new CrazyOrange folder within the Solution Explorer and select Add New Item. From the resulting dialog box, add a new `*.skin` file. Update the `CrazyOrange.skin` file to define a unique UI look and feel for the same web controls. For example:

```
<asp:Button runat="server" BackColor="#FF8000"/>
<asp:TextBox runat="server" BackColor="#FF8000"/>
<asp:Calendar BackColor="White" BorderColor="Black"
  BorderStyle="Solid" CellSpacing="1"
  Font-Names="Verdana" Font-Size="9pt" ForeColor="Black" Height="250px"
  NextPrevFormat="ShortMonth" Width="330px" runat="server">
  <SelectedDayStyle BackColor="#333399" ForeColor="White" />
  <OtherMonthDayStyle ForeColor="#999999" />
  <TodayDayStyle BackColor="#999999" ForeColor="White" />
  <DayStyle BackColor="#CCCCCC" />
  <NextPrevStyle Font-Bold="True" Font-Size="8pt" ForeColor="White" />
  <DayHeaderStyle Font-Bold="True" Font-Size="8pt"
    ForeColor="#333333" Height="8pt" />
  <TitleStyle BackColor="#333399" BorderStyle="Solid"
    Font-Bold="True" Font-Size="12pt"
    ForeColor="White" Height="12pt" />
</asp:Calendar>
```

At this point, your Solution Explorer should like Figure 32-23.

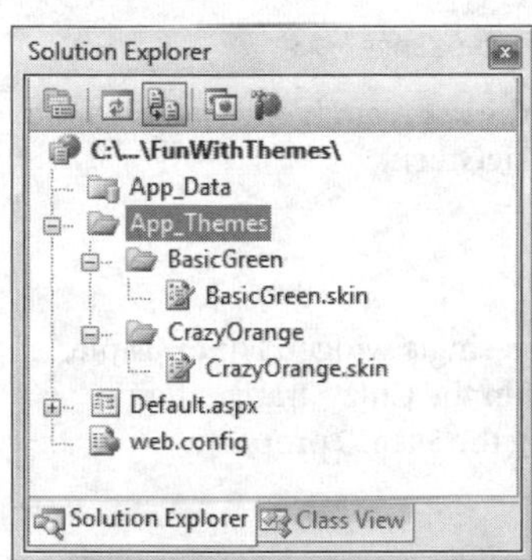

Figure 32-23. *A single website with multiple themes*

So now that your site has a few themes defined, the next logical question is how to apply them to your pages? As you might guess, there are many ways to do so.

■ **Note** To be sure, these example themes are quite bland. Feel free to spruce things up to your liking.

Applying Sitewide Themes

If you wish to make sure that every page in your site adheres to the same theme, the simplest way to do so is to update your `web.config` file. Open your current `web.config` file and locate the `<pages>` element within the scope of your `<system.web>` root element. If you add a theme attribute to the

<pages> element, this will ensure that every page in your website is assigned the selected theme (which is, of course, the name of one of the subdirectories under App_Theme). Here is the core update:

```
<configuration>
  <system.web>
    ...
    <pages theme="BasicGreen">
      ...
    </pages>
  </system.web>
</configuration>
```

If you were to now place various Buttons, Calendars, and TextBoxes onto your Default.aspx file and run the application, you would find each widget has the UI of BasicGreen. If you were to update the theme attribute to CrazyOrange and run the page again, you would find the UI defined by this theme is used instead.

Applying Themes at the Page Level

It is also possible to assign themes on a page-by-page level. This can be helpful in a variety of circumstances. For example, perhaps your web.config file defines a sitewide theme (as described in the previous section); however, you wish to assign a different theme to a specific page. To do so, you can simply update the <%@Page%> directive. If you are using Visual Studio 2008 to do so, you will be happy to find that IntelliSense will display each defined theme within your App_Theme folder.

```
<%@ Page Language="C#" AutoEventWireup="true"
    CodeFile="Default.aspx.cs" Inherits="_Default" Theme ="CrazyOrange" %>
```

Because we assigned the CrazyOrange theme to this page, but the Web.config file specified the BasicGreen theme, all pages *but this page* will be rendered using BasicGreen.

The SkinID Property

Sometimes you wish to define a set of possible UI look and feels for a single widget. For example, assume you want to define two possible UIs for the Button type within the CrazyOrange theme. When you wish do so, you may differentiate each look and feel using the SkinID property:

```
<asp:Button runat="server" BackColor="#FF8000"/>
<asp:Button runat="server" SkinID = "BigFontButton"
  Font-Size="30pt" BackColor="#FF8000"/>
```

Now, if you have a page that makes use of the CrazyOrange theme, each Button will by default be assigned the unnamed Button skin. If you wish to have various buttons within the *.aspx file make use of the BigFontButton skin, simply specify the SkinID property within the markup:

```
<asp:Button ID="Button2" runat="server"
  SkinID="BigFontButton" Text="Button" /><br />
```

As an example, Figure 32-24 shows a page that is making use of the CrazyOrange theme. The topmost Button is assigned the unnamed Button skin, while the Button on the bottom of the page has been assigned the SkinID of BigFontButton.

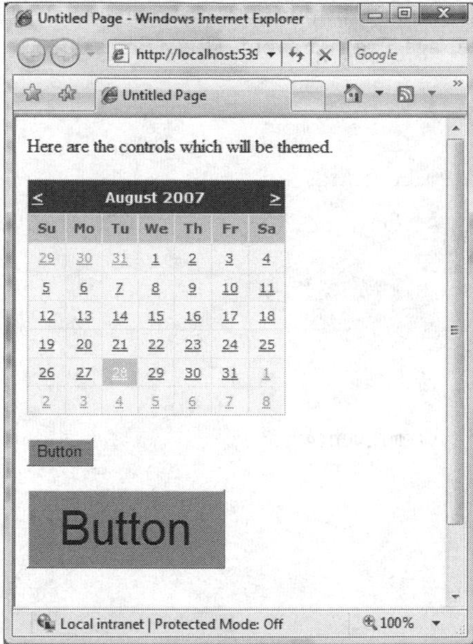

Figure 32-24. *Fun with* `SkinIDs`

Assigning Themes Programmatically

Last but not least, it is possible to assign a theme in code. This can be helpful when you wish to provide a way for end users to select a theme for their current session. Of course, we have not yet examined how to build stateful web applications, so the current theme selection will be forgotten between postbacks. In a production-level site, you may wish to store the user's current theme selection within a session variable, or persist the theme selection to a database.

Although we really have not examined the use of session variables at this point in the text, to illustrate how to assign a theme programmatically, update the UI of your `Default.aspx` file with three new `Button` types as shown in Figure 32-25. Once you have done so, handle the `Click` event for each `Button` type.

Figure 32-25. *The updated UI*

Now be aware that you can only assign a theme programmatically during specific phases of your page's life cycle. Typically, this will be done within the `Page_PreInit` event. This being said, update your code file as follows:

```
partial class _Default : System.Web.UI.Page
{
  protected void btnNoTheme_Click(object sender, System.EventArgs e)
  {
    // Empty strings result in no theme being applied.
    Session["UserTheme"] = "";

    // Triggers the PreInit event again.
    Server.Transfer(Request.FilePath);
  }

  protected void btnGreenTheme_Click(object sender, System.EventArgs e)
  {
    Session["UserTheme"] = "BasicGreen";

    // Triggers the PreInit event again.
    Server.Transfer(Request.FilePath);
  }

  protected void btnOrangeTheme_Click(object sender, System.EventArgs e)
  {
    Session["UserTheme"] = "CrazyOrange";

    // Triggers the PreInit event again.
    Server.Transfer(Request.FilePath);
  }

  protected void Page_PreInit(object sender, System.EventArgs e)
  {
    try
    {
      Theme = Session["UserTheme"].ToString();
    }
    catch
    {
      Theme = "";
    }
  }
}
```

Notice that we are storing the selected theme within a session variable (see Chapter 33 for details) named `UserTheme`, which is formally assigned within the `Page_PreInit()` event handler. Also note that when the user clicks a given `Button`, we programmatically force the `PreInit` event to fire by calling `Server.Transfer()` and requesting the current page once again. If you were to run this page, you would now find that you can establish your theme via various `Button` clicks.

Source Code The FunWithThemes project is included under the Chapter 32 subdirectory.

Positioning Controls Using HTML Tables

If you are new to web development, you may have quickly noticed that positioning controls on a designer surface is far from intuitive. For example, unlike with Windows Forms, you cannot (by default) drag a UI element from the Toolbox and position it *exactly* where you want to (which as you might agree is quite frustrating).

Earlier versions of ASP.NET provided two modes of positioning (`GridLayout` and `FlowLayout`) that could be set via the `pageLayout` attribute of the `DOCUMENT`. When set to `GridLayout`, absolute positioning was possible using DHTML. This, however, made ASP.NET 1.*x* web pages limited to browsers that supported dynamic HTML. `FlowLayout` (the current default mode for ASP.NET) does *not* provide for absolute position . . . which can be frustrating to develop with; however, it does ensure every browser can correctly display the web content.

Strictly speaking, ASP.NET does still allow developers to define controls (manually) using `GridLayout` semantics. However, the designers will complain, as the necessary infrastructure is not considered valid within the XHTML specification. For example, consider the following `*.aspx` file, which makes use of the `style` attribute to provide absolute position to a `Button` type using the `style` attribute of the `Button` type:

```
<body MS_POSITIONING="GridLayout">
  <form id="Form2" method="post" runat="server">

    <asp:Button id="Button1" runat="server" Text="Button"
      style="Z-INDEX: 101; LEFT: 106px; POSITION: absolute; TOP: 79px">
    </asp:Button>

    <asp:TextBox id="TextBox1" runat="server">
    </asp:TextBox>
  </form>
</body>
```

Rather than making use of non–XHTML-compliant code (and risk the chance of not working within every browser), many web developers place widgets within HTML tables. The HTML table is not literally visible in the browser; however, at design time, controls may be placed within the cells to provide a level of absolute positioning.

Better yet, Visual Studio 2008 allows you to edit and manipulate these cells visually in a manner similar to an Excel spreadsheet. For example, the Tab key moves you between each cell, and selecting multiple cells allows you to merge/resize them via the context menu. Furthermore, each cell can be customized with various styles via the Properties window. By way of a quick example, consider the designer snapshot of an HTML table control on an arbitrary `*.aspx` file shown in Figure 32-26.

Once you have configured the cells of your table (which typically include other nested tables), you are then able to arrange the ASP.NET web controls in a manner of your choice. The benefit is that as the user resizes the web browser, the controls retain their relative positioning.

Note The remaining examples of this section of the book do not require you to design pages using HTML tables; however, you should be aware of their usefulness in web development.

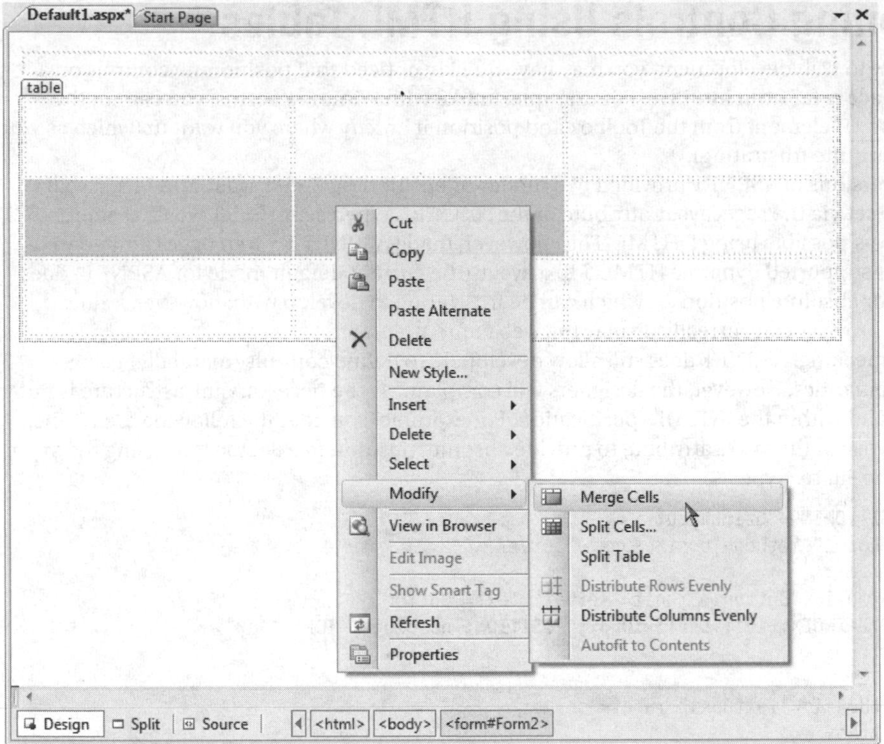

Figure 32-26. *Visual Studio 2008 provides excellent HTML table configuration support.*

Summary

This chapter examined how to make use of various ASP.NET web controls. We began by examining the role of the `Control` and `WebControl` base classes, and you came to learn how to dynamically interact with a panel's internal controls collection. Along the way, you were exposed to the new site navigation model (`*.sitemap` files and the `SiteMapDataSource` component), the new data binding engine (via the `SqlDataSource` component and the new `GridView` type), and various validation controls.

The latter half of this chapter examined the role of master pages and themes. Recall that master pages can be used to define a common frame for a set of pages on your site. Also recall that the `*.master` file defines any number of "content placeholders" to which content pages plug in their custom UI content. Finally, as you were shown, the ASP.NET theme engine allows you to declaratively or programmatically apply a common UI look and feel to your widgets on the web server.

CHAPTER 33

ASP.NET State Management Techniques

The previous two chapters concentrated on the composition and behavior of ASP.NET pages and the web controls they contain. This chapter builds on that information by examining the role of the Global.asax file and the underlying HttpApplication type. As you will see, the functionality of HttpApplication allows you to intercept numerous events that enable you to treat your web applications as a cohesive unit, rather than a set of stand-alone *.aspx files.

In addition to investigating the HttpApplication type, this chapter also addresses the all-important topic of state management. Here you will learn the role of view state, session and application variables (including the application cache), cookie data, and the ASP.NET Profile API.

The Issue of State

At the beginning of the Chapter 31, I pointed out that HTTP on the Web results in a *stateless* wire protocol. This very fact makes web development extremely different from the process of building an executable assembly. For example, when you are building a Windows Forms application, you can rest assured that any member variables defined in the Form-derived class will typically exist in memory until the user explicitly shuts down the executable:

```
public partial class MainWindow : System.Windows.Forms.Form
{
  // State data!
  private string userFavoriteCar = "Yugo";
}
```

In the world of the World Wide Web, however, you are not afforded the same luxurious assumption. To prove the point, create a new ASP.NET website named SimpleStateExample. Within the code-behind file of your initial *.aspx file, define a page-level string variable named userFavoriteCar:

```
public partial class _Default : System.Web.UI.Page
{
  // State data?
  private string userFavoriteCar = "Yugo";

  protected void Page_Load(object sender, EventArgs e)
  {

  }
}
```

Next, construct the web UI as shown in Figure 33-1.

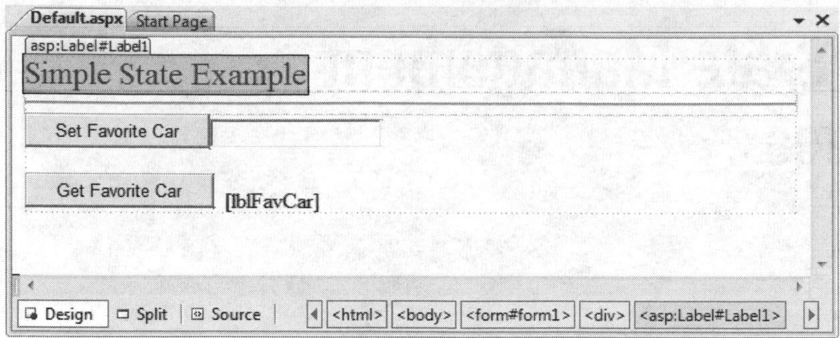

Figure 33-1. *The UI for the simple state page*

The server-side `Click` event handler for the Set button (named `btnSetCar`) will allow the user to assign the `string` member variable to the value within the `TextBox` (named `txtFavCar`):

```
protected void btnSetCar_Click(object sender, EventArgs e)
{
  // Store fave car in member variable.
  userFavoriteCar = txtFavCar.Text;
}
```

while the `Click` event handler for the Get button (`btnGetCar`) will display the current value of the member variable within the page's `Label` widget (`lblFavCar`):

```
protected void btnGetCar_Click(object sender, EventArgs e)
{
  // Show value of member variable.
  lblFavCar.Text = userFavoriteCar;
}
```

Now, if you were building a Windows Forms application, you would be right to assume that once the user sets the initial value, it would be remembered throughout the life of the desktop application. Sadly, when you run this web application, you will find that each time you post back to the web server (by clicking either button), the value of the `userFavoriteCar` string variable is set back to the initial value of "Yugo"; therefore, the `Label`'s text is continuously fixed.

Again, given that HTTP has no clue how to automatically remember data once the HTTP response has been sent, it stands to reason that the `Page` object is destroyed almost instantly. Therefore, when the client posts back to the `*.aspx` file, a new `Page` object is constructed that will reset any page-level member variables. This is clearly a major dilemma. Imagine how useless online shopping would be if every time you posted back to the web server, any and all information you previously entered (such as the items you wished to purchase) were discarded. When you wish to remember information regarding the users who are logged on to your site, you need to make use of various state management techniques.

■ **Note** This issue is in no way limited to ASP.NET. Java servlets, CGI applications, classic ASP, and PHP applications all must contend with the thorny issue of state management.

To remember the value of the userFavoriteCar string type between postbacks, you are required to store the value of this string type within a *session variable*. You will examine the exact details of session state in the pages that follow. For the sake of completion, however, here are the necessary updates for the current page (note that you are no longer using the private string member variable, therefore feel free to comment out or remove the definition altogether):

```
public partial class _Default : System.Web.UI.Page
{
  // State data?
  // private string userFavoriteCar = "Yugo";

  protected void Page_Load(object sender, EventArgs e)
  {

  }

  protected void btnSetCar_Click(object sender, EventArgs e)
  {
    // Store value to be remembered in session variable.
    Session["UserFavCar"] = txtFavCar.Text;
  }

  protected void btnGetCar_Click(object sender, EventArgs e)
  {
    // Get session variable value.
    lblFavCar.Text = (string)Session["UserFavCar"];
  }
}
```

If you now run the application, the value of your favorite automobile will be preserved across postbacks, thanks to the HttpSessionState object manipulated indirectly by the inherited Session property.

Source Code The SimpleStateExample project is included under the Chapter 33 subdirectory.

ASP.NET State Management Techniques

ASP.NET provides several mechanisms that you can use to maintain stateful information in your web applications. Specifically, you have the following options:

- Make use of ASP.NET view state.
- Make use of ASP.NET control state.
- Define application-level variables.
- Make use of the cache object.
- Define session-level variables.
- Define cookie data.

The one thing these approaches have in common is that they each demand that a given user is in session and that the web application is loaded into memory. As soon as a user logs off (or times out) from your site (or your website is shut down), your site is once again stateless. If you wish to persist user data in a permanent manner, ASP.NET provides an out-of-the-box Profile API. We'll examine the details of each approach in turn, beginning with the topic of ASP.NET view state.

Understanding the Role of ASP.NET View State

The term *view state* has been thrown out a few times here and in the previous two chapters without a formal definition, so let's demystify this term once and for all. Under classic (COM-based) ASP, web developers were required to manually repopulate the values of the incoming form widgets during the process of constructing the outgoing HTTP response. For example, if the incoming HTTP request contained five text boxes with specific values, the `*.asp` file required script code to extract the current values (via the `Form` or `QueryString` collections of the `Request` object) and manually place them back into the HTTP response stream (needless to say, this was a drag). If the developer failed to do so, the caller was presented with a set of five empty text boxes!

Under ASP.NET, we are no longer required to manually scrape out and repopulate the values contained within the HTML widgets because the ASP.NET runtime will automatically embed a hidden form field (named `__VIEWSTATE`), which will flow between the browser and a specific page. The data assigned to this field is a Base64-encoded string that contains a set of name/value pairs that represent the values of each GUI widget on the page at hand.

The `System.Web.UI.Page` base class's `Init` event handler is the entity in charge of reading the incoming values found within the `__VIEWSTATE` field to populate the appropriate member variables in the derived class (which is why it is risky at best to access the state of a web widget within the scope of a page's `Init` event handler).

Also, just before the outgoing response is emitted back to the requesting browser, the `__VIEWSTATE` data is used to repopulate the form's widgets, to ensure that the current values of the HTML widgets appear as they did prior to the previous postback.

Clearly, the best thing about this aspect of ASP.NET is that it just happens without any work on your part. Of course, you are always able to interact with, alter, or disable this default functionality if you so choose. To understand how to do this, let's see a concrete view state example.

Demonstrating View State

First, create a new ASP.NET web application called ViewStateApp. On your initial `*.aspx` page, add a single ASP.NET `ListBox` web control (named `myListBox`) and a single `Button` type (named `btnPostback`). Handle the `Click` event for the `Button` to provide a way for the user to post back to the web server:

```
public partial class _Default : System.Web.UI.Page
{
  protected void Page_Load(object sender, EventArgs e)
  {
  }
  protected void btnPostback_Click(object sender, EventArgs e)
  {
    // No-op. This is just here to allow a postback.
  }
}
```

Now, using the Visual Studio 2008 Properties window, access the `Items` property and add four `ListItems` to the `ListBox` using the associated dialog box. The resulting markup looks like this:

```
<asp:ListBox ID="myListBox" runat="server">
  <asp:ListItem>Item One</asp:ListItem>
  <asp:ListItem>Item Two</asp:ListItem>
```

```
  <asp:ListItem>Item Three</asp:ListItem>
  <asp:ListItem>Item Four</asp:ListItem>
</asp:ListBox>
```

Note that you are hard-coding the items in the ListBox directly within the *.aspx file. As you already know, all <asp:> definitions found within an HTML form will automatically render back their HTML representation before the final HTTP response (provided they have the runat="server" attribute).

The <%@Page%> directive has an optional attribute called EnableViewState that by default is set to true. To disable this behavior, simply update the <%@Page%> directive as follows:

```
<%@ Page Language="C#" AutoEventWireup="true"
  CodeFile="Default.aspx.cs" Inherits="_Default"
  EnableViewState ="false" %>
```

So, what exactly does it mean to disable view state? The answer is, it depends. Given the previous definition of the term, you would think that if you disable view state for an *.aspx file, the values within your ListBox would not be remembered between postbacks to the web server. However, if you were to run this application as is, you might be surprised to find that the information in the ListBox is retained regardless of how many times you post back to the page.

In fact, if you examine the source HTML returned to the browser (by right-clicking the page within the browser and selecting View Source), you may be further surprised to see that the hidden __VIEWSTATE field is *still present*:

```
<input type="hidden" name="__VIEWSTATE" id="__VIEWSTATE"
 value="/wEPDwUKLTM4MTM2MDM4NGRkqGC6gjEV25JnddkJiRmoIc1OSIA=" />
```

The reason the view state string is still visible is the fact that the *.aspx file has explicitly defined the ListBox items within the scope of the HTML <form> tags. Thus, the ListBox items will be autogenerated each time the web server responds to the client.

However, assume that your ListBox is dynamically populated within the code-behind file rather than within the HTML <form> definition. First, remove the <asp:ListItem> declarations from the current *.aspx file:

```
<asp:ListBox ID="myListBox" runat="server">
</asp:ListBox>
```

Next, fill the list items within the Load event handler within your code-behind file:

```
protected void Page_Load(object sender, EventArgs e)
{
  if (!IsPostBack)
  {
    // Fill ListBox dynamically!
    myListBox.Items.Add("Item One");
    myListBox.Items.Add("Item Two");
    myListBox.Items.Add("Item Three");
    myListBox.Items.Add("Item Four");
  }
}
```

If you post to this updated page, you will find that the first time the browser requests the page, the values in the ListBox are present and accounted for. However, on postback, the ListBox is suddenly empty. The first rule of ASP.NET view state is that its effect is only realized when you have widgets whose values are dynamically generated through code. If you hard-code values within the *.aspx file's <form> tags, the state of these items is always remembered across postbacks (even when you set EnableViewState to false for a given page).

Furthermore, view state is most useful when you have a dynamically populated web widget that always needs to be repopulated for each and every postback (such as an ASP.NET GridView, which is always filled using a database hit). If you did not disable view state for pages that contain such widgets, the entire state of the grid is represented within the hidden __VIEWSTATE field. Given that complex pages may contain numerous ASP.NET web controls, you can imagine how large this string would become. As the payload of the HTTP request/response cycle could become quite heavy, this may become a problem for the dial-up web surfers of the world. In cases such as these, you may find faster throughput if you disable view state for the page.

If the idea of disabling view state for the entire *.aspx file seems a bit too aggressive, do know that every descendent of the System.Web.UI.Control base class inherits the EnableViewState property, which makes it very simple to disable view state on a control-by-control basis:

```
<asp:GridView id="myHugeDynamicallyFilledGridOfData" runat="server"
 EnableViewState="false">
</asp:GridView>
```

■ **Note** ASP.NET pages reserve a small part of the __VIEWSTATE string for internal use. Given this, you will find that the __VIEWSTATE field will still appear in the client-side source even when the entire page (and all the controls) have disabled view state.

Adding Custom View State Data

In addition to the EnableViewState property, the System.Web.UI.Control base class provides an inherited property named ViewState. Under the hood, this property provides access to a System.Web.UI.StateBag type, which represents all the data contained within the __VIEWSTATE field. Using the indexer of the StateBag type, you can embed custom information within the hidden __VIEWSTATE form field using a set of name/value pairs. Here's a simple example:

```
protected void btnAddToVS_Click(object sender, EventArgs e)
{
  ViewState["CustomViewStateItem"] = "Some user data";
  lblVSValue.Text = (string)ViewState["CustomViewStateItem"];
}
```

Because the System.Web.UI.StateBag type has been designed to operate on any type-derived System.Object, when you wish to access the value of a given key, you should explicitly cast it into the correct underlying data type (in this case, a System.String). Be aware, however, that values placed within the __VIEWSTATE field cannot literally be any object. Specifically, the only valid types are Strings, Integers, Booleans, ArrayLists, Hashtables, or an array of these types.

So, given that *.aspx pages may insert custom bits of information into the __VIEWSTATE string, the next logical question is when you would want to do so. Most of the time, custom view state data is best suited for user-specific preferences. For example, you may establish a point of view state data that specifies how a user wishes to view the UI of a GridView (such as a sort order). View state data is not well suited for full-blown user data, such as items in a shopping cart or cached DataSets. When you need to store this sort of complex information, you are required to work with session or application data. Before we get to that point, you need to understand the role of the Global.asax file.

■ **Source Code** The ViewStateApp project is included under the Chapter 33 subdirectory.

A BRIEF WORD REGARDING CONTROL STATE

Since the release of .NET 2.0, a control's state data can now be persisted via *control state* rather than view state. This technique is most helpful if you have written a custom ASP.NET web control that must remember data between round-trips. While the `ViewState` property can be used for this purpose, if view state is disabled at a page level, the custom control is effectively broken. For this very reason, web controls now support a `ControlState` property.

Control state works identically to view state; however, it will not be disabled if view state is disabled at the page level. As mentioned, this feature is most useful for those who are developing custom web controls (a topic not covered in this text). Consult the .NET Framework 3.5 SDK documentation for further details.

The Role of the Global.asax File

At this point, an ASP.NET application may seem to be little more than a set of `*.aspx` files and their respective web controls. While you could build a web application by simply linking a set of related web pages, you will most likely need a way to interact with the web application as a whole. To this end, your ASP.NET web applications may choose to include an optional `Global.asax` file via the Web Site ➤ Add New Item menu option, as shown in Figure 33-2 (notice you are selecting the Global Application Class icon).

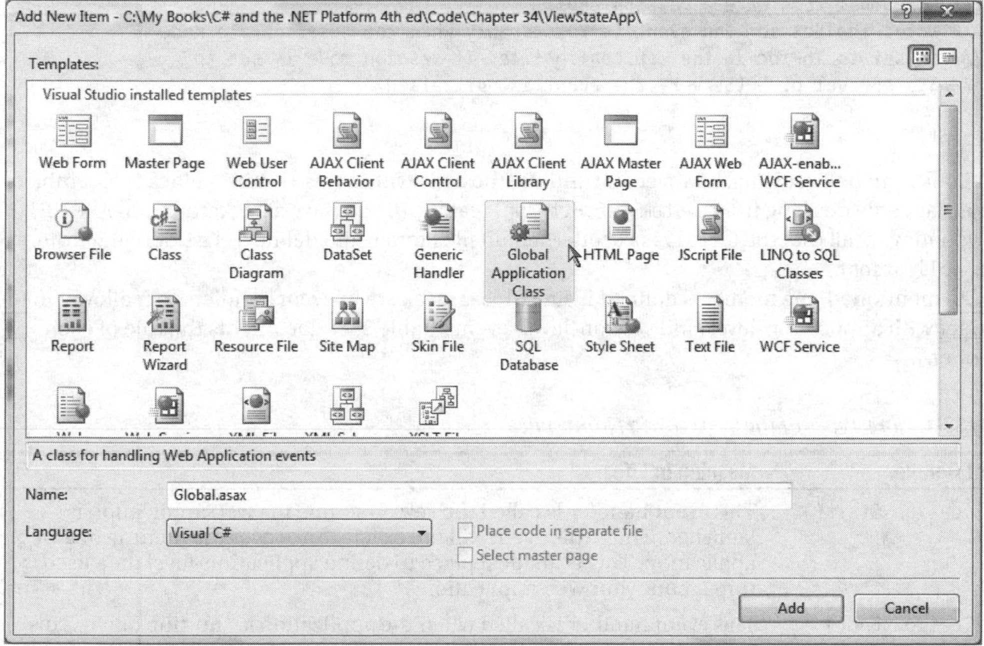

Figure 33-2. *The* `Global.asax` *file*

Simply put, `Global.asax` is just about as close to a traditional double-clickable `*.exe` that we can get in the world of ASP.NET, meaning this type represents the runtime behavior of the website itself. Once you insert a `Global.asax` file into a web project, you will notice it is little more than a `<script>` block containing a set of event handlers:

```
<%@ Application Language="C#" %>

<script runat="server">
  void Application_Start(object sender, EventArgs e)
  {
    // Code that runs on application startup.
  }

  void Application_End(object sender, EventArgs e)
  {
    //  Code that runs on application shutdown.
  }

  void Application_Error(object sender, EventArgs e)
  {
    // Code that runs when an unhandled error occurs.
  }

  void Session_Start(object sender, EventArgs e)
  {
    // Code that runs when a new session is started.
  }

  void Session_End(object sender, EventArgs e)
  {
    // Code that runs when a session ends.
    // Note: The Session_End event is raised only when the sessionstate mode
    // is set to InProc in the Web.config file. If session mode is set to
    // StateServer or SQLServer, the event is not raised.
  }
</script>
```

Looks can be deceiving, however. At runtime, the code within this `<script>` block is assembled into a class type deriving from `System.Web.HttpApplication` (if you have a background in ASP.NET 1.x, you may recall that the `Global.asax` code-behind file literally did define a class deriving from `HttpApplication`).

As mentioned, the members defined inside `Global.asax` are in event handlers that allow you to interact with application-level (and session-level) events. Table 33-1 documents the role of each member.

Table 33-1. *Core Types of the* `System.Web` *Namespace*

Event Handler	Meaning in Life
`Application_Start()`	This event handler is called the very first time the web application is launched. Thus, this event will fire exactly once over the lifetime of a web application. This is an ideal place to define application-level data used throughout your web application.
`Application_End()`	This event handler is called when the application is shutting down. This will occur when the last user times out or if you manually shut down the application via IIS.
`Session_Start()`	This event handler is fired when a new user logs on to your application. Here you may establish any user-specific data points.

Event Handler	Meaning in Life
Session_End()	This event handler is fired when a user's session has terminated (typically through a predefined timeout).
Application_Error()	This is a global error handler that will be called when an unhandled exception is thrown by the web application.

The Global Last-Chance Exception Event Handler

First, let me point out the role of the Application_Error() event handler. Recall that a specific page may handle the Error event to process any unhandled exception that occurred within the scope of the page itself. In a similar light, the Application_Error() event handler is the final place to handle an exception that was not handled by a given page. As with the page-level Error event, you are able to access the specific System.Exception using the inherited Server property:

```
void Application_Error(object sender, EventArgs e)
{
  // Obtain the unhandled error.
  Exception ex = Server.GetLastError();

  // Process error here...

  // Clear error when finished.
  Server.ClearError();
}
```

Given that the Application_Error() event handler is the last-chance exception handler for your web application, it is quite common to implement this method in such a way that the user is transferred to a predefined error page on the server. Other common duties may include sending an e-mail to the web administrator or writing to an external error log.

The HttpApplication Base Class

As mentioned, the Global.asax script is dynamically generated into a class deriving from the System.Web.HttpApplication base class, which supplies some of the same sort of functionality as the System.Web.UI.Page type (without a visible user interface). Table 33-2 documents the key members of interest.

Table 33-2. *Key Members Defined by the* System.Web.HttpApplication *Type*

Property	Meaning in Life
Application	This property allows you to interact with application-level variables, using the exposed HttpApplicationState type.
Request	This property allows you to interact with the incoming HTTP request, using the underlying HttpRequest object.
Response	This property allows you to interact with the incoming HTTP response, using the underlying HttpResponse object.
Server	This property gets the intrinsic server object for the current request, using the underlying HttpServerUtility object.
Session	This property allows you to interact with session-level variables, using the underlying HttpSessionState object.

Again, given that the `Global.asax` file does not explicitly document that `HttpApplication` is the underlying base class, it is important to remember that all of the rules of the "is-a" relationship do indeed apply. For example, if you were to apply the dot operator to the `base` keyword within any of the members within `Global.asax`, you would find you have immediate access to all members of the chain of inheritance, as you see in Figure 33-3.

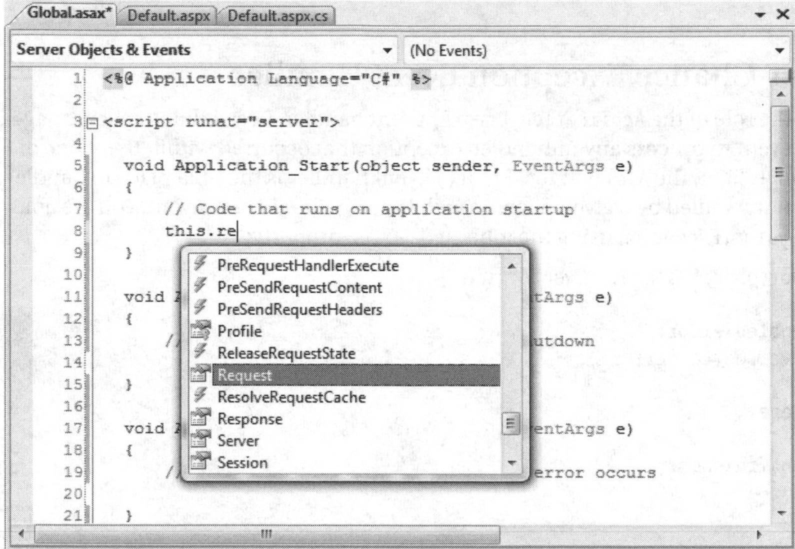

Figure 33-3. *Remember that* `HttpApplication` *is the parent of the type lurking within* `Global.asax`.

Understanding the Application/Session Distinction

Under ASP.NET, application state is maintained by an instance of the `HttpApplicationState` type. This class enables you to share global information across all users (and all pages) who are logged on to your ASP.NET application. Not only can application data be shared by all users on your site, but also if the value of an application-level data point changes, the new value is seen by all users on their next postback.

On the other hand, session state is used to remember information for a specific user (again, such as items in a shopping cart). Physically, a user's session state is represented by the `HttpSessionState` class type. When a new user logs on to an ASP.NET web application, the runtime will automatically assign that user a new session ID, which by default will expire after 20 minutes of inactivity. Thus, if 20,000 users are logged on to your site, you have 20,000 distinct `HttpSessionState` objects, each of which is automatically assigned a unique session ID. The relationship between a web application and web sessions is shown in Figure 33-4.

As you may remember based on past experience, under classic ASP, application- and session-state data is represented using distinct COM objects (e.g., `Application` and `Session`). Under ASP.NET, `Page`-derived types as well as the `HttpApplication` type make use of identically named properties (i.e., `Application` and `Session`), which expose the underlying `HttpApplicationState` and `HttpSessionState` types.

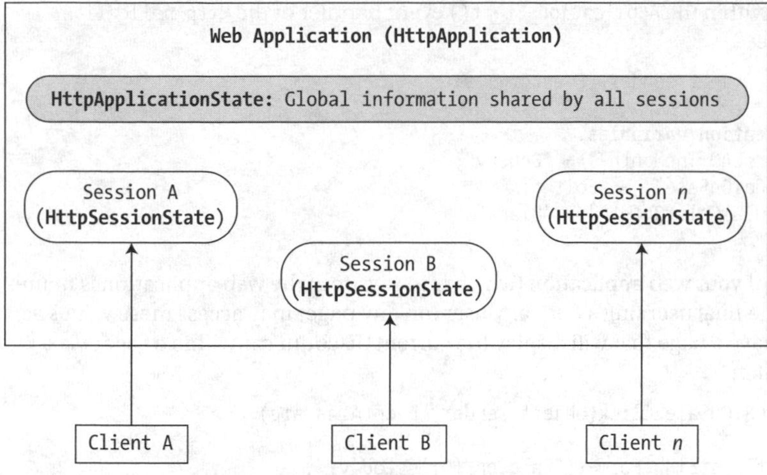

Figure 33-4. *The application/session state distinction*

Maintaining Application-Level State Data

The `HttpApplicationState` type enables developers to share global information across multiple sessions in an ASP.NET application. For example, you may wish to maintain an application-wide connection string that can be used by all pages, a common `DataSet` used by multiple pages, or any other piece of data that needs to be accessed on an application-wide scale. Table 33-3 describes some core members of this type.

Table 33-3. *Members of the* `HttpApplicationState` *Type*

Members	Meaning in Life
`Add()`	This method allows you to add a new name/value pair into the `HttpApplicationState` type. Do note that this method is typically *not* used in favor of the indexer of the `HttpApplicationState` class.
`AllKeys`	This property returns an array of `System.String` types that represent all the names in the `HttpApplicationState` type.
`Clear()`	This method deletes all items in the `HttpApplicationState` type. This is functionally equivalent to the `RemoveAll()` method.
`Count`	This property gets the number of item objects in the `HttpApplicationState` type.
`Lock()`, `Unlock()`	These two methods are used when you wish to alter a set of application variables in a thread-safe manner.
`RemoveAll()`, `Remove()`, `RemoveAt()`	These methods remove a specific item (by string name) within the `HttpApplicationState` type. `RemoveAt()` removes the item via a numerical indexer.

To illustrate working with application state, create a new ASP.NET web application named AppState and insert a new `Global.asax` file. When you create data members that can be shared among all active sessions, you need to establish a set of name/value pairs. In most cases, the most natural place to do so is within the Application_Start() event handler of the HttpApplication-derived type, for example:

```
void Application_Start(Object sender, EventArgs e)
{
  // Set up some application variables.
  Application["SalesPersonOfTheMonth"] = "Chucky";
  Application["CurrentCarOnSale"] = "Colt";
  Application["MostPopularColorOnLot"] = "Black";
}
```

During the lifetime of your web application (which is to say, until the web application is manually shut down or until the final user times out), any user (on any page) may access these values as necessary. Assume you have a page that will display the current discount car within a Label via a button Click event handler:

```
protected void btnShowCarOnSale_Click(object sender, EventArgs arg)
{
  lblCurrCarOnSale.Text = string.Format("Sale on {0}'s today!",
    (string)Application["CurrentCarOnSale"]);
}
```

Like the ViewState property, notice how you should cast the value returned from the HttpApplicationState type into the correct underlying type as the Application property operates on general System.Object types.

Now, given that the HttpApplicationState type can hold any type, it should stand to reason that you can place custom types (or any .NET object) within your site's application state. Assume you would rather maintain the three current application variables within a strongly typed class named CarLotInfo:

```
public class CarLotInfo
{
  public CarLotInfo(string s, string c, string m)
  {
    salesPersonOfTheMonth = s;
    currentCarOnSale = c;
    mostPopularColorOnLot = m;
  }
  // Public for easy access, could also make use of automatic
  // property syntax.
  public string salesPersonOfTheMonth;
  public string currentCarOnSale;
  public string mostPopularColorOnLot;
}
```

With this helper class in place, you could modify the Application_Start() event handler as follows:

```
void Application_Start(Object sender, EventArgs e)
{
  // Place a custom object in the application data sector.
  Application["CarSiteInfo"] =
    new CarLotInfo("Chucky", "Colt", "Black");
}
```

and then access the information using the public field data within a server-side Click event handler for a Button type named btnShowAppVariables:

```
protected void btnShowAppVariables_Click(object sender, EventArgs e)
{
  CarLotInfo appVars =
    ((CarLotInfo)Application["CarSiteInfo"]);
  string appState =
    string.Format("<li>Car on sale: {0}</li>",
    appVars.currentCarOnSale);
  appState +=
    string.Format("<li>Most popular color: {0}</li>",
    appVars.mostPopularColorOnLot);
  appState +=
    string.Format("<li>Big shot SalesPerson: {0}</li>",
    appVars.salesPersonOfTheMonth);
  lblAppVariables.Text = appState;
}
```

Given that the current car-on-sale data is now exposed from a custom class type, your btnShowCarOnSale Click event handler would also need to be updated like so:

```
protected void btnShowCarOnSale_Click1(object sender, EventArgs e)
{
  lblCurrCarOnSale.Text = String.Format("Sale on {0}'s today!",
    ((CarLotInfo)Application["CarSiteInfo"]).currentCarOnSale);
}
```

If you now run this page, you will find that a list of each application variable is displayed on the page's Label types, as displayed in Figure 33-5.

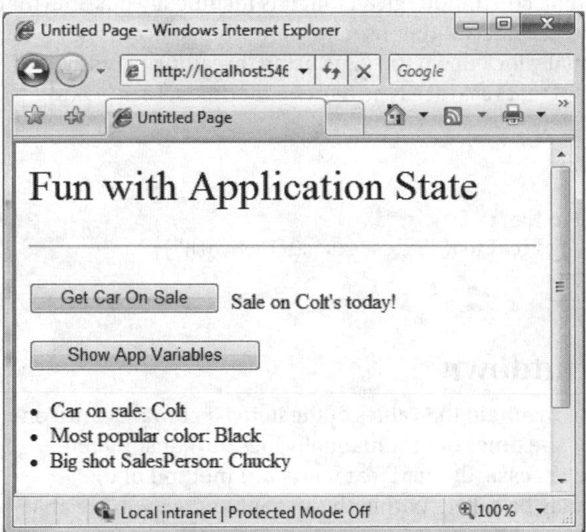

Figure 33-5. *Displaying application data*

Modifying Application Data

You may programmatically update or delete any or all members using members of the HttpApplicationState type during the execution of your web application. For example, to delete a specific item, simply call the Remove() method. If you wish to destroy all application-level data, call RemoveAll():

```
private void CleanAppData()
{
  // Remove a single item via string name.
  Application.Remove["SomeItemIDontNeed"];

  // Destroy all application data!
  Application.RemoveAll();
}
```

If you wish to simply change the value of an existing application-level variable, you only need to make a new assignment to the data item in question. Assume your page now supports a new Button type that allows your user to change the current hotshot salesperson by reading in a value from a TextBox named txtNewSP. The Click event handler is as you would expect:

```
protected void btnSetNewSP_Click(object sender, EventArgs e)
{
  // Set the new Salesperson.
  ((CarLotInfo)Application["CarSiteInfo"]).salesPersonOfTheMonth
    = txtNewSP.Text;
}
```

If you run the web application, you will find that the application-level variable has been updated. Furthermore, given that application variables are accessible from all user sessions, if you were to launch three or four instances of your web browser, you would find that if one instance changes the current hotshot salesperson, each of the other browsers displays the new value on postback.

Understand that if you have a situation where a set of application-level variables must be updated as a unit, you risk the possibility of data corruption (given that it is technically possible that an application-level data point may be changed while another user is attempting to access it!). While you could take the long road and manually lock down the logic using threading primitives of the System.Threading namespace, the HttpApplicationState type has two methods, Lock() and Unlock(), that automatically ensure thread safety:

```
// Safely access related application data.
Application.Lock();
Application["SalesPersonOfTheMonth"] = "Maxine";
Application["CurrentBonusedEmployee"] = Application("SalesPersonOfTheMonth");
Application.Unlock();
```

Handling Web Application Shutdown

The HttpApplicationState type is designed to maintain the values of the items it contains until one of two situations occurs: the last user on your site times out (or manually logs out) or someone manually shuts down the website via IIS. In each case, the Application_End() method of the HttpApplication-derived type will automatically be called. Within this event handler, you are able to perform whatever sort of cleanup code is necessary:

```
void Application_End(Object sender, EventArgs e)
{
  // Write current application variables
  // to a database or whatever else you need to do...
}
```

Source Code The AppState project is included under the Chapter 33 subdirectory.

Working with the Application Cache

ASP.NET provides a second and more flexible manner to handle application-wide data. As you recall, the values within the HttpApplicationState object remain in memory as long as your web application is alive and kicking. Sometimes, however, you may wish to maintain a piece of application data only for a specific period of time. For example, you may wish to obtain an ADO.NET DataSet that is valid for only five minutes. After that time, you may want to obtain a fresh DataSet to account for possible database updates. While it is technically possible to build this infrastructure using HttpApplicationState and some sort of handcrafted monitor, your task is greatly simplified using the ASP.NET application cache.

As suggested by its name, the ASP.NET System.Web.Caching.Cache object (which is accessible via the Context.Cache property) allows you to define an object that is accessible by all users (from all pages) for a fixed amount of time. In its simplest form, interacting with the cache looks identical to interacting with the HttpApplicationState type:

```
// Add an item to the cache.
// This item will *not* expire.
Context.Cache["SomeStringItem"] = "This is the string item";

// Get item from the cache.
string s = (string)Context.Cache["SomeStringItem"]
```

Note If you wish to access the Cache from within Global.asax, you are required to use the Context property. However, if you are within the scope of a System.Web.UI.Page-derived type, you can make use of the Cache object directly.

Now, understand that if you have no interest in automatically updating (or removing) an application-level data point (as seen here), the Cache object is of little benefit, as you can directly use the HttpApplicationState type. However, when you do wish to have a data point destroyed after a fixed point of time—and optionally be informed when this occurs—the Cache type is extremely helpful.

The System.Web.Caching.Cache class defines only a small number of members beyond the type's indexer. For example, the Add() method can be used to insert a new item into the cache that is not currently defined (if the specified item is already present, Add() effectively does nothing). The Insert() method will also place a member into the cache. If, however, the item is currently defined, Insert() will replace the current item with the new type. Given that this is most often the behavior you will desire, I'll focus on the Insert() method exclusively.

Fun with Data Caching

Let's see an example. To begin, create a new ASP.NET web application named CacheState and insert a Global.asax file. Like an application-level variable maintained by the HttpApplicationState type, the Cache may hold any System.Object-derived type and is often populated within the Application_Start() event handler. For this example, the goal is to automatically update the contents of a DataSet every 15 seconds. The DataSet in question will contain the current set of records from the Inventory table of the AutoLot database created during our discussion of ADO.NET.

Given these design notes, set a reference to AutoLotDAL.dll (see Chapter 22) and update your Global class type like so (code analysis to follow):

```
<%@ Application Language="C#" %>
<%@ Import Namespace = "AutoLotConnectedLayer" %>
<%@ Import Namespace = "System.Data" %>
```

```
<script runat="server">
  // Define a static-level Cache member variable.
  static Cache theCache;

  void Application_Start(Object sender, EventArgs e)
  {
    // First assign the static 'theCache' variable.
    theCache = Context.Cache;

    // When the application starts up,
    // read the current records in the
    // Inventory table of the AutoLot DB.
    InventoryDAL dal = new InventoryDAL();
    dal.OpenConnection(@"Data Source=(local)\SQLEXPRESS;" +
      "Initial Catalog=AutoLot;Integrated Security=True");
    DataTable theCars = dal.GetAllInventory();
    dal.CloseConnection();

    // Now store DataTable in the cache.
    theCache.Insert("AppDataTable",
      theCars, null,
      DateTime.Now.AddSeconds(15),
      Cache.NoSlidingExpiration,
      CacheItemPriority.Default,
      new CacheItemRemovedCallback(UpdateCarInventory));
  }

  // The target for the CacheItemRemovedCallback delegate.
  static void UpdateCarInventory(string key, object item,
    CacheItemRemovedReason reason)
  {
    InventoryDAL  dal = new InventoryDAL();
    dal.OpenConnection(@"Data Source=(local)\SQLEXPRESS;" +
      "Initial Catalog=AutoLot;Integrated Security=True");
    DataTable theCars = dal.GetAllInventory();
    dal.CloseConnection();

    // Now store in the cache.
    theCache.Insert("AppDataTable",
      theCars, null,
      DateTime.Now.AddSeconds(15),
      Cache.NoSlidingExpiration,
      CacheItemPriority.Default,
      new CacheItemRemovedCallback(UpdateCarInventory));
  }
...
</script>
```

First, notice that the `Global` type has defined a static `Cache` member variable. The reason is that you have defined two shared members that need to access the `Cache` object. Recall that static members do not have access to inherited members, therefore you can't use the `Context` property!

Inside the `Application_Start()` event handler, you fill a `DataTable` and place the object within the application cache. As you would guess, the `Context.Cache.Insert()` method has been overloaded a number of times. Here, you supply a value for each possible parameter. Consider the following commented call to `Add()`:

```
theCache.Add("AppDataTable",         // Name used to identify item in the cache.
  theCars,                           // Object to put in the cache.
  null,                              // Any dependencies for this object?
  DateTime.Now.AddSeconds(15),       // How long item will be in cache.
  Cache.NoSlidingExpiration,         // Fixed or sliding time?
  CacheItemPriority.Default,         // Priority level of cache item.
  // Delegate for CacheItemRemove event.
  new CacheItemRemovedCallback(UpdateCarInventory));
```

The first two parameters simply make up the name/value pair of the item. The third parameter allows you to define a CacheDependency type (which is null in this case, as you do not have any other entities in the cache that are dependent on the DataTable).

Note The ability to define a CacheDependency type is quite interesting. For example, you could establish a dependency between a member and an external file. If the contents of the file were to change, the type can be automatically updated. Check out the .NET Framework 3.5 SDK documentation for further details.

The next three parameters are used to define the amount of time the item will be allowed to remain in the application cache and its level of priority. Here, you specify the read-only Cache.NoSlidingExpiration field, which informs the cache that the specified time limit (15 seconds) is absolute. Finally, and most important for this example, you create a new CacheItemRemovedCallback delegate type, and pass in the name of the method to call when the DataSet is purged. As you can see from the signature of the UpdateCarInventory() method, the CacheItemRemovedCallback delegate can only call methods that match the following signature:

```
static void UpdateCarInventory(string key, object item,
  CacheItemRemovedReason reason)
{
}
```

So, at this point, when the application starts up, the DataTable is populated and cached. Every 15 seconds, the DataTable is purged, updated, and reinserted into the cache. To see the effects of doing this, you need to create a Page that allows for some degree of user interaction.

Modifying the *.aspx File

Update the UI of your initial *.aspx file as shown in Figure 33-6.

In the page's Load event handler, configure your GridView to display the current contents of the cached DataTable the first time the user posts to the page (be sure to import the AutoLotConnectedLayer namespace within your code file):

```
protected void Page_Load(object sender, EventArgs e)
{
  if (!IsPostBack)
  {
    carsGridView.DataSource = (DataTable)Cache["AppDataTable"];
    carsGridView.DataBind();
  }
}
```

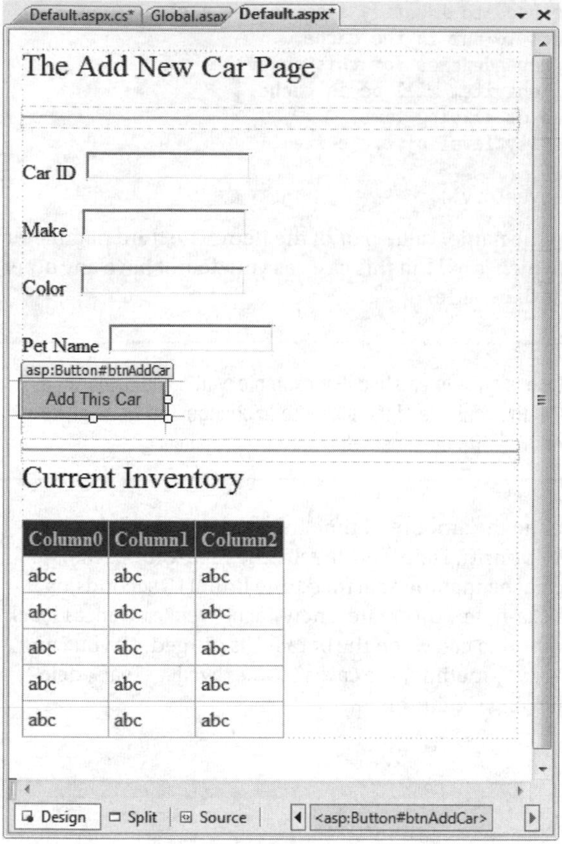

Figure 33-6. *The cache application GUI*

In the Click event handler of the Add This Car button, insert the new record into the AutoLot database using the InventoryDAL type. Once the record has been inserted, call a helper function named RefreshGrid(), which will update the UI:

```
protected void btnAddCar_Click(object sender, EventArgs e)
{
  // Update the Inventory table
  // and call RefreshGrid().
  InventoryDAL dal = new InventoryDAL();
  dal.OpenConnection(@"Data Source=(local)\SQLEXPRESS;" +
    "Initial Catalog=AutoLot;Integrated Security=True");
  dal.InsertAuto(int.Parse(txtCarID.Text), txtCarColor.Text,
    txtCarMake.Text, txtCarPetName.Text);
  dal.CloseConnection();
  RefreshGrid();
}

private void RefreshGrid()
{
  InventoryDAL dal = new InventoryDAL();
  dal.OpenConnection(@"Data Source=(local)\SQLEXPRESS;" +
    "Initial Catalog=AutoLot;Integrated Security=True");
```

```
    DataTable theCars = dal.GetAllInventory();
    dal.CloseConnection();

    carsGridView.DataSource = theCars;
    carsGridView.DataBind();
}
```

Now, to test the use of the cache, begin by running the current program (Ctrl+F5) and copy the URL appearing in the browser to your clipboard. Next, launch a second instance of Internet Explorer (using the Start button) and paste the URL into this instance. At this point you should have two instances of your web browser, both viewing `Default.aspx` and showing identical data.

In one instance of the browser, add a new automobile entry. Obviously, this results in an updated `GridView` viewable from the browser that initiated the postback.

In the second browser instance, click the Refresh button (F5). You should not see the new item, given that the `Page_Load` event handler is reading directly from the cache. (If you did see the value, the 15 seconds had already expired. Either type faster or increase the amount of time the `DataTable` will remain in the cache.) Wait a few seconds and click the Refresh button from the second browser instance one more time. Now you should see the new item, given that the `DataTable` in the cache has expired and the `CacheItemRemovedCallback` delegate target method has automatically updated the cached `DataTable`.

As you can see, the major benefit of the `Cache` type is that you can ensure that when a member is removed, you have a chance to respond. In this example, you certainly could avoid using the `Cache` and simply have the `Page_Load()` event handler always read directly from the AutoLot database. Nevertheless, the point should be clear: the cache allows you to automatically refresh data using the cache mechanism.

■ **Source Code** The CacheState project is included under the Chapter 33 subdirectory.

Maintaining Session Data

So much for our examination of application-level and cached data. Next, let's check out the role of per-user data. As mentioned earlier, a *session* is little more than a given user's interaction with a web application, which is represented via a unique `HttpSessionState` object. To maintain stateful information for a particular user, the `HttpApplication`-derived type and any `System.Web.UI.Page`-derived types may access the `Session` property. The classic example of the need to maintain per-user data would be an online shopping cart. Again, if 10 people all log on to an online store, each individual will maintain a unique set of items that she (may) intend to purchase.

When a new user logs on to your web application, the .NET runtime will automatically assign the user a unique session ID, which is used to identify the user in question. Each session ID is assigned a custom instance of the `HttpSessionState` type to hold on to user-specific data. Inserting or retrieving session data is syntactically identical to manipulating application data, for example:

```
// Add/retrieve a session variable for current user.
Session["DesiredCarColor"] = "Green";
string color = (string) Session["DesiredCarColor"];
```

The `HttpApplication`-derived type allows you to intercept the beginning and end of a session via the `Session_Start()` and `Session_End()` event handlers. Within `Session_Start()`, you can freely create any per-user data items, while `Session_End()` allows you to perform any work you may need to do when the user's session has terminated:

```
<%@ Application Language="C#" %>
...
void Session_Start(Object sender, EventArgs e)
{
  // New session! Prep if required.
}

void Session_End(Object sender, EventArgs e)
{
  // User logged off/timed out. Tear down if needed.
}
```

Like the HttpApplicationState type, HttpSessionState may hold any System.Object-derived type, including your custom classes. For example, assume you have a new web application (SessionState) that defines a class named UserShoppingCart:

```
public class UserShoppingCart
{
  public string desiredCar;
  public string desiredCarColor;
  public float downPayment;
  public bool isLeasing;
  public DateTime dateOfPickUp;

  public override string ToString()
  {
    return string.Format
     ("Car: {0}<br>Color: {1}<br>$ Down: {2}<br>Lease: {3}<br>Pick-up Date: {4}",
      desiredCar, desiredCarColor, downPayment, isLeasing,
      dateOfPickUp.ToShortDateString());
  }
}
```

Within the Session_Start() event handler, you can now assign each user a new instance of the UserShoppingCart class:

```
void Session_Start(Object sender, EventArgs e)
{
  Session["UserShoppingCartInfo"]
    = new UserShoppingCart();
}
```

As the user traverses your web pages, you are able to pluck out the UserShoppingCart instance and fill the fields with user-specific data. For example, assume you have a simple *.aspx page that defines a set of input widgets that correspond to each field of the UserShoppingCart type and a Button used to set the values and two Labels that will be used to display the user's session ID and session information (see Figure 33-7).

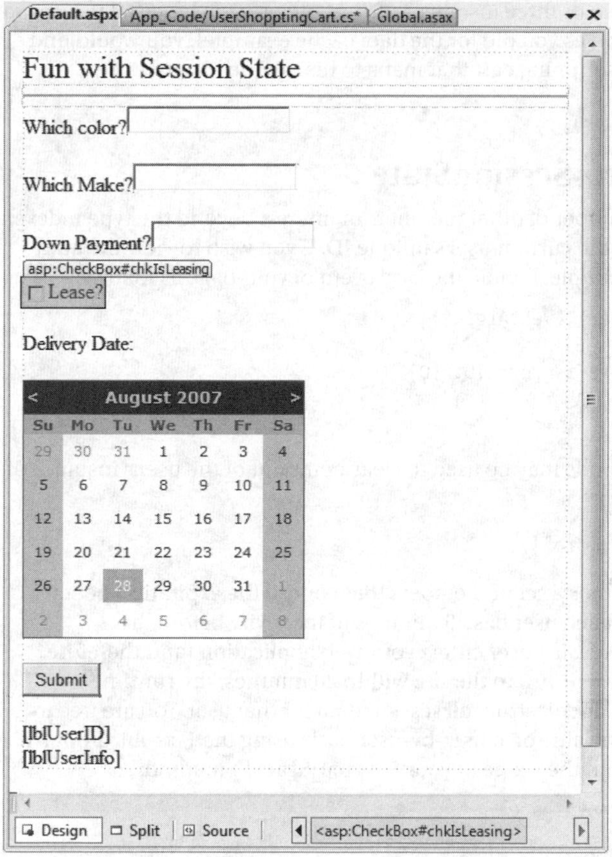

Figure 33-7. *The session application GUI*

The server-side `Click` event handler for the `Button` type is straightforward (scrape out values from `TextBoxes` and display the shopping cart data on a `Label` type):

```
protected void btnSubmit_Click(object sender, EventArgs e)
{
  // Set current user prefs.
  UserShoppingCart cart =
    (UserShoppingCart)Session["UserShoppingCartInfo"];
  cart.dateOfPickUp = myCalendar.SelectedDate;
  cart.desiredCar = txtCarMake.Text;
  cart.desiredCarColor = txtCarColor.Text;
  cart.downPayment = float.Parse(txtDownPayment.Text);
  cart.isLeasing = chkIsLeasing.Checked;
  lblUserInfo.Text = cart.ToString();
  Session["UserShoppingCartInfo"] = cart;
}
```

Within `Session_End()`, you may wish to persist the fields of the `UserShoppingCart` to a database or whatnot (however, as you will see at the conclusion of this chapter, the ASP.NET Profile API will do so automatically). As well, you may wish to implement `Session_Error()` to trap any faulty input (or perhaps make use of various validation controls on the `Default.aspx` page to account for such user errors).

In any case, if you were to launch two or three instances of your browser of choice all posting to the same URL (via a copy/paste operation as you did for the data cache example), you would find that each user is able to build a custom shopping cart that maps to his unique instance of `HttpSessionState`.

Additional Members of HttpSessionState

The `HttpSessionState` class defines a number of other members of interest beyond the type indexer. First, the `SessionID` property will return the current user's unique ID. If you wish to view the automatically assigned session ID for this example, handle the `Load` event of your page as follows:

```
protected void Page_Load(object sender, EventArgs e)
{
  lblUserID.Text = string.Format("Here is your ID: {0}",
    Session.SessionID);
}
```

The `Remove()` and `RemoveAll()` methods may be used to clear items out of the user's instance of `HttpSessionState`:

```
Session.Remove["SomeItemWeDontNeedAnymore"];
```

The `HttpSessionState` type also defines a set of members that control the expiration policy of the current session. Again, by default each user has 20 minutes of inactivity before the `HttpSessionState` object is destroyed. Thus, if a user enters your web application (and therefore obtains a unique session ID), but does not return to the site within 20 minutes, the runtime assumes the user is no longer interested and destroys all session data for that user. You are free to change this default 20-minute expiration value on a user-by-user basis using the `Timeout` property. The most common place to do so is within the scope of your `Session_Start()` method:

```
void Session_Start(Object sender, EventArgs e)
{
  // Each user has 5 minutes of inactivity.
  Session.Timeout = 5;
  Session["UserShoppingCartInfo"]
    = new UserShoppingCart();
}
```

■Note If you do not need to tweak each user's `Timeout` value, you are able to alter the 20-minute default for all users via the `Timeout` attribute of the `<sessionState>` element within the `Web.config` file (examined at the end of this chapter).

The benefit of the `Timeout` property is that you have the ability to assign specific timeout values discretely for each user. For example, imagine you have created a web application that allows users to pay cash for a given membership level. You may say that Gold members should time out within one hour, while Wood members should get only 30 seconds. This possibility begs the question, how can you remember user-specific information (such as the current membership level) across web visits? One possible answer is through the user of the `HttpCookie` type. (And speaking of cookies . . .)

■Source Code The SessionState project is included under the Chapter 33 subdirectory.

Understanding Cookies

The next state management technique examined here is the act of persisting data within a *cookie*, which is often realized as a text file (or set of files) on the user's machine. When a user logs on to a given site, the browser checks to see whether the user's machine has a cookie file for the URL in question and, if so, appends this data to the HTTP request.

The receiving server-side web page could then read the cookie data to create a GUI that may be based on the current user preferences. I'm sure you've noticed that when you visit one of your favorite websites, it somehow "just knows" the sort of content you wish to see. The reason (in part) may have to do with a cookie stored on your computer that contains information relevant to a given website.

■ **Note** The exact location of your cookie files will depend on which browser and operating system you happen to be using.

The contents of a given cookie file will obviously vary among URLs, but keep in mind that they are ultimately text files. Thus, cookies are a horrible choice when you wish to maintain sensitive information about the current user (such as a credit card number, password, or whatnot). Even if you take the time to encrypt the data, a crafty hacker could decrypt the value and use it for purely evil pursuits. In any case, cookies do play a role in the development of web applications, so let's check out how ASP.NET handles this particular state management technique.

Creating Cookies

First of all, understand that ASP.NET cookies can be configured to be either persistent or temporary. A *persistent* cookie is typically regarded as the classic definition of cookie data, in that the set of name/value pairs is physically saved to the user's hard drive. A *temporary* cookie (also termed a *session cookie*) contains the same data as a persistent cookie, but the name/value pairs are never saved to the user's hard drive; rather, they exist *only* within the HTTP header. Once the user shuts down the browser, all data contained within the session cookie is destroyed.

■ **Note** Most browsers support cookies of up to 4,096 bytes. Because of this size limit, cookies are best used to store small amounts of data, such as a user ID that can be used to identify the user and pull details from a database.

The `System.Web.HttpCookie` type is the class that represents the server side of the cookie data (persistent or temporary). When you wish to create a new cookie, you access the `Response.Cookies` property. Once the new `HttpCookie` is inserted into the internal collection, the name/value pairs flow back to the browser within the HTTP header.

To check out cookie behavior firsthand, create a new ASP.NET web application (CookieStateApp) and create the UI displayed in Figure 33-8.

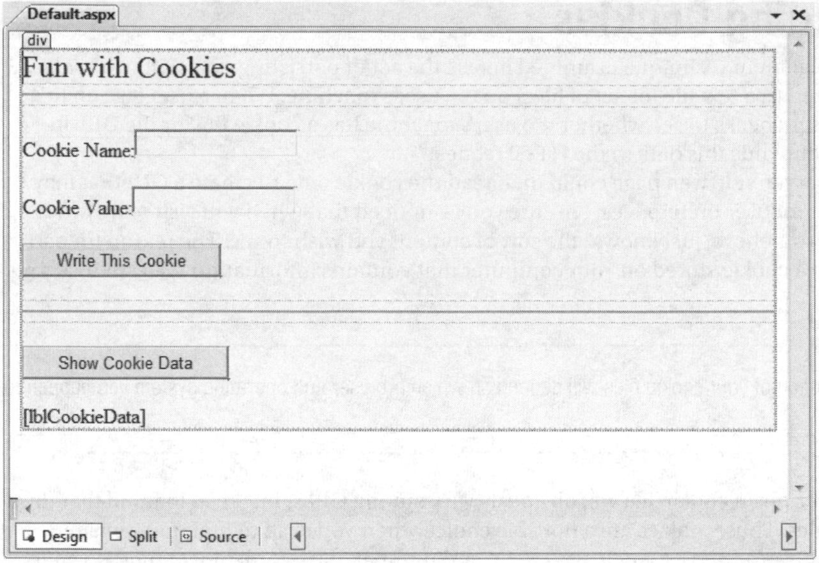

Figure 33-8. *The UI of CookieStateApp*

Within the first button's `Click` event handler, build a new `HttpCookie` and insert it into the `Cookie` collection exposed from the `HttpRequest.Cookies` property. Be very aware that the data will not persist itself to the user's hard drive unless you explicitly set an expiration date using the `HttpCookie.Expires` property. Thus, the following implementation will create a temporary cookie that is destroyed when the user shuts down the browser:

```
protected void btnCookie_Click(object sender, EventArgs e)
{
  // Make a temp cookie.
  HttpCookie theCookie =
    new HttpCookie(txtCookieName.Text,
    txtCookieValue.Text);
  Response.Cookies.Add(theCookie);
}
```

However, the following generates a persistent cookie that will expire on March 24, 2009:

```
protected void btnCookie_Click(object sender, EventArgs e)
{
  HttpCookie theCookie =
    new HttpCookie(txtCookieName.Text,
    txtCookieValue.Text);
  theCookie.Expires = DateTime.Parse("03/24/2009");
  Response.Cookies.Add(theCookie);
}
```

Reading Incoming Cookie Data

Recall that the browser is the entity in charge of accessing persisted cookies when navigating to a previously visited page. To interact with the incoming cookie data under ASP.NET, access the `HttpRequest.Cookies` property. To illustrate, implement the `Click` event handler for the second button as so:

```
protected void btnShowCookie_Click(object sender, EventArgs e)
{
  string cookieData = "";
  foreach (string s in Request.Cookies)
  {
    cookieData +=
     string.Format("<li><b>Name</b>: {0}, <b>Value</b>: {1}</li>",
     s, Request.Cookies[s].Value);
  }
  lblCookieData.Text = cookieData;
}
```

If you now run the application and click your new button, you will find that the cookie data has indeed been sent by your browser (see Figure 33-9).

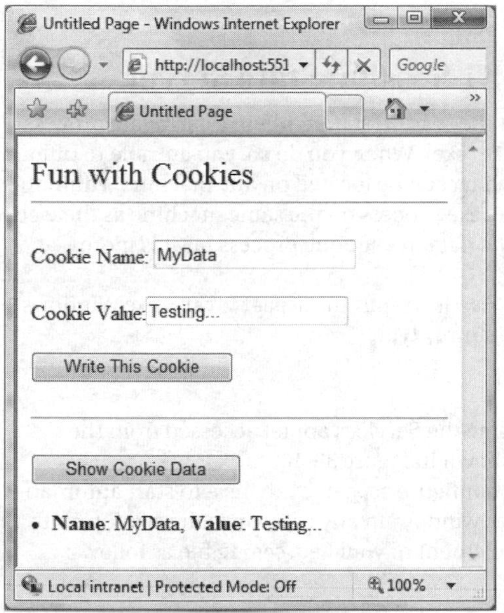

Figure 33-9. *Viewing cookie data*

■ **Source Code** The CookieStateApp project is included under the Chapter 33 subdirectory.

The Role of the <sessionState> Element

At this point in the chapter, you have examined numerous ways to remember information about your users. As you have seen, view state and application, cache, session, and cookie data are manipulated in more or less the same way (via a class indexer). As you have also seen, the `HttpApplication` type is often used to intercept and respond to events that occur during your web application's lifetime.

By default, ASP.NET will store session state using an in-process `*.dll` hosted by the ASP.NET worker process (`aspnet_wp.exe`). Like any `*.dll`, the plus side is that access to the information is as fast as possible. However, the downside is that if this AppDomain crashes (for whatever reason), all of the user's state data is destroyed. Furthermore, when you store state data as an in-process `*.dll`, you cannot interact with a networked web farm. This default behavior is recorded in the `<sessionState>` element of your `machine.config` file like so:

```
<sessionState
  mode="InProc"
  stateConnectionString="tcpip=127.0.0.1:42626"
  sqlConnectionString="data source=127.0.0.1;Trusted_Connection=yes"
  cookieless="false"
  timeout="20"
/>
```

This default mode of storage works just fine if your web application is hosted by a single web server. As you might guess, however, this model is not ideal for a farm of web servers, given that session state is "trapped" within a given AppDomain.

Storing Session Data in the ASP.NET Session State Server

Under ASP.NET, you can instruct the runtime to host the session state `*.dll` in a surrogate process named the ASP.NET session state server (`aspnet_state.exe`). When you do so, you are able to offload the `*.dll` from `aspnet_wp.exe` into a unique `*.exe`, which can be located on any machine within the web farm. Even if you intend to run the `aspnet_state.exe` process on the same machine as the web server, you do gain the benefit of partitioning the state data in a unique process (as it is more durable).

To make use of the session state server, the first step is to start the `aspnet_state.exe` Windows service on the target machine. At the command line, simply type

```
net start aspnet_state
```

Alternatively, you can start `aspnet_state.exe` using the Services applet accessed from the Administrative Tools folder of the Control Panel, as shown in Figure 33-10.

The key benefit of this approach is that you can configure `aspnet_state.exe` to start automatically when the machine boots up using the Properties window. In any case, once the session state server is running, add the following `<sessionState>` element of your `Web.config` file as follows:

```
<sessionState
  mode="StateServer"
  stateConnectionString="tcpip=127.0.0.1:42626"
  sqlConnectionString="data source=127.0.0.1;Trusted_Connection=yes"
  cookieless="false"
  timeout="20"
/>
```

Here, the `mode` attribute has been set to `StateServer`. That's it! At this point, the CLR will host session-centric data within `aspnet_state.exe`. In this way, if the AppDomain hosting the web application crashes, the session data is preserved. Notice as well that the `<sessionState>` element can also support a `stateConnectionString` attribute. The default TCP/IP address value (127.0.0.1) points to the local machine. If you would rather have the .NET runtime use the `aspnet_state.exe` service located on another networked machine (again, think web farms), you are free to update this value.

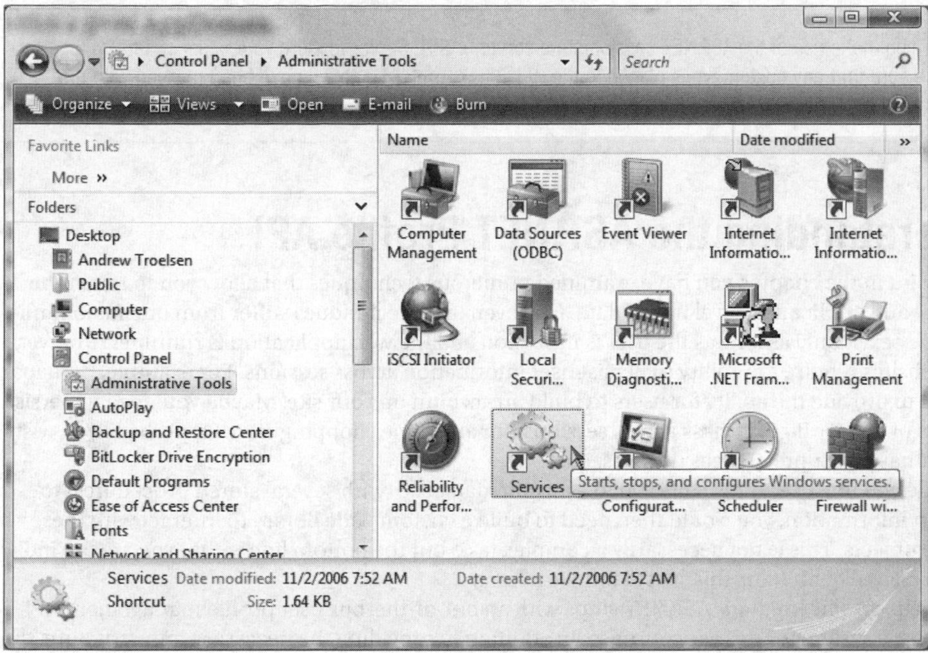

Figure 33-10. *Starting* `aspnet_state.exe` *using the Services applet*

Storing Session Data in a Dedicated Database

Finally, if you require the highest degree of isolation and durability for your web application, you may choose to have the runtime store all your session state data within Microsoft SQL Server. The appropriate update to the `Web.config` file is simple:

```
<sessionState
  mode="SQLServer"
  stateConnectionString="tcpip=127.0.0.1:42626"
  sqlConnectionString="data source=127.0.0.1;Trusted_Connection=yes"
  cookieless="false"
  timeout="20"
/>
```

However, before you attempt to run the associated web application, you need to ensure that the target machine (specified by the `sqlConnectionString` attribute) has been properly configured. When you install the .NET Framework 3.5 SDK (or Visual Studio 2008), you will be provided with two files named `InstallSqlState.sql` and `UninstallSqlState.sql`, located by default under C:\Windows\Microsoft.NET\Framework\<*version*>. On the target machine, you must run the `InstallSqlState.sql` file using a tool such as the Microsoft SQL Server Management Studio (which ships with Microsoft SQL Server 2005).

Once this SQL script has executed, you will find a new SQL Server database has been created (ASPState) that contains a number of stored procedures called by the ASP.NET runtime and a set of tables used to store the session data itself (also, the tempdb database has been updated with a set of tables for swapping purposes). As you would guess, configuring your web application to store session data within SQL Server is the slowest of all possible options. The benefit is that user data is as durable as possible (even if the web server is rebooted).

■Note If you make use of the ASP.NET session state server or SQL Server to store your session data, you must make sure that any custom types placed in the `HttpSessionState` object have been marked with the `[Serializable]` attribute.

Understanding the ASP.NET Profile API

At this point in the chapter, you have examined numerous techniques that allow you to remember user-level and application-level bits of data. However, these techniques suffer from one major limitation: they exist only as long as the user is in session and the web application is running! However, many websites require the ability to persist user information across sessions. For example, perhaps you need to provide the ability for users to build an account on your site. Maybe you need to persist instances of a `ShoppingCart` class across sessions (for an online shopping site). Or perhaps you wish to persist basic user preferences (themes, etc.).

While you most certainly could build a custom database (with several stored procedures) to hold such information, you would then need to build a custom code library to interact with these database objects. This is not necessarily a complex task, but the bottom line is that *you* are the individual in charge of building this sort of infrastructure.

To help simplify matters, ASP.NET ships with an out-of-the-box user profile management API and database system for this very purpose. In addition to providing the necessary infrastructure, the Profile API also allows you to define the data to be persisted directly within your `Web.config` file (for purposes of simplification); however, you are also able to persist any `[Serializable]` type. Before we get too far ahead of ourselves, let's check out where the Profile API will be storing the specified data.

The ASPNETDB.mdf Database

Every ASP.NET website built with Visual Studio 2008 automatically provides an App_Data subdirectory. By default, the Profile API (as well as other services, such as the ASP.NET role membership API; not examined in this text) is configured to make use of a local SQL Server 2008 database named `ASPNETDB.mdf`, located within the App_Data folder. This default behavior is due to settings within the `machine.config` file for the current .NET installation on your machine. In fact, when your code base makes use of any ASP.NET service requiring the App_Data folder, the `ASPNETDB.mdf` data file will be automatically created on the fly if a copy does not currently exist.

If you would rather have the ASP.NET runtime communicate with an `ASPNETDB.mdf` file located on another networked machine, or you would rather install this database on an instance of SQL Server 7.0 (or higher), you will need to manually build `ASPNETDB.mdf` using the `aspnet_regsql.exe` command-line utility. Like any good command-line tool, `aspnet_regsql.exe` provides numerous options; however, if you run the tool with no arguments, as so:

```
aspnet_regsql
```

you will launch a GUI-based wizard to help walk you through the process of creating and installing `ASPNETDB.mdf` on your machine (and version of SQL Server) of choice.

Now, assuming your site is not making use of a local copy of the database under the App_Data folder, the final step is to update your `Web.config` file to point to the unique location of your `ASPNETDB.mdf`. Assume you have installed `ASPNETDB.mdf` on a machine named ProductionServer. The following (partial) `Web.config` file (for a website named ShoppingCart) could be used to instruct the Profile API where to find the necessary database items:

```
<configuration>
  <connectionStrings>
    <add name="SqlServices"
         connectionString ="Data Source=ProductionServer;Integrated
         Security=SSPI;Initial Catalog=aspnetdb;"
         providerName="System.Data.SqlClient"/>
  </connectionStrings>
  <system.web>
    <profile defaultProvider ="SqlProvider">
      <providers>
        <clear/>
        <add name="AspNetSqlProfileProvider"
             connectionStringName="LocalSqlServer"
             applicationName="ShoppingCart"
             type="System.Web.Profile.SqlProfileProvider, System.Web,
             Version=2.0.0.0,
             Culture=neutral, PublicKeyToken=b03f5f7f11d50a3a" />
      </providers>
    </profile>
  </system.web>
</configuration>
```

Like most *.config files, this looks much worse than it is. Basically we are defining a <connectionString> element with the necessary data, followed by a named instance of the SqlProfileProvider (this is the default provider used regardless of physical location of the ASPNETDB.mdf). If you require further information regarding this configuration syntax, be sure to check out the .NET Framework 3.5 SDK documentation.

Note For simplicity, I will assume that you will simply make use of the autogenerated ASPNETDB.mdf database located under your web application's App_Data subdirectory.

Defining a User Profile Within Web.config

As mentioned, a user profile is defined within a Web.config file. The really nifty aspect of this approach is that you can interact with this profile in a strongly typed manner using the inherited Profile property. To illustrate this, create a new website named FunWithProfiles and open your Web.config file for editing.

Our goal is to make a profile that models the home address of the users who are in session as well as the total number of times they have posted to this site. Not surprisingly, profile data is defined within a <profile> element using a set of name/data type pairs. Consider the following profile, which is created within the scope of the <system.web> element:

```
<profile>
  <properties>
    <add name="StreetAddress" type="System.String" />
    <add name="City" type="System.String" />
    <add name="State" type="System.String" />
    <add name="TotalPost" type="System.Int32" />
  </properties>
</profile>
```

Here, we have specified a name and CLR data type for each item in the profile (of course, we could add additional items for zip code, name, and so forth, but I am sure you get the idea). Strictly speaking, the type attribute is optional; however, the default is a System.String. As you would guess, there are many other attributes that can be specified in a profile entry to further qualify how this information should be persisted in ASPNETDB.mdf. Table 33-4 illustrates some of the core attributes.

Table 33-4. *Select Attributes of Profile Data*

Attribute	Example Values	Meaning in Life
allowAnonymous	True | False	Restricts or allows anonymous access to this value. If it is set to false, anonymous users won't have access to this profile value.
defaultValue	String	The value to return if the property has not been explicitly set.
name	String	A unique identifier for this property.
provider	String	The provider used to manage this value. It overrides the defaultProvider setting in Web.config or machine.config.
readOnly	True | False	Restricts or allows write access.
serializeAs	String | XML | Binary	The format of a value when persisting in the data store.
type	Primitive | User-defined type	A .NET primitive type or class. Class names must be fully qualified (e.g., MyApp.UserData.ColorPrefs).

We will see some of these attributes in action as we modify the current profile. For now, let's see how to access this data programmatically from within our pages.

Accessing Profile Data Programmatically

Recall that the whole purpose of the ASP.NET Profile API is to automate the process of writing data to (and reading data from) a dedicated database. To test this out for yourself, update the UI of your Default.aspx file with a set of TextBoxes (and descriptive Labels) to gather the street address, city, and state of the user. As well, add a Button type (named btnSubmit) and a final Label (named lblUserData) that will be used to display the persisted data, as shown in Figure 33-11.

Now, within the Click event handler of the button, make use of the inherited Profile property to persist each point of profile data based on what the user has entered in the related TextBox. As you can see from Figure 33-12, Visual Studio 2008 will expose each bit of profile data as a strongly typed property. In effect, the Web.config file has been used to define a custom structure!

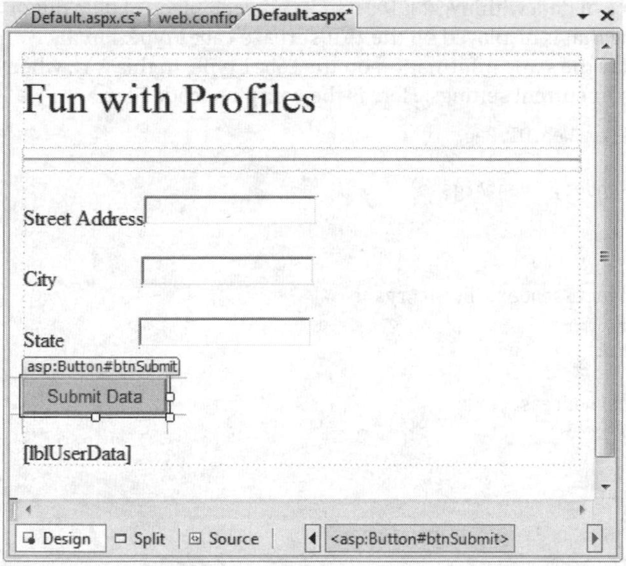

Figure 33-11. *The UI of the FunWithProfiles* `Default.aspx` *page*

Figure 33-12. *Profile data is strongly typed*

Once you have persisted each piece of data within ASPNETDB.mdf, read each piece of data out of the database and format it into a String that is displayed on the lblUserData Label type. Finally, handle the page's Load event, and display the same information on the Label type. In this way, when users come to the page, they can see their current settings. Here is the complete code file:

```
public partial class _Default : System.Web.UI.Page
{
  protected void Page_Load(object sender, EventArgs e)
  {
    GetUserAddress();
  }
  protected void btnSubmit_Click(object sender, EventArgs e)
  {
    // Database writes happening here!
    Profile.City = txtCity.Text;
    Profile.StreetAddress = txtStreetAddress.Text;
    Profile.State = txtState.Text;

    // Get settings from database.
    GetUserAddress();
  }

  private void GetUserAddress()
  {
    // Database reads happening here!
    lblUserData.Text = String.Format("You live here: {0}, {1}, {2}",
        Profile.StreetAddress, Profile.City, Profile.State);
  }
}
```

Now if you run this page, you will notice a lengthy delay the first time Default.aspx is requested. The reason is that the ASPNETDB.mdf file is being created on the fly and placed within your App_Data file. You can verify this for yourself by refreshing Solution Explorer (see Figure 33-13).

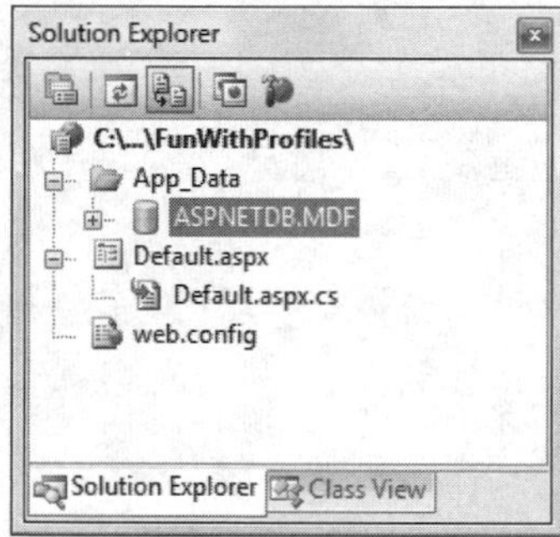

Figure 33-13. *Behold* ASPNETDB.mdf*!*

You will also find that the first time you come to this page, the lblUserData Label does not display any profile data, as you have not yet entered your data into the correct table of ASPNETDB.mdf. Once you enter values in the TextBox controls and post back to the server, you will find this Label is formatted with the persisted data, as shown in Figure 33-14.

Figure 33-14. *Our persisted user data*

Now, for the really interesting aspect of this technology. If you shut down your browser and rerun your website, you will find that your previously entered profile data has indeed been persisted, as the `Label` displays the correct information. This begs the obvious question, how were you remembered?

For this example, the Profile API made use of your Windows network identity, which was obtained by your current login credentials. However, when you are building public websites (where the users are not part of a given domain), rest assured that the Profile API integrates with the Forms-based authentication model of ASP.NET and also supports the notion of "anonymous profiles," which allow you to persist profile data for users who do not currently have an active identity on your site.

■ **Note** This edition of the text does not address ASP.NET security topics (such as Forms-based authentication or anonymous profiles). Consult the .NET Framework 3.5 SDK documentation for details.

Grouping Profile Data and Persisting Custom Objects

To wrap up this chapter, allow me to make a few additional comments on how profile data may be defined within a `Web.config` file. The current profile simply defined four pieces of data that were exposed directly from the profile type. When you build more complex profiles, it can be helpful to group related pieces of data under a unique name. Consider the following update:

```
<profile>
  <properties>
    <group name ="Address">
      <add name="StreetAddress" type="String" />
      <add name="City" type="String" />
      <add name="State" type="String" />
```

```
    </group>
    <add name="TotalPost" type="Integer" />
  </properties>
</profile>
```

This time we have defined a custom group named Address to expose the street address, city, and state of our user. To access this data in our pages would now require us to update our code base by specifying Profile.Address to get each subitem. For example, here is the updated GetUserAddress() method (the Click event handler for the Button type would need to be updated in a similar manner):

```
private void GetUserAddress()
{
  // Database reads happening here!
  lblUserData.Text = String.Format("You live here: {0}, {1}, {2}",
    Profile.Address.StreetAddress,
    Profile.Address.City, Profile.Address.State);
}
```

■Note A profile can contain as many groups as you feel are necessary. Simply define multiple <group> elements within your <properties> scope.

Finally, it is worth pointing out that a profile may also persist (and obtain) custom objects to and from ASPNETDB.mdf. To illustrate, assume that you wanted to build a custom class (or structure) that will represent the user's address data. The only requirement expected by the Profile API is that the type be marked with the [Serializable] attribute, for example:

```
[Serializable]
public class UserAddress
{
  public string Street = string.Empty;
  public string City = string.Empty;
  public string State = string.Empty;
}
```

With this class in place, our profile definition can now be updated as follows (notice I removed the custom group, although this is not mandatory):

```
<profile>
  <properties>
    <add name="AddressInfo" type="UserAddress" serializeAs ="Binary"/>
    <add name="TotalPost" type="Integer" />
  </properties>
</profile>
```

Notice that when you are adding [Serializable] types to a profile, the type attribute is the fully qualified named of the type being persisted. Thus, if you were adding an ArrayList to a profile, type would be set to System.Collections.ArrayList. As well, you can control how this state data should be persisted into ASPNETDB.mdf using the serializeAs attribute. As you will see from the Visual Studio 2008 IntelliSense, your core choices are binary, XML, or string data.

Now that we are capturing street address information as a custom class type, we (once again) need to update our code base:

```
private void GetUserAddress()
{
  // Database reads happening here!
  lblUserData.Text = String.Format("You live here: {0}, {1}, {2}",
    Profile.AddressInfo.Street, Profile.AddressInfo.City,
    Profile.AddressInfo.State);
}
```

To be sure, there is much more to the Profile API than I have had space to cover here. For example, the `Profile` property actually encapsulates a type named `ProfileCommon`. Using this type, you are able to programmatically obtain all information for a given user, delete (or add) profiles to `ASPNETDB.mdf`, update aspects of a profile, and so forth.

As well, the Profile API has numerous points of extensibility that can allow you to optimize how the profile manager accesses the tables of the `ASPNETDB.mdf` database. As you would expect, there are numerous ways to decrease the number of "hits" this database takes. Interested readers are encouraged to consult the .NET Framework 3.5 SDK documentation for further details.

Source Code The FunWithProfiles project is included under the Chapter 33 subdirectory.

Summary

In this chapter, you rounded out your knowledge of ASP.NET by examining how to leverage the `HttpApplication` type. As you have seen, this type provides a number of default event handlers that allow you to intercept various application- and session-level events. The bulk of this chapter was spent examining a number of state management techniques. Recall that view state is used to automatically repopulate the values of HTML widgets between postbacks to a specific page. Next, you checked out the distinction of application- and session-level data, cookie management, and the ASP.NET application cache.

The remainder of this chapter exposed you to the ASP.NET Profile API. As you have seen, this technology provides an out-of-the-box solution to the issue of persisting user data across sessions. Using your website's `Web.config` file, you are able to define any number of profile items (including groups of items and `[Serializable]` types) that will automatically be persisted into `ASPNETDB.mdf`.

PART 8

Appendixes

APPENDIX A

COM and .NET Interoperability

The goal of this book was to provide you with a solid foundation in the C# language and the core services provided by the .NET platform. I suspect that when you contrast the object model provided by .NET to that of Microsoft's previous component architecture (COM), you'll no doubt be convinced that these are two entirely unique systems. Regardless of the fact that COM is now considered to be a legacy framework, you may have existing COM-based systems that you would like to integrate into your new .NET applications.

Thankfully, the .NET platform provides various types, tools, and namespaces that make the process of COM and .NET interoperability quite straightforward. This appendix begins by examining the process of .NET to COM interoperability and the related Runtime Callable Wrapper (RCW). The latter part of this appendix examines the opposite situation: a COM type communicating with a .NET type using a COM Callable Wrapper (CCW).

Note A full examination of the .NET interoperability layer would require a book unto itself. If you require more details than presented in this appendix, check out my book *COM and .NET Interoperability* (Apress, 2002).

The Scope of .NET Interoperability

Recall that when you build assemblies using a .NET-aware compiler, you are creating *managed code* that can be hosted by the common language runtime (CLR). Managed code offers a number of benefits such as automatic memory management, a unified type system (the CTS), self-describing assemblies, and so forth. As you have also seen, .NET assemblies have a particular internal composition. In addition to CIL instructions and type metadata, assemblies contain a manifest that fully documents any required external assemblies as well as other file-related details (strong naming, version number, etc.).

On the other side of the spectrum are legacy COM servers (which are, of course, *unmanaged code*). These binaries bear no relationship to .NET assemblies beyond a shared file extension (`*.dll` or `*.exe`). First of all, COM servers contain platform-specific machine code, not platform-agnostic CIL instructions, and work with a unique set of data types (often termed *oleautomation* or *variant-compliant* data types), none of which are directly understood by the CLR.

In addition to the necessary COM-centric infrastructure required by all COM binaries (such as registry entries and support for core COM interfaces like `IUnknown`) is the fact that COM types demand to be *reference counted* in order to correctly control the lifetime of a COM object. This is in stark contrast, of course, to a .NET object, which is allocated on a managed heap and handled by the CLR garbage collector.

Given that .NET types and COM types have so little in common, you may wonder how these two architectures can make use of each others' services. Unless you are lucky enough to work for a company dedicated to "100% Pure .NET" development, you will most likely need to build .NET solutions that use legacy COM types. As well, you may find that a legacy COM server might like to communicate with the types contained within a shiny new .NET assembly.

The bottom line is that for some time to come, COM and .NET must learn how to get along. This appendix examines the process of managed and unmanaged types living together in harmony using the .NET interoperability layer. In general, the .NET Framework supports two core flavors of interoperability:

- .NET applications using COM types
- COM applications using .NET types

As you'll see throughout this appendix, the .NET Framework 3.5 SDK and Visual Studio 2008 supply a number of tools that help bridge the gap between these unique architectures. As well, the .NET base class library defines a namespace (`System.Runtime.InteropServices`) dedicated solely to the issue of interoperability. However, before diving in too far under the hood, let's look at a very simple example of a .NET class communicating with a COM server.

■ **Note** The .NET platform also makes it very simple for a .NET assembly to call into the underlying API of the operating system (as well as any C-based unmanaged `*.dll`) using a technology termed *platform invocation* (or simply PInvoke). From a C# point of view, working with PInvoke involves at absolute minimum applying the `[DllImport]` attribute to the external method to be executed. Although PInvoke is not examined in this appendix, check out the `[DllImport]` attribute using the .NET Framework 3.5 SDK documentation for further details.

A Simple Example of .NET to COM Interop

To begin our exploration of interoperability services, let's see just how simple things appear on the surface. The goal of this section is to build a Visual Basic 6.0 ActiveX `*.dll` server, which is then consumed by a C# application.

■ **Note** There are many COM frameworks in existence beyond VB6 (such as the Active Template Library [ATL] and the Microsoft Foundation Classes [MFC]). VB6 has been chosen to build the COM servers in this appendix, as it provides the most user-friendly syntax to build COM applications. Feel free to make use of ATL/MFC if you so choose.

Fire up VB6, and create a new ActiveX `*.dll` project named SimpleComServer, rename your initial class file to `ComCalc.cls`, and name the class itself `ComCalc`. As you may know, the name of your project and the names assigned to the contained classes will be used to define the programmatic identifier (ProgID) of the COM types (`SimpleComServer.ComCalc`, in this case). Finally, define the following methods within `ComCalc.cls`:

```
' The VB6 COM object
Option Explicit

Public Function Add(ByVal x As Integer, ByVal y As Integer) As Integer
  Add = x + y
End Function
```

```
Public Function Subtract(ByVal x As Integer, ByVal y As Integer) As Integer
  Subtract = x - y
End Function
```

At this point, compile your *.dll (via the File ➤ Make menu option) and, just to keep things peaceful in the world of COM, establish binary compatibility (via the Component tab of the project's Property page) before you exit the VB6 IDE. This will ensure that if you recompile the application, VB6 will preserve the assigned globally unique identifiers (GUIDs).

Source Code The SimpleComServer project is located under the Appendix A subdirectory.

Building the C# Client

Now open up Visual Studio 2008 and create a new C# Console Application named CSharpComClient. When you are building a .NET application that needs to communicate with a legacy COM application, the first step is to reference the COM server within your project (much like you reference a .NET assembly).

To do so, simply access the Project ➤ Add Reference menu selection and select the COM tab from the Add Reference dialog box. The name of your COM server will be listed alphabetically, as the VB6 compiler updated the system registry with the necessary listings when you compiled your project. Go ahead and select the SimpleComServer.dll as shown in Figure A-1 and close the dialog box.

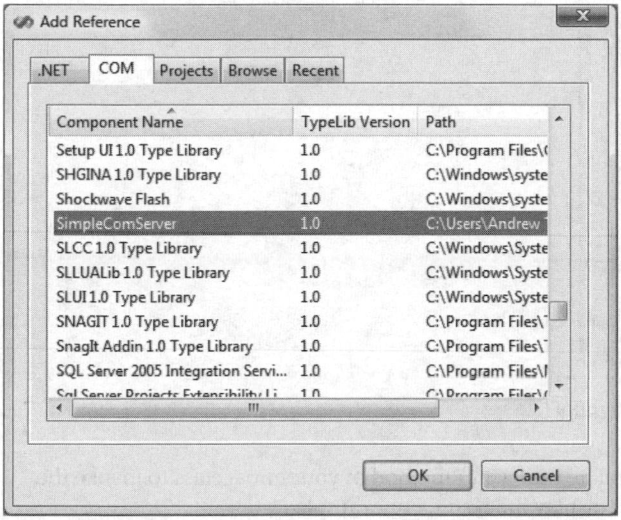

Figure A-1. *Referencing a COM server using Visual Studio 2008*

Now, if you examine the References folder of the Solution Explorer, you see what looks to be a new .NET assembly reference added to your project, as illustrated in Figure A-2. Formally speaking, assemblies that are generated when referencing a COM server are termed *interop assemblies*. Without getting too far ahead of ourselves at this point, simply understand that interop assemblies contain .NET descriptions of COM types.

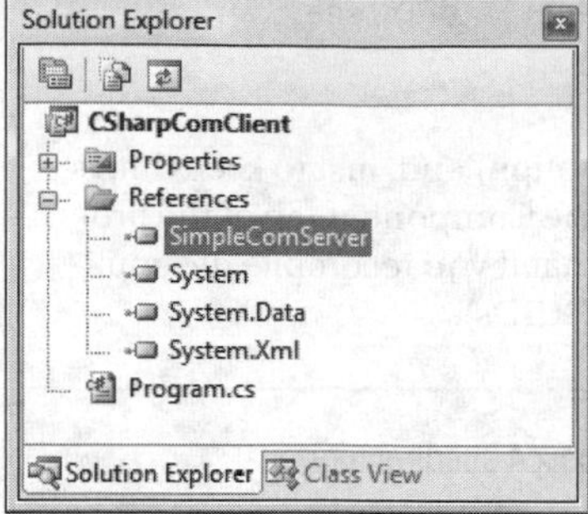

Figure A-2. *The referenced interop assembly*

Although we have not added any code to our initial C# class type, if you compile your application and examine the project's bin\Debug directory, you will find that a local copy of the generated interop assembly has been placed in the application directory (see Figure A-3). Notice that Visual Studio 2008 automatically prefixes `Interop.` to interop assemblies generated when using the Add Reference dialog box—however, this is only a convention; the CLR does not demand that interop assemblies follow this particular naming convention.

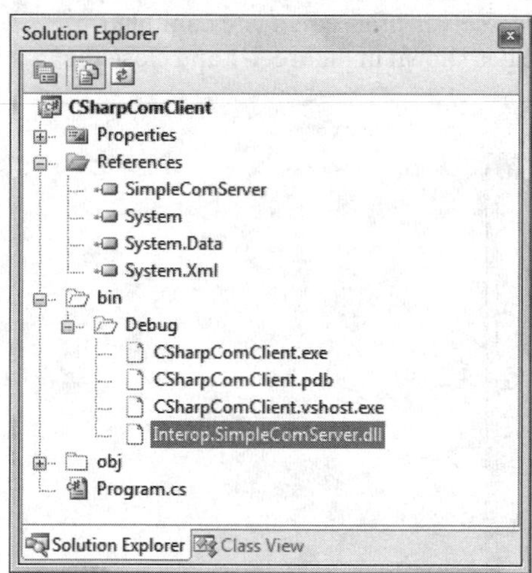

Figure A-3. *The autogenerated interop assembly*

To complete this initial example, update the `Main()` method of your initial class to invoke the `Add()` method from a `ComCalc` object and display the result. For example:

```
using System;
using SimpleComServer;

namespace CSharpComClient
{
  class Program
  {
    static void Main(string[] args)
    {
```

```
      Console.WriteLine("***** The .NET COM Client App *****");
      ComCalc comObj  = new ComCalc();
      Console.WriteLine("COM server says 10 + 832 is {0}",
        comObj.Add(10, 832));
      Console.ReadLine();
    }
  }
}
```

As you can see from the previous code example, the namespace that contains the ComCalc COM object is named identically to the original VB6 project (notice the using statement). The output shown in Figure A-4 is as you would expect.

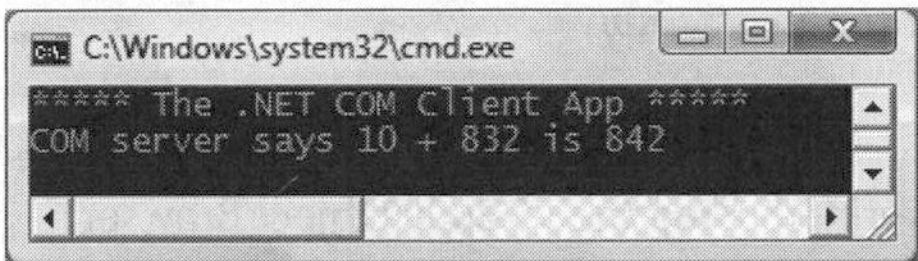

Figure A-4. *Behold! .NET to COM interoperability*

As you can see, consuming a COM type from a .NET application can be a very transparent operation indeed. As you might imagine, however, a number of details are occurring behind the scenes to make this communication possible, the gory details of which you will explore throughout this appendix, beginning with taking a deeper look into the interop assembly itself.

Investigating a .NET Interop Assembly

As you have just seen, when you reference a COM server using the Visual Studio 2008 Add Reference dialog box, the IDE responds by generating a brand-new .NET assembly taking an Interop. prefix (such as Interop.SimpleComServer.dll). Just like an assembly that you would create yourself, interop assemblies contain type metadata, an assembly manifest, and under some circumstances *may* contain CIL code. As well, just like a "normal" assembly, interop assemblies can be deployed privately (e.g., within the directory of the client assembly) or assigned a strong name to be deployed to the GAC.

Interop assemblies are little more than containers to hold .NET metadata descriptions of the original COM types. In many cases, interop assemblies do not contain CIL instructions to implement their methods, as the real work is taking place in the COM server itself. The only time an interop assembly contains executable CIL instructions is if the COM server contains COM objects that have the ability to fire events to the client. In this case, the CIL code within the interop assembly is used by the CLR to translate the event-handling logic from COM connection points into .NET delegates.

At first glance, it may seem that interop assemblies are not entirely useful, given that they do not contain any implementation logic. However, the metadata descriptions within an interop assembly are extremely important, as it will be consumed by the CLR at runtime to build a runtime proxy (termed the *Runtime Callable Wrapper*, or simply *RCW*) that forms a bridge between the .NET application and the COM object it is communicating with.

You'll examine the details of the RCW in the next several sections; however, for the time being, open up the Interop.SimpleComServer.dll assembly using ildasm.exe, as you see in Figure A-5.

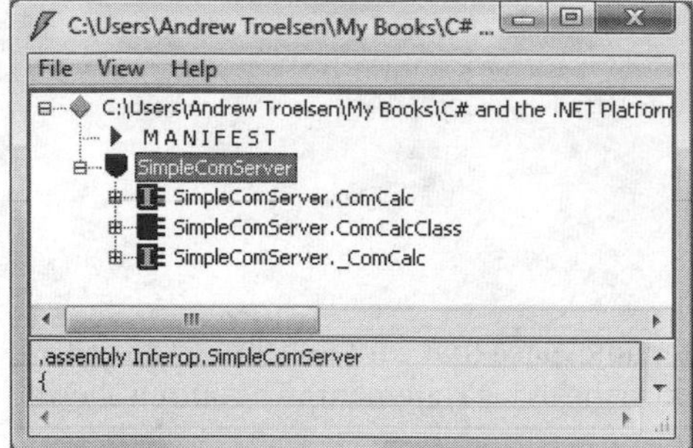

Figure A-5. *The guts of the* `Interop.SimpleComServer.dll` *interop assembly*

As you can see, although the original VB6 project only defined a single COM class (`ComCalc`), the interop assembly contains *three* types. This can also be verified using the VS 2008 Object Browser (see Figure A-6).

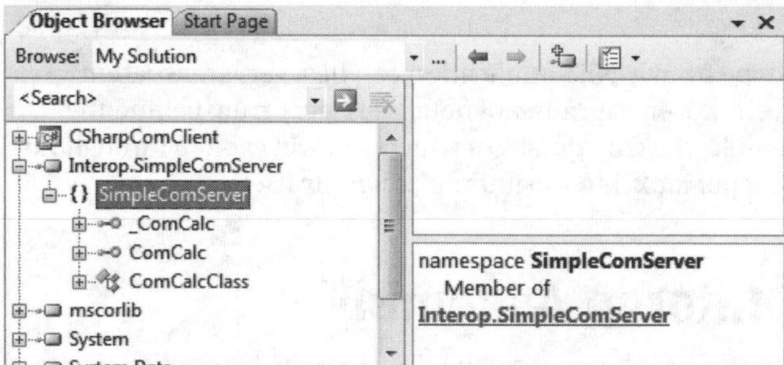

Figure A-6. *Hmm, how does a single COM type yield three .NET types?*

Simply put, each COM class is represented by three distinct .NET types. First, you have a .NET type that is identically named to the original COM type (`ComCalc`, in this case). Next, you have a second .NET type that takes a `Class` suffix (`ComCalcClass`). These types are very helpful when you have a COM type that implements several custom interfaces, in that the `Class`-suffixed types expose *all* members from *each* interface supported by the COM type. Thus, from a .NET programmer's point of view, there is no need to manually obtain a reference to a specific COM interface before invoking its functionality. Although `ComCalc` did not implement multiple custom interfaces, we are able to invoke the `Add()` and `Subtract()` methods from a `ComCalcClass` object (rather than a `ComCalc` object) as follows:

```
static void Main(string[] args)
{
  Console.WriteLine("***** The .NET COM Client App *****");

  // Now using the Class-suffixed type.
  ComCalcClass comObj = new ComCalcClass();
  Console.WriteLine("COM server says 10 + 832 is {0}",
    comObj.Add(10, 832));
  Console.ReadLine();
}
```

Finally, interop assemblies define .NET equivalents of any original COM interfaces defined within the COM server. In this case, we find a .NET interface named `_ComCalc`. Unless you are well versed in the mechanics of VB6 COM, this is certain to appear strange, given that we never directly created an interface in our SimpleComServer project (let alone the oddly named `_ComCalc` interface). The role of these underscore-prefixed interfaces will become clear as you move throughout this appendix; for now, simply know that if you really wanted to, you could make use of interface-based programming techniques to invoke `Add()` or `Subtract()`:

```
static void Main(string[] args)
{
  Console.WriteLine("***** The .NET COM Client App *****");

  // Now manually obtain the hidden interface.
  ComCalc itfComInterface = null;
  ComCalcClass comObj = new ComCalcClass();
  itfComInterface = (_ComCalc)comObj;

  Console.WriteLine("COM server says 10 + 832 is {0}",
    itfComInterface.Add(10, 832));
  Console.ReadLine();
}
```

Now, do understand that invoking a method using the `Class`-suffixed or underscore-prefixed interface is seldom necessary. However, as you build more complex .NET applications that need to work with COM types in more sophisticated manners, having knowledge of these types is critical.

Source Code The CSharpComClient project is located under the Appendix A subdirectory.

Understanding the Runtime Callable Wrapper

As mentioned, at runtime the CLR will make use of the metadata contained within a .NET interop assembly to build a proxy type that will manage the process of .NET to COM communication. The proxy to which I am referring is the Runtime Callable Wrapper, which is little more than a bridge to the real COM class (officially termed a *coclass*). Every coclass accessed by a .NET client requires a corresponding RCW. Thus, if you have a single .NET application that uses three COM coclasses, you end up with three distinct RCWs that map .NET calls into COM requests. Figure A-7 illustrates the big picture.

Note There is always a single RCW per COM object, regardless of how many interfaces the .NET client has obtained from the COM type (you'll examine a multi-interfaced VB6 COM object a bit later in this appendix). Using this technique, the RCW can maintain the correct COM identity (and reference count) of the COM object.

Again, the good news is that the RCW is created automatically when required by the CLR. The other bit of good news is that legacy COM servers do not require any modifications to be consumed by a .NET-aware language. The intervening RCW takes care of the internal work. To see how this is achieved, let's formalize some core responsibilities of the RCW.

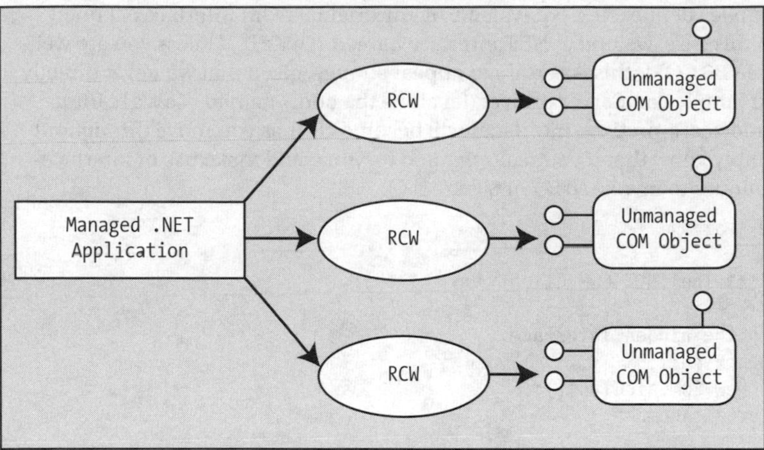

Figure A-7. *RCWs sit between the .NET caller and the COM object.*

The RCW: Exposing COM Types As .NET Types

The RCW is in charge of transforming COM data types into .NET equivalents (and vice versa). As a simple example, assume you have a VB6 COM subroutine defined as follows:

```
' VB6 COM method definition.
Public Sub DisplayThisString(ByVal s as String)
```

The interop assembly defines the method parameter as a .NET `System.String`:

```
' C# mapping of COM method.
public void DisplayThisString(string s)
```

When this method is invoked by the .NET code base, the RCW automatically takes the incoming `System.String` and transforms it into a VB6 `String` data type (which, as you may know, is in fact a COM `BSTR`). As you would guess, all COM data types have a corresponding .NET equivalent. To help you gain your bearings, Table A-1 documents the mapping taking place between COM IDL (interface definition language) data types, the related .NET `System` data types, and the corresponding C# keyword (if applicable).

Table A-1. *Mapping Intrinsic COM Types to .NET Types*

COM IDL Data Type	System Types	C# Keyword
wchar_t, short	System.Int16	short
long, int	System.Int32	int
Hyper	System.Int64	long
unsigned char, byte	System.Byte	byte
single	System.Single	-
double	System.Double	double
VARIANT_BOOL	System.Boolean	bool

COM IDL Data Type	System Types	C# Keyword
BSTR	System.String	string
VARIANT	System.Object	object
DECIMAL	System.Decimal	-
DATE	System.DateTime	-
GUID	System.Guid	-
CURRENCY	System.Decimal	-
IUnknown	System.Object	object
IDispatch	System.Object	object

The RCW: Managing a Coclass's Reference Count

Another important duty of the RCW is to manage the reference count of the COM object. As you may know from your experience with COM, the COM reference-counting scheme is a joint venture between coclass and client and revolves around the proper use of `AddRef()` and `Release()` calls. COM objects self-destruct when they detect that they have no outstanding references.

However, .NET types do not use the COM reference-counting scheme, and therefore a .NET client should not be forced to call `Release()` on the COM types it uses. To keep each participant happy, the RCW caches all interface references internally and triggers the final release when the type is no longer used by the .NET client. The bottom line is that similar to VB6, .NET clients never explicitly call `AddRef()`, `Release()`, or `QueryInterface()`.

Note If you wish to directly interact with a COM object's reference count from a .NET application, the `System.Runtime.InteropServices` namespace provides a type named `Marshal`. This class defines a number of static methods, many of which can be used to manually interact with a COM object's lifetime. Although you will typically not need to make use of `Marshal` in most of your applications, consult the .NET Framework 3.5 SDK documentation for further details.

The RCW: Hiding Low-Level COM Interfaces

The final core service provided by the RCW is to consume a number of low-level COM interfaces. Because the RCW tries to do everything it can to fool the .NET client into thinking it is directly communicating with a native .NET type, the RCW must hide various low-level COM interfaces from view.

For example, when you build a COM class that supports `IConnectionPointContainer` (and maintains a subobject or two supporting `IConnectionPoint`), the coclass in question is able to fire events back to the COM client. VB6 hides this entire process from view using the `Event` and `RaiseEvent` keywords. In the same vein, the RCW also hides such COM "goo" from the .NET client. Table A-2 outlines the role of these hidden COM interfaces consumed by the RCW.

Table A-2. *Hidden COM Interfaces*

Hidden COM Interface	Meaning in Life
IConnectionPointContainer IConnectionPoint	Enable a coclass to send events back to an interested client. VB6 automatically provides a default implementation of each of these interfaces.
IDispatch IProvideClassInfo	Facilitate "late binding" to a coclass. Again, when you are building VB6 COM types, these interfaces are automatically supported by a given COM type.
IErrorInfo ISupportErrorInfo ICreateErrorInfo	These interfaces enable COM clients and COM objects to send and respond to COM errors.
IUnknown	The granddaddy of COM. Manages the reference count of the COM object and allows clients to obtain interfaces from the coclass.

The Role of COM IDL

At this point, you hopefully have a solid understanding of the role of the interop assembly and the RCW. Before you go much further into the COM to .NET conversion process, it is necessary to review some of the finer details of COM IDL. Understand, of course, that this appendix is *not* intended to function as a complete COM IDL tutorial; however, to better understand the interop layer, you only need to be aware of a few IDL constructs.

All .NET assemblies contain *metadata*. Formally speaking, metadata is used to describe each and every aspect of a .NET assembly, including the internal types (their members, base class, and so on), assembly version, and optional assembly-level information (strong name, culture, and so on).

In many ways, .NET metadata is the big brother of an earlier metadata format used to describe classic COM servers. Classic ActiveX COM servers (`*.dlls` or `*.exes`) document their internal types using a *type library*, which may be realized as a stand-alone `*.tlb` file or bundled into the COM server as an internal resource (which is the default behavior of VB6). COM type libraries are typically created using a metadata language called the Interface Definition Language and a special compiler named `midl.exe` (the Microsoft IDL compiler).

VB6 does a fantastic job of hiding type libraries and IDL from view. In fact, many skilled VB COM programmers can live a happy and productive life ignoring the syntax of IDL altogether. Nevertheless, whenever you compile ActiveX project workspace types, VB automatically generates and embeds the type library within the physical `*.dll` or `*.exe` COM server. Furthermore, VB6 ensures that the type library is automatically registered under a very particular part of the system registry: HKEY_CLASSES_ROOT\TypeLib (see Figure A-8).

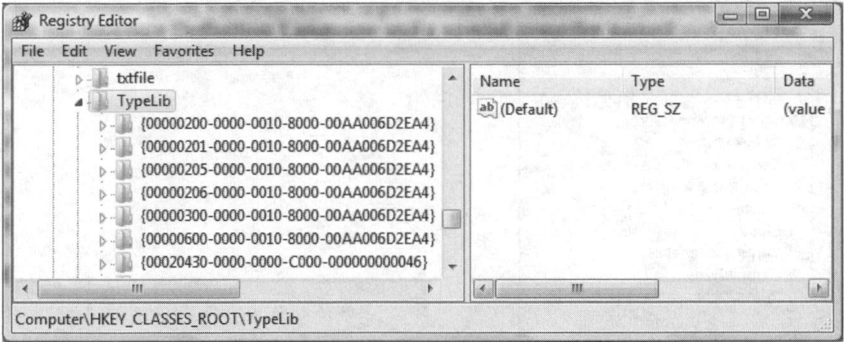

Figure A-8. *HKCR\TypeLib lists all registered type libraries on a given machine.*

Type libraries are referenced all the time by numerous IDEs. For example, whenever you access the Project ➤ References menu selection of VB6, the IDE consults HKCR\TypeLib to determine each and every registered type library, as shown in Figure A-9.

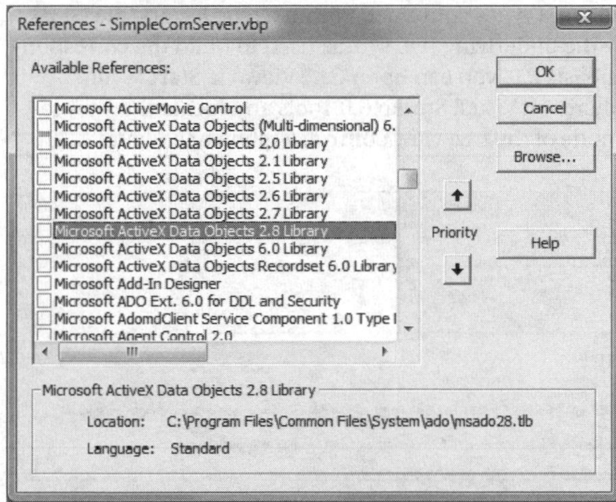

Figure A-9. *Referencing COM type information from VB6*

Likewise, when you open the VB6 Object Browser, the VB6 IDE reads the type information and displays the contents of the COM server using a friendly GUI, as shown in Figure A-10.

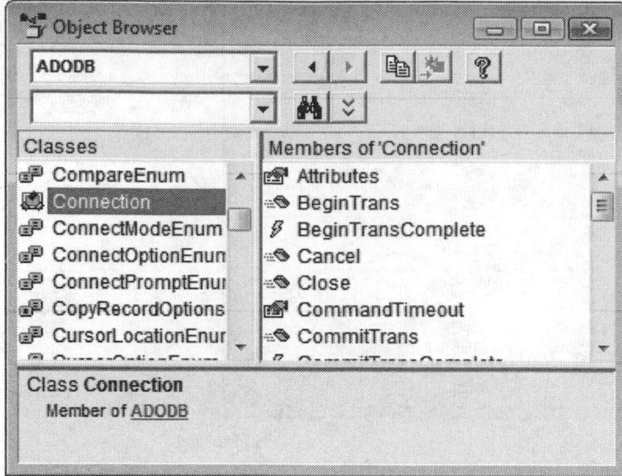

Figure A-10. *Viewing type libraries using the VB6 Object Browser*

Observing the Generated IDL for Your VB COM Server

Although the VB6 Object Browser displays all COM types contained within a type library, the OLE View utility (`oleview.exe`) allows you to view the underlying IDL syntax used to build the corresponding type library. If you have installed Visual Basic 6.0, you can open OLE View via Start ➤ All Programs ➤ Microsoft Visual Studio 6.0 ➤ Microsoft Visual Studio 6.0 Tools and locate the SimpleComServer server under the Type Libraries node of the tree view control, as shown in Figure A-11.

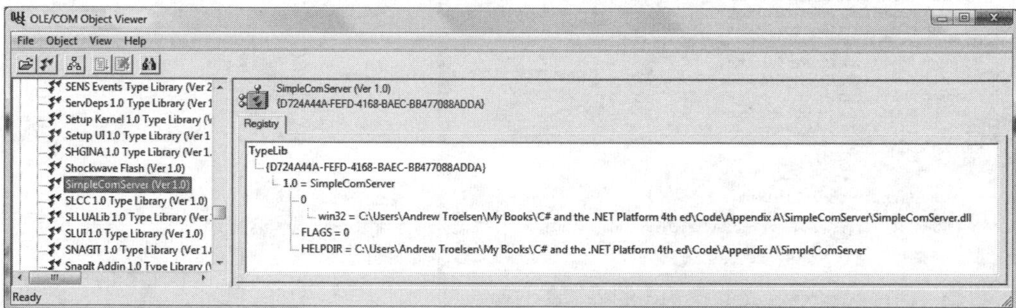

Figure A-11. *Hunting down SimpleComServer using the OLE/COM object viewer*

If you were to double-click the type library icon, you would open a new window that shows you all of the IDL tokens that constitute the type library generated by the VB6 compiler. Here is the relevant—and slightly reformatted—IDL (your `[uuid]` values will differ):

```
[uuid(8AED93CB-7832-4699-A2FC-CAE08693E720), version(1.0)]
library SimpleComServer
{
  importlib("stdole2.tlb");
  interface _ComCalc;

  [odl, uuid(5844CD28-2075-4E77-B619-9B65AA0761A3), version(1.0),
   hidden, dual, nonextensible, oleautomation]
  interface _ComCalc : IDispatch {
    [id(0x60030000)]
```

```
    HRESULT Add([in] short x, [in] short y, [out, retval] short* );
    [id(0x60030001)]
    HRESULT Subtract([in] short x, [in] short y, [out, retval] short* );
    };

    [uuid(012B1485-6834-47FF-8E53-3090FE85050C), version(1.0)]
    coclass ComCalc {
        [default] interface _ComCalc;
    };
};
```

IDL Attributes

To begin parsing out this IDL, notice that IDL syntax contains blocks of code placed in square brackets ([...]). Within these brackets is a comma-delimited set of IDL keywords, which are used to disambiguate the "very next thing" (the item to the right of the block or the item directly below the block). These blocks are IDL *attributes* that serve the same purpose as .NET attributes (i.e., they describe something). One key IDL attribute is [uuid], which is used to assign the GUID of a given COM type. As you may already know, just about everything in COM is assigned a GUID (interfaces, COM classes, type libraries, and so on), which is used to uniquely identify a given item.

The IDL Library Statement

Starting at the top, you have the COM *library statement*, which is marked using the IDL library keyword. Contained within the library statement are each and every interface and COM class, and any enumeration and user-defined type. In the case of SimpleComServer, the type library lists exactly one COM class, ComCalc, which is marked using the coclass (i.e., COM class) keyword.

The Role of the [default] Interface

According to the laws of COM, the only possible way in which a COM client can communicate with a COM class is to use an interface reference (not an object reference). If you have created C++-based COM clients, you are well aware of the process of querying for a given interface, releasing the interface when it is no longer used, and so forth. However, when you make use of VB6 to build COM clients, you receive a *default interface* on the COM class automatically.

When you build VB6 COM servers, any public member on a *.cls file (such as your Add() function) is placed onto the "default interface" of the COM class. Now, if you examine the class definition of ComCalc, you can see that the name of the default interface is _ComCalc:

```
[uuid(012B1485-6834-47FF-8E53-3090FE85050C), version(1.0)]
coclass ComCalc {
  [default] interface _ComCalc;
};
```

In case you are wondering, the name of the default interface VB6 constructs in the background is always _NameOfTheClass (the underscore is a naming convention used to specify a hidden interface). Thus, if you have a class named Car, the default interface is _Car, a class named DataConnector has a default interface named _DataConnector, and so forth.

Under VB6, the default interface is completely hidden from view. However, when you write the following VB6 code:

```
' VB 6.0 COM client code.
Dim c As ComCalc
Set c = New ComCalc ' [default] _ComCalc interface returned automatically!
```

the VB runtime automatically queries the object for the default interface (as specified by the type library) and returns it to the client. Because VB always returns the default interface on a COM class, you can pretend that you have a true object reference. However, this is only a bit of syntactic sugar provided by VB6. In COM, there is no such thing as a direct object reference. You always have an interface reference (even if it happens to be the default).

The Role of IDispatch

If you examine the IDL description of the default `_ComCalc` interface, you see that this interface derives from a standard COM interface named `IDispatch`. While a full discussion concerning the role of `IDispatch` is well outside of the scope of this appendix, simply understand that this is the interface that makes it possible to interact with COM objects on the Web from within a classic Active Server Page, as well as anywhere else where late binding is required.

IDL Parameter Attributes

The final bit of IDL that you need to be aware of is how VB6 parameters are expressed under the hood. Under VB6 all parameters are passed by reference, unless the `ByVal` keyword is used explicitly, which is represented using the IDL `[in]` attribute. Furthermore, a function's return value is marked using the `[out, retval]` attributes. Thus, the following VB6 function:

```
' VB6 function
Public Function Add(ByVal x as Integer, ByVal y as Integer) as Integer
  Add = x + y
End Function
```

would be expressed in IDL like so:

```
HRESULT Add([in] short* x, [in] short* y, [out, retval] short*);
```

On the other hand, if you do not mark a parameter using the VB6 `ByVal` keyword, `ByRef` is assumed:

```
' These parameters are passed ByRef under VB6!
Public Function Subtract(x As Integer, y As Integer) As Integer
  Subtract = x - y
End Function
```

`ByRef` parameters are marked in IDL via the `[in, out]` attributes:

```
HRESULT Subtract([in, out] short x,  [in, out] short y,  [out, retval] short*);
```

Using a Type Library to Build an Interop Assembly

To be sure, the VB6 compiler generates many other IDL attributes under the hood, and you will see additional bits and pieces where appropriate. However, at this point, I am sure you are wondering exactly why I spent the last several pages describing COM IDL. The reason is simple: when you add a reference to a COM server using Visual Studio 2008, the IDE reads the type library to build the corresponding interop assembly. While VS 2008 does a very good job of generating an interop assembly, the Add Reference dialog box follows a default set of rules regarding how the interop assembly will be constructed and does not allow you to fine-tune this construction.

If you require a greater level of flexibility, you have the option of generating interop assemblies at the command prompt, using a .NET tool named `tlbimp.exe` (the type library importer utility). Among other things, `tlbimp.exe` allows you to control the name of the .NET namespace that will contain the types and the name of the output file. Furthermore, if you wish to assign a strong name to your interop assembly in order to deploy it to the GAC, `tlbimp.exe` provides the `/keyfile` flag to specify the `*.snk` file (see Chapter 15 for details regarding strong names). To view all of your options, simply type **tlbimp** at a Visual Studio 2008 command prompt and hit the Enter key, as shown in Figure A-12.

```
Administrator: Visual Studio 2008 Beta 2 Command Prompt
Setting environment for using Microsoft Visual Studio 2008 Beta2 x86 tools.

C:\Program Files\Microsoft Visual Studio 9.0\VC>tlbimp
Microsoft (R) .NET Framework Type Library to Assembly Converter 2.0.50727.312
Copyright (C) Microsoft Corporation.  All rights reserved.

Syntax: TlbImp TypeLibName [Options]
Options:
    /out:FileName             File name of assembly to be produced
    /namespace:Namespace      Namespace of the assembly to be produced
    /asmversion:Version       Version number of the assembly to be produced
    /reference:FileName       File name of assembly to use to resolve references
    /tlbreference:FileName    File name of typelib to use to resolve references
    /publickey:FileName       File containing strong name public key
    /keyfile:FileName         File containing strong name key pair
    /keycontainer:FileName    Key container holding strong name key pair
    /delaysign                Force strong name delay signing
    /unsafe                   Produce interfaces without runtime security checks
    /noclassmembers           Prevents TlbImp from adding members to classes
    /nologo                   Prevents TlbImp from displaying logo
    /silent                   Suppresses all output except for errors
    /verbose                  Displays extra information
    /primary                  Produce a primary interop assembly
```

Figure A-12. *Options of* `tlbimp.exe`

While this tool has numerous options, the following command could be used to generate a strongly named interop assembly (assuming you have generated a `*.snk` file named `myKeyPair.snk`) named `CalcInteropAsm.dll`:

```
tlbimp SimpleComServer.dll /keyfile:myKeyPair.snk /out:CalcInteropAsm.dll
```

Again, if you are happy with the interop assembly created by Visual Studio 2008, you are not required to directly make use of `tlbimp.exe`.

Late Binding to the CoCalc Coclass

Once you have generated an interop assembly, your .NET applications are now able to make use of their types using early binding or late binding techniques. Given that you have already seen how to create a COM type using early binding at the opening of this appendix (via the C# `new` keyword), let's turn our attention to activating a COM object using late binding.

As you recall from Chapter 16, the `System.Reflection` namespace provides a way for you to programmatically inspect the types contained in a given assembly at runtime. In COM, the same sort of functionality is supported through the use of a set of standard interfaces (e.g., `ITypeLib`, `ITypeInfo`, and so on). When a client binds to a member at runtime (rather than at compile time), the client is said to exercise "late" binding.

By and large, you should always prefer the early binding technique using the C# `new` keyword. There are times, however, when you must use late binding to a coclass. For example, some legacy COM servers may have been constructed in such a way that they provide no type information whatsoever. If this is the case, it should be clear that you cannot run the `tlbimp.exe` utility in the first place. For these rare occurrences, you can access classic COM types using .NET reflection services.

The process of late binding begins with a client obtaining the IDispatch interface from a given coclass. This standard COM interface defines a total of four methods, only two of which you need to concern yourself with at the moment. First, you have GetIDsOfNames(). This method allows a caller to use late binding by obtaining the numerical value (called the dispatch ID, or DISPID) used to identify the method it is attempting to invoke.

In COM IDL, a member's DISPID is assigned using the [id] attribute. If you examine the IDL code generated by VB6 (using the OLE View tool), you will see that the DISPID of the Add() method has been assigned a DISPID such as the following:

```
[id(0x60030000)] HRESULT Add( [in] short x, [in] short y, [out, retval] short* );
```

This is the value that GetIDsOfNames() returns to the late-bound client. Once the client obtains this value, it makes a call to the next method of interest, Invoke(). This method of IDispatch takes a number of arguments, one of which is the DISPID obtained using GetIDsOfNames(). In addition, the Invoke() method takes an array of COM VARIANT types that represent the parameters passed to the function. In the case of the Add() method, this array contains two shorts (of some value). The final argument of Invoke() is another VARIANT that holds the return value of the method invocation (again, a short).

Although a .NET client using late binding does not directly use the IDispatch interface, the same general functionality comes through using the System.Reflection namespace. To illustrate, the following is another C# client that uses late binding to trigger the Add() logic. Notice that this application does *not* make reference to the assembly in any way and therefore does not require the use of the tlbimp.exe utility.

```
// Be sure to use the System.Reflection namespace.
static void Main(string[] args)
{
  Console.WriteLine("***** The Late Bound .NET Client *****");

  // First get IDispatch reference from coclass.
  Type calcObj =
    Type.GetTypeFromProgID("SimpleCOMServer.ComCalc");
  object calcDisp = Activator.CreateInstance(calcObj);

  // Make the array of args.
  object[] addArgs = { 100, 24 };

  // Invoke the Add() method and obtain summation.
  object sum = null;
  sum = calcObj.InvokeMember("Add", BindingFlags.InvokeMethod,
    null, calcDisp, addArgs);

  // Display result.
  Console.WriteLine("Late bound adding: 100 + 24 is: {0}", sum);
  Console.ReadLine();
}
```

Source Code The CSharpComLateBinding application is included under the Appendix A subdirectory.

Building a More Elaborate COM Server

So much for Math 101. It's time to build a VB6 ActiveX server that makes use of more elaborate COM programming techniques. Create a brand-new ActiveX *.dll workspace named Vb6ComCarServer. Rename your initial class to CoCar, which is implemented like so:

```
Option Explicit

' A COM enum.
Enum CarType
  Viper
  Colt
  BMW
End Enum

' A COM Event.
Public Event BlewUp()

' Member variables.
Private currSp As Integer
Private maxSp As Integer
Private Make As CarType

' Remember! All Public members
' are exposed by the default interface!
Public Property Get CurrentSpeed() As Integer
  CurrentSpeed = currSp
End Property

Public Property Get CarMake() As CarType
  CarMake = Make
End Property

Public Sub SpeedUp()
  currSp = currSp + 10
  If currSp >= maxSp Then
    RaiseEvent BlewUp ' Fire event if you max out the engine.
  End If
End Sub

Private Sub Class_Initialize()
  MsgBox "Init COM car"
End Sub

Public Sub Create(ByVal max As Integer, _
  ByVal cur As Integer, ByVal t As CarType)
  maxSp = max
  currSp = cur
  Make = t
End Sub
```

As you can see, this is a simple COM class that mimics the functionality of the C# Car class used throughout this text. The only point of interest is the Create() subroutine, which allows the caller to pass in the state data representing the Car object.

Supporting an Additional COM Interface

Now that you have fleshed out the details of building a COM class with a single (default) interface, insert a new `*.cls` file that defines the following `IDriverInfo` interface:

```
Option Explicit

' Driver has a name
Public Property Let DriverName(ByVal s As String)
End Property
Public Property Get DriverName() As String
End Property
```

If you have created COM objects supporting multiple interfaces, you are aware that VB6 provides the `Implements` keyword. Once you specify the interfaces implemented by a given COM class, you are able to make use of the VB6 code window to build the method stubs. Assume you have added a private `String` variable (`driverName`) to the `CoCar` class type and implemented the `IDriverInfo` interface as follows:

```
' Implemented interfaces
' [General][Declarations]
Implements IDriverInfo
...
' ***** IDriverInfo impl ***** '
Private Property Let IDriverInfo_DriverName(ByVal RHS As String)
  driverName = RHS
End Property

Private Property Get IDriverInfo_DriverName() As String
  IDriverInfo_driverName = driverName
End Property
```

To wrap up this interface implementation, set the `Instancing` property of `IDriverInfo` to `PublicNotCreatable` (given that the outside world should not be able to allocate interface types).

Exposing an Inner Object

Under VB6 (as well as COM itself), we do not have the luxury of classical implementation inheritance. Rather, we're limited to the use of the containment/delegation model (the "has-a" relationship). For testing purposes, add a final `*.cls` file to your current VB6 project named `Engine`, and set its instancing property to `PublicNotCreatable` (as you want to prevent the user from directly creating an `Engine` object).

The default public interface of `Engine` is short and sweet. Define a single function that returns an array of strings to the outside world representing pet names for each cylinder of the engine (okay, no right-minded person gives friendly names to his or her cylinders, but hey . . .):

```
Option Explicit

Public Function GetCylinders() As String()
  Dim c(3) As String
  c(0) = "Grimey"
  c(1) = "Thumper"
  c(2) = "Oily"
  c(3) = "Crusher"
  GetCylinders = c
End Function
```

Finally, add a method to the default interface of CoCar named GetEngine(), which returns an instance of the contained Engine (I assume you will create a Private member variable named eng of type Engine for this purpose):

```
' Return the Engine to the world.
Public Function GetEngine() As Engine
  Set GetEngine = eng
End Function
```

At this point, you have an ActiveX server that contains a COM class supporting two interfaces. As well, you are able to return an internal COM type using the [default] interface of the CoCar and interact with some common programming constructs (enums and COM arrays). Go ahead and compile your sever (setting binary compatibility, once finished), and then close down your current VB6 workspace.

Source Code The Vb6ComCarServer project is included under the Appendix A subdirectory.

Examining the Interop Assembly

Rather than making use of the tlbimp.exe utility to generate our interop assembly, simply create a new console project (named CSharpCarClient) using Visual Studio 2008 and set a reference to the Vb6ComCarServer.dll using the COM tab of the Add Reference dialog box. Now, examine the interop assembly using the VS 2008 Object Browser utility, as shown in Figure A-13.

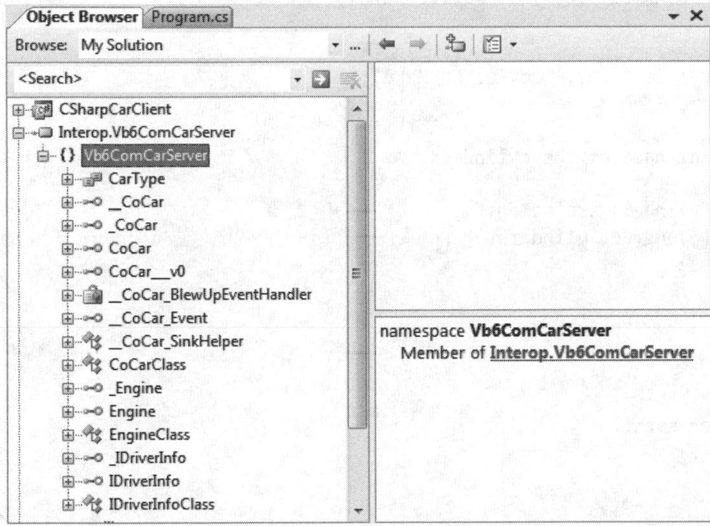

Figure A-13. *The* Interop.VbComCarServer.dll *assembly*

Once again we have a number of Class-suffixed and underscore-prefixed interface types, as well as a number of new items we have not yet examined, whose names suggest they may be used to handle COM to .NET event notifications (__CoCar_Event, __CoCar_SinkHelper, and __CoCarBlewUpEventHandler in particular). Recall from earlier in this appendix, I mentioned that when a COM object exposes COM events, the interop assembly will contain additional CIL code that is used by the CLR to map COM events to .NET events (you'll see them in action in just a bit).

Building Our C# Client Application

Given that the CLR will automatically create the necessary RCW at runtime, our C# application can program directly against the CoCar, CarType, Engine, and IDriveInfo types as if they were all implemented using managed code. Here is the complete implementation, with analysis to follow:

```
// Be sure to import the Vb6ComCarServer namespace.
class Program
{
  static void Main(string[] args)
  {
    Console.WriteLine("***** CoCar Client App *****");

    // Create the COM class using early binding.
    CoCar myCar = new CoCar();

    // Handle the BlewUp event.
    myCar.BlewUp += new __CoCar_BlewUpEventHandler(myCar_BlewUp);

    // Call the Create() method.
    myCar.Create(50, 10, CarType.BMW);

    // Set name of driver.
    IDriverInfo itf = (IDriverInfo)myCar;
    itf.DriverName = "Fred";
    Console.WriteLine("Drive is named: {0}", itf.DriverName);

    // Print type of car.
    Console.WriteLine("Your car is a {0}.", myCar.CarMake);
    Console.WriteLine();

    // Get the Engine and print name of the cylinders.
    Engine eng = myCar.GetEngine();
    Console.WriteLine("Your Cylinders are named:");
    string[] names = (string[])eng.GetCylinders();
    foreach (string s in names)
    {
      Console.WriteLine(s);
    }
    Console.WriteLine();

    // Speed up car to trigger event.
    for (int i = 0; i < 5; i++)
    {
      myCar.SpeedUp();
    }
  }

  // Handler for the BlewUp event.
  static void myCar_BlewUp()
  {
    Console.WriteLine("Your car is toast!");
  }
}
```

Notice that when we call GetCylinders(), we are casting the return value into an array of strings. The reason is the fact that COM arrays are (most often) represented by the SAFEARRAY COM type (which is always the case when building COM applications using VB6). The RCW will map SAFEARRAY types into a System.Array object, rather than automatically mapping SAFEARRAYs into an array represented with C# syntax. Thus, by casting the Array object into a string[], we can process the array more naturally.

Interacting with the CoCar Type

Recall that when we created the VB6 CoCar, we defined and implemented a custom COM interface named IDriverInfo, in addition to the automatically generated default interface (_CoCar) created by the VB6 compiler. When our Main() method creates an instance of CoCar, we only have direct access to the members of the _CoCar interface, which as you recall will be composed by each public member of the COM class:

```
// Here, you are really working with the [default] interface.
myCar.Create(50, 10, CarType.BMW);
```

Given this fact, in order to invoke the DriverName property of the IDriverInfo interface, we must explicitly cast the CoCar object to an IDriverInfo interface as follows:

```
// Set name of driver.
IDriverInfo itf = (IDriverInfo)myCar;
itf.DriverName = "Fred";
Console.WriteLine("Drive is named: {0}", itf.DriverName);
```

Recall, however, that when a type library is converted into an interop assembly, it will contain Class-suffixed types that expose every member of every interface. Therefore, if you so choose, you could simplify your programming if you create and make use of a CoCarClass object, rather than a CoCar object. For example, consider the following subroutine, which makes use of members of the default interface of CoCar as well as members of IDriverInfo:

```
static void UseCar()
{
  // -Class suffix types expose all
  // members from all interfaces.
  CoCarClass c = new CoCarClass();

  // This property is a member of IDriverInfo.
  c.DriverName = "Mary";

  // This method is a member of _CoCar.
  c.SpeedUp();
}
```

If you are wondering exactly how this single type is exposing members of each implemented interface, check out the list of implemented interfaces and the base class of CoCarClass using the Visual Studio 2008 Object Browser (see Figure A-14).

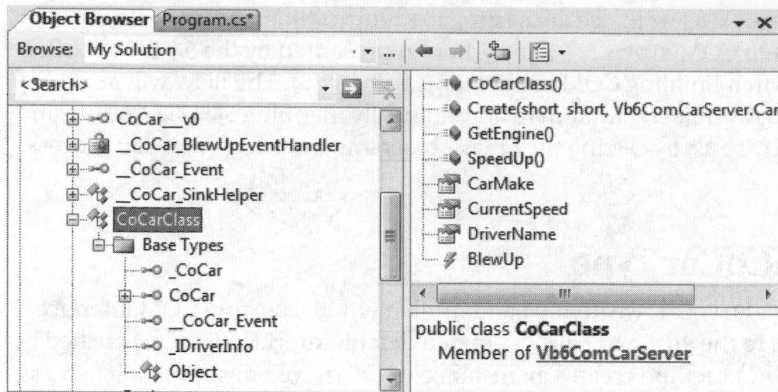

Figure A-14. *The composition of* `CoCarClass`

As you can see, this type implements the `_CoCar` and `_IDriverInfo` interfaces and exposes them as "normal" public members.

Intercepting COM Events

In Chapter 11, you learned about the .NET event model. Recall that this architecture is based on delegating the flow of logic from one part of the application to another. The entity in charge of forwarding a request is a type deriving from `System.MulticastDelegate`, which we create indirectly in C# using the `delegate` keyword.

When the `tlbimp.exe` utility encounters event definitions in the COM server's type library, it responds by creating a number of managed types that wrap the low-level COM connection point architecture. Using these types, you can pretend to add a member to a `System.MulticastDelegate`'s internal list of methods. Under the hood, of course, the proxy is mapping the incoming COM event to their managed equivalents. Table A-3 briefly describes these types.

Table A-3. *COM Event Helper Types*

Generated Type (Based on the _CarEvents [source] Interface)	Meaning in Life
`__CoCar_Event`	This is a managed interface that defines the add and remove members used to add (or remove) a method to (or from) the `System.MulticastDelegate`'s linked list.
`__CoCar_BlewUpEventHandler`	This is the managed delegate (which derives from `System.MulticastDelegate`).
`__CoCar_SinkHelper`	This generated class implements the outbound interface in a .NET-aware sink object.

As you would hope, you are able to handle the incoming COM events in the same way you handle events based on the .NET delegation architecture:

```
class Program
{
  static void Main(string[] args)
  {
    Console.WriteLine("***** CoCar Client App *****");
    CoCar myCar = new CoCar();
```

```
    // Handle the BlewUp event.
    myCar.BlewUp += new __CoCar_BlewUpEventHandler(myCar_BlewUp);
    ...
  }

  // Handler for the BlewUp event.
  static void myCar_BlewUp()
  {
    Console.WriteLine("Your car is toast!");
  }
}
```

It is also worth pointing out if your C# code base is able to make use of all of the event-centric notations (anonymous methods, method group conversion, lambda expressions, etc.) when intercepting events from COM objects.

Source Code The CSharpCarClient project is included under the Appendix A subdirectory.

That wraps up our investigation of how a .NET application can communicate with a legacy COM application. Now be aware that the techniques you have just learned would work for *any* COM server at all. This is important to remember, given that many COM servers might never be rewritten as native .NET applications. For example, the object model of Microsoft Outlook is currently exposed as a COM library. Thus, if you needed to build a .NET program that interacted with this product, the interoperability layer is (currently) mandatory.

Understanding COM to .NET Interoperability

The next topic of this appendix is to examine the process of a COM application communicating with a .NET type. This "direction" of interop allows legacy COM code bases (such as an existing VB6 project) to make use of functionality contained within newer .NET assemblies. As you might imagine, this situation is less likely to occur than .NET to COM interop; however, it is still worth exploring.

For a COM application to make use of a .NET type, we somehow need to fool the COM program into believing that the managed .NET type is in fact *unmanaged*. In essence, you need to allow the COM application to interact with the .NET type using the functionality required by the COM architecture. For example, the COM type should be able to obtain new interfaces through `QueryInterface()` calls, simulate unmanaged memory management using `AddRef()` and `Release()`, make use of the COM connection point protocol, and so on.

Beyond fooling the COM client, COM to .NET interoperability also involves fooling the COM runtime. A COM server is activated using the COM runtime rather than the CLR. For this to happen, the COM runtime must look up numerous bits of information in the system registry (ProgIDs, CLSIDs, IIDs, and so forth). The problem, of course, is that .NET assemblies are not registered in the registry in the first place!

Given these points, to make your .NET assemblies available to COM clients, you must take the following steps:

1. Register your .NET assembly in the system registry to allow the COM runtime to locate it.
2. Generate a COM type library (`*.tlb`) file (based on the .NET metadata) to allow the COM client to interact with the public types.
3. Deploy the assembly in the same directory as the COM client or (more typically) install it into the GAC.

As you will see, these steps can be performed using Visual Studio 2008 or at the command line using various tools that ship with the .NET Framework 3.5 SDK.

The Attributes of System.Runtime.InteropServices

In addition to performing these steps, you will typically also need to decorate your C# types with various .NET attributes, all of which are defined in the `System.Runtime.InteropServices` namespace. These attributes ultimately control how the COM type library is created and therefore control how the COM application is able to interact with your managed types. Table A-4 documents some (but not all) of the attributes you can use to control the generated COM type library.

Table A-4. *Select Attributes of* `System.Runtime.InteropServices`

.NET Interop Attribute	Meaning in Life
`[ClassInterface]`	Used to create a default COM interface for a .NET class type.
`[ComClass]`	This attribute is similar to `[ClassInterface]`, except it also provides the ability to establish the GUIDs used for the class ID (CLSID) and interface IDs of the COM types within the type library.
`[DispId]`	Used to hard-code the DISPID values assigned to a member for purposes of late binding.
`[Guid]`	Used to hard-code a GUID value in the COM type library.
`[In]`	Exposes a member parameter as an input parameter in COM IDL.
`[InterfaceType]`	Used to control how a .NET interface should be exposed to COM (`IDispatch`-only, dual, or `IUnknown`-only).
`[Out]`	Exposes a member parameter as an output parameter in COM IDL.

Now do be aware that for simple COM to .NET interop scenarios, you are not required to adorn your .NET code with dozens of attributes in order to control how the underlying COM type library is defined. However, when you need to be very specific regarding how your .NET types will be exposed to COM, the more you understand COM IDL attributes the better, given that the attributes defined in `System.Runtime.InteropServices` are little more than managed definitions of these IDL keywords.

The Role of the CCW

Before we walk through the steps of exposing a .NET type to COM, let's take a look at exactly how COM programs interact with .NET types using a COM Callable Wrapper, or CCW. As you have seen, when a .NET program communicates with a COM type, the CLR creates a Runtime Callable Wrapper. In a similar vein, when a COM client accesses a .NET type, the CLR makes use of an intervening proxy termed the COM Callable Wrapper to negotiate the COM to .NET conversion (see Figure A-15).

Like any COM object, the CCW is a reference-counted entity. This should make sense, given that the COM client is assuming that the CCW is a real COM type and thus must abide by the rules of `AddRef()` and `Release()`. When the COM client has issued the final release, the CCW releases its reference to the real .NET type, at which point it is ready to be garbage collected.

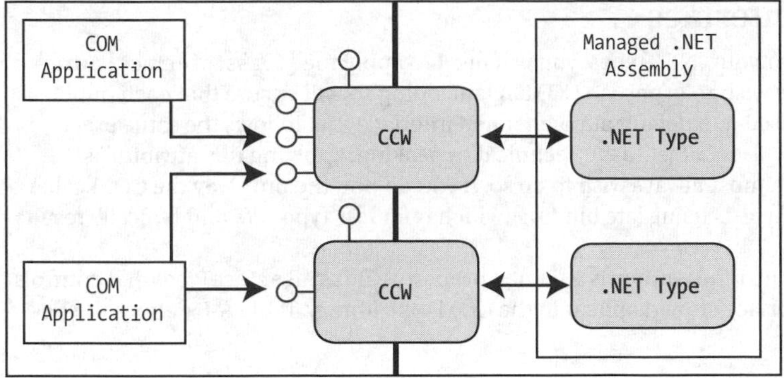

Figure A-15. *COM types talk to .NET types using a CCW.*

The CCW implements a number of COM interfaces automatically to further the illusion that the proxy represents a genuine coclass. In addition to the set of custom interfaces defined by the .NET type (including an entity termed the *class interface* that you examine in just a moment), the CCW provides support for the standard COM behaviors described in Table A-5.

Table A-5. *The CCW Supports Many Core COM Interfaces*

CCW-Implemented Interface	Meaning in Life
`IConnectionPoint` `IConnectionPointContainer`	If the .NET type supports any events, they are represented as COM connection points.
`IEnumVariant`	If the .NET type supports the `IEnumerable` interface, it appears to the COM client as a standard COM enumerator.
`IErrorInfo` `ISupportErrorInfo`	These interfaces allow coclasses to send COM error objects.
`ITypeInfo` `IProvideClassInfo`	These interfaces allow the COM client to pretend to manipulate an assembly's COM type information. In reality, the COM client is interacting with .NET metadata.

`IUnknown`
`IDispatch`
`IDispatchEx`
	These core COM interfaces provide support for early and late binding to the .NET type.

The Role of the .NET Class Interface

In classic COM, the only way a COM client can communicate with a COM object is to use an interface reference. In contrast, .NET types do not need to support any interfaces whatsoever, which is clearly a problem for a COM caller. Given that classic COM clients cannot work with object references, another responsibility of the CCW is to expose a *class interface* to represent each member defined by the type's public sector. As you can see, the CCW is taking the same approach as Visual Basic 6.0!

Defining a Class Interface

To define a class interface for your .NET types, you will need to apply the [ClassInterface] attribute on each public class you wish to expose to COM. Again, doing so will ensure that each public member of the class is exposed to a default autogenerated interface that follows the same exact naming convention as VB6 (_NameOfTheClass). Technically speaking, applying this attribute is optional; however, you will almost always wish to do so. If you do not, the only way the COM caller can communicate with the type is using late binding (which is far less type safe and typically results in slower performance).

The [ClassInterface] attribute supports a named property (ClassInterfaceType) that controls exactly how this default interface should appear in the COM type library. Table A-6 defines the possible settings.

Table A-6. *Values of the* ClassInterfaceType *Enumeration*

ClassInterfaceType Member Name	Meaning in Life
AutoDispatch	Indicates the autogenerated default interface will only support late binding, and is equivalent to not applying the [ClassInterface] attribute at all.
AutoDual	Indicates that the autogenerated default interface is a "dual interface" and can therefore be interacted with using early binding or late binding. This would be the same behavior taken by VB6 when it defines a default COM interface.
None	Indicates that no interface will be generated for the class. This can be helpful when you have defined your own strongly typed .NET interfaces that will be exposed to COM, and do not wish to have the "freebie" interface.

In the next example, you specify ClassInterfaceType.AutoDual as the class interface designation. In this way, late-binding clients such as VBScript can access the Add() and Subtract() methods using IDispatch, while early-bound clients (such as VB6 or C++) can use the class interface (named _VbDotNetCalc).

Building Your .NET Types

To illustrate a COM type communicating with managed code, assume you have created a simple C# Class Library project named ComCallableDotNetServer, which defines a class named DotNetCalc. This class will define two simple methods named Add() and Subtract(). The implementation logic is trivial; however, notice the use of the [ClassInterface] attribute:

```
// We need this to obtain the necessary
// interop attributes.
using System.Runtime.InteropServices;

namespace ComCallableDotNetServer
{
  [ClassInterface(ClassInterfaceType.AutoDual)]
  public class DotNetCalc
  {
    public int Add(int x, int y)
    { return x + y; }
```

```
    public int Subtract(int x, int y)
    { return x - y; }
  }
}
```

As mentioned earlier in this appendix, in the world of COM, just about everything is identified using a 128-bit number termed a GUID. These values are recorded into the system registry in order to define an identity of the COM type. Here, we have not specifically defined GUID values for our DotNetCalc class, and therefore the type library exporter tool (tlbexp.exe) will generate GUIDs on the fly. The problem with this approach, of course, is that each time you generate the type library (which we will do shortly), you receive unique GUID values, which can break existing COM clients.

To define specific GUID values, you may make use of the guidgen.exe utility, which is accessible from the Tools ➤ Create Guid menu item of Visual Studio 2008. Although this tool provides four GUID formats, the [Guid] attribute demands the GUID value be defined using the Registry Format option, as shown in Figure A-16.

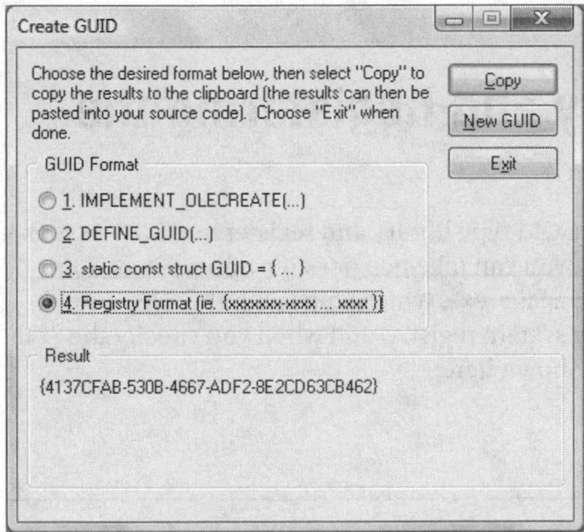

Figure A-16. *Obtaining a GUID value*

Once you copy this value to your clipboard (via the Copy GUID button), you can then paste it in as an argument to the [Guid] attribute. Be aware that you must remove the curly brackets from the GUID value! This being said, here is our updated DotNetCalc class type (your GUID value will differ):

```
[ClassInterface(ClassInterfaceType.AutoDual)]
[Guid("4137CFAB-530B-4667-ADF2-8E2CD63CB462")]
public class DotNetCalc
{
  public int Add(int x, int y)
  { return x + y; }

  public int Subtract(int x, int y)
  { return x - y; }
}
```

On a related note, click the Show All Files button on the Solution Explorer and open up the AssemblyInfo.cs file located under the Properties icon. By default, all Visual Studio 2008 project workspaces are provided with an assembly-level [Guid] attribute used to identify the GUID of the type library generated based on the .NET server (if exposed to COM).

```
// The following GUID is for the ID of the typelib if this project is exposed to COM
[Assembly: Guid("EB268C4F-EB36-464C-8A25-93212C00DC89")]
```

Defining a Strong Name

As a best practice, all .NET assemblies that are exposed to COM should be assigned a strong name and installed into the global assembly cache (the GAC). Technically speaking, this is not required; however, if you do not deploy the assembly to the GAC, you will need to copy this assembly into the same folder as the COM application making use of it.

Given that Chapter 15 already walked you through the details of defining a strongly named assembly, simply generate a new `*.snk` file for signing purposes using the Signing tab of the Properties editor. At this point, you can compile your assembly and install `ComCallableDotNetServer.dll` into the GAC using `gacutil.exe` (again, see Chapter 15 for details).

```
gacutil -i ComCallableDotNetServer.dll
```

Generating the Type Library and Registering the .NET Types

At this point, we are ready to generate the necessary COM type library and register our .NET assembly into the system registry for use by COM. Do to so, you can take two possible approaches. Your first approach is to use a command-line tool named `regasm.exe`, which ships with the .NET Framework 3.5 SDK. This tool will add several listings to the system registry, and when you specify the `/tlb` flag, it will also generate the required type library, as shown here:

```
regasm ComCallableDotNetServer.dll /tlb
```

■ **Note** The .NET Framework 3.5 SDK also provides a tool named `tlbexp.exe`. Like `regasm.exe`, this tool will generate type libraries from a .NET assembly; however, it does not add the necessary registry entries. Given this, it is more common to simply use `regasm.exe` to perform each required step.

While `regasm.exe` provides the greatest level of flexibility regarding how the COM type library is to be generated, Visual Studio 2008 provides a handy alternative. Using the Properties editor, simply check the Register for COM interop option on the Compile tab, as shown in Figure A-17, and recompile your assembly.

Once you have run `regasm.exe` or enabled the Register for COM Interop option, you will find that your bin\Debug folder now contains a COM type library file (taking a `*.tlb` file extension).

■ **Source Code** ComCallableDotNetServer application is included under the Appendix A subdirectory.

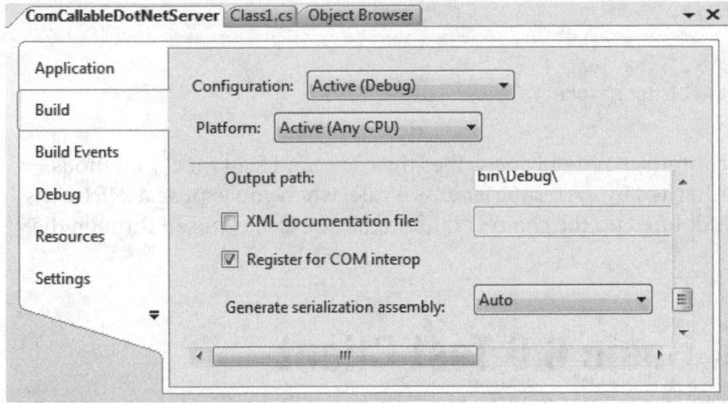

Figure A-17. *Registering an assembly for COM interop using Visual Studio 2008*

Examining the Exported Type Information

Now that you have generated the corresponding COM type library, you can view its contents using the OLE View utility by loading the `*.tlb` file. If you load `ComCallableDotNetServer.tlb` (via the File ➤ View Type Library menu option), you will find the COM type descriptions for each of your .NET class types. For example, the `DotNetCalc` class has been defined to support the default `_DotNetClass` interface due to the `[ClassInterface]` attribute, as well as an interface named (surprise, surprise) `_Object`. As you would guess, this is an unmanaged definition of the functionality defined by `System.Object`:

```
[uuid(88737214-2E55-4D1B-A354-7A538BD9AB2D),
 version(1.0), custom({0F21F359-AB84-41E8-9A78-36D110E6D2F9},
 "ComCallableDotNetServer.DotNetCalc")]
coclass DotNetCalc {
  [default] interface _DotNetCalc;
  interface _Object;
};
```

As specified by the `[ClassInterface]` attribute, the default interface has been configured as a dual interface, and can therefore be accessed using early or late binding:

```
[odl, uuid(AC807681-8C59-39A2-AD49-3072994C1EB1), hidden,
 dual, nonextensible, oleautomation,
 custom({0F21F359-AB84-41E8-9A78-36D110E6D2F9},
 "ComCallableDotNetServer.DotNetCalc")]
interface _DotNetCalc : IDispatch {
  [id(00000000), propget,
   custom({54FC8F55-38DE-4703-9C4E-250351302B1C}, "1")]
  HRESULT ToString([out, retval] BSTR* pRetVal);
  [id(0x60020001)]
  HRESULT Equals( [in] VARIANT obj,
                  [out, retval] VARIANT_BOOL* pRetVal);
  [id(0x60020002)]
  HRESULT GetHashCode([out, retval] long* pRetVal);
  [id(0x60020003)]
  HRESULT GetType([out, retval] _Type** pRetVal);
  [id(0x60020004)]
  HRESULT Add([in] long x, [in] long y,
```

```
      [out, retval] long* pRetVal);
    [id(0x60020005)]
    HRESULT Subtract( [in] long x, [in] long y,
                      [out, retval] long* pRetVal);
};
```

Notice that the _DotNetCalc interface not only describes the Add() and Subtract() methods, but also exposes the members inherited by System.Object. As a rule, when you expose a .NET class type to COM, all public methods defined up the chain of inheritance are also exposed through the autogenerated class interface.

Building a Visual Basic 6.0 Test Client

Now that the .NET assembly has been properly configured to interact with the COM runtime, you can build some COM clients. You can create a simple VB6 Standard *.exe project type (named VB6DotNetClient) and set a reference to the new generated type library (see Figure A-18).

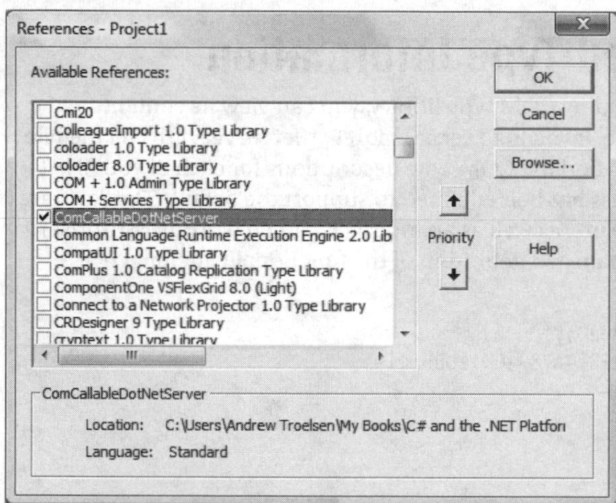

Figure A-18. *Referencing your .NET server from VB6*

As for the GUI front end, keep things really simple. A single Button object will be used to manipulate the DotNetCalc .NET type. Here is the code (notice that you are also invoking ToString(), defined by the _Object interface):

```
Private Sub btnUseDotNetObject_Click()
  ' Create the .NET object.
  Dim c As New DotNetCalc
  MsgBox c.Add(10, 10), , "Adding with .NET"

  ' Invoke some members of System.Object.
  MsgBox c.ToString, , "ToString value"
End Sub
```

Source Code The VB6DotNetClient application is included under the Appendix A subdirectory.

So, at this point you have seen the process of building .NET applications that talk to COM types and COM applications that talk to .NET types. Again, while there are many additional topics regarding the role of interop services, you should be in a solid position for further exploration.

Summary

.NET is a wonderful thing. Nevertheless, managed and unmanaged code must learn to work together for some time to come. Given this fact, the .NET platform provides various techniques that allow you to blend the best of both worlds.

A major section of this appendix focused on the details of .NET types using legacy COM components. As you have seen, the process begins by generating an assembly proxy for your COM types. The RCW forwards calls to the underlying COM binary and takes care of the details of mapping COM types to their .NET equivalents.

The appendix concluded by examining how COM types can call on the services of newer .NET types. As you have seen, this requires that the creatable types in the .NET assembly are registered for use by COM, and that the .NET types are described via a COM type library.

APPENDIX B

Platform-Independent .NET Development with Mono

This appendix introduces you to the topic of cross-platform C# and .NET development using an open source implementation of .NET named *Mono* (in case you are wondering about the name, "Mono" is a Spanish word for monkey, as in "code monkey," a term often used to describe individuals who author code for a living). In this appendix, you will come to understand the role of the Common Language Infrastructure (CLI), the overall scope of Mono, and numerous Mono development tools. Given your work over the course of this text, you will be in a perfect position to dig further into Mono development as you see fit at the conclusion of this appendix.

Note If you require a detailed treatment of cross-platform .NET development, I recommend picking up a copy of *Cross-Platform .NET Development: Using Mono, Portable .NET, and Microsoft .NET* by Mark Easton and Jason King (Apress, 2004).

The Platform-Independent Nature of .NET

Historically speaking, when programmers made use of a Microsoft development language or programming framework (VB6, MFC, COM, ATL, etc.), they had to resign themselves to building software that (by and large) only executed on the Windows family of operating systems. Many .NET developers, accustomed to previous Microsoft development options, are quite surprised when they learn that .NET is *platform-independent*. But it's true. You can compile and execute .NET assemblies on operating systems other than Microsoft Windows.

Using open source .NET implementations such as Mono, Mac OS X, Solaris, AIX, as well as numerous flavors of Unix/Linux can be happy homes for your .NET binaries. Furthermore, Mono provides an installation package for (surprise, surprise) Microsoft Windows. Thus, it is possible to build and run .NET assemblies on the Windows operating system, without ever installing the Microsoft .NET Framework 3.5 SDK or the Visual Studio 2008 IDE.

Note Be aware, however, that if you are only interested in building .NET software for the Windows operating system, the Microsoft .NET Framework 3.5 SDK and Visual Studio 2008 provide the best options for doing so.

Even after developers are made aware of .NET code's cross-platform capabilities, they often assume that the scope of platform-independent .NET development is limited to little more than

"Hello World" console applications. In reality, however, you can build production-ready assemblies that make use of ADO.NET, Windows Forms (in addition to alternative GUI toolkits such as GTK# and Cocoa#), ASP.NET, and XML web services using many of the core namespaces and language features you have seen used throughout this text.

The way in which .NET's cross-platform nature is achieved is different from the approach taking by Sun Microsystems with the handling of the Java programming platform. Unlike Java, Microsoft itself does not provide installers of .NET for Mac, Linux, etc. Rather, Microsoft has released a set of formalized specifications that other entities can use as a road map for building .NET distributions for their platform(s) of choice. Collectively, these specifications are termed the CLI.

The Role of the CLI

As briefly mentioned in Chapter 1, when C# and the .NET platform were released to the world at large, Microsoft Corporation submitted two formal specifications to ECMA (European Computer Manufacturers Association). Once approved, these same specifications were submitted to the International Organization for Standardization (ISO) and ratified shortly thereafter.

So, why on earth should you care? Again, these two specifications provide a road map for other companies, developers, universities, and other such organizations to build their own custom distributions of the C# programming language and the .NET platform. The two specifications in question are

- *ECMA-334*, which defines the syntax and semantics of the C# programming language
- *ECMA-335*, which defines numerous details of the .NET platform, collectively termed the *Common Language Infrastructure*

ECMA-334 tackles the lexical grammar of C# in an extremely rigorous and scientific manner (as you might guess, this level of detail is quite important to those implementing their own C# compiler). However, ECMA-335 is the meatier of the two specifications, so much so that it has been broken down into six partitions, as listed in Table B-1.

Table B-1. *ECMA-335 Specification Partitions*

ECMA-335 Partition	Meaning in Life
Partition I: Architecture	Describes the overall architecture of the CLI, including the rules of the Common Type System, the Common Language Specification, and the mechanics of the .NET runtime engine.
Partition II: Metadata	Describes the details of the .NET metadata format.
Partition III: CIL	Describes the syntax and semantics of the common intermediate language (CIL) programming language.
Partition IV: Libraries	Gives a high-level overview of the minimal and complete class libraries that must be supported by a CLI-compatible .NET distribution.
Partition V: Binary Formats	Provides details of the portable debug interchange format (CILDB). Portable CILDB files provide a standard way to interchange debugging information between CLI producers and consumers.
Partition VI: Annexes	Represents a collection of "odds and ends" examining topics such as class library design guidelines and the implementation details of a CIL compiler.

The point of this appendix is not to dive into the details of the ECMA-334 and ECMA-335 specifications—nor are you required to know the ins-and-outs of these documents to understand how to build platform-independent .NET assemblies. However, if you are interested, you can download both of these specifications for free from the ECMA website (`http://www.ecma-international.org/publications/standards`).

Note Even if you have no interest in the cross-platform aspects of .NET, I would recommend reading the ECMA-334 and ECMA-335 specifications, as they provide a number of insights regarding the C# language and the .NET platform.

The Mainstream CLI Distributions

To date, there are two mainstream implementations of the CLI, beyond Microsoft's CLR, Microsoft Silverlight, and the Microsoft NET Compact Framework (see Table B-2).

Table B-2. *Mainstream .NET CLI Distributions*

CLI Distribution	Supporting Website	Meaning in Life
Mono	`http://www.mono-project.com`	Mono is an open source and commercially supported distribution of .NET sponsored by Novell Corporation. Mono is targeted to run on many popular flavors of Unix/Linux, Mac OS X, Solaris, and Windows.
Portable .NET	`http://www.dotgnu.org`	Portable .NET is distributed under the GNU General Public License. As the name implies, Portable .NET intends to function on as many operation systems and architectures as possible, including many esoteric platforms such as BeOS, Microsoft Xbox, and Sony PlayStation (no, I'm not kidding about those last two!).

Each of the CLI implementations shown in Table B-2 provide a fully function C# compiler, numerous command-line development tools, a global assembly cache (GAC) implementation, sample code, useful documentation, and dozens of assemblies that constitute the base class libraries.

Beyond implementing the core libraries defined by Partition IV of ECMA-335, Mono and Portable .NET provide Microsoft-compatible implementations of `mscorlib.dll`, `System.Data.dll`, `System.Web.dll`, `System.Drawing.dll`, and `System.Windows.Forms.dll` (among many others). Furthermore, the Mono and Portable .NET distribution also ship with a handful of assemblies specifically targeted at Unix/Linux and Mac OS X operating systems. For example, Cocoa# is a .NET wrapper around the Mac OX GUI toolkit, Cocoa. In this appendix, I will not dig into these OS-specific binaries and instead stay focused on making use of the OS-agonistic programming stacks.

Note Portable .NET will not be examined in this appendix. However, it is important to know that Mono is not the only platform-independent distribution of the .NET platform available today. I would recommend you take some time to play around with Portable .NET in addition to the Mono platform.

The Scope of Mono

Given that Mono is an API built on existing ECMA specifications that originated from Microsoft Corporation, you would be correct in assuming that Mono is playing a constant game of catch up as newer versions of Microsoft's .NET platform are released. At the time of this writing, Mono is compatible with C# 2.0/.NET 2.0. Therefore, you are able to build ASP.NET websites, Windows Forms applications, database-centric applications using ADO.NET, and (of course) simple console applications.

Currently, Mono is *not* completely compatible with C# 2008 or .NET 3.0/3.5. What that means is your Mono applications are currently unable (again, at the time of this writing) to make use of the following APIs:

- Windows Presentation Foundation (WPF)
- Windows Communication Foundation (WCF)
- Windows Workflow Foundation (WF)
- The LINQ APIs
- C# 2008–specific language features

Rest assured that the Novell-based Mono team is already working on incorporating these APIs and C# 2008 programming features into the Mono project. In fact, many C# 2008 language features are already part of the latest build of Mono (1.2.5), including implicit typing, object initialization syntax, and anonymous types.

■ **Note** The C# 2008 support is enabled by passing the `-langversion:linq` option to the Mono C# compiler.

In addition, the Olive project, which plans to bring WPF, WCF, and WF into the Mono platform, is currently underway. LINQ support, you will be happy to know, is also moving along nicely.

■ **Note** The Mono website maintains a page that describes the overall road map of Mono's functionality and plans for future releases (`http://www.mono-project.com/plans`).

The final point of interest regarding the Mono feature set is that much like Microsoft's .NET Framework 3.5 SDK, the Mono SDK supports a number of .NET programming languages. While this appendix will stay focused on C#, Mono does provide support for a Visual Basic .NET–compatible compiler, as well as support for many other .NET-aware programming languages.

Obtaining and Installing Mono

With this basic primer behind us, we can turn our attention to obtaining and installing Mono on your operating system of choice. Navigate to the Mono website (`http://www.mono-project.com`) and click the Download Now button to navigate to the downloads page. Here you are able to download a variety of installers.

I am assuming that you are installing the Windows distribution of Mono (note that installing Mono will not interfere whatsoever with any existing installation of Microsoft .NET or Visual Studio IDEs). Begin by downloading the current stable Mono installation package for Microsoft Windows and saving the setup program to your local hard drive.

Note If you are installing Mono on a Linux-based OS, I'd suggest doing so using the Linux Installer for x86 package, which will allow you to install Mono using a friendly setup wizard (rather than forcing you to install Mono from source; be sure to read the supplied installation notes on the Mono website). If you make use of the Mac OS X Mono installer, the installation process will be identical to installing other Mac-based software.

When you run the setup program, you will be given a chance to install a variety of Mono development tools beyond the expected base class libraries and the C# programming tools. Specifically, the installer will ask you whether you wish to include GTK# (an open source .NET GUI API based on the Linux-centric GTK toolkit) and XSP (a stand-alone web server, similar to Microsoft's `webdev.webserver.exe`). In this appendix, I will assume you have opted for a full installation, so be sure you have checked each option in the setup script (see Figure B-1).

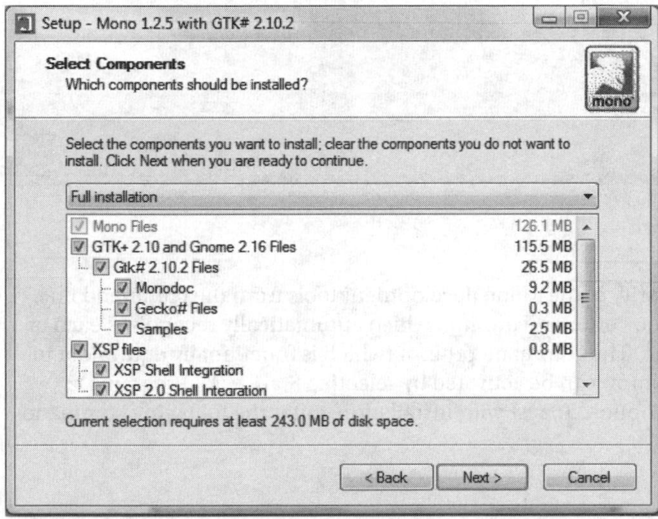

Figure B-1. *Select all options for your Mono installation.*

All of the remaining options of the Mono installer can be left using the suggested default values.

Examining Mono's Directory Structure

By default, Mono installs under `C:\Program Files\Mono-`*`<version>`* (at the time of this writing, the latest and greatest version of Mono is 1.2.5). Beneath that root you will find a number of subdirectories (see Figure B-2).

For this appendix, you need only concern yourself with the following subdirectories:

- *bin*: Contains a majority of the Mono development tools including the C# command-line compilers
- *lib\mono\gac*: The location of Mono's global assembly cache

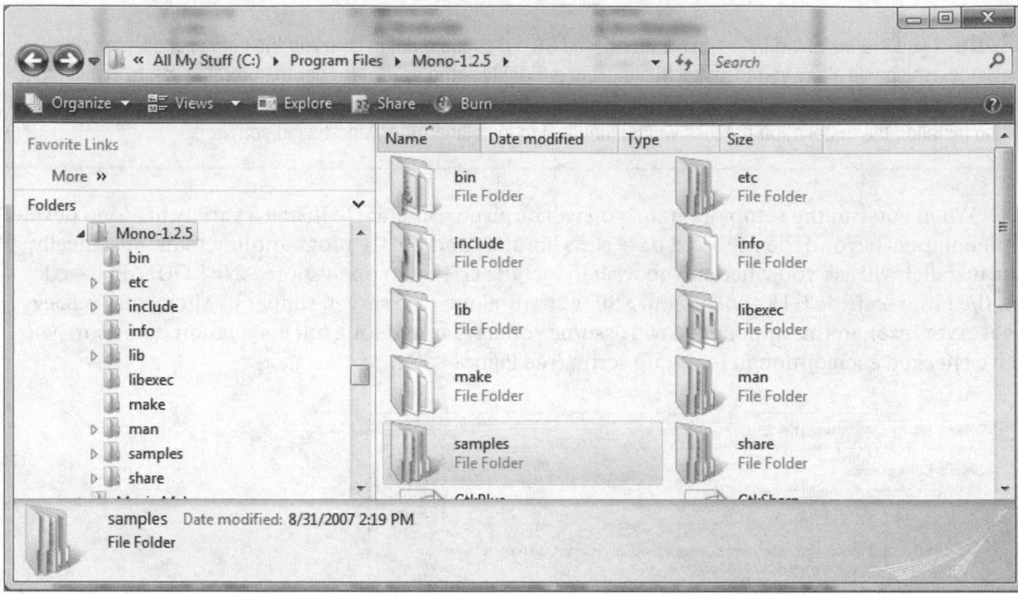

Figure B-2. *The Mono directory structure*

Given that you run the vast majority of the Mono development tools from the command line, you will want to make use of the Mono command prompt, which automatically recognizes each of the command-line development tools. The command prompt (which is functionally equivalent to the Visual Studio 2008 command prompt) can be activated by selecting Start ➤ All Programs ➤ Mono <*version*> For Windows menu option. To test your installation, enter the following command and press the Enter key:

```
mono --version
```

If all is well, you should see various details regarding the Mono runtime environment (see Figure B-3).

```
Administrator: Mono-1.2.5 Command Prompt
Mono version 1.2.5 Build 5
Prepending 'C:\PROGRA~1\MONO-1~1.5\bin' to PATH
C:\Windows\system32>mono --version
Mono JIT compiler version 1.2.5 (tarball)
Copyright (C) 2002-2007 Novell, Inc and Contributors. www.mono-project.com
        TLS:           normal
        GC:            Included Boehm (with typed GC)
        SIGSEGV:       normal
        Architecture:  x86
        Disabled:      none

C:\Windows\system32>
```

Figure B-3. *The Mono runtime environment*

The Mono Development Tools

Similar to the Microsoft's CLR distribution, Mono ships with a number of managed compilers:

- `mcs/gmcs`: The C# compilers
- `vbnc`: The Mono Visual Basic compiler
- `booc`: The Boo language compiler
- `ilasm/ilasm2`: The Mono CIL compilers

While this appendix focuses only on the C# compilers, again recall that the Mono project does ship with a Visual Basic .NET compiler. While this tool is currently under development, the intended goal is to bring the world of human-readable keywords (`Inherits`, `MustOverride`, `Implements`, etc.) to the world of Unix/Linux and Mac OS X (see `http://www.mono-project.com/Visual_Basic` for more detail).

Boo is an object-oriented statically typed programming language for the CLI that sports a Python-based syntax. Check out `http://boo.codehaus.org` for more details on the Boo programming language. Finally, as you might have guessed, `ilasm/ilasm2` are the Mono CIL compilers (the second of which supports .NET 2.0 programming constructs).

Working with the C# Compilers

The first C# compiler for the Mono project was `mcs`, and it's fully compatible with C# 1.1 (in fact, `mcs` is written in C#). Like the Microsoft C# command-line compiler (`csc.exe`), `mcs` supports response files, a `/target:` flag (to define the assembly type), an `/out:` flag (to define the name of the compiled assembly), and a `/reference:` flag (to update the manifest of the current assembly with external dependencies). You can view all the options of `mcs` using the following command:

```
mcs -?
```

The "generic mono C# compiler," or `gmcs`, as the name implies, is a version of `mcs` that has support for .NET 2.0–specific C# language features (generics, covariance/contravariance, nullable types, partial types, anonymous methods, etc.) and references the .NET 2.0–based base class libraries. The command-line options of `gmcs` are identical to `mcs`, which you can verify with the following command:

```
gmcs -?
```

Given the presence of two C# compilers, you might naturally assume that only `gmcs` can be used to build .NET applications that make use of the C# 2.0 language enhancements. In reality, `mcs` was the first of the two compilers to support 2.0 features, which were perfected and ported to `gmcs`. The code examples in this appendix can be compiled using either of the two C# compilers, so pick your poison.

Microsoft-Compatible Mono Development Tools

In addition to various managed compilers, Mono ships with various development tools that are functionally equivalent to tools found in the Microsoft .NET SDK (some of which are identically named). Table B-3 enumerates the mappings between some of the commonly used Mono/Microsoft .NET utilities.

Table B-3. *Mono Command-Line Tools and Their Microsoft .NET Counterparts*

Mono Utility	Microsoft .NET Utility	Meaning in Life
`al`	`al.exe`	Manipulates assembly manifests and builds multifile assemblies (among other things)
`gacutil`	`gacutil.exe`	Interacts with the GAC
`mono` when run with the `-aot` option	`ngen.exe`	Performs a precompilation of an assembly's CIL code
`wsdl`	`wsdl.exe`	Generates client-side proxy code for XML web services
`disco`	`disco.exe`	Discovers the URLs of XML web services located on a web server
`xsd`	`xsd.exe`	Generates type definitions from an XSD schema file
`sn`	`sn.exe`	Generates key data for a strongly named assembly
`monodis`	`ildasm.exe`	The CIL disassembler
`ilasm`	`ilasm.exe`	The CIL assembler
`xsp2`	`webdev.webserver.exe`	A testing and development ASP.NET web server

Mono-Specific Development Tools

In addition, there are Mono development tools for which no direct Microsoft .NET Framework 3.5 SDK equivalents exist, and these are listed in Table B-4.

Table B-4. *Mono Tools That Have No Direct Microsoft .NET SDK Equivalent*

Mono-Specific Development Tool	Meaning in Life
`monop/monop2`	The `monop` (mono print) utility will display the definition of a specified type in the syntax of C#.
`SQL#`	The Mono Project ships with a graphical front end (`SQL#`) to allow you to interact with relational databases using a variety of ADO.NET data providers.
`Glade 3`	This tool is a visual development IDE for building GTK# graphical applications.

■ **Note** You can load SQL# and Glade by using Windows's Start button and navigating to the Applications folder within the Mono installation directory. Be sure to do so, as it will clearly illustrate how rich the Mono platform has become.

Using monop(2)

The `monop` and `monop2` utilities (both of which are shorthand for *mono print*) can be used to display the C# definition of a given type within a specified assembly. The distinction between these two utilities is that monop is programmed to only display types compatible with Microsoft .NET 1.1, whereas monop2 will also display types compatible with Microsoft .NET 2.0. As you might suspect, these tools can be quite helpful when you wish to quickly view a method signature, rather than digging through the formal documentation. By way of a quick test, enter the following command within a Mono command prompt:

```
monop2 System.Object
```

Figure B-4 shows the definition of our good friend `System.Object`.

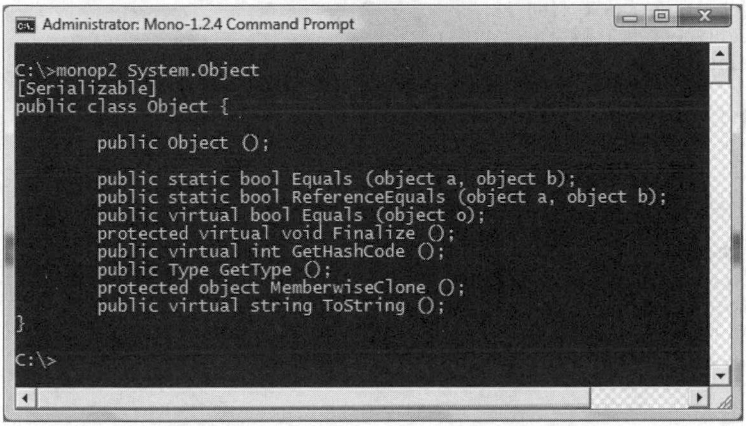

```
Administrator: Mono-1.2.4 Command Prompt
C:\>monop2 System.Object
[Serializable]
public class Object {

        public Object ();

        public static bool Equals (object a, object b);
        public static bool ReferenceEquals (object a, object b);
        public virtual bool Equals (object o);
        protected virtual void Finalize ();
        public virtual int GetHashCode ();
        public Type GetType ();
        protected object MemberwiseClone ();
        public virtual string ToString ();
}

C:\>
```

Figure B-4. `monop`*(2) displays C# code definitions for compiled types.*

You'll see the use of additional Mono tools over the course of this appendix; however, you may wish to specify -? as an argument to a tool of interest to see the available command set.

Building .NET Applications with Mono

To illustrate Mono in action, you will begin by building a code library named `CoreLibDumper.dll`. This assembly contains a single class type named `CoreLibDumper` that supports a static method named `DumpTypeToFile()`. The method takes a string parameter that represents the fully qualified name of any type within `mscorlib.dll` and obtains the related type information via the reflection API (see Chapter 16), dumping the class member signatures to a local file on the hard drive.

Building a Mono Code Library

Create a new folder on your C drive named MonoCode. Within this new folder, create a subfolder named CoreLibDumper that contains the following C# file (named `CorLibDumper.cs`):

```
// CoreLibDumper.cs
using System;
using System.Reflection;
using System.IO;

// Define assembly version.
[assembly:AssemblyVersion("1.0.0.0")]
```

```
namespace CoreLibDumper
{
  public class TypeDumper
  {
    public static bool DumpTypeToFile(string typeToDisplay)
    {
      // Attempt to load type into memory.
      Type theType = null;
      try
      {
        // Throw exception if we can't find it.
        theType = Type.GetType(typeToDisplay, true);
      } catch { return false; }

      // Create local *.txt file.
      using(StreamWriter sw =
        File.CreateText(string.Format("{0}.txt",
        theType.FullName)))
      {
        // Now dump type to file.
        sw.WriteLine("Type Name: {0}", theType.FullName);
        sw.WriteLine("Members:");
        foreach(MemberInfo mi in theType.GetMembers())
          sw.WriteLine("\t-> {0}", mi.ToString());

      }
      return true;
    }
  }
}
```

Like the Microsoft C# compiler, the Mono C# compilers support the use of response files (see Chapter 2). While you could compile this file by specifying each required argument manually at the command line, instead create a new file named `LibraryBuild.rsp` (in the same location as `CoreLibDumper.cs`) that contains the following command set:

```
/target:library
/out:CoreLibDumper.dll
CoreLibDumper.cs
```

You can now compile your library at the command line as follows:

```
gmcs @LibraryBuild.rsp
```

This approach is functionally equivalent to the following (more verbose) command set:

```
gmcs /target:library /out:CoreLibDumper.dll CoreLibDumper.cs
```

Assigning CoreLibDumper.dll a Strong Name

Mono supports the notion of deploying strongly named and shared assemblies (see Chapter 15) to the Mono GAC. To generate the necessary public/private key data, Mono provides the `sn` command-line utility, which functions more or less identically to Microsoft's tool of the same name. For example, the following command generates a new `*.snk` file (specify the `-?` option to view all possible commands):

```
sn -k myTestKeyPair.snk
```

To inform the C# compiler to make use of this key data to assign a strong name to `CoreLibDumper.dll`, simply update your `LibraryBuild.rsp` file with the following additional command:

```
/target:library
/out:CoreLibDumper.dll
/keyfile:myTestKeyPair.snk
CoreLibDumper.cs
```

Now recompile your assembly:

```
gmcs @LibraryBuild.rsp
```

Viewing the Updated Manifest with monodis

Before deploying the assembly to the Mono GAC, allow me to introduce the `monodis` command-line tool, which is the functional equivalent of Microsoft's `ildasm.exe` (without the GUI front end). Using `monodis`, you can view the CIL code, manifest, and type metadata for a specified assembly. In this case, we're interested in viewing the core details of our (now strongly named) assembly via the `--assembly` flag. Figure B-5 shows the result of the following command set:

```
monodis --assembly CoreLibDumper.dll
```

```
Administrator: Mono-1.2.4 Command Prompt
C:\My Books\C# and the .NET Platform 4th ed\Code\Appendix B\CoreLibDumper>monodi
s --assembly CoreLibDumper.dll
Assembly Table
Name:          CoreLibDumper
Hash Algoritm: 0x00008004
Version:       1.0.0.0
Flags:         0x00000000
PublicKey:     BlobPtr (0x00000036)
       Dump:
0x00000000: 00 24 00 00 04 80 00 00 94 00 00 00 06 02 00 00
0x00000010: 00 24 00 00 52 53 41 31 00 04 00 00 11 00 00 00
0x00000020: 03 5B 79 36 3E 97 38 E8 46 D7 D7 7B E8 5A 70 DB
0x00000030: C3 0F E8 E0 57 2E A5 D4 CF 51 D9 1A 2C 86 CC 26
0x00000040: E8 2E 80 0C 7A 11 0C 79 09 FA 36 6F 1A A6 80 39
0x00000050: 2A 0A 26 44 FB 34 E0 D8 49 F7 57 EF 30 BD 8F 90
0x00000060: 0F 66 A0 23 FD 1C 71 5E FC 25 53 49 E1 71 EA 7F
0x00000070: 37 85 D8 7F 4C 9D 71 E3 31 18 68 FE F2 10 41 4D
0x00000080: BA 63 94 00 82 BB D8 AB DC 11 7D F2 CA F4 11 34
0x00000090: 31 FB 7E 32 DF 26 7A CE 1D DE DE 31 AC C3 83 EB
Culture:

C:\My Books\C# and the .NET Platform 4th ed\Code\Appendix B\CoreLibDumper>
```

Figure B-5. `monodis` *allows you to view the CIL code, metadata, and manifest of an assembly.*

As you can see, the assembly's manifest now exposes the public key value defined within `myTestKeyPair.snk`.

Installing Assemblies into the Mono GAC

Now that you have provided `CoreLibDumper.dll` with a strong name, you install it into the Mono GAC using `gacutil`. Like Microsoft's tool of the same name, Mono's `gacutil` supports options to install, uninstall, and list the current assemblies installed under C:\Program Files\Mono-<*version*>\lib\mono\gac. The following command deploys `CoreLibDumper.dll` to the GAC and sets it up as a shared assembly on the machine.

```
gacutil -i CoreLibDumper.dll
```

Note Be sure to use a Mono command prompt to install this binary to the Mono GAC! If you use the Microsoft gacutil.exe program, you'll install CoreLibDumper.dll into the Microsoft GAC!

After running the command, if you open the \gac directory, you should find a new folder named CoreLibDumper (see Figure B-6), which defines a subdirectory that follows the same naming conventions as Microsoft's GAC (*versionOfAssembly__publicKeyToken*).

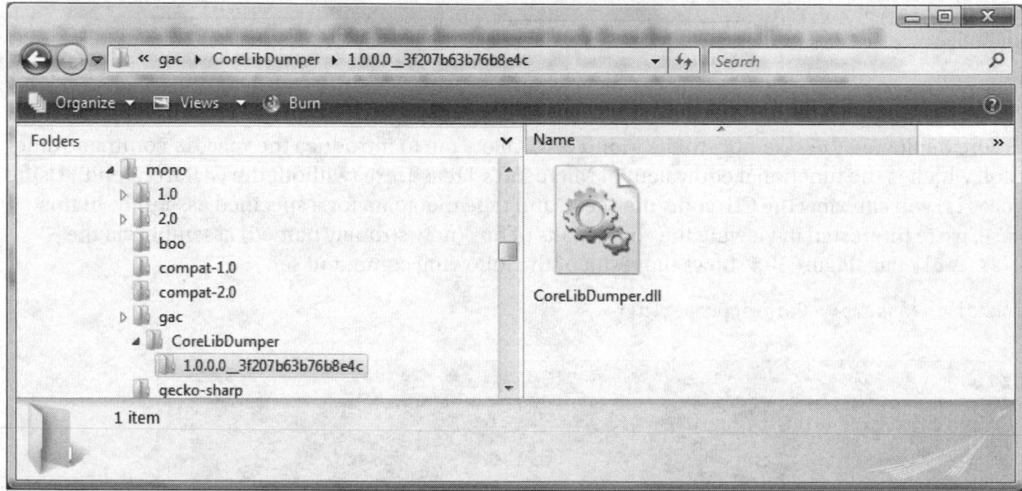

Figure B-6. *Deploying our code library to the Mono GAC*

Note Supplying the -l option to gacutil will list out each assembly in the Mono GAC.

Building a Console Application in Mono

Your first Mono client will be a simple console-based application named ConsoleClientApp.exe. Create a new file in your C:\MonoCode\CorLibDumper folder, ConsoleClientApp.cs, that contains the following Program type:

```
// This client app makes use of the CoreLibDumper.dll
// to dump types to a file.
using System;
using CoreLibDumper;

namespace ConsoleClientApp
{
  public class Program
  {
    public static void Main()
    {
      Console.WriteLine(
        "***** The Type Dumper App *****\n");
```

```
      // Ask user for name of type.
      string typeName = "";
      Console.Write("Please enter type name: ");
      typeName = Console.ReadLine();

      // Now send it to the helper library.
      if(TypeDumper.DumpTypeToFile(typeName))
         Console.WriteLine("Data saved into {0}.txt",
         typeName);
      else
        Console.WriteLine("Error!  Can't find that type...");
    }
  }
}
```

Notice that the Main() method simply prompts the user for a fully qualified type name. The TypeDumper.DumpTypeToFile() method uses the user-entered name to dump the type's members to a local file. Next, create a ClientBuild.rsp file for this client application that references CoreLibDumper.dll:

```
/target:exe
/out:ConsoleClientApp.exe
/reference:CoreLibDumper.dll
ConsoleClientApp.cs
```

Now, using a Mono command prompt, change to the folder containing your client files and compile the executable using gmcs as shown here:

```
gmcs @ClientBuild.rsp
```

Loading Our Client Application in the Mono Runtime

At this point, you can load ConsoleClientApp.exe into the Mono runtime engine by specifying the name of the executable (with the *.exe file extension) as an argument to mono:

```
mono ConsoleClientApp.exe
```

As a test, enter System.Threading.Thread at the prompt, and press the Enter key. You will now find a new file named System.Threading.Thread.txt containing the type's metadata definition (see Figure B-7).

Before moving on to a Windows Forms–based client, try the following experiment. Using the Windows Explorer, rename the CoreLibDumper.dll assembly from the folder containing the client application to DontUseCoreLibDumper.dll. You should be able to still successfully run the client application, as the only reason we needed access to this assembly when building the client was to update the client manifest. At runtime, the Mono runtime will load the version of CoreLibDumper.dll you deployed to the Mono GAC.

However, if you open Windows Explorer and attempt to run your client application by double-clicking ConsoleClientApp.exe, you might be surprised to find a FileNotFoundException is thrown. At first glance, you might assume this is due to the fact that you renamed CoreLibDumper.dll from the location of the client application. However, the true reason is because you just loaded ConsoleClientApp.exe into the Microsoft CLR!

To run an application under Mono, you must pass it into the Mono runtime via mono. If you do not, you will be loading your assembly into the Microsoft CLR, which assumes all shared assemblies are installed into the Microsoft GAC located in the <%windir%>\Assembly directory.

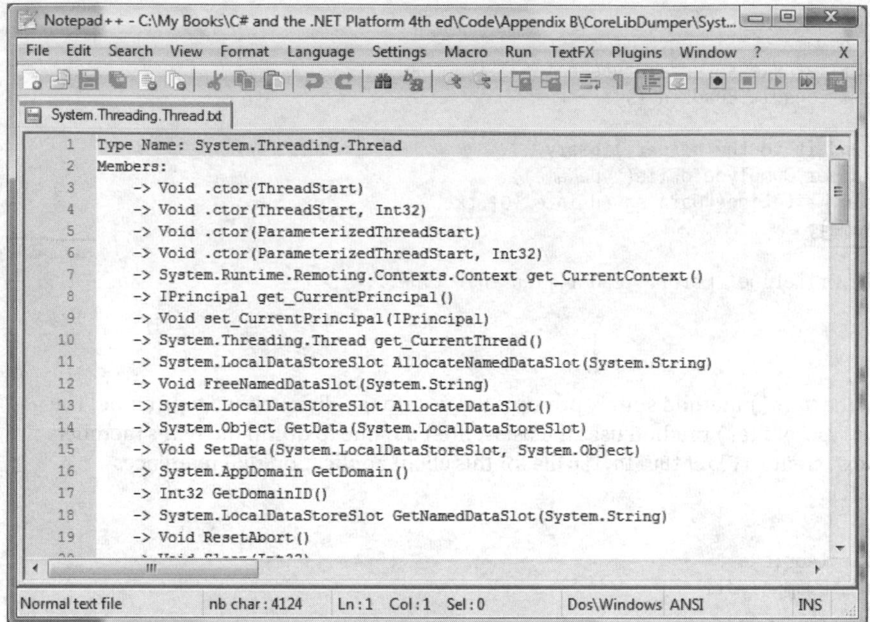

Figure B-7. *Result of running our client application*

Building a Windows Forms Client Program

Before continuing, be sure to rename `DontUseCoreLibDumper.dll` back to `CoreLibDumper.dll`. Next, create a new C# file named `WinFormsClientApp.cs` saved in the same location as your current project files. This file defines two types, both of which make use of a few C# 2.0 language features, including static classes and anonymous methods:

```
using System;
using System.Windows.Forms;
using CoreLibDumper;
using System.Drawing;

namespace WinFormsClientApp
{
  // Application object.
  public static class Program
  {
    public static void Main()
    {
      Application.Run(new MainWindow());
    }
  }

  // Our simple Window.
  public class MainWindow : Form
  {
    private Button btnDumpToFile = new Button();
    private TextBox txtTypeName = new TextBox();
```

```
    public MainWindow()
    {
      // Config the UI.
      ConfigControls();
    }

    private void ConfigControls()
    {
      // Configure the Form.
      Text = "My Mono Win Forms App!";
      ClientSize = new System.Drawing.Size(366, 90);
      StartPosition = FormStartPosition.CenterScreen;
      AcceptButton = btnDumpToFile;

      // Configure the Button.
      btnDumpToFile.Text = "Dump";
      btnDumpToFile.Location = new System.Drawing.Point(13, 40);

      // Handle click event anonymously.
      btnDumpToFile.Click += delegate
      {
        if(TypeDumper.DumpTypeToFile(txtTypeName.Text))
          MessageBox.Show(string.Format(
            "Data saved into {0}.txt",
            txtTypeName.Text));
        else
          MessageBox.Show("Error!  Can't find that type...");
      };
      Controls.Add(btnDumpToFile);

      // Configure the TextBox.
      txtTypeName.Location = new System.Drawing.Point(13, 13);
      txtTypeName.Size = new System.Drawing.Size(341, 20);
      Controls.Add(txtTypeName);
    }
  }
}
```

To compile this Windows Forms application using a response file, create a file named `WinFormsClientApp.rsp` (the contents of which follow) and supply that as an argument to `gmcs` as shown previously.

```
/target:winexe
/out:WinFormsClientApp.exe
/r:CoreLibDumper.dll
/r:System.Windows.Forms.dll
/r:System.Drawing.dll
WinFormsClientApp.cs
```

Finally, run your Windows Forms application via `mono`:

```
mono WinFormsClientApp.exe
```

Figure B-8 shows the output.

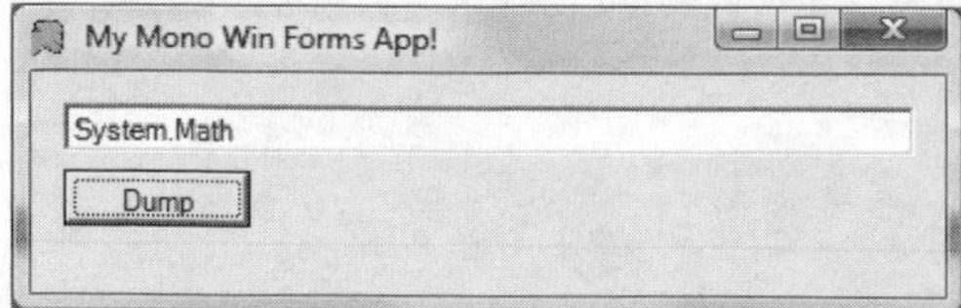

Figure B-8. *A Windows Forms application build using Mono*

Executing Our Windows Forms Application Under Linux

Up until now, this appendix has created a few assemblies that could have been compiled using the Microsoft .NET Framework 3.5 SDK. However, the importance of Mono becomes quite clear when you view Figure B-9, which shows the same exact Windows Forms application running under SuSe Linux. Notice how our Windows Forms application has taken on the correct look and feel of my current theme.

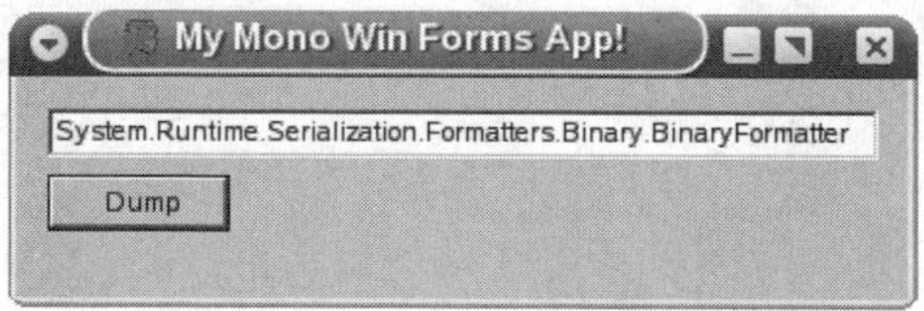

Figure B-9. *Our Windows Forms application executing under SuSe Linux!*

Source Code The CorLibDumper project can be found under the Appendix B subdirectory.

So, you can compile and execute the same exact C# code shown during this appendix on Linux (or any OS supported by Mono) using the same Mono development tools. In fact, you can deploy or recompile any of the assemblies created in this text that *do not use* 3.0 or 3.5 programming constructs to a new Mono-aware OS and run them directly using the mono runtime utility. Because all assemblies simply contain platform-agonistic CIL code, you are not required to recompile the applications whatsoever.

Note Do recall that Mono 1.2.5 does have limited support for C# 2008 language features, so *some* of the examples from Chapter 13 should work as-is.

Suggestions for Further Study

If you followed along with the materials presented in this book, you already know a great deal about Mono, given that it is an ECMA-compatible implementation of the CLI. If you are interested in learning more about Mono particulars, the first place to begin is the official Mono website (`http://www.mono-project.com`). Specifically, you should be sure to examine `http://www.mono-project.com/Use`, as this page is an entry point to a number of important topics including database access using ADO.NET, web development using ASP.NET, and so forth.

As well, I have authored some Mono-centric articles on the DevX website (`http://www.devx.com`) that may be of interest to you:

- "Mono IDEs: Going Beyond the Command Line": Examines numerous Mono-aware IDEs
- "Building Robust UIs in Mono with Gtk#": Examines building desktop applications using the GTK# toolkit as an alternative to Windows Forms

Last but not least, be aware of the Mono documentation website (`http://www.go-mono.com/docs`). Here you will find documentation on the Mono base class libraries, development tools, and other topics (see Figure B-10).

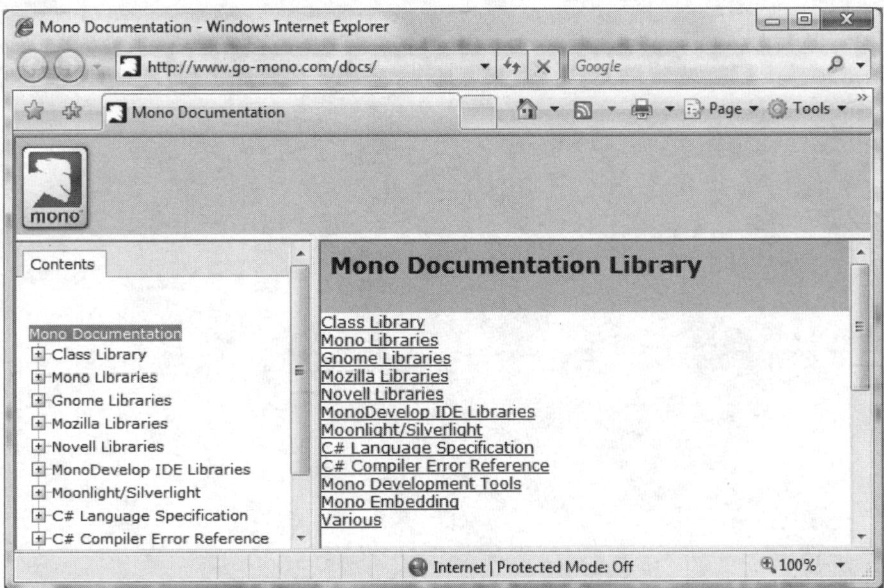

Figure B-10. *The online Mono documentation*

Note Mono's online documentation website is community supported; therefore, don't be too surprised if you find some incomplete documentation links! Given that Mono is an ECMA-compatible distribution of Microsoft .NET, you may prefer to make use of the feature-rich MSDN online documentation when exploring Mono.

Summary

The point of this appendix was to provide an introduction to the cross-platform nature of the C# programming language and the .NET platform using the Mono framework. As you have seen, Mono ships with a number of command-line tools that allow you to build any variety of .NET assembly, including strongly named assemblies deployed to the GAC, Windows Forms applications, and .NET code libraries.

As explained, Mono is not fully compatible with the .NET 3.0 or .NET 3.5 programming APIs (WPF, WCF, WF, or LINQ) or the C# 2008 language features (however, Mono 1.2.5 has some limited

C# 2008 language support). Efforts are underway (via the Olive project) to bring these aspects of the Microsoft .NET platform to Mono. In any case, if you need to build .NET applications that can execute under a variety of operating systems, the Mono project is a wonderful choice to do so.

Index

Special Characters

Numbers

A

D

E

H

Q

R

T

U

X

Y